THE SPORT AMERICANA®

Basketball Card PRICE GUIDE and Alphabetical Checklist

By

DR. JAMES BECKETT

NUMBER 2

EDGEWATER BOOK COMPANY • CLEVELAND

 Prices in this guide reflect current retail rates determined just prior to printing. They do not reflect *for sale* prices by the author, publisher, distributors, advertisers, or any card dealers associated with this guide. Every effort has been made to eliminate errors. Readers are invited to write us noting any errors which may be researched and corrected in subsequent printings. The publisher will not be held responsible for losses which may occur in the sale or purchase of cards because of information contained herein.

SPORT AMERICANA is a registered trademark of

EDGEWATER BOOK COMPANY
P.O. BOX 40238
CLEVELAND, OHIO 44140

Manufactured in the United States of America

First Printing

ISBN 0-937424-64-1

THE SPORT AMERICANA BASKETBALL CARD PRICE GUIDE

Table of Contents

Pro Basketball

College

Late-Breaking Sets

Index to Advertisers

ABOUT THE AUTHOR

Dr. Jim Beckett, the leading authority on sport card values in the United States, maintains a wide range of activities in the world of sports. He possesses one of the finest collections of sports cards and autographs in the world, has made numerous appearances on radio and television, and frequently has been cited in many national publications. He was awarded the first "Special Achievement Award" for Contributions to the Hobby by the National Sports Collectors Convention in 1980, the "Jock-Jasperson Award" for Hobby Dedication in 1983, and the "Buck Barker, Spirit of the Hobby" Award in 1991.

Dr. Beckett is the author of The Sport Americana Baseball Card Price Guide, The Official Price Guide to Baseball Cards, The Sport Americana Price Guide to Baseball Collectibles, The Sport Americana Baseball Memorabilia and Autograph Price Guide, The Sport Americana Football Card Price Guide, The Official Price Guide to Football Cards, The Sport Americana Hockey Card Price Guide, The Official Price Guide to Hockey Cards, The Sport Americana Basketball Card Price Guide and Alphabetical Checklist, The Official Price Guide to Basketball Cards, and The Sport Americana Baseball Card Alphabetical Checklist. In addition, he is the founder, publisher, and editor of Beckett Baseball Card Monthly, Beckett Basketball Monthly, Beckett Football Card Monthly, Beckett Hockey Monthly, and Beckett Focus on Future Stars, magazines dedicated to advancing the card collecting hobby.

Jim Beckett received his Ph.D. in Statistics from Southern Methodist University in 1975. Prior to starting Beckett Publications in 1984, Dr. Beckett served as an Associate Professor of Statistics at Bowling Green State University and as a Vice President of a consulting firm in Dallas, Texas. He currently resides in Dallas with his wife Patti and their daughters, Christina, Rebecca, and Melissa.

ACKNOWLEDGMENTS

A great deal of diligence, hard work, and dedicated effort went into this year's volume. However, the high standards to which we hold ourselves could not have been met without the expert input and generous time contributed by many people. Our sincere thanks are extended to each and every one of you.

I believe this year's Price Guide is our best yet. For that, you can thank all of the contributors nationwide (listed below) as well as our staff here in Dallas. Our company now boasts a substantial Technical Services team which has made (and is continuing to make) direct and important contributions to this work. Technical Services capably handled numerous technical details and provided able assistance in pricing for this edition of the annual guide. That effort was directed by Technical Services manager Pepper Hastings. He was assisted by Technical Services coordinator Mary Gregory, Price Guide analysts Theo Chen, Mike Hersh, Dan Hitt, Mary Huston, Rich Klein, Tom Layberger, Allan Muir, Grant Sandground, Dave Sliepka, and Steve Smith. Also contributing to our Technical Services functions were Scott Layton, Margaret Mall, Peter Tepp, and Jana Threatt, whose special assistance was invaluable in making this project a success. The price gathering and analytical talents of this fine group of hobbyists has helped make our Beckett team stronger, while making this guide and its companion monthly Price Guides more widely recognized as the hobby's most reliable and relied upon sources of pricing information.

Granted, the production of any book is a total staff effort. However, I owe special thanks to the members of our Book Team who demonstrated extraordinary contributions to this basketball book.

Scott Layton, our research associate, served as point man in the demanding area of new set entry and was a key person in the organization of both technological and people resources for the book. Margaret Mall and Kent Lawrence ensured the proper administration of our contributor price guide surveys. Pricing analysts Theo Chen, Rich Klein, and Grant Sandground track the basketball card market year round, and their baseline analysis and careful proofreading were key contributions to the accuracy of this annual.

Airey Baringer spent many late-night hours paginating and typesetting the text layout. Gayla Newberry was responsible for many of the card photos you see throughout the book. Maria Gonzalez-Davis again was meticulous in her work on the paste-up table. Wendy Kizer spent tireless hours on the phone attending to the wishes of our dealer advertisers. Once the ad specifications were delivered to our offices, John Marshall used his computer skills to turn raw copy into attractive display advertisements that

were carefully proofed by Bruce Felps. Finally, Managing Editor of Special Projects, Susan K. Elliott, set up initial schedules and ensured that all deadlines were met.

My sincere thanks to everyone on our Book Team and to all at Beckett Publications, who are listed below, for another job well done.

It is very difficult to be "accurate" — one can only do one's best. But this job is especially difficult since we're shooting at a moving target: Prices are fluctuating all the time. Having several full-time pricing experts has definitely proven to be better than just one, and I thank all of them for working together to provide you, our readers, with the most accurate prices possible.

Those who have worked closely with us on this and many other books, have again proven themselves invaluable in every aspect of producing this book: Rich Altman, Mike Aronstein, Baseball Hobby News (Frank and Vivian Barning), Jerry Bell, Chris Benjamin, Sy Berger (Topps Chewing Gum), Mike Blaisdell, Bill Bossert (Mid-Atlantic Coin Exchange), Barry Colla, Mike Cramer (Pacific Trading Cards), Todd Crosner (California Sportscard Exchange), Bud Darland, Bill and Diane Dodge, Willie Erving, Gervise Ford, Steve Freedman, Larry and Jeff Fritsch, Steve Galletta, Tony Galovich, Jim Galusha, Dick Gariepy, Dick Gilkeson, Mike and Howard Gordon, George Grauer, John Greenwald, Wayne Grove, Bill Haber, Bill Henderson, George Henn, Jerry Hersh, Steve Johnson, Edward J. Kabala, Judy and Norman Kay, Alan Kaye (Sports Card News), Lesnik Public Relations (Timm Boyle and Bob Ibach), Robert Levin (The Star Company), Lew Lipset, Dave Lucey, Jim Macie, Paul Marchant, Brian Marcy (Scottsdale Baseball Cards), Dr. John McCue, Michael Moretto, Brian Morris, B.A. Murry, Jack Pollard, Tom Reid, Gavin Riley, Alan Rosen (Mr. Mint), John Rumierz, San Diego Sport Collectibles (Bill Goepner and Nacho Arredondo), Kevin Savage (Sports Gallery), Mike Schechter (MSA), Bill Shonscheck, John Spalding, Nigel Spill (Oldies and Goodies), Sports Collectors Store (Pat Quinn and Don Steinbach), Frank Steele, Murvin Sterling, Dan Stickney, Steve Taft, Ed Taylor, Paul S. Taylor, Lee Temanson, Bill Wesslund, Kit Young, Robert Zanze, and Bill Zimpleman.

Many other individuals have provided price input, illustrative material, checklist verifications, errata, and/or background information. At the risk of inadvertently overlooking or omitting these many contributors, we should like to personally thank Jerry Adamic, Tom Akins, Dennis Anderson, Ellis Anmuth, Arkansas Sports Distributing, Toni Axtell, Douglas Baker, Baseball Cards Plus, Josh Baver, Bay State Cards (Lenny DeAngelico), Chris Becirel, Klaus Becker, Darrell E. Benjamin Jr., Andy Bergman, Carl Bergstrom, Adrian Betts, Beulah Sports, Brian Bigelow (Candl), Walter Bird, Brian Black, Keith and Ryan Bonner, Gary Boyd, Michael Boyd, Terry Brock, Fritz Brogan, Scott Brondyke, Karen Sue Brown, Dan Bruner (The Card King), Buckhead Baseball Cards (Marc Spector), Shawn Burke, Zac Burke, Curtis H. Butler, California Card Co., Mark Cantin, Danny Cariseo, Phil Carpenter, Cee Tim's Cards, Dwight Chapin, Rich Chavez, Dennis Chin, Bradley Clark, Shane Cohen (Grand Slam), Aaron Cole, Matt Collett, Danny Collins, H. William Cook, Ben Coulter, Enrique Cuenca, Robert Curtis, Herb Dallas Jr., Kenneth Dean, Matt DeBrabant, David Diehl, Cliff Dolgins, Discount Dorothy, Bill Eckle, David Edwards, Robert Ehnert, Robin Emmerling, Ed Emmitt, Mark Enger, David Erickson, Jonathan R. Farmer, Andy Feinstein, James Fendley, Terry Fennell, L.V. Fischer (The Collectors Den), Steve Foster, Doug French, Donny Frost, Dick Fuisz, Rob Gagnon, Robby Gantt, Steve Gerber, Michael R. Gionet, Steve Gold (AU Sports), Jeff Goldstein, Brandon Goodloe, Darin Goodwin, Gary W. Graber (Minden Games), David Grauf (Cards for the Connoisseur), Nick Grier, Erik Griggs, Don Guilbert, Hall's Nostalgia, Sean Hank, Chad Harris, Jacob Harrison, Lenny Helicer, Vaughn Hickman, Clay Hill, Alisa Hills, H.L.T. and T. Sports (Harold and Todd Nelkin), Will Ho, Russell Hoffman, Verdeen Hogan, Home Plate of Provo (Ken Edick), Keith Hora, Gene Horvath, Thomas James, Andy Jenkins, Kevin Jeu, Richard Johnson, Darryl Jordan, Tom Judd, Patricia Kaleihehana, Kevin Kamel, Bruce Kangas, Jay Kasper, Kim Kellogg, Joe Kelly, Dan Kent, Jeff Kluger, Roger Krafve, Paul Krasinkewicz, Mayank Keshaviah, Nicholas Krupke, Thomas Kunnecke, Vasin Laiteerapong, Ted Larkins (The Card Clubhouse), Dan Lavin, John F. Law, Stephen M. Lawson, A.B. Leo, Nathan Leon, Irv Lerner, Howie Levy of Blue Chip, Scott M. Lewandowski, Craig Lightcap, Dan Linroth, Jim Loeffler, Cody Lorance, R.J. Lyons, Jack Maiden, Larry Marks, Maurice Massey, Robert Matonis, Gary O. May, Jack Mayes, Leonard McClure, Anthony McCoy, Mike McDonald (Sports Page), Lou

McDonough, Timothy McElroy, Erik McKenzie, Jay F. McLain, James McNaughton, Dale C. Meek, Steve Melnick, Blake Meyer, Darren Milbrandt, Alan Miller, Richard Mold, Sean Moody, William Moorhead, Joe Morano, Joe Morris, Paul Morrison, Jeff Mowers, David Mowett, Fred Muollo, Dave Murray, Funz Napolitano, Cory T. Neu, No Gum Just Cards, Brad Norwood, John O'Hara, Trace Ono, Jeremy Opperman, Paul Orlick, G. Michael Oyster, Ricky Parker, Clay Pasternack, Earl Petersen, Troy Peterson, Tom Pfirrmann, John Pollack, Darren Porter, Ben Powers, Jonathan Ramos, Josh Randall, Phil Regli, David Renshaw, Louis Rene Reyes, Emily Rice, Mark Risk, Juan Rivera, Richard Robinson, Chuck Roethel, Steven Roeglin, Barry J. Rossheim, Ted Russo, Terry Sack, Joe Sak, Garret Salomon, Arnold Sanchez, Ron Sanders, Michael Sang, Bob Santos, Nathan Schank, Michael Seaman, Sebring Sports, Steven Senft, Mark Shields, Terry C. Shook, Ryan D. Shrimplin, Glen Sidler, Darrin Silverman, Gail Smith, Raymond Smith, Ron Smith, Bob Snyder, Luke Somers, William Soung, Carl Specht, Sports Legends, Doug Stauduhar, Paul M. Stefani, Allen Stengel (Perfect Image), Cary Stephenson, Scott Stucki, Michael Stuy, Doug Such, Mark Tanaka (Front Row), Chris Tateosian, Robert Taylor, Steve Taylor, Nick Teresi, Craig Thomas, Melanie Thomas, Mike Thompson, Emerson Tongco, Jeffrey K. Tsai, Peter Tsang, Jessie Turner, Warren Utsunomiya, Mark Velger (Trade Mark SportsCards), Eric Ware, Matthew Waten, David Weber, Jennifer Wegner, Richard West, Gregory Wiggins, Bob Wilke (The Shoe Box), Brian Wilkie, Shawn Williacy, Jeff Williams, Mark Williams, Matt Winters, Mike Woods (The Dugout), World Series Cards (Neil Armstrong), Mike Yost, and Zards Cards.

Every year, we make active solicitations for expert input. We are particularly appreciative of help (however extensive or cursory) provided for this volume. We receive many inquiries, comments and questions regarding material within this book. In fact, each and every one is read and digested. Time constraints, however, prevent us from personally replying. But keep sharing your knowledge. Your letters and input are part of the "big picture" of hobby information we can pass along to readers in our books and magazines. Even though we cannot respond to each letter, you are making significant contributions to the hobby through your interest and comments.

In the years since this guide debuted, Beckett Publications has grown beyond any rational expectation. A great many talented and hard working individuals have been instrumental in this growth and success. Our whole team is to be congratulated for what we together have accomplished.

Our Beckett Publications team is led by Associate Publisher Claire Backus, Vice Presidents Joe Galindo and Fred Reed, and Director of Marketing Jeff Amano. They are ably assisted by Fernando Albieri, Theresa Anderson, Gena Andrews, Jeff Anthony, Airey Baringer II, Barbara Barry, Nancy Bassi, Therese Bellar, Louise Bird, Wendy Bird, Cathryn Black, Terry Bloom, Lisa Borden, Dianne Boudreaux, Amy Brougher, Anthony Brown, Chris Calandro, Emily Camp, Mary Campana, Renata Campos, Becky Cann, Sammy Cantrell, Susan Catka, Jose Chavez, Theo Chen, Lynne Chinn, Tommy Collins, Belinda Cross, Billy Culbert, Randy Cummings, Patrick Cunningham, Gail Docekal, Andrew Drago, Louise Ebaugh, Alejandro Egusquiza, Mila Egusquiza, Susan Elliott, Daniel Evans, Bruce Felps, Jorge Field, Sara Field, Jean Paul Figari, Jeany Finch, Robson Fonseca, Kim Ford, Jeannie Fulbright, Gayle Gasperin, Anita Gonzalez, Mary Gonzalez-Davis, Jeff Greer, Mary Gregory, Julie Grove, Marcio Guimaraes, Karen Hall, Carmen Hand, Sabrina Harbour, Lori Harmeyer, Vivian Harmon, Patti Harris, Beth Harwell, Jenny Harwell, Mark Harwell, Pepper Hastings, Joanna Hayden, Cindy Herbert, Mike Hersh, Barbara Hinkle, Tracy Hinton, Dan Hitt, Heather Holland, E.J. Hradek, Rex Hudson, Mary Huston, Don James, Sara Jenks, Julia Jernigan, Wendy Jewell, Jay Johnson, Matt Keifer, Fran Keng, Monte King, Debbie Kingsbury, Amy Kirk, Sheri Kirk, Rudy Klancnik, Rich Klein, Frances Knight, John Knotts, Kent Lawrence, Tom Layberger, Jane Ann Layton, Scott Layton, Lori Lindsey, Cheryl Lingenfelter, Margaret Mall, Mark Manning, Louis Marroquin, John Marshall, Laura Massey, Kaki Matheson, Teri McGahey, Kirk McKinney, Mary McNertney, Omar Mediano, Edras Mendez, Sherry Monday, Robert Montenegro, Stephen Moore, Glen Morante, Elizabeth Morris, Daniel Moscoso, Daniel Moscoso Jr., Mike Moss, Randy Mosty, Allan Muir, Hugh Murphy, Shawn Murphy, Marie Neubauer, Wendy Neumann, Allen Neumann, Gayla Newberry, Rosanna Olaechea, Lisa O'Neill, Rich Olivieri, Abraham Pacheco, Guillermo Pacheco, Michael Patton, Mike Payne, Suzee Payton, Ronda Pearson, Julie Polomis, Tim Polzer,

Reed Poole, Roberto Ramirez, Roger Randall, Nikki Renshaw, Patrick Richard, Cristina Riojas, Jamile Romero, Stephen Rueckhaus, Grant Sandground, Gary Santaniello, Gabriel Santos, Manuel Santos, Stacy Schreiner, Maggie Seward, Elaine Simmons, Carol Slawson, Steve Slawson, Dave Sliepka, Judi Smalling, Steve Smith, Lisa Spaight, Margaret Steele, Mark Stokes, Jason Stone, Cindy Struble, Doree Tate, Peter Tepp, Jim Tereschuk, Christiann Thomas, Becky Thompson, Jana Threatt, Jason Todd, Brett Tulloss, Valerie Voigt, Steve Wilson, Carol Ann Wurster, and Robert Yearby. In addition, our consultants James and Sandi Beane and Dan Swanson performed several major system programming jobs for us again this year, to help us accomplish our work faster and more accurately. The whole Beckett Publications team has my thanks for jobs well done. Thank you, everyone.

I also thank my family, especially my wife, Patti, and daughters, Christina, Rebecca, and Melissa, for putting up with me again.

PREFACE

Isn't it great? Every year this book gets bigger and bigger, packed with all the new sets coming out. But even more exciting is that every year there are more collectors, more shows, more stores, and more interest in the cards we love so much. This edition has been enhanced and expanded from the previous edition. The cards you collect — who they depict, what they look like, where they are from, and (most important to many of you) what their current values are — are enumerated within. Many of the features contained in the other Beckett Price Guides have been incorporated into this volume since condition grading, nomenclature, and many other aspects of collecting are common to the card hobby in general. We hope you find the book both interesting and useful in your collecting pursuits.

Everyone knows about the tremendous growth in interest in baseball cards, but basketball cards are quite popular as well. In fact, interest in basketball cards is currently at an all-time high. They are becoming increasingly visible at the nation's card shows and stores.

The reason for the emergence of these cards in particular is due in large part to the continuing and increasing popularity of the sport itself. This increased popularity has made basketball superstars well known to millions of fans who watch them during the winter and spring and read about them all year. Megastars such as Michael Jordan, Clyde Drexler and David Robinson are among the most famous and recognizeable athletes in the world. Finally, the comparatively high cost of premium baseball cards has persuaded many collectors to pursue cards of other sports as a more affordable means of pursuing the sports collectibles hobby. Nevertheless, as you can see from the prices in this book, basketball cards are valuable — and they are perceived by a growing number of collectors as being good values for their hobby dollar.

Basketball cards are also typically produced in smaller sets than baseball, football and hockey sets, making it easier for collectors to complete them. The small size of all except the most recent basketball card sets has another positive aspect: There are more star cards and fewer commons.

The Beckett Guide has been successful where other attempts have failed because it is complete, current, and valid. This Price Guide contains not just one, but three prices by condition for all the football cards listed. These account for almost every football card in existence. The prices were added to the card lists just prior to printing and reflect not the author's opinions or desires but the going retail prices for each card, based on the marketplace (sports memorabilia conventions and shows, sports card shops, hobby papers, current mail-order catalogs, computer trading networks, auction results, and other firsthand reportings of actual realized prices).

What is the best price guide on the market today? Of course card sellers will consider the price guide with the highest prices as the best — while card buyers will naturally prefer the one with the lowest prices. Accuracy, however, is the true test. Use the price guide used by more collectors and dealers than all the others combined. Look for the Beckett name. I won't put my name on anything I won't stake my reputation on. Not the lowest and not the highest — but the most accurate, with integrity.

To facilitate your use of this book, read the complete introductory section in the pages following before going to the pricing pages. Every collectible field has its own terminology; we've tried to capture most of these terms and definitions in our glossary. Please read carefully the section on grading and the condition of your cards, as you will not be able to determine which price column is appropriate for a given card without first assessing its condition. Welcome to the world of basketball cards.

Sincerely, Dr. James Beckett

INTRODUCTION

Welcome to the exciting world of sports card collecting, America's fastest-growing avocation. You have made a good choice in buying this book, since it will open up to you the entire panorama of this field in the simplest, most concise way.

Hundreds of thousands of different sports cards have been issued during the past century. And the number of total sports cards produced by all manufacturers last year has been estimated at several billion, with an initial wholesale value of more than $1 billion. Sales of older cards by dealers may account for an equal or greater amount. With all that cardboard available in the marketplace, it should be no surprise that several million sports fans like you collect sports cards today, and that number is growing each year.

The growth of Beckett Baseball Card Monthly, Beckett Basketball Monthly, Beckett Football Card Monthly, Beckett Hockey Monthly, and Beckett Focus on Future Stars is another indication of this rising crescendo of popularity for sports cards. Founded in 1984 by Dr. James Beckett, the author of this Price Guide, Beckett Baseball Card Monthly has reached the pinnacle of the sports card hobby, with nearly two million readers anxiously awaiting each enjoyable and informative issue. The other four magazines have met similar success, with hundreds of thousands of readers devoted to each publication.

So collecting sports cards — while still pursued as a hobby with youthful exuberance by kids in your neighborhood — has also taken on the trappings of an industry, with thousands of full- and part-time card dealers, as well as vendors of supplies, clubs and conventions. In fact, each year since 1980, thousands of hobbyists have assembled for a National Sports Collectors Convention, at which hundreds of dealers have displayed their wares, seminars have been conducted, autographs penned by sports notables, and millions of cards changed hands. These colossal affairs have been staged in Los Angeles, Detroit, St. Louis, Chicago, New York, Anaheim, Arlington (Texas), San Francisco, Atlantic City, Chicago, Arlington (Texas), Anaheim, and this year in Atlanta. So sports card collecting really is national in scope!

This increasing interest is reflected in card values. As more collectors compete for available supplies, card prices rise (especially for older premium-grade cards). A perusal of the prices in this book, compared to the figures in earlier editions of this Price Guide, will quickly confirm this. Which brings us back around to the book you have in your hands. It is the best guide available to the exciting world of your favorite sport's cards. Read it and use it. May your enjoyment and your card collection increase in the coming months and years.

HOW TO COLLECT

Each collection is personal and reflects the individuality of its owner. There are no set rules on how to collect cards. Since card collecting is a hobby or leisure pastime, what you collect, how much you collect, and how much time and money you spend collecting, are entirely up to you. The funds you have available for collecting and your own personal taste should determine how you collect. Information and ideas presented here are intended to help you get the most enjoyment from this hobby.

It is impossible to collect every card ever produced. Therefore, beginners as well as intermediate and advanced collectors usually specialize in some way. One of the most popular aspects of this hobby is that individual collectors can define and tailor their collecting methods to match their own tastes. To give you some ideas of the various approaches to collecting, we will list some of the more popular areas of specialization.

Many collectors select complete sets from particular years. For example, they may concentrate on assembling complete sets from all the years since their birth or since they became avid sports fans. They may try to collect a card for every player during that specified period of time. Many others wish to acquire only certain players. Usually such players are the superstars of the sport, but occasionally collectors will specialize in all the cards of players who attended a particular college or came from a certain town. Some collectors are only interested in the first cards or rookie cards of certain players.

Another fun way to collect cards is by team. Most fans have a favorite team, and it is natural for that loyalty to be translated into a desire for cards of the players on that favorite team. For most of the recent years, team sets (all the cards from a given team for that year) are readily available at a reasonable price. This concept can also be applied to your favorite college's products. For instance, Maryland collectors would pursue cards of Brad Davis, Albert King, Tom McMillen, John Lucas, Tony Massenburg, Jerrod Mustaf and Walt Williams — or Georgia Tech collectors would pursue cards of Mark Price, John Salley, Tom Hammonds, Dennis Scott, Kenny Anderson, etc.

Obtaining Cards

Several avenues are open to card collectors to seek their favorite issues. Cards can be purchased in the traditional way at the local candy, grocery, or drug stores, with the bubble gum or other products included. For many years, it has been possible to purchase complete sets of cards through mail-order advertisers found in traditional sports media publications, such as The Sporting News, Basketball Digest, Street & Smith yearbooks, and others. These sets are also advertised in card collecting periodicals. Many collectors will begin by subscribing to at least one of the hobby periodicals. In fact, subscription offers can be found in the advertising section of this book. In addition, a great variety of cards (typically from all eras and all sports) are available through the growing number of hobby retail stores dedicated to sports cards and memorabilia around the country.

Most serious card collectors obtain old (and new) cards from one or more of several main sources: (1) trading or buying from other collectors or dealers; (2) responding to buy, sell or auction ads in hobby publications; (3) buying at a local hobby store; and/or (4) attending sports collectibles shows or conventions.
We advise that you try all four methods since each has its own distinct advantages: (1) trading is a great way to make new friends; (2) hobby periodicals help you keep up with what's going on in the hobby (including when and where the conventions are happening); (3) stores provide the opportunity for considering (any day of the week) a great diversity of material in a relaxed sports-oriented atmosphere most fans love; and (4) shows provide enjoyment and the opportunity to view thousands of collectibles under one roof, in addition to meeting some of the hundreds or even thousands of other collectors with similar interests, who also attend the shows.

Preserving Your Cards

Cards are fragile. They must be handled properly in order to retain their value. Careless handling can easily result in creased or bent cards. It is, however, not recommended that tweezers or tongs be used to pick up your cards since such utensils might mar or indent card surfaces and thus reduce those cards' conditions and values. In general, your cards should be handled directly as little as possible. This is sometimes easier to say than to do. Although there are many who use custom boxes, storage trays, or even shoe boxes, plastic sheets represent an inexpensive method to store and display cards. A collection stored in plastic pages in a three-ring album allows you to view your collection at any time without the need to touch the card itself. Cards can also be kept in single holders (of various types and thickness) designed for the enjoyment of each card individually. Most experienced collectors use a combination of the above methods.
When purchasing plastic sheets for your cards, be sure that you find the pocket size that fits the cards snugly. Don't put your oversized 1969-70 Topps basketball cards in a sheet designed to fit standard 2 1/2" by 3 1/2" cards. Most hobby and collectibles shops and virtually all collectors' conventions will have these plastic pages available in quantity, or you can purchase them directly from the advertisers in this book. Also remember that pocket size isn't the only factor to consider when looking for plastic sheets. Some collectors concerned with long-term storage of their cards in plastic sheets are cautious to avoid sheets containing PVC and request non-PVC sheets from their dealer.

Damp, sunny and/or hot conditions — no, this is not a weather forecast — are three elements to avoid in extremes if you are interested in preserving your collection. Too much (or less frequently, too little) humidity can cause gradual deterioration of a card. Direct sunlight (or fluorescent light) will bleach out the color of a card. Extreme heat accelerates the decomposition of the card. On the other hand, many cards have lasted more than 50 years with minimal scientific intervention. So be cautious, even if the above factors typically present a problem only when present in the extreme. It never hurts to be prudent.

Collecting/Investing

Collecting individual players and collecting complete sets are both popular vehicles for investment and speculation. Most investors and speculators stock up on complete sets or on quantities of players they think have good investment potential.

There is obviously no guarantee in this book, or anywhere else for that matter, that cards will outperform the stock market or other investment alternatives in the future. After all, sports cards do not pay quarterly dividends and cards cannot be sold at their "current values" as easily as stocks or bonds.

Nevertheless, investors have noticed a favorable long-term trend in the past performance of many sports collectibles, and certain cards and sets have outperformed just about any other investment in some years. Many hobbyists maintain that the best investment is, and always will be, the building of a collection, which traditionally has held up better than outright speculation.

Some of the obvious questions are: Which cards? When to buy? When to sell? The best investment you can make is in your own education. The more you know about your collection, the hobby and the players depicted on the cards, the more informed the decisions you will be able to make. We're not selling investment tips. We're selling information about the current value of sports cards. It's up to you to use that information to your best advantage.

NOMENCLATURE

Basketball sets, generally having been produced in the modern era from 1948 to present, can be described and identified by their year, maker, type of issue, and any other distinguishing characteristic. Regional issues are usually referred to by year, maker, and sometimes by title or theme of the set.

The following abbreviations are used for identifying major basketball sets:

B - Bowman (1948)
F - Fleer (1961-62, 1986-87 to 1991-92)
H - NBA Hoops (1989-90 to 1991-92)
S - Star Company (1983-84 to 1985-86)
SB - SkyBox (1990-91 to 1991-92)
T - Topps (1957-58, 1969-70 to 1981-82)
UD - Upper Deck (1991-92)

GLOSSARY / LEGEND

Our glossary defines terms frequently used in the card collecting hobby. Many of these terms are also common to other types of sports memorabilia collecting. Some terms may have several meanings, depending on use and context.

ABA - American Basketball Association.

ACC - American Card Catalog.

ACO - Assistant coach card.

AL - Active Leader.

ART - All-Rookie Team.

AS - All-Star card.

ALP - Alphabetical.

BRICK - A group of cards, usually 50 or more having common characteristics, that is intended to be bought, sold, or traded as a unit.

CBA - Continental Basketball Association.

CC - Classic Confrontations.

CHECKLIST - A list of the cards contained in a particular set. The list is always in numerical order if the cards are numbered. Some unnumbered sets are artificially numbered in alphabetical order, or by team and alphabetically within the team for convenience.

CL - Checklist card. A card that lists in order the cards and players in the set or series. Older checklist cards in Mint condition that have not been checked off are very desirable and command large premiums.

CO - Coach card.

COIN - A small disc of metal or plastic portraying a player in its center.

COLLECTOR - A person who engages in the hobby of collecting cards primarily for his own enjoyment, with any profit motive being secondary.

COLLECTOR ISSUE - A set produced for

the sake of the card itself with no product or service sponsor. It derives its name from the fact that most of these sets are produced for sale directly to the hobby market.

COMBINATION CARD - A single card depicting two or more players (but not a team card).

COMMON CARD - The typical card of any set; it has no premium value accruing from subject matter, numerical scarcity, popular demand or anomaly.

CONVENTION ISSUE - A set produced in conjunction with a sports collectibles convention to commemorate or promote the show. Most recent convention issues could also be classified as promo sets.

COR - Corrected card. A version of an error card that was fixed by the manufacturer.

COUPON - See Tab.

DEALER - A person who engages in buying, selling, and trading sports collectibles or supplies. A dealer may also be a collector, but as a dealer, he anticipates a profit.

DFO - Don't Foul Out.

DIE-CUT - A card with part of its stock partially cut, allowing one or more parts to be folded or removed. After removal or appropriate folding, the remaining part of the card can frequently be made to stand up.

DISC - A circular-shaped card.

DISPLAY CARD - A sheet, usually containing three to nine cards, that is printed and used by the manufacturer to advertise and/or display the packages containing his products and cards. The backs of display cards are blank or contain advertisements.

DISPLAY SHEET - A clear, plastic page that is punched for insertion into a binder (with standard three-ring spacing) containing pockets for displaying cards. Many different styles of sheets exist with pockets of varying sizes to hold the many differing card formats. The vast majority of current cards measure 2 1/2 by 3 1/2 inches and fit in nine-pocket sheets.

DP - Double-printed card. A card that is approximately twice as common as a regular card in the same set.

ERR - Error card. A card with erroneous information, spelling, or depiction on either side of the card. Most errors are never corrected by the producing card company.

FULL SHEET - A complete sheet of cards that has not been cut up into individual cards by the manufacturer. Also called an uncut sheet.

GQ - Gentleman's Quarterly.

HL - Highlight card.

HOF - Hall of Fame.

HOR - Horizontal pose on card as opposed to the standard vertical orientation found on most cards.

IA - In Action card. A special type of card depicting a player in an action photo, such as the 1982 Topps cards.

INSERT - A special card or other collectible (often a poster or sticker) contained and sold in the same package along with cards of a major set. Sometimes called a BONUS CARD.

IS - Inside Stuff.

ISSUE - Synonymous with set, but usually used in conjunction with a manufacturer, e.g., a Topps issue.

LEGITIMATE ISSUE - A set produced to promote or boost sales of a product or service, e.g., bubble gum, cereal, cigarettes, etc. Most collector issues are not legitimate issues in this sense.

LID - A circular-shaped card (possibly with tab) that forms the top of the container for the product being promoted.

LL - League leader card. A card depicting the leader or leaders in a specific statistical category form the previous season. Not to be confused with Team Leader (TL).

MAG - Magic of SkyBox card.

MAJOR SET - A set produced by a national manufacturer of cards containing a large number of cards. Usually 100 or more different cards comprise a major set.

MS - Milestone card.

MINI - A small card or stamp (the 1991-92 SkyBox Canadian set, for example).

MVP - Most Valuable Player.

NY - New York.

OBVERSE - The front, face, or pictured side of the card.

OLY - Olympic team card (1984-85 Star Company subset).

PANEL - An extended card composed of multiple individual cards. The most obvious basketball panels are found in the 1980-81 Topps set.

PERIPHERAL SET - A loosely defined term that applies to any non-regular issue set. This term is most often used to describe food issue, giveaway, regional or sendaway sets that contain a fairly small number of cards and are not accepted by the hobby as major sets.

PREMIUM - A card, sometimes on photographic stock, that is purchased or obtained in conjunction with (or redeemed for) another card or product. This term applies mainly to older products, as newer cards distributed in this manner are generally lumped together as peripheral sets.

PREMIUM CARDS - A class of products introduced recently that are intended to have higher quality card stock and photography than regular cards, but more limited production and higher cost. Defining what is and isn't a premium card is somewhat subjective.

PROMOTIONAL SET - A set, usually containing a small number of cards, issued by a national card producer and distributed in limited quantities or to a select group of people such as major show attendees or dealers with wholesale accounts. Presumably, the purpose of a promo set is to stir up demand for an upcoming set. Also called a preview, prototype or test set.

RARE - A card or series of cards of very limited availability. Unfortunately, "rare" is a subjective term sometimes used indiscriminately. Using the strict definitions, rare cards are harder to obtain than scarce cards.

RB - Record Breaker card.

RC - Rookie Card. A player's first appearance on a regular issue card from one of the major card companies. Each company has only one regular issue set per season, and that is the traditional set that is widely available. With a few exceptions, each player has only one RC in any given set. A Rookie Card cannot be an All-Star, Highlight, In Action, league leader, Super Action or team leader card. It can, however, be a coach card, draft pick or top prospect card.

REGIONAL - A card issued and distributed only in a limited geographical area of the country. The producer may or may not be a major, national producer of trading cards. The key is whether the set was distributed nationally in any form or not.

REVERSE - The back side of the card.

REV NEG - Reversed or flopped photo side of the card. This is a major type of error card, but only some are corrected.

RIS - Rising Star.

ROY - Rookie of the Year.

SA - Super Action.

SAL - SkyBox Salutes.

SASE - Self-addressed, stamped envelope.

SC - Supreme Court.

SCARCE - A card or series of cards of limited availability. This subjective term is sometimes used indiscriminately to promote or hype value. Using strict definitions, scarce cards are not as difficult to obtain as rare cards.

SD - Slam Dunk.

SERIES - The entire set of cards issued by a particular producer in a particular year, e.g., the 1978-79 Topps series. Also, within a particular set, series can refer to a group of (consecutively numbered) cards printed at the same time, e.g., the first series of the 1972-73 Topps set (#1 through #132).

SET - One each of the entire run of cards of the same type produced by a particular manufacturer during a single season. In other words, if you have a complete set of 1988-89 Fleer basketball cards, then you have every card from #1 up to and including #132; i.e., all the different cards that were produced.

SHOW - A large gathering of dealers and collectors at a single location for the purpose of buying, selling, and trading sorts cards and memorabilia. Conventions are open to the public and sometimes also feature autograph guests, door prizes, films, contests, etc.

SM - Sky Masters.

SMALL - Small School Sensation.

SP - Single or Short Print. A card which was printed in lesser quantity compared to the other cards in the same series (also see DP). This term can only be used in a relative sense and in reference to one particular set. For instance, the shortprinted 1989-90 Hoops Pistons Championship card (#353A) is less common than the other cards in that set, but it isn't necessarily scarcer than regular cards of any other set.

SPECIAL CARD - Generic term that applies to any card that portrays something other than a single player or team.

SS - Shooting Star.

STAR CARD - A card that portrays a player of some repute, usually determined by his ability, but sometimes referring to sheer popularity.

STAY - Stay in School.

STICKER - A card with a removable layer that can be affixed to another surface, for example the 1986-87 through 1989-90 Fleer bonus cards.

STOCK - The cardboard or paper on which the card is printed.

SUPERSTAR CARD - A card that portrays a superstar, e.g., a Hall of Fame member or a player whose current performance likely will eventually warrant serious Hall of Fame consideration.

TC - Team checklist card.

TEAM CARD - A card that depicts or represents an entire team, notably the 1989-90 and 1990-91 NBA Hoops Detroit Pistons championship cards and the 1991-92 NBA Hoops subset.

TEST SET - A set, usually containing a small number of cards, issued by a national producer and distributed in a limited section of the country or to a select group of people. Presumably, the purpose of a test set is to measure market appeal for a particular type of card. Also called a promo or prototype set.

THEN - Then and Now.

TL - Team Leader card.

TP - Top Prospect.

TR - Traded card.

TW - Teamwork.

UER - Uncorrected error card.

USA - Team USA card.

VARIATION - One of two or more cards from the same series with the same number (or player with identical pose if the series is unnumbered) differing from one another in some aspect, including the printing, stock or other feature of the card. This is usually caused when the manufacturer becomes aware of an error or inconsistency in a particular card, fixes the mistake and resumes the print run. In this case there will be two variations of the same card. Sometimes one of the variations is relatively scarce. Variations can also result from accidental or deliberate design changes, information updates, photo substitutions, etc.

VERT - Vertical pose on a card.

XRC - Extended Rookie Card. A player's first appearance on a card, but issued in a limited distribution, major set not distributed nationally nor in packs. In basketball sets, this term refers only to 1983-84, 1984-85 and 1985-86 Star Company sets.

YB - Yearbook.

6M - Sixth Man.

BASKETBALL CARD HISTORY

Basketball cards have been produced on and off since 1948 with the scarce 72-card Bowman set of that year. However, one must skip ahead to 1957-58 to find the next basketball set, this time an 80-card set issued by Topps. Then skip ahead to 1961-62 to the 66-card Fleer issue. Finally in 1969, Topps began a 13-year run of producing basketball card sets which ended in 1981-82. Ironically, this was about the time the league's popularity had bottomed out and was about to begin its ascent to the lofty level it's at today.

Topps' run included several sets that are troublesome for today's collectors. The 1969-70, 1970-71 and 1976-77 sets are larger than standard size, thus making them hard to store and preserve. The 1980-81 set consists of standard-size panels containing three cards each. Completing and cataloging the 1980-81 set (which features the classic Larry Bird RC/ Magic Johnson RC/Julius Erving panel) is challenging, to say the least.

In 1983, this basketball card void was filled by the Star Company, a small company which issued three attractive sets of basketball cards, along with a plethora of peripheral sets. Star's 1983-84 premiere offering was issued in four groups, with the first series (cards 1-100) very difficult to obtain, as many of the early team subsets were miscut and destroyed before release. The 1984-85 and 1985-86 sets were more widely and evenly distributed. Even so, players' initial appearances on any of the three Star Company sets are considered Extended Rookie Cards, not regular Rookie Cards, because of the relatively limited distribution. Chief among these is Michael Jordan's 1984-85 Star XRC, the most valuable sports card issued in a 1980s major set.

Then, in 1986, Fleer took over the rights to produce cards for the NBA. Their 1986-87, 1987-88 and 1988-89 sets each contain 132 attractive, colorful cards depicting mostly stars and superstars. They were sold in the familiar wax pack format (12 cards and one sticker per pack). Fleer increased its set size to 168 in 1989-90, and was joined by NBA Hoops, which produced a 300-card first series (containing David Robinson's only Rookie Card) and a 52-card second series. The demand for all three Star Company sets, along with the first four Fleer sets and the premiere NBA Hoops set, skyrocketed during the early part of 1990.

The basketball card market stabilized somewhat in 1990-91, with both Fleer and Hoops stepping up production tremendously. A new major set, SkyBox, also made a splash in the market with its unique "high-tech" cards featuring computer-generated backgrounds. Because of overproduction, none of the three major 1990-91 sets have experienced significant price growth, although the increased competition apparently has led to higher quality and more innovative products.

Another milestone in 1990-91 was the first-time inclusion of current rookies in update sets

(NBA Hoops and SkyBox Series II, Fleer Update). The NBA Hoops and SkyBox issues contain just the 11 lottery picks, while Fleer's 100-card boxed set includes all rookies of any significance. A small company called "Star Pics" (not to be confused with Star Company) tried to fill this niche by printing a 70-card set in late 1990, but because the set was not licensed by the NBA, it is not considered a major set by the majority of collectors. It does, however, contain the first nationally distributed cards of 1990-91 rookies such as Derrick Coleman, Kendall Gill, Dee Brown and others.

In 1991-92, the draft pick set market that Star Pics opened in 1990-91 now has expanded to include several competitors. More significantly, that season brought with it the three established NBA card brands plus Upper Deck, known throughout the hobby for its high quality card stock and photography in other sports. Upper Deck's first basketball set probably captured NBA action better than any previous set. But its value — like all other major 1990-91 and 1991-92 NBA sets — declined because of overproduction.

On the bright side, the historic entrance of NBA players to Olympic competition kept interest in basketball cards going long after the Chicago Bulls won their second straight NBA championship. So for at least one year, the basketball card market — probably the most seasonal of the four major team sports — remained in the spotlight for an extended period of time.

BUSINESS OF SPORTS CARD COLLECTING

Determining Value

Why are some cards more valuable than others? Obviously, the economic law of supply and demand is applicable to sports card collecting, just as it is to any other field where a commodity is bought, sold, or traded in a free, unregulated market.

Supply (the number of cards available on the market) is less than the total number of cards originally produced, since attrition diminishes that original quantity. Each year a percentage of cards is typically thrown away, destroyed, or otherwise lost to collectors. This percentage is much smaller today than it was in the past because more and more people have become increasingly aware of the value of sports cards.

For those who collect only Mint condition cards, the supply of older cards can be quite small indeed. Until recently, collectors were not so conscious of the need to preserve the condition of their cards. For this reason, it is difficult to know exactly how many 1948 Bowman basketball cards are currently available, Mint or otherwise. It is generally accepted that there are many fewer 1948 Bowmans available than 1969-70 Topps or 1987-88 Fleer basketball cards. If demand were equal for each of these sets, the law of supply and demand would increase the price for the least available sets. Demand, however, is never equal for all sets, so price correlations can be complicated.

The total number of cards produced for any given issue can only be approximated, as compared to other collectibles such as coins and stamps. The reason is simple: Card manufacturers are predominantly private companies which are not required to reveal such internal information, while governments are required to release figures regarding currency and postage stamp production.

The demand for any given card is influenced by many factors. These include: (1) the age of the card; (2) the number of cards printed; (3) the player(s) portrayed on the card; (4) the attractiveness and popularity of the set; and perhaps most importantly, (5) the physical condition of the card.

In general, (1) the older the card, (2) the fewer the number of the cards printed, (3) the more famous the player, (4) the more attractive and popular the set, or (5) the better the condition of the card, the higher the value of the card will be. There are exceptions to all but one of these factors: the condition of the card. Given two cards similar in all respects except condition, the one in the best condition will always be valued higher.

While there are certain guidelines that help to establish the value of a card, the numerous exceptions and peculiarities make any simple, direct mathematical formula to determine card values impossible.

One certainty in the sports card hobby is the high demand for Rookie Cards, specifically for RCs of superstar players. A Rookie Card is defined as the first card from a major set of a particular player. Because minor league baseball players have signed contracts and are therefore professionals, baseball Rookie Cards often are issued before or during a player's first major league season. These cards usually are designated "Future Stars," "Major League Prospects," "Rated Rookies," or something similar on the front.

Basketball Rookie Cards, on the other hand, cannot be issued when a player is still in college. They can only be printed once a player has no more collegiate eligibility. Therefore, until 1990-91, basketball Rookie Cards were generally released in the year after the player's first (or even second or third, for late bloomers) professional season. And until recently, the fronts of basketball Rookie Cards did not have any special notation. But in the 1990-91 NBA Hoops set, rookies of the previous year have "Rookie Star" designations on the fronts. Also in 1990-91, the three major NBA card manufacturers (Fleer, NBA Hoops and SkyBox) each issued RCs for current rookies. The 1990-91 and 1991-92 NBA Hoops and SkyBox Series II sets contain only the 11 lottery picks, while the Fleer Update sets from both seasons depict all 1990-91 rookies of any significance. Upper Deck's 1991-92 set was the first to include June's draftees in its first series set, which immediately set it apart from the competition.

Regional Variation

Two types of price variations exist among the sections of the country where a card is bought or sold. The first is the general price variation on all cards bought and sold in one geographical area as compared to another. Card prices are slightly higher on the East and West coasts, and slightly lower in the middle of the country. Although prices may vary from the East to the West, or from the Southwest to the Midwest, the prices listed in this guide are nonetheless presented as a consensus of all sections of this large and diverse country.

Still, prices for a particular player's cards are usually higher in his home team's area than in other regions. This represents the second type of regional price variation in which local players are favored over those from distant areas. For example, a John Havlicek card is valued higher in Boston than in Los Angeles because Havlicek played in Boston; therefore, the demand there for Havlicek cards is higher than it is in Los Angeles. On the other hand, a Jerry West card is priced higher in Los Angeles where he played and is still the Lakers general manager, than in Boston, for similar reasons. Frequently, even common player cards command such a premium from hometown collectors.

Set Prices

A somewhat paradoxical situation exists in the price of a complete set versus the combined cost of the individual cards in the set. In nearly every case, the sum of the prices for the individual cards is higher than the cost for the complete set. This is especially prevalent in the cards of the past few years. The reasons for this apparent anomaly stem from the habits of collectors, and from the carrying costs to dealers. Today, each card in a set is normally produced in the same quantity as all others in its set.

However, many collectors pick up only stars, superstars, and particular teams. As a result, the dealer is left with a shortage of certain player cards and an abundance of others. He therefore incurs an expense in simply "carrying" these less desirable cards in stock. On the other hand, if he sells a complete set, he gets rid of large numbers of cards at one time. For this reason, he is generally willing to receive less money for a complete set. By doing this, he recovers all of his costs and also makes a profit.

The disparity between the price of the complete set and that for the sum of the individual cards has also been influenced by the fact that some major manufacturers are now pre-collating card sets. To date, the only pre-collated basketball set produced was the 1991-92 Upper Deck factory set.

Set prices also do not include rare card varieties, unless specifically stated. Of course, the prices for sets do include one example of each type for the given set, but this is the least expensive variety.

Scarce Series

Only a select few basketball sets contain scarce series: 1948 Bowman, 1970-71 and 1972-73 Topps and 1983-84 Star Company. The 1948 Bowman set was printed on two 36-card sheets, the second of which was issued in significantly lower quantities. The two Topps scarce series are only marginally tougher than the set as a whole. The Star Company scarcity actually is for particular team sets (the 76ers, Lakers, Celtics, Bucks and Mavericks) which, to different extents, were less widely distributed.

Grading Your Cards

Each hobby has its own grading terminology — stamps, coins, comic books, beer cans, right down the line. Collectors of sports cards are no exception. The one invariable criterion for determining the value of a card is its condition. The better the condition of the card, the more valuable it is. However, condition grading is very subjective. Individual card dealers and collectors differ in the strictness of their grading, but the stated condition of a card should be determined without regard to whether it is being bought or sold.

The physical defects that lower the condition of a card are usually quite apparent, but each individual places his own estimation (negative value, in this case) on these defects. We present the condition guide for use in determining values listed in this Price Guide in the hopes that excess subjectivity can be minimized.

The defects listed in the condition guide below are those either created at the time of printing, such as uneven borders, or those defects that occur to a card under normal handling — corner sharpness, gloss, edge wear, light creases — and finally, environmental conditions, such as browning. Other defects to cards are caused by human carelessness, and in all cases should be noted separately and in addition to the condition grade. Among the more common alterations are tape, tape stains, heavy creases, rubber band marks, water damage, smoke damage, trimming, paste, tears, writing, pin or tack holes, any back damage, and missing parts (tabs, tops, coupons, backgrounds).

Centering

It is important to define in words and pictures what is meant by frequently used hobby terms relating to grading cards. The adjacent pictures portray various stages of centering. Centering can range from well-centered to slightly off-center to off-center to badly off-center to miscut.

Slightly Off-Center (60/40): A slightly off-center card is one which is found to have one border bigger than the opposite border. This degree once was only offensive to purists, but now some hobbyists try to avoid cards that are anything other than perfectly centered.

Off-Center (70/30): An off-center card has one border which is noticeably more than twice as wide as the opposite border.

Badly Off-Center (80/20 or worse): A badly off-center card has virtually no border on one side of the card.

Miscut: A miscut card actually shows part of the adjacent card in its larger border and consequently a corresponding amount of its card is cut off.

Corner Wear

Degrees of corner wear generate several common terms used to facilitate accurate grading. The wear on card corners can be expressed as fuzzy corners, corner wear or slightly rounded corners, rounded corners, or badly rounded corners.

Fuzzy Corners: Fuzzy corners still come to a right angle (to a point) but the point has begun to fray slightly.

Corner Wear or Slightly Rounded Corners: The slight fraying of corners has increased to where there is no longer a point to the corner. Nevertheless, the corner is still reasonably sharp. There may be evidence of some slight loss of color in the corner also.

Rounded Corners: The corner is no longer sharp but is not badly rounded.

Badly Rounded Corners: The corner is rounded to an objectionable degree. Excessive wear and rough handling are evident.

Creases

A third common defect is the crease. The degree of creasing in a card is very difficult to show in a drawing or picture. On giving the specific condition of an expensive card for sale, the seller should note any creases additionally. Creases can be categorized as to severity according to the following scale.

Light Crease: A light crease is a crease which is barely noticeable on close inspection. In fact when cards are in plastic sheets or holders, a light crease may not be seen (until the card is taken out of the holder). A light crease on the front is much more serious than a light crease on the card back only.

Medium Crease: A medium crease is noticeable when held and studied at arm's length by the naked eye, but does not overly detract from the appearance of the card. It is an obvious crease, but not one that breaks the picture surface of the card.

Heavy Crease: A heavy crease is one which has torn or broken through the card's picture surface, e.g., puts a tear in the photo surface.

CENTERING

WELL-CENTERED

SLIGHTLY OFF-CENTERED

OFF-CENTERED

BADLY OFF-CENTERED

MISCUT

Alterations

Deceptive Trimming: This occurs when someone alters the card in order (1) to shave off edge wear, (2) to improve the sharpness of the corners, or (3) to improve centering — obviously their objective is to falsely increase the perceived value of the card to an unsuspecting buyer. The shrinkage is usually only evident if the trimmed card is compared to an adjacent full-sized card or if the trimmed card is itself measured.

Obvious Trimming: Obvious trimming is noticeable and unfortunate. It is usually performed by non-collectors who give no thought to the present or future value of their cards.

Deceptively Retouched Borders: This occurs when the borders (especially on those cards with dark borders) are touched up on the edges and corners with magic marker of appropriate color in order to make the card appear to be Mint.

Categorization of Defects

A "Micro Defect" would be fuzzy corners, slight off-centering, printers' lines, printers' spots, slightly out of focus, or slight loss of original gloss. A NrMt card may have one micro defect. An ExMt card may have two or more micro defects.

A "Minor Defect" would be corner wear or slight rounding, off-centering, light crease on back, wax or gum stains on reverse, loss of original gloss, writing or tape marks on back, or rubber band marks. An Excellent card may have minor defects.

A "Major Defect" would be rounded corner(s), badly off-centering, crease(s), deceptive trimming, deceptively retouched borders, pin hole, staple hole, incidental writing or tape marks on front, severe warping, water stains, medium crease(s), or sun fading. A Vg card may have one major defect. A Good card may have two or more major defects.

A "Catastrophic Defect" is the worst kind of defect and would include such defects as badly rounded corner(s), miscutting, heavy crease(s), obvious trimming, punch hole, tack hole, tear(s), corner missing or clipped, destructive writing on front. A Fair card may have one catastrophic defect. A Poor card has two or more catastrophic defects.

Condition Guide

Mint (Mt) - A card with no defects. The card has sharp corners, even borders, original gloss or shine on the surface, sharp focus of the picture, smooth edges, no signs of wear, and white borders. A Mint card does NOT have printers' lines or other printing defects, or other serious quality control problems that should have been discovered by the card company before distribution. Note also that there is no allowance made for the age of the card.

Near Mint (NrMt) - A card with a micro defect. Any of the following would be sufficient to lower the grade of a card from Mint to the Near Mint category: layering at some of the corners (fuzzy corners), a very small amount of the original gloss lost, very minor wear on the edges, slightly off-center borders, slight wear visible only on close inspection, slight off-whiteness of the borders.

Excellent to Mint (ExMt) - A card with micro defects, but no minor defects. Two or three of the following would be sufficient to lower the grade of a card from Mint to the ExMt category: layering at some of the corners (fuzzy corners), a very small amount of the original gloss lost, minor wear on the edges, slightly off-center borders, slight wear visible only on close inspection, slight off-whiteness of the borders.

Excellent (Ex) - A card with minor defects. Any of the following would be sufficient to lower the grade of a card from Mint to the Excellent category: slight rounding at some of the corners, a small amount of the original gloss lost, minor wear on the edges, off-center borders, wear visible only on close inspection, off-whiteness of the borders.

Very Good (Vg) - A card that has been handled but not abused. Some rounding at all corners, slight layering or scuffing at one or two corners, slight notching on edges, gloss lost from the surface but not scuffed, borders might be somewhat uneven but some white is visible on all borders, noticeable yellowing or browning of borders, light crease(s), pictures may be slightly off focus.

Good (G) - A well-handled card, rounding and some layering at the corners, scuffing at the corners and minor scuffing on the face, borders noticeably uneven and browning, loss of gloss on the face, medium crease(s), notching on the edges.

Fair (F) - Round and layering corners, brown and dirty borders, frayed edges, noticeable scuffing on the face, white not visible on one or more borders, medium to heavy creases, cloudy focus.

Poor (P) - An abused card: The lowest grade

of card, frequently some major physical alteration has been performed on the card, collectible only as a filler until a better-condition replacement can be obtained.

Categories between these major condition grades are frequently used, such as Very Good to Excellent (VgEx), Fair to Good (F-G), etc. Such grades indicate a card with all qualities at least in the lower of the two categories, but with several qualities in the higher of the two categories. In the case of ExMt, it essentially refers to a card which is halfway between Excellent and Mint.

Unopened packs, boxes and factory-collated sets are considered Mint in their unknown (and presumed perfect) state. However, once opened or broken out, each of these cards is graded (and valued) in its own right by taking into account any quality control defects (such as off-centering, printers' lines, machine creases, or gum stains) present in spite of the fact that the card has never been handled.

Cards before 1980 that are priced in the Price Guide in top condition of NrMt are obviously worth an additional premium when offered in strict Mint condition. This additional premium increases relative to the age and scarcity of the card. For example, Mint cards from the late 1970s may bring only a 10 percent premium for Mint (above NrMt), whereas high demand (or condition rarity) cards from early vintage sets can be sold for as much as double (and occasionally even more) the NrMt price when offered in strict Mint condition.

Selling Your Cards

Just about every collector sells cards or will sell cards eventually. Someday you may be interested in selling your duplicates or maybe even your whole collection. You may sell to other collectors, friends, or dealers. You may even sell cards you purchased from a certain dealer back to that same dealer. In any event, it helps to know some of the mechanics of the typical transaction between buyer and seller.

Dealers will buy cards in order to resell them to other collectors who are interested in the cards. Dealers will always pay a higher percentage for items which (in their opinion) can be resold quickly, and a much lower percentage for those items which are perceived as having low demand and hence are slow moving. In either case, dealers must buy at a price that allows for the expense of doing business and a margin for profit.

If you have cards for sale, the best advice we can give is that you get several offers for your cards — either from card shops or at a card show — and take the best offer, all things considered. Note, the "best" offer may not be the one for the highest amount. And remember, if a dealer really wants your cards, he won't let you get away without making his best competitive offer. Another alternative is to place your cards in an auction as one or several lots.

Many people think nothing of going into a department store and paying $15 for an item of clothing the store paid $5. But, if you were selling your $15 card to a dealer and he offered you only $5 for it, you might think his mark-up unreasonable. To complete the analogy: most department stores (and card dealers) that consistently pay $10 for $15 items eventually go out of business. An exception is when the dealer has a willing buyer for the item(s) you are attempting to sell lined up, or if the cards are so Hot that it's likely he'll only have to hold the cards for a short period of time.

In those cases, an offer of up to 75 percent of book value will still allow the dealer to make a reasonable profit considering the short time he will need to hold the merchandise. In general, however, most cards and collections will bring offers in the range of 25 to 50 percent of retail price. Also consider that most material from the past five to 10 years is very plentiful. If that's what you're selling, expect even less or no offer at all unless you have Hot cards that the dealer can move easily.

INTERESTING NOTES

The numerically first card of an issue is the single card most likely to obtain excessive wear. Consequently, you will typically find the price on the No. 1 card (in NrMt or Mint condition) somewhat higher than might otherwise be the case. Similarly, but to a lesser extent (because normally the less important, reverse side of the card is the one exposed), the numerically last card in an issue is also prone to abnormal wear. This extra wear and tear occurs because the first and last cards are exposed to the elements (human element included) more than any other cards. They are generally end cards in any brick formations, rubber bandings, stackings on wet surfaces, and like activities.

Sports cards have no intrinsic value. The

value of a card, like the value of other collectibles, can only be determined by you and your enjoyment in viewing and possessing these cardboard swatches.

Remember, the buyer ultimately determines the price of each baseball card. You are the determining price factor because you have the ability to say "No" to the price of any card by not exchanging your hard-earned money for a given card. When the cost of a trading card exceeds the enjoyment you will receive from it, your answer should be "No." We assess and report the prices. You set them!

We are always interested in receiving the price input of collectors and dealers from around the country. We happily credit major contributors. We welcome your opinions, since your contributions assist us in ensuring a better guide each year. If you would like to join our survey list for the next editions of this book and others authored by Dr. Beckett, please send your name and address to Dr. James Beckett, 4887 Alpha Road, Suite 200, Dallas, Texas 75244.

ADVERTISING

Within this guide you will find advertisements for sports memorabilia material, mail order, and retail sports collectibles establishments. All advertisements were accepted in good faith based on the reputation of the advertiser; however, neither the author, the publisher, the distributors, nor the other advertisers in the Price Guide accept any responsibility for any particular advertiser not complying with the terms of his or her ad.

Readers should also be aware that prices in advertisements are subject to change over the annual period before a new edition of this volume is issued each fall. When replying to an advertisement late in the sporting year following the fall release of this volume, the reader should take this into account, and contact the dealer by phone or in writing for up-to-date price quotes and availability. Should you come into contact with any of the advertisers in this guide as a result of their advertisement herein, please mention to them this source as your contact.

RECOMMENDED READING

With the increase in popularity of the hobby in recent years, there has been a corresponding increase in available literature. Below is a list of the books and periodicals that receive our highest recommendation and that we hope will further your knowledge and enjoyment of our great hobby.

The Sport Americana Baseball Card Price Guide by Dr. James Beckett (Fourteenth Edition, $15.95, released 1992, published by Edgewater Book Company) — the most informative, up-to-date, and reliable Price Guide/checklist on its subject matter ever compiled. No serious hobbyist should be without it.

The Official Price Guide to Baseball Cards by Dr. James Beckett (Twelfth Edition, $5.99, released 1992, published by The House of Collectibles) — this work is an abridgment of *The Sport Americana Baseball Card Price Guide* immediately above, published in a convenient and economical pocket-size format and provides Dr. Beckett's pricing of the major baseball sets since 1948.

The Sport Americana Football Card Price Guide by Dr. James Beckett (Ninth Edition, $14.95, released 1992, published by Edgewater Book Company) — the most comprehensive price guide/checklist ever issued on football cards. No serious football card hobbyist should be without it.

The Official Price Guide to Football Cards by Dr. James Beckett (Twelfth Edition, $5.99, released 1992, published by The House of Collectibles) — an abridgement of *The Sport Americana Football Card Price Guide* listed above in a convenient and economical pocket-size format providing Dr. Beckett's pricing of the major football sets since 1948.

The Sport Americana Hockey Card Price Guide by Dr. James Beckett (Second Edition, $12.95, released 1992, published by Edgewater Book Company) — the most informative, up-to-date, and reliable Price Guide/checklist on its subject matter ever compiled. The introductory section is presented in both English and French. No serious hobbyist should be without it.

The Official Price Guide to Hockey Cards by Dr. James Beckett (Second Edition, $5.99, released 1992, published by The House of Collectibles) — this work is an abridgment of

The Sport Americana Hockey Card Price Guide immediately above, published in a convenient and economical pocket-size format and provides Dr. Beckett's pricing of the major hockey sets since 1951. The introductory section and the set descriptions are presented in both English and French.

The Official Price Guide to Basketball Cards by Dr. James Beckett (Second Edition, $5.99, released 1992, published by The House of Collectibles) — this book is essentially an abridgement of the *Sports Americana Basketball Card Price Guide and Alphabetical Checklist*, published in a convenient and economical pocket-size format that provides Dr. Beckett's pricing of the major basketball sets since 1948.

The Sport Americana Price Guide to Baseball Collectibles by Dr. James Beckett (Second Edition, $12.95, released 1988, published by Edgewater Book Company) — the complete guide and checklist with up-to-date values for box cards, coins, decals, R-cards, bread labels, exhibits, discs, lids, fabric, pins, Canadian cards, stamps, stickers, and miscellaneous Topps issues.

The Sport Americana Baseball Card Alphabetical Checklist by Dr. James Beckett (Fifth Edition, $14.95, released 1992, published by Edgewater Book Company) — an alphabetical listing, by the last name of the player portrayed on the card. Virtually all major and minor league baseball cards produced through the 1991 major sets are listed.

The Sport Americana Price Guide to the Non-Sports Cards 1930-1960 by Christopher Benjamin and Dennis W. Eckes ($14.95, released 1991, published by Edgewater Book Company) — the definitive guide to virtually all popular non-sports American tobacco and bubblegum cards issued between 1930 and 1960. In addition to cards, illustrations and prices for wrappers are also included.

The Sport Americana Price Guide to the Non-Sports Cards by Christopher Benjamin (Fourth Edition, $14.95, released 1992, published by Edgewater Book Company) — the definitive guide to all popular non-sports American cards. In addition to cards, illustrations and prices for wrappers are also included. This volume covers non-sports cards from 1961 to 1992.

The Sport Americana Baseball Address List by Jack Smalling and Dennis W. Eckes (Sixth Edition, $12.95, released 1990, published by Edgewater Book Company) — the definitive guide for autograph hunters, giving addresses and deceased information for virtually all major league baseball players, managers, and even umpires, past and present.

The Sport Americana Team Baseball Card Checklist by Jeff Fritsch (Sixth Edition, $12.95, released 1992, published by Edgewater Book Company) — includes all Topps, Bowman, Fleer, Play Ball, Goudey, Upper Deck and Donruss cards, with the players portrayed on the cards listed by their team. The book is invaluable to the collector who specializes in an individual team because it is the most complete baseball card team checklist available.

The Sport Americana Team Football and Basketball Card Checklist by Jane Fritsch, Jeff Fritsch, and Dennis W. Eckes (First Edition, $10.95, released 1990, published by Edgewater Book Company) — The book is invaluable to the collector who specializes in an individual team because it is the most complete football and basketball card team checklist available.

Beckett Baseball Card Monthly, published and edited by Dr. James Beckett — contains the most extensive and accepted monthly Price Guide, collectible glossy superstar covers, colorful feature articles, "who's Hot and who's not" section, Convention Calendar, tips for beginners, "Readers Write" letters to and responses from the editor, information on errors and varieties, autograph collecting tips, and profiles of the sport's Hottest stars. Published every month, BBCM is the hobby's largest paid circulation periodical.

Beckett Football Card Monthly, Beckett Basketball Monthly, Beckett Hockey Monthly, and *Beckett Focus on Future Stars* were built on the success of BBCM. These other publications contain many of the same features as BBCM, and contain the most relied upon Price Guides to their respective segments of the sports card hobby.

PRICES IN THIS GUIDE

Prices found in this guide reflect current retail rates just prior to the printing of this book. They do not reflect the FOR SALE prices of the author, the publisher, the distributors, the advertisers, or any card dealers associated with this guide. No one is obligated in any way to buy, sell, or trade his or her cards based on these prices. The price listings were compiled by the author from actual buy/sell transactions at sports conventions, buy/sell advertisements in the hobby papers, for sale prices from dealer catalogs and price lists, and discussions with leading hobbyists in the U.S. and Canada. All prices are in U.S. dollars.

ERRATA

There are thousands of names, more than 100,000 prices, and untold other words in this book. There are going to be a few typographical errors, a few misspellings, and possibly, a number or three out of place. If you catch a blooper, drop me a note directly and we will fix it in next year's edition.

1992 ACC Basketball Tournament Champions

This 40-card boxed set was offered by the Atlantic Coast Conference in conjunction with Spectator Sports Services. It features 36 championship teams from 1954 to 1989, including 19 NCAA Final Four teams and three national championship teams. Only 10,000 of this first edition set were produced, with the set number indicated on a sequentially numbered gold card of authenticity. Also each set includes a randomly inserted bonus card, which is a duplicate of one of the championship team cards but portrays the official ACC seal in gold foil. The standard-size (2 1/2" by 3 1/2") cards display on the front reproductions of the original black and white or color team photos as taken during the respective ACC championship seasons. The information presented on the backs includes a synopsis of the championship game, the box score, a listing of players and coaches appearing in the team photo, and the winner of the MVP award of the ACC Tournament. The cards are numbered on the back.

	MINT	EXC	G-VG
COMPLETE SET (40)	12.50	6.25	1.25
COMMON PLAYER (1-36)	.35	.17	.03
☐ 1 '54 NC State Wolfpack	.35	.17	.03
☐ 2 '55 NC State Wolfpack	.35	.17	.03
☐ 3 '56 NC State Wolfpack	.35	.17	.03
☐ 4 '57 UNC Tar Heels	.35	.17	.03
☐ 5 '58 Maryland Terrapins	.35	.17	.03
☐ 6 '59 NC State Wolfpack	.35	.17	.03
☐ 7 '60 Duke Blue Devils	.35	.17	.03
☐ 8 '61 Wake Forest Demon Deacons	.35	.17	.03
☐ 9 '62 Wake Forest Demon Deacons	.35	.17	.03
☐ 10 '63 Duke Blue Devils	.35	.17	.03
☐ 11 '64 Duke Blue Devils	.35	.17	.03
☐ 12 '65 NC State Wolfpack	.35	.17	.03
☐ 13 '66 Duke Blue Devils	.35	.17	.03
☐ 14 '67 UNC Tar Heels	.35	.17	.03
☐ 15 '68 UNC Tar Heels	.35	.17	.03
☐ 16 '69 UNC Tar Heels	.35	.17	.03
☐ 17 '70 NC State Wolfpack	.35	.17	.03
☐ 18 '71 SC Gamecocks	.35	.17	.03
☐ 19 '72 UNC Tar Heels	.35	.17	.03
☐ 20 '73 NC State Wolfpack	.35	.17	.03
☐ 21 '74 NC State Wolfpack	.50	.25	.05
☐ 22 '75 UNC Tar Heels	.35	.17	.03
☐ 23 '76 Virginia Cavaliers	.35	.17	.03
☐ 24 '77 UNC Tar Heels	.35	.17	.03
☐ 25 '78 Duke Blue Devils	.35	.17	.03
☐ 26 '79 UNC Tar Heels	.35	.17	.03
☐ 27 '80 Duke Blue Devils	.35	.17	.03
☐ 28 '81 UNC Tar Heels	.35	.17	.03
☐ 29 '82 UNC Tar Heels	.50	.25	.05
☐ 30 '83 NC State Wolfpack	.50	.25	.05
☐ 31 '84 Maryland Terrapins	.50	.25	.05
☐ 32 '85 Georgia Tech Yellow Jackets	.35	.17	.03
☐ 33 '86 Duke Blue Devils	.35	.17	.03
☐ 34 '87 NC State Wolfpack	.35	.17	.03
☐ 35 '88 Duke Blue Devils	.35	.17	.03
☐ 36 '89 UNC Tar Heels	.35	.17	.03
☐ xx '91 FSU Joins ACC	.35	.17	.03
☐ xx ACC Seal Original	.35	.17	.03
☐ xx ACC Seal Revised (includes Florida State)	.35	.17	.03
☐ xx Certificate of Authenticity	.35	.17	.03

1991 Arena Holograms 12th National Promos *

These standard-size (2 1/2" by 3 1/2") cards have on their fronts a 3-D silver-colored emblem on a white background with orange borders. Though the back of each card salutes a different superstar, the players themselves are not pictured; instead, one finds pictures of a football; hockey stick and puck; basketball; and baseball in glove respectively. The cards are numbered on the front.

	MINT	EXC	G-VG
COMPLETE SET (4)	30.00	15.00	3.00
COMMON PLAYER (1-4)	10.00	5.00	1.00
☐ 1 Joe Montana	10.00	5.00	1.00
☐ 2 Wayne Gretzky	10.00	5.00	1.00
☐ 3 Michael Jordan	12.00	6.00	1.20
☐ 4 Nolan Ryan	12.00	6.00	1.20

1955 Ashland/Aetna Oil

The 1955 Ashland/Aetna Oil Basketball set contains 96 black and white, unnumbered cards each measuring 2 5/8" by 3 3/4". There are two different backs for each card front, one with an Ashland Oil ad, the other with an Aetna Oil ad. Aetna cards are considered to be worth an additional premium of 25 percent above the prices listed below. The backs contain a player's vital statistics, his home town, and his graduation class. These thin-stocked cards are relatively difficult to obtain and have been numbered in the checklist below, by team and alphabetically within each team. The set contains 12 players each from eight colleges: Eastern Kentucky 1-12, Kentucky 13-24, Louisville 25-36, Marshall 37-48, Morehead 49-60, Murray 61-72, Western Kentucky 73-84, and West Virginia 85-96. The cards of smaller school players within this set might well be in shorter supply than the cards of the larger schools. However, the prices below reflect the smaller demand for the cards of players from the smaller schools. The key card in the set is the first card of Adolph Rupp, Hall of Famer and legendary coach of the Kentucky Wildcats. The catalog designation for this set is U018.

	NRMT	VG-E	GOOD
COMPLETE SET (96)	4000.00	2000.00	500.00
COMMON PLAYER (1-96)	40.00	20.00	4.00
☐ 1 Jack Adams	40.00	20.00	4.00
☐ 2 William Baxter	40.00	20.00	4.00
☐ 3 Jeffrey Brock	40.00	20.00	4.00
☐ 4 Paul Collins	40.00	20.00	4.00
☐ 5 Richard Culbertson	40.00	20.00	4.00
☐ 6 James Floyd	40.00	20.00	4.00
☐ 7 Harold Fraler	40.00	20.00	4.00
☐ 8 George Francis Jr.	40.00	20.00	4.00
☐ 9 Paul McBrayer CO	40.00	20.00	4.00
☐ 10 James Mitchell	40.00	20.00	4.00
☐ 11 Ronald Pellegrinon	40.00	20.00	4.00
☐ 12 Guy Strong	40.00	20.00	4.00
☐ 13 Earl Adkins	40.00	20.00	4.00
☐ 14 William Bibb	40.00	20.00	4.00
☐ 15 Jerry Bird	40.00	20.00	4.00
☐ 16 John Brewer	40.00	20.00	4.00
☐ 17 Robert Burrow	40.00	20.00	4.00
☐ 18 Gerry Calvert	40.00	20.00	4.00
☐ 19 William Evans	40.00	20.00	4.00
☐ 20 Phillip Grawemeyer	40.00	20.00	4.00
☐ 21 Ray Mills	40.00	20.00	4.00
☐ 22 Linville Puckett	40.00	20.00	4.00
☐ 23 Gayle Rose	60.00	30.00	6.00
☐ 24 Adolph Rupp CO	350.00	175.00	35.00
☐ 25 William Darrah	40.00	20.00	4.00
☐ 26 Vladimir Gastevich	40.00	20.00	4.00
☐ 27 Allan Glaza	40.00	20.00	4.00
☐ 28 Herbert Harrah	40.00	20.00	4.00
☐ 29 Bernard Hickman CO	80.00	40.00	8.00
☐ 30 Richard Keffer	40.00	20.00	4.00
☐ 31 Gerald Moreman	40.00	20.00	4.00
☐ 32 James Morgan	40.00	20.00	4.00
☐ 33 John Prudhoe	40.00	20.00	4.00
☐ 34 Phillip Rollins	40.00	20.00	4.00
☐ 35 Roscoe Shackelford	40.00	20.00	4.00
☐ 36 Charles Tyra	60.00	30.00	6.00
☐ 37 Robert Ashley	40.00	20.00	4.00
☐ 38 Lewis Burns	40.00	20.00	4.00
☐ 39 Francis Crum	40.00	20.00	4.00
☐ 40 Raymond Frazier	40.00	20.00	4.00
☐ 41 Cam Henderson CO	60.00	30.00	6.00
☐ 42 Joseph Hunnicutt	40.00	20.00	4.00
☐ 43 Clarence Parkins	40.00	20.00	4.00
☐ 44 Jerry Pierson	40.00	20.00	4.00
☐ 45 David Robinson	40.00	20.00	4.00
☐ 46 Paul Underwood	40.00	20.00	4.00
☐ 47 Cebert Price	40.00	20.00	4.00
☐ 48 Charles Slack	40.00	20.00	4.00
☐ 49 David Breeze	40.00	20.00	4.00
☐ 50 Leonard Carpenter	40.00	20.00	4.00
☐ 51 Omar Fannin	40.00	20.00	4.00
☐ 52 Donnie Gaunce	40.00	20.00	4.00
☐ 53 Steve Hamilton	40.00	20.00	4.00
☐ 54 Bobby Laughlin CO	40.00	20.00	4.00
☐ 55 Jesse Mayabb	40.00	20.00	4.00
☐ 56 Jerry Riddle	40.00	20.00	4.00
☐ 57 Howard Shumate	40.00	20.00	4.00
☐ 58 Dan Swartz	40.00	20.00	4.00
☐ 59 Harlan Tolle	40.00	20.00	4.00
☐ 60 Donald Whitehouse	40.00	20.00	4.00
☐ 61 Rex Alexander CO	40.00	20.00	4.00
☐ 62 Jorgen Anderson	40.00	20.00	4.00
☐ 63 Jack Clutter	40.00	20.00	4.00
☐ 64 Howard Crittenden	40.00	20.00	4.00
☐ 65 James Gainey	40.00	20.00	4.00
☐ 66 Richard Kinder	40.00	20.00	4.00
☐ 67 Theo. Koenigsmark	40.00	20.00	4.00
☐ 68 Joseph Mikez	40.00	20.00	4.00
☐ 69 John Powless	60.00	30.00	6.00
☐ 70 Dolph Regelsky	60.00	30.00	6.00
☐ 71 Reinhard Tauck	40.00	20.00	4.00
☐ 72 Francis Watrous	40.00	20.00	4.00
☐ 73 Forrest Able	40.00	20.00	4.00
☐ 74 Tom Benbrook	40.00	20.00	4.00
☐ 75 Ronald Clark	40.00	20.00	4.00
☐ 76 Lynn Cole	40.00	20.00	4.00
☐ 77 Robert Daniels	40.00	20.00	4.00
☐ 78 Ed Diddle CO	200.00	100.00	20.00
☐ 79 Victor Harned	40.00	20.00	4.00
☐ 80 Dencil Miller	40.00	20.00	4.00
☐ 81 Ferrel Miller	40.00	20.00	4.00
☐ 82 George Orr	40.00	20.00	4.00
☐ 83 Jerry Weber	40.00	20.00	4.00
☐ 84 Jerry Whitsell	40.00	20.00	4.00
☐ 85 William Bergines	40.00	20.00	4.00
☐ 86 James Brennan	40.00	20.00	4.00
☐ 87 Marc Constantine	40.00	20.00	4.00
☐ 88 Michael Holt	40.00	20.00	4.00
☐ 89 Hot Rod Hundley	250.00	125.00	25.00
☐ 90 Clayce Kishbaugh	40.00	20.00	4.00
☐ 91 Ronald LaNeve	40.00	20.00	4.00
☐ 92 Gary Mullins	40.00	20.00	4.00
☐ 93 Fred Schaus CO	80.00	40.00	8.00
☐ 94 Frank Spadafore	40.00	20.00	4.00
☐ 95 Peter White	40.00	20.00	4.00
☐ 96 Paul Witting	40.00	20.00	4.00

1948 Bowman

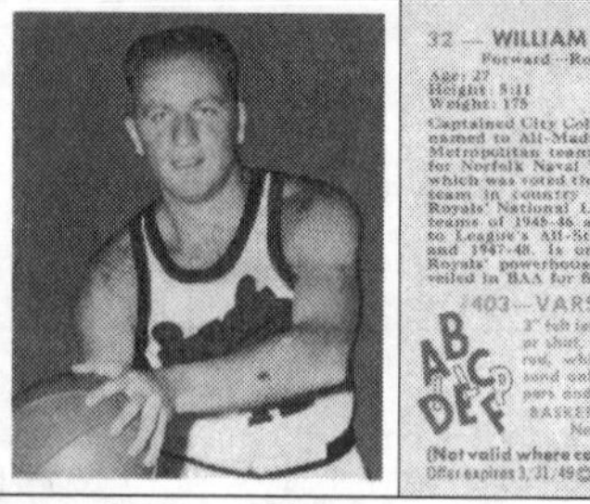

The 1948 Bowman basketball card set of 72 cards was Bowman's only basketball issue. It was also the only major basketball issue until 1958. Cards in the set measure 2 1/16" by 2 1/2". The set is in color and features both player cards and diagram cards. The player cards in the second series are sometimes found without the red or blue printing on the card front, leaving only a gray background. These gray-front cards are more difficult to find, as they are printing errors where the printer apparently ran out of red or blue ink that was supposed to print on the player's uniform. The key rookie cards in this set are Joe Fulks, William "Red" Holzman, George Mikan, Jim Pollard, and Max Zaslofsky.

	NRMT	VG-E	GOOD
COMPLETE SET (72)	6000.00	2750.00	750.00
COMMON PLAYER (1-36)	36.00	18.00	3.60
COMMON PLAYER (37-72)	60.00	30.00	6.00
☐ 1 Ernie Calverley	100.00	30.00	6.00
Providence Steamrollers			
☐ 2 Ralph Hamilton	36.00	18.00	3.60
Ft. Wayne Pistons			
☐ 3 Gale Bishop	36.00	18.00	3.60
Philadelphia Warriors			
☐ 4 Fred Lewis CO	42.00	21.00	4.20
Indianapolis Jets			
☐ 5 Basketball Play	25.00	12.50	2.50
Single cut off post			
☐ 6 Bob Ferrick	45.00	22.50	4.50
Washington Capitols			
☐ 7 John Logan	36.00	18.00	3.60
St. Louis Bombers			
☐ 8 Mel Riebe	36.00	18.00	3.60
Boston Celtics			
☐ 9 Andy Phillip	80.00	40.00	8.00
Chicago Stags			
☐ 10 Bob Davies	80.00	40.00	8.00
Rochester Royals			
☐ 11 Basketball Play	25.00	12.50	2.50
Single cut with return pass to post			
☐ 12 Kenny Sailors	36.00	18.00	3.60
Providence Steamrollers			
☐ 13 Paul Armstrong	36.00	18.00	3.60
Ft. Wayne Pistons			
☐ 14 Howard Dallmar	45.00	22.50	4.50
Philadelphia Warriors			
☐ 15 Bruce Hale	45.00	22.50	4.50
Indianapolis Jets			
☐ 16 Sid Hertzberg	36.00	18.00	3.60
Washington Capitols			
☐ 17 Basketball Play	25.00	12.50	2.50
Single cut			
☐ 18 Red Rocha	36.00	18.00	3.60
St. Louis Bombers			
☐ 19 Eddie Ehlers	36.00	18.00	3.60
Boston Celtics			
☐ 20 Ellis(Gene) Vance	36.00	18.00	3.60

		NRMT	VG-E	GOOD
	Chicago Stags			
☐ 21	Andrew(Fuzzy) Levane	45.00	22.50	4.50
	Rochester Royals			
☐ 22	Earl Shannon	36.00	18.00	3.60
	Providence Steamrollers			
☐ 23	Basketball Play	25.00	12.50	2.50
	Double cut off post			
☐ 24	Leo(Crystal) Klier	36.00	18.00	3.60
	Ft. Wayne Pistons			
☐ 25	George Senesky	36.00	18.00	3.60
	Philadelphia Warriors			
☐ 26	Price Brookfield	36.00	18.00	3.60
	Indianapolis Jets			
☐ 27	John Norlander	36.00	18.00	3.60
	Washington Capitols			
☐ 28	Don Putman	36.00	18.00	3.60
	St. Louis Bombers			
☐ 29	Basketball Play	25.00	12.50	2.50
	Double post			
☐ 30	Jack Garfinkel	36.00	18.00	3.60
	Boston Celtics			
☐ 31	Chuck Gilmur	36.00	18.00	3.60
	Chicago Stags			
☐ 32	William Holzman	250.00	125.00	25.00
	Rochester Royals			
☐ 33	Jack Smiley	36.00	18.00	3.60
	Ft. Wayne Pistons			
☐ 34	Joe Fulks	225.00	110.00	22.00
	Philadelphia Warriors			
☐ 35	Basketball Play	25.00	12.50	2.50
	Screen play			
☐ 36	Hal Tidrick	36.00	18.00	3.60
	Indianapolis Jets			
☐ 37	Don(Swede) Carlson	60.00	30.00	6.00
	Minneapolis Lakers			
☐ 38	Buddy Jeanette CO	70.00	35.00	7.00
	Baltimore Bullets			
☐ 39	Ray Kuka	60.00	30.00	6.00
	New York Knicks			
☐ 40	Stan Miasek	60.00	30.00	6.00
	Chicago Stags			
☐ 41	Basketball Play	36.00	18.00	3.60
	Double screen			
☐ 42	George Nostrand	60.00	30.00	6.00
	Providence Steamrollers			
☐ 43	Chuck Halbert	70.00	35.00	7.00
	Boston Celtics			
☐ 44	Arnie Johnson	60.00	30.00	6.00
	Rochester Royals			
☐ 45	Bob Doll	60.00	30.00	6.00
	St. Louis Bombers			
☐ 46	Horace McKinney	85.00	42.50	8.50
	Washington Capitols			
☐ 47	Basketball Play	36.00	18.00	3.60
	Out of bounds			
☐ 48	Ed Sadowski	60.00	30.00	6.00
	Philadelphia Warriors			
☐ 49	Bob Kinney	60.00	30.00	6.00
	Ft. Wayne Pistons			
☐ 50	Charles(Hawk) Black	60.00	30.00	6.00
	Indianapolis Jets			
☐ 51	Jack Dwan	60.00	30.00	6.00
	Minneapolis Lakers			
☐ 52	Cornelius Simmons	60.00	30.00	6.00
	Baltimore Bullets			
☐ 53	Basketball Play	36.00	18.00	3.60
	Out of bounds			
☐ 54	Bud Palmer	75.00	37.50	7.50
	New York Knicks			
☐ 55	Max Zaslofsky	180.00	90.00	18.00
	Chicago Stags			
☐ 56	Lee Roy Robbins	60.00	30.00	6.00
	Providence Steamrollers			
☐ 57	Arthur Spector	60.00	30.00	6.00
	Boston Celtics			
☐ 58	Arnie Risen	75.00	37.50	7.50
	Rochester Royals			
☐ 59	Basketball Play	36.00	18.00	3.60
	Out of bounds play			
☐ 60	Ariel Maughan	60.00	30.00	6.00
	St. Louis Bombers			
☐ 61	Dick O'Keefe	60.00	30.00	6.00
	Washington Capitols			
☐ 62	Herman Schaefer	60.00	30.00	6.00
	Minneapolis Lakers			
☐ 63	John Mahnken	60.00	30.00	6.00
	Baltimore Bullets			
☐ 64	Tommy Byrnes	60.00	30.00	6.00
	New York Knicks			
☐ 65	Basketball Play	36.00	18.00	3.60
	Held ball			
☐ 66	Jim Pollard	250.00	125.00	25.00
	Minneapolis Lakers			
☐ 67	Lee Mogus	60.00	30.00	6.00
	Baltimore Bullets			
☐ 68	Lee Knorek	60.00	30.00	6.00
	New York Knicks			
☐ 69	George Mikan	3000.00	1250.00	400.00
	Minneapolis Lakers			
☐ 70	Walter Budko	60.00	30.00	6.00
	Baltimore Bullets			
☐ 71	Basketball Play	36.00	18.00	3.60
	Guards Play			
☐ 72	Carl Braun	125.00	40.00	8.00
	New York Knicks			

1952 Bread for Health

The 1952 Bread for Health basketball set consists of 32 bread end labels (each measuring approximately 2 3/4" by 2 3/4") of players in the National Basketball Association. While all the bakeries who issued this set are not at present known, Fisher's Bread in the New Jersey, New York and Pennsylvania area and NBC Bread in the Michigan area are two of the bakeries that have been confirmed to date. As with many of the bread label sets of the early '50s, an album to house the set was probably issued. Each label contains the B.E.B. copyright found on so many of the labels of this period. Labels which contain "Bread for Energy" at the bottom are not a part of the set but part of a series of movie, western and sports stars issued during the same approximate time period. The American Card Catalog does not designate a number to this series; however, based on its similarity to a corresponding football issue, it is referenced as D290-15A.

		NRMT	VG-E	GOOD
	COMPLETE SET (32)	6500.00	3250.00	750.00
	COMMON PLAYER (1-32)	150.00	75.00	15.00
☐ 1	Paul Armstrong	150.00	75.00	15.00
	Ft.Wayne Pistons			
☐ 2	Vince Boryla	150.00	75.00	15.00
	New York Knicks			
☐ 3	Donald Boven	150.00	75.00	15.00
	Tri-Cities Blackhawks			
☐ 4	Walter Budko	150.00	75.00	15.00
	Baltimore Bullets			
☐ 5	Al Cervi	150.00	75.00	15.00
	Syracuse Nats			
☐ 6	Bob Davies	250.00	125.00	25.00
	Rochester Royals			
☐ 7	Dwight Eddleman	150.00	75.00	15.00
	Tri-Cities Blackhawks			
☐ 8	Arnold Ferrin	150.00	75.00	15.00
	Minneapolis Lakers			
☐ 9	Joe Fulks	300.00	150.00	30.00
	Philadelphia Warriors			
☐ 10	Harry Gallatin	250.00	125.00	25.00
	New York Knicks			
☐ 11	Chuck Gilmur	150.00	75.00	15.00
	Washington Caps			
☐ 12	Alex Groza	175.00	85.00	18.00
	Indianapolis Olympians			
☐ 13	Bruce Hale	150.00	75.00	15.00
	Indianapolis Olympians			
☐ 14	Paul Hoffman	150.00	75.00	15.00
	Baltimore Bullets			
☐ 15	Buddy Jeanette	175.00	85.00	18.00
	Baltimore Bullets			
☐ 16	Bob Kinney	150.00	75.00	15.00
	Boston Celtics			
☐ 17	Dante Lavelli	250.00	125.00	25.00

	Boston Celtics			
☐ 18	Ron Livingstone	150.00	75.00	15.00
	Philadelphia Warriors			
☐ 19	Horace McKinney	175.00	85.00	18.00
	Washington Caps			
☐ 20	Stan Miasek	150.00	75.00	15.00
	Chicago Stags			
☐ 21	George Mikan	1500.00	600.00	200.00
	Minneapolis Lakers			
☐ 22	Vern Mikkelsen	250.00	125.00	25.00
	Minneapolis Lakers			
☐ 23	Andy Phillip	250.00	125.00	25.00
	Chicago Stags			
☐ 24	Arnie Risen	175.00	85.00	18.00
	Rochester Royals			
☐ 25	Fred Schaus	175.00	85.00	18.00
	Ft.Wayne Pistons			
☐ 26	Fred Scolari	150.00	75.00	15.00
	Washington Caps			
☐ 27	George Senesky	150.00	75.00	15.00
	Philadelphia Warriors			
☐ 28	Paul Seymour	150.00	75.00	15.00
	Syracuse Nats			
☐ 29	Cornelius Simmons	150.00	75.00	15.00
	New York Knicks			
☐ 30	Gene Vance	150.00	75.00	15.00
	Tri-Cities Blackhawks			
☐ 31	Brady Walker	150.00	75.00	15.00
	Boston Celtics			
☐ 32	Max Zaszlofsky	250.00	125.00	25.00
	New York Knicks			

1976 Buckman Discs

The 1976 Buckman Discs set contains 20 unnumbered discs approximately 3 3/8" in diameter. The discs have various color borders, and feature black and white drawings of the players with fascimile signatures. This set was distributed through Buckman's Ice Cream Village in Rochester, New York.

	NRMT	VG-E	GOOD
COMPLETE SET (20)	60.00	30.00	6.00
COMMON PLAYER (1-20)	1.00	.50	.10
☐ 1 Nate Archibald	4.00	2.00	.40
☐ 2 Rick Barry	6.00	3.00	.60
☐ 3 Tom Boerwinkle	1.00	.50	.10
☐ 4 Bill Bradley	9.00	4.50	.90
☐ 5 Dave Cowens	4.00	2.00	.40
☐ 6 Bob Dandridge	1.00	.50	.10
☐ 7 Walt Frazier	4.00	2.00	.40
☐ 8 Gail Goodrich	2.50	1.25	.25
☐ 9 John Havlicek	6.00	3.00	.60
☐ 10 Connie Hawkins	4.00	2.00	.40
☐ 11 Lou Hudson	1.50	.75	.15
☐ 12 Kareem Abdul-Jabbar	15.00	7.50	1.50
☐ 13 Sam Lacey	1.00	.50	.10
☐ 14 Bob Lanier	3.00	1.50	.30
☐ 15 Bob Love	1.50	.75	.15
☐ 16 Bob McAdoo	2.00	1.00	.20
☐ 17 Earl Monroe	3.00	1.50	.30
☐ 18 Jerry Sloan	1.50	.75	.15
☐ 19 Norm Van Lier	1.00	.50	.10
☐ 20 Jo Jo White	1.50	.75	.15

1971-72 Bucks Linnett

These 10 charcoal drawings are skillfully executed facial portraits of Milwaukee Bucks players. They were drawn by noted sports artist Charles Linnett and measure approximately 8 1/2" by 11". In the lower right corner, a facsimile autograph of the player is written across the portrait. The backs are blank. The drawings are unnumbered and we have checklisted them below in alphabetical order.

	NRMT	VG-E	GOOD
COMPLETE SET (10)	20.00	10.00	2.00
COMMON PLAYER (1-10)	1.00	.50	.10
☐ 1 Kareem Abdul-Jabbar	12.50	6.25	1.25
☐ 2 Gary Brokaw	1.50	.75	.15
☐ 3 Bob Dandridge	2.00	1.00	.20
☐ 4 Mickey Davis	1.00	.50	.10
☐ 5 Steve Kuberski	1.00	.50	.10
☐ 6 Jon McGlocklin	1.50	.75	.15
☐ 7 Jim Price	1.00	.50	.10
☐ 8 Kevin Restani	1.00	.50	.10
☐ 9 George Thompson	1.00	.50	.10
☐ 10 Cornell Warner	1.00	.50	.10

1977-78 Bucks Action Photos

These glossy action photos (of Milwaukee Bucks) measure approximately 5" by 7" and are printed on very thin paper. The photos are in full color and borderless. The players are identified only by their facsimile autographs inscribed across the picture. The backs are blank.

	NRMT	VG-E	GOOD
COMPLETE SET (10)	18.00	9.00	1.80
COMMON PLAYER (1-10)	1.00	.50	.10
☐ 1 Kent Benson	2.00	1.00	.20
☐ 2 Junior Bridgeman	2.00	1.00	.20
☐ 3 Quinn Buckner	2.50	1.25	.25
☐ 4 Alex English	7.50	3.75	.75
☐ 5 John Gianelli	1.00	.50	.10
☐ 6 Ernie Grunfeld	2.00	1.00	.20
☐ 7 Marques Johnson	4.00	2.00	.40

☐ 8 Dave Meyers	2.00	1.00	.20
☐ 9 Lloyd Walton	1.00	.50	.10
☐ 10 Brian Winters	2.00	1.00	.20

1979 Bucks Open Pantry *

This set is an unnumbered, 12-card set featuring players from Milwaukee area professional sports teams with five Brewers baseball (1-5), five Bucks basketball (6-10), and two Packers football (11-12). Cards are black and white with red trim and measure approximately 5" by 6". Cards were sponsored by Open Pantry, Lake to Lake, and MACC (Milwaukee Athletes against Childhood Cancer). The cards are unnumbered and hence are listed and numbered below alphabetically within sport.

	NRMT	VG-E	GOOD
COMPLETE SET (12)	30.00	15.00	3.00
COMMON BASEBALL (1-5)	2.00	1.00	.20
COMMON BASKETBALL (6-10)	2.00	1.00	.20
COMMON FOOTBALL (11-12)	2.00	1.00	.20
☐ 1 Jerry Augustine	2.00	1.00	.20
☐ 2 Sal Bando	4.00	2.00	.40
☐ 3 Cecil Cooper	3.00	1.50	.30
☐ 4 Larry Hisle	2.00	1.00	.20
☐ 5 Lary Sorensen	2.00	1.00	.20
☐ 6 Kent Benson	3.00	1.50	.30
☐ 7 Junior Bridgeman	3.00	1.50	.30
☐ 8 Quinn Buckner	4.00	2.00	.40
☐ 9 Marques Johnson	5.00	2.50	.50
☐ 10 Jon McGlocklin	3.00	1.50	.30
☐ 11 Rich McGeorge	2.00	1.00	.20
☐ 12 Steve Wagner	2.00	1.00	.20

1979-80 Bucks Police/Spic'n'Span

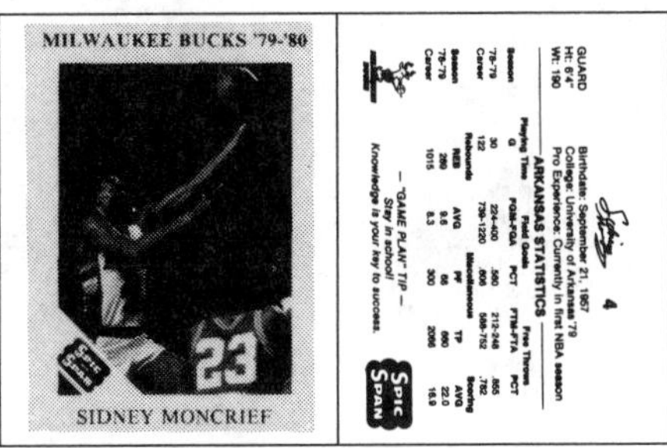

This set contains 12 cards measuring 2 1/2" by 3 1/2" featuring the Milwaukee Bucks. Backs contain safety tips ("Game Plan Tip"). The cards are numbered on the back next to the facsimile autograph. The cards feature full-color fronts and black printing on a white card stock back. The set was sponsored by Spic'N'Span. A coupon card was also available.

	MINT	EXC	G-VG
COMPLETE SET (12)	100.00	50.00	10.00
COMMON PLAYER	6.00	3.00	.60
☐ 2 Junior Bridgeman	10.00	5.00	1.00
☐ 4 Sidney Moncrief	20.00	10.00	2.00
☐ 6 Pat Cummings	7.50	3.75	.75
☐ 7 Dave Meyers	10.00	5.00	1.00
☐ 8 Marques Johnson	15.00	7.50	1.50
☐ 11 Lloyd Walton	6.00	3.00	.60
☐ 21 Quinn Buckner	10.00	5.00	1.00
☐ 31 Richard Washington	9.00	4.50	.90
☐ 32 Brian Winters	7.50	3.75	.75
☐ 42 Harvey Catchings	6.00	3.00	.60
☐ 54 Kent Benson	7.50	3.75	.75
☐ xx Coach Don Nelson and John Killilea, Assistant Coach	9.00	4.50	.90

1987-88 Bucks Polaroid

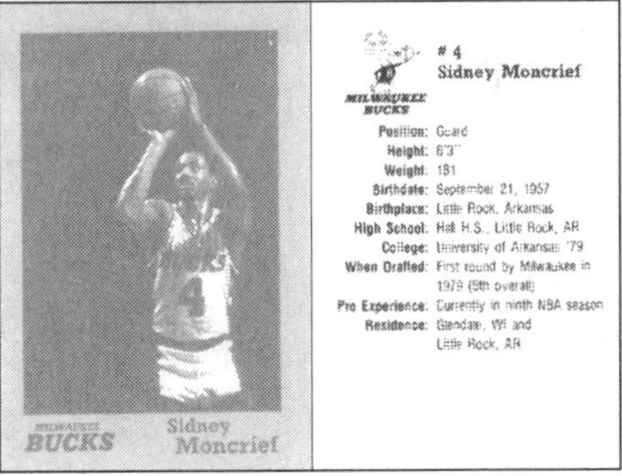

The 1987-88 Polaroid Milwaukee Bucks set contains 16 cards each measuring approximately 2 3/4" by 4". There are 14 player cards plus one coaching staff card and one title card. The cards were distributed in sheet form with perforations. The front borders are deep green and the backs feature biographical information.

	MINT	EXC	G-VG
COMPLETE SET (16)	25.00	12.50	2.50
COMMON PLAYER	1.00	.50	.10
☐ 2 Junior Bridgeman	2.00	1.00	.20

☐ 3 Pace Mannion	1.00	.50	.10
☐ 4 Sidney Moncrief	4.50	2.25	.45
☐ 10 John Lucas	2.50	1.25	.25
☐ 15 Craig Hodges	3.00	1.50	.30
☐ 21 Conner Henry	1.00	.50	.10
☐ 25 Paul Pressey	3.00	1.50	.30
☐ 34 Terry Cummings	5.00	2.50	.50
☐ 35 Jerry Reynolds	1.50	.75	.15
☐ 42 Larry Krystkowiak	1.50	.75	.15
☐ 43 Jack Sikma	3.50	1.75	.35
☐ 44 Paul Mokeski	1.00	.50	.10
☐ 45 Randy Breuer	1.00	.50	.10
☐ 54 John Stroeder	1.00	.50	.10
☐ xx Bucks Coaches Del Harris HEAD Frank Hamblen ASST Mack Calvin ASST Mike Dunleavy ASST Jeff Snedeker TR	1.00	.50	.10
☐ xx Title Card (discount offer detailed on back)	1.00	.50	.10

1988-89 Bucks Green Border

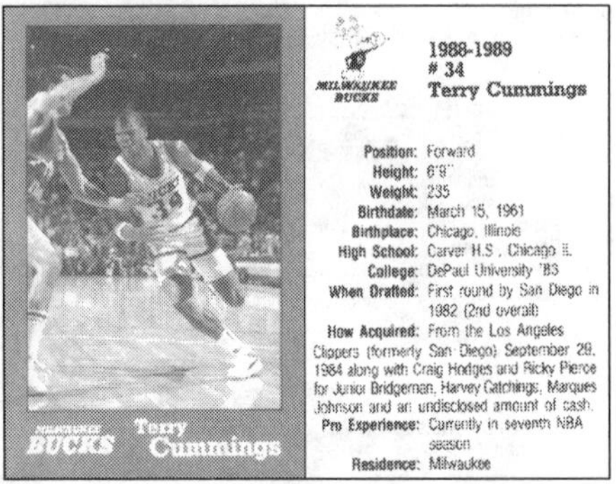

This 16-card set was issued in a panel of four rows of four cards each; after perforation, the cards measure approximately 2 3/4" by 4". The fronts feature a color action player photo, with a thin black border on medium green background. In white lettering the team and player name are given below the picture. The back has the Milwaukee Bucks logo in the upper left corner and biographical information given in tabular format.

	MINT	EXC	G-VG
COMPLETE SET (16)	20.00	10.00	2.00
COMMON PLAYER (1-16)	.90	.45	.09
☐ 1 Kareem Abdul-Jabbar	6.00	3.00	.60
☐ 2 Randy Breuer	.90	.45	.09
☐ 3 Terry Cummings	2.50	1.25	.25
☐ 4 Jeff Grayer	1.50	.75	.15
☐ 5 Del Harris CO	1.25	.60	.12
☐ 6 Tito Horford	1.25	.60	.12
☐ 7 Jay Humphries	2.00	1.00	.20
☐ 8 Larry Krystkowiak	1.25	.60	.12
☐ 9 Paul Mokeski	.90	.45	.09
☐ 10 Sidney Moncrief	2.00	1.00	.20
☐ 11 Ricky Pierce	2.50	1.25	.25
☐ 12 Paul Pressey	1.50	.75	.15
☐ 13 Fred Roberts	1.50	.75	.15
☐ 14 Jack Sikma	2.00	1.00	.20
☐ 15 The Bradley Center	.90	.45	.09
☐ 16 1988-89 Coaching Staff Del Harris Frank Hamblen Mack Calvin Mike Dunleavy Jeff Snedeker (Trainer)	.90	.45	.09

1954-55 Bullets Gunther Beer

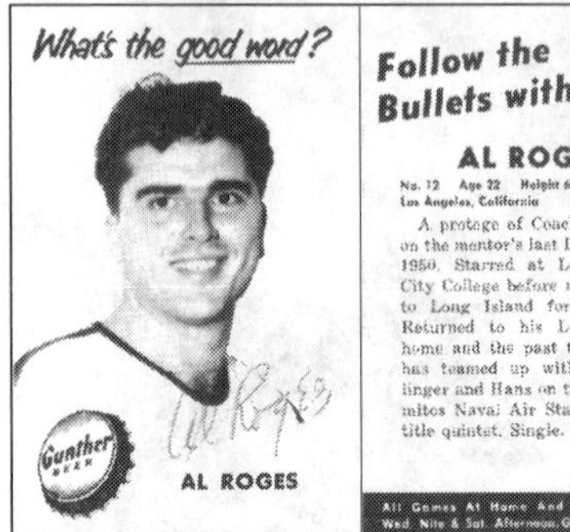

This 11-card set of Baltimore Bullets was sponsored by Gunther Beer. These black and white cards measure approximately 2 5/8" by 3 5/8". The fronts feature a black and white posed player photo. The question "What's the good word," is written across the card top. A Gunther Beer bottle cap and the player's name are superimposed on the player's chest. The back has the words "Follow the Bullets with Guntner Beer" at the top, with biographical information and career summary below. A radio and TV notice on the bottom round out the card back. The cards are unnumbered and are checklisted below in alphabetical order. The cards are frequently found personally autographed. The catalog designation for this set is H805.

	NRMT	VG-E	GOOD
COMPLETE SET (11)	1400.00	650.00	150.00
COMMON PLAYER (1-11)	100.00	50.00	10.00
☐ 1 Leo Barnhorst	100.00	50.00	10.00
☐ 2 Clair Bee CO	300.00	150.00	30.00
☐ 3 Bill Bolger	100.00	50.00	10.00
☐ 4 Ray Felix	150.00	75.00	15.00
☐ 5 Jim Fritsche	100.00	50.00	10.00
☐ 6 Rollen Hans	100.00	50.00	10.00
☐ 7 Paul Hoffman	100.00	50.00	10.00
☐ 8 Bob Houbregs	225.00	110.00	22.00
☐ 9 Ed Miller	100.00	50.00	10.00
☐ 10 Al Roges	100.00	50.00	10.00
☐ 11 Harold Uplinger	100.00	50.00	10.00

1973-74 Bullets Standups

These 12 player cards are issued in an album, with six players per 11 1/4" by 14" sheet. After perforation, the cards measure approximately 3 3/4" by 7 1/16". The cards are die cut, allowing the player pictures and bases to be pushed out and displayed as stand-ups. The fronts feature a color photo of the player, either dribbling or shooting the ball. The backs are blank. The cards are unnumbered and are checklisted below in alphabetical order. A card set, still intact in the album, would be valued at triple the values listed below.

	MINT	EXC	G-VG
COMPLETE SET (12)	30.00	15.00	3.00
COMMON PLAYER (1-12)	2.00	1.00	.20
☐ 1 Phil Chenier	3.50	1.75	.35
☐ 2 Archie Clark	4.00	2.00	.40
☐ 3 Elvin Hayes	12.00	6.00	1.20
☐ 4 Tom Kozelko	2.00	1.00	.20
☐ 5 Manny Leaks	2.00	1.00	.20
☐ 6 Louie Nelson	2.50	1.25	.25
☐ 7 Kevin Porter	4.00	2.00	.40
☐ 8 Mike Riordan	3.00	1.50	.30
☐ 9 Dave Stallworth	3.00	1.50	.30
☐ 10 Wes Unseld	9.00	4.50	.90

☐ 11 Nick Weatherspoon	2.00	1.00	.20
☐ 12 Walt Wesley	2.00	1.00	.20

1970-71 Bulls Hawthorne Milk

This five-card set was issued on the side panels of Hawthorne Milk cartons. The cards were intended to be cut from the carton and measure approximately 3 1/4" by 3 3/8" and feature on the front a posed head shot of the player within a circular picture frame. The second Weiss card measures 4 11/16" by 2 7/8". The backs are blank. The cards are unnumbered and are checklisted below in alphabetical order. The player photo is printed in blue but the outer border of the card is bright red.

	NRMT	VG-E	GOOD
COMPLETE SET (5)	300.00	150.00	30.00
COMMON PLAYER (1-5)	60.00	30.00	6.00
☐ 1 Bob Love	90.00	45.00	9.00
☐ 2 Jerry Sloan	90.00	45.00	9.00
☐ 3 Chet Walker	90.00	45.00	9.00
☐ 4 Bob Weiss (regular size)	60.00	30.00	6.00
☐ 5 Bob Weiss (large size)	75.00	37.50	7.50

1977-78 Bulls White Hen Pantry

These high gloss player photos are printed on very thin paper and measure approximately 5" by 7". The fronts feature borderless color game action photos with a facsimile autograph; the backs are blank. The photos are unnumbered and we have checklisted them below in alphabetical order.

	NRMT	VG-E	GOOD
COMPLETE SET (7)	15.00	7.50	1.50
COMMON PLAYER (1-7)	2.00	1.00	.20
☐ 1 Tom Boerwinkle	2.00	1.00	.20
☐ 2 Artis Gilmore	5.00	2.50	.50
☐ 3 Wilbur Holland	2.00	1.00	.20
☐ 4 Mickey Johnson	2.50	1.25	.25
☐ 5 Scott May	3.00	1.50	.30
☐ 6 John Mengelt	2.50	1.25	.25
☐ 7 Norm Van Lier	3.00	1.50	.30

1979-80 Bulls Police

This set contains 16 cards measuring approximately 2 5/8" by 4 1/8" featuring the Chicago Bulls. Cards in the set have rounded corners. Backs contain safety tips and are written in black ink with blue accent. The set was also sponsored by La Margarita Mexican Restaurants and Azteca Tortillas. The card backs are subtitled Kiwanis Cue Cards. Cards are unnumbered except for uniform number; they are checklisted below by uniform number. The cards of Coby Dietrick and Reggie Theus are considered more difficult to find and are marked as SP in the listings below.

	MINT	EXC	G-VG
COMPLETE SET (16)	90.00	45.00	9.00
COMMON PLAYER	4.00	2.00	.40
☐ 1 Delmer Beshore	4.00	2.00	.40
☐ 13 Dwight Jones	5.00	2.50	.50

☐ 15 John Mengelt	7.50	3.75	.75
☐ 17 Scott May	7.50	3.75	.75
☐ 20 Dennis Awtrey	5.00	2.50	.50
☐ 24 Reggie Theus SP	15.00	7.50	1.50
☐ 26 Coby Dietrick SP	7.50	3.75	.75
☐ 27 Ollie Johnson	4.00	2.00	.40
☐ 28 Sam Smith	4.00	2.00	.40
☐ 34 David Greenwood	7.50	3.75	.75
☐ 40 Ricky Sobers	7.50	3.75	.75
☐ 53 Artis Gilmore	12.00	6.00	1.20
☐ 54 Mark Landsberger	4.00	2.00	.40
☐ xx Jerry Sloan CO	6.00	3.00	.60
☐ xx Phil Johnson, assistant coach	4.00	2.00	.40
☐ xx Luv-A-Bull	7.50	3.75	.75

1985 Bulls Interlake

These glossy color action photos measure approximately 5" by 7" and are printed on thin card stock. The player photo image has rounded corners and a red border on a white card face. Player information appears beneath the picture, between two circles. The left circle has a Boy Scout emblem, while the right one has the words "An Interlake Youth Incentive Program." Supposedly the cards were given out in the fall of 1985 as an incentive to join the Boy Scouts. The Chicago Bulls sponsored a dinner for the Boy Scouts and Michael Jordan was the guest speaker. The backs are blank.

	MINT	EXC	G-VG
COMPLETE SET (2)	135.00	65.00	13.50
COMMON PLAYER	20.00	10.00	2.00
☐ 1 Michael Jordan	125.00	60.00	12.50
☐ 2 Orlando Woolridge	20.00	10.00	2.00

1987-88 Bulls Entenmann's

The 1987-88 Entenmann's Chicago Bulls set contains 12 blank-backed cards measuring approximately 2 5/8" by 4". There are 11 player cards and one coach card in this set. The cards are unnumbered except for uniform number; they are ordered and numbered below by uniform number. The set features the first professional cards of Horace Grant and Scottie Pippen.

	MINT	EXC	G-VG
COMPLETE SET (12)	90.00	45.00	9.00
COMMON PLAYER (1-12)	1.00	.50	.10
☐ 2 Rory Sparrow 2	1.00	.50	.10
☐ 3 Sedale Threatt 3	2.50	1.25	.25
☐ 5 John Paxson 5	3.50	1.75	.35
☐ 6 Brad Sellers 6	1.50	.75	.15
☐ 17 Mike Brown 17	1.25	.60	.12
☐ 23 Michael Jordan 23	50.00	25.00	5.00
☐ 31 Granville Waiters 31	1.00	.50	.10
☐ 33 Scottie Pippen 33	30.00	15.00	3.00
☐ 34 Charles Oakley 34	2.50	1.25	.25
☐ 40 Dave Corzine 40	1.00	.50	.10
☐ 54 Horace Grant 54	10.00	5.00	1.00
☐ xx Doug Collins CO	2.50	1.25	.25

1988-89 Bulls Entenmann's

The 1988-89 Entenmann's Chicago Bulls set contains 12 blank-backed player cards each measuring approximately 2 5/8" by 4". The cards are unnumbered except for uniform number; they are ordered and numbered below by uniform number.

	MINT	EXC	G-VG
COMPLETE SET (12)	50.00	25.00	5.00
COMMON PLAYER	.90	.45	.09
☐ 2 Brad Sellers	.90	.45	.09
☐ 5 John Paxson	2.25	1.10	.22
☐ 11 Sam Vincent	1.50	.75	.15
☐ 14 Craig Hodges	1.75	.85	.17
☐ 15 Jack Haley	.90	.45	.09
☐ 22 Charles Davis	.90	.45	.09
☐ 23 Michael Jordan	30.00	15.00	3.00
☐ 24 Bill Cartwright	1.75	.85	.17

☐ 32 Will Perdue	1.50	.75	.15
☐ 33 Scottie Pippen	15.00	7.50	1.50
☐ 40 Dave Corzine	.90	.45	.09
☐ 54 Horace Grant	4.00	2.00	.40

1989-90 Bulls Equal

This 11-card set was sponsored by Equal Brand sweetener, and its company logo appears in the lower right corner of the card face. It has been reported that 10,000 sets were given away to fans attending the April 17th Chicago Bulls home game. These oversized cards measure approximately 3" by 4 1/4". The fronts feature a borderless color action photo. The player's number, name, height, and position are given in the white stripe below the picture. Except for the sponsor's trademark notice, the backs are blank. The cards are unnumbered and checklisted below in alphabetical order, with jersey number after the player's name.

	MINT	EXC	G-VG
COMPLETE SET (11)	30.00	15.00	3.00
COMMON PLAYER (1-11)	.75	.35	.07
☐ 1 B.J. Armstrong 10	2.00	1.00	.20
☐ 2 Bill Cartwright 24	1.50	.75	.15
☐ 3 Charles Davis 22	.75	.35	.07
☐ 4 Horace Grant 54	2.50	1.25	.25
☐ 5 Craig Hodges 14	1.50	.75	.15
☐ 6 Michael Jordan 23	15.00	7.50	1.50
☐ 7 Stacey King 34	2.50	1.25	.25
☐ 8 Ed Nealy 45	.75	.35	.07
☐ 9 John Paxson 5	1.50	.75	.15
☐ 10 Will Perdue 32	1.25	.60	.12
☐ 11 Scottie Pippen 33	6.00	3.00	.60
☐ 12 Jeff Sanders 42	1.00	.50	.10

1990-91 Bulls Equal/Star

This 16-card set was sponsored by Equal brand sweetener and celebrates the 25th anniversary of the Chicago Bulls franchise. The set was produced (reportedly 10,000 complete sets) by Star Company and was distributed at the April 9th Chicago Bulls home game. The cards measure the standard size (2 1/2" by 3 1/2"). The fronts feature color action player photos for current Bull players, and blue-tinted photos for past Bull players. The team logo and the words "The Silver Season" overlay the top of the picture. The card background is in silver, and the player's name appears in a gray diagonal stripe traversing the bottom of the picture. The sponsor logo appears in blue print at the card bottom. The back has brief biographical information and statistics, in black print on a pink background. The cards are numbered on the back.

	MINT	EXC	G-VG
COMPLETE SET (16)	18.00	9.00	1.80
COMMON PLAYER (1-16)	.60	.30	.06
☐ 1 Michael Jordan	9.00	4.50	.90
☐ 2 Tom Boerwinkle	.60	.30	.06
☐ 3 Bob Boozer	.60	.30	.06
☐ 4 Bill Cartwright	1.00	.50	.10
☐ 5 Artis Gilmore	1.50	.75	.15
☐ 6 Horace Grant	1.75	.85	.17
☐ 7 Phil Jackson CO	1.00	.50	.10
☐ 8 Johnny(Red) Kerr	1.00	.50	.10
☐ 9 Bob Love	1.00	.50	.10
☐ 10 Dick Motta CO	.60	.30	.06
☐ 11 John Paxson	1.25	.60	.12
☐ 12 Scottie Pippen	4.00	2.00	.40
☐ 13 Guy Rodgers	.60	.30	.06
☐ 14 Jerry Sloan	.75	.35	.07
☐ 15 Norm Van Lier	.75	.35	.07
☐ 16 Chet Walker	1.00	.50	.10

1956 Busch Bavarian Hawks

These black and white photo-like cards were sponsored by Busch Bavarian Beer and feature members of the St. Louis Hawks. The cards are blank backed and measure approximately 4" by 5". The cards show a facsimile autograph of the player on a drop-out background.

	NRMT	VG-E	GOOD
COMPLETE SET (4)	400.00	200.00	40.00
COMMON PLAYER (1-4)	50.00	25.00	5.00
☐ 1 Cliff Hagan	100.00	50.00	10.00
☐ 2 Clyde Lovellette	100.00	50.00	10.00
☐ 3 John McCarthy	50.00	25.00	5.00
☐ 4 Bob Pettit	200.00	100.00	20.00

1975 Carvel Discs

The 1975 Carvel NBA Basketball Discs set contains 36 unnumbered discs approximately 3 3/8" in diameter. The blank-backed discs have various color borders, and feature black and white drawings of the players with fascimile signatures. Since the discs are unnumbered, they are checklisted below in alphabetical order.

	NRMT	VG-E	GOOD
COMPLETE SET (36)	100.00	50.00	10.00
COMMON PLAYER (1-36)	1.00	.50	.10
☐ 1 Nate Archibald	5.00	2.50	.50
☐ 2 Bill Bradley	12.00	6.00	1.20
☐ 3 Don Chaney	1.50	.75	.15
☐ 4 Dave Cowens	5.00	2.50	.50
☐ 5 Bob Dandridge	1.25	.60	.12
☐ 6 Ernie DiGregorio	1.25	.60	.12
☐ 7 Walt Frazier	5.00	2.50	.50
☐ 8 John Gianelli	1.00	.50	.10
☐ 9 Gail Goodrich	2.50	1.25	.25
☐ 10 Happy Hairston	1.25	.60	.12
☐ 11 John Havlicek	8.00	4.00	.80
☐ 12 Spencer Haywood	1.50	.75	.15
☐ 13 Garfield Heard	1.00	.50	.10
☐ 14 Lou Hudson	1.25	.60	.12
☐ 15 Kareem Abdul-Jabbar	20.00	10.00	2.00
☐ 16 Phil Jackson	2.50	1.25	.25
☐ 17 Sam Lacey	1.00	.50	.10
☐ 18 Bob Lanier	4.00	2.00	.40
☐ 19 Bob Love	1.50	.75	.15
☐ 20 Bob McAdoo	3.00	1.50	.30
☐ 21 Jim McMillian	1.00	.50	.10
☐ 22 Dean Meminger	1.25	.60	.12
☐ 23 Earl Monroe	5.00	2.50	.50
☐ 24 Don Nelson	2.50	1.25	.25
☐ 25 Jim Price	1.00	.50	.10
☐ 26 Clifford Ray	1.00	.50	.10
☐ 27 Charlie Scott	1.25	.60	.12
☐ 28 Paul Silas	2.00	1.00	.20
☐ 29 Jerry Sloan	1.25	.60	.12
☐ 30 Randy Smith	1.25	.60	.12
☐ 31 Dick Van Arsdale	1.25	.60	.12
☐ 32 Norm Van Lier	1.25	.60	.12
☐ 33 Chet Walker	1.50	.75	.15
☐ 34 Paul Westphal	2.00	1.00	.20
☐ 35 JoJo White	2.00	1.00	.20
☐ 36 Hawthorne Wingo	2.00	1.00	.20

1992 Center Court

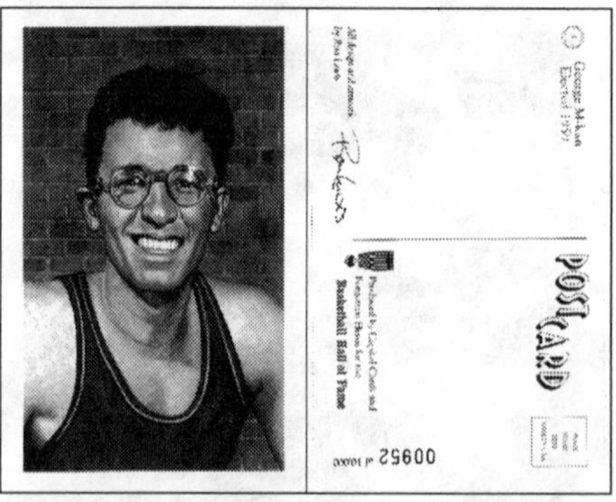

This 26-card set was produced by Capital Cards and Forgotten Heroes for the Basketball Hall of Fame. The production run was limited to 10,000 (each card of the set is numbered "X of 10,000" on the back). The cards are postcard size and measure 3 1/2" by 5 1/2". Inside white borders, the fronts display glossy color player portraits by noted sports artist Ron Lewis. The horizontally oriented backs have the player's name and the year he was elected to the Hall of Fame. The cards are numbered on the back.

	MINT	EXC	G-VG
COMPLETE SET (26)	40.00	20.00	4.00
COMMON PLAYER (1-26)	2.00	1.00	.20

☐ 1 George Mikan	4.00	2.00	.40
☐ 2 Bill Bradley	3.00	1.50	.30
☐ 3 Bobby Wanzer	2.00	1.00	.20
☐ 4 Ed Macauley	2.00	1.00	.20
☐ 5 Harry Gallatin	2.00	1.00	.20
☐ 6 William(Pop) Gates	2.00	1.00	.20
☐ 7 Bobby Knight CO	4.00	2.00	.40
☐ 8 Dolph Schayes	2.00	1.00	.20
☐ 9 Bob Pettit	3.00	1.50	.30
☐ 10 Walt Frazier	3.00	1.50	.30
☐ 11 Elvin Hayes	3.00	1.50	.30
☐ 12 Paul Arizin	2.00	1.00	.20
☐ 13 Forrest(Phog) Allen CO	2.00	1.00	.20
☐ 14 Oscar Robertson	4.00	2.00	.40
☐ 15 John Wooden CO	3.00	1.50	.30
☐ 16 Red Holzman CO	2.00	1.00	.20
☐ 17 Jack Twyman	2.00	1.00	.20
☐ 18 Dean Smith CO	3.00	1.50	.30
☐ 19 John Nucatola	2.00	1.00	.20
☐ 20 Elgin Baylor	3.00	1.50	.30
☐ 21 Dave Bing	2.00	1.00	.20
☐ 22 Lester Harrison	2.00	1.00	.20
☐ 23 Joe Lapchick	2.00	1.00	.20
☐ 24 Rick Barry	3.00	1.50	.30
☐ 25 Lou Carnesecca CO	2.00	1.00	.20
☐ 26 Checklist	2.00	1.00	.20

1991 Classic Draft

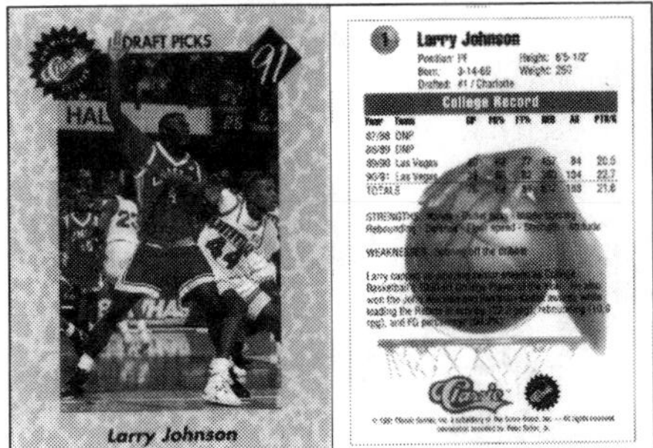

This 50-card set was produced by Classic Games, Inc. and features 48 players picked in the first two rounds of the 1991 NBA draft. A total of 450,000 sets were issued, and each set is accompanied by a letter of limited edition. The cards measure the standard size (2 1/2" by 3 1/2"). The fronts feature a glossy color action photo of each player. The backs have statistics and biographical information. Special cards included in the set are a commemorative number one draft choice card of Larry Johnson and a "One-on-One" card of Billy Owens slam-dunking over Johnson.

	MINT	EXC	G-VG
COMPLETE SET (50)	12.00	6.00	1.20
COMMON PLAYER (1-50)	.05	.02	.00
☐ 1 Larry Johnson UNLV	5.00	2.50	.50
☐ 2 Billy Owens Syracuse	3.50	1.75	.35
☐ 3 Dikembe Mutombo Georgetown	2.50	1.25	.25
☐ 4 Mark Macon Temple	.35	.17	.03
☐ 5 Brian Williams Arizona	.60	.30	.06
☐ 6 Terrell Brandon Oregon	.40	.20	.04
☐ 7 Greg Anthony UNLV	.40	.20	.04
☐ 8 Dale Davis Clemson	.35	.17	.03
☐ 9 Anthony Avent Seton Hall	.20	.10	.02
☐ 10 Chris Gatling Old Dominion	.40	.20	.04
☐ 11 Victor Alexander Iowa State	.30	.15	.03
☐ 12 Kevin Brooks Southwest Louisiana	.15	.07	.01
☐ 13 Eric Murdock Providence	.30	.15	.03
☐ 14 LeRon Ellis Syracuse	.12	.06	.01
☐ 15 Stanley Roberts LSU	1.00	.50	.10
☐ 16 Rick Fox North Carolina	1.00	.50	.10
☐ 17 Pete Chilcutt North Carolina	.20	.10	.02
☐ 18 Kevin Lynch Minnesota	.15	.07	.01
☐ 19 George Ackles UNLV	.08	.04	.01
☐ 20 Rodney Monroe North Carolina State	.35	.17	.03
☐ 21 Randy Brown New Mexico State	.15	.07	.01
☐ 22 Chad Gallagher Creighton	.08	.04	.01
☐ 23 Donald Hodge Temple	.35	.17	.03
☐ 24 Myron Brown Slippery Rock	.10	.05	.01
☐ 25 Mike Iuzzolino St. Francis	.35	.17	.03
☐ 26 Chris Corchiani North Carolina State	.15	.07	.01
☐ 27 Elliott Perry UER Memphis State	.15	.07	.01
☐ 28 Joe Wylie Miami (FL)	.08	.04	.01
☐ 29 Jimmy Oliver Purdue	.20	.10	.02
☐ 30 Doug Overton LaSalle	.08	.04	.01
☐ 31 Sean Green Iona	.15	.07	.01
☐ 32 Steve Hood James Madison	.10	.05	.01
☐ 33 Lamont Strothers Chris. Newport	.15	.07	.01
☐ 34 Alvaro Teheran Houston	.05	.02	.00
☐ 35 Bobby Phills Southern	.10	.05	.01
☐ 36 Richard Dumas DNP (Spain/Okla.St.)	.08	.04	.01
☐ 37 Keith Hughes Rutgers	.08	.04	.01
☐ 38 Isaac Austin Arizona State	.15	.07	.01
☐ 39 Greg Sutton Oral Roberts	.20	.10	.02
☐ 40 Joey Wright Texas	.08	.04	.01
☐ 41 Anthony Jones Oral Roberts	.05	.02	.00
☐ 42 Von McDade Milwaukee/Wisconsin	.08	.04	.01
☐ 43 Marcus Kennedy E. Michigan	.08	.04	.01
☐ 44 Larry Johnson UNLV Top Pick	.75	.35	.07
☐ 45 Larry Johnson and Billy Owens UNLV and Syracuse	.75	.35	.07
☐ 46 Anderson Hunt UNLV	.10	.05	.01
☐ 47 Darrin Chancellor S. Mississippi	.08	.04	.01
☐ 48 Damon Lopez Fordham	.05	.02	.00
☐ 49 Thomas Jordan DNP (Spain/Okla.St.)	.05	.02	.00
☐ 50 Tony Farmer Nebraska	.08	.04	.01

1991 Classic Draft Pick Collection *

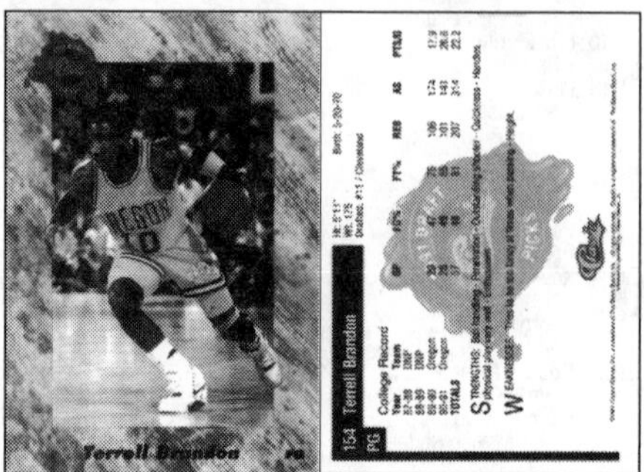

This 230-card multisport set includes all 200 draft pick players from the four Classic Draft Picks sets (football, baseball, basketball, and hockey), plus an additional 30 draft picks not previously found in these other sets. The standard-size (2 1/2" by 3 1/2") cards display new color player photos, with blue-gray marbled borders. The "1991 Classic Draft Picks" emblem appears as a wine-colored wax seal. The full color backs present biographical information and statistics. Appended to the 230-card set is a special ten-card bonus subset, with nine silver bordered cards and a tenth "Gold Card" featuring Raghib "Rocket" Ismail. A five-card Ismail subset is also to be found within the nine silver bordered cards. A final special subset within the 230 cards consists of five cards highlighting the famous one-on-one game between Billy Owens and Larry Johnson. As an additional incentive to collectors, Classic has randomly inserted over 60,000 autographed cards into the foil packs; it is claimed that each case should contain two or more autographed cards. The autographed cards were 61 different players, approximately two-thirds of whom were hockey players. The production run for the English version was 25,000 cases, and a bilingual version of the set was also produced at 20 percent of the English production. The major subdivisions of set are according to sport: hockey (2-50), baseball (51-101), football (102-148), and basketball (149-202). The cards are numbered on the back and checklisted below accordingly.

	MINT	EXC	G-VG
COMPLETE SET (230)	27.00	13.50	2.70
COMMON PLAYER (1-230)	.05	.02	.00
☐ 1 Future Stars	4.00	2.00	.40
Larry Johnson			
Brien Taylor			
Russell Maryland			
Eric Lindros			
☐ 2 Pat Falloon	1.75	.85	.17
☐ 3 Scott Niedermayer	1.00	.50	.10
☐ 4 Scott Lachance	1.00	.50	.10
☐ 5 Peter Forsberg	.35	.17	.03
☐ 6 Alex Stojanov	.15	.07	.01
☐ 7 Richard Matvichuk	.12	.06	.01
☐ 8 Patrick Poulin	.25	.12	.02
☐ 9 Martin Lapointe	.30	.15	.03
☐ 10 Tyler Wright	.20	.10	.02
☐ 11 Philippe Boucher	.15	.07	.01
☐ 12 Pat Peake	.20	.10	.02
☐ 13 Markus Naslund	.35	.17	.03
☐ 14 Brent Bilodeau	.15	.07	.01
☐ 15 Glen Murray	.35	.17	.03
☐ 16 Niklas Sundblad	.10	.05	.01
☐ 17 Martin Rucinsky	.30	.15	.03
☐ 18 Trevor Halverson	.20	.10	.02
☐ 19 Dean McAmmond	.25	.12	.02
☐ 20 Ray Whitney	.50	.25	.05
☐ 21 Rene Corbet	.20	.10	.02
☐ 22 Eric Lavigne	.12	.06	.01
☐ 23 Zigmund Palffy	.25	.12	.02
☐ 24 Steve Staios	.15	.07	.01
☐ 25 Jim Campbell	.15	.07	.01
☐ 26 Jassen Cullimore	.12	.06	.01
☐ 27 Martin Hamrlik	.25	.12	.02
☐ 28 Jamie Pushor	.12	.06	.01
☐ 29 Donevan Hextall	.15	.07	.01
☐ 30 Andrew Verner	.15	.07	.01
☐ 31 Jason Dawe	.20	.10	.02
☐ 32 Jeff Nelson	.20	.10	.02
☐ 33 Darcy Werenka	.12	.06	.01
☐ 34 Jozef Stumpel	.35	.17	.03
☐ 35 Francois Groleau	.12	.06	.01
☐ 36 Guy Leveque	.12	.06	.01
☐ 37 Jamie Matthews	.15	.07	.01
☐ 38 Dody Wood	.12	.06	.01
☐ 39 Yanic Perreault	.50	.25	.05
☐ 40 Jamie McLennan	.15	.07	.01
☐ 41 Yanick Dupre UER	.20	.10	.02
(Yanic misspelled on both sides of card)			
☐ 42 Sandy McCarthy	.12	.06	.01
☐ 43 Chris Osgood	.20	.10	.02
☐ 44 Fredrik Lindquist	.20	.10	.02
☐ 45 Jason Young	.12	.06	.01
☐ 46 Steve Konowalchuk	.15	.07	.01
☐ 47 Michael Nylander UER	.25	.12	.02
☐ 48 Shane Peacock	.12	.06	.01
☐ 49 Yves Sarault	.10	.05	.01
☐ 50 Marcel Cousineau	.15	.07	.01
☐ 51 Brien Taylor	3.00	1.50	.30
☐ 52 Mike Kelly	2.25	1.10	.22
☐ 53 David McCarty	2.25	1.10	.22
☐ 54 Dmitri Young	1.25	.60	.12
☐ 55 Joe Vitiello	.75	.35	.07
☐ 56 Mark Smith	.60	.30	.06
☐ 57 Tyler Green	.90	.45	.09
☐ 58 Shawn Estes UER	.35	.17	.03
(Reversed negative)			
☐ 59 Doug Glanville	.50	.25	.05
☐ 60 Manny Ramirez	.90	.45	.09
☐ 61 Cliff Floyd	.75	.35	.07
☐ 62 Tyrone Hill	.50	.25	.05
☐ 63 Eduardo Perez	1.00	.50	.10
☐ 64 Al Shirley	.50	.25	.05
☐ 65 Benji Gil	.60	.30	.06
☐ 66 Calvin Reese	.40	.20	.04
☐ 67 Allen Watson	.20	.10	.02
☐ 68 Brian Barber	.30	.15	.03
☐ 69 Aaron Sele	.50	.25	.05
☐ 70 Jon Farrell UER	.15	.07	.01
☐ 71 Scott Ruffcorn	.35	.17	.03
☐ 72 Brent Gates	.40	.20	.04
☐ 73 Scott Stahoviak	.40	.20	.04
☐ 74 Tom McKinnon	.15	.07	.01
☐ 75 Shawn Livsey	.20	.10	.02
☐ 76 Jason Pruitt	.15	.07	.01
☐ 77 Greg Anthony	.15	.07	.01
(Baseball)			
☐ 78 Justin Thompson	.20	.10	.02
☐ 79 Steve Whitaker	.15	.07	.01
☐ 80 Jorge Fabregas	.20	.10	.02
☐ 81 Jeff Ware	.30	.15	.03
☐ 82 Bobby Jones	.35	.17	.03
☐ 83 J.J. Johnson	.15	.07	.01
☐ 84 Mike Rossiter	.12	.06	.01
☐ 85 Dan Cholowsky	.75	.35	.07
☐ 86 Jimmy Gonzalez	.12	.06	.01
☐ 87 Trever Miller UER	.20	.10	.02
☐ 88 Scott Hatteberg	.30	.15	.03
☐ 89 Mike Groppuso	.15	.07	.01
☐ 90 Ryan Long	.15	.07	.01
☐ 91 Eddie Williams	.30	.15	.03
☐ 92 Mike Durant	.20	.10	.02
☐ 93 Buck McNabb	.12	.06	.01
☐ 94 Jimmy Lewis	.15	.07	.01
☐ 95 Eddie Ramos	.08	.04	.01
☐ 96 Terry Horn	.10	.05	.01
☐ 97 Jon Barnes	.08	.04	.01
☐ 98 Shawn Curran	.08	.04	.01
☐ 99 Tommy Adams	.40	.20	.04
☐ 100 Trevor Mallory	.15	.07	.01
☐ 101 Frankie Rodriguez	1.25	.60	.12
☐ 102 Raghib(Rocket) Ismail	2.00	1.00	.20
☐ 103 Russell Maryland	.90	.45	.09
☐ 104 Eric Turner	.40	.20	.04
☐ 105 Bruce Pickens	.20	.10	.02
☐ 106 Mike Croel	.90	.45	.09
☐ 107 Todd Lyght	.75	.35	.07
☐ 108 Eric Swann	.30	.15	.03
☐ 109 Antone Davis	.15	.07	.01
☐ 110 Stanley Richard	.20	.10	.02
("Sheriff")			
☐ 111 Pat Harlow	.20	.10	.02
☐ 112 Alvin Harper	.60	.30	.06
☐ 113 Mike Pritchard	.90	.45	.09
☐ 114 Leonard Russell	1.00	.50	.10
☐ 115 Dan McGwire	.90	.45	.09
☐ 116 Bobby Wilson	.25	.12	.02

☐ 117 Vinnie Clark	.20	.10	.02
☐ 118 Kelvin Pritchett	.20	.10	.02
☐ 119 Harvey Williams	.90	.45	.09
☐ 120 Stan Thomas	.10	.05	.01
☐ 121 Randal Hill	.75	.35	.07
☐ 122 Todd Marinovich	1.00	.50	.10
☐ 123 Henry Jones	.10	.05	.01
☐ 124 Mike Dumas	.20	.10	.02
☐ 125 Ed King	.12	.06	.01
☐ 126 Reggie Johnson	.15	.07	.01
☐ 127 Roman Phifer	.20	.10	.02
☐ 128 Mike Jones	.10	.05	.01
☐ 129 Brett Favre	.60	.30	.06
☐ 130 Browning Nagle	1.25	.60	.12
☐ 131 Esera Tuaolo	.20	.10	.02
☐ 132 George Thornton	.08	.04	.01
☐ 133 Dixon Edwards	.15	.07	.01
☐ 134 Darryl Lewis UER	.25	.12	.02
☐ 135 Eric Bieniemy	.20	.10	.02
☐ 136 Shane Curry	.05	.02	.00
☐ 137 Jerome Henderson	.08	.04	.01
☐ 138 Wesley Carroll	.35	.17	.03
☐ 139 Nick Bell	.60	.30	.06
☐ 140 John Flannery	.08	.04	.01
☐ 141 Ricky Watters	.40	.20	.04
☐ 142 Jeff Graham	.30	.15	.03
☐ 143 Eric Moten	.10	.05	.01
☐ 144 Jesse Campbell	.08	.04	.01
☐ 145 Chris Zorich	.35	.17	.03
☐ 146 Doug Thomas	.10	.05	.01
☐ 147 Phil Hansen	.10	.05	.01
☐ 148 Reggie Barrett	.15	.07	.01
☐ 149 Larry Johnson	3.50	1.75	.35
☐ 150 Billy Owens	3.00	1.50	.30
☐ 151 Dikembe Mutombo	1.75	.85	.17
☐ 152 Mark Macon	.25	.12	.02
☐ 153 Brian Williams	.50	.25	.05
☐ 154 Terrell Brandon	.30	.15	.03
☐ 155 Greg Anthony (Basketball)	.30	.15	.03
☐ 156 Dale Davis	.25	.12	.02
☐ 157 Anthony Avent	.12	.06	.01
☐ 158 Chris Gatling	.30	.15	.03
☐ 159 Victor Alexander	.20	.10	.02
☐ 160 Kevin Brooks	.12	.06	.01
☐ 161 Eric Murdock	.20	.10	.02
☐ 162 LeRon Ellis	.10	.05	.01
☐ 163 Stanley Roberts	.90	.45	.09
☐ 164 Rick Fox	.90	.45	.09
☐ 165 Pete Chilcutt	.15	.07	.01
☐ 166 Kevin Lynch	.12	.06	.01
☐ 167 George Ackles	.08	.04	.01
☐ 168 Rodney Monroe	.25	.12	.02
☐ 169 Randy Brown	.10	.05	.01
☐ 170 Chad Gallagher	.08	.04	.01
☐ 171 Donald Hodge	.25	.12	.02
☐ 172 Myron Brown	.08	.04	.01
☐ 173 Mike Iuzzolino	.25	.12	.02
☐ 174 Chris Corchiani	.12	.06	.01
☐ 175 Elliot Perry UER	.12	.06	.01
☐ 176 Joe Wylie	.08	.04	.01
☐ 177 Jimmy Oliver	.15	.07	.01
☐ 178 Doug Overton	.08	.04	.01
☐ 179 Sean Green	.12	.06	.01
☐ 180 Steve Hood	.08	.04	.01
☐ 181 Lamont Strothers	.12	.06	.01
☐ 182 Alvaro Teheran	.05	.02	.00
☐ 183 Bobby Phills	.08	.04	.01
☐ 184 Richard Dumas	.08	.04	.01
☐ 185 Keith Hughes	.08	.04	.01
☐ 186 Isaac Austin	.12	.06	.01
☐ 187 Greg Sutton	.15	.07	.01
☐ 188 Joey Wright	.08	.04	.01
☐ 189 Anthony Jones	.08	.04	.01
☐ 190 Von McDade	.08	.04	.01
☐ 191 Marcus Kennedy	.08	.04	.01
☐ 192 Larry Johnson (Number One Pick)	1.00	.50	.10
☐ 193 Classic One on One II	.25	.12	.02
☐ 194 Anderson Hunt	.08	.04	.01
☐ 195 Darrin Chancellor	.08	.04	.01
☐ 196 Damon Lopez	.08	.04	.01
☐ 197 Thomas Jordan	.08	.04	.01
☐ 198 Tony Farmer	.08	.04	.01
☐ 199 Billy Owens (Number Three Pick)	.90	.45	.09
☐ 200 Owens Takes 4-3 Lead (Billy Owens)	.25	.12	.02
☐ 201 Johnson Slams for 6-6 Tie (Larry Johnson)	.25	.12	.02
☐ 202 Score Tied with :49 Left	.25	.12	.02
☐ 203 Gary Brown	.15	.07	.01
☐ 204 Rob Carpenter	.25	.12	.02
☐ 205 Ricky Ervins	2.00	1.00	.20
☐ 206 Donald Hollas	.25	.12	.02
☐ 207 Greg Lewis	.60	.30	.06
☐ 208 Darren Lewis	.35	.17	.03
☐ 209 Anthony Morgan	.30	.15	.03
☐ 210 Chris Smith	.08	.04	.01
☐ 211 Perry Carter	.08	.04	.01
☐ 212 Melvin Cheatum	.08	.04	.01
☐ 213 Jerome Harmon	.08	.04	.01
☐ 214 Keith(Mr.) Jennings	.12	.06	.01
☐ 215 Brian Shorter	.08	.04	.01
☐ 216 Dexter Davis	.08	.04	.01
☐ 217 Ed McCaffrey	.30	.15	.03
☐ 218 Joey Hamilton	.90	.45	.09
☐ 219 Marc Kroon	.20	.10	.02
☐ 220 Moe Gardner	.20	.10	.02
☐ 221 Jon Vaughn	.30	.15	.03
☐ 222 Lawrence Dawsey	.75	.35	.07
☐ 223 Michael Stonebreaker	.10	.05	.01
☐ 224 Shawn Moore	.30	.15	.03
☐ 225 Shawn Green	1.00	.50	.10
☐ 226 Scott Pisciotta	.20	.10	.02
☐ 227 Checklist 1	.05	.02	.00
☐ 228 Checklist 2	.05	.02	.00
☐ 229 Checklist 3	.05	.02	.00
☐ 230 Checklist 4	.05	.02	.00

1991 Classic Draft Pick Collection LP Inserts *

Cards from this ten-card bonus subset were randomly inserted in 1991 Classic Draft Pick Collection foil packs. The cards are distinguished from the regular issue in that nine of them have a silver inner border while one has a gold inner border. A five-card Ismail subset is also to be found within the nine silver-bordered cards. The "1991 Classic Draft Picks" emblem appears as a wine-colored wax seal at the upper left corner. The horizontally oriented backs carry brief comments superimposed over a dusted version of Classic's wax seal emblem. The cards are numbered on the back.

	MINT	EXC	G-VG
COMPLETE SET (10)	40.00	20.00	4.00
COMMON PLAYER (1-10)	3.00	1.50	.30
☐ LP1 Rocket Lands In Canada	3.00	1.50	.30
☐ LP2 Rocket Surveys The Future	3.00	1.50	.30
☐ LP3 Rocket Launch	3.00	1.50	.30
☐ LP4 Track Star (Rocket Ismail)	3.00	1.50	.30
☐ LP5 Rocket Knows Classic	3.00	1.50	.30
☐ LP6 Johnson's Guns (Larry Johnson)	6.00	3.00	.60
☐ LP7 Brien Taylor	6.00	3.00	.60
☐ LP8 Classic Gold Card SP	12.00	6.00	1.20
☐ LP9 The Final Shot (Larry Johnson and Billy Owens)	5.00	2.50	.50
☐ LP10 Russell Maryland (Number One Pick)	4.00	2.00	.40

1992 Classic Draft Picks

The 1992 Classic Draft Pick set contains 100 standard-size (2 1/2" by 3 1/2") cards, including all 54 drafted players. The set features the only 1992 trading card of NBA first overall pick Shaquille O'Neal as well as the only draft cards of second pick Alonzo Mourning and fourth pick Jimmy Jackson. The set also includes a Flashback (95-98) subset. The fronts feature glossy color action photos bordered in white. The player's name appears in a silver stripe beneath the picture, which intersects the Classic logo at the lower left corner. The backs have a second color player photo and present biographical information, complete college statistics, and a scouting report. The cards are numbered on the back. Cards 61-100 were only available in foil packs as the blister sets contained only cards 1-60.

	MINT	EXC	G-VG
COMPLETE SET (100)	15.00	7.50	1.50
COMMON PLAYER (1-60)	.07	.03	.01
COMMON PLAYER (61-100)	.07	.03	.01
☐ 1 Shaquille O'Neal LSU	6.00	3.00	.60
☐ 2 Walt Williams Maryland	.50	.25	.05
☐ 3 Lee Mayberry Arkansas	.25	.12	.02
☐ 4 Tony Bennett Wisconsin (Green Bay)	.15	.07	.01
☐ 5 Litterial Green Georgia	.25	.12	.02
☐ 6 Chris Smith Connecticut	.20	.10	.02
☐ 7 Henry Williams NC (Charlotte)	.15	.07	.01
☐ 8 Terrell Lowery Loyola	.12	.06	.01
☐ 9 Radenko Dobras South Florida	.10	.05	.01
☐ 10 Curtis Blair Richmond	.15	.07	.01
☐ 11 Randy Woods La Salle	.25	.12	.02
☐ 12 Todd Day Arkansas	.60	.30	.06
☐ 13 Anthony Peeler Missouri	.40	.20	.04
☐ 14 Darin Archbold Butler	.07	.03	.01
☐ 15 Benford Williams Texas	.07	.03	.01
☐ 16 Terrence Lewis Washington State	.07	.03	.01
☐ 17 James McCoy Massachusetts	.07	.03	.01
☐ 18 Damon Patterson Oklahoma	.07	.03	.01
☐ 19 Bryant Stith Virginia	.30	.15	.03
☐ 20 Doug Christie Pepperdine	.25	.12	.02
☐ 21 Latrell Sprewell Alabama	.20	.10	.02
☐ 22 Hubert Davis North Carolina	.35	.17	.03
☐ 23 David Booth DePaul	.10	.05	.01
☐ 24 David Johnson Syracuse	.35	.17	.03
☐ 25 Jon Barry Georgia Tech	.35	.17	.03
☐ 26 Everick Sullivan Louisville	.10	.05	.01
☐ 27 Brian Davis Duke	.20	.10	.02
☐ 28 Clarence Weatherspoon Southern Mississippi	.40	.20	.04
☐ 29 Malik Sealy St. John's	.35	.17	.03
☐ 30 Matt Geiger Georgia Tech	.15	.07	.01
☐ 31 Jimmy Jackson Ohio State	1.50	.75	.15
☐ 32 Matt Steigenga Michigan State	.20	.10	.02
☐ 33 Robert Horry Alabama	.25	.12	.02
☐ 34 Marlon Maxey UTEP	.15	.07	.01
☐ 35 Reggie Slater Wyoming	.07	.03	.01
☐ 36 Lucius Davis Cal (Santa Barbara)	.07	.03	.01
☐ 37 Chris King Wake Forest	.15	.07	.01
☐ 38 Dexter Cambridge Texas	.07	.03	.01
☐ 39 Alonzo Jamison Kansas	.07	.03	.01
☐ 40 Anthony Tucker Wake Forest	.07	.03	.01
☐ 41 Tracy Murray UCLA	.35	.17	.03
☐ 42 Vernel Singleton LSU	.07	.03	.01
☐ 43 Christian Laettner Duke	1.25	.60	.12
☐ 44 Don MacLean UCLA	.35	.17	.03
☐ 45 Adam Keefe Stanford	.30	.15	.03
☐ 46 Tom Gugliotta North Carolina State	.35	.17	.03
☐ 47 LaPhonso Ellis Notre Dame	.50	.25	.05
☐ 48 Byron Houston Oklahoma	.35	.17	.03
☐ 49 Oliver Miller Arkansas	.25	.12	.02
☐ 50 Ron"Popeye" Jones Murray State	.15	.07	.01
☐ 51 P.J. Brown Louisiana Tech	.15	.07	.01
☐ 52 Eric Anderson Indiana	.10	.05	.01
☐ 53 Darren Morningstar Pittsburgh	.20	.10	.02
☐ 54 Isaiah Morris Arkansas	.15	.07	.01
☐ 55 Stephen Howard DePaul	.07	.03	.01
☐ 56 Reggie Smith TCU	.20	.10	.02
☐ 57 Elmore Spencer UNLV	.20	.10	.02
☐ 58 Sean Rooks Arizona	.20	.10	.02
☐ 59 Robert Werdann St. John's	.15	.07	.01
☐ 60 Alonzo Mourning Georgetown	1.75	.85	.17
☐ 61 Steve Rogers Alabama State	.15	.07	.01
☐ 62 Tim Burroughs Jacksonville	.15	.07	.01
☐ 63 Ed Book Canisius	.07	.03	.01
☐ 64 Herb Jones Cincinnati	.10	.05	.01
☐ 65 Mik Kilgore Temple	.07	.03	.01
☐ 66 Ken Leeks Central Florida	.07	.03	.01
☐ 67 Sam Mack Houston	.07	.03	.01
☐ 68 Sean Miller Pittsburgh	.07	.03	.01
☐ 69 Craig Upchurch Houston	.07	.03	.01
☐ 70 Van Usher Tennessee Tech	.07	.03	.01

☐ 71 Corey Williams Oklahoma State	.20	.10	.02
☐ 72 Duane Cooper USC	.20	.10	.02
☐ 73 Brett Roberts Morehead State	.15	.07	.01
☐ 74 Elmer Bennett Notre Dame	.20	.10	.02
☐ 75 Brent Price Oklahoma	.20	.10	.02
☐ 76 Daimon Sweet Notre Dame	.10	.05	.01
☐ 77 Darrick Martin UCLA	.10	.05	.01
☐ 78 Gerald Madkins UCLA	.10	.05	.01
☐ 79 Jo Jo English South Carolina	.07	.03	.01
☐ 80 Alex Blackwell Monmouth	.07	.03	.01
☐ 81 Anthony Dade Louisiana Tech	.07	.03	.01
☐ 82 Matt Fish NC (Wilmington)	.15	.07	.01
☐ 83 Byron Tucker George Mason	.07	.03	.01
☐ 84 Harold Miner USC	.60	.30	.06
☐ 85 Greg Dennis East Tennessee State	.07	.03	.01
☐ 86 Jeff Roulston South Carolina	.07	.03	.01
☐ 87 Keir Rogers Loyola (Illinois)	.07	.03	.01
☐ 88 Billy Law Colorado	.07	.03	.01
☐ 89 Geoff Lear Pepperdine	.07	.03	.01
☐ 90 Lambert Shell Bridgeport	.07	.03	.01
☐ 91 Elbert Rogers Alabama (Birmingham)	.07	.03	.01
☐ 92 Ron Ellis Louisiana Tech	.15	.07	.01
☐ 93 Predrag Danilovic	.15	.07	.01
☐ 94 Calvin Talford East Tennessee State	.07	.03	.01
☐ 95 Stacey Augmon UNLV Flashback 1	.12	.06	.01
☐ 96 Steve Smith Michigan State Flashback 2	.15	.07	.01
☐ 97 Billy Owens Syracuse Flashback 3	.25	.12	.02
☐ 98 Dikembe Mutombo Georgetown Flashback 4	.25	.12	.02
☐ 99 Checklist 1 (1-50)	.07	.03	.01
☐ 100 Checklist 2 (51-100)	.07	.03	.01
☐ BC Christian Laettner (bonus card only in blister sets)	2.00	1.00	.20

1992 Classic Draft Pick LP Inserts

This 10-card set, subtitled "Top Ten Pick", features the top ten picks of the 1992 NBA Draft. These standard size (2 1/2" by 3 1/2") cards were inserted in 1992 Classic Draft Pick foil packs. The fronts feature glossy color action photos enclosed by white borders. The player's name appears in a silver foil stripe beneath the picture, which intersects the Classic logo at the lower left corner. The production figures "1 of 56,000" and the "Top Ten Pick" emblem at the card top are also silver foil. The horizontally oriented backs have a silver background and feature a second color player photo and player profile. The cards are numbered on the back with an LP (limited print) prefix.

	MINT	EXC	G-VG
COMPLETE SET (10)	45.00	22.50	4.50
COMMON PLAYER (1-10)	3.00	1.50	.30
☐ LP1 Shaquille O'Neal LSU	18.00	9.00	1.80
☐ LP2 Alonzo Mourning Georgetown	8.00	4.00	.80
☐ LP3 Christian Laettner Duke	6.00	3.00	.60
☐ LP4 Jimmy Jackson Ohio State	7.00	3.50	.70
☐ LP5 LaPhonso Ellis Notre Dame	4.00	2.00	.40
☐ LP6 Tom Gugliotta North Carolina State	3.00	1.50	.30
☐ LP7 Walt Williams Maryland	4.00	2.00	.40
☐ LP8 Todd Day Arkansas	4.00	2.00	.40
☐ LP9 Clarence Weatherspoon Southern Mississippi	3.00	1.50	.30
☐ LP10 Adam Keefe Stanford	3.00	1.50	.30

1992 Classic BK Previews

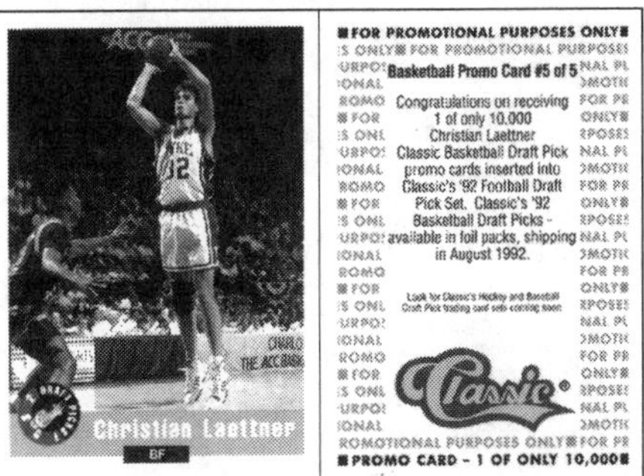

These Classic Basketball Draft Pick preview cards were randomly inserted in the 1992 Classic Football Draft Pick packs. Only 10,000 of each card were produced. The standard-size cards (2 1/2" by 3 1/2") cards feature on the front glossy color action player photos enclosed by white borders. The Classic logo, player's name, and position appear in a silver stripe beneath the picture. The backs read repeatedly "For Promotional Purposes Only" as well as bearing an advertisement and the Classic logo. The cards are numbered on the back.

	MINT	EXC	G-VG
COMPLETE SET (5)	40.00	20.00	4.00
COMMON PLAYER (1-5)	4.00	2.00	.40
☐ 1 Shaquille O'Neal LSU	25.00	12.50	2.50
☐ 2 Alonzo Mourning Georgetown	10.00	5.00	1.00
☐ 3 Don McLean UCLA	4.00	2.00	.40
☐ 4 Walt Williams Maryland	6.00	3.00	.60
☐ 5 Christian Laettner Duke	8.00	4.00	.80

1978-79 Clippers Handyman

The 1978-79 San Diego Clippers Handyman set contains nine cards measuring approximately 2" by 4 1/4". The cards are "3-D" and are similar to the 1970s Kelloggs baseball sets. Each card has a coupon tab attached (included in the dimensions given above). Coach Gene Shue's card was apparently not distributed (as it was the grand prize winner of the contest) with the other cards but does exist. Some veteran collectors and dealers also consider Kunnert to be somewhat tougher to find. In addition there is a second version of the Lloyd Free card.

	NRMT	VG-E	GOOD
COMPLETE SET (9)	35.00	17.50	3.50
COMMON PLAYER (1-9)	3.00	1.50	.30
□ 1 Randy Smith 9	4.50	2.25	.45
□ 2 Nick Weatherspoon 12	3.50	1.75	.35
□ 3 Freeman Williams 20	3.50	1.75	.35
□ 4 Sidney Wicks 21	7.50	3.75	.75
□ 5 Lloyd Free 24	5.00	2.50	.50
□ 6 Swen Nater 31	5.00	2.50	.50
□ 7 Jerome Whitehead 33	3.00	1.50	.30
□ 8 Kermit Washington 42	3.50	1.75	.35
□ 9 Kevin Kunnert 44	7.50	3.75	.75
□ xx Gene Shue CO	750.00	375.00	75.00

1990-91 Clippers Star

This 12-card set of Los Angeles Clippers was produced by the Star Company and measures the standard size (2 1/2" and 3 1/2"). The fronts feature color action shots, with red borders that wash out in the middle of the card face. The horizontally oriented backs are printed in red and blue on white and have biographical as well as statistical information. The cards are unnumbered and are checklisted below in alphabetical order. Benoit Benjamin and Mike Smrek were apparently planned for the set but were not released with the other cards listed below.

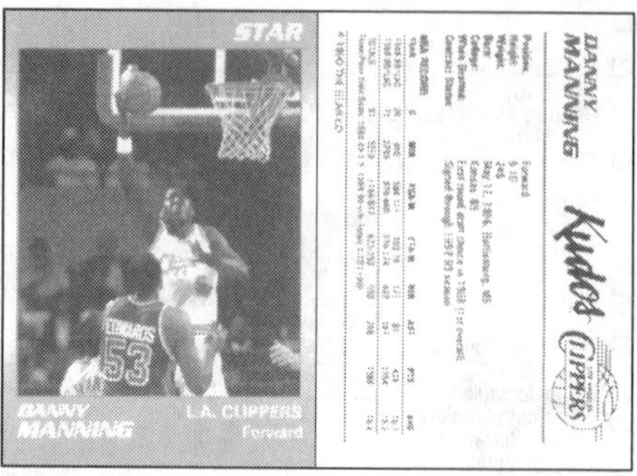

	MINT	EXC	G-VG
COMPLETE SET (12)	9.00	4.50	.90
COMMON PLAYER (1-12)	.60	.30	.06
□ 1 Ken Bannister	.60	.30	.06
□ 2 Winston Garland	.60	.30	.06
□ 3 Tom Garrick	.60	.30	.06
□ 4 Gary Grant	.75	.35	.07
□ 5 Ron Harper	1.50	.75	.15
□ 6 Bo Kimble	1.00	.50	.10
□ 7 Danny Manning	2.00	1.00	.20
□ 8 Jeff Martin	.60	.30	.06
□ 9 Ken Norman	1.25	.60	.12
□ 10 Mike Schuler CO	.60	.30	.06
□ 11 Charles Smith	1.50	.75	.15
□ 12 Loy Vaught	1.00	.50	.10

1971 Colonels Marathon Oil

This set of Marathon Oil Pro Star Portraits consists of colorful portraits by distinguished artist Nicholas Volpe. Each (ABA Kentucky Colonels) portrait measures approximately 7 1/2" by 9 7/8" and features a painting of the player's face on a black background, with an action painting superimposed to the side. A facsimile autograph in white appears at the bottom of the portrait. At the bottom of each portrait is a postcard measuring 7 1/2" by 4" after perforation. While the back of the portrait has offers for a basketball photo album, autographed tumblers, and a poster, the postcard itself could also be used to apply for a Marathon credit card. The portraits are unnumbered and checklisted below in alphabetical order.

	NRMT	VG-E	GOOD
COMPLETE SET (11)	45.00	22.50	4.50
COMMON PLAYER (1-11)	3.50	1.75	.35
□ 1 Darrell Carrier	4.50	2.25	.45
□ 2 Bobby Croft	3.50	1.75	.35
□ 3 Louie Dampier	6.00	3.00	.60
□ 4 Les Hunter	4.50	2.25	.45
□ 5 Dan Issel	15.00	7.50	1.50
□ 6 Jim Ligon	3.50	1.75	.35
□ 7 Cincy Powell	3.50	1.75	.35
□ 8 Mike Pratt	3.50	1.75	.35
□ 9 Walt Simon	3.50	1.75	.35
□ 10 Sam Smith	3.50	1.75	.35
□ 11 Howard Wright	3.50	1.75	.35

1989 Converse

This 14-card set was sponsored by Converse and measures the standard size (2 1/2" by 3 1/2"). The color action player photo on the front is outlined by a thin black border against a white background. At the top, the words "Converse, Official Shoe of the NBA" is printed in blue lettering, as is the player's name and number below the picture. The NBA logo in the upper right corner rounds out the card face. The back presents a brief biography, career highlights, and a tip from the player and Converse in the form of an anti-drug or alcohol message. The cards are unnumbered and checklisted below in alphabetical order. Mark Aguirre is misspelled Aquirre on the checklist card.

	MINT	EXC	G-VG
COMPLETE SET (14)	20.00	10.00	2.00
COMMON PLAYER (1-14)	.60	.30	.06
☐ 1 Mark Aguirre	.60	.30	.06
☐ 2 Larry Bird	7.50	3.75	.75
☐ 3 Rolando Blackman	.60	.30	.06
☐ 4 Tyrone Bogues	.60	.30	.06
☐ 5 Rex Chapman	1.00	.50	.10
☐ 6 Magic Johnson	10.00	5.00	1.00
☐ 7 Bernard King	1.00	.50	.10
☐ 8 Bill Laimbeer	.75	.35	.07
☐ 9 Karl Malone	2.50	1.25	.25
☐ 10 Kevin McHale	1.25	.60	.12
☐ 11 Mark Price	2.00	1.00	.20
☐ 12 Jack Sikma	.75	.35	.07
☐ 13 Reggie Theus	.75	.35	.07
☐ 14 Title Card (checklist back)	.60	.30	.06

1991 Courtside Draft Pix

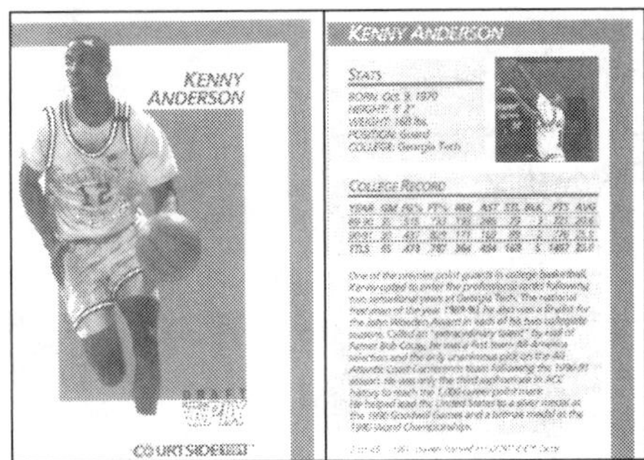

The 1991 Courtside Draft Pix basketball set consists of 45 cards measuring the standard size (2 1/2" by 3 1/2"). All 198,000 sets produced are numbered and distributed as complete sets in their own custom boxes each accompanied by a certificate with a unique serial number. It has also been reported that 30,000 autographed cards were randomly inserted in the 9,900 cases. The card front features a color action player photo. The design of the card fronts features a color rectangle (either pearlized red, blue, or green) on a pearlized white background, with two border stripes in the same color intersecting at the upper right corner. The player's name appears at the upper right corner of the card face, with the words "Courtside 1991" at the bottom. The backs reflect the color on the fronts and present stats (biographical), college record (year by year statistics), and player profile. The cards are numbered on the back. The unnumbered Larry Johnson sendaway card is not included in the complete set price below.

	MINT	EXC	G-VG
COMPLETE SET (45)	10.00	5.00	1.00
COMMON PLAYER (1-45)	.05	.02	.00
☐ 1 Larry Johnson First Draft Pick UNLV	2.00	1.00	.20
☐ 2 George Ackles UNLV	.08	.04	.01
☐ 3 Kenny Anderson Georgia Tech	1.50	.75	.15
☐ 4 Greg Anthony UNLV	.40	.20	.04
☐ 5 Anthony Avent Seton Hall	.20	.10	.02
☐ 6 Terrell Brandon Oregon	.40	.20	.04
☐ 7 Kevin Brooks Southwestern Louisiana	.15	.07	.01
☐ 8 Marc Brown Siena	.12	.06	.01
☐ 9 Myron Brown Slippery Rock	.10	.05	.01
☐ 10 Randy Brown New Mexico State	.15	.07	.01
☐ 11 Darrin Chancellor Southern Mississippi	.08	.04	.01
☐ 12 Pete Chilcutt North Carolina	.20	.10	.02
☐ 13 Chris Corchiani North Carolina St.	.15	.07	.01
☐ 14 John Crotty Virginia	.10	.05	.01
☐ 15 Dale Davis Clemson	.35	.17	.03
☐ 16 Marty Dow San Diego State	.08	.04	.01
☐ 17 Richard Dumas Oklahoma State	.08	.04	.01
☐ 18 LeRon Ellis Syracuse	.12	.06	.01
☐ 19 Tony Farmer Nebraska	.08	.04	.01
☐ 20 Roy Fisher California	.08	.04	.01
☐ 21 Rick Fox North Carolina	1.00	.50	.10
☐ 22 Chad Gallagher Creighton	.08	.04	.01
☐ 23 Chris Gatling Old Dominion	.40	.20	.04
☐ 24 Sean Green Iona	.15	.07	.01
☐ 25 Reggie Hanson Kentucky	.08	.04	.01
☐ 26 Donald Hodge Temple	.35	.17	.03
☐ 27 Steve Hood James Madison	.10	.05	.01
☐ 28 Keith Hughes Rutgers	.08	.04	.01
☐ 29 Mike Iuzzolino St.Francis	.35	.17	.03
☐ 30 Keith Jennings East Tenn. State	.15	.07	.01
☐ 31 Larry Johnson UNLV	5.00	2.50	.50
☐ 32 Treg Lee Ohio State	.08	.04	.01
☐ 33 Cedric Lewis Maryland	.08	.04	.01
☐ 34 Kevin Lynch Minnesota	.15	.07	.01
☐ 35 Mark Macon Temple	.35	.17	.03
☐ 36 Jason Matthews Pittsburgh	.08	.04	.01
☐ 37 Eric Murdock Providence	.30	.15	.03
☐ 38 Jimmy Oliver Purdue	.20	.10	.02
☐ 39 Doug Overton LaSalle	.08	.04	.01
☐ 40 Elliot Perry Memphis State	.15	.07	.01
☐ 41 Brian Shorter Pittsburgh	.08	.04	.01
☐ 42 Alvaro Teheran Houston	.05	.02	.00
☐ 43 Joey Wright Texas	.08	.04	.01
☐ 44 Joe Wylie Miami (FL)	.08	.04	.01

		MINT	EXC	G-VG
☐ 45	Larry Johnson Collegiate Player of the Year	1.50	.75	.15
☐ NNO	Larry Johnson SP (Sendaway)	5.00	2.50	.50

1991 Courtside Holograms

These three holograms were issued in a plastic sleeve within a paper envelope. According to information printed on the envelope, 99,000 sets were produced. Each hologram features the player photo against a parquet basketball floor background, with a subtitle at the bottom of the card face. Framed by turquoise borders above and on the right, the backs present stats (biographical), college record (year by year statistics), and profile. The cards are unnumbered and checklisted below in alphabetical order.

	MINT	EXC	G-VG
COMPLETE SET (3)	5.00	2.50	.50
COMMON PLAYER (1-3)	.60	.30	.06
☐ 1 Greg Anthony 1990 National Champions	.80	.40	.08
☐ 2 Larry Johnson 1990 Player of the Year	4.50	2.25	.45
☐ 3 Mark Macon First Round Draft Pick	.60	.30	.06

1992 Courtside College Flashback

As a tribute to 100 years of basketball, Courtside released this 45-card standard-size (2 1/2" by 3 1/2") set, featuring some of the greatest players and coaches of the sport. It is reported that the production run was 199,000 sets, with 20 sets per individually numbered (from 1 to 9,950) case. Ten thousand autographed cards were randomly included with the sets. In exchange for the Courtside certificate found within each set, the collector received one of 25,000 promotional strips, featuring Larry Bird, David Robinson, and Kareem Abdul-Jabbar. The front features a color player photo cut out and superimposed on a background consisting of white and either red, green, or blue blocks. The backs carry a second color player photo and a brief career summary. The cards are numbered on the back.

	MINT	EXC	G-VG
COMPLETE SET (45)	8.00	4.00	.80
COMMON PLAYER (1-45)	.10	.05	.01
☐ 1 Tommy Amaker Duke	.10	.05	.01
☐ 2 Charles Barkley Auburn	.50	.25	.05
☐ 3 Rick Barry Miami (FL)	.25	.12	.02
☐ 4 Larry Bird Indiana State	1.00	.50	.10
☐ 5 Larry Brown CO	.10	.05	.01
☐ 6 Quinn Buckner Indiana	.15	.07	.01
☐ 7 Tom Burleson North Carolina State	.10	.05	.01
☐ 8 Austin Carr Notre Dame	.15	.07	.01
☐ 9 Phil Ford North Carolina	.15	.07	.01
☐ 10 Andrew Gaze Seton Hall	.10	.05	.01
☐ 11 Artis Gilmore Jacksonville	.20	.10	.02
☐ 12 Jack Givens Kentucky	.10	.05	.01
☐ 13 Gail Goodrich UCLA	.20	.10	.02
☐ 14 Kevin Grevey Kentucky	.10	.05	.01
☐ 15 Ernie Grunfeld Tennessee	.10	.05	.01
☐ 16 Elvin Hayes Houston	.35	.17	.03
☐ 17 Walt Hazzard UCLA	.15	.07	.01
☐ 18 Kareem Abdul-Jabbar UCLA	.75	.35	.07
☐ 19 Marques Johnson UCLA	.15	.07	.01
☐ 20 John Lucas Maryland	.15	.07	.01
☐ 21 Kyle Macy Kentucky	.10	.05	.01
☐ 22 Rollie Massimino CO Villanova	.10	.05	.01
☐ 23 Cedric Maxwell N. Carolina-Charlotte	.10	.05	.01
☐ 24 Bob McAdoo North Carolina	.20	.10	.02
☐ 25 Al McGuire CO Marquette	.20	.10	.02
☐ 26 George Mikan DePaul	.35	.17	.03
☐ 27 Sidney Moncrief Arkansas	.15	.07	.01
☐ 28 Chris Mullin St. John's	.40	.20	.04
☐ 29 Calvin Murphy Niagara	.20	.10	.02
☐ 30 Sam Perkins North Carolina	.20	.10	.02
☐ 31 David Robinson Navy	1.00	.50	.10
☐ 32 Curtis Rowe UCLA	.15	.07	.01
☐ 33 Cazzie Russell Michigan	.15	.07	.01
☐ 34 Charlie Scott North Carolina	.10	.05	.01
☐ 35 Dean Smith CO North Carolina	.15	.07	.01
☐ 36 Jerry Tarkanian CO UNLV	.20	.10	.02
☐ 37 David Thompson North Carolina State	.15	.07	.01
☐ 38 Nate Thurmond Bowling Green	.15	.07	.01
☐ 39 Monte Towe North Carolina State	.10	.05	.01
☐ 40 Jim Valvano CO	.20	.10	.02

North Carolina State			
☐ 41 Bill Walton	.25	.12	.02
UCLA			
☐ 42 Paul Westphal	.15	.07	.01
USC			
☐ 43 Dereck Whittenburg	.10	.05	.01
North Carolina State			
☐ 44 Sidney Wicks	.15	.07	.01
North Carolina State			
☐ 45 John Wooden CO	.20	.10	.02
UCLA			

1991 Cousy Collection Preview

This five-card "preview" set was issued to honor Bob Cousy, who sparked the Boston Celtics to six world championships during his thirteen year career. The cards measure 2 1/2" by 3 1/2". The front features vintage black and white photos that highlight Bob Cousy's career. The lettering is in green and white on a black background. The back presents biographical information and is printed in black lettering on gray, with black and green stripes traversing the top of the card. The cards are numbered on the back.

	MINT	EXC	G-VG
COMPLETE SET (5)	10.00	5.00	1.00
COMMON PLAYER (1-5)	2.00	1.00	.20
☐ 1 Rookie Card	4.00	2.00	.40
☐ 2 High School 1945-46	2.00	1.00	.20
☐ 3 1940-50 Senior Year Holy Cross	2.00	1.00	.20
☐ 4 1962-63 Season	2.00	1.00	.20
☐ 5 Coaching Boston College	2.00	1.00	.20

1991 Cousy Collection

Publicist Milton Kahn produced this 25-card set to chronicle the career of former Boston Celtic great and Basketball Hall of Famer Bob Cousy. Production quantities of the standard-size (2 1/2" by 3 1/2") cards were limited to 100,000 sets. The fronts feature black and white photos that capture various moments in Cousy's career. The photos are bordered on the top by a green stripe and by black on the other three sides. The backs have a similar design to the fronts. On a gray background, they have captions for the photos and a card number in the upper left corner. On the back, each card of the set bears a unique serial number.

	MINT	EXC	G-VG
COMPLETE SET (25)	20.00	10.00	2.00
COMMON PLAYER (1-25)	1.00	.50	.10
☐ 1 Rookie Card	2.00	1.00	.20
☐ 2 "1st Year" Card 1929	1.00	.50	.10

☐ 3 Playground 1944-1945	1.00	.50	.10
☐ 4 High School 1945-1946	1.00	.50	.10
☐ 5 NCAA Kings 1946-1947	1.00	.50	.10
☐ 6 Holy Cross, Senior Year 1949-1950	1.00	.50	.10
☐ 7 Double Trouble 1951-1952	1.00	.50	.10
☐ 8 Star of Stars 1954	1.00	.50	.10
☐ 9 Stan the Man 1955	1.00	.50	.10
☐ 10 Timely Idea 1955	1.00	.50	.10
☐ 11 "Star" Again 1957	1.00	.50	.10
☐ 12 The MVP 1957	1.00	.50	.10
☐ 13 The Deal 1959	1.00	.50	.10
☐ 14 "Four" Plan 1958-1959	1.00	.50	.10
☐ 15 At Home 1960	1.00	.50	.10
☐ 16 Victory Watch 1961-1962	1.00	.50	.10
☐ 17 Visit with J.F.K. 1961-1962	1.00	.50	.10
☐ 18 Master and Mentor 1963	1.00	.50	.10
☐ 19 His "Day" 1963	1.00	.50	.10
☐ 20 A Career 1963	1.00	.50	.10
☐ 21 Author 1965	1.00	.50	.10
☐ 22 "Podnuhs" 1965	1.00	.50	.10
☐ 23 Coaching, Boston College 1968-1969	1.00	.50	.10
☐ 24 Coaching, Cincinnati Royals 1969-1970	1.00	.50	.10
☐ 25 Made for TV 1990-1991	1.00	.50	.10

1977-78 Dell Flipbooks

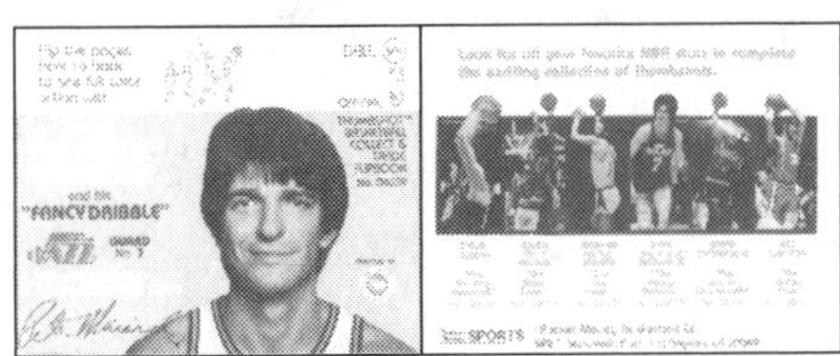

This set of flipbooks was produced by Pocket Money Basketball Co. These flipbooks measure approximately 4" by 3 1/8" and are 24 pages in length. They have color action player photos and career statistics. The booklets are unnumbered and are checklisted below in alphabetical order by subject. The front has a white stripe at the top, and a color head and shoulders shot of the player on a color background. The inside front cover has a table of contents, while the inside back cover has the logos of all 22 NBA teams. Each flipbook features a different play or move by the player; e.g., the Maravich flipbook is titled, "Pete The Pistol Maravich and his Fancy Dribble." When the odd-numbered pages are flipped in a smooth movement from front to back, they form a color "motion picture" of Maravich crossing over his dribble through his legs. The even-numbered pages present a variety of information on Maravich, his team (New Orleans Jazz), and the 1976-77 NBA season.

	NRMT	VG-E	GOOD
COMPLETE SET (6)	100.00	50.00	10.00
COMMON PLAYER (1-6)	10.00	5.00	1.00
☐ 1 Kareem Abdul-Jabbar	35.00	17.50	3.50
☐ 2 Dave Cowens	12.00	6.00	1.20
☐ 3 Julius Erving	25.00	12.50	2.50
☐ 4 Pete Maravich	20.00	10.00	2.00
☐ 5 David Thompson	10.00	5.00	1.00
☐ 6 Bill Walton	16.00	8.00	1.60

1948-49 Exhibits Sports Champions

This multi-sport 1948-49 Sports Champions Exhibits issue contains 49 cards. The cards measure 3 1/4" by 5 3/8". The cards are identifiable by a line of agate type below the facsimile autograph relating some information about the player's accomplishments. The cards, as with most exhibits, are blank backed. The catalog designation for this exhibit set is W469. The cards issued in 1949 are reportedly twice as difficult to find as those issued in 1948. Cards issued only in 1949 are indicated with (49) in the checklist. Variations on Button and Scott exist in the agate line of type found on the bottom of the card.

	NRMT	VG-E	GOOD
COMPLETE SET (49)	1700.00	850.00	200.00
COMMON FOOTBALL	12.00	6.00	1.20
COMMON HOCKEY	18.00	9.00	1.80
COMMON BOXER	12.00	6.00	1.20
COMMON BASKETBALL	30.00	15.00	3.00
COMMON OTHER SPORTS	4.00	2.00	.40
☐ 1 Ted Allen horseshoes (49)	8.00	4.00	.80
☐ 2 Sammy Baugh football	50.00	25.00	5.00
☐ 3 Doug and Max Bentley hockey	35.00	17.50	3.50
☐ 4 Buddy Bomar bowling	4.00	2.00	.40
☐ 5A Richard Button skating (white coat; signature in white)	12.00	6.00	1.20
☐ 5B Richard Button skating (dark coat; signature in black)	12.00	6.00	1.20
☐ 6 Citation racehorse (49)	8.00	4.00	.80
☐ 7 John Cobb auto racing	15.00	7.50	1.50
☐ 8 Roy Conacher hockey (49)	30.00	15.00	3.00
☐ 9 Bob(Tarmac) Cook basketball	30.00	15.00	3.00
☐ 10 Ann Curtis swimming	4.00	2.00	.40
☐ 11 Ned Day (49)	8.00	4.00	.80
☐ 12 Jack Dempsey boxing	35.00	17.50	3.50
☐ 13 Harrison Dillard track (49)	12.00	6.00	1.20
☐ 14 Glenn Dobbs football (49)	30.00	15.00	3.00
☐ 15 Gil Dodds track	4.00	2.00	.40
☐ 16 Bill Durnan hockey	35.00	17.50	3.50
☐ 17 Chalmers(Bump) Elliott football	12.00	6.00	1.20
☐ 18 Joe Fulks basketball (49)	150.00	75.00	15.00
☐ 19 Edward Gauden track (49)	8.00	4.00	.80
☐ 20 Lucien Goudin fencing (49)	8.00	4.00	.80
☐ 21 Otto Graham football	35.00	17.50	3.50
☐ 22 Pat Harder football	15.00	7.50	1.50
☐ 23 Sonja Heine skating	6.00	3.00	.60
☐ 24 Ben Hogan golf (49)	30.00	15.00	3.00
☐ 25 Willie Hoppe billiards	4.00	2.00	.40
☐ 26 Jack Jacobs football	15.00	7.50	1.50
☐ 27 Jack Kramer tennis	8.00	4.00	.80
☐ 28 Gus Lewis handball (49)	8.00	4.00	.80
☐ 29 Guy Lombardo boat racing (49)	10.00	5.00	1.00
☐ 30 Joe Louis boxing	60.00	30.00	6.00
☐ 31 Sid Luckman football	35.00	17.50	3.50
☐ 32 Johnny Lujack football	30.00	15.00	3.00
☐ 33 Man of War racehorse	4.00	2.00	.40
☐ 34 Bob Mathias track (49)	25.00	12.50	2.50
☐ 35 Bob McDermott basketball	30.00	15.00	3.00
☐ 36 Gretchen Merrill skating	4.00	2.00	.40
☐ 37 George Mikan basketball	500.00	250.00	50.00
☐ 38 Dick Miles table tennis	4.00	2.00	.40
☐ 39 Marion Motley football (49)	40.00	20.00	4.00
☐ 40 Andy Phillip basketball (49)	100.00	50.00	10.00
☐ 41 Bobby Riggs tennis	8.00	4.00	.80
☐ 42A Barbara Ann Scott skating (looking to side; signature in white)	6.00	3.00	.60
☐ 42A Barbara Ann Scott skating (looking straight; signature in black)	6.00	3.00	.60
☐ 43 Ben Sklar marbles	4.00	2.00	.40
☐ 44 Clyde(Bulldog) Turner football	20.00	10.00	2.00
☐ 45 Steve Van Buren football	25.00	12.50	2.50
☐ 46 Andy Veripapa bowling	8.00	4.00	.80
☐ 47 Bob Waterfield football (49)	40.00	20.00	4.00
☐ 48 Murray Weir basketball (49)	100.00	50.00	10.00
☐ 49 Claude(Buddy) Young (hands on knees) football	12.00	6.00	1.20

1961-62 Fleer

The 1961 Fleer set was Fleer's only major basketball issue until the 1986-87 season. The cards in the set measure the standard, 2 1/2" by 3 1/2". Cards numbered 45 to 66 are action shots (designated IA) of players elsewhere in the set. Both the regular cards and the IA cards are numbered alphabetically within that

particular subgroup. No known scarcities exist, although the set is quite popular since it contains the first basketball cards of many of the game's all-time greats including Elgin Baylor, Wilt Chamberlain, Oscar Robertson, and Jerry West. Many of the cards are frequently found with centering problems.

	NRMT	VG-E	GOOD
COMPLETE SET (66)	4500.00	2100.00	500.00
COMMON PLAYER (1-44)	15.00	7.50	1.50
COMMON PLAYER IA (45-66)	11.00	5.50	1.10
☐ 1 Al Attles Philadelphia Warriors	70.00	15.00	3.00
☐ 2 Paul Arizin Philadelphia Warriors	27.00	13.50	2.70
☐ 3 Elgin Baylor Los Angeles Lakers	300.00	150.00	30.00
☐ 4 Walt Bellamy Chicago Packers	36.00	18.00	3.60
☐ 5 Arlen Bockhorn Cincinnati Royals	15.00	7.50	1.50
☐ 6 Bob Boozer Cincinnati Royals	18.00	9.00	1.80
☐ 7 Carl Braun Boston Celtics	18.00	9.00	1.80
☐ 8 Wilt Chamberlain Philadelphia Warriors	1500.00	600.00	175.00
☐ 9 Larry Costello Syracuse Nationals	20.00	10.00	2.00
☐ 10 Bob Cousy Boston Celtics	135.00	60.00	12.00
☐ 11 Walter Dukes Detroit Pistons	15.00	7.50	1.50
☐ 12 Wayne Embry Cincinnati Royals	35.00	17.50	3.50
☐ 13 Dave Gambee Syracuse Nationals	15.00	7.50	1.50
☐ 14 Tom Gola Philadelphia Warriors	27.00	13.50	2.70
☐ 15 Sihugo Green St. Louis Hawks	20.00	10.00	2.00
☐ 16 Hal Greer Syracuse Nationals	45.00	22.50	4.50
☐ 17 Richie Guerin New York Knicks	28.00	14.00	2.80
☐ 18 Cliff Hagan St. Louis Hawks	27.00	13.50	2.70
☐ 19 Tom Heinsohn Boston Celtics	50.00	25.00	5.00
☐ 20 Bailey Howell Detroit Pistons	25.00	12.50	2.50
☐ 21 Rod Hundley Los Angeles Lakers	27.00	13.50	2.70
☐ 22 K.C. Jones Boston Celtics	50.00	25.00	5.00
☐ 23 Sam Jones Boston Celtics	50.00	25.00	5.00
☐ 24 Phil Jordan New York Knicks	15.00	7.50	1.50
☐ 25 John Kerr Syracuse Nationals	25.00	12.50	2.50
☐ 26 Rudy LaRusso Los Angeles Lakers	25.00	12.50	2.50
☐ 27 George Lee Detroit Pistons	15.00	7.50	1.50
☐ 28 Bob Leonard Chicago Packers	15.00	7.50	1.50
☐ 29 Clyde Lovellette St. Louis Hawks	25.00	12.50	2.50
☐ 30 John McCarthy St. Louis Hawks	15.00	7.50	1.50
☐ 31 Tom Meschery Philadelphia Warriors	21.00	10.50	2.10
☐ 32 Willie Naulls New York Knicks	18.00	9.00	1.80
☐ 33 Don Ohl Detroit Pistons	20.00	10.00	2.00
☐ 34 Bob Pettit St. Louis Hawks	65.00	32.50	6.50
☐ 35 Frank Ramsey Boston Celtics	27.00	13.50	2.70
☐ 36 Oscar Robertson Cincinnati Royals	450.00	225.00	45.00
☐ 37 Guy Rodgers Philadelphia Warriors	21.00	10.50	2.10
☐ 38 Bill Russell Boston Celtics	500.00	250.00	50.00
☐ 39 Dolph Schayes Syracuse Nationals	30.00	15.00	3.00
☐ 40 Frank Selvy Los Angeles Lakers	15.00	7.50	1.50
☐ 41 Gene Shue Detroit Pistons	20.00	10.00	2.00
☐ 42 Jack Twyman Cincinnati Royals	25.00	12.50	2.50
☐ 43 Jerry West Los Angeles Lakers	675.00	325.00	65.00
☐ 44 Len Wilkens UER St. Louis Hawks (Misspelled Wilkins on card front)	65.00	32.50	6.50
☐ 45 Paul Arizin IA Philadelphia Warriors	15.00	7.50	1.50
☐ 46 Elgin Baylor IA Los Angeles Lakers	85.00	42.50	8.50
☐ 47 Wilt Chamberlain IA Philadelphia Warriors	300.00	150.00	30.00
☐ 48 Larry Costello IA Syracuse Nationals	12.00	6.00	1.20
☐ 49 Bob Cousy IA Boston Celtics	50.00	25.00	5.00
☐ 50 Walter Dukes IA Detroit Pistons	11.00	5.50	1.10
☐ 51 Tom Gola IA Philadelphia Warriors	15.00	7.50	1.50
☐ 52 Richie Guerin IA New York Knicks	15.00	7.50	1.50
☐ 53 Cliff Hagan IA St. Louis Hawks	16.00	8.00	1.60
☐ 54 Tom Heinsohn IA Boston Celtics	25.00	12.50	2.50
☐ 55 Bailey Howell IA Detroit Pistons	12.00	6.00	1.20
☐ 56 John Kerr IA Syracuse Nationals	14.00	7.00	1.40
☐ 57 Rudy LaRusso IA Los Angeles Lakers	14.00	7.00	1.40
☐ 58 Clyde Lovellette IA St. Louis Hawks	14.00	7.00	1.40
☐ 59 Bob Pettit IA St. Louis Hawks	30.00	15.00	3.00
☐ 60 Frank Ramsey IA Boston Celtics	14.00	7.00	1.40
☐ 61 Oscar Robertson IA Cincinnati Royals	125.00	60.00	12.50
☐ 62 Bill Russell IA Boston Celtics	200.00	100.00	20.00
☐ 63 Dolph Schayes IA Syracuse Nationals	17.00	8.50	1.70
☐ 64 Gene Shue IA Detroit Pistons	12.00	6.00	1.20
☐ 65 Jack Twyman IA Cincinnati Royals	14.00	7.00	1.40
☐ 66 Jerry West IA Los Angeles Lakers	210.00	75.00	15.00

1973-74 Fleer "The Shots"

This 21-card set was produced by artist R.G. Laughlin for Fleer. The cards measure approximately 2 1/2" by 4". The cards were distributed in packs with one "Shots" card along with two team logo cloth patches and one stick of gum. The fronts feature an illustration of the shot depicted on the card. The illustration is in color, although crudely drawn. The back has a discussion of the shot. The cards are numbered on the back.

	NRMT	VG-E	GOOD
COMPLETE SET (21)	35.00	17.50	3.50
COMMON PLAYER (1-21)	2.00	1.00	.20
☐ 1 Two-Hand Set	3.00	1.50	.30
☐ 2 Overhead Set	2.00	1.00	.20
☐ 3 One-Hand Set	2.00	1.00	.20
☐ 4 Two-Hand Jumper	2.00	1.00	.20
☐ 5 One-Hand Jumper	2.00	1.00	.20
☐ 6 Twisting Jumper	2.00	1.00	.20
☐ 7 Hook Shot	2.00	1.00	.20
☐ 8 Driving Hook	2.00	1.00	.20
☐ 9 Layup	2.00	1.00	.20
☐ 10 Reverse Layup	2.00	1.00	.20
☐ 11 Underhand Layup	2.00	1.00	.20
☐ 12 Pivot Shots	2.00	1.00	.20
☐ 13 Step-Away	2.00	1.00	.20
☐ 14 Running One-Hander	2.00	1.00	.20
☐ 15 Stuff or Dunk	3.00	1.50	.30
☐ 16 Tap-In	2.00	1.00	.20
☐ 17 Bank Shot	2.00	1.00	.20
☐ 18 Free Throw	2.00	1.00	.20
☐ 19 Desperation Shot	2.00	1.00	.20
☐ 20 Blocked Shot	2.00	1.00	.20
☐ 21 The "Good" Shot	3.00	1.50	.30

1986-87 Fleer

This 132-card set features prominent players in the NBA. Cards measure the standard 2 1/2" by 3 1/2". The photo on the front is inside a red, white, and blue frame. A Fleer "Premier" logo is pictured in the upper corner of the obverse. The card backs are printed in red and blue on white card stock. The card numbers correspond to the alphabetical order of the player's names. Each retail wax pack contained 12 player cards, a piece of gum, and an insert sticker card. Several cards have special "Traded" notations on them if the player was traded after his picture was selected. Since only the Star Company had been issuing basketball cards nationally since 1983, most of the players in this Fleer set already had cards which are considered XRC's, extended rookie cards. However, since this Fleer set was the first nationally available set in packs since the 1981-82 Topps issue, most of the players in the set could be considered rookie cards. Therefore, the key rookie cards in this set, who had already had cards in previous Star sets are Charles Barkley, Clyde Drexler, Patrick Ewing, Michael Jordan, Hakeem Olajuwon, Isiah Thomas, and Dominique Wilkins. The key rookie cards in this set, who had not previously appeared on cards, are Karl Malone and Chris Mullin. It's important to note that some of the more expensive cards in this set (especially Michael Jordan) have been counterfeited in the past few years. Checking key detailed printing areas such as the "Fleer Premier" logo on the front and the players' association logo on the back under eight or ten power magnification usually detects the legitimate from the counterfeits.

	MINT	EXC	G-VG
COMPLETE SET (132)	900.00	450.00	90.00
COMMON PLAYER (1-132)	1.25	.60	.12
☐ 1 Kareem Abdul-Jabbar Los Angeles Lakers	12.00	6.00	1.20
☐ 2 Alvan Adams Phoenix Suns	1.25	.60	.12
☐ 3 Mark Aguirre Dallas Mavericks	4.00	2.00	.40
☐ 4 Danny Ainge Boston Celtics	6.00	3.00	.60
☐ 5 John Bagley Cleveland Cavaliers	2.50	1.25	.25
☐ 6 Thurl Bailey Utah Jazz	1.50	.75	.15
☐ 7 Charles Barkley Philadelphia 76ers	65.00	32.50	6.50
☐ 8 Benoit Benjamin Los Angeles Clippers	4.00	2.00	.40
☐ 9 Larry Bird Boston Celtics	20.00	10.00	2.00
☐ 10 Otis Birdsong New Jersey Nets	1.25	.60	.12
☐ 11 Rolando Blackman Dallas Mavericks	6.50	3.25	.65
☐ 12 Manute Bol Washington Bullets	3.00	1.50	.30
☐ 13 Sam Bowie Portland Trail Blazers	3.00	1.50	.30
☐ 14 Joe Barry Carroll Golden State Warriors	1.25	.60	.12
☐ 15 Tom Chambers Seattle Supersonics	12.50	6.25	1.25
☐ 16 Maurice Cheeks Philadelphia 76ers	1.50	.75	.15
☐ 17 Michael Cooper Los Angeles Lakers	1.50	.75	.15
☐ 18 Wayne Cooper Denver Nuggets	1.25	.60	.12
☐ 19 Pat Cummings New York Knicks	1.25	.60	.12
☐ 20 Terry Cummings Milwaukee Bucks	7.00	3.50	.70
☐ 21 Adrian Dantley Utah Jazz	1.50	.75	.15
☐ 22 Brad Davis Dallas Mavericks	1.50	.75	.15
☐ 23 Walter Davis Phoenix Suns	1.50	.75	.15
☐ 24 Darryl Dawkins New Jersey Nets	1.50	.75	.15
☐ 25 Larry Drew Sacramento Kings	1.50	.75	.15
☐ 26 Clyde Drexler Portland Trail Blazers	80.00	40.00	8.00
☐ 27 Joe Dumars Detroit Pistons	25.00	12.50	2.50
☐ 28 Mark Eaton Utah Jazz	2.00	1.00	.20
☐ 29 James Edwards Phoenix Suns	1.50	.75	.15
☐ 30 Alex English Denver Nuggets	2.25	1.10	.22
☐ 31 Julius Erving Philadelphia 76ers	12.00	6.00	1.20
☐ 32 Patrick Ewing New York Knicks	70.00	35.00	7.00
☐ 33 Vern Fleming Indiana Pacers	1.50	.75	.15
☐ 34 Sleepy Floyd Golden State Warriors	1.50	.75	.15

☐ 35 World B. Free Cleveland Cavaliers	1.50	.75	.15
☐ 36 George Gervin Chicago Bulls	2.50	1.25	.25
☐ 37 Artis Gilmore San Antonio Spurs	1.75	.85	.17
☐ 38 Mike Gminski New Jersey Nets	1.25	.60	.12
☐ 39 Rickey Green Utah Jazz	1.50	.75	.15
☐ 40 Sidney Green Chicago Bulls	1.25	.60	.12
☐ 41 David Greenwood San Antonio Spurs	1.25	.60	.12
☐ 42 Darrell Griffith Utah Jazz	1.50	.75	.15
☐ 43 Bill Hanzlik Denver Nuggets	1.25	.60	.12
☐ 44 Derek Harper Dallas Mavericks	4.00	2.00	.40
☐ 45 Gerald Henderson Seattle Supersonics	1.25	.60	.12
☐ 46 Roy Hinson Philadelphia 76ers	1.50	.75	.15
☐ 47 Craig Hodges Milwaukee Bucks	2.50	1.25	.25
☐ 48 Phil Hubbard Cleveland Cavaliers	1.25	.60	.12
☐ 49 Jay Humphries Phoenix Suns	2.50	1.25	.25
☐ 50 Dennis Johnson Boston Celtics	1.75	.85	.17
☐ 51 Eddie Johnson Sacramento Kings	3.50	1.75	.35
☐ 52 Frank Johnson Washington Bullets	1.25	.60	.12
☐ 53 Magic Johnson Los Angeles Lakers	36.00	18.00	3.60
☐ 54 Marques Johnson Los Angeles Clippers (Decimal point missing, rookie year scoring avg.)	1.50	.75	.15
☐ 55 Steve Johnson UER San Antonio Spurs (photo actually David Greenwood)	1.25	.60	.12
☐ 56 Vinnie Johnson Detroit Pistons	1.50	.75	.15
☐ 57 Michael Jordan Chicago Bulls	550.00	275.00	55.00
☐ 58 Clark Kellogg Indiana Pacers	1.50	.75	.15
☐ 59 Albert King New Jersey Nets	1.25	.60	.12
☐ 60 Bernard King New York Knicks	2.00	1.00	.20
☐ 61 Bill Laimbeer Detroit Pistons	2.00	1.00	.20
☐ 62 Allen Leavell Houston Rockets	1.25	.60	.12
☐ 63 Lafayette Lever Denver Nuggets	1.75	.85	.17
☐ 64 Alton Lister Seattle Supersonics	1.50	.75	.15
☐ 65 Lewis Lloyd Houston Rockets	1.25	.60	.12
☐ 66 Maurice Lucas Los Angeles Lakers	1.50	.75	.15
☐ 67 Jeff Malone Washington Bullets	10.00	5.00	1.00
☐ 68 Karl Malone Utah Jazz	65.00	32.50	6.50
☐ 69 Moses Malone Washington Bullets	4.00	2.00	.40
☐ 70 Cedric Maxwell Los Angeles Clippers	1.50	.75	.15
☐ 71 Rodney McCray Houston Rockets	1.75	.85	.17
☐ 72 Xavier McDaniel Seattle Supersonics	13.00	6.50	1.30
☐ 73 Kevin McHale Boston Celtics	3.00	1.50	.30
☐ 74 Mike Mitchell San Antonio Spurs	1.25	.60	.12
☐ 75 Sidney Moncrief Milwaukee Bucks	1.75	.85	.17
☐ 76 Johnny Moore San Antonio Spurs	1.25	.60	.12
☐ 77 Chris Mullin Golden State Warriors	55.00	27.50	5.50
☐ 78 Larry Nance Phoenix Suns	11.00	5.50	1.10
☐ 79 Calvin Natt Denver Nuggets	1.25	.60	.12
☐ 80 Norm Nixon Los Angeles Clippers	1.25	.60	.12
☐ 81 Charles Oakley Chicago Bulls	3.00	1.50	.30
☐ 82 Hakeem Olajuwon Houston Rockets	45.00	22.50	4.50
☐ 83 Louis Orr New York Knicks	1.25	.60	.12
☐ 84 Robert Parish UER Boston Celtics	4.00	2.00	.40
☐ 85 Jim Paxson Portland Trail Blazers	1.25	.60	.12
☐ 86 Sam Perkins Dallas Mavericks	8.00	4.00	.80
☐ 87 Ricky Pierce Milwaukee Bucks	8.00	4.00	.80
☐ 88 Paul Pressey Milwaukee Bucks	1.50	.75	.15
☐ 89 Kurt Rambis Los Angeles Lakers	1.50	.75	.15
☐ 90 Robert Reid Houston Rockets	1.25	.60	.12
☐ 91 Doc Rivers Atlanta Hawks	2.75	1.35	.27
☐ 92 Alvin Robertson San Antonio Spurs	4.00	2.00	.40
☐ 93 Cliff Robinson Philadelphia 76ers	1.25	.60	.12
☐ 94 Tree Rollins Atlanta Hawks	1.25	.60	.12
☐ 95 Dan Roundfield Washington Bullets	1.25	.60	.12
☐ 96 Jeff Ruland Philadelphia 76ers	1.50	.75	.15
☐ 97 Ralph Sampson Houston Rockets	1.75	.85	.17
☐ 98 Danny Schayes Denver Nuggets	1.50	.75	.15
☐ 99 Byron Scott Los Angeles Lakers	5.00	2.50	.50
☐ 100 Purvis Short Golden State Warriors	1.25	.60	.12
☐ 101 Jerry Sichting Boston Celtics	1.25	.60	.12
☐ 102 Jack Sikma Milwaukee Bucks	1.50	.75	.15
☐ 103 Derek Smith Los Angeles Clippers	1.50	.75	.15
☐ 104 Larry Smith Golden State Warriors	1.25	.60	.12
☐ 105 Rory Sparrow New York Knicks	1.25	.60	.12
☐ 106 Steve Stipanovich Indiana Pacers	1.50	.75	.15
☐ 107 Terry Teagle Golden State Warriors	2.00	1.00	.20
☐ 108 Reggie Theus Sacramento Kings	1.50	.75	.15
☐ 109 Isiah Thomas Detroit Pistons	30.00	15.00	3.00
☐ 110 LaSalle Thompson Sacramento Kings	1.50	.75	.15
☐ 111 Mychal Thompson Portland Trail Blazers	1.50	.75	.15
☐ 112 Sedale Threatt Philadelphia 76ers	4.50	2.25	.45
☐ 113 Wayman Tisdale Indiana Pacers	5.00	2.50	.50
☐ 114 Andrew Toney Philadelphia 76ers	1.50	.75	.15
☐ 115 Kelly Tripucka Detroit Pistons	1.50	.75	.15
☐ 116 Mel Turpin Cleveland Cavaliers	1.50	.75	.15
☐ 117 Kiki Vandeweghe Portland Trail Blazers	1.50	.75	.15
☐ 118 Jay Vincent Dallas Mavericks	1.25	.60	.12
☐ 119 Bill Walton Boston Celtics (Missing decimal points on four lines of FG Percentage)	3.25	1.60	.32
☐ 120 Spud Webb Atlanta Hawks	6.50	3.25	.65
☐ 121 Dominique Wilkins Atlanta Hawks	30.00	15.00	3.00
☐ 122 Gerald Wilkins New York Knicks	5.00	2.50	.50
☐ 123 Buck Williams New Jersey Nets	11.00	5.50	1.10
☐ 124 Gus Williams Washington Bullets	1.50	.75	.15
☐ 125 Herb Williams	1.50	.75	.15

		MINT	EXC	G-VG
	Indiana Pacers			
☐ 126	Kevin Willis	8.00	4.00	.80
	Atlanta Hawks			
☐ 127	Randy Wittman	1.25	.60	.12
	Atlanta Hawks			
☐ 128	Al Wood	1.25	.60	.12
	Seattle Supersonics			
☐ 129	Mike Woodson	1.25	.60	.12
	Sacramento Kings			
☐ 130	Orlando Woolridge	3.50	1.75	.35
	Chicago Bulls			
☐ 131	James Worthy	25.00	12.50	2.50
	Los Angeles Lakers			
☐ 132	Checklist 1-132	1.50	.75	.15

1986-87 Fleer Sticker Inserts

This set of 11 stickers was distributed in the wax packs (one per pack) with the Fleer regular 132-card issue. The stickers are 2 1/2" by 3 1/2". The backs of the sticker cards are printed in blue and red on white card stock. The set numbering of the stickers is alphabetical by player's name.

		MINT	EXC	G-VG
COMPLETE SET (11)		75.00	37.50	7.50
COMMON PLAYER (1-11)		1.00	.50	.10
☐ 1	Kareem Abdul-Jabbar	5.00	2.50	.50
	Los Angeles Lakers			
☐ 2	Larry Bird	9.00	4.50	.90
	Boston Celtics			
☐ 3	Adrian Dantley	1.00	.50	.10
	Utah Jazz			
☐ 4	Alex English	1.00	.50	.10
	Denver Nuggets			
☐ 5	Julius Erving	5.00	2.50	.50
	Philadelphia 76ers			
☐ 6	Patrick Ewing	12.00	6.00	1.20
	New York Knicks			
☐ 7	Magic Johnson	13.50	6.50	1.35
	Los Angeles Lakers			
☐ 8	Michael Jordan	50.00	25.00	5.00
	Chicago Bulls			
☐ 9	Hakeem Olajuwon	6.50	3.25	.65
	Houston Rockets			
☐ 10	Isiah Thomas	5.00	2.50	.50
	Detroit Pistons			
☐ 11	Dominique Wilkins	5.00	2.50	.50
	Atlanta Hawks			

1987-88 Fleer

The 1987-88 Fleer basketball set contains 132 standard size (2 1/2" by 3 1/2") cards featuring 131 of the NBA's better-known players, plus a checklist. The fronts are white with gray horizontal stripes. The backs are red, white, and blue and show each player's complete NBA statistics. The cards are numbered essentially in alphabetical order. This set was issued in wax packs, each containing 12 cards. The key "pure" rookie cards in this set are Brad Daugherty, A.C. Green, Ron Harper, Chuck Person, Terry Porter, Detlef Schrempf, and Hot Rod Williams. Other key rookie cards in this set, who had already had cards in previous Star sets, are Jerome Kersey, John Paxson, and Otis Thorpe.

		MINT	EXC	G-VG
COMPLETE SET (132)		265.00	115.00	22.00
COMMON PLAYER (1-132)		.50	.25	.05
☐ 1	Kareem Abdul-Jabbar	8.00	4.00	.80
	Los Angeles Lakers			
☐ 2	Alvan Adams	.50	.25	.05
	Phoenix Suns			
☐ 3	Mark Aguirre	1.00	.50	.10
	Dallas Mavericks			
☐ 4	Danny Ainge	1.50	.75	.15
	Boston Celtics			
☐ 5	John Bagley	.75	.35	.07
	Cleveland Cavaliers			
☐ 6	Thurl Bailey UER	.50	.25	.05
	Utah Jazz			
	(reverse negative)			
☐ 7	Greg Ballard	.50	.25	.05
	Golden State Warriors			
☐ 8	Gene Banks	.50	.25	.05
	Chicago Bulls			
☐ 9	Charles Barkley	17.00	8.50	1.70
	Philadelphia 76ers			
☐ 10	Benoit Benjamin	1.00	.50	.10
	Los Angeles Clippers			
☐ 11	Larry Bird	13.00	6.50	1.30
	Boston Celtics			
☐ 12	Rolando Blackman	1.50	.75	.15
	Dallas Mavericks			
☐ 13	Manute Bol	.75	.35	.07
	Washington Bullets			
☐ 14	Tony Brown	.50	.25	.05
	New Jersey Nets			
☐ 15	Michael Cage	1.50	.75	.15
	Los Angeles Clippers			
☐ 16	Joe Barry Carroll	.50	.25	.05
	Golden State Warriors			
☐ 17	Bill Cartwright	.75	.35	.07
	New York Knicks			
☐ 18	Terry Catledge	1.50	.75	.15
	Washington Bullets			
☐ 19	Tom Chambers	3.50	1.75	.35
	Seattle Supersonics			
☐ 20	Maurice Cheeks	.75	.35	.07
	Philadelphia 76ers			
☐ 21	Michael Cooper	.75	.35	.07
	Los Angeles Lakers			
☐ 22	Dave Corzine	.50	.25	.05
	Chicago Bulls			
☐ 23	Terry Cummings	1.75	.85	.17
	Milwaukee Bucks			
☐ 24	Adrian Dantley	.75	.35	.07
	Detroit Pistons			
☐ 25	Brad Daugherty	24.00	12.00	2.40
	Cleveland Cavaliers			
☐ 26	Walter Davis	.75	.35	.07
	Phoenix Suns			
☐ 27	Johnny Dawkins	3.00	1.50	.30
	San Antonio Spurs			
☐ 28	James Donaldson	.75	.35	.07
	Dallas Mavericks			
☐ 29	Larry Drew	.50	.25	.05
	Los Angeles Clippers			
☐ 30	Clyde Drexler	20.00	10.00	2.00

Portland Trail Blazers
☐ 31 Joe Dumars .... 7.00 3.50 .70
Detroit Pistons
☐ 32 Mark Eaton .... .75 .35 .07
Utah Jazz
☐ 33 Dale Ellis .... 3.00 1.50 .30
Seattle Supersonics
☐ 34 Alex English .... 1.00 .50 .10
Denver Nuggets
☐ 35 Julius Erving .... 8.00 4.00 .80
Philadelphia 76ers
☐ 36 Mike Evans .... .50 .25 .05
Denver Nuggets
☐ 37 Patrick Ewing 18.00 9.00 1.80
New York Knicks
☐ 38 Vern Fleming .... .50 .25 .05
Indiana Pacers
☐ 39 Sleepy Floyd .... .50 .25 .05
Golden State Warriors
☐ 40 Artis Gilmore .... 1.00 .50 .10
San Antonio Spurs
☐ 41 Mike Gminski UER .... .50 .25 .05
New Jersey Nets
(reversed negative)
☐ 42 A.C. Green .... 4.50 2.25 .45
Los Angeles Lakers
☐ 43 Rickey Green .... .50 .25 .05
Utah Jazz
☐ 44 Sidney Green .... .50 .25 .05
Detroit Pistons
☐ 45 David Greenwood .... .50 .25 .05
San Antonio Spurs
☐ 46 Darrell Griffith .... .50 .25 .05
Utah Jazz
☐ 47 Bill Hanzlik .... .50 .25 .05
Denver Nuggets
☐ 48 Derek Harper .... 1.00 .50 .10
Dallas Mavericks
☐ 49 Ron Harper .... 6.00 3.00 .60
Cleveland Cavaliers
☐ 50 Gerald Henderson .... .50 .25 .05
New York Knicks
☐ 51 Roy Hinson .... .50 .25 .05
Philadelphia 76ers
☐ 52 Craig Hodges .... .75 .35 .07
Milwaukee Bucks
☐ 53 Phil Hubbard .... .50 .25 .05
Cleveland Cavaliers
☐ 54 Dennis Johnson .... .75 .35 .07
Boston Celtics
☐ 55 Eddie Johnson .... 1.00 .50 .10
Sacramento Kings
☐ 56 Magic Johnson 22.00 11.00 2.20
Los Angeles Lakers
☐ 57 Steve Johnson .... .50 .25 .05
Portland Trail Blazers
☐ 58 Vinnie Johnson .... .75 .35 .07
Detroit Pistons
☐ 59 Michael Jordan 125.00 60.00 12.50
Chicago Bulls
☐ 60 Jerome Kersey 12.50 6.25 1.25
Portland Trail Blazers
☐ 61 Bill Laimbeer .... 1.00 .50 .10
Detroit Pistons
☐ 62 Lafayette Lever UER .... .75 .35 .07
Denver Nuggets
(Photo actually
Otis Smith)
☐ 63 Cliff Levingston .... 1.50 .75 .15
Atlanta Hawks
☐ 64 Alton Lister .... .50 .25 .05
Seattle Supersonics
☐ 65 John Long .... .50 .25 .05
Indiana Pacers
☐ 66 John Lucas .... .50 .25 .05
Milwaukee Bucks
☐ 67 Jeff Malone .... 2.50 1.25 .25
Washington Bullets
☐ 68 Karl Malone 17.00 8.50 1.70
Utah Jazz
☐ 69 Moses Malone .... 3.00 1.50 .30
Washington Bullets
☐ 70 Cedric Maxwell .... .75 .35 .07
Houston Rockets
☐ 71 Tim McCormick .... .75 .35 .07
Philadelphia 76ers
☐ 72 Rodney McCray .... .75 .35 .07
Houston Rockets
☐ 73 Xavier McDaniel .... 3.50 1.75 .35
Seattle Supersonics
☐ 74 Kevin McHale .... 2.00 1.00 .20
Boston Celtics
☐ 75 Nate McMillan .... 1.25 .60 .12
Seattle Supersonics
☐ 76 Sidney Moncrief .... .75 .35 .07
Milwaukee Bucks
☐ 77 Chris Mullin 15.00 7.50 1.50
Golden State Warriors
☐ 78 Larry Nance .... 2.50 1.25 .25
Phoenix Suns
☐ 79 Charles Oakley .... .75 .35 .07
Chicago Bulls
☐ 80 Hakeem Olajuwon 12.50 6.25 1.25
Houston Rockets
☐ 81 Robert Parish UER .... 3.00 1.50 .30
Boston Celtics
(Misspelled Parrish
on both sides)
☐ 82 Jim Paxson .... .50 .25 .05
Portland Trail Blazers
☐ 83 John Paxson .... 7.00 3.50 .70
Chicago Bulls
☐ 84 Sam Perkins .... 2.00 1.00 .20
Dallas Mavericks
☐ 85 Chuck Person .... 6.50 3.25 .65
Indiana Pacers
☐ 86 Jim Peterson .... .75 .35 .07
Houston Rockets
☐ 87 Ricky Pierce .... 1.75 .85 .17
Milwaukee Bucks
☐ 88 Ed Pinckney .... 1.75 .85 .17
Phoenix Suns
☐ 89 Terry Porter 17.00 8.50 1.70
Portland Trail Blazers
(College Wisconsin,
should be Wisconsin -
Stevens Point)
☐ 90 Paul Pressey .... .50 .25 .05
Milwaukee Bucks
☐ 91 Robert Reid .... .50 .25 .05
Houston Rockets
☐ 92 Doc Rivers .... .75 .35 .07
Atlanta Hawks
☐ 93 Alvin Robertson .... 1.00 .50 .10
San Antonio Spurs
☐ 94 Tree Rollins .... .50 .25 .05
Atlanta Hawks
☐ 95 Ralph Sampson .... .75 .35 .07
Houston Rockets
☐ 96 Mike Sanders .... .75 .35 .07
Phoenix Suns
☐ 97 Detlef Schrempf .... 8.00 4.00 .80
Dallas Mavericks
☐ 98 Byron Scott .... 1.25 .60 .12
Los Angeles Lakers
☐ 99 Jerry Sichting .... .50 .25 .05
Boston Celtics
☐ 100 Jack Sikma .... .75 .35 .07
Milwaukee Bucks
☐ 101 Larry Smith .... .50 .25 .05
Golden State Warriors
☐ 102 Rory Sparrow .... .50 .25 .05
New York Knicks
☐ 103 Steve Stipanovich .... .50 .25 .05
Indiana Pacers
☐ 104 Jon Sundvold .... .75 .35 .07
San Antonio Spurs
☐ 105 Reggie Theus .... .75 .35 .07
Sacramento Kings
☐ 106 Isiah Thomas .... 9.00 4.50 .90
Detroit Pistons
☐ 107 LaSalle Thompson .... .50 .25 .05
Sacramento Kings
☐ 108 Mychal Thompson .... .75 .35 .07
Los Angeles Lakers
☐ 109 Otis Thorpe .... 7.00 3.50 .70
Sacramento Kings
☐ 110 Sedale Threatt .... 1.00 .50 .10
Chicago Bulls
☐ 111 Waymon Tisdale .... 1.25 .60 .12
Indiana Pacers
☐ 112 Kelly Tripucka .... .75 .35 .07
Utah Jazz
☐ 113 Trent Tucker .... .75 .35 .07
New York Knicks
☐ 114 Terry Tyler .... .50 .25 .05
Sacramento Kings
☐ 115 Darnell Valentine .... .50 .25 .05
Los Angeles Clippers
☐ 116 Kiki Vandeweghe .... .75 .35 .07
Portland Trail Blazers
☐ 117 Darrell Walker .... .75 .35 .07
Denver Nuggets
☐ 118 Dominique Wilkins .... 9.00 4.50 .90
Atlanta Hawks
☐ 119 Gerald Wilkins .... 1.00 .50 .10
New York Knicks
☐ 120 Buck Williams .... 3.00 1.50 .30

New Jersey Nets			
☐ 121 Herb Williams	.75	.35	.07
Indiana Pacers			
☐ 122 John Williams	.75	.35	.07
Washington Bullets			
☐ 123 John Williams	5.00	2.50	.50
Cleveland Cavaliers			
☐ 124 Kevin Willis	2.00	1.00	.20
Atlanta Hawks			
☐ 125 David Wingate	.75	.35	.07
Philadelphia 76ers			
☐ 126 Randy Wittman	.50	.25	.05
Atlanta Hawks			
☐ 127 Leon Wood	.50	.25	.05
New Jersey Nets			
☐ 128 Mike Woodson	.50	.25	.05
Los Angeles Clippers			
☐ 129 Orlando Woolridge	1.00	.50	.10
New Jersey Nets			
☐ 130 James Worthy	7.00	3.50	.70
Los Angeles Lakers			
☐ 131 Danny Young	.75	.35	.07
Seattle Supersonics			
☐ 132 Checklist Card	.75	.35	.07

1987-88 Fleer Sticker Inserts

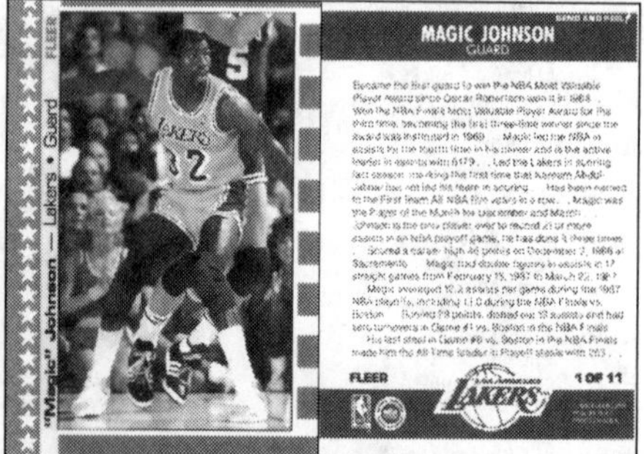

The 1987-88 Fleer Stickers set is an 11-card standard size (2 1/2" by 3 1/2") set issued as an insert with the regular 132-card set. The fronts are red, white, blue, and yellow. The backs are white and blue, and contain career highlights. One sticker was included in each wax pack. Virtually all cards from this set have wax-stained backs as a result of the packaging.

	MINT	EXC	G-VG
COMPLETE SET (11)	35.00	17.50	3.50
COMMON PLAYER (1-11)	.50	.25	.05
☐ 1 Magic Johnson	9.00	4.50	.90
Los Angeles Lakers			
☐ 2 Michael Jordan	25.00	12.50	2.50
Chicago Bulls (In text, votes misspelled as voites)			
☐ 3 Hakeem Olajuwon UER	3.75	1.85	.37
Houston Rockets (Misspelled Olajuwan on card back)			
☐ 4 Larry Bird	5.00	2.50	.50
Boston Celtics			
☐ 5 Kevin McHale	.75	.35	.07
Boston Celtics			
☐ 6 Charles Barkley	5.50	2.75	.55
Philadelphia 76ers			
☐ 7 Dominique Wilkins	3.00	1.50	.30
Atlanta Hawks			
☐ 8 Kareem Abdul-Jabbar	3.00	1.50	.30
Los Angeles Lakers			
☐ 9 Mark Aguirre	.50	.25	.05
Dallas Mavericks			
☐ 10 Chuck Person	1.00	.50	.10
Indiana Pacers			
☐ 11 Alex English	.50	.25	.05
Denver Nuggets			

1988-89 Fleer

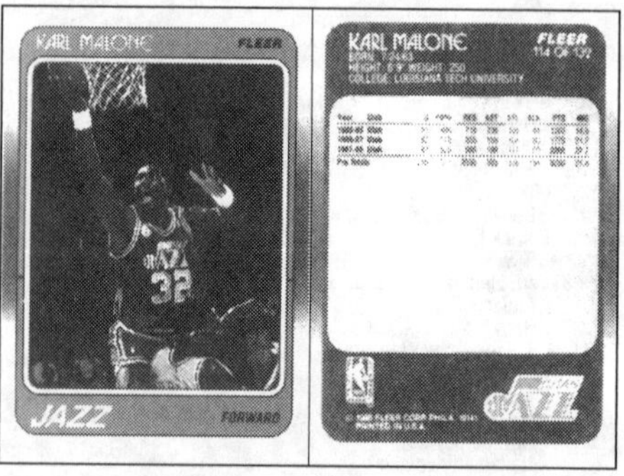

The 1988-89 Fleer basketball set contains 132 standard size (2 1/2" by 3 1/2") cards. There are 119 regular cards, plus 12 All-Star cards and a checklist. The outer borders are white and gray, while the inner borders correspond to the team colors. The backs are greenish, and show full NBA statistics with limited biographical information. The set is ordered alphabetically in team subsets (with a few exceptions due to late trades). The teams themselves are also presented in alphabetical order, Atlanta Hawks (1-6, 98, and 118), Boston Celtics (8-12), Charlotte Hornets (13-14), Chicago Bulls (15-17 and 19-21), Cleveland Cavaliers (22-26), Dallas Mavericks (27-32), Denver Nuggets (33-38), Detroit Pistons (39-45), Golden State Warriors (46-49), Houston Rockets (50-54 and 63), Indiana Pacers (55-60), Los Angeles Clippers (61), Los Angeles Lakers (64-70), Miami Heat (71-72), Milwaukee Bucks (73-76), New Jersey Nets (77-79 and 102), New York Knicks (18 and 80-84), Philadelphia 76ers (85-88), Phoenix Suns (89-91 and 106), Portland Trail Blazers (92-96), Sacramento Kings (7, 97, and 99-100), San Antonio Spurs (101 and 103-105), Seattle Supersonics (62 and 107-110), Utah Jazz (111-115), Washington Bullets (116-117 and 119), and All-Stars (120-131). This set was issued in wax packs of 12 cards. The key rookie cards in this set are Michael Adams, Kevin Duckworth, Horace Grant, Reggie Miller, Derrick McKey, Scottie Pippen, Mark Price, Dennis Rodman, and Kenny Smith. There is also a rookie card of John Stockton who had previously only appeared in Star Company sets.

	MINT	EXC	G-VG
COMPLETE SET (132)	150.00	75.00	15.00
COMMON PLAYER (1-132)	.20	.10	.02
☐ 1 Antoine Carr	1.00	.30	.06
☐ 2 Cliff Levingston	.30	.15	.03
☐ 3 Doc Rivers	.30	.15	.03
☐ 4 Spud Webb	.75	.35	.07
☐ 5 Dominique Wilkins	3.50	1.75	.35
☐ 6 Kevin Willis	1.00	.50	.10
☐ 7 Randy Wittman	.20	.10	.02
☐ 8 Danny Ainge	.75	.35	.07
☐ 9 Larry Bird	6.00	3.00	.60
☐ 10 Dennis Johnson	.30	.15	.03
☐ 11 Kevin McHale	1.00	.50	.10
☐ 12 Robert Parish	1.25	.60	.12
☐ 13 Tyrone Bogues	1.00	.50	.10
☐ 14 Dell Curry	1.50	.75	.15
☐ 15 Dave Corzine	.20	.10	.02
☐ 16 Horace Grant	12.00	6.00	1.20
☐ 17 Michael Jordan	36.00	18.00	3.60
☐ 18 Charles Oakley	.30	.15	.03
☐ 19 John Paxson	1.00	.50	.10
☐ 20 Scottie Pippen UER	55.00	27.50	5.50
(Misspelled Pippin on card back)			
☐ 21 Brad Sellers	.30	.15	.03
☐ 22 Brad Daugherty	6.00	3.00	.60
☐ 23 Ron Harper	1.00	.50	.10
☐ 24 Larry Nance	1.25	.60	.12
☐ 25 Mark Price	9.00	4.50	.90

☐ 26 Hot Rod Williams	.75	.35	.07
☐ 27 Mark Aguirre	.50	.25	.05
☐ 28 Rolando Blackman	.75	.35	.07
☐ 29 James Donaldson	.20	.10	.02
☐ 30 Derek Harper	.50	.25	.05
☐ 31 Sam Perkins	1.00	.50	.10
☐ 32 Roy Tarpley	.60	.30	.06
☐ 33 Michael Adams	3.50	1.75	.35
☐ 34 Alex English	.60	.30	.06
☐ 35 Lafayette Lever	.30	.15	.03
☐ 36 Blair Rasmussen	.60	.30	.06
☐ 37 Danny Schayes	.30	.15	.03
☐ 38 Jay Vincent	.20	.10	.02
☐ 39 Adrian Dantley	.40	.20	.04
☐ 40 Joe Dumars	3.00	1.50	.30
☐ 41 Vinnie Johnson	.30	.15	.03
☐ 42 Bill Laimbeer	.40	.20	.04
☐ 43 Dennis Rodman	9.00	4.50	.90
☐ 44 John Salley	2.00	1.00	.20
☐ 45 Isiah Thomas	3.25	1.60	.32
☐ 46 Winston Garland	.50	.25	.05
☐ 47 Rod Higgins	.30	.15	.03
☐ 48 Chris Mullin	5.50	2.75	.55
☐ 49 Ralph Sampson	.30	.15	.03
☐ 50 Joe Barry Carroll	.20	.10	.02
☐ 51 Sleepy Floyd	.30	.15	.03
☐ 52 Rodney McCray	.30	.15	.03
☐ 53 Hakeem Olajuwon	4.00	2.00	.40
☐ 54 Purvis Short	.20	.10	.02
☐ 55 Vern Fleming	.20	.10	.02
☐ 56 John Long	.20	.10	.02
☐ 57 Reggie Miller	9.00	4.50	.90
☐ 58 Chuck Person	1.00	.50	.10
☐ 59 Steve Stipanovich	.30	.15	.03
☐ 60 Waymon Tisdale	.60	.30	.06
☐ 61 Benoit Benjamin	.50	.25	.05
☐ 62 Michael Cage	.30	.15	.03
☐ 63 Mike Woodson	.20	.10	.02
☐ 64 Kareem Abdul-Jabbar	4.00	2.00	.40
☐ 65 Michael Cooper	.40	.20	.04
☐ 66 A.C. Green	.75	.35	.07
☐ 67 Magic Johnson	10.00	5.00	1.00
☐ 68 Byron Scott	.60	.30	.06
☐ 69 Mychal Thompson	.30	.15	.03
☐ 70 James Worthy	3.00	1.50	.30
☐ 71 Duane Washington	.30	.15	.03
☐ 72 Kevin Williams	.20	.10	.02
☐ 73 Randy Breuer	.30	.15	.03
☐ 74 Terry Cummings	.75	.35	.07
☐ 75 Paul Pressey	.20	.10	.02
☐ 76 Jack Sikma	.30	.15	.03
☐ 77 John Bagley	.30	.15	.03
☐ 78 Roy Hinson	.20	.10	.02
☐ 79 Buck Williams	1.25	.60	.12
☐ 80 Patrick Ewing	6.50	3.25	.65
☐ 81 Sidney Green	.20	.10	.02
☐ 82 Mark Jackson	2.25	1.10	.22
☐ 83 Kenny Walker	.30	.15	.03
☐ 84 Gerald Wilkins	.50	.25	.05
☐ 85 Charles Barkley	5.50	2.75	.55
☐ 86 Maurice Cheeks	.40	.20	.04
☐ 87 Mike Gminski	.20	.10	.02
☐ 88 Cliff Robinson	.20	.10	.02
☐ 89 Armon Gilliam	1.75	.85	.17
☐ 90 Eddie Johnson	.40	.20	.04
☐ 91 Mark West	.50	.25	.05
☐ 92 Clyde Drexler	7.00	3.50	.70
☐ 93 Kevin Duckworth	2.50	1.25	.25
☐ 94 Steve Johnson	.20	.10	.02
☐ 95 Jerome Kersey	3.00	1.50	.30
☐ 96 Terry Porter	4.50	2.25	.45
(College Wisconsin, should be Wisconsin - Stevens Point)			
☐ 97 Joe Kleine	.35	.17	.03
☐ 98 Reggie Theus	.30	.15	.03
☐ 99 Otis Thorpe	1.00	.50	.10
☐ 100 Kenny Smith	2.00	1.00	.20
(College NC State, should be North Carolina)			
☐ 101 Greg Anderson	.90	.45	.09
☐ 102 Walter Berry	.35	.17	.03
☐ 103 Frank Brickowski	.35	.17	.03
☐ 104 Johnny Dawkins	.35	.17	.03
☐ 105 Alvin Robertson	.50	.25	.05
☐ 106 Tom Chambers	1.00	.50	.10
(Born 6/2/59, should be 6/21/59)			
☐ 107 Dale Ellis	.40	.20	.04
☐ 108 Xavier McDaniel	1.00	.50	.10
☐ 109 Derrick McKey	2.00	1.00	.20
☐ 110 Nate McMillan UER	.30	.15	.03
(Photo actually Kevin Williams)			
☐ 111 Thurl Bailey	.20	.10	.02
☐ 112 Mark Eaton	.30	.15	.03
☐ 113 Bobby Hansen	.30	.15	.03
☐ 114 Karl Malone	5.50	2.75	.55
☐ 115 John Stockton	22.00	11.00	2.20
☐ 116 Bernard King	.60	.30	.06
☐ 117 Jeff Malone	1.00	.50	.10
☐ 118 Moses Malone	1.00	.50	.10
☐ 119 John Williams	.30	.15	.03
☐ 120 Michael Jordan AS	12.00	6.00	1.20
Chicago Bulls			
☐ 121 Mark Jackson AS	.50	.25	.05
New York Knicks			
☐ 122 Byron Scott AS	.30	.15	.03
Los Angeles Lakers			
☐ 123 Magic Johnson AS	4.50	2.25	.45
Los Angeles Lakers			
☐ 124 Larry Bird AS	2.75	1.35	.27
Boston Celtics			
☐ 125 Dominique Wilkins AS	1.50	.75	.15
Atlanta Hawks			
☐ 126 Hakeem Olajuwon AS	1.75	.85	.17
Houston Rockets			
☐ 127 John Stockton AS	5.50	2.75	.55
Utah Jazz			
☐ 128 Alvin Robertson AS	.30	.15	.03
San Antonio Spurs			
☐ 129 Charles Barkley AS	2.50	1.25	.25
Philadelphia 76ers (Back says Buck Williams is member of Jets, should be Nets)			
☐ 130 Patrick Ewing AS	2.50	1.25	.25
New York Knicks			
☐ 131 Mark Eaton AS	.30	.15	.03
Utah Jazz			
☐ 132 Checklist Card	.30	.15	.03

1988-89 Fleer Sticker Inserts

The 1988-89 Fleer Sticker set is an 11-card standard size (2 1/2" by 3 1/2") set issued as an insert with the regular 132-card set. The fronts are baby blue, red, and white. The backs are blue and pink and contain career highlights. The stickers were packed randomly in the wax packs. The set is ordered alphabetically. Virtually all cards from this set have wax-stained backs as a result of the packaging.

	MINT	EXC	G-VG
COMPLETE SET (11)	12.50	6.25	1.25
COMMON PLAYER (1-11)	.30	.15	.03
☐ 1 Mark Aguirre	.30	.15	.03
Dallas Mavericks			
☐ 2 Larry Bird	2.00	1.00	.20
Boston Celtics			
☐ 3 Clyde Drexler	2.00	1.00	.20
Portland Trail Blazers			
☐ 4 Alex English	.30	.15	.03
Denver Nuggets			
☐ 5 Patrick Ewing	1.75	.85	.17
New York Knicks			
☐ 6 Magic Johnson	3.00	1.50	.30
Los Angeles Lakers			
☐ 7 Michael Jordan	8.00	4.00	.80

	MINT	EXC	G-VG
Chicago Bulls			
☐ 8 Karl Malone	1.50	.75	.15
Utah Jazz			
☐ 9 Kevin McHale	.40	.20	.04
Boston Celtics			
☐ 10 Isiah Thomas	1.00	.50	.10
Detroit Pistons			
☐ 11 Dominique Wilkins	1.00	.50	.10
Atlanta Hawks			

1989-90 Fleer

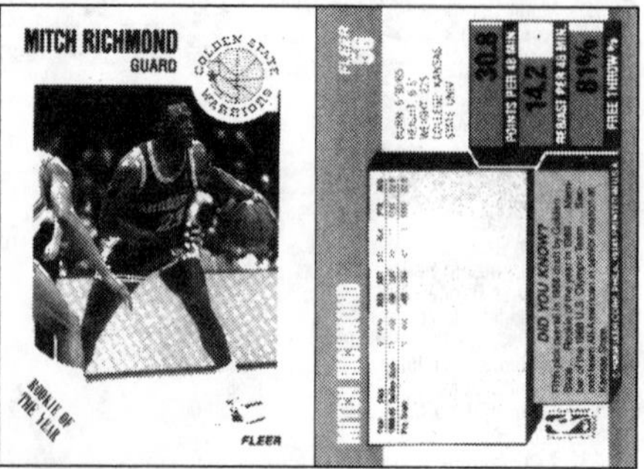

The 1989-90 Fleer basketball set consists of 168 cards measuring the standard size (2 1/2" by 3 1/2"). The fronts feature color action player photos, with various color borders between white inner and outer borders. The player's name and position appear in the upper left corner, with the team logo superimposed over the upper right corner of the picture. The horizontally oriented backs have black lettering on red, pink, and white background and present career statistics, biographical information, and a performance index. The set is ordered alphabetically in team subsets (with a few exceptions due to late trades). The teams themselves are also presented in alphabetical order, Atlanta Hawks (1-7), Boston Celtics (8-14), Charlotte Hornets (15-18), Chicago Bulls (19-23), Cleveland Cavaliers (25-31), Dallas Mavericks (32-37), Denver Nuggets (38-43), Detroit Pistons (44-51), Golden State Warriors (52-57), Houston Rockets (58-63), Indiana Pacers (64-68), Los Angeles Clippers (69-74), Los Angeles Lakers (75-80), Miami Heat (81-84), Milwaukee Bucks (85-91), Minnesota Timberwolves (92-94), New Jersey Nets (95-99), New York Knicks (100-107), Orlando Magic (108-111), Philadelphia 76ers (112-118), Phoenix Suns (119-125), Portland Trail Blazers (126-132), Sacramento Kings (133-139), San Antonio Spurs (140-144), Seattle Supersonics (24 and 145-150), Utah Jazz (151-156), Washington Bullets (157-162), and All-Star Game Combos (163-167). Rookie Cards included in this set are Willie Anderson, Rex Chapman, Hersey Hawkins, Jeff Hornacek, Kevin Johnson, Reggie Lewis, Dan Majerle, Danny Manning, Vernon Maxwell, Ken Norman, Mitch Richmond, Rony Seikaly, Brian Shaw, Scott Skiles, Charles Smith, and Rod Strickland.

	MINT	EXC	G-VG
COMPLETE SET (168)	35.00	17.50	3.50
COMMON PLAYER (1-168)	.06	.03	.00
☐ 1 John Battle	.30	.15	.03
☐ 2 Jon Koncak	.10	.05	.01
☐ 3 Cliff Levingston	.06	.03	.00
☐ 4 Moses Malone	.40	.20	.04
☐ 5 Glenn Rivers	.10	.05	.01
☐ 6 Spud Webb UER	.25	.12	.02
(Points per 48 minutes incorrect at 2.6)			
☐ 7 Dominique Wilkins	.90	.45	.09
☐ 8 Larry Bird	2.25	1.10	.22
☐ 9 Dennis Johnson	.12	.06	.01
☐ 10 Reggie Lewis	5.50	2.75	.55
☐ 11 Kevin McHale	.40	.20	.04
☐ 12 Robert Parish	.50	.25	.05
☐ 13 Ed Pinckney	.10	.05	.01
☐ 14 Brian Shaw	.75	.35	.07
☐ 15 Rex Chapman	.50	.25	.05
☐ 16 Kurt Rambis	.10	.05	.01
☐ 17 Robert Reid	.06	.03	.00
☐ 18 Kelly Tripucka	.10	.05	.01
☐ 19 Bill Cartwright UER	.10	.05	.01
(First season 1978-80, should be 1979-80)			
☐ 20 Horace Grant	1.50	.75	.15
☐ 21 Michael Jordan	8.00	4.00	.80
☐ 22 John Paxson	.35	.17	.03
☐ 23 Scottie Pippen	8.00	4.00	.80
☐ 24 Brad Sellers	.06	.03	.00
☐ 25 Brad Daugherty	1.75	.85	.17
☐ 26 Craig Ehlo	1.25	.60	.12
☐ 27 Ron Harper	.25	.12	.02
☐ 28 Larry Nance	.35	.17	.03
☐ 29 Mark Price	1.25	.60	.12
☐ 30 Mike Sanders	.10	.05	.01
☐ 31A John Williams ERR	1.00	.50	.10
Washington Bullets			
☐ 31B John Williams COR	.25	.12	.02
Cleveland Cavaliers			
☐ 32 Rolando Blackman UER	.25	.12	.02
(Career blocks and points listed as 1961 and 2127, should be 196 and 12,127)			
☐ 33 Adrian Dantley	.20	.10	.02
☐ 34 James Donaldson	.06	.03	.00
☐ 35 Derek Harper	.15	.07	.01
☐ 36 Sam Perkins	.30	.15	.03
☐ 37 Herb Williams	.10	.05	.01
☐ 38 Michael Adams	.50	.25	.05
☐ 39 Walter Davis	.12	.06	.01
☐ 40 Alex English	.20	.10	.02
☐ 41 Lafayette Lever	.10	.05	.01
☐ 42 Blair Rasmussen	.06	.03	.00
☐ 43 Dan Schayes	.10	.05	.01
☐ 44 Mark Aguirre	.12	.06	.01
☐ 45 Joe Dumars	.60	.30	.06
☐ 46 James Edwards	.10	.05	.01
☐ 47 Vinnie Johnson	.12	.06	.01
☐ 48 Bill Laimbeer	.15	.07	.01
☐ 49 Dennis Rodman	1.25	.60	.12
☐ 50 Isiah Thomas	.90	.45	.09
☐ 51 John Salley	.15	.07	.01
☐ 52 Manute Bol	.12	.06	.01
☐ 53 Winston Garland	.06	.03	.00
☐ 54 Rod Higgins	.06	.03	.00
☐ 55 Chris Mullin	1.50	.75	.15
☐ 56 Mitch Richmond	3.00	1.50	.30
☐ 57 Terry Teagle	.10	.05	.01
☐ 58 Derrick Chievous UER	.12	.06	.01
(Stats correctly say 81 games in '88-89, text says 82)			
☐ 59 Sleepy Floyd	.10	.05	.01
☐ 60 Tim McCormick	.06	.03	.00
☐ 61 Hakeem Olajuwon	1.25	.60	.12
☐ 62 Otis Thorpe	.35	.17	.03
☐ 63 Mike Woodson	.06	.03	.00
☐ 64 Vern Fleming	.10	.05	.01
☐ 65 Reggie Miller	1.25	.60	.12
☐ 66 Chuck Person	.35	.17	.03
☐ 67 Detlef Schrempf	1.00	.50	.10
☐ 68 Rik Smits	.50	.25	.05
☐ 69 Benoit Benjamin	.15	.07	.01
☐ 70 Gary Grant	.40	.20	.04
☐ 71 Danny Manning	3.50	1.75	.35
☐ 72 Ken Norman	.75	.35	.07
☐ 73 Charles Smith	1.50	.75	.15
☐ 74 Reggie Williams	.75	.35	.07
☐ 75 Michael Cooper	.12	.06	.01
☐ 76 A.C. Green	.25	.12	.02
☐ 77 Magic Johnson	4.50	2.25	.45
☐ 78 Byron Scott	.20	.10	.02
☐ 79 Mychal Thompson	.10	.05	.01
☐ 80 James Worthy	.60	.30	.06
☐ 81 Kevin Edwards	.30	.15	.03
☐ 82 Grant Long	1.00	.50	.10
☐ 83 Rony Seikaly	2.00	1.00	.20
☐ 84 Rory Sparrow	.06	.03	.00
☐ 85 Greg Anderson UER	.10	.05	.01
(Stats show 1988-89 as 19888-89)			
☐ 86 Jay Humphries	.10	.05	.01
☐ 87 Larry Krystkowiak	.20	.10	.02
☐ 88 Ricky Pierce	.30	.15	.03
☐ 89 Paul Pressey	.10	.05	.01
☐ 90 Alvin Robertson	.10	.05	.01
☐ 91 Jack Sikma	.10	.05	.01
☐ 92 Steve Johnson	.06	.03	.00

☐ 93 Rick Mahorn	.10	.05	.01
☐ 94 David Rivers	.10	.05	.01
☐ 95 Joe Barry Carroll	.06	.03	.00
☐ 96 Lester Conner UER	.10	.05	.01
(Garden State in stats, should be Golden State)			
☐ 97 Roy Hinson	.06	.03	.00
☐ 98 Mike McGee	.10	.05	.01
☐ 99 Chris Morris	.50	.25	.05
☐ 100 Patrick Ewing	1.75	.85	.17
☐ 101 Mark Jackson	.30	.15	.03
☐ 102 Johnny Newman	.50	.25	.05
☐ 103 Charles Oakley	.12	.06	.01
☐ 104 Rod Strickland	1.00	.50	.10
☐ 105 Trent Tucker	.06	.03	.00
☐ 106 Kiki Vandeweghe	.10	.05	.01
☐ 107A Gerald Wilkins	.12	.06	.01
(U. of Tennessee)			
☐ 107B Gerald Wilkins	.12	.06	.01
(U. of Tenn.)			
☐ 108 Terry Catledge	.12	.06	.01
☐ 109 Dave Corzine	.06	.03	.00
☐ 110 Scott Skiles	.75	.35	.07
☐ 111 Reggie Theus	.12	.06	.01
☐ 112 Ron Anderson	.30	.15	.03
☐ 113 Charles Barkley	1.50	.75	.15
☐ 114 Scott Brooks	.20	.10	.02
☐ 115 Maurice Cheeks	.15	.07	.01
☐ 116 Mike Gminski	.10	.05	.01
☐ 117 Hersey Hawkins UER	3.50	1.75	.35
(Born 9/29/65, should be 9/9/65)			
☐ 118 Chris Welp	.10	.05	.01
☐ 119 Tom Chambers	.35	.17	.03
☐ 120 Armon Gilliam	.20	.10	.02
☐ 121 Jeff Hornacek	2.00	1.00	.20
☐ 122 Eddie Johnson	.12	.06	.01
☐ 123 Kevin Johnson	9.00	4.50	.90
☐ 124 Dan Majerle	2.00	1.00	.20
☐ 125 Mark West	.06	.03	.00
☐ 126 Richard Anderson	.10	.05	.01
☐ 127 Mark Bryant	.30	.15	.03
☐ 128 Clyde Drexler	2.00	1.00	.20
☐ 129 Kevin Duckworth	.25	.12	.02
☐ 130 Jerome Kersey	.90	.45	.09
☐ 131 Terry Porter	1.25	.60	.12
☐ 132 Buck Williams	.40	.20	.04
☐ 133 Danny Ainge	.25	.12	.02
☐ 134 Ricky Berry	.10	.05	.01
☐ 135 Rodney McCray	.10	.05	.01
☐ 136 Jim Petersen	.06	.03	.00
☐ 137 Harold Pressley	.10	.05	.01
☐ 138 Kenny Smith	.20	.10	.02
☐ 139 Wayman Tisdale	.20	.10	.02
☐ 140 Willie Anderson	.75	.35	.07
☐ 141 Frank Brickowski	.10	.05	.01
☐ 142 Terry Cummings	.25	.12	.02
☐ 143 Johnny Dawkins	.12	.06	.01
☐ 144 Vern Maxwell	.75	.35	.07
☐ 145 Michael Cage	.06	.03	.00
☐ 146 Dale Ellis	.12	.06	.01
☐ 147 Alton Lister	.06	.03	.00
☐ 148 Xavier McDaniel UER	.40	.20	.04
(All-Rookie team inx 1985, not 1988)			
☐ 149 Derrick McKey	.25	.12	.02
☐ 150 Nate McMillan	.06	.03	.00
☐ 151 Thurl Bailey	.10	.05	.01
☐ 152 Mark Eaton	.10	.05	.01
☐ 153 Darrell Griffith	.10	.05	.01
☐ 154 Eric Leckner	.10	.05	.01
☐ 155 Karl Malone	1.50	.75	.15
☐ 156 John Stockton	3.00	1.50	.30
☐ 157 Mark Alarie	.10	.05	.01
☐ 158 Ledell Eackles	.60	.30	.06
☐ 159 Bernard King	.20	.10	.02
☐ 160 Jeff Malone	.35	.17	.03
☐ 161 Darrell Walker	.06	.03	.00
☐ 162A John Williams ERR	.75	.35	.07
Cleveland Cavaliers			
☐ 162B John Williams COR	.10	.05	.01
Washington Bullets			
☐ 163 All Star Game	.40	.20	.04
Karl Malone			
John Stockton			
☐ 164 All Star Game	.40	.20	.04
Hakeem Olajuwon			
Clyde Drexler			
☐ 165 All Star Game	.30	.15	.03
Dominique Wilkins			
Moses Malone			
☐ 166 All Star Game UER	.40	.20	.04
Brad Daugherty			
Mark Price			
(Bio says Nance had 204 blocks, should be 206)			
☐ 167 All Star Game	.40	.20	.04
Patrick Ewing			
Mark Jackson			
☐ 168 Checklist Card	.10	.01	.00

1989-90 Fleer All-Stars

This set of 11 insert stickers features NBA All-Stars and measures the standard size (2 1/2" by 3 1/2"). The front has a color action player photo in the shape of a cup silhouette. An aqua stripe with dark blue stars traverses the card top, and the same pattern reappears about halfway down the card face. The words "Fleer '89 All-Stars" appear at the top of the picture, with the player's name and position immediately below the picture. The back has a star pattern similar to the front. A career summary is printed in blue on a white background. The stickers are numbered on the back and checklisted below accordingly. One was inserted in each wax pack.

	MINT	EXC	G-VG
COMPLETE SET (11)	5.00	2.50	.50
COMMON STICKER (1-11)	.10	.05	.01
☐ 1 Karl Malone	.75	.35	.07
Utah Jazz			
☐ 2 Hakeem Olajuwon	.50	.25	.05
Houston Rockets			
☐ 3 Michael Jordan	2.50	1.25	.25
Chicago Bulls			
☐ 4 Charles Barkley	.75	.35	.07
Philadelphia 76ers			
☐ 5 Magic Johnson	1.50	.75	.15
Los Angeles Lakers			
☐ 6 Isiah Thomas	.40	.20	.04
Detroit Pistons			
☐ 7 Patrick Ewing	.75	.35	.07
New York Knicks			
☐ 8 Dale Ellis	.10	.05	.01
Seattle Supersonics			
☐ 9 Chris Mullin	.75	.35	.07
Golden State Warriors			
☐ 10 Larry Bird	1.00	.50	.10
Boston Celtics			
☐ 11 Tom Chambers	.15	.07	.01
Phoenix Suns			

1990-91 Fleer

The 1990-91 Fleer set contains 198 cards measuring the standard size (2 1/2" by 3 1/2"). The fronts feature a color action player photo, with a white inner border and a two-color (red on top and bottom, blue on sides) outer border on a white card face. The team logo is superimposed at the upper left corner of the picture, with the player's name and position appearing

below the picture. The backs are printed in black, gray, and yellow, and present biographical and statistical information. The cards are numbered on the back. The set is ordered alphabetically in team subsets (with a few exceptions due to late trades). The teams themselves are also presented in alphabetical order, Atlanta Hawks (1-7), Boston Celtics (8-15), Charlotte Hornets (16-21), Chicago Bulls (22-30 and 120), Cleveland Cavaliers (31-37), Dallas Mavericks (38-45 and 50), Denver Nuggets (46-53), Detroit Pistons (54-61), Golden State Warriors (62-68), Houston Rockets (69-75), Indiana Pacers (76-83), Los Angeles Clippers (84-89), Los Angeles Lakers (90-97), Miami Heat (98-103), Milwaukee Bucks (104-110), Minnesota Timberwolves (111-116 and 140), New Jersey Nets (117-123 and 136), New York Knicks (124-131), Orlando Magic (132-135 and 137), Philadelphia 76ers (138-139 and 141-145), Phoenix Suns (146-153), Portland Trail Blazers (154-161), Sacramento Kings (162-167 and 186-187), San Antonio Spurs (168-174), Seattle Supersonics (175-181), Utah Jazz (182-189 and 195), and Washington Bullets (164, 190-194, and 196). The description, All-American, is properly capitalized on the back of cards 134 and 144, but is not capitalized on cards 20, 29, 51, 53, 59, 70, 119, 130, 178, and 192. The key rookies in this set are Nick Anderson, B.J. Armstrong, Vlade Divac, Sherman Douglas, Sean Elliott, Pervis Ellison, Danny Ferry, Tim Hardaway, Shawn Kemp, Sarunas Marciulionis, Glen Rice, Pooh Richardson, and Cliff Robinson.

	MINT	EXC	G-VG
COMPLETE SET (198)	10.00	5.00	1.00
COMMON PLAYER (1-198)	.03	.01	.00
☐ 1 John Battle UER	.06	.03	.00
(Drafted in '84, should be '85)			
☐ 2 Cliff Levingston	.03	.01	.00
☐ 3 Moses Malone	.10	.05	.01
☐ 4 Kenny Smith	.06	.03	.00
☐ 5 Spud Webb	.06	.03	.00
☐ 6 Dominique Wilkins	.15	.07	.01
☐ 7 Kevin Willis	.10	.05	.01
☐ 8 Larry Bird	.35	.17	.03
☐ 9 Dennis Johnson	.08	.04	.01
☐ 10 Joe Kleine	.03	.01	.00
☐ 11 Reggie Lewis	.25	.12	.02
☐ 12 Kevin McHale	.10	.05	.01
☐ 13 Robert Parish	.12	.06	.01
☐ 14 Jim Paxson	.03	.01	.00
☐ 15 Ed Pinckney	.03	.01	.00
☐ 16 Tyrone Bogues	.03	.01	.00
☐ 17 Rex Chapman	.06	.03	.00
☐ 18 Dell Curry	.03	.01	.00
☐ 19 Armon Gilliam	.03	.01	.00
☐ 20 J.R. Reid	.15	.07	.01
☐ 21 Kelly Tripucka	.03	.01	.00
☐ 22 B.J. Armstrong	.40	.20	.04
☐ 23A Bill Cartwright ERR	.50	.25	.05
(No decimal points in FGP and FTP)			
☐ 23B Bill Cartwright COR	.06	.03	.00
☐ 24 Horace Grant	.20	.10	.02
☐ 25 Craig Hodges	.03	.01	.00
☐ 26 Michael Jordan UER	1.50	.75	.15
(Led NBA in scoring 4 years, not 3)			
☐ 27 Stacey King UER	.25	.12	.02
(Comma missing between progressed and Stacy)			
☐ 28 John Paxson	.06	.03	.00
☐ 29 Will Perdue	.10	.05	.01
☐ 30 Scottie Pippen UER	.60	.30	.06
(Born AR, not AK)			
☐ 31 Brad Daugherty	.20	.10	.02
☐ 32 Craig Ehlo	.06	.03	.00
☐ 33 Danny Ferry	.20	.10	.02
☐ 34 Steve Kerr	.03	.01	.00
☐ 35 Larry Nance	.10	.05	.01
☐ 36 Mark Price UER	.20	.10	.02
(Drafted by Cleveland, should be Dallas)			
☐ 37 Hot Rod Williams	.08	.04	.01
☐ 38 Rolando Blackman	.06	.03	.00
☐ 39A Adrian Dantley ERR	.50	.25	.05
(No decimal points in FGP and FTP)			
☐ 39B Adrian Dantley COR	.08	.04	.01
☐ 40 Brad Davis	.03	.01	.00
☐ 41 James Donaldson UER	.03	.01	.00
(Text says in committed, should be is committed)			
☐ 42 Derek Harper	.06	.03	.00
☐ 43 Sam Perkins UER	.10	.05	.01
(First line of text should be intact)			
☐ 44 Bill Wennington	.03	.01	.00
☐ 45 Herb Williams	.03	.01	.00
☐ 46 Michael Adams	.08	.04	.01
☐ 47 Walter Davis	.06	.03	.00
☐ 48 Alex English UER	.08	.04	.01
(Stats missing from '76-77 through '79-80)			
☐ 49 Bill Hanzlik	.03	.01	.00
☐ 50 Lafayette Lever UER	.06	.03	.00
(Born AR, not AK)			
☐ 51 Todd Lichti	.10	.05	.01
☐ 52 Blair Rasmussen	.03	.01	.00
☐ 53 Dan Schayes	.03	.01	.00
☐ 54 Mark Aguirre	.06	.03	.00
☐ 55 Joe Dumars	.12	.06	.01
☐ 56 James Edwards	.03	.01	.00
☐ 57 Vinnie Johnson	.06	.03	.00
☐ 58 Bill Laimbeer	.08	.04	.01
☐ 59 Dennis Rodman UER	.20	.10	.02
(College misspelled as coilege on back)			
☐ 60 John Salley	.06	.03	.00
☐ 61 Isiah Thomas	.15	.07	.01
☐ 62 Manute Bol	.03	.01	.00
☐ 63 Tim Hardaway	1.50	.75	.15
☐ 64 Rod Higgins	.03	.01	.00
☐ 65 Sarunas Marciulionis	.40	.20	.04
☐ 66 Chris Mullin	.25	.12	.02
☐ 67 Mitch Richmond	.15	.07	.01
☐ 68 Terry Teagle	.03	.01	.00
☐ 69 Anthony Bowie UER	.15	.07	.01
(Seasons, not seeasons)			
☐ 70 Eric Floyd	.06	.03	.00
☐ 71 Buck Johnson	.03	.01	.00
☐ 72 Vernon Maxwell	.06	.03	.00
☐ 73 Hakeem Olajuwon	.25	.12	.02
☐ 74 Otis Thorpe	.06	.03	.00
☐ 75 Mitchell Wiggins	.03	.01	.00
☐ 76 Vern Fleming	.03	.01	.00
☐ 77 George McCloud	.10	.05	.01
☐ 78 Reggie Miller	.20	.10	.02
☐ 79 Chuck Person	.08	.04	.01
☐ 80 Mike Sanders	.06	.03	.00
☐ 81 Detlef Schrempf	.10	.05	.01
☐ 82 Rik Smits	.08	.04	.01
☐ 83 LaSalle Thompson	.03	.01	.00
☐ 84 Benoit Benjamin	.06	.03	.00
☐ 85 Winston Garland	.03	.01	.00
☐ 86 Ron Harper	.06	.03	.00
☐ 87 Danny Manning	.15	.07	.01
☐ 88 Ken Norman	.08	.04	.01
☐ 89 Charles Smith	.10	.05	.01
☐ 90 Michael Cooper	.06	.03	.00
☐ 91 Vlade Divac	.30	.15	.03
☐ 92 A.C. Green	.06	.03	.00
☐ 93 Magic Johnson	.75	.35	.07
☐ 94 Byron Scott	.06	.03	.00
☐ 95 Mychal Thompson UER	.03	.01	.00
(Missing '78-79 stats from Portland)			
☐ 96 Orlando Woolridge	.03	.01	.00
☐ 97 James Worthy	.15	.07	.01
☐ 98 Sherman Douglas	.20	.10	.02
☐ 99 Kevin Edwards	.03	.01	.00

☐ 100 Grant Long	.06	.03	.00
☐ 101 Glen Rice	.90	.45	.09
☐ 102 Rony Seikaly UER (Ron on front)	.15	.07	.01
☐ 103 Billy Thompson	.06	.03	.00
☐ 104 Jeff Grayer	.15	.07	.01
☐ 105 Jay Humphries	.03	.01	.00
☐ 106 Ricky Pierce	.06	.03	.00
☐ 107 Paul Pressey	.03	.01	.00
☐ 108 Fred Roberts	.06	.03	.00
☐ 109 Alvin Robertson	.06	.03	.00
☐ 110 Jack Sikma	.06	.03	.00
☐ 111 Randy Breuer	.03	.01	.00
☐ 112 Tony Campbell	.10	.05	.01
☐ 113 Tyrone Corbin	.06	.03	.00
☐ 114 Sam Mitchell UER (Mercer University, not Mercer College)	.15	.07	.01
☐ 115 Tod Murphy UER (Born Long Beach, not Lakewood)	.06	.03	.00
☐ 116 Pooh Richardson	.40	.20	.04
☐ 117 Mookie Blaylock	.20	.10	.02
☐ 118 Sam Bowie	.06	.03	.00
☐ 119 Lester Conner	.03	.01	.00
☐ 120 Dennis Hopson	.06	.03	.00
☐ 121 Chris Morris	.06	.03	.00
☐ 122 Charles Shackleford	.06	.03	.00
☐ 123 Purvis Short	.03	.01	.00
☐ 124 Maurice Cheeks	.06	.03	.00
☐ 125 Patrick Ewing	.30	.15	.03
☐ 126 Mark Jackson	.06	.03	.00
☐ 127A Johnny Newman ERR (Jr. misprinted as J. on card back)	.50	.25	.05
☐ 127B Johnny Newman COR	.06	.03	.00
☐ 128 Charles Oakley	.06	.03	.00
☐ 129 Trent Tucker	.03	.01	.00
☐ 130 Kenny Walker	.03	.01	.00
☐ 131 Gerald Wilkins	.06	.03	.00
☐ 132 Nick Anderson	.40	.20	.04
☐ 133 Terry Catledge	.03	.01	.00
☐ 134 Sidney Green	.03	.01	.00
☐ 135 Otis Smith	.06	.03	.00
☐ 136 Reggie Theus	.06	.03	.00
☐ 137 Sam Vincent	.03	.01	.00
☐ 138 Ron Anderson	.06	.03	.00
☐ 139 Charles Barkley UER (FG Percentage .545.)	.25	.12	.02
☐ 140 Scott Brooks UER ('89-89 Philadelphia in wrong typeface)	.03	.01	.00
☐ 141 Johnny Dawkins	.03	.01	.00
☐ 142 Mike Gminski	.03	.01	.00
☐ 143 Hersey Hawkins	.15	.07	.01
☐ 144 Rick Mahorn	.06	.03	.00
☐ 145 Derek Smith	.03	.01	.00
☐ 146 Tom Chambers	.10	.05	.01
☐ 147 Jeff Hornacek	.15	.07	.01
☐ 148 Eddie Johnson	.06	.03	.00
☐ 149 Kevin Johnson	.25	.12	.02
☐ 150A Dan Majerle ERR (Award in 1988; three-time selection)	.50	.25	.05
☐ 150B Dan Majerle COR (Award in 1989; three-time selection)	.15	.07	.01
☐ 151 Tim Perry	.20	.10	.02
☐ 152 Kurt Rambis	.06	.03	.00
☐ 153 Mark West	.03	.01	.00
☐ 154 Clyde Drexler	.30	.15	.03
☐ 155 Kevin Duckworth	.03	.01	.00
☐ 156 Byron Irvin	.08	.04	.01
☐ 157 Jerome Kersey	.10	.05	.01
☐ 158 Terry Porter	.15	.07	.01
☐ 159 Cliff Robinson	.40	.20	.04
☐ 160 Buck Williams	.10	.05	.01
☐ 161 Danny Young	.03	.01	.00
☐ 162 Danny Ainge	.06	.03	.00
☐ 163 Antoine Carr	.03	.01	.00
☐ 164 Pervis Ellison	.60	.30	.06
☐ 165 Rodney McCray	.03	.01	.00
☐ 166 Harold Pressley	.03	.01	.00
☐ 167 Wayman Tisdale	.08	.04	.01
☐ 168 Willie Anderson	.08	.04	.01
☐ 169 Frank Brickowski	.03	.01	.00
☐ 170 Terry Cummings	.08	.04	.01
☐ 171 Sean Elliott	.40	.20	.04
☐ 172 David Robinson	1.50	.75	.15
☐ 173 Rod Strickland	.08	.04	.01
☐ 174 David Wingate	.03	.01	.00
☐ 175 Dana Barros	.20	.10	.02
☐ 176 Michael Cage UER (Born AR, not AK)	.03	.01	.00
☐ 177 Dale Ellis	.06	.03	.00
☐ 178 Shawn Kemp	1.50	.75	.15
☐ 179 Xavier McDaniel	.10	.05	.01
☐ 180 Derrick McKey	.06	.03	.00
☐ 181 Nate McMillan	.03	.01	.00
☐ 182 Thurl Bailey	.03	.01	.00
☐ 183 Mike Brown	.06	.03	.00
☐ 184 Mark Eaton	.03	.01	.00
☐ 185 Blue Edwards	.20	.10	.02
☐ 186 Bob Hansen	.03	.01	.00
☐ 187 Eric Leckner	.03	.01	.00
☐ 188 Karl Malone	.25	.12	.02
☐ 189 John Stockton	.25	.12	.02
☐ 190 Mark Alarie	.03	.01	.00
☐ 191 Ledell Eackles	.06	.03	.00
☐ 192A Harvey Grant (First name on card front in black)	1.00	.50	.10
☐ 192B Harvey Grant (First name on card front in white)	.15	.07	.01
☐ 193 Tom Hammonds	.15	.07	.01
☐ 194 Bernard King	.06	.03	.00
☐ 195 Jeff Malone	.10	.05	.01
☐ 196 Darrell Walker	.03	.01	.00
☐ 197 Checklist Card	.06	.01	.00
☐ 198 Checklist Card	.06	.01	.00

1990-91 Fleer All-Stars

These All-Star inserts measure the standard size (2 1/2" by 3 1/2"). The fronts feature a color action photo, framed by a basketball hoop and net on an aqua background. An orange stripe at the top represents the bottom of the backboard and has the words "Fleer '90 All-Stars." The player's name and position are given at the bottom between stars. The backs are printed in blue and pink with white borders and have career summaries. The cards are numbered on the back. These inserts were not included in every wax pack and hence they are a little more difficult to find than the Fleer All-Star inserts of the previous years.

	MINT	EXC	G-VG
COMPLETE SET (12)	6.00	3.00	.60
COMMON PLAYER (1-12)	.30	.15	.03
☐ 1 Charles Barkley, Philadelphia 76ers	.60	.30	.06
☐ 2 Larry Bird, Boston Celtics	.90	.45	.09
☐ 3 Hakeem Olajuwon, Houston Rockets	.50	.25	.05
☐ 4 Magic Johnson, Los Angeles Lakers	1.50	.75	.15
☐ 5 Michael Jordan, Chicago Bulls	2.50	1.25	.25
☐ 6 Isiah Thomas, Detroit Pistons	.40	.20	.04
☐ 7 Karl Malone, Utah Jazz	.60	.30	.06
☐ 8 Tom Chambers, Phoenix Suns	.30	.15	.03
☐ 9 John Stockton, Utah Jazz	.60	.30	.06
☐ 10 David Robinson	2.00	1.00	.20

	MINT	EXC	G-VG
San Antonio Spurs			
☐ 11 Clyde Drexler	.75	.35	.07
Portland Trail Blazers			
☐ 12 Patrick Ewing	.75	.35	.07
New York Knicks			

1990-91 Fleer Rookie Sensations

These rookie sensation cards measure the standard size (2 1/2" by 3 1/2"). The fronts feature color action player photos, with white and red borders on an aqua background. A basketball overlays the lower left corner of the picture, with the words "Rookie Sensation" in yellow lettering, and the player's name appearing in white lettering in the bottom red border. The backs are printed in black and red on gray background (with white borders), and present summaries of their college careers and rookie seasons. The cards are numbered on the back. These inserts were distributed intermittently in cello packs and thus are considered a tough insert set to complete.

	MINT	EXC	G-VG
COMPLETE SET (10)	80.00	40.00	8.00
COMMON PLAYER (1-10)	2.50	1.25	.25
☐ 1 David Robinson UER	35.00	17.50	3.50
San Antonio Spurs (Text has 1988-90 season, should be 1989-90)			
☐ 2 Sean Elliott UER	6.00	3.00	.60
San Antonio Spurs (Misspelled Elliot on card front)			
☐ 3 Glen Rice	16.00	8.00	1.60
Miami Heat			
☐ 4 J.R.Reid	2.50	1.25	.25
Charlotte Hornets			
☐ 5 Stacey King	4.00	2.00	.40
Chicago Bulls			
☐ 6 Pooh Richardson	6.00	3.00	.60
Minnesota Timberwolves			
☐ 7 Nick Anderson	6.00	3.00	.60
Orlando Magic			
☐ 8 Tim Hardaway	35.00	17.50	3.50
Golden State Warriors			
☐ 9 Vlade Divac	4.00	2.00	.40
Los Angeles Lakers			
☐ 10 Sherman Douglas	3.50	1.75	.35
Miami Heat			

1990-91 Fleer Update

The cards are the same size (2 1/2" by 3 1/2") and design as the regular issue. The set numbering is arranged alphabetically by team as follows: Atlanta Hawks (1-5), Boston Celtics (6-10), Charlotte Hornets (11-13), Chicago Bulls (14-15), Cleveland Cavaliers (16-18), Dallas Mavericks (19-23), Cleveland Cavaliers (24-27), Detroit Pistons (28-30), Golden State Warriors (31-

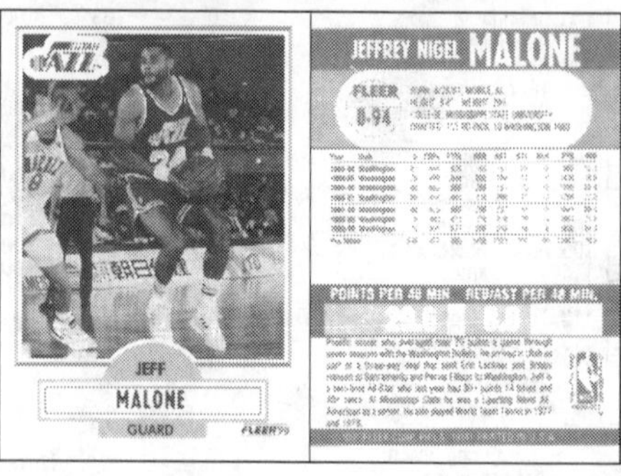

34), Houston Rockets (35-36), Indiana Pacers (37-39), Los Angeles Clippers (40-42), Los Angeles Lakers (43-46), Miami Heat (47-50), Milwaukee Bucks (51-55), Minnesota Timberwolves (56-58), New Jersey Nets (59-62), New York Knicks (63-66), Orlando Magic (67), Philadelphia 76ers (68-73), Phoenix Suns (74-77), Portland Trail Blazers (78-81), Sacramento Kings (82-87), San Antonio Spurs (88-91), Seattle Supersonics (92-93), Utah Jazz (94-96), and Washington Bullets (97-99). The key rookies in this set are Dee Brown, Derrick Coleman, Kendall Gill, Gary Payton, Drazen Petrovic, Dennis Scott, and Lionel Simmons.

	MINT	EXC	G-VG
COMPLETE SET (100)	14.00	7.00	1.40
COMMON PLAYER (1-100)	.04	.02	.00
☐ U1 Jon Koncak	.07	.03	.01
☐ U2 Tim McCormick	.04	.02	.00
☐ U3 Glenn Rivers	.07	.03	.01
☐ U4 Rumeal Robinson	.35	.17	.03
☐ U5 Trevor Wilson	.07	.03	.01
☐ U6 Dee Brown	1.50	.75	.15
☐ U7 Dave Popson	.07	.03	.01
☐ U8 Kevin Gamble	.12	.06	.01
☐ U9 Brian Shaw	.07	.03	.01
☐ U10 Michael Smith	.07	.03	.01
☐ U11 Kendall Gill	5.00	2.50	.50
☐ U12 Johnny Newman	.07	.03	.01
☐ U13 Steve Scheffler	.07	.03	.01
☐ U14 Dennis Hopson	.07	.03	.01
☐ U15 Cliff Levingston	.04	.02	.00
☐ U16 Chucky Brown	.10	.05	.01
☐ U17 John Morton	.07	.03	.01
☐ U18 Gerald Paddio	.07	.03	.01
☐ U19 Alex English	.07	.03	.01
☐ U20 Fat Lever	.07	.03	.01
☐ U21 Rodney McCray	.04	.02	.00
☐ U22 Roy Tarpley	.07	.03	.01
☐ U23 Randy White	.10	.05	.01
☐ U24 Anthony Cook	.07	.03	.01
☐ U25 Chris Jackson	.40	.20	.04
☐ U26 Marcus Liberty	.60	.30	.06
☐ U27 Orlando Woolridge	.04	.02	.00
☐ U28 William Bedford	.10	.05	.01
☐ U29 Lance Blanks	.10	.05	.01
☐ U30 Scott Hastings	.04	.02	.00
☐ U31 Tyrone Hill	.40	.20	.04
☐ U32 Les Jepsen	.10	.05	.01
☐ U33 Steve Johnson	.04	.02	.00
☐ U34 Kevin Pritchard	.07	.03	.01
☐ U35 Dave Jamerson	.10	.05	.01
☐ U36 Kenny Smith	.07	.03	.01
☐ U37 Greg Dreiling	.07	.03	.01
☐ U38 Kenny Williams	.20	.10	.02
☐ U39 Micheal Williams UER	.30	.15	.03
☐ U40 Gary Grant	.04	.02	.00
☐ U41 Bo Kimble	.10	.05	.01
☐ U42 Loy Vaught	.40	.20	.04
☐ U43 Elden Campbell	.50	.25	.05
☐ U44 Sam Perkins	.10	.05	.01
☐ U45 Tony Smith	.15	.07	.01
☐ U46 Terry Teagle	.04	.02	.00
☐ U47 Willie Burton	.40	.20	.04
☐ U48 Bimbo Coles	.40	.20	.04
☐ U49 Terry Davis	.25	.12	.02
☐ U50 Alec Kessler	.10	.05	.01
☐ U51 Greg Anderson	.04	.02	.00

☐ U52 Frank Brickowski	.04	.02	.00
☐ U53 Steve Henson	.07	.03	.01
☐ U54 Brad Lohaus	.07	.03	.01
☐ U55 Dan Schayes	.04	.02	.00
☐ U56 Gerald Glass	.40	.20	.04
☐ U57 Felton Spencer	.25	.12	.02
☐ U58 Doug West	.40	.20	.04
☐ U59 Jud Buechler	.15	.07	.01
☐ U60 Derrick Coleman	3.00	1.50	.30
☐ U61 Tate George	.07	.03	.01
☐ U62 Reggie Theus	.07	.03	.01
☐ U63 Greg Grant	.07	.03	.01
☐ U64 Jerrod Mustaf	.25	.12	.02
☐ U65 Eddie Lee Wilkins	.07	.03	.01
☐ U66 Michael Ansley	.07	.03	.01
☐ U67 Jerry Reynolds	.07	.03	.01
☐ U68 Dennis Scott	.90	.45	.09
☐ U69 Manute Bol	.04	.02	.00
☐ U70 Armon Gilliam	.04	.02	.00
☐ U71 Brian Oliver	.10	.05	.01
☐ U72 Kenny Payne	.10	.05	.01
☐ U73 Jayson Williams	.15	.07	.01
☐ U74 Kenny Battle	.12	.06	.01
☐ U75 Cedric Ceballos	.75	.35	.07
☐ U76 Negele Knight	.40	.20	.04
☐ U77 Xavier McDaniel	.10	.05	.01
☐ U78 Alaa Abdelnaby	.30	.15	.03
☐ U79 Danny Ainge	.10	.05	.01
☐ U80 Mark Bryant	.04	.02	.00
☐ U81 Drazen Petrovic	1.25	.60	.12
☐ U82 Anthony Bonner	.30	.15	.03
☐ U83 Duane Causwell	.30	.15	.03
☐ U84 Bobby Hansen	.04	.02	.00
☐ U85 Eric Leckner	.07	.03	.01
☐ U86 Travis Mays	.25	.12	.02
☐ U87 Lionel Simmons	1.50	.75	.15
☐ U88 Sidney Green	.04	.02	.00
☐ U89 Tony Massenburg	.07	.03	.01
☐ U90 Paul Pressey	.04	.02	.00
☐ U91 Dwayne Schintzius	.07	.03	.01
☐ U92 Gary Payton	.90	.45	.09
☐ U93 Olden Polynice	.04	.02	.00
☐ U94 Jeff Malone	.10	.05	.01
☐ U95 Walter Palmer	.07	.03	.01
☐ U96 Delaney Rudd	.10	.05	.01
☐ U97 Pervis Ellison	1.25	.60	.12
☐ U98 A.J. English	.35	.17	.03
☐ U99 Greg Foster	.07	.03	.01
☐ U100 Checklist Card	.07	.01	.00

1991-92 Fleer

The 1991-92 Fleer basketball card set contains 240 cards measuring the standard size (2 1/2" by 3 1/2"). The fronts features color action player photos, bordered by a red stripe on the bottom, and gray and red stripes on the top. A 3/4" blue stripe checkered with black NBA logos runs the length of the card and serves as the left border of the picture. The team logo, player's name, and position are printed in white lettering in this stripe. The picture is bordered on the right side by a thin gray stripe and a thicker blue one. The backs present career summaries and are printed with black lettering on various pastel colors, superimposed over a wooden basketball floor background. The cards are numbered and checklisted below alphabetically within and according to teams as follows: Atlanta Hawks (1-7), Boston Celtics (8-16), Charlotte Hornets (17-24), Chicago Bulls (25-33), Cleveland Cavaliers (34-41), Dallas Mavericks (42-48), Denver Nuggets (49-56), Detroit Pistons (57-64), Golden State Warriors (65-72), Houston Rockets (73-80), Indiana Pacers (81-88), L.A. Clippers (86-96), L.A. Lakers (97-104), Miami Heat (105-112), Milwaukee Bucks (113-120), Minnesota Timberwolves (121-127), New Jersey Nets (128-134), New York Knicks (135-142), Orlando Magic (143-149), Philadelphia 76ers (150-157), Phoenix Suns (158-165), Portland Trail Blazers (166-173), Sacramento Kings (174-181), San Antonio Spurs (182-188), Seattle Supersonics (189-196), Utah Jazz (197-203), and Washington Bullets (204-209). Other subsets within the set are All-Stars (210-219), League Leaders (220-226), Slam Dunk (227-232), and All Star Game Highlights (233-238). There are no key Rookie Cards in this first series.

	MINT	EXC	G-VG
COMPLETE SET (240)	6.00	3.00	.60
COMMON PLAYER (1-240)	.03	.01	.00
☐ 1 John Battle	.06	.03	.00
☐ 2 Jon Koncak	.03	.01	.00
☐ 3 Rumeal Robinson	.06	.03	.00
☐ 4 Spud Webb	.06	.03	.00
☐ 5 Bob Weiss CO	.03	.01	.00
☐ 6 Dominique Wilkins	.12	.06	.01
☐ 7 Kevin Willis	.08	.04	.01
☐ 8 Larry Bird	.25	.12	.02
☐ 9 Dee Brown	.20	.10	.02
☐ 10 Chris Ford CO	.03	.01	.00
☐ 11 Kevin Gamble	.06	.03	.00
☐ 12 Reggie Lewis	.12	.06	.01
☐ 13 Kevin McHale	.08	.04	.01
☐ 14 Robert Parish	.10	.05	.01
☐ 15 Ed Pinckney	.03	.01	.00
☐ 16 Brian Shaw	.06	.03	.00
☐ 17 Tyrone Bogues	.03	.01	.00
☐ 18 Rex Chapman	.06	.03	.00
☐ 19 Dell Curry	.03	.01	.00
☐ 20 Kendall Gill	.50	.25	.05
☐ 21 Eric Leckner	.03	.01	.00
☐ 22 Gene Littles CO	.03	.01	.00
☐ 23 Johnny Newman	.03	.01	.00
☐ 24 J.R. Reid	.06	.03	.00
☐ 25 B.J. Armstrong	.10	.05	.01
☐ 26 Bill Cartwright	.06	.03	.00
☐ 27 Horace Grant	.10	.05	.01
☐ 28 Phil Jackson CO	.03	.01	.00
☐ 29 Michael Jordan	1.00	.50	.10
☐ 30 Cliff Levingston	.03	.01	.00
☐ 31 John Paxson	.06	.03	.00
☐ 32 Will Perdue	.06	.03	.00
☐ 33 Scottie Pippen	.30	.15	.03
☐ 34 Brad Daugherty	.12	.06	.01
☐ 35 Craig Ehlo	.06	.03	.00
☐ 36 Danny Ferry	.06	.03	.00
☐ 37 Larry Nance	.08	.04	.01
☐ 38 Mark Price	.12	.06	.01
☐ 39 Darnell Valentine	.03	.01	.00
☐ 40 Hot Rod Williams	.06	.03	.00
☐ 41 Lenny Wilkens CO	.06	.03	.00
☐ 42 Richie Adubato CO	.03	.01	.00
☐ 43 Rolando Blackman	.06	.03	.00
☐ 44 James Donaldson	.03	.01	.00
☐ 45 Derek Harper	.06	.03	.00
☐ 46 Rodney McCray	.03	.01	.00
☐ 47 Randy White	.06	.03	.00
☐ 48 Herb Williams	.03	.01	.00
☐ 49 Chris Jackson	.08	.04	.01
☐ 50 Marcus Liberty	.15	.07	.01
☐ 51 Todd Lichti	.03	.01	.00
☐ 52 Blair Rasmussen	.03	.01	.00
☐ 53 Paul Westhead CO	.03	.01	.00
☐ 54 Reggie Williams	.06	.03	.00
☐ 55 Joe Wolf	.03	.01	.00
☐ 56 Orlando Woolridge	.03	.01	.00
☐ 57 Mark Aguirre	.06	.03	.00
☐ 58 Chuck Daly CO	.06	.03	.00
☐ 59 Joe Dumars	.10	.05	.01
☐ 60 James Edwards	.03	.01	.00
☐ 61 Vinnie Johnson	.03	.01	.00
☐ 62 Bill Laimbeer	.06	.03	.00
☐ 63 Dennis Rodman	.10	.05	.01
☐ 64 Isiah Thomas	.12	.06	.01
☐ 65 Tim Hardaway	.50	.25	.05
☐ 66 Rod Higgins	.03	.01	.00
☐ 67 Tyrone Hill	.08	.04	.01
☐ 68 Sarunas Marciulionis	.12	.06	.01
☐ 69 Chris Mullin	.15	.07	.01

☐ 70 Don Nelson CO .03 .01 .00
☐ 71 Mitch Richmond .10 .05 .01
☐ 72 Tom Tolbert .03 .01 .00
☐ 73 Don Chaney CO .03 .01 .00
☐ 74 Eric(Sleepy) Floyd .03 .01 .00
☐ 75 Buck Johnson .03 .01 .00
☐ 76 Vernon Maxwell .06 .03 .00
☐ 77 Hakeem Olajuwon .12 .06 .01
☐ 78 Kenny Smith .03 .01 .00
☐ 79 Larry Smith .03 .01 .00
☐ 80 Otis Thorpe .06 .03 .00
☐ 81 Vern Fleming .03 .01 .00
☐ 82 Bob Hill CO .06 .03 .00
☐ 83 Reggie Miller .10 .05 .01
☐ 84 Chuck Person .06 .03 .00
☐ 85 Detlef Schrempf .06 .03 .00
☐ 86 Rik Smits .06 .03 .00
☐ 87 LaSalle Thompson .03 .01 .00
☐ 88 Micheal Williams .06 .03 .00
☐ 89 Gary Grant .03 .01 .00
☐ 90 Ron Harper .06 .03 .00
☐ 91 Bo Kimble .06 .03 .00
☐ 92 Danny Manning .10 .05 .01
☐ 93 Ken Norman .06 .03 .00
☐ 94 Olden Polynice .03 .01 .00
☐ 95 Mike Schuler CO .03 .01 .00
☐ 96 Charles Smith .08 .04 .01
☐ 97 Vlade Divac .08 .04 .01
☐ 98 Mike Dunleavy CO .03 .01 .00
☐ 99 A.C. Green .06 .03 .00
☐ 100 Magic Johnson .60 .30 .06
☐ 101 Sam Perkins .08 .04 .01
☐ 102 Byron Scott .06 .03 .00
☐ 103 Terry Teagle .03 .01 .00
☐ 104 James Worthy .10 .05 .01
☐ 105 Willie Burton .06 .03 .00
☐ 106 Bimbo Coles .10 .05 .01
☐ 107 Sherman Douglas .06 .03 .00
☐ 108 Kevin Edwards .03 .01 .00
☐ 109 Grant Long .03 .01 .00
☐ 110 Kevin Loughery CO .03 .01 .00
☐ 111 Glen Rice .25 .12 .02
☐ 112 Rony Seikaly .08 .04 .01
☐ 113 Frank Brickowski .03 .01 .00
☐ 114 Dale Ellis .06 .03 .00
☐ 115 Del Harris CO .03 .01 .00
☐ 116 Jay Humphries .03 .01 .00
☐ 117 Fred Roberts .03 .01 .00
☐ 118 Alvin Robertson .06 .03 .00
☐ 119 Dan Schayes .03 .01 .00
☐ 120 Jack Sikma .06 .03 .00
☐ 121 Tony Campbell .06 .03 .00
☐ 122 Tyrone Corbin .06 .03 .00
☐ 123 Sam Mitchell .03 .01 .00
☐ 124 Tod Murphy .03 .01 .00
☐ 125 Pooh Richardson .10 .05 .01
☐ 126 Jim Rodgers CO .03 .01 .00
☐ 127 Felton Spencer .06 .03 .00
☐ 128 Mookie Blaylock .06 .03 .00
☐ 129 Sam Bowie .06 .03 .00
☐ 130 Derrick Coleman .30 .15 .03
☐ 131 Chris Dudley .03 .01 .00
☐ 132 Bill Fitch CO .03 .01 .00
☐ 133 Chris Morris .06 .03 .00
☐ 134 Drazen Petrovic .15 .07 .01
☐ 135 Maurice Cheeks .06 .03 .00
☐ 136 Patrick Ewing .20 .10 .02
☐ 137 Mark Jackson .06 .03 .00
☐ 138 Charles Oakley .06 .03 .00
☐ 139 Pat Riley CO .06 .03 .00
☐ 140 Trent Tucker .03 .01 .00
☐ 141 Kiki Vandeweghe .06 .03 .00
☐ 142 Gerald Wilkins .06 .03 .00
☐ 143 Nick Anderson .10 .05 .01
☐ 144 Terry Catledge .03 .01 .00
☐ 145 Matt Guokas CO .03 .01 .00
☐ 146 Jerry Reynolds .03 .01 .00
☐ 147 Dennis Scott .10 .05 .01
☐ 148 Scott Skiles .06 .03 .00
☐ 149 Otis Smith .03 .01 .00
☐ 150 Ron Anderson .03 .01 .00
☐ 151 Charles Barkley .15 .07 .01
☐ 152 Johnny Dawkins .03 .01 .00
☐ 153 Armon Gilliam .03 .01 .00
☐ 154 Hersey Hawkins .08 .04 .01
☐ 155 Jim Lynam CO .03 .01 .00
☐ 156 Rick Mahorn .06 .03 .00
☐ 157 Brian Oliver .06 .03 .00
☐ 158 Tom Chambers .08 .04 .01
☐ 159 Cotton Fitzsimmons CO .03 .01 .00
☐ 160 Jeff Hornacek .10 .05 .01
☐ 161 Kevin Johnson .15 .07 .01
☐ 162 Negele Knight .06 .03 .00
☐ 163 Dan Majerle .10 .05 .01
☐ 164 Xavier McDaniel .08 .04 .01
☐ 165 Mark West .03 .01 .00
☐ 166 Rick Adelman CO .03 .01 .00
☐ 167 Danny Ainge .06 .03 .00
☐ 168 Clyde Drexler .20 .10 .02
☐ 169 Kevin Duckworth .03 .01 .00
☐ 170 Jerome Kersey .08 .04 .01
☐ 171 Terry Porter .10 .05 .01
☐ 172 Cliff Robinson .10 .05 .01
☐ 173 Buck Williams .08 .04 .01
☐ 174 Antoine Carr .03 .01 .00
☐ 175 Duane Causwell .06 .03 .00
☐ 176 Jim Les .08 .04 .01
☐ 177 Travis Mays .06 .03 .00
☐ 178 Dick Motta CO .03 .01 .00
☐ 179 Lionel Simmons .15 .07 .01
☐ 180 Rory Sparrow .03 .01 .00
☐ 181 Wayman Tisdale .06 .03 .00
☐ 182 Willie Anderson .06 .03 .00
☐ 183 Larry Brown CO .03 .01 .00
☐ 184 Terry Cummings .08 .04 .01
☐ 185 Sean Elliott .10 .05 .01
☐ 186 Paul Pressey .03 .01 .00
☐ 187 David Robinson .60 .30 .06
☐ 188 Rod Strickland .06 .03 .00
☐ 189 Benoit Benjamin .03 .01 .00
☐ 190 Eddie Johnson .06 .03 .00
☐ 191 K.C. Jones CO .03 .01 .00
☐ 192 Shawn Kemp .50 .25 .05
☐ 193 Derrick McKey .06 .03 .00
☐ 194 Gary Payton .10 .05 .01
☐ 195 Ricky Pierce .06 .03 .00
☐ 196 Sedale Threatt .06 .03 .00
☐ 197 Thurl Bailey .03 .01 .00
☐ 198 Mark Eaton .03 .01 .00
☐ 199 Blue Edwards .03 .01 .00
☐ 200 Jeff Malone .08 .04 .01
☐ 201 Karl Malone .15 .07 .01
☐ 202 Jerry Sloan CO .03 .01 .00
☐ 203 John Stockton .15 .07 .01
☐ 204 Ledell Eackles .03 .01 .00
☐ 205 Pervis Ellison .15 .07 .01
☐ 206 A.J. English .10 .05 .01
☐ 207 Harvey Grant .06 .03 .00
☐ 208 Bernard King .08 .04 .01
☐ 209 Wes Unseld CO .06 .03 .00
☐ 210 Kevin Johnson AS .10 .05 .01
☐ 211 Michael Jordan AS .40 .20 .04
☐ 212 Dominique Wilkins AS .08 .04 .01
☐ 213 Charles Barkley AS .10 .05 .01
☐ 214 Hakeem Olajuwon AS .08 .04 .01
☐ 215 Patrick Ewing AS .10 .05 .01
☐ 216 Tim Hardaway AS .20 .10 .02
☐ 217 John Stockton AS .10 .05 .01
☐ 218 Chris Mullin AS .10 .05 .01
☐ 219 Karl Malone AS .10 .05 .01
☐ 220 Michael Jordan LL .40 .20 .04
☐ 221 John Stockton LL .10 .05 .01
☐ 222 Alvin Robertson LL .06 .03 .00
☐ 223 Hakeem Olajuwon LL .08 .04 .01
☐ 224 Buck Williams LL .06 .03 .00
☐ 225 David Robinson LL .25 .12 .02
☐ 226 Reggie Miller LL .08 .04 .01
☐ 227 Blue Edwards SD .03 .01 .00
☐ 228 Dee Brown SD .15 .07 .01
☐ 229 Rex Chapman SD .06 .03 .00
☐ 230 Kenny Smith SD .03 .01 .00
☐ 231 Shawn Kemp SD .20 .10 .02
☐ 232 Kendall Gill SD .25 .12 .02
☐ 233 '91 All Star Game .06 .03 .00
Enemies - A Love Story
(East Bench Scene)
☐ 234 '91 All Star Game .06 .03 .00
A Game of Contrasts
(Drexler over McHale)
☐ 235 '91 All Star Game .03 .01 .00
Showtime
(Alvin Robertson)
☐ 236 '91 All Star Game .06 .03 .00
Unstoppable Force
vs. Unbeatable Man
(Ewing rejects K.Malone)
☐ 237 '91 All Star Game .06 .03 .00
Just Me and the Boys
(Rebounding Scene)
☐ 238 '91 All Star Game .10 .05 .01
Unforgettable
(Jordan reverse lay-in)
☐ 239 Checklist 1-120 .06 .01 .00
☐ 240 Checklist 121-240 .06 .01 .00

1991-92 Fleer Pro Visions

This six-card set measures the standard size (2 1/2" by 3 1/2") and showcases outstanding NBA players. The set was distributed as a random insert in 1991-92 Fleer wax packs. The fronts feature a color player portrait by sports artist Terry Smith. The portrait is bordered on all sides by white, with the player's name in red lettering below the picture. The backs present biographical information and career summary in black lettering on a color background (with white borders). The cards are numbered on the back.

	MINT	EXC	G-VG
COMPLETE SET (6)	1.50	.75	.15
COMMON PLAYER (1-6)	.25	.12	.02
☐ 1 David Robinson San Antonio Spurs	.60	.30	.06
☐ 2 Michael Jordan Chicago Bulls	.75	.35	.07
☐ 3 Charles Barkley Philadelphia 76ers	.25	.12	.02
☐ 4 Patrick Ewing New York Knicks	.25	.12	.02
☐ 5 Karl Malone Utah Jazz	.25	.12	.02
☐ 6 Magic Johnson Los Angeles Lakers	.60	.30	.06

1991-92 Fleer Rookie Sensations

This ten-card set showcases outstanding rookies from the 1990-91 season and measures the standard size (2 1/2" by 3 1/2"). The set was distributed as a random insert in 1991-92 Fleer cello packs. The fronts feature a color player photo inside a basketball rim and net. The picture is bordered in magenta on all sides. The words "Rookie Sensations" appear above the picture, and player information is given below the picture. An orange basketball with the words "Fleer '91" appears in the upper left corner on both sides of the card. The back has a magenta border and includes highlights of the player's rookie season. The cards are numbered on the back.

	MINT	EXC	G-VG
COMPLETE SET (10)	20.00	10.00	2.00
COMMON PLAYER (1-10)	.75	.35	.07
☐ 1 Lionel Simmons	3.00	1.50	.30
☐ 2 Dennis Scott	2.00	1.00	.20
☐ 3 Derrick Coleman	4.50	2.25	.45
☐ 4 Kendall Gill	8.00	4.00	.80
☐ 5 Travis Mays	.75	.35	.07
☐ 6 Felton Spencer	.75	.35	.07
☐ 7 Willie Burton	.75	.35	.07
☐ 8 Chris Jackson	1.00	.50	.10
☐ 9 Gary Payton	2.00	1.00	.20
☐ 10 Dee Brown	3.00	1.50	.30

1991-92 Fleer Schoolyard Stars

This six-card set measures the standard size (2 1/2" by 3 1/2"). The set was distributed only in 1991-92 Fleer rak packs (one per pack). The front features color action player photos. The photos are bordered on the left and bottom by a black stripe and a broken pink stripe. Yellow stripes traverse the card top and bottom, and the background is a gray cement-colored design. The back has a similar layout and presents a basketball tip in black lettering on white. The cards are numbered on the back.

	MINT	EXC	G-VG
COMPLETE SET (6)	2.50	1.25	.25
COMMON PLAYER (1-6)	.30	.15	.03
☐ 1 Chris Mullin Golden State Warriors	1.00	.50	.10
☐ 2 Isiah Thomas Detroit Pistons	.75	.35	.07
☐ 3 Kevin McHale Boston Celtics	.40	.20	.04
☐ 4 Kevin Johnson Phoenix Suns	1.00	.50	.10
☐ 5 Karl Malone Utah Jazz	1.00	.50	.10
☐ 6 Alvin Robertson Milwaukee Bucks	.30	.15	.03

1991-92 Fleer Update

The 1991-92 Fleer Update basketball set contains 160 standard-size (2 1/2" by 3 1/2") cards and features hot rookies and traded veterans. The set was only distributed in wax packs. Special Dikembe Mutombo and Dominique Wilkins cards were randomly and intermittently inserted in the packs, and each player signed over 2,000 of his cards. The fronts feature the same design as the first series, with color player photos and a 3/4" blue

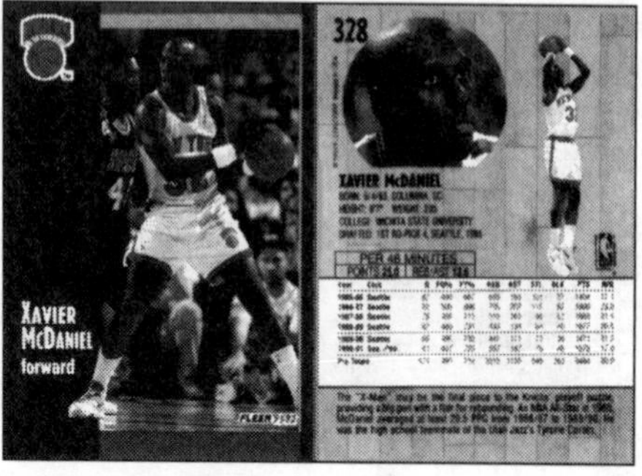

checkered stripe serving as a left border. The backs have a close-up photo, biography, and statistics on a wooden basketball floor background. The cards are numbered on the back and checklisted below alphabetically according to teams as follows: Atlanta Hawks (241-246), Boston Celtics (247-251), Charlotte Hornets (252-255), Chicago Bulls (256-259), Cleveland Cavaliers (260-265), Dallas Mavericks (266-271), Denver Nuggets (272-277), Detroit Pistons (278-283), Golden State Warriors (284-288), Houston Rockets (289-292), Indiana Pacers (293-295), Los Angeles Clippers (296-299), Los Angeles Lakers (300-304), Miami Heat (305-309), Milwaukee Bucks (310-315), Minnesota Timberwolves (316-321), New Jersey Nets (322-325), New York Knicks (326-330), Orlando Magic (331-334), Philadelphia 76ers (335-338), Phoenix Suns (339-343), Portland Trail Blazers (344-346), Sacramento Kings (347-352), San Antonio Spurs (353-356), Seattle Supersonics (357-361), Utah Jazz (362-366), and Washington Bullets (367-371). Team Leaders (372-398) and checklist cards (399-400) round out the set. The key rookie cards in this extended set are Stacey Augmon, Larry Johnson, Dikembe Mutumbo, Billy Owens, and Steve Smith.

	MINT	EXC	G-VG
COMPLETE SET (160)	8.00	4.00	.80
COMMON PLAYER (241-400)	.03	.01	.00
☐ 241 Stacey Augmon	.75	.35	.07
☐ 242 Maurice Cheeks	.06	.03	.00
☐ 243 Paul Graham	.20	.10	.02
☐ 244 Rodney Monroe	.15	.07	.01
☐ 245 Blair Rasmussen	.03	.01	.00
☐ 246 Alexander Volkov	.08	.04	.01
☐ 247 John Bagley	.06	.03	.00
☐ 248 Rick Fox	.75	.35	.07
☐ 249 Rickey Green	.03	.01	.00
☐ 250 Joe Kleine	.03	.01	.00
☐ 251 Stojko Vrankovic	.10	.05	.01
☐ 252 Allan Bristow CO	.03	.01	.00
☐ 253 Kenny Gattison	.10	.05	.01
☐ 254 Mike Gminski	.03	.01	.00
☐ 255 Larry Johnson	4.00	2.00	.40
☐ 256 Bobby Hansen	.03	.01	.00
☐ 257 Craig Hodges	.03	.01	.00
☐ 258 Stacey King	.06	.03	.00
☐ 259 Scott Williams	.25	.12	.02
☐ 260 John Battle	.03	.01	.00
☐ 261 Winston Bennett	.03	.01	.00
☐ 262 Terrell Brandon	.35	.17	.03
☐ 263 Henry James	.08	.04	.01
☐ 264 Steve Kerr	.03	.01	.00
☐ 265 Jimmy Oliver	.10	.05	.01
☐ 266 Brad Davis	.03	.01	.00
☐ 267 Terry Davis	.06	.03	.00
☐ 268 Donald Hodge	.25	.12	.02
☐ 269 Mike Iuzzolino	.20	.10	.02
☐ 270 Fat Lever	.06	.03	.00
☐ 271 Doug Smith	.35	.17	.03
☐ 272 Greg Anderson	.03	.01	.00
☐ 273 Kevin Brooks	.08	.04	.01
☐ 274 Walter Davis	.06	.03	.00
☐ 275 Winston Garland	.03	.01	.00
☐ 276 Mark Macon	.30	.15	.03
☐ 277A Dikembe Mutombo (Fleer '91 on front)	2.00	1.00	.20
☐ 277A Dikembe Mutombo (Fleer '91-92 on front)	2.00	1.00	.20
☐ 278 William Bedford	.03	.01	.00
☐ 279 Lance Blanks	.06	.03	.00
☐ 280 John Salley	.06	.03	.00
☐ 281 Charles Thomas	.08	.04	.01
☐ 282 Darrell Walker	.03	.01	.00
☐ 283 Orlando Woolridge	.06	.03	.00
☐ 284 Victor Alexander	.15	.07	.01
☐ 285 Vincent Askew	.10	.05	.01
☐ 286 Mario Elie	.15	.07	.01
☐ 287 Alton Lister	.03	.01	.00
☐ 288 Billy Owens	2.00	1.00	.20
☐ 289 Matt Bullard	.12	.06	.01
☐ 290 Carl Herrera	.12	.06	.01
☐ 291 Tree Rollins	.03	.01	.00
☐ 292 John Turner	.08	.04	.01
☐ 293 Dale Davis UER (Photo on back actually Sean Green)	.20	.10	.02
☐ 294 Sean Green	.08	.04	.01
☐ 295 Kenny Williams	.06	.03	.00
☐ 296 James Edwards	.03	.01	.00
☐ 297 LeRon Ellis	.08	.04	.01
☐ 298 Doc Rivers	.06	.03	.00
☐ 299 Loy Vaught	.08	.04	.01
☐ 300 Elden Campbell	.10	.05	.01
☐ 301 Jack Haley	.03	.01	.00
☐ 302 Keith Owens	.08	.04	.01
☐ 303 Tony Smith	.06	.03	.00
☐ 304 Sedale Threatt	.06	.03	.00
☐ 305 Keith Askins	.08	.04	.01
☐ 306 Alec Kessler	.06	.03	.00
☐ 307 John Morton	.03	.01	.00
☐ 308 Alan Ogg	.08	.04	.01
☐ 309 Steve Smith	.90	.45	.09
☐ 310 Lester Conner	.03	.01	.00
☐ 311 Jeff Grayer	.03	.01	.00
☐ 312 Frank Hamblen CO	.06	.03	.00
☐ 313 Steve Henson	.03	.01	.00
☐ 314 Larry Krystkowiak	.03	.01	.00
☐ 315 Moses Malone	.10	.05	.01
☐ 316 Thurl Bailey	.03	.01	.00
☐ 317 Randy Breuer	.03	.01	.00
☐ 318 Scott Brooks	.03	.01	.00
☐ 319 Gerald Glass	.10	.05	.01
☐ 320 Luc Longley	.15	.07	.01
☐ 321 Doug West	.08	.04	.01
☐ 322 Kenny Anderson	.75	.35	.07
☐ 323 Tate George	.06	.03	.00
☐ 324 Terry Mills	.12	.06	.01
☐ 325 Greg Anthony	.30	.15	.03
☐ 326 Anthony Mason	.25	.12	.02
☐ 327 Tim McCormick	.03	.01	.00
☐ 328 Xavier McDaniel	.08	.04	.01
☐ 329 Brian Quinnett	.03	.01	.00
☐ 330 John Starks	.50	.25	.05
☐ 331 Stanley Roberts	.60	.30	.06
☐ 332 Jeff Turner	.03	.01	.00
☐ 333 Sam Vincent	.03	.01	.00
☐ 334 Brian Williams	.30	.15	.03
☐ 335 Manute Bol	.03	.01	.00
☐ 336 Kenny Payne	.03	.01	.00
☐ 337 Charles Shackleford	.03	.01	.00
☐ 338 Jayson Williams	.06	.03	.00
☐ 339 Cedric Ceballos	.12	.06	.01
☐ 340 Andrew Lang	.10	.05	.01
☐ 341 Jerrod Mustaf	.08	.04	.01
☐ 342 Tim Perry	.06	.03	.00
☐ 343 Kurt Rambis	.06	.03	.00
☐ 344 Alaa Abdelnaby	.08	.04	.01
☐ 345 Robert Pack	.50	.25	.05
☐ 346 Danny Young	.03	.01	.00
☐ 347 Anthony Bonner	.06	.03	.00
☐ 348 Pete Chilcutt	.10	.05	.01
☐ 349 Rex Hughes	.06	.03	.00
☐ 350 Mitch Richmond	.10	.05	.01
☐ 351 Dwayne Schintzius	.06	.03	.00
☐ 352 Spud Webb	.06	.03	.00
☐ 353 Antoine Carr	.03	.01	.00
☐ 354 Sidney Green	.03	.01	.00
☐ 355 Vinnie Johnson	.03	.01	.00
☐ 356 Greg Sutton	.08	.04	.01
☐ 357 Dana Barros	.03	.01	.00
☐ 358 Michael Cage	.03	.01	.00
☐ 359 Marty Conlon	.08	.04	.01
☐ 360 Rich King	.10	.05	.01
☐ 361 Nate McMillan	.03	.01	.00
☐ 362 David Benoit	.30	.15	.03
☐ 363 Mike Brown	.03	.01	.00
☐ 364 Tyrone Corbin	.06	.03	.00
☐ 365 Eric Murdock	.15	.07	.01
☐ 366 Delaney Rudd	.03	.01	.00
☐ 367 Michael Adams	.08	.04	.01

□ 368 Tom Hammonds	.06	.03	.00
□ 369 Larry Stewart	.25	.12	.02
□ 370 Andre Turner	.08	.04	.01
□ 371 David Wingate	.03	.01	.00
□ 372 Dominique Wilkins TL Atlanta Hawks	.08	.04	.01
□ 373 Larry Bird TL Boston Celtics	.15	.07	.01
□ 374 Rex Chapman TL Charlotte Hornets	.06	.03	.00
□ 375 Michael Jordan TL Chicago Bulls	.40	.20	.04
□ 376 Brad Daugherty TL Cleveland Cavaliers	.08	.04	.01
□ 377 Derek Harper TL Dallas Mavericks	.06	.03	.00
□ 378 Dikembe Mutombo TL Denver Nuggets	.30	.15	.03
□ 379 Joe Dumars TL Detroit Pistons	.08	.04	.01
□ 380 Chris Mullin TL Golden State Warriors	.10	.05	.01
□ 381 Hakeem Olajuwon TL Houston Rockets	.08	.04	.01
□ 382 Chuck Person TL Indiana Pacers	.06	.03	.00
□ 383 Charles Smith TL Los Angeles Clippers	.06	.03	.00
□ 384 James Worthy TL Los Angeles Lakers	.08	.04	.01
□ 385 Glen Rice TL Miami Heat	.15	.07	.01
□ 386 Alvin Robertson TL Milwaukee Bucks	.03	.01	.00
□ 387 Tony Campbell TL Minnesota Timberwolves	.03	.01	.00
□ 388 Derrick Coleman TL New Jersey Nets	.20	.10	.02
□ 389 Patrick Ewing TL New York Knicks	.10	.05	.01
□ 390 Scott Skiles TL Orlando Magic	.03	.01	.00
□ 391 Charles Barkley TL Philadelphia 76ers	.10	.05	.01
□ 392 Kevin Johnson TL Phoenix Suns	.10	.05	.01
□ 393 Clyde Drexler TL Portland Trail Blazers	.12	.06	.01
□ 394 Lionel Simmons TL Sacramento Kings	.10	.05	.01
□ 395 David Robinson TL San Antonio Spurs	.25	.12	.02
□ 396 Ricky Pierce TL Seattle Supersonics	.03	.01	.00
□ 397 John Stockton TL Utah Jazz	.10	.05	.01
□ 398 Michael Adams TL Washington Bullets	.03	.01	.00
□ 399 Checklist	.06	.01	.00
□ 400 Checklist	.06	.01	.00

1991-92 Fleer Dikembe Mutombo Inserts

This 12-card subset was randomly inserted in 1991-92 Fleer Update wax packs. Mutombo autographed over 2,000 of these cards. The cards measure the standard size (2 1/2" by 3 1/2"). The front borders are dark red and checkered with miniature black NBA logos. The background of the color action photo is ghosted so that the featured player stands out, and the color of the lettering on the front is mustard. On a pink background, the back has a color close-up photo and a summary of the player's performance. The cards are numbered on the back.

	MINT	EXC	G-VG
COMPLETE SET (12)	12.00	6.00	1.20
COMMON PLAYER (1-12)	1.50	.75	.15
□ 1 Dikembe Mutombo Childhood in Zaire	1.50	.75	.15
□ 2 Dikembe Mutombo Georgetown Start	1.50	.75	.15
□ 3 Dikembe Mutombo Arrival on college scene	1.50	.75	.15
□ 4 Dikembe Mutombo Capping college career	1.50	.75	.15
□ 5 Dikembe Mutombo NBA Draft	1.50	.75	.15
□ 6 Dikembe Mutombo First NBA games	1.50	.75	.15
□ 7 Dikembe Mutombo Offensive skills	1.50	.75	.15
□ 8 Dikembe Mutombo What he has meant to Nuggets	1.50	.75	.15
□ 9 Dikembe Mutombo Work habits	1.50	.75	.15
□ 10 Dikembe Mutombo Charmed Denver	1.50	.75	.15
□ 11 Dikembe Mutombo The future	1.50	.75	.15
□ 12 Dikembe Mutombo The Mutombo legend	1.50	.75	.15

1991-92 Fleer Dominique Wilkins Inserts

Cards from this 12-card subset were randomly inserted in 1991-92 Fleer Update wax packs. Wilkins autographed over 2,000 of these cards. The cards measure the standard size (2 1/2" by 3 1/2"). The front borders are dark red and checkered with miniature black NBA logos. The background of the color action photo is ghosted so that the featured player stands out, and the color of the lettering on the front is mustard. On a pink background, the back has a color close-up photo and a summary of the player's performance. The cards are numbered on the back.

	MINT	EXC	G-VG
COMPLETE SET (12)	8.00	4.00	.80
COMMON PLAYER (1-12)	1.00	.50	.10
□ 1 Dominique Wilkins Overview	1.00	.50	.10
□ 2 Dominique Wilkins College	1.00	.50	.10
□ 3 Dominique Wilkins Early years	1.00	.50	.10
□ 4 Dominique Wilkins Early Career	1.00	.50	.10

☐ 5 Dominique Wilkins Dominique emerges	1.00	.50	.10
☐ 6 Dominique Wilkins Another milestone	1.00	.50	.10
☐ 7 Dominique Wilkins Wilkins continues shine	1.00	.50	.10
☐ 8 Dominique Wilkins Best all-round season	1.00	.50	.10
☐ 9 Dominique Wilkins Charitable causes	1.00	.50	.10
☐ 10 Dominique Wilkins Durability	1.00	.50	.10
☐ 11 Dominique Wilkins Career numbers	1.00	.50	.10
☐ 12 Dominique Wilkins Future	1.00	.50	.10

1971-72 Floridians McDonald's

This nine-card set of ABA Miami Floridians was sponsored by McDonald's. The cards measure approximately 2 1/2" by 4", including a 1/2" tear-off tab at the bottom. The bottom tab admitted one 14-or-under child to the game with each regular price adult ticket. The fronts feature color action player photos with rounded corners and black borders. The backs have player information, rules governing the free youth tickets, and an offer to receive an ABA basketball in exchange for a set of ten different Floridian tickets. The cards are unnumbered and are checklisted below in alphabetical order.

	NRMT	VG-E	GOOD
COMPLETE SET (9)	650.00	325.00	65.00
COMMON PLAYER (1-9)	75.00	37.50	7.50
☐ 1 Warren Armstrong	90.00	45.00	9.00
☐ 2 Mack Calvin	150.00	75.00	15.00
☐ 3 Ron Franz	75.00	37.50	7.50
☐ 4 Ira Harge	75.00	37.50	7.50
☐ 5 Larry Jones	75.00	37.50	7.50
☐ 6 Willie Long	75.00	37.50	7.50
☐ 7 Sam Robinson	75.00	37.50	7.50
☐ 8 George Tinsley	75.00	37.50	7.50
☐ 9 Lonnie Wright	75.00	37.50	7.50

1988 Foot Locker Slam Fest *

This nine-card set was produced by Foot Locker to commemorate the "Foot Locker Slam Fest" slam dunk contest, televised on ESPN on May 17, 1988. These standard size cards (2 1/2" by 3 1/2") feature color posed shots of the participants, who were professional athletes from sports other than basketball. The pictures have magenta and blue borders on a white card face. A colored banner with the words "Foot Locker" overlays the top of the picture. A line drawing of a referee overlays the

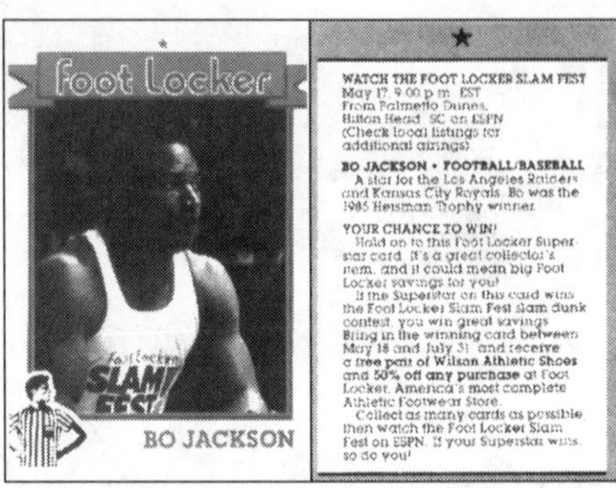

lower left corner of the picture. The backs are printed in blue on white and promote the slam dunk contest and an in-store contest. The cards were given out in May at participating Foot Locker stores to customers. Between May 18 and July 31, customers could turn in the winner's card (Mike Conley) and receive a free pair of Wilson athletic shoes and 50 percent off any purchase at Foot Locker. The cards are unnumbered and checklisted below in alphabetical order. Bo Jackson is obviously the key card in the set.

	MINT	EXC	G-VG
COMPLETE SET (9)	30.00	15.00	3.00
COMMON PLAYER (1-9)	1.25	.60	.12
☐ 1 Carl Banks Football	2.50	1.25	.25
☐ 2 Mike Conley Track and Field	3.50	1.75	.35
☐ 3 Thomas Hearns Boxing	1.25	.60	.12
☐ 4 Bo Jackson Baseball/Football	12.50	6.25	1.25
☐ 5 Keith Jackson Football	3.00	1.50	.30
☐ 6 Karch Kiraly Volleyball	4.00	2.00	.40
☐ 7 Ricky Sanders Football	1.50	.75	.15
☐ 8 Dwight Stones Track and Field	1.50	.75	.15
☐ 9 Devon White Baseball	2.00	1.00	.20

1989 Foot Locker Slam Fest *

This ten-card set was produced by Foot Locker and Nike to commemorate the "Foot Locker Slam Fest" slam dunk contest, which was televised during halftimes of NBC college basketball games through March 12, 1989. These standard size cards (2 1/2" by 3 1/2") feature color posed shots of the participants, who were professional athletes from sports other than basketball. A banner with the words "Foot Locker" traverses the top of the card face. The cards were wrapped in cellophane and issued with one stick of gum. They were given out at participating Foot Locker stores upon request with a purchase. The cards are unnumbered and checklisted below in alphabetical order.

	MINT	EXC	G-VG
COMPLETE SET (10)	9.00	4.50	.90
COMMON PLAYER (1-10)	.50	.25	.05
☐ 1 Mike Conley Track and Field	1.00	.50	.10
☐ 2 Keith Jackson Football	1.00	.50	.10
☐ 3 Vince Coleman Baseball	1.00	.50	.10
☐ 4 Eric Dickerson Football	1.50	.75	.15
☐ 5 Steve Timmons Volleyball	1.50	.75	.15
☐ 6 Matt Biondi Swimming	1.00	.50	.10
☐ 7 Carl Lewis Track and Field	1.50	.75	.15
☐ 8 Mike Quick Football	.50	.25	.05
☐ 9 Mike Powell Track and Field	2.00	1.00	.20
☐ 10 Checklist Card	.50	.25	.05

1991 Foot Locker Slam Fest *

This 30-card set was issued by Footlocker in three ten-card series to commemorate the "Foot Locker Slam Fest" dunk contest televised during halftimes of NBC college basketball games through March 10, 1991. The fronts of these standard-size cards (2 1/2" by 3 1/2") feature both posed and action photos enclosed in an arch like double red borders. The card top carries a blue border with "Foot Locker" in blue print on a white background. Beneath the photo appears "Limited Edition" and the player's name. The backs present career highlights, card series, and numbers placed within an arch of double red borders. The player's name and team name appear in black lettering at the bottom. Each set contained two Domino's Pizza coupons and a 5.00 discount coupon on any purchase of 50.00 or more at Foot Locker. The set was released in quantity after the promotional coupons expired. The cards are numbered on the back; the card numbering below adds the number 10 to each card number in the second series and 20 to each card number in the third series.

	MINT	EXC	G-VG
COMPLETE SET (30)	7.00	3.50	.70
COMMON PLAYER (1-10)	.15	.07	.01
COMMON PLAYER (11-20)	.15	.07	.01
COMMON PLAYER (21-30)	.15	.07	.01
☐ 1 Ken Griffey Jr. Baseball	.75	.35	.07
☐ 2 Delino Deshields Baseball	.40	.20	.04
☐ 3 Barry Bonds Baseball	.50	.25	.05
☐ 4 Jack Armstrong Baseball	.15	.07	.01
☐ 5 Dave Justice Baseball	.50	.25	.05
☐ 6 Deion Sanders Baseball/Football	.50	.25	.05
☐ 7 Michael Dean Perry Football	.25	.12	.02
☐ 8 Tim Brown Football	.25	.12	.02
☐ 9 Mike Conley Track and Field	.25	.12	.02
☐ 10 Mike Powell Track and Field	.25	.12	.02
☐ 11 Wilt Chamberlain Basketball	.35	.17	.03
☐ 12 Cal Ramsey Basketball	.15	.07	.01
☐ 13 Bobby Jones Basketball	.15	.07	.01
☐ 14 John Havlicek Basketball	.35	.17	.03
☐ 15 Calvin Murphy Basketball	.25	.12	.02
☐ 16 Nate Thurmond Basketball	.25	.12	.02
☐ 17 John Havlicek Basketball	.35	.17	.03
☐ 18 Series 1 Checklist The Dunkers	.25	.12	.02
☐ 19 Series 2 Checklist The Judges	.25	.12	.02
☐ 20 Series 3 Checklist Fest Moments	.25	.12	.02
☐ 21 Jerry Lucas Basketball	.25	.12	.02
☐ 22 Bo Jackson Basketball/Football	.50	.25	.05
☐ 23 Elvin Hayes Basketball	.25	.12	.02
☐ 24 Thomas Hearns Boxing	.15	.07	.01
☐ 25 Matt Biondi Swimming	.25	.12	.02
☐ 26 Earl Monroe Basketball	.25	.12	.02
☐ 27 Eric Dickerson Football	.35	.17	.03
☐ 28 Carl Lewis Track and Field	.35	.17	.03
☐ 29 Wilt and Company Basketball	.25	.12	.02
☐ 30 TV Slam Fest Schedule	.15	.07	.01

1988 Fournier NBA Estrellas

The 32-card set was produced in Spain by Fournier and showcases many of the NBA hottest stars. The cards measure approximately 2 1/8" by 3 7/16" and have rounded corners. The fronts feature borderless high glossy action player photos; in the white stripe below the picture, player statistics are given. The entire area of the card backs displays the NBA logo in red, white, and blue (indicating that the set was licensed by the NBA for distribution in Spain). The cards are numbered on the front in the upper left corner. The card backs were written in Spanish. The set features Danny Manning's first professional card.

	MINT	EXC	G-VG
COMPLETE SET (32)	20.00	10.00	2.00
COMMON PLAYER (1-32)	.75	.35	.07
☐ 1 Larry Bird	3.50	1.75	.35
☐ 2 Robert Parish	1.00	.50	.10
☐ 3 Kevin McHale	.90	.45	.09
☐ 4 Magic Johnson	4.00	2.00	.40
☐ 5 Kareem Abdul-Jabbar	2.50	1.25	.25
☐ 6 Byron Scott	.75	.35	.07
☐ 7 Isiah Thomas	2.00	1.00	.20
☐ 8 Adrian Dantley	1.00	.50	.10
☐ 9 Dominique Wilkins	2.00	1.00	.20
☐ 10 Spud Webb	.75	.35	.07
☐ 11 Clyde Drexler	2.50	1.25	.25
☐ 12 Terry Porter	1.25	.60	.12
☐ 13 Mark Aguirre	.90	.45	.09
☐ 14 Muggsy Bogues	.75	.35	.07
☐ 15 Patrick Ewing	2.50	1.25	.25
☐ 16 Karl Malone	2.00	1.00	.20
☐ 17 Charles Barkley	2.00	1.00	.20
☐ 18 Ron Harper	.75	.35	.07
☐ 19 Alex English	1.00	.50	.10
☐ 20 Xavier McDaniel	1.00	.50	.10
☐ 21 Jeff Malone	.90	.45	.09
☐ 22 Michael Jordan	6.50	3.25	.65
☐ 23 Hakeem Olajuwon	2.00	1.00	.20
☐ 24 Ralph Sampson	.75	.35	.07
☐ 25 Buck Williams	.90	.45	.09
☐ 26 Chuck Person	.90	.45	.09
☐ 27 Alvin Robertson	.75	.35	.07
☐ 28 Tom Chambers	.90	.45	.09
☐ 29 Paul Pressey	.75	.35	.07
☐ 30 Danny Manning	2.50	1.25	.25
☐ 31 Lasalle Thompson	.75	.35	.07
☐ 32 John Stockton	2.00	1.00	.20

1988 Fournier NBA Estrellas Stickers

The 10-sticker set was produced in Spain by Fournier as a random insert with its regular set. Only a portion of the sets contained a sticker insert. The stickers measure approximately 1" by 1 1/4" and picture the player from the chest up. The stickers come in a sealed pouch which is semi-transparent. The easiest stickers to find are Larry Bird, Magic Johnson, and Michael Jordan. The stickers are unnumbered and are listed below in alphabetical order.

	MINT	EXC	G-VG
COMPLETE SET (10)	100.00	50.00	10.00
COMMON PLAYER (1-10)	5.00	2.50	.50
☐ 1 Kareem Abdul-Jabbar	15.00	7.50	1.50
☐ 2 Mark Aguirre	5.00	2.50	.50
☐ 3 Larry Bird DP	15.00	7.50	1.50
☐ 4 Magic Johnson DP	20.00	10.00	2.00
☐ 5 Michael Jordan DP	25.00	12.50	2.50
☐ 6 Moses Malone	10.00	5.00	1.00
☐ 7 Kevin McHale	6.00	3.00	.60
☐ 8 Robert Parish	7.00	3.50	.70
☐ 9 Isiah Thomas	10.00	5.00	1.00
☐ 10 James Worthy	8.00	4.00	.80

1991 Front Row 50

The 1991 Front Row Basketball Draft Pick set contains 50 cards measuring the standard-size (2 1/2" by 3 1/2"). For the American version, Front Row produced approximately 150,000 factory sets and 600 wax cases, for a total press run of about 187,000 sets. The factory sets come with an official certificate of authenticity that bears a unique serial number. Two bilingual versions were also printed. The Japanese/English version features the same players as in the American version, but with different production quantities (62,000 factory sets and 600 wax cases). The Italian/English version features many different players and has 100 cards, with production quantities of 30,000 factory sets and 3,000 wax cases. Finally the bonus card in the American version could be redeemed for two Italian Promotional cards and an additional card number 50 to replace the returned bonus card. The front design features glossy color action player photos with white borders. The player's name appears in a green stripe beneath the picture. The backs have different smaller color photos (upper right corner) as well as biography, college statistics, and achievements superimposed on a gray background with an orange basketball. The set also includes a second (career highlights) card of some players (39-43), and a subset devoted to Larry Johnson (44-49). The cards are numbered on the back.

	MINT	EXC	G-VG
COMPLETE SET (50)	10.00	5.00	1.00
COMMON PLAYER (1-50)	.05	.02	.00
☐ 1 Larry Johnson UNLV	5.00	2.50	.50
☐ 2 Kenny Anderson Georgia Tech	1.50	.75	.15
☐ 3 Rick Fox North Carolina	1.00	.50	.10
☐ 4 Pete Chilcutt North Carolina	.20	.10	.02
☐ 5 George Ackles UNLV	.08	.04	.01
☐ 6 Mark Macon Temple	.35	.17	.03
☐ 7 Greg Anthony UNLV	.40	.20	.04
☐ 8 Mike Iuzzolino St. Francis	.35	.17	.03
☐ 9 Anthony Avent Seton Hall	.20	.10	.02
☐ 10 Terrell Brandon Oregon	.40	.20	.04
☐ 11 Kevin Brooks SW Louisiana	.15	.07	.01
☐ 12 Myron Brown Slippery Rock	.10	.05	.01
☐ 13 Chris Corchiani North Carolina State	.15	.07	.01
☐ 14 Chris Gatling	.40	.20	.04

Card	MINT	EXC	G-VG
Old Dominion			
☐ 15 Marcus Kennedy	.08	.04	.01
Eastern Michigan			
☐ 16 Eric Murdock	.30	.15	.03
Providence			
☐ 17 Tony Farmer	.08	.04	.01
Nebraska			
☐ 18 Keith Hughes	.08	.04	.01
Rutgers			
☐ 19 Kevin Lynch	.15	.07	.01
Minnesota			
☐ 20 Chad Gallagher	.08	.04	.01
Creighton			
☐ 21 Darrin Chancellor	.08	.04	.01
Southern Mississippi			
☐ 22 Jimmy Oliver	.20	.10	.02
Purdue			
☐ 23 Von McDade	.08	.04	.01
Wisconsin-Milwaukee			
☐ 24 Donald Hodge	.35	.17	.03
Temple			
☐ 25 Randy Brown	.15	.07	.01
New Mexico State			
☐ 26 Doug Overton	.08	.04	.01
LaSalle			
☐ 27 LeRon Ellis	.12	.06	.01
Syracuse			
☐ 28 Sean Green	.15	.07	.01
Iona			
☐ 29 Elliot Perry	.15	.07	.01
Memphis State			
☐ 30 Richard Dumas	.08	.04	.01
Oklahoma State			
☐ 31 Dale Davis	.35	.17	.03
Clemson			
☐ 32 Lamont Strothers	.15	.07	.01
Christopher Newport			
☐ 33 Steve Hood	.10	.05	.01
James Madison			
☐ 34 Joey Wright	.08	.04	.01
Texas			
☐ 35 Patrick Eddie	.12	.06	.01
Mississippi			
☐ 36 Joe Wylie	.08	.04	.01
Miami			
☐ 37 Bobby Phills	.10	.05	.01
Southern			
☐ 38 Alvaro Teheran	.05	.02	.00
Houston			
☐ 39 Dale Davis	.10	.05	.01
Career Highlights			
☐ 40 Rick Fox	.30	.15	.03
Career Highlights			
☐ 41 Terrell Brandon	.12	.06	.01
Career Highlights			
☐ 42 Greg Anthony	.12	.06	.01
Career Highlights			
☐ 43 Mark Macon	.10	.05	.01
Career Highlights			
☐ 44 Larry Johnson	.50	.25	.05
Career Highlights			
☐ 45 Larry Johnson	.50	.25	.05
First in the Nation			
☐ 46 Larry Johnson	.50	.25	.05
Power			
☐ 47 Larry Johnson	.50	.25	.05
A Class Act			
☐ 48 Larry Johnson	.50	.25	.05
Flashback			
☐ 49 Larry Johnson	.50	.25	.05
Up Close and Personal			
☐ 50A Bonus Card	.75	.35	.07
☐ 50B Marty Conlon	.25	.12	.02
Providence			

1991 Front Row Update

The 1991 Front Row Update basketball set completes the 1991 Front Row Draft Picks set. Each set was accompanied by a certificate of authenticity that bears a unique serial number, with the production run reported to be 50,000 sets. The cards measure the standard size (2 1/2" by 3 1/2"). The fronts feature glossy color action player photos enclosed by white borders. A basketball backboard and rim with the words "Update 92" appears in the lower left corner, with the player's name and

position in a dark green stripe beneath the picture. On a gray background with an orange basketball, the backs carry biography, color close-up photo, statistics, and achievements. The cards are numbered on the back.

	MINT	EXC	G-VG
COMPLETE SET (50)	9.00	4.50	.90
COMMON PLAYER (51-100)	.05	.02	.00
☐ 51 Billy Owens	2.50	1.25	.25
Syracuse			
☐ 52 Dikembe Mutombo	1.75	.85	.17
Georgetown			
☐ 53 Steve Smith	1.50	.75	.15
Michigan State			
☐ 54 Luc Longley	.25	.12	.02
New Mexico			
☐ 55 Doug Smith	.40	.20	.04
Missouri			
☐ 56 Stacey Augmon	1.00	.50	.10
UNLV			
☐ 57 Brian Williams	.50	.25	.05
Arizona			
☐ 58 Stanley Roberts	.90	.45	.09
LSU			
☐ 59 Rodney Monroe	.25	.12	.02
North Carolina State			
☐ 60 Isaac Austin	.10	.05	.01
Arizona State			
☐ 61 Rich King	.10	.05	.01
Nebraska			
☐ 62 Victor Alexander	.20	.10	.02
Iowa State			
☐ 63 LaBradford Smith	.20	.10	.02
Louisville			
☐ 64 Greg Sutton	.12	.06	.01
Oklahoma City			
☐ 65 John Turner	.10	.05	.01
Phillips			
☐ 66 Joao Viana	.10	.05	.01
Nassuna			
☐ 67 Charles Thomas	.08	.04	.01
Eastern Michigan			
☐ 68 Carl Thomas	.08	.04	.01
Eastern Michigan			
☐ 69 Tharon Mayes	.08	.04	.01
Florida State			
☐ 70 David Benoit	.35	.17	.03
Alabama			
☐ 71 Corey Crowder	.08	.04	.01
Kentucky Wesleyan			
☐ 72 Larry Stewart	.35	.17	.03
Coppin State			
☐ 73 Steve Bardo	.08	.04	.01
Illinois			
☐ 74 Paris McCurdy	.05	.02	.00
Ball State			
☐ 75 Robert Pack	.50	.25	.05
USC			
☐ 76 Doug Lee	.08	.04	.01
Purdue			
☐ 77 Tom Copa	.05	.02	.00
Marquette			
☐ 78 Keith Owens	.10	.05	.01
UCLA			
☐ 79 Mike Goodson	.05	.02	.00
Pittsburgh			
☐ 80 John Crotty	.10	.05	.01
Virginia			
☐ 81 Sean Muto	.05	.02	.00

	MINT	EXC	G-VG
St. John's			
☐ 82 Chancellor Nichols	.05	.02	.00
James Madison			
☐ 83 Stevie Thompson	.08	.04	.01
Syracuse			
☐ 84 Demetrius Calip	.08	.04	.01
Michigan			
☐ 85 Clifford Martin	.05	.02	.00
Idaho			
☐ 86 Andy Kennedy	.08	.04	.01
Alabama (Birmingham)			
☐ 87 Oliver Taylor	.05	.02	.00
Seton Hall			
☐ 88 Gary Waites	.05	.02	.00
Alabama			
☐ 89 Matt Roe	.08	.04	.01
Maryland			
☐ 90 Cedric Lewis	.08	.04	.01
Maryland			
☐ 91 Emanuel Davis	.05	.02	.00
Deleware State			
☐ 92 Jackie Jones	.08	.04	.01
Oklahoma			
☐ 93 Clifford Scales	.05	.02	.00
Nebraska			
☐ 94 Cameron Burns	.05	.02	.00
Mississippi State			
☐ 95 Clinton Venable	.08	.04	.01
Bowling Green			
☐ 96 Ken Redfield	.08	.04	.01
Michigan State			
☐ 97 Melvin Newbern	.08	.04	.01
Minnesota			
☐ 98 Chris Harris	.05	.02	.00
Illinois (Chicago)			
☐ 99 Bonus Card	.75	.35	.07
☐ 100 Checklist	.05	.02	.00

1991 Front Row Italian/English 100

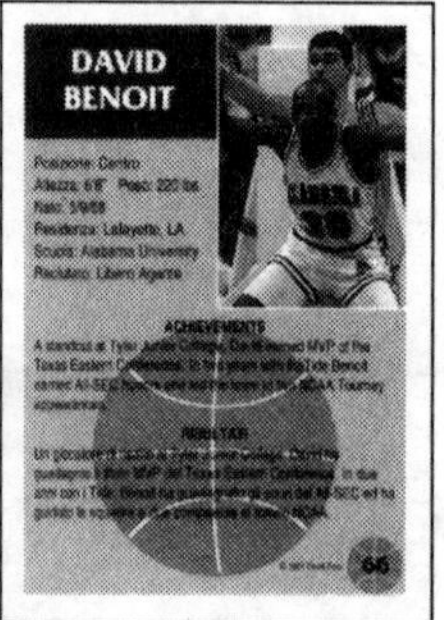

The 1991 Front Row Italian/English Basketball Draft Pick set contains 100 cards measuring standard size (2 1/2" by 3 1/2"). Each factory set comes with an official certificate of authenticity that bears a unique serial number. This set is distinguished from the American version by length (100 instead of 50 cards), different production quantities (30,000 factory sets and 3,000 wax cases), and a red stripe on the card front. The front design features glossy color action player photos with white borders. The player's name appears in a red stripe beneath the picture. The backs have different smaller color photos (upper right corner) as well as biography, college statistics, and achievements superimposed on a gray background with an orange basketball. The set also includes a second (career highlights) card of some players (39-43), a subset devoted to Larry Johnson (44-49), and two "Retrospect" cards (96-97). The cards are numbered on the back.

	MINT	EXC	G-VG
COMPLETE SET (100)	12.00	6.00	1.20
COMMON PLAYER (1-50)	.05	.02	.00
COMMON PLAYER (51-100)	.05	.02	.00
☐ 1 Larry Johnson	5.00	2.50	.50
UNLV			
☐ 2 Kenny Anderson	1.50	.75	.15
Georgia Tech			
☐ 3 Rick Fox	1.00	.50	.10
North Carolina			
☐ 4 Pete Chilcutt	.20	.10	.02
North Carolina			
☐ 5 George Ackles	.08	.04	.01
UNLV			
☐ 6 Mark Macon	.35	.17	.03
Temple			
☐ 7 Greg Anthony	.40	.20	.04
UNLV			
☐ 8 Mike Iuzzolino	.35	.17	.03
St. Francis			
☐ 9 Anthony Avent	.20	.10	.02
Seton Hall			
☐ 10 Terrell Brandon	.40	.20	.04
Oregon			
☐ 11 Kevin Brooks	.15	.07	.01
SW Louisiana			
☐ 12 Myron Brown	.10	.05	.01
Slippery Rock			
☐ 13 Chris Corchiani	.15	.07	.01
North Carolina State			
☐ 14 Chris Gatling	.40	.20	.04
Old Dominion			
☐ 15 Marcus Kennedy	.08	.04	.01
Eastern Michigan			
☐ 16 Eric Murdock	.30	.15	.03
Providence			
☐ 17 Tony Farmer	.08	.04	.01
Nebraska			
☐ 18 Keith Hughes	.08	.04	.01
Rutgers			
☐ 19 Kevin Lynch	.15	.07	.01
Minnesota			
☐ 20 Chad Gallagher	.08	.04	.01
Creighton			
☐ 21 Darrin Chancellor	.08	.04	.01
Southern Mississippi			
☐ 22 Jimmy Oliver	.20	.10	.02
Purdue			
☐ 23 Von McDade	.08	.04	.01
Wisconsin-Milwaukee			
☐ 24 Donald Hodge	.35	.17	.03
Temple			
☐ 25 Randy Brown	.15	.07	.01
New Mexico State			
☐ 26 Doug Overton	.08	.04	.01
LaSalle			
☐ 27 LeRon Ellis	.12	.06	.01
Syracuse			
☐ 28 Sean Green	.15	.07	.01
Iona			
☐ 29 Elliot Perry	.15	.07	.01
Memphis State			
☐ 30 Richard Dumas	.08	.04	.01
Oklahoma State			
☐ 31 Dale Davis	.35	.17	.03
Clemson			
☐ 32 Lamont Strothers	.15	.07	.01
Christopher Newport			
☐ 33 Steve Hood	.10	.05	.01
James Madison			
☐ 34 Joey Wright	.08	.04	.01
Texas			
☐ 35 Patrick Eddie	.12	.06	.01
Mississippi			
☐ 36 Joe Wylie	.08	.04	.01
Miami			
☐ 37 Bobby Phills	.10	.05	.01
Southern			
☐ 38 Alvaro Teheran	.05	.02	.00
Houston			
☐ 39 Dale Davis	.10	.05	.01
Career Highlights			
☐ 40 Rick Fox	.30	.15	.03
Career Highlights			
☐ 41 Terrell Brandon	.12	.06	.01
Career Highlights			
☐ 42 Greg Anthony	.12	.06	.01
Career Highlights			
☐ 43 Mark Macon	.10	.05	.01
Career Highlights			
☐ 44 Larry Johnson	.50	.25	.05
Career Highlights			
☐ 45 Larry Johnson	.50	.25	.05
First in the Nation			
☐ 46 Larry Johnson	.50	.25	.05
Power			
☐ 47 Larry Johnson	.50	.25	.05
A Class Act			

☐ 48 Larry Johnson	.50	.25	.05
Flashback			
☐ 49 Larry Johnson	.50	.25	.05
Up Close and Personal			
☐ 50A Bonus Card	.75	.35	.07
☐ 50B Marty Conlon	.25	.12	.02
Providence			
☐ 51 Mike Goodson	.05	.02	.00
Pittsburgh			
☐ 52 Drexel Deveaux	.05	.02	.00
Tampa			
☐ 53 Sean Muto	.05	.02	.00
St. John's			
☐ 54 Keith Owens	.15	.07	.01
UCLA			
☐ 55 Joao Viana	.05	.02	.00
Nassuna			
☐ 56 Chancellor Nichols	.05	.02	.00
James Madison			
☐ 57 Charles Thomas	.12	.06	.01
Eastern Michigan			
☐ 58 Carl Thomas	.08	.04	.01
Eastern Michigan			
☐ 59 Anthony Blakley	.05	.02	.00
Panhandle State			
☐ 60 Demetrius Calip	.12	.06	.01
Michigan			
☐ 61 Dale Turnquist	.05	.02	.00
Bethel College			
☐ 62 Carlos Funchess	.05	.02	.00
Northeast Louisiana			
☐ 63 Tharon Mayes	.12	.06	.01
Florida State			
☐ 64 Andy Kennedy	.08	.04	.01
Alabama - Birmingham			
☐ 65 Oliver Taylor	.05	.02	.00
Seton Hall			
☐ 66 David Benoit	.50	.25	.05
Alabama			
☐ 67 Gary Waites	.05	.02	.00
Alabama			
☐ 68 Corey Crowder	.10	.05	.01
Kentucky Wesleyan			
☐ 69 Sydney Grider	.05	.02	.00
Southwestern Louisiana			
☐ 70 Derek Strong	.08	.04	.01
Xavier			
☐ 71 Larry Stewart	.50	.25	.05
Coppin State			
☐ 72 Matt Roe	.08	.04	.01
Maryland			
☐ 73 Cedric Lewis	.08	.04	.01
Maryland			
☐ 74 Anthony Houston	.05	.02	.00
St. Mary's			
☐ 75 Steve Bardo	.08	.04	.01
Illinois			
☐ 76 Marc Brown	.12	.06	.01
Siena			
☐ 77 Michael Cutright	.05	.02	.00
McNeese State			
☐ 78 Emanuel Davis	.05	.02	.00
Deleware State			
☐ 79 Paris McCurdy	.05	.02	.00
Ball State			
☐ 80 Jackie Jones	.08	.04	.01
Oklahoma State			
☐ 81 Mark Peterson	.05	.02	.00
Rutgers			
☐ 82 Clifford Scales	.05	.02	.00
Nebraska			
☐ 83 Robert Pack	.75	.35	.07
USC			
☐ 84 Doug Lee	.12	.06	.01
Purdue			
☐ 85 Cameron Burns	.05	.02	.00
Mississippi State			
☐ 86 Tom Copa	.05	.02	.00
Marquette			
☐ 87 Clinton Venable	.08	.04	.01
Bowling Green State			
☐ 88 Ken Redfield	.08	.04	.01
Michigan State			
☐ 89 Melvin Newbern	.08	.04	.01
Minnesota			
☐ 90 Darren Henrie	.05	.02	.00
David Lipscomb			
☐ 91 Chris Harris	.05	.02	.00
Illinois (Chicago)			
☐ 92 John Crotty	.10	.05	.01
Virginia			
☐ 93 Paul Graham	.40	.20	.04
Ohio			
☐ 94 Stevie Thompson	.10	.05	.01
Syracuse			
☐ 95 Clifford Martin	.05	.02	.00
Idaho			
☐ 96 Brian Shaw	.12	.06	.01
UC Santa Barbara			
☐ 97 Danny Ferry	.12	.06	.01
Duke			
☐ 98 Doug Loescher	.05	.02	.00
☐ 99 Checklist	.05	.02	.00
☐ 100 Bonus Card	.75	.35	.07

1991 Front Row Italian Promos

The American version of the 1991 Front Row Draft Pick set (50) included a bonus card that could be redeemed for two Italian promo cards through a mail-in offer. This promo set consists of ten cards measuring the standard size (2 1/2" by 3 1/2"). The color player photos on the front are bordered in white, and the player's name appears in a red stripe beneath the picture. On a gray background with an orange Front Row basketball logo, the backs read "Italian Promo Card" and "20,000 Ten Card Sets Produced" although the back of the Bonus Card says "50,000 Sets Produced". The cards are unnumbered and checklisted below in alphabetical order.

	MINT	EXC	G-VG
COMPLETE SET (10)	3.00	1.50	.30
COMMON PLAYER (1-10)	.15	.07	.01
☐ 1 Steve Bardo	.15	.07	.01
Illinois			
☐ 2 Corey Crowder	.20	.10	.02
Kentucky Wesleyan			
☐ 3 Danny Ferry	.30	.15	.03
Duke			
☐ 4 Doug Lee	.25	.12	.02
Purdue			
☐ 5 Tharon Mayes	.25	.12	.02
Florida State			
☐ 6 Robert Pack	1.00	.50	.10
USC			
☐ 7 Brian Shaw	.35	.17	.03
Cal (Santa Barbara)			
☐ 8 Larry Stewart	.75	.35	.07
Coppen State			
☐ 9 Carl Thomas	.15	.07	.01
Eastern Michigan			
☐ 10 Charles Thomas	.25	.12	.02
Eastern Michigan			

1991 Front Row Larry Johnson

These ten standard-size (2 1/2" by 3 1/2") cards feature different action shots of Larry Johnson. According to Front Row, there were 50,000 sets produced. The cards are numbered on the back.

	MINT	EXC	G-VG
COMPLETE SET (10)	7.00	3.50	.70

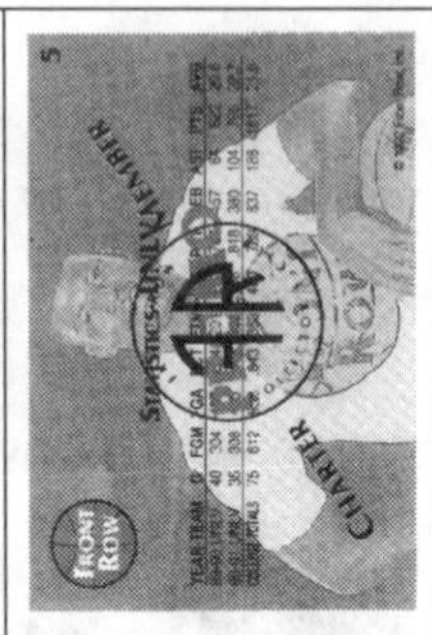

	MINT	EXC	G-VG
COMMON PLAYER (1-10)	1.00	.50	.10
☐ 1 Larry Johnson Accomplishments	1.00	.50	.10
☐ 2 Larry Johnson Career Highlights	1.00	.50	.10
☐ 3 Larry Johnson High School Highlights	1.00	.50	.10
☐ 4 Larry Johnson Statistics - Odessa Jr. College	1.00	.50	.10
☐ 5 Larry Johnson Statistics - UNLV	1.00	.50	.10
☐ 6 Larry Johnson Personal Biography	1.00	.50	.10
☐ 7 Larry Johnson Vital Statistics	1.00	.50	.10
☐ 8 Larry Johnson Sharks' Rebel	1.00	.50	.10
☐ 9 Larry Johnson Scouting Report	1.00	.50	.10
☐ 10 Larry Johnson Olympic Hopeful	1.00	.50	.10

1991 Front Row Stacey Augmon

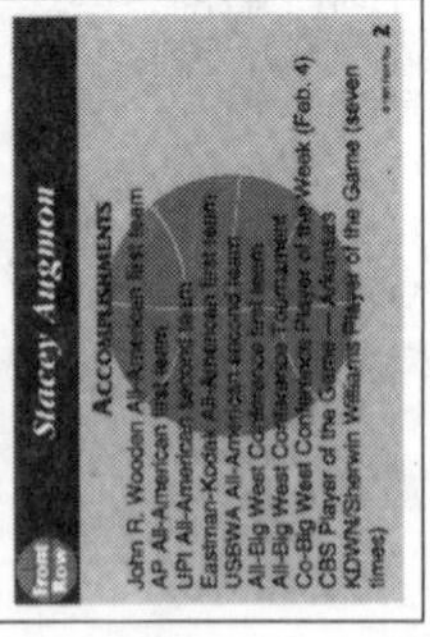

These seven standard-size (2 1/2" by 3 1/2") cards feature seven different action shots of Stacey Augmon. The glossy color photos are enclosed by white borders, while the player's name appears in a purple stripe beneath the picture. Issued with each set, a certificate of authenticity gives the individual serial number of the set and the total production run (25,000). The words "Limited Edition" are gold-foil stamped across the card top. On a gray background with an orange basketball, the horizontally oriented backs summarize Augmon's career. Only card number 7 includes a second photo on its back. The cards are numbered on the back.

	MINT	EXC	G-VG
COMPLETE SET (7)	5.00	2.50	.50
COMMON PLAYER (1-7)	1.00	.50	.10
☐ 1 Stacey Augmon Profile	1.00	.50	.10
☐ 2 Stacey Augmon Accomplishments	1.00	.50	.10
☐ 3 Stacey Augmon Career Highs	1.00	.50	.10
☐ 4 Stacey Augmon Tarkanian on Augmon	1.00	.50	.10
☐ 5 Stacey Augmon Defensive POY	1.00	.50	.10
☐ 6 Stacey Augmon Statistics	1.00	.50	.10
☐ 7 Stacey Augmon Style	1.00	.50	.10

1991 Front Row Dikembe Mutombo

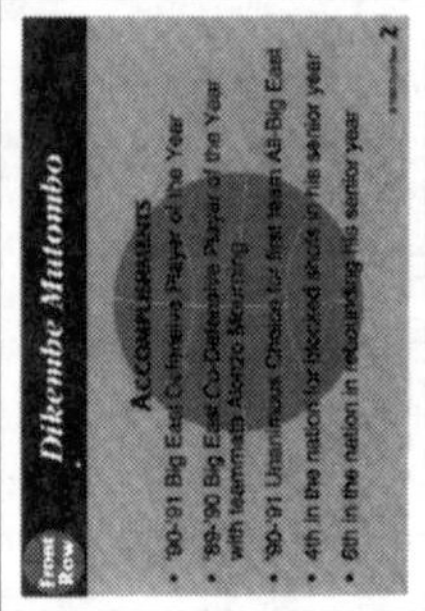

These seven standard-size (2 1/2" by 3 1/2") cards feature seven different action shots of Dikembe Mutombo. The glossy color photos are enclosed by white borders, while the player's name appears in a purple stripe beneath the picture. Issued with each set, a certificate of authenticity gives the individual serial number of the set and the total production run (50,000). The words "Limited Edition" are gold-foil stamped across the card top. On a gray background with an orange basketball, the horizontally oriented backs summarize Mutombo's collegiate career. The cards are numbered on the back.

	MINT	EXC	G-VG
COMPLETE SET (7)	5.00	2.50	.50
COMMON PLAYER (1-7)	1.00	.50	.10
☐ 1 Dikembe Mutombo Profile	1.00	.50	.10
☐ 2 Dikembe Mutombo Accomplishments	1.00	.50	.10
☐ 3 Dikembe Mutombo Career Highs	1.00	.50	.10
☐ 4 Dikembe Mutombo The Experts on Mutombo	1.00	.50	.10
☐ 5 Dikembe Mutombo Admirable Hoya	1.00	.50	.10
☐ 6 Dikembe Mutombo Statistics	1.00	.50	.10
☐ 7 Dikembe Mutombo Name Card	1.00	.50	.10

1991 Front Row Billy Owens

These seven standard-size (2 1/2" by 3 1/2") cards feature seven different action shots of Billy Owens. The glossy color photos are enclosed by white borders, while the player's name appears in a purple stripe beneath the picture. Issued with each set, a certificate of authenticity gives the individual serial number of

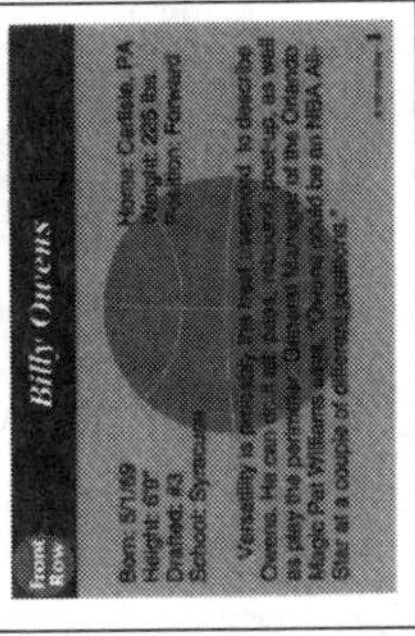

the set and the total production run (25,000). The words "Limited Edition" are gold-foil stamped across the card top. On a gray background with an orange basketball, the horizontally oriented backs summarize Owens' collegiate career. The cards are numbered on the back.

	MINT	EXC	G-VG
COMPLETE SET (7)	5.00	2.50	.50
COMMON PLAYER (1-7)	1.00	.50	.10
☐ 1 Billy Owens Profile	1.00	.50	.10
☐ 2 Billy Owens Accomplishments	1.00	.50	.10
☐ 3 Billy Owens Career Highs	1.00	.50	.10
☐ 4 Billy Owens The Experts on Owens	1.00	.50	.10
☐ 5 Billy Owens High School	1.00	.50	.10
☐ 6 Billy Owens Statistics	1.00	.50	.10
☐ 7 Billy Owens Career Highlights	1.00	.50	.10

1991 Front Row Steve Smith

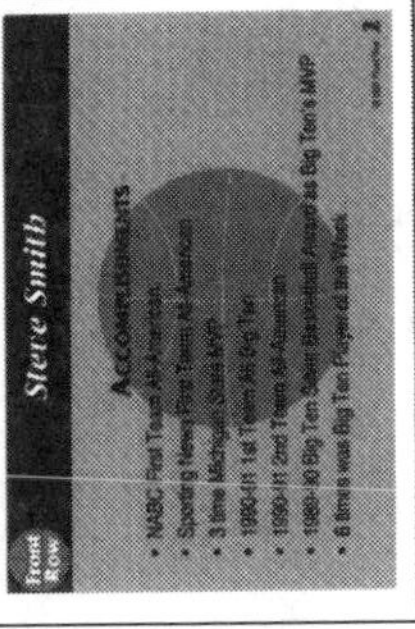

These seven standard-size (2 1/2" by 3 1/2") cards feature seven different action shots of Steve Smith. The glossy color photos are enclosed by white borders, while the player's name appears in a purple stripe beneath the picture. Issued with each set, a certificate of authenticity gives the individual serial number of the set and the total production run (25,000). The words "Limited Edition" are gold-foil stamped across the card top. On a gray background with an orange basketball, the horizontally oriented backs summarize Smith's collegiate career. Only card number 5 includes a second photo on its back.The cards are numbered on the back.

	MINT	EXC	G-VG
COMPLETE SET (7)	5.00	2.50	.50
COMMON PLAYER (1-7)	1.00	.50	.10
☐ 1 Steve Smith Profile	1.00	.50	.10
☐ 2 Steve Smith Accomplishments	1.00	.50	.10
☐ 3 Steve Smith Career Highlights	1.00	.50	.10
☐ 4 Steve Smith What's in a Nickname	1.00	.50	.10
☐ 5 Steve Smith Dr.Heckle and Mr.Jive	1.00	.50	.10
☐ 6 Steve Smith Statistics	1.00	.50	.10
☐ 7 Steve Smith The Magic is Back	1.00	.50	.10

1991-92 Front Row Premier

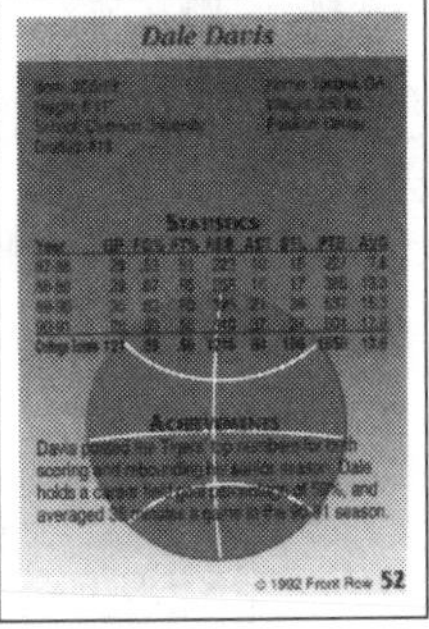

The 1991-92 Front Row Premier set contains 120 standard-size (2 1/2" by 3 1/2") cards. No factory sets were made, and the production run was limited to 2,500 waxbox cases, with 360 cards per box. The set included five bonus cards (86, 88, 90, 91, 93) that were redeemable through a mail-in offer for unnamed player cards. Moreover, limited edition cards as well as gold, silver, and autographed cards were randomly inserted in the wax packs. The glossy color player photos on the fronts are enclosed by borders with different shades of white and blue. The player's name appears in a silver stripe beneath the picture. The backs have biography, statistics, and achievements superimposed on an orange basketball icon. The cards are numbered on the back.

	MINT	EXC	G-VG
COMPLETE SET (120)	14.00	7.00	1.40
COMMON PLAYER (1-120)	.05	.02	.00
☐ 1 Rich King Nebraska	.10	.05	.01
☐ 2 Kenny Anderson Georgia Tech	1.00	.50	.10
☐ 3 Billy Owens ACC Syracuse	.60	.30	.06
☐ 4 Ken Redfield Michigan State	.08	.04	.01
☐ 5 Robert Pack USC	.50	.25	.05
☐ 6 Clinton Venable Bowling Green	.08	.04	.01
☐ 7 Tom Copa Marquette	.05	.02	.00
☐ 8 Rick Fox HL North Carolina	.15	.07	.01
☐ 9 Cameron Burns Mississippi State	.05	.02	.00
☐ 10 Doug Lee Purdue	.08	.04	.01
☐ 11 LaBradford Smith Louisville	.20	.10	.02
☐ 12 Clifford Scales Nebraska	.05	.02	.00
☐ 13 Mark Peterson	.05	.02	.00

Rutgers
☐ 14 Jackie Jones .... .05 .02 .00
Oklahoma
☐ 15 Paris McCurdy .... .05 .02 .00
Ball State
☐ 16 Dikembe Mutombo ACC .... .50 .25 .05
Georgetown
☐ 17 Emanuel Davis .... .05 .02 .00
Delaware State
☐ 18 Michael Cutright .... .05 .02 .00
McNeese State
☐ 19 Marc Brown .... .08 .04 .01
Siena
☐ 20 Steve Bardo .... .08 .04 .01
Illinois
☐ 21 John Turner .... .10 .05 .01
Phillips
☐ 22 Anthony Houston .... .05 .02 .00
St. Mary's
☐ 23 Cedric Lewis .... .08 .04 .01
Maryland
☐ 24 Matt Roe .... .08 .04 .01
Maryland
☐ 25 Larry Stewart .... .35 .17 .03
Coppin State
☐ 26 Derek Strong .... .08 .04 .01
Xavier
☐ 27 Sydney Grider .... .05 .02 .00
Southwestern Louisiana
☐ 28 Corey Crowder .... .08 .04 .01
Kentucky Wesleyan
☐ 29 Gary Waites .... .05 .02 .00
Alabama
☐ 30 David Benoit .... .35 .17 .03
Alabama
☐ 31 Larry Johnson ACC .... .75 .35 .07
UNLV
☐ 32 Oliver Taylor UER .... .05 .02 .00
Seton Hall
(Chris Corchiani's name
on back)
☐ 33 Andy Kennedy .... .08 .04 .01
Alabama-Birmingham
☐ 34 Tharon Mayes .... .08 .04 .01
Florida State
☐ 35 Carlos Funchess .... .05 .02 .00
Northeast Louisiana
☐ 36 Dale Turnquist .... .05 .02 .00
Bethel
☐ 37 Luc Longley .... .25 .12 .02
New Mexico
☐ 38 Demetrius Calip .... .08 .04 .01
Michigan
☐ 39 Anthony Blakley .... .05 .02 .00
Panhandle State
☐ 40 Carl Thomas .... .08 .04 .01
Eastern Michigan
☐ 41 Charles Thomas .... .08 .04 .01
Eastern Michigan
☐ 42 Chancellor Nichols .... .05 .02 .00
James Madison
☐ 43 Joao Viana .... .10 .05 .01
Nassuna
☐ 44 Keith Owens .... .10 .05 .01
UCLA
☐ 45 Sean Muto .... .05 .02 .00
St. Johns
☐ 46 Drexel Deveaux .... .05 .02 .00
Tampa
☐ 47 Stacey Augmon ACC .... .25 .12 .02
UNLV
☐ 48 Mike Goodson .... .05 .02 .00
Pittsburgh
☐ 49 Marty Conlon .... .08 .04 .01
Providence
☐ 50 Mark Macon .... .25 .12 .02
Temple
☐ 51 Greg Anthony .... .30 .15 .03
UNLV
☐ 52 Dale Davis .... .25 .12 .02
Clemson
☐ 53 Isaac Austin .... .10 .05 .01
Arizona State
☐ 54 Alvaro Teheran .... .05 .02 .00
Houston
☐ 55 Bobby Phills .... .08 .04 .01
Southern
☐ 56 Joe Wylie .... .08 .04 .01
Miami
☐ 57 Patrick Eddie .... .08 .04 .01
Mississippi
☐ 58 Joey Wright .... .08 .04 .01
Texas
☐ 59 Steve Hood .... .08 .04 .01
James Maidson
☐ 60 Lamont Strothers .... .10 .05 .01
Christopher Newport
☐ 61 Victor Alexander .... .20 .10 .02
Iowa State
☐ 62 Richard Dumas .... .08 .04 .01
Oklahoma State
☐ 63 Elliot Perry .... .10 .05 .01
Memphis State
☐ 64 Sean Green .... .10 .05 .01
Iona
☐ 65 Rick Fox .... .90 .45 .09
North Carolina
☐ 66 LeRon Ellis .... .10 .05 .01
Syracuse
☐ 67 Doug Overton .... .08 .04 .01
LaSalle
☐ 68 Randy Brown .... .10 .05 .01
New Mexico State
☐ 69 Donald Hodge .... .25 .12 .02
Temple
☐ 70 Von McDade .... .08 .04 .01
Wisconsin-Milwaukee
☐ 71 Greg Sutton .... .12 .06 .01
Oral Roberts
☐ 72 Jimmy Oliver .... .15 .07 .01
Purdue
☐ 73 Terrell Brandon HL .... .10 .05 .01
Oregon
☐ 74 Darrin Chancellor .... .05 .02 .00
Southern Mississippi
☐ 75 Chad Gallagher .... .05 .02 .00
Creighton
☐ 76 Kevin Lynch .... .10 .05 .01
Minnesota
☐ 77 Keith Hughes .... .08 .04 .01
Rutgers
☐ 78 Tony Farmer .... .05 .02 .00
Nebraska
☐ 79 Eric Murdock .... .20 .10 .02
Providence
☐ 80 Marcus Kennedy .... .08 .04 .01
Eastern Michigan
☐ 81 Larry Johnson .... 4.00 2.00 .40
UNLV
☐ 82 Stacey Augmon .... 1.00 .50 .10
UNLV
☐ 83 Dikembe Mutombo .... 1.75 .85 .17
Georgetown
☐ 84 Steve Smith .... 1.50 .75 .15
Michigan State
☐ 85 Billy Owens .... 2.50 1.25 .25
Syracuse
☐ 86 Bonus Card 1 .... .30 .15 .03
Stanley Roberts
LSU
☐ 87 Brian Shaw .... .10 .05 .01
UC Santa Barbara
☐ 88 Bonus Card 2 .... .20 .10 .02
Rodney Monroe
North Carolina State
☐ 89 LaBradford Smith HL .... .08 .04 .01
Louisville
☐ 90 Bonus Card 3 .... .15 .07 .01
Mark Randall
Kansas
☐ 91 Bonus Card 4 .... .25 .12 .02
Brian Williams
Arizona
☐ 92 Danny Ferry .... .08 .04 .01
(Flashback)
Duke
☐ 93 Bonus Card 5 .... .15 .07 .01
Shawn Vandiver
Colorado
☐ 94 Doug Smith HL .... .10 .05 .01
Missouri
☐ 95 Luc Longley HL .... .10 .05 .01
New Mexico
☐ 96 Billy Owens HL .... .60 .30 .06
Syracuse
☐ 97 Steve Smith HL .... .35 .17 .03
Michigan State
☐ 98 Dikembe Mutombo HL .... .50 .25 .05
Georgetown
☐ 99 Stacey Augmon HL .... .25 .12 .02
UNLV
☐ 100 Larry Johnson HL .... .75 .35 .07
UNLV
☐ 101 Chris Gatling .... .30 .15 .03
Old Dominion
☐ 102 Chris Corchiani .... .10 .05 .01
North Carolina State
☐ 103 Myron Brown .... .08 .04 .01

Slippery Rock			
☐ 104 Kevin Brooks	.10	.05	.01
Southwestern Louisiana			
☐ 105 Anthony Avent	.12	.06	.01
Seton Hall			
☐ 106 Steve Smith ACC	.35	.17	.03
Michigan State			
☐ 107 Mike Iuzzolino	.25	.12	.02
Saint Francis			
☐ 108 George Ackles	.08	.04	.01
UNLV			
☐ 109 Melvin Newbern	.08	.04	.01
Minnesota			
☐ 110 Robert Pack HL	.20	.10	.02
USC			
☐ 111 Darren Henrie	.05	.02	.00
David Lipscomb			
☐ 112 Chris Harris	.05	.02	.00
Illinois-Chicago			
☐ 113 John Crotty	.08	.04	.01
Virginia			
☐ 114 Terrell Brandon	.30	.15	.03
Oregon			
☐ 115 Paul Graham	.25	.12	.02
Ohio			
☐ 116 Stevie Thompson	.08	.04	.01
Syracuse			
☐ 117 Clifford Martin	.05	.02	.00
Idaho			
☐ 118 Doug Smith	.40	.20	.04
Missouri			
☐ 119 Pete Chilcutt	.12	.06	.01
North Carolina			
☐ 120 Checklist Card	.05	.02	.00

1971-72 Globetrotters Cocoa Puffs 28

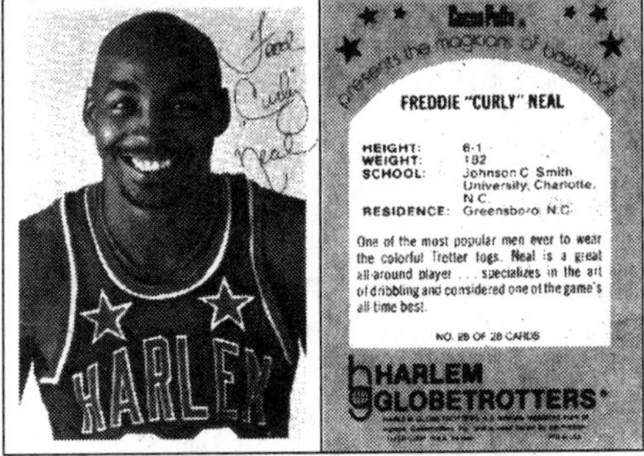

This 1971-72 Harlem Globetrotters set was produced for Cocoa Puffs cereal by Fleer and contains 28 standard size (2 1/2" by 3 1/2") cards. The card fronts have full color pictures with facsimile autographs. The card backs have black printing on gray card stock and feature biographical sketches and other interesting information about the Globetrotters. The cards are numbered on back out of 28.

	NRMT	VG-E	GOOD
COMPLETE SET (28)	125.00	60.00	12.50
COMMON CARD (1-28)	3.50	1.75	.35
☐ 1 Geese Ausbie and Curly Neal	7.50	3.75	.75
☐ 2 Neal and Meadowlark	5.50	2.75	.55
☐ 3 Meadowlark is Safe	5.50	2.75	.55
☐ 4 Meadowlark, Neal, and Geese Ausbie	5.50	2.75	.55
☐ 5 Mel Davis and Bill Meggett	3.50	1.75	.35
☐ 6 Ausbie, Meadowlark, and Curly Neal	5.50	2.75	.55
☐ 7 Ausbie, Meadowlark, and Curly Neal	5.50	2.75	.55
☐ 8 Mel Davis and Curly Neal	3.50	1.75	.35
☐ 9 Meadowlark, Neal, and Geese Ausbie	5.50	2.75	.55
☐ 10 Curly, Meadowlark, and Mel Davis	5.50	2.75	.55
☐ 11 Football Routine	3.50	1.75	.35
☐ 12 1970-71 Highlights	3.50	1.75	.35
☐ 13 Pabs Robertson	3.50	1.75	.35
☐ 14 Bobby Joe Mason	3.50	1.75	.35
☐ 15 Pabs Robertson	3.50	1.75	.35
☐ 16 Clarence Smith	3.50	1.75	.35
☐ 17 Clarence Smith	3.50	1.75	.35
☐ 18 Hubert(Geese) Ausbie	4.50	2.25	.45
☐ 19 Hubert(Geese) Ausbie (Two balls)	4.50	2.25	.45
☐ 20 Bobby Hunter	4.50	2.25	.45
☐ 21 Bobby Hunter (One leg up)	4.50	2.25	.45
☐ 22 Meadowlark Lemon (Three balls)	5.50	2.75	.55
☐ 23 Meadowlark Lemon	5.50	2.75	.55
☐ 24 Freddie(Curly) Neal	5.50	2.75	.55
☐ 25 Freddie(Curly) Neal (Three paint brushes)	5.50	2.75	.55
☐ 26 Meadowlark Lemon (Palming two balls)	5.50	2.75	.55
☐ 27 Mel Davis (Leaning over with ball)	3.50	1.75	.35
☐ 28 Freddie"Curly" Neal	5.50	2.75	.55

1971-72 Globetrotters 84

The 1971-72 Harlem Globetrotters set was produced by Fleer and sold in wax packs. The set contains 84 standard size (2 1/2" by 3 1/2") cards. The card fronts have full color pictures. The card backs have black printing on gray card stock and feature biographical sketches and other interesting information about the Globetrotters. The cards are numbered on back out of 84.

	NRMT	VG-E	GOOD
COMPLETE SET (85)	200.00	100.00	20.00
COMMON CARD (1-84)	1.50	.75	.15
☐ 1 Bob"Showboat" Hall (full length)	7.50	3.75	.75
☐ 2 Bob"Showboat" Hall (kicking ball)	1.50	.75	.15
☐ 3 Bob"Showboat" Hall (passing behind back)	1.50	.75	.15
☐ 4 Pablo"Pabs" Robertson (ball in front)	1.50	.75	.15
☐ 5 Pablo"Pabs" Robertson (smiling)	1.50	.75	.15
☐ 6 Pablo"Pabs" Robertson (dribbling down)	1.50	.75	.15
☐ 7 Pablo"Pabs" Robertson (dribbling up)	1.50	.75	.15
☐ 8 Pablo"Pabs" Robertson (back-side)	1.50	.75	.15
☐ 9 Meadowlark Lemon (kicking behind back)	3.50	1.75	.35
☐ 10 Meadowlark Lemon (rolling ball on arm)	3.50	1.75	.35
☐ 11 Meadowlark Lemon (palming two balls)	3.50	1.75	.35
☐ 12 Meadowlark Lemon (ball on neck)	3.50	1.75	.35
☐ 13 Meadowlark Lemon (three balls)	3.50	1.75	.35

☐ 14 Meadowlark Lemon (three balls in front)	3.50	1.75	.35
☐ 15 Meadowlark Lemon (three balls)	3.50	1.75	.35
☐ 16 Meadowlark Lemon (dribbling two balls)	3.50	1.75	.35
☐ 17 Meadowlark Lemon (with cap)	3.50	1.75	.35
☐ 18 Curley, Meadowlark, and Mel	3.50	1.75	.35
☐ 19 Football Play (Meadowlark centering)	3.50	1.75	.35
☐ 20 Meadowlark Lemon (hooking)	3.50	1.75	.35
☐ 21 Hubert"Geese" Ausbie (balls between legs)	2.50	1.25	.25
☐ 22 Hubert"Geese" Ausbie (ball under arm)	2.50	1.25	.25
☐ 23 Hubert"Geese" Ausbie (ball on finger)	2.50	1.25	.25
☐ 24 Hubert"Geese" Ausbie (ball behind back)	2.50	1.25	.25
☐ 25 Hubert"Geese" Ausbie (no ball)	2.50	1.25	.25
☐ 26 Ausbie and Neal (with confetti)	3.50	1.75	.35
☐ 27 Freddie"Curly" Neal (artist)	3.50	1.75	.35
☐ 28 Freddie"Curly" Neal (sitting on ball)	3.50	1.75	.35
☐ 29 Freddie"Curly" Neal (two balls on head)	3.50	1.75	.35
☐ 30 Mel Davis and "Curly" Neal	2.50	1.25	.25
☐ 31 Freddie"Curly" Neal (smiling)	3.50	1.75	.35
☐ 32 Freddie"Curly" Neal (looking to side)	3.50	1.75	.35
☐ 33 Mel Davis (looking down)	1.50	.75	.15
☐ 34 Mel Davis (ready to shoot)	1.50	.75	.15
☐ 35 Mel Davis (ball in hand)	1.50	.75	.15
☐ 36 Mel Davis (ball over head)	1.50	.75	.15
☐ 37 Mel Davis and Bill Meggett (leap frog)	1.50	.75	.15
☐ 38 Mel Davis (ball on knee)	1.50	.75	.15
☐ 39 Bobby Joe Mason (ball under arm)	1.50	.75	.15
☐ 40 Bobby Joe Mason (ball between legs)	1.50	.75	.15
☐ 41 Bobby Joe Mason (passing behind back)	1.50	.75	.15
☐ 42 Mason and Stephens	1.50	.75	.15
☐ 43 Bobby Joe Mason (ball to side)	1.50	.75	.15
☐ 44 Bobby Joe Mason (ready to shoot)	1.50	.75	.15
☐ 45 Clarence Smith (three balls between legs)	1.50	.75	.15
☐ 46 Clarence Smith (on bike)	1.50	.75	.15
☐ 47 Clarence Smith (ball at ear)	1.50	.75	.15
☐ 48 Clarence Smith (dribbling on side)	1.50	.75	.15
☐ 49 Jerry Venable	1.50	.75	.15
☐ 50 Frank Stephens (hands in front)	1.50	.75	.15
☐ 51 Frank Stephens (ball on finger)	1.50	.75	.15
☐ 52 Frank Stephens (waiting for ball)	1.50	.75	.15
☐ 53 Frank Stephens (ball in hand)	1.50	.75	.15
☐ 54 Theodis Ray Lee (ball on hip)	1.50	.75	.15
☐ 55 Theodis Ray Lee (ball between knees)	1.50	.75	.15
☐ 56 Jerry Venable (palming ball)	1.50	.75	.15
☐ 57 Doug Himes (ball in air)	1.50	.75	.15
☐ 58 Doug Himes (ball behind back)	1.50	.75	.15
☐ 59 Bill Meggett (dribbling two balls)	1.50	.75	.15
☐ 60 Bill Meggett (ready to shoot)	1.50	.75	.15
☐ 61 Vincent White (ball on hip)	1.50	.75	.15
☐ 62 Vincent White (kicking ball)	1.50	.75	.15
☐ 63 Pablo and "Showboat" (arm in arm)	1.50	.75	.15
☐ 64 Meadowlark, Neal, and Ausbie (balls behind back)	3.50	1.75	.35
☐ 65 Curley Neal, Quarterback	3.50	1.75	.35
☐ 66 Ausbie, Meadowlark, and Neal (looking at ball)	3.50	1.75	.35
☐ 67 Neal and Meadowlark	3.50	1.75	.35
☐ 68 Football Routine	2.50	1.25	.25
☐ 69 Meadowlark To Neal To Ausbie	3.50	1.75	.35
☐ 70 Meadowlark Is Safe At The Plate	3.50	1.75	.35
☐ 71 1970-71 Highlights (baseball act)	2.50	1.25	.25
☐ 72 1970-71 Highlights (Lemon and Neal)	3.50	1.75	.35
☐ 73 Bobby Hunter (ball on hip)	2.00	1.00	.20
☐ 74 Bobby Hunter (ball in hand)	2.00	1.00	.20
☐ 75 Bobby Hunter (ball on shoulder)	2.00	1.00	.20
☐ 76 Bobby Hunter (ball in air)	2.00	1.00	.20
☐ 77 Bobby Hunter (passing between legs)	2.00	1.00	.20
☐ 78 Jackie Jackson (ball on hip)	2.50	1.25	.25
☐ 79 Jackie Jackson (ball behind back)	2.50	1.25	.25
☐ 80 Jackie Jackson (ball in air)	2.50	1.25	.25
☐ 81 Jackie Jackson (ball on finger)	2.50	1.25	.25
☐ 82 The Globetrotters	2.50	1.25	.25
☐ 83 The Globetrotters	2.50	1.25	.25
☐ 84 Dallas Thornton	4.50	2.25	.45
☐ xx Globetrotter Official Peel-off Team Emblem Sticker (unnumbered)	12.00	6.00	1.20

1968-74 Hall of Fame Bookmarks

These bookmarks commemorate individuals who were elected to the Basketball Hall of Fame. They measure approximately 2 7/16" by 6 3/8". The top of the front has a blue-tinted 2 1/8" by 2 5/16 "mug shot" of the individual on paper stock. In blue lettering the individual's name and a brief biography are printed below the picture. The backs are blank and the cards are unnumbered. The cards were probably issued year after year (with additions) by the Hall of Fame book store. The last seven cards listed below were inducted in 1969 (47-48), 1970 (49-51), 1972 (52), and 1974 (53); there are some slight style and size differences in these later issue cards compared to the first 46 cards in the set.

	NRMT	VG-E	GOOD
COMPLETE SET (53)	40.00	20.00	4.00
COMMON PLAYER (1-46)	.30	.15	.03
COMMON PLAYER (47-53)	1.00	.50	.10
☐ 1 Forrest C. Allen	.50	.25	.05
☐ 2 Arnold J. Auerbach	1.00	.50	.10
☐ 3 Clair F. Bee	.75	.35	.07
☐ 4 Bernhard Borgmann	.30	.15	.03
☐ 5 Walter A. Brown	.30	.15	.03
☐ 6 John W. Bunn	.30	.15	.03
☐ 7 Howard G. Cann	.30	.15	.03
☐ 8 H. Clifford Carlson	.30	.15	.03
☐ 9 Everett S. Dean	.30	.15	.03
☐ 10 Forrest S. DeBernardi	.30	.15	.03
☐ 11 Henry G. Dehnert	.30	.15	.03
☐ 12 Harold E. Foster	.30	.15	.03
☐ 13 Amory T. Gill	.30	.15	.03
☐ 14 Victor A. Hanson	.30	.15	.03
☐ 15 Edward J. Hickox	.30	.15	.03

JOHN R. WOODEN
(1910-)

ELECTED 1959-COLLEGE PLAYER

Graduated from Martinsville (Ind.) H.S. 1928 and Purdue 1932. High School All-State 1926-27-28. All-Big 10 1930-31-32. All-American 1930-31-32 Captain 1931, 1932; set Conference scoring record 1932. Led Nat'l. Champions 1932. Star in semi-pro Basketball. Made 138 consecutive free throws in competition. Member All-time All-American Team. Became outstanding high school and university coach.

☐ 16 Paul D. Hinkle	.30	.15	.03
☐ 17 Howard A. Hobson	.30	.15	.03
☐ 18 Nat Holman	.50	.25	.05
☐ 19 Charles D. Hyatt	.30	.15	.03
☐ 20 Henry P. Iba	1.00	.50	.10
☐ 21 Edward S. Irish	.50	.25	.05
☐ 22 Alvin F. Julian	.30	.15	.03
☐ 23 Matthew P. Kennedy	.30	.15	.03
☐ 24 Robert A. Kurland	.75	.35	.07
☐ 25 Ward L. Lambert	.30	.15	.03
☐ 26 Joe Lapchick	.75	.35	.07
☐ 27 Kenneth D. Loeffler	.30	.15	.03
☐ 28 Angelo Luisetti	.75	.35	.07
☐ 29 Ed Macauley	.50	.25	.05
☐ 30 Branch McCracken	.30	.15	.03
☐ 31 George Mikan	3.50	1.75	.35
☐ 32 William G. Mokray	.30	.15	.03
☐ 33 Charles C. Murphy	.30	.15	.03
☐ 34 James Naismith	1.50	.75	.15
☐ 35 Andy Phillip	.50	.25	.05
☐ 36 John S. Roosma	.30	.15	.03
☐ 37 Adolph F. Rupp	1.50	.75	.15
☐ 38 John D. Russell	.30	.15	.03
☐ 39 Arthur A. Schabinger	.30	.15	.03
☐ 40 Amos Alonzo Stagg	1.00	.50	.10
☐ 41 Charles H. Taylor	.30	.15	.03
☐ 42 John A. Thompson	.30	.15	.03
☐ 43 David Tobey	.30	.15	.03
☐ 44 Oswald Tower	.30	.15	.03
☐ 45 David H. Walsh	.30	.15	.03
☐ 46 John R. Wooden	1.25	.60	.12
☐ 47 Bernard Carnevale	1.00	.50	.10
☐ 48 Bob Davies	2.00	1.00	.20
☐ 49 Bob Cousy	3.00	1.50	.30
☐ 50 Bob Pettit	3.00	1.50	.30
☐ 51 Abraham M. Saperstein	2.00	1.00	.20
☐ 52 Adolph Schayes	2.00	1.00	.20
☐ 53 Bill Russell	5.00	2.50	.50

1961 Hawks Essex Meats

The 1961 Essex Meats set contains 13 cards featuring the St. Louis Hawks. These cards measure the standard 2 1/2" by 3 1/2". The fronts picture a posed black and white photo of the player with his name at the bottom of the card in bold-faced type. The backs of this white-stock card feature the player's name, brief physical data and biographical information. The cards are unnumbered and give no indication of the producer

ROBERT E. LEE PETTIT, JR.
Age: 28 Hgt. 6-9 Wgt. 225

Last year was the finest in Pettit's illustrious career as he led the Hawks to a 5th straight Western Division title. He was named to the first All-NBA team and played in the annual E-W All-Star game, both for the 7th year in a row. Bob has won the NBA's most valuable player award twice and led the Hawks last year in all but four departments. Missed only 3 of the Hawks' 79 regular games. His career total of 12,896 pts. ranks 4th among active players in the NBA today. He came to the Hawks in 1954. He won All-America honors the previous two years at LSU where he is regarded as the greatest player in the annals of Louisiana basketball. His high game as a pro came last Feb. 18 in Detroit when he scored 57 points in a winning effort. Bob is Hawks player representative and team captain and is one of sports' most eligible bachelors. He has an insurance business in Baton Rouge and varied other interests.

on the card. The cards were distributed by Bonnie Brands. The catalog designation for the set is F175.

	NRMT	VG-E	GOOD
COMPLETE SET (13)	250.00	125.00	25.00
COMMON PLAYER (1-13)	12.00	6.00	1.20
☐ 1 Barney Cable	12.00	6.00	1.20
☐ 2 Al Ferrari	12.00	6.00	1.20
☐ 3 Larry Foust	18.00	9.00	1.80
☐ 4 Cliff Hagen	35.00	17.50	3.50
☐ 5 Vern Hatton	12.00	6.00	1.20
☐ 6 Cleo Hill	12.00	6.00	1.20
☐ 7 Fred LaCour	12.00	6.00	1.20
☐ 8 Andrew(Fuzzy) Levane	12.00	6.00	1.20
☐ 9 Clyde Lovellette	35.00	17.50	3.50
☐ 10 John McCarthy	12.00	6.00	1.20
☐ 11 Shellie McMillon	12.00	6.00	1.20
☐ 12 Bob Pettit	100.00	50.00	10.00
☐ 13 Bobby Sims	12.00	6.00	1.20

1978-79 Hawks Coke/WPLO

TOM McMILLEN 52

Three-time All-American at Maryland where he established an all-time scoring mark of 1,807 points in three varsity seasons. Averaged 20.5 points and 9.8 rebounds per game. Led Maryland to the 1972 NIT Championship and was the MVP of the tournament. Played on the 1972 American Olympic team. Played a year in Italy while a Rhodes Scholar student in Oxford, England.

Drafted by Buffalo on the first round (9th pick) of the 1974 Draft. Traded with Bob McAdoo to the New York Knicks for John Gianelli and cash, December 9, 1976. Traded to Atlanta for a second round draft choice, November 1, 1977.

Injured in Knicks training camp and did not play prior to joining the Hawks. Broke into starting lineup after an injury benched John Brown. As a starter in 31 games during 1977-78 season, he averaged 12.5 points and 7.9 rebounds per game while shooting .523 from the field. Led the Hawks in field goal percentage with a .493 mark and had a 9.9 scoring average for the entire year.

V-103
DISCO STEREO

This 14-card set was sponsored by V-103/WPLO radio and Coca-Cola, and they were given out at 7-Eleven stores. The cards are printed on thin cardboard stock and measure approximately 3 by 4 1/4". The fronts feature a black and white pen and ink drawing of the player's head, with the Hawks' and Coke logos in the lower corners in red. The back has a career summary and the sponsor's "V-103 Disco Stereo" at the bottom. The cards are unnumbered and are checklisted below in alphabetical order.

	NRMT	VG-E	GOOD
COMPLETE SET (14)	50.00	25.00	5.00
COMMON PLAYER (1-14)	2.50	1.25	.25
☐ 1 Hubie Brown CO	3.50	1.75	.35
☐ 2 Charlie Criss	4.50	2.25	.45
☐ 3 John Drew	5.00	2.50	.50
☐ 4 Mike Fratello CO	5.00	2.50	.50

	MINT	EXC	G-VG
☐ 5 Jack Givens	4.50	2.25	.45
☐ 6 Steve Hawes	2.50	1.25	.25
☐ 7 Armond Hill	3.50	1.75	.35
☐ 8 Eddie Johnson	3.00	1.50	.30
☐ 9 Frank Layden CO	5.00	2.50	.50
☐ 10 Butch Lee	3.50	1.75	.35
☐ 11 Tom McMillen	6.00	3.00	.60
☐ 12 Tree Rollins	5.00	2.50	.50
☐ 13 Dan Roundfield	4.00	2.00	.40
☐ 14 Rick Wilson	2.50	1.25	.25

1979-80 Hawks Majik Market

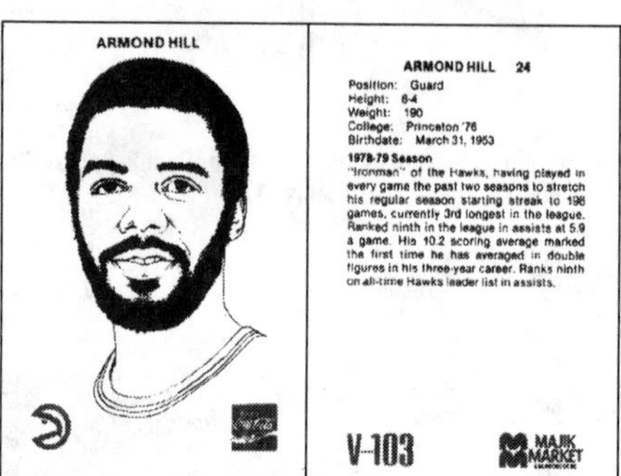

The 1979-80 Majik Market/Coca-Cola Atlanta Hawks set contains 15 cards on thin white stock. Cards are approximately 3" by 4 1/4". The fronts of the cards include a crude, black line drawing of the player, the player's name and, in red, a Coke logo and a stylized Hawks logo. The backs contain biographical data and a summary of the player's activity during the 1978-79 season. The Majik Market logo and the call letters V-103/WPLO are printed in red on the back of the cards. Most collectors consider the set quite unattractive and poorly produced. The cards are unnumbered and are checklisted below in alphabetical order.

	MINT	EXC	G-VG
COMPLETE SET (15)	50.00	25.00	5.00
COMMON PLAYER (1-15)	2.50	1.25	.25
☐ 1 Hubie Brown CO	3.50	1.75	.35
☐ 2 John Brown	3.50	1.75	.35
☐ 3 Charlie Criss	4.50	2.25	.45
☐ 4 John Drew	5.00	2.50	.50
☐ 5 Mike Fratello ACO	5.00	2.50	.50
☐ 6 Jack Givens	4.50	2.25	.45
☐ 7 Steve Hawes	2.50	1.25	.25
☐ 8 Armond Hill	3.50	1.75	.35
☐ 9 Eddie Johnson	3.00	1.50	.30
☐ 10 Jimmy McElroy	2.50	1.25	.25
☐ 11 Tom McMillen	6.00	3.00	.60
☐ 12 Sam Pellom	2.50	1.25	.25
☐ 13 Tree Rollins	5.00	2.50	.50
☐ 14 Dan Roundfield	4.00	2.00	.40
☐ 15 Brendan Suhr ACO	2.50	1.25	.25

1987-88 Hawks Pizza Hut

The 1987-88 Atlanta Hawks Team Photo Night (March 11, 1988) set was sponsored by Pizza Hut. This photo album was distributed to fans attending the Atlanta Hawks home game. It consists of three sheets, each measuring approximately 8 1/4" by 11" and joined together to form one continuous sheet. The first sheet features a team photo of the Hawks. While the second sheet presents two rows of five cards each, the third sheet presents seven additional player cards, with the remaining three slots filled in by Pizza Hut coupons. After perforation, the

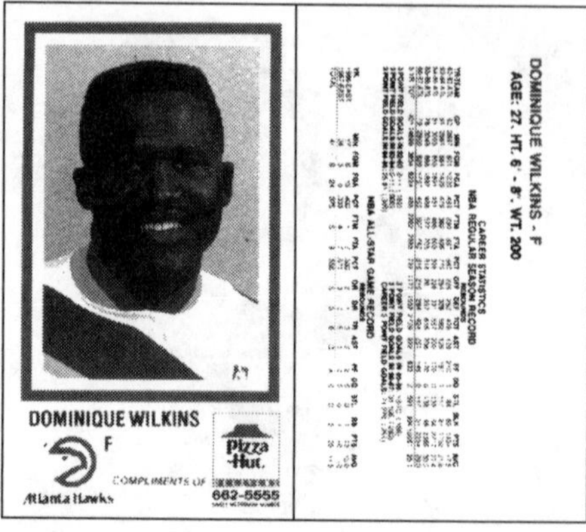

cards measure approximately 2 3/16" by 3 3/4". The card front features a color action player photo, with a red border on white card stock. The player's name and position are given below the picture, along with the team and Pizza Hut logos. The back presents career statistics in a horizontal format. The cards are unnumbered and checklisted below in the order they appear in the album.

	MINT	EXC	G-VG
COMPLETE SET (17)	20.00	10.00	2.00
COMMON PLAYER (1-17)	.90	.45	.09
☐ 1 Mike Fratello CO	1.50	.75	.15
☐ 2 Brendan Suhr ASST	.90	.45	.09
☐ 3 Brian Hill ASST	.90	.45	.09
☐ 4 Don Chaney ASST	1.25	.60	.12
☐ 5 Joe O'Toole TR	.90	.45	.09
☐ 6 John Battle	1.50	.75	.15
☐ 7 Antoine Carr	2.00	1.00	.20
☐ 8 Scott Hastings	.90	.45	.09
☐ 9 Jon Koncak	1.50	.75	.15
☐ 10 Cliff Levingston	1.50	.75	.15
☐ 11 Doc Rivers	2.00	1.00	.20
☐ 12 Tree Rollins	1.25	.60	.12
☐ 13 Chris Washburn	1.25	.60	.12
☐ 14 Spud Webb	2.00	1.00	.20
☐ 15 Dominique Wilkins	4.50	2.25	.45
☐ 16 Kevin Willis	3.00	1.50	.30
☐ 17 Randy Wittman	.90	.45	.09

1989-90 Heat Publix

This 15-card set was distributed in Publix stores in the greater Miami area. The cards measure approximately 2" by 3 1/2". The fronts feature a color action player photo, with the player's name and position in the stripe below the picture. The back has biographical and statistical information. The cards are unnumbered and are checklisted below in alphabetical order. The set features early cards of Glen Rice and Rony Seikaly among others.

	MINT	EXC	G-VG
COMPLETE SET (15)	45.00	22.50	4.50
COMMON PLAYER (1-15)	2.00	1.00	.20
☐ 1 Terry Davis	3.00	1.50	.30
☐ 2 Sherman Douglas	4.00	2.00	.40
☐ 3 Kevin Edwards	3.00	1.50	.30
☐ 4 Tony Fiorentino CO	2.00	1.00	.20
☐ 5 Tellis Frank	2.00	1.00	.20
☐ 6 Scott Haffner	2.00	1.00	.20
☐ 7 Grant Long	5.00	2.50	.50
☐ 8 Heat Mascot	2.00	1.00	.20
☐ 9 Glen Rice	12.00	6.00	1.20
☐ 10 Ron Rothstein CO	3.00	1.50	.30
☐ 11 Rony Seikaly	6.00	3.00	.60
☐ 12 Rory Sparrow	2.00	1.00	.20

	MINT	EXC	G-VG
☐ 13 Jon Sundvold	2.00	1.00	.20
☐ 14 Billy Thompson	3.00	1.50	.30
☐ 15 Dave Wohl CO	2.00	1.00	.20

1990-91 Heat Publix

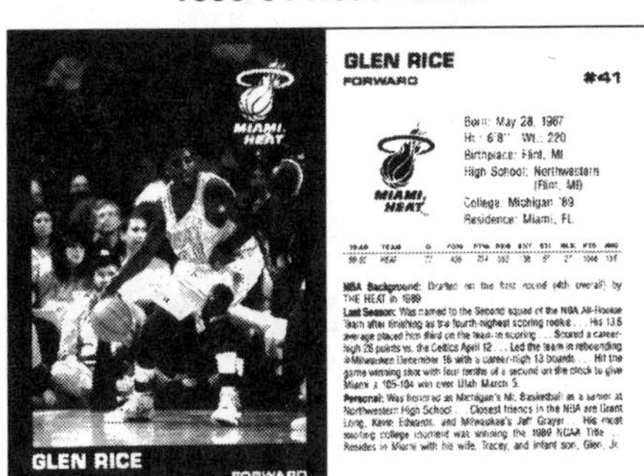

This 16-card set of Miami Heat was sponsored by Domino's, Dixie, and Bumble Bee. The cards were issued in a sheet that contains 16 player cards and four manufacturers' coupons; after perforation, the cards and coupons alike measure the standard size (2 1/2" by 3 1/2"). The front features a color action player photo on a black background. The team logo appears in the upper right corner, while the player's name appears in white lettering below the picture. The back has biographical and statistical information. The cards are unnumbered and are checklisted below as they are listed on the panel, in alphabetical order with coaches at the end.

	MINT	EXC	G-VG
COMPLETE SET (16)	20.00	10.00	2.00
COMMON PLAYER (1-16)	1.00	.50	.10
☐ 1 Keith Askins	1.00	.50	.10
☐ 2 Willie Burton	2.50	1.25	.25
☐ 3 Bimbo Coles	2.50	1.25	.25
☐ 4 Terry Davis	1.50	.75	.15
☐ 5 Sherman Douglas	2.50	1.25	.25
☐ 6 Kevin Edwards	1.50	.75	.15
☐ 7 Alec Kessler	1.50	.75	.15
☐ 8 Grant Long	1.50	.75	.15
☐ 9 Alan Ogg	1.25	.60	.12
☐ 10 Glen Rice	4.50	2.25	.45
☐ 11 Rony Seikaly	3.00	1.50	.30
☐ 12 Jon Sundvold	1.00	.50	.10
☐ 13 Billy Thompson	1.25	.60	.12
☐ 14 Ron Rothstein CO	1.25	.60	.12
☐ 15 Dave Wohl CO	1.00	.50	.10
☐ 16 Tony Fiorentino CO	1.00	.50	.10

1989-90 Hoops I

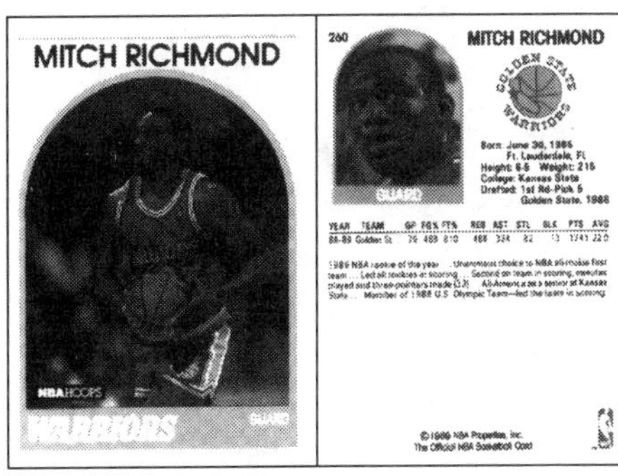

The 1989-90 Hoops sets contains 300 cards measuring the standard size (2 1/2" by 3 1/2"). The fronts feature color action player photos, bordered by a basketball lane in one of the team's colors. On a white card face the player's name appears in black lettering above the picture. The backs have head shots of the players, biographical information, and statistics, all printed on a pale yellow background with white borders. The cards are numbered on the backs. The key rookie in this set is David Robinson's card number 138, which only appeared in this first series of Hoops. Other Rookie Cards included in this series are Willie Anderson, Rex Chapman, Harvey Grant, Hersey Hawkins, Jeff Hornacek, Kevin Johnson, Reggie Lewis, Dan Majerle, Danny Manning, Vernon Maxwell, Ken Norman, Mitch Richmond, Rony Seikaly, Brian Shaw, Scott Skiles, Charles Smith, Rod Strickland, and Micheal Williams. Beware of David Robinson counterfeit cards which are distinguishable primarily by comparison to a real card or under magnification.

	MINT	EXC	G-VG
COMPLETE SET (300)	45.00	22.50	4.50
COMMON PLAYER (1-300)	.03	.01	.00
COMMON PLAYER SP (1-300)	.20	.10	.02
☐ 1 Joe Dumars Detroit Pistons	.25	.12	.02
☐ 2 Wayne Rollins Cleveland Cavaliers	.03	.01	.00
☐ 3 Kenny Walker New York Knicks	.03	.01	.00
☐ 4 Mychal Thompson Los Angeles Lakers	.03	.01	.00
☐ 5 Alvin Robertson SP San Antonio Spurs	.20	.10	.02
☐ 6 Vinny Del Negro Sacramento Kings	.10	.05	.01
☐ 7 Greg Anderson SP San Antonio Spurs	.20	.10	.02
☐ 8 Rod Strickland New York Knicks	.40	.20	.04
☐ 9 Ed Pinckney Boston Celtics	.06	.03	.00
☐ 10 Dale Ellis Seattle Supersonics	.06	.03	.00
☐ 11 Chuck Daly CO Detroit Pistons	.20	.10	.02
☐ 12 Eric Leckner Utah Jazz	.08	.04	.01
☐ 13 Charles Davis Chicago Bulls	.03	.01	.00
☐ 14 Cotton Fitzsimmons CO Phoenix Suns (No NBA logo on back in bottom right)	.03	.01	.00
☐ 15 Byron Scott Los Angeles Lakers	.08	.04	.01
☐ 16 Derrick Chievous Houston Rockets	.08	.04	.01
☐ 17 Reggie Lewis Boston Celtics	1.75	.85	.17
☐ 18 Jim Paxson Boston Celtics	.03	.01	.00
☐ 19 Tony Campbell Los Angeles Lakers	.35	.17	.03
☐ 20 Rolando Blackman Dallas Mavericks	.10	.05	.01
☐ 21 Michael Jordan AS Chicago Bulls	.75	.35	.07
☐ 22 Cliff Levingston Atlanta Hawks	.06	.03	.00
☐ 23 Roy Tarpley Dallas Mavericks	.06	.03	.00
☐ 24 Harold Pressley UER Sacramento Kings (Cinderella misspelled as cindarella)	.08	.04	.01
☐ 25 Larry Nance Cleveland Cavaliers	.15	.07	.01
☐ 26 Chris Morris New Jersey Nets	.20	.10	.02
☐ 27 Bob Hansen UER Utah Jazz (Drafted in '84, should say '83)	.03	.01	.00

☐ 28 Mark Price AS Cleveland Cavaliers	.10	.05	.01
☐ 29 Reggie Miller Indiana Pacers	.40	.20	.04
☐ 30 Karl Malone Utah Jazz	.40	.20	.04
☐ 31 Sidney Lowe SP Charlotte Hornets	.20	.10	.02
☐ 32 Ron Anderson Philadelphia 76ers	.03	.01	.00
☐ 33 Mike Gminski Philadelphia 76ers	.03	.01	.00
☐ 34 Scott Brooks Philadelphia 76ers	.10	.05	.01
☐ 35 Kevin Johnson Phoenix Suns	2.50	1.25	.25
☐ 36 Mark Bryant Portland Trail Blazers	.12	.06	.01
☐ 37 Rik Smits Indiana Pacers	.20	.10	.02
☐ 38 Tim Perry Phoenix Suns	.35	.17	.03
☐ 39 Ralph Sampson Golden State Warriors	.06	.03	.00
☐ 40 Danny Manning UER Los Angeles Clippers (Missing 1988 in draft info)	1.00	.50	.10
☐ 41 Kevin Edwards Miami Heat	.15	.07	.01
☐ 42 Paul Mokeski Milwaukee Bucks	.03	.01	.00
☐ 43 Dale Ellis AS Seattle Supersonics	.06	.03	.00
☐ 44 Walter Berry Houston Rockets	.03	.01	.00
☐ 45 Chuck Person Indiana Pacers	.12	.06	.01
☐ 46 Rick Mahorn SP Detroit Pistons	.20	.10	.02
☐ 47 Joe Kleine Boston Celtics	.03	.01	.00
☐ 48 Brad Daugherty AS Cleveland Cavaliers	.20	.10	.02
☐ 49 Mike Woodson Houston Rockets	.03	.01	.00
☐ 50 Brad Daugherty Cleveland Cavaliers	.50	.25	.05
☐ 51 Shelton Jones SP Philadelphia 76ers	.25	.12	.02
☐ 52 Michael Adams Denver Nuggets	.20	.10	.02
☐ 53 Wes Unseld CO Washington Bullets	.10	.05	.01
☐ 54 Rex Chapman Charlotte Hornets	.20	.10	.02
☐ 55 Kelly Tripucka Charlotte Hornets	.03	.01	.00
☐ 56 Rickey Green Milwaukee Bucks	.03	.01	.00
☐ 57 Frank Johnson SP Houston Rockets	.20	.10	.02
☐ 58 Johnny Newman New York Knicks	.20	.10	.02
☐ 59 Billy Thompson Miami Heat	.10	.05	.01
☐ 60 Stu Jackson CO New York Knicks	.06	.03	.00
☐ 61 Walter Davis Denver Nuggets	.06	.03	.00
☐ 62 Brian Shaw SP UER Boston Celtics (Gary Grant led rookies in assists, not Shaw)	.50	.25	.05
☐ 63 Gerald Wilkins New York Knicks	.06	.03	.00
☐ 64 Armon Gilliam Phoenix Suns	.10	.05	.01
☐ 65 Maurice Cheeks SP Philadelphia 76ers	.25	.12	.02
☐ 66 Jack Sikma Milwaukee Bucks	.06	.03	.00
☐ 67 Harvey Grant Washington Bullets	.90	.45	.09
☐ 68 Jim Lynam CO Philadelphia 76ers	.03	.01	.00
☐ 69 Clyde Drexler AS Portland Trail Blazers	.25	.12	.02
☐ 70 Xavier McDaniel Seattle Supersonics	.15	.07	.01
☐ 71 Danny Young Portland Trail Blazers	.03	.01	.00
☐ 72 Fennis Dembo Detroit Pistons	.08	.04	.01
☐ 73 Mark Acres SP Boston Celtics	.20	.10	.02
☐ 74 Brad Lohaus SP Sacramento Kings	.25	.12	.02
☐ 75 Manute Bol Golden State Warriors	.06	.03	.00
☐ 76 Purvis Short Houston Rockets	.03	.01	.00
☐ 77 Allen Leavell Houston Rockets	.03	.01	.00
☐ 78 Johnny Dawkins SP San Antonio Spurs	.20	.10	.02
☐ 79 Paul Pressey Milwaukee Bucks	.03	.01	.00
☐ 80 Patrick Ewing New York Knicks	.50	.25	.05
☐ 81 Bill Wennington Dallas Mavericks	.10	.05	.01
☐ 82 Danny Schayes Denver Nuggets	.06	.03	.00
☐ 83 Derek Smith Philadelphia 76ers	.03	.01	.00
☐ 84 Moses Malone AS Atlanta Hawks	.08	.04	.01
☐ 85 Jeff Malone Washington Bullets	.15	.07	.01
☐ 86 Otis Smith SP Golden State Warriors	.25	.12	.02
☐ 87 Trent Tucker New York Knicks	.03	.01	.00
☐ 88 Robert Reid Charlotte Hornets	.03	.01	.00
☐ 89 John Paxson Chicago Bulls	.15	.07	.01
☐ 90 Chris Mullin Golden State Warriors	.40	.20	.04
☐ 91 Tom Garrick Los Angeles Clippers	.08	.04	.01
☐ 92 Willis Reed CO SP UER New Jersey Nets (Gambling, should be Grambling)	.30	.15	.03
☐ 93 Dave Corzine SP Chicago Bulls	.20	.10	.02
☐ 94 Mark Alarie Washington Bullets	.08	.04	.01
☐ 95 Mark Aguirre Detroit Pistons	.08	.04	.01
☐ 96 Charles Barkley AS Philadelphia 76ers	.20	.10	.02
☐ 97 Sidney Green SP New York Knicks	.20	.10	.02
☐ 98 Kevin Willis Atlanta Hawks	.20	.10	.02
☐ 99 Dave Hoppen Charlotte Hornets	.08	.04	.01
☐ 100 Terry Cummings SP Milwaukee Bucks	.30	.15	.03
☐ 101 Dwayne Washington SP Miami Heat	.20	.10	.02
☐ 102 Larry Brown CO San Antonio Spurs	.03	.01	.00
☐ 103 Kevin Duckworth Portland Trail Blazers	.08	.04	.01
☐ 104 Uwe Blab SP Dallas Mavericks	.30	.15	.03
☐ 105 Terry Porter Portland Trail Blazers	.35	.17	.03
☐ 106 Craig Ehlo Cleveland Cavaliers	.50	.25	.05
☐ 107 Don Casey CO Los Angeles Clippers	.03	.01	.00
☐ 108 Pat Riley CO Los Angeles Lakers	.06	.03	.00
☐ 109 John Salley Detroit Pistons	.08	.04	.01
☐ 110 Charles Barkley Philadelphia 76ers	.40	.20	.04
☐ 111 Sam Bowie SP Portland Trail Blazers	.25	.12	.02
☐ 112 Earl Cureton Charlotte Hornets	.08	.04	.01
☐ 113 Craig Hodges UER Chicago Bulls (3-pointing shooting)	.06	.03	.00
☐ 114 Benoit Benjamin Los Angeles Clippers	.06	.03	.00
☐ 115A Spud Webb ERR SP Atlanta Hawks (Signed 9/27/89)	.35	.17	.03
☐ 115B Spud Webb COR Atlanta Hawks (Second series;	.15	.07	.01

signed 9/26/85)

☐ 116 Karl Malone AS Utah Jazz	.20	.10	.02
☐ 117 Sleepy Floyd Houston Rockets	.06	.03	.00
☐ 118 John Williams Cleveland Cavaliers	.10	.05	.01
☐ 119 Michael Holton Charlotte Hornets	.03	.01	.00
☐ 120 Alex English Denver Nuggets	.10	.05	.01
☐ 121 Dennis Johnson Boston Celtics	.08	.04	.01
☐ 122 Wayne Cooper SP Denver Nuggets	.20	.10	.02
☐ 123A Don Chaney CO Houston Rockets (Line next to NBA coaching record)	.30	.15	.03
☐ 123B Don Chaney CO Houston Rockets (No line)	.06	.03	.00
☐ 124 A.C. Green Los Angeles Lakers	.08	.04	.01
☐ 125 Adrian Dantley Dallas Mavericks	.12	.06	.01
☐ 126 Del Harris CO Milwaukee Bucks	.03	.01	.00
☐ 127 Dick Harter CO Charlotte Hornets	.03	.01	.00
☐ 128 Reggie Williams Los Angeles Clippers	.30	.15	.03
☐ 129 Bill Hanzlik Denver Nuggets	.03	.01	.00
☐ 130 Dominique Wilkins Atlanta Hawks	.30	.15	.03
☐ 131 Herb Williams Dallas Mavericks	.06	.03	.00
☐ 132 Steve Johnson SP Portland Trail Blazers	.20	.10	.02
☐ 133 Alex English AS Denver Nuggets	.06	.03	.00
☐ 134 Darrell Walker Washington Bullets	.03	.01	.00
☐ 135 Bill Laimbeer Detroit Pistons	.08	.04	.01
☐ 136 Fred Roberts Milwaukee Bucks	.10	.05	.01
☐ 137 Hersey Hawkins Philadelphia 76ers	1.00	.50	.10
☐ 138 David Robinson SP San Antonio Spurs	33.00	15.00	3.00
☐ 139 Brad Sellers SP Chicago Bulls	.20	.10	.02
☐ 140 John Stockton Utah Jazz	.75	.35	.07
☐ 141 Grant Long Miami Heat	.35	.17	.03
☐ 142 Marc Iavaroni SP Utah Jazz	.20	.10	.02
☐ 143 Steve Alford SP Golden State Warriors	.25	.12	.02
☐ 144 Jeff Lamp SP Los Angeles Lakers	.20	.10	.02
☐ 145 Buck Williams SP UER New Jersey Nets (Won ROY in '81, should say '82)	.35	.17	.03
☐ 146 Mark Jackson AS New York Knicks	.06	.03	.00
☐ 147 Jim Petersen Sacramento Kings	.03	.01	.00
☐ 148 Steve Stipanovich SP Indiana Pacers	.20	.10	.02
☐ 149 Sam Vincent SP Chicago Bulls	.30	.15	.03
☐ 150 Larry Bird Boston Celtics	.60	.30	.06
☐ 151 Jon Koncak Atlanta Hawks	.08	.04	.01
☐ 152 Olden Polynice Seattle Supersonics	.25	.12	.02
☐ 153 Randy Breuer Milwaukee Bucks	.03	.01	.00
☐ 154 John Battle Atlanta Hawks	.15	.07	.01
☐ 155 Mark Eaton Utah Jazz	.06	.03	.00
☐ 156 Kevin McHale AS UER Boston Celtics (No TM on Celtics logo on back)	.08	.04	.01
☐ 157 Jerry Sichting SP Portland Trail Blazers	.20	.10	.02
☐ 158 Pat Cummings SP Miami Heat	.20	.10	.02
☐ 159 Patrick Ewing AS New York Knicks	.20	.10	.02
☐ 160 Mark Price Cleveland Cavaliers	.40	.20	.04
☐ 161 Jerry Reynolds CO Sacramento Kings	.03	.01	.00
☐ 162 Ken Norman Los Angeles Clippers	.30	.15	.03
☐ 163 John Bagley SP UER New Jersey Nets (Picked in '83, should say '82)	.25	.12	.02
☐ 164 Christian Welp SP Philadelphia 76ers	.25	.12	.02
☐ 165 Reggie Theus SP Atlanta Hawks	.25	.12	.02
☐ 166 Magic Johnson AS Los Angeles Lakers	.75	.35	.07
☐ 167 John Long UER Detroit Pistons (Picked in '79, should say '78)	.03	.01	.00
☐ 168 Larry Smith SP Golden State Warriors	.20	.10	.02
☐ 169 Charles Shackleford New Jersey Nets	.10	.05	.01
☐ 170 Tom Chambers Phoenix Suns	.12	.06	.01
☐ 171A John MacLeod CO SP Dallas Mavericks ERR (NBA logo in wrong place)	.30	.15	.03
☐ 171B John MacLeod CO Dallas Mavericks COR (Second series)	.06	.03	.00
☐ 172 Ron Rothstein CO Miami Heat	.03	.01	.00
☐ 173 Joe Wolf Los Angeles Clippers	.08	.04	.01
☐ 174 Mark Eaton AS Utah Jazz	.03	.01	.00
☐ 175 Jon Sundvold Miami Heat	.03	.01	.00
☐ 176 Scott Hastings SP Miami Heat	.20	.10	.02
☐ 177 Isiah Thomas AS Detroit Pistons	.12	.06	.01
☐ 178 Hakeem Olajuwon AS Houston Rockets	.15	.07	.01
☐ 179 Mike Fratello CO Atlanta Hawks	.03	.01	.00
☐ 180 Hakeem Olajuwon Houston Rockets	.35	.17	.03
☐ 181 Randolph Keys Cleveland Cavaliers	.08	.04	.01
☐ 182 Richard Anderson UER Portland Trail Blazers (Trail Blazers on front should be all caps)	.03	.01	.00
☐ 183 Dan Majerle Phoenix Suns	.75	.35	.07
☐ 184 Derek Harper Dallas Mavericks	.08	.04	.01
☐ 185 Robert Parish Boston Celtics	.20	.10	.02
☐ 186 Ricky Berry SP Sacramento Kings	.20	.10	.02
☐ 187 Michael Cooper Los Angeles Lakers	.08	.04	.01
☐ 188 Vinnie Johnson Detroit Pistons	.06	.03	.00
☐ 189 James Donaldson Dallas Mavericks	.03	.01	.00
☐ 190 Clyde Drexler UER Portland Trail Blazers (4th pick, should be 14th)	.50	.25	.05
☐ 191 Jay Vincent SP San Antonio Spurs	.20	.10	.02
☐ 192 Nate McMillan Seattle Supersonics	.03	.01	.00
☐ 193 Kevin Duckworth AS Portland Trail Blazers	.06	.03	.00
☐ 194 Ledell Eackles Washington Bullets	.25	.12	.02
☐ 195 Eddie Johnson Phoenix Suns	.06	.03	.00
☐ 196 Terry Teagle Golden State Warriors	.06	.03	.00
☐ 197 Tom Chambers AS Phoenix Suns	.08	.04	.01
☐ 198 Joe Barry Carroll	.03	.01	.00

New Jersey Nets			
☐ 199 Dennis Hopson	.12	.06	.01
New Jersey Nets			
☐ 200 Michael Jordan	2.50	1.25	.25
Chicago Bulls			
☐ 201 Jerome Lane	.10	.05	.01
Denver Nuggets			
☐ 202 Greg Kite	.06	.03	.00
Charlotte Hornets			
☐ 203 David Rivers SP	.25	.12	.02
Los Angeles Lakers			
☐ 204 Sylvester Gray	.08	.04	.01
Miami Heat			
☐ 205 Ron Harper	.12	.06	.01
Cleveland Cavaliers			
☐ 206 Frank Brickowski	.03	.01	.00
San Antonio Spurs			
☐ 207 Rory Sparrow	.03	.01	.00
Miami Heat			
☐ 208 Gerald Henderson	.03	.01	.00
Philadelphia 76ers			
☐ 209 Rod Higgins UER	.03	.01	.00
Golden State Warriors ('85-86 stats should also include San Antonio and Seattle)			
☐ 210 James Worthy	.25	.12	.02
Los Angeles Lakers			
☐ 211 Dennis Rodman	.40	.20	.04
Detroit Pistons			
☐ 212 Ricky Pierce	.15	.07	.01
Milwaukee Bucks			
☐ 213 Charles Oakley	.08	.04	.01
New York Knicks			
☐ 214 Steve Colter	.03	.01	.00
Washington Bullets			
☐ 215 Danny Ainge	.10	.05	.01
Sacramento Kings			
☐ 216 Lenny Wilkens CO UER	.08	.04	.01
Cleveland Cavaliers (No NBA logo on back in bottom right)			
☐ 217 Larry Nance AS	.08	.04	.01
Cleveland Cavaliers			
☐ 218 Muggsy Bogues	.06	.03	.00
Charlotte Hornets			
☐ 219 James Worthy AS	.12	.06	.01
Los Angeles Lakers			
☐ 220 Lafayette Lever	.06	.03	.00
Denver Nuggets			
☐ 221 Quintin Dailey SP	.20	.10	.02
Los Angeles Clippers			
☐ 222 Lester Conner	.03	.01	.00
New Jersey Nets			
☐ 223 Jose Ortiz	.10	.05	.01
Utah Jazz			
☐ 224 Micheal Williams SP	1.00	.50	.10
Detroit Pistons UER (Misspelled Michael on card)			
☐ 225 Wayman Tisdale	.10	.05	.01
Sacramento Kings			
☐ 226 Mike Sanders SP	.20	.10	.02
Cleveland Cavaliers			
☐ 227 Jim Farmer SP	.25	.12	.02
Utah Jazz			
☐ 228 Mark West	.03	.01	.00
Phoenix Suns			
☐ 229 Jeff Hornacek	.75	.35	.07
Phoenix Suns			
☐ 230 Chris Mullin AS	.20	.10	.02
Golden State Warriors			
☐ 231 Vern Fleming	.06	.03	.00
Indiana Pacers			
☐ 232 Kenny Smith	.10	.05	.01
Sacramento Kings			
☐ 233 Derrick McKey	.15	.07	.01
Seattle Supersonics			
☐ 234 Dominique Wilkins AS	.15	.07	.01
Atlanta Hawks			
☐ 235 Willie Anderson	.30	.15	.03
San Antonio Spurs			
☐ 236 Keith Lee SP	.25	.12	.02
New Jersey Nets			
☐ 237 Buck Johnson	.15	.07	.01
Houston Rockets			
☐ 238 Randy Wittman	.03	.01	.00
Indiana Pacers			
☐ 239 Terry Catledge SP	.20	.10	.02
Washington Bullets			
☐ 240 Bernard King	.10	.05	.01
Washington Bullets			
☐ 241 Darrell Griffith	.03	.01	.00
Utah Jazz			
☐ 242 Horace Grant	.50	.25	.05
Chicago Bulls			
☐ 243 Rony Seikaly	.75	.35	.07
Miami Heat			
☐ 244 Scottie Pippen	2.50	1.25	.25
Chicago Bulls			
☐ 245 Michael Cage UER	.03	.01	.00
Seattle Supersonics (Picked in '85, should say '84)			
☐ 246 Kurt Rambis	.06	.03	.00
Charlotte Hornets			
☐ 247 Morlon Wiley SP	.25	.12	.02
Dallas Mavericks			
☐ 248 Ronnie Grandison	.08	.04	.01
Boston Celtics			
☐ 249 Scott Skiles SP	.75	.35	.07
Indiana Pacers			
☐ 250 Isiah Thomas	.30	.15	.03
Detroit Pistons			
☐ 251 Thurl Bailey	.03	.01	.00
Utah Jazz			
☐ 252 Doc Rivers	.06	.03	.00
Atlanta Hawks			
☐ 253 Stuart Gray SP	.20	.10	.02
Indiana Pacers			
☐ 254 John Williams	.06	.03	.00
Washington Bullets			
☐ 255 Bill Cartwright	.06	.03	.00
Chicago Bulls			
☐ 256 Terry Cummings AS	.06	.03	.00
Milwaukee Bucks			
☐ 257 Rodney McCray	.06	.03	.00
Sacramento Kings			
☐ 258 Larry Krystkowiak	.10	.05	.01
Milwaukee Bucks			
☐ 259 Will Perdue	.40	.20	.04
Chicago Bulls			
☐ 260 Mitch Richmond	1.25	.60	.12
Golden State Warriors			
☐ 261 Blair Rasmussen	.03	.01	.00
Denver Nuggets			
☐ 262 Charles Smith	.60	.30	.06
Los Angeles Clippers			
☐ 263 Tyrone Corbin SP	.40	.20	.04
Phoenix Suns			
☐ 264 Kelvin Upshaw	.08	.04	.01
Boston Celtics			
☐ 265 Otis Thorpe	.20	.10	.02
Houston Rockets			
☐ 266 Phil Jackson CO	.06	.03	.00
Chicago Bulls			
☐ 267 Jerry Sloan CO	.03	.01	.00
Utah Jazz			
☐ 268 John Shasky	.08	.04	.01
Miami Heat			
☐ 269A B. Bickerstaff CO SP	.30	.15	.03
Seattle Supersonics ERR (Born 2/11/44)			
☐ 269B B. Bickerstaff CO	.08	.04	.01
Seattle Supersonics COR (Second series; Born 11/2/43)			
☐ 270 Magic Johnson	1.50	.75	.15
Los Angeles Lakers			
☐ 271 Vernon Maxwell	.30	.15	.03
San Antonio Spurs			
☐ 272 Tim McCormick	.03	.01	.00
Houston Rockets			
☐ 273 Don Nelson CO	.03	.01	.00
Golden State Warriors			
☐ 274 Gary Grant	.15	.07	.01
Los Angeles Clippers			
☐ 275 Sidney Moncrief SP	.30	.15	.03
Milwaukee Bucks			
☐ 276 Roy Hinson	.03	.01	.00
New Jersey Nets			
☐ 277 Jimmy Rodgers CO	.03	.01	.00
Boston Celtics			
☐ 278 Antoine Carr	.06	.03	.00
Atlanta Hawks			
☐ 279A Orlando Woolridge SP	.30	.15	.03
Los Angeles Lakers ERR (No Trademark)			
☐ 279B Orlando Woolridge	.08	.04	.01
Los Angeles Lakers COR (Second series)			
☐ 280 Kevin McHale	.15	.07	.01
Boston Celtics			
☐ 281 LaSalle Thompson	.03	.01	.00
Indiana Pacers			
☐ 282 Detlef Schrempf	.30	.15	.03
Indiana Pacers			
☐ 283 Doug Moe CO	.03	.01	.00

	No.	Player / Team	MINT	EXC	G-VG
		Denver Nuggets			
☐	284A	James Edwards Detroit Pistons (Small black line next to card number)	.30	.15	.03
☐	284B	James Edwards Detroit Pistons (No small black line)	.06	.03	.00
☐	285	Jerome Kersey Portland Trail Blazers	.30	.15	.03
☐	286	Sam Perkins Dallas Mavericks	.15	.07	.01
☐	287	Sedale Threatt Seattle Supersonics	.08	.04	.01
☐	288	Tim Kempton SP Charlotte Hornets	.25	.12	.02
☐	289	Mark McNamara Los Angeles Lakers	.03	.01	.00
☐	290	Moses Malone Atlanta Hawks	.15	.07	.01
☐	291	Rick Adelman CO UER Portland Trail Blazers (Chemekata misspelled as Chemketa)	.06	.03	.00
☐	292	Dick Versace CO Indiana Pacers	.03	.01	.00
☐	293	Alton Lister SP Seattle Supersonics	.20	.10	.02
☐	294	Winston Garland Golden State Warriors	.03	.01	.00
☐	295	Kiki Vandeweghe New York Knicks	.06	.03	.00
☐	296	Brad Davis Dallas Mavericks	.03	.01	.00
☐	297	John Stockton AS Utah Jazz	.20	.10	.02
☐	298	Jay Humphries Milwaukee Bucks	.06	.03	.00
☐	299	Dell Curry Charlotte Hornets	.06	.03	.00
☐	300	Mark Jackson New York Knicks	.12	.06	.01

1989-90 Hoops II

The design of the cards in the 53-card Hoops II set is identical to that of the first series. This set features the expansion teams (Minnesota and Orlando), traded players, a special NBA Championship card of the Detroit Pistons, and a David Robinson In Action card. The cards are standard size (2 1/2" by 3 1/2") and numbered on the back in continuation of the first series. Cards numbered 301, 305, 307, 308, 318, 322, 328, 339, and 343 all have basketball misspelled as baasketball on the bottom of the card back. The key rookie in this set is Kevin Gamble. Since the original card number 353 Detroit Pistons World Champs was so difficult for collectors to find in packs, Hoops produced another edition of the card that was available direct from the company for free with additional copies available for only 35 cents per card.

	MINT	EXC	G-VG
COMPLETE SET (53)	6.00	3.00	.60
COMMON PLAYER (301-352)	.05	.02	.00

	No.	Player / Team	MINT	EXC	G-VG
☐	301	Morlon Wiley Orlando Magic	.08	.04	.01
☐	302	Reggie Theus Orlando Magic	.08	.04	.01
☐	303	Otis Smith Orlando Magic	.08	.04	.01
☐	304	Tod Murphy Minnesota Timberwolves	.10	.05	.01
☐	305	Sidney Green Orlando Magic	.05	.02	.00
☐	306	Shelton Jones Milwaukee Bucks	.08	.04	.01
☐	307	Mark Acres Orlando Magic	.05	.02	.00
☐	308	Terry Catledge Orlando Magic	.08	.04	.01
☐	309	Larry Smith Houston Rockets	.05	.02	.00
☐	310	David Robinson IA San Antonio Spurs	5.00	2.50	.50
☐	311	Johnny Dawkins Philadelphia 76ers	.08	.04	.01
☐	312	Terry Cummings San Antonio Spurs	.15	.07	.01
☐	313	Sidney Lowe Minnesota Timberwolves	.05	.02	.00
☐	314	Bill Musselman CO Minnesota Timberwolves	.05	.02	.00
☐	315	Buck Williams UER Portland Trail Blazers (Won ROY in '81, should say '82)	.15	.07	.01
☐	316	Mel Turpin Washington Bullets	.05	.02	.00
☐	317	Scott Hastings Detroit Pistons	.05	.02	.00
☐	318	Scott Skiles Orlando Magic	.20	.10	.02
☐	319	Tyrone Corbin Minnesota Timberwolves	.12	.06	.01
☐	320	Maurice Cheeks San Antonio Spurs	.08	.04	.01
☐	321	Matt Goukas CO Orlando Magic	.05	.02	.00
☐	322	Jeff Turner Orlando Magic	.08	.04	.01
☐	323	David Wingate San Antonio Spurs	.05	.02	.00
☐	324	Steve Johnson Minnesota Timberwolves	.05	.02	.00
☐	325	Alton Lister Golden State Warriors	.05	.02	.00
☐	326	Ken Bannister Los Angeles Clippers	.08	.04	.01
☐	327	Bill Fitch CO UER New Jersey Nets (Copyright missing on bottom of back)	.05	.02	.00
☐	328	Sam Vincent Orlando Magic	.08	.04	.01
☐	329	Larry Drew Los Angeles Lakers	.05	.02	.00
☐	330	Rick Mahorn Minnesota Timberwolves	.08	.04	.01
☐	331	Christian Welp San Antonio Spurs	.05	.02	.00
☐	332	Brad Lohaus Minnesota Timberwolves	.08	.04	.01
☐	333	Frank Johnson Orlando Magic	.05	.02	.00
☐	334	Jim Farmer Minnesota Timberwolves	.08	.04	.01
☐	335	Wayne Cooper Portland Trail Blazers	.05	.02	.00
☐	336	Mike Brown Utah Jazz	.12	.06	.01
☐	337	Sam Bowie New Jersey Nets	.10	.05	.01
☐	338	Kevin Gamble Boston Celtics	.50	.25	.05
☐	339	Jerry Ice Reynolds Orlando Magic	.15	.07	.01
☐	340	Mike Sanders Indiana Pacers	.08	.04	.01
☐	341	Bill Jones UER New Jersey Nets (Center on front, should be F)	.08	.04	.01
☐	342	Greg Anderson Milwaukee Bucks	.08	.04	.01
☐	343	Dave Corzine Orlando Magic	.05	.02	.00
☐	344	Micheal Williams UER Phoenix Suns	.35	.17	.03

Card	MINT	EXC	G-VG
(Misspelled Michael on card)			
☐ 345 Jay Vincent .... Philadelphia 76ers	.05	.02	.00
☐ 346 David Rivers .... Minnesota Timberwolves	.08	.04	.01
☐ 347 Caldwell Jones UER .... San Antonio Spurs (He was not starting center on '83 Sixers)	.08	.04	.01
☐ 348 Brad Sellers .... Seattle Supersonics	.05	.02	.00
☐ 349 Scott Roth .... Minnesota Timberwolves	.08	.04	.01
☐ 350 Alvin Robertson .... Milwaukee Bucks	.08	.04	.01
☐ 351 Steve Kerr .... Cleveland Cavaliers	.20	.10	.02
☐ 352 Stuart Gray .... Charlotte Hornets	.05	.02	.00
☐ 353A World Champions SP .... Detroit Pistons	7.50	3.75	.75
☐ 353B World Champions UER .... Detroit Pistons (George Blaha misspelled Blanha)	.40	.20	.04

1990 Hoops 100 Superstars

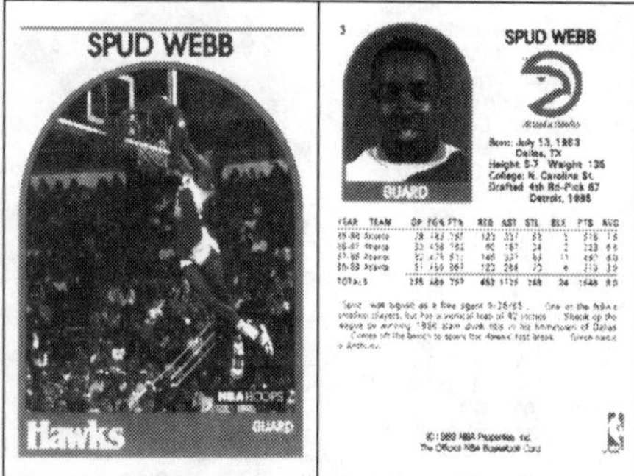

This 100-card set is a partial remake of the 1989-90 Hoops set, still measuring the standard size (2 1/2" by 3 1/2"). The pictures used are the same. The backs have a head shot in the same format as the front, as well as biographical and statistical information (only up through the 1988-89 season) on a pale yellow background. However, they differ from the Hoops issue in the yellow coloring on the card fronts and a new card numbering system. The cards are numbered on the back and arranged alphabetically according to teams as follows: Atlanta Hawks (1-4), Boston Celtics (5-8), Charlotte Hornets (9-11), Chicago Bulls (12-15), Cleveland Cavaliers (16-19), Dallas Mavericks (20-23), Denver Nuggets (24-26), Detroit Pistons (27-30), Golden State Warriors (31-34), Houston Rockets (35-38), Indiana Pacers (39-42), Los Angeles Clippers (43-46), Los Angeles Lakers (47-50), Miami Heat (51-53), Milwaukee Bucks (54-57), Minnesota Timberwolves (58-60), New Jersey Nets (61-63), New York Knicks (64-67), Orlando Magic (68-70), Philadelphia 76ers (71-74), Phoenix Suns (75-78), Portland Trail Blazers (79-82), Sacramento Kings (83-85), San Antonio Spurs (86-88), Seattle Supersonics (89-92), Utah Jazz (93-96), and Washington Bullets (97-100). This set was primarily sold through the Sears catalog.

	MINT	EXC	G-VG
COMPLETE SET (100)	15.00	7.50	1.50
COMMON PLAYER (1-100)	.05	.02	.00
☐ 1 Doc Rivers	.10	.05	.01
☐ 2 Dominique Wilkins	.35	.17	.03
☐ 3 Spud Webb	.10	.05	.01
☐ 4 Moses Malone	.20	.10	.02
☐ 5 Reggie Lewis	.90	.45	.09
☐ 6 Larry Bird	1.00	.50	.10
☐ 7 Kevin McHale	.12	.06	.01
☐ 8 Robert Parish	.15	.07	.01
☐ 9 Muggsy Bogues	.05	.02	.00
☐ 10 Rex Chapman	.30	.15	.03
☐ 11 Kelly Tripucka	.05	.02	.00
☐ 12 Michael Jordan	3.50	1.75	.35
☐ 13 Scottie Pippen	.90	.45	.09
☐ 14 John Paxson	.12	.06	.01
☐ 15 Bill Cartwright	.08	.04	.01
☐ 16 Mark Price	.25	.12	.02
☐ 17 Larry Nance	.15	.07	.01
☐ 18 Hot Rod Williams	.12	.06	.01
☐ 19 Brad Daugherty	.25	.12	.02
☐ 20 Derek Harper	.10	.05	.01
☐ 21 Rolando Blackman	.15	.07	.01
☐ 22 Sam Perkins	.15	.07	.01
☐ 23 James Donaldson	.05	.02	.00
☐ 24 Michael Adams	.12	.06	.01
☐ 25 Lafayette Lever	.08	.04	.01
☐ 26 Alex English	.10	.05	.01
☐ 27 Isiah Thomas	.35	.17	.03
☐ 28 Joe Dumars	.25	.12	.02
☐ 29 Bill Laimbeer	.08	.04	.01
☐ 30 Dennis Rodman	.25	.12	.02
☐ 31 Mitch Richmond	1.00	.50	.10
☐ 32 Chris Mullin	.45	.22	.04
☐ 33 Manute Bol	.05	.02	.00
☐ 34 Rod Higgins	.05	.02	.00
☐ 35 Eric Floyd	.08	.04	.01
☐ 36 Otis Thorpe	.10	.05	.01
☐ 37 Buck Johnson	.08	.04	.01
☐ 38 Hakeem Olajuwon	.35	.17	.03
☐ 39 Vern Fleming	.08	.04	.01
☐ 40 Reggie Miller	.40	.20	.04
☐ 41 Chuck Person	.20	.10	.02
☐ 42 Rik Smits	.10	.05	.01
☐ 43 Benoit Benjamin	.08	.04	.01
☐ 44 Charles Smith	.35	.17	.03
☐ 45 Gary Grant	.10	.05	.01
☐ 46 Danny Manning	.75	.35	.07
☐ 47 Magic Johnson	1.50	.75	.15
☐ 48 Byron Scott	.12	.06	.01
☐ 49 A.C. Green	.10	.05	.01
☐ 50 James Worthy	.30	.15	.03
☐ 51 Kevin Edwards	.10	.05	.01
☐ 52 Rory Sparrow	.05	.02	.00
☐ 53 Rony Seikaly	.25	.12	.02
☐ 54 Jay Humphries	.08	.04	.01
☐ 55 Alvin Robertson	.10	.05	.01
☐ 56 Ricky Pierce	.12	.06	.01
☐ 57 Jack Sikma	.10	.05	.01
☐ 58 Tyrone Corbin	.08	.04	.01
☐ 59 Sidney Lowe	.05	.02	.00
☐ 60 Steve Johnson	.05	.02	.00
☐ 61 Dennis Hopson	.08	.04	.01
☐ 62 Chris Morris	.15	.07	.01
☐ 63 Roy Hinson	.05	.02	.00
☐ 64 Mark Jackson	.10	.05	.01
☐ 65 Gerald Wilkins	.08	.04	.01
☐ 66 Charles Oakley	.08	.04	.01
☐ 67 Patrick Ewing	.75	.35	.07
☐ 68 Reggie Theus	.08	.04	.01
☐ 69 Sam Vincent	.05	.02	.00
☐ 70 Terry Catledge	.08	.04	.01
☐ 71 Hersey Hawkins	.45	.22	.04
☐ 72 Johnny Dawkins	.10	.05	.01
☐ 73 Charles Barkley	.50	.25	.05
☐ 74 Mike Gminski	.08	.04	.01
☐ 75 Kevin Johnson	.90	.45	.09
☐ 76 Jeff Hornacek	.40	.20	.04
☐ 77 Tom Chambers	.20	.10	.02
☐ 78 Eddie Johnson	.10	.05	.01
☐ 79 Terry Porter	.25	.12	.02
☐ 80 Clyde Drexler	.60	.30	.06
☐ 81 Jerome Kersey	.20	.10	.02
☐ 82 Kevin Duckworth	.08	.04	.01
☐ 83 Danny Ainge	.15	.07	.01
☐ 84 Rodney McCray	.08	.04	.01
☐ 85 Wayman Tisdale	.15	.07	.01
☐ 86 Willie Anderson	.30	.15	.03
☐ 87 Terry Cummings	.15	.07	.01
☐ 88 David Robinson	3.00	1.50	.30
☐ 89 Dale Ellis	.08	.04	.01
☐ 90 Derrick McKey	.10	.05	.01
☐ 91 Xavier McDaniel	.15	.07	.01
☐ 92 Michael Cage	.05	.02	.00
☐ 93 John Stockton	.50	.25	.05
☐ 94 Karl Malone	.50	.25	.05
☐ 95 Thurl Bailey	.08	.04	.01
☐ 96 Mark Eaton	.08	.04	.01
☐ 97 Jeff Malone	.15	.07	.01
☐ 98 Darrell Walker	.05	.02	.00

☐ 99 Bernard King	.12	.06	.01
☐ 100 John Williams	.08	.04	.01

1990-91 Hoops I

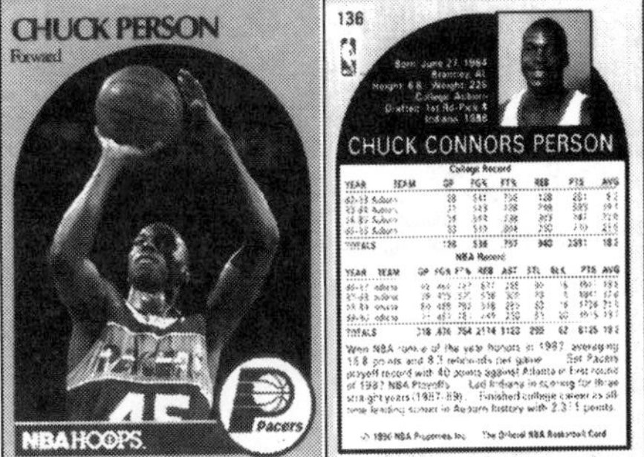

The 1990-91 Hoops basketball set contains 336 cards measuring the standard size (2 1/2" by 3 1/2). On the front the color action player photo appears in the shape of a basketball lane, bordered by gold on the All-Star cards (1-26) and by silver on the regular issues (27-331, 336). The player's name and the stripe below the picture are printed in one of the team's colors. The team logo at the lower right corner rounds out the card face. The back of the regular issue has a color head shot and biographical information as well as college and pro statistics, framed by a basketball lane. The cards are numbered on the back and arranged alphabetically according to teams as follows: Atlanta Hawks (27-37), Boston Celtics (38-48), Charlotte Hornets (49-59), Chicago Bulls (60-69), Cleveland Cavaliers (70-80), Dallas Mavericks (81-90), Denver Nuggets (91-100), Detroit Pistons (101-111), Golden State Warriors (112-122), Houston Rockets (123-131), Indiana Pacers (132-141), Los Angeles Clippers (142-152), Los Angeles Lakers (153-163), Miami Heat (164-172), Milwaukee Bucks (173-183), Minnesota Timberwolves (184-192), New Jersey Nets (193-201), New York Knicks (202-212), Orlando Magic (213-223), Philadelphia 76ers (224-232), Phoenix Suns (233-242), Portland Trail Blazers (243-252), Sacramento Kings (253-262), San Antonio Spurs (263-273), Seattle Supersonics (274-284), Utah Jazz (285-294), and Washington Bullets (295-304). The coaches cards number 305-331. Some of the All-Star cards (card numbers 2, 6, and 8) can be found with or without a printing mistake, i.e., no T in the the trademark logo on the card back. A few of the cards (card numbers 14, 66, 144, and 279) refer to the player as "all America" rather than "All America". The following cards can be found with or without a black line under the card number, height, and birthplace: 20, 23, 24, 29, and 87. Rookie Cards included in this set are Nick Anderson, B.J. Armstrong, Vlade Divac, Sherman Douglas, Sean Elliott, Pervis Ellison, Danny Ferry, Tim Hardaway, Shawn Kemp, Sarunas Marciulionis, Drazen Petrovic, Glen Rice, Pooh Richardson, and Cliff Robinson.

	MINT	EXC	G-VG
COMPLETE SET (336)	8.00	4.00	.80
COMMON PLAYER (1-336)	.03	.01	.00
COMMON AS PLAYER (1-26)	.06	.03	.00
COMMON PLAYER SP	.06	.03	.00
☐ 1 Charles Barkley AS SP Philadelphia 76ers	.25	.12	.02
☐ 2 Larry Bird AS SP Boston Celtics	.30	.15	.03
☐ 3 Joe Dumars AS SP Detroit Pistons	.12	.06	.01
☐ 4 Patrick Ewing AS SP New York Knicks (A-S blocks listed as 1, should be 5) UER	.30	.15	.03
☐ 5 Michael Jordan AS SP Chicago Bulls (Won Slam Dunk in '87 and '88, not '86 and '88) UER	1.25	.60	.12
☐ 6 Kevin McHale AS SP Boston Celtics	.10	.05	.01
☐ 7 Reggie Miller AS SP Indiana Pacers	.12	.06	.01
☐ 8 Robert Parish AS SP Boston Celtics	.12	.06	.01
☐ 9 Scottie Pippen AS SP Chicago Bulls	.40	.20	.04
☐ 10 Dennis Rodman AS SP Detroit Pistons	.12	.06	.01
☐ 11 Isiah Thomas AS SP Detroit Pistons	.15	.07	.01
☐ 12 Dominique Wilkins AS SP Atlanta Hawks	.15	.07	.01
☐ 13A All-Star Checklist SP ERR (No card number)	.40	.20	.04
☐ 13B All-Star Checklist SP COR (Card number on back)	.10	.05	.01
☐ 14 Rolando Blackman AS SP Dallas Mavericks	.08	.04	.01
☐ 15 Tom Chambers AS SP Phoenix Suns	.08	.04	.01
☐ 16 Clyde Drexler AS SP Portland Trail Blazers	.30	.15	.03
☐ 17 A.C. Green AS SP Los Angeles Lakers	.06	.03	.00
☐ 18 Magic Johnson AS SP Los Angeles Lakers	.75	.35	.07
☐ 19 Kevin Johnson AS SP Phoenix Suns	.25	.12	.02
☐ 20 Lafayette Lever AS SP Denver Nuggets	.06	.03	.00
☐ 21 Karl Malone AS SP Utah Jazz	.25	.12	.02
☐ 22 Chris Mullin AS SP Golden State Warriors	.25	.12	.02
☐ 23 Hakeem Olajuwon AS SP Houston Rockets	.20	.10	.02
☐ 24 David Robinson AS SP San Antonio Spurs	1.00	.50	.10
☐ 25 John Stockton AS SP Utah Jazz	.25	.12	.02
☐ 26 James Worthy AS SP Los Angeles Lakers	.12	.06	.01
☐ 27 John Battle Atlanta Hawks	.03	.01	.00
☐ 28 Jon Koncak Atlanta Hawks	.03	.01	.00
☐ 29 Cliff Levingston SP Atlanta Hawks	.06	.03	.00
☐ 30 John Long SP Atlanta Hawks	.06	.03	.00
☐ 31 Moses Malone Atlanta Hawks	.12	.06	.01
☐ 32 Doc Rivers Atlanta Hawks	.06	.03	.00
☐ 33 Kenny Smith SP Atlanta Hawks	.06	.03	.00
☐ 34 Alexander Volkov Atlanta Hawks	.12	.06	.01
☐ 35 Spud Webb Atlanta Hawks	.06	.03	.00
☐ 36 Dominique Wilkins Atlanta Hawks	.15	.07	.01
☐ 37 Kevin Willis Atlanta Hawks	.10	.05	.01
☐ 38 John Bagley Boston Celtics	.06	.03	.00
☐ 39 Larry Bird Boston Celtics	.35	.17	.03
☐ 40 Kevin Gamble Boston Celtics	.10	.05	.01
☐ 41 Dennis Johnson SP Boston Celtics	.10	.05	.01
☐ 42 Joe Kleine Boston Celtics	.03	.01	.00
☐ 43 Reggie Lewis Boston Celtics	.25	.12	.02
☐ 44 Kevin McHale Boston Celtics	.10	.05	.01
☐ 45 Robert Parish Boston Celtics	.12	.06	.01
☐ 46 Jim Paxson SP Boston Celtics	.06	.03	.00
☐ 47 Ed Pinckney Boston Celtics	.03	.01	.00
☐ 48 Brian Shaw Boston Celtics	.08	.04	.01

☐ 49 Richard Anderson SP .... .06 .03 .00
Charlotte Hornets
☐ 50 Muggsy Bogues .... .03 .01 .00
Charlotte Hornets
☐ 51 Rex Chapman .... .06 .03 .00
Charlotte Hornets
☐ 52 Dell Curry .... .03 .01 .00
Charlotte Hornets
☐ 53 Kenny Gattison .... .20 .10 .02
Charlotte Hornets
☐ 54 Armon Gilliam .... .03 .01 .00
Charlotte Hornets
☐ 55 Dave Hoppen .... .03 .01 .00
Charlotte Hornets
☐ 56 Randolph Keys .... .03 .01 .00
Charlotte Hornets
☐ 57 J.R. Reid .... .15 .07 .01
Charlotte Hornets
☐ 58 Robert Reid SP .... .06 .03 .00
Charlotte Hornets
☐ 59 Kelly Tripucka .... .03 .01 .00
Charlotte Hornets
☐ 60 B.J. Armstrong .... .40 .20 .04
Chicago Bulls
☐ 61 Bill Cartwright .... .06 .03 .00
Chicago Bulls
☐ 62 Charles Davis SP .... .06 .03 .00
Chicago Bulls
☐ 63 Horace Grant .... .20 .10 .02
Chicago Bulls
☐ 64 Craig Hodges .... .03 .01 .00
Chicago Bulls
☐ 65 Michael Jordan .... 1.50 .75 .15
Chicago Bulls
☐ 66 Stacey King .... .25 .12 .02
Chicago Bulls
☐ 67 John Paxson .... .08 .04 .01
Chicago Bulls
☐ 68 Will Perdue .... .06 .03 .00
Chicago Bulls
☐ 69 Scottie Pippen .... .60 .30 .06
Chicago Bulls
☐ 70 Winston Bennett .... .08 .04 .01
Cleveland Cavaliers
☐ 71 Chucky Brown .... .08 .04 .01
Cleveland Cavaliers
☐ 72 Derrick Chievous .... .03 .01 .00
Cleveland Cavaliers
☐ 73 Brad Daugherty .... .20 .10 .02
Cleveland Cavaliers
☐ 74 Craig Ehlo .... .06 .03 .00
Cleveland Cavaliers
☐ 75 Steve Kerr .... .03 .01 .00
Cleveland Cavaliers
☐ 76 Paul Mokeski SP .... .06 .03 .00
Cleveland Cavaliers
☐ 77 John Morton .... .08 .04 .01
Cleveland Cavaliers
☐ 78 Larry Nance .... .10 .05 .01
Cleveland Cavaliers
☐ 79 Mark Price .... .20 .10 .02
Cleveland Cavaliers
☐ 80 Hot Rod Williams .... .08 .04 .01
Cleveland Cavaliers
☐ 81 Steve Alford .... .06 .03 .00
Dallas Mavericks
☐ 82 Rolando Blackman .... .08 .04 .01
Dallas Mavericks
☐ 83 Adrian Dantley SP .... .10 .05 .01
Dallas Mavericks
☐ 84 Brad Davis .... .03 .01 .00
Dallas Mavericks
☐ 85 James Donaldson .... .03 .01 .00
Dallas Mavericks
☐ 86 Derek Harper .... .06 .03 .00
Dallas Mavericks
☐ 87 Sam Perkins SP .... .12 .06 .01
Dallas Mavericks
☐ 88 Roy Tarpley .... .06 .03 .00
Dallas Mavericks
☐ 89 Bill Wennington SP .... .06 .03 .00
Dallas Mavericks
☐ 90 Herb Williams .... .03 .01 .00
Dallas Mavericks
☐ 91 Michael Adams .... .08 .04 .01
Denver Nuggets
☐ 92 Joe Barry Carroll SP .... .08 .04 .01
Denver Nuggets
☐ 93 Walter Davis UER .... .06 .03 .00
Denver Nuggets
(Born NC, not PA)
☐ 94 Alex English SP .... .10 .05 .01
Denver Nuggets
☐ 95 Bill Hanzlik .... .03 .01 .00
Denver Nuggets
☐ 96 Jerome Lane .... .03 .01 .00
Denver Nuggets
☐ 97 Lafayette Lever SP .... .08 .04 .01
Denver Nuggets
☐ 98 Todd Lichti .... .10 .05 .01
Denver Nuggets
☐ 99 Blair Rasmussen .... .03 .01 .00
Denver Nuggets
☐ 100 Danny Schayes SP .... .06 .03 .00
Denver Nuggets
☐ 101 Mark Aguirre .... .06 .03 .00
Detroit Pistons
☐ 102 William Bedford .... .08 .04 .01
Detroit Pistons
☐ 103 Joe Dumars .... .12 .06 .01
Detroit Pistons
☐ 104 James Edwards .... .03 .01 .00
Detroit Pistons
☐ 105 Scott Hastings .... .03 .01 .00
Detroit Pistons
☐ 106 Gerald Henderson SP .... .06 .03 .00
Detroit Pistons
☐ 107 Vinnie Johnson .... .06 .03 .00
Detroit Pistons
☐ 108 Bill Laimbeer .... .08 .04 .01
Detroit Pistons
☐ 109 Dennis Rodman .... .20 .10 .02
Detroit Pistons
☐ 110 John Salley .... .06 .03 .00
Detroit Pistons
☐ 111 Isiah Thomas UER .... .15 .07 .01
Detroit Pistons
(No position listed
on the card)
☐ 112 Manute Bol SP .... .08 .04 .01
Golden State Warriors
☐ 113 Tim Hardaway .... 1.50 .75 .15
Golden State Warriors
☐ 114 Rod Higgins .... .03 .01 .00
Golden State Warriors
☐ 115 Sarunas Marciulionis .... .40 .20 .04
Golden State Warriors
☐ 116 Chris Mullin UER .... .25 .12 .02
Golden State Warriors
(Born Brooklyn, NY,
not New York, NY)
☐ 117 Jim Petersen .... .03 .01 .00
Golden State Warriors
☐ 118 Mitch Richmond .... .15 .07 .01
Golden State Warriors
☐ 119 Mike Smrek .... .10 .05 .01
Golden State Warriors
☐ 120 Terry Teagle SP .... .06 .03 .00
Golden State Warriors
☐ 121 Tom Tolbert .... .08 .04 .01
Golden State Warriors
☐ 122 Christian Welp SP .... .06 .03 .00
Golden State Warriors
☐ 123 Byron Dinkins SP .... .10 .05 .01
Houston Rockets
☐ 124 Eric(Sleepy) Floyd .... .06 .03 .00
Houston Rockets
☐ 125 Buck Johnson .... .06 .03 .00
Houston Rockets
☐ 126 Vernon Maxwell .... .06 .03 .00
Houston Rockets
☐ 127 Hakeem Olajuwon .... .25 .12 .02
Houston Rockets
☐ 128 Larry Smith .... .03 .01 .00
Houston Rockets
☐ 129 Otis Thorpe .... .06 .03 .00
Houston Rockets
☐ 130 Mitchell Wiggins SP .... .06 .03 .00
Houston Rockets
☐ 131 Mike Woodson .... .03 .01 .00
Houston Rockets
☐ 132 Greg Dreiling .... .08 .04 .01
Indiana Pacers
☐ 133 Vern Fleming .... .03 .01 .00
Indiana Pacers
☐ 134 Rickey Green SP .... .06 .03 .00
Indiana Pacers
☐ 135 Reggie Miller .... .20 .10 .02
Indiana Pacers
☐ 136 Chuck Person .... .08 .04 .01
Indiana Pacers
☐ 137 Mike Sanders .... .06 .03 .00
Indiana Pacers
☐ 138 Detlef Schrempf .... .10 .05 .01
Indiana Pacers
☐ 139 Rik Smits .... .08 .04 .01
Indiana Pacers
☐ 140 LaSalle Thompson .... .03 .01 .00

Indiana Pacers
☐ 141 Randy Wittman .03 .01 .00
Indiana Pacers
☐ 142 Benoit Benjamin .06 .03 .00
Los Angeles Clippers
☐ 143 Winston Garland .03 .01 .00
Los Angeles Clippers
☐ 144 Tom Garrick .03 .01 .00
Los Angeles Clippers
☐ 145 Gary Grant .03 .01 .00
Los Angeles Clippers
☐ 146 Ron Harper .06 .03 .00
Los Angeles Clippers
☐ 147 Danny Manning .15 .07 .01
Los Angeles Clippers
☐ 148 Jeff Martin .08 .04 .01
Los Angeles Clippers
☐ 149 Ken Norman .08 .04 .01
Los Angeles Clippers
☐ 150 David Rivers SP .06 .03 .00
Los Angeles Clippers
☐ 151 Charles Smith .12 .06 .01
Los Angeles Clippers
☐ 152 Joe Wolf SP .06 .03 .00
Los Angeles Clippers
☐ 153 Michael Cooper SP .10 .05 .01
Los Angeles Lakers
☐ 154 Vlade Divac UER .30 .15 .03
Los Angeles Lakers
(Height 6'11",
should be 7'1")
☐ 155 Larry Drew .03 .01 .00
Los Angeles Lakers
☐ 156 A.C. Green .06 .03 .00
Los Angeles Lakers
☐ 157 Magic Johnson .75 .35 .07
Los Angeles Lakers
☐ 158 Mark McNamara SP .06 .03 .00
Los Angeles Lakers
☐ 159 Byron Scott .06 .03 .00
Los Angeles Lakers
☐ 160 Mychal Thompson .03 .01 .00
Los Angeles Lakers
☐ 161 Jay Vincent SP .06 .03 .00
Los Angeles Lakers
☐ 162 Orlando Woolridge SP .08 .04 .01
Los Angeles Lakers
☐ 163 James Worthy .12 .06 .01
Los Angeles Lakers
☐ 164 Sherman Douglas .20 .10 .02
Miami Heat
☐ 165 Kevin Edwards .03 .01 .00
Miami Heat
☐ 166 Tellis Frank SP .10 .05 .01
Miami Heat
☐ 167 Grant Long .06 .03 .00
Miami Heat
☐ 168 Glen Rice .90 .45 .09
Miami Heat
☐ 169A Rony Seikaly .15 .07 .01
Miami Heat
(Athens)
☐ 169B Rony Seikaly .15 .07 .01
Miami Heat
(Beirut)
☐ 170 Rory Sparrow SP .06 .03 .00
Miami Heat
☐ 171A Jon Sundvold .06 .03 .00
Miami Heat
(First series)
☐ 171B Billy Thompson .06 .03 .00
Miami Heat
(Second series)
☐ 172A Billy Thompson .06 .03 .00
Miami Heat
(First series)
☐ 172B Jon Sundvold .06 .03 .00
Miami Heat
(Second series)
☐ 173 Greg Anderson .03 .01 .00
Milwaukee Bucks
☐ 174 Jeff Grayer .15 .07 .01
Milwaukee Bucks
☐ 175 Jay Humphries .03 .01 .00
Milwaukee Bucks
☐ 176 Frank Kornet .08 .04 .01
Milwaukee Bucks
☐ 177 Larry Krystkowiak .03 .01 .00
Milwaukee Bucks
☐ 178 Brad Lohaus .06 .03 .00
Milwaukee Bucks
☐ 179 Ricky Pierce .06 .03 .00
Milwaukee Bucks
☐ 180 Paul Pressey SP .06 .03 .00
Milwaukee Bucks
☐ 181 Fred Roberts .06 .03 .00
Milwaukee Bucks
☐ 182 Alvin Robertson .06 .03 .00
Milwaukee Bucks
☐ 183 Jack Sikma .06 .03 .00
Milwaukee Bucks
☐ 184 Randy Breuer .03 .01 .00
Minnesota Timberwolves
☐ 185 Tony Campbell .06 .03 .00
Minnesota Timberwolves
☐ 186 Tyrone Corbin .06 .03 .00
Minnesota Timberwolves
☐ 187 Sidney Lowe SP .06 .03 .00
Minnesota Timberwolves
☐ 188 Sam Mitchell .15 .07 .01
Minnesota Timberwolves
☐ 189 Tod Murphy .06 .03 .00
Minnesota Timberwolves
☐ 190 Pooh Richardson .35 .17 .03
Minnesota Timberwolves
☐ 191 Scott Roth SP .06 .03 .00
Minnesota Timberwolves
☐ 192 Brad Sellers SP .06 .03 .00
Minnesota Timberwolves
☐ 193 Mookie Blaylock .25 .12 .02
New Jersey Nets
☐ 194 Sam Bowie .06 .03 .00
New Jersey Nets
☐ 195 Lester Conner .03 .01 .00
New Jersey Nets
☐ 196 Derrick Gervin .08 .04 .01
New Jersey Nets
☐ 197 Jack Haley .08 .04 .01
New Jersey Nets
☐ 198 Roy Hinson .03 .01 .00
New Jersey Nets
☐ 199 Dennis Hopson SP .06 .03 .00
New Jersey Nets
☐ 200 Chris Morris .06 .03 .00
New Jersey Nets
☐ 201 Purvis Short SP .06 .03 .00
New Jersey Nets
☐ 202 Maurice Cheeks .08 .04 .01
New York Knicks
☐ 203 Patrick Ewing .30 .15 .03
New York Knicks
☐ 204 Stuart Gray .03 .01 .00
New York Knicks
☐ 205 Mark Jackson .06 .03 .00
New York Knicks
☐ 206 Johnny Newman SP .08 .04 .01
New York Knicks
☐ 207 Charles Oakley .06 .03 .00
New York Knicks
☐ 208 Trent Tucker .03 .01 .00
New York Knicks
☐ 209 Kiki Vandeweghe .06 .03 .00
New York Knicks
☐ 210 Kenny Walker .03 .01 .00
New York Knicks
☐ 211 Eddie Lee Wilkins .03 .01 .00
New York Knicks
☐ 212 Gerald Wilkins .06 .03 .00
New York Knicks
☐ 213 Mark Acres .03 .01 .00
Orlando Magic
☐ 214 Nick Anderson .50 .25 .05
Orlando Magic
☐ 215 Michael Ansley UER .08 .04 .01
Orlando Magic
(Ranked first, not third)
☐ 216 Terry Catledge .06 .03 .00
Orlando Magic
☐ 217 Dave Corzine SP .06 .03 .00
Orlando Magic
☐ 218 Sidney Green SP .06 .03 .00
Orlando Magic
☐ 219 Jerry Reynolds .03 .01 .00
Orlando Magic
☐ 220 Scott Skiles .08 .04 .01
Orlando Magic
☐ 221 Otis Smith .03 .01 .00
Orlando Magic
☐ 222 Reggie Theus SP .08 .04 .01
Orlando Magic
☐ 223A Sam Vincent .50 .25 .05
Orlando Magic
(First series, shows
12 Michael Jordan)
☐ 223B Sam Vincent .06 .03 .00
Orlando Magic
(Second series, shows
Sam dribbling)

☐ 224 Ron Anderson Philadelphia 76ers	.03	.01	.00
☐ 225 Charles Barkley Philadelphia 76ers	.25	.12	.02
☐ 226 Scott Brooks SP UER Philadelphia 76ers (Born French Camp, not Lathron, Cal.)	.06	.03	.00
☐ 227 Johnny Dawkins Philadelphia 76ers	.03	.01	.00
☐ 228 Mike Gminski Philadelphia 76ers	.03	.01	.00
☐ 229 Hersey Hawkins Philadelphia 76ers	.15	.07	.01
☐ 230 Rick Mahorn Philadelphia 76ers	.06	.03	.00
☐ 231 Derek Smith SP Philadelphia 76ers	.06	.03	.00
☐ 232 Bob Thornton Philadelphia 76ers	.08	.04	.01
☐ 233 Kenny Battle Phoenix Suns	.10	.05	.01
☐ 234A Tom Chambers Phoenix Suns (First series; Forward on front)	.10	.05	.01
☐ 234B Tom Chambers Phoenix Suns (Second series; Guard on front)	.10	.05	.01
☐ 235 Greg Grant SP Phoenix Suns	.10	.05	.01
☐ 236 Jeff Hornacek Phoenix Suns	.15	.07	.01
☐ 237 Eddie Johnson Phoenix Suns	.06	.03	.00
☐ 238A Kevin Johnson Phoenix Suns (First series; Guard on front)	.30	.15	.03
☐ 238B Kevin Johnson Phoenix Suns (Second series; Forward on front)	.30	.15	.03
☐ 239 Dan Majerle Phoenix Suns	.15	.07	.01
☐ 240 Tim Perry Phoenix Suns	.08	.04	.01
☐ 241 Kurt Rambis Phoenix Suns	.06	.03	.00
☐ 242 Mark West Phoenix Suns	.03	.01	.00
☐ 243 Mark Bryant Portland Trail Blazers	.03	.01	.00
☐ 244 Wayne Cooper Portland Trail Blazers	.03	.01	.00
☐ 245 Clyde Drexler Portland Trail Blazers	.30	.15	.03
☐ 246 Kevin Duckworth Portland Trail Blazers	.03	.01	.00
☐ 247 Jerome Kersey Portland Trail Blazers	.12	.06	.01
☐ 248 Drazen Petrovic Portland Trail Blazers	.50	.25	.05
☐ 249A Terry Porter ERR Portland Trail Blazers (No NBA symbol on back)	.50	.25	.05
☐ 249B Terry Porter COR Portland Trail Blazers	.15	.07	.01
☐ 250 Cliff Robinson Portland Trail Blazers	.40	.20	.04
☐ 251 Buck Williams Portland Trail Blazers	.10	.05	.01
☐ 252 Danny Young Portland Trail Blazers	.03	.01	.00
☐ 253 Danny Ainge SP UER Sacramento Kings (Middle name Ray misspelled as Rae on back)	.08	.04	.01
☐ 254 Randy Allen SP Sacramento Kings	.10	.05	.01
☐ 255 Antoine Carr Sacramento Kings	.06	.03	.00
☐ 256 Vinny Del Negro SP Sacramento Kings	.08	.04	.01
☐ 257 Pervis Ellison SP Sacramento Kings	.75	.35	.07
☐ 258 Greg Kite SP Sacramento Kings	.06	.03	.00
☐ 259 Rodney McCray SP Sacramento Kings	.08	.04	.01
☐ 260 Harold Pressley SP Sacramento Kings	.08	.04	.01
☐ 261 Ralph Sampson Sacramento Kings	.06	.03	.00
☐ 262 Wayman Tisdale Sacramento Kings	.08	.04	.01
☐ 263 Willie Anderson San Antonio Spurs	.08	.04	.01
☐ 264 Uwe Blab SP San Antonio Spurs	.06	.03	.00
☐ 265 Frank Brickowski SP San Antonio Spurs	.06	.03	.00
☐ 266 Terry Cummings San Antonio Spurs	.08	.04	.01
☐ 267 Sean Elliott San Antonio Spurs	.40	.20	.04
☐ 268 Caldwell Jones SP San Antonio Spurs	.06	.03	.00
☐ 269 Johnny Moore SP San Antonio Spurs	.06	.03	.00
☐ 270 David Robinson San Antonio Spurs	1.25	.60	.12
☐ 271 Rod Strickland San Antonio Spurs	.08	.04	.01
☐ 272 Reggie Williams San Antonio Spurs	.06	.03	.00
☐ 273 David Wingate SP San Antonio Spurs	.06	.03	.00
☐ 274 Dana Barros UER Seattle Supersonics (Born April, not March)	.20	.10	.02
☐ 275 Michael Cage UER Seattle Supersonics (Drafted '84, not '85)	.03	.01	.00
☐ 276 Quintin Dailey Seattle Supersonics	.03	.01	.00
☐ 277 Dale Ellis Seattle Supersonics	.06	.03	.00
☐ 278 Steve Johnson SP Seattle Supersonics	.06	.03	.00
☐ 279 Shawn Kemp Seattle Supersonics	1.50	.75	.15
☐ 280 Xavier McDaniel Seattle Supersonics	.10	.05	.01
☐ 281 Derrick McKey Seattle Supersonics	.06	.03	.00
☐ 282 Nate McMillan Seattle Supersonics	.03	.01	.00
☐ 283 Olden Polynice Seattle Supersonics	.03	.01	.00
☐ 284 Sedale Threatt Seattle Supersonics	.06	.03	.00
☐ 285 Thurl Bailey Utah Jazz	.06	.03	.00
☐ 286 Mike Brown Utah Jazz	.03	.01	.00
☐ 287 Mark Eaton UER Utah Jazz (72nd pick, not 82nd)	.06	.03	.00
☐ 288 Blue Edwards Utah Jazz	.20	.10	.02
☐ 289 Darrell Griffith Utah Jazz	.03	.01	.00
☐ 290 Robert Hansen SP Utah Jazz	.06	.03	.00
☐ 291 Eric Leckner SP Utah Jazz	.08	.04	.01
☐ 292 Karl Malone Utah Jazz	.25	.12	.02
☐ 293 Delaney Rudd Utah Jazz	.08	.04	.01
☐ 294 John Stockton Utah Jazz	.25	.12	.02
☐ 295 Mark Alarie Washington Bullets	.03	.01	.00
☐ 296 Ledell Eackles SP Washington Bullets	.10	.05	.01
☐ 297 Harvey Grant Washington Bullets	.06	.03	.00
☐ 298A Tom Hammonds Washington Bullets (No rookie logo on front)	.15	.07	.01
☐ 298B Tom Hammonds Washington Bullets (Rookie logo on front)	.15	.07	.01
☐ 299 Charles Jones Washington Bullets	.03	.01	.00
☐ 300 Bernard King Washington Bullets	.08	.04	.01
☐ 301 Jeff Malone SP Washington Bullets	.12	.06	.01
☐ 302 Mel Turpin SP Washington Bullets	.08	.04	.01
☐ 303 Darrell Walker Washington Bullets	.03	.01	.00
☐ 304 John Williams Washington Bullets	.03	.01	.00

Card	MINT	EXC	G-VG
☐ 305 Bob Weiss CO Atlanta Hawks	.03	.01	.00
☐ 306 Chris Ford CO Boston Celtics	.03	.01	.00
☐ 307 Gene Littles CO Charlotte Hornets	.03	.01	.00
☐ 308 Phil Jackson CO Chicago Bulls	.03	.01	.00
☐ 309 Lenny Wilkens CO Cleveland Cavaliers	.08	.04	.01
☐ 310 Richie Adubato CO Dallas Mavericks	.03	.01	.00
☐ 311 Doug Moe CO SP Denver Nuggets	.10	.05	.01
☐ 312 Chuck Daly CO Detroit Pistons	.06	.03	.00
☐ 313 Don Nelson CO Golden State Warriors	.03	.01	.00
☐ 314 Don Chaney CO Houston Rockets	.03	.01	.00
☐ 315 Dick Versace CO Indiana Pacers	.03	.01	.00
☐ 316 Mike Schuler CO Los Angeles Clippers	.03	.01	.00
☐ 317 Pat Riley CO SP Los Angeles Lakers	.10	.05	.01
☐ 318 Ron Rothstein CO Miami Heat	.03	.01	.00
☐ 319 Del Harris CO Milwaukee Bucks	.03	.01	.00
☐ 320 Bill Musselman CO Minnesota Timberwolves	.03	.01	.00
☐ 321 Bill Fitch CO New Jersey Nets	.03	.01	.00
☐ 322 Stu Jackson CO New York Knicks	.03	.01	.00
☐ 323 Matt Guokas CO Orlando Magic	.03	.01	.00
☐ 324 Jim Lynam CO Philadelphia 76ers	.03	.01	.00
☐ 325 Cotton Fitzsimmons CO Phoenix Suns	.03	.01	.00
☐ 326 Rick Adelman CO Portland Trail Blazers	.06	.03	.00
☐ 327 Dick Motta CO Sacramento Kings	.03	.01	.00
☐ 328 Larry Brown CO San Antonio Spurs	.03	.01	.00
☐ 329 K.C. Jones CO Seattle Supersonics	.08	.04	.01
☐ 330 Jerry Sloan CO Utah Jazz	.03	.01	.00
☐ 331 Wes Unseld CO Washington Bullets	.06	.03	.00
☐ 332 Checklist 1 SP	.08	.04	.01
☐ 333 Checklist 2 SP	.08	.04	.01
☐ 334 Checklist 3 SP	.08	.04	.01
☐ 335 Checklist 4 SP	.08	.04	.01
☐ 336 Danny Ferry SP Cleveland Cavaliers	.25	.12	.02
☐ NNO David Robinson and All-Rookie Team (No stats on back)	2.25	1.10	.22
☐ NNO David Robinson and All-Rookie Team (Stats on back)	15.00	7.50	1.50

1990-91 Hoops II

The design of the cards in the 104-card Hoops II set is identical to that of the first series. This set features NBA finals (337-342), coaches (343-354), team checklists (355-381), inside stuff (382-385), stay in school (386-387), don't foul out (388-389), lottery selections (390-400), and updates (401-438). The cards are standard size (2 1/2" by 3 1/2") and are numbered on the back in continuation of the first series. The key rookies in the set are the eleven lottery picks (390-400) led by Derrick Coleman, Kendall Gill, and Lionel Simmons.

	MINT	EXC	G-VG
COMPLETE SET (104)	6.00	3.00	.60
COMMON PLAYER (337-440)	.03	.01	.00
☐ 337 NBA Final Game 1	.06	.03	.00
☐ 338 NBA Final Game 2	.06	.03	.00

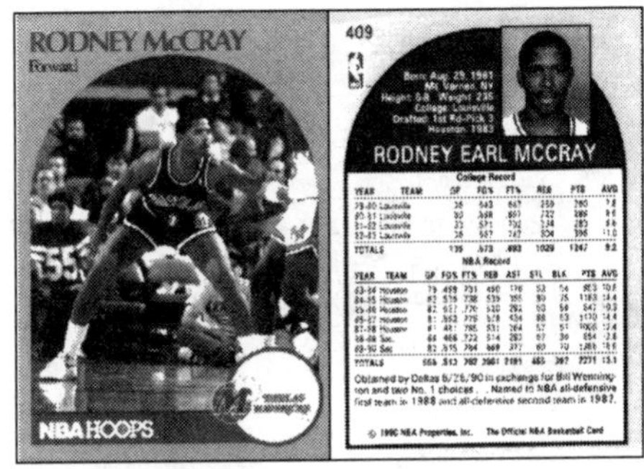

Card	MINT	EXC	G-VG
☐ 339 NBA Final Game 3	.06	.03	.00
☐ 340 NBA Final Game 4	.06	.03	.00
☐ 341A NBA Final Game 5 ERR (No headline on back)	.10	.05	.01
☐ 341B NBA Final Game 5 COR	.10	.05	.01
☐ 342 Championship Card UER (Player named as Sidney Green is really David Greenwood)	.10	.05	.01
☐ 343 K.C. Jones CO Seattle Supersonics	.06	.03	.00
☐ 344 Wes Unseld CO Washington Bullets	.06	.03	.00
☐ 345 Don Nelson CO Golden State Warriors	.03	.01	.00
☐ 346 Bob Weiss CO Atlanta Hawks	.03	.01	.00
☐ 347 Chris Ford CO Boston Celtics	.03	.01	.00
☐ 348 Phil Jackson CO Chicago Bulls	.06	.03	.00
☐ 349 Lenny Wilkens CO Cleveland Cavaliers	.06	.03	.00
☐ 350 Don Chaney CO Houston Rockets	.03	.01	.00
☐ 351 Mike Dunleavy CO Los Angeles Lakers	.03	.01	.00
☐ 352 Matt Guokas CO Orlando Magic	.03	.01	.00
☐ 353 Rick Adelman CO Portland Trail Blazers	.06	.03	.00
☐ 354 Jerry Sloan CO Utah Jazz	.03	.01	.00
☐ 355 Dominique Wilkins TC Atlanta Hawks	.08	.04	.01
☐ 356 Larry Bird TC Boston Celtics	.15	.07	.01
☐ 357 Rex Chapman TC Charlotte Hornets	.06	.03	.00
☐ 358 Michael Jordan TC Chicago Bulls	.50	.25	.05
☐ 359 Mark Price TC Cleveland Cavaliers	.08	.04	.01
☐ 360 Rolando Blackman TC Dallas Mavericks	.06	.03	.00
☐ 361 Michael Adams TC UER Denver Nuggets (Westhead should be card 422, not 440)	.06	.03	.00
☐ 362 Joe Dumars TC UER Detroit Pistons (Gerald Henderson's name and number not listed)	.08	.04	.01
☐ 363 Chris Mullin TC Golden State Warriors	.12	.06	.01
☐ 364 Hakeem Olajuwon TC Houston Rockets	.12	.06	.01
☐ 365 Reggie Miller TC Indiana Pacers	.08	.04	.01
☐ 366 Danny Manning TC Los Angeles Clippers	.08	.04	.01
☐ 367 Magic Johnson TC UER Los Angeles Lakers (Dunleavy listed as 439, should be 351)	.35	.17	.03
☐ 368 Rony Seikaly TC Miami Heat	.08	.04	.01
☐ 369 Alvin Robertson TC Milwaukee Bucks	.06	.03	.00
☐ 370 Pooh Richardson TC Minnesota Timberwolves	.10	.05	.01
☐ 371 Chris Morris TC	.06	.03	.00

New Jersey Nets			
☐ 372 Patrick Ewing TC	.15	.07	.01
New York Knicks			
☐ 373 Nick Anderson TC	.12	.06	.01
Orlando Magic			
☐ 374 Charles Barkley TC	.12	.06	.01
Philadelphia 76ers			
☐ 375 Kevin Johnson TC	.12	.06	.01
Phoenix Suns			
☐ 376 Clyde Drexler TC	.15	.07	.01
Portland Trail Blazers			
☐ 377 Wayman Tisdale TC	.06	.03	.00
Sacramento Kings			
☐ 378A David Robinson TC	.50	.25	.05
San Antonio Spurs			
(basketball fully			
visible)			
☐ 378A David Robinson TC	.50	.25	.05
San Antonio Spurs			
(basketball partially			
visible)			
☐ 379 Xavier McDaniel TC	.06	.03	.00
Seattle Supersonics			
☐ 380 Karl Malone TC	.12	.06	.01
Utah Jazz			
☐ 381 Bernard King TC	.06	.03	.00
Washington Bullets			
Inside Stuff			
☐ 382 Michael Jordan	.75	.35	.07
Playground			
☐ 383 Lights, Camera,	.12	.06	.01
NBA Action			
(Karl Malone			
on horseback)			
☐ 384 European Imports	.10	.05	.01
(Vlade Divac and			
Sarunas Marciulionis)			
☐ 385 Super Streaks	1.00	.50	.10
Stay In School			
(Magic Johnson and			
Michael Jordan)			
☐ 386 Johnny Newman	.06	.03	.00
Charlotte Hornets			
(Stay in School)			
☐ 387 Dell Curry	.06	.03	.00
Charlotte Hornets			
(Stay in School)			
☐ 388 Patrick Ewing	.15	.07	.01
New York Knicks			
(Don't Foul Out)			
☐ 389 Isiah Thomas	.08	.04	.01
Detroit Pistons			
(Don't Foul Out)			
☐ 390 Derrick Coleman LS	1.50	.75	.15
New Jersey Nets			
☐ 391 Gary Payton LS	.50	.25	.05
Seattle Supersonics			
☐ 392 Chris Jackson LS	.25	.12	.02
Denver Nuggets			
☐ 393 Dennis Scott LS	.50	.25	.05
Los Angeles Lakers			
☐ 394 Kendall Gill LS	2.00	1.00	.20
Charlotte Hornets			
☐ 395 Felton Spencer LS	.15	.07	.01
Minnesota Timberwolves			
☐ 396 Lionel Simmons LS	.75	.35	.07
Sacramento Kings			
☐ 397 Bo Kimble LS	.10	.05	.01
Los Angeles Clippers			
☐ 398 Willie Burton LS	.20	.10	.02
Miami Heat			
☐ 399 Rumeal Robinson LS	.20	.10	.02
Atlanta Hawks			
☐ 400 Tyrone Hill LS	.20	.10	.02
Golden State Warriors			
☐ 401 Tim McCormick	.03	.01	.00
Atlanta Hawks			
☐ 402 Sidney Moncrief	.06	.03	.00
Atlanta Hawks			
☐ 403 Johnny Newman	.06	.03	.00
Charlotte Hornets			
☐ 404 Dennis Hopson	.06	.03	.00
Chicago Bulls			
☐ 405 Cliff Levingston	.03	.01	.00
Chicago Bulls			
☐ 406A Danny Ferry ERR	.15	.07	.01
Cleveland Cavaliers			
(No position on			
front of card)			
☐ 406B Danny Ferry COR	.08	.04	.01
Cleveland Cavaliers			
☐ 407 Alex English	.08	.04	.01
Dallas Mavericks			
☐ 408 Lafayette Lever	.06	.03	.00
Dallas Mavericks			
☐ 409 Rodney McCray	.03	.01	.00
Dallas Mavericks			
☐ 410 Mike Dunleavy CO	.03	.01	.00
Los Angeles Lakers			
☐ 411 Orlando Woolridge	.06	.03	.00
Denver Nuggets			
☐ 412 Joe Wolf	.03	.01	.00
Denver Nuggets			
☐ 413 Tree Rollins	.03	.01	.00
Detroit Pistons			
☐ 414 Kenny Smith	.06	.03	.00
Houston Rockets			
☐ 415 Sam Perkins	.10	.05	.01
Los Angeles Lakers			
☐ 416 Terry Teagle	.03	.01	.00
Los Angeles Lakers			
☐ 417 Frank Brickowski	.03	.01	.00
Milwaukee Bucks			
☐ 418 Danny Schayes	.03	.01	.00
Milwaukee Bucks			
☐ 419 Scott Brooks	.03	.01	.00
Minnesota Timberwolves			
☐ 420 Reggie Theus	.06	.03	.00
New Jersey Nets			
☐ 421 Greg Grant	.03	.01	.00
New York Knicks			
☐ 422 Paul Westhead CO	.03	.01	.00
Denver Nuggets			
☐ 423 Greg Kite	.03	.01	.00
Orlando Magic			
☐ 424 Manute Bol	.03	.01	.00
Philadelphia 76ers			
☐ 425 Rickey Green	.03	.01	.00
Philadelphia 76ers			
☐ 426 Ed Nealy	.03	.01	.00
Phoenix Suns			
☐ 427 Danny Ainge	.06	.03	.00
Portland Trail Blazers			
☐ 428 Bobby Hansen	.03	.01	.00
Sacramento Kings			
☐ 429 Eric Leckner	.06	.03	.00
Charlotte Hornets			
☐ 430 Rory Sparrow	.03	.01	.00
Sacramento Kings			
☐ 431 Bill Wennington	.03	.01	.00
Sacramento Kings			
☐ 432 Paul Pressey	.03	.01	.00
San Antonio Spurs			
☐ 433 David Greenwood	.03	.01	.00
San Antonio Spurs			
☐ 434 Mark McNamara	.03	.01	.00
Orlando Magic			
☐ 435 Sidney Green	.03	.01	.00
Orlando Magic			
☐ 436 Dave Corzine	.03	.01	.00
Orlando Magic			
☐ 437 Jeff Malone	.10	.05	.01
Utah Jazz			
☐ 438 Pervis Ellison	.35	.17	.03
Washington Bullets			
☐ 439 Checklist 5	.06	.01	.00
☐ 440 Checklist 6	.06	.01	.00

1990-91 Hoops CollectABooks

These card-size "books" measure approximately 2 1/2" by 3 3/8". Each book consists of eight pages, including the front and back covers. The front cover features a borderless color player photo, with the player's above the picture in the team's color stripe. Pages 2 and 3 have a color "mug shot" of the player, biographical information, team logo, and career highlights. A color stripe runs across the bottom of each page, with the team name in white lettering. Pages 4 and 5 has a "personal story" about the player. Page 6 has career statistics (college and pro), while page 7 features a borderless color action photo. The top half of the back cover has another color player photo, with a player quote below the picture. The set was issued in four different boxes, with 12 different mini-books in each box.

	MINT	EXC	G-VG
COMPLETE SET (48)	10.00	5.00	1.00
COMMON PLAYER (1-48)	.20	.10	.02

☐ 1 Sam Bowie .... New Jersey Nets	.20	.10	.02
☐ 2 Tom Chambers .... Phoenix Suns	.25	.12	.02
☐ 3 Clyde Drexler .... Portland Trail Blazers	.75	.35	.07
☐ 4 Michael Jordan .... Chicago Bulls	1.50	.75	.15
☐ 5 Karl Malone .... Utah Jazz	.50	.25	.05
☐ 6 Kevin McHale .... Boston Celtics	.30	.15	.03
☐ 7 Reggie Miller .... Indiana Pacers	.30	.15	.03
☐ 8 Mark Price .... Cleveland Cavaliers	.30	.15	.03
☐ 9 Mitch Richmond .... Golden State Warriors	.35	.17	.03
☐ 10 Doc Rivers .... Atlanta Hawks	.20	.10	.02
☐ 11 Rony Seikaly .... Miami Heat	.35	.17	.03
☐ 12 Wayman Tisdale .... Sacramento Kings	.20	.10	.02
☐ 13 Charles Barkley .... Philadelphia 76ers	.60	.30	.06
☐ 14 Terry Cummings .... San Antonio Spurs	.30	.15	.03
☐ 15 Patrick Ewing .... New York Knicks	.60	.30	.06
☐ 16 Terry Porter .... Portland Trail Blazers	.35	.17	.03
☐ 17 Danny Manning .... Los Angeles Clippers	.40	.20	.04
☐ 18 Larry Nance .... Cleveland Cavaliers	.25	.12	.02
☐ 19 Robert Parish .... Boston Celtics	.35	.17	.03
☐ 20 Chuck Person .... Indiana Pacers	.30	.15	.03
☐ 21 Ricky Pierce .... Milwaukee Bucks	.25	.12	.02
☐ 22 John Stockton .... Utah Jazz	.50	.25	.05
☐ 23 Isiah Thomas .... Detroit Pistons	.45	.22	.04
☐ 24 Anthony(Spud) Webb .... Atlanta Hawks	.25	.12	.02
☐ 25 Michael Adams .... Denver Nuggets	.25	.12	.02
☐ 26 Muggsy Bogues .... Charlotte Hornets	.20	.10	.02
☐ 27 Joe Dumars .... Detroit Pistons	.35	.17	.03
☐ 28 Hersey Hawkins .... Philadelphia 76ers	.35	.17	.03
☐ 29 Magic Johnson .... Los Angeles Lakers	1.00	.50	.10
☐ 30 Bernard King .... Washington Bullets	.30	.15	.03
☐ 31 Chris Mullin .... Golden State Warriors	.50	.25	.05
☐ 32 Charles Oakley .... New York Knicks	.20	.10	.02
☐ 33 Alvin Robertson .... Milwaukee Bucks	.20	.10	.02
☐ 34 David Robinson .... San Antonio Spurs	1.00	.50	.10
☐ 35 Dominique Wilkins .... Atlanta Hawks	.35	.17	.03
☐ 36 Buck Williams .... Portland Trail Blazers	.25	.12	.02
☐ 37 Larry Bird .... Boston Celtics	.75	.35	.07
☐ 38 Rolando Blackman .... Dallas Mavericks	.20	.10	.02
☐ 39 Mark Eaton .... Utah Jazz	.20	.10	.02
☐ 40 Kevin Johnson .... Phoenix Suns	.50	.25	.05
☐ 41 J.R. Reid .... Charlotte Hornets	.20	.10	.02
☐ 42 Xavier McDaniel .... Seattle Supersonics	.25	.12	.02
☐ 43 Hakeem Olajuwon .... Houston Rockets	.50	.25	.05
☐ 44 Scottie Pippen .... Chicago Bulls	.75	.35	.07
☐ 45 Pooh Richardson .... Minnesota Timberwolves	.50	.25	.05
☐ 46 Dennis Rodman .... Detroit Pistons	.35	.17	.03
☐ 47 Charles Smith .... Los Angeles Clippers	.35	.17	.03
☐ 48 James Worthy .... Los Angeles Lakers	.40	.20	.04

1991 Hoops 100 Superstars

This 100-card set is a partial remake of the 1990-91 Hoops set, and it was primarily sold through the Sears catalog. The standard-size (2 1/2" by 3 1/2") cards use the same pictures. The backs have a color headshot, with biographical and statistical information (only up through the 1989-90 season) in a basketball lane format. However, these cards differ from the regular Hoops issue in the gold coloring on the card fronts and a new numbering system. The players are arranged alphabetically within teams, and the teams are arranged alphabetically as follows: Atlanta Hawks (1-4), Boston Celtics (5-9), Charlotte Hornets (10-11), Chicago Bulls (12-16), Cleveland Cavaliers (17-19), Dallas Mavericks (20-24), Denver Nuggets (25-26), Detroit Pistons (27-31), Golden State Warriors (32-34), Houston Rockets (35-38), Indiana Pacers (39-41), Los Angeles Clippers (42-45), Los Angeles Lakers (46-51), Miami Heat (52-54), Milwaukee Bucks (55-57), Minnesota Timberwolves (58-60), New Jersey Nets (61-63), New York Knicks (64-67), Orlando Magic (68-70), Philadelphia 76ers (71-74), Phoenix Suns (75-79), Portland Trail Blazers (80-83), Sacramento Kings (84-85), San Antonio Spurs (86-90), Seattle Supersonics (91-93), Utah Jazz (94-97), and Washington Bullets (98-100).

	MINT	EXC	G-VG
COMPLETE SET (100)	15.00	7.50	1.50
COMMON PLAYER (1-100)	.05	.02	.00
☐ 1 Moses Malone	.12	.06	.01
☐ 2 Doc Rivers	.08	.04	.01
☐ 3 Spud Webb	.08	.04	.01
☐ 4 Dominique Wilkins	.30	.15	.03
☐ 5 Larry Bird	.75	.35	.07
☐ 6 Reggie Lewis	.40	.20	.04
☐ 7 Kevin McHale	.12	.06	.01
☐ 8 Robert Parish	.15	.07	.01

☐ 9 Brian Shaw	.10	.05	.01
☐ 10 Muggsy Bogues	.08	.04	.01
☐ 11 Johnny Newman	.08	.04	.01
☐ 12 Horace Grant	.25	.12	.02
☐ 13 Michael Jordan	2.00	1.00	.20
☐ 14 Scottie Pippen	.60	.30	.06
☐ 15 Brad Daugherty	.25	.12	.02
☐ 16 Craig Ehlo	.08	.04	.01
☐ 17 Larry Nance	.10	.05	.01
☐ 18 Mark Price	.20	.10	.02
☐ 19 Hot Rod Williams	.10	.05	.01
☐ 20 Rolando Blackman	.10	.05	.01
☐ 21 James Donaldson	.05	.02	.00
☐ 22 Derek Harper	.08	.04	.01
☐ 23 Fat Lever	.08	.04	.01
☐ 24 Roy Tarpley	.08	.04	.01
☐ 25 Michael Adams	.10	.05	.01
☐ 26 Orlando Woolridge	.08	.04	.01
☐ 27 Joe Dumars	.20	.10	.02
☐ 28 Bill Laimbeer	.08	.04	.01
☐ 29 Vinnie Johnson	.08	.04	.01
☐ 30 Dennis Rodman	.15	.07	.01
☐ 31 Isiah Thomas	.25	.12	.02
☐ 32 Chris Mullin	.35	.17	.03
☐ 33 Tim Hardaway	1.00	.50	.10
☐ 34 Mitch Richmond	.30	.15	.03
☐ 35 Eric(Sleepy) Floyd	.08	.04	.01
☐ 36 Hakeem Olajuwon	.20	.10	.02
☐ 37 Kenny Smith	.08	.04	.01
☐ 38 Otis Thorpe	.10	.05	.01
☐ 39 Reggie Miller	.15	.07	.01
☐ 40 Chuck Person	.12	.06	.01
☐ 41 Detlef Schrempf	.12	.06	.01
☐ 42 Danny Manning	.20	.10	.02
☐ 43 Ken Norman	.12	.06	.01
☐ 44 Ron Harper	.12	.06	.01
☐ 45 Charles Smith	.15	.07	.01
☐ 46 Vlade Divac	.35	.17	.03
☐ 47 A.C. Green	.08	.04	.01
☐ 48 Magic Johnson	1.00	.50	.10
☐ 49 Byron Scott	.10	.05	.01
☐ 50 James Worthy	.25	.12	.02
☐ 51 Sam Perkins	.12	.06	.01
☐ 52 Rony Seikaly	.25	.12	.02
☐ 53 Sherman Douglas	.30	.15	.03
☐ 54 Glen Rice	.75	.35	.07
☐ 55 Jay Humphries	.08	.04	.01
☐ 56 Alvin Robertson	.08	.04	.01
☐ 57 Jack Sikma	.08	.04	.01
☐ 58 Tony Campbell	.10	.05	.01
☐ 59 Tyrone Corbin	.08	.04	.01
☐ 60 Pooh Richardson	.40	.20	.04
☐ 61 Roy Hinson	.05	.02	.00
☐ 62 Chris Morris	.08	.04	.01
☐ 63 Reggie Theus	.08	.04	.01
☐ 64 Maurice Cheeks	.10	.05	.01
☐ 65 Patrick Ewing	.35	.17	.03
☐ 66 Mark Jackson	.10	.05	.01
☐ 67 Charles Oakley	.08	.04	.01
☐ 68 Nick Anderson	.30	.15	.03
☐ 69 Terry Catledge	.10	.05	.01
☐ 70 Scott Skiles	.10	.05	.01
☐ 71 Charles Barkley	.40	.20	.04
☐ 72 Johnny Dawkins	.08	.04	.01
☐ 73 Hersey Hawkins	.12	.06	.01
☐ 74 Rick Mahorn	.08	.04	.01
☐ 75 Tom Chambers	.15	.07	.01
☐ 76 Jeff Hornacek	.15	.07	.01
☐ 77 Kevin Johnson	.40	.20	.04
☐ 78 Dan Majerle	.15	.07	.01
☐ 79 Mark West	.05	.02	.00
☐ 80 Clyde Drexler	.60	.30	.06
☐ 81 Terry Porter	.20	.10	.02
☐ 82 Jerome Kersey	.15	.07	.01
☐ 83 Buck Williams	.08	.04	.01
☐ 84 Antoine Carr	.08	.04	.01
☐ 85 Wayman Tisdale	.10	.05	.01
☐ 86 Willie Anderson	.08	.04	.01
☐ 87 Terry Cummings	.15	.07	.01
☐ 88 Paul Pressey	.05	.02	.00
☐ 89 David Robinson	.75	.35	.07
☐ 90 Rod Strickland	.12	.06	.01
☐ 91 Michael Cage	.05	.02	.00
☐ 92 Shawn Kemp	1.00	.50	.10
☐ 93 Derrick McKey	.08	.04	.01
☐ 94 Thurl Bailey	.05	.02	.00
☐ 95 Jeff Malone	.12	.06	.01
☐ 96 Karl Malone	.35	.17	.03
☐ 97 John Stockton	.35	.17	.03
☐ 98 Harvey Grant	.15	.07	.01
☐ 99 Bernard King	.10	.05	.01
☐ 100 Darrell Walker	.05	.02	.00

1991 Hoops Larry Bird Video

This standard-size (2 1/2" by 3 1/2") card was enclosed in cellophane and included as an insert with the "Larry Bird - Basketball Legend" VHS video tape. The front has a color photo of Bird shooting the basketball, with the Boston Garden parquet floor serving as the border on the front and back. The lower right corner of the picture is cut off to allow space for the team logo. The back has a color close-up photo, a street sign from the intersection of Main St. and Larry Bird Blvd., and career highlights within a drawing of Indiana's borders. The NBA Hoops logo appears on the card front. The card is unnumbered.

	MINT	EXC	G-VG
☐ NNO Larry Bird	15.00	7.50	1.50

1991-92 Hoops Prototypes

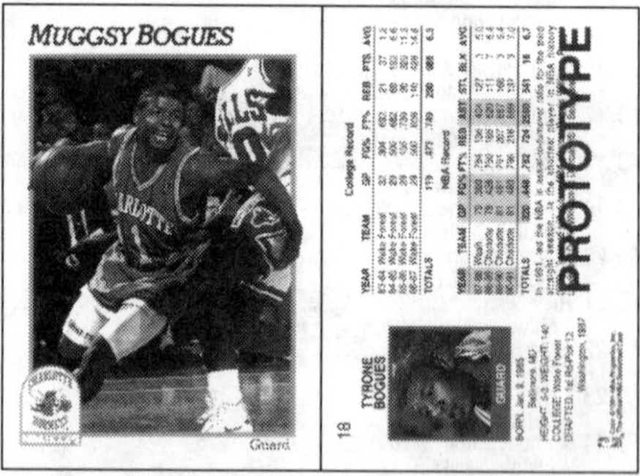

This four-card set measures the standard size (2 1/2" by 3 1/2"). The fronts features color action player photos, with differing color borders in one of the team's colors. The player's name appears above the picture, and the team logo overlays the lower left corner of the picture. In a horizontal format the back has a head shot of the player, biographical information, and college and pro statistics. The words "Prototype" are written in block lettering across the back. The cards are numbered on the back.

	MINT	EXC	G-VG
COMPLETE SET (4)	30.00	15.00	3.00
COMMON PLAYER	6.00	3.00	.60
☐ 9 Larry Bird	20.00	10.00	2.00
☐ 18 Muggsy Bogues	6.00	3.00	.60
☐ 142 Charles Oakley	6.00	3.00	.60
☐ 159 Armon Gilliam	6.00	3.00	.60

1991-92 Hoops Prototypes 00

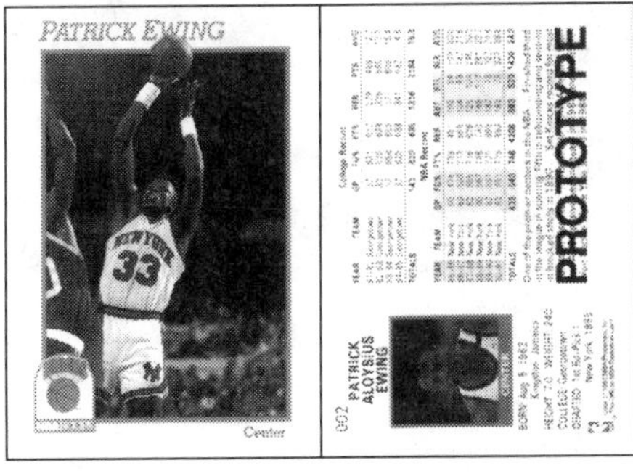

This six-card set measures the standard size (2 1/2" by 3 1/2"). The fronts features color action player photos, with differing color borders in one of the team's colors. The player's name appears above the picture, and the team logo overlays the lower left corner of the picture. In a horizontal format the back has a head shot of the player, biographical information, and college and pro statistics. The words "Prototype" are written in block lettering across the back. The cards are numbered on the back as 001, 002, etc.

	MINT	EXC	G-VG
COMPLETE SET (6)	125.00	60.00	12.50
COMMON PLAYER (001-006)	12.00	6.00	1.20
☐ 001 Clyde Drexler	25.00	12.50	2.50
☐ 002 Patrick Ewing	25.00	12.50	2.50
☐ 003 Magic Johnson	35.00	17.50	3.50
☐ 004 Michael Jordan	50.00	25.00	5.00
☐ 005 Karl Malone	12.00	6.00	1.20
☐ 006 Hakeem Olajuwon	12.00	6.00	1.20

1991-92 Hoops I

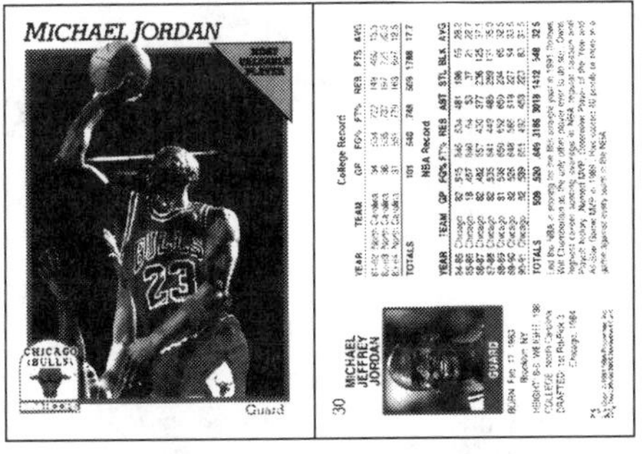

The 1991-92 Hoops I basketball set contains 330 cards measuring the standard size (2 1/2" by 3 1/2"). The fronts feature color action player photos, with different color borders on a white card face. The player's name is printed in black lettering in the upper left corner, and the team logo is superimposed over the lower left corner of the picture. In a horizontal format the backs have color head shots and biographical information on the left side, while the right side presents college and pro statistics. The cards are numbered on the back and checklisted below alphabetically within and according to teams as follows: Atlanta Hawks (1-8), Boston Celtics (9-17), Charlotte Hornets (18-25), Chicago Bulls (26-34), Cleveland Cavaliers (35-42), Dallas Mavericks (43-50), Denver Nuggets (51-58), Detroit Pistons (59-66), Golden State Warriors (67-74), Houston Rockets (75-82), Indiana Pacers (83-90), Los Angeles Clippers (91-98), Los Angeles Lakers (99-106), Miami Heat (107-114), Milwaukee Bucks (115-122), Minnesota Timberwolves (123-130), New Jersey Nets (131-138), New York Knicks (139-146), Orlando Magic (147-154), Philadelphia 76ers (155-162), Phoenix Suns (163-170), Portland Trail Blazers (171-179), Sacramento Kings (180-187), San Antonio Spurs (188-196), Seattle Supersonics (197-204), Utah Jazz (205-212), and Washington Bullets (213-220). Other subsets included in this set are coaches (221-247), All-Stars East (248-260), All-Stars West (261-273), teams (274-300), Centennial Card honoring James Naismith (301), Inside Stuff (302-305), League Leaders (306-313), Milestones (314-318), NBA yearbook (319-324), Stay in School (325-326), Don't Drive and Drink (327), and Checklists (328-330). There are no key rookie cards in this series. A special short-printed Naismith card, numbered CC1, was inserted into wax packs. It features a colorized photo of Dr. Naismith standing between two peach baskets like those used in the first basketball game. The back narrates the invention of the game of basketball. An unnumbered Centennial Card featuring the Centennial Logo was also available via a mail-in offer.

	MINT	EXC	G-VG
COMPLETE SET (330)	8.00	4.00	.80
COMMON PLAYER (1-330)	.03	.01	.00
☐ 1 John Battle	.06	.03	.00
☐ 2 Moses Malone UER	.10	.05	.01
(119 rebounds 1982-83, should be 1194)			
☐ 3 Sidney Moncrief	.06	.03	.00
☐ 4 Doc Rivers	.06	.03	.00
☐ 5 Rumeal Robinson UER	.06	.03	.00
(Back says 11th pick in 1990, should be 10th)			
☐ 6 Spud Webb	.06	.03	.00
☐ 7 Dominique Wilkins	.12	.06	.01
☐ 8 Kevin Willis	.08	.04	.01
☐ 9 Larry Bird	.25	.12	.02
☐ 10 Dee Brown	.25	.12	.02
☐ 11 Kevin Gamble	.06	.03	.00
☐ 12 Joe Kleine	.03	.01	.00
☐ 13 Reggie Lewis	.12	.06	.01
☐ 14 Kevin McHale	.08	.04	.01
☐ 15 Robert Parish	.10	.05	.01
☐ 16 Ed Pinckney	.03	.01	.00
☐ 17 Brian Shaw	.06	.03	.00
☐ 18 Muggsy Bogues	.03	.01	.00
☐ 19 Rex Chapman	.06	.03	.00
☐ 20 Dell Curry	.03	.01	.00
☐ 21 Kendall Gill	.50	.25	.05
☐ 22 Mike Gminski	.03	.01	.00
☐ 23 Johnny Newman	.03	.01	.00
☐ 24 J.R. Reid	.06	.03	.00
☐ 25 Kelly Tripucka	.03	.01	.00
☐ 26 B.J. Armstrong	.10	.05	.01
(B.J. on front, Benjamin Roy on back)			
☐ 27 Bill Cartwright	.06	.03	.00
☐ 28 Horace Grant	.10	.05	.01
☐ 29 Craig Hodges	.03	.01	.00
☐ 30 Michael Jordan	1.00	.50	.10
☐ 31 Stacey King	.06	.03	.00
☐ 32 Cliff Levingston	.03	.01	.00
☐ 33 John Paxson	.06	.03	.00
☐ 34 Scottie Pippen	.30	.15	.03
☐ 35 Chucky Brown	.03	.01	.00
☐ 36 Brad Daugherty	.12	.06	.01
☐ 37 Craig Ehlo	.06	.03	.00
☐ 38 Danny Ferry	.06	.03	.00
☐ 39 Larry Nance	.08	.04	.01
☐ 40 Mark Price	.12	.06	.01
☐ 41 Darnell Valentine	.03	.01	.00
☐ 42 Hot Rod Williams	.06	.03	.00
☐ 43 Rolando Blackman	.06	.03	.00
☐ 44 Brad Davis	.03	.01	.00
☐ 45 James Donaldson	.03	.01	.00
☐ 46 Derek Harper	.06	.03	.00
☐ 47 Fat Lever	.06	.03	.00
☐ 48 Rodney McCray	.03	.01	.00
☐ 49 Roy Tarpley	.06	.03	.00
☐ 50 Herb Williams	.03	.01	.00
☐ 51 Michael Adams	.06	.03	.00

☐ 52 Chris Jackson UER .08 .04 .01
(Born in Mississippi,
not Michigan)
☐ 53 Jerome Lane .03 .01 .00
☐ 54 Todd Lichti .03 .01 .00
☐ 55 Blair Rasmussen .03 .01 .00
☐ 56 Reggie Williams .06 .03 .00
☐ 57 Joe Wolf .03 .01 .00
☐ 58 Orlando Woolridge .06 .03 .00
☐ 59 Mark Aguirre .06 .03 .00
☐ 60 Joe Dumars .10 .05 .01
☐ 61 James Edwards .03 .01 .00
☐ 62 Vinnie Johnson .03 .01 .00
☐ 63 Bill Laimbeer .06 .03 .00
☐ 64 Dennis Rodman .10 .05 .01
☐ 65 John Salley .06 .03 .00
☐ 66 Isiah Thomas .12 .06 .01
☐ 67 Tim Hardaway .50 .25 .05
☐ 68 Rod Higgins .03 .01 .00
☐ 69 Tyrone Hill .08 .04 .01
☐ 70 Alton Lister .03 .01 .00
☐ 71 Sarunas Marciulionis .12 .06 .01
☐ 72 Chris Mullin .15 .07 .01
☐ 73 Mitch Richmond .10 .05 .01
☐ 74 Tom Tolbert .03 .01 .00
☐ 75 Eric(Sleepy) Floyd .06 .03 .00
☐ 76 Buck Johnson .03 .01 .00
☐ 77 Vernon Maxwell .06 .03 .00
☐ 78 Hakeem Olajuwon .12 .06 .01
☐ 79 Kenny Smith .03 .01 .00
☐ 80 Larry Smith .03 .01 .00
☐ 81 Otis Thorpe .06 .03 .00
☐ 82 David Wood .08 .04 .01
☐ 83 Vern Fleming .03 .01 .00
☐ 84 Reggie Miller .10 .05 .01
☐ 85 Chuck Person .06 .03 .00
☐ 86 Mike Sanders .06 .03 .00
☐ 87 Detlef Schrempf .06 .03 .00
☐ 88 Rik Smits .06 .03 .00
☐ 89 LaSalle Thompson .03 .01 .00
☐ 90 Micheal Williams .06 .03 .00
☐ 91 Winston Garland .03 .01 .00
☐ 92 Gary Grant .03 .01 .00
☐ 93 Ron Harper .06 .03 .00
☐ 94 Danny Manning .10 .05 .01
☐ 95 Jeff Martin .03 .01 .00
☐ 96 Ken Norman .06 .03 .00
☐ 97 Olden Polynice .03 .01 .00
☐ 98 Charles Smith .08 .04 .01
☐ 99 Vlade Divac .10 .05 .01
☐ 100 A.C. Green .06 .03 .00
☐ 101 Magic Johnson .60 .30 .06
☐ 102 Sam Perkins .08 .04 .01
☐ 103 Byron Scott .06 .03 .00
☐ 104 Terry Teagle .03 .01 .00
☐ 105 Mychal Thompson .03 .01 .00
☐ 106 James Worthy .10 .05 .01
☐ 107 Willie Burton .06 .03 .00
☐ 108 Bimbo Coles .10 .05 .01
☐ 109 Terry Davis .06 .03 .00
☐ 110 Sherman Douglas .06 .03 .00
☐ 111 Kevin Edwards .03 .01 .00
☐ 112 Alec Kessler .06 .03 .00
☐ 113 Glen Rice .25 .12 .02
☐ 114 Rony Seikaly .08 .04 .01
☐ 115 Frank Brickowski .03 .01 .00
☐ 116 Dale Ellis .06 .03 .00
☐ 117 Jay Humphries .03 .01 .00
☐ 118 Brad Lohaus .03 .01 .00
☐ 119 Fred Roberts .03 .01 .00
☐ 120 Alvin Robertson .06 .03 .00
☐ 121 Danny Schayes .03 .01 .00
☐ 122 Jack Sikma .06 .03 .00
☐ 123 Randy Breuer .03 .01 .00
☐ 124 Tony Campbell .03 .01 .00
☐ 125 Tyrone Corbin .03 .01 .00
☐ 126 Gerald Glass .12 .06 .01
☐ 127 Sam Mitchell .03 .01 .00
☐ 128 Tod Murphy .03 .01 .00
☐ 129 Pooh Richardson .10 .05 .01
☐ 130 Felton Spencer .06 .03 .00
☐ 131 Mookie Blaylock .06 .03 .00
☐ 132 Sam Bowie .06 .03 .00
☐ 133 Jud Buechler .03 .01 .00
☐ 134 Derrick Coleman .30 .15 .03
☐ 135 Chris Dudley .03 .01 .00
☐ 136 Chris Morris .06 .03 .00
☐ 137 Drazen Petrovic .15 .07 .01
☐ 138 Reggie Theus .06 .03 .00
☐ 139 Maurice Cheeks .06 .03 .00
☐ 140 Patrick Ewing .20 .10 .02
☐ 141 Mark Jackson .06 .03 .00
☐ 142 Charles Oakley .06 .03 .00
☐ 143 Trent Tucker .03 .01 .00
☐ 144 Kiki Vandeweghe .06 .03 .00
☐ 145 Kenny Walker .03 .01 .00
☐ 146 Gerald Wilkins .06 .03 .00
☐ 147 Nick Anderson .12 .06 .01
☐ 148 Michael Ansley .03 .01 .00
☐ 149 Terry Catledge .03 .01 .00
☐ 150 Jerry Reynolds .03 .01 .00
☐ 151 Dennis Scott .10 .05 .01
☐ 152 Scott Skiles .06 .03 .00
☐ 153 Otis Smith .03 .01 .00
☐ 154 Sam Vincent .03 .01 .00
☐ 155 Ron Anderson .03 .01 .00
☐ 156 Charles Barkley .15 .07 .01
☐ 157 Manute Bol .03 .01 .00
☐ 158 Johnny Dawkins .06 .03 .00
☐ 159 Armon Gilliam .03 .01 .00
☐ 160 Rickey Green .03 .01 .00
☐ 161 Hersey Hawkins .08 .04 .01
☐ 162 Rick Mahorn .06 .03 .00
☐ 163 Tom Chambers .08 .04 .01
☐ 164 Jeff Hornacek .10 .05 .01
☐ 165 Kevin Johnson .15 .07 .01
☐ 166 Andrew Lang .10 .05 .01
☐ 167 Dan Majerle .10 .05 .01
☐ 168 Xavier McDaniel .08 .04 .01
☐ 169 Kurt Rambis .06 .03 .00
☐ 170 Mark West .03 .01 .00
☐ 171 Danny Ainge .06 .03 .00
☐ 172 Mark Bryant .03 .01 .00
☐ 173 Walter Davis .06 .03 .00
☐ 174 Clyde Drexler .20 .10 .02
☐ 175 Kevin Duckworth .03 .01 .00
☐ 176 Jerome Kersey .08 .04 .01
☐ 177 Terry Porter .10 .05 .01
☐ 178 Cliff Robinson .10 .05 .01
☐ 179 Buck Williams .08 .04 .01
☐ 180 Anthony Bonner .08 .04 .01
☐ 181 Antoine Carr .03 .01 .00
☐ 182 Duane Causwell .06 .03 .00
☐ 183 Bobby Hansen .03 .01 .00
☐ 184 Travis Mays .06 .03 .00
☐ 185 Lionel Simmons .20 .10 .02
☐ 186 Rory Sparrow .03 .01 .00
☐ 187 Wayman Tisdale .06 .03 .00
☐ 188 Willie Anderson .06 .03 .00
☐ 189 Terry Cummings .08 .04 .01
☐ 190 Sean Elliott .12 .06 .01
☐ 191 Sidney Green .03 .01 .00
☐ 192 David Greenwood .03 .01 .00
☐ 193 Paul Pressey .03 .01 .00
☐ 194 David Robinson .60 .30 .06
☐ 195 Dwayne Schintzius .06 .03 .00
☐ 196 Rod Strickland .06 .03 .00
☐ 197 Benoit Benjamin .03 .01 .00
☐ 198 Michael Cage .03 .01 .00
☐ 199 Eddie Johnson .06 .03 .00
☐ 200 Shawn Kemp .50 .25 .05
☐ 201 Derrick McKey .06 .03 .00
☐ 202 Gary Payton .10 .05 .01
☐ 203 Ricky Pierce .06 .03 .00
☐ 204 Sedale Threatt .06 .03 .00
☐ 205 Thurl Bailey .03 .01 .00
☐ 206 Mike Brown .03 .01 .00
☐ 207 Mark Eaton .03 .01 .00
☐ 208 Blue Edwards UER .03 .01 .00
(Forward/guard on
front, guard on back)
☐ 209 Darrell Griffith .03 .01 .00
☐ 210 Jeff Malone .08 .04 .01
☐ 211 Karl Malone .15 .07 .01
☐ 212 John Stockton .15 .07 .01
☐ 213 Ledell Eackles .03 .01 .00
☐ 214 Pervis Ellison .15 .07 .01
☐ 215 A.J. English .10 .05 .01
☐ 216 Harvey Grant .08 .04 .01
(Shown boxing out
twin brother Horace)
☐ 217 Charles Jones .03 .01 .00
☐ 218 Bernard King .06 .03 .00
☐ 219 Darrell Walker .03 .01 .00
☐ 220 John Williams .03 .01 .00
☐ 221 Bob Weiss CO .03 .01 .00
☐ 222 Chris Ford CO .03 .01 .00
☐ 223 Gene Littles CO .03 .01 .00
☐ 224 Phil Jackson CO .06 .03 .00
☐ 225 Lenny Wilkens CO .06 .03 .00
☐ 226 Richie Adubato CO .03 .01 .00
☐ 227 Paul Westhead CO .03 .01 .00
☐ 228 Chuck Daly CO .06 .03 .00
☐ 229 Don Nelson CO .03 .01 .00
☐ 230 Don Chaney CO .03 .01 .00
☐ 231 Bob Hill CO UER .06 .03 .00
(Coached under Ted
Owens, not Ted Owen)

☐ 232 Mike Schuler CO	.03	.01	.00
☐ 233 Mike Dunleavy CO	.03	.01	.00
☐ 234 Kevin Loughery CO	.03	.01	.00
☐ 235 Del Harris CO	.03	.01	.00
☐ 236 Jimmy Rodgers CO	.03	.01	.00
☐ 237 Bill Fitch CO	.03	.01	.00
☐ 238 Pat Riley CO	.06	.03	.00
☐ 239 Matt Guokas CO	.03	.01	.00
☐ 240 Jim Lynam CO	.03	.01	.00
☐ 241 Cotton Fitzsimmons CO	.03	.01	.00
☐ 242 Rick Adelman CO	.06	.03	.00
☐ 243 Dick Motta CO	.03	.01	.00
☐ 244 Larry Brown CO	.06	.03	.00
☐ 245 K.C. Jones CO	.06	.03	.00
☐ 246 Jerry Sloan CO	.03	.01	.00
☐ 247 Wes Unseld CO	.06	.03	.00
☐ 248 Charles Barkley AS	.10	.05	.01
☐ 249 Brad Daugherty AS	.08	.04	.01
☐ 250 Joe Dumars AS	.08	.04	.01
☐ 251 Patrick Ewing AS	.10	.05	.01
☐ 252 Hersey Hawkins AS	.06	.03	.00
☐ 253 Michael Jordan AS	.40	.20	.04
☐ 254 Bernard King AS	.06	.03	.00
☐ 255 Kevin McHale AS	.08	.04	.01
☐ 256 Robert Parish AS	.08	.04	.01
☐ 257 Ricky Pierce AS	.06	.03	.00
☐ 258 Alvin Robertson AS	.03	.01	.00
☐ 259 Dominique Wilkins AS	.08	.04	.01
☐ 260 Chris Ford CO AS	.03	.01	.00
☐ 261 Tom Chambers AS	.06	.03	.00
☐ 262 Clyde Drexler AS	.12	.06	.01
☐ 263 Kevin Duckworth AS	.03	.01	.00
☐ 264 Tim Hardaway AS	.20	.10	.02
☐ 265 Kevin Johnson AS	.10	.05	.01
☐ 266 Magic Johnson AS	.30	.15	.03
☐ 267 Karl Malone AS	.10	.05	.01
☐ 268 Chris Mullen AS	.10	.05	.01
☐ 269 Terry Porter AS	.06	.03	.00
☐ 270 David Robinson AS	.20	.10	.02
☐ 271 John Stockton AS	.10	.05	.01
☐ 272 James Worthy AS	.08	.04	.01
☐ 273 Rick Adelman CO AS	.03	.01	.00
☐ 274 Atlanta Hawks Team Card UER (Actually began as Tri-Cities Blackhawks)	.06	.03	.00
☐ 275 Boston Celtics Team Card UER (No NBA Hoops logo on card front)	.06	.03	.00
☐ 276 Charlotte Hornets Team Card	.06	.03	.00
☐ 277 Chicago Bulls Team Card	.06	.03	.00
☐ 278 Cleveland Cavaliers Team Card	.06	.03	.00
☐ 279 Dallas Mavericks Team Card	.06	.03	.00
☐ 280 Denver Nuggets Team Card	.06	.03	.00
☐ 281 Detroit Pistons Team Card UER (Pistons not NBA Finalists until 1988; Ft. Wayne Pistons in Finals in 1955 and 1956)	.06	.03	.00
☐ 282 Golden State Warriors Team Card	.06	.03	.00
☐ 283 Houston Rockets Team Card	.06	.03	.00
☐ 284 Indiana Pacers Team Card	.06	.03	.00
☐ 285 Los Angeles Clippers Team Card	.06	.03	.00
☐ 286 Los Angeles Lakers Team Card	.06	.03	.00
☐ 287 Miami Heat Team Card	.06	.03	.00
☐ 288 Milwaukee Bucks Team Card	.06	.03	.00
☐ 289 Minnesota Timberwolves Team Card	.06	.03	.00
☐ 290 New Jersey Nets Team Card	.06	.03	.00
☐ 291 New York Knicks Team Card UER (Golden State not mentioned as an active charter member of NBA)	.06	.03	.00
☐ 292 Orlando Magic Team Card	.06	.03	.00
☐ 293 Philadelphia 76ers Team Card	.06	.03	.00
☐ 294 Phoenix Suns Team Card	.06	.03	.00
☐ 295 Portland Trail Blazers Team Card	.06	.03	.00
☐ 296 Sacramento Kings Team Card	.06	.03	.00
☐ 297 San Antonio Spurs Team Card	.06	.03	.00
☐ 298 Seattle Supersonics Team Card	.06	.03	.00
☐ 299 Utah Jazz Team Card	.06	.03	.00
☐ 300 Washington Bullets Team Card	.06	.03	.00
☐ 301 Centennial Card James Naismith	.10	.05	.01
☐ 302 Kevin Johnson IS	.10	.05	.01
☐ 303 Reggie Miller IS	.08	.04	.01
☐ 304 Hakeem Olajuwon IS	.08	.04	.01
☐ 305 Robert Parish IS	.08	.04	.01
☐ 306 Scoring Leaders Michael Jordan Karl Malone	.35	.17	.03
☐ 307 3-Point FG Percent League Leaders Jim Les Trent Tucker	.06	.03	.00
☐ 308 Free Throw Percent League Leaders Reggie Miller Jeff Malone	.06	.03	.00
☐ 309 Blocks League Leaders Hakeem Olajuwon David Robinson	.20	.10	.02
☐ 310 Steals League Leaders Alvin Robertson John Stockton	.06	.03	.00
☐ 311 Rebounds LL UER David Robinson Dennis Rodman (Robinson credited as playing for Houston)	.15	.07	.01
☐ 312 Assists League Leaders John Stockton Magic Johnson	.20	.10	.02
☐ 313 Field Goal Percent League Leaders Buck Williams Robert Parish	.06	.03	.00
☐ 314 Larry Bird UER Milestone (Should be card 315 to fit Milestone sequence)	.15	.07	.01
☐ 315 A.English/M.Malone Milestone UER (Should be card 314 and be a League Leader card)	.08	.04	.01
☐ 316 Magic Johnson Milestone	.30	.15	.03
☐ 317 Michael Jordan Milestone	.40	.20	.04
☐ 318 Moses Malone Milestone	.08	.04	.01
☐ 319 Larry Bird NBA Yearbook Look Back	.15	.07	.01
☐ 320 Maurice Cheeks NBA Yearbook Look Back	.06	.03	.00
☐ 321 Magic Johnson NBA Yearbook Look Back	.30	.15	.03
☐ 322 Bernard King NBA Yearbook Look Back	.06	.03	.00
☐ 323 Moses Malone NBA Yearbook Look Back	.08	.04	.01
☐ 324 Robert Parish NBA Yearbook Look Back	.08	.04	.01
☐ 325 All-Star Jam Jammin' With Will Smith (Stay in School)	.06	.03	.00
☐ 326 All-Star Jam Jammin' With The Boys and Will Smith (Stay in School)	.06	.u3	.00
☐ 327 David Robinson Leave Alcohol Out	.25	.12	.02
☐ 328 Checklist 1	.06	.01	.00
☐ 329 Checklist 2 UER (Card front is from 330)	.06	.01	.00
☐ 330 Checklist 3 UER	.06	.01	.00

		MINT	EXC	G-VG
	(Card front is from 329; card 327 listed operation, should be celebration)			
☐ CC1	Dr.James Naismith SP	5.00	2.50	.50
☐ NNO	Centennial Card (Sendaway)	.50	.25	.05

1991-92 Hoops Slam Dunk Champions

The six-card subset features the winners of the All-Star weekend slam dunk competition from 1986 to 1991. The cards measure the standard size (2 1/2" by 3 1/2") and were only available in first series 47-card rack packs. The front has a color photo of the player dunking the ball, with royal blue borders on a white card face. The player's name appears in orange lettering in a purple stripe above the picture, and the year the player won is given in a "Slam Dunk Champion" emblem overlaying the lower left corner of the picture. The design of the back is similar to the front, only with an extended caption on a yellow-green background. A drawing of a basketball entering a rim appears at the upper left corner. The cards are numbered on the back by Roman numerals.

	MINT	EXC	G-VG
COMPLETE SET (6)	4.00	2.00	.40
COMMON PLAYER (1-6)	.30	.15	.03
☐ 1 Larry Nance (Numbered I)	.40	.20	.04
☐ 2 Dominique Wilkins (Numbered II)	1.00	.50	.10
☐ 3 Spud Webb (Numbered III)	.30	.15	.03
☐ 4 Michael Jordan (Numbered IV)	3.00	1.50	.30
☐ 5 Kenny Walker (Numbered V)	.30	.15	.03
☐ 6 Dee Brown (Numbered VI)	1.00	.50	.10

1991-92 Hoops II

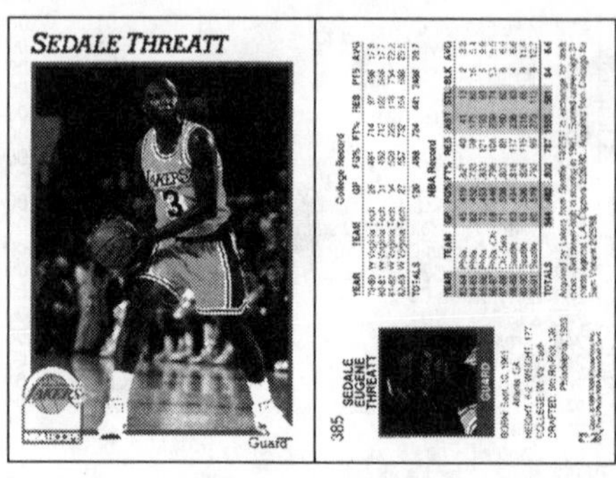

The 1991-92 Hoops II basketball set contains 260 cards measuring the standard size (2 1/2" by 3 1/2"). Series II packs also featured a randomly packed Gold Foil USA Basketball logo card. On a white card face, the fronts feature color player photos inside different color frames. The player's name appears above the picture, while the team logo appears at the lower left corner. In a horizontal format, the backs have a color head shot, biography, and complete statistics (college and pro). The cards are numbered on the back and checklisted below alphabetically according to and within teams as follows: Atlanta Hawks (331-337), Boston Celtics (338-341), Charlotte Hornets (342-344), Chicago Bulls (345-346), Cleveland Cavaliers (347-351), Dallas Mavericks (352-353), Denver Nuggets (354-359), Detroit Pistons (360-367), Houston Rockets (368-371), Indiana Pacers (372-375), Los Angeles Clippers (376-381), Los Angeles Lakers (382-385), Miami Heat (386-389), Milwaukee Bucks (390-394), Minnesota Timberwolves (395-397), New Jersey Nets (398-401), New York Knicks (402-406), Orlando Magic (407-410), Philadelphia 76ers (411-416), Phoenix Suns (417-422), Portland Trail Blazers (423-425), Sacramento Kings (426-431), San Antonio Spurs (432-437), Seattle Supersonics (438-441), Utah Jazz (442), and Washington Bullets (443-448). The set includes the following special cards and subsets: Supreme Court (449-502), Art Cards (503-529), Active Leaders (530-537), NBA Hoops Tribune (538-543), Stay in School (544-545), Draft Picks (546-556), USA Basketball 1976 (557), USA Basketball 1984 (558-564), USA Basketball 1988 (565-574), and USA Basketball 1992 (575-588). The key rookie cards in this series are Stacey Augmon, Larry Johnson, Dikembe Mutumbo, Billy Owens, and Steve Smith. A special individually numbered (out of 10,000) "Head of the Class" (showing the top six draft picks from 1991) card was made available to the first 10,000 fans requesting one along with three wrappers from each series of 1991-92 Hoops cards.

	MINT	EXC	G-VG
COMPLETE SET (260)	16.00	8.00	1.60
COMMON PLAYER (331-590)	.03	.01	.00
☐ 331 Maurice Cheeks	.06	.03	.00
☐ 332 Duane Ferrell	.03	.01	.00
☐ 333 Jon Koncak	.03	.01	.00
☐ 334 Gary Leonard	.08	.04	.01
☐ 335 Travis Mays	.06	.03	.00
☐ 336 Blair Rasmussen	.03	.01	.00
☐ 337 Alexander Volkov	.06	.03	.00
☐ 338 John Bagley	.06	.03	.00
☐ 339 Rickey Green UER (Ricky on front)	.03	.01	.00
☐ 340 Derek Smith	.03	.01	.00
☐ 341 Stojko Vrankovic	.10	.05	.01
☐ 342 Anthony Frederick	.15	.07	.01
☐ 343 Kenny Gattison	.06	.03	.00
☐ 344 Eric Leckner	.03	.01	.00
☐ 345 Will Perdue	.03	.01	.00
☐ 346 Scott Williams	.25	.12	.02
☐ 347 John Battle	.03	.01	.00
☐ 348 Winston Bennett	.03	.01	.00
☐ 349 Henry James	.08	.04	.01
☐ 350 Steve Kerr	.03	.01	.00
☐ 351 John Morton	.03	.01	.00
☐ 352 Terry Davis	.06	.03	.00
☐ 353 Randy White	.03	.01	.00
☐ 354 Greg Anderson	.03	.01	.00
☐ 355 Anthony Cook	.06	.03	.00
☐ 356 Walter Davis	.06	.03	.00
☐ 357 Winston Garland	.03	.01	.00
☐ 358 Scott Hastings	.03	.01	.00
☐ 359 Marcus Liberty	.15	.07	.01
☐ 360 William Bedford	.03	.01	.00
☐ 361 Lance Blanks	.06	.03	.00
☐ 362 Brad Sellers	.03	.01	.00
☐ 363 Darrell Walker	.03	.01	.00

☐ 364	Orlando Woolridge	.06	.03	.00
☐ 365	Vincent Askew	.10	.05	.01
☐ 366	Mario Elie	.15	.07	.01
☐ 367	Jim Petersen	.03	.01	.00
☐ 368	Matt Bullard	.12	.06	.01
☐ 369	Gerald Henderson	.03	.01	.00
☐ 370	Dave Jamerson	.06	.03	.00
☐ 371	Tree Rollins	.03	.01	.00
☐ 372	Greg Dreiling	.03	.01	.00
☐ 373	George McCloud	.06	.03	.00
☐ 374	Kenny Williams	.03	.01	.00
☐ 375	Randy Wittman	.03	.01	.00
☐ 376	Tony Brown	.03	.01	.00
☐ 377	Lanard Copeland	.03	.01	.00
☐ 378	James Edwards	.03	.01	.00
☐ 379	Bo Kimble	.06	.03	.00
☐ 380	Doc Rivers	.06	.03	.00
☐ 381	Loy Vaught	.10	.05	.01
☐ 382	Elden Campbell	.10	.05	.01
☐ 383	Jack Haley	.03	.01	.00
☐ 384	Tony Smith	.06	.03	.00
☐ 385	Sedale Threatt	.06	.03	.00
☐ 386	Keith Askins	.08	.04	.01
☐ 387	Grant Long	.03	.01	.00
☐ 388	Alan Ogg	.08	.04	.01
☐ 389	Jon Sundvold	.03	.01	.00
☐ 390	Lester Conner	.03	.01	.00
☐ 391	Jeff Grayer	.03	.01	.00
☐ 392	Steve Henson	.03	.01	.00
☐ 393	Larry Krystkowiak	.03	.01	.00
☐ 394	Moses Malone	.10	.05	.01
☐ 395	Scott Brooks	.03	.01	.00
☐ 396	Tellis Frank	.03	.01	.00
☐ 397	Doug West	.06	.03	.00
☐ 398	Rafael Addison	.10	.05	.01
☐ 399	Dave Feitl	.08	.04	.01
☐ 400	Tate George	.06	.03	.00
☐ 401	Terry Mills	.12	.06	.01
☐ 402	Tim McCormick	.03	.01	.00
☐ 403	Xavier McDaniel	.08	.04	.01
☐ 404	Anthony Mason	.25	.12	.02
☐ 405	Brian Quinnett	.03	.01	.00
☐ 406	John Starks	.50	.25	.05
☐ 407	Mark Acres	.03	.01	.00
☐ 408	Greg Kite	.03	.01	.00
☐ 409	Jeff Turner	.03	.01	.00
☐ 410	Morlon Wiley	.03	.01	.00
☐ 411	Dave Hoppen	.03	.01	.00
☐ 412	Brian Oliver	.06	.03	.00
☐ 413	Kenny Payne	.03	.01	.00
☐ 414	Charles Shackleford	.03	.01	.00
☐ 415	Mitchell Wiggins	.03	.01	.00
☐ 416	Jayson Williams	.06	.03	.00
☐ 417	Cedric Ceballos	.12	.06	.01
☐ 418	Negele Knight	.08	.04	.01
☐ 419	Andrew Lang	.06	.03	.00
☐ 420	Jerrod Mustaf	.08	.04	.01
☐ 421	Ed Nealy	.03	.01	.00
☐ 422	Tim Perry	.06	.03	.00
☐ 423	Alaa Abdelnaby	.08	.04	.01
☐ 424	Wayne Cooper	.03	.01	.00
☐ 425	Danny Young	.03	.01	.00
☐ 426	Dennis Hopson	.06	.03	.00
☐ 427	Les Jepsen	.03	.01	.00
☐ 428	Jim Les	.08	.04	.01
☐ 429	Mitch Richmond	.10	.05	.01
☐ 430	Dwayne Schintzius	.06	.03	.00
☐ 431	Spud Webb	.06	.03	.00
☐ 432	Jud Buechler	.06	.03	.00
☐ 433	Antoine Carr	.03	.01	.00
☐ 434	Tom Garrick	.03	.01	.00
☐ 435	Sean Higgins	.10	.05	.01
☐ 436	Avery Johnson	.03	.01	.00
☐ 437	Tony Massenburg	.03	.01	.00
☐ 438	Dana Barros	.06	.03	.00
☐ 439	Quintin Dailey	.03	.01	.00
☐ 440	Bart Kofoed	.08	.04	.01
☐ 441	Nate McMillan	.03	.01	.00
☐ 442	Delaney Rudd	.03	.01	.00
☐ 443	Michael Adams	.08	.04	.01
☐ 444	Mark Alarie	.03	.01	.00
☐ 445	Greg Foster	.03	.01	.00
☐ 446	Tom Hammonds	.06	.03	.00
☐ 447	Andre Turner	.08	.04	.01
☐ 448	David Wingate	.03	.01	.00
☐ 449	Dominique Wilkins SC	.08	.04	.01
☐ 450	Kevin Willis SC	.06	.03	.00
☐ 451	Larry Bird SC	.15	.07	.01
☐ 452	Robert Parish SC	.08	.04	.01
☐ 453	Rex Chapman SC	.06	.03	.00
☐ 454	Kendall Gill SC	.25	.12	.02
☐ 455	Michael Jordan SC	.40	.20	.04
☐ 456	Scottie Pippen SC	.15	.07	.01
☐ 457	Brad Daugherty SC	.08	.04	.01
☐ 458	Larry Nance SC	.06	.03	.00
☐ 459	Rolando Blackman SC	.06	.03	.00
☐ 460	Derek Harper SC	.06	.03	.00
☐ 461	Chris Jackson SC	.06	.03	.00
☐ 462	Todd Lichti SC	.03	.01	.00
☐ 463	Joe Dumars SC	.08	.04	.01
☐ 464	Isiah Thomas SC	.08	.04	.01
☐ 465	Tim Hardaway SC	.20	.10	.02
☐ 466	Chris Mullin SC	.10	.05	.01
☐ 467	Hakeem Olajuwon SC	.08	.04	.01
☐ 468	Otis Thorpe SC	.03	.01	.00
☐ 469	Reggie Miller SC	.08	.04	.01
☐ 470	Detlef Schrempf SC	.06	.03	.00
☐ 471	Ron Harper SC	.06	.03	.00
☐ 472	Charles Smith SC	.06	.03	.00
☐ 473	Magic Johnson SC	.30	.15	.03
☐ 474	James Worthy SC	.08	.04	.01
☐ 475	Sherman Douglas SC	.06	.03	.00
☐ 476	Rony Seikaly SC	.08	.04	.01
☐ 477	Jay Humphries SC	.03	.01	.00
☐ 478	Alvin Robertson SC	.03	.01	.00
☐ 479	Tyrone Corbin SC	.03	.01	.00
☐ 480	Pooh Richardson SC	.08	.04	.01
☐ 481	Sam Bowie SC	.03	.01	.00
☐ 482	Derrick Coleman SC	.15	.07	.01
☐ 483	Patrick Ewing SC	.10	.05	.01
☐ 484	Charles Oakley SC	.03	.01	.00
☐ 485	Dennis Scott SC	.08	.04	.01
☐ 486	Scott Skiles SC	.03	.01	.00
☐ 487	Charles Barkley SC	.10	.05	.01
☐ 488	Hersey Hawkins SC	.06	.03	.00
☐ 489	Tom Chambers SC	.06	.03	.00
☐ 490	Kevin Johnson SC	.10	.05	.01
☐ 491	Clyde Drexler SC	.12	.06	.01
☐ 492	Terry Porter SC	.08	.04	.01
☐ 493	Lionel Simmons SC	.10	.05	.01
☐ 494	Wayman Tisdale SC	.06	.03	.00
☐ 495	Terry Cummings SC	.06	.03	.00
☐ 496	David Robinson SC	.20	.10	.02
☐ 497	Shawn Kemp SC	.20	.10	.02
☐ 498	Ricky Pierce SC	.06	.03	.00
☐ 499	Karl Malone SC	.10	.05	.01
☐ 500	John Stockton SC	.10	.05	.01
☐ 501	Harvey Grant SC	.06	.03	.00
☐ 502	Bernard King SC	.06	.03	.00
☐ 503	Travis Mays Art	.06	.03	.00
☐ 504	Kevin McHale Art	.08	.04	.01
☐ 505	Muggsy Bogues Art	.03	.01	.00
☐ 506	Scottie Pippen Art	.15	.07	.01
☐ 507	Brad Daugherty Art	.08	.04	.01
☐ 508	Derek Harper Art	.06	.03	.00
☐ 509	Chris Jackson Art	.06	.03	.00
☐ 510	Isiah Thomas Art	.08	.04	.01
☐ 511	Tim Hardaway Art	.20	.10	.02
☐ 512	Otis Thorpe Art	.03	.01	.00
☐ 513	Chuck Person Art	.06	.03	.00
☐ 514	Ron Harper Art	.06	.03	.00
☐ 515	James Worthy Art	.08	.04	.01
☐ 516	Sherman Douglas Art	.06	.03	.00
☐ 517	Dale Ellis Art	.06	.03	.00
☐ 518	Tony Campbell Art	.03	.01	.00
☐ 519	Derrick Coleman Art	.15	.07	.01
☐ 520	Gerald Wilkins Art	.03	.01	.00
☐ 521	Scott Skiles Art	.03	.01	.00
☐ 522	Manute Bol Art	.03	.01	.00
☐ 523	Tom Chambers Art	.06	.03	.00
☐ 524	Terry Porter Art	.08	.04	.01
☐ 525	Lionel Simmons Art	.10	.05	.01
☐ 526	Sean Elliott Art	.10	.05	.01
☐ 527	Shawn Kemp Art	.20	.10	.02
☐ 528	John Stockton Art	.10	.05	.01
☐ 529	Harvey Grant Art	.06	.03	.00
☐ 530	Michael Adams All-Time Active Leader Three-Point Field Goals	.06	.03	.00
☐ 531	Charles Barkley All-Time Active Leader Field Goal Percentage	.10	.05	.01
☐ 532	Larry Bird All-Time Active Leader Free Throw Percentage	.15	.07	.01
☐ 533	Maurice Cheeks All-Time Active Leader Steals	.06	.03	.00
☐ 534	Mark Eaton All-Time Active Leader Blocks	.03	.01	.00
☐ 535	Magic Johnson All-Time Active Leader Assists	.30	.15	.03
☐ 536	Michael Jordan All-Time Active Leader Scoring Average	.40	.20	.04

☐ 537 Moses Malone All-Time Active Leader Rebounds	.08	.04	.01
☐ 538 NBA Finals Game 1 Perkins' Three Pointer (Sam Perkins)	.06	.03	.00
☐ 539 NBA Finals Game 2 Bulls Rout Lakers (Pippen against Worthy)	.08	.04	.01
☐ 540 NBA Finals Game 3 Bulls Win OT Thriller (Vlade Divac lay-in)	.06	.03	.00
☐ 541 NBA Finals Game 4 Bulls One Game Away (John Paxson jumper)	.06	.03	.00
☐ 542 NBA Finals Game 5 Jordan, Bulls Win First Title (Jordan reverses over Vlade Divac)	.10	.05	.01
☐ 543 Championship Card Chicago Bulls Champs (Michael Jordan kissing trophy)	.10	.05	.01
☐ 544 Otis Smith Stay in School	.03	.01	.00
☐ 545 Jeff Turner Stay in School	.03	.01	.00
☐ 546 Larry Johnson	4.00	2.00	.40
☐ 547 Kenny Anderson	.75	.35	.07
☐ 548 Billy Owens	2.00	1.00	.20
☐ 549 Dikembe Mutombo	2.00	1.00	.20
☐ 550 Steve Smith	.90	.45	.09
☐ 551 Doug Smith	.35	.17	.03
☐ 552 Luc Longley	.15	.07	.01
☐ 553 Mark Macon	.30	.15	.03
☐ 554 Stacey Augmon	.75	.35	.07
☐ 555 Brian Williams	.30	.15	.03
☐ 556 Terrell Brandon	.35	.17	.03
☐ 557 Walter Davis Team USA 1976	.06	.03	.00
☐ 558 Vern Fleming Team USA 1984	.06	.03	.00
☐ 559 Joe Kleine Team USA 1984	.06	.03	.00
☐ 560 Jon Koncak Team USA 1984	.06	.03	.00
☐ 561 Sam Perkins Team USA 1984	.10	.05	.01
☐ 562 Alvin Robertson Team USA 1984	.06	.03	.00
☐ 563 Wayman Tisdale Team USA 1984	.06	.03	.00
☐ 564 Jeff Turner Team USA 1984	.06	.03	.00
☐ 565 Willie Anderson Team USA 1988	.06	.03	.00
☐ 566 Stacey Augmon Team USA 1988	.40	.20	.04
☐ 567 Bimbo Coles Team USA 1988	.10	.05	.01
☐ 568 Jeff Grayer Team USA 1988	.06	.03	.00
☐ 569 Hersey Hawkins Team USA 1988	.12	.06	.01
☐ 570 Dan Majerle Team USA 1988	.10	.05	.01
☐ 571 Danny Manning Team USA 1988	.10	.05	.01
☐ 572 J.R. Reid Team USA 1988	.06	.03	.00
☐ 573 Mitch Richmond Team USA 1988	.10	.05	.01
☐ 574 Charles Smith Team USA 1988	.10	.05	.01
☐ 575 Charles Barkley Team USA 1992	.50	.25	.05
☐ 576 Larry Bird Team USA 1992	.75	.35	.07
☐ 577 Patrick Ewing Team USA 1992	.60	.30	.06
☐ 578 Magic Johnson Team USA 1992	1.50	.75	.15
☐ 579 Michael Jordan Team USA 1992	2.00	1.00	.20
☐ 580 Karl Malone Team USA 1992	.50	.25	.05
☐ 581 Chris Mullin Team USA 1992	.50	.25	.05
☐ 582 Scottie Pippen Team USA 1992	.90	.45	.09
☐ 583 David Robinson Team USA 1992	1.50	.75	.15
☐ 584 John Stockton Team USA 1992	.50	.25	.05
☐ 585 Chuck Daly CO Team USA 1992	.15	.07	.01
☐ 586 Lenny Wilkens CO Team USA 1992	.12	.06	.01
☐ 587 P.J. Carlesimo CO Team USA 1992	.15	.07	.01
☐ 588 Mike Krzyzewski CO Team USA 1992	.30	.15	.03
☐ 589 Checklist Card 1	.06	.01	.00
☐ 590 Checklist Card 2	.06	.01	.00
☐ NNO Team USA SP Title Card	10.00	5.00	1.00
☐ xx Head of the Class SP Kenny Anderson Larry Johnson Dikembe Mutombo Billy Owens Doug Smith Steve Smith	25.00	12.50	2.50

1991-92 Hoops All-Star MVP's

This six-card standard-size (2 1/2" by 3 1/2") set commemorates the most valuable player of the NBA All-Star games from 1986 to 1991. One card was inserted in each series II rack pack. On a white card face, the front features non-action color photos framed by either a blue (7, 9, 12) or red (8, 10, 11) border. The top thicker border is jagged and displays the player's name, while the year the award was received appears in a colored box in the lower left corner. The backs have the same design and feature a color action photo from the All-Star game. The cards are numbered on the back by Roman numerals.

	MINT	EXC	G-VG
COMPLETE SET (6)	7.00	3.50	.70
COMMON PLAYER (7-12)	.30	.15	.03
☐ 7 Isiah Thomas (Numbered VII)	1.00	.50	.10
☐ 8 Tom Chambers (Numbered VIII)	.30	.15	.03
☐ 9 Michael Jordan (Numbered IX)	3.00	1.50	.30
☐ 10 Karl Malone (Numbered X)	1.50	.75	.15
☐ 11 Magic Johnson (Numbered XI)	2.00	1.00	.20
☐ 12 Charles Barkley (Numbered XII)	1.50	.75	.15

1991-92 Hoops McDonald's

Four-card cello packs, featuring three NBA cards and one Olympic team card, were distributed at participating McDonald's restaurants with the purchase of any Extra Value Meal, or for 49 cents with any other purchase. A specially marked instant

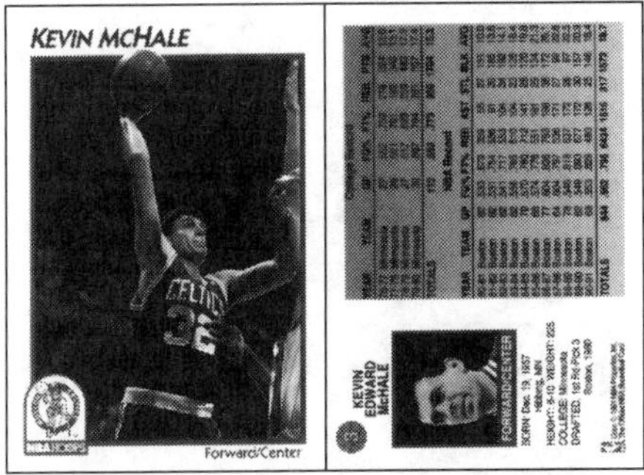

winner card replaced a regular card in one in 20,000 packs, and the holder of this card received the complete 70-card "Superstar" set. The standard-size (2 1/2" by 3 1/2") cards display color action photos enclosed by different color borders on a white card face. The horizontally oriented backs have a color head shot as well as biographical and statistical information. The set divides into three sections and is checklisted below as follows: player cards (1-50 listed alphabetically according to teams), USA Olympic basketball team (51-62), and Chicago Bulls (63-70 available only in the Chicago area). The cards are numbered on the back.

	MINT	EXC	G-VG
COMPLETE SET (70)	18.00	9.00	1.80
COMMON PLAYER (1-50)	.05	.02	.00
COMMON PLAYER (51-62)	.10	.05	.01
COMMON PLAYER (63-70)	.50	.25	.05
☐ 1 Dominique Wilkins Atlanta Hawks	.25	.12	.02
☐ 2 Larry Bird Boston Celtics	.75	.35	.07
☐ 3 Kevin McHale Boston Celtics	.12	.06	.01
☐ 4 Robert Parish Boston Celtics	.15	.07	.01
☐ 5 Rex Chapman Charlotte Hornets	.12	.06	.01
☐ 6 Michael Jordan Chicago Bulls	1.50	.75	.15
☐ 7 John Paxson Chicago Bulls	.10	.05	.01
☐ 8 Scottie Pippen Chicago Bulls	.50	.25	.05
☐ 9 Brad Daugherty Cleveland Cavaliers	.20	.10	.02
☐ 10 Rolando Blackman Dallas Mavericks	.10	.05	.01
☐ 11 Derek Harper Dallas Mavericks	.08	.04	.01
☐ 12 Joe Dumars Detroit Pistons	.15	.07	.01
☐ 13 Bill Laimbeer Detroit Pistons	.08	.04	.01
☐ 14 Isiah Thomas Detroit Pistons	.25	.12	.02
☐ 15 Tim Hardaway Golden State Warriors	.35	.17	.03
☐ 16 Chris Mullin Golden State Warriors	.30	.15	.03
☐ 17 Hakeem Olajuwon Houston Rockets	.25	.12	.02
☐ 18 Reggie Miller Indiana Pacers	.15	.07	.01
☐ 19 Chuck Person Indiana Pacers	.12	.06	.01
☐ 20 Charles Smith Los Angeles Clippers	.15	.07	.01
☐ 21 Vlade Divac Los Angeles Lakers	.15	.07	.01
☐ 22 James Worthy Los Angeles Lakers	.20	.10	.02
☐ 23 Rony Seikaly Miami Heat	.15	.07	.01
☐ 24 Pooh Richardson Minnesota Timberwolves	.20	.10	.02
☐ 25 Derrick Coleman New Jersey Nets	.50	.25	.05
☐ 26 Patrick Ewing New York Knicks	.35	.17	.03
☐ 27 Xavier McDaniel New York Knicks	.10	.05	.01
☐ 28 Dennis Scott Orlando Magic	.20	.10	.02
☐ 29 Scott Skiles Orlando Magic	.08	.04	.01
☐ 30 Charles Barkley Philadelphia 76ers	.35	.17	.03
☐ 31 Hersey Hawkins Philadelphia 76ers	.12	.06	.01
☐ 32 Tom Chambers Phoenix Suns	.12	.06	.01
☐ 33 Kevin Johnson Phoenix Suns	.40	.20	.04
☐ 34 Clyde Drexler Portland Trail Blazers	.50	.25	.05
☐ 35 Terry Porter Portland Trail Blazers	.15	.07	.01
☐ 36 Buck Williams Portland Trail Blazers	.08	.04	.01
☐ 37 Mitch Richmond Sacramento Kings	.20	.10	.02
☐ 38 Lionel Simmons Sacramento Kings	.25	.12	.02
☐ 39 Terry Cummings San Antonio Spurs	.12	.06	.01
☐ 40 Sean Elliott San Antonio Spurs	.15	.07	.01
☐ 41 David Robinson San Antonio Spurs	.75	.35	.07
☐ 42 Shawn Kemp Seattle Supersonics	.50	.25	.05
☐ 43 Ricky Pierce Seattle Supersonics	.08	.04	.01
☐ 44 Karl Malone Utah Jazz	.25	.12	.02
☐ 45 John Stockton Utah Jazz	.25	.12	.02
☐ 46 Bernard King Washington Bullets	.10	.05	.01
☐ 47 Larry Johnson Charlotte Hornets	1.50	.75	.15
☐ 48 Dikembe Mutombo Denver Nuggets	1.00	.50	.10
☐ 49 Billy Owens Golden State Warriors	1.00	.50	.10
☐ 50 Kenny Anderson New Jersey Nets	.75	.35	.07
☐ 51 Charles Barkley USA	.35	.17	.03
☐ 52 Larry Bird USA	.75	.35	.07
☐ 53 Patrick Ewing USA	.35	.17	.03
☐ 54 Magic Johnson USA	1.00	.50	.10
☐ 55 Michael Jordan USA	1.50	.75	.15
☐ 56 Karl Malone USA	.20	.10	.02
☐ 57 Chris Mullin USA	.30	.15	.03
☐ 58 Scottie Pippen USA	.40	.20	.04
☐ 59 David Robinson USA	.75	.35	.07
☐ 60 John Stockton USA	.20	.10	.02
☐ 61 Chuck Daly CO USA	.10	.05	.01
☐ 62 USAB Team	.35	.17	.03
☐ 63 B.J. Armstrong	.75	.35	.07
☐ 64 Bill Cartwright	.50	.25	.05
☐ 65 Horace Grant	1.00	.50	.10
☐ 66 Craig Hodges	.50	.25	.05
☐ 67 Stacey King	.50	.25	.05
☐ 68 Cliff Levingston	.50	.25	.05
☐ 69 Will Perdue	.50	.25	.05
☐ 70 Scott Williams	.60	.30	.06

1972-73 Icee Bear

The 1972-73 Icee Bear set contains 20 player cards each measuring approximately 3" by 5". The cards are printed on thin stock. The fronts feature color facial pictures, and the backs show brief biographical information. The set may have been printed in 1973-74 or perhaps later. There are three cards that are more difficult to find than the other 17; these three are listed as SP's in the checklist below.

	NRMT	VG-E	GOOD
COMPLETE SET (20)	200.00	100.00	20.00
COMMON PLAYER (1-20)	2.50	1.25	.25
COMMON PLAYER SP	15.00	7.50	1.50

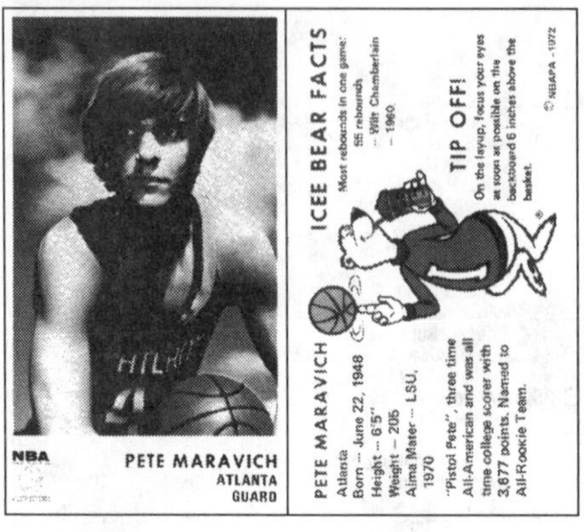

□ 1 Dennis Awtrey	2.50	1.25	.25
□ 2 Tom Boerwinkle	2.50	1.25	.25
□ 3 Austin Carr SP	15.00	7.50	1.50
□ 4 Wilt Chamberlain	35.00	17.50	3.50
□ 5 Archie Clark SP	15.00	7.50	1.50
□ 6 Dave DeBusschere	7.50	3.75	.75
□ 7 Walt Frazier SP	35.00	17.50	3.50
□ 8 John Havlicek	15.00	7.50	1.50
□ 9 Connie Hawkins	7.50	3.75	.75
□ 10 Kareem Abdul-Jabbar	35.00	17.50	3.50
□ 11 Bob Love	3.50	1.75	.35
□ 12 Jerry Lucas	7.50	3.75	.75
□ 13 Pete Maravich	20.00	10.00	2.00
□ 14 Calvin Murphy	4.00	2.00	.40
□ 15 Oscar Robertson	16.00	8.00	1.60
□ 16 Jerry Sloan	2.50	1.25	.25
□ 17 Wes Unseld	6.00	3.00	.60
□ 18 Dick Van Arsdale	2.50	1.25	.25
□ 19 Jerry West	21.00	10.50	2.10
□ 20 Sidney Wicks	4.50	2.25	.45

1988-89 Jazz Smokey

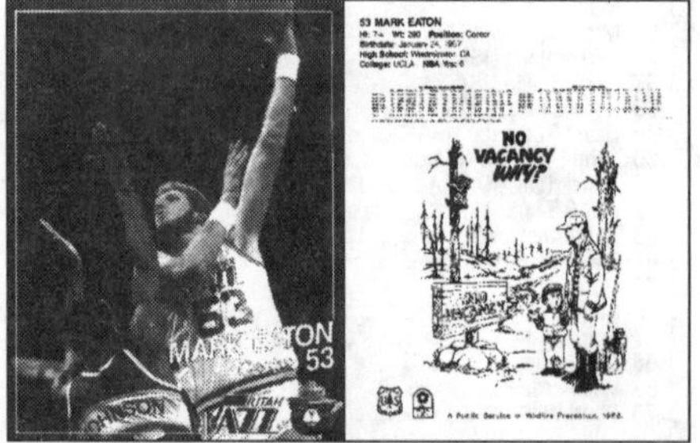

The 1988-89 Smokey Utah Jazz set contains eight 8" by 10" (approximately) cards featuring color action photos. The card backs feature a large fire safety cartoon and player information in the form of year-by-year statistics for each NBA regular season and playoffs. The cards are unnumbered and are ordered below alphabetically. The set was sponsored by the Utah Department of State Lands and Forestry and U.S.D.A. Forest Service. The player's name, number, and position are overprinted in white in the lower right corner of each obverse.

	MINT	EXC	G-VG
COMPLETE SET (8)	45.00	22.50	4.50
COMMON PLAYER (1-8)	4.00	2.00	.40
□ 1 Thurl Bailey	5.00	2.50	.50
□ 2 Mark Eaton	6.00	3.00	.60
□ 3 Frank Layden CO	4.00	2.00	.40
□ 4 Karl Malone	15.00	7.50	1.50
□ 5 Marc Iavaroni	4.00	2.00	.40
□ 6 John Stockton	15.00	7.50	1.50
□ 7 Smokey Bear	4.00	2.00	.40
□ 8 Bobby Hansen	4.00	2.00	.40

1989 Jazz Old Home

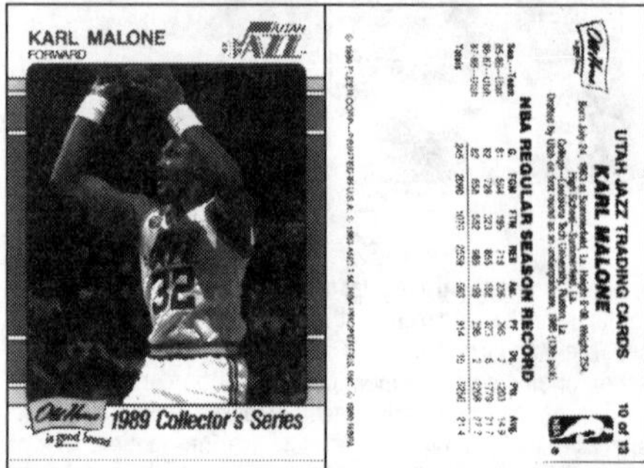

This 13-card set of Utah Jazz was sponsored by Old Home bread, and its company logo appears on both sides of the card. The cards measure the standard size (2 1/2" by 3 1/2"). The color action player photo on the front has rounded corners, and it is superimposed on a background of yellow, green, and purple stripes of varying width. The player's name and team logo appear above the picture, and the words "1989 Collector's Series" below. The horizontally-oriented backs are printed in pink and red and present biographical and statistical information. The cards are numbered on the back.

	MINT	EXC	G-VG
COMPLETE SET (13)	65.00	32.50	6.50
COMMON PLAYER (1-13)	2.50	1.25	.25
□ 1 Thurl Bailey	3.50	1.75	.35
□ 2 Mike Brown	2.50	1.25	.25
□ 3 Mark Eaton	4.50	2.25	.45
□ 4 Darrell Griffith	3.50	1.75	.35
□ 5 Bobby Hansen	2.50	1.25	.25
□ 6 Marc Iavaroni	2.50	1.25	.25
□ 7 Frank Layden CO	3.50	1.75	.35
□ 8 Eric Leckner	2.50	1.25	.25
□ 9 Jim Les	3.50	1.75	.35
□ 10 Karl Malone	20.00	10.00	2.00
□ 11 Jose Ortiz	3.50	1.75	.35
□ 12 Scott Roth	2.50	1.25	.25
□ 13 John Stockton	20.00	10.00	2.00

1990-91 Jazz Star

This 12-card set of Utah Jazz measures the standard size (2 1/2" and 3 1/2"). The fronts feature color action shots, with purple borders that wash out in the middle of the card face. The horizontally oriented backs are printed in purple on white and have various kinds of player information. The cards are numbered on the back and checklisted below accordingly.

	MINT	EXC	G-VG
COMPLETE SET (12)	10.00	5.00	1.00
COMMON PLAYER (1-12)	.60	.30	.06
□ 1 Karl Malone	2.50	1.25	.25
□ 2 John Stockton	2.50	1.25	.25
□ 3 Mark Eaton	.90	.45	.09
□ 4 Blue Edwards	.90	.45	.09
□ 5 Thurl Bailey	.75	.35	.07
□ 6 Mike Brown	.60	.30	.06
□ 7 Jeff Malone	.90	.45	.09

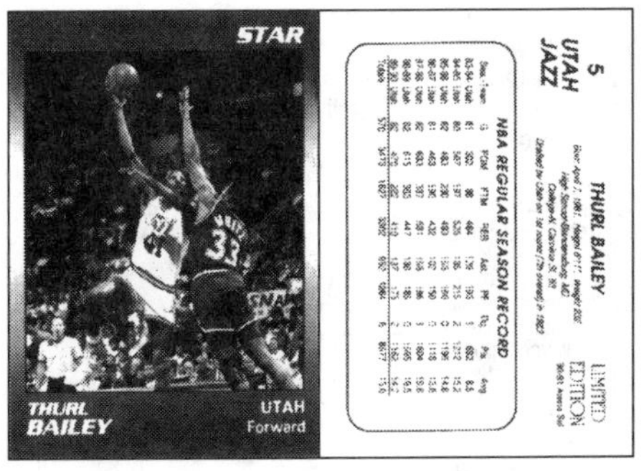

☐ 8 Andy Toolson	.60	.30	.06
☐ 9 Darrell Griffith	.75	.35	.07
☐ 10 Delaney Rudd	.60	.30	.06
☐ 11 Walter Palmer	.60	.30	.06
☐ 12 Jerry Sloan CO	.75	.35	.07

1985-86 JMS Game

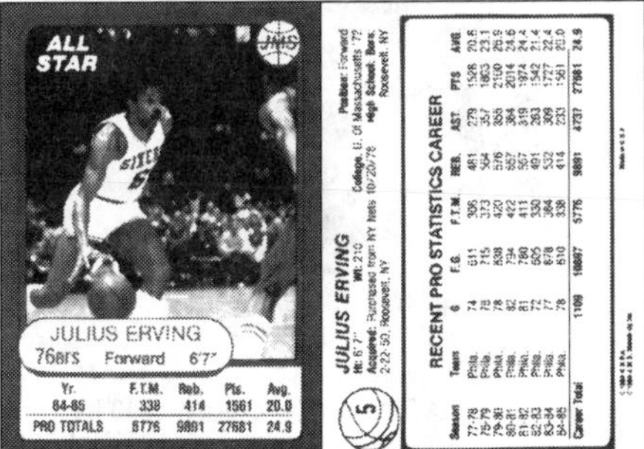

These standard size (2 1/2" by 3 1/2") cards were issued by J.M.S. in uncut team sheets as part of a table top game and featured nine players each from the Philadelphia 76ers (1-9), Boston Celtics (10-18), and Los Angeles Lakers (19-27). The front features a color action player photo, with a blue border on red background. Player information appears in a white capsule, and statistics are given below the picture in a pink box. In a horizontal format the back has a statistical breakdown year by year and brief biographical information. The cards are numbered on the back.

	MINT	EXC	G-VG
COMPLETE SET (27)	250.00	125.00	25.00
COMMON 76ERS (1-9)	4.00	2.00	.40
COMMON CELTICS (10-18)	4.00	2.00	.40
COMMON LAKERS (19-27)	4.00	2.00	.40
☐ 1 Maurice Cheeks	8.00	4.00	.80
☐ 2 Moses Malone	15.00	7.50	1.50
☐ 3 Bobby Jones	8.00	4.00	.80
☐ 4 Charles Barkley	40.00	20.00	4.00
☐ 5 Julius Erving	25.00	12.50	2.50
☐ 6 Clint Richardson	4.00	2.00	.40
☐ 8 Sedale Threatt	8.00	4.00	.80
☐ 7 Andrew Toney	6.00	3.00	.60
☐ 9 Clem Johnson	4.00	2.00	.40
☐ 10 Bill Walton	12.00	6.00	1.20
☐ 11 Danny Ainge	8.00	4.00	.80
☐ 12 Robert Parish	15.00	7.50	1.50
☐ 13 Kevin McHale	12.00	6.00	1.20
☐ 14 Larry Bird	45.00	22.50	4.50
☐ 15 Dennis Johnson	6.00	3.00	.60
☐ 16 Ray Williams	4.00	2.00	.40
☐ 17 Scott Wedman	4.00	2.00	.40
☐ 18 Greg Kite	4.00	2.00	.40
☐ 19 Michael Cooper	8.00	4.00	.80
☐ 20 Kareem Abdul-Jabbar	25.00	12.50	2.50
☐ 21 Jamaal Wilkes	8.00	4.00	.80
☐ 22 Bob McAdoo	8.00	4.00	.80
☐ 23 James Worthy	20.00	10.00	2.00
☐ 24 Magic Johnson	60.00	30.00	6.00
☐ 25 Michael McGee	4.00	2.00	.40
☐ 26 Kurt Rambis	6.00	3.00	.60
☐ 27 Byron Scott	8.00	4.00	.80

1957-58 Kahn's

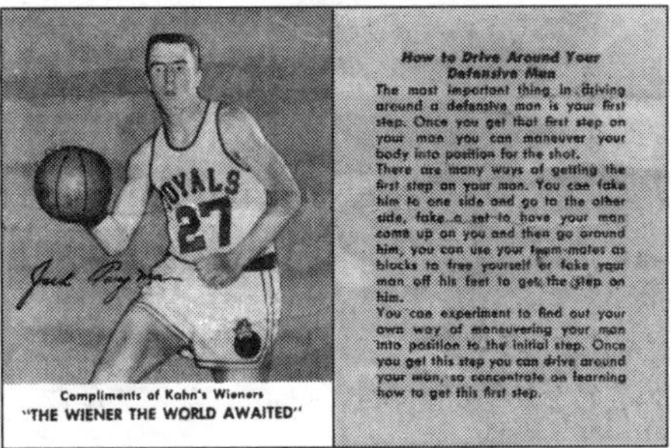

The 1957-58 Kahn's Basketball set contains 11 black and white cards. Cards are approximately 3 3/16" by 3 15/16". The backs contain "How To" articles and instructional text. Only Cincinnati Royals players are depicted.

	NRMT	VG-E	GOOD
COMPLETE SET (11)	1250.00	600.00	135.00
COMMON PLAYER (1-11)	90.00	45.00	9.00
☐ 1 Richard Duckett	90.00	45.00	9.00
☐ 2 George King	90.00	45.00	9.00
☐ 3 Clyde Lovelette	175.00	85.00	18.00
☐ 4 Tom Marshall	90.00	45.00	9.00
☐ 5 Jim Paxson	100.00	50.00	10.00
☐ 6 Dave Piontek	90.00	45.00	9.00
☐ 7 Richard Regan	90.00	45.00	9.00
☐ 8 Richard(Dick) Ricketts	100.00	50.00	10.00
☐ 9 Maurice Stokes	225.00	110.00	22.00
☐ 10 Jack Twyman	175.00	85.00	18.00
☐ 11 Bobby Wanzer	125.00	60.00	12.50

1958-59 Kahn's

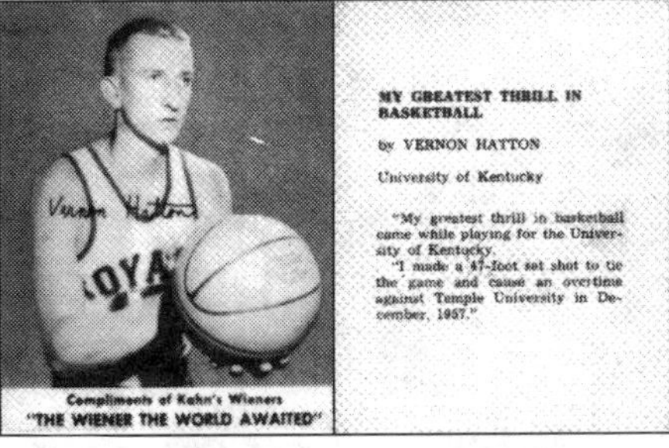

The 1958-59 Kahn's Basketball set contains 10 black and white cards. Cards measure approximately 3 1/4" by 3 15/16". The backs feature a short narrative entitled "My Greatest Thrill in Basketball" allegedly written by the player depicted on the front. Only Cincinnati Royals players are depicted. The Sihugo Green card is supposedly a little tougher to find than the other cards in the set.

	NRMT	VG-E	GOOD
COMPLETE SET (10)	750.00	350.00	90.00
COMMON PLAYER (1-10)	70.00	35.00	7.00
☐ 1 Arlen Bockhorn	70.00	35.00	7.00
☐ 2 Archie Dees	70.00	35.00	7.00
☐ 3 Sihugo Green	100.00	50.00	10.00
☐ 4 Vern Hatton	70.00	35.00	7.00
☐ 5 Tom Marshall	70.00	35.00	7.00
☐ 6 Jack Paar	80.00	40.00	8.00
☐ 7 George Palmer	70.00	35.00	7.00
☐ 8 Jim Palmer	70.00	35.00	7.00
☐ 9 Dave Piontek	70.00	35.00	7.00
☐ 10 Jack Twyman	135.00	65.00	13.50

1959-60 Kahn's

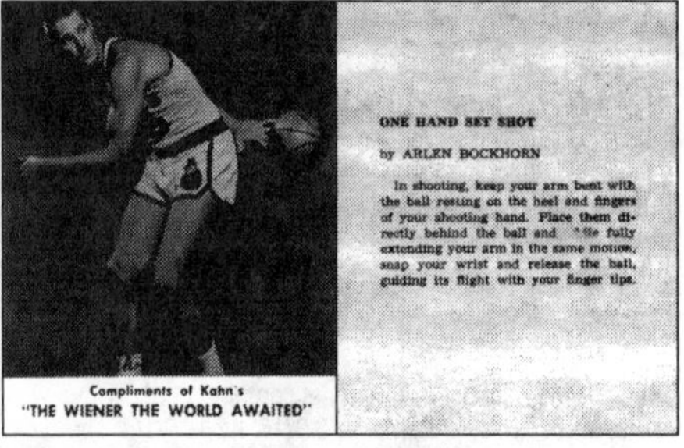

The 1959-60 Kahn's Basketball set features 10 black and white cards. Cards are approximately 3 1/4" by 4". The backs feature descriptive narratives allegedly written by the player depicted on the front. No statistics are featured on the backs. Only Cincinnati Royals players are depicted.

	NRMT	VG-E	GOOD
COMPLETE SET (10)	550.00	275.00	55.00
COMMON PLAYER (1-10)	50.00	25.00	5.00
☐ 1 Arlen Bockhorn	50.00	25.00	5.00
☐ 2 Wayne Embry	70.00	35.00	7.00
☐ 3 Tom Marshall	50.00	25.00	5.00
☐ 4 Med Park	50.00	25.00	5.00
☐ 5 Dave Piontek	50.00	25.00	5.00
☐ 6 Hub Reed	50.00	25.00	5.00
☐ 7 Phil Rollins	50.00	25.00	5.00
☐ 8 Larry Staverman	50.00	25.00	5.00
☐ 9 Jack Twyman	100.00	50.00	10.00
☐ 10 Win Wilfong	50.00	25.00	5.00

1960-61 Kahn's

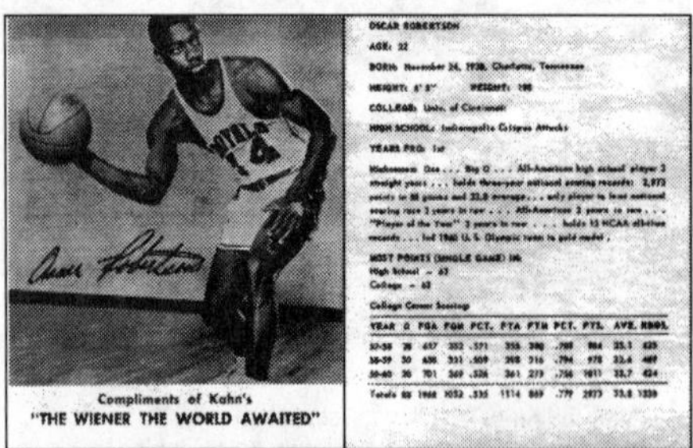

The 1960-61 Kahn's Basketball set features 12 black and white cards. Cards are approximately 3 1/4" by 3 15/16". The backs contain statistical season-by-season records up through the 1959-60 season, player vital statistics, and a short biography of the player's career. The key cards in the set are the first professional cards of Hall of Famers Oscar Robertson and Jerry West. The Lakers' Jerry West is the only non-Cincinnati Royals player depicted and his card does not have any statistical breakdown.

	NRMT	VG-E	GOOD
COMPLETE SET (12)	1800.00	900.00	200.00
COMMON PLAYER (1-12)	35.00	17.50	3.50
☐ 1 Arlen Bockhorn	35.00	17.50	3.50
☐ 2 Robert L. Boozer	40.00	20.00	4.00
☐ 3 Ralph E. Davis	35.00	17.50	3.50
☐ 4 Wayne Embry	45.00	22.50	4.50
☐ 5 Mike Farmer	35.00	17.50	3.50
☐ 6 Phil Jordan	35.00	17.50	3.50
☐ 7 Hub Reed	35.00	17.50	3.50
☐ 8 Oscar Robertson	600.00	300.00	60.00
☐ 9 Larry Staverman	35.00	17.50	3.50
☐ 10 Jack Twyman	75.00	37.50	7.50
☐ 11 Jerry West	900.00	450.00	90.00
☐ 12 Win Wilfong	35.00	17.50	3.50

1961-62 Kahn's

The 1961-62 Kahn's Basketball set consists of 13 black and white cards. Cards measure approximately 3 3/16" by 4 1/16". The Lakers' Jerry West is the only non-Cincinnati Royals player depicted and there is also a card of coach Charley Wolf. The backs of the cards are blank; this was the only year the Kahn's basketball cards were blank backed.

	NRMT	VG-E	GOOD
COMPLETE SET (13)	900.00	450.00	90.00
COMMON PLAYER (1-13)	25.00	12.50	2.50
☐ 1 Arlen Bockhorn	25.00	12.50	2.50
☐ 2 Bob Boozer	30.00	15.00	3.00
☐ 3 Joe Buckhalter	25.00	12.50	2.50
☐ 4 Wayne Embry	35.00	17.50	3.50
☐ 5 Bob Nordmann	25.00	12.50	2.50
☐ 6 Hub Reed	25.00	12.50	2.50
☐ 7 Oscar Robertson	250.00	125.00	25.00
☐ 8 Adrian Smith	30.00	15.00	3.00
☐ 9 Jack Twyman	50.00	25.00	5.00
☐ 10 Bob Wesenhahn	25.00	12.50	2.50
☐ 11 Jerry West	375.00	175.00	40.00
☐ 12 Charley Wolf CO	25.00	12.50	2.50
☐ 13 Dave Zeller	25.00	12.50	2.50

1962-63 Kahn's

The 1962-63 Kahn's Basketball set contains 11 black and white cards. Cards measure approximately 3 1/4" by 4 3/16". Jerry West of the Lakers is the only non-Cincinnati Royals player depicted and there is also a card of Royals' coach Charley Wolf. The backs feature a short biography of the player depicted on the front of the card. The Jerry West card has a picture with no

border around it. Cards of Bockhorn, Boozer, Reed, and Twyman are oriented horizontally.

	NRMT	VG-E	GOOD
COMPLETE SET (11)	650.00	325.00	65.00
COMMON PLAYER (1-11)	25.00	12.50	2.50
☐ 1 Arlen Bockhorn HOR	25.00	12.50	2.50
☐ 2 Bob Boozer HOR	30.00	15.00	3.00
☐ 3 Wayne Embry	35.00	17.50	3.50
☐ 4 Tom Hawkins	35.00	17.50	3.50
☐ 5 Bud Olsen	25.00	12.50	2.50
☐ 6 Hub Reed HOR	25.00	12.50	2.50
☐ 7 Oscar Robertson	175.00	85.00	18.00
☐ 8 Adrian Smith	30.00	15.00	3.00
☐ 9 Jack Twyman HOR	50.00	25.00	5.00
☐ 10 Jerry West	250.00	125.00	25.00
☐ 11 Charley Wolf CO	25.00	12.50	2.50

1963-64 Kahn's

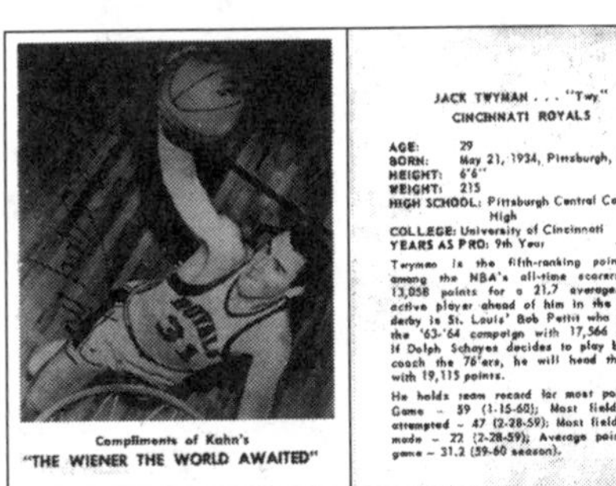

The 1963-64 Kahn's Basketball set contains 13 black and white cards. Cards measure approximately 3 1/4" by 4 3/16". This is the only Kahn's basketball set on which there is a distinctive white border on the fronts of the cards; in this respect the set is similar to the 1963 Kahn's baseball and football sets. A brief biography of the player is contained on the back of the card. Jerry West of the Lakers is the only non-Cincinnati Royals player depicted and there is also a card of coach Jack McMahon. The Jerry West card is identical to that of the previous year except set in smaller type and with the distinctive white border on the front. The cards of Bob Boozer and Jack Twyman are oriented horizontally.

	NRMT	VG-E	GOOD
COMPLETE SET (13)	600.00	300.00	60.00
COMMON PLAYER (1-13)	20.00	10.00	2.00
☐ 1 Jay Arnette	20.00	10.00	2.00
☐ 2 Arlen Bockhorn	20.00	10.00	2.00
☐ 3 Bob Boozer HOR	25.00	12.50	2.50
☐ 4 Wayne Embry	30.00	15.00	3.00
☐ 5 Tom Hawkins	30.00	15.00	3.00
☐ 6 Jerry Lucas	100.00	50.00	10.00
☐ 7 Jack McMahon CO	20.00	10.00	2.00
☐ 8 Bud Olsen	20.00	10.00	2.00
☐ 9 Oscar Robertson	125.00	60.00	12.50
☐ 10 Adrian Smith	20.00	10.00	2.00
☐ 11 Thomas P. Thacker	25.00	12.50	2.50
☐ 12 Jack Twyman HOR	40.00	20.00	4.00
☐ 13 Jerry West	175.00	85.00	18.00

1964-65 Kahn's

The 1964-65 Kahn's Basketball set contains 12 full-color subjects on 14 distinct cards. Cards measure approximately 3" by 3 5/8". These cards come in two types distinguishable by the color of the printing on the backs. Type I cards (1-3) have light maroon printing on the backs, while type II (4-12) have black printing on the backs. The fronts are completely devoid of any written material. There are two poses each of Jerry Lucas and Oscar Robertson.

	NRMT	VG-E	GOOD
COMPLETE SET (14)	550.00	275.00	55.00
COMMON PLAYER (1-3)	20.00	10.00	2.00
COMMON PLAYER (4-12)	20.00	10.00	2.00
☐ 1 Harold(Happy) Hairston	25.00	12.50	2.50
☐ 2 Jack McMahon CO	20.00	10.00	2.00
☐ 3 George(Jif) Wilson	20.00	10.00	2.00
☐ 4 Jay Arnette	20.00	10.00	2.00
☐ 5 Arlen Bockhorn	20.00	10.00	2.00
☐ 6 Wayne Embry	25.00	12.50	2.50
☐ 7 Tom Hawkins	25.00	12.50	2.50
☐ 8A Jerry Lucas (windows open; right thumb hidden)	50.00	25.00	5.00
☐ 8B Jerry Lucas (no windows visible; right thumb barely visible)	50.00	25.00	5.00
☐ 9 Bud Olsen	20.00	10.00	2.00
☐ 10A Oscar Robertson (facing side)	125.00	60.00	12.50
☐ 10B Oscar Robertson (facing front)	125.00	60.00	12.50
☐ 11 Adrian Smith	20.00	10.00	2.00
☐ 12 Jack Twyman	40.00	20.00	4.00

1965-66 Kahn's

The 1965-66 Kahn's Basketball set contains four full-color cards featuring players of the Cincinnati Royals. Cards in this set measure approximately 3" by 3 9/16". This was the last of the Kahn's Basketball issues and the second in full color. The fronts are devoid of all written material, and the backs are printed in red ink. The "Compliments of Kahn's, The Wiener the World Awaited" slogan appears on the backs of the cards. The set is presumed complete with the following cards.

	NRMT	VG-E	GOOD
COMPLETE SET (4)	250.00	125.00	25.00
COMMON PLAYER (1-4)	30.00	15.00	3.00

☐ 1 Wayne Embry	30.00	15.00	3.00
☐ 2 Jerry Lucas	75.00	37.50	7.50
☐ 3 Oscar Robertson	125.00	60.00	12.50
☐ 4 Jack Twyman	50.00	25.00	5.00

1971 Keds KedKards *

This set is composed of crude artistic renditions of popular subjects from various sports from 1971 who were apparently celebrity endorsers of Keds shoes. The cards actually form a complete panel on the Keds tennis shoes box. The two different panels are actually different sizes; the Bing panel contains smaller cards. The smaller Bubba Smith shows him without beard and standing straight; the large Bubba shows him leaning over, with beard, and jersey number partially visible. The individual player card portions of the card panels measure approximately 2 15/16" by 2 3/4" and 2 5/16" by 2 3/16" respectively, although it should noted that there are slight size differences among the individual cards even on the same panel. The panel background is colored in black and yellow.

	NRMT	VG-E	GOOD
COMPLETE SET (2)	60.00	30.00	6.00
COMMON PLAYER (1-2)	25.00	12.50	2.50
☐ 1 Dave Bing (Basketball) Clark Graebner (Tennis) Bubba Smith (Football) Jim Maloney (Baseball)	50.00	25.00	5.00
☐ 2 Willis Reed (Basketball) Stan Smith (Tennis) Bubba Smith (Football) Johnny Bench (Baseball)	25.00	12.50	2.50

1948 Kellogg's Pep *

These rather unattractive cards measure 1 7/16" by 1 5/8". The card front presents a black and white head-and-shoulders shot of the player, with a white border. The back has the player's

name and a brief description of his accomplishments. The cards are unnumbered. There is only one basketball card in the set. The catalog designation for this set is F273-19.

	NRMT	VG-E	GOOD
COMPLETE SET (20)	1000.00	500.00	125.00
COMMON BASEBALL (1-5)	20.00	10.00	2.00
COMMON FOOTBALL (6-10)	30.00	15.00	3.00
COMMON OTHERS (11-18)	10.00	5.00	1.00
☐ 1 Phil Cavaretta (baseball)	30.00	15.00	3.00
☐ 2 Orval Grove (baseball)	20.00	10.00	2.00
☐ 3 Mike Tresh (baseball)	20.00	10.00	2.00
☐ 4 Paul(Dizzy) Trout (baseball)	20.00	10.00	2.00
☐ 5 Dick Wakefield (baseball)	20.00	10.00	2.00
☐ 6 Lou Groza (football)	100.00	50.00	10.00
☐ 7 George McAfee (football)	60.00	30.00	6.00
☐ 8 Norm Standlee (football)	30.00	15.00	3.00
☐ 9A Charlie Trippi ERR (reversed negative)	75.00	37.50	7.50
☐ 9B Charlie Trippi COR (football)	60.00	30.00	6.00
☐ 10 Bob Waterfield (football)	100.00	50.00	10.00
☐ 11 Donald Budge (tennis)	15.00	7.50	1.50
☐ 12 James Ferrier (golf)	10.00	5.00	1.00
☐ 13 Mary Hardwick (tennis)	10.00	5.00	1.00
☐ 14 Adolph Kiefer (swimming)	10.00	5.00	1.00
☐ 15 Lloyd Mangrum (golf)	10.00	5.00	1.00
☐ 16 George Mikan (basketball)	350.00	175.00	35.00
☐ 17 Samuel Jackson Snead (golf)	25.00	12.50	2.50
☐ 18A Tony Zale ERR (reversed negative)	30.00	15.00	3.00
☐ 18B Tony Zale COR (boxing)	20.00	10.00	2.00

1991-92 Kellogg's College Greats

The 1992 Kellogg's College Basketball Greats set contains 18 cards measuring the standard-size (2 1/2" by 3 1/2"). The front design features a color action photo with the player in his college uniform. The pictures are bordered in different colors on different cards, and the words "College Basketball Greats" is written vertically along the left of each card. In a horizontal format, the back presents outstanding achievements of the player and his college statistics. The cards are numbered on the back. The cards were inserted into boxes of Kellogg's Raisin Bran through the end of March, 1992. The complete set, including a special card holder, was also available for 2.99 with three proofs of purchase from any size box of Kellogg's Raisin Bran.

	MINT	EXC	G-VG
COMPLETE SET (19)	7.00	3.50	.70
COMMON PLAYER (1-18)	.20	.10	.02
☐ 1 Kenny Anderson Georgia Tech	.75	.35	.07
☐ 2 Wayman Tisdale Oklahoma	.20	.10	.02
☐ 3 Clyde Drexler Houston	.60	.30	.06
☐ 4 Horace Grant Clemson	.30	.15	.03
☐ 5 Kevin Johnson California	.50	.25	.05
☐ 6 Karl Malone Louisiana Tech	.40	.20	.04
☐ 7 Larry Bird Indiana State	.75	.35	.07
☐ 8 John Stockton Gonzaga	.40	.20	.04
☐ 9 Doug Smith Missouri	.40	.20	.04
☐ 10 Mark Price Georgia Tech	.30	.15	.03
☐ 11 Hakeem Olajuwon Houston	.40	.20	.04
☐ 12 Charles Smith Pittsburgh	.20	.10	.02
☐ 13 Bernard King Tennessee	.20	.10	.02
☐ 14 Tim Hardaway UTEP	.40	.20	.04
☐ 15 Spud Webb North Carolina State	.20	.10	.02
☐ 16 Mark Macon Temple	.30	.15	.03
☐ 17 Scottie Pippen Central Arkansas	.50	.25	.05
☐ 18 Gary Payton Oregon State	.30	.15	.03
☐ x Album/Holder	1.25	.60	.12

1985-86 Kings Smokey

This 15-card set features members of the Sacramento Kings of the NBA. The cards were originally distributed as a perforated sheet along with (and perforated to) a large team photo. The cards are numbered on the back in the upper right corner. The cards measure approximately 4" by 5 1/2". The card backs contain a fire safety cartoon but minimal information about the player.

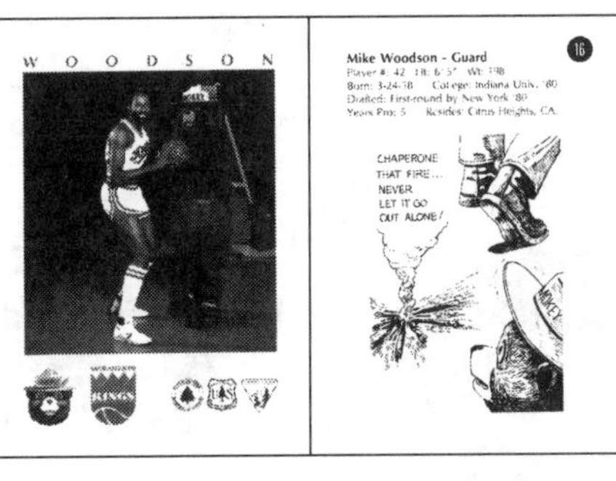

	MINT	EXC	G-VG
COMPLETE SET (16)	20.00	10.00	2.00
COMMON PLAYER (1-16)	.90	.45	.09
☐ 1 Smokey Emblem	.90	.45	.09
☐ 2 Phil Johnson CO	.90	.45	.09
☐ 3 Frank Hamblen ASST Jerry Reynolds ASST Bill Jones TR	.90	.45	.09
☐ 4 Smokey Bear	.90	.45	.09
☐ 5 Michael Adams	3.50	1.75	.35
☐ 6 Larry Drew	1.25	.60	.12
☐ 7 Carl Henry	.90	.45	.09
☐ 8 Eddie Johnson	2.00	1.00	.20
☐ 9 Rich Kelley	.90	.45	.09
☐ 10 Joe Kleine	1.25	.60	.12
☐ 11 Mark Olberding	.90	.45	.09
☐ 12 Reggie Theus	1.50	.75	.15
☐ 13 LaSalle Thompson	1.50	.75	.15
☐ 14 Otis Thorpe	4.00	2.00	.40
☐ 15 Terry Tyler	.90	.45	.09
☐ 16 Mike Woodson	1.25	.60	.12

1986-87 Kings Smokey

This 15-card set features members of the Sacramento Kings of the NBA. The cards were originally distributed as a perforated sheet along with (and perforated to) a large team photo. Since the cards are unnumbered, they are listed below in alphabetical order. The player's uniform number (given on both sides of the card) is also listed below. The cards measure approximately 2 3/8" by 3". The card backs contain a fire safety cartoon but minimal information about the player.

	MINT	EXC	G-VG
COMPLETE SET (15)	18.00	9.00	1.80
COMMON PLAYER	1.00	.50	.10
☐ 1 Don Buse ASST	1.00	.50	.10
☐ 2 Franklin Edwards 10	1.00	.50	.10
☐ 3 Eddie Johnson 8	2.25	1.10	.22
☐ 4 Bill Jones TR	1.00	.50	.10
☐ 5 Joe Kleine 35	1.50	.75	.15
☐ 6 Mark Olberding 53	1.00	.50	.10
☐ 7 Harold Pressley 21	1.50	.75	.15
☐ 8 Jerry Reynolds CO	1.00	.50	.10
☐ 9 Johnny Rogers 32	1.00	.50	.10
☐ 10 Derek Smith 18	1.50	.75	.15
☐ 11 Reggie Theus 24	2.00	1.00	.20
☐ 12 LaSalle Thompson 41	2.00	1.00	.20
☐ 13 Otis Thorpe 33	3.00	1.50	.30
☐ 14 Terry Tyler 40	1.00	.50	.10
☐ 15 Othell Wilson 2	1.25	.60	.12

1988-89 Kings Carl's Jr.

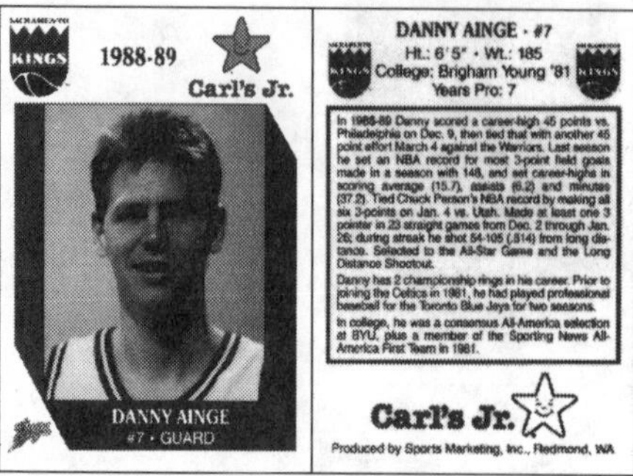

The 1988-89 Carl's Jr. Sacramento Kings set contains 12 cards each measuring approximately 2 1/2" by 3 1/2". There are 11 player cards and one coach card in this set. The cards are unnumbered except for uniform number; they are ordered below by uniform number. The cards were issued in three strips of four players plus a coupon for savings at Carl's Jr. restaurants before May 31, 1989. Since this set was issued in late spring of 1989, it includes comments and statistics about the 1988-89 season. The set was produced for Carl's Jr. by Sports Marketing Inc. of Redmond, Washington.

	MINT	EXC	G-VG
COMPLETE SET (12)	12.00	6.00	1.20
COMMON PLAYER (1-12)	.75	.35	.07
☐ 2 Michael Jackson	.75	.35	.07
☐ 7 Danny Ainge	1.75	.85	.17
☐ 15 Vinnie Del Negro	1.00	.50	.10
☐ 21 Harold Pressley	.75	.35	.07
☐ 22 Rodney McCray	1.00	.50	.10
☐ 23 Wayman Tisdale	1.50	.75	.15
☐ 30 Kenny Smith	1.50	.75	.15
☐ 34 Ricky Berry	.75	.35	.07
☐ 43 Jim Petersen	.75	.35	.07
☐ 50 Ben Gillery	.75	.35	.07
☐ 54 Brad Lohaus	1.00	.50	.10
☐ xx Jerry Reynolds CO	.75	.35	.07

1989-90 Kings Carl's Jr.

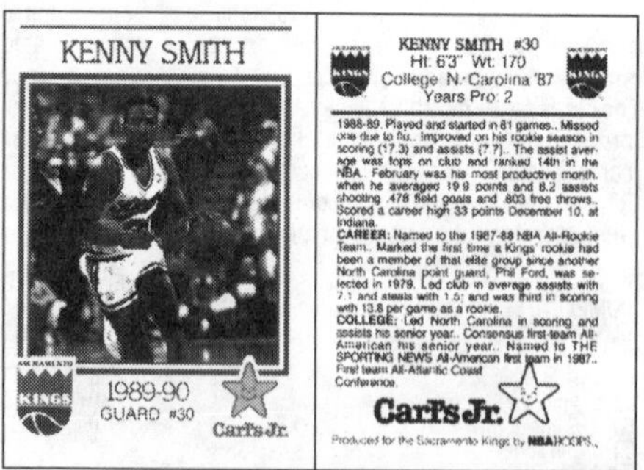

This 12-card set of Sacramento Kings was sponsored by Carl's Jr. restaurants and issued in three panels, each containing four player cards and one sponsor's coupon. After perforation, the player cards measure the standard size (2 1/2" by 3 1/2"). The front features a color action player photo, with red, white, and blue borders on white card stock. The player's name is written between a thin blue stripe and the top border. The team and sponsors' logos overlay the lower corners of the picture, with the year, position, and uniform number below the picture. The back has two team logos in the upper corners, with biographical information and career summary. The cards are unnumbered and checklisted below by uniform number. The cards were given away at three different games in strips of four player cards each. The set includes an early professional card of Pervis Ellison, the first pick of the 1989 NBA draft. The player groups on the panels were as follows: Michael Jackson, Vinny Del Negro, Wayman Tisdale, and Pervis Ellison; Danny Ainge, Kenny Smith, Randy Allen, and Ralph Sampson; and Harold Pressley, Rodney McCray, Greg Kite, and Jerry Reynolds.

	MINT	EXC	G-VG
COMPLETE SET (12)	8.00	4.00	.80
COMMON PLAYER	.50	.25	.05
☐ 2 Michael Jackson	.50	.25	.05
☐ 7 Danny Ainge	1.25	.60	.12
☐ 15 Vinny Del Negro	.75	.35	.07
☐ 21 Harold Pressley	.50	.25	.05
☐ 22 Rodney McCray	.75	.35	.07
☐ 23 Wayman Tisdale	1.00	.50	.10
☐ 30 Kenny Smith	1.00	.50	.10
☐ 32 Greg Kite	.50	.25	.05
☐ 40 Randy Allen	.50	.25	.05
☐ 42 Pervis Ellison	2.00	1.00	.20
☐ 50 Ralph Sampson	.75	.35	.07
☐ xx Jerry Reynolds CO	.50	.25	.05

1990-91 Kings Safeway

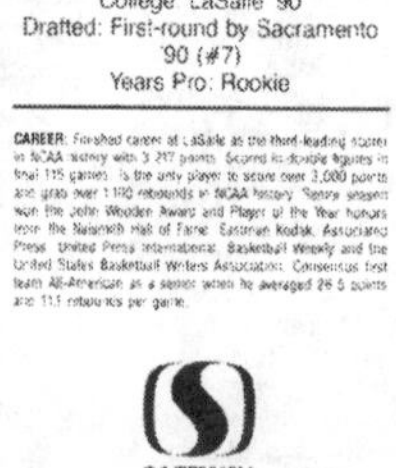

This 12-card set of Sacramento Kings was sponsored by Safeway stores and issued in three panels, each containing four player cards and one sponsor's coupon. After perforation, the player cards measure the standard size (2 1/2" by 3 1/2"). The front features a color action player photo, with red, white, and blue borders on white card stock. The player's name is written between a thin blue stripe and the top border. The team and sponsors' logos overlay the lower corners of the picture, with the year, position, and uniform number below the picture. The back has two team logos in the upper corners, with biographical information and career summary. The cards are unnumbered and are checklisted below in alphabetical order, with the uniform number after the player's name.

	MINT	EXC	G-VG
COMPLETE SET (12)	10.00	5.00	1.00
COMMON PLAYER (1-12)	.50	.25	.05
☐ 1 Anthony Bonner 24	1.00	.50	.10
☐ 2 Antoine Carr 35	.75	.35	.07
☐ 3 Duane Causwell 31	1.25	.60	.12
☐ 4 Steve Colter 21	.50	.25	.05
☐ 5 Bobby Hansen 20	.50	.25	.05
☐ 6 Eric Leckner 45	.50	.25	.05
☐ 7 Travis Mays 1	1.25	.60	.12
☐ 8 Dick Motta CO	.50	.25	.05
☐ 9 Lionel Simmons 22	2.50	1.25	.25
☐ 10 Rory Sparrow 2	.50	.25	.05
☐ 11 Wayman Tisdale 23	1.00	.50	.10
☐ 12 Bill Wennington 34	.50	.25	.05

1988-89 Knicks Frito Lay

This 15-card set was sponsored by Frito Lay. The cards were issued in two sheets; after perforation, the cards measure approximately 2 1/2" by 3 1/2". The front design has color action player photos with white borders. The team logo appears in the lower left corner, with the player's name to the right in a yellow stripe. The horizontally oriented backs have blank print on a gray and white background and present biographical and statistical information. The cards are unnumbered and checklisted below in alphabetical order.

	MINT	EXC	G-VG
COMPLETE SET (15)	25.00	12.50	2.50
COMMON PLAYER (1-15)	1.00	.50	.10
☑ 1 Greg Butler	1.00	.50	.10
☐ 2 Patrick Ewing	10.00	5.00	1.00
☐ 3 Sidney Green	1.50	.75	.15
☐ 4 Mark Jackson	3.00	1.50	.30
☐ 5 Pete Myers	1.00	.50	.10
☐ 6 Johnny Newman	1.50	.75	.15
☐ 7 Charles Oakley	2.00	1.00	.20
☐ 8 Rick Pitino CO	2.00	1.00	.20
☐ 9 Rod Strickland	3.00	1.50	.30
☐ 10 Trent Tucker	1.50	.75	.15
☐ 11 Kiki Vandeweghe	2.00	1.00	.20
☐ 12 Kenny Walker	1.50	.75	.15
☐ 13 Eddie Lee Wilkins	1.00	.50	.10
☐ 14 Gerald Wilkins	2.00	1.00	.20
☐ 15 Frito Lay Manufacturer's Coupon	1.00	.50	.10

1989-90 Knicks Marine Midland

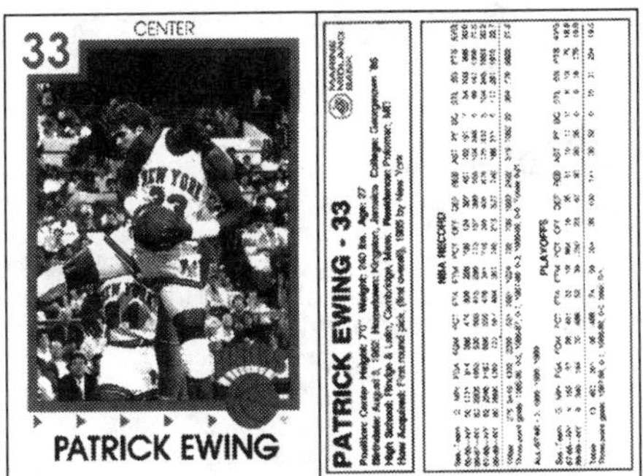

This 14-card set of New York Knicks was sponsored by Marine Midland Bank. The cards were issued in one sheet with three rows of five cards each, and they measure the standard size (2 1/2" by 3 1/2") after perforation. The 15th slot is filled by the sponsor's advertisement. The front features a color action photo of the player, with orange borders. The upper left corner of the picture is cut out to provide space for the uniform number. The team logo overlays the lower right corner of the picture, and a row of miniature blue triangles run beneath the bottom orange border. In a horizontal format the back is divided into two boxes and presents biographical (on blue) and statistical information. The cards are unnumbered and are checklisted below in alphabetical order, with the uniform number after the player's name.

	MINT	EXC	G-VG
COMPLETE SET (14)	20.00	10.00	2.00
COMMON PLAYER (1-14)	1.00	.50	.10
☐ 1 Greg Butler 54	1.00	.50	.10
☐ 2 Patrick Ewing 33	6.50	3.25	.65
☐ 3 Mark Jackson 13	2.00	1.00	.20
☐ 4 Stu Jackson CO	2.00	1.00	.20
☐ 5 Charles Oakley 34	1.50	.75	.15
☐ 6 Pete Myers 8	1.00	.50	.10
☐ 7 Johnny Newman 4	2.00	1.00	.20
☐ 8 Brian Quinnett 23	1.00	.50	.10
☐ 9 Rod Strickland 11	2.50	1.25	.25
☐ 10 Trent Tucker 6	1.00	.50	.10
☐ 11 Kiki Vandeweghe 55	2.00	1.00	.20
☐ 12 Kenny Walker 7	1.50	.75	.15
☐ 13 Gerald Wilkins 21	1.50	.75	.15
☐ 14 Eddie Lee Wilkins 45	1.00	.50	.10

1961-62 Lakers Bell Brand

The unattractive cards within this ten-card set measure approximately 6" by 3 1/2" and feature members of the Los Angeles Lakers basketball team. Each player has two versions of his card, once in blue ink on white stock and again in brown ink on brown-tinted stock. The left half of the card features the player whereas the right side features a Laker schedule. The catalog designation is F391-2.

	NRMT	VG-E	GOOD
COMPLETE SET (10)	3500.00	1650.00	400.00
COMMON PLAYER (1-10)	200.00	100.00	20.00
☐ 1 Elgin Baylor	750.00	375.00	75.00
☐ 2 Ray Felix	200.00	100.00	20.00
☐ 3 Tom Hawkins	300.00	150.00	30.00
☐ 4 Rod Hundley	400.00	200.00	40.00
☐ 5 Howard Joliff	200.00	100.00	20.00
☐ 6 Rudy LaRusso	250.00	125.00	25.00
☐ 7 Fred Schaus CO	200.00	100.00	20.00

☐ 8 Frank Selvy	200.00	100.00	20.00
☐ 9 Jerry West	1250.00	600.00	150.00
☐ 10 Wayne Yates	200.00	100.00	20.00

1979-80 Lakers/Kings Alta-Dena*

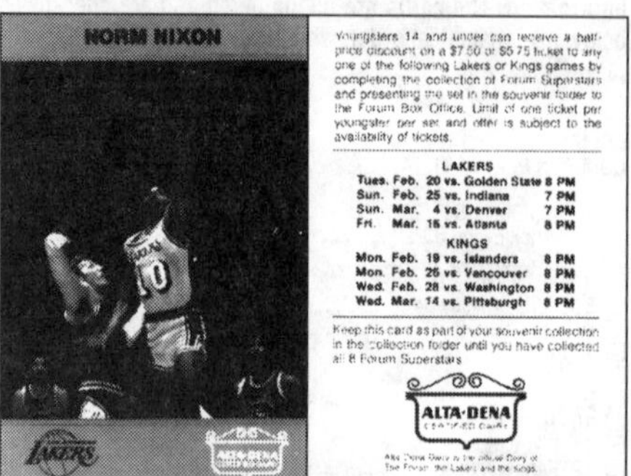

This 8-card set was sponsored by Alta-Dena Dairy, and its logo adorns the bottom of both sides of the card. The cards measure approximately 2 3/4" by 4" and feature color action player photos on the fronts. While the sides of the picture have no borders, green and red-orange stripes border the picture on its top and bottom. The player's name appears in black lettering in the top red-orange stripe. The team logo appears in the bottom red-orange stripe. The back has an offer for youngsters 14-and-under, who could present the complete eight-card set in the souvenir folder to the Forum Box Office and receive a half-price discount on certain tickets to any one of the Lakers and Kings games listed on the reverse of the card. The cards are unnumbered and are checklisted below in alphabetical order. This small set features Los Angeles Kings and Los Angeles Lakers as they were both owned by Jerry Buss. Cards 1-4 are Los Angeles Lakers (NBA) and Cards 5-8 are Los Angeles Kings (NHL).

	NRMT	VG-E	GOOD
COMPLETE SET (8)	24.00	12.00	2.40
COMMON PLAYER (1-8)	1.00	.50	.10
☐ 1 Adrian Dantley	3.00	1.50	.30
☐ 2 Don Ford	1.00	.50	.10
☐ 3 Kareem Abdul-Jabbar	10.00	5.00	1.00
☐ 4 Norm Nixon	1.50	.75	.15
☐ 5 Marcel Dionne	6.00	3.00	.60
☐ 6 Butch Goring	1.25	.60	.12
☐ 7 Mike Murphy	1.00	.50	.10
☐ 8 Dave Taylor	3.00	1.50	.30
☐ x Souvenir Folder	5.00	2.50	.50

1982-83 Lakers BASF

This 13-card set was produced by BASF audio and video tapes in a promotional tie-in with the Los Angeles Lakers. The cards measure approximately 5" by 7" and are unnumbered except for uniform number; they are listed below in alphabetical order for convenience. This set can be distinguished from the other two years of BASF Lakers sets in that it is the only year the set was also sponsored by Big Ben's and the only year there were no facsimile autographs on the back. The cards were distributed by Big Ben's and The Wherehouse (both chain record and tape stores in southern California), one player per week, with the final card scheduled for distribution during the week of the NBA

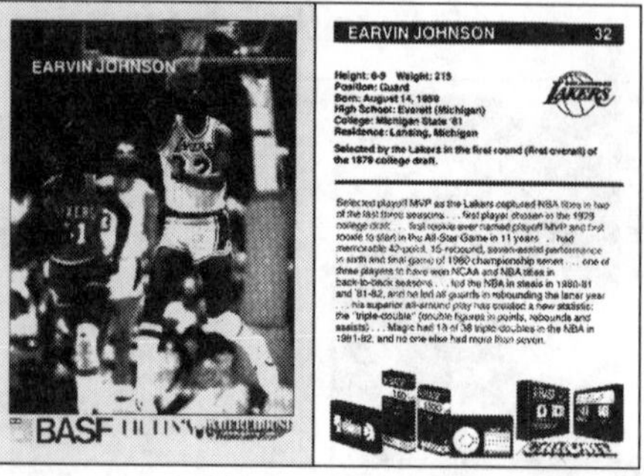

championship series. The set features James Worthy's first professional card.

	MINT	EXC	G-VG
COMPLETE SET (13)	16.00	7.50	1.50
COMMON CARD (1-13)	.75	.35	.07
☐ 1 Kareem Abdul-Jabbar	5.00	2.50	.50
☐ 2 Michael Cooper	1.25	.60	.12
☐ 3 Clay Johnson	.75	.35	.07
☐ 4 Magic Johnson	7.50	3.75	.75
☐ 5 Eddie Jordan	.75	.35	.07
☐ 6 Mark Landsberger	.75	.35	.07
☐ 7 Bob McAdoo	1.25	.60	.12
☐ 8 Mike McGee	.75	.35	.07
☐ 9 Norm Nixon	1.25	.60	.12
☐ 10 Kurt Rambis	1.00	.50	.10
☐ 11 Jamaal Wilkes	1.25	.60	.12
☐ 12 James Worthy	3.00	1.50	.30
☐ 13 Team Card (team roster on back)	.75	.35	.07

1983-84 Lakers BASF

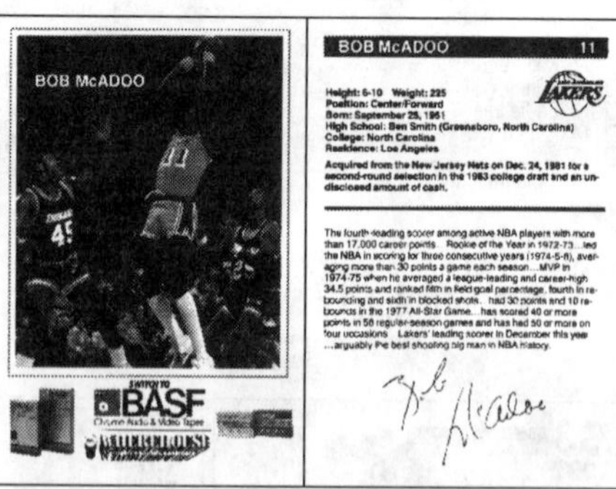

This 14-card set was produced by BASF audio and video tapes in a promotional tie-in with the Los Angeles Lakers. The cards measure approximately 5" by 7" and are unnumbered except for uniform number; they are listed below in alphabetical order for convenience. This set can be distinguished from the other two years of BASF Lakers sets in that it is the only year the set was referenced on the front of the card as "Switch to BASF". The set features Byron Scott's first professional card.

	MINT	EXC	G-VG
COMPLETE SET (14)	16.00	7.50	1.50
COMMON PLAYER (1-14)	.75	.35	.07
☐ 1 Kareem Abdul-Jabbar 33	5.00	2.50	.50
☐ 2 Michael Cooper 21	1.25	.60	.12
☐ 3 Calvin Garrett 00	.75	.35	.07
☐ 4 Magic Johnson 32	7.50	3.75	.75
☐ 5 Mitch Kupchak 25	1.00	.50	.10

☐ 6 Bob McAdoo 11	1.25	.60	.12
☐ 7 Mike McGee 40	1.00	.50	.10
☐ 8 Swen Nater 41	1.00	.50	.10
☐ 9 Kurt Rambis 31	1.25	.60	.12
☐ 10 Byron Scott 4	1.50	.75	.15
☐ 11 Larry Spriggs 35	.75	.35	.07
☐ 12 Jamaal Wilkes 52	1.25	.60	.12
☐ 13 James Worthy 42	2.50	1.25	.25
☐ 14 Team Photo (team roster on back)	.75	.35	.07

1984-85 Lakers BASF

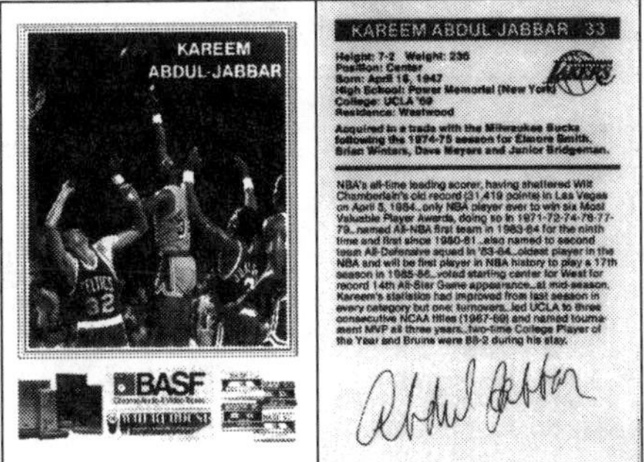

This 12-card set was produced by BASF audio and video tapes in a promotional tie-in with the Los Angeles Lakers. The cards measure approximately 5" by 7" and are unnumbered except for uniform number; they are listed below in alphabetical order for convenience.

	MINT	EXC	G-VG
COMPLETE SET (12)	16.00	7.50	1.50
COMMON PLAYER (1-12)	.75	.35	.07
☐ 1 Kareem Abdul-Jabbar 33	5.00	2.50	.50
☐ 2 Michael Cooper 21	1.25	.60	.12
☐ 3 Magic Johnson 32	7.50	3.75	.75
☐ 4 Mitch Kupchak 25	1.00	.50	.10
☐ 5 Ronnie Lester 12	.75	.35	.07
☐ 6 Bob McAdoo 14	1.25	.60	.12
☐ 7 Mike McGee 40	.75	.35	.07
☐ 8 Kurt Rambis 31	1.00	.50	.10
☐ 9 Byron Scott 4	1.25	.60	.12
☐ 10 Larry Spriggs 35	.75	.35	.07
☐ 11 James Worthy 42	2.00	1.00	.20
☐ 12 Team Photo (team roster on back)	.75	.35	.07

1992 Lime Rock Larry Bird

This three-card hologram set was produced by Lime Rock Productions and packaged in a black folder displaying a three-dimensional embossed etching of Larry Bird. According to Lime Rock, the production run was limited to 10,000 cases or 250,000 sets, and that 2,500 autographed cards were randomly inserted throughout the packaging process (one in every 100 sets). A numbered certificate of authenticity was included with each set. The cards measure the standard size (2 1/2" by 3 1/2") and depict three stages in his career: 1) his passing skill at Indiana State; 2) his patented shooting style at Boston; and 3) posed in a red, white, and blue warm-up in anticipation of his participation in the Summer Olympic games in Barcelona. The backs have color photos and an extended caption summarizing Bird's career. The cards are numbered on the back.

	MINT	EXC	G-VG
COMPLETE SET (3)	9.00	4.50	.90
COMMON PLAYER (1-3)	4.00	2.00	.40

☐ 1 Larry Bird (Passing Skill developed at Indiana State)	4.00	2.00	.40
☐ 2 Larry Bird (Legendary shooting style at Boston)	4.00	2.00	.40
☐ 3 Larry Bird (Posed in patriotic warm-up for Summer Olympic Games)	4.00	2.00	.40

1989-90 Magic Pepsi

This eight-card set of Orlando Magic was sponsored by Pepsi. The cards measure the standard size (2 1/2" by 3 1/2") and feature on the front a posed color player photo, without borders on the sides. While the player's name and team logo appears in the aqua stripe above the picture, the Pepsi logo and the words "'89/'90 Inaugural Season Collector's Card" appear in red stripe below the picture. Also an official sweepstakes entry sticker is attached to each card face. This sticker was to be peeled off and affixed to an official entry form available at participating stores. By collecting four stickers, one was entitled to enter the sweepstakes. The back presents 1988-89 statistics and career highlights, and is printed in black lettering on blue background, with a white stripe at the card bottom. The cards are unnumbered and are checklisted below in alphabetical order. The set features Nick Anderson's first professional card.

	MINT	EXC	G-VG
COMPLETE SET (8)	50.00	25.00	5.00
COMMON PLAYER (1-8)	5.00	2.50	.50
☐ 1 Nick Anderson	16.00	8.00	1.60
☐ 2 Michael Ansley	7.50	3.75	.75
☐ 3 Terry Catledge	7.50	3.75	.75
☐ 4 Dave Corzine	5.00	2.50	.50
☐ 5 Sidney Green	6.00	3.00	.60
☐ 6 Otis Smith	5.00	2.50	.50
☐ 7 Sam Vincent	6.00	3.00	.60
☐ 8 Stuff the Magic Dragon Mascot	6.00	3.00	.60

1988-89 Mavs Bud Light BLC

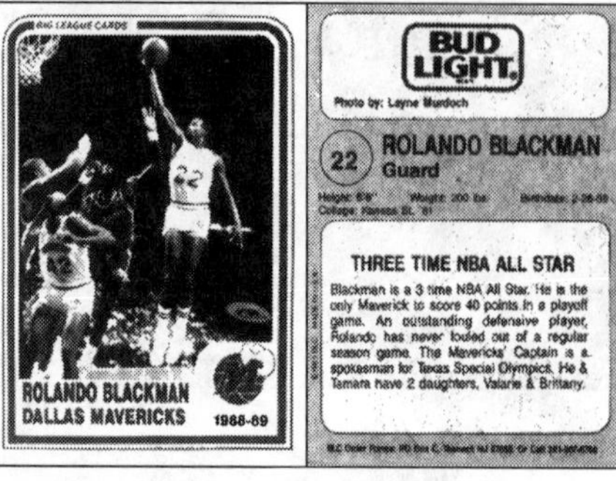

The 1988-89 Bud Light Dallas Mavericks set contains 14 cards comprised of 12 players and two coaches. The cards are standard sized (2 1/2" by 3 1/2"). The set is unnumbered except for uniform numbers on the card backs. This set was produced for distribution at the Mavericks "card night" promotion but may not have actually been used by the Mavericks. However the sets do exist within the hobby as the cards were not all destroyed. The set may have been rejected by the Mavericks because of the inclusion of Roy Tarpley and Mark Aguirre; however there is no indication that either the Tarpley or Aguirre cards is any harder to find than the others in the set. The set was produced for the Mavericks by Big League Cards of New Jersey.

	MINT	EXC	G-VG
COMPLETE SET (14)	15.00	7.50	1.50
COMMON PLAYER	.60	.30	.06
☐ 12 Derek Harper	1.25	.60	.12
☐ 15 Brad Davis	1.00	.50	.10
☐ 20 Morlon Wiley	.60	.30	.06
☐ 22 Rolando Blackman	1.75	.85	.17
☐ 23 Bill Wennington	.60	.30	.06
☐ 24 Mark Aguirre	1.50	.75	.15
☐ 32 Detlef Schrempf	1.50	.75	.15
☐ 33 Uwe Blab	.60	.30	.06
☐ 40 James Donaldson	.75	.35	.07
☐ 41 Terry Tyler	.60	.30	.06
☐ 42 Roy Tarpley	3.50	1.75	.35
☐ 44 Sam Perkins	1.75	.85	.17
☐ xx Coaching Staff Richie Adubato Garfield Heard (unnumbered)	.60	.30	.06
☐ xx John MacLeod CO (unnumbered)	.75	.35	.07

1988-89 Mavs Bud Light Card Night

The 1988-89 Bud Light Dallas Mavericks set contains 13 cards comprised of 12 players and Head Coach John MacLeod. The cards are standard sized (2 1/2" by 3 1/2"). The set is unnumbered except for uniform numbers on the card backs. This set was produced for distribution at the Mavericks "card night" promotion and is apparently a rework of the set immediately above since Roy Tarpley and Mark Aguirre are not even in this set and many late season acquisitions are noted. It is not known what company produced these cards for the Mavericks and Bud Light.

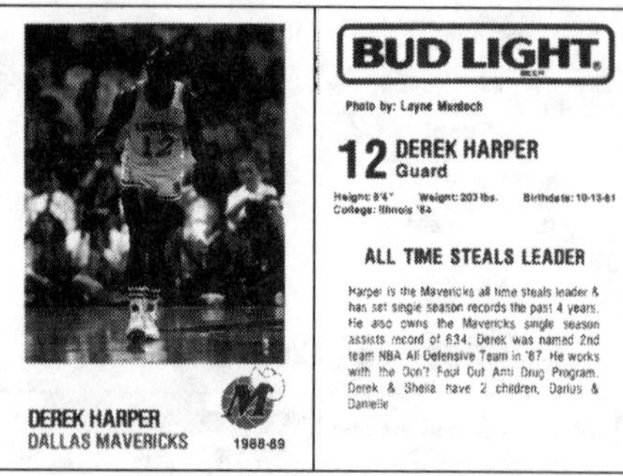

	MINT	EXC	G-VG
COMPLETE SET (13)	12.00	6.00	1.20
COMMON PLAYER	.60	.30	.06
☐ 4 Adrian Dantley	1.50	.75	.15
☐ 12 Derek Harper	1.25	.60	.12
☐ 15 Brad Davis	1.00	.50	.10
☐ 20 Morlon Wiley	.60	.30	.06
☐ 21 Anthony Jones	.60	.30	.06
☐ 22 Rolando Blackman	1.75	.85	.17
☐ 23 Bill Wennington	.60	.30	.06
☐ 32 Herb Williams	1.00	.50	.10
☐ 33 Uwe Blab	.60	.30	.06
☐ 40 James Donaldson	.75	.35	.07
☐ 41 Terry Tyler	.60	.30	.06
☐ 44 Sam Perkins	1.75	.85	.17
☐ xx John MacLeod CO (unnumbered)	.75	.35	.07

1990-91 McDonald's Michael Jordan/ Jackie Joyner-Kersee*

This 16-card set featuring Michael Jordan and Jackie Joyner-Kersee was sponsored by McDonald's restaurants as part of their "Sports Tips" series. The cards of each subject were issued on a 10 7/8" by 8 1/8" perforated sheet (two rows of four cards each) as a special insert in Sports Illustrated for Kids. The two sheets were attached connecting Michael Jordan and 1988 Olympic gold medalist Jackie Joyner-Kersee. After perforation, the cards measure the standard size (2 1/2" by 3 1/2"). The front has a color action photo of Jordan, with four different border stripes on each side of the picture: red above, green below, yellow with black dots on the left, and black , blue candy-stripe on the right. Jordan's autograph is inscribed on the red border, while the card title appears in the green border. The back has a hint on how to perform the move, a training tip, and a nutrition tip. A pink top border stripe and a green bottom border stripe frame this information. The Joyner-Kersee cards are styled similarly. The cards are numbered on both sides; the Joyner-Kersee cards are numbered below using a "JK" prefix to distinguish from the similarly numbered Jordan cards.

	MINT	EXC	G-VG
COMPLETE SET (16)	6.00	3.00	.60
COMMON PLAYER (1-8)	.75	.35	.07
COMMON PLAYER (JK1-JK8)	.15	.07	.01
☐ 1 Michael Jordan The Lay-up	.75	.35	.07
☐ 2 Michael Jordan The Blocked Shot	.75	.35	.07
☐ 3 Michael Jordan The Chest Pass	.75	.35	.07
☐ 4 Michael Jordan The Drive	.75	.35	.07
☐ 5 Michael Jordan The Speed Dribble	.75	.35	.07
☐ 6 Michael Jordan The Backup Dribble	.75	.35	.07
☐ 7 Michael Jordan The Jump Shot	.75	.35	.07
☐ 8 Michael Jordan The Free Throw	.75	.35	.07
☐ JK1 Jackie Joyner-Kersee The 200 Meters	.15	.07	.01
☐ JK2 Jackie Joyner-Kersee The Javelin	.15	.07	.01
☐ JK3 Jackie Joyner-Kersee The 800 Meters	.15	.07	.01
☐ JK4 Jackie Joyner-Kersee The 100M Hurdles	.15	.07	.01
☐ JK5 Jackie Joyner-Kersee The Long Jump	.15	.07	.01
☐ JK6 Jackie Joyner-Kersee The High Jump	.15	.07	.01
☐ JK7 Jackie Joyner-Kersee The Shot Put	.15	.07	.01
☐ JK8 Jackie Joyner-Kersee The Heptathlon	.15	.07	.01

1974 Nabisco Sugar Daddy *

This set of 25 tiny (approximately 1" by 2 3/4") cards features athletes from a variety of popular pro sports. The set is referred to as Pro Faces as the cards show an enlarged head photo with a small caricature body. Cards 1-10 are football players, cards 11-16 and 22 are hockey players, and cards 17-21 and 23-25 are basketball players.

	NRMT	VG-E	GOOD
COMPLETE SET (25)	120.00	60.00	12.50
COMMON PLAYER (1-25)	2.00	1.00	.20
☐ 1 Roger Staubach	20.00	10.00	2.00
☐ 2 Floyd Little	4.00	2.00	.40
☐ 3 Steve Owen	3.00	1.50	.30
☐ 4 Roman Gabriel	4.00	2.00	.40
☐ 5 Bobby Douglass	2.00	1.00	.20
☐ 6 John Gilliam	2.00	1.00	.20
☐ 7 Bob Lilly	7.50	3.75	.75
☐ 8 John Brockington	3.00	1.50	.30
☐ 9 Jim Plunkett	5.00	2.50	.50
☐ 10 Greg Landry	2.00	1.00	.20
☐ 11 Phil Esposito	7.50	3.75	.75
☐ 12 Dennis Hull	3.00	1.50	.30
☐ 13 Reg Fleming	2.00	1.00	.20
☐ 14 Garry Unger	3.00	1.50	.30
☐ 15 Derek Sanderson	3.50	1.75	.35
☐ 16 Jerry Korab	2.00	1.00	.20
☐ 17 Oscar Robertson	12.50	6.25	1.25
☐ 18 Spencer Haywood	4.00	2.00	.40
☐ 19 Jo Jo White	3.00	1.50	.30
☐ 20 Connie Hawkins	6.00	3.00	.60
☐ 21 Nate Thurmond	4.00	2.00	.40
☐ 22 Mickey Redmond	2.50	1.25	.25
☐ 23 Chet Walker	3.00	1.50	.30
☐ 24 Calvin Murphy	3.00	1.50	.30
☐ 25 Kareem Abdul-Jabbar	20.00	10.00	2.00

1975 Nabisco Sugar Daddy *

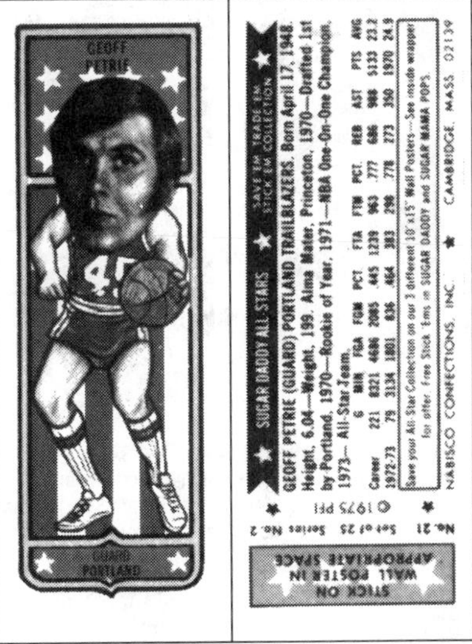

This set of 25 tiny (approximately 1" by 2 3/4") cards features athletes from a variety of popular pro sports. The set is referred to as Sugar Daddy All-Stars. As with the set of the previous year, the cards show an enlarged head photo with a small caricature body with a flag background of stars and stripes. This set is referred on the back as Series No. 2 and has a red, white, and blue background behind the picture on the front of the card. Cards 1-10 are pro football players and the remainder are pro basketball (17-21, 23-25) and hockey (11-16, 22) players.

	NRMT	VG-E	GOOD
COMPLETE SET (25)	120.00	60.00	12.50
COMMON PLAYER (1-25)	2.00	1.00	.20
☐ 1 Roger Staubach	20.00	10.00	2.00
☐ 2 Floyd Little	4.00	2.00	.40
☐ 3 Alan Page	5.00	2.50	.50
☐ 4 Merlin Olson	7.50	3.75	.75
☐ 5 Wally Chambers	2.00	1.00	.20
☐ 6 John Gilliam	2.00	1.00	.20
☐ 7 Bob Lilly	7.50	3.75	.75
☐ 8 John Brockington	3.00	1.50	.30
☐ 9 Jim Plunkett	5.00	2.50	.50
☐ 10 Willie Lanier	5.00	2.50	.50
☐ 11 Phil Esposito	7.50	3.75	.75

☐ 13 Brad Park	5.00	2.50	.50
☐ 14 Tom Lysiak	2.00	1.00	.20
☐ 15 Bernie Parent	6.00	3.00	.60
☐ 16 Mickey Redmond	2.50	1.25	.25
☐ 17 Jerry Sloan	2.00	1.00	.20
☐ 18 Spencer Haywood	3.00	1.50	.30
☐ 19 Bob Lanier	4.00	2.00	.40
☐ 20 Connie Hawkins	5.00	2.50	.50
☐ 21 Geoff Petrie	2.00	1.00	.20
☐ 22 Don Awrey	2.00	1.00	.20
☐ 23 Chet Walker	3.00	1.50	.30
☐ 24 Bob McAdoo	4.00	2.00	.40
☐ 25 Kareem Abdul-Jabbar	20.00	10.00	2.00

1976 Nabisco Sugar Daddy *

This set of 25 tiny (approximately 1" by 2 3/4") cards features action scenes from a variety of popular sports from around the world. The set is referred to as Sugar Daddy Sports World on the backs of the cards. The cards are in color with a relatively wide white border around the front of the cards.

	NRMT	VG-E	GOOD
COMPLETE SET (25)	60.00	30.00	6.00
COMMON PLAYER (1-25)	2.00	1.00	.20
☐ 1 Cricket	2.00	1.00	.20
☐ 2 Yachting	2.00	1.00	.20
☐ 3 Diving	2.00	1.00	.20
☐ 4 Football (Sonny Jurgensen)	5.00	2.50	.50
☐ 5 Soccer	4.00	2.00	.40
☐ 6 Lacrosse	2.00	1.00	.20
☐ 7 Track and Field	2.00	1.00	.20
☐ 8 Motorcycle	2.00	1.00	.20
☐ 9 Hang Gliding	2.00	1.00	.20
☐ 10 Tennis	2.00	1.00	.20
☐ 11 Hockey	5.00	2.50	.50
☐ 12 Shot Put	2.00	1.00	.20
☐ 13 Basketball	5.00	2.50	.50
☐ 14 Track and Field	2.00	1.00	.20
☐ 15 Gymnastics	2.00	1.00	.20
☐ 16 Power Boat Racing	2.00	1.00	.20
☐ 17 Bike Racing	2.00	1.00	.20
☐ 18 Golf	3.00	1.50	.30
☐ 19 Hot Dog Ski	2.00	1.00	.20
☐ 20 Fishing	2.00	1.00	.20
☐ 21 Jai Alai	2.00	1.00	.20
☐ 22 Canoeing	2.00	1.00	.20
☐ 23 Gymnastics (Cathy Rigby)	3.00	1.50	.30
☐ 24 Steeple Chase	2.00	1.00	.20
☐ 25 Baseball (Bobby Murcer)	5.00	2.50	.50

1973-74 NBA Players Assn.

This set contains 40 full-color postcard format cards measuring approximately 3 3/8" by 5 5/8". The front features a borderless posed "action" shot of the player. The back has the player's name at the top, and the NBA Players Association logo. The cards are unnumbered and are checklisted below in alphabetical order. There are ten tougher cards which are marked as SP in the checklist below. The two toughest of these are Mike Newlin and Paul Silas. Walt Bellamy was listed on the checklist, but was never issued, having been replaced by Lou Hudson.

	NRMT	VG-E	GOOD
COMPLETE SET (40)	450.00	225.00	45.00
COMMON PLAYER (1-40)	2.50	1.25	.25
COMMON PLAYER SP	12.00	6.00	1.20
☐ 1 Lucius Allen	2.50	1.25	.25
☐ 2 Dave Bing SP	25.00	12.50	2.50
☐ 3 Bill Bradley	15.00	7.50	1.50
☐ 4 Fred Carter SP	12.00	6.00	1.20
☐ 5 Austin Carr	2.50	1.25	.25
☐ 6 Dave Cowens	10.00	5.00	1.00
☐ 7 Dave DeBusschere	10.00	5.00	1.00
☐ 8 Ernie DiGregorio	2.50	1.25	.25
☐ 9 Gail Goodrich	5.00	2.50	.50
☐ 10 Hal Greer	5.00	2.50	.50
☐ 11 John Havlicek	12.00	6.00	1.20
☐ 12 Connie Hawkins	5.00	2.50	.50
☐ 13 Spencer Haywood	3.50	1.75	.35
☐ 14 Lou Hudson	3.00	1.50	.30
☐ 15 Bob Kauffman	2.50	1.25	.25
☐ 16 Bob Lanier	6.00	3.00	.60
☐ 17 Bob Love	3.50	1.75	.35
☐ 18 Jack Marin	2.50	1.25	.25
☐ 19 Jim McMillian	2.50	1.25	.25
☐ 20 Earl Monroe SP	30.00	15.00	3.00
☐ 21 Calvin Murphy	5.00	2.50	.50
☐ 22 Mike Newlin SP	75.00	37.50	7.50
☐ 23 Geoff Petrie	2.50	1.25	.25
☐ 24 Willis Reed SP	25.00	12.50	2.50
☐ 25 Rich Rinaldi	2.50	1.25	.25
☐ 26 Mike Riordan SP	12.00	6.00	1.20
☐ 27 Oscar Robertson SP	50.00	25.00	5.00
☐ 28 Cazzie Russell	3.50	1.75	.35
☐ 29 Paul Silas SP	75.00	37.50	7.50
☐ 30 Jerry Sloan	3.50	1.75	.35
☐ 31 Elmore Smith	2.50	1.25	.25
☐ 32 Dick Snyder	2.50	1.25	.25
☐ 33 Nate Thurmond	5.00	2.50	.50
☐ 34 Rudy Tomjanovich	2.50	1.25	.25
☐ 35 Wes Unseld	6.50	3.25	.65
☐ 36 Dick Van Arsdale SP	12.00	6.00	1.20
☐ 37 Tom Van Arsdale	2.50	1.25	.25
☐ 38 Chet Walker SP	15.00	7.50	1.50
☐ 39 Jo Jo White	3.50	1.75	.35
☐ 40 Len Wilkens	6.50	3.25	.65

1984-85 Nets Getty

This 12-card set was produced by Getty and issued in four sheets, with three player cards per sheet. The sheets measure approximately 8" by 11". Although the sheets are not actually perforated, the black broken lines indicate that the cut cards measure 3 5/8" by 6 3/4". The front features a borderless color action shot, with the player's facsimile autograph below the picture. The player's name and number appear above the picture in block lettering. The New Jersey Nets and Getty logos appear at the bottom of each sheet. The cards are unnumbered and we have checklisted them below in alphabetical order.

	MINT	EXC	G-VG
COMPLETE SET (12)	40.00	20.00	4.00
COMMON PLAYER (1-12)	2.50	1.25	.25
☐ 1 Stan Albeck CO	2.50	1.25	.25
☐ 2 Otis Birdsong 10	3.50	1.75	.35
☐ 3 Darwin Cook 12	2.50	1.25	.25

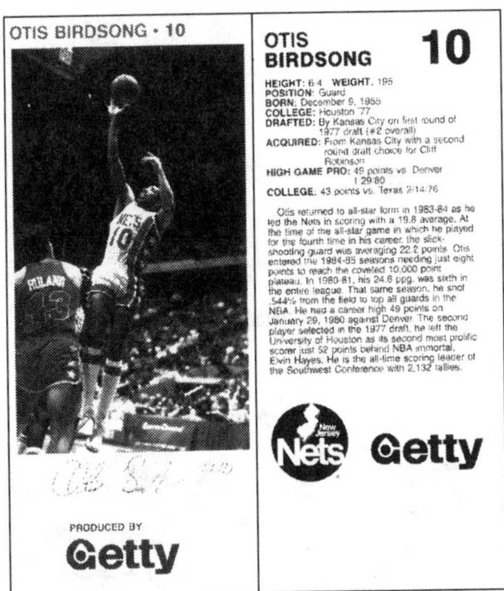

☐ 4 Darryl Dawkins 53	5.00	2.50	.50
☐ 5 Mike Gminski 42	4.00	2.00	.40
☐ 6 Albert King 55	3.50	1.75	.35
☐ 7 Mike O'Koren 31	3.50	1.75	.35
☐ 8 Kelvin Ransey 14	2.50	1.25	.25
☐ 9 M.R. Richardson 20	3.50	1.75	.35
☐ 10 Jeff Turner 35	2.50	1.25	.25
☐ 11 Buck Williams 52	8.00	4.00	.80
☐ 12 Duncan (Mascot)	2.50	1.25	.25

1990-91 Nets Kayo/Breyers

This 14-card set of New Jersey Nets was sponsored by Kayo Cards and Breyers Ice Cream and measures the standard size (2 1/2" by 3 1/2"). The front features a color action player photo, with a thin red border. The left corner is cut out, and the word "Kayo" appears. The team logo overlays the left bottom corner of the picture, and the player's position and name are given below the picture in black and white lettering on red. The outer border is blue, which washes out as one moves toward the card bottom. The back has biographical information as well as college and pro statistics, enframed by a black border. As on the front, the red outer border washes out. The cards are numbered on the back. The set features an early professional card of Derrick Coleman.

	MINT	EXC	G-VG
COMPLETE SET (14)	9.00	4.50	.90
COMMON PLAYER (1-14)	.50	.25	.05

☐ 1 Mookie Blaylock	1.00	.50	.10
☐ 2 Sam Bowie	.75	.35	.07
☐ 3 Jud Buechler	.75	.35	.07
☐ 4 Derrick Coleman	3.00	1.50	.30
☐ 5 Lester Conner	.50	.25	.05
☐ 6 Chris Dudley	.50	.25	.05
☐ 7 Tate George	.75	.35	.07
☐ 8 Derrick Gervin	.75	.35	.07
☐ 9 Jack Haley	.50	.25	.05
☐ 10 Kirk Lee	.50	.25	.05
☐ 11 Chris Morris	.75	.35	.07
☐ 12 Reggie Theus	.75	.35	.07
☐ 13 Bill Fitch CO	.50	.25	.05
☐ 14 Nets Home Schedule	.50	.25	.05

1991 Nike Michael Jordan/Spike Lee

This six-card set was issued by Nike to depict memorable Nike commercials starring Michael Jordan and Spike Lee. Nike plans to produce an additional set of cards every three months featuring other world famous athletes in Nike commercials. The standard-size cards (2 1/2" by 3 1/2") all have the same horizontally oriented front, with oval-shapped photos of Michael Jordan and Mars Blackmon (the character played by Spike Lee) and a Nike Trading Cards logo. A different quote appears at the top of each card front. The backs are either horizontally or vertically oriented and have either a black and white photo or a commercial advertisement. The cards are numbered on the front.

	MINT	EXC	G-VG
COMPLETE SET (6)	5.00	2.50	.50
COMMON PLAYER (1-6)	1.00	.50	.10
☐ 1 Earth/Mars 1988	1.00	.50	.10
☐ 2 High Flying 1989	1.00	.50	.10
☐ 3 Do You Know 1990	1.00	.50	.10
☐ 4 Stay in School 1991	1.00	.50	.10
☐ 5 Genie 1991 With Little Richard	1.00	.50	.10
☐ 6 Michael Jordan Flight School	1.00	.50	.10

1982-83 Nuggets Police

This set contains 14 cards measuring 2 5/8" by 4 1/8" featuring the Denver Nuggets. Backs contain safety tips and are printed with black ink. The set was sponsored by Colorado National Banks, the Denver Nuggets, and the metropolitan area police Juvenile Crime Prevention Bureaus. The cards are unnumbered except for uniform number.

	MINT	EXC	G-VG
COMPLETE SET (14)	7.00	3.50	.70
COMMON PLAYER	.35	.17	.03
☐ 2 Alex English	1.50	.75	.15
☐ 7 Billy McKinney	.50	.25	.05
☐ 21 Rob Williams	.35	.17	.03
☐ 22 Glen Gondrezick	.35	.17	.03
☐ 23 T.R. Dunn	.35	.17	.03
☐ 24 Bill Hanzlik	.50	.25	.05
☐ 25 Dave Robisch	.35	.17	.03
☐ 43 James Ray	.35	.17	.03
☐ 44 Dan Issel	1.25	.60	.12
☐ 53 Rich Kelley	.35	.17	.03
☐ 55 Kiki Vandeweghe	1.00	.50	.10
☐ xx Carl Scheer, Pres. and General Mgr.	.35	.17	.03
☐ xx Doug Moe CO	.75	.35	.07
☐ xx Bill Ficke, Assistant Coach and Bob Travaglini TR	.35	.17	.03

1983-84 Nuggets Police

This set contains 14 cards measuring 2 5/8" by 4 1/8" featuring the Denver Nuggets. Backs contain safety tips with black printing. The team name written vertically on the front is distinctive in that "Denver" is in red and "Nuggets" is in blue. The cards are unnumbered except for uniform number.

	MINT	EXC	G-VG
COMPLETE SET (14)	7.00	3.50	.70
COMMON PLAYER	.35	.17	.03
☐ 2 Alex English	1.00	.50	.10
☐ 5 Mike Evans	.35	.17	.03
☐ 21 Rob Williams	.35	.17	.03
☐ 23 T.R. Dunn	.35	.17	.03
☐ 24 Bill Hanzlik	.50	.25	.05
☐ 32 Howard Carter	.35	.17	.03
☐ 33 Ken Dennard	.35	.17	.03
☐ 34 Danny Schayes	.90	.45	.09
☐ 35 Richard Anderson	.50	.25	.05
☐ 44 Dan Issel	1.00	.50	.10
☐ 55 Kiki Vandeweghe	.75	.35	.07
☐ xx Carl Scheer, Pres. and General Mgr.	.35	.17	.03
☐ xx Bill Ficke, Assistant Coach	.35	.17	.03
☐ xx Doug Moe CO	.75	.35	.07

1985-86 Nuggets Police/Wendy's

The 1985-86 Wendy's Denver Nuggets set contains 12 cards each measuring approximately 2 1/2" by 5". A contest entry form tab is attached to each card (included in the dimensions above). The card fronts have color photos with navy and beige borders. The backs are black and white and have safety tips.

	MINT	EXC	G-VG
COMPLETE SET (12)	8.00	4.00	.80
COMMON PLAYER (1-12)	.50	.25	.05
☐ 1 Alex English	1.25	.60	.12
☐ 2 Mike Evans	.50	.25	.05
☐ 3 Bill Hanzlik	.60	.30	.06
☐ 4 Pete Williams	.50	.25	.05
☐ 5 Danny Schayes	1.00	.50	.10
☐ 6 Wayne Cooper	.50	.25	.05
☐ 7 Blair Rasmussen	.75	.35	.07
☐ 8 Elston Turner	.50	.25	.05
☐ 9 Lafayette(Fat) Lever	1.00	.50	.10
☐ 10 T.R. Dunn	.50	.25	.05
☐ 11 Willie White	.50	.25	.05
☐ 12 Calvin Natt	.75	.35	.07

1988-89 Nuggets Police/Pepsi

This 12-card set was sponsored by Pepsi, Pizza Hut, and The Children's Hospital of Denver. The cards measure approximately 2 5/8" by 4 1/8". The front features a borderless color action player photo. The player's number and name appear in white lettering in a purple stripe at the top of the card face, while team and sponsor logos appear in the white stripe at the bottom. The back is printed in blue on white and presents a safety tip from the player. The English and Lever variation cards differ only in the safety tip found on the back. The cards are unnumbered but they are numbered on the card front at the top by uniform number. The two Alex English cards and two Fat Lever cards are exactly the same except for the safety tip.

	MINT	EXC	G-VG
COMPLETE SET (12)	6.00	3.00	.60
COMMON PLAYER	.30	.15	.03

☐ 2A Alex English "If someone is hurt in an accident ..."	.75	.35	.07
☐ 2B Alex English "You should never run around ..."	.75	.35	.07
☐ 6 Walter Davis	.75	.35	.07
☐ 12A Fat Lever "Always wear a helmet when you're ..."	.60	.30	.06
☐ 12B Fat Lever "If you're ever in danger, the most ..."	.60	.30	.06
☐ 14 Michael Adams	.75	.35	.07
☐ 20 Elston Turner	.30	.15	.03
☐ 24 Bill Hanzlik	.30	.15	.03
☐ 34 Danny Schayes	.60	.30	.06
☐ 35 Jerome Lane	.50	.25	.05
☐ 41 Blair Rasmussen	.50	.25	.05
☐ 42 Wayne Cooper	.30	.15	.03

1989-90 Nuggets Police/Pepsi

This 12-card set was sponsored by Pepsi, 7/Eleven, and The Children's Hospital of Denver. Beginning in early February, the cards were given out in 7/Eleven stores with Pepsi products. They measure approximately 2 5/8" by 4 1/8". The front features a borderless color action player photo. Two stripes descend from the top of the picture on the right. The longer of the two has alternating black and yellow diagonal sections. In the white stripe appears the player's name and number. The team logo and sponsors' logos appear in the white stripe at the bottom of the card face. The back is printed in lavender on white card stock and presents a safety tip from the player. The cards are unnumbered and checklisted below in alphabetical order, with jersey number after the player's name.

	MINT	EXC	G-VG
COMPLETE SET (12)	5.00	2.50	.50
COMMON PLAYER (1-12)	.30	.15	.03
☐ 1 Michael Adams 14	.75	.35	.07
☐ 2 Walter Davis 6	.60	.30	.06
☐ 3 T.R. Dunn 23	.30	.15	.03
☐ 4 Alex English 2	.75	.35	.07
☐ 5 Bill Hanzlik 24	.40	.20	.04
☐ 6 Eddie Hughes 1	.30	.15	.03
☐ 7 Tim Kempton 45	.30	.15	.03
☐ 8 Jerome Lane 35	.40	.20	.04
☐ 9 Lafayette Lever 12	.60	.30	.06
☐ 10 Todd Lichti 21	.60	.30	.06
☐ 11 Blair Rasmussen 41	.50	.25	.05
☐ 12 Danny Schayes 34	.60	.30	.06

1971 Pacers Marathon Oil

This set of Marathon Oil Pro Star Portraits consists of colorful portraits by distinguished artist Nicholas Volpe. Each portrait measures approximately 7 1/2" by 9 7/8" and features a painting of the player's face on a black background, with an action painting superimposed to the side. A facsimile autograph in white appears at the bottom of the portrait. At the bottom of each portrait is a postcard measuring 7 1/2" by 4" after perforation. While the back of the portrait has offers for a basketball photo album, autographed tumblers, and a poster, the postcard itself may be used to apply for a Marathon credit card. The portraits are unnumbered and checklisted below according to alphabetical order.

	NRMT	VG-E	GOOD
COMPLETE SET (9)	40.00	20.00	4.00
COMMON PLAYER (1-9)	3.50	1.75	.35
☐ 1 Roger Brown	5.00	2.50	.50
☐ 2 Mel Daniels	6.50	3.25	.65
☐ 3 Earle Higgins	3.50	1.75	.35
☐ 4 Bill Keller	5.00	2.50	.50
☐ 5 Bob Leonard CO	4.50	2.25	.45
☐ 6 Freddie Lewis	5.00	2.50	.50
☐ 7 Rick Mount	6.50	3.25	.65
☐ 8 Bob Netolicky	4.50	2.25	.45
☐ 9 Howard Wright	3.50	1.75	.35

1990-91 Panini NBA

This set of 180 basketball stickers was produced and distributed by Panini. The stickers measure 1 7/8" by 2 15/16" and are issued in sheets consisting of three rows of four stickers each. The sheets were included with the sticker album itself. The stickers feature color action photos of the players on a white background. The team name is given in a light blue stripe below the picture, with a basketball icon to the right. The player's name appears at the bottom of the sticker. The stickers are numbered on the back. Stickers 1-162 showcase NBA players according to their teams as follows: Los Angeles Lakers (1-6), Portland Trail Blazers (7-12), Phoenix Suns (13-18), Seattle Supersonics (19-24), Golden State Warriors (25-30), Los Angeles Clippers (31-36), Sacramento Kings (37-42), San Antonio Spurs (43-48), Utah Jazz (49-54), Dallas Mavericks (55-60), Denver Nuggets (61-66), Houston Rockets (67-72), Minnesota Timberwolves (73-78), Charlotte Hornets (79-84), Detroit Pistons (85-90), Chicago Bulls (91-96), Milwaukee Bucks (97-102), Cleveland Cavaliers (103-108), Indiana Pacers (109-114), Atlanta Hawks (115-120), Orlando Magic (121-126), Philadelphia 76ers (127-132), Boston Celtics (133-138), New York Knicks (139-144), Washington Bullets (145-150), Miami Heat (151-156), and New Jersey Nets (157-162). The remaining 18 stickers are lettered A-R and feature 1990 NBA All-Stars (A-J); Jordan, Bird, and Olajuwon (K-M); and the 1990 NBA Finals (N-R).

	MINT	EXC	G-VG
COMPLETE SET (180)	9.00	4.50	.90
COMMON PLAYER (1-162)	.03	.01	.00
COMMON STICKER (A-R)	.05	.02	.00
☐ 1 Magic Johnson	.60	.30	.06
☐ 2 Mychal Thompson	.03	.01	.00
☐ 3 Vlade Divac	.12	.06	.01
☐ 4 Byron Scott	.06	.03	.00
☐ 5 James Worthy	.12	.06	.01
☐ 6 A.C. Green	.06	.03	.00
☐ 7 Jerome Kersey	.08	.04	.01
☐ 8 Clyde Drexler	.30	.15	.03
☐ 9 Buck Williams	.06	.03	.00
☐ 10 Kevin Duckworth	.06	.03	.00
☐ 11 Terry Porter	.12	.06	.01
☐ 12 Cliff Robinson	.08	.04	.01
☐ 13 Tom Chambers	.10	.05	.01
☐ 14 Dan Majerle	.10	.05	.01
☐ 15 Mark West	.03	.01	.00
☐ 16 Kevin Johnson	.30	.15	.03
☐ 17 Jeff Hornacek	.10	.05	.01
☐ 18 Kurt Rambis	.06	.03	.00
☐ 19 Nate McMillan	.03	.01	.00
☐ 20 Shawn Kemp	.40	.20	.04
☐ 21 Dale Ellis	.06	.03	.00
☐ 22 Michael Cage	.03	.01	.00
☐ 23 Xavier McDaniel	.06	.03	.00
☐ 24 Derrick McKey	.03	.01	.00
☐ 25 Manute Bol	.03	.01	.00
☐ 26 Chris Mullin	.15	.07	.01
☐ 27 Terry Teagle	.03	.01	.00
☐ 28 Tim Hardaway	.40	.20	.04
☐ 29 Sarunas Marciulionis	.15	.07	.01
☐ 30 Mitch Richmond	.15	.07	.01
☐ 31 Gary Grant	.03	.01	.00
☐ 32 Danny Manning	.12	.06	.01
☐ 33 Benoit Benjamin	.06	.03	.00
☐ 34 Ron Harper	.06	.03	.00
☐ 35 Ken Norman	.06	.03	.00
☐ 36 Charles Smith	.06	.03	.00
☐ 37 Harold Pressley	.03	.01	.00
☐ 38 Antoine Carr	.03	.01	.00
☐ 39 Danny Ainge	.08	.04	.01
☐ 40 Wayman Tisdale	.06	.03	.00
☐ 41 Ralph Sampson	.06	.03	.00
☐ 42 Vinny Del Negro	.03	.01	.00
☐ 43 David Robinson	.60	.30	.06
☐ 44 Sean Elliott	.15	.07	.01
☐ 45 Terry Cummings	.06	.03	.00
☐ 46 Willie Anderson	.06	.03	.00
☐ 47 Rod Strickland	.06	.03	.00
☐ 48 Frank Brickowski	.03	.01	.00
☐ 49 Karl Malone	.20	.10	.02
☐ 50 Darrell Griffith	.06	.03	.00
☐ 51 John Stockton	.20	.10	.02
☐ 52 Blue Edwards	.08	.04	.01
☐ 53 Mark Eaton	.03	.01	.00
☐ 54 Thurl Bailey	.03	.01	.00
☐ 55 Rolando Blackman	.08	.04	.01
☐ 56 Sam Perkins	.08	.04	.01
☐ 57 James Donaldson	.03	.01	.00
☐ 58 Herb Williams	.03	.01	.00
☐ 59 Roy Tarpley	.06	.03	.00
☐ 60 Derek Harper	.06	.03	.00
☐ 61 Michael Adams	.08	.04	.01
☐ 62 Blair Rasmussen	.03	.01	.00
☐ 63 Jerome Lane	.03	.01	.00
☐ 64 Walter Davis	.06	.03	.00
☐ 65 Todd Lichti	.06	.03	.00
☐ 66 Joe Barry Carroll	.03	.01	.00
☐ 67 Vernon Maxwell	.06	.03	.00
☐ 68 Otis Thorpe	.06	.03	.00
☐ 69 Hakeem Olajuwon	.20	.10	.02
☐ 70 Buck Johnson	.03	.01	.00
☐ 71 Eric(Sleepy) Floyd	.03	.01	.00
☐ 72 Mitchell Wiggins	.03	.01	.00
☐ 73 Tony Campbell	.08	.04	.01
☐ 74 Tod Murphy	.06	.03	.00
☐ 75 Tyrone Corbin	.06	.03	.00
☐ 76 Sam Mitchell	.06	.03	.00
☐ 77 Randy Breuer	.03	.01	.00
☐ 78 Pooh Richardson	.25	.12	.02
☐ 79 Rex Chapman	.12	.06	.01
☐ 80 Dell Curry	.03	.01	.00
☐ 81 Tyrone Bogues	.03	.01	.00
☐ 82 J.R. Reid	.10	.05	.01
☐ 83 Armon Gilliam	.03	.01	.00
☐ 84 Kelly Tripucka	.03	.01	.00
☐ 85 Dennis Rodman	.08	.04	.01
☐ 86 Joe Dumars	.10	.05	.01
☐ 87 Isiah Thomas	.15	.07	.01
☐ 88 Bill Laimbeer	.06	.03	.00
☐ 89 Vinnie Johnson	.03	.01	.00
☐ 90 James Edwards	.03	.01	.00
☐ 91 Michael Jordan	1.00	.50	.10
☐ 92 Stacey King	.08	.04	.01
☐ 93 Scottie Pippen	.30	.15	.03
☐ 94 John Paxson	.08	.04	.01
☐ 95 Horace Grant	.12	.06	.01
☐ 96 Craig Hodges	.06	.03	.00
☐ 97 Brad Lohaus	.06	.03	.00
☐ 98 Jack Sikma	.06	.03	.00
☐ 99 Ricky Pierce	.08	.04	.01
☐ 100 Greg Anderson	.03	.01	.00
☐ 101 Alvin Robertson	.06	.03	.00
☐ 102 Jay Humphries	.06	.03	.00
☐ 103 Mark Price	.12	.06	.01
☐ 104 Winston Bennett	.06	.03	.00
☐ 105 Brad Daugherty	.15	.07	.01
☐ 106 Craig Ehlo	.06	.03	.00
☐ 107 Larry Nance	.08	.04	.01
☐ 108 Hot Rod Williams	.06	.03	.00
☐ 109 Rik Smits	.06	.03	.00
☐ 110 Chuck Person	.08	.04	.01
☐ 111 Reggie Miller	.12	.06	.01
☐ 112 LaSalle Thompson	.03	.01	.00
☐ 113 Detlef Schrempf	.10	.05	.01
☐ 114 Vern Fleming	.03	.01	.00
☐ 115 Moses Malone	.15	.07	.01
☐ 116 Glenn Rivers	.06	.03	.00
☐ 117 Dominique Wilkins	.20	.10	.02
☐ 118 Spud Webb	.06	.03	.00
☐ 119 Kevin Willis	.10	.05	.01
☐ 120 Kenny Smith	.06	.03	.00

☐ 121 Otis Smith	.03	.01	.00
☐ 122 Sidney Green	.03	.01	.00
☐ 123 Nick Anderson	.15	.07	.01
☐ 124 Scott Skiles	.08	.04	.01
☐ 125 Jerry Reynolds	.03	.01	.00
☐ 126 Terry Catledge	.06	.03	.00
☐ 127 Charles Barkley	.25	.12	.02
☐ 128 Ron Anderson	.06	.03	.00
☐ 129 Hersey Hawkins	.10	.05	.01
☐ 130 Mike Gminski	.03	.01	.00
☐ 131 Johnny Dawkins	.03	.01	.00
☐ 132 Rick Mahorn	.06	.03	.00
☐ 133 Michael Smith	.06	.03	.00
☐ 134 Reggie Lewis	.25	.12	.02
☐ 135 Larry Bird	.40	.20	.04
☐ 136 Kevin McHale	.10	.05	.01
☐ 137 Joe Kleine	.03	.01	.00
☐ 138 Robert Parish	.12	.06	.01
☐ 139 Maurice Cheeks	.06	.03	.00
☐ 140 Patrick Ewing	.30	.15	.03
☐ 141 Charles Oakley	.06	.03	.00
☐ 142 Gerald Wilkins	.06	.03	.00
☐ 143 Kenny Walker	.03	.01	.00
☐ 144 Mark Jackson	.06	.03	.00
☐ 145 Mark Alarie	.03	.01	.00
☐ 146 John Williams	.03	.01	.00
☐ 147 Darrell Walker	.03	.01	.00
☐ 148 Bernard King	.08	.04	.01
☐ 149 Harvey Grant	.08	.04	.01
☐ 150 Ledell Eackles	.06	.03	.00
☐ 151 Glen Rice	.25	.12	.02
☐ 152 Kevin Edwards	.03	.01	.00
☐ 153 Tellis Frank	.03	.01	.00
☐ 154 Rony Seikaly	.10	.05	.01
☐ 155 Billy Thompson	.06	.03	.00
☐ 156 Sherman Douglas	.08	.04	.01
☐ 157 Roy Hinson	.03	.01	.00
☐ 158 Chris Morris	.06	.03	.00
☐ 159 Lester Conner	.03	.01	.00
☐ 160 Sam Bowie	.06	.03	.00
☐ 161 Purvis Short	.03	.01	.00
☐ 162 Mookie Blaylock	.08	.04	.01
☐ A John Stockton AS	.25	.12	.02
☐ B Magic Johnson AS	.50	.25	.05
☐ C A.C. Green AS	.05	.02	.00
☐ D Hakeem Olajuwon AS	.20	.10	.02
☐ E James Worthy AS	.15	.07	.01
☐ F Isiah Thomas AS	.15	.07	.01
☐ G Michael Jordan AS	.75	.35	.07
☐ H Larry Bird AS	.35	.17	.03
☐ I Patrick Ewing AS	.25	.12	.02
☐ J Charles Barkley AS	.25	.12	.02
☐ K Michael Jordan	.75	.35	.07
☐ L Larry Bird	.35	.17	.03
☐ M Hakeem Olajuwon	.20	.10	.02
☐ N NBA Finals	.05	.02	.00
☐ O NBA Finals	.05	.02	.00
☐ P NBA Finals	.05	.02	.00
☐ Q NBA Finals	.05	.02	.00
☐ R NBA Finals	.05	.02	.00

1991-92 Panini

This set of 192 basketball stickers was produced and distributed by Panini. Unlike the previous year's issue, these were distributed only in the usual Panini packet of six stickers with 100 packets per box. The stickers measure approximately 1 7/8" by 2 15/16". The fronts feature player action shots. The stickers are numbered on the back and checklisted below alphabetically according to teams within the divisions (Midwest, Pacific, Central, and Atlantic): Golden State Warriors (3-8), Los Angeles Clippers (9-14), Los Angeles Lakers (15-20), Phoenix Suns (21-26), Portland Trail Blazers (27-32), Sacramento Kings (33-38), Seattle Supersonics (39-44), Dallas Mavericks (45-50), Denver Nuggets (51-56), Houston Rockets (57-62), Minnesota Timberwolves (63-68), Orlando Magic (69-74), San Antonio Spurs (75-80), Utah Jazz (81-86), Atlanta Hawks (101-106), Charlotte Hornets (107-112), Chicago Bulls (113-118), Cleveland Cavaliers (119-124), Detroit Pistons (125-130), Indiana Pacers (131-136), Milwaukee Bucks (137-142), Boston Celtics (143-148), Miami Heat (149-154), New Jersey Nets (155-160), New York Knicks (161-166), Philadelphia 76ers (167-172), and Washington Bullets (173-178). The set closes with the All-Rookie Team (179-186) and All-NBA 1st Team (187-192).

	MINT	EXC	G-VG
COMPLETE SET (192)	12.00	6.00	1.20
COMMON PLAYER (1-192)	.03	.01	.00
☐ 1 NBA Official Licensed Product Logo	.03	.01	.00
☐ 2 1991 NBA Finals Logo	.03	.01	.00
☐ 3 Chris Mullin	.20	.10	.02
☐ 4 Mitch Richmond	.15	.07	.01
☐ 5 Alton Lister	.03	.01	.00
☐ 6 Tim Hardaway	.25	.12	.02
☐ 7 Tom Tolbert	.03	.01	.00
☐ 8 Rod Higgins	.03	.01	.00
☐ 9 Charles Smith	.06	.03	.00
☐ 10 Ron Harper	.06	.03	.00
☐ 11 Olden Polynice	.03	.01	.00
☐ 12 Ken Norman	.06	.03	.00
☐ 13 Gary Grant	.06	.03	.00
☐ 14 Danny Manning	.08	.04	.01
☐ 15 Sam Perkins	.06	.03	.00
☐ 16 Vlade Divac	.08	.04	.01
☐ 17 James Worthy	.15	.07	.01
☐ 18 Magic Johnson	.50	.25	.05
☐ 19 A.C. Green	.06	.03	.00
☐ 20 Byron Scott	.06	.03	.00
☐ 21 Kevin Johnson	.25	.12	.02
☐ 22 Mark West	.03	.01	.00
☐ 23 Dan Majerle	.08	.04	.01
☐ 24 Jeff Hornacek	.08	.04	.01
☐ 25 Xavier McDaniel	.06	.03	.00
☐ 26 Tom Chambers	.08	.04	.01
☐ 27 Terry Porter	.08	.04	.01
☐ 28 Kevin Duckworth	.03	.01	.00
☐ 29 Clyde Drexler	.25	.12	.02
☐ 30 Jerome Kersey	.08	.04	.01
☐ 31 Buck Williams	.06	.03	.00
☐ 32 Danny Ainge	.08	.04	.01
☐ 33 Wayman Tisdale	.06	.03	.00
☐ 34 Antoine Carr	.06	.03	.00
☐ 35 Lionel Simmons	.15	.07	.01
☐ 36 Travis Mays	.06	.03	.00
☐ 37 Rory Sparrow	.03	.01	.00
☐ 38 Duane Causwell	.06	.03	.00
☐ 39 Benoit Benjamin	.06	.03	.00
☐ 40 Michael Cage	.03	.01	.00
☐ 41 Derrick McKey	.06	.03	.00
☐ 42 Shawn Kemp	.25	.12	.02
☐ 43 Gary Payton	.08	.04	.01
☐ 44 Ricky Pierce	.06	.03	.00
☐ 45 Derek Harper	.06	.03	.00
☐ 46 James Donaldson	.03	.01	.00
☐ 47 Randy White	.06	.03	.00
☐ 48 Rodney McCray	.03	.01	.00
☐ 49 Alex English	.08	.04	.01
☐ 50 Rolando Blackman	.08	.04	.01
☐ 51 Orlando Woolridge	.06	.03	.00
☐ 52 Todd Lichti	.06	.03	.00
☐ 53 Chris Jackson	.08	.04	.01
☐ 54 Blair Rasmussen	.03	.01	.00
☐ 55 Reggie Williams	.08	.04	.01
☐ 56 Marcus Liberty	.12	.06	.01
☐ 57 Hakeem Olajuwon	.20	.10	.02
☐ 58 Kenny Smith	.06	.03	.00
☐ 59 Vernon Maxwell	.06	.03	.00
☐ 60 Otis Thorpe	.06	.03	.00
☐ 61 Buck Johnson	.03	.01	.00
☐ 62 Larry Smith	.03	.01	.00
☐ 63 Pooh Richardson	.12	.06	.01
☐ 64 Felton Spencer	.06	.03	.00
☐ 65 Tod Murphy	.03	.01	.00
☐ 66 Tyrone Corbin	.03	.01	.00
☐ 67 Tony Campbell	.06	.03	.00
☐ 68 Sam Mitchell	.03	.01	.00
☐ 69 Dennis Scott	.10	.05	.01
☐ 70 Nick Anderson	.12	.06	.01
☐ 71 Terry Catledge	.06	.03	.00
☐ 72 Scott Skiles	.06	.03	.00
☐ 73 Otis Smith	.03	.01	.00
☐ 74 Greg Kite	.03	.01	.00
☐ 75 Terry Cummings	.08	.04	.01
☐ 76 Rod Strickland	.08	.04	.01
☐ 77 David Robinson	.40	.20	.04
☐ 78 Willie Anderson	.06	.03	.00
☐ 79 Sean Elliott	.10	.05	.01
☐ 80 Paul Pressey	.03	.01	.00
☐ 81 John Stockton	.20	.10	.02
☐ 82 Jeff Malone	.08	.04	.01
☐ 83 Mark Eaton	.03	.01	.00
☐ 84 Thurl Bailey	.03	.01	.00
☐ 85 Karl Malone	.20	.10	.02

☐ 86 Blue Edwards	.06	.03	.00
☐ 87 Kevin Johnson	.25	.12	.02
☐ 88 '91 Western Division All-Stars	.03	.01	.00
☐ 89 NBA All-Star Weekend Logo	.03	.01	.00
☐ 90 Magic Johnson AS	.30	.15	.03
☐ 91 Karl Malone AS	.15	.07	.01
☐ 92 David Robinson AS	.20	.10	.02
☐ 93 Chris Mullin AS	.15	.07	.01
☐ 94 Charles Barkley AS	.15	.07	.01
☐ 95 '91 Eastern Division All-Stars	.03	.01	.00
☐ 96 Michael Jordan AS	.40	.20	.04
☐ 97 Isiah Thomas AS	.10	.05	.01
☐ 98 Charles Barkley AS	.15	.07	.01
☐ 99 Patrick Ewing AS	.15	.07	.01
☐ 100 Larry Bird AS	.20	.10	.02
☐ 101 Dominique Wilkins	.15	.07	.01
☐ 102 Kevin Willis	.08	.04	.01
☐ 103 John Battle	.03	.01	.00
☐ 104 Doc Rivers	.06	.03	.00
☐ 105 Spud Webb	.06	.03	.00
☐ 106 Moses Malone	.12	.06	.01
☐ 107 J.R. Reid	.06	.03	.00
☐ 108 Johnny Newman	.06	.03	.00
☐ 109 Rex Chapman	.08	.04	.01
☐ 110 Muggsy Bogues	.03	.01	.00
☐ 111 Mike Gminski	.03	.01	.00
☐ 112 Kendall Gill	.40	.20	.04
☐ 113 Scottie Pippen	.25	.12	.02
☐ 114 Bill Cartwright	.06	.03	.00
☐ 115 John Paxson	.08	.04	.01
☐ 116 Michael Jordan	.50	.25	.05
☐ 117 Horace Grant	.15	.07	.01
☐ 118 B.J. Armstrong	.08	.04	.01
☐ 119 Brad Daugherty	.15	.07	.01
☐ 120 Larry Nance	.08	.04	.01
☐ 121 John Williams	.06	.03	.00
☐ 122 Craig Ehlo	.06	.03	.00
☐ 123 Darnell Valentine	.03	.01	.00
☐ 124 Danny Ferry	.08	.04	.01
☐ 125 Isiah Thomas	.15	.07	.01
☐ 126 James Edwards	.03	.01	.00
☐ 127 Bill Laimbeer	.06	.03	.00
☐ 128 Vinnie Johnson	.03	.01	.00
☐ 129 Joe Dumars	.10	.05	.01
☐ 130 Dennis Rodman	.08	.04	.01
☐ 131 Reggie Miller	.08	.04	.01
☐ 132 Detlef Schrempf	.08	.04	.01
☐ 133 Chuck Person	.08	.04	.01
☐ 134 LaSalle Thompson	.03	.01	.00
☐ 135 Vern Fleming	.03	.01	.00
☐ 136 Rik Smits	.06	.03	.00
☐ 137 Dale Ellis	.06	.03	.00
☐ 138 Frank Brickowski	.03	.01	.00
☐ 139 Jay Humphries	.06	.03	.00
☐ 140 Jack Sikma	.06	.03	.00
☐ 141 Fred Roberts	.03	.01	.00
☐ 142 Alvin Robertson	.06	.03	.00
☐ 143 Robert Parish	.10	.05	.01
☐ 144 Kevin McHale	.08	.04	.01
☐ 145 Kevin Gamble	.06	.03	.00
☐ 146 Larry Bird	.40	.20	.04
☐ 147 Reggie Lewis	.20	.10	.02
☐ 148 Brian Shaw	.06	.03	.00
☐ 149 Sherman Douglas	.08	.04	.01
☐ 150 Rony Seikaly	.12	.06	.01
☐ 151 Glen Rice	.20	.10	.02
☐ 152 Grant Long	.06	.03	.00
☐ 153 Billy Thompson	.03	.01	.00
☐ 154 Willie Burton	.06	.03	.00
☐ 155 Reggie Theus	.06	.03	.00
☐ 156 Sam Bowie	.06	.03	.00
☐ 157 Derrick Coleman	.25	.12	.02
☐ 158 Drazen Petrovic	.12	.06	.01
☐ 159 Mookie Blaylock	.06	.03	.00
☐ 160 Chris Morris	.06	.03	.00
☐ 161 Gerald Wilkins	.06	.03	.00
☐ 162 Charles Oakley	.06	.03	.00
☐ 163 Patrick Ewing	.25	.12	.02
☐ 164 Kiki Vandeweghe	.06	.03	.00
☐ 165 Maurice Cheeks	.06	.03	.00
☐ 166 John Starks	.25	.12	.02
☐ 167 Hersey Hawkins	.08	.04	.01
☐ 168 Rick Mahorn	.06	.03	.00
☐ 169 Charles Barkley	.25	.12	.02
☐ 170 Rickey Green	.03	.01	.00
☐ 171 Ron Anderson	.03	.01	.00
☐ 172 Armon Gilliam	.03	.01	.00
☐ 173 Bernard King	.06	.03	.00
☐ 174 Ledell Eackles	.03	.01	.00
☐ 175 John Williams	.03	.01	.00
☐ 176 Darrell Walker	.03	.01	.00
☐ 177 Haywoode Workman	.03	.01	.00
☐ 178 Harvey Grant	.08	.04	.01
☐ 179 Derrick Coleman ART	.20	.10	.02
☐ 180 Dee Brown ART	.15	.07	.01
☐ 181 Lionel Simmons ART	.15	.07	.01
☐ 182 Felton Spencer ART	.08	.04	.01
☐ 183 Dennis Scott ART	.08	.04	.01
☐ 184 Gary Payton ART	.08	.04	.01
☐ 185 Travis Mays ART	.06	.03	.00
☐ 186 Kendall Gill ART	.25	.12	.02
☐ 187 All-NBA 1st Team	.03	.01	.00
☐ 188 Charles Barkley AS	.15	.07	.01
☐ 189 Patrick Ewing AS	.15	.07	.01
☐ 190 Michael Jordan AS	.30	.15	.03
☐ 191 Karl Malone AS	.15	.07	.01
☐ 192 Magic Johnson AS	.25	.12	.02

1968-70 Partridge Meats *

This black and white (with a little bit of red trim) photo-like card set features players from all three Cincinnati major league sports teams of that time, Reds baseball (1-8), Bengals football (9-12), and Royals basketball (13-14). The cards measure approximately 4" by 5", although there are other sizes sometimes found which are attributable to other years of issue. The cards are blank backed.

	NRMT	VG-E	GOOD
COMPLETE SET (14)	750.00	375.00	75.00
COMMON BASEBALL (1-8)	15.00	7.50	1.50
COMMON FOOTBALL (9-12)	20.00	10.00	2.00
COMMON BASKETBALL (13-14)	30.00	15.00	3.00
☐ 1 Johnny Bench	250.00	125.00	25.00
☐ 2 Jimmy Bragan	15.00	7.50	1.50
☐ 3 Tommy Helms	15.00	7.50	1.50
☐ 4 Gary Nolan	15.00	7.50	1.50
☐ 5 Don Pavletich	15.00	7.50	1.50
☐ 6 Mel Queen	15.00	7.50	1.50
☐ 7 Pete Rose	250.00	125.00	25.00
☐ 8 Jim Stewart	15.00	7.50	1.50
☐ 9 Bob Johnson	25.00	12.50	2.50
☐ 10 Paul Robinson	25.00	12.50	2.50
☐ 11 John Stofa	20.00	10.00	2.00
☐ 12 Bob Trumpy	30.00	15.00	3.00
☐ 13 Adrian Smith	30.00	15.00	3.00
☐ 14 Tom Van Arsdale	40.00	20.00	4.00

1977-78 Pepsi All-Stars

This set of eight photos was sponsored by Pepsi. The borderless color player photos measure approximately 8" by 10" and are printed on thick cardboard stock. All the photos depict players either shooting or dunking the ball. The Pepsi logo and the player's name appear in the upper right corner. In blue print the back presents various statistics. The photos are unnumbered and are checklisted below in alphabetical order.

	NRMT	VG-E	GOOD
COMPLETE SET (8)	50.00	25.00	5.00
COMMON PLAYER (1-8)	5.00	2.50	.50
☐ 1 Rick Barry	7.00	3.50	.70
☐ 2 Dave Cowens	7.00	3.50	.70
☐ 3 Julius Erving	15.00	7.50	1.50
☐ 4 Kareem Abdul-Jabbar	18.00	9.00	1.80
☐ 5 Pete Maravich	14.00	7.00	1.40
☐ 6 Bob McAdoo	5.00	2.50	.50
☐ 7 David Thompson	6.00	3.00	.60
☐ 8 Bill Walton	9.00	4.50	.90

1981-82 Philip Morris *

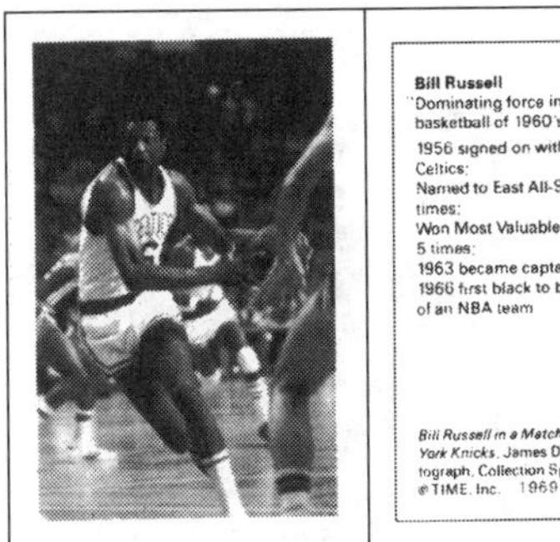

This 18-card set was included in the Champions of American Sport program and features major stars from a variety of sports. The program was issued in conjunction with a traveling exhibition organized by the National Portrait Gallery and the Smithsonian Institution and sponsored by Philip Morris and Miller Brewing Company. The cards are standard size, 2 1/2" by 3 1/2". The cards are either reproductions of works of art (paintings) or famous photographs of the time. The cards are frequently found with a perforated edge on at least one side. The cards were actually obtained from two perforated pages in the program. There is no recognition anywhere on the cards with respect to who produced them.

	MINT	EXC	G-VG
COMPLETE SET (18)	60.00	30.00	6.00
COMMON CARD (1-18)	1.00	.50	.10
☐ 1 Muhammed Ali	6.00	3.00	.60
☐ 2 Arthur Ashe	3.00	1.50	.30
☐ 3 Peggy Fleming	1.00	.50	.10
☐ 4 A.J. Foyt	5.00	2.50	.50
☐ 5 Eric Heiden	1.00	.50	.10
☐ 6 Bobby Hull	8.00	4.00	.80
☐ 7 Sandy Koufax	9.00	4.50	.90
☐ 8 Joe Louis	3.00	1.50	.30
☐ 9 Bob Mathias	1.00	.50	.10
☐ 10 Willie Mays	9.00	4.50	.90
☐ 11 Joe Namath	9.00	4.50	.90
☐ 12 Jack Nicklaus	4.00	2.00	.40
☐ 13 Knute Rockne	5.00	2.50	.50
☐ 14 Bill Russell	12.00	6.00	1.20
☐ 15 Jim Ryun	1.00	.50	.10
☐ 16 Willie Shoemaker	3.00	1.50	.30
☐ 17 Casey Stengel	4.00	2.00	.40
☐ 18 Johnny Unitas	8.00	4.00	.80

1990-91 Pistons Unocal

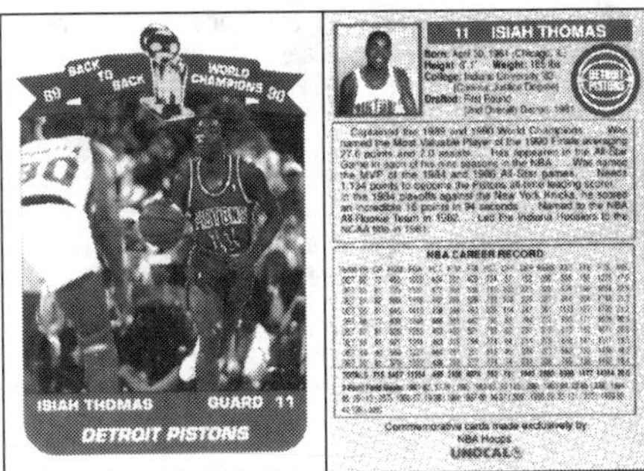

This 16-card set was produced by Hoops for UNOCAL 76 to commemorate the Piston's back to back championship seasons. A photo album to hold the cards was available for 2.76 at all participating UNOCAL 76 filling stations. Beginning on December 1, 1990 and continuing through the end of March, one card was given away each week with a fuel purchase at participating stations. The cards measure the standard size (2 1/2" by 3 1/2") and feature color action player photos on white card stock. A blue banner is draped along the top of the picture, and it reads "89-90 Back to Back World Champions." A Lawrence O'Brien trophy is superimposed at the middle of the banner. Player information and the team name are given in a reddish-orange stripe below the picture. On a blue background, the backs have a head shot of the player in the upper left corner, biographical information, and statistics for the player's NBA career. The cards are unnumbered.

	MINT	EXC	G-VG
COMPLETE SET (16)	12.00	6.00	1.20
COMMON PLAYER (1-16)	.60	.30	.06
☐ 1 Mark Aguirre	.75	.35	.07
☐ 2 Chuck Daly CO	.75	.35	.07
☐ 3 Joe Dumars	1.50	.75	.15
☐ 4 James Edwards	.75	.35	.07
☐ 5 Vinnie Johnson	.75	.35	.07
☐ 6 Vinnie Johnson (The Shot)	.75	.35	.07
☐ 7 Bill Laimbeer	1.00	.50	.10
☐ 8 Lawrence O'Brien Trophy	.60	.30	.06
☐ 9 Dennis Rodman	1.50	.75	.15
☐ 10 John Salley	1.00	.50	.10
☐ 11 Isiah Thomas	2.00	1.00	.20
☐ 12 Isiah Thomas MVP	1.50	.75	.15
☐ 13 Celebration Card	.60	.30	.06
☐ 14 Team Photo	.75	.35	.07
☐ 15 Two Championship Rings	.60	.30	.06
☐ 16 1990 World Champions	.60	.30	.06

1990-91 Pistons Star

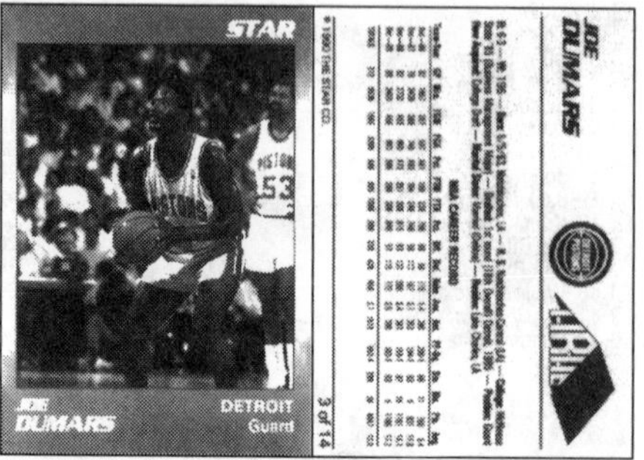

This 14-card set was produced by Star Company and sponsored by Home Respiratory Health Care, Inc., and the HRHC logo adorns the top of each card back. The cards measure the standard size (2 1/2" by 3 1/2"). The front features a color action photo of the player, on a royal blue background that washes out in the middle of the card. In white lettering the player's name, team, and position appear below the picture. In blue lettering the back presents biographical and statistical information in a horizontal format. The cards are numbered on the back.

	MINT	EXC	G-VG
COMPLETE SET (14)	9.00	4.50	.90
COMMON PLAYER (1-14)	.50	.25	.05
☐ 1 Mark Aguirre	.75	.35	.07
☐ 2 William Bedford	.50	.25	.05
☐ 3 Joe Dumars	1.25	.60	.12
☐ 4 James Edwards	.50	.25	.05
☐ 5 David Greenwood	.50	.25	.05
☐ 6 Scott Hastings	.50	.25	.05
☐ 7 Gerald Henderson	.50	.25	.05
☐ 8 Vinnie Johnson	.75	.35	.07
☐ 9 Bill Laimbeer	1.00	.50	.10
☐ 10 Dennis Rodman	1.25	.60	.12
☐ 11 John Salley	.75	.35	.07
☐ 12 Isiah Thomas	1.50	.75	.15
☐ 13 Chuck Daly CO	.75	.35	.07
☐ 14 Maia A. Porche PRES	.50	.25	.05

1991-92 Pistons Unocal

This 16-card standard size (2 1/2" by 3 1/2") set marks the second straight year that Hoops has produced a set for UNOCAL 76. The production run was reported to be 2.5 million cards or roughly 157,000 sets. The cards were distributed two per week with a fill up as part of a promotion that began November 28 and ran through March 1992. In addition, 125,000 vinyl photo albums were produced, and collectors who purchased one for $2.76 at participating UNOCAL filling stations received a redemption card that could be exchanged for a complete set. The fronts feature color action player photos framed in yellow on a blue card face. The upper left and lower right corners of the pictures are cut out. On various color panels, the backs carry a color head shot, biography, career summary, and complete statistics. The cards are unnumbered and checklisted below in alphabetical order, with the multi-player cards listed at the end.

	MINT	EXC	G-VG
COMPLETE SET (16)	10.00	5.00	1.00
COMMON PLAYER (1-16)	.50	.25	.05
☐ 1 Mark Aguirre	.75	.35	.07
☐ 2 Dave Bing 1989 HOF Inductee	1.00	.50	.10
☐ 3 Chuck Daly CO	.75	.35	.07
☐ 4 Joe Dumars	1.00	.50	.10
☐ 5 Joe Dumars 1991 Pistons MVP	1.00	.50	.10
☐ 6 Bill Laimbeer	.75	.35	.07
☐ 7 Bill Laimbeer All-Time Leading Rebounder	.75	.35	.07
☐ 8 Dennis Rodman	1.00	.50	.10
☐ 9 John Salley	.75	.35	.07
☐ 10 Isiah Thomas	1.25	.60	.12
☐ 11 Isiah Thomas All-Time Leading Scorer	1.25	.60	.12
☐ 12 Darrell Walker	.50	.25	.05
☐ 13 Orlando Woolridge	.60	.30	.06
☐ 14 Team Photo 1989 World Champs	.75	.35	.07
☐ 15 All-Stars Mark Aguirre Joe Dumars Bill Laimbeer Dennis Rodman Isiah Thomas Chuck Daly CO	.75	.35	.07
☐ 16 Role Players Brad Sellers Bob McCann Charles Thomas William Bedford Lance Blanks	.50	.25	.05

1985 Prism Stickers

These gaudy metallic stickers measure approximately 2 11/16" by 4". The front features a colorful drawn picture of the player, with the player's name in block lettering, and a facsimile autograph. The picture has rounded corners and a silver border. The backs are blank. The stickers are unnumbered and are checklisted below in alphabetical order by subject.

	MINT	EXC	G-VG
COMPLETE SET (9)	75.00	37.50	7.50
COMMON PLAYER (1-9)	2.00	1.00	.20
☐ 1 Bird vs. Worthy	10.00	5.00	1.00
☐ 2 Patrick Ewing	10.00	5.00	1.00
☐ 3 Michael Jordan	35.00	17.50	3.50
☐ 3 Moses Malone	5.00	2.50	.50
☐ 4 Malone vs. Jabbar	7.50	3.75	.75
☐ 5 Sidney Moncrief	3.00	1.50	.30
☐ 6 Isiah Thomas	6.00	3.00	.60
☐ 7 Kelly Tripucka	2.00	1.00	.20
☐ 8 Buck Williams	3.00	1.50	.30

1989-90 ProCards CBA

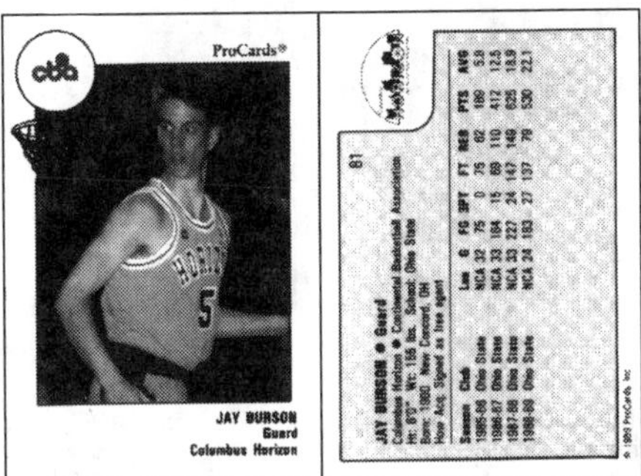

The 1989-90 ProCards CBA basketball set contains 207 cards measuring the standard size (2 1/2" by 3 1/2"). The fronts feature posed or action color player photos on a light tan background. Overlaying the upper left corner of the picture is a white circle (representing a basketball), with the CBA logo on it. Just below the circle a basketball rim and net are drawn. The player's name, position, and team are given in black lettering in the lower right corner of the card face. On a gray background with black borders and lettering the horizontally oriented backs present biographical and statistical information. The team logo appears in the cut-out section at the upper right corner. The cards are numbered on the back and arranged according to teams as follows: Sioux Falls SkyForce (1-13), Wichita Falls Texans (14-25), Rapid City Thrillers (26-37), Quad City Thunder (38-50), Pensacola Tornados (51-60), Omaha Racers (61-74, 206-7), Columbus Horizon (75-86), Rockford Lightning (87-100), Albany Patroons (101-114), Santa Barbara Islanders (115-127), Grand Rapids Hoops (128-140), Tulsa Fast Breakers (141-153), LaCrosse Catbirds (154-165), Topeka Sizzlers (166-178), Cedar Rapids Silver Bullets (179-192), and San Jose Jammers (193-205). The set features the first professional card of John Starks.

	MINT	EXC	G-VG
COMPLETE SET (207)	75.00	37.50	7.50
COMMON PLAYER (1-207)	.25	.12	.02
☐ 1 Sioux Falls Checklist	.35	.17	.03
☐ 2 Ben Wilson	.35	.17	.03
☐ 3 Leonard Harris	.35	.17	.03
☐ 4 Laurent Crawford	.25	.12	.02
☐ 5 Steve Grayer	.35	.17	.03
☐ 6 Jim Lampley	.50	.25	.05
☐ 7 Eric Brown	.25	.12	.02
☐ 8 Dennis Nutt	.35	.17	.03
☐ 9 Ralph Lewis	.25	.12	.02
☐ 10 Lashun McDaniel	.25	.12	.02
☐ 11 Leo Parent	.25	.12	.02
☐ 12 Ron Ekker	.35	.17	.03
☐ 13 Terry Gould	.25	.12	.02
☐ 14 Wichita Falls Checklist	.35	.17	.03
☐ 15 Mark Peterson	.25	.12	.02
☐ 16 Greg Van Soelen	.25	.12	.02
☐ 17 Maurice Selvin	.25	.12	.02
☐ 18 Michael Tait	.35	.17	.03
☐ 19 Deon Hunter	.35	.17	.03
☐ 20 Randy Henry	.25	.12	.02
☐ 21 Kenny McClary	.25	.12	.02
☐ 22 Earl Walker	.25	.12	.02
☐ 23 Jeff Hodge	.25	.12	.02
☐ 24 Martin Nessley	.35	.17	.03
☐ 25 On Court Staff	.25	.12	.02
☐ 26 Rapid City Checklist	.35	.17	.03
☐ 27 Daren Queenan	.25	.12	.02
☐ 28 Carey Scurry	.25	.12	.02
☐ 29 Keith Smart	1.50	.75	.15
☐ 30 Jim Thomas	.50	.25	.05
☐ 31 Pearl Washington	.50	.25	.05
☐ 32 Chris Childs	.25	.12	.02
☐ 33 Jarvis Basnight	.50	.25	.05
☐ 34 Dwight Boyd	.25	.12	.02
☐ 35 Raymond Brown	.25	.12	.02
☐ 36 Sylvester Gray	.35	.17	.03
☐ 37 Eric Musselman	.35	.17	.03
☐ 38 Quad City Checklist	.35	.17	.03
☐ 39 Kenny Gattison	1.00	.50	.10
☐ 40 Lafester Rhodes	.35	.17	.03
☐ 41 Perry Young	.50	.25	.05
☐ 42 Wiley Brown	.35	.17	.03
☐ 43 Jose Slaughter	.35	.17	.03
☐ 44 Gerald Greene	.25	.12	.02
☐ 45 Lloyd Daniels	3.50	1.75	.35
☐ 46 Bill Jones	.35	.17	.03
☐ 47 Sean Couch	.25	.12	.02
☐ 48 Marty Eggleston	.25	.12	.02
☐ 49 Mauro Panaggio	.35	.17	.03
☐ 50 Dan Panaggio	.25	.12	.02
☐ 51 Pensacola Checklist	.35	.17	.03
☐ 52 Joe Mullaney	.35	.17	.03
☐ 53 Mark Wade	.50	.25	.05
☐ 54 Larry Houzer	.25	.12	.02
☐ 55 Clifford Lett	.35	.17	.03
☐ 56 Tony Dawson	.25	.12	.02
☐ 57 Johnathan Edwards	.25	.12	.02
☐ 58 Jim Farmer	.75	.35	.07
☐ 59 Dwayne Taylor	.25	.12	.02
☐ 60 Bob McCann	.35	.17	.03
☐ 61 Omaha Checklist	.35	.17	.03
☐ 62 Silks/Rodie	.25	.12	.02
☐ 63 Racers Front Office	.25	.12	.02
☐ 64 Rodie-Team Mascot	.25	.12	.02
☐ 65 Tim Price	.25	.12	.02
☐ 66 Barry Glanzer	.25	.12	.02
☐ 67 Greg Wiltjer	.25	.12	.02
☐ 68 Ron Kellogg	.25	.12	.02
☐ 69 Tat Hunter	.25	.12	.02
☐ 70 Reginald Turner	.25	.12	.02
☐ 71 Jerry Adams	.25	.12	.02
☐ 72 Roland Gray	.25	.12	.02
☐ 73 Tim Legler	.35	.17	.03
☐ 74 Corey Gaines	.35	.17	.03
☐ 75 Columbus Checklist	.35	.17	.03
☐ 76 Gary Youmans	.25	.12	.02
☐ 77 Kelvin Ransey	.50	.25	.05
☐ 78 Chip Engelland	.35	.17	.03
☐ 79 Brian Martin	.25	.12	.02
☐ 80 Ray Hall	.25	.12	.02
☐ 81 Jay Burson	1.00	.50	.10
☐ 82 Bill Martin	.35	.17	.03
☐ 83 Eric Mudd	.25	.12	.02
☐ 84 Tom Schafer	.35	.17	.03
☐ 85 Steve Harris	.35	.17	.03
☐ 86 Eric Newsome	.25	.12	.02
☐ 87 Rockford Checklist	.35	.17	.03
☐ 88 Charley Rosen	.25	.12	.02
☐ 89 Tom Hart	.25	.12	.02
☐ 90 Team Picture	.35	.17	.03
☐ 91 Brent Carmichael	.25	.12	.02
☐ 92 Fred Cofield	.25	.12	.02
☐ 93 Darren Guest	.25	.12	.02
☐ 94 Bobby Parks	.35	.17	.03
☐ 95 Elston Turner	.50	.25	.05
☐ 96 Adrian McKinnon	.25	.12	.02
☐ 97 Gary Massey	.25	.12	.02
☐ 98 Tim Dillon	.25	.12	.02
☐ 99 Herb Blunt	.25	.12	.02
☐ 100 Greg Grissom	.35	.17	.03
☐ 101 Albany Checklist	.35	.17	.03
☐ 102 Leroy Witherspoon	.25	.12	.02
☐ 103 Vincent Askew	1.50	.75	.15
☐ 104 Clinton Smith	.25	.12	.02
☐ 105 Andre Patterson	.25	.12	.02
☐ 106 Jim Ferrer	.25	.12	.02
☐ 107 Willie Glass	.50	.25	.05
☐ 108 Darryl Joe	.35	.17	.03
☐ 109 Mario Elie	2.50	1.25	.25
☐ 110 Dave Popson	.50	.25	.05

	Card	MINT	EXC	G-VG
☐	111 Danny Pearson	.25	.12	.02
☐	112 Doc Nunnally	.25	.12	.02
☐	113 Gene Espeland	.25	.12	.02
☐	114 Gerald Oliver	.25	.12	.02
☐	115 Santa Barbara CL	.35	.17	.03
☐	116 Luther Burks	.25	.12	.02
☐	117 Brian Christensen	.35	.17	.03
☐	118 Kevin Francewar	.25	.12	.02
☐	119 Leon Wood	.50	.25	.05
☐	120 Derrick Gervin	1.25	.60	.12
☐	121 Larry Spriggs	.75	.35	.07
☐	122 Michael Phelps	.50	.25	.05
☐	123 Mike Ratliff	.35	.17	.03
☐	124 Steffond Johnson	.50	.25	.05
☐	125 Mitch McMullen	.25	.12	.02
☐	126 Sonny Allen	.35	.17	.03
☐	127 Don Ford	.35	.17	.03
☐	128 Grand Rapids Checklist	.35	.17	.03
☐	129 Lorenzo Sutton	.35	.17	.03
☐	130 Willie Simmons	.25	.12	.02
☐	131 Kenny Fields	.50	.25	.05
☐	132 Winston Crite	.35	.17	.03
☐	133 Eric McLaughlin	.25	.12	.02
☐	134 Tony Brown	.35	.17	.03
☐	135 Ricky Wilson	.35	.17	.03
☐	136 Milt Newton	.50	.25	.05
☐	137 Albert Springs	.25	.12	.02
☐	138 Herbert Crook	.50	.25	.05
☐	139 Mike Mashak	.25	.12	.02
☐	140 Jim Sleeper	.25	.12	.02
☐	141 Tulsa Checklist	.35	.17	.03
☐	142 Terry Faggins	.25	.12	.02
☐	143 Ozell Jones	.35	.17	.03
☐	144 Brian Rahilly	.25	.12	.02
☐	145 Duane Washington	.35	.17	.03
☐	146 Ron Spivey	.25	.12	.02
☐	147 Henry Bibby CO	.50	.25	.05
☐	148 Al Gipson	.35	.17	.03
☐	149 Greg Jones	.25	.12	.02
☐	150 Andre Moore	.25	.12	.02
☐	151 Tracy Moore	.50	.25	.05
☐	152 Steve Bontranger	.25	.12	.02
☐	153 Bubby Breaker Team Mascot	.25	.12	.02
☐	154 Lacrosse Checklist	.35	.17	.03
☐	155 Mike Williams	.25	.12	.02
☐	156 Vince Hamilton	.25	.12	.02
☐	157 John Harris	.25	.12	.02
☐	158 Tony White	.25	.12	.02
☐	159 Todd Alexander	.25	.12	.02
☐	160 Richard Johnson	.35	.17	.03
☐	161 Leo Rautins	.35	.17	.03
☐	162 Dwayne McClain	.50	.25	.05
☐	163 Carlos Clark	.35	.17	.03
☐	164 Vada Martin	.25	.12	.02
☐	165 Flip Saunders	.35	.17	.03
☐	166 Topeka Checklist	.35	.17	.03
☐	167 Cedric Hunter	.35	.17	.03
☐	168 Elfrem Jackson	.25	.12	.02
☐	169 Glen Clem	.25	.12	.02
☐	170 Mike Richmond	.25	.12	.02
☐	171 Jim Rowinski	.35	.17	.03
☐	172 Craig Jackson	.25	.12	.02
☐	173 Tony Mack	.25	.12	.02
☐	174 Hubert Henderson	.25	.12	.02
☐	175 Kevin Nixon	.25	.12	.02
☐	176 Haywoode Workman	.50	.25	.05
☐	177 Porter Cutrell	.25	.12	.02
☐	178 Mike Riley	.25	.12	.02
☐	179 Cedar Rapids Checklist	.35	.17	.03
☐	180 Bullet Bear	.25	.12	.02
☐	181 George Whittaker	.25	.12	.02
☐	182 Tom Domako	.25	.12	.02
☐	183 Al Lorenzen	.35	.17	.03
☐	184 Darryl Johnson	.25	.12	.02
☐	185 Mel Braxton	.25	.12	.02
☐	186 Orlando Graham	.25	.12	.02
☐	187 Reggie Owens	.35	.17	.03
☐	188 John Starks	4.00	2.00	.40
☐	189 Kenny Drummond	.25	.12	.02
☐	190 Mark Plansky	.35	.17	.03
☐	191 Anthony Blakley	.35	.17	.03
☐	192 Everette Stephens	.35	.17	.03
☐	193 San Jose Checklist	.35	.17	.03
☐	194 Cory Russell	.25	.12	.02
☐	195 Jim Ellis	.25	.12	.02
☐	196 Butch Hays	.25	.12	.02
☐	197 Mike Doktorczyk	.25	.12	.02
☐	198 Scooter Barry	1.00	.50	.10
☐	199 Monroe Douglass	.35	.17	.03
☐	200 Scott Fisher	.25	.12	.02
☐	201 David Boone	.25	.12	.02
☐	202 Jervis Cole	.25	.12	.02
☐	203 Freddie Banks	.35	.17	.03
☐	204 Richard Morton	.25	.12	.02
☐	205 Dan Williams	.25	.12	.02
☐	206 Mike Thibault CO	.25	.12	.02
☐	207 Omaha Coaches Omaha Racers	.25	.12	.02

1990-91 ProCards CBA

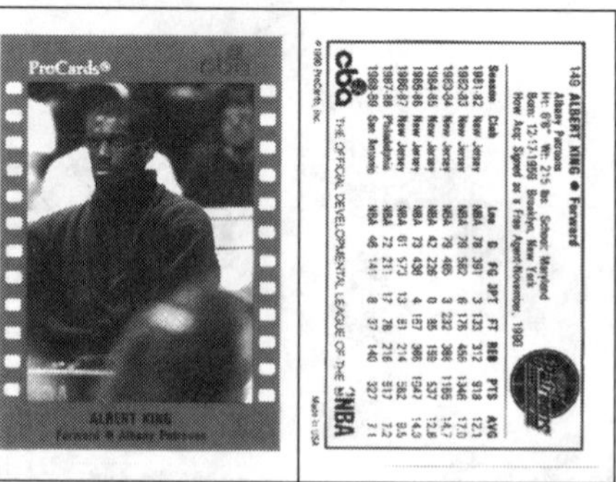

The 1990-91 ProCards CBA basketball set contains 203 cards measuring the standard size (2 1/2" by 3 1/2"). The color player photos on the fronts are framed by a filmstrip design in red on a white card face. The horizontally oriented backs are printed in black on light purple and feature biographical as well as statistical information. The cards are checklisted below according to teams as follows: Omaha Racers (1-16), Cedar Rapids Silver Bullets (17-29), Pensacola Tornados (30-44), Rockford Lightning (45-59), Lacrosse Catbirds (60-71), Rapid City Thrillers (72-81), Sioux Falls Skyforce (82-96), Oklahoma City Cavalry (97-107), Tulsa Fast Breakers (108-118), Wichita Falls Texans (119-134), Quad City Thunder (135-148), Albany Patroons (149-162), Grand Rapids Hoops (163-171), Columbus Horizon (172-183), Yakima Sun Kings (184-192), and San Jose Jammers (193-203).

		MINT	EXC	G-VG
	COMPLETE SET (203)	60.00	30.00	6.00
	COMMON PLAYER (1-203)	.25	.12	.02
☐	1 Jim Les	1.00	.50	.10
☐	2 Ron Moore	.25	.12	.02
☐	3 Rod Mason	.25	.12	.02
☐	4 Paul Weakly	.25	.12	.02
☐	5 Brian Howard	.25	.12	.02
☐	6 Pat Bolden	.25	.12	.02
☐	7 Mike Thibault	.25	.12	.02
☐	8 Tim Legler	.35	.17	.03
☐	9 Cedric Hunter	.35	.17	.03
☐	10 Mark Peterson	.25	.12	.02
☐	11 Greg Wiltjer	.25	.12	.02
☐	12 The Idelman's	.25	.12	.02
☐	13 The Silks and Rodie	.25	.12	.02
☐	14 Basketball Staff	.25	.12	.02
☐	15 Front Office Staff	.25	.12	.02
☐	16 Omaha Checklist	.35	.17	.03
☐	17 Calvin Duncan	.25	.12	.02
☐	18 Pat Durham	.35	.17	.03
☐	19 Steve Grayer	.35	.17	.03
☐	20 Roy Marble	1.00	.50	.10
☐	21 Tony Martin	.35	.17	.03
☐	22 Shawn McDaniel	.25	.12	.02
☐	23 Peter Thibeaux	.35	.17	.03
☐	24 Clarence Thompson	.25	.12	.02
☐	25 Demone Webster	.25	.12	.02
☐	26 A.J. Wynder	.25	.12	.02
☐	27 Steve Kahl	.25	.12	.02
☐	28 Steve Bontrager	.25	.12	.02
☐	29 Cedar Rapids Checklist	.35	.17	.03
☐	30 Skeeter Henry	.35	.17	.03
☐	31 Eugene McDowell	.35	.17	.03

Card	Player			
☐ 32	Bruce Wheatley	.25	.12	.02
☐ 33	Mark Wade	.35	.17	.03
☐ 34	Cheyenne Gibson	.25	.12	.02
☐ 35	Clifford Lett	.35	.17	.03
☐ 36	Larry Houzer	.25	.12	.02
☐ 37	Tony Dawson	.35	.17	.03
☐ 38	Richard Hollis	.35	.17	.03
☐ 39	Ed Leonard and Joe Corona	.25	.12	.02
☐ 40	Front Office Staff	.25	.12	.02
☐ 41	Torry the Tornado	.25	.12	.02
☐ 42	Fred Bryan	.25	.12	.02
☐ 43	Jim Goodman	.25	.12	.02
☐ 44	Pensacola Checklist	.35	.17	.03
☐ 45	Joe Fredrick	.25	.12	.02
☐ 46	Everette Stephens	.35	.17	.03
☐ 47	Mario Donaldson	.25	.12	.02
☐ 48	Dan Godfread	.25	.12	.02
☐ 49	Haakon Austefjord	.25	.12	.02
☐ 50	Gary Massey	.25	.12	.02
☐ 51	Chris Childs	.25	.12	.02
☐ 52	Gerry Wright	.25	.12	.02
☐ 53	Marty Conlon	.35	.17	.03
☐ 54	Tony Costner	.25	.12	.02
☐ 55	Steve Hayes	.35	.17	.03
☐ 56	Tom Hart	.25	.12	.02
☐ 57	Paul Kulick	.25	.12	.02
☐ 58	Rockford Team Photo	.25	.12	.02
☐ 59	Rockford Checklist	.35	.17	.03
☐ 60	Mike Williams	.25	.12	.02
☐ 61	Brian Rahilly	.25	.12	.02
☐ 62	Bill Martin	.35	.17	.03
☐ 63	Vince Hamilton	.25	.12	.02
☐ 64	Dwayne McClain	.50	.25	.05
☐ 65	Bart Kofoed	.35	.17	.03
☐ 66	Dominic Pressley	.35	.17	.03
☐ 67	Herb Dixon	.25	.12	.02
☐ 68	Todd Mitchell	.50	.25	.05
☐ 69	Ben Mitchell	.25	.12	.02
☐ 70	Flip Saunders	.35	.17	.03
☐ 71	Lacrosse Checklist	.35	.17	.03
☐ 72	Keith Smart	1.25	.60	.12
☐ 73	Stephen Thompson	1.50	.75	.15
☐ 74	Brian Rowsom	.35	.17	.03
☐ 75	Tony Martin	.25	.12	.02
☐ 76	Joe Ward	.25	.12	.02
☐ 77	Fennis Dembo	.75	.35	.07
☐ 78	Glenn Puddy	.35	.17	.03
☐ 79	Lanard Copeland	.75	.35	.07
☐ 80	Carl Brown	.25	.12	.02
☐ 81	Rapid City Checklist	.35	.17	.03
☐ 82	Dennis Nutt	.35	.17	.03
☐ 83	Leonard Harris	.25	.12	.02
☐ 84	Tharon Mayes	.35	.17	.03
☐ 85	Melvin McCants	.50	.25	.05
☐ 86	Tracy Mitchell	.50	.25	.05
☐ 87	Ken Redfield	.35	.17	.03
☐ 88	Frank Ross	.25	.12	.02
☐ 89	Michael Phelps	.35	.17	.03
☐ 90	Brian Christensen	.25	.12	.02
☐ 91	Kevin McKenna	.25	.12	.02
☐ 92	Steve Raab	.25	.12	.02
☐ 93	Clay Moser	.25	.12	.02
☐ 94	Tony Khing	.25	.12	.02
☐ 95	Little Dude	.25	.12	.02
☐ 96	Sioux Falls Checklist	.35	.17	.03
☐ 97	Perry Young	.35	.17	.03
☐ 98	Ozell Jones	.35	.17	.03
☐ 99	Willie Simmons	.25	.12	.02
☐ 100	Alvin Heggs	.25	.12	.02
☐ 101	Kelsey Weems	.35	.17	.03
☐ 102	Anthony Frederick	.35	.17	.03
☐ 103	Royce Jeffries	.25	.12	.02
☐ 104	Darryl McDonald	.25	.12	.02
☐ 105	Sgt. Slammer	.35	.17	.03
☐ 106	Charley Rosen	.25	.12	.02
☐ 107	Oklahoma City Checklist	.35	.17	.03
☐ 108	Keith Wilson	.35	.17	.03
☐ 109	James Carter	.25	.12	.02
☐ 110	Tracy Moore	.50	.25	.05
☐ 111	Mark Plansky	.35	.17	.03
☐ 112	Charles Bradley	.25	.12	.02
☐ 113	Leroy Combs	.25	.12	.02
☐ 114	Anthony Mason	1.25	.60	.12
☐ 115	Gary Voce	.25	.12	.02
☐ 116	Jim Lampley	.35	.17	.03
☐ 117	Henry Bibby CO	.50	.25	.05
☐ 118	Tulsa Checklist	.35	.17	.03
☐ 119	Texans Logo	.25	.12	.02
☐ 120	Ennis Whatley	1.25	.60	.12
☐ 121	Mike Mitchell	.35	.17	.03
☐ 122	Derrick Taylor	.35	.17	.03
☐ 123	Kenny Atkinson	.25	.12	.02
☐ 124	Jaren Jackson	.35	.17	.03
☐ 125	Cedric Ball	.25	.12	.02
☐ 126	Chris Munk	.25	.12	.02
☐ 127	Mark Becker	.25	.12	.02
☐ 128	Rodney Blake	.25	.12	.02
☐ 129	Kurt Portmann	.25	.12	.02
☐ 130	Henry James	1.00	.50	.10
☐ 131	John Treloar	.25	.12	.02
☐ 132	Dave Whitney	.35	.17	.03
☐ 133	Mike Davis	.25	.12	.02
☐ 134	Wichita Falls Checklist	.35	.17	.03
☐ 135	Milt Wagner	.50	.25	.05
☐ 136	Phil Henderson	.75	.35	.07
☐ 137	Tony Harris	.25	.12	.02
☐ 138	Steve Bardo	.50	.25	.05
☐ 139	A.J. Wynder	.25	.12	.02
☐ 140	Joel DeBortoli	.25	.12	.02
☐ 141	Tim Anderson	.25	.12	.02
☐ 142	Ron Draper	.25	.12	.02
☐ 143	Barry Sumpter	.35	.17	.03
☐ 144	Demone Webster	.25	.12	.02
☐ 145	Thunderbird Dance Team	.25	.12	.02
☐ 146	Mauro Panaggio	.35	.17	.03
☐ 147	Dan Panaggio	.25	.12	.02
☐ 148	Quad City Checklist	.35	.17	.03
☐ 149	Albert King	.50	.25	.05
☐ 150	Keith Smith	.25	.12	.02
☐ 151	Mario Elie	2.00	1.00	.20
☐ 152	Albert Springs	.25	.12	.02
☐ 153	Jeff Fryer	.35	.17	.03
☐ 154	Clinton Smith	.25	.12	.02
☐ 155	Vincent Askew	1.00	.50	.10
☐ 156	Paul Graham	1.00	.50	.10
☐ 157	Ben McDonald	.35	.17	.03
☐ 158	Willie McDuffie	.25	.12	.02
☐ 159	George Karl	.50	.25	.05
☐ 160	Terry Stotts	.35	.17	.03
☐ 161	Doc Nunnally	.25	.12	.02
☐ 162	Albany Checklist	.35	.17	.03
☐ 163	Reggie Fox	.25	.12	.02
☐ 164	Ron Draper	.25	.12	.02
☐ 165	Sedric Toney	.25	.12	.02
☐ 166	Alex Austin	.25	.12	.02
☐ 167	Robert Brickey	.50	.25	.05
☐ 168	Ricky Blanton	.50	.25	.05
☐ 169	Stan Kimbrough	.25	.12	.02
☐ 170	Ron Cavenall	.35	.17	.03
☐ 171	Grand Rapids Checklist	.35	.17	.03
☐ 172	Darren Henrie	.25	.12	.02
☐ 173	Duane Washington	.35	.17	.03
☐ 174	Barry Stevens	.25	.12	.02
☐ 175	Craig Neal	.35	.17	.03
☐ 176	Ron Spivey	.25	.12	.02
☐ 177	Kerry Hammonds	.25	.12	.02
☐ 178	Brian Martin	.25	.12	.02
☐ 179	Jerome Henderson	.25	.12	.02
☐ 180	John McIntyre	.25	.12	.02
☐ 181	Chris Childs	.25	.12	.02
☐ 182	The Jacobson's	.25	.12	.02
☐ 183	Columbus Checklist	.35	.17	.03
☐ 184	Luther Burks	.25	.12	.02
☐ 185	Lee Campbell	.25	.12	.02
☐ 186	Corey Gaines	.35	.17	.03
☐ 187	Mike Higgins	.25	.12	.02
☐ 188	Ron Kellogg	.25	.12	.02
☐ 189	Bart Kofoed	.35	.17	.03
☐ 190	Jim Rowinski	.25	.12	.02
☐ 191	Riley Smith	.25	.12	.02
☐ 192	Yakima Checklist	.35	.17	.03
☐ 193	Mike Yoest	.25	.12	.02
☐ 194	Freddie Banks	.35	.17	.03
☐ 195	Scooter Barry	.75	.35	.07
☐ 196	Richard Morton	.35	.17	.03
☐ 197	Kelby Stuckey	.25	.12	.02
☐ 198	Jervis Cole	.25	.12	.02
☐ 199	Kenny McClary	.25	.12	.02
☐ 200	Joe Wallace	.25	.12	.02
☐ 201	Mark Tillmon	.50	.25	.05
☐ 202	Greg Butler	.50	.25	.05
☐ 203	San Jose Checklist	.35	.17	.03

1991-92 ProCards CBA

The 1991-92 ProCards CBA basketball set contains 206 cards measuring the standard size (2 1/2" by 3 1/2"). The fronts

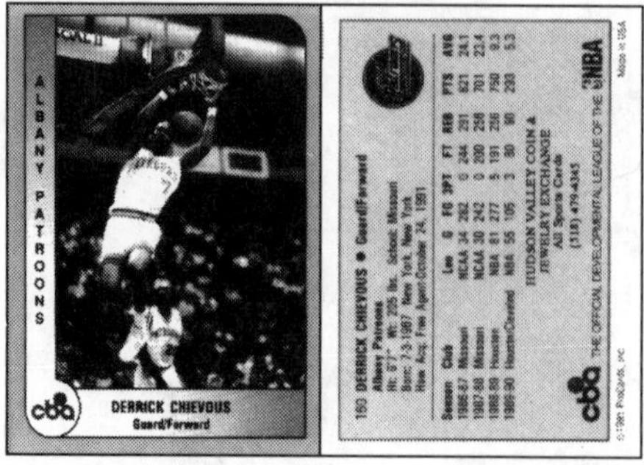

feature a mix of posed and action color player photos, bordered in silver. Two stripes that shade from pink to white accent the pictures on the left and bottom; the CBA logo appears in a circle at their intersection. On a gray background with black borders and lettering, the backs present biographical and statistical information. Seven teams found sponsors that listed their business on the card back, of which four were sports card shops. The cards are numbered on the back and checklisted below according to teams as follows: Bakersfield Jammers (1-11, 72), Wichita Texans (12-24), Rockford Lightning (25-35), Quad City Thunder (36-48), Oklahoma City Cavalry (49-60), Rapid City Thrillers (61-71), Fort Wayne Fury (73-85), Yakima Sun Kings (86-97), Grand Rapids Hoops (98-109), Sioux Falls Skyforce (110-121, 206), Tri-City Chinook (122-135), Columbus Horizon (136-147), LaCrosse Catbirds (148-159), Albany Patroons (160-171), Tulsa Zone (172-183), Omaha Racers (184-195), and Birmingham Bandits (196-205).

	MINT	EXC	G-VG
COMPLETE SET (206)	45.00	22.50	4.50
COMMON PLAYER (1-206)	.25	.12	.02
□ 1 Chris Childs	.25	.12	.02
□ 2 Mark Tillmon	.35	.17	.03
□ 3 Greg Butler	.35	.17	.03
□ 4 Keith Hill	.25	.12	.02
□ 5 Jean Derouillere	.25	.12	.02
□ 6 Levy Middlebrooks	.25	.12	.02
□ 7 Tank Collins	.25	.12	.02
□ 8 Sam Williams	.25	.12	.02
□ 9 Herman Kull CO	.25	.12	.02
□ 10 Don Ford ACO	.35	.17	.03
□ 11 Charles Charlesworth Trainer	.25	.12	.02
□ 12 Calvin Oldham	.25	.12	.02
□ 13 Larry Smith	.25	.12	.02
□ 14 Trent Jackson	.25	.12	.02
□ 15 Rob Rose	.25	.12	.02
□ 16 Walter Bond	.25	.12	.02
□ 17 Jeff Majerle	.25	.12	.02
□ 18 Brad Baldridge	.25	.12	.02
□ 19 Kurt Portman	.25	.12	.02
□ 20 Cedric Jenkins	.25	.12	.02
□ 21 John Treloar CO	.25	.12	.02
□ 22 Mike Davis ACO	.25	.12	.02
□ 23 Dave Whitney ACO	.25	.12	.02
□ 24 Wichita Falls CL	.35	.17	.03
□ 25 Tim Dillon	.25	.12	.02
□ 26 Kenny Miller	.25	.12	.02
□ 27 Stevie Wise	.25	.12	.02
□ 28 Dan Godfread	.25	.12	.02
□ 29 Mario Donaldson	.25	.12	.02
□ 30 Steve Berger	.25	.12	.02
□ 31 Corey Beasley	.25	.12	.02
□ 32 Danny Jones	.25	.12	.02
□ 33 Lanny Van Eman CO	.25	.12	.02
□ 34 Tony Morocco ACO	.25	.12	.02
□ 35 Rockford CL	.35	.17	.03
□ 36 Bobby Martin	.35	.17	.03
□ 37 Dwight Moody	.35	.17	.03
□ 38 Tim Anderson	.25	.12	.02
□ 39 A.J. Wynder	.25	.12	.02
□ 40 Keith Robinson	.35	.17	.03
□ 41 Steve Scheffler	.50	.25	.05
□ 42 Anthony Bowie	.50	.25	.05
□ 43 Tony Harris	.25	.12	.02
□ 44 Barry Mitchell	.35	.17	.03
□ 45 Tom Sheehey	.25	.12	.02
□ 46 Dan Panaggio CO	.25	.12	.02
□ 47 Mike Mashak ACO	.25	.12	.02
□ 48 Quad City CL	.25	.12	.02
□ 49 Bernard Thompson	.35	.17	.03
□ 50 Daryll Walker	.25	.12	.02
□ 51 Darryl Kennedy	.35	.17	.03
□ 52 Stevie Thompson	.75	.35	.07
□ 53 Kelsey Weems	.35	.17	.03
□ 54 Steve Burtt	.50	.25	.05
□ 55 Junie Lewis	.25	.12	.02
□ 56 Chris Harris	.25	.12	.02
□ 57 Jeff Hodge	.25	.12	.02
□ 58 Demone Webster	.25	.12	.02
□ 59 Henry Bibby CO	.35	.17	.03
□ 60 Oklahoma City CL	.25	.12	.02
□ 61 Jarvis Basnight	.35	.17	.03
□ 62 Ed Horton	.50	.25	.05
□ 63 Irving Thomas	.35	.17	.03
□ 64 Stanley Brundy	.25	.12	.02
□ 65 Nate Johnson	.25	.12	.02
□ 66 Keith Smart	1.00	.50	.10
□ 67 Larry Robinson	.35	.17	.03
□ 68 Michael Anderson	.25	.12	.02
□ 69 Eric Musselman CO	.35	.17	.03
□ 70 Duane Ticknor ACO	.25	.12	.02
□ 71 Rapid City CL	.35	.17	.03
□ 72 Bakersfield CL	.35	.17	.03
□ 73 Lyndon Jones	.50	.25	.05
□ 74 Warren Bradley	.25	.12	.02
□ 75 Anthony Corbitt	.25	.12	.02
□ 76 Tony Karasek	.25	.12	.02
□ 77 Mark Peterson	.25	.12	.02
□ 78 Dan Palombizio	.35	.17	.03
□ 79 Ricky Hall	.25	.12	.02
□ 80 John Cooper	.25	.12	.02
□ 81 Carl Thomas	.35	.17	.03
□ 82 Travis Williams	.25	.12	.02
□ 83 Gerald Oliver CO	.25	.12	.02
□ 84 Coaching Staff Kevin Kacer TR Terry Stotts ACO Dave Carrington ACO Walter Jordan ACO	.25	.12	.02
□ 85 Fort Wayne CL	.25	.12	.02
□ 86 Ronn McMahon	.25	.12	.02
□ 87 Sean Tyson	.25	.12	.02
□ 88 McKinley Singleton	.25	.12	.02
□ 89 Teo Alibegovic	.25	.12	.02
□ 90 Joey Johnson	.25	.12	.02
□ 91 Riley Smith	.25	.12	.02
□ 92 Alex Austin	.25	.12	.02
□ 93 Dennis Williams	.25	.12	.02
□ 94 Luther Banks	.25	.12	.02
□ 95 Bill Klucas CO	.25	.12	.02
□ 96 Jack Miller ACO	.25	.12	.02
□ 97 Yakima CL	.25	.12	.02
□ 98 Roy Fisher	.35	.17	.03
□ 99 Reggie Isaac	.25	.12	.02
□ 100 Reggie Jordan	.25	.12	.02
□ 101 Cedric Lewis	.25	.12	.02
□ 102 Jeff Martin	.50	.25	.05
□ 103 Dyron Nix	.50	.25	.05
□ 104 Walter Watts	.25	.12	.02
□ 105 Gary Waites	.25	.12	.02
□ 106 Gerald Paddio	.35	.17	.03
□ 107 Bruce Stewart CO	.25	.12	.02
□ 108 Jeff Burkhamer ACO	.25	.12	.02
□ 109 Grand Rapids CL	.25	.12	.02
□ 110 Petur Gundmundsson	.35	.17	.03
□ 111 Ralph Lewis	.25	.12	.02
□ 112 John Smith	.25	.12	.02
□ 113 Tony Farmer	.50	.25	.05
□ 114 Matt Roe	.35	.17	.03
□ 115 Darryl McDonald	.25	.12	.02
□ 116 Corey Gaines	.35	.17	.03
□ 117 Richard Rellford	.35	.17	.03
□ 118 Ken Redfield	.25	.12	.02
□ 119 Chuckie White	.35	.17	.03
□ 120 Kevin McKenna CO	.25	.12	.02
□ 121 Clay Moser ACO	.25	.12	.02
□ 122 Donald Royal	.50	.25	.05
□ 123 Wayne Tinkle	.25	.12	.02
□ 124 Jim Usevitch	.25	.12	.02
□ 125 Eric Dunn	.25	.12	.02
□ 126 Jeffty Connelly	.25	.12	.02
□ 127 Alan Pollard	.25	.12	.02
□ 128 Clifford Scales	.35	.17	.03
□ 129 Harold Wright	.25	.12	.02
□ 130 Willie Simms	.25	.12	.02
□ 131 Michael Holton	.50	.25	.05
□ 132 Terrill Hall	.25	.12	.02
□ 133 Calvin Duncan Guard/Assistant CO	.25	.12	.02

☐ 134 Steve Hayes CO	.35	.17	.03
☐ 135 Yakima CL	.35	.17	.03
☐ 136 Duane Washington	.25	.12	.02
☐ 137 Kermit Holmes	.25	.12	.02
☐ 138 Mike Goodson	.25	.12	.02
☐ 139 Byron Dinkins	.50	.25	.05
☐ 140 Leonard Harris	.25	.12	.02
☐ 141 Louis Banks	.25	.12	.02
☐ 142 James Bradley	.25	.12	.02
☐ 143 Jeff King	.25	.12	.02
☐ 144 Ron Spivey	.25	.12	.02
☐ 145 Orlando Graham	.25	.12	.02
☐ 146 Vincent Chickerella CO	.25	.12	.02
☐ 147 Columbus CL	.35	.17	.03
☐ 148 Daron Hoges	.25	.12	.02
☐ 149 Von McDade	.35	.17	.03
☐ 150 Byron Irvin	.75	.35	.07
☐ 151 Patrick Tompkins	.25	.12	.02
☐ 152 Brian Rahilly	.25	.12	.02
☐ 153 Kenny Battle	.50	.25	.05
☐ 154 Jaren Jackson	.35	.17	.03
☐ 155 Troy Truvillion	.25	.12	.02
☐ 156 Mark Davis	.25	.12	.02
☐ 157 Vince Hamilton	.25	.12	.02
☐ 158 Don Zierden ACO and Mike McCollow ACO	.25	.12	.02
☐ 159 LaCrosse CL	.35	.17	.03
☐ 160 Derrick Chievous	1.00	.50	.10
☐ 161 Jeff Sanders	.50	.25	.05
☐ 162 Marc Brown	.25	.12	.02
☐ 163 Johnnie Hilliad	.25	.12	.02
☐ 164 Jerry Johnson	.25	.12	.02
☐ 165 Dave Popson	.50	.25	.05
☐ 166 Derrick Rowland	.25	.12	.02
☐ 167 Jose Slaughter	.35	.17	.03
☐ 168 Steve Wright	.25	.12	.02
☐ 169 Charley Rosen CO	.25	.12	.02
☐ 170 Lowes Moore ACO	.50	.25	.05
☐ 171 Albany CL	.35	.17	.03
☐ 172 Jasper Hooks	.25	.12	.02
☐ 173 Tracy Moore	.50	.25	.05
☐ 174 Keith Wilson	.35	.17	.03
☐ 175 Shawn McDaniel	.25	.12	.02
☐ 176 Sam Johnson	.25	.12	.02
☐ 177 Jeff Fryer	.35	.17	.03
☐ 178 A.C. Carver	.25	.12	.02
☐ 179 Jawann Oldham	.50	.25	.05
☐ 180 Lefty Moore	.25	.12	.02
☐ 181 Anthony Blakley	.25	.12	.02
☐ 182 Steve Bontrager CO	.25	.12	.02
☐ 183 Tulsa CL	.25	.12	.02
☐ 184 Cedric Hunter	.35	.17	.03
☐ 185 Ronnie Grandison	.35	.17	.03
☐ 186 Ricky Jones	.25	.12	.02
☐ 187 Tim Legler	.35	.17	.03
☐ 188 Chip Engelland	.35	.17	.03
☐ 189 Brian Howard	.25	.12	.02
☐ 190 Greg Wiltjer	.25	.12	.02
☐ 191 Rod Mason	.25	.12	.02
☐ 192 Roland Gray	.25	.12	.02
☐ 193 Tat Hunter	.25	.12	.02
☐ 194 Mike Thibault CO	.25	.12	.02
☐ 195 Omaha CL	.35	.17	.03
☐ 196 Chris Collier	.25	.12	.02
☐ 197 Skeeter Henry	.35	.17	.03
☐ 198 Emmitt Smith	.25	.12	.02
☐ 199 Anthony Houston	.25	.12	.02
☐ 200 Michael Cutright	.35	.17	.03
☐ 201 Michael Ansley	.50	.25	.05
☐ 202 Eugene McDowell	.25	.12	.02
☐ 203 Eric Johnson	.25	.12	.02
☐ 204 Moe McHone CO	.25	.12	.02
☐ 205 Birmingham CL	.35	.17	.03
☐ 206 Sioux Falls CL	.35	.17	.03

1954 Quaker Sports Oddities *

This 27-card set features strange moments in sports and was issued as an insert inside Quaker Puffed Rice cereal boxes. Fronts of the cards are drawings depicting the person or the event. In a stripe at the top of the card face appear the words "Sports Oddities." Two colorful drawings fill the remaining space: the left half is a portrait, while the right half is action-oriented. A variety of sports are included. The cards measure approximately 2 1/4" by 3 1/2" and have rounded corners. The

last line on the back of each card declares, "It's Odd but True."

	NRMT	VG-E	GOOD
COMPLETE SET (27)	250.00	125.00	25.00
COMMON CARD (1-27)	3.00	1.50	.30
☐ 1 Johnny Miller (Incredible Punt)	7.50	3.75	.75
☐ 2 Fred Snite Sr. (Two Holes-In-One)	3.00	1.50	.30
☐ 3 George Quam (One Arm Handball)	3.00	1.50	.30
☐ 4 John B. Maypole (Speedboating)	3.00	1.50	.30
☐ 5 Harold(Bunny) Levitt (Free Throws)	15.00	7.50	1.50
☐ 6 Wake Forest College (Six Forward Passes)	7.50	3.75	.75
☐ 7 Amos Alonzo Stagg (Three TD's No Score)	25.00	12.50	2.50
☐ 8 Catherine Fellmuth	3.00	1.50	.30
☐ 9 Bill Wilson	3.00	1.50	.30
☐ 10 Chicago Blackhawks	9.00	4.50	.90
☐ 11 Betty Robinson	3.00	1.50	.30
☐ 12 Dartmouth College/ University of Utah (1944 NCAA Basketball)	9.00	4.50	.90
☐ 13 Ab Jenkins	3.00	1.50	.30
☐ 14 Capt.Eddie Rickenbacker	5.00	2.50	.50
☐ 15 Jackie LaVine	3.00	1.50	.30
☐ 16 Jackie Riley	3.00	1.50	.30
☐ 17 Carol Stokholm	3.00	1.50	.30
☐ 18 Jimmy Smilgoff	3.00	1.50	.30
☐ 19 George Halas	30.00	15.00	3.00
☐ 20 Joyce Rosenblom	3.00	1.50	.30
☐ 21 Squatter's Rights	3.00	1.50	.30
☐ 22 Richard Dwyer	3.00	1.50	.30
☐ 23 Harlem Globetrotters	35.00	17.50	3.50
☐ 24 Everett Dean (basketball)	18.00	9.00	1.80
☐ 25 Texas University/ Northwestern University	6.00	3.00	.60
☐ 26 Bronko Nagurski (All-American Team)	90.00	45.00	9.00
☐ 27 Yankee Stadium (No Homers Out)	9.00	4.50	.90

1968-69 Rockets Jack in the Box

This 14-card set of San Diego Rockets was sponsored by Jack-in-the-Box and available at their restaurants in the greater San Diego area. There is some question of whether or not this set was substantially reissued the following year. The cards measure approximately 2" by 3" and have the appearance of wallet-size photos. The fronts have posed color head and shoulders shots, with the player's name, team name, team logo, and sponsor's logo below the picture. The backs are blank. The cards are unnumbered and are checklisted below in alphabetical order. The two cards in the set that are more difficult to find are marked by SP in the checklist below. The set features the first professional cards of Rick Adelman, Elvin Hayes, and Pat Riley among others.

	NRMT	VG-E	GOOD
COMPLETE SET (14)	80.00	40.00	8.00
COMMON PLAYER (1-14)	2.00	1.00	.20
COMMON PLAYER SP	20.00	10.00	2.00
☐ 1 Rick Adelman	7.50	3.75	.75
☐ 2 Harry Barnes SP	20.00	10.00	2.00
☐ 3 Jim Barnett	3.00	1.50	.30
☐ 4 John Block	2.00	1.00	.20
☐ 5 Henry Finkel SP	20.00	10.00	2.00
☐ 6 Elvin Hayes	20.00	10.00	2.00
☐ 7 Toby Kimball	2.00	1.00	.20
☐ 8 Don Kojis	2.00	1.00	.20
☐ 9 Stu Lantz	2.00	1.00	.20
☐ 10 Pat Riley	15.00	7.50	1.50
☐ 11 Bobby Smith	4.00	2.00	.40
☐ 12 John Q. Trapp	2.00	1.00	.20
☐ 13 Art Williams	2.00	1.00	.20
☐ 14 Bernie Williams	3.00	1.50	.30

1978-79 Royal Crown Cola

This 40-card set was sponsored by RC Cola, and its logo appears at the top of the card face. The cards were supposedly only issued in the southern New England area. The cards were intended to be placed in six-packs of Royal Crown Cola, one per six-pack. The cards measure approximately 3 1/8" by 6". The front features a black and white head shot of the player framed by a basketball hoop net with red and blue trim. The cards are unnumbered and are checklisted below in alphabetical order. The cards were apparently only licensed by the NBA Players Association since there are no team logos or team markings anywhere on the cards. The set features an early professional card of Bernard King.

	NRMT	VG-E	GOOD
COMPLETE SET (40)	500.00	250.00	50.00
COMMON PLAYER (1-40)	7.50	3.75	.75
☐ 1 Kareem Abdul-Jabbar	60.00	30.00	6.00
☐ 2 Nate Archibald	20.00	10.00	2.00
☐ 3 Rick Barry	25.00	12.50	2.50
☐ 4 Jim Chones	7.50	3.75	.75
☐ 5 Doug Collins	10.00	5.00	1.00
☐ 6 Dave Cowens	20.00	10.00	2.00
☐ 7 Adrian Dantley	15.00	7.50	1.50
☐ 8 Walter Davis	12.50	6.25	1.25
☐ 9 John Drew	9.00	4.50	.90
☐ 10 Julius Erving	50.00	25.00	5.00
☐ 11 Walt Frazier	25.00	12.50	2.50
☐ 12 George Gervin	15.00	7.50	1.50
☐ 13 Artis Gilmore	15.00	7.50	1.50
☐ 14 Elvin Hayes	20.00	10.00	2.00
☐ 15 Dan Issel	20.00	10.00	2.00
☐ 16 Marques Johnson	9.00	4.50	.90
☐ 17 Bernard King	15.00	7.50	1.50
☐ 18 Bob Lanier	15.00	7.50	1.50
☐ 19 Maurice Lucas	9.00	4.50	.90
☐ 20 Pete Maravich	30.00	15.00	3.00
☐ 21 Bob McAdoo	9.00	4.50	.90
☐ 22 George McGinnis	9.00	4.50	.90
☐ 23 Eric Money	7.50	3.75	.75
☐ 24 Earl Monroe	15.00	7.50	1.50
☐ 25 Calvin Murphy	12.00	6.00	1.20
☐ 26 Robert Parish	25.00	12.50	2.50
☐ 27 Billy Paultz	7.50	3.75	.75
☐ 28 Jack Sikma	9.00	4.50	.90
☐ 29 Ricky Sobers	7.50	3.75	.75
☐ 30 David Thompson	10.00	5.00	1.00
☐ 31 Rudy Tomjanovich	9.00	4.50	.90
☐ 32 Wes Unseld	12.00	6.00	1.20
☐ 33 Norm Van Lier	7.50	3.75	.75
☐ 34 Bill Walton	15.00	7.50	1.50
☐ 35 Marvin Webster	7.50	3.75	.75
☐ 36 Scott Wedman	7.50	3.75	.75
☐ 37 Paul Westphal	9.00	4.50	.90
☐ 38 Jo Jo White	9.00	4.50	.90
☐ 39 John Williamson	7.50	3.75	.75
☐ 40 Brian Winters	7.50	3.75	.75

1952 Royal Desserts

The 1952 Royal Desserts Stars of Basketball set contains eight horizontally oriented cards. The cards formed the backs of Royal Desserts packages of the period; consequently many cards are found with uneven edges stemming from the method of cutting the cards off the box. Each card has its number and the statement "Royal Stars of Basketball" in a red rectangle at the top. Cards measure approximately 2 5/8" by 3 1/4". The cards fronts have a stripe at the top and are divided into halves. The left half has a light-blue tinted head shot of the player and a facsimile autograph, while the right half has career summary. The blue tinted picture contains a facsimile autograph of the player. An album was presumably available as it is advertised on the card. The catalog designation for this scarce set is F219-2.

	NRMT	VG-E	GOOD
COMPLETE SET (8)	3000.00	1500.00	350.00
COMMON PLAYER (1-8)	200.00	100.00	20.00

☐ 1 Fred Schaus	250.00	125.00	25.00
☐ 2 Dick McGuire	300.00	150.00	30.00
☐ 3 Jack Nichols	200.00	100.00	20.00
☐ 4 Frank Brian	200.00	100.00	20.00
☐ 5 Joe Fulks	400.00	200.00	40.00
☐ 6 George Mikan	1500.00	650.00	165.00
☐ 7 Jim Pollard	400.00	200.00	40.00
☐ 8 Harry E. Jeanette	200.00	100.00	20.00

1975-76 76ers McDonald's Standups

The 1975-76 McDonalds Philadelphia 76ers set contains six blank-backed cards measuring approximately 3 3/4" by 7". The cards are die cut, allowing the player pictures to be punched out and displayed. The cards are unnumbered and checklisted below in alphabetical order.

	NRMT	VG-E	GOOD
COMPLETE SET (6)	20.00	10.00	2.00
COMMON PLAYER (1-6)	2.00	1.00	.20
☐ 1 Fred Carter	2.00	1.00	.20
☐ 2 Harvey Catchings	2.00	1.00	.20
☐ 3 Doug Collins	5.00	2.50	.50
☐ 4 Billy Cunningham	7.50	3.75	.75
☐ 5 George McGinnis	5.00	2.50	.50
☐ 6 Steve Mix	2.00	1.00	.20

1989-90 76ers Kodak

This team photo album was jointly sponsored by Jack's Cameras and Kodak. The photo album consists of three sheets, each measuring approximately 8" by 11" and joined together to form one continuous sheet. The first sheet features a team photo of the Philadelphia 76ers. While the second sheet presents two rows of five cards each, the third sheet presents six additional player cards, with the remaining four slots filled in by coupons redeemable at Jack's Cameras. After perforation, the cards measure 2 3/16" by 3 3/4". The card front features a color action

player photo, with a red border on white card stock. The player's name and position are given below the picture, and the 76ers logo is sandwiched between the sponsors' logos. The backs have the Philadelphia 76ers logo in blue and red print. The cards are presented in the album in alphabetical order, with coaches at the end, and we have checklisted them below accordingly, placing the uniform number to the right of the name. The set features an early professional card of Hersey Hawkins.

	MINT	EXC	G-VG
COMPLETE SET (16)	8.00	4.00	.80
COMMON PLAYER (1-16)	.40	.20	.04
☐ 1 Ron Anderson 20	.50	.25	.05
☐ 2 Charles Barkley 34	2.50	1.25	.25
☐ 3 Scott Brooks 1	.50	.25	.05
☐ 4 Lanard Copeland 7	.40	.20	.04
☐ 5 Johnny Dawkins 12	.60	.30	.06
☐ 6 Mike Gminski 42	.50	.25	.05
☐ 7 Hersey Hawkins 33	2.00	1.00	.20
☐ 8 Rick Mahorn 44	.60	.30	.06
☐ 9 Kurt Nimphius 40	.40	.20	.04
☐ 10 Kenny Payne 21	.40	.20	.04
☐ 11 Derek Smith 18	.50	.25	.05
☐ 12 Bob Thornton 23	.40	.20	.04
☐ 13 Big Shot Team Mascot	.40	.20	.04
☐ 14 Jim Lynam CO	.40	.20	.04
☐ 15 Fred Carter CO	.40	.20	.04
☐ 16 Buzz Braman CO	.40	.20	.04

1990-91 SkyBox Prototypes

This ten-card set of prototypes was issued singly as well as in a complete sheet. The cards were mailed out to prospective dealers and members of the media to show the unique new design of the inaugural SkyBox issue. The cards are distinguishable by the presence of a red diagonal "prototype" line cutting across the upper left corner of the front. The cards are standard size, 2 1/2" by 3 1/2" and are numbered on the back.

	MINT	EXC	G-VG
COMPLETE SET (10)	225.00	110.00	22.00
COMMON PLAYER	6.00	3.00	.60

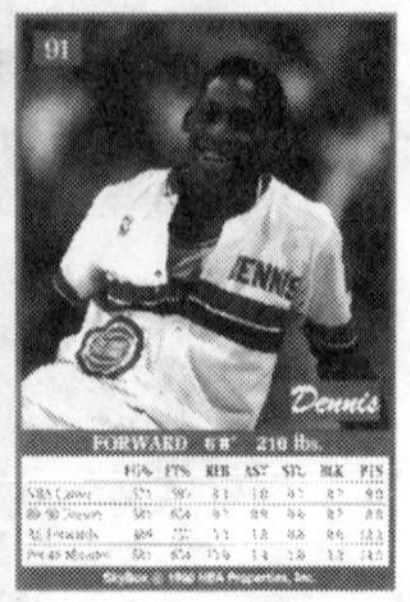

	MINT	EXC	G-VG
☐ 41 Michael Jordan	65.00	32.50	6.50
☐ 91 Dennis Rodman	7.50	3.75	.75
☐ 138 Magic Johnson	45.00	22.50	4.50
☐ 151 Rony Seikaly	10.00	5.00	1.00
☐ 162 Ricky Pierce	6.00	3.00	.60
☐ 173 Pooh Richardson	12.00	6.00	1.20
☐ 224 Kevin Johnson	15.00	7.50	1.50
☐ 233 Clyde Drexler	30.00	15.00	3.00
☐ 260 David Robinson	35.00	17.50	3.50
☐ 282 Karl Malone	20.00	10.00	2.00

1990-91 SkyBox I

The 1990-91 SkyBox set contains 300 cards featuring NBA players. The cards measure the standard size (2 1/2" by 3 1/2"). The front features an action shot of the player on a computer-generated background consisting of various color stripes and geometric shapes. The player's name appears in a black stripe below the photo, with the team logo superimposed at the left lower corner. The photo is bordered in gold. The back presents head shots of the player, with gold borders on white background. Player statistics are given in a box below the photo. The cards are numbered on the back and checklisted below alphabetically according to team names as follows: Atlanta Hawks (1-12), Boston Celtics (13-24), Charlotte Hornets (25-36), Chicago Bulls (37-47), Cleveland Cavaliers (48-58), Dallas Mavericks (59-70), Denver Nuggets (71-81), Detroit Pistons (82-93), Golden State Warriors (94-104), Houston Rockets (105-113), Indiana Pacers (114-123), Los Angeles Clippers (124-133), Los Angeles Lakers (134-143), Miami Heat (144-154), Milwaukee Bucks (155-166), Minnesota Timberwolves (167-175), New Jersey Nets (176-185), New York Knicks (186-197), Orlando Magic (198-209), Philadelphia 76ers (210-219), Phoenix Suns (220-230), Portland Trail Blazers (231-241), Sacramento Kings (242-251), San Antonio Spurs (252-262), Seattle Supersonics (263-273), Utah Jazz (274-284), and Washington Bullets (285-294). Rookie Cards included in this set are Nick Anderson, B.J. Armstrong, Vlade Divac, Sherman Douglas, Sean Elliott, Pervis Ellison, Danny Ferry, Tim Hardaway, Shawn Kemp, Sarunas Marciulionis, Drazen Petrovic, Glen Rice, Pooh Richardson, and Cliff Robinson. Cards that were deleted by SkyBox for the second series are marked in the checklist below by SP.

	MINT	EXC	G-VG
COMPLETE SET (300)	15.00	7.50	1.50
COMMON PLAYER (1-300)	.04	.02	.00
COMMON PLAYER SP	.07	.03	.01
☐ 1 John Battle Atlanta Hawks	.07	.03	.01
☐ 2 Duane Ferrell SP Atlanta Hawks	.20	.10	.02
☐ 3 Jon Koncak Atlanta Hawks	.04	.02	.00
☐ 4 Cliff Levingston SP Atlanta Hawks	.07	.03	.01
☐ 5 John Long SP Atlanta Hawks	.07	.03	.01
☐ 6 Moses Malone Atlanta Hawks	.15	.07	.01
☐ 7 Glenn Rivers Atlanta Hawks	.07	.03	.01
☐ 8 Kenny Smith SP Atlanta Hawks	.07	.03	.01
☐ 9 Alexander Volkov Atlanta Hawks	.15	.07	.01
☐ 10 Spud Webb Atlanta Hawks	.10	.05	.01
☐ 11 Dominique Wilkins Atlanta Hawks	.20	.10	.02
☐ 12 Kevin Willis Atlanta Hawks	.12	.06	.01
☐ 13 John Bagley Boston Celtics	.07	.03	.01
☐ 14 Larry Bird Boston Celtics	.50	.25	.05
☐ 15 Kevin Gamble Boston Celtics	.12	.06	.01
☐ 16 Dennis Johnson SP Boston Celtics	.12	.06	.01
☐ 17 Joe Kleine Boston Celtics	.04	.02	.00
☐ 18 Reggie Lewis Boston Celtics	.35	.17	.03
☐ 19 Kevin McHale Boston Celtics	.15	.07	.01
☐ 20 Robert Parish Boston Celtics	.15	.07	.01
☐ 21 Jim Paxson SP Boston Celtics	.07	.03	.01
☐ 22 Ed Pinckney Boston Celtics	.04	.02	.00
☐ 23 Brian Shaw Boston Celtics	.10	.05	.01
☐ 24 Michael Smith Boston Celtics	.07	.03	.01
☐ 25 Richard Anderson SP Charlotte Hornets	.07	.03	.01
☐ 26 Tyrone Bogues Charlotte Hornets	.04	.02	.00
☐ 27 Rex Chapman Charlotte Hornets	.10	.05	.01
☐ 28 Dell Curry Charlotte Hornets	.07	.03	.01
☐ 29 Armon Gilliam Charlotte Hornets	.04	.02	.00
☐ 30 Michael Holton SP Charlotte Hornets	.07	.03	.01
☐ 31 Dave Hoppen Charlotte Hornets	.04	.02	.00
☐ 32 J.R. Reid Charlotte Hornets	.20	.10	.02
☐ 33 Robert Reid SP Charlotte Hornets	.07	.03	.01
☐ 34 Brian Rowsom SP Charlotte Hornets	.20	.10	.02
☐ 35 Kelly Tripucka Charlotte Hornets	.04	.02	.00
☐ 36 Micheal Williams SP Charlotte Hornets UER (Misspelled Michael on card)	.35	.17	.03
☐ 37 B.J. Armstrong Chicago Bulls	.60	.30	.06
☐ 38 Bill Cartwright Chicago Bulls	.07	.03	.01
☐ 39 Horace Grant Chicago Bulls	.30	.15	.03
☐ 40 Craig Hodges	.04	.02	.00

Chicago Bulls

☐ 41 Michael Jordan .... 2.50 1.25 .25
Chicago Bulls

☐ 42 Stacey King .... .35 .17 .03
Chicago Bulls

☐ 43 Ed Nealy SP .... .07 .03 .01
Chicago Bulls

☐ 44 John Paxson .... .10 .05 .01
Chicago Bulls

☐ 45 Will Perdue .... .10 .05 .01
Chicago Bulls

☐ 46 Scottie Pippen .... 1.00 .50 .10
Chicago Bulls

☐ 47 Jeff Sanders SP .... .10 .05 .01
Chicago Bulls

☐ 48 Winston Bennett .... .07 .03 .01
Cleveland Cavaliers

☐ 49 Chucky Brown .... .10 .05 .01
Cleveland Cavaliers

☐ 50 Brad Daugherty .... .30 .15 .03
Cleveland Cavaliers

☐ 51 Craig Ehlo .... .12 .06 .01
Cleveland Cavaliers

☐ 52 Steve Kerr .... .04 .02 .00
Cleveland Cavaliers

☐ 53 Paul Mokeski SP .... .07 .03 .01
Cleveland Cavaliers

☐ 54 John Morton .... .07 .03 .01
Cleveland Cavaliers

☐ 55 Larry Nance .... .12 .06 .01
Cleveland Cavaliers

☐ 56 Mark Price .... .30 .15 .03
Cleveland Cavaliers

☐ 57 Tree Rollins SP .... .07 .03 .01
Cleveland Cavaliers

☐ 58 Hot Rod Williams .... .10 .05 .01
Cleveland Cavaliers

☐ 59 Steve Alford .... .07 .03 .01
Dallas Mavericks

☐ 60 Rolando Blackman .... .10 .05 .01
Dallas Mavericks

☐ 61 Adrian Dantley SP .... .12 .06 .01
Dallas Mavericks

☐ 62 Brad Davis .... .04 .02 .00
Dallas Mavericks

☐ 63 James Donaldson .... .04 .02 .00
Dallas Mavericks

☐ 64 Derek Harper .... .07 .03 .01
Dallas Mavericks

☐ 65 Anthony Jones SP .... .10 .05 .01
Dallas Mavericks

☐ 66 Sam Perkins SP .... .15 .07 .01
Dallas Mavericks

☐ 67 Roy Tarpley .... .07 .03 .01
Dallas Mavericks

☐ 68 Bill Wennington SP .... .07 .03 .01
Dallas Mavericks

☐ 69 Randy White .... .10 .05 .01
Dallas Mavericks

☐ 70 Herb Williams .... .04 .02 .00
Dallas Mavericks

☐ 71 Michael Adams .... .10 .05 .01
Denver Nuggets

☐ 72 Joe Barry Carroll SP .... .07 .03 .01
Denver Nuggets

☐ 73 Walter Davis .... .07 .03 .01
Denver Nuggets

☐ 74 Alex English SP .... .12 .06 .01
Denver Nuggets

☐ 75 Bill Hanzlik .... .04 .02 .00
Denver Nuggets

☐ 76 Tim Kempton SP .... .07 .03 .01
Denver Nuggets

☐ 77 Jerome Lane .... .04 .02 .00
Denver Nuggets

☐ 78 Lafayette Lever SP .... .10 .05 .01
Denver Nuggets

☐ 79 Todd Lichti .... .12 .06 .01
Denver Nuggets

☐ 80 Blair Rasmussen .... .04 .02 .00
Denver Nuggets

☐ 81 Dan Schayes SP .... .07 .03 .01
Denver Nuggets

☐ 82 Mark Aguirre .... .10 .05 .01
Detroit Pistons

☐ 83 William Bedford .... .07 .03 .01
Detroit Pistons

☐ 84 Joe Dumars .... .20 .10 .02
Detroit Pistons

☐ 85 James Edwards .... .04 .02 .00
Detroit Pistons

☐ 86 David Greenwood SP .... .07 .03 .01
Detroit Pistons

☐ 87 Scott Hastings .... .04 .02 .00
Detroit Pistons

☐ 88 Gerald Henderson SP .... .07 .03 .01
Detroit Pistons

☐ 89 Vinnie Johnson .... .07 .03 .01
Detroit Pistons

☐ 90 Bill Laimbeer .... .10 .05 .01
Detroit Pistons

☐ 91A Dennis Rodman .... .30 .15 .03
Detroit Pistons
(SkyBox logo in upper
right corner)

☐ 91B Dennis Rodman .... .30 .15 .03
Detroit Pistons
(SkyBox logo in upper
left corner)

☐ 92 John Salley .... .10 .05 .01
Detroit Pistons

☐ 93 Isiah Thomas .... .20 .10 .02
Detroit Pistons

☐ 94 Manute Bol SP .... .10 .05 .01
Golden State Warriors

☐ 95 Tim Hardaway .... 2.50 1.25 .25
Golden State Warriors

☐ 96 Rod Higgins .... .04 .02 .00
Golden State Warriors

☐ 97 Sarunas Marciulionis .... .60 .30 .06
Golden State Warriors

☐ 98 Chris Mullin .... .35 .17 .03
Golden State Warriors

☐ 99 Jim Petersen .... .04 .02 .00
Golden State Warriors

☐ 100 Mitch Richmond .... .20 .10 .02
Golden State Warriors

☐ 101 Mike Smrek .... .12 .06 .01
Golden State Warriors

☐ 102 Terry Teagle SP .... .07 .03 .01
Golden State Warriors

☐ 103 Tom Tolbert .... .10 .05 .01
Golden State Warriors

☐ 104 Kelvin Upshaw SP .... .10 .05 .01
Golden State Warriors

☐ 105 Anthony Bowie SP .... .25 .12 .02
Houston Rockets

☐ 106 Adrian Caldwell .... .10 .05 .01
Houston Rockets

☐ 107 Eric(Sleepy) Floyd .... .07 .03 .01
Houston Rockets

☐ 108 Buck Johnson .... .04 .02 .00
Houston Rockets

☐ 109 Vernon Maxwell .... .07 .03 .01
Houston Rockets

☐ 110 Hakeem Olajuwon .... .30 .15 .03
Houston Rockets

☐ 111 Larry Smith .... .04 .02 .00
Houston Rockets

☐ 112A Otis Thorpe ERR .... .75 .35 .07
Houston Rockets
(Front photo actually
Mitchell Wiggins)

☐ 112B Otis Thorpe COR .... .12 .06 .01
Houston Rockets

☐ 113A M. Wiggins SP ERR .... .75 .35 .07
Houston Rockets
(Front photo actually
Otis Thorpe)

☐ 113B M. Wiggins SP COR .... .10 .05 .01
Houston Rockets

☐ 114 Vern Fleming .... .04 .02 .00
Indiana Pacers

☐ 115 Rickey Green SP .... .07 .03 .01
Indiana Pacers

☐ 116 George McCloud .... .12 .06 .01
Indiana Pacers

☐ 117 Reggie Miller .... .30 .15 .03
Indiana Pacers

☐ 118A Dyron Nix SP ERR .... 2.50 1.25 .25
Indiana Pacers
(Back photo actually
Wayman Tisdale)

☐ 118B Dyron Nix SP COR .... .10 .05 .01
Indiana Pacers

☐ 119 Chuck Person .... .10 .05 .01
Indiana Pacers

☐ 120 Mike Sanders .... .07 .03 .01
Indiana Pacers

☐ 121 Detlef Schrempf .... .15 .07 .01
Indiana Pacers

☐ 122 Rik Smits .... .10 .05 .01
Indiana Pacers

☐ 123 LaSalle Thompson .... .04 .02 .00
Indiana Pacers

☐ 124 Benoit Benjamin .... .07 .03 .01
Los Angeles Clippers

☐ 125 Winston Garland .... .04 .02 .00

Los Angeles Clippers
☐ 126 Tom Garrick .07 .03 .01
Los Angeles Clippers
☐ 127 Gary Grant .04 .02 .00
Los Angeles Clippers
☐ 128 Ron Harper .10 .05 .01
Los Angeles Clippers
☐ 129 Danny Manning .25 .12 .02
Los Angeles Clippers
☐ 130 Jeff Martin .10 .05 .01
Los Angeles Clippers
☐ 131 Ken Norman .10 .05 .01
Los Angeles Clippers
☐ 132 Charles Smith .15 .07 .01
Los Angeles Clippers
☐ 133 Joe Wolf SP .07 .03 .01
Los Angeles Clippers
☐ 134 Michael Cooper SP .12 .06 .01
Los Angeles Lakers
☐ 135 Vlade Divac .40 .20 .04
Los Angeles Lakers
☐ 136 Larry Drew .04 .02 .00
Los Angeles Lakers
☐ 137 A.C. Green .07 .03 .01
Los Angeles Lakers
☐ 138 Magic Johnson 1.00 .50 .10
Los Angeles Lakers
☐ 139 Mark McNamara SP .07 .03 .01
Los Angeles Lakers
☐ 140 Byron Scott .07 .03 .01
Los Angeles Lakers
☐ 141 Mychal Thompson .04 .02 .00
Los Angeles Lakers
☐ 142 Orlando Woolridge SP .10 .05 .01
Los Angeles Lakers
☐ 143 James Worthy .20 .10 .02
Los Angeles Lakers
☐ 144 Terry Davis .20 .10 .02
Miami Heat
☐ 145 Sherman Douglas .30 .15 .03
Miami Heat
☐ 146 Kevin Edwards .07 .03 .01
Miami Heat
☐ 147 Tellis Frank SP .10 .05 .01
Miami Heat
☐ 148 Scott Haffner SP .10 .05 .01
Miami Heat
☐ 149 Grant Long .10 .05 .01
Miami Heat
☐ 150 Glen Rice 1.50 .75 .15
Miami Heat
☐ 151 Rony Seikaly .20 .10 .02
Miami Heat
☐ 152 Rory Sparrow SP .07 .03 .01
Miami Heat
☐ 153 Jon Sundvold .04 .02 .00
Miami Heat
☐ 154 Billy Thompson .04 .02 .00
Miami Heat
☐ 155 Greg Anderson .04 .02 .00
Milwaukee Bucks
☐ 156 Ben Coleman SP .10 .05 .01
Milwaukee Bucks
☐ 157 Jeff Grayer .20 .10 .02
Milwaukee Bucks
☐ 158 Jay Humphries .04 .02 .00
Milwaukee Bucks
☐ 159 Frank Kornet .07 .03 .01
Milwaukee Bucks
☐ 160 Larry Krystkowiak .04 .02 .00
Milwaukee Bucks
☐ 161 Brad Lohaus .07 .03 .01
Milwaukee Bucks
☐ 162 Ricky Pierce .07 .03 .01
Milwaukee Bucks
☐ 163 Paul Pressey SP .07 .03 .01
Milwaukee Bucks
☐ 164 Fred Roberts .07 .03 .01
Milwaukee Bucks
☐ 165 Alvin Robertson .07 .03 .01
Milwaukee Bucks
☐ 166 Jack Sikma .07 .03 .01
Milwaukee Bucks
☐ 167 Randy Breuer .04 .02 .00
Minnesota Timberwolves
☐ 168 Tony Campbell .07 .03 .01
Minnesota Timberwolves
☐ 169 Tyrone Corbin .07 .03 .01
Minnesota Timberwolves
☐ 170 Sidney Lowe SP .07 .03 .01
Minnesota Timberwolves
☐ 171 Sam Mitchell .20 .10 .02
Minnesota Timberwolves
☐ 172 Tod Murphy .07 .03 .01

Minnesota Timberwolves
☐ 173 Pooh Richardson .60 .30 .06
Minnesota Timberwolves
☐ 174 Donald Royal SP .10 .05 .01
Minnesota Timberwolves
☐ 175 Brad Sellers SP .07 .03 .01
Minnesota Timberwolves
☐ 176 Mookie Blaylock .25 .12 .02
New Jersey Nets
☐ 177 Sam Bowie .07 .03 .01
New Jersey Nets
☐ 178 Lester Conner .04 .02 .00
New Jersey Nets
☐ 179 Derrick Gervin .10 .05 .01
New Jersey Nets
☐ 180 Jack Haley .10 .05 .01
New Jersey Nets
☐ 181 Roy Hinson .04 .02 .00
New Jersey Nets
☐ 182 Dennis Hopson SP .10 .05 .01
New Jersey Nets
☐ 183 Chris Morris .07 .03 .01
New Jersey Nets
☐ 184 Pete Myers SP .10 .05 .01
New Jersey Nets
☐ 185 Purvis Short SP .07 .03 .01
New Jersey Nets
☐ 186 Maurice Cheeks .10 .05 .01
New York Knicks
☐ 187 Patrick Ewing .35 .17 .03
New York Knicks
☐ 188 Stuart Gray .04 .02 .00
New York Knicks
☐ 189 Mark Jackson .07 .03 .01
New York Knicks
☐ 190 Johnny Newman SP .10 .05 .01
New York Knicks
☐ 191 Charles Oakley .07 .03 .01
New York Knicks
☐ 192 Brian Quinnett .10 .05 .01
New York Knicks
☐ 193 Trent Tucker .04 .02 .00
New York Knicks
☐ 194 Kiki Vandeweghe .07 .03 .01
New York Knicks
☐ 195 Kenny Walker .04 .02 .00
New York Knicks
☐ 196 Eddie Lee Wilkins .04 .02 .00
New York Knicks
☐ 197 Gerald Wilkins .07 .03 .01
New York Knicks
☐ 198 Mark Acres .04 .02 .00
Orlando Magic
☐ 199 Nick Anderson .60 .30 .06
Orlando Magic
☐ 200 Michael Ansley .07 .03 .01
Orlando Magic
☐ 201 Terry Catledge .07 .03 .01
Orlando Magic
☐ 202 Dave Corzine SP .07 .03 .01
Orlando Magic
☐ 203 Sidney Green SP .07 .03 .01
Orlando Magic
☐ 204 Jerry Reynolds .07 .03 .01
Orlando Magic
☐ 205 Scott Skiles .10 .05 .01
Orlando Magic
☐ 206 Otis Smith .07 .03 .01
Orlando Magic
☐ 207 Reggie Theus SP .10 .05 .01
Orlando Magic
☐ 208 Jeff Turner .04 .02 .00
Orlando Magic
☐ 209 Sam Vincent .07 .03 .01
Orlando Magic
☐ 210 Ron Anderson .04 .02 .00
Philadelphia 76ers
☐ 211 Charles Barkley .35 .17 .03
Philadelphia 76ers
☐ 212 Scott Brooks SP .07 .03 .01
Philadelphia 76ers
☐ 213 Lanard Copeland SP .07 .03 .01
Philadelphia 76ers
☐ 214 Johnny Dawkins .04 .02 .00
Philadelphia 76ers
☐ 215 Mike Gminski .04 .02 .00
Philadelphia 76ers
☐ 216 Hersey Hawkins .20 .10 .02
Philadelphia 76ers
☐ 217 Rick Mahorn .07 .03 .01
Philadelphia 76ers
☐ 218 Derek Smith SP .07 .03 .01
Philadelphia 76ers
☐ 219 Bob Thornton .07 .03 .01

	Philadelphia 76ers			
☐ 220	Tom Chambers	.12	.06	.01
	Phoenix Suns			
☐ 221	Greg Grant SP	.12	.06	.01
	Phoenix Suns			
☐ 222	Jeff Hornacek	.20	.10	.02
	Phoenix Suns			
☐ 223	Eddie Johnson	.07	.03	.01
	Phoenix Suns			
☐ 224A	Kevin Johnson	.40	.20	.04
	Phoenix Suns			
	(SkyBox logo in lower			
	right corner)			
☐ 224B	Kevin Johnson	.40	.20	.04
	Phoenix Suns			
	(SkyBox logo in upper			
	right corner)			
☐ 225	Andrew Lang	.30	.15	.03
	Phoenix Suns			
☐ 226	Dan Majerle	.20	.10	.02
	Phoenix Suns			
☐ 227	Mike McGee SP	.07	.03	.01
	Phoenix Suns			
☐ 228	Tim Perry	.07	.03	.01
	Phoenix Suns			
☐ 229	Kurt Rambis	.07	.03	.01
	Phoenix Suns			
☐ 230	Mark West	.04	.02	.00
	Phoenix Suns			
☐ 231	Mark Bryant	.07	.03	.01
	Portland Trail Blazers			
☐ 232	Wayne Cooper	.04	.02	.00
	Portland Trail Blazers			
☐ 233	Clyde Drexler	.40	.20	.04
	Portland Trail Blazers			
☐ 234	Kevin Duckworth	.04	.02	.00
	Portland Trail Blazers			
☐ 235	Byron Irvin SP	.12	.06	.01
	Portland Trail Blazers			
☐ 236	Jerome Kersey	.15	.07	.01
	Portland Trail Blazers			
☐ 237	Drazen Petrovic	.75	.35	.07
	Portland Trail Blazers			
☐ 238	Terry Porter	.20	.10	.02
	Portland Trail Blazers			
☐ 239	Cliff Robinson	.60	.30	.06
	Portland Trail Blazers			
☐ 240	Buck Williams	.12	.06	.01
	Portland Trail Blazers			
☐ 241	Danny Young	.04	.02	.00
	Portland Trail Blazers			
☐ 242	Danny Ainge SP	.10	.05	.01
	Sacramento Kings			
☐ 243	Randy Allen SP	.10	.05	.01
	Sacramento Kings			
☐ 244A	Antoine Carr SP	.12	.06	.01
	Sacramento Kings			
	(Wearing Atlanta			
	jersey on back)			
☐ 244B	Antoine Carr	.07	.03	.01
	Sacramento Kings			
	(Wearing Sacramento			
	jersey on back)			
☐ 245	Vinny Del Negro SP	.10	.05	.01
	Sacramento Kings			
☐ 246	Pervis Ellison	1.25	.60	.12
	Sacramento Kings			
☐ 247	Greg Kite SP	.07	.03	.01
	Sacramento Kings			
☐ 248	Rodney McCray SP	.07	.03	.01
	Sacramento Kings			
☐ 249	Harold Pressley SP	.07	.03	.01
	Sacramento Kings			
☐ 250	Ralph Sampson	.07	.03	.01
	Sacramento Kings			
☐ 251	Wayman Tisdale	.10	.05	.01
	Sacramento Kings			
☐ 252	Willie Anderson	.10	.05	.01
	San Antonio Spurs			
☐ 253	Uwe Blab SP	.07	.03	.01
	San Antonio Spurs			
☐ 254	Frank Brickowski SP	.07	.03	.01
	San Antonio Spurs			
☐ 255	Terry Cummings	.10	.05	.01
	San Antonio Spurs			
☐ 256	Sean Elliott	.60	.30	.06
	San Antonio Spurs			
☐ 257	Caldwell Jones SP	.07	.03	.01
	San Antonio Spurs			
☐ 258	Johnny Moore SP	.07	.03	.01
	San Antonio Spurs			
☐ 259	Zarko Paspalj SP	.12	.06	.01
	San Antonio Spurs			
☐ 260	David Robinson	2.00	1.00	.20
	San Antonio Spurs			
☐ 261	Rod Strickland	.10	.05	.01
	San Antonio Spurs			
☐ 262	David Wingate SP	.07	.03	.01
	San Antonio Spurs			
☐ 263	Dana Barros	.30	.15	.03
	Seattle Supersonics			
☐ 264	Michael Cage	.04	.02	.00
	Seattle Supersonics			
☐ 265	Quintin Dailey	.04	.02	.00
	Seattle Supersonics			
☐ 266	Dale Ellis	.07	.03	.01
	Seattle Supersonics			
☐ 267	Steve Johnson SP	.07	.03	.01
	Seattle Supersonics			
☐ 268	Shawn Kemp	2.50	1.25	.25
	Seattle Supersonics			
☐ 269	Xavier McDaniel	.12	.06	.01
	Seattle Supersonics			
☐ 270	Derrick McKey	.07	.03	.01
	Seattle Supersonics			
☐ 271A	Nate McMillan SP ERR	.12	.06	.01
	Seattle Supersonics			
	(Back photo actually			
	Olden Polynice;			
	first series)			
☐ 271B	Nate McMillan COR	.07	.03	.01
	Seattle Supersonics			
	(second series)			
☐ 272	Olden Polynice	.07	.03	.01
	Seattle Supersonics			
☐ 273	Sedale Threatt	.07	.03	.01
	Seattle Supersonics			
☐ 274	Thurl Bailey	.07	.03	.01
	Utah Jazz			
☐ 275	Mike Brown	.07	.03	.01
	Utah Jazz			
☐ 276	Mark Eaton	.04	.02	.00
	Utah Jazz			
☐ 277	Blue Edwards	.30	.15	.03
	Utah Jazz			
☐ 278	Darrell Griffith	.07	.03	.01
	Utah Jazz			
☐ 279	Bobby Hansen SP	.07	.03	.01
	Utah Jazz			
☐ 280	Eric Johnson	.07	.03	.01
	Utah Jazz			
☐ 281	Eric Leckner SP	.07	.03	.01
	Utah Jazz			
☐ 282	Karl Malone	.30	.15	.03
	Utah Jazz			
☐ 283	Delaney Rudd	.10	.05	.01
	Utah Jazz			
☐ 284	John Stockton	.30	.15	.03
	Utah Jazz			
☐ 285	Mark Alarie	.04	.02	.00
	Washington Bullets			
☐ 286	Steve Colter SP	.07	.03	.01
	Washington Bullets			
☐ 287	Ledell Eackles SP	.10	.05	.01
	Washington Bullets			
☐ 288	Harvey Grant	.20	.10	.02
	Washington Bullets			
☐ 289	Tom Hammonds	.25	.12	.02
	Washington Bullets			
☐ 290	Charles Jones	.04	.02	.00
	Washington Bullets			
☐ 291	Bernard King	.10	.05	.01
	Washington Bullets			
☐ 292	Jeff Malone SP	.15	.07	.01
	Washington Bullets			
☐ 293	Darrell Walker	.04	.02	.00
	Washington Bullets			
☐ 294	John Williams	.04	.02	.00
	Washington Bullets			
☐ 295	Checklist 1 SP	.07	.01	.00
☐ 296	Checklist 2 SP	.07	.01	.00
☐ 297	Checklist 3 SP	.07	.01	.00
☐ 298	Checklist 4 SP	.07	.01	.00
☐ 299	Checklist 5 SP	.07	.01	.00
☐ 300	Danny Ferry SP	.30	.15	.03
	Cleveland Cavaliers			

1990-91 SkyBox II

This 123-card set measures the standard size (2 1/2" by 3 1/2") and has the same design as the regular issue 1990-91 SkyBox.

The backs of the coaches' cards each feature a quote. The cards are numbered on the back in continuation of the first series and checklisted below as follows: coaches (301-327), team checklists (328-354), lottery picks (355-365), updates (366-420), and card checklists (421-423). The key rookies in the second series are the eleven lottery picks (355-365) led by Derrick Coleman, Kendall Gill, Gary Payton, Dennis Scott, and Lionel Simmons.

	MINT	EXC	G-VG
COMPLETE SET (123)	9.00	4.50	.90
COMMON PLAYER (301-423)	.04	.02	.00
☐ 301 Bob Weiss CO Atlanta Hawks	.04	.02	.00
☐ 302 Chris Ford CO Boston Celtics	.04	.02	.00
☐ 303 Gene Littles CO Charlotte Hornets	.04	.02	.00
☐ 304 Phil Jackson CO Chicago Bulls	.07	.03	.01
☐ 305 Lenny Wilkens CO Cleveland Cavaliers	.07	.03	.01
☐ 306 Richie Adubato CO Dallas Mavericks	.04	.02	.00
☐ 307 Paul Westhead CO Denver Nuggets	.04	.02	.00
☐ 308 Chuck Daly CO Detroit Pistons	.07	.03	.01
☐ 309 Don Nelson CO Golden State Warriors	.04	.02	.00
☐ 310 Don Chaney CO Houston Rockets	.04	.02	.00
☐ 311 Dick Versace CO Indiana Pacers	.04	.02	.00
☐ 312 Mike Schuler CO Los Angeles Clippers	.04	.02	.00
☐ 313 Mike Dunleavy CO Los Angeles Lakers	.04	.02	.00
☐ 314 Ron Rothstein CO Miami Heat	.04	.02	.00
☐ 315 Del Harris CO Milwaukee Bucks	.04	.02	.00
☐ 316 Bill Musselman CO Minnesota Timberwolves	.04	.02	.00
☐ 317 Bill Fitch CO Houston Rockets	.04	.02	.00
☐ 318 Stu Jackson CO New York Knicks	.04	.02	.00
☐ 319 Matt Guokas CO Orlando Magic	.04	.02	.00
☐ 320 Jim Lynam CO Philadelphia 76ers	.04	.02	.00
☐ 321 Cotton Fitzsimmons CO Phoenix Suns	.04	.02	.00
☐ 322 Rick Adelman CO Portland Trail Blazers	.07	.03	.01
☐ 323 Dick Motta CO Sacramento Kings	.04	.02	.00
☐ 324 Larry Brown CO San Antonio Spurs	.04	.02	.00
☐ 325 K.C. Jones CO Seattle Supersonics	.04	.02	.00
☐ 326 Jerry Sloan CO Utah Jazz	.04	.02	.00
☐ 327 Wes Unseld CO Washington Bullets	.07	.03	.01
☐ 328 Atlanta Hawks TC	.04	.02	.00
☐ 329 Boston Celtics TC	.04	.02	.00
☐ 330 Charlotte Hornets TC	.04	.02	.00
☐ 331 Chicago Bulls TC	.04	.02	.00
☐ 332 Cleveland Cavaliers TC	.04	.02	.00
☐ 333 Dallas Mavericks TC	.04	.02	.00
☐ 334 Denver Nuggets TC	.04	.02	.00
☐ 335 Detroit Pistons TC	.04	.02	.00
☐ 336 Golden State Warriors TC	.04	.02	.00
☐ 337 Houston Rockets TC	.04	.02	.00
☐ 338 Indiana Pacers TC	.04	.02	.00
☐ 339 Los Angeles Clippers TC	.04	.02	.00
☐ 340 Los Angeles Lakers TC	.04	.02	.00
☐ 341 Miami Heat TC	.04	.02	.00
☐ 342 Milwaukee Bucks TC	.04	.02	.00
☐ 343 Minnesota Timberwolves TC	.04	.02	.00
☐ 344 New Jersey Nets TC	.04	.02	.00
☐ 345 New York Knicks TC	.04	.02	.00
☐ 346 Orlando Magic TC	.04	.02	.00
☐ 347 Philadelphia 76ers TC	.04	.02	.00
☐ 348 Phoenix Suns TC	.04	.02	.00
☐ 349 Portland Trail BlazersTC	.04	.02	.00
☐ 350 Sacramento Kings TC	.04	.02	.00
☐ 351 San Antonio Spurs TC	.04	.02	.00
☐ 352 Seattle SuperSonics TC	.04	.02	.00
☐ 353 Utah Jazz TC	.04	.02	.00
☐ 354 Washington Bullets TC	.04	.02	.00
☐ 355 Rumeal Robinson LP Atlanta Hawks	.30	.15	.03
☐ 356 Kendall Gill LP Charlotte Hornets	3.00	1.50	.30
☐ 357 Chris Jackson LP Denver Nuggets	.35	.17	.03
☐ 358 Tyrone Hill LP Golden State Warriors	.30	.15	.03
☐ 359 Bo Kimble LP Los Angeles Clippers	.10	.05	.01
☐ 360 Willie Burton LP Miami Heat	.30	.15	.03
☐ 361 Felton Spencer LP Minnesota Timberwolves	.20	.10	.02
☐ 362 Derrick Coleman LP New Jersey Nets	2.00	1.00	.20
☐ 363 Dennis Scott LP Orlando Magic	.75	.35	.07
☐ 364 Lionel Simmons LP Sacramento Kings	1.00	.50	.10
☐ 365 Gary Payton LP Seattle Supersonics	.75	.35	.07
☐ 366 Tim McCormick Atlanta Hawks	.04	.02	.00
☐ 367 Sidney Moncrief Atlanta Hawks	.07	.03	.01
☐ 368 Kenny Gattison Charlotte Hornets	.20	.10	.02
☐ 369 Randolph Keys Charlotte Hornets	.04	.02	.00
☐ 370 Johnny Newman Charlotte Hornets	.07	.03	.01
☐ 371 Dennis Hopson Chicago Bulls	.07	.03	.01
☐ 372 Cliff Levingston Chicago Bulls	.04	.02	.00
☐ 373 Derrick Chievous Cleveland Cavaliers	.04	.02	.00
☐ 374 Danny Ferry Cleveland Cavaliers	.10	.05	.01
☐ 375 Alex English Dallas Mavericks	.07	.03	.01
☐ 376 Lafayette Lever Dallas Mavericks	.07	.03	.01
☐ 377 Rodney McCray Dallas Mavericks	.04	.02	.00
☐ 378 T.R. Dunn Denver Nuggets	.04	.02	.00
☐ 379 Corey Gaines Denver Nuggets	.07	.03	.01
☐ 380 Avery Johnson San Antonio Spurs	.10	.05	.01
☐ 381 Joe Wolf Denver Nuggets	.04	.02	.00
☐ 382 Orlando Woolridge Denver Nuggets	.07	.03	.01
☐ 383 Wayne Rollins Detroit Pistons	.04	.02	.00
☐ 384 Steve Johnson Seattle Supersonics	.04	.02	.00
☐ 385 Kenny Smith Houston Rockets	.07	.03	.01
☐ 386 Mike Woodson Cleveland Cavaliers	.04	.02	.00
☐ 387 Greg Dreiling Indiana Pacers	.07	.03	.01
☐ 388 Micheal Williams Indiana Pacers	.20	.10	.02
☐ 389 Randy Wittman	.04	.02	.00

	Indiana Pacers			
☐ 390	Ken Bannister Los Angeles Clippers	.04	.02	.00
☐ 391	Sam Perkins Los Angeles Lakers	.10	.05	.01
☐ 392	Terry Teagle Los Angeles Lakers	.04	.02	.00
☐ 393	Milt Wagner Miami Heat	.07	.03	.01
☐ 394	Frank Brickowski Milwaukee Bucks	.04	.02	.00
☐ 395	Dan Schayes Milwaukee Bucks	.04	.02	.00
☐ 396	Scott Brooks Minnesota Timberwolves	.04	.02	.00
☐ 397	Doug West Minnesota Timberwolves	.30	.15	.03
☐ 398	Chris Dudley New Jersey Nets	.12	.06	.01
☐ 399	Reggie Theus New Jersey Nets	.07	.03	.01
☐ 400	Greg Grant New York Knicks	.04	.02	.00
☐ 401	Greg Kite Orlando Magic	.04	.02	.00
☐ 402	Mark McNamara Orlando Magic	.04	.02	.00
☐ 403	Manute Bol Philadelphia 76ers	.04	.02	.00
☐ 404	Rickey Green Philadelphia 76ers	.04	.02	.00
☐ 405	Kenny Battle Denver Nuggets	.12	.06	.01
☐ 406	Ed Nealy Phoenix Suns	.04	.02	.00
☐ 407	Danny Ainge Portland Trail Blazers	.10	.05	.01
☐ 408	Steve Colter Sacramento Kings	.04	.02	.00
☐ 409	Bobby Hansen Sacramento Kings	.04	.02	.00
☐ 410	Eric Leckner Charlotte Hornets	.07	.03	.01
☐ 411	Rory Sparrow Sacramento Kings	.04	.02	.00
☐ 412	Bill Wennington Sacramento Kings	.04	.02	.00
☐ 413	Sidney Green San Antonio Spurs	.04	.02	.00
☐ 414	David Greenwood San Antonio Spurs	.04	.02	.00
☐ 415	Paul Pressey San Antonio Spurs	.04	.02	.00
☐ 416	Reggie Williams San Antonio Spurs	.07	.03	.01
☐ 417	Dave Corzine Orlando Magic	.04	.02	.00
☐ 418	Jeff Malone Utah Jazz	.12	.06	.01
☐ 419	Pervis Ellison Washington Bullets	.40	.20	.04
☐ 420	Byron Irvin Washington Bullets	.10	.05	.01
☐ 421	Checklist 1	.07	.01	.00
☐ 422	Checklist 2	.07	.01	.00
☐ 423	Checklist 3	.07	.01	.00
☐ NNO	SkyBox Salutes the NBA SP	4.50	2.00	.40

1991 SkyBox Magic Johnson Video

This standard-size (2 1/2" by 3 1/2") card was enclosed in cellophane and included as an insert with the "Magic Johnson - Always Showtime" VHS video tape. The front features a cut-out action shot of Johnson superimposed on the familiar SkyBox bright colored computer-generated geometric background. In a horizontal format, the backs carry a close-up photo and career highlights. The SkyBox logo and copyright appear on the back only. The card is unnumbered.

	MINT	EXC	G-VG
☐ NNO Magic Johnson	20.00	10.00	2.00

1991-92 SkyBox Prototypes

Cards from this 20-card set of prototypes were mailed out to prospective dealers and members of the media to show the new design of the 1991-92 SkyBox issue. The cards are distinguishable by the presence of a black diagonal "prototype" line cutting across the upper left corner of the back. The cards are standard size, 2 1/2" by 3 1/2". Dennis Rodman and Chris Mullin are supposed to be the two toughest as they were withdrawn early.

	MINT	EXC	G-VG
COMPLETE SET (20)	150.00	75.00	15.00
COMMON PLAYER	6.00	3.00	.60
☐ 24 Rex Chapman	6.00	3.00	.60
☐ 86 Dennis Rodman SP	40.00	20.00	4.00
☐ 95 Chris Mullin SP	30.00	15.00	3.00
☐ 97 Mitch Richmond	7.50	3.75	.75
☐ 114 Reggie Miller	6.00	3.00	.60
☐ 130 Charles Smith	6.00	3.00	.60
☐ 137 Magic Johnson	25.00	12.50	2.50
☐ 143 James Worthy	7.50	3.75	.75
☐ 173 Pooh Richardson	7.50	3.75	.75
☐ 205 Dennis Scott	6.00	3.00	.60

☐ 216 Hersey Hawkins	6.00	3.00	.60
☐ 223 Tom Chambers	6.00	3.00	.60
☐ 237 Clyde Drexler	15.00	7.50	1.50
☐ 240 Terry Porter	7.50	3.75	.75
☐ 242 Buck Williams	6.00	3.00	.60
☐ 269 Ricky Pierce	6.00	3.00	.60
☐ 294 Bernard King	6.00	3.00	.60

1991-92 SkyBox I

The 1991-92 SkyBox Series I basketball set contains 350 cards measuring the standard size (2 1/2" by 3 1/2"). The fronts feature color action player photos overlaying multi-colored computer-generated geometric shapes and stripes. The pictures are borderless and the card face is white. The player's name appears in different color lettering at the bottom of each card, with the team logo in the lower right corner. In a trapezoid shape, the backs have non-action color player photos. At the bottom biographical and statistical information appear inside a color-striped diagonal. The cards are numbered and checklisted below alphabetically within and according to teams as follows: Atlanta Hawks (1-11), Boston Celtics (12-22), Charlotte Hornets (23-33), Chicago Bulls (34-44), Cleveland Cavaliers (45-55), Dallas Mavericks (56-66), Denver Nuggets (67-77), Detroit Pistons (78-88), Golden State Warriors (89-99), Houston Rockets (100-110), Indiana Pacers (111-121), Los Angeles Clippers (122-132), Los Angeles Lakers (133-143), Miami Heat (144-154), Milwaukee Bucks (155-165), Minnesota Timberwolves (166-176), New Jersey Nets (177-187), New York Knicks (188-198), Orlando Magic (199-209), Philadelphia 76ers (210-220), Phoenix Suns (221-231), Portland Trail Blazers (232-242), Sacramento Kings (243-253), San Antonio Spurs (254-264), Seattle Supersonics (265-275), Utah Jazz (276-286), and Washington Bullets (287-297). Other subsets included in this set are Stats (298-307), Best Single Game Performance (308-312), NBA All-Star Weekend Highlights (313-317), NBA All-Rookie Team (318-322), GQ's "NBA All-Star Style Team" (323-327), Centennial Highlights (328-332), Great Moments from the NBA Finals (333-337), Stay in School (338-344), and Checklists (345-350). The key rookie card in the first series is John Starks. The cards were available in 15-card fin-sealed foil packs that feature four different mail-in offers on the back, or 62-card blister packs that contain two (of four) SkyBox logo cards not available in the 15-card foil packs. As part of a promotion with Cheerios, four SkyBox cards were inserted into specially marked 10-ounce and 15-ounce cereal boxes. These cereal boxes appeared on store shelves in December 1991 and January 1992, and they depicted images of SkyBox cards on the front, back, and side panels.

	MINT	EXC	G-VG
COMPLETE SET (350)	13.00	6.50	1.30
COMMON PLAYER (1-350)	.03	.01	.00

☐ 1 John Battle	.06	.03	.00
☐ 2 Duane Ferrell	.03	.01	.00
☐ 3 Jon Koncak	.03	.01	.00
☐ 4 Moses Malone	.12	.06	.01
☐ 5 Tim McCormick	.03	.01	.00
☐ 6 Sidney Moncrief	.06	.03	.00
☐ 7 Doc Rivers	.06	.03	.00
☐ 8 Rumeal Robinson UER (Drafted 11th, should say 10th)	.06	.03	.00
☐ 9 Spud Webb	.06	.03	.00
☐ 10 Dominique Wilkins	.15	.07	.01
☐ 11 Kevin Willis	.08	.04	.01
☐ 12 Larry Bird	.35	.17	.03
☐ 13 Dee Brown	.35	.17	.03
☐ 14 Kevin Gamble	.06	.03	.00
☐ 15 Joe Kleine	.03	.01	.00
☐ 16 Reggie Lewis	.15	.07	.01
☐ 17 Kevin McHale	.10	.05	.01
☐ 18 Robert Parish	.12	.06	.01
☐ 19 Ed Pinckney	.03	.01	.00
☐ 20 Brian Shaw	.06	.03	.00
☐ 21 Michael Smith	.03	.01	.00
☐ 22 Stojko Vrankovic	.12	.06	.01
☐ 23 Muggsy Bogues	.03	.01	.00
☐ 24 Rex Chapman	.06	.03	.00
☐ 25 Dell Curry	.03	.01	.00
☐ 26 Kenny Gattison	.06	.03	.00
☐ 27 Kendall Gill	.90	.45	.09
☐ 28 Mike Gminski	.03	.01	.00
☐ 29 Randolph Keys	.03	.01	.00
☐ 30 Eric Leckner	.03	.01	.00
☐ 31 Johnny Newman	.03	.01	.00
☐ 32 J.R. Reid	.06	.03	.00
☐ 33 Kelly Tripucka	.03	.01	.00
☐ 34 B.J. Armstrong	.15	.07	.01
☐ 35 Bill Cartwright	.06	.03	.00
☐ 36 Horace Grant	.12	.06	.01
☐ 37 Craig Hodges	.03	.01	.00
☐ 38 Dennis Hopson	.06	.03	.00
☐ 39 Michael Jordan	1.25	.60	.12
☐ 40 Stacey King	.06	.03	.00
☐ 41 Cliff Levingston	.03	.01	.00
☐ 42 John Paxson	.08	.04	.01
☐ 43 Will Perdue	.03	.01	.00
☐ 44 Scottie Pippen	.40	.20	.04
☐ 45 Winston Bennett	.03	.01	.00
☐ 46 Chucky Brown	.03	.01	.00
☐ 47 Brad Daugherty	.15	.07	.01
☐ 48 Craig Ehlo	.06	.03	.00
☐ 49 Danny Ferry	.06	.03	.00
☐ 50 Steve Kerr	.03	.01	.00
☐ 51 John Morton	.03	.01	.00
☐ 52 Larry Nance	.08	.04	.01
☐ 53 Mark Price	.15	.07	.01
☐ 54 Darnell Valentine	.03	.01	.00
☐ 55 John Williams	.06	.03	.00
☐ 56 Steve Alford	.06	.03	.00
☐ 57 Rolando Blackman	.06	.03	.00
☐ 58 Brad Davis	.03	.01	.00
☐ 59 James Donaldson	.03	.01	.00
☐ 60 Derek Harper	.06	.03	.00
☐ 61 Fat Lever	.06	.03	.00
☐ 62 Rodney McCray	.03	.01	.00
☐ 63 Roy Tarpley	.06	.03	.00
☐ 64 Kelvin Upshaw	.03	.01	.00
☐ 65 Randy White	.03	.01	.00
☐ 66 Herb Williams	.03	.01	.00
☐ 67 Michael Adams	.08	.04	.01
☐ 68 Greg Anderson	.03	.01	.00
☐ 69 Anthony Cook	.03	.01	.00
☐ 70 Chris Jackson	.08	.04	.01
☐ 71 Jerome Lane	.03	.01	.00
☐ 72 Marcus Liberty	.25	.12	.02
☐ 73 Todd Lichti	.03	.01	.00
☐ 74 Blair Rasmussen	.03	.01	.00
☐ 75 Reggie Williams	.06	.03	.00
☐ 76 Joe Wolf	.03	.01	.00
☐ 77 Orlando Woolridge	.06	.03	.00
☐ 78 Mark Aguirre	.06	.03	.00
☐ 79 William Bedford	.03	.01	.00
☐ 80 Lance Blanks	.06	.03	.00
☐ 81 Joe Dumars	.12	.06	.01
☐ 82 James Edwards	.03	.01	.00
☐ 83 Scott Hastings	.03	.01	.00
☐ 84 Vinnie Johnson	.03	.01	.00
☐ 85 Bill Laimbeer	.06	.03	.00
☐ 86 Dennis Rodman	.12	.06	.01
☐ 87 John Salley	.06	.03	.00
☐ 88 Isiah Thomas	.15	.07	.01
☐ 89 Mario Elie	.20	.10	.02
☐ 90 Tim Hardaway	.75	.35	.07
☐ 91 Rod Higgins	.03	.01	.00
☐ 92 Tyrone Hill	.10	.05	.01

☐ 93	Les Jepsen	.03	.01	.00
☐ 94	Alton Lister	.03	.01	.00
☐ 95	Sarunas Marciulionis	.20	.10	.02
☐ 96	Chris Mullin	.20	.10	.02
☐ 97	Jim Petersen	.03	.01	.00
☐ 98	Mitch Richmond	.12	.06	.01
☐ 99	Tom Tolbert	.03	.01	.00
☐ 100	Adrian Caldwell	.03	.01	.00
☐ 101	Eric(Sleepy) Floyd	.03	.01	.00
☐ 102	Dave Jamerson	.06	.03	.00
☐ 103	Buck Johnson	.03	.01	.00
☐ 104	Vernon Maxwell	.06	.03	.00
☐ 105	Hakeem Olajuwon	.20	.10	.02
☐ 106	Kenny Smith	.03	.01	.00
☐ 107	Larry Smith	.03	.01	.00
☐ 108	Otis Thorpe	.06	.03	.00
☐ 109	Kennard Winchester	.10	.05	.01
☐ 110	David Wood	.08	.04	.01
☐ 111	Greg Dreiling	.03	.01	.00
☐ 112	Vern Fleming	.03	.01	.00
☐ 113	George McCloud	.06	.03	.00
☐ 114	Reggie Miller	.12	.06	.01
☐ 115	Chuck Person	.06	.03	.00
☐ 116	Mike Sanders	.06	.03	.00
☐ 117	Detlef Schrempf	.06	.03	.00
☐ 118	Rik Smits	.06	.03	.00
☐ 119	LaSalle Thompson	.03	.01	.00
☐ 120	Kenny Williams	.03	.01	.00
☐ 121	Micheal Williams	.06	.03	.00
☐ 122	Ken Bannister	.03	.01	.00
☐ 123	Winston Garland	.03	.01	.00
☐ 124	Gary Grant	.03	.01	.00
☐ 125	Ron Harper	.06	.03	.00
☐ 126	Bo Kimble	.06	.03	.00
☐ 127	Danny Manning	.12	.06	.01
☐ 128	Jeff Martin	.03	.01	.00
☐ 129	Ken Norman	.08	.04	.01
☐ 130	Olden Polynice	.03	.01	.00
☐ 131	Charles Smith	.10	.05	.01
☐ 132	Loy Vaught	.12	.06	.01
☐ 133	Elden Campbell	.15	.07	.01
☐ 134	Vlade Divac	.12	.06	.01
☐ 135	Larry Drew	.03	.01	.00
☐ 136	A.C. Green	.06	.03	.00
☐ 137	Magic Johnson	.90	.45	.09
☐ 138	Sam Perkins	.08	.04	.01
☐ 139	Byron Scott	.06	.03	.00
☐ 140	Tony Smith	.06	.03	.00
☐ 141	Terry Teagle	.03	.01	.00
☐ 142	Mychal Thompson	.03	.01	.00
☐ 143	James Worthy	.12	.06	.01
☐ 144	Willie Burton	.06	.03	.00
☐ 145	Bimbo Coles	.12	.06	.01
☐ 146	Terry Davis	.06	.03	.00
☐ 147	Sherman Douglas	.06	.03	.00
☐ 148	Kevin Edwards	.03	.01	.00
☐ 149	Alec Kessler	.06	.03	.00
☐ 150	Grant Long	.03	.01	.00
☐ 151	Glen Rice	.40	.20	.04
☐ 152	Rony Seikaly	.12	.06	.01
☐ 153	Jon Sundvold	.03	.01	.00
☐ 154	Billy Thompson	.03	.01	.00
☐ 155	Frank Brickowski	.03	.01	.00
☐ 156	Lester Conner	.03	.01	.00
☐ 157	Jeff Grayer	.03	.01	.00
☐ 158	Jay Humphries	.03	.01	.00
☐ 159	Larry Krystkowiak	.03	.01	.00
☐ 160	Brad Lohaus	.03	.01	.00
☐ 161	Dale Ellis	.06	.03	.00
☐ 162	Fred Roberts	.03	.01	.00
☐ 163	Alvin Robertson	.06	.03	.00
☐ 164	Danny Schayes	.03	.01	.00
☐ 165	Jack Sikma	.06	.03	.00
☐ 166	Randy Breuer	.03	.01	.00
☐ 167	Scott Brooks	.03	.01	.00
☐ 168	Tony Campbell	.03	.01	.00
☐ 169	Tyrone Corbin	.03	.01	.00
☐ 170	Gerald Glass	.15	.07	.01
☐ 171	Sam Mitchell	.03	.01	.00
☐ 172	Tod Murphy	.03	.01	.00
☐ 173	Pooh Richardson	.15	.07	.01
☐ 174	Felton Spencer	.06	.03	.00
☐ 175	Bob Thornton	.06	.03	.00
☐ 176	Doug West	.10	.05	.01
☐ 177	Mookie Blaylock	.06	.03	.00
☐ 178	Sam Bowie	.06	.03	.00
☐ 179	Jud Buechler	.06	.03	.00
☐ 180	Derrick Coleman	.50	.25	.05
☐ 181	Chris Dudley	.03	.01	.00
☐ 182	Tate George	.06	.03	.00
☐ 183	Jack Haley	.03	.01	.00
☐ 184	Terry Mills	.20	.10	.02
☐ 185	Chris Morris	.06	.03	.00
☐ 186	Drazen Petrovic	.25	.12	.02
☐ 187	Reggie Theus	.06	.03	.00
☐ 188	Maurice Cheeks	.06	.03	.00
☐ 189	Patrick Ewing	.25	.12	.02
☐ 190	Mark Jackson	.06	.03	.00
☐ 191	Jerrod Mustaf	.10	.05	.01
☐ 192	Charles Oakley	.06	.03	.00
☐ 193	Brian Quinnett	.03	.01	.00
☐ 194	John Starks	.75	.35	.07
☐ 195	Trent Tucker	.03	.01	.00
☐ 196	Kiki Vandeweghe	.06	.03	.00
☐ 197	Kenny Walker	.03	.01	.00
☐ 198	Gerald Wilkins	.06	.03	.00
☐ 199	Mark Acres	.03	.01	.00
☐ 200	Nick Anderson	.15	.07	.01
☐ 201	Michael Ansley	.06	.03	.00
☐ 202	Terry Catledge	.03	.01	.00
☐ 203	Greg Kite	.03	.01	.00
☐ 204	Jerry Reynolds	.03	.01	.00
☐ 205	Dennis Scott	.15	.07	.01
☐ 206	Scott Skiles	.06	.03	.00
☐ 207	Otis Smith	.03	.01	.00
☐ 208	Jeff Turner	.03	.01	.00
☐ 209	Sam Vincent	.03	.01	.00
☐ 210	Ron Anderson	.03	.01	.00
☐ 211	Charles Barkley	.20	.10	.02
☐ 212	Manute Bol	.03	.01	.00
☐ 213	Johnny Dawkins	.03	.01	.00
☐ 214	Armon Gilliam	.03	.01	.00
☐ 215	Rickey Green	.03	.01	.00
☐ 216	Hersey Hawkins	.10	.05	.01
☐ 217	Rick Mahorn	.06	.03	.00
☐ 218	Brian Oliver	.06	.03	.00
☐ 219	Andre Turner	.08	.04	.01
☐ 220	Jayson Williams	.06	.03	.00
☐ 221	Joe Barry Carroll	.03	.01	.00
☐ 222	Cedric Ceballos	.20	.10	.02
☐ 223	Tom Chambers	.08	.04	.01
☐ 224	Jeff Hornacek	.12	.06	.01
☐ 225	Kevin Johnson	.20	.10	.02
☐ 226	Negele Knight	.10	.05	.01
☐ 227	Andrew Lang	.06	.03	.00
☐ 228	Dan Majerle	.12	.06	.01
☐ 229	Xavier McDaniel	.08	.04	.01
☐ 230	Kurt Rambis	.06	.03	.00
☐ 231	Mark West	.03	.01	.00
☐ 232	Alaa Abdelnaby	.10	.05	.01
☐ 233	Danny Ainge	.08	.04	.01
☐ 234	Mark Bryant	.03	.01	.00
☐ 235	Wayne Cooper	.03	.01	.00
☐ 236	Walter Davis	.06	.03	.00
☐ 237	Clyde Drexler	.30	.15	.03
☐ 238	Kevin Duckworth	.03	.01	.00
☐ 239	Jerome Kersey	.08	.04	.01
☐ 240	Terry Porter	.12	.06	.01
☐ 241	Cliff Robinson	.20	.10	.02
☐ 242	Buck Williams	.10	.05	.01
☐ 243	Anthony Bonner	.10	.05	.01
☐ 244	Antoine Carr	.03	.01	.00
☐ 245	Duane Causwell	.06	.03	.00
☐ 246	Bobby Hansen	.03	.01	.00
☐ 247	Jim Les	.10	.05	.01
☐ 248	Travis Mays	.06	.03	.00
☐ 249	Ralph Sampson	.06	.03	.00
☐ 250	Lionel Simmons	.20	.10	.02
☐ 251	Rory Sparrow	.03	.01	.00
☐ 252	Wayman Tisdale	.06	.03	.00
☐ 253	Bill Wennington	.03	.01	.00
☐ 254	Willie Anderson	.06	.03	.00
☐ 255	Terry Cummings	.08	.04	.01
☐ 256	Sean Elliott	.15	.07	.01
☐ 257	Sidney Green	.03	.01	.00
☐ 258	David Greenwood	.03	.01	.00
☐ 259	Avery Johnson	.03	.01	.00
☐ 260	Paul Pressey	.03	.01	.00
☐ 261	David Robinson	.90	.45	.09
☐ 262	Dwayne Schintzius	.06	.03	.00
☐ 263	Rod Strickland	.06	.03	.00
☐ 264	David Wingate	.03	.01	.00
☐ 265	Dana Barros	.03	.01	.00
☐ 266	Benoit Benjamin	.03	.01	.00
☐ 267	Michael Cage	.03	.01	.00
☐ 268	Quintin Dailey	.03	.01	.00
☐ 269	Ricky Pierce	.06	.03	.00
☐ 270	Eddie Johnson	.06	.03	.00
☐ 271	Shawn Kemp	.75	.35	.07
☐ 272	Derrick McKey	.06	.03	.00
☐ 273	Nate McMillan	.03	.01	.00
☐ 274	Gary Payton	.15	.07	.01
☐ 275	Sedale Threatt	.06	.03	.00
☐ 276	Thurl Bailey	.03	.01	.00
☐ 277	Mike Brown	.03	.01	.00
☐ 278	Tony Brown	.03	.01	.00
☐ 279	Mark Eaton	.03	.01	.00
☐ 280	Blue Edwards	.03	.01	.00

☐ 281 Darrell Griffith	.03	.01	.00
☐ 282 Jeff Malone	.08	.04	.01
☐ 283 Karl Malone	.20	.10	.02
☐ 284 Delaney Rudd	.03	.01	.00
☐ 285 John Stockton	.20	.10	.02
☐ 286 Andy Toolson	.08	.04	.01
☐ 287 Mark Alarie	.03	.01	.00
☐ 288 Ledell Eackles	.06	.03	.00
☐ 289 Pervis Ellison	.25	.12	.02
☐ 290 A.J. English	.12	.06	.01
☐ 291 Harvey Grant	.06	.03	.00
☐ 292 Tom Hammonds	.06	.03	.00
☐ 293 Charles Jones	.03	.01	.00
☐ 294 Bernard King	.08	.04	.01
☐ 295 Darrell Walker	.03	.01	.00
☐ 296 John Williams	.03	.01	.00
☐ 297 Haywoode Workman	.10	.05	.01
☐ 298 Muggsy Bogues Charlotte Hornets Assist-to-Turnover Ratio Leader	.03	.01	.00
☐ 299 Lester Conner Milwaukee Bucks Steal-to Turnover Ratio Leader	.03	.01	.00
☐ 300 Michael Adams Denver Nuggets Largest One-Year Scoring Improvement	.06	.03	.00
☐ 301 Chris Mullin Golden State Warriors Most Minutes Per Game	.10	.05	.01
☐ 302 Otis Thorpe Houston Rockets Most Consecutive Games Played	.06	.03	.00
☐ 303 Mitch Richmond Chris Mullin Tim Hardaway Highest Scoring Trio	.12	.06	.01
☐ 304 Darrell Walker Washington Bullets Top Rebounding Guard	.03	.01	.00
☐ 305 Jerome Lane Denver Nuggets Rebounds Per 48 Minutes	.03	.01	.00
☐ 306 John Stockton Utah Jazz Assists Per 48 Minutes	.10	.05	.01
☐ 307 Michael Jordan Chicago Bulls Points Per 48 Minutes	.60	.30	.06
☐ 308 Michael Adams Denver Nuggets Best Single Game Performance: Points	.06	.03	.00
☐ 309 Larry Smith Houston Rockets Jerome Lane Denver Nuggets Best Single Game Performance: Rebounds	.03	.01	.00
☐ 310 Scott Skiles Orlando Magic Best Single Game Performance: Assists	.03	.01	.00
☐ 311 Hakeem Olajuwon David Robinson Best Single Game Performance: Blocks	.20	.10	.02
☐ 312 Alvin Robertson Milwaukee Bucks Best Single Game Performance: Steals	.03	.01	.00
☐ 313 Stay In School Jam	.03	.01	.00
☐ 314 Craig Hodges Chicago Bulls Three-Point Shootout	.03	.01	.00
☐ 315 Dee Brown Boston Celtics Slam-Dunk Championship	.20	.10	.02
☐ 316 Charles Barkley Philadelphia 76ers All-Star Game MVP	.10	.05	.01
☐ 317 Behind the Scenes Charles Barkley Joe Dumars Kevin McHale	.06	.03	.00
☐ 318 Derrick Coleman ART New Jersey Nets	.25	.12	.02
☐ 319 Lionel Simmons ART Sacramento Kings	.12	.06	.01
☐ 320 Dennis Scott ART Orlando Magic	.10	.05	.01
☐ 321 Kendall Gill ART Charlotte Hornets	.40	.20	.04
☐ 322 Dee Brown ART Boston Celtics	.15	.07	.01
☐ 323 Magic Johnson GQ All-Star Style Team	.40	.20	.04
☐ 324 Hakeem Olajuwon GQ All-Star Style Team	.10	.05	.01
☐ 325 Kevin Willis Dominique Wilkins GQ All-Star Style Team	.15	.07	.01
☐ 326 Kevin Willis Dominique Wilkins GQ All-Star Style Team	.15	.07	.01
☐ 327 Gerald Wilkins GQ All-Star Style Team	.06	.03	.00
☐ 328 1891-1991 Basketball Centennial Logo	.08	.04	.01
☐ 329 Old-Fashioned Ball	.03	.01	.00
☐ 330 Women Take the Court	.06	.03	.00
☐ 331 The Peach Basket	.03	.01	.00
☐ 332 James A. Naismith Founder of Basketball	.15	.07	.01
☐ 333 Magic Johnson and Michael Jordan Great Moments from the NBA Finals	1.00	.50	.10
☐ 334 Michael Jordan Chicago Bulls Great Moments from the NBA Finals	.60	.30	.06
☐ 335 Vlade Divac Los Angeles Lakers Great Moments from the NBA Finals	.08	.04	.01
☐ 336 John Paxson Chicago Bulls Great Moments from the NBA Finals	.06	.03	.00
☐ 337 Bulls Starting Five Great Moments from the NBA Finals	.15	.07	.01
☐ 338 Language Arts Stay in School	.03	.01	.00
☐ 339 Mathematics Stay in School	.03	.01	.00
☐ 340 Vocational Education Stay in School	.03	.01	.00
☐ 341 Social Studies Stay in School	.03	.01	.00
☐ 342 Physical Education Stay in School	.03	.01	.00
☐ 343 Art Stay in School	.03	.01	.00
☐ 344 Science Stay in School	.03	.01	.00
☐ 345 Checklist 1 (1-60)	.06	.01	.00
☐ 346 Checklist 2 (61-120)	.06	.01	.00
☐ 347 Checklist 3 (121-180)	.06	.01	.00
☐ 348 Checklist 4 (181-244)	.06	.01	.00
☐ 349 Checklist 5 (245-305)	.06	.01	.00
☐ 350 Checklist 6 (306-350)	.06	.01	.00

1991-92 SkyBox Blister Inserts

The first four inserts were featured in series one blister packs, while the last two were inserted in series two blister packs. The cards measure the standard size (2 1/2" by 3 1/2"). The first four have logos on their front and comments on the back. The last two are double-sided cards and display most valuable players from the same team for two consecutive years. The cards are numbered on the back with Roman numerals.

	MINT	EXC	G-VG
COMPLETE SET (6)	2.00	1.00	.20
COMMON PLAYER (1-4)	.25	.12	.02
COMMON PLAYER (5-6)	.25	.12	.02
☐ 1 USA Basketball (Numbered I)	.25	.12	.02
☐ 2 Stay in School It's Your Best Move (Numbered II)	.25	.12	.02
☐ 3 Orlando All-Star Weekend (Numbered III)	.25	.12	.02

	MINT	EXC	G-VG
☐ 4 Inside Stuff (Numbered IV)	.25	.12	.02
☐ 5 Magic Johnson and James Worthy Back to Back NBA Finals MVP 1987/1988 (Numbered V)	.75	.35	.07
☐ 6 Joe Dumars and Isiah Thomas Back to Back NBA Finals MVP 1989/1990 (Numbered VI)	.25	.12	.02

1991-92 SkyBox II

The 1991-92 SkyBox II basketball set contains 309 cards, measuring the standard size (2 1/2" by 3 1/2"). An unnumbered gold foil-stamped 1992 USA Basketball Team card was randomly inserted into series II foil packs, while the blister packs featured two-card sets of NBA MVPs from the same team for consecutive years. Also the foil packs carry one of four different direct mail offers. On a white card face, the fronts feature color player photos cut out and superimposed on colorful computer-generated geometric shapes and stars. The cards are numbered on the back and checklisted below as follows: Team Logos (351-377), Coaches (378-404), Game Frames (405-431), Sixth Man (432-458), Teamwork (459-485), Rising Stars (486-512), Lottery Picks (513-523), Centennial (524-529), 1992 USA Basketball Team (530-546), 1988 USA Basketball Team (547-556), 1984 USA Basketball Team (557-563), The Magic of SkyBox (564-571), SkyBox Salutes (572-576), Skymasters (577-588), Shooting Stars (589-602), Small School Sensations (603-609), NBA Stay in School (610-614), Player Updates (615-653), and Checklists (654-659). The key rookie cards in this series are Stacey Augmon, Larry Johnson, Dikembe Mutumbo, Billy Owens, and Steve Smith.

	MINT	EXC	G-VG
COMPLETE SET (309)	27.00	13.50	2.70
COMMON PLAYER (351-659)	.03	.01	.00
☐ 351 Atlanta Hawks Team Logo	.03	.01	.00
☐ 352 Boston Celtics Team Logo	.03	.01	.00
☐ 353 Charlotte Hornets Team Logo	.03	.01	.00
☐ 354 Chicago Bulls Team Logo	.03	.01	.00
☐ 355 Cleveland Cavaliers Team Logo	.03	.01	.00
☐ 356 Dallas Mavericks Team Logo	.03	.01	.00
☐ 357 Denver Nuggets Team Logo	.03	.01	.00
☐ 358 Detroit Pistons Team Logo	.03	.01	.00
☐ 359 Golden State Warriors Team Logo	.03	.01	.00
☐ 360 Houston Rockets Team Logo	.03	.01	.00
☐ 361 Indiana Pacers Team Logo	.03	.01	.00
☐ 362 Los Angeles Clippers Team Logo	.03	.01	.00
☐ 363 Los Angeles Lakers Team Logo	.03	.01	.00
☐ 364 Miami Heat Team Logo	.03	.01	.00
☐ 365 Milwaukee Bucks Team Logo	.03	.01	.00
☐ 366 Minnesota Timberwolves Team Logo	.03	.01	.00
☐ 367 New Jersey Nets Team Logo	.03	.01	.00
☐ 368 New York Knicks Team Logo	.03	.01	.00
☐ 369 Orlando Magic Team Logo	.03	.01	.00
☐ 370 Philadelphia 76ers Team Logo	.03	.01	.00
☐ 371 Phoenix Suns Team Logo	.03	.01	.00
☐ 372 Portland Trail Blazers Team Logo	.03	.01	.00
☐ 373 Sacramento Kings Team Logo	.03	.01	.00
☐ 374 San Antonio Spurs Team Logo	.03	.01	.00
☐ 375 Seattle Supersonics Team Logo	.03	.01	.00
☐ 376 Utah Jazz Team Logo	.03	.01	.00
☐ 377 Washington Bullets Team Logo	.03	.01	.00
☐ 378 Bob Weiss CO Atlanta Hawks	.03	.01	.00
☐ 379 Chris Ford CO Boston Celtics	.03	.01	.00
☐ 380 Allan Bristow CO Charlotte Hornets	.03	.01	.00
☐ 381 Phil Jackson CO Chicago Bulls	.03	.01	.00
☐ 382 Lenny Wilkens CO Cleveland Cavaliers	.06	.03	.00
☐ 383 Richie Adubato CO Dallas Mavericks	.03	.01	.00
☐ 384 Paul Westhead CO Denver Nuggets	.03	.01	.00
☐ 385 Chuck Daly CO Detroit Pistons	.06	.03	.00
☐ 386 Don Nelson CO Golden State Warriors	.03	.01	.00
☐ 387 Don Chaney CO Houston Rockets	.03	.01	.00
☐ 388 Bob Hill CO Indiana Pacers	.06	.03	.00
☐ 389 Mike Schuler CO Los Angeles Clippers	.03	.01	.00
☐ 390 Mike Dunleavy CO Los Angeles Lakers	.03	.01	.00
☐ 391 Kevin Loughery CO Miami Heat	.03	.01	.00
☐ 392 Del Harris CO Milwaukee Bucks	.03	.01	.00
☐ 393 Jimmy Rodgers CO Minnesota Timberwolves	.03	.01	.00
☐ 394 Bill Fitch CO New Jersey Nets	.03	.01	.00
☐ 395 Pat Riley CO New York Knicks	.06	.03	.00
☐ 396 Matt Guokas CO Orlando Magic	.03	.01	.00

☐ 397 Jim Lynam CO .03 .01 .00
Philadelphia 76ers
☐ 398 Cotton Fitzsimmons CO .03 .01 .00
Phoenix Suns
☐ 399 Rick Adelman CO .06 .03 .00
Portland Trail Blazers
☐ 400 Dick Motta CO .03 .01 .00
Sacramento Kings
☐ 401 Larry Brown CO .03 .01 .00
San Antonio Spurs
☐ 402 K.C. Jones CO .03 .01 .00
Seattle Supersonics
☐ 403 Jerry Sloan CO .03 .01 .00
Utah Jazz
☐ 404 Wes Unseld CO .06 .03 .00
Washington Bullets
☐ 405 Atlanta Hawks .03 .01 .00
Game Frame
(Mo Cheeks drives
around pick)
☐ 406 Boston Celtics .03 .01 .00
Game Frame
(Dee Brown drives
and shoots)
☐ 407 Charlotte Hornets .03 .01 .00
Game Frame
(Rex Chapman dunking)
☐ 408 Chicago Bulls .08 .04 .01
Game Frame
(Michael Jordan swipes
Reggie Lewis)
☐ 409 Cleveland Cavaliers .03 .01 .00
Game Frame
(John Williams ties
up Eddie Lee Wilkins)
☐ 410 Dallas Mavericks .03 .01 .00
Game Frame
(James Donaldson block)
☐ 411 Denver Nuggets .03 .01 .00
Game Frame
(Dikembe Mutombo
blocking Kenny Smith)
☐ 412 Detroit Pistons .06 .03 .00
Game Frame
(Isiah Thomas)
☐ 413 Golden State Warriors .08 .04 .01
Game Frame
(Tim Hardaway and
Magic Johnson)
☐ 414 Houston Rockets .03 .01 .00
Game Frame
(Hakeem Olajuwon
sets pick)
☐ 415 Indiana Pacers .03 .01 .00
Game Frame
(Detlef Schrempf block)
☐ 416 Los Angeles Clippers .03 .01 .00
Game Frame
(Danny Manning
sets pick)
☐ 417 Los Angeles Lakers .08 .04 .01
Game Frame
(Magic Johnson
no-look pass)
☐ 418 Miami Heat .03 .01 .00
Game Frame
(Bimbo Coles rebounds)
☐ 419 Milwaukee Bucks .03 .01 .00
Game Frame
(Alvin Robertson
rebounds)
☐ 420 Minnesota Timberwolves .03 .01 .00
Game Frame
(Sam Mitchell drives)
☐ 421 New Jersey Nets .03 .01 .00
Game Frame
(Sam Bowie blocking
Mark Eaton's shot)
☐ 422 New York Knicks .03 .01 .00
Game Frame
(Mark Jackson
dribbles between legs)
☐ 423 Orlando Magic .03 .01 .00
Game Frame
☐ 424 Philadelphia 76ers .03 .01 .00
Game Frame
(Charles Barkley
in rebounding position)
☐ 425 Phoenix Suns .06 .03 .00
Game Frame
(Dan Majerle drives)
☐ 426 Portland Trail Blazers .06 .03 .00
Game Frame
(Robert Pack drives)
☐ 427 Sacramento Kings .03 .01 .00
Game Frame
(Wayman Tisdale drives)
☐ 428 San Antonio Spurs .06 .03 .00
Game Frame
(David Robinson scoop)
☐ 429 Seattle Supersonics .03 .01 .00
Game Frame
(Nate McMillan
protecting ball)
☐ 430 Utah Jazz .03 .01 .00
Game Frame
(Karl Malone
blocks out)
☐ 431 Washington Bullets .03 .01 .00
Game Frame
(Michael Adams drives)
☐ 432 Duane Ferrell 6M .03 .01 .00
Atlanta Hawks
☐ 433 Kevin McHale 6M .08 .04 .01
Boston Celtics
☐ 434 Dell Curry 6M .03 .01 .00
Charlotte Hornets
☐ 435 B.J. Armstrong 6M .08 .04 .01
Chicago Bulls
☐ 436 John Williams 6M .06 .03 .00
Cleveland Cavaliers
☐ 437 Brad Davis 6M .03 .01 .00
Dallas Mavericks
☐ 438 Marcus Liberty 6M .12 .06 .01
Denver Nuggets
☐ 439 Mark Aguirre 6M .06 .03 .00
Detroit Pistons
☐ 440 Rod Higgins 6M .03 .01 .00
Golden State Warriors
☐ 441 Eric(Sleepy) Floyd 6M .03 .01 .00
Houston Rockets
☐ 442 Detlef Schrempf 6M .06 .03 .00
Indiana Pacers
☐ 443 Loy Vaught 6M .08 .04 .01
Los Angeles Clippers
☐ 444 Terry Teagle 6M .03 .01 .00
Los Angeles Lakers
☐ 445 Kevin Edwards 6M .03 .01 .00
Miami Heat
☐ 446 Dale Ellis 6M .06 .03 .00
Milwaukee Bucks
☐ 447 Tod Murphy 6M .03 .01 .00
Minnesota Timberwolves
☐ 448 Chris Dudley 6M .03 .01 .00
New Jersey Nets
☐ 449 Mark Jackson 6M .06 .03 .00
New York Knicks
☐ 450 Jerry Reynolds 6M .03 .01 .00
Orlando Magic
☐ 451 Ron Anderson 6M .03 .01 .00
Philadelphia 76ers
☐ 452 Dan Majerle 6M .08 .04 .01
Phoenix Suns
☐ 453 Danny Ainge 6M .06 .03 .00
Portland Trail Blazers
☐ 454 Jim Les 6M .06 .03 .00
Sacramento Kings
☐ 455 Paul Pressey 6M .03 .01 .00
San Antonio Spurs
☐ 456 Ricky Pierce 6M .06 .03 .00
Seattle Supersonics
☐ 457 Mike Brown 6M .03 .01 .00
Utah Jazz
☐ 458 Ledell Eackles 6M .03 .01 .00
Washington Bullets
☐ 459 Atlanta Hawks .08 .04 .01
Teamwork
(Dominique Wilkins
and Kevin Willis)
☐ 460 Boston Celtics .12 .06 .01
Teamwork
(Larry Bird and
Robert Parish)
☐ 461 Charlotte Hornets .15 .07 .01
Teamwork
(Rex Chapman and
Kendall Gill)
☐ 462 Chicago Bulls .50 .25 .05
Teamwork
(Michael Jordan and
Scottie Pippen)
☐ 463 Cleveland Cavaliers .06 .03 .00
Teamwork
(Craig Ehlo and
Mark Price)
☐ 464 Dallas Mavericks .06 .03 .00
Teamwork
(Derek Harper and

	No.	Card			
		Rolando Blackman)			
☐	465	Denver Nuggets Teamwork (Reggie Williams and Chris Jackson)	.06	.03	.00
☐	466	Detroit Pistons Teamwork (Isiah Thomas and Bill Laimbeer)	.08	.04	.01
☐	467	Golden State Warriors Teamwork (Tim Hardaway and Chris Mullin)	.15	.07	.01
☐	468	Houston Rockets Teamwork (Vernon Maxwell and Kenny Smith)	.03	.01	.00
☐	469	Indiana Pacers Teamwork (Detlef Schrempf and Reggie Miller)	.06	.03	.00
☐	470	Los Angeles Clippers Teamwork (Charles Smith and Danny Manning)	.06	.03	.00
☐	471	Los Angeles Lakers Teamwork (Magic Johnson and James Worthy)	.25	.12	.02
☐	472	Miami Heat Teamwork (Glen Rice and Rony Seikaly)	.10	.05	.01
☐	473	Milwaukee Bucks Teamwork (Jay Humphries and Alvin Robertson)	.03	.01	.00
☐	474	Minnesota Timberwolves Teamwork (Tony Campbell and Pooh Richardson)	.06	.03	.00
☐	475	New Jersey Nets Teamwork (Derrick Coleman and Sam Bowie)	.12	.06	.01
☐	476	New York Knicks Teamwork (Patrick Ewing and Charles Oakley)	.10	.05	.01
☐	477	Orlando Magic Teamwork (Dennis Scott and Scott Skiles)	.06	.03	.00
☐	478	Philadelphia 76ers Teamwork (Charles Barkley and Hersey Hawkins)	.10	.05	.01
☐	479	Phoenix Suns Teamwork (Kevin Johnson and Tom Chambers)	.08	.04	.01
☐	480	Portland Trail Blazers Teamwork (Clyde Drexler and Terry Porter)	.15	.07	.01
☐	481	Sacramento Kings Teamwork (Lionel Simmons and Wayman Tisdale)	.08	.04	.01
☐	482	San Antonio Spurs Teamwork (Terry Cummings and Sean Elliott)	.06	.03	.00
☐	483	Seattle Supersonics Teamwork (Eddie Johnson and Ricky Pierce)	.03	.01	.00
☐	484	Utah Jazz Teamwork (Karl Malone and John Stockton)	.15	.07	.01
☐	485	Washington Bullets Teamwork (Harvey Grant and Bernard King)	.06	.03	.00
☐	486	Rumeal Robinson RS Atlanta Hawks	.06	.03	.00
☐	487	Dee Brown RS Boston Celtics	.20	.10	.02
☐	488	Kendall Gill RS Charlotte Hornets	.40	.20	.04
☐	489	B.J. Armstrong RS Chicago Bulls	.10	.05	.01
☐	490	Danny Ferry RS Cleveland Cavaliers	.06	.03	.00
☐	491	Randy White RS Dallas Mavericks	.03	.01	.00
☐	492	Chris Jackson RS Denver Nuggets	.06	.03	.00
☐	493	Lance Blanks RS Detroit Pistons	.03	.01	.00
☐	494	Tim Hardaway RS Golden State Warriors	.40	.20	.04
☐	495	Vernon Maxwell RS Houston Rockets	.06	.03	.00
☐	496	Micheal Williams RS Indiana Pacers	.06	.03	.00
☐	497	Charles Smith RS Los Angeles Clippers	.06	.03	.00
☐	498	Vlade Divac RS Los Angeles Lakers	.08	.04	.01
☐	499	Willie Burton RS Miami Heat	.06	.03	.00
☐	500	Jeff Grayer RS Milwaukee Bucks	.03	.01	.00
☐	501	Pooh Richardson RS Minnesota Timberwolves	.08	.04	.01
☐	502	Derrick Coleman RS New Jersey Nets	.25	.12	.02
☐	503	John Starks RS New York Knicks	.20	.10	.02
☐	504	Dennis Scott RS Orlando Magic	.10	.05	.01
☐	505	Hersey Hawkins RS Philadelphia 76ers	.06	.03	.00
☐	506	Negele Knight RS Phoenix Suns	.06	.03	.00
☐	507	Cliff Robinson RS Portland Trail Blazers	.10	.05	.01
☐	508	Lionel Simmons RS Sacramento Kings	.12	.06	.01
☐	509	David Robinson RS San Antonio Spurs	.40	.20	.04
☐	510	Gary Payton RS Seattle Supersonics	.10	.05	.01
☐	511	Blue Edwards RS Utah Jazz	.06	.03	.00
☐	512	Harvey Grant RS Washington Bullets	.06	.03	.00
☐	513	Larry Johnson Charlotte Hornets	6.00	3.00	.60
☐	514	Kenny Anderson New Jersey Nets	1.00	.50	.10
☐	515	Billy Owens Golden State Warriors	3.50	1.75	.35
☐	516	Dikembe Mutombo Denver Nuggets	3.50	1.75	.35
☐	517	Steve Smith Miami Heat	1.25	.60	.12
☐	518	Doug Smith Dallas Mavericks	.40	.20	.04
☐	519	Luc Longley Minnesota Timberwolves	.20	.10	.02
☐	520	Mark Macon Denver Nuggets	.40	.20	.04
☐	521	Stacey Augmon Atlanta Hawks	1.00	.50	.10
☐	522	Brian Williams Orlando Magic	.40	.20	.04
☐	523	Terrell Brandon Cleveland Cavaliers	.50	.25	.05
☐	524	The Ball	.03	.01	.00
☐	525	The Basket	.03	.01	.00
☐	526	The 24-second Shot Clock	.03	.01	.00
☐	527	The Game Program	.03	.01	.00
☐	528	The Championship Gift	.03	.01	.00
☐	529	Championship Trophy	.03	.01	.00
☐	530	Charles Barkley USA	.75	.35	.07
☐	531	Larry Bird USA	1.00	.50	.10
☐	532	Patrick Ewing USA	.90	.45	.09
☐	533	Magic Johnson USA	1.75	.85	.17
☐	534	Michael Jordan USA	2.50	1.25	.25
☐	535	Karl Malone USA	.75	.35	.07
☐	536	Chris Mullin USA	.75	.35	.07
☐	537	Scottie Pippen USA	1.25	.60	.12
☐	538	David Robinson USA	1.75	.85	.17
☐	539	John Stockton USA	.75	.35	.07
☐	540	Chuck Daly CO USA	.25	.12	.02
☐	541	P.J. Carlesimo CO USA	.25	.12	.02
☐	542	Mike Krzyzewski CO USA	.40	.20	.04
☐	543	Lenny Wilkens CO USA	.20	.10	.02
☐	544	Team USA Card 1	1.50	.75	.15
☐	545	Team USA Card 2	1.50	.75	.15
☐	546	Team USA Card 3	1.50	.75	.15
☐	547	Willie Anderson USA	.06	.03	.00
☐	548	Stacey Augmon USA	.75	.35	.07
☐	549	Bimbo Coles USA	.12	.06	.01

	Card			
☐ 550	Jeff Grayer USA	.06	.03	.00
☐ 551	Hersey Hawkins USA	.15	.07	.01
☐ 552	Dan Majerle USA	.12	.06	.01
☐ 553	Danny Manning USA	.15	.07	.01
☐ 554	J.R. Reid USA	.06	.03	.00
☐ 555	Mitch Richmond USA	.12	.06	.01
☐ 556	Charles Smith USA	.12	.06	.01
☐ 557	Vern Fleming USA	.06	.03	.00
☐ 558	Joe Kleine USA	.06	.03	.00
☐ 559	Jon Koncak USA	.06	.03	.00
☐ 560	Sam Perkins USA	.12	.06	.01
☐ 561	Alvin Robertson USA	.06	.03	.00
☐ 562	Wayman Tisdale USA	.06	.03	.00
☐ 563	Jeff Turner USA	.06	.03	.00
☐ 564	Tony Campbell	.03	.01	.00
	Minnesota Timberwolves			
	Magic of SkyBox			
☐ 565	Joe Dumars	.08	.04	.01
	Detroit Pistons			
	Magic of SkyBox			
☐ 566	Horace Grant	.08	.04	.01
	Chicago Bulls			
	Magic of SkyBox			
☐ 567	Reggie Lewis	.10	.05	.01
	Boston Celtics			
	Magic of SkyBox			
☐ 568	Hakeem Olajuwon	.10	.05	.01
	Houston Rockets			
	Magic of SkyBox			
☐ 569	Sam Perkins	.06	.03	.00
	Los Angeles Lakers			
	Magic of SkyBox			
☐ 570	Chuck Person	.06	.03	.00
	Indiana Pacers			
	Magic of SkyBox			
☐ 571	Buck Williams	.08	.04	.01
	Portland Trail Blazers			
	Magic of SkyBox			
☐ 572	Michael Jordan	.60	.30	.06
	Chicago Bulls			
	SkyBox Salutes			
☐ 573	Bernard King	.06	.03	.00
	NBA All-Star			
	SkyBox Salutes			
☐ 574	Moses Malone	.08	.04	.01
	Milwaukee Bucks			
	SkyBox Salutes			
☐ 575	Robert Parish	.08	.04	.01
	Boston Celtics			
	SkyBox Salutes			
☐ 576	Pat Riley CO	.06	.03	.00
	Los Angeles Lakers			
	SkyBox Salutes			
☐ 577	Dee Brown	.15	.07	.01
	Boston Celtics			
	SkyMaster			
☐ 578	Rex Chapman	.06	.03	.00
	Charlotte Hornets			
	SkyMaster			
☐ 579	Clyde Drexler	.15	.07	.01
	Portland Trail Blazers			
	SkyMaster			
☐ 580	Blue Edwards	.03	.01	.00
	Utah Jazz			
	SkyMaster			
☐ 581	Ron Harper	.06	.03	.00
	Los Angeles Clippers			
	SkyMaster			
☐ 582	Kevin Johnson	.10	.05	.01
	Phoenix Suns			
	SkyMaster			
☐ 583	Michael Jordan	.60	.30	.06
	Chicago Bulls			
	SkyMaster			
☐ 584	Shawn Kemp	.30	.15	.03
	Seattle Supersonics			
	SkyMaster			
☐ 585	Xavier McDaniel	.08	.04	.01
	New York Knicks			
	SkyMaster			
☐ 586	Scottie Pippen	.25	.12	.02
	Chicago Bulls			
	SkyMaster			
☐ 587	Kenny Smith	.03	.01	.00
	Houston Rockets			
	SkyMaster			
☐ 588	Dominique Wilkins	.08	.04	.01
	Atlanta Hawks			
	SkyMaster			
☐ 589	Michael Adams	.06	.03	.00
	Denver Nuggets			
	Shooting Star			
☐ 590	Danny Ainge	.06	.03	.00
	Denver Nuggets			
	Shooting Star			
☐ 591	Larry Bird	.20	.10	.02
	Boston Celtics			
	Shooting Star			
☐ 592	Dale Ellis	.06	.03	.00
	Milwaukee Bucks			
	Shooting Star			
☐ 593	Hersey Hawkins	.06	.03	.00
	Philadelphia 76ers			
	Shooting Star			
☐ 594	Jeff Hornacek	.08	.04	.01
	Phoenix Suns			
	Shooting Star			
☐ 595	Jeff Malone	.08	.04	.01
	Utah Jazz			
	Shooting Star			
☐ 596	Reggie Miller	.08	.04	.01
	Indiana Pacers			
	Shooting Star			
☐ 597	Chris Mullin	.10	.05	.01
	Golden State Warriors			
	Shooting Star			
☐ 598	John Paxson	.06	.03	.00
	Chicago Bulls			
	Shooting Star			
☐ 599	Drazen Petrovic	.12	.06	.01
	New Jersey Nets			
	Shooting Star			
☐ 600	Ricky Pierce	.06	.03	.00
	Milwaukee Bucks			
	Shooting Star			
☐ 601	Mark Price	.08	.04	.01
	Cleveland Cavaliers			
	Shooting Star			
☐ 602	Dennis Scott	.08	.04	.01
	Orlando Magic			
	Shooting Star			
☐ 603	Manute Bol	.03	.01	.00
	Philadelphia 76ers			
	Small School Sensation			
☐ 604	Jerome Kersey	.08	.04	.01
	Portland Trail Blazers			
	Small School Sensation			
☐ 605	Charles Oakley	.03	.01	.00
	New York Knicks			
	Small School Sensation			
☐ 606	Scottie Pippen	.20	.10	.02
	Chicago Bulls			
	Small School Sensation			
☐ 607	Terry Porter	.08	.04	.01
	Portland Trail Blazers			
	Small School Sensation			
☐ 608	Dennis Rodman	.08	.04	.01
	Detroit Pistons			
	Small School Sensation			
☐ 609	Sedale Threatt	.06	.03	.00
	Los Angeles Lakers			
	Small School Sensation			
☐ 610	Business	.03	.01	.00
	Stay in School			
☐ 611	Engineering	.03	.01	.00
	Stay in School			
☐ 612	Law	.03	.01	.00
	Stay in School			
☐ 613	Liberal Arts	.03	.01	.00
	Stay in School			
☐ 614	Medicine	.03	.01	.00
	Stay in School			
☐ 615	Maurice Cheeks	.06	.03	.00
	Atlanta Hawks			
☐ 616	Travis Mays	.06	.03	.00
	Atlanta Hawks			
☐ 617	Blair Rasmussen	.03	.01	.00
	Atlanta Hawks			
☐ 618	Alexander Volkov	.06	.03	.00
	Atlanta Hawks			
☐ 619	Rickey Green	.03	.01	.00
	Boston Celtics			
☐ 620	Bobby Hansen	.03	.01	.00
	Chicago Bulls			
☐ 621	John Battle	.03	.01	.00
	Cleveland Cavaliers			
☐ 622	Terry Davis	.08	.04	.01
	Dallas Mavericks			
☐ 623	Walter Davis	.06	.03	.00
	Denver Nuggets			
☐ 624	Winston Garland	.03	.01	.00
	Denver Nuggets			
☐ 625	Scott Hastings	.03	.01	.00
	Denver Nuggets			
☐ 626	Brad Sellers	.03	.01	.00
	Denver Nuggets			
☐ 627	Darrell Walker	.03	.01	.00
	Detroit Pistons			

☐ 628	Orlando Woolridge Detroit Pistons	.06	.03	.00
☐ 629	Tony Brown Los Angeles Clippers	.03	.01	.00
☐ 630	James Edwards Los Angeles Clippers	.03	.01	.00
☐ 631	Doc Rivers Los Angeles Clippers	.06	.03	.00
☐ 632	Jack Haley Los Angeles Lakers	.03	.01	.00
☐ 633	Sedale Threatt Los Angeles Lakers	.06	.03	.00
☐ 634	Moses Malone Milwaukee Bucks	.12	.06	.01
☐ 635	Thurl Bailey Minnesota Timberwolves	.03	.01	.00
☐ 636	Rafael Addison New Jersey Nets	.15	.07	.01
☐ 637	Tim McCormick New York Knicks	.03	.01	.00
☐ 638	Xavier McDaniel New York Knicks	.08	.04	.01
☐ 639	Charles Shackleford Philadelphia 76ers	.03	.01	.00
☐ 640	Mitchell Wiggins Philadelphia 76ers	.03	.01	.00
☐ 641	Jerrod Mustaf Phoenix Suns	.08	.04	.01
☐ 642	Dennis Hopson Sacramento Kings	.06	.03	.00
☐ 643	Les Jepsen Sacramento Kings	.06	.03	.00
☐ 644	Mitch Richmond Sacramento Kings	.12	.06	.01
☐ 645	Dwayne Schintzius Sacramento Kings	.06	.03	.00
☐ 646	Spud Webb Sacramento Kings	.06	.03	.00
☐ 647	Jud Buechler San Antonio Spurs	.03	.01	.00
☐ 648	Antoine Carr San Antonio Spurs	.03	.01	.00
☐ 649	Tyrone Corbin Utah Jazz	.03	.01	.00
☐ 650	Michael Adams Washington Bullets	.08	.04	.01
☐ 651	Ralph Sampson Washington Bullets	.06	.03	.00
☐ 652	Andre Turner Washington Bullets	.06	.03	.00
☐ 653	David Wingate Washington Bullets	.03	.01	.00
☐ 654	Checklist "S" (351-404)	.06	.01	.00
☐ 655	Checklist "K" (405-458)	.06	.01	.00
☐ 656	Checklist "Y" (459-512)	.06	.01	.00
☐ 657	Checklist "B" (513-563)	.06	.01	.00
☐ 658	Checklist "O" (564-614)	.06	.01	.00
☐ 659	Checklist "X" (615-659)	.06	.01	.00
☐ NNO	Clyde Drexler USA SP (Send-away)	25.00	12.50	2.50
☐ NNO	Team USA Card SP	20.00	10.00	2.00

1991-92 SkyBox Canadian Minis

This set of 50 mini-trading cards was a sports promotion in Canada involving SkyBox and Hostess/Frito Lay. The miniature cards measure 1 1/4" by 1 3/4," and one was inserted in specially marked bags of Hostess/Frito Lay products, including Doritos, Ruffles, Cheetos, O'Ryans, and Hostess. It was claimed that 9 out of every 10 bags contained a trading card, and in the event that the consumer purchased a bag without a card, a card could be obtained without charge through a mail-in offer. The promotion ran January 20 through March, and it was supported by colorful displays at more than 75,000 locations in Canada as well as televisions ads. The card design was identical to the regular issue, with the exception that the backs feature bilingual information.

		MINT	EXC	G-VG
COMPLETE SET (50)		20.00	10.00	2.00
COMMON PLAYER (1-50)		.20	.10	.02
☐ 1	Kevin Willis Atlanta Hawks	.25	.12	.02
☐ 2	Larry Bird Boston Celtics	1.25	.60	.12
☐ 3	Kevin McHale Boston Celtics	.25	.12	.02
☐ 4	Robert Parish Boston Celtics	.30	.15	.03
☐ 5	Kendall Gill Charlotte Hornets	.75	.35	.07
☐ 6	J.R. Reid Charlotte Hornets	.20	.10	.02
☐ 7	Michael Jordan Chicago Bulls	2.50	1.25	.25
☐ 8	Scottie Pippen Chicago Bulls	.90	.45	.09
☐ 9	Brad Daugherty Cleveland Cavaliers	.35	.17	.03
☐ 10	Larry Nance Cleveland Cavaliers	.25	.12	.02
☐ 11	Rolando Blackman Dallas Mavericks	.25	.12	.02
☐ 12	Derek Harper Dallas Mavericks	.20	.10	.02
☐ 13	Chris Jackson Denver Nuggets	.30	.15	.03
☐ 14	Jerome Lane Denver Nuggets	.20	.10	.02
☐ 15	Joe Dumars Detroit Pistons	.30	.15	.03
☐ 16	Dennis Rodman Detroit Pistons	.30	.15	.03
☐ 17	Tim Hardaway Golden State Warriors	.90	.45	.09
☐ 18	Chris Mullin Golden State Warriors	.60	.30	.06
☐ 19	Hakeem Olajuwon Houston Rockets	.50	.25	.05
☐ 20	Otis Thorpe Houston Rockets	.20	.10	.02
☐ 21	Reggie Miller Indiana Pacers	.25	.12	.02
☐ 22	Detlef Schrempf Indiana Pacers	.25	.12	.02
☐ 23	Danny Manning Los Angeles Clippers	.30	.15	.03
☐ 24	Charles Smith Los Angeles Clippers	.25	.12	.02
☐ 25	Magic Johnson Los Angeles Lakers	1.50	.75	.15
☐ 26	James Worthy Los Angeles Lakers	.40	.20	.04
☐ 27	Sherman Douglas Miami Heat	.25	.12	.02
☐ 28	Rony Seikaly Miami Heat	.30	.15	.03
☐ 29	Alvin Robertson Milwaukee Bucks	.20	.10	.02
☐ 30	Tony Campbell Minnesota Timberwolves	.20	.10	.02
☐ 31	Derrick Coleman New Jersey Nets	.90	.45	.09
☐ 32	Charles Oakley New York Knicks	.20	.10	.02
☐ 33	Dennis Scott Orlando Magic	.30	.15	.03
☐ 34	Scott Skiles Orlando Magic	.20	.10	.02

	MINT	EXC	G-VG
□ 35 Charles Barkley Philadelphia 76ers	.60	.30	.06
□ 36 Hersey Hawkins Philadelphia 76ers	.35	.17	.03
□ 37 Jeff Hornacek Phoenix Suns	.30	.15	.03
□ 38 Kevin Johnson Phoenix Suns	.60	.30	.06
□ 39 Clyde Drexler Portland Trail Blazers	.75	.35	.07
□ 40 Terry Porter Portland Trail Blazers	.30	.15	.03
□ 41 Wayman Tisdale Sacramento Kings	.25	.12	.02
□ 42 Terry Cummings San Antonio Spurs	.25	.12	.02
□ 43 David Robinson San Antonio Spurs	1.25	.60	.12
□ 44 Shawn Kemp Seattle Supersonics	.90	.45	.09
□ 45 Ricky Pierce Seattle Supersonics	.20	.10	.02
□ 46 Karl Malone Utah Jazz	.50	.25	.05
□ 47 John Stockton Utah Jazz	.50	.25	.05
□ 48 Harvey Grant Washington Bullets	.25	.12	.02
□ 49 Bernard King Washington Bullets	.30	.15	.03
□ 50 Checklist	.20	.10	.02

1992 SkyBox USA

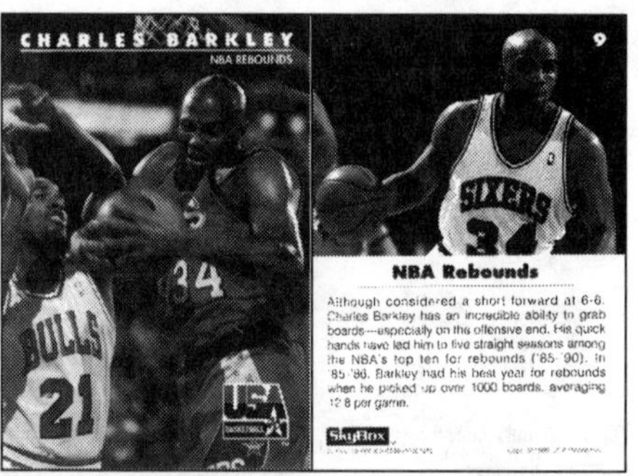

The 1992 SkyBox USA basketball set contains 110 cards, including nine cards of each of the first 10 NBA players named to the team, two cards of each coach, and two checklist cards. The set concludes with a "Magic On" subset, representing Johnson's thoughts on his teammates. The wax packs included randomly inserted cards autographed by Johnson and Robinson as well as a plastic trading card featuring a team photo. The standard-size (2 1/2" by 3 1/2") cards feature on the fronts full-bleed glossy color action shots, with the player's name and the card's subtitle printed across the top of the picture. On the upper portion, the backs feature a color close-up photo, while the lower portion presents statistics or summarizes the player's professional career. The cards are numbered on the back.

	MINT	EXC	G-VG
COMPLETE SET (110)	24.00	12.00	2.40
COMMON PLAYER (1-110)	.15	.07	.01
□ 1 Charles Barkley NBA Update	.45	.22	.04
□ 2 Charles Barkley NBA Rookie	.45	.22	.04
□ 3 Charles Barkley Game Strategy	.45	.22	.04
□ 4 Charles Barkley NBA Best Game	.45	.22	.04
□ 5 Charles Barkley Off the Court	.45	.22	.04
□ 6 Charles Barkley NBA Playoffs	.45	.22	.04
□ 7 Charles Barkley NBA All-Star Record	.45	.22	.04
□ 8 Charles Barkley NBA Shooting	.45	.22	.04
□ 9 Charles Barkley NBA Rebounds	.45	.22	.04
□ 10 Larry Bird NBA Update	.75	.35	.07
□ 11 Larry Bird NBA Rookie	.75	.35	.07
□ 12 Larry Bird Game Strategy	.75	.35	.07
□ 13 Larry Bird NBA Best Game	.75	.35	.07
□ 14 Larry Bird Off the Court	.75	.35	.07
□ 15 Larry Bird NBA Playoffs	.75	.35	.07
□ 16 Larry Bird NBA All-Star Record	.75	.35	.07
□ 17 Larry Bird NBA Shooting	.75	.35	.07
□ 18 Larry Bird NBA Rebounds	.75	.35	.07
□ 19 Patrick Ewing NBA Update	.45	.22	.04
□ 20 Patrick Ewing NBA Rookie	.45	.22	.04
□ 21 Patrick Ewing Game Strategy	.45	.22	.04
□ 22 Patrick Ewing NBA Best Game	.45	.22	.04
□ 23 Patrick Ewing Off the Court	.45	.22	.04
□ 24 Patrick Ewing NBA Playoffs	.45	.22	.04
□ 25 Patrick Ewing NBA All-Star Record	.45	.22	.04
□ 26 Patrick Ewing NBA Shooting	.45	.22	.04
□ 27 Patrick Ewing NBA Rebounds	.45	.22	.04
□ 28 Magic Johnson NBA Update	1.00	.50	.10
□ 29 Magic Johnson NBA Rookie	1.00	.50	.10
□ 30 Magic Johnson Game Strategy	1.00	.50	.10
□ 31 Magic Johnson NBA Best Game	1.00	.50	.10
□ 32 Magic Johnson Off the Court	1.00	.50	.10
□ 33 Magic Johnson NBA Playoffs	1.00	.50	.10
□ 34 Magic Johnson NBA All-Star Record	1.00	.50	.10
□ 35 Magic Johnson NBA Shooting	1.00	.50	.10
□ 36 Magic Johnson NBA Assists	1.00	.50	.10
□ 37 Michael Jordan NBA Update	1.25	.60	.12
□ 38 Michael Jordan NBA Rookie	1.25	.60	.12
□ 39 Michael Jordan Game Strategy	1.25	.60	.12
□ 40 Michael Jordan NBA Best Game	1.25	.60	.12
□ 41 Michael Jordan Off the Court	1.25	.60	.12
□ 42 Michael Jordan NBA Playoffs	1.25	.60	.12
□ 43 Michael Jordan NBA All-Star Record	1.25	.60	.12
□ 44 Michael Jordan NBA Shooting	1.25	.60	.12
□ 45 Michael Jordan NBA All-Time Records	1.25	.60	.12
□ 46 Karl Malone NBA Update	.45	.22	.04
□ 47 Karl Malone NBA Rookie	.45	.22	.04
□ 48 Karl Malone Game Strategy	.45	.22	.04
□ 49 Karl Malone NBA Best Game	.45	.22	.04
□ 50 Karl Malone Off the Court	.45	.22	.04
□ 51 Karl Malone NBA Playoffs	.45	.22	.04
□ 52 Karl Malone NBA All-Star Record	.45	.22	.04
□ 53 Karl Malone	.45	.22	.04

NBA Shooting			
☐ 54 Karl Malone	.45	.22	.04
NBA Rebounds			
☐ 55 Chris Mullin	.35	.17	.03
NBA Update			
☐ 56 Chris Mullin	.35	.17	.03
NBA Rookie			
☐ 57 Chris Mullin	.35	.17	.03
Game Strategy			
☐ 58 Chris Mullin	.35	.17	.03
NBA Best Game			
☐ 59 Chris Mullin	.35	.17	.03
Off the Court			
☐ 60 Chris Mullin	.35	.17	.03
NBA Playoffs			
☐ 61 Chris Mullin	.35	.17	.03
NBA All-Star Record			
☐ 62 Chris Mullin	.35	.17	.03
NBA Shooting			
☐ 63 Chris Mullin	.35	.17	.03
NBA Minutes			
☐ 64 Scottie Pippen	.45	.22	.04
NBA Update			
☐ 65 Scottie Pippen	.45	.22	.04
NBA Rookie			
☐ 66 Scottie Pippen	.45	.22	.04
Game Strategy			
☐ 67 Scottie Pippen	.45	.22	.04
NBA Best Game			
☐ 68 Scottie Pippen	.45	.22	.04
Off the Court			
☐ 69 Scottie Pippen	.45	.22	.04
NBA Playoffs			
☐ 70 Scottie Pippen	.45	.22	.04
NBA All-Star Record			
☐ 71 Scottie Pippen	.45	.22	.04
NBA Shooting			
☐ 72 Scottie Pippen	.45	.22	.04
NBA Steals and Blocks			
☐ 73 David Robinson	.75	.35	.07
NBA Update			
☐ 74 David Robinson	.75	.35	.07
NBA Rookie			
☐ 75 David Robinson	.75	.35	.07
Game Strategy			
☐ 76 David Robinson	.75	.35	.07
NBA Best Game			
☐ 77 David Robinson	.75	.35	.07
Off the Court			
☐ 78 David Robinson	.75	.35	.07
NBA Playoffs			
☐ 79 David Robinson	.75	.35	.07
NBA All-Star			
☐ 80 David Robinson	.75	.35	.07
NBA Shooting			
☐ 81 David Robinson	.75	.35	.07
NBA All-Around			
☐ 82 John Stockton	.45	.22	.04
NBA Update			
☐ 83 John Stockton	.45	.22	.04
NBA Rookie			
☐ 84 John Stockton	.45	.22	.04
Game Strategy			
☐ 85 John Stockton	.45	.22	.04
NBA Best Game			
☐ 86 John Stockton	.45	.22	.04
Off the Court			
☐ 87 John Stockton	.45	.22	.04
NBA Playoffs			
☐ 88 John Stockton	.45	.22	.04
NBA All-Star Record			
☐ 89 John Stockton	.45	.22	.04
NBA Shooting			
☐ 90 John Stockton	.45	.22	.04
NBA Assists			
☐ 91 P.J. Carlesimo CO	.15	.07	.01
College Coaching			
☐ 92 P.J. Carlesimo CO	.15	.07	.01
NCAA Coaching Record			
☐ 93 Chuck Daly CO	.15	.07	.01
NBA Coaching			
☐ 94 Chuck Daly CO	.15	.07	.01
NCAA Coaching Record			
☐ 95 Mike Krzyzewski CO	.15	.07	.01
College Coaching			
☐ 96 Mike Krzyzewski CO	.15	.07	.01
College Coaching Record			
☐ 97 Lenny Wilkens CO	.15	.07	.01
NBA Coaching			
☐ 98 Lenny Wilkens CO	.15	.07	.01
NBA Coaching Record			
☐ 99 Checklist 1-54	.15	.07	.01
☐ 100 Checklist 55-110	.15	.07	.01
☐ 101 Magic on Barkley	.35	.17	.03
☐ 102 Magic on Bird	.45	.22	.04
☐ 103 Magic on Ewing	.35	.17	.03
☐ 104 Magic on Magic	.75	.35	.07
☐ 105 Magic on Jordan	1.00	.50	.10
☐ 106 Magic on Malone	.35	.17	.03
☐ 107 Magic on Mullin	.35	.17	.03
☐ 108 Magic on Pippen	.35	.17	.03
☐ 109 Magic on Robinson	.45	.22	.04
☐ 110 Magic on Stockton	.35	.17	.03

1991 Smokey's Larry Johnson

This seven-card set was sponsored by Smokey's, Inc. (Las Vegas, Nevada) in honor of Larry Johnson, the 1990-91 NCAA Player of the Year. Set production was limited to 49,500, and the unique set number appears on a cardboard picture frame that accompanies the seven cards. The standard-size (2 1/2" by 3 1/2") cards have high gloss color action photos on the front, with gold borders on a black card face. Johnson's name is written in aqua and white lettering at the bottom of the card. Inside a gold border, the glossy backs have a black marble design. A color mugshot of Johnson appears at the top of each back, and an extended caption to the card appears in a pale green rectangle. The cards are numbered on the backs.

	MINT	EXC	G-VG
COMPLETE SET (7)	8.00	4.00	.80
COMMON PLAYER (1-7)	1.25	.60	.12
☐ 1 Rebel Rookie	1.50	.75	.15
☐ 2 89-90 Champs	1.25	.60	.12
☐ 3 All American	1.25	.60	.12
☐ 4 Undefeated Season	1.25	.60	.12
☐ 5 Tough Loss	1.25	.60	.12
☐ 6 1990 NCAA Player of the Year	1.25	.60	.12
☐ 7 Checklist Card	1.50	.75	.15

1979-80 Spurs Police

This set contains 15 cards measuring approximately 2 5/8" by 4 1/8" featuring the San Antonio Spurs. Backs contain safety tips, "Tips from the Spurs." The set was also sponsored by Handy Dan and were put out by Express News and Handy Dan in conjunction with the Police Department.

	MINT	EXC	G-VG
COMPLETE SET (15)	5.00	2.50	.50
COMMON PLAYER	.30	.15	.03
☐ 1 Mike Evans	.30	.15	.03
☐ 2 Billy Paultz	.40	.20	.04
☐ 12 Mike Gale	.30	.15	.03
☐ 13 James Silas	.40	.20	.04
☐ 21 Irv Kiffin	.30	.15	.03
☐ 30 Paul Griffin	.30	.15	.03
☐ 31 Kevin Restani	.30	.15	.03

#44 George Gervin

6-7 Guard
185 lbs. Eastern Michigan '72

TIPS from the SPURS

Baseline:

The endline area of the floor — an area where good defensive players never allow their opponents to go when they have the ball.

There are places where you and your friends should not play. Streets, vacant houses and construction areas are dangerous.

Courtesy of

EXPRESS-NEWS

and

Handy Dan

☐ 35 Larry Kenon	.50	.25	.05
☐ 44 George Gervin	1.50	.75	.15
☐ 53 Mark Olberding	.30	.15	.03
☐ 54 Wiley Peck	.30	.15	.03
☐ xx Bob Bass	.30	.15	.03
☐ xx George Karl CO	.50	.25	.05
☐ xx Bernie LaReau	.30	.15	.03
☐ xx Doug Moe CO	.60	.30	.06

1988-89 Spurs Police/Diamond Shamrock

This eight-card set of San Antonio Spurs is one of two that were sponsored by Diamond Shamrock, a regional oil retailer and convenience store chain headquartered in San Antonio. One set had a tear-off tab, and one card was given out each week at San Antonio Diamond Shamrock CornerStore locations with each 3.00 purchase or purchase of eight gallons of gas. It is reported that 100,000 sets were printed. This promotion included weekly drawings for pairs of tickets and a final drawing to determine the winners of the Grand Prize and other prizes. The other set was donated to the San Antonio Police Department and distributed to kids in the San Antonio area by patrolmen on the night shift; 50,000 sets were produced. The cards measure approximately 2 1/2" by 3 9/16" and except for the tear-off tab, the two sets are identical. The front features a color action player photo with a white border (only the Robinson card has a posed shot). The card front has a distinctive black background with a white pinstripe pattern. Three color bands (aqua, red, and orange) overlay the top of the picture, with the team logo in the middle. The player's name is given in the aqua band below the picture. The back has biographical information and a player safety tip in a gray box. The San Antonio Police and sponsor logos appear at the bottom. The cards are unnumbered and checklisted below in alphabetical order, with jersey number after the player's name. The set may have received additional multiple printings in order to capitalize on the popularity of the David Robinson card, which was printed a year earlier than his 1989-90 Hoops Rookie Card.

	MINT	EXC	G-VG
COMPLETE SET (8)	12.00	6.00	1.20
COMMON PLAYER (1-8)	.50	.25	.05
☐ 1 Greg Anderson 33	.50	.25	.05
☐ 2 Willie Anderson 40	1.25	.60	.12
☐ 3 Frank Brickowski 43	.60	.30	.06
☐ 4 Larry Brown CO	.75	.35	.07
☐ 5 Dallas Comegys 22	.60	.30	.06
☐ 6 Johnny Dawkins 24	.75	.35	.07
☐ 7 Alvin Robertson 21	.75	.35	.07
☐ 8 David Robinson 50	7.50	3.75	.75

1983-84 Star NBA

This set of 276 cards was issued in four series during the first six months of 1984. The set features players by team throughout the NBA. Several teams in the first series (1-100) are difficult to obtain due to extensive miscuts (all of which were destroyed according to the company) in the original production process for those teams. Cards measure 2 1/2" by 3 1/2" and have a colored border around the fronts of the cards according to the team with corresponding color printing on the backs. Cards are numbered according to team order, e.g., Philadelphia 76ers (1-12), Los Angeles Lakers (13-25), Boston Celtics (26-37), Milwaukee Bucks (38-48), Dallas Mavericks (49-60), New York Knicks (61-72), Houston Rockets (73-84), Detroit Pistons (85-96), Portland Trail Blazers (97-108), Phoenix Suns (109-120), San Diego Clippers (121-132), Utah Jazz (133-144), New Jersey Nets (145-156), Indiana Pacers (157-168), Chicago Bulls (169-180), Denver Nuggets (181-192), Seattle Supersonics (193-203), Washington Bullets (204-215), Kansas City Kings (216-227), Cleveland Cavaliers (228-240), San Antonio Spurs (241-251), Golden State Warriors (252-263), and Atlanta Hawks (264-275). The key extended rookie cards in this set are Mark Aguirre, Rolando Blackman, Tom Chambers, Clyde Drexler, Dale Ellis, Derek Harper, Isiah Thomas, Dominique Wilkins, and James Worthy. A promotional card of Sidney Moncrief was produced in limited quantities, but it was numbered 39 rather than 38 as it was in the regular set.

	MINT	EXC	G-VG
COMPLETE SET (276)	2700.00	1250.00	325.00
COMMON 76ER (1-12)	5.00	2.50	.50
COMMON LAKERS (13-25)	3.50	1.75	.35
COMMON CELTICS (26-37)	11.00	5.50	1.10
COMMON BUCKS (38-48)	3.50	1.75	.35
COMMON MAVS (49-60)	30.00	15.00	3.00
COMMON PLAYER (61-275)	1.50	.75	.15
☐ 1 Julius Erving	90.00	45.00	9.00
☐ 2 Maurice Cheeks	14.00	7.00	1.40
☐ 3 Franklin Edwards	5.00	2.50	.50
☐ 4 Marc Iavaroni	5.00	2.50	.50
☐ 5 Clemon Johnson	5.00	2.50	.50
☐ 6 Bobby Jones	7.50	3.75	.75

☐ 7 Moses Malone 35.00 17.50 3.50
☐ 8 Leo Rautins 5.00 2.50 .50
☐ 9 Clint Richardson 5.00 2.50 .50
☐ 10 Sedale Threatt 25.00 12.50 2.50
☐ 11 Andrew Toney 9.00 4.50 .90
☐ 12 Sam Williams 5.00 2.50 .50
☐ 13 Magic Johnson 180.00 90.00 18.00
☐ 14 Kareem Abdul-Jabbar 55.00 27.50 5.50
☐ 15 Michael Cooper 8.00 4.00 .80
☐ 16 Calvin Garrett 3.50 1.75 .35
☐ 17 Mitch Kupchak 3.50 1.75 .35
☐ 18 Bob McAdoo 9.00 4.50 .90
☐ 19 Mike McGee 4.50 2.25 .45
☐ 20 Swen Nater 4.00 2.00 .40
☐ 21 Kurt Rambis 10.00 5.00 1.00
☐ 22 Byron Scott 30.00 15.00 3.00
☐ 23 Larry Spriggs 4.00 2.00 .40
☐ 24 Jamaal Wilkes 5.00 2.50 .50
☐ 25 James Worthy 110.00 55.00 11.00
☐ 26 Larry Bird 150.00 75.00 15.00
☐ 27 Danny Ainge 50.00 25.00 5.00
☐ 28 Quinn Buckner 12.00 6.00 1.20
☐ 29 M.L. Carr 12.00 6.00 1.20
☐ 30 Carlos Clark 11.00 5.50 1.10
☐ 31 Gerald Henderson 11.00 5.50 1.10
☐ 32 Dennis Johnson 15.00 7.50 1.50
☐ 33 Cedric Maxwell 13.50 6.50 1.35
☐ 34 Kevin McHale 45.00 22.50 4.50
☐ 35 Robert Parish 60.00 30.00 6.00
☐ 36 Scott Wedman 12.00 6.00 1.20
☐ 37 Greg Kite 12.00 6.00 1.20
☐ 38 Sidney Moncrief 13.50 6.50 1.35
☐ 39A Sidney Moncrief 100.00 50.00 10.00
(Promotional card)
☐ 39B Nate Archibald 13.50 6.50 1.35
☐ 40 Randy Breuer 5.50 2.75 .55
☐ 41 Junior Bridgeman 4.00 2.00 .40
☐ 42 Harvey Catchings 3.50 1.75 .35
☐ 43 Kevin Grevey 3.50 1.75 .35
☐ 44 Marques Johnson 6.00 3.00 .60
☐ 45 Bob Lanier 13.50 6.50 1.35
☐ 46 Alton Lister 6.00 3.00 .60
☐ 47 Paul Mokeski 4.50 2.25 .45
☐ 48 Paul Pressey 9.00 4.50 .90
☐ 49 Mark Aguirre 75.00 37.50 7.50
☐ 50 Rolando Blackman 100.00 50.00 10.00
☐ 51 Pat Cummings 35.00 17.50 3.50
☐ 52 Brad Davis 40.00 20.00 4.00
☐ 53 Dale Ellis 75.00 37.50 7.50
☐ 54 Bill Garnett 30.00 15.00 3.00
☐ 55 Derek Harper 80.00 40.00 8.00
☐ 56 Kurt Nimphius 30.00 15.00 3.00
☐ 57 Jim Spanarkel 30.00 15.00 3.00
☐ 58 Elston Turner 30.00 15.00 3.00
☐ 59 Jay Vincent 35.00 17.50 3.50
☐ 60 Mark West 45.00 22.50 4.50
☐ 61 Bernard King 12.00 6.00 1.20
☐ 62 Bill Cartwright 6.50 3.25 .65
☐ 63 Len Elmore 2.50 1.25 .25
☐ 64 Eric Fernsten 1.50 .75 .15
☐ 65 Ernie Grunfeld 2.50 1.25 .25
☐ 66 Louis Orr 1.50 .75 .15
☐ 67 Leonard Robinson 2.50 1.25 .25
☐ 68 Rory Sparrow 3.50 1.75 .35
☐ 69 Trent Tucker 3.00 1.50 .30
☐ 70 Darrell Walker 5.00 2.50 .50
☐ 71 Marvin Webster 1.50 .75 .15
☐ 72 Ray Williams 1.50 .75 .15
☐ 73 Ralph Sampson 6.00 3.00 .60
☐ 74 James Bailey 1.50 .75 .15
☐ 75 Phil Ford 2.00 1.00 .20
☐ 76 Elvin Hayes 9.00 4.50 .90
☐ 77 Caldwell Jones 2.00 1.00 .20
☐ 78 Major Jones 1.50 .75 .15
☐ 79 Allen Leavell 1.50 .75 .15
☐ 80 Lewis Lloyd 1.50 .75 .15
☐ 81 Rodney McCray 7.00 3.50 .70
☐ 82 Robert Reid 1.50 .75 .15
☐ 83 Terry Teagle 8.00 4.00 .80
☐ 84 Wally Walker 1.50 .75 .15
☐ 85 Kelly Tripucka 3.50 1.75 .35
☐ 86 Kent Benson 2.00 1.00 .20
☐ 87 Earl Cureton 2.50 1.25 .25
☐ 88 Lionel Hollins 2.00 1.00 .20
☐ 89 Vinnie Johnson 4.00 2.00 .40
☐ 90 Bill Laimbeer 7.00 3.50 .70
☐ 91 Cliff Levingston 8.00 4.00 .80
☐ 92 John Long 1.50 .75 .15
☐ 93 David Thirdkill 1.50 .75 .15
☐ 94 Isiah Thomas 150.00 75.00 15.00
☐ 95 Ray Tolbert 2.50 1.25 .25
☐ 96 Terry Tyler 1.50 .75 .15
☐ 97 Jim Paxson 2.00 1.00 .20
☐ 98 Kenny Carr 1.50 .75 .15
☐ 99 Wayne Cooper 1.50 .75 .15
☐ 100 Clyde Drexler 350.00 175.00 35.00
☐ 101 Jeff Lamp 2.00 1.00 .20
☐ 102 Lafayette Lever 8.00 4.00 .80
☐ 103 Calvin Natt 2.00 1.00 .20
☐ 104 Audie Norris 1.50 .75 .15
☐ 105 Tom Piotrowski 1.50 .75 .15
☐ 106 Mychal Thompson 3.00 1.50 .30
☐ 107 Darnell Valentine 2.00 1.00 .20
☐ 108 Pete Verhoeven 1.50 .75 .15
☐ 109 Walter Davis 3.00 1.50 .30
☐ 110 Alvan Adams 2.00 1.00 .20
☐ 111 James Edwards 3.00 1.50 .30
☐ 112 Rod Foster 2.00 1.00 .20
☐ 113 Maurice Lucas 3.00 1.50 .30
☐ 114 Kyle Macy 2.00 1.00 .20
☐ 115 Larry Nance 40.00 20.00 4.00
☐ 116 Charles Pittman 1.50 .75 .15
☐ 117 Rick Robey 2.00 1.00 .20
☐ 118 Mike Sanders 4.50 2.25 .45
☐ 119 Alvin Scott 1.50 .75 .15
☐ 120 Paul Westphal 3.00 1.50 .30
☐ 121 Bill Walton 9.00 4.50 .90
☐ 122 Michael Brooks 1.50 .75 .15
☐ 123 Terry Cummings 30.00 15.00 3.00
☐ 124 James Donaldson 3.50 1.75 .35
☐ 125 Craig Hodges 10.00 5.00 1.00
☐ 126 Greg Kelser 2.00 1.00 .20
☐ 127 Hank McDowell 1.50 .75 .15
☐ 128 Billy McKinney 2.00 1.00 .20
☐ 129 Norm Nixon 2.50 1.25 .25
☐ 130 Ricky Pierce 33.00 15.00 3.00
☐ 131 Derek Smith 3.00 1.50 .30
☐ 132 Jerome Whitehead 1.50 .75 .15
☐ 133 Adrian Dantley 5.50 2.75 .55
☐ 134 Mitch Anderson 1.50 .75 .15
☐ 135 Thurl Bailey 7.00 3.50 .70
☐ 136 Tom Boswell 1.50 .75 .15
☐ 137 John Drew 2.00 1.00 .20
☐ 138 Mark Eaton 9.00 4.50 .90
☐ 139 Jerry Eaves 1.50 .75 .15
☐ 140 Rickey Green 3.50 1.75 .35
☐ 141 Darrell Griffith 2.50 1.25 .25
☐ 142 Bobby Hansen 3.50 1.75 .35
☐ 143 Rich Kelley 1.50 .75 .15
☐ 144 Jeff Wilkins 1.50 .75 .15
☐ 145 Buck Williams 40.00 20.00 4.00
☐ 146 Otis Birdsong 2.00 1.00 .20
☐ 147 Darwin Cook 1.50 .75 .15
☐ 148 Darryl Dawkins 3.50 1.75 .35
☐ 149 Mike Gminski 2.50 1.25 .25
☐ 150 Reggie Johnson 1.50 .75 .15
☐ 151 Albert King 2.50 1.25 .25
☐ 152 Mike O'Koren 2.00 1.00 .20
☐ 153 Kelvin Ransey 1.50 .75 .15
☐ 154 M.R. Richardson 2.00 1.00 .20
☐ 155 Clarence Walker 1.50 .75 .15
☐ 156 Bill Willoughby 1.50 .75 .15
☐ 157 Steve Stipanovich 2.50 1.25 .25
☐ 158 Butch Carter 1.50 .75 .15
☐ 159 Edwin Leroy Combs 1.50 .75 .15
☐ 160 George L. Johnson 1.50 .75 .15
☐ 161 Clark Kellogg 3.00 1.50 .30
☐ 162 Sidney Lowe 2.50 1.25 .25
☐ 163 Kevin McKenna 1.50 .75 .15
☐ 164 Jerry Sichting 2.50 1.25 .25
☐ 165 Brook Steppe 1.50 .75 .15
☐ 166 Jimmy Thomas 1.50 .75 .15
☐ 167 Granville Waiters 1.50 .75 .15
☐ 168 Herb Williams 7.00 3.50 .70
☐ 169 Dave Corzine 1.50 .75 .15
☐ 170 Wallace Bryant 1.50 .75 .15
☐ 171 Quintin Dailey 2.50 1.25 .25
☐ 172 Sidney Green 2.50 1.25 .25
☐ 173 David Greenwood 1.50 .75 .15
☐ 174 Rod Higgins 3.50 1.75 .35
☐ 175 Clarence Johnson 1.50 .75 .15
☐ 176 Ronnie Lester 1.50 .75 .15
☐ 177 Jawann Oldham 1.50 .75 .15
☐ 178 Ennis Whatley 3.00 1.50 .30
☐ 179 Mitchell Wiggins 2.50 1.25 .25
☐ 180 Orlando Woolridge 20.00 10.00 2.00
☐ 181 Kiki Vandeweghe 9.00 4.50 .90
☐ 182 Richard Anderson 2.00 1.00 .20
☐ 183 Howard Carter 1.50 .75 .15
☐ 184 T.R. Dunn 1.50 .75 .15
☐ 185 Keith Edmonson 1.50 .75 .15
☐ 186 Alex English 9.00 4.50 .90
☐ 187 Mike Evans 1.50 .75 .15
☐ 188 Bill Hanzlik 3.00 1.50 .30
☐ 189 Dan Issel 7.00 3.50 .70
☐ 190 Anthony Roberts 1.50 .75 .15
☐ 191 Danny Schayes 7.00 3.50 .70
☐ 192 Rob Williams 1.50 .75 .15

No.	Player	MINT	EXC	G-VG
193	Jack Sikma	3.50	1.75	.35
194	Fred Brown	2.00	1.00	.20
195	Tom Chambers	60.00	30.00	6.00
196	Steve Hawes	1.50	.75	.15
197	Steve Hayes	1.50	.75	.15
198	Reggie King	1.50	.75	.15
199	Scooter McCray	2.00	1.00	.20
200	Jon Sundvold	2.50	1.25	.25
201	Danny Vranes	2.00	1.00	.20
202	Gus Williams	2.00	1.00	.20
203	Al Wood	2.00	1.00	.20
204	Jeff Ruland	3.50	1.75	.35
205	Greg Ballard	1.50	.75	.15
206	Charles Davis	1.50	.75	.15
207	Darren Daye	2.00	1.00	.20
208	Michael Gibson	1.50	.75	.15
209	Frank Johnson	1.50	.75	.15
210	Joe Kopicki	1.50	.75	.15
211	Rick Mahorn	2.50	1.25	.25
212	Jeff Malone	35.00	17.50	3.50
213	Tom McMillen	4.25	2.10	.42
214	Ricky Sobers	1.50	.75	.15
215	Bryan Warrick	1.50	.75	.15
216	Billy Knight	1.50	.75	.15
217	Don Buse	1.50	.75	.15
218	Larry Drew	2.50	1.25	.25
219	Eddie Johnson	17.00	8.50	1.70
220	Joe Meriweather	1.50	.75	.15
221	Larry Micheaux	1.50	.75	.15
222	Ed Nealy	3.00	1.50	.30
223	Mark Olberding	1.50	.75	.15
224	Dave Robisch	1.50	.75	.15
225	Reggie Theus	3.50	1.75	.35
226	LaSalle Thompson	4.00	2.00	.40
227	Mike Woodson	2.00	1.00	.20
228	World B. Free	3.00	1.50	.30
229	John Bagley	9.00	4.50	.90
230	Jeff Cook	1.50	.75	.15
231	Geoff Crompton	1.50	.75	.15
232	John Garris	1.50	.75	.15
233	Stewart Granger	1.50	.75	.15
234	Roy Hinson	3.00	1.50	.30
235	Phil Hubbard	1.50	.75	.15
236	Geoff Huston	1.50	.75	.15
237	Ben Poquette	1.50	.75	.15
238	Cliff Robinson	2.00	1.00	.20
239	Lonnie Shelton	1.50	.75	.15
240	Paul Thompson	1.50	.75	.15
241	George Gervin	8.00	4.00	.80
242	Gene Banks	1.50	.75	.15
243	Ron Brewer	1.50	.75	.15
244	Artis Gilmore	5.50	2.75	.55
245	Edgar Jones	1.50	.75	.15
246	John Lucas	2.50	1.25	.25
247A	Mike Mitchell ERR (Photo actually Mark McNamara)	6.00	3.00	.60
247B	Mike Mitchell COR	2.00	1.00	.20
248A	Mark McNamara ERR (Photo actually Mike Mitchell)	6.00	3.00	.60
248B	Mark McNamara COR	2.00	1.00	.20
249	Johnny Moore	2.00	1.00	.20
250	John Paxson	25.00	12.50	2.50
251	Fred Roberts	6.00	3.00	.60
252	Joe Barry Carroll	2.00	1.00	.20
253	Mike Bratz	1.50	.75	.15
254	Don Collins	1.50	.75	.15
255	Lester Conner	1.50	.75	.15
256	Chris Engler	1.50	.75	.15
257	Sleepy Floyd	7.00	3.50	.70
258	Wallace Johnson	1.50	.75	.15
259	Pace Mannion	1.50	.75	.15
260	Purvis Short	2.00	1.00	.20
261	Larry Smith	2.00	1.00	.20
262	Darren Tillis	1.50	.75	.15
263	Dominique Wilkins	150.00	75.00	15.00
264	Rickey Brown	1.50	.75	.15
265	Johnny Davis	1.50	.75	.15
266	Mike Glenn	1.50	.75	.15
267	Scott Hastings	2.50	1.25	.25
268	Eddie Johnson	1.50	.75	.15
269	Mark Landsberger	1.50	.75	.15
270	Billy Paultz	1.50	.75	.15
271	Doc Rivers	12.00	6.00	1.20
272	Tree Rollins	2.00	1.00	.20
273	Dan Roundfield	2.00	1.00	.20
274	Sly Williams	1.50	.75	.15
275	Randy Wittman	2.50	1.25	.25

1984-85 Star NBA

This set of 288 cards was issued in three series during the first five months of 1985 by the Star Company. The set features players by team throughout the NBA. Cards measure 2 1/2" by 3 1/2" and have a colored border around the fronts of the cards according to the team with corresponding color printing on the backs. Card are organized numerically by team, i.e., Boston Celtics (1-12), Los Angeles Clippers (13-24), New York Knicks (25-37), Phoenix Suns (38-51), Indiana Pacers (52-63), San Antonio Spurs (64-75), Atlanta Hawks (76-87), New Jersey Nets (88-100), Chicago Bulls (101-112), Seattle Supersonics (113-124), Milwaukee Bucks (125-136), Denver Nuggets (137-148), Golden State Warriors (149-160), Portland Trail Blazers (161-171), Los Angeles Lakers (172-184), Washington Bullets (185-194), Philadelphia 76ers (201-212), Cleveland Cavaliers (213-224), Utah Jazz (225-236), Houston Rockets (237-249), Dallas Mavericks (250-260), Detroit Pistons (261-269), and Sacramento Kings (270-280). The set also features a special subseries (195-200) honoring Gold Medal-winning players from the 1984 Olympic basketball competition as well as a subseries of NBA specials (281-288). The key extended rookies cards in this set are Charles Barkley, Michael Jordan, Hakeem Olajuwon and John Stockton.

No.	Player	MINT	EXC	G-VG
	COMPLETE SET (288)	4000.00	1800.00	500.00
	COMMON PLAYER (1-288)	1.50	.75	.15
1	Larry Bird	75.00	37.50	7.50
2	Danny Ainge	8.50	4.25	.85
3	Quinn Buckner	2.50	1.25	.25
4	Rick Carlisle	2.00	1.00	.20
5	M.L. Carr	2.00	1.00	.20
6	Dennis Johnson	4.50	2.25	.45
7	Greg Kite	2.00	1.00	.20
8	Cedric Maxwell	2.50	1.25	.25
9	Kevin McHale	12.00	6.00	1.20
10	Robert Parish	15.00	7.50	1.50
11	Scott Wedman	2.00	1.00	.20
12	Larry Bird 1983-84 NBA MVP	35.00	17.50	3.50
13	Marques Johnson	3.00	1.50	.30
14	Junior Bridgeman	2.00	1.00	.20
15	Michael Cage	8.00	4.00	.80
16	Harvey Catchings	1.50	.75	.15
17	James Donaldson	2.00	1.00	.20
18	Lancaster Gordon	2.00	1.00	.20
19	Jay Murphy	1.50	.75	.15
20	Norm Nixon	2.50	1.25	.25
21	Derek Smith	2.00	1.00	.20
22	Bill Walton	7.50	3.75	.75
23	Bryan Warrick	1.50	.75	.15
24	Rory White	1.50	.75	.15
25	Bernard King	7.00	3.50	.70
26	James Bailey	1.50	.75	.15
27	Ken Bannister	1.50	.75	.15
28	Butch Carter	1.50	.75	.15
29	Bill Cartwright	5.50	2.75	.55
30	Pat Cummings	2.00	1.00	.20
31	Ernie Grunfeld	2.00	1.00	.20
32	Louis Orr	1.50	.75	.15
33	Leonard Robinson	2.00	1.00	.20
34	Rory Sparrow	2.00	1.00	.20

☐	35	Trent Tucker	2.00	1.00	.20
☐	36	Darrell Walker	2.50	1.25	.25
☐	37	Eddie Lee Wilkins	2.00	1.00	.20
☐	38	Alvan Adams	2.00	1.00	.20
☐	39	Walter Davis	2.50	1.25	.25
☐	40	James Edwards	2.50	1.25	.25
☐	41	Rod Foster	1.50	.75	.15
☐	42	Michael Holton	2.00	1.00	.20
☐	43	Jay Humphries	8.00	4.00	.80
☐	44	Charles Jones	1.50	.75	.15
☐	45	Maurice Lucas	2.50	1.25	.25
☐	46	Kyle Macy	2.00	1.00	.20
☐	47	Larry Nance	14.00	7.00	1.40
☐	48	Charles Pittman	1.50	.75	.15
☐	49	Rick Robey	2.00	1.00	.20
☐	50	Mike Sanders	3.00	1.50	.30
☐	51	Alvin Scott	1.50	.75	.15
☐	52	Clark Kellogg	2.50	1.25	.25
☐	53	Tony Brown	1.75	.85	.17
☐	54	Devin Durrant	1.75	.85	.17
☐	55	Vern Fleming	7.50	3.75	.75
☐	56	Bill Garnett	1.75	.85	.17
☐	57	Stuart Gray UER (Photo actually Tony Brown)	2.50	1.25	.25
☐	58	Jerry Sichting	2.50	1.25	.25
☐	59	Terence Stansbury	2.50	1.25	.25
☐	60	Steve Stipanovich	2.50	1.25	.25
☐	61	Jimmy Thomas	1.75	.85	.17
☐	62	Granville Waiters	1.75	.85	.17
☐	63	Herb Williams	3.00	1.50	.30
☐	64	Artis Gilmore	4.50	2.25	.45
☐	65	Gene Banks	1.50	.75	.15
☐	66	Ron Brewer	1.50	.75	.15
☐	67	George Gervin	6.50	3.25	.65
☐	68	Edgar Jones	1.50	.75	.15
☐	69	Ozell Jones	1.50	.75	.15
☐	70	Mark McNamara	1.50	.75	.15
☐	71	Mike Mitchell	1.50	.75	.15
☐	72	Johnny Moore	1.50	.75	.15
☐	73	John Paxson	10.00	5.00	1.00
☐	74	Fred Roberts	2.50	1.25	.25
☐	75	Alvin Robertson	20.00	10.00	2.00
☐	76	Dominique Wilkins	50.00	25.00	5.00
☐	77	Rickey Brown	1.50	.75	.15
☐	78	Antoine Carr	10.00	5.00	1.00
☐	79	Mike Glenn	1.50	.75	.15
☐	80	Scott Hastings	2.00	1.00	.20
☐	81	Eddie Johnson	1.50	.75	.15
☐	82	Cliff Levingston	3.00	1.50	.30
☐	83	Leo Rautins	1.50	.75	.15
☐	84	Doc Rivers	5.00	2.50	.50
☐	85	Tree Rollins	2.00	1.00	.20
☐	86	Randy Wittman	1.50	.75	.15
☐	87	Sly Williams	1.50	.75	.15
☐	88	Darryl Dawkins	3.00	1.50	.30
☐	89	Otis Birdsong	2.00	1.00	.20
☐	90	Darwin Cook	1.50	.75	.15
☐	91	Mike Gminski	2.00	1.00	.20
☐	92	George L. Johnson	1.50	.75	.15
☐	93	Albert King	1.50	.75	.15
☐	94	Mike O'Koren	1.50	.75	.15
☐	95	Kelvin Ransey	1.50	.75	.15
☐	96	M.R. Richardson	2.00	1.00	.20
☐	97	Wayne Sappleton	1.50	.75	.15
☐	98	Jeff Turner	2.50	1.25	.25
☐	99	Buck Williams	16.00	8.00	1.60
☐	100	Michael Wilson	1.50	.75	.15
☐	101	Michael Jordan	2000.00	800.00	250.00
☐	102	Dave Corzine	1.50	.75	.15
☐	103	Quintin Dailey	1.50	.75	.15
☐	104	Sidney Green	1.50	.75	.15
☐	105	David Greenwood	1.50	.75	.15
☐	106	Rod Higgins	2.00	1.00	.20
☐	107	Steve Johnson	2.00	1.00	.20
☐	108	Caldwell Jones	2.00	1.00	.20
☐	109	Wes Matthews	1.50	.75	.15
☐	110	Jawann Oldham	1.50	.75	.15
☐	111	Ennis Whatley	2.50	1.25	.25
☐	112	Orlando Woolridge	6.50	3.25	.65
☐	113	Tom Chambers	20.00	10.00	2.00
☐	114	Cory Blackwell	2.00	1.00	.20
☐	115	Frank Brickowski	4.50	2.25	.45
☐	116	Gerald Henderson	1.50	.75	.15
☐	117	Reggie King	1.50	.75	.15
☐	118	Tim McCormick	2.50	1.25	.25
☐	119	John Schweitz	1.50	.75	.15
☐	120	Jack Sikma	2.50	1.25	.25
☐	121	Ricky Sobers	1.50	.75	.15
☐	122	Jon Sundvold	1.50	.75	.15
☐	123	Danny Vranes	1.50	.75	.15
☐	124	Al Wood	1.50	.75	.15
☐	125	Terry Cummings UER (Robert Cummings on card back)	11.00	5.50	1.10
☐	126	Randy Breuer	2.00	1.00	.20
☐	127	Charles Davis	1.50	.75	.15
☐	128	Mike Dunleavy	3.50	1.75	.35
☐	129	Kenny Fields	2.00	1.00	.20
☐	130	Kevin Grevey	1.50	.75	.15
☐	131	Craig Hodges	4.00	2.00	.40
☐	132	Alton Lister	2.00	1.00	.20
☐	133	Larry Micheaux	1.50	.75	.15
☐	134	Paul Mokeski	1.50	.75	.15
☐	135	Sidney Moncrief	4.00	2.00	.40
☐	136	Paul Pressey	2.50	1.25	.25
☐	137	Alex English	6.00	3.00	.60
☐	138	Wayne Cooper	1.50	.75	.15
☐	139	T.R. Dunn	1.50	.75	.15
☐	140	Mike Evans	1.50	.75	.15
☐	141	Bill Hanzlik	2.00	1.00	.20
☐	142	Dan Issel	6.00	3.00	.60
☐	143	Joe Kopicki	1.50	.75	.15
☐	144	Lafayette Lever	2.50	1.25	.25
☐	145	Calvin Natt	2.00	1.00	.20
☐	146	Danny Schayes	2.50	1.25	.25
☐	147	Elston Turner	1.50	.75	.15
☐	148	Willie White	1.50	.75	.15
☐	149	Purvis Short	2.00	1.00	.20
☐	150	Chuck Aleksinas	1.50	.75	.15
☐	151	Mike Bratz	1.50	.75	.15
☐	152	Steve Burtt	1.50	.75	.15
☐	153	Lester Conner	1.50	.75	.15
☐	154	Sleepy Floyd	3.00	1.50	.30
☐	155	Mickey Johnson	1.50	.75	.15
☐	156	Gary Plummer	1.50	.75	.15
☐	157	Larry Smith	2.00	1.00	.20
☐	158	Peter Thibeaux	1.50	.75	.15
☐	159	Jerome Whitehead	1.50	.75	.15
☐	160	Othell Wilson	1.50	.75	.15
☐	161	Kiki Vandeweghe	3.00	1.50	.30
☐	162	Sam Bowie	11.00	5.50	1.10
☐	163	Kenny Carr	1.50	.75	.15
☐	164	Steve Colter	2.00	1.00	.20
☐	165	Clyde Drexler	110.00	55.00	11.00
☐	166	Audie Norris	1.50	.75	.15
☐	167	Jim Paxson	1.50	.75	.15
☐	168	Tom Scheffler	1.50	.75	.15
☐	169	Bernard Thompson	1.50	.75	.15
☐	170	Mychal Thompson	2.50	1.25	.25
☐	171	Darnell Valentine	1.50	.75	.15
☐	172	Magic Johnson	110.00	55.00	11.00
☐	173	Kareem Abdul-Jabbar	30.00	15.00	3.00
☐	174	Michael Cooper	3.00	1.50	.30
☐	175	Earl Jones	1.50	.75	.15
☐	176	Mitch Kupchak	2.00	1.00	.20
☐	177	Ronnie Lester	1.50	.75	.15
☐	178	Bob McAdoo	4.50	2.25	.45
☐	179	Mike McGee	1.50	.75	.15
☐	180	Kurt Rambis	3.25	1.60	.32
☐	181	Byron Scott	8.00	4.00	.80
☐	182	Larry Spriggs	1.50	.75	.15
☐	183	Jamaal Wilkes	2.50	1.25	.25
☐	184	James Worthy	35.00	17.50	3.50
☐	185	Gus Williams	2.50	1.25	.25
☐	186	Greg Ballard	1.50	.75	.15
☐	187	Dudley Bradley	1.50	.75	.15
☐	188	Darren Daye	1.50	.75	.15
☐	189	Frank Johnson	1.50	.75	.15
☐	190	Charles Jones	1.50	.75	.15
☐	191	Rick Mahorn	2.00	1.00	.20
☐	192	Jeff Malone	14.00	7.00	1.40
☐	193	Tom McMillen	3.50	1.75	.35
☐	194	Jeff Ruland	2.50	1.25	.25
☐	195	Michael Jordan	450.00	225.00	45.00
☐	196	Vern Fleming	3.50	1.75	.35
☐	197	Sam Perkins	12.00	6.00	1.20
☐	198	Alvin Robertson	8.00	4.00	.80
☐	199	Jeff Turner	2.00	1.00	.20
☐	200	Leon Wood	2.00	1.00	.20
☐	201	Moses Malone	12.50	6.25	1.25
☐	202	Charles Barkley	225.00	110.00	22.00
☐	203	Maurice Cheeks	4.50	2.25	.45
☐	204	Julius Erving	30.00	15.00	3.00
☐	205	Clemon Johnson	1.50	.75	.15
☐	206	George Johnson	1.50	.75	.15
☐	207	Bobby Jones	2.50	1.25	.25
☐	208	Clint Richardson	1.50	.75	.15
☐	209	Sedale Threatt	6.50	3.25	.65
☐	210	Andrew Toney	2.50	1.25	.25
☐	211	Sam Williams	1.50	.75	.15
☐	212	Leon Wood	2.00	1.00	.20
☐	213	Mel Turpin	2.50	1.25	.25
☐	214	Ron Anderson	7.50	3.75	.75
☐	215	John Bagley	2.50	1.25	.25
☐	216	Johnny Davis	1.50	.75	.15
☐	217	World B. Free	2.50	1.25	.25
☐	218	Roy Hinson	2.00	1.00	.20

	MINT	EXC	G-VG
☐ 219 Phil Hubbard	1.50	.75	.15
☐ 220 Edgar Jones	1.50	.75	.15
☐ 221 Ben Poquette	1.50	.75	.15
☐ 222 Lonnie Shelton	1.50	.75	.15
☐ 223 Mark West	2.50	1.25	.25
☐ 224 Kevin Williams	1.50	.75	.15
☐ 225 Mark Eaton	3.50	1.75	.35
☐ 226 Mitchell Anderson	1.50	.75	.15
☐ 227 Thurl Bailey	2.50	1.25	.25
☐ 228 Adrian Dantley	4.50	2.25	.45
☐ 229 Rickey Green	2.00	1.00	.20
☐ 230 Darrell Griffith	2.50	1.25	.25
☐ 231 Rich Kelley	1.50	.75	.15
☐ 232 Pace Mannion	1.50	.75	.15
☐ 233 Billy Paultz	1.50	.75	.15
☐ 234 Fred Roberts	2.50	1.25	.25
☐ 235 John Stockton	225.00	110.00	22.00
☐ 236 Jeff Wilkins	1.50	.75	.15
☐ 237 Hakeem Olajuwon	160.00	80.00	16.00
☐ 238 Craig Ehlo	18.00	9.00	1.80
☐ 239 Lionel Hollins	1.50	.75	.15
☐ 240 Allen Leavell	1.50	.75	.15
☐ 241 Lewis Lloyd	1.50	.75	.15
☐ 242 John Lucas	2.00	1.00	.20
☐ 243 Rodney McCray	2.50	1.25	.25
☐ 244 Hank McDowell	1.50	.75	.15
☐ 245 Larry Micheaux	1.50	.75	.15
☐ 246 Jim Peterson	3.00	1.50	.30
☐ 247 Robert Reid	1.50	.75	.15
☐ 248 Ralph Sampson	2.50	1.25	.25
☐ 249 Mitchell Wiggins	1.50	.75	.15
☐ 250 Mark Aguirre	6.00	3.00	.60
☐ 251 Rolando Blackman	9.00	4.50	.90
☐ 252 Wallace Bryant	1.50	.75	.15
☐ 253 Brad Davis	2.50	1.25	.25
☐ 254 Dale Ellis	4.50	2.25	.45
☐ 255 Derek Harper	7.00	3.50	.70
☐ 256 Kurt Nimphius	1.50	.75	.15
☐ 257 Sam Perkins	30.00	15.00	3.00
☐ 258 Charlie Sitton	1.50	.75	.15
☐ 259 Tom Sluby	1.50	.75	.15
☐ 260 Jay Vincent	2.00	1.00	.20
☐ 261 Isiah Thomas	50.00	25.00	5.00
☐ 262 Kent Benson	2.00	1.00	.20
☐ 263 Earl Cureton	1.50	.75	.15
☐ 264 Vinnie Johnson	3.00	1.50	.30
☐ 265 Bill Laimbeer	6.00	3.00	.60
☐ 266 John Long	1.50	.75	.15
☐ 267 Dan Roundfield	2.00	1.00	.20
☐ 268 Kelly Tripucka	2.00	1.00	.20
☐ 269 Terry Tyler	1.50	.75	.15
☐ 270 Reggie Theus	2.50	1.25	.25
☐ 271 Don Buse	1.50	.75	.15
☐ 272 Larry Drew	2.00	1.00	.20
☐ 273 Eddie Johnson	6.50	3.25	.65
☐ 274 Billy Knight	1.50	.75	.15
☐ 275 Joe Meriweather	1.50	.75	.15
☐ 276 Mark Olberding	1.50	.75	.15
☐ 277 LaSalle Thompson	2.50	1.25	.25
☐ 278 Otis Thorpe	25.00	12.50	2.50
☐ 279 Pete Verhoeven	1.50	.75	.15
☐ 280 Mike Woodson	2.00	1.00	.20
☐ 281 Julius Erving	20.00	10.00	2.00
☐ 282 Kareem Abdul-Jabbar	20.00	10.00	2.00
☐ 283 Dan Issel	4.00	2.00	.40
☐ 284 Bernard King	4.00	2.00	.40
☐ 285 Moses Malone	6.00	3.00	.60
☐ 286 Mark Eaton	2.50	1.25	.25
☐ 287 Isiah Thomas	22.00	11.00	2.20
☐ 288 Michael Jordan	450.00	225.00	45.00

1985-86 Star NBA

This 172-card set was produced by the Star Company and features players in the NBA. Cards are numbered in team order and measure the standard 2 1/2" by 3 1/2". The team ordering is as follows, Philadelphia 76ers (1-9), Detroit Pistons (10-17), Houston Rockets (18-25), Los Angeles Lakers (26-33), Phoenix Suns (34-41), Atlanta Hawks (42-49), Denver Nuggets (50-57), New Jersey Nets (58-65), Seattle Supersonics (66-73), Sacramento Kings (74-80), Indiana Pacers (81-87), Los Angeles Clippers (88-94), Boston Celtics (95-102), Portland Trail Blazers (103-109), Washington Bullets (110-116), Chicago Bulls (117-123), Milwaukee Bucks (124-130), Golden State Warriors (131-136), Utah Jazz (137-144), San Antonio Spurs (145-151), Cleveland Cavaliers (152-158), Dallas Mavericks (159-165), and New York Knicks (166-172). Players on each team have the same color border on the front. Cards were issued in two series, 1-94 and 95-172. Card backs are very similar to the other Star basketball sets except that the player statistics go up through the 1984-85 season. The key extended rookie cards in this set are Patrick Ewing, Jerome Kersey, and Kevin Willis.

	MINT	EXC	G-VG
COMPLETE SET (172)	1500.00	650.00	175.00
COMMON PLAYER (1-172)	1.50	.75	.15
☐ 1 Maurice Cheeks	3.50	1.75	.35
☐ 2 Charles Barkley	75.00	37.50	7.50
☐ 3 Julius Erving	25.00	12.50	2.50
☐ 4 Clemon Johnson	1.50	.75	.15
☐ 5 Bobby Jones	2.50	1.25	.25
☐ 6 Moses Malone	9.00	4.50	.90
☐ 7 Sedale Threatt	4.50	2.25	.45
☐ 8 Andrew Toney	2.50	1.25	.25
☐ 9 Leon Wood	1.50	.75	.15
☐ 10 Isiah Thomas UER (No Pistons logo on card front)	35.00	17.50	3.50
☐ 11 Kent Benson	2.00	1.00	.20
☐ 12 Earl Cureton	1.50	.75	.15
☐ 13 Vinnie Johnson	2.50	1.25	.25
☐ 14 Bill Laimbeer	4.00	2.00	.40
☐ 15 John Long	1.50	.75	.15
☐ 16 Rick Mahorn	2.00	1.00	.20
☐ 17 Kelly Tripucka	2.00	1.00	.20
☐ 18 Hakeem Olajuwon	50.00	25.00	5.00
☐ 19 Allen Leavell	1.50	.75	.15
☐ 20 Lewis Lloyd	1.50	.75	.15
☐ 21 John Lucas	2.00	1.00	.20
☐ 22 Rodney McCray	2.00	1.00	.20
☐ 23 Robert Reid	1.50	.75	.15
☐ 24 Ralph Sampson	2.50	1.25	.25
☐ 25 Mitchell Wiggins	1.50	.75	.15
☐ 26 Kareem Abdul-Jabbar	30.00	15.00	3.00
☐ 27 Michael Cooper	3.00	1.50	.30
☐ 28 Magic Johnson	120.00	60.00	12.00
☐ 29 Mitch Kupchak	1.75	.85	.17
☐ 30 Maurice Lucas	2.50	1.25	.25
☐ 31 Kurt Rambis	2.75	1.35	.27
☐ 32 Byron Scott	6.00	3.00	.60
☐ 33 James Worthy	30.00	15.00	3.00
☐ 34 Larry Nance	11.00	5.50	1.10
☐ 35 Alvan Adams	2.00	1.00	.20
☐ 36 Walter Davis	2.50	1.25	.25
☐ 37 James Edwards	2.50	1.25	.25
☐ 38 Jay Humphries	3.00	1.50	.30
☐ 39 Charles Pittman	1.50	.75	.15
☐ 40 Rick Robey	2.00	1.00	.20
☐ 41 Mike Sanders	2.50	1.25	.25
☐ 42 Dominique Wilkins	35.00	17.50	3.50
☐ 43 Scott Hastings	2.00	1.00	.20
☐ 44 Eddie Johnson	1.50	.75	.15
☐ 45 Cliff Levingston	2.50	1.25	.25
☐ 46 Tree Rollins	2.00	1.00	.20
☐ 47 Doc Rivers	3.50	1.75	.35
☐ 48 Kevin Willis	27.00	13.50	2.70
☐ 49 Randy Wittman	2.00	1.00	.20
☐ 50 Alex English	4.00	2.00	.40
☐ 51 Wayne Cooper	1.50	.75	.15
☐ 52 T.R. Dunn	1.50	.75	.15
☐ 53 Mike Evans	1.50	.75	.15
☐ 54 Lafayette Lever	2.50	1.25	.25
☐ 55 Calvin Natt	2.00	1.00	.20

☐ 56	Danny Schayes	2.00	1.00	.20
☐ 57	Elston Turner	1.50	.75	.15
☐ 58	Buck Williams	12.00	6.00	1.20
☐ 59	Otis Birdsong	1.50	.75	.15
☐ 60	Darwin Cook	1.50	.75	.15
☐ 61	Darryl Dawkins	2.50	1.25	.25
☐ 62	Mike Gminski	2.00	1.00	.20
☐ 63	Mickey Johnson	1.50	.75	.15
☐ 64	Mike O'Koren	1.50	.75	.15
☐ 65	Micheal R. Richardson	2.00	1.00	.20
☐ 66	Tom Chambers	16.00	8.00	1.60
☐ 67	Gerald Henderson	2.00	1.00	.20
☐ 68	Tim McCormick	2.00	1.00	.20
☐ 69	Jack Sikma	2.50	1.25	.25
☐ 70	Ricky Sobers	1.50	.75	.15
☐ 71	Danny Vranes	1.50	.75	.15
☐ 72	Al Wood	1.50	.75	.15
☐ 73	Danny Young	3.00	1.50	.30
☐ 74	Reggie Theus	2.50	1.25	.25
☐ 75	Larry Drew	2.00	1.00	.20
☐ 76	Eddie Johnson	4.50	2.25	.45
☐ 77	Mark Olberding	1.50	.75	.15
☐ 78	LaSalle Thompson	2.50	1.25	.25
☐ 79	Otis Thorpe	9.00	4.50	.90
☐ 80	Mike Woodson	1.50	.75	.15
☐ 81	Clark Kellogg	2.00	1.00	.20
☐ 82	Quinn Buckner	2.00	1.00	.20
☐ 83	Vern Fleming	2.50	1.25	.25
☐ 84	Bill Garnett	1.50	.75	.15
☐ 85	Terence Stansbury	1.50	.75	.15
☐ 86	Steve Stipanovich	2.00	1.00	.20
☐ 87	Herb Williams	2.50	1.25	.25
☐ 88	Marques Johnson	2.50	1.25	.25
☐ 89	Michael Cage	2.50	1.25	.25
☐ 90	Franklin Edwards	1.50	.75	.15
☐ 91	Cedric Maxwell	2.50	1.25	.25
☐ 92	Derek Smith	2.00	1.00	.20
☐ 93	Rory White	1.50	.75	.15
☐ 94	Jamaal Wilkes	2.50	1.25	.25
☐ 95A	Larry Bird (Green border)	55.00	27.50	5.50
☐ 95B	Larry Bird (White border)	55.00	27.50	5.50
☐ 96A	Danny Ainge (Green border)	7.00	3.50	.70
☐ 96B	Danny Ainge (White border)	7.00	3.50	.70
☐ 97A	Dennis Johnson (Green border)	3.50	1.75	.35
☐ 97B	Dennis Johnson (White border)	3.50	1.75	.35
☐ 98A	Kevin McHale (Green border)	10.00	5.00	1.00
☐ 98B	Kevin McHale (White border)	10.00	5.00	1.00
☐ 99A	Robert Parish ERR (Green border; no number on back)	12.00	6.00	1.20
☐ 99B	Robert Parish COR (White border)	12.00	6.00	1.20
☐ 100A	Jerry Sichting (Green border)	1.50	.75	.15
☐ 100B	Jerry Sichting (White border)	1.50	.75	.15
☐ 101A	Bill Walton (Green border)	6.50	3.25	.65
☐ 101B	Bill Walton (White border)	6.50	3.25	.65
☐ 102A	Scott Wedman (Green border)	2.00	1.00	.20
☐ 102B	Scott Wedman (White border)	2.00	1.00	.20
☐ 103	Kiki Vandeweghe	2.50	1.25	.25
☐ 104	Sam Bowie	4.00	2.00	.40
☐ 105	Kenny Carr	1.50	.75	.15
☐ 106	Clyde Drexler	90.00	45.00	9.00
☐ 107	Jerome Kersey	36.00	18.00	3.60
☐ 108	Jim Paxson	1.50	.75	.15
☐ 109	Mychal Thompson	2.50	1.25	.25
☐ 110	Gus Williams	2.00	1.00	.20
☐ 111	Darren Daye	1.50	.75	.15
☐ 112	Jeff Malone	11.00	5.50	1.10
☐ 113	Tom McMillen	3.00	1.50	.30
☐ 114	Cliff Robinson	1.50	.75	.15
☐ 115	Dan Roundfield	2.00	1.00	.20
☐ 116	Jeff Ruland	2.50	1.25	.25
☐ 117	Michael Jordan	600.00	300.00	60.00
☐ 118	Gene Banks	1.50	.75	.15
☐ 119	Dave Corzine	1.50	.75	.15
☐ 120	Quintin Dailey	1.50	.75	.15
☐ 121	George Gervin	6.00	3.00	.60
☐ 122	Jawann Oldham	1.50	.75	.15
☐ 123	Orlando Woolridge	4.00	2.00	.40
☐ 124	Terry Cummings	9.00	4.50	.90
☐ 125	Craig Hodges	3.50	1.75	.35
☐ 126	Alton Lister	1.50	.75	.15
☐ 127	Paul Mokeski	1.50	.75	.15
☐ 128	Sidney Moncrief	3.50	1.75	.35
☐ 129	Ricky Pierce	9.00	4.50	.90
☐ 130	Paul Pressey	2.50	1.25	.25
☐ 131	Purvis Short	2.00	1.00	.20
☐ 132	Joe Barry Carroll	2.00	1.00	.20
☐ 133	Lester Conner	1.50	.75	.15
☐ 134	Sleepy Floyd	2.50	1.25	.25
☐ 135	Geoff Huston	1.50	.75	.15
☐ 136	Larry Smith	2.00	1.00	.20
☐ 137	Jerome Whitehead	1.50	.75	.15
☐ 138	Adrian Dantley	3.00	1.50	.30
☐ 139	Mitchell Anderson	1.50	.75	.15
☐ 140	Thurl Bailey	2.00	1.00	.20
☐ 141	Mark Eaton	3.00	1.50	.30
☐ 142	Rickey Green	2.00	1.00	.20
☐ 143	Darrell Griffith	2.50	1.25	.25
☐ 144	John Stockton	75.00	37.50	7.50
☐ 145	Artis Gilmore	4.00	2.00	.40
☐ 146	Marc Iavaroni	1.50	.75	.15
☐ 147	Steve Johnson	1.50	.75	.15
☐ 148	Mike Mitchell	1.50	.75	.15
☐ 149	Johnny Moore	1.50	.75	.15
☐ 150	Alvin Robertson	5.00	2.50	.50
☐ 151	Jon Sundvold	1.50	.75	.15
☐ 152	World B. Free	2.50	1.25	.25
☐ 153	John Bagley	2.50	1.25	.25
☐ 154	Johnny Davis	1.50	.75	.15
☐ 155	Roy Hinson	2.00	1.00	.20
☐ 156	Phil Hubbard	1.50	.75	.15
☐ 157	Ben Poquette	1.50	.75	.15
☐ 158	Mel Turpin	2.00	1.00	.20
☐ 159	Rolando Blackman	7.00	3.50	.70
☐ 160	Mark Aguirre	4.00	2.00	.40
☐ 161	Brad Davis	2.00	1.00	.20
☐ 162	Dale Ellis	4.00	2.00	.40
☐ 163	Derek Harper	5.00	2.50	.50
☐ 164	Sam Perkins	10.00	5.00	1.00
☐ 165	Jay Vincent	2.00	1.00	.20
☐ 166	Patrick Ewing	240.00	100.00	20.00
☐ 167	Bill Cartwright	4.00	2.00	.40
☐ 168	Pat Cummings	1.50	.75	.15
☐ 169	Ernie Grunfeld	2.00	1.00	.20
☐ 170	Rory Sparrow	1.50	.75	.15
☐ 171	Trent Tucker	1.50	.75	.15
☐ 172	Darrell Walker	2.00	1.00	.20

1983 Star All-Star Game

This was the first NBA set issued by the Star Company. The set contains 30 cards measuring 2 1/2" by 3 1/2". The cards have a blue border on the front of each card and blue print is used on the back of each card. The set commemorates the 1983 NBA All-Star Game held in Los Angeles. Many of the cards feature players in their special all-star uniforms. There are two unnumbered cards in the set listed at the end of the list below. The cards are numbered on the backs with the order of the numbering essentially alphabetical according to the name of the subject. The set features the first professional card of Isiah Thomas.

	MINT	EXC	G-VG
COMPLETE SET (32)	80.00	40.00	8.00

COMMON PLAYER (1-30)	1.50	.75	.15
☐ 1 Checklist (Julius Erving on front)	7.50	3.75	.75
☐ 2 Larry Bird	18.00	9.00	1.80
☐ 3 Maurice Cheeks	2.25	1.10	.22
☐ 4 Julius Erving	10.00	5.00	1.00
☐ 5 Marques Johnson	2.25	1.10	.22
☐ 6 Bill Laimbeer	3.50	1.75	.35
☐ 7 Moses Malone	4.50	2.25	.45
☐ 8 Sidney Moncrief	2.25	1.10	.22
☐ 9 Robert Parish	4.50	2.25	.45
☐ 10 Reggie Theus	2.25	1.10	.22
☐ 11 Isiah Thomas	30.00	15.00	3.00
☐ 12 Andrew Toney	1.50	.75	.15
☐ 13 Buck Williams	7.50	3.75	.75
☐ 14 Kareem Abdul-Jabbar	10.00	5.00	1.00
☐ 15 Alex English	3.00	1.50	.30
☐ 16 George Gervin	3.00	1.50	.30
☐ 17 Artis Gilmore	3.00	1.50	.30
☐ 18 Magic Johnson	25.00	12.50	2.50
☐ 19 Maurice Lucas	1.50	.75	.15
☐ 20 Jim Paxson	1.50	.75	.15
☐ 21 Jack Sikma	1.50	.75	.15
☐ 22 David Thompson	2.25	1.10	.22
☐ 23 Kiki Vandeweghe	2.00	1.00	.20
☐ 24 Jamaal Wilkes	2.00	1.00	.20
☐ 25 Gus Williams	2.00	1.00	.20
☐ 26 All-Star MVPs (Dr. J, '77, '83)	6.00	3.00	.60
☐ 27 One Player, Single Game Records (Theus and Malone)	2.25	1.10	.22
☐ 28 All-Star All-Time Leaders (East Coast Line)	2.25	1.10	.22
☐ 29 East Box Score (Boston Bombers: Bird and Parish)	9.00	4.50	.90
☐ 30 West Box Score (Moncrief Soars)	1.50	.75	.15
☐ xx Gilmore and English (Ad on back)	2.25	1.10	.22
☐ xx Kareem Abdul-Jabbar (Uncut sheet offer on back)	7.50	3.75	.75

1983-84 Star All-Rookies

This set features the 10 members of the 1982-83 NBA All-Rookie Team. Cards measure 2 1/2" by 3 1/2" and have a yellow border around the fronts of the cards. The set was issued in late Summer of 1983 and features the Star '84 logo on the front of each card. The cards are numbered on the backs with the order of the numbering essentially alphabetical according to the name of the subject.

	MINT	EXC	G-VG
COMPLETE SET (10)	75.00	37.50	7.50
COMMON PLAYER (1-10)	2.00	1.00	.20
☐ 1 Terry Cummings	30.00	15.00	3.00
☐ 2 Quintin Dailey	2.00	1.00	.20
☐ 3 Roderick Higgins	2.00	1.00	.20
☐ 4 Clark Kellogg	3.00	1.50	.30
☐ 5 Lafayette Lever	8.00	4.00	.80
☐ 6 Paul Pressey	4.00	2.00	.40
☐ 7 Trent Tucker	2.50	1.25	.25
☐ 8 Dominique Wilkins	35.00	17.50	3.50
☐ 9 Rob Williams	2.00	1.00	.20
☐ 10 James Worthy	30.00	15.00	3.00

1983-84 Star Sixers Champs

This set of 25 cards is devoted to Philadelphia's NBA Championship victory over the Los Angeles Lakers in 1983. Cards measure 2 1/2" by 3 1/2" and have a red border around the fronts of the cards and red printing on the backs. The set was issued in late Summer of 1983 and features the Star '84 logo on the front of each card.

	MINT	EXC	G-VG
COMPLETE SET (25)	40.00	20.00	4.00
COMMON PLAYER (1-25)	1.50	.75	.15
☐ 1 Sixers 1982-83 NBA World Champs (Checklist back)	3.00	1.50	.30
☐ 2 Billy Cunningham Head Coach	2.25	1.10	.22
☐ 3 Clash of the Titans Malone vs. Abdul-Jabbar	6.00	3.00	.60
☐ 4 The Quest Begins Julius Erving	6.00	3.00	.60
☐ 5 Philly Super-Sub Clint Richardson	1.50	.75	.15
☐ 6 Laker Killer Andrew Toney	1.50	.75	.15
☐ 7 Phila. 113, LA 107 Game 1 Boxscore	1.50	.75	.15
☐ 8 Secretary of Defense Bobby Jones	2.25	1.10	.22
☐ 9 Mo Can Go Maurice Cheeks	2.25	1.10	.22
☐ 10 Doc for 2 Julius Erving	6.00	3.00	.60
☐ 11 Toney on the Drive Andrew Toney	1.50	.75	.15
☐ 12 Phila. 103, LA 93 Game 2 Boxscore	1.50	.75	.15
☐ 13 Serious Sixers (Pre-Game Lineup)	1.50	.75	.15
☐ 14 Moses Leads Sixers Moses Malone	4.00	2.00	.40
☐ 15 Bench Strength Clemon Johnson	1.50	.75	.15
☐ 16 One Mo Time Maurice Cheeks	2.25	1.10	.22
☐ 17 Phila. 111, LA 94 Game 3 Boxscore	1.50	.75	.15
☐ 18 Julius Scoops Julius Erving	6.00	3.00	.60
☐ 19 Sixth Man of Year Bobby Jones	2.25	1.10	.22
☐ 20 Coast to Coast Moses Malone	4.00	2.00	.40
☐ 21 World Champs Phila. 115, LA 108 Game 4 Boxscore	1.50	.75	.15
☐ 22 Doc Gets the Ring (Julius Erving) Series Stats	4.00	2.00	.40

	MINT	EXC	G-VG
☐ 23 Philly in a Sweep Prior World Champs	1.50	.75	.15
☐ 24 Basking in Glory Profile: Dr.J	6.00	3.00	.60
☐ 25 The NBA's MVP Profile: Moses Malone	4.00	2.00	.40

1984 Star All-Star Game

This set of 25 cards features players in the 34th Annual 1984 NBA All-Star Game held in Denver. Cards measure 2 1/2" by 3 1/2" and have a white border around the fronts of the cards and blue printing on the backs. Cards feature the Star '84 logo on the front. The cards are ordered with the East All-Stars on cards 2-13 and the West All-Stars on cards 14-25. The cards are numbered on the backs with the order of the numbering essentially alphabetical according to the name of the subject within division.

	MINT	EXC	G-VG
COMPLETE SET (25)	85.00	42.50	8.50
COMMON PLAYER (1-25)	1.50	.75	.15
☐ 1 1984 NBA All-Star Game Checklist (Isiah Thomas)	4.50	2.25	.45
☐ 2 Larry Bird	20.00	10.00	2.00
☐ 3 Otis Birdsong	1.50	.75	.15
☐ 4 Julius Erving	8.00	4.00	.80
☐ 5 Bernard King	3.50	1.75	.35
☐ 6 Bill Laimbeer	2.50	1.25	.25
☐ 7 Kevin McHale	3.50	1.75	.35
☐ 8 Sidney Moncrief	2.00	1.00	.20
☐ 9 Robert Parish	4.50	2.25	.45
☐ 10 Jeff Ruland	2.00	1.00	.20
☐ 11 Isiah Thomas (Magic Johnson also shown on card)	12.00	6.00	1.20
☐ 12 Andrew Toney	1.50	.75	.15
☐ 13 Kelly Tripucka	1.50	.75	.15
☐ 14 Kareem Abdul-Jabbar	8.00	4.00	.80
☐ 15 Mark Aguirre	2.00	1.00	.20
☐ 16 Adrian Dantley	3.00	1.50	.30
☐ 17 Walter Davis	2.50	1.25	.25
☐ 18 Alex English	3.00	1.50	.30
☐ 19 George Gervin	4.00	2.00	.40
☐ 20 Rickey Green	1.50	.75	.15
☐ 21 Magic Johnson	30.00	15.00	3.00
☐ 22 Jim Paxson	1.50	.75	.15
☐ 23 Ralph Sampson	2.00	1.00	.20
☐ 24 Jack Sikma	2.00	1.00	.20
☐ 25 Kiki Vandeweghe	2.00	1.00	.20

1984 Star Police Denver ASG

This 34-card set was distributed as individual cards by the Denver Police in the months following the NBA All-Star Game (ASG) held in Denver. The set was composed of participants in the All-Star Game (1-25) and the Slam Dunk contest (26-34). Cards measure 2 1/2" by 3 1/2" and have a white border around the fronts of the cards and blue printing on the backs. Cards feature Star '84 logo on the fronts and safety tips on the backs. Supposedly 10,000 sets were produced.

	MINT	EXC	G-VG
COMPLETE SET (34)	200.00	100.00	20.00
COMMON PLAYER (1-34)	3.00	1.50	.30
☐ 1 Checklist Card	5.00	2.50	.50
☐ 2 Larry Bird	40.00	20.00	4.00
☐ 3 Otis Birdsong	3.00	1.50	.30
☐ 4 Julius Erving	15.00	7.50	1.50
☐ 5 Bernard King	7.50	3.75	.75
☐ 6 Bill Laimbeer	5.00	2.50	.50
☐ 7 Kevin McHale	7.50	3.75	.75
☐ 8 Sidney Moncrief	4.50	2.25	.45
☐ 9 Robert Parish	9.00	4.50	.90
☐ 10 Jeff Ruland	3.00	1.50	.30
☐ 11 Isiah Thomas (Magic Johnson also shown on card)	25.00	12.50	2.50
☐ 12 Andrew Toney	3.00	1.50	.30
☐ 13 Kelly Tripucka	3.00	1.50	.30
☐ 14 Kareem Abdul-Jabbar	16.00	8.00	1.60
☐ 15 Mark Aguirre	4.00	2.00	.40
☐ 16 Adrian Dantley	6.00	3.00	.60
☐ 17 Walter Davis	4.00	2.00	.40
☐ 18 Alex English	6.00	3.00	.60
☐ 19 George Gervin	7.50	3.75	.75
☐ 20 Rickey Green	3.00	1.50	.30
☐ 21 Magic Johnson	60.00	30.00	6.00
☐ 22 Jim Paxson	3.00	1.50	.30
☐ 23 Ralph Sampson	4.00	2.00	.40
☐ 24 Jack Sikma	4.00	2.00	.40
☐ 25 Kiki Vandeweghe	4.00	2.00	.40
☐ 26 Michael Cooper	6.00	3.00	.60
☐ 27 Clyde Drexler	40.00	20.00	4.00
☐ 28 Julius Erving	15.00	7.50	1.50
☐ 29 Darrell Griffith	4.00	2.00	.40
☐ 30 Edgar Jones	3.00	1.50	.30
☐ 31 Larry Nance	9.00	4.50	.90
☐ 32 Ralph Sampson	4.00	2.00	.40
☐ 33 Dominique Wilkins	18.00	9.00	1.80
☐ 34 Orlando Woolridge	5.00	2.50	.50

1984 Star Slam Dunk

An 11-card set highlighting the revival of the Slam Dunk contest (during the 1984 All-Star Weekend in Denver) was produced by the Star Company in 1984. Cards measure 2 1/2" by 3 1/2" and have a white border around the fronts of the cards and blue printing on the backs. Cards feature the Star '84 logo on the front. The cards are numbered on the backs with the order of the numbering essentially alphabetical according to the name of the subject.

	MINT	EXC	G-VG
COMPLETE SET (11)	85.00	42.50	8.50
COMMON PLAYER (1-11)	2.00	1.00	.20

☐ 1 Group Photo (checklist back)	12.00	6.00	1.20
☐ 2 Michael Cooper	5.00	2.50	.50
☐ 3 Clyde Drexler	50.00	25.00	5.00
☐ 4 Julius Erving	20.00	10.00	2.00
☐ 5 Darrell Griffith	3.00	1.50	.30
☐ 6 Edgar Jones	2.00	1.00	.20
☐ 7 Larry Nance	9.00	4.50	.90
☐ 8 Ralph Sampson	3.00	1.50	.30
☐ 9 Dominique Wilkins	25.00	12.50	2.50
☐ 10 Orlando Woolridge	4.00	2.00	.40
☐ 11 Larry Nance, 1984 Slam Dunk Champ	7.50	3.75	.75

1984 Star Celtics Champs

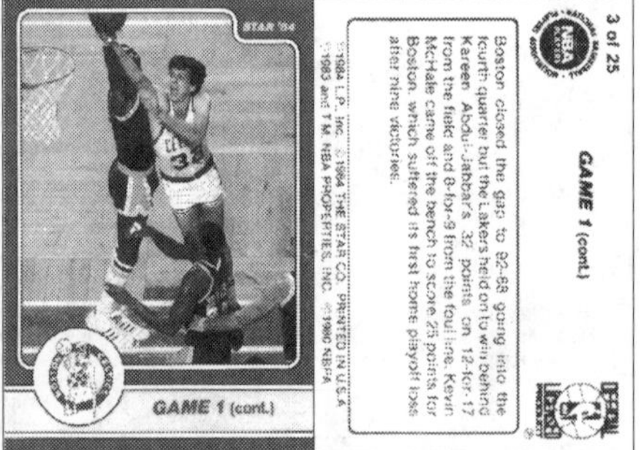

This set of 25 cards is devoted to Boston's NBA Championship victory over the Los Angeles Lakers in 1984. Cards measure 2 1/2" by 3 1/2" and have a green border around the fronts of the cards and green printing on the backs. The set was issued in Summer of 1984 and features the Star '84 logo on the front of each card. The set includes two of the three Red Auerbach cards ever printed.

	MINT	EXC	G-VG
COMPLETE SET (25)	65.00	32.50	6.50
COMMON PLAYER (1-25)	1.50	.75	.15
☐ 1 Celtics Champs (Red Auerbach/Maxwell) (Checklist back)	2.50	1.25	.25
☐ 2 Game 1 (Abdul-Jabbar over Parish)	4.00	2.00	.40
☐ 3 Game 1 (McHale drives)	3.50	1.75	.35
☐ 4 LA 115, Boston 109 (Larry Bird)	7.50	3.75	.75
☐ 5 Game 2 (Magic Johnson)	12.00	6.00	1.20
☐ 6 Game 2 (K.C. Jones and Danny Ainge)	2.50	1.25	.25
☐ 7 Boston 124, LA 121 (OT) (Larry Bird)	7.50	3.75	.75
☐ 8 Game 3 (Abdul-Jabbar and McHale)	4.00	2.00	.40
☐ 9 Game 3 (J.Worthy)	4.00	2.00	.40
☐ 10 LA 137, Boston 104 (Magic Johnson)	12.00	6.00	1.20
☐ 11 Game 4 (Magic blocks Bird)	15.00	7.50	1.50
☐ 12 Game 4 (Ainge scuffle)	2.00	1.00	.20
☐ 13 Boston 129, LA 125 Overtime (Carr and Maxwell)	1.50	.75	.15
☐ 14 Game 5 (Larry Bird)	7.50	3.75	.75
☐ 15 Game 5 (Pat Riley)	2.50	1.25	.25
☐ 16 Boston 121, LA 103 (Kareem Abdul-Jabbar)	4.00	2.00	.40
☐ 17 Game 6 (Parish sandwich)	3.00	1.50	.30
☐ 18 Game 6 (Kareem Abdul-Jabbar)	4.00	2.00	.40
☐ 19 LA 119, Boston 108 (Dennis Johnson)	2.50	1.25	.25
☐ 20 Game 7 (Kareem sky hook)	5.00	2.50	.50
☐ 21 Game 7 (K.C. Jones)	1.50	.75	.15
☐ 22 World Champs; Boston 111, LA 102 (M.L. Carr)	1.50	.75	.15
☐ 23 Prior Celtic Championships (Red Auerbach)	2.50	1.25	.25
☐ 24 Bird: Championship Series MVP	9.00	4.50	.90
☐ 25 The Road to the Title (Boston Garden)	2.25	1.10	.22

1984 Star Award Winners

This 24-card set was produced for the NBA to be given away at the Awards Banquet which took place following the conclusion of the 1983-84 season. Cards highlighted award winners from the 1983-84 season. Cards measure 2 1/2" by 3 1/2" and have a blue border around the fronts of the cards and pink and blue printing on the backs. The set was issued in June of 1984 and features the Star '84 logo on the front of each card.

	MINT	EXC	G-VG
COMPLETE SET (24)	60.00	30.00	6.00
COMMON PLAYER (1-24)	1.50	.75	.15
☐ 1 1984 Award Winners Checklist	2.50	1.25	.25
☐ 2 Frank Layden CO	1.50	.75	.15
☐ 3 Ralph Sampson ROY	2.00	1.00	.20
☐ 4 Comeback Player of the Year; Adrian Dantley	2.25	1.10	.22
☐ 5 Sixth Man: Kevin McHale	4.00	2.00	.40
☐ 6 Pivotal Player of the Year; Magic Johnson	20.00	10.00	2.00
☐ 7 Defensive Player: Sidney Moncrief	2.50	1.25	.25
☐ 8 MVP: Larry Bird	12.50	6.25	1.25
☐ 9 Slam Dunk Champ; Larry Nance	5.00	2.50	.50
☐ 10 Statistical Leaders	2.50	1.25	.25

		MINT	EXC	G-VG
☐ 11	Statistical Leaders II	2.50	1.25	.25
☐ 12	All-Star Game MVP; Isiah Thomas	6.00	3.00	.60
☐ 13	Leading Scorer; Adrian Dantley	2.25	1.10	.22
☐ 14	Field Goal Percent Leader; Artis Gilmore	2.25	1.10	.22
☐ 15	Free Throw Percent Leader; Larry Bird	10.00	5.00	1.00
☐ 16	Three Point Field Goal Percent Leader; Darrell Griffith	2.25	1.10	.22
☐ 17	Assists Leader; Magic Johnson	15.00	7.50	1.50
☐ 18	Steals Leader; Rickey Green	1.50	.75	.15
☐ 19	Most Blocked Shots; Mark Eaton	1.50	.75	.15
☐ 20	Leading Rebounder; Moses Malone	3.50	1.75	.35
☐ 21	Most Career Points; Kareem Abdul-Jabbar	6.00	3.00	.60
☐ 22	NBA All-Defensive Team	3.00	1.50	.30
☐ 23	NBA All-Rookie Team	3.00	1.50	.30
☐ 24	NBA All-NBA Team	7.50	3.75	.75

1984 Star Larry Bird

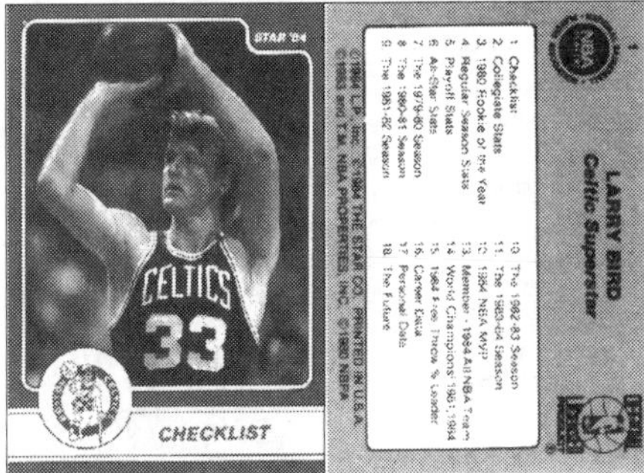

This set contains 18 cards highlighting the career of basketball great Larry Bird. Cards measure 2 1/2" by 3 1/2" and have a green border around the fronts of the cards and green printing on the backs. Cards feature Star '84 logo on the front as they were released in May of 1984.

	MINT	EXC	G-VG
COMPLETE SET (18)	75.00	37.50	7.50
COMMON PLAYER (1-18)	5.00	2.50	.50
☐ 1 Checklist	7.50	3.75	.75
☐ 2 Collegiate Stats	5.00	2.50	.50
☐ 3 1980 Rookie of the Year	5.00	2.50	.50
☐ 4 Regular Season Stats	5.00	2.50	.50
☐ 5 Playoff Stats	5.00	2.50	.50
☐ 6 All-Star Stats	5.00	2.50	.50
☐ 7 The 1979-80 Season	5.00	2.50	.50
☐ 8 The 1980-81 Season	5.00	2.50	.50
☐ 9 The 1981-82 Season	5.00	2.50	.50
☐ 10 The 1982-83 Season	5.00	2.50	.50
☐ 11 The 1983-84 Season	5.00	2.50	.50
☐ 12 The 1984 NBA MVP	5.00	2.50	.50
☐ 13 Member - 1984 All NBA Team	5.00	2.50	.50
☐ 14 World Champions 1981, 1984	5.00	2.50	.50
☐ 15 1984 Free Throw Percentage Leader	5.00	2.50	.50
☐ 16 Career Data	5.00	2.50	.50
☐ 17 Personal Data	5.00	2.50	.50
☐ 18 The Future	10.00	5.00	1.00

1984 Star Mr. Z's Trail Blazers

This five-card set was produced by Star Co. as a promotion for Mr. Z's frozen pizzas. The cards measure approximately 5" by 7" and feature on the fronts glossy color action player photos, with rounded corners as well as white and black borders on a dark red background. The team logo is superimposed over the picture at the intersection of the left side and bottom borders. The sponsor logo "Mr. Z's" appears in the upper right corner of the front, and player information is given below the picture. The backs have an advertisement for Blazer merchandise. The cards are unnumbered and are checklisted below in alphabetical order. Originally the set was planned to feature the whole team (12 players) but only five players were issued. Individual cards were given out in Mr. Z's frozen pizzas. Supposedly 10,000 cards of each player were produced. The cards were issued beginning in January 1984.

	MINT	EXC	G-VG
COMPLETE SET (5)	400.00	200.00	40.00
COMMON PLAYER (1-5)	50.00	25.00	5.00
☐ 1 Kenny Carr	50.00	25.00	5.00
☐ 2 Clyde Drexler	250.00	125.00	25.00
☐ 3 Audie Norris	50.00	25.00	5.00
☐ 4 Mychal Thompson	60.00	30.00	6.00
☐ 5 Darnell Valentine	50.00	25.00	5.00

1984-85 Star Arena

These sets were produced to be sold in the arena of each of the five teams. Each set is different from the team's regular issue set in that the photography and and card backs are different. Shortly after distribution began, Bob Lanier announced his retirement plans and hence his cards were withdrawn from the Milwaukee set. Cards measure 2 1/2" by 3 1/2" and have a colored border around the fronts of the cards according to the team with corresponding color printing on the backs. Celtics feature Star '85 logo on the front while the other four teams feature the Star '84 logo on the front. The cards are ordered below by teams, for example, Boston Celtics A, Dallas Mavericks B, Milwaukee Bucks C, Los Angeles Lakers D, and Philadelphia 76ers E.

	MINT	EXC	G-VG
COMPLETE SET (49)	225.00	110.00	22.00
COMMON PLAYER	1.50	.75	.15
☐ A1 Larry Bird	35.00	17.50	3.50
☐ A2 Danny Ainge	5.00	2.50	.50
☐ A3 Rick Carlisle	1.50	.75	.15
☐ A4 Dennis Johnson	3.50	1.75	.35
☐ A5 Cedric Maxwell	3.00	1.50	.30
☐ A6 Kevin McHale	7.00	3.50	.70
☐ A7 Robert Parish	8.00	4.00	.80
☐ A8 Scott Wedman	1.50	.75	.15
☐ A9 World Champs 1981, 1984 Robert Parish Larry Bird Kevin McHale Jimmy Rodgers CO K.C. Jones CO Chris Ford CO	15.00	7.50	1.50
☐ B1 Mark Aguirre	4.00	2.00	.40
☐ B2 Rolando Blackman	5.00	2.50	.50
☐ B3 Brad Davis	1.50	.75	.15
☐ B4 Dale Ellis	4.00	2.00	.40
☐ B5 Bill Garnett	1.50	.75	.15
☐ B6 Derek Harper UER (Mike Harper on both sides with Mike's birthdate, etc.)	3.50	1.75	.35
☐ B7 Kurt Nimphius	1.50	.75	.15
☐ B8 Jim Spanarkel	1.50	.75	.15
☐ B9 Elston Turner	1.50	.75	.15
☐ B10 Jay Vincent	2.50	1.25	.25
☐ B11 Mark West	3.50	1.75	.35
☐ C1 Nate Archibald	6.00	3.00	.60
☐ C2 Junior Bridgeman	2.50	1.25	.25
☐ C3 Mike Dunleavy	3.50	1.75	.35
☐ C4 Kevin Grevey	2.25	1.10	.22
☐ C5 Marques Johnson	4.00	2.00	.40
☐ C6 Bob Lanier SP	600.00	300.00	60.00
☐ C7 Alton Lister	1.50	.75	.15
☐ C8 Sidney Moncrief	3.50	1.75	.35
☐ C9 Paul Pressey	2.50	1.25	.25
☐ D1 Kareem Abdul-Jabbar	14.00	7.00	1.40
☐ D2 Michael Cooper	5.00	2.50	.50
☐ D3 Magic Johnson	50.00	25.00	5.00
☐ D4 Mike McGee	1.50	.75	.15
☐ D5 Swen Nater	2.25	1.10	.22
☐ D6 Kurt Rambis	3.50	1.75	.35
☐ D7 Byron Scott	6.00	3.00	.60
☐ D8 James Worthy	12.00	6.00	1.20
☐ D9 Laker All-Stars (Magic Johnson and Kareem Abdul-Jabbar)	35.00	17.50	3.50
☐ D10 Kareem Abdul-Jabbar NBA Scoring Leader	12.00	6.00	1.20
☐ E1 Julius Erving	14.00	7.00	1.40
☐ E2 Maurice Cheeks	3.50	1.75	.35
☐ E3 Franklin Edwards	1.50	.75	.15
☐ E4 Marc Iavaroni	1.50	.75	.15
☐ E5 Clemon Johnson	1.50	.75	.15
☐ E6 Bobby Jones	3.50	1.75	.35
☐ E7 Moses Malone	8.00	4.00	.80
☐ E8 Clint Richardson	1.50	.75	.15
☐ E9 Andrew Toney	1.50	.75	.15
☐ E10 Sam Williams	1.50	.75	.15

1984-85 Star Court Kings

This 50-card set was issued as two series of 25. Cards measure 5" by 7" and have a yellow (first series 1-25) or blue (second series 26-50) colored border around the fronts of the cards and blue and yellow printing on the backs. These large cards feature the Star '85 logo on the front. The set features early professional cards of Charles Barkley, Michael Jordan, Hakeem Olajuwon, and Sam Perkins.

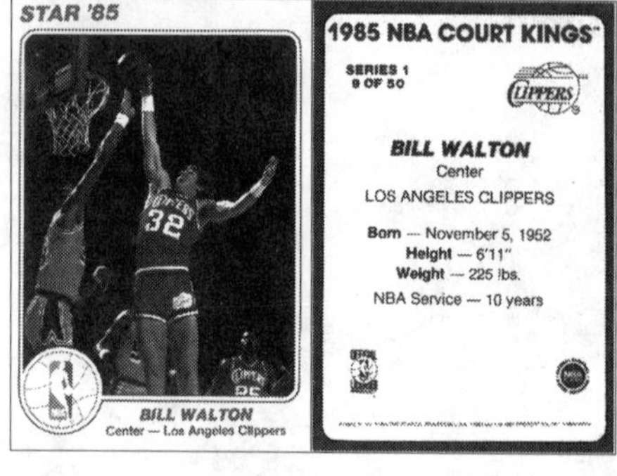

	MINT	EXC	G-VG
COMPLETE SET (50)	300.00	150.00	30.00
COMMON PLAYER (1-25)	2.50	1.25	.25
COMMON PLAYER (26-50)	3.00	1.50	.30
☐ 1 Kareem Abdul-Jabbar	15.00	7.50	1.50
☐ 2 Jeff Ruland	3.50	1.75	.35
☐ 3 Mark Aguirre	5.00	2.50	.50
☐ 4 Julius Erving	14.00	7.00	1.40
☐ 5 Kelly Tripucka	2.50	1.25	.25
☐ 6 Buck Williams	7.50	3.75	.75
☐ 7 Sidney Moncrief	5.00	2.50	.50
☐ 8 World B. Free	4.00	2.00	.40
☐ 9 Bill Walton	7.50	3.75	.75
☐ 10 Purvis Short	2.50	1.25	.25
☐ 11 Rickey Green	2.50	1.25	.25
☐ 12 Dominique Wilkins	12.00	6.00	1.20
☐ 13 Jim Paxson	2.50	1.25	.25
☐ 14 Ralph Sampson	3.50	1.75	.35
☐ 15 Magic Johnson	40.00	20.00	4.00
☐ 16 Reggie Theus	3.50	1.75	.35
☐ 17 Moses Malone	9.00	4.50	.90
☐ 18 Larry Bird	30.00	15.00	3.00
☐ 19 Larry Nance	6.00	3.00	.60
☐ 20 Clark Kellogg	2.50	1.25	.25
☐ 21 Jack Sikma	3.50	1.75	.35
☐ 22 Alex English	6.00	3.00	.60
☐ 23 Bernard King	6.00	3.00	.60
☐ 24 Dave Corzine	2.50	1.25	.25
☐ 25 George Gervin	6.00	3.00	.60
☐ 26 Michael Jordan	125.00	60.00	12.50
☐ 27 Rolando Blackman	5.00	2.50	.50
☐ 28 Dan Issel	6.00	3.00	.60
☐ 29 Maurice Cheeks	4.00	2.00	.40
☐ 30 Isiah Thomas	12.00	6.00	1.20
☐ 31 Robert Parish	8.00	4.00	.80
☐ 32 Mark Eaton	4.00	2.00	.40
☐ 33 Sam Perkins	12.00	6.00	1.20
☐ 34 Artis Gilmore	5.00	2.50	.50
☐ 35 Andrew Toney	3.00	1.50	.30
☐ 36 Adrian Dantley	6.00	3.00	.60
☐ 37 Terry Cummings	12.00	6.00	1.20
☐ 38 Orlando Woolridge	6.00	3.00	.60
☐ 39 Tom Chambers	12.00	6.00	1.20
☐ 40 Gus Williams	4.00	2.00	.40
☐ 41 Charles Barkley	40.00	20.00	4.00
☐ 42 Kevin McHale	7.00	3.50	.70
☐ 43 Otis Birdsong	3.00	1.50	.30
☐ 44 Sam Bowie	5.00	2.50	.50
☐ 45 Darrell Griffith	4.00	2.00	.40
☐ 46 Kiki Vandeweghe	4.00	2.00	.40
☐ 47 Hakeem Olajuwon	30.00	15.00	3.00
☐ 48 Marques Johnson	4.00	2.00	.40
☐ 49 James Worthy	10.00	5.00	1.00
☐ 50 Mel Turpin	3.00	1.50	.30

1984-85 Star Julius Erving

This set contains 18 cards highlighting the career of basketball great Julius Erving. Cards measure 2 1/2" by 3 1/2" and have a red border around the fronts of the cards and red printing on the backs. Cards feature Star '85 logo on the front although they were released in the Summer of 1984.

	MINT	EXC	G-VG
COMPLETE SET (18)	50.00	25.00	5.00
COMMON PLAYER (1-18)	4.00	2.00	.40
□ 1 Checklist	5.00	2.50	.50
□ 2 NBA Regular Season Stats	4.00	2.00	.40
□ 3 ABA Regular Season Stats	4.00	2.00	.40
□ 4 NBA All-Star Eight Times	4.00	2.00	.40
□ 5 ABA All-Star Five Times	4.00	2.00	.40
□ 6 NBA Playoff Stats	4.00	2.00	.40
□ 7 ABA Playoff Stats	4.00	2.00	.40
□ 8 NBA MVP, 1981	4.00	2.00	.40
□ 9 ABA MVP, 1974, 1975, and 1976	4.00	2.00	.40
□ 10 Collegiate Stats	4.00	2.00	.40
□ 11 NBA All-Star MVP, 1977 and 1983	4.00	2.00	.40
□ 12 NBA Career Highlights	4.00	2.00	.40
□ 13 ABA Career Highlights	4.00	2.00	.40
□ 14 1983 World Champs	4.00	2.00	.40
□ 15 ABA Champions 1974 and 1976	4.00	2.00	.40
□ 16 All-Time Scoring	4.00	2.00	.40
□ 17 Personal Data	4.00	2.00	.40
□ 18 The Future	5.00	2.50	.50

1985 Star Bucks Card Night

This 13-card set was given away during the Milwaukee Bucks "Card Night" on January 21, 1985. Card number 10 Larry Micheaux was withdrawn at the request of the Bucks management due to his Free Agent signing after the printing of the cards. Cards measure 2 1/2" by 3 1/2" and have a green border around the fronts of the cards and green printing on the backs. Cards feature Star '85 logo on the fronts.

	MINT	EXC	G-VG
COMPLETE SET (13)	75.00	37.50	7.50
COMMON PLAYER (1-13)	1.50	.75	.15
□ 1 Don Nelson CO	3.50	1.75	.35
□ 2 Randy Breuer	2.00	1.00	.20
□ 3 Terry Cummings	9.00	4.50	.90
□ 4 Charlie Davis	1.50	.75	.15
□ 5 Mike Dunleavy	3.50	1.75	.35
□ 6 Kenny Fields	2.00	1.00	.20
□ 7 Kevin Grevey	2.00	1.00	.20
□ 8 Craig Hodges	4.00	2.00	.40
□ 9 Alton Lister	2.00	1.00	.20
□ 10 Larry Micheaux SP	50.00	25.00	5.00
□ 11 Paul Mokeski	2.00	1.00	.20
□ 12 Sidney Moncrief	6.00	3.00	.60
□ 13 Paul Pressey	3.00	1.50	.30

1985 Star Slam Dunk Supers

This ten-card set uses actual photography from the 1985 Slam Dunk contest in Indianapolis held during the NBA All-Star Weekend. Cards measure 5" by 7" and have a red border around the fronts of the cards and red printing on the backs. Cards feature Star '85 logo on the fronts. The set ordering for these numbered cards is alphabetical by subject's name.

	MINT	EXC	G-VG
COMPLETE SET (10)	200.00	100.00	20.00
COMMON PLAYER (1-10)	3.00	1.50	.30
□ 1 Checklist Card	6.00	3.00	.60
□ 2 Clyde Drexler	45.00	22.50	4.50
□ 3 Julius Erving	15.00	7.50	1.50
□ 4 Darrell Griffith	4.00	2.00	.40
□ 5 Michael Jordan	125.00	60.00	12.50
□ 6 Larry Nance	7.50	3.75	.75
□ 7 Terence Stansbury	3.00	1.50	.30
□ 8 Dominique Wilkins	18.00	9.00	1.80
□ 9 Orlando Woolridge	4.00	2.00	.40
□ 10 Dominique Wilkins (1985 Slam Dunk Champion)	12.50	6.25	1.25

1985 Star Gatorade Slam Dunk

This nine-card set was given to the people who attended the 1985 All-Star Weekend Banquet at Indianapolis. Since Terence Stansbury was a late substitute in the Slam Dunk contest for Charles Barkley, both cards were produced, but the Barkley card was never released. Cards measure 2 1/2" by 3 1/2" and have a green border around the fronts of the cards and green printing on the backs. Cards feature the Star '85 and Gatorade logos on the fronts.

	MINT	EXC	G-VG
COMPLETE SET (9)	200.00	100.00	20.00
COMMON PLAYER (1-9)	3.00	1.50	.30
□ 1 Gatorade 2nd Annual Slam Dunk Championship	6.00	3.00	.60

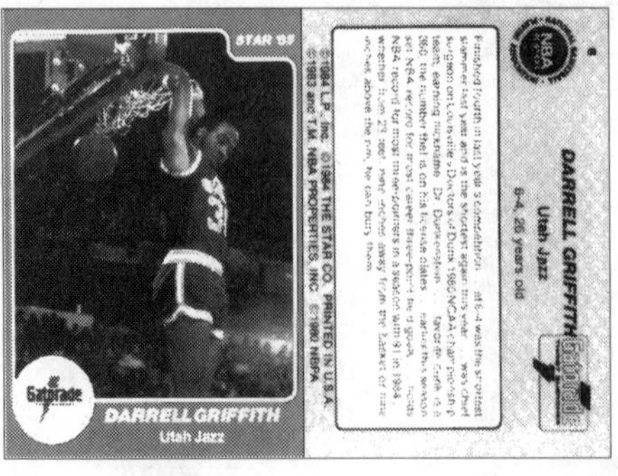

(checklist back)			
☐ 2 Larry Nance	7.50	3.75	.75
☐ 3 Terence Stansbury	3.00	1.50	.30
☐ 4 Clyde Drexler	45.00	22.50	4.50
☐ 5 Julius Erving	15.00	7.50	1.50
☐ 6 Darrell Griffith	4.00	2.00	.40
☐ 7 Michael Jordan	125.00	60.00	12.50
☐ 8 Dominique Wilkins	18.00	9.00	1.80
☐ 9 Orlando Woolridge	4.00	2.00	.40

1985 Star Lite All-Stars

This 13-card set was given to the people who attended the 1985 All-Star Weekend Banquet at Indianapolis. Cards measure 2 1/2" by 3 1/2" and have a blue border around the fronts of the cards and blue printing on the backs. Cards feature the Star '85 and Lite Beer logos on the fronts. Players featured are the 1985 NBA All-Star starting line-ups and coaches.

	MINT	EXC	G-VG
COMPLETE SET (13)	200.00	100.00	20.00
COMMON PLAYER (1-13)	3.00	1.50	.30
☐ 1 1985 NBA All-Stars Starting Line-Ups	3.00	1.50	.30
☐ 2 Larry Bird	30.00	15.00	3.00
☐ 3 Julius Erving	12.00	6.00	1.20
☐ 4 Michael Jordan	125.00	60.00	12.50
☐ 5 Moses Malone	6.00	3.00	.60
☐ 6 Isiah Thomas	12.00	6.00	1.20
☐ 7 K.C. Jones CO	3.00	1.50	.30
☐ 8 Kareem Abdul-Jabbar	12.00	6.00	1.20
☐ 9 Adrian Dantley	4.00	2.00	.40
☐ 10 George Gervin	6.00	3.00	.60
☐ 11 Magic Johnson	40.00	20.00	4.00
☐ 12 Ralph Sampson	3.00	1.50	.30
☐ 13 Pat Riley CO	4.00	2.00	.40

1985 Star Schick Legends

This 24-card set was given to the people who attended the 1985 All-Star Weekend Banquet at Indianapolis. Cards measure 2 1/2" by 3 1/2" and have a yellow border around the fronts of the cards and yellow and black printing on the backs. Cards feature the Star '85 and Schick logos on the fronts. Players featured were participants in the Schick NBA Legends Classic. The cards are numbered on the back; the numbering corresponds to alphabetical order by player.

	MINT	EXC	G-VG
COMPLETE SET (25)	50.00	25.00	5.00
COMMON PLAYER (1-25)	1.50	.75	.15
☐ 1 Schick NBA Legends Checklist	2.50	1.25	.25
☐ 2 Rick Barry	7.50	3.75	.75
☐ 3 Zelmo Beaty	1.50	.75	.15
☐ 4 Walt Bellamy	1.50	.75	.15
☐ 5 Dave Bing	4.00	2.00	.40
☐ 6 Roger Brown	1.50	.75	.15
☐ 7 Bob Cousy	9.00	4.50	.90
☐ 8 Mel Daniels	1.50	.75	.15
☐ 9 Bob Davies	2.00	1.00	.20
☐ 10 Dave DeBusschere	4.00	2.00	.40
☐ 11 Walt Frazier	6.00	3.00	.60
☐ 12 John Havlicek	9.00	4.50	.90
☐ 13 Connie Hawkins	4.00	2.00	.40
☐ 14 Tom Heinsohn	4.00	2.00	.40
☐ 15 Red Holzman CO	2.00	1.00	.20
☐ 16 Johnny Kerr	1.50	.75	.15
☐ 17 Bobby Leonard	1.50	.75	.15
☐ 18 Pete Maravich	18.00	9.00	1.80
☐ 19 Earl Monroe	5.00	2.50	.50
☐ 20 Bob Pettit	6.00	3.00	.60
☐ 21 Oscar Robertson	10.00	5.00	1.00
☐ 22 Nate Thurmond	4.00	2.00	.40
☐ 23 Dick Van Arsdale	1.50	.75	.15
☐ 24 Tom Van Arsdale	1.50	.75	.15
☐ 25 George Yardley	1.50	.75	.15

1985 Star Team Supers

This 40-card set is actually eight team sets of five each except for the Sixers having 10 players included. Cards measure 5" by 7" and have a colored border around the fronts of the cards according to the team with corresponding color printing on the backs. Cards feature Star '85 logo on the front. Cards are numbered below by assigning a team prefix based on the initials of the team, for example, BC for Boston Celtics.

	MINT	EXC	G-VG
COMPLETE SET (40)	400.00	200.00	40.00
COMMON PLAYER	3.00	1.50	.30
☐ BC1 Larry Bird	35.00	17.50	3.50
☐ BC2 Robert Parish	8.00	4.00	.80
☐ BC3 Kevin McHale	7.00	3.50	.70
☐ BC4 Dennis Johnson	5.00	2.50	.50
☐ BC5 Danny Ainge	6.00	3.00	.60

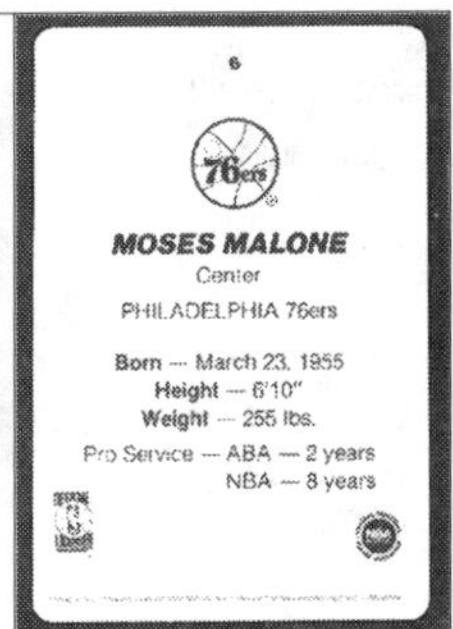

☐ CB1 Michael Jordan	125.00	60.00	12.50
☐ CB2 Orlando Woolridge	4.50	2.25	.45
☐ CB3 Quintin Dailey	3.00	1.50	.30
☐ CB4 Dave Corzine	3.00	1.50	.30
☐ CB5 Steve Johnson	3.00	1.50	.30
☐ DP1 Isiah Thomas	15.00	7.50	1.50
☐ DP2 Kelly Tripucka	4.00	2.00	.40
☐ DP3 Vinnie Johnson	5.00	2.50	.50
☐ DP4 Bill Laimbeer	6.50	3.25	.65
☐ DP5 John Long	3.00	1.50	.30
☐ HR1 Ralph Sampson	4.00	2.00	.40
☐ HR2 Hakeem Olajuwon	35.00	17.50	3.50
☐ HR3 Lewis Lloyd	3.00	1.50	.30
☐ HR4 Rodney McCray	5.00	2.50	.50
☐ HR5 Lionel Hollins	4.00	2.00	.40
☐ LA1 Kareem Abdul-Jabbar	16.00	8.00	1.60
☐ LA2 Magic Johnson	45.00	22.50	4.50
☐ LA3 James Worthy	12.00	6.00	1.20
☐ LA4 Byron Scott	6.00	3.00	.60
☐ LA5 Bob McAdoo	5.00	2.50	.50
☐ MB1 Terry Cummings	11.00	5.50	1.10
☐ MB2 Sidney Moncrief	6.00	3.00	.60
☐ MB3 Paul Pressey	5.00	2.50	.50
☐ MB4 Mike Dunleavy	4.00	2.00	.40
☐ MB5 Alton Lister	3.00	1.50	.30
☐ PS1 Julius Erving	16.00	8.00	1.60
☐ PS2 Maurice Cheeks	4.00	2.00	.40
☐ PS3 Bobby Jones	5.00	2.50	.50
☐ PS4 Clemon Johnson	3.00	1.50	.30
☐ PS5 Leon Wood	3.00	1.50	.30
☐ PS6 Moses Malone	9.00	4.50	.90
☐ PS7 Andrew Toney	3.00	1.50	.30
☐ PS8 Charles Barkley	60.00	30.00	6.00
☐ PS9 Clint Richardson	3.00	1.50	.30
☐ PS10 Sedale Threatt	7.00	3.50	.70

1985 Star Coaches

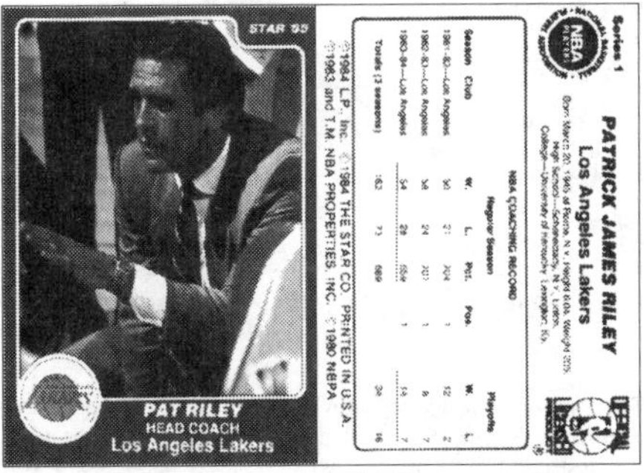

The 1984-85 Star NBA Coaches set is a ten-card set depicting some of the NBA's best known coaches. The set's basic design is identical to those of the Star Company's regular NBA sets. The cards measure approximately 2 1/2" by 3 1/2". The front borders are royal blue, and the backs show each man's coaching records. Statistics for ex-players are NOT included. The cards show a Star '85 logo in the upper right corner. Coaching statistics on the card backs only go up through the 1983-84 NBA season. The cards are numbered on the back; the numbering is essentially alphabetical by name.

	MINT	EXC	G-VG
COMPLETE SET (10)	18.00	9.00	1.80
COMMON PLAYER (1-10)	1.50	.75	.15
☐ 1 John Bach	1.50	.75	.15
☐ 2 Hubie Brown	2.00	1.00	.20
☐ 3 Cotton Fitzsimmons	2.00	1.00	.20
☐ 4 Kevin Loughery	2.00	1.00	.20
☐ 5 John MacLeod	1.50	.75	.15
☐ 6 Doug Moe	2.50	1.25	.25
☐ 7 Don Nelson	3.00	1.50	.30
☐ 8 Jack Ramsey	2.00	1.00	.20
☐ 9 Pat Riley	5.00	2.50	.50
☐ 10 Lenny Wilkens UER (Name misspelled on card back)	3.50	1.75	.35

1985 Star Crunch'n'Munch All-Stars

The 1985 Star Crunch 'n Munch NBA All-Stars set is an 11-card set featuring the ten starting players in the 1985 NBA All-Star Game, plus a checklist card. The set's basic design is identical to those of the Star Company's regular NBA sets. The cards measure approximately 2 1/2" by 3 1/2". The cards show a Star '85 logo in the upper right corner. The front borders are yellowish orange, and the backs show each player's All-Star Game record.

	MINT	EXC	G-VG
COMPLETE SET (11)	200.00	100.00	20.00
COMMON PLAYER (1-11)	2.00	1.00	.20
☐ 1 Checklist Card	5.00	2.50	.50
☐ 2 Larry Bird	30.00	15.00	3.00
☐ 3 Julius Erving	12.00	6.00	1.20
☐ 4 Michael Jordan	125.00	60.00	12.50
☐ 5 Moses Malone	8.00	4.00	.80
☐ 6 Isiah Thomas	12.00	6.00	1.20
☐ 7 Kareem Abdul-Jabbar	12.00	6.00	1.20
☐ 8 Adrian Dantley	4.00	2.00	.40
☐ 9 George Gervin	6.00	3.00	.60
☐ 10 Magic Johnson	40.00	20.00	4.00
☐ 11 Ralph Sampson	2.00	1.00	.20

1985 Star Kareem

The 1985 Star Kareem Abdul-Jabbar set is an 18-card tribute highlighting the career of Abdul-Jabbar. Most of the pictures on the fronts show recent pictures of Kareem, but the backs provide various statistics and tidbits of information about Abdul-Jabbar. The set's basic design is identical to those of the

Star Company's regular NBA sets. The cards show a Star '85 logo in the upper right corner. The cards measure approximately 2 1/2" by 3 1/2". The front borders are Lakers' purple.

	MINT	EXC	G-VG
COMPLETE SET (18)	50.00	25.00	5.00
COMMON PLAYER (1-18)	4.00	2.00	.40
☐ 1 Checklist Card	5.00	2.50	.50
☐ 2 Collegiate Stats	4.00	2.00	.40
☐ 3 Regular Season Stats	4.00	2.00	.40
☐ 4 Playoff Stats	4.00	2.00	.40
☐ 5 All Star Stats	4.00	2.00	.40
☐ 6 All-Time Scoring King	4.00	2.00	.40
☐ 7 NBA MVP 71/72/74	4.00	2.00	.40
☐ 8 NBA MVP 76/77/80	4.00	2.00	.40
☐ 9 Defensive Star	4.00	2.00	.40
☐ 10 World Champs 71	4.00	2.00	.40
☐ 11 World Champs 80/82/85	4.00	2.00	.40
☐ 12 All-Time Records	4.00	2.00	.40
☐ 13 Rookie-of-the-Year 70	4.00	2.00	.40
☐ 14 Playoff MVP 71/85	4.00	2.00	.40
☐ 15 The League Leader	4.00	2.00	.40
☐ 16 Career Highlights	4.00	2.00	.40
☐ 17 Personal Data	4.00	2.00	.40
☐ 18 The Future	5.00	2.50	.50

1985 Star ROY's

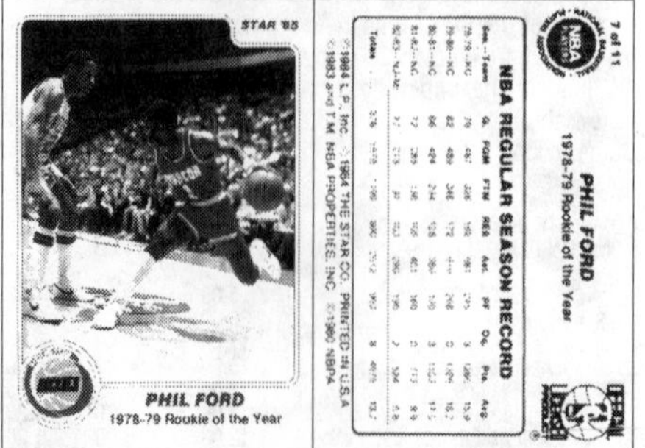

The 1985 Star Rookies of the Year set is an 11-card set depicting each of the NBA's ROY award winners from the 1974-75 through 1984-85 seasons. Michael Jordan's card only shows his collegiate statistics; all others provide NBA statistics (but only up through the 1983-84 NBA season). Cards of Darrell Griffith and Keith Wilkes show the Star '86 logo in the upper right corner; all others in the set show Star '85. The set's basic design is identical to those of the Star Company's regular NBA sets, and the front borders are off-white. The cards measure approximately 2 1/2" by 3 1/2". The cards are numbered on the back in reverse chronological order according to when each player won the ROY.

	MINT	EXC	G-VG
COMPLETE SET (11)	200.00	100.00	20.00
COMMON PLAYER (1-11)	1.50	.75	.15
☐ 1 Michael Jordan	135.00	60.00	13.50
☐ 2 Ralph Sampson	2.50	1.25	.25
☐ 3 Terry Cummings	14.00	7.00	1.40
☐ 4 Buck Williams	12.00	6.00	1.20
☐ 5 Darrell Griffith	3.00	1.50	.30
☐ 6 Larry Bird	45.00	22.50	4.50
☐ 7 Phil Ford	2.00	1.00	.20
☐ 8 Walter Davis	4.00	2.00	.40
☐ 9 Adrian Dantley	4.50	2.25	.45
☐ 10 Alvan Adams	1.50	.75	.15
☐ 11 Keith Wilkes	3.50	1.75	.35

1985-86 Star All-Rookie Team

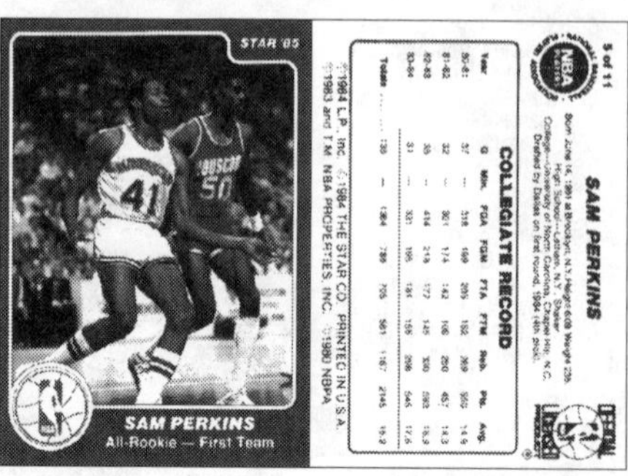

The 1985-86 Star NBA All-Rookie Team is an 11-card set features 11 top rookies from the previous (1984-85) season. The set's basic design is identical to those of the Star Company's regular NBA sets. The cards measure approximately 2 1/2" by 3 1/2". The front borders are red, and the backs include each player's collegiate statistics. Alvin Robertson's card shows the Star '86 logo in the upper right corner; all others in the set show Star '85. The statistics on the card backs provide only college records.

	MINT	EXC	G-VG
COMPLETE SET (11)	300.00	150.00	30.00
COMMON PLAYER (1-11)	1.50	.75	.15
☐ 1 Hakeem Olajuwon	45.00	22.50	4.50
☐ 2 Michael Jordan	135.00	60.00	13.50
☐ 3 Charles Barkley	75.00	37.50	7.50
☐ 4 Sam Bowie	6.00	3.00	.60
☐ 5 Sam Perkins	12.50	6.25	1.25
☐ 6 Vern Fleming	3.00	1.50	.30
☐ 7 Otis Thorpe	12.50	6.25	1.25
☐ 8 John Stockton	75.00	37.50	7.50
☐ 9 Kevin Willis	10.00	5.00	1.00
☐ 10 Tim McCormick	1.50	.75	.15
☐ 11 Alvin Robertson	7.50	3.75	.75

1985-86 Star Lakers Champs

The 1985-86 Star Lakers NBA Champs set is an 18-card set commemorating the Los Angeles Lakers' 1985 NBA Championship. Each card depicts one scene from the Championship series. The front borders are off-white. The backs feature game and series summaries, plus other related information. The set's basic design is identical to those of the Star Company's regular NBA sets. The cards show a Star '86 logo in the upper right corner. The cards measure approximately 2 1/2" by 3 1/2". The cards are numbered in the upper left corner of the reverse.

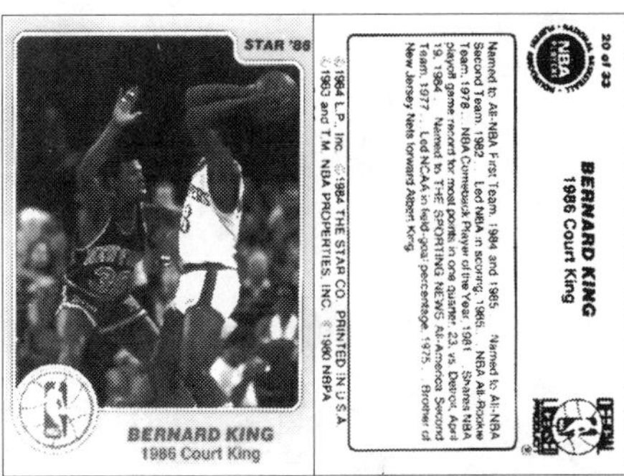

	MINT	EXC	G-VG
COMPLETE SET (18)	75.00	37.50	7.50
COMMON PLAYER (1-18)	1.50	.75	.15
☐ 1 Lakers 1985 NBA Champs (Kareem and Buss with trophy)	7.50	3.75	.75
☐ 2 Boston 148, L.A. 114 (Bird under basket)	10.00	5.00	1.00
☐ 3 L.A. 109, Boston 102 (Dennis Johnson)	3.50	1.75	.35
☐ 4 L.A. 136, Boston 111 (Danny Ainge)	3.50	1.75	.35
☐ 5 Boston 107, L.A. 105 (Byron Scott driving)	3.00	1.50	.30
☐ 6 L.A. 120, Boston 111 (McHale under basket)	4.00	2.00	.40
☐ 7 L.A. 111, Boston 100 (Magic driving)	12.50	6.25	1.25
☐ 8 Kareem 1985 Series MVP	6.00	3.00	.60
☐ 9 Playoff Highs (Larry Bird)	10.00	5.00	1.00
☐ 10 Top Playoff Scorers (Kareem holding ball)	6.00	3.00	.60
☐ 11 Title Fight (Ainge/Michael Cooper)	3.00	1.50	.30
☐ 12 Laker Series Stats (Riley in huddle)	3.00	1.50	.30
☐ 13 Boston Series Stats (K.C. Jones in huddle)	2.25	1.10	.22
☐ 14 L.A. Playoff Stats (Magic driving)	12.50	6.25	1.25
☐ 15 Boston Playoff Stats (action under basket)	1.50	.75	.15
☐ 16 Road To The Title	1.50	.75	.15
☐ 17 Prior World Champs I (riding on float)	2.50	1.25	.25
☐ 18 Prior World Champs II (with Ronald Reagan)	20.00	10.00	2.00

1986 Star Court Kings

The 1986 Star Court Kings set contains 33 cards which feature many of the NBA's top players. The set's basic design is identical to those of the Star Company's regular NBA sets. The front borders are yellow, and the backs have career narrative summaries of each player but no statistics. The cards show a Star '86 logo in the upper right corner. The cards measure approximately 2 1/2" by 3 1/2". The cards are numbered in the upper left corner of the reverse; the numbering corresponds to alphabetical order by subject.

	MINT	EXC	G-VG
COMPLETE SET (33)	275.00	135.00	27.00
COMMON PLAYER (1-33)	1.50	.75	.15
☐ 1 Mark Aguirre	3.00	1.50	.30
☐ 2 Kareem Abdul-Jabbar	12.00	6.00	1.20
☐ 3 Charles Barkley	35.00	17.50	3.50
☐ 4 Larry Bird	30.00	15.00	3.00
☐ 5 Rolando Blackman	3.50	1.75	.35
☐ 6 Tom Chambers	6.50	3.25	.65
☐ 7 Maurice Cheeks	2.50	1.25	.25
☐ 8 Terry Cummings	7.50	3.75	.75
☐ 9 Adrian Dantley	3.50	1.75	.35
☐ 10 Darryl Dawkins	2.50	1.25	.25
☐ 11 Mark Eaton	2.50	1.25	.25
☐ 12 Alex English	5.00	2.50	.50
☐ 13 Julius Erving	12.00	6.00	1.20
☐ 14 Patrick Ewing	50.00	25.00	5.00
☐ 15 George Gervin	6.00	3.00	.60
☐ 16 Darrell Griffith	3.00	1.50	.30
☐ 17 Magic Johnson	40.00	20.00	4.00
☐ 18 Michael Jordan	125.00	60.00	12.50
☐ 19 Clark Kellogg	1.50	.75	.15
☐ 20 Bernard King	4.00	2.00	.40
☐ 21 Moses Malone	6.00	3.00	.60
☐ 22 Kevin McHale	5.00	2.50	.50
☐ 23 Sidney Moncrief	3.50	1.75	.35
☐ 24 Larry Nance	5.00	2.50	.50
☐ 25 Hakeem Olajuwon	20.00	10.00	2.00
☐ 26 Robert Parish	7.50	3.75	.75
☐ 27 Ralph Sampson	3.00	1.50	.30
☐ 28 Isiah Thomas	10.00	5.00	1.00
☐ 29 Andrew Toney	1.50	.75	.15
☐ 30 Kelly Tripucka	1.50	.75	.15
☐ 31 Kiki Vandeweghe	2.50	1.25	.25
☐ 32 Dominique Wilkins	12.00	6.00	1.20
☐ 33 James Worthy	10.00	5.00	1.00

1986 Star Michael Jordan

The 1986 Star Michael Jordan set contains 10 cards highlighting the career of Michael Jordan. The card backs contain various information about Jordan. The set's basic design is identical to those of the Star Company's regular NBA sets. The front borders are red. The cards show a Star '86 logo in the upper right corner. The cards measure approximately 2 1/2" by 3 1/2". The cards are numbered in the upper left corner of the reverse.

	MINT	EXC	G-VG
COMPLETE SET (10)	500.00	250.00	50.00
COMMON PLAYER (1-10)	75.00	37.50	7.50
☐ 1 Michael Jordan	75.00	37.50	7.50

☐ 2 Collegiate Stats	75.00	37.50	7.50
☐ 3 1984 Olympian	75.00	37.50	7.50
☐ 4 Pro Stats	75.00	37.50	7.50
☐ 5 1985 All-Star	75.00	37.50	7.50
☐ 6 1985 Rookie of Year	75.00	37.50	7.50
☐ 7 Career Highlights	75.00	37.50	7.50
☐ 8 The 1986 Playoffs	75.00	37.50	7.50
☐ 9 Personal Data	75.00	37.50	7.50
☐ 10 The Future	75.00	37.50	7.50

1986 Star Lifebuoy Bucks

The 1986 Star Lifebuoy Milwaukee Bucks set contains 13 cards, one for each of the 12 players plus a coaching staff card. The set's basic design is identical to those of the Star Company's regular NBA sets. The front borders are lime green, and the backs show each player's NBA statistics (collegiate for number 13 Jerry Reynolds). The cards show a Star '86 logo in the upper right corner. The cards measure approximately 2 1/2" by 3 1/2". The cards are numbered in the upper left corner of the reverse; the numbering corresponds to alphabetical order by player.

	MINT	EXC	G-VG
COMPLETE SET (13)	15.00	7.50	1.50
COMMON PLAYER (1-13)	1.50	.75	.15
☐ 1 Don Nelson CO	2.50	1.25	.25
☐ 2 Randy Breuer	2.00	1.00	.20
☐ 3 Terry Cummings	6.00	3.00	.60
☐ 4 Charlie Davis	1.50	.75	.15
☐ 5 Kenny Fields	2.00	1.00	.20
☐ 6 Craig Hodges	3.00	1.50	.30
☐ 7 Jeff Lamp	1.50	.75	.15
☐ 8 Alton Lister	2.00	1.00	.20
☐ 9 Paul Mokeski	1.50	.75	.15
☐ 10 Sidney Moncrief	4.00	2.00	.40
☐ 11 Ricky Pierce	6.00	3.00	.60
☐ 12 Paul Pressey	2.50	1.25	.25
☐ 13 Jerry Reynolds	1.50	.75	.15

1986 Star Lifebuoy Nets

The 1986 Star Lifebuoy New Jersey Nets set contains 14 cards, one for each of the 12 players, one for Head Coach Dave Wohl, and a checklist card. The set's basic design is identical to those of the Star Company's regular NBA sets. The front borders are royal blue, and the backs show each player's NBA statistics. The cards show a Star '86 logo in the upper right corner. The cards measure approximately 2 1/2" by 3 1/2". The cards are numbered in the upper left corner of the reverse; the numbering corresponds to alphabetical order by player.

	MINT	EXC	G-VG
COMPLETE SET (14)	15.00	7.50	1.50
COMMON PLAYER (1-14)	1.50	.75	.15
☐ 1 Dave Wohl CO	1.50	.75	.15

☐ 2 Otis Birdsong	2.00	1.00	.20
☐ 3 Bobby Cattage	1.50	.75	.15
☐ 4 Darwin Cook	1.50	.75	.15
☐ 5 Darryl Dawkins	3.00	1.50	.30
☐ 6 Mike Gminski	2.50	1.25	.25
☐ 7 Mickey Johnson	2.00	1.00	.20
☐ 8 Albert King	2.00	1.00	.20
☐ 9 Mike O'Koren	2.00	1.00	.20
☐ 10 Kelvin Ransey	1.50	.75	.15
☐ 11 Micheal Ray Richardson	2.50	1.25	.25
☐ 12 Jeff Turner	1.50	.75	.15
☐ 13 Buck Williams	6.00	3.00	.60
☐ 14 Title Card (checklist on back)	1.50	.75	.15

1986 Star Best of the Old/New

According to the producer, only 440 of these sets were produced by Star Company, who distributed them to dealers who bought 1985-86 complete sets. Dealers received one set for every five regular sets purchased. The cards measure the standard size (2 1/2" by 3 1/2"). The cards are unnumbered and checklisted below in alphabetical order. The Best of the New are numbered 1-4 and the Best of the Old are numbered 5-8. The numbering is alphabetical within each group.

	MINT	EXC	G-VG
COMPLETE SET (8)	1900.00	900.00	225.00
COMMON PLAYER (1-4)	40.00	20.00	4.00
COMMON PLAYER (5-8)	40.00	20.00	4.00
☐ 1 Patrick Ewing	300.00	150.00	30.00
☐ 2 Michael Jordan	1000.00	450.00	100.00
☐ 3 Hakeem Olajuwon	225.00	110.00	22.00
☐ 4 Ralph Sampson	40.00	20.00	4.00
☐ 5 Kareem Abdul-Jabbar	125.00	60.00	12.50
☐ 6 Julius Erving	125.00	60.00	12.50
☐ 7 George Gervin	40.00	20.00	4.00
☐ 8 Bill Walton	60.00	30.00	6.00

1990 Star Pics

This premier edition showcases sixty of college basketball's top pro prospects. The cards measure the standard size (2 1/2" by 3 1/2"). The front features a color action player photo, with the player shown in his college uniform. A white border separates the picture from the surrounding "basketball" background. The player's name appears in an aqua box at the bottom. The back has a head shot of the player in the upper left corner and the card number in a red star in the upper right corner. On a tan-colored basketball court design, the back presents biography, accomplishments, and a mini-scouting report that assesses a player's strengths and weaknesses. The more limited "Medallion" edition (supposedly only 25,000 Medallion sets

were produced, each with its own serial number) is valued at approximately double the prices listed below. The Medallion cards are distinguished by their more glossy feel and gold metallic print. The Medallion sets did not contain any random autographed cards inserted.

	MINT	EXC	G-VG
COMPLETE SET (70)	27.00	13.50	2.70
COMMON PLAYER (1-70)	.05	.02	.00
☐ 1 Checklist Card	.05	.02	.00
☐ 2 David Robinson (Mr. Robinson)	4.00	2.00	.40
☐ 3 Antonio Davis UTEP	.05	.02	.00
☐ 4 Steve Bardo Illinois	.12	.06	.01
☐ 5 Jayson Williams St. John's	.15	.07	.01
☐ 6 Alaa Abdelnaby Duke	.20	.10	.02
☐ 7 Trevor Wilson UCLA	.08	.04	.01
☐ 8 Dee Brown Jacksonville	2.50	1.25	.25
☐ 9 Dennis Scott Georgia Tech	1.25	.60	.12
☐ 10 Danny Ferry (Flashback)	.15	.07	.01
☐ 11 Stevie Thompson Syracuse	.12	.06	.01
☐ 12 Anthony Bonner St. Louis	.50	.25	.05
☐ 13 Keith Robinson Notre Dame	.05	.02	.00
☐ 14 Sean Higgins Michigan	.35	.17	.03
☐ 15 Bo Kimble Loyola Marymount	.15	.07	.01
☐ 16 David Jamerson Ohio University	.15	.07	.01
☐ 17 Anthony Pullard McNeese State	.05	.02	.00
☐ 18 Phil Henderson Duke	.08	.04	.01
☐ 19 Mike Mitchell Colorado State	.05	.02	.00
☐ 20 Vanderbilt Team	.05	.02	.00
☐ 21 Gary Payton Oregon State	1.25	.60	.12
☐ 22 Tony Massenburg Maryland	.15	.07	.01
☐ 23 Cedric Ceballos Cal State-Fullerton	1.00	.50	.10
☐ 24 Dwayne Schintzius Florida	.12	.06	.01
☐ 25 Bimbo Coles Virginia Tech	.60	.30	.06
☐ 26 Scott Williams North Carolina	.50	.25	.05
☐ 27 Willie Burton Minnesota	.50	.25	.05
☐ 28 Tate George U Conn	.15	.07	.01
☐ 29 Mark Stevenson Duquesne	.05	.02	.00
☐ 30 UNLV Team	1.00	.50	.10
☐ 31 Earl Wise Tennessee Tech	.05	.02	.00
☐ 32 Alec Kessler Georgia	.15	.07	.01
☐ 33 Les Jepsen Iowa	.15	.07	.01
☐ 34 Boo Harvey St. John's	.08	.04	.01
☐ 35 Elden Campbell Clemson	.75	.35	.07
☐ 36 Jud Buechler Arizona	.15	.07	.01
☐ 37 Loy Vaught Michigan	.40	.20	.04
☐ 38 Tyrone Hill Xavier	.40	.20	.04
☐ 39 Toni Kukoc Jugoplastika	.75	.35	.07
☐ 40 Jim Calhoun CO U Conn	.08	.04	.01
☐ 41 Felton Spencer Louisville	.35	.17	.03
☐ 42 Dan Godfread Evansville	.05	.02	.00
☐ 43 Derrick Coleman Syracuse	5.00	2.50	.50
☐ 44 Terry Mills Michigan	.50	.25	.05
☐ 45 Kendall Gill Illinois	7.00	3.50	.70
☐ 46 A.J. English Virginia Union	.50	.25	.05
☐ 47 Duane Causwell Temple	.40	.20	.04
☐ 48 Jerrod Mustaf Maryland	.25	.12	.02
☐ 49 Alan Ogg Alabama Birmingham	.12	.06	.01
☐ 50 Pervis Ellison (Flashback)	1.00	.50	.10
☐ 51 Matt Bullard Iowa	.25	.12	.02
☐ 52 Melvin Newbern Minnesota	.08	.04	.01
☐ 53 Marcus Liberty Ilinois	.60	.30	.06
☐ 54 Walter Palmer Dartmouth	.05	.02	.00
☐ 55 Negele Knight Dayton	.50	.25	.05
☐ 56 Steve Henson Kansas State	.15	.07	.01
☐ 57 Greg Foster UTEP	.12	.06	.01
☐ 58 Brian Oliver Georgia Tech	.12	.06	.01
☐ 59 Travis Mays Texas	.30	.15	.03
☐ 60 All-Rookie Team	.60	.30	.06
☐ 61 Steve Scheffler Purdue	.10	.05	.01
☐ 62 Chris Jackson LSU	.60	.30	.06
☐ 63 Derek Strong Xavier	.10	.05	.01
☐ 64 David Butler UNLV	.08	.04	.01
☐ 65 Kevin Pritchard Kansas	.15	.07	.01
☐ 66 Lionel Simmons LaSalle	1.75	.85	.17
☐ 67 Gerald Glass Mississippi	.50	.25	.05
☐ 68 Tony Harris New Orleans	.10	.05	.01
☐ 69 Lance Blanks Texas	.12	.06	.01
☐ 70 Draft Overview	.05	.02	.00
☐ 71 Medallion special card (Only available as part of Medallion set)	1.00	.50	.10
☐ 72 Medallion special card (Only available as part of Medallion set)	1.00	.50	.10

1991 Star Pics

This 73-card set was produced by Star Pics, subtitled "Pro Prospects," and features 45 of the 54 players picked in the 1991 NBA draft. The cards measure the standard size (2 1/2" by 3 1/

2"). The front features a color action photo of player in his college uniform. This picture overlays a black background with a basketball partially in view. The back has a color head shot of the player in the upper left corner and an orange border. On a two color jersey background, the back presents biographical information, accomplishments, and a mini scouting report assessing the player's strengths and weaknesses. The cards are numbered on the back. The Medallion version of this set is tougher to find than that of the previous year and is valued at triple the prices listed below. The Medallion sets again did not contain any random autographed cards inserted.

	MINT	EXC	G-VG
COMPLETE SET (73)	8.00	4.00	.80
COMMON PLAYER (1-72)	.05	.02	.00
☐ 1 Draft Overview	.05	.02	.00
☐ 2 Derrick Coleman Flashback	.30	.15	.03
☐ 3 Treg Lee Ohio State	.08	.04	.01
☐ 4 Rich King Nebraska	.15	.07	.01
☐ 5 Kenny Anderson Georgia Tech	1.50	.75	.15
☐ 6 John Crotty Virginia	.10	.05	.01
☐ 7 Mark Randall Kansas	.20	.10	.02
☐ 8 Kevin Brooks Southwestern Lousiana	.15	.07	.01
☐ 9 Lamont Strothers Christopher Newport	.10	.05	.01
☐ 10 Tim Hardaway Flashback	.25	.12	.02
☐ 11 Eric Murdock Providence	.30	.15	.03
☐ 12 Melvin Cheatum Alabama	.08	.04	.01
☐ 13 Pete Chilcutt North Carolina	.20	.10	.02
☐ 14 Zan Tabak Jugoplastika	.12	.06	.01
☐ 15 Greg Anthony UNLV	.40	.20	.04
☐ 16 George Ackles UNLV	.08	.04	.01
☐ 17 Stacey Augmon UNLV	1.25	.60	.12
☐ 18 Larry Johnson UNLV	5.00	2.50	.50
☐ 19 Alvaro Teheran Houston	.05	.02	.00
☐ 20 Reggie Miller Flashback	.12	.06	.01
☐ 21 Steve Smith Michigan State	2.00	1.00	.20
☐ 22 Sean Green Iona	.15	.07	.01
☐ 23 Johnny Pittman Oklahoma State	.08	.04	.01
☐ 24 Anthony Avent Seton Hall	.20	.10	.02
☐ 25 Chris Gatling Old Dominion	.40	.20	.04
☐ 26 Mark Macon Temple	.35	.17	.03
☐ 27 Joey Wright Texas	.08	.04	.01
☐ 28 Von McDade Wisconsin (Milwaukee)	.08	.04	.01
☐ 29 Bobby Phills Southern U	.10	.05	.01
☐ 30 Larry Fleisher HOF and Lawyer (In Memoriam)	.05	.02	.00
☐ 31 Luc Longley New Mexico	.35	.17	.03
☐ 32 Jean Derouillere Kansas State	.05	.02	.00
☐ 33 Doug Smith Missouri	.60	.30	.06
☐ 34 Chad Gallagher Creighton	.08	.04	.01
☐ 35 Marty Dow San Diego State	.08	.04	.01
☐ 36 Tony Farmer Nebraska	.08	.04	.01
☐ 37 John Taft Marshall	.08	.04	.01
☐ 38 Reggie Hanson Kentucky	.08	.04	.01
☐ 39 Terrell Brandon Oregon	.40	.20	.04
☐ 40 Dee Brown Flashback	.20	.10	.02
☐ 41 Doug Overton La Salle	.08	.04	.01
☐ 42 Joe Wylie Miami	.08	.04	.01
☐ 43 Myron Brown Slippery Rock	.10	.05	.01
☐ 44 Steve Hood James Madison	.10	.05	.01
☐ 45 Randy Brown New Mexico State	.15	.07	.01
☐ 46 Chris Corchiani NC State	.15	.07	.01
☐ 47 Kevin Lynch Minnesota	.15	.07	.01
☐ 48 Donald Hodge Temple	.35	.17	.03
☐ 49 LaBradford Smith Louisville	.30	.15	.03
☐ 50 Shawn Kemp Flashback	.25	.12	.02
☐ 51 Brian Shorter Pittsburgh	.08	.04	.01
☐ 52 Gary Waites Alabama	.05	.02	.00
☐ 53 Mike Iuzzolino St. Francis	.35	.17	.03
☐ 54 LeRon Ellis Syracuse	.12	.06	.01
☐ 55 Perry Carter Ohio State	.08	.04	.01
☐ 56 Keith Hughes Rutgers	.08	.04	.01
☐ 57 John Turner Phillips University	.15	.07	.01
☐ 58 Marcus Kennedy Eastern Michigan	.08	.04	.01
☐ 59 Randy Ayers CO Ohio State	.10	.05	.01
☐ 60 All Rookie Team	.35	.17	.03
☐ 61 Jackie Jones Oklahoma	.08	.04	.01
☐ 62 Shaun Vandiver Colorado	.12	.06	.01
☐ 63 Dale Davis Clemson	.35	.17	.03
☐ 64 Jimmy Oliver Purdue	.20	.10	.02
☐ 65 Elliot Perry Memphis State	.15	.07	.01
☐ 66 Jerome Harmon Louisville	.08	.04	.01
☐ 67 Darrin Chancellor Southern Mississippi	.08	.04	.01
☐ 68 Roy Fisher California (Berkeley)	.08	.04	.01
☐ 69 Rick Fox North Carolina	1.00	.50	.10
☐ 70 Kenny Anderson Special Second Card	.50	.25	.05
☐ 71 Richard Dumas Oklahoma State	.08	.04	.01
☐ 72 Checklist Card	.05	.02	.00
☐ NNO Salute/American Flag	.08	.04	.01

1968-69 Suns Carnation Milk

This 12-card set of Phoenix Suns was sponsored by Carnation Milk and was issued as panels on the sides of milk cartons. The fronts feature a player pose and brief biographical information near the photo. The bottom of the panels indicate "WIN, 440 Home Game tickets to be given away." The cards measure approximately 3 1/2" by 7 1/2" and are blank backed. The cards are unnumbered and are checklisted below in alphabetical order. Bob Warlick was only with the Phoenix Suns during the last half of the 1968-69 season. The set features the first professional card of Gail Goodrich.

	NRMT	VG-E	GOOD
COMPLETE SET (12)	300.00	150.00	30.00
COMMON PLAYER (1-12)	20.00	10.00	2.00
☐ 1 Jim Fox	20.00	10.00	2.00
☐ 2 Gail Goodrich	60.00	30.00	6.00
☐ 3 Gary Gregor	20.00	10.00	2.00
☐ 4 Neil Johnson	20.00	10.00	2.00
☐ 5 John Kerr CO	25.00	12.50	2.50
☐ 6 Dave Lattin	25.00	12.50	2.50
☐ 7 Stan McKenzie	20.00	10.00	2.00
☐ 8 McCoy McLemore	20.00	10.00	2.00
☐ 9 Dick Snyder	20.00	10.00	2.00
☐ 10 Dick Van Arsdale	30.00	15.00	3.00
☐ 11 Bob Warlick	20.00	10.00	2.00
☐ 12 George Wilson	20.00	10.00	2.00

1969-70 Suns Carnation Milk

This ten-card set features members of the Phoenix Suns and was produced by Carnation Milk. The cards show white backgrounds with blue and white drawings of the players. Playing tips (in red type) are found at the bottom of each card. Player statistics were on the opposite milk carton panel and hence were not saved in most cases. The cards measure approximately 3 1/2" by 7 1/2". The backs are blank. The cards are unnumbered and are checklisted below in alphabetical order. The set features the first professional card of Connie Hawkins.

	NRMT	VG-E	GOOD
COMPLETE SET (10)	300.00	150.00	30.00
COMMON PLAYER (1-10)	20.00	10.00	2.00
☐ 1 Jerry Chambers	20.00	10.00	2.00
☐ 2 Jim Fox	20.00	10.00	2.00
☐ 3 Gail Goodrich	60.00	30.00	6.00
☐ 4 Connie Hawkins	60.00	30.00	6.00
☐ 5 Stan McKenzie	20.00	10.00	2.00
☐ 6 Paul Silas	40.00	20.00	4.00
☐ 7 Dick Snyder	20.00	10.00	2.00
☐ 8 Dick Van Arsdale	30.00	15.00	3.00
☐ 9 Neal Walk	25.00	12.50	2.50
☐ 10 Gene Williams	20.00	10.00	2.00

1970-71 Suns Carnation Milk

This 11-card set features members of the Phoenix Suns and was produced by Carnation Milk. The cards have solid red backgrounds or orange backgrounds if the cards were from diet milk cartons. Apparently the entire set was issued in both color backgrounds. The cards measure approximately 3 1/2" by 7 1/2". The backs are blank. The cards are unnumbered and are checklisted below in alphabetical order.

	NRMT	VG-E	GOOD
COMPLETE SET (11)	300.00	150.00	30.00
COMMON PLAYER (1-11)	20.00	10.00	2.00
☐ 1 Mel Counts	25.00	12.50	2.50
☐ 2 Lamar Green	20.00	10.00	2.00
☐ 3 Art Harris	20.00	10.00	2.00
☐ 4 Clem Haskins	30.00	15.00	3.00
☐ 5 Connie Hawkins	55.00	27.50	5.50
☐ 6 Gus Johnson	40.00	20.00	4.00
☐ 7 Otto Moore	20.00	10.00	2.00
☐ 8 Paul Silas	40.00	20.00	4.00
☐ 9 Dick Van Arsdale	30.00	15.00	3.00
☐ 10 Bill VanBredaKolff CO	20.00	10.00	2.00
☐ 11 Neal Walk	25.00	12.50	2.50

1970-71 Suns A1 Premium Beer

These scarce cards are black and white and come with unperforated tabs. The cards were actually the price tabs for six-packs of beer. Apparently the 98 cent variations are tougher to find. The set features members of the Phoenix Suns. There are three variations primarily based on the price marked on the tab. The cards are unnumbered and are checklisted below in alphabetical order.

	NRMT	VG-E	GOOD
COMPLETE SET (13)	1200.00	600.00	125.00
COMMON PLAYER (1-10)	75.00	37.50	7.50
☐ 1A Mel Counts (95 cents)	90.00	45.00	9.00
☐ 1B Mel Counts (98 cents)	125.00	60.00	12.50
☐ 2 Lamar Green	75.00	37.50	7.50
☐ 3 Clem Haskins	100.00	50.00	10.00
☐ 4 Connie Hawkins	150.00	75.00	15.00
☐ 5 Greg Howard	75.00	37.50	7.50
☐ 6 Paul Silas	100.00	50.00	10.00
☐ 7 Fred Taylor	75.00	37.50	7.50
☐ 8A Dick Van Arsdale ERR (reversed negative)	150.00	75.00	15.00
☐ 8B Dick Van Arsdale COR	100.00	50.00	10.00
☐ 9A Neal Walk (95 cents)	90.00	45.00	9.00
☐ 9B Neal Walk (no price)	125.00	60.00	12.50
☐ 10 John Wetzel	75.00	37.50	7.50

1975-76 Suns Phoenix

The 1975-76 Phoenix Suns set contains 16 cards, including 12 player cards. The fronts feature black and white pictures, and the backs are blank. The dimensions are approximately 3 1/2" by 4 3/8". The set commemorates the Suns' Western Conference Championship. The cards are unnumbered and are checklisted below in alphabetical order. The set features Alvan Adams' first professional card.

	NRMT	VG-E	GOOD
COMPLETE SET (16)	15.00	7.50	1.50
COMMON PLAYER (1-16)	.60	.30	.06
☐ 1 Alvan Adams	2.50	1.25	.25
☐ 2 Dennis Awtrey	.75	.35	.07
☐ 3 Al Bianchi GM	.75	.35	.07
☐ 4 Jerry Colangelo VP	.60	.30	.06
☐ 5 Keith Erickson	1.00	.50	.10
☐ 6 Nate Hawthorne	.60	.30	.06
☐ 7 Garfield Heard	1.00	.50	.10
☐ 8 Phil Lumpkin	.60	.30	.06
☐ 9 John MacLeod CO	1.25	.60	.12
☐ 10 Curtis Perry	1.00	.50	.10
☐ 11 Joe Proski TR	.60	.30	.06
☐ 12 Pat Riley	3.00	1.50	.30
☐ 13 Ricky Sobers	1.25	.60	.12
☐ 14 Dick Van Arsdale	1.00	.50	.10
☐ 15 Paul Westphal	3.00	1.50	.30
☐ 16 John Wetzel	.60	.30	.06

1976-77 Suns Phoenix

The 1976-77 Phoenix Suns set contains 12 horizontal player cards measuring 3 1/2" by 4 3/8". The fronts have circular black and white photos framed by the Suns' orange and purple logo. The backs are blank.

	NRMT	VG-E	GOOD
COMPLETE SET (12)	12.00	6.00	1.20
COMMON PLAYER (1-12)	.60	.30	.06
☐ 1 Alvan Adams	1.50	.75	.15
☐ 2 Dennis Awtrey	.75	.35	.07
☐ 3 Keith Erickson	1.00	.50	.10
☐ 4 Butch Feher	.60	.30	.06
☐ 5 Garfield Heard	1.00	.50	.10
☐ 6 Ron Lee	.60	.30	.06
☐ 7 Curtis Perry	.75	.35	.07
☐ 8 Ricky Sobers	1.00	.50	.10
☐ 9 Ira Terrell	1.00	.50	.10
☐ 10 Dick Van Arsdale	1.00	.50	.10
☐ 11 Tom Van Arsdale	1.00	.50	.10
☐ 12 Paul Westphal	2.50	1.25	.25

1977-78 Suns Humpty Dumpty Discs

The 1977-78 Humpty Dumpty Phoenix Suns set contains 12 discs measuring approximately 3 1/4" in diameter. The blankbacked discs are printed on thick stock. The fronts feature small black and white facial photos surrounded by a purple border with orange trim. Players are numbered below in alphabetical order by subject. The set features Walter Davis' first professional card.

	NRMT	VG-E	GOOD
COMPLETE SET (12)	15.00	7.50	1.50
COMMON PLAYER	.75	.35	.07
☐ 1 Alvan Adams	2.00	1.00	.20
☐ 2 Dennis Awtrey	.75	.35	.07
☐ 3 Mike Bratz	1.00	.50	.10
☐ 4 Don Buse	1.00	.50	.10
☐ 5 Walter Davis	4.50	2.25	.45
☐ 6 Bayard Forrest	.75	.35	.07
☐ 7 Garfield Heard	1.25	.60	.12
☐ 8 Ron Lee	.75	.35	.07
☐ 9 Curtis Perry	1.00	.50	.10
☐ 10 Alvin Scott	.75	.35	.07
☐ 11 Ira Terrell	1.00	.50	.10
☐ 12 Paul Westphal	3.00	1.50	.30

1980-81 Suns Pepsi

The 1980-81 Pepsi Phoenix Suns set contains 12 numbered cards attached to a bumper sticker-sized promotional flyer/ entry blank. The cards themselves are approximately 2 1/2" by 3 1/2". The fronts feature color photos, and the backs include statistics and biographical information. The cards were part of a promotion featuring the fans' selection of their Suns' dream team.

	MINT	EXC	G-VG
COMPLETE SET (12)	15.00	7.50	1.50
COMMON PLAYER (1-12)	.75	.35	.07
☐ 1 Walter Davis	2.50	1.25	.25
☐ 2 Alvin Scott	.75	.35	.07
☐ 3 Johnny High	1.00	.50	.10
☐ 4 Dennis Johnson	3.00	1.50	.30
☐ 5 Alvan Adams	1.50	.75	.15
☐ 6 Rich Kelley	1.00	.50	.10
☐ 7 Truck Robinson	1.50	.75	.15
☐ 8 Joel Kramer	.75	.35	.07
☐ 9 Jeff Cook	.75	.35	.07
☐ 10 Mike Niles	.75	.35	.07
☐ 11 Kyle Macy	1.25	.60	.12
☐ 12 John MacLeod CO	1.00	.50	.10

1982-83 Suns Giant Service

The 1982-83 Giant Self Service Stations Phoenix Suns set contains three cards each measuring approximately 3 1/4" by 4 1/2". The fronts have color photos while the backs show detailed career highlights and statistics. Each card has a safety tip on back. Apparently during the course of the promotion, one card was given out each month until the end of the season, Walter Davis in January, Maurice Lucas in February, and Larry Nance in March. In addition to being available at gas stations, the cards were also distributed at the Phoenix Suns' Arena on "Giant Service Station Night". The set features Larry Nance's first professional card.

	MINT	EXC	G-VG
COMPLETE SET (3)	16.00	8.00	1.60
COMMON PLAYER (1-3)	5.00	2.50	.50
☐ 1 Walter Davis January	6.00	3.00	.60
☐ 2 Maurice Lucas February	5.00	2.50	.50
☐ 3 Larry Nance March	10.00	5.00	1.00

1984-85 Suns Police

This set contains 16 cards measuring 2 5/8" by 4 1/8" featuring the Phoenix Suns. This set was issued in the Summer of 1984. Backs contain safety tips ("Suns Tips") and are written in purple print with an orange accent color. The set was sponsored by Kiwanis, the Suns, the NBA, and the Phoenix Police. The cards are unnumbered except for uniform number.

	MINT	EXC	G-VG
COMPLETE SET (16)	30.00	15.00	3.00
COMMON PLAYER	1.25	.60	.12
☐ 4 Kyle Macy	2.00	1.00	.20
☐ 6 Walter Davis	3.50	1.75	.35
☐ 7 Mike Sanders	2.50	1.25	.25
☐ 8 Rick Robey	2.00	1.00	.20
☐ 10 Rod Foster	1.50	.75	.15
☐ 14 Alvin Scott	1.25	.60	.12
☐ 21 Maurice Lucas	2.00	1.00	.20
☐ 22 Larry Nance	5.00	2.50	.50
☐ 32 Charles Pittman	1.25	.60	.12
☐ 33 Alvan Adams	2.50	1.25	.25
☐ 44 Paul Westphal	3.50	1.75	.35
☐ 53 James Edwards	3.00	1.50	.30
☐ xx Suns Mascot	1.25	.60	.12
☐ xx John MacLeod CO	2.00	1.00	.20
☐ xx Al Bianchi ACO	1.25	.60	.12
☐ xx Joe Proski TR	1.25	.60	.12

1987-88 Suns Circle K

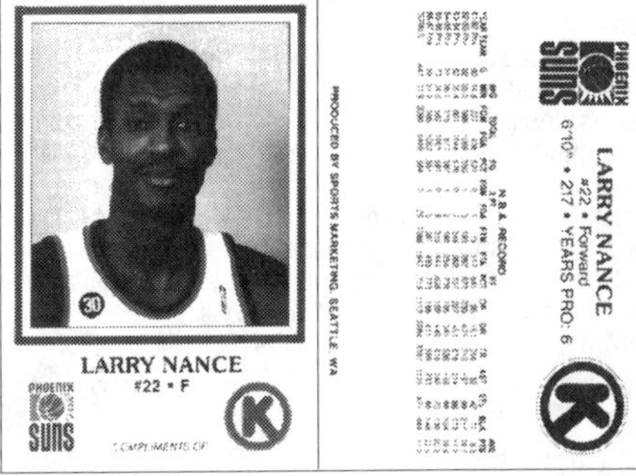

This ten-card set was sponsored by Circle K stores. The cards were issued in two strips of five player cards each, plus a coupon. After perforation, the cards measure the standard size (2 1/2" by 3 1/2"). The front features a posed color player photo, with white and purple borders on white card stock. Player information is given below the picture, and team and sponsor logos in the lower corners round out the card face. In a horizontal format the back has biographical and statistical information. The cards are unnumbered and are checklist below in alphabetical order, with the uniform number after the player's name. The set features Jeff Hornacek's first professional card.

	MINT	EXC	G-VG
COMPLETE SET (10)	24.00	12.00	2.40
COMMON PLAYER (1-10)	1.25	.60	.12
☐ 1 Alvan Adams 33	2.50	1.25	.25
☐ 2 Herb Brown ACO	1.25	.60	.12
☐ 3 Jeff Cook 45	1.25	.60	.12
☐ 4 Walter Davis 6	3.00	1.50	.30
☐ 5 James Edwards 53	2.50	1.25	.25
☐ 6 Jeff Hornacek 14	9.00	4.50	.90
☐ 7 Larry Nance 22	3.50	1.75	.35
☐ 8 Mike Sanders 11	2.00	1.00	.20
☐ 9 Bernard Thompson 7	1.25	.60	.12
☐ 10 John Wetzel CO	1.25	.60	.12

1990-91 Suns Smokey

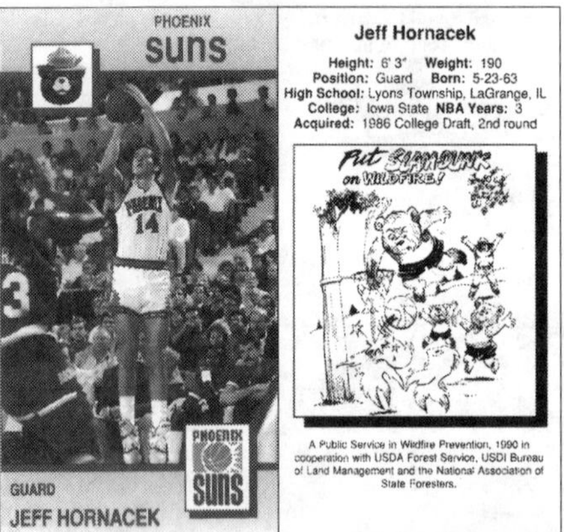

This five-card set of Phoenix Suns was sponsored by the USDA Forest Service in cooperation with several other federal agencies. The cards are oversized and measure approximately 3" by 5". The front features a color action player photo, with the Smokey Bear logo superimposed on the top left edge of the picture and the team logo on the bottom right edge. The picture is bordered in purple and has a shadow format. The team name and player's name are given in purple lettering on a peach-colored background. The back presents brief biographical information and features a fire prevention cartoon starring Smokey the Bear. The cards are unnumbered and are checklisted below in alphabetical order. Eddie Johnson was apparently pulled from distribution after he was traded and hence his card is a little tougher to find than the other four players.

	MINT	EXC	G-VG
COMPLETE SET (5)	20.00	10.00	2.00
COMMON PLAYER (1-5)	4.50	2.25	.45
☐ 1 Tom Chambers	4.50	2.25	.45
☐ 2 Jeff Hornacek	4.50	2.25	.45
☐ 3 Eddie Johnson SP	7.50	3.75	.75
☐ 4 Kevin Johnson	6.00	3.00	.60
☐ 5 Dan Majerle	4.50	2.25	.45

1969-70 Supersonics Sunbeam Bread

This 11-card set consists of cards measuring 2 3/4" by 2 3/4". The cards were attached to plastic bread ties and issued on loafs of Sunbeam Bread. The front features a color posed photo of each player shot from the waist up. The team and player name are given in white lettering in the picture. The photo has a thin red border, with the words "Sunbeam Enriched Bread" across the top of the card face. The words "Sonic Stars" are written vertically along the right side of the picture. Cards show the team's schedule for the 1969-70 season. Cards are unnumbered so they are listed below in alphabetical order.

	NRMT	VG-E	GOOD
COMPLETE SET (11)	90.00	45.00	9.00
COMMON PLAYER (1-11)	7.50	3.75	.75
☐ 1 Lucius Allen	12.00	6.00	1.20
☐ 2 Bob Boozer	7.50	3.75	.75
☐ 3 Barry Clemens	7.50	3.75	.75
☐ 4 Art Harris	7.50	3.75	.75
☐ 5 Tom Meschery	7.50	3.75	.75
☐ 6 Erwin Mueller	7.50	3.75	.75
☐ 7 Dorie Murrey	7.50	3.75	.75
☐ 8 Bob Rule	7.50	3.75	.75
☐ 9 John Tresvant	7.50	3.75	.75
☐ 10 Len Wilkens (Player/coach)	20.00	10.00	2.00
☐ 11 Sonics Coliseum	7.50	3.75	.75

1970-71 Supersonics Sunbeam Bread

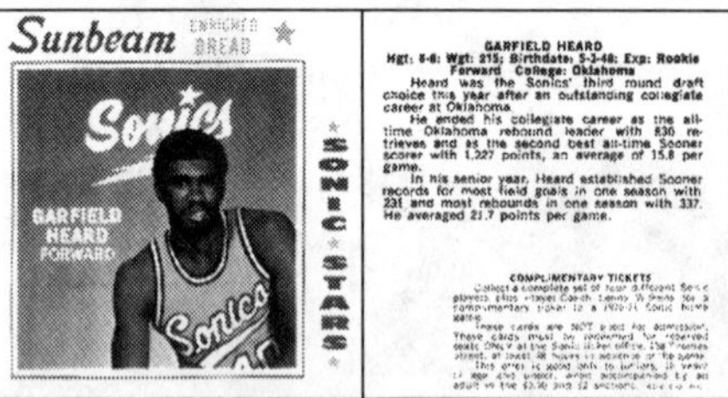

This 11-card set consists of cards measuring 2 3/4" by 2 3/4". The cards were attached to plastic bread ties and issued on loafs of Sunbeam Bread. The front features a color posed photo of each player shot from the waist up. The team and player name are given in white lettering in the picture. The photo has a thin red border, with the words "Sunbeam Enriched Bread" across the top of the card face. The words "Sonic Stars" are written vertically along the right side of the picture. The back has a career summary of the player and an offer to complete a set of four different Sonic players (including Wilkens) for a complimentary ticket to a 1970-71 Seattle Supersonics home game. Cards are unnumbered so they are listed below in alphabetical order.

	NRMT	VG-E	GOOD
COMPLETE SET (11)	90.00	45.00	9.00
COMMON PLAYER (1-11)	7.50	3.75	.75
☐ 1 Tom Black	7.50	3.75	.75
☐ 2 Barry Clemens	7.50	3.75	.75
☐ 3 Pete Cross	7.50	3.75	.75
☐ 4 Jake Ford	7.50	3.75	.75
☐ 5 Garfield Heard	10.00	5.00	1.00
☐ 6 Don Kojis	7.50	3.75	.75
☐ 7 Tom Meschery	7.50	3.75	.75
☐ 8 Dick Snyder	7.50	3.75	.75
☐ 9 Len Wilkens (Player/Coach)	20.00	10.00	2.00
☐ 10 Lee Winfield	7.50	3.75	.75
☐ 11 Seattle Coliseum	7.50	3.75	.75

1971-72 Supersonics Sunbeam Bread

This 11-card set consists of cards measuring 2 3/4" by 2 3/4". The cards were attached to plastic bread ties and issued on loafs of Sunbeam Bread. The front features a color posed photo of each player shot from the waist up. The team and player name are given in white lettering in the picture. The photo has a thin red border, with the words "Sunbeam Enriched Bread" across the top of the card face. The words "Sonic Stars" are written vertically along the right side of the picture. Cards are unnumbered so they are listed below in alphabetical order.

	NRMT	VG-E	GOOD
COMPLETE SET (11)	90.00	45.00	9.00
COMMON PLAYER (1-11)	7.50	3.75	.75
☐ 1 Pete Cross	7.50	3.75	.75
☐ 2 Jake Ford	7.50	3.75	.75
☐ 3 Spencer Haywood	15.00	7.50	1.50
☐ 4 Garfield Heard	10.00	5.00	1.00
☐ 5 Don Kojis	7.50	3.75	.75
☐ 6 Bob Rule	7.50	3.75	.75
☐ 7 Don Smith	7.50	3.75	.75
☐ 8 Dick Snyder	7.50	3.75	.75
☐ 9 Len Wilkens (Player/Coach)	20.00	10.00	2.00
☐ 10 Lee Winfield	7.50	3.75	.75
☐ 11 Sonics Coliseum	7.50	3.75	.75

1973-74 Supersonics Shur-Fresh

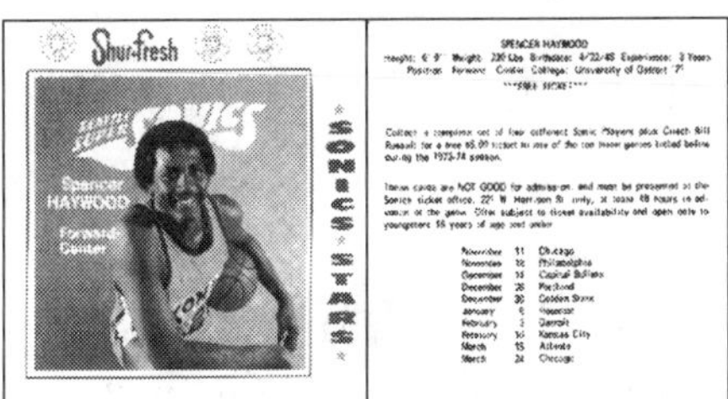

The 1973-74 Shur-Fresh Seattle Supersonics set contains 12 cards measuring 2 3/4" square. There are ten player cards and two coach cards. The cards have plastic bread ties attached to them. The fronts have color photos and the backs have biographical information. Cards are unnumbered so they are listed below in alphabetical order. The set features one of the few cards of Hall of Famer Bill Russell.

	NRMT	VG-E	GOOD
COMPLETE SET (12)	125.00	60.00	12.50
COMMON PLAYER (1-12)	7.50	3.75	.75
☐ 1 John Brisker	7.50	3.75	.75
☐ 2 Fred Brown	15.00	7.50	1.50
☐ 3 Emmette Bryant ACO	7.50	3.75	.75
☐ 4 Jim Fox	7.50	3.75	.75
☐ 5 Dick Gibbs	7.50	3.75	.75
☐ 6 Spencer Haywood	12.00	6.00	1.20
☐ 7 Bill Russell CO	50.00	25.00	5.00
☐ 8 Jim McDaniels	7.50	3.75	.75
☐ 9 Kennedy McIntosh	7.50	3.75	.75
☐ 10 Dick Snyder	7.50	3.75	.75
☐ 11 Bud Stallworth	7.50	3.75	.75
☐ 12 Lee Winfield	7.50	3.75	.75

1978-79 Supersonics Police

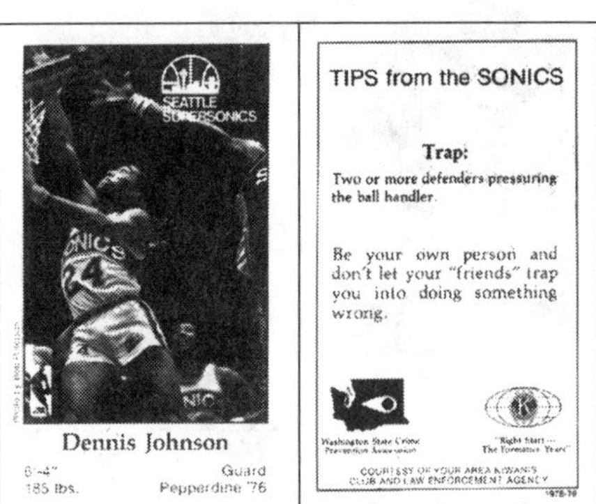

This set contains 16 unnumbered cards measuring 2 5/8" by 4 1/8" featuring the Seattle Supersonics. The set was sponsored by the Washington State Crime Prevention Association, Kiwanis Club, and local law enforcement agencies. The year of issue is printed in the lower right corner of the reverse. Backs contain safety tips ("Tips from the Sonics") and are written in black ink with blue accent. The cards are listed below in alphabetical order; the uniform number is added parenthetically in the checklist below where applicable. The set features early professional cards of Dennis Johnson and Jack Sikma.

	NRMT	VG-E	GOOD
COMPLETE SET (16)	15.00	7.50	1.50
COMMON PLAYER (1-16)	.75	.35	.07
☐ 1 Fred Brown (32)	1.50	.75	.15
☐ 2 Joe Hassett (10)	.75	.35	.07
☐ 3 Dennis Johnson (24)	2.00	1.00	.20
☐ 4 John Johnson (27)	1.00	.50	.10
☐ 5 Tom LaGarde (23)	.75	.35	.07
☐ 6 Lonnie Shelton (8)	1.00	.50	.10
☐ 7 Jack Sikma (43)	1.50	.75	.15
☐ 8 Paul Silas (35)	1.25	.60	.12
☐ 9 Dick Snyder (11)	.75	.35	.07
☐ 10 Wally Walker (42)	.75	.35	.07
☐ 11 Gus Williams (1)	1.50	.75	.15
☐ 12 Len Wilkens CO	2.00	1.00	.20
☐ 13 Les Habegger ASST	.75	.35	.07
☐ 14 Frank Furtado TR	.75	.35	.07
☐ 15 T. Wheedle, mascot	.75	.35	.07
☐ 16 Team Photo	1.00	.50	.10

1979-80 Supersonics Police

This set contains 16 numbered cards measuring 2 5/8" by 4 1/8" featuring the Seattle Supersonics. Backs contain safety tips ("Tips for the Sonics") and are written in blue ink with red accent. The cards are numbered and dated in the lower right corner of the obverse. The set was sponsored by the Washington State Crime Prevention Association, Kiwanis, Coca Cola, Rainier Bank, and local area law enforcement agencies. The set features the first professional card of Vinnie Johnson.

	MINT	EXC	G-VG
COMPLETE SET (16)	12.00	6.00	1.20
COMMON PLAYER (1-16)	.50	.25	.05
☐ 1 Gus Williams	1.25	.60	.12
☐ 2 James Bailey	.75	.35	.07
☐ 3 Jack Sikma	1.25	.60	.12
☐ 4 Tom LaGarde	.50	.25	.05
☐ 5 Paul Silas	1.00	.50	.10
☐ 6 Lonnie Shelton	.75	.35	.07
☐ 7 T. Wheedle (mascot)	.50	.25	.05
☐ 8 Vinnie Johnson	3.00	1.50	.30

☐ 9 Dennis Johnson	1.50	.75	.15
☐ 10 Wally Walker	.50	.25	.05
☐ 11 Les Habegger ASST	.50	.25	.05
☐ 12 Frank Furtado TR	.50	.25	.05
☐ 13 Fred Brown	1.00	.50	.10
☐ 14 John Johnson	.75	.35	.07
☐ 15 Team Photo	.75	.35	.07
☐ 16 Len Wilkens CO	1.50	.75	.15

1983-84 Supersonics Police

This set contains 16 cards measuring 2 5/8" by 4 1/8" featuring the Seattle Supersonics. Backs contain safety tips ("Tips from the Sonics") and are written in blue ink with a red accent. Set was also sponsored by the Washington State Crime Prevention Association, Kiwanis, Coca Cola, Ernst Home Centers, and area law enforcement agencies. The year of issue is given at the bottom right corner of the obverse. The cards are numbered on the back. The set features an early professional card of Tom Chambers.

	MINT	EXC	G-VG
COMPLETE SET (16)	7.00	3.50	.70
COMMON PLAYER (1-16)	.35	.17	.03
☐ 1 Reggie King	.35	.17	.03
☐ 2 Frank Furtado TR	.35	.17	.03
☐ 3 Tom Chambers	1.50	.75	.15
☐ 4 Dave Harshman ASST	.35	.17	.03
☐ 5 Gus Williams	.75	.35	.07
☐ 6 T. Wheedle, mascot	.35	.17	.03
☐ 7 Scooter McCray	.35	.17	.03
☐ 8 Jack Sikma	.75	.35	.07
☐ 9 Al Wood	.35	.17	.03
☐ 10 Bob Blackburn, Voice of the Sonics	.35	.17	.03
☐ 11 Danny Vranes	.35	.17	.03
☐ 12 Charles Bradley	.35	.17	.03
☐ 13 Steve Hawes	.35	.17	.03
☐ 14 Jon Sundvold	.50	.25	.05
☐ 15 Fred Brown	.75	.35	.07
☐ 16 Lenny Wilkens CO	1.25	.60	.12

1990-91 Supersonics Kayo

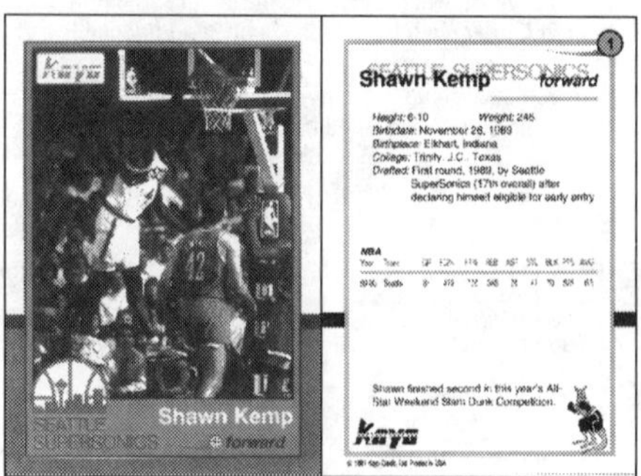

This 14-card set was produced by Kayo Cards as a give-away to fans attending the April 13, 1991 Seattle Supersonics home game. A total of 10,000 sets supposedly were produced. The cards are numbered on the back. Cards are standard size, 2 1/2" by 3 1/2". The set features early professional cards of Shawn Kemp and Gary Payton.

	MINT	EXC	G-VG
COMPLETE SET (14)	8.00	4.00	.80
COMMON PLAYER (1-14)	.30	.15	.03
☐ 1 Shawn Kemp	3.50	1.75	.35
☐ 2 Scott Meents	.30	.15	.03
☐ 3 Derrick McKey	.75	.35	.07
☐ 4 Michael Cage	.30	.15	.03
☐ 5 Benoit Benjamin	.50	.25	.05
☐ 6 Dave Corzine	.30	.15	.03
☐ 7 K.C. Jones CO	.50	.25	.05
☐ 8 Quintin Dailey	.30	.15	.03
☐ 9 Ricky Pierce	.75	.35	.07
☐ 10 Eddie Johnson	.60	.30	.06
☐ 11 Nate McMillan	.40	.20	.04
☐ 12 Gary Payton	1.25	.60	.12
☐ 13 Sedale Threatt	.50	.25	.05
☐ 14 Dana Barros	.40	.20	.04

1990-91 Supersonics Smokey

This 16-card set was sponsored by the USDA Forest Service in conjunction with other federal agencies. The cards were issued in a sheet of four rows of four cards each. After perforation, they measure the standard size (2 1/2" by 3 1/2"). The front features a color action player photo, with the Smokey the Bear logo in the lower left corner. The front is done in the team's colors: border and lettering in yellow on a green background. The team name is inscribed above the picture, with the player's name below. The back presents biographical information and a fire prevention cartoon starring Smokey. The set features early professional cards of Shawn Kemp and Gary Payton.

	MINT	EXC	G-VG
COMPLETE SET (16)	15.00	7.50	1.50
COMMON PLAYER (1-16)	.50	.25	.05
☐ 1 Dana Barros	.75	.35	.07
☐ 2 Michael Cage	.60	.30	.06
☐ 3 Dave Corzine	.50	.25	.05
☐ 4 Quintin Dailey	.50	.25	.05
☐ 5 Dale Ellis	1.00	.50	.10
☐ 6 K.C. Jones CO	1.00	.50	.10
☐ 7 Shawn Kemp	4.50	2.25	.45
☐ 8 Bob Kloppenburg CO	.50	.25	.05
☐ 9 Xavier McDaniel	1.50	.75	.15
☐ 10 Derrick McKey	1.00	.50	.10
☐ 11 Nate McMillan	.75	.35	.07
☐ 12 Scott Meents	.60	.30	.06
☐ 13 Kip Moota CO	.50	.25	.05
☐ 14 Gary Payton	1.50	.75	.15
☐ 15 Olden Polynice	.50	.25	.05
☐ 16 Sedale Threatt	1.00	.50	.10

☐ 19 Ken Jones	.75	.35	.07
☐ 20 Rory Sparrow	3.50	1.75	.35
☐ 21 Mauro Panaggio (Coach Rochester)	1.00	.50	.10
☐ 22 Glenn Hagan	.75	.35	.07
☐ 23 Larry Fogle	1.25	.60	.12
☐ 24 Wayne Abrams	.75	.35	.07
☐ 25 Jerry Christian	.75	.35	.07
☐ 26 Edgar Jones	1.50	.75	.15
☐ 27 Jerry Radocha	.75	.35	.07
☐ 28 Greg Jackson	.75	.35	.07
☐ 29 Eddie Mast (Player/Coach, Lehigh Valley)	.75	.35	.07
☐ 30 Ron Davis	.75	.35	.07
☐ 31 Tico Brown	.75	.35	.07
☐ 32 Freeman Blade	.75	.35	.07
☐ 33 Bill Klucas (Coach Anchorage)	.75	.35	.07
☐ 34 Melvin Davis	1.25	.60	.12
☐ 35 James Hardy	.75	.35	.07
☐ 36 Brad Davis	4.00	2.00	.40
☐ 37 Andre Wakefield	.75	.35	.07
☐ 38 Brett Vroman	.75	.35	.07
☐ 39 Larry Knight	.75	.35	.07
☐ 40 Mel Bennett	.75	.35	.07
☐ 41 Stan Eckwood	.75	.35	.07
☐ 42 Andrew Parker	.75	.35	.07
☐ 43 Billy Ray(Dunk) Bates	3.50	1.75	.35
☐ 44 Matt Teahan	.75	.35	.07
☐ 45 Carlton Green	.75	.35	.07

1980-81 TCMA CBA

The 1980-81 Continental Basketball Association set, produced by TCMA, features 45 black and white photos of the players along with the team name in red along the side of the front of the card. The backs contain brief biographical data and statistics, the CBA logo, the team logo and the card number. A 1981 TCMA copyright date also appears on the back. The cards are numbered on back and are printed on white cardboard backs. Cards measure the standard 2 1/2" by 3 1/2".

	MINT	EXC	G-VG
COMPLETE SET (45)	50.00	25.00	5.00
COMMON PLAYER (1-45)	.75	.35	.07
☐ 1 Chubby Cox	1.50	.75	.15
☐ 2 Sylvester Cuyler	.75	.35	.07
☐ 3 Harry Davis	.75	.35	.07
☐ 4 Danny Salisbury	.75	.35	.07
☐ 5 Cazzie Russell	5.00	2.50	.50
☐ 6 Al Green	.75	.35	.07
☐ 7 Rick Wilson	.75	.35	.07
☐ 8 Jim Brogan	.75	.35	.07
☐ 9 Andre McCarter	1.50	.75	.15
☐ 10 Jerry Baskerville	.75	.35	.07
☐ 11 James Woods	.75	.35	.07
☐ 12 Geoff Crompton	1.50	.75	.15
☐ 13 Korky Nelson	.75	.35	.07
☐ 14 George Karl (Coach Montana)	2.50	1.25	.25
☐ 15 Stan Pietkiewicz	.75	.35	.07
☐ 16 Raymond Townsend	1.50	.75	.15
☐ 17 Lenny Horton	.75	.35	.07
☐ 18 Carl Bailey	.75	.35	.07

1981 TCMA NBA

This 44-card set features some of the all-time great basketball players. The fronts feature a color posed photo of the player, while the back has name, career summary, and career highlights. The cards are numbered on the back and checklisted below accordingly. The cards are standard size, 2 1/2" by 3 1/2".

	MINT	VG-E	F-G
COMPLETE SET (44)	100.00	50.00	10.00
COMMON PLAYER (1-44)	1.00	.50	.10
☐ 1 Alex Hannum	1.00	.50	.10
☐ 2 Larry Foust	1.00	.50	.10
☐ 3 George Mikan	12.00	6.00	1.20
☐ 4 Mel(Hutch) Hutchins	1.00	.50	.10
☐ 5 Bob Pettit	5.00	2.50	.50
☐ 6 Willis Reed	5.00	2.50	.50
☐ 7 Adolph Schayes	3.00	1.50	.30
☐ 8 Vern Mikkelsen	2.00	1.00	.20
☐ 9 Cazzie Russell	2.00	1.00	.20
☐ 10 Dick Van Arsdale	1.00	.50	.10
☐ 11 Lenny Wilkens	3.50	1.75	.35
☐ 12 Ray Felix	1.00	.50	.10
☐ 13 Ed Macauley	2.00	1.00	.20
☐ 14 Clyde Lovellette	2.00	1.00	.20
☐ 15 Slater(Dugie) Martin	2.00	1.00	.20
☐ 16 Bill Russell	20.00	10.00	2.00
☐ 17 Oscar Robertson	7.50	3.75	.75
☐ 18 Bill Bradley	7.50	3.75	.75
☐ 19 Elgin Baylor	6.00	3.00	.60
☐ 20 Bill Sharman	3.00	1.50	.30
☐ 21 Tom(Satch) Sanders	1.00	.50	.10
☐ 22 Dave Bing	3.00	1.50	.30
☐ 23 Carl Braun	1.00	.50	.10

☐ 24 Frank Selvy	1.00	.50	.10
☐ 25 George Yardley	1.00	.50	.10
☐ 26 Dick McGuire	1.00	.50	.10
☐ 27 Leroy Ellis	1.00	.50	.10
☐ 28 Jack Twyman	2.00	1.00	.20
☐ 29 Nate Thurmond	3.00	1.50	.30
☐ 30 Walt Frazier	4.00	2.00	.40
☐ 31 John(Red) Kerr	1.00	.50	.10
☐ 32 Jerry West	12.00	6.00	1.20
☐ 33 John Egan	1.00	.50	.10
☐ 34 Jim Loscutoff	1.00	.50	.10
☐ 35 Bob Leonard	1.00	.50	.10
☐ 36 Rick Barry	5.00	2.50	.50
☐ 37 Gene Shue	1.00	.50	.10
☐ 38 Jerry Lucas	4.00	2.00	.40
☐ 39 Dave DeBusschere	3.00	1.50	.30
☐ 40 John Green, Charles Tyra, Carl Braun, Richie Guerin, and John George	1.00	.50	.10
☐ 41 Bob Cousy	7.50	3.75	.75
☐ 42 Walter Bellamy	1.00	.50	.10
☐ 43 Billy Cunningham	3.00	1.50	.30
☐ 44 Wilt Chamberlain	16.00	8.00	1.60

1981-82 TCMA CBA

This 90-card set features black and white photos surrounded by a red frame line in which the player's name and team are printed. The Continental Basketball Association (CBA) logo appears in black on the front of the card. The back of the card contains the card number, career statistics, brief biographical data, and the team and CBA logos. A TCMA copyright date appears on the back. Cards measure the standard 2 1/2" by 3 1/2".

	MINT	EXC	G-VG
COMPLETE SET (90)	75.00	37.50	7.50
COMMON PLAYER (1-90)	.75	.35	.07
☐ 1 1981 CBA Champions Rochester Zeniths (previous champions listed on back)	2.00	1.00	.20
☐ 2 Wayne Abrams	.75	.35	.07
☐ 3 Pete Taylor	.75	.35	.07
☐ 4 George Torres	.75	.35	.07
☐ 5 Henry Bibby	3.00	1.50	.30
☐ 6 Rufus Harris	.75	.35	.07
☐ 7 Donnie Koonce	.75	.35	.07
☐ 8 Jeff Wilkins	1.50	.75	.15
☐ 9 Kurt Nimphius	2.00	1.00	.20
☐ 10 Billy Ray Bates	3.50	1.75	.35
☐ 11 James Lee	1.50	.75	.15
☐ 12 Marlon Redmond	.75	.35	.07
☐ 13 Gary Mazza (Coach Alberta)	.75	.35	.07
☐ 14 Tony Fuller	.75	.35	.07
☐ 15 Brad Davis	3.50	1.75	.35
☐ 16 Joe Cooper	1.25	.60	.12
☐ 17 Andra Griffin	.75	.35	.07
☐ 18 Rudy White	1.50	.75	.15
☐ 19 Ricky Williams	.75	.35	.07
☐ 20 Glenn Hagan	.75	.35	.07
☐ 21 Ernie Graham	.75	.35	.07
☐ 22 Kevin Graham	.75	.35	.07
☐ 23 Billy Reid	.75	.35	.07
☐ 24 Mauro Panaggio (Coach Rochester)	1.00	.50	.10
☐ 25 Bo Ellis	3.50	1.75	.35
☐ 26 Ollie Matson	.75	.35	.07
☐ 27 Tony Turner	.75	.35	.07
☐ 28 Leo Papile (Coach Quincy)	.75	.35	.07
☐ 29 Larry Holmes	.75	.35	.07
☐ 30 Steve Hayes	2.00	1.00	.20
☐ 31 Carl Bailey	.75	.35	.07
☐ 32 Tico Brown	.75	.35	.07
☐ 33 Percy Davis	.75	.35	.07
☐ 34 Al Leslie	.75	.35	.07
☐ 35 Ken Dennard	1.50	.75	.15
☐ 36 Larry Spriggs	3.50	1.75	.35
☐ 37 John Smith	.75	.35	.07
☐ 38 Kenny Natt	1.50	.75	.15
☐ 39 Harry Heineken	.75	.35	.07
☐ 40 Lowes Moore	1.50	.75	.15
☐ 41 Curtis Berry	1.25	.60	.12
☐ 42 Freeman Blade (Coach Anchorage)	.75	.35	.07
☐ 43 Larry Lawrence	.75	.35	.07
☐ 44 Purvis Miller	1.25	.60	.12
☐ 45 Ron Valentine	.75	.35	.07
☐ 46 Charles Floyd	.75	.35	.07
☐ 47 Greg Cornelius	.75	.35	.07
☐ 48 Clay Johnson	1.50	.75	.15
☐ 49 Bill Klucas (Coach Billings)	.75	.35	.07
☐ 50 Cazzie Russell (Player/Coach Lancaster)	3.00	1.50	.30
☐ 51 Craig Shelton	2.00	1.00	.20
☐ 52 Dave Britton	.75	.35	.07
☐ 53 Ken Green	.75	.35	.07
☐ 54 Stan Pawlak (Coach Atlantic City)	.75	.35	.07
☐ 55 Rich Yonakor	1.50	.75	.15
☐ 56 Darryl Gladden	.75	.35	.07
☐ 57 Norman Black	.75	.35	.07
☐ 58 Pete Harris	.75	.35	.07
☐ 59 Anthony Roberts	1.50	.75	.15
☐ 60 Jawann Oldham	3.00	1.50	.30
☐ 61 Sam Clancy	3.00	1.50	.30
☐ 62 Andre McCarter	1.25	.60	.12
☐ 63 Joe Merten	.75	.35	.07
☐ 64 Eddie Moss	.75	.35	.07
☐ 65 Brad Branson	.75	.35	.07
☐ 66 Lenny Horton	.75	.35	.07
☐ 67 Jerome Henderson	.75	.35	.07
☐ 68 Terry Stotts	.75	.35	.07
☐ 69 Tony Wells	.75	.35	.07
☐ 70 Rickey Green	4.00	2.00	.40
☐ 71 Don Newman	.75	.35	.07
☐ 72 Randy Owens	.75	.35	.07
☐ 73 Erv Giddings	.75	.35	.07
☐ 74 Barry Young	1.00	.50	.10
☐ 75 Jim Brogan	.75	.35	.07
☐ 76 Richard Johnson	.75	.35	.07
☐ 77 George Karl (Coach Montana)	2.50	1.25	.25
☐ 78 U.S. Reed	1.50	.75	.15
☐ 79 Fran Greenberg (Public Relations Director)	1.00	.50	.10
☐ 80 Ron Davis	.75	.35	.07
☐ 81 Larry Fogle	1.25	.60	.12
☐ 82 Clarence Kea	.75	.35	.07
☐ 83 Steve Craig	.75	.35	.07
☐ 84 Harry Davis	.75	.35	.07
☐ 85 Jacky Dorsey	1.50	.75	.15
☐ 86 Herb Gray	.75	.35	.07
☐ 87 Randy Johnson	.75	.35	.07
☐ 88 Jim Drucker (Commissioner)	1.50	.75	.15
☐ 89 Lynbert Johnson	1.25	.60	.12
☐ 90 Checklist 1-90	1.50	.75	.15

1982-83 TCMA CBA

This third Continental Basketball Association set from TCMA features 90 black and white cards with red frame lines. The CBA logo, the player's name, physical data, team name, and team logo appear on the front, as does the card number. The back of

the cards form a large puzzle. The cards were apparently issued in two series of 45 cards each. Cards measure the standard 2 1/2" by 3 1/2".

	MINT	EXC	G-VG
COMPLETE SET (90)	75.00	37.50	7.50
COMMON PLAYER (1-45)	.75	.35	.07
COMMON PLAYER (46-90)	.75	.35	.07

	MINT	EXC	G-VG
☐ 1 Cazzie Russell (Coach Lancaster)	3.00	1.50	.30
☐ 2 Boot Bond	.75	.35	.07
☐ 3 Ron Charles	.75	.35	.07
☐ 4 Charles Pittman	1.50	.75	.15
☐ 5 Calvin Garrett	1.50	.75	.15
☐ 6 Willie Jones	.75	.35	.07
☐ 7 Riley Clarida	.75	.35	.07
☐ 8 Jim Johnstone	.75	.35	.07
☐ 9 Bobby Potts	.75	.35	.07
☐ 10 Lowes Moore	1.50	.75	.15
☐ 11 Dwight Anderson	3.50	1.75	.35
☐ 12 John Coughran	.75	.35	.07
☐ 13 Mike Evans	1.50	.75	.15
☐ 14 Alan Hardy	.75	.35	.07
☐ 15 Willie Smith	.75	.35	.07
☐ 16 Oliver Mack	1.25	.60	.12
☐ 17 Checklist 1-45	1.50	.75	.15
☐ 18 Picture 1 (action under basket)	.75	.35	.07
☐ 19 James Lee	1.50	.75	.15
☐ 20 Kenny Natt	1.50	.75	.15
☐ 21 Cyrus Mann	.75	.35	.07
☐ 22 Bobby Cattage	.75	.35	.07
☐ 23 Garry Witts	.75	.35	.07
☐ 24 Bill Klucas (Coach Billings)	.75	.35	.07
☐ 25 Al Smith	.75	.35	.07
☐ 26 B.B. Fontenet	.75	.35	.07
☐ 27 Chris Giles	.75	.35	.07
☐ 28 Barry Young	1.00	.50	.10
☐ 29 Horace Wyatt	.75	.35	.07
☐ 30 Robert Smith	1.25	.60	.12
☐ 31 Ron Baxter	1.50	.75	.15
☐ 32 Charlie Jones	.75	.35	.07
☐ 33 Tico Brown	.75	.35	.07
☐ 34 John McCullough	.75	.35	.07
☐ 35 Dan Callandrillo	1.50	.75	.15
☐ 36 John Leonard	.75	.35	.07
☐ 37 Sam Worthen	1.25	.60	.12
☐ 38 Dale Wilkinson	.75	.35	.07
☐ 39 Gary Johnson	.75	.35	.07
☐ 40 Dean Meminger (Coach Albany)	1.50	.75	.15
☐ 41 Lloyd Terry	.75	.35	.07
☐ 42 Mike Schultz	.75	.35	.07
☐ 43 Darryl Gladden	.75	.35	.07
☐ 44 Clarence Kea	.75	.35	.07
☐ 45 Charlie Floyd	.75	.35	.07
☐ 46 Skip Dillard	1.25	.60	.12
☐ 47 Craig Tucker	.75	.35	.07
☐ 48 Gib Hinz	.75	.35	.07
☐ 49 Tom Sienkiewicz	1.00	.50	.10
☐ 50 Larry Spriggs	2.50	1.25	.25
☐ 51 Perry Moss	.75	.35	.07
☐ 52 Gerald Sims	.75	.35	.07
☐ 53 Alan Taylor	.75	.35	.07
☐ 54 James Terry	.75	.35	.07
☐ 55 John Nillen (Coach Ohio)	.75	.35	.07
☐ 56 Steve Burks	.75	.35	.07
☐ 57 Anthony Martin	.75	.35	.07
☐ 58 Purvis Miller	1.25	.60	.12
☐ 59 Kevin Smith	.75	.35	.07
☐ 60 John Neumann (Coach Maine)	1.50	.75	.15
☐ 61 Mike Davis	.75	.35	.07
☐ 62 Gary Carter	.75	.35	.07
☐ 63 Checklist 46-90	1.50	.75	.15
☐ 64 Picture 2 (action under basket)	.75	.35	.07
☐ 65 Charles Thompson	.75	.35	.07
☐ 66 John Douglas	1.00	.50	.10
☐ 67 John Schweitz	.75	.35	.07
☐ 68 Kevin Figaro	.75	.35	.07
☐ 69 John Smith	.75	.35	.07
☐ 70 Joe Cooper	1.25	.60	.12
☐ 71 Tony Brown	.75	.35	.07
☐ 72 Mike Wilson	.75	.35	.07
☐ 73 Wayne Abrams	.75	.35	.07
☐ 74 T.X. Martin	.75	.35	.07
☐ 75 Joe Merten	.75	.35	.07
☐ 76 Joe Kopicki	.75	.35	.07
☐ 77 Carl Nicks	1.50	.75	.15
☐ 78 Wayne Kreklow	.75	.35	.07
☐ 79 Tony Guy	1.50	.75	.15
☐ 80 Dave Harshman (Coach Wisconsin)	1.00	.50	.10
☐ 81 Bob Davis	.75	.35	.07
☐ 82 Gary Mazza (Coach Detroit)	.75	.35	.07
☐ 83 Randy Owens	.75	.35	.07
☐ 84 David Burns	.75	.35	.07
☐ 85 Erv Giddings	.75	.35	.07
☐ 86 JoJo Hunter	1.50	.75	.15
☐ 87 Frankie Sanders	.75	.35	.07
☐ 88 Dave Richardson	.75	.35	.07
☐ 89 Lionel Garrett	.75	.35	.07
☐ 90 Marvin Barnes	3.00	1.50	.30

1982-83 TCMA Lancaster CBA

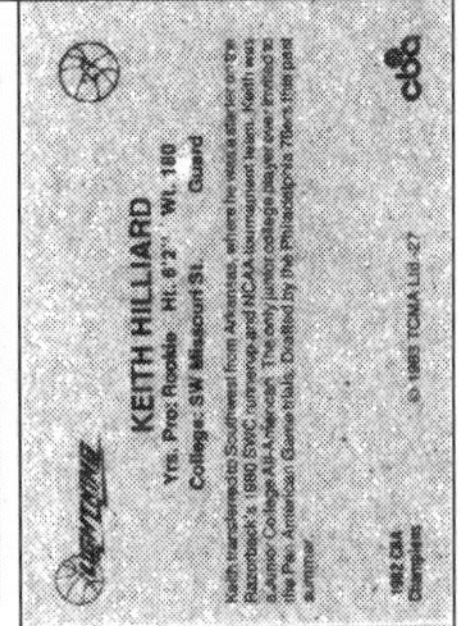

This set features 30 black and white standard-sized (2 1/2" by 3 1/2") cards with blue border on front. The card backs contain statistics and are numbered on the back. Many of the poses are in action shots. The set is printed on dark cardboard. All cards feature players or personnel of the Lancaster Lightning (Continental Basketball Association) team which won the 1981-82 CBA Championship. The set was produced by TCMA.

	MINT	EXC	G-VG
COMPLETE SET (30)	30.00	15.00	3.00
COMMON PLAYER (1-30)	1.00	.50	.10

	MINT	EXC	G-VG
☐ 1 Lightning Wins 1982 CBA Championship	2.00	1.00	.20
☐ 2 1982-83 Lancaster Lightning Team Picture	1.00	.50	.10
☐ 3 Dr. Seymour Kilstein, President	1.00	.50	.10
☐ 4 Cazzie Russell, Head Coach	4.00	2.00	.40
☐ 5 Coach Russell IA	4.00	2.00	.40
☐ 6 Ed Koback, Operations	3.00	1.50	.30
☐ 7 Bob Danforth, Marketing	1.00	.50	.10
☐ 8 Henry Bibby In Action	2.00	1.00	.20

☐ 9 Joe Cooper, Center	1.50	.75	.15
☐ 10 Joe Cooper IA	1.50	.75	.15
☐ 11 Curtis Berry	1.50	.75	.15
☐ 12 Curtis Berry IA	1.50	.75	.15
☐ 13 James Lee	1.50	.75	.15
☐ 14 James Lee IA	1.50	.75	.15
☐ 15 Ed Sherod IA	1.50	.75	.15
☐ 16 Charlie Floyd	1.00	.50	.10
☐ 17 Charlie Floyd IA	1.00	.50	.10
☐ 18 Darryl Gladden	1.00	.50	.10
☐ 19 Gladden In Action	1.00	.50	.10
☐ 20 Tom Sienkiewicz	1.50	.75	.15
☐ 21 Tom Sienkiewicz IA	1.50	.75	.15
☐ 22 Stan Williams	1.00	.50	.10
☐ 23 Willie Redden	1.00	.50	.10
☐ 24 Reginald Gaines	1.00	.50	.10
☐ 25 Gary(Cat) Johnson	1.50	.75	.15
☐ 26 Cat Johnson IA	1.50	.75	.15
☐ 27 Keith Hilliard	1.00	.50	.10
☐ 28 Keith Hilliard IA	1.00	.50	.10
☐ 29 Donald Seals	1.00	.50	.10
☐ 30 Rufus Harris	1.00	.50	.10

1989-90 Timberwolves Burger King

This seven-card set was sponsored by Burger King to commemorate the inaugural season of the Minnesota Timberwolves. The cards were issued with a (9" by 12") Player Cards Collector Set, which included on the inside a 1989-90 game schedule and slots to hold the cards. The standard size (2 1/2" by 3 1/2") cards feature on the fronts color action player photos, with dark blue borders on white card stock. A banner reading "Inaugural Season" overlays the top of the picture. The team name and logo at the top and player identification below the picture round out the card face. The backs have biographical and statistical information, with the team logo and a blue stripe (with player's name in white) appearing at the top of the cards. The cards are unnumbered. Brad Lohaus is considered somewhat tougher to find since he was supposedly pulled from the set and replaced by Randy Breuer during the promotion. The set features the first professional card of Jerome "Pooh" Richardson.

	MINT	EXC	G-VG
COMPLETE SET (7)	8.00	4.00	.80
COMMON PLAYER	.75	.35	.07
☐ 19 Tony Campbell	1.25	.60	.12
☐ 23 Tyrone Corbin	1.00	.50	.10
☐ 24 Pooh Richardson	4.00	2.00	.40
☐ 35 Sidney Lowe	.75	.35	.07
☐ 42 Sam Mitchell	1.00	.50	.10
☐ 45 Randy Breuer	1.00	.50	.10
☐ 54 Brad Lohaus	1.25	.60	.12

1948 Topps Magic Photos *

The 1948 Topps Magic Photos set contains 252 small (approximately 7/8" by 1 7/16") individual cards featuring sport and non-sport subjects. They were issued in 19 lettered series with cards numbered within each series. The fronts were developed from a "blank" appearance by using moisture and sunlight. Due to varying degrees of photographic sensitivity, the clarity of these cards ranges from fully developed to poorly developed. This set contains Topps' first baseball cards. A premium album holding 126 cards was also issued. The set is sometimes confused with Topps' 1956 Hocus-Focus set, although the cards in this set are slightly smaller than those in the Hocus-Focus set. The checklist below is presented by series. Poorly developed cards are considered in lesser condition and hence have lesser value. The catalog designation for this set is R714-27. Each type of card subject has a letter prefix as follows: Boxing Champions (A), All-American Basketball (B), All-American Football (C), Wrestling Champions (D), Track and Field Champions (E), Stars of Stage and Screen (F), American

Dogs (G), General Sports (H), Movie Stars (J), Baseball Hall of Fame (K), Aviation Pioneers (L), Famous Landmarks (M), American Inventors (N), American Military Leaders (O), American Explorers (P), Basketball Thrills (Q), Football Thrills (R), Figures of the Wild West (S), and General Sports (T).

	NRMT	VG-E	GOOD
COMPLETE SET	3200.00	1600.00	375.00
COMMON CARD A/B/C/D/K	15.00	7.50	1.50
COMMON CARD Q/R	10.00	5.00	1.00
COMMON CARD E/F/J/L	6.00	3.00	.60
COMMON CARD OTHERS	2.50	1.25	.25
☐ A1 Tommy Burns	15.00	7.50	1.50
☐ A2 John L. Sullivan	40.00	20.00	4.00
☐ A3 James J. Corbett	35.00	17.50	3.50
☐ A4 Bob Fitzsimmons	20.00	10.00	2.00
☐ A5 James J. Jeffries	30.00	15.00	3.00
☐ A6 Jack Johnson	35.00	17.50	3.50
☐ A7 Jess Willard	20.00	10.00	2.00
☐ A8 Jack Dempsey	40.00	20.00	4.00
☐ A9 Gene Tunney	40.00	20.00	4.00
☐ A10 Max Schmeling	20.00	10.00	2.00
☐ A11 Jack Sharkey	15.00	7.50	1.50
☐ A12 Primo Carnera	15.00	7.50	1.50
☐ A13 Max Baer	20.00	10.00	2.00
☐ A14 James J. Braddock	20.00	10.00	2.00
☐ A15 Joe Louis	40.00	20.00	4.00
☐ A16 Gus Lesnevich	15.00	7.50	1.50
☐ A17 Tony Zale	15.00	7.50	1.50
☐ A18 Ike Williams	15.00	7.50	1.50
☐ A19 Ray Robinson	35.00	17.50	3.50
☐ A20 Willie Pep	15.00	7.50	1.50
☐ A21 Rinty Monaghan	15.00	7.50	1.50
☐ A22 Manuel Ortiz	15.00	7.50	1.50
☐ A23 Marcel Cerdan	15.00	7.50	1.50
☐ A24 Buddy Baer	15.00	7.50	1.50
☐ B1 Ralph Beard	30.00	15.00	3.00
☐ B2 Murray Weir	30.00	15.00	3.00
☐ B3 Ed Macauley	50.00	25.00	5.00
☐ B4 Kevin O'Shea	20.00	10.00	2.00
☐ B5 Jim McIntyre	20.00	10.00	2.00
☐ B6 Manhattan Beats Dartmouth	20.00	10.00	2.00
☐ C1 Barney Poole	20.00	10.00	2.00
☐ C2 Pete Elliott	20.00	10.00	2.00
☐ C3 Doak Walker	40.00	20.00	4.00
☐ C4 Bill Swiacki	20.00	10.00	2.00
☐ C5 Bill Fischer	20.00	10.00	2.00
☐ C6 Johnny Lujack	40.00	20.00	4.00
☐ C7 Chuck Bednarik	40.00	20.00	4.00
☐ C8 Joe Steffy	20.00	10.00	2.00
☐ C9 George Connor	30.00	15.00	3.00
☐ C10 Steve Suhey	25.00	12.50	2.50
☐ C11 Bob Chappins	20.00	10.00	2.00
☐ C12 Columbia 23/Navy 14	20.00	10.00	2.00
☐ C13 Army-Notre Dame	25.00	12.50	2.50
☐ D1 Frank Gotch	25.00	12.50	2.50
☐ D2 Hackenschmidt	15.00	7.50	1.50
☐ D3 Stanuslaus Zbyszko	15.00	7.50	1.50
☐ D4 Jim Browning	25.00	12.50	2.50
☐ D5 Jim Londos	25.00	12.50	2.50
☐ D6 Strangler Lewis	25.00	12.50	2.50
☐ D7 George Becker	15.00	7.50	1.50
☐ D8 Ernie Dusek	15.00	7.50	1.50
☐ D9 Rudy Dusek	15.00	7.50	1.50
☐ D10 Dean Detton	15.00	7.50	1.50
☐ D11 Masked Marvel	25.00	12.50	2.50
☐ D12 Maurice Tillet	15.00	7.50	1.50
☐ D13 Olaf Swenson	15.00	7.50	1.50
☐ D14 Tony Galento	25.00	12.50	2.50
☐ D15 Frank Sexton	15.00	7.50	1.50
☐ D16 George Calza	15.00	7.50	1.50
☐ D17 Arm Lock	15.00	7.50	1.50
☐ D18 Flying Dropkick	15.00	7.50	1.50
☐ D19 Primo Carnera	20.00	10.00	2.00
☐ D20 Gino Garabaldi	15.00	7.50	1.50
☐ D21 "Lord"Jan Blears	30.00	15.00	3.00
☐ D22 Joe Savoldi	15.00	7.50	1.50
☐ D23 Dick Shikat	15.00	7.50	1.50
☐ D24 Wadleslaw	20.00	10.00	2.00
☐ D25 Steinke	15.00	7.50	1.50
☐ E1 Jesse Owens	25.00	12.50	2.50
☐ E2 Leo Steers	6.00	3.00	.60
☐ E3 Ben Eastman	6.00	3.00	.60
☐ E4 Harrison Dillard	10.00	5.00	1.00
☐ E5 Greg Rice	6.00	3.00	.60
☐ E6 Kolehmainen	6.00	3.00	.60
☐ E7 Gunner Hagg	8.00	4.00	.80
☐ E8 Chas. Pores	6.00	3.00	.60
☐ E9 Grover Kelmmer	6.00	3.00	.60
☐ E10 Boyd Brown	6.00	3.00	.60
☐ E11 Pat Ryan	6.00	3.00	.60
☐ E12 Charlie Fonville	6.00	3.00	.60
☐ E13 Cornelius Warmerdam	10.00	5.00	1.00
☐ E14 Army-Navy Tie	6.00	3.00	.60
☐ E15 Haaken Lidman (Sweden)	6.00	3.00	.60
☐ E16 Morris-Army Wins	6.00	3.00	.60
☐ E17 M. Jarvinen, Javelin	6.00	3.00	.60
☐ F1 Clark Gable	25.00	12.50	2.50
☐ F2 Barbara Stanwyck	12.00	6.00	1.20
☐ F3 Lana Turner	12.00	6.00	1.20
☐ F4 Ingrid Bergman	12.00	6.00	1.20
☐ F5 Betty Grable	12.00	6.00	1.20
☐ F6 Tyrone Power	12.00	6.00	1.20
☐ F7 Olivia DeHavilland	8.00	4.00	.80
☐ F8 Joan Fontaine	8.00	4.00	.80
☐ F9 June Allyson	8.00	4.00	.80
☐ F10 Dorothy Lamour	8.00	4.00	.80
☐ F11 William Powell	8.00	4.00	.80
☐ F12 Sylvia Sidney	6.00	3.00	.60
☐ F13 Van Johnson	8.00	4.00	.80
☐ F14 Virginia Mayo	8.00	4.00	.80
☐ F15 Claudette Colbert	8.00	4.00	.80
☐ F16 Eve Arden	8.00	4.00	.80
☐ F17 Lynn Bari	6.00	3.00	.60
☐ F18 Maureen O'Hara	8.00	4.00	.80
☐ F19 Jean Arthur	8.00	4.00	.80
☐ F20 Hazel Brooks	6.00	3.00	.60
☐ F21 Martha Vickers	8.00	4.00	.80
☐ F22 Noreen Nash	6.00	3.00	.60
☐ G1 Terrier	2.50	1.25	.25
☐ G2 Chow	2.50	1.25	.25
☐ G3 Cairn Terrier	2.50	1.25	.25
☐ G4 White Sealyham	2.50	1.25	.25
☐ G5 St. Bernard	3.50	1.75	.35
☐ G6 Boston Bull	2.50	1.25	.25
☐ G7 Greyhound	2.50	1.25	.25
☐ G8 Dalmation	3.50	1.75	.35
☐ G9 Pointer	2.50	1.25	.25
☐ G10 Cocker Spaniel	2.50	1.25	.25
☐ G11 English Bulldog	2.50	1.25	.25
☐ G12 Champion Pointer	2.50	1.25	.25
☐ G13 Setter	2.50	1.25	.25
☐ G14 Boxer	2.50	1.25	.25
☐ G15 Russian Wolfhound	2.50	1.25	.25
☐ G16 Doberman	3.50	1.75	.35
☐ G17 Collie	3.50	1.75	.35
☐ H1 Mr. and Mrs. George Remington	2.50	1.25	.25
☐ H2 Bernice Dossey	2.50	1.25	.25
☐ J1 Johnny Mack Brown	8.00	4.00	.80
☐ J2 Andy Clyde	6.00	3.00	.60
☐ J3 Roddy McDowall	10.00	5.00	1.00
☐ J4 Keye Luke	8.00	4.00	.80
☐ J5 Jackie Coogan	8.00	4.00	.80
☐ J6 Joe Kirkwood Jr.	6.00	3.00	.60
☐ J7 Jackie Cooper	8.00	4.00	.80
☐ J8 Arthur Lake	6.00	3.00	.60
☐ J9 Sam Levine	8.00	4.00	.80
☐ J10 Binnie Barnes	6.00	3.00	.60
☐ J11 Gertrude Niesen	6.00	3.00	.60
☐ J12 Rory Calhoun	8.00	4.00	.80
☐ J13 June Lockhart	8.00	4.00	.80
☐ J14 Hedy Lamarr	8.00	4.00	.80
☐ J15 Robert Cummings	8.00	4.00	.80
☐ J16 Brian Aherne	6.00	3.00	.60
☐ J17 William Bendix	8.00	4.00	.80
☐ J18 Roland Winters	6.00	3.00	.60
☐ J19 Michael O'Shea	6.00	3.00	.60
☐ J20 Lois Butler	6.00	3.00	.60
☐ J21 Renie Riano	6.00	3.00	.60
☐ J22 Jimmy Wakely	6.00	3.00	.60
☐ J23 Audie Murphy	12.00	6.00	1.20
☐ J24 Leo Gorcey	8.00	4.00	.80
☐ J25 Leon Errol	8.00	4.00	.80
☐ J26 Lon Chaney	12.00	6.00	1.20
☐ J27 William Frawley	8.00	4.00	.80
☐ J28 Billy Benedict	6.00	3.00	.60
☐ J29 Rod Cameron	6.00	3.00	.60
☐ J30 James Gleason	6.00	3.00	.60
☐ J31 Gilbert Roland	8.00	4.00	.80
☐ J32 Raymond Hatton	6.00	3.00	.60
☐ J33 Joe Yule	8.00	4.00	.80
☐ J34 Eddie Albert	8.00	4.00	.80
☐ J35 Barry Sullivan	8.00	4.00	.80
☐ J36 Richard Basehart	8.00	4.00	.80
☐ J37 Claire Trevor	8.00	4.00	.80
☐ J38 Constance Bennett	8.00	4.00	.80
☐ J39 Gale Storm	8.00	4.00	.80
☐ J40 Elyse Knox	6.00	3.00	.60
☐ J41 Jane Wyatt	8.00	4.00	.80
☐ J42 Whip Wilson	6.00	3.00	.60
☐ J43 Charles Bickford	8.00	4.00	.80

☐ J44 Guy Madison	10.00	5.00	1.00
☐ J45 Barton MacLane	6.00	3.00	.60
☐ K1 Lou Boudreau	35.00	17.50	3.50
☐ K2 Cleveland Indians	15.00	7.50	1.50
☐ K3 Bob Elliott	15.00	7.50	1.50
☐ K4 Cleveland Indians 4-3	15.00	7.50	1.50
☐ K5 Cleveland Indians 4-1 (Boudreau scoring)	20.00	10.00	2.00
☐ K6 Babe Ruth 714	200.00	100.00	20.00
☐ K7 Tris Speaker 793	35.00	17.50	3.50
☐ K8 Rogers Hornsby	50.00	25.00	5.00
☐ K9 Connie Mack	40.00	20.00	4.00
☐ K10 Christy Mathewson	50.00	25.00	5.00
☐ K11 Hans Wagner	60.00	30.00	6.00
☐ K12 Grover Alexander	35.00	17.50	3.50
☐ K13 Ty Cobb	100.00	50.00	10.00
☐ K14 Lou Gehrig	100.00	50.00	10.00
☐ K15 Walter Johnson	50.00	25.00	5.00
☐ K16 Cy Young	50.00	25.00	5.00
☐ K17 George Sisler 257	30.00	15.00	3.00
☐ K18 Tinker and Evers	25.00	12.50	2.50
☐ K19 Third Base, Cleveland Indians	15.00	7.50	1.50
☐ L1 Colonial Airlines	6.00	3.00	.60
☐ L2 James Doolittle	10.00	5.00	1.00
☐ L3 Wiley Post	10.00	5.00	1.00
☐ L4 Eddie Rickenbacker	10.00	5.00	1.00
☐ L5 Amelia Earhart	12.00	6.00	1.20
☐ L6 Charles Lindbergh	15.00	7.50	1.50
☐ L7 Doug Corrigan	8.00	4.00	.80
☐ L8 Chas. A. Levine	6.00	3.00	.60
☐ L9 Wright Brothers	8.00	4.00	.80
☐ M1 Niagara Falls	3.50	1.75	.35
☐ M2 Empire State Building	3.50	1.75	.35
☐ M3 Leaning Tower of Pisa	2.50	1.25	.25
☐ M4 Eiffel Tower	2.50	1.25	.25
☐ M5 Lincoln Memorial	2.50	1.25	.25
☐ M6 Statue of Liberty	3.50	1.75	.35
☐ M7 Geyser, Yellowstone	2.50	1.25	.25
☐ M8 Sphinx	2.50	1.25	.25
☐ M9 Washington Monument	2.50	1.25	.25
☐ N1 Eli Whitney	2.50	1.25	.25
☐ N2 Thomas A. Edison	3.50	1.75	.35
☐ N3 C.E. Duryea	2.50	1.25	.25
☐ N4 Benjamin Franklin	5.00	2.50	.50
☐ N5 V.K. Zworykin	3.50	1.75	.35
☐ N6 Robert Fulton	2.50	1.25	.25
☐ N7 Samuel Morse	2.50	1.25	.25
☐ N8 Alexander Graham Bell	5.00	2.50	.50
☐ O1 Joseph Stillwell	2.50	1.25	.25
☐ O2 Adm. Chester Nimitz	3.50	1.75	.35
☐ O3 George Patton	6.00	3.00	.60
☐ O4 General John Pershing	3.50	1.75	.35
☐ O5 Adm. David Farragut	3.50	1.75	.35
☐ O6 Jonathan Wainwright	2.50	1.25	.25
☐ O7 Douglas MacArthur	6.00	3.00	.60
☐ O8 General Omar Bradley	3.50	1.75	.35
☐ O9 George Dewey	2.50	1.25	.25
☐ O10 Gen.Dwight Eisenhower	9.00	4.50	.90
☐ P1 Adm. Robert Peary	2.50	1.25	.25
☐ P2 Richard E. Byrd	2.50	1.25	.25
☐ Q1 St. Louis Univ.	10.00	5.00	1.00
☐ Q2 Long Island Univ.	10.00	5.00	1.00
☐ Q3 Notre Dame	20.00	10.00	2.00
☐ Q4 Kentucky 58-42	12.00	6.00	1.20
☐ Q5 DePaul 75-64	10.00	5.00	1.00
☐ R1 Wally Triplett	10.00	5.00	1.00
☐ R2 Gil Stevenson	12.00	6.00	1.20
☐ R3 Northwestern	10.00	5.00	1.00
☐ R4 Yale vs. Columbia	10.00	5.00	1.00
☐ R5 Cornell	10.00	5.00	1.00
☐ S1 General Custer	6.00	3.00	.60
☐ S2 Buffalo Bill Cody	6.00	3.00	.60
☐ S3 Sitting Bull	3.50	1.75	.35
☐ S4 Annie Oakley	5.00	2.50	.50
☐ S5 Jessie James	6.00	3.00	.60
☐ S6 Geronimo	3.50	1.75	.35
☐ S7 Billy the Kid	5.00	2.50	.50
☐ T1 Soccer	5.00	2.50	.50
☐ T2 Motor Boat Racing	3.50	1.75	.35
☐ T3 Ice Hockey	10.00	5.00	1.00
☐ T4 Water Skiing	3.50	1.75	.35
☐ T5 Gallorette	2.50	1.25	.25
☐ T6 Headlock	2.50	1.25	.25
☐ T7 Tennis	5.00	2.50	.50

1957-58 Topps

The 1957-58 Topps basketball set of 80 cards was Topps first basketball issue. Topps did not release another basketball set until 1969. Cards in the set measure approximately 2 1/2" by 3 1/2". A number of the cards in the set were double printed and hence more plentiful; these are designated DP in the checklist below. In fact there are 49 double prints, 30 single prints, and one quadruple print in the set. Card backs give statistical information from the 1956-57 NBA season. The key rookie cards in this set are Bob Cousy, Tom Heinsohn, Bob Pettit, and Bill Russell. The set contains the only card of Maurice Stokes.

	NRMT	VG-E	GOOD
COMPLETE SET (80)	5000.00	2250.00	600.00
COMMON PLAYER (1-80)	30.00	15.00	3.00
COMMON PLAYER DP	21.00	10.50	2.10
☐ 1 Nat Clifton DP Detroit Pistons	150.00	35.00	7.00
☐ 2 George Yardley DP Detroit Pistons	48.00	24.00	4.80
☐ 3 Neil Johnston DP Philadelphia Warriors	48.00	24.00	4.80
☐ 4 Carl Braun DP New York Knicks	32.00	16.00	3.20
☐ 5 Bill Sharman DP Boston Celtics	125.00	60.00	12.50
☐ 6 George King DP Cincinnati Royals	32.00	16.00	3.20
☐ 7 Kenny Sears DP New York Knicks	32.00	16.00	3.20
☐ 8 Dick Ricketts DP Cincinnati Royals	27.00	13.50	2.70
☐ 9 Jack Nichols DP Boston Celtics	21.00	10.50	2.10
☐ 10 Paul Arizin DP Philadelphia Warriors	65.00	32.50	6.50
☐ 11 Chuck Noble DP Detroit Pistons	21.00	10.50	2.10
☐ 12 Slater Martin DP St. Louis Hawks	48.00	24.00	4.80
☐ 13 Dolph Schayes DP Syracuse Nationals	85.00	42.50	8.50
☐ 14 Dick Atha DP Detroit Pistons	21.00	10.50	2.10
☐ 15 Frank Ramsey DP Boston Celtics	65.00	32.50	6.50
☐ 16 Dick McGuire DP Detroit Pistons	40.00	20.00	4.00
☐ 17 Bob Cousy DP Boston Celtics	375.00	175.00	37.00
☐ 18 Larry Foust DP Minneapolis Lakers	32.00	16.00	3.20
☐ 19 Tom Heinsohn Boston Celtics	200.00	100.00	20.00
☐ 20 Bill Thieben DP Detroit Pistons	21.00	10.50	2.10
☐ 21 Don Meineke DP Cincinnati Royals	32.00	16.00	3.20
☐ 22 Tom Marshall Cincinnati Royals	30.00	15.00	3.00
☐ 23 Dick Garmaker Minneapolis Lakers	30.00	15.00	3.00
☐ 24 Bob Pettit QP St. Louis Hawks	165.00	75.00	15.00
☐ 25 Jim Krebs DP Minneapolis Lakers	32.00	16.00	3.20

☐ 26 Gene Shue DP Detroit Pistons	50.00	25.00	5.00
☐ 27 Ed Macauley DP St. Louis Hawks	48.00	24.00	4.80
☐ 28 Vern Mikkelsen Minneapolis Lakers	42.00	21.00	4.20
☐ 29 Willie Naulls New York Knicks	42.00	21.00	4.20
☐ 30 Walter Dukes DP Detroit Pistons	35.00	17.50	3.50
☐ 31 Dave Piontek DP Cincinnati Royals	21.00	10.50	2.10
☐ 32 John Kerr Syracuse Nationals	60.00	30.00	6.00
☐ 33 Larry Costello DP Syracuse Nationals	42.00	21.00	4.20
☐ 34 Woody Sauldsberry DP Philadelphia Warriors	32.00	16.00	3.20
☐ 35 Ray Felix New York Knicks	36.00	18.00	3.60
☐ 36 Ernie Beck Philadelphia Warriors	30.00	15.00	3.00
☐ 37 Cliff Hagan St. Louis Hawks	80.00	40.00	8.00
☐ 38 Guy Sparrow DP New York Knicks	21.00	10.50	2.10
☐ 39 Jim Loscutoff Boston Celtics	45.00	22.50	4.50
☐ 40 Arnie Risen DP Boston Celtics	32.00	16.00	3.20
☐ 41 Joe Graboski Philadelphia Warriors	30.00	15.00	3.00
☐ 42 Maurice Stokes DP UER Cincinnati Royals (Text refers to N.F.L. Record)	90.00	45.00	9.00
☐ 43 Rod Hundley DP Minneapolis Lakers	70.00	35.00	7.00
☐ 44 Tom Gola DP Philadelphia Warriors	65.00	32.50	6.50
☐ 45 Med Park St. Louis Hawks	32.00	16.00	3.20
☐ 46 Mel Hutchins DP New York Knicks	21.00	10.50	2.10
☐ 47 Larry Friend DP New York Knicks	21.00	10.50	2.10
☐ 48 Lennie Rosenbluth DP Philadelphia Warriors	40.00	20.00	4.00
☐ 49 Walt Davis Philadelphia Warriors	30.00	15.00	3.00
☐ 50 Richie Regan Cincinnati Royals	32.00	16.00	3.20
☐ 51 Frank Selvy DP St. Louis Hawks	36.00	18.00	3.60
☐ 52 Art Spoelstra DP Minneapolis Lakers	21.00	10.50	2.10
☐ 53 Bob Hopkins Syracuse Nationals	36.00	18.00	3.60
☐ 54 Earl Lloyd Syracuse Nationals	36.00	18.00	3.60
☐ 55 Phil Jordan DP New York Knicks	21.00	10.50	2.10
☐ 56 Bob Houbregs DP Detroit Pistons	36.00	18.00	3.60
☐ 57 Lou Tsioropoulas DP Boston Celtics	21.00	10.50	2.10
☐ 58 Ed Conlin Syracuse Nationals	32.00	16.00	3.20
☐ 59 Al Bianchi Syracuse Nationals	45.00	22.50	4.50
☐ 60 George Dempsey Philadelphia Warriors	32.00	16.00	3.20
☐ 61 Chuck Share St. Louis Hawks	30.00	15.00	3.00
☐ 62 Harry Gallatin DP Detroit Pistons	45.00	22.50	4.50
☐ 63 Bob Harrison Syracuse Nationals	30.00	15.00	3.00
☐ 64 Bob Burrow DP Minneapolis Lakers	21.00	10.50	2.10
☐ 65 Win Wilfong DP St. Louis Hawks	21.00	10.50	2.10
☐ 66 Jack McMahon DP St. Louis Hawks	36.00	18.00	3.60
☐ 67 Jack George Philadelphia Warriors	30.00	15.00	3.00
☐ 68 Charlie Tyra DP New York Knicks	21.00	10.50	2.10
☐ 69 Ron Sobie New York Knicks	30.00	15.00	3.00
☐ 70 Jack Coleman St. Louis Hawks	30.00	15.00	3.00
☐ 71 Jack Twyman DP Cincinnati Royals	75.00	37.50	7.50
☐ 72 Paul Seymour Syracuse Nationals	36.00	18.00	3.60
☐ 73 Jim Paxson DP Cincinnati Royals	40.00	20.00	4.00
☐ 74 Bob Leonard Minneapolis Lakers	36.00	18.00	3.60
☐ 75 Andy Phillip Boston Celtics	36.00	18.00	3.60
☐ 76 Joe Holup Syracuse Nationals	30.00	15.00	3.00
☐ 77 Bill Russell Boston Celtics	2000.00	800.00	250.00
☐ 78 Clyde Lovellette DP Cincinnati Royals	80.00	40.00	8.00
☐ 79 Ed Fleming DP Minneapolis Lakers	21.00	10.50	2.10
☐ 80 Dick Schnittker Minneapolis Lakers	70.00	20.00	4.00

1968-69 Topps Test

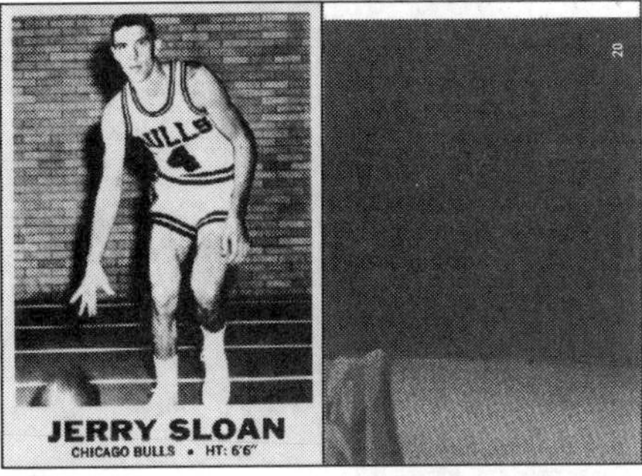

This set was apparently a limited test issue produced by Topps. The cards measure the standard size (2 1/2" by 3 1/2"). The fronts feature a black and white "action" pose of the player, on white card stock. The player's name, team, and height are given below the picture. The horizontally oriented card backs form a composite of Wilt Chamberlain. The cards are numbered on the back. The set is dated as 1968-69 since Earl Monroe's first season was 1967-68. The set features the first professional cards of Dave Bing, Bill Bradley, Dave DeBusschere, John Havlicek, Earl Monroe, and Willis Reed, among others.

	NRMT	VG-E	GOOD
COMPLETE SET (24)	12000.00	5500.00	1350.00
COMMON PLAYER (1-24)	225.00	110.00	22.00
☐ 1 Wilt Chamberlain	1800.00	900.00	200.00
☐ 2 Hal Greer Philadelphia 76ers	400.00	200.00	40.00
☐ 3 Chet Walker Philadelphia 76ers	275.00	135.00	27.00
☐ 4 Bill Russell	1800.00	900.00	200.00
☐ 5 John Havlicek UER Boston Celtics (Misspelled Havilcek)	700.00	350.00	70.00
☐ 6 Cazzie Russell New York Knicks	275.00	135.00	27.00
☐ 7 Willis Reed New York Knicks	450.00	225.00	45.00
☐ 8 Bill Bradley New York Knicks	800.00	400.00	80.00
☐ 9 Odie Smith Cincinnati Royals	225.00	110.00	22.00
☐ 10 Dave Bing Detroit Pistons	450.00	225.00	45.00
☐ 11 Dave DeBusschere Detroit Pistons	500.00	250.00	50.00
☐ 12 Earl Monroe Baltimore Bullets	450.00	225.00	45.00
☐ 13 Nate Thurmond San Francisco Warriors	400.00	200.00	40.00
☐ 14 Jim King San Francisco Warriors	225.00	110.00	22.00
☐ 15 Len Wilkens St. Louis Hawks	450.00	225.00	45.00

☐ 16 Bill Bridges St. Louis Hawks	225.00	110.00	22.00
☐ 17 Zelmo Beaty St. Louis Hawks	225.00	110.00	22.00
☐ 18 Elgin Baylor Los Angeles Lakers	600.00	300.00	60.00
☐ 19 Jerry West Los Angeles Lakers	1200.00	600.00	135.00
☐ 20 Jerry Sloan Chicago Bulls	275.00	135.00	27.00
☐ 21 Jerry Lucas Cincinnati Royals	600.00	300.00	60.00
☐ 22 Oscar Robertson Cincinnati Royals	800.00	400.00	80.00

1969-70 Topps

The 1969-70 Topps set of 99 cards was Topps' first basketball issue since 1958. These tall cards measure 2 1/2" by 4 11/16". The cards are much larger than the standard card size, perhaps rather appropriate considering the dimensions of most basketball players. The set features the first card of Lew Alcindor (later Kareem Abdul-Jabbar). Other notable rookie cards in the set are Bill Bradley, Billy Cunningham, Dave DeBusschere, Walt Frazier, John Havlicek, Elvin Hayes, Jerry Lucas, Earl Monroe, Willis Reed, and Wes Unseld. The set was printed on a sheet of 99 cards (nine rows of eleven across) with the checklist card occupying the lower right corner of the sheet.

	NRMT	VG-E	GOOD
COMPLETE SET (99)	2000.00	900.00	225.00
COMMON PLAYER (1-99)	4.00	2.00	.40
☐ 1 Wilt Chamberlain Los Angeles Lakers	225.00	75.00	25.00
☐ 2 Gail Goodrich Phoenix Suns	21.00	10.50	2.10
☐ 3 Cazzie Russell New York Knicks	11.00	5.50	1.10
☐ 4 Darrall Imhoff Philadelphia 76ers	4.50	2.25	.45
☐ 5 Bailey Howell Boston Celtics	4.50	2.25	.45
☐ 6 Lucius Allen Seattle Supersonics	7.50	3.75	.75
☐ 7 Tom Boerwinkle Chicago Bulls	5.50	2.75	.55
☐ 8 Jimmy Walker Detroit Pistons	5.00	2.50	.50
☐ 9 John Block San Diego Rockets	4.50	2.25	.45
☐ 10 Nate Thurmond San Francisco Warriors	27.00	13.50	2.70
☐ 11 Gary Gregor Atlanta Hawks	4.00	2.00	.40
☐ 12 Gus Johnson Baltimore Bullets	11.00	5.50	1.10
☐ 13 Luther Rackley Cincinnati Royals	4.00	2.00	.40
☐ 14 Jon McGlocklin Milwaukee Bucks	5.00	2.50	.50
☐ 15 Connie Hawkins Phoenix Suns	30.00	15.00	3.00
☐ 16 Johnny Egan Los Angeles Lakers	4.00	2.00	.40
☐ 17 Jim Washington Philadelphia 76ers	4.00	2.00	.40
☐ 18 Dick Barnett New York Knicks	7.00	3.50	.70
☐ 19 Tom Meschery Seattle Supersonics	4.00	2.00	.40
☐ 20 John Havlicek Boston Celtics	165.00	75.00	15.00
☐ 21 Eddie Miles Detroit Pistons	4.00	2.00	.40
☐ 22 Walt Wesley Chicago Bulls	4.00	2.00	.40
☐ 23 Rick Adelman San Diego Rockets	12.50	6.25	1.25
☐ 24 Al Attles San Francisco Warriors	4.50	2.25	.45
☐ 25 Lew Alcindor Milwaukee Bucks	700.00	350.00	70.00
☐ 26 Jack Marin Baltimore Bullets	5.50	2.75	.55
☐ 27 Walt Hazzard Atlanta Hawks	9.00	4.50	.90
☐ 28 Connie Dierking Cincinnati Royals	4.00	2.00	.40
☐ 29 Keith Erickson Los Angeles Lakers	5.50	2.75	.55
☐ 30 Bob Rule Seattle Supersonics	5.00	2.50	.50
☐ 31 Dick Van Arsdale Phoenix Suns	5.50	2.75	.55
☐ 32 Archie Clark Philadelphia 76ers	7.50	3.75	.75
☐ 33 Terry Dischinger Detroit Pistons	5.50	2.75	.55
☐ 34 Henry Finkel Boston Celtics	4.50	2.25	.45
☐ 35 Elgin Baylor Los Angeles Lakers	55.00	27.50	5.50
☐ 36 Ron Williams San Francisco Warriors	4.50	2.25	.45
☐ 37 Loy Petersen Chicago Bulls	4.00	2.00	.40
☐ 38 Guy Rodgers Milwaukee Bucks	4.50	2.25	.45
☐ 39 Toby Kimball San Diego Rockets	4.00	2.00	.40
☐ 40 Billy Cunningham Philadelphia 76ers	45.00	22.50	4.50
☐ 41 Joe Caldwell Atlanta Hawks	5.00	2.50	.50
☐ 42 Leroy Ellis Baltimore Bullets	5.00	2.50	.50
☐ 43 Bill Bradley New York Knicks	200.00	100.00	20.00
☐ 44 Len Wilkens UER Seattle Supersonics (Misspelled Wilkins on card back)	16.00	8.00	1.60
☐ 45 Jerry Lucas San Francisco Warriors	45.00	22.50	4.50
☐ 46 Neal Walk Phoenix Suns	4.50	2.25	.45
☐ 47 Emmette Bryant Boston Celtics	4.50	2.25	.45
☐ 48 Bob Kauffman Chicago Bulls	4.50	2.25	.45
☐ 49 Mel Counts Los Angeles Lakers	4.50	2.25	.45
☐ 50 Oscar Robertson Cincinnati Royals	70.00	35.00	7.00
☐ 51 Jim Barnett San Diego Rockets	4.50	2.25	.45
☐ 52 Don Smith Milwaukee Bucks	4.00	2.00	.40
☐ 53 Jim Davis Atlanta Hawks	4.00	2.00	.40
☐ 54 Wally Jones Philadelphia 76ers	4.50	2.25	.45
☐ 55 Dave Bing Detroit Pistons	25.00	12.50	2.50
☐ 56 Wes Unseld Baltimore Bullets	36.00	18.00	3.60
☐ 57 Joe Ellis San Francisco Warriors	4.00	2.00	.40
☐ 58 John Tresvant Seattle Supersonics	4.00	2.00	.40
☐ 59 Larry Siegfried	5.50	2.75	.55

Boston Celtics			
□ 60 Willis Reed New York Knicks	45.00	22.50	4.50
□ 61 Paul Silas Phoenix Suns	11.00	5.50	1.10
□ 62 Bob Weiss Chicago Bulls	7.00	3.50	.70
□ 63 Willie McCarter Los Angeles Lakers	4.00	2.00	.40
□ 64 Don Kojis San Diego Rockets	4.50	2.25	.45
□ 65 Lou Hudson Atlanta Hawks	11.00	5.50	1.10
□ 66 Jim King Cincinnati Royals	4.00	2.00	.40
□ 67 Luke Jackson Philadelphia 76ers	4.50	2.25	.45
□ 68 Len Chappell Milwaukee Bucks	5.00	2.50	.50
□ 69 Ray Scott Baltimore Bullets	4.50	2.25	.45
□ 70 Jeff Mullins San Francisco Warriors	7.00	3.50	.70
□ 71 Howie Komives Detroit Pistons	4.50	2.25	.45
□ 72 Tom Sanders Boston Celtics	5.50	2.75	.55
□ 73 Dick Snyder Seattle Supersonics	4.00	2.00	.40
□ 74 Dave Stallworth New York Knicks	5.00	2.50	.50
□ 75 Elvin Hayes San Diego Rockets	70.00	35.00	7.00
□ 76 Art Harris Phoenix Suns	4.00	2.00	.40
□ 77 Don Ohl Atlanta Hawks	4.00	2.00	.40
□ 78 Bob Love Chicago Bulls	11.00	5.50	1.10
□ 79 Tom Van Arsdale Cincinnati Royals	5.50	2.75	.55
□ 80 Earl Monroe Baltimore Bullets	45.00	22.50	4.50
□ 81 Greg Smith Milwaukee Bucks	4.00	2.00	.40
□ 82 Don Nelson Boston Celtics	21.00	10.50	2.10
□ 83 Happy Hairston Detroit Pistons	7.50	3.75	.75
□ 84 Hal Greer Philadelphia 76ers	9.00	4.50	.90
□ 85 Dave DeBusschere New York Knicks	45.00	22.50	4.50
□ 86 Bill Bridges Atlanta Hawks	5.50	2.75	.55
□ 87 Herm Gilliam Cincinnati Royals	4.50	2.25	.45
□ 88 Jim Fox Phoenix Suns	4.00	2.00	.40
□ 89 Bob Boozer Seattle Supersonics	4.50	2.25	.45
□ 90 Jerry West Los Angeles Lakers	100.00	50.00	10.00
□ 91 Chet Walker Chicago Bulls	11.00	5.50	1.10
□ 92 Flynn Robinson Milwaukee Bucks	4.50	2.25	.45
□ 93 Clyde Lee San Francisco Warriors	4.50	2.25	.45
□ 94 Kevin Loughery Baltimore Bullets	11.00	5.50	1.10
□ 95 Walt Bellamy Detroit Pistons	7.00	3.50	.70
□ 96 Art Williams San Diego Rockets	4.00	2.00	.40
□ 97 Adrian Smith Cincinnati Royals	4.50	2.25	.45
□ 98 Walt Frazier New York Knicks	75.00	37.50	7.50
□ 99 Checklist Card	265.00	30.00	6.00

1969-70 Topps Rulers

The 1969-70 Topps basketball cartoon poster inserts are clever color cartoon drawings of NBA players, with "ruler" markings on the left edge of the insert. These paper-thin posters measure approximately 2 1/2" by 9 7/8". The player's height is indicated

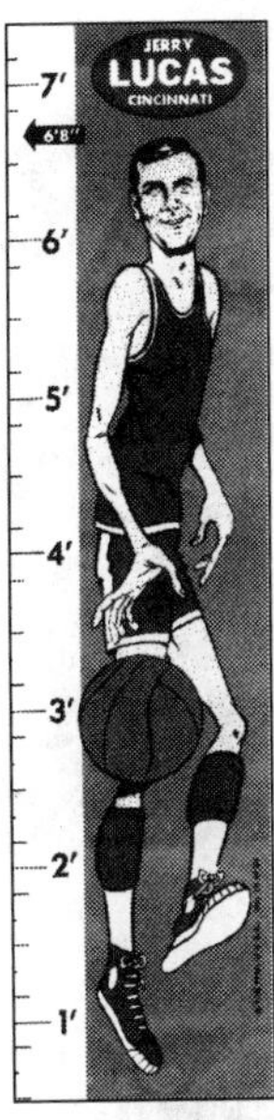

in an arrow pointing towards the ruler, and the top of the player's head corresponds to this line on the ruler. The inserts are numbered and contain the player's name and team in an oval near the bottom of the insert. As might be expected, these inserts make the players look both taller and thinner than they actually are. Insert number 5 was never issued; it was intended to be Bill Russell. The inserts came with gum packages of Topps regular issue basketball cards of that year.

	NRMT	VG-E	GOOD
COMPLETE SET (23)	400.00	200.00	40.00
COMMON PLAYER (1-24)	5.00	2.50	.50
□ 1 Walt Bellamy Detroit Pistons	5.00	2.50	.50
□ 2 Jerry West Los Angeles Lakers	35.00	17.50	3.50
□ 3 Bailey Howell Boston Celtics	5.00	2.50	.50
□ 4 Elvin Hayes San Diego Rockets	20.00	10.00	2.00
□ 5 Never Issued	0.00	0.00	.00
□ 6 Bob Rule Seattle Supersonics	5.00	2.50	.50
□ 7 Gail Goodrich Phoenix Suns	8.00	4.00	.80
□ 8 Jeff Mullins San Francisco Warriors	5.00	2.50	.50
□ 9 John Havlicek Boston Celtics	30.00	15.00	3.00
□ 10 Lew Alcindor Milwaukee Bucks	90.00	45.00	9.00
□ 11 Wilt Chamberlain Los Angeles Lakers	80.00	40.00	8.00
□ 12 Nate Thurmond San Francisco Warriors	9.00	4.50	.90
□ 13 Hal Greer Philadelphia 76ers	7.00	3.50	.70
□ 14 Lou Hudson Atlanta Hawks	5.00	2.50	.50
□ 15 Jerry Lucas San Francisco Warriors	15.00	7.50	1.50
□ 16 Dave Bing Detroit Pistons	12.00	6.00	1.20
□ 17 Walt Frazier New York Knicks	20.00	10.00	2.00
□ 18 Gus Johnson Baltimore Bullets	5.00	2.50	.50
□ 19 Willis Reed New York Knicks	15.00	7.50	1.50
□ 20 Earl Monroe Baltimore Bullets	15.00	7.50	1.50
□ 21 Billy Cunningham	12.00	6.00	1.20

Philadelphia 76ers			
☐ 22 Wes Unseld	12.00	6.00	1.20
Baltimore Bullets			
☐ 23 Bob Boozer	5.00	2.50	.50
Seattle Supersonics			
☐ 24 Oscar Robertson	30.00	15.00	3.00
Cincinnati Royals			

1970-71 Topps

The 1970-71 Topps basketball card set of 175 full-color cards continued the larger-size card format established the previous year. These tall cards measure approximately 2 1/2" by 4 11/16". Cards numbered 106 to 115 contained the previous season's NBA first and second team All-Star selections. The first six cards in the set (1-6) feature the statistical league leaders from the previous season. The last eight cards in the set (168-175) summarize the results of the previous season's NBA championship playoff series won by the Knicks over the Lakers. The key rookie cards in this set are Pete Maravich, Calvin Murphy, and Pat Riley.

	NRMT	VG-E	GOOD
COMPLETE SET (175)	1200.00	500.00	150.00
COMMON PLAYER (1-110)	2.50	1.25	.25
COMMON PLAYER (111-175)	3.00	1.50	.30
☐ 1 NBA Scoring Leaders	30.00	7.50	1.50
Lew Alcindor			
Jerry West			
Elvin Hayes			
☐ 2 NBA Scoring Average Leaders	18.00	9.00	1.80
Jerry West			
Lew Alcindor			
Elvin Hayes			
☐ 3 NBA FG Pct Leaders	5.00	2.50	.50
Johnny Green			
Darrall Imhoff			
Lou Hudson			
☐ 4 NBA FT Pct Leaders	6.00	3.00	.60
Flynn Robinson			
Chet Walker			
Jeff Mullins			
☐ 5 NBA Rebound Leaders	15.00	7.50	1.50
Elvin Hayes			
Wes Unseld			
Lew Alcindor			
☐ 6 NBA Assist Leaders	6.00	3.00	.60
Len Wilkens			
Walt Frazier			
Clem Haskins			
☐ 7 Bill Bradley	90.00	45.00	9.00
New York Knicks			
☐ 8 Ron Williams	2.50	1.25	.25
San Francisco Warriors			
☐ 9 Otto Moore	2.50	1.25	.25
Detroit Pistons			
☐ 10 John Havlicek	80.00	40.00	8.00
Boston Celtics			
☐ 11 George Wilson	3.00	1.50	.30
Buffalo Braves			
☐ 12 John Trapp	2.50	1.25	.25
San Diego Rockets			
☐ 13 Pat Riley	45.00	22.50	4.50
Portland Trail Blazers			
☐ 14 Jim Washington	2.50	1.25	.25
Philadelphia 76ers			
☐ 15 Bob Rule	2.50	1.25	.25
Seattle Supersonics			
☐ 16 Bob Weiss	3.00	1.50	.30
Chicago Bulls			
☐ 17 Neil Johnson	2.50	1.25	.25
Phoenix Suns			
☐ 18 Walt Bellamy	4.50	2.25	.45
Atlanta Hawks			
☐ 19 McCoy McLemore	2.50	1.25	.25
Cleveland Cavaliers			
☐ 20 Earl Monroe	15.00	7.50	1.50
Baltimore Bullets			
☐ 21 Wally Anderzunas	2.50	1.25	.25
Cincinnati Royals			
☐ 22 Guy Rodgers	3.00	1.50	.30
Milwaukee Bucks			
☐ 23 Rick Roberson	2.50	1.25	.25
Los Angeles Lakers			
☐ 24 Checklist 1-110	45.00	4.50	.90
☐ 25 Jimmy Walker	2.50	1.25	.25
Detroit Pistons			
☐ 26 Mike Riordan	4.00	2.00	.40
New York Knicks			
☐ 27 Henry Finkel	2.50	1.25	.25
Boston Celtics			
☐ 28 Joe Ellis	2.50	1.25	.25
San Francisco Warriors			
☐ 29 Mike Davis	2.50	1.25	.25
Buffalo Braves			
☐ 30 Lou Hudson	4.00	2.00	.40
Atlanta Hawks			
☐ 31 Lucius Allen	3.25	1.60	.32
Seattle Supersonics			
☐ 32 Toby Kimball	2.50	1.25	.25
San Diego Rockets			
☐ 33 Luke Jackson	2.50	1.25	.25
Philadelphia 76ers			
☐ 34 Johnny Egan	2.50	1.25	.25
Cleveland Cavaliers			
☐ 35 Leroy Ellis	3.00	1.50	.30
Portland Trail Blazers			
☐ 36 Jack Marin	3.00	1.50	.30
Baltimore Bullets			
☐ 37 Joe Caldwell	3.00	1.50	.30
Atlanta Hawks			
☐ 38 Keith Erickson	3.00	1.50	.30
Los Angeles Lakers			
☐ 39 Don Smith	2.50	1.25	.25
Milwaukee Bucks			
☐ 40 Flynn Robinson	2.50	1.25	.25
Cincinnati Royals			
☐ 41 Bob Boozer	2.50	1.25	.25
Seattle Supersonics			
☐ 42 Howie Komives	2.50	1.25	.25
Detroit Pistons			
☐ 43 Dick Barnett	3.25	1.60	.32
New York Knicks			
☐ 44 Stu Lantz	3.00	1.50	.30
San Diego Rockets			
☐ 45 Dick Van Arsdale	3.00	1.50	.30
Phoenix Suns			
☐ 46 Jerry Lucas	15.00	7.50	1.50
San Francisco Warriors			
☐ 47 Don Chaney	7.50	3.75	.75
Boston Celtics			
☐ 48 Ray Scott	2.50	1.25	.25
Buffalo Braves			
☐ 49 Dick Cunningham	2.50	1.25	.25
Milwaukee Bucks			
☐ 50 Wilt Chamberlain	120.00	60.00	12.00
Los Angeles Lakers			
☐ 51 Kevin Loughery	4.00	2.00	.40
Baltimore Bullets			
☐ 52 Stan McKenzie	2.50	1.25	.25
Portland Trail Blazers			
☐ 53 Fred Foster	2.50	1.25	.25
Cincinnati Royals			
☐ 54 Jim Davis	2.50	1.25	.25
Atlanta Hawks			
☐ 55 Walt Wesley	2.50	1.25	.25
Cleveland Cavaliers			
☐ 56 Bill Hewitt	2.50	1.25	.25
Detroit Pistons			
☐ 57 Darrall Imhoff	2.50	1.25	.25

Philadelphia 76ers
☐ 58 John Block 2.50 1.25 .25
San Diego Rockets
☐ 59 Al Attles 3.00 1.50 .30
San Francisco Warriors
☐ 60 Chet Walker 4.25 2.10 .42
Chicago Bulls
☐ 61 Luther Rackley 2.50 1.25 .25
Cleveland Cavaliers
☐ 62 Jerry Chambers 3.00 1.50 .30
Atlanta Hawks
☐ 63 Bob Dandridge 7.50 3.75 .75
Milwaukee Bucks
☐ 64 Dick Snyder 2.50 1.25 .25
Seattle Supersonics
☐ 65 Elgin Baylor 35.00 17.50 3.50
Los Angeles Lakers
☐ 66 Connie Dierking 2.50 1.25 .25
Cincinnati Royals
☐ 67 Steve Kuberski 3.00 1.50 .30
Boston Celtics
☐ 68 Tom Boerwinkle 2.50 1.25 .25
Chicago Bulls
☐ 69 Paul Silas 4.25 2.10 .42
Phoenix Suns
☐ 70 Elvin Hayes 28.00 14.00 2.80
San Diego Rockets
☐ 71 Bill Bridges 3.00 1.50 .30
Atlanta Hawks
☐ 72 Wes Unseld 10.00 5.00 1.00
Baltimore Bullets
☐ 73 Herm Gilliam 2.50 1.25 .25
Buffalo Braves
☐ 74 Bobby Smith 3.25 1.60 .32
Cleveland Cavaliers
☐ 75 Lew Alcindor 180.00 90.00 18.00
Milwaukee Bucks
☐ 76 Jeff Mullins 3.25 1.60 .32
San Francisco Warriors
☐ 77 Happy Hairston 3.25 1.60 .32
Los Angeles Lakers
☐ 78 Dave Stallworth 3.00 1.50 .30
New York Knicks
☐ 79 Fred Hetzel 2.50 1.25 .25
Portland Trail Blazers
☐ 80 Len Wilkens 9.00 4.50 .90
Seattle Supersonics
☐ 81 Johnny Green 3.25 1.60 .32
Cincinnati Royals
☐ 82 Erwin Mueller 2.50 1.25 .25
Detroit Pistons
☐ 83 Wally Jones 2.50 1.25 .25
Philadelphia 76ers
☐ 84 Bob Love 4.25 2.10 .42
Chicago Bulls
☐ 85 Dick Garrett 3.00 1.50 .30
Buffalo Braves
☐ 86 Don Nelson 7.50 3.75 .75
Boston Celtics
☐ 87 Neal Walk 2.50 1.25 .25
Phoenix Suns
☐ 88 Larry Siegfried 3.00 1.50 .30
San Diego Rockets
☐ 89 Gary Gregor 2.50 1.25 .25
Portland Trail Blazers
☐ 90 Nate Thurmond 7.50 3.75 .75
San Francisco Warriors
☐ 91 John Warren 2.50 1.25 .25
Cleveland Cavaliers
☐ 92 Gus Johnson 4.25 2.10 .42
Baltimore Bullets
☐ 93 Gail Goodrich 6.00 3.00 .60
Los Angeles Lakers
☐ 94 Dorrie Murrey 2.50 1.25 .25
Portland Trail Blazers
☐ 95 Cazzie Russell 4.25 2.10 .42
New York Knicks
☐ 96 Terry Dischinger 3.00 1.50 .30
Detroit Pistons
☐ 97 Norm Van Lier 5.50 2.75 .55
Cincinnati Royals
☐ 98 Jim Fox 2.50 1.25 .25
Chicago Bulls
☐ 99 Tom Meschery 2.50 1.25 .25
Seattle Supersonics
☐ 100 Oscar Robertson 42.00 21.00 4.20
Milwaukee Bucks
☐ 101A Checklist 111-175 30.00 3.00 .60
(1970-71 in black)
☐ 101B Checklist 111-175 30.00 3.00 .60
(1970-71 in white)
☐ 102 Rich Johnson 2.50 1.25 .25
Boston Celtics
☐ 103 Mel Counts 2.50 1.25 .25

Phoenix Suns
☐ 104 Bill Hosket 3.00 1.50 .30
Buffalo Braves
☐ 105 Archie Clark 3.00 1.50 .30
Philadelphia 76ers
☐ 106 Walt Frazier AS 11.00 5.50 1.10
New York Knicks
☐ 107 Jerry West AS 28.00 14.00 2.80
Los Angeles Lakers
☐ 108 Bill Cunningham AS 6.00 3.00 .60
Philadelphia 76ers
☐ 109 Connie Hawkins AS 4.00 2.00 .40
Phoenix Suns
☐ 110 Willis Reed AS 7.00 3.50 .70
New York Knicks
☐ 111 Nate Thurmond AS 5.00 2.50 .50
San Francisco Warriors
☐ 112 John Havlicek AS 27.00 13.50 2.70
Boston Celtics
☐ 113 Elgin Baylor AS 16.00 8.00 1.60
Los Angeles Lakers
☐ 114 Oscar Robertson AS 21.00 10.50 2.10
Milwaukee Bucks
☐ 115 Lou Hudson AS 4.00 2.00 .40
Atlanta Hawks
☐ 116 Emmette Bryant 3.00 1.50 .30
Buffalo Braves
☐ 117 Greg Howard 3.00 1.50 .30
Phoenix Suns
☐ 118 Rick Adelman 5.00 2.50 .50
Portland Trail Blazers
☐ 119 Barry Clemens 3.00 1.50 .30
Seattle Supersonics
☐ 120 Walt Frazier 30.00 15.00 3.00
New York Knicks
☐ 121 Jim Barnes 3.50 1.75 .35
Boston Celtics
☐ 122 Bernie Williams 3.00 1.50 .30
San Diego Rockets
☐ 123 Pete Maravich 160.00 75.00 15.00
Atlanta Hawks
☐ 124 Matt Guokas 6.00 3.00 .60
Philadelphia 76ers
☐ 125 Dave Bing 8.50 4.25 .85
Detroit Pistons
☐ 126 John Tresvant 3.00 1.50 .30
Los Angeles Lakers
☐ 127 Shaler Halimon 3.00 1.50 .30
Chicago Bulls
☐ 128 Don Ohl 3.00 1.50 .30
Cleveland Cavaliers
☐ 129 Fred Carter 3.50 1.75 .35
Baltimore Bullets
☐ 130 Connie Hawkins 9.00 4.50 .90
Phoenix Suns
☐ 131 Jim King 3.00 1.50 .30
Cincinnati Royals
☐ 132 Ed Manning 3.50 1.75 .35
Portland Trail Blazers
☐ 133 Adrian Smith 3.00 1.50 .30
San Francisco Warriors
☐ 134 Walt Hazzard 4.50 2.25 .45
Atlanta Hawks
☐ 135 Dave DeBusschere 16.50 7.50 1.50
New York Knicks
☐ 136 Don Kojis 3.00 1.50 .30
Seattle Supersonics
☐ 137 Calvin Murphy 25.00 12.50 2.50
San Diego Rockets
☐ 138 Nate Bowman 3.00 1.50 .30
Buffalo Braves
☐ 139 Jon McGlocklin 3.50 1.75 .35
Milwaukee Bucks
☐ 140 Billy Cunningham 13.50 6.50 1.25
Philadelphia 76ers
☐ 141 Willie McCarter 3.00 1.50 .30
Los Angeles Lakers
☐ 142 Jim Barnett 3.50 1.75 .35
Portland Trail Blazers
☐ 143 JoJo White 16.00 8.00 1.60
Boston Celtics
☐ 144 Clyde Lee 3.00 1.50 .30
San Francisco Warriors
☐ 145 Tom Van Arsdale 3.50 1.75 .35
Cincinnati Royals
☐ 146 Len Chappell 3.00 1.50 .30
Cleveland Cavaliers
☐ 147 Lee Winfield 3.00 1.50 .30
Seattle Supersonics
☐ 148 Jerry Sloan 9.00 4.50 .90
Chicago Bulls
☐ 149 Art Harris 3.00 1.50 .30
Phoenix Suns
☐ 150 Willis Reed 16.50 7.50 1.50

	New York Knicks			
☐ 151	Art Williams	3.00	1.50	.30
	San Diego Rockets			
☐ 152	Don May	3.00	1.50	.30
	Buffalo Braves			
☐ 153	Loy Petersen	3.00	1.50	.30
	Cleveland Cavaliers			
☐ 154	Dave Gambee	3.00	1.50	.30
	San Francisco Warriors			
☐ 155	Hal Greer	5.00	2.50	.50
	Philadelphia 76ers			
☐ 156	Dave Newmark	3.00	1.50	.30
	Atlanta Hawks			
☐ 157	Jimmy Collins	3.50	1.75	.35
	Chicago Bulls			
☐ 158	Bill Turner	3.00	1.50	.30
	Cincinnati Royals			
☐ 159	Eddie Miles	3.00	1.50	.30
	Baltimore Bullets			
☐ 160	Jerry West	65.00	32.50	6.50
	Los Angeles Lakers			
☐ 161	Bob Quick	3.00	1.50	.30
	Detroit Pistons			
☐ 162	Fred Crawford	3.00	1.50	.30
	Buffalo Braves			
☐ 163	Tom Sanders	3.50	1.75	.35
	Boston Celtics			
☐ 164	Dale Schlueter	3.00	1.50	.30
	Portland Trail Blazers			
☐ 165	Clem Haskins	5.00	2.50	.50
	Phoenix Suns			
☐ 166	Greg Smith	3.00	1.50	.30
	Milwaukee Bucks			
☐ 167	Rod Thorn	5.00	2.50	.50
	Seattle Supersonics			
☐ 168	Playoff Game 1	6.00	3.00	.60
	(Willis Reed)			
☐ 169	Playoff Game 2	4.50	2.25	.45
	(Dick Garrett)			
☐ 170	Playoff Game 3	6.00	3.00	.60
	(Dave DeBusschere)			
☐ 171	Playoff Game 4	12.00	6.00	1.20
	(Jerry West)			
☐ 172	Playoff Game 5	12.00	6.00	1.20
	(Bill Bradley)			
☐ 173	Playoff Game 6	14.00	7.00	1.40
	(Wilt Chamberlain)			
☐ 174	Playoff Game 7	8.00	4.00	.80
	(Walt Frazier)			
☐ 175	Knicks Celebrate (New York Knicks, World Champs)	20.00	5.00	1.00

1970-71 Topps Poster Inserts

This set of 24 large (8" by 10") thin paper posters was issued with the 1970-71 Topps regular basketball cards. The posters are in full color and contain the player's name and his team near the upper left of the poster. The number appears in the border at the lower right, and a Topps copyright date and a 1968 National Basketball Player's Association copyright date appears in the border at the left.

		NRMT	VG-E	GOOD
COMPLETE SET (24)		150.00	75.00	15.00
COMMON PLAYER (1-24)		1.50	.75	.15
☐ 1	Walt Frazier	7.50	3.75	.75
	New York Knicks			
☐ 2	Joe Caldwell	1.50	.75	.15
	Atlanta Hawks			
☐ 3	Willis Reed	7.50	3.75	.75
	New York Knicks			
☐ 4	Elvin Hayes	10.00	5.00	1.00
	San Diego Rockets			
☐ 5	Jeff Mullins	1.50	.75	.15
	San Francisco Warriors			
☐ 6	Oscar Robertson	20.00	10.00	2.00
	Cincinnati Royals			
☐ 7	Dave Bing	5.00	2.50	.50
	Detroit Pistons			
☐ 8	Jerry Sloan	1.50	.75	.15
	Chicago Bulls			
☐ 9	Leroy Ellis	1.50	.75	.15
	Portland Trail Blazers			
☐ 10	Hal Greer	3.50	1.75	.35
	Philadelphia 76ers			
☐ 11	Emmette Bryant	1.50	.75	.15
	Buffalo Braves			
☐ 12	Bob Rule	1.50	.75	.15
	Seattle Supersonics			
☐ 13	Lew Alcindor	45.00	22.50	4.50
	Milwaukee Bucks			
☐ 14	Chet Walker	2.00	1.00	.20
	Chicago Bulls			
☐ 15	Jerry West	25.00	12.50	2.50
	Los Angeles Lakers			
☐ 16	Billy Cunningham	5.00	2.50	.50
	Philadelphia 76ers			
☐ 17	Wilt Chamberlain	35.00	17.50	3.50
	Los Angeles Lakers			
☐ 18	John Havlicek	20.00	10.00	2.00
	Boston Celtics			
☐ 19	Lou Hudson	1.50	.75	.15
	Atlanta Hawks			
☐ 20	Earl Monroe	6.00	3.00	.60
	Baltimore Bullets			
☐ 21	Wes Unseld	5.00	2.50	.50
	Baltimore Bullets			
☐ 22	Connie Hawkins	5.00	2.50	.50
	Phoenix Suns			
☐ 23	Tom Van Arsdale	1.50	.75	.15
	Cincinnati Royals			
☐ 24	Len Chappell	1.50	.75	.15
	Cleveland Cavaliers			

1971-72 Topps

The 1971-72 Topps basketball set of 233 witnessed a return to the standard-sized card, i.e., 2 1/2" by 3 1/2". National Basketball Association (NBA) players are depicted on cards 1 to 144 and American Basketball Association (ABA) players are depicted on cards 145 to 233. The set was produced on two sheets. The second production sheet contained the ABA players (145-233) as well as 31 double-printed cards (essentially NBA players) from the first sheet. These DP's are indicated in the checklist below. Special subseries within this set include NBA Playoffs (133-137), NBA Statistical Leaders (138-143), and ABA Statistical Leaders (146-151). The key rookie cards in this set are Nate Archibald, Rick Barry, Dave Cowens, Dan Issel, and Bob Lanier.

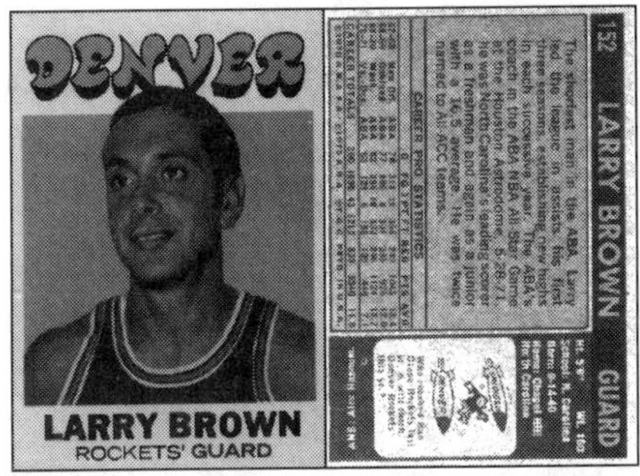

	NRMT	VG-E	GOOD
COMPLETE SET (233)	850.00	425.00	85.00
COMMON PLAYER (1-144)	1.25	.60	.12
COMMON PLAYER (145-233)	1.50	.75	.15
□ 1 Oscar Robertson Milwaukee Bucks	50.00	15.00	3.00
□ 2 Bill Bradley New York Knicks	48.00	24.00	4.80
□ 3 Jim Fox Chicago Bulls	1.25	.60	.12
□ 4 John Johnson Cleveland Cavaliers	2.00	1.00	.20
□ 5 Luke Jackson Philadelphia 76ers	1.25	.60	.12
□ 6 Don May DP Atlanta Hawks	.90	.45	.09
□ 7 Kevin Loughery Baltimore Bullets	2.50	1.25	.25
□ 8 Terry Dischinger Detroit Pistons	1.50	.75	.15
□ 9 Neal Walk Phoenix Suns	1.25	.60	.12
□ 10 Elgin Baylor Los Angeles Lakers	25.00	12.50	2.50
□ 11 Rick Adelman Portland Trail Blazers	3.00	1.50	.30
□ 12 Clyde Lee Golden State Warriors	1.25	.60	.12
□ 13 Jerry Chambers Buffalo Braves	1.25	.60	.12
□ 14 Fred Carter Baltimore Bullets	1.25	.60	.12
□ 15 Tom Boerwinkle DP Chicago Bulls	.90	.45	.09
□ 16 John Block Houston Rockets	1.25	.60	.12
□ 17 Dick Barnett New York Knicks	1.75	.85	.17
□ 18 Henry Finkel Boston Celtics	1.25	.60	.12
□ 19 Norm Van Lier Cincinnati Royals	1.75	.85	.17
□ 20 Spencer Haywood Seattle Supersonics	10.00	5.00	1.00
□ 21 George Johnson Baltimore Bullets	1.25	.60	.12
□ 22 Bobby Lewis Cleveland Cavaliers	1.25	.60	.12
□ 23 Bill Hewitt Detroit Pistons	1.25	.60	.12
□ 24 Walt Hazzard DP Buffalo Braves	2.50	1.25	.25
□ 25 Happy Hairston Los Angeles Lakers	1.75	.85	.17
□ 26 George Wilson Buffalo Braves	1.25	.60	.12
□ 27 Lucius Allen Milwaukee Bucks	1.75	.85	.17
□ 28 Jim Washington Philadelphia 76ers	1.25	.60	.12
□ 29 Nate Archibald Cincinnati Royals	30.00	15.00	3.00
□ 30 Willis Reed New York Knicks	10.00	5.00	1.00
□ 31 Erwin Mueller Detroit Pistons	1.25	.60	.12
□ 32 Art Harris Phoenix Suns	1.25	.60	.12
□ 33 Pete Cross Seattle Supersonics	1.25	.60	.12
□ 34 Geoff Petrie Portland Trail Blazers	4.50	2.25	.45
□ 35 John Havlicek Boston Celtics	35.00	17.50	3.50
□ 36 Larry Siegfried Houston Rockets	1.50	.75	.15
□ 37 John Tresvant DP Baltimore Bullets	.90	.45	.09
□ 38 Ron Williams Golden State Warriors	1.25	.60	.12
□ 39 Lamar Green DP Phoenix Suns	.90	.45	.09
□ 40 Bob Rule DP Seattle Supersonics	.90	.45	.09
□ 41 Jim McMillian Los Angeles Lakers	2.50	1.25	.25
□ 42 Wally Jones Philadelphia 76ers	1.25	.60	.12
□ 43 Bob Boozer Milwaukee Bucks	1.25	.60	.12
□ 44 Eddie Miles Baltimore Bullets	1.25	.60	.12
□ 45 Bob Love DP Chicago Bulls	2.50	1.25	.25
□ 46 Claude English Portland Trail Blazers	1.25	.60	.12
□ 47 Dave Cowens Boston Celtics	45.00	22.50	4.50
□ 48 Emmette Bryant Buffalo Braves	1.25	.60	.12
□ 49 Dave Stallworth New York Knicks	1.50	.75	.15
□ 50 Jerry West Los Angeles Lakers	42.00	21.00	4.20
□ 51 Joe Ellis Golden State Warriors	1.25	.60	.12
□ 52 Walt Wesley DP Cleveland Cavaliers	.90	.45	.09
□ 53 Howie Komives Detroit Pistons	1.25	.60	.12
□ 54 Paul Silas Phoenix Suns	3.00	1.50	.30
□ 55 Pete Maravich DP Atlanta Hawks	40.00	20.00	4.00
□ 56 Gary Gregor Portland Trail Blazers	1.25	.60	.12
□ 57 Sam Lacey Cincinnati Royals	2.00	1.00	.20
□ 58 Calvin Murphy DP Houston Rockets	5.50	2.75	.55
□ 59 Bob Dandridge Milwaukee Bucks	2.00	1.00	.20
□ 60 Hal Greer Philadelphia 76ers	4.00	2.00	.40
□ 61 Keith Erickson Los Angeles Lakers	1.50	.75	.15
□ 62 Joe Cooke Cleveland Cavaliers	1.25	.60	.12
□ 63 Bob Lanier Detroit Pistons	35.00	17.50	3.50
□ 64 Don Kojis Seattle Supersonics	1.25	.60	.12
□ 65 Walt Frazier New York Knicks	15.00	7.50	1.50
□ 66 Chet Walker DP Chicago Bulls	2.50	1.25	.25
□ 67 Dick Garrett Buffalo Braves	1.25	.60	.12
□ 68 John Trapp Houston Rockets	1.25	.60	.12
□ 69 JoJo White Boston Celtics	5.50	2.75	.55
□ 70 Wilt Chamberlain Los Angeles Lakers	70.00	35.00	7.00
□ 71 Dave Sorenson Cleveland Cavaliers	1.25	.60	.12
□ 72 Jim King Chicago Bulls	1.25	.60	.12
□ 73 Cazzie Russell Golden State Warriors	3.00	1.50	.30
□ 74 Jon McGlocklin Milwaukee Bucks	1.50	.75	.15
□ 75 Tom Van Arsdale Cincinnati Royals	1.50	.75	.15
□ 76 Dale Schlueter Portland Trail Blazers	1.25	.60	.12
□ 77 Gus Johnson DP Baltimore Bullets	1.75	.85	.17
□ 78 Dave Bing Detroit Pistons	5.50	2.75	.55
□ 79 Billy Cunningham Philadelphia 76ers	7.50	3.75	.75
□ 80 Len Wilkens Seattle Supersonics	5.50	2.75	.55
□ 81 Jerry Lucas DP	8.50	4.25	.85

New York Knicks			
☐ 82 Don Chaney	2.50	1.25	.25
Boston Celtics			
☐ 83 McCoy McLemore	1.25	.60	.12
Milwaukee Bucks			
☐ 84 Bob Kauffman DP	.90	.45	.09
Buffalo Braves			
☐ 85 Dick Van Arsdale	1.50	.75	.15
Phoenix Suns			
☐ 86 Johnny Green	1.25	.60	.12
Cincinnati Royals			
☐ 87 Jerry Sloan	3.00	1.50	.30
Chicago Bulls			
☐ 88 Luther Rackley DP	.90	.45	.09
Cleveland Cavaliers			
☐ 89 Shaler Halimon	1.25	.60	.12
Portland Trail Blazers			
☐ 90 Jimmy Walker	1.25	.60	.12
Detroit Pistons			
☐ 91 Rudy Tomjanovich	6.00	3.00	.60
Houston Rockets			
☐ 92 Levi Fontaine	1.25	.60	.12
Golden State Warriors			
☐ 93 Bobby Smith	1.50	.75	.15
Cleveland Cavaliers			
☐ 94 Bob Arnzen	1.25	.60	.12
Cincinnati Royals			
☐ 95 Wes Unseld DP	6.00	3.00	.60
Baltimore Bullets			
☐ 96 Clem Haskins DP	1.25	.60	.12
Phoenix Suns			
☐ 97 Jim Davis	1.25	.60	.12
Atlanta Hawks			
☐ 98 Steve Kuberski	1.25	.60	.12
Boston Celtics			
☐ 99 Mike Davis DP	.90	.45	.09
Buffalo Braves			
☐ 100 Lew Alcindor	90.00	45.00	9.00
Milwaukee Bucks			
☐ 101 Willie McCarter	1.25	.60	.12
Los Angeles Lakers			
☐ 102 Charlie Paulk	1.25	.60	.12
Chicago Bulls			
☐ 103 Lee Winfield	1.25	.60	.12
Seattle Supersonics			
☐ 104 Jim Barnett	1.50	.75	.15
Golden State Warriors			
☐ 105 Connie Hawkins DP	6.00	3.00	.60
Phoenix Suns			
☐ 106 Archie Clark DP	1.25	.60	.12
Philadelphia 76ers			
☐ 107 Dave DeBusschere	10.00	5.00	1.00
New York Knicks			
☐ 108 Stu Lantz DP	.90	.45	.09
Houston Rockets			
☐ 109 Don Smith	1.25	.60	.12
Seattle Supersonics			
☐ 110 Lou Hudson	2.50	1.25	.25
Atlanta Hawks			
☐ 111 Leroy Ellis	1.25	.60	.12
Portland Trail Blazers			
☐ 112 Jack Marin	1.50	.75	.15
Baltimore Bullets			
☐ 113 Matt Guokas	2.25	1.10	.22
Cincinnati Royals			
☐ 114 Don Nelson	4.50	2.25	.45
Boston Celtics			
☐ 115 Jeff Mullins DP	1.50	.75	.15
Golden State Warriors			
☐ 116 Walt Bellamy	3.25	1.60	.32
Atlanta Hawks			
☐ 117 Bob Quick	1.25	.60	.12
Detroit Pistons			
☐ 118 John Warren	1.25	.60	.12
Cleveland Cavaliers			
☐ 119 Barry Clemens	1.25	.60	.12
Seattle Supersonics			
☐ 120 Elvin Hayes DP	14.00	7.00	1.40
Houston Rockets			
☐ 121 Gail Goodrich	2.50	1.25	.25
Los Angeles Lakers			
☐ 122 Ed Manning	1.50	.75	.15
Portland Trail Blazers			
☐ 123 Herm Gilliam DP	.90	.45	.09
Atlanta Hawks			
☐ 124 Dennis Awtrey	1.50	.75	.15
Philadelphia 76ers			
☐ 125 John Hummer DP	.90	.45	.09
Buffalo Braves			
☐ 126 Mike Riordan	1.50	.75	.15
New York Knicks			
☐ 127 Mel Counts	1.25	.60	.12
Phoenix Suns			
☐ 128 Bob Weiss DP	1.50	.75	.15
Chicago Bulls			
☐ 129 Greg Smith DP	.90	.45	.09
Milwaukee Bucks			
☐ 130 Earl Monroe	10.00	5.00	1.00
Baltimore Bullets			
☐ 131 Nate Thurmond DP	5.00	2.50	.50
Golden State Warriors			
☐ 132 Bill Bridges DP	1.25	.60	.12
Atlanta Hawks			
☐ 133 NBA Playoffs G1	9.00	4.50	.90
Alcindor scores 31			
☐ 134 NBA Playoffs G2	2.50	1.25	.25
Bucks make it			
Two Straight			
☐ 135 NBA Playoffs G3	2.50	1.25	.25
Dandridge makes			
It Three in a Row			
☐ 136 NBA Playoffs G4	6.50	3.25	.65
A Clean Sweep			
(Oscar Robertson)			
☐ 137 NBA Champs Celebrate	2.50	1.25	.25
Bucks sweep Bullets			
☐ 138 NBA Scoring Leaders	12.00	6.00	1.20
Lew Alcindor			
Elvin Hayes			
John Havlicek			
☐ 139 NBA Scoring Average	12.00	6.00	1.20
Leaders			
Lew Alcindor			
John Havlicek			
Elvin Hayes			
☐ 140 NBA FG Pct Leaders	10.00	5.00	1.00
Johnny Green			
Lew Alcindor			
Wilt Chamberlain			
☐ 141 NBA FT Pct Leaders	3.50	1.75	.35
Chet Walker			
Oscar Robertson			
Ron Williams			
☐ 142 NBA Rebound Leaders	17.00	8.50	1.70
Wilt Chamberlain			
Elvin Hayes			
Lew Alcindor			
☐ 143 NBA Assist Leaders	7.00	3.50	.70
Norm Van Lier			
Oscar Robertson			
Jerry West			
☐ 144A NBA Checklist 1-144	15.00	7.50	1.50
(copyright notation			
extends up to			
card 110)			
☐ 144B NBA Checklist 1-144	15.00	7.50	1.50
(copyright notation			
extends up to			
card 108)			
☐ 145 ABA Checklist 145-233	15.00	7.50	1.50
☐ 146 ABA Scoring Leaders	4.50	2.25	.45
Dan Issel			
John Brisker			
Charlie Scott			
☐ 147 ABA Scoring Average	9.00	4.50	.90
Leaders			
Dan Issel			
Rick Barry			
John Brisker			
☐ 148 ABA 2pt FG Pct Leaders	2.75	1.35	.27
Zelmo Beaty			
Bill Paultz			
Roger Brown			
☐ 149 ABA FT Pct Leaders	8.00	4.00	.80
Rick Barry			
Darrell Carrier			
Billy Keller			
☐ 150 ABA Rebound Leaders	2.75	1.35	.27
Mel Daniels			
Julius Keye			
Mike Lewis			
☐ 151 ABA Assist Leaders	2.75	1.35	.27
Bill Melchionni			
Mack Calvin			
Charlie Scott			
☐ 152 Larry Brown	11.00	5.50	1.10
Denver Rockets			
☐ 153 Bob Bedell	1.50	.75	.15
Dallas Chaparrals			
☐ 154 Merv Jackson	1.50	.75	.15
Utah Stars			
☐ 155 Joe Caldwell	2.00	1.00	.20
Carolina Cougars			
☐ 156 Billy Paultz	2.50	1.25	.25
New York Nets			
☐ 157 Les Hunter	1.50	.75	.15
Kentucky Colonels			
☐ 158 Charlie Williams	1.50	.75	.15

	Memphis Pros			
☐ 159	Stew Johnson	1.50	.75	.15
	Pittsburgh Condors			
☐ 160	Mack Calvin	4.50	2.25	.45
	Florida Floridians			
☐ 161	Don Sidle	1.50	.75	.15
	Indiana Pacers			
☐ 162	Mike Barrett	1.50	.75	.15
	Virginia Squires			
☐ 163	Tom Workman	1.50	.75	.15
	Denver Rockets			
☐ 164	Joe Hamilton	1.50	.75	.15
	Dallas Chaparrals			
☐ 165	Zelmo Beaty	4.00	2.00	.40
	Utah Stars			
☐ 166	Dan Hester	1.50	.75	.15
	Kentucky Colonels			
☐ 167	Bob Verga	1.50	.75	.15
	Carolina Cougars			
☐ 168	Wilbert Jones	1.50	.75	.15
	Memphis Pros			
☐ 169	Skeeter Swift	1.50	.75	.15
	Pittsburgh Condors			
☐ 170	Rick Barry	75.00	37.50	7.50
	New York Nets			
☐ 171	Billy Keller	2.50	1.25	.25
	Indiana Pacers			
☐ 172	Ron Franz	1.50	.75	.15
	Florida Floridians			
☐ 173	Roland Taylor	2.00	1.00	.20
	Virginia Squires			
☐ 174	Julian Hammond	1.50	.75	.15
	Denver Rockets			
☐ 175	Steve Jones	3.50	1.75	.35
	Dallas Chaparrals			
☐ 176	Gerald Govan	1.50	.75	.15
	Memphis Pros			
☐ 177	Darrell Carrier	2.50	1.25	.25
	Kentucky Colonels			
☐ 178	Ron Boone	3.00	1.50	.30
	Utah Stars			
☐ 179	George Peeples	1.50	.75	.15
	Carolina Cougars			
☐ 180	John Brisker	2.00	1.00	.20
	Pittsburgh Condors			
☐ 181	Doug Moe	12.50	6.25	1.25
	Virginia Squires			
☐ 182	Ollie Taylor	2.00	1.00	.20
	New York Nets			
☐ 183	Bob Netolicky	2.00	1.00	.20
	Indiana Pacers			
☐ 184	Sam Robinson	1.50	.75	.15
	Florida Floridians			
☐ 185	James Jones	2.00	1.00	.20
	Memphis Pros			
☐ 186	Julius Keye	1.50	.75	.15
	Denver Rockets			
☐ 187	Wayne Hightower	1.50	.75	.15
	Dallas Chaparrals			
☐ 188	Warren Armstrong	2.00	1.00	.20
	Indiana Pacers			
☐ 189	Mike Lewis	2.00	1.00	.20
	Pittsburgh Condors			
☐ 190	Charlie Scott	5.50	2.75	.55
	Virginia Squires			
☐ 191	Jim Ard	1.50	.75	.15
	New York Nets			
☐ 192	George Lehmann	1.50	.75	.15
	Carolina Cougars			
☐ 193	Ira Harge	1.50	.75	.15
	Florida Floridians			
☐ 194	Willie Wise	3.00	1.50	.30
	Utah Stars			
☐ 195	Mel Daniels	6.00	3.00	.60
	Indiana Pacers			
☐ 196	Larry Cannon	1.50	.75	.15
	Denver Rockets			
☐ 197	Jim Eakins	1.50	.75	.15
	Virginia Squires			
☐ 198	Rich Jones	1.50	.75	.15
	Dallas Chaparrals			
☐ 199	Bill Melchionni	2.50	1.25	.25
	New York Nets			
☐ 200	Dan Issel	36.00	18.00	3.60
	Kentucky Colonels			
☐ 201	George Stone	1.50	.75	.15
	Utah Stars			
☐ 202	George Thompson	1.50	.75	.15
	Pittsburgh Condors			
☐ 203	Craig Raymond	1.50	.75	.15
	Memphis Pros			
☐ 204	Freddie Lewis	2.50	1.25	.25
	Indiana Pacers			
☐ 205	George Carter	1.50	.75	.15
	Virginia Squires			
☐ 206	Lonnie Wright	1.50	.75	.15
	Florida Floridians			
☐ 207	Cincy Powell	1.50	.75	.15
	Kentucky Colonels			
☐ 208	Larry Miller	2.00	1.00	.20
	Carolina Cougars			
☐ 209	Sonny Dove	2.00	1.00	.20
	New York Nets			
☐ 210	Byron Beck	2.00	1.00	.20
	Denver Rockets			
☐ 211	John Beasley	1.50	.75	.15
	Dallas Chaparrals			
☐ 212	Lee Davis	1.50	.75	.15
	Memphis Pros			
☐ 213	Rick Mount	6.00	3.00	.60
	Indiana Pacers			
☐ 214	Walt Simon	1.50	.75	.15
	Kentucky Colonels			
☐ 215	Glen Combs	2.00	1.00	.20
	Utah Stars			
☐ 216	Neil Johnson	1.50	.75	.15
	Virginia Squires			
☐ 217	Manny Leaks	2.00	1.00	.20
	New York Nets			
☐ 218	Chuck Williams	1.50	.75	.15
	Pittsburgh Condors			
☐ 219	Warren Davis	1.50	.75	.15
	Florida Floridians			
☐ 220	Donnie Freeman	2.50	1.25	.25
	Dallas Chaparrals			
☐ 221	Randy Mahaffey	1.50	.75	.15
	Carolina Cougars			
☐ 222	John Barnhill	1.50	.75	.15
	Denver Rockets			
☐ 223	Al Cueto	1.50	.75	.15
	Memphis Pros			
☐ 224	Louie Dampier	4.25	2.10	.42
	Kentucky Colonels			
☐ 225	Roger Brown	3.00	1.50	.30
	Indiana Pacers			
☐ 226	Joe DePre	1.50	.75	.15
	New York Nets			
☐ 227	Ray Scott	1.50	.75	.15
	Virginia Squires			
☐ 228	Arvesta Kelly	1.50	.75	.15
	Pittsburgh Condors			
☐ 229	Vann Williford	1.50	.75	.15
	Carolina Cougars			
☐ 230	Larry Jones	2.00	1.00	.20
	Florida Floridians			
☐ 231	Gene Moore	1.50	.75	.15
	Dallas Chaparrals			
☐ 232	Ralph Simpson	3.00	1.50	.30
	Denver Rockets			
☐ 233	Red Robbins	2.50	1.00	.20
	Utah Stars			

1971-72 Topps Trios

The 1971-72 Topps Trios (insert sticker panels) set contains 26 card-sized (2 1/2" by 3 1/2") panels each with three player stickers. There are also three logo sticker panels. Each player sticker has a black border surrounding a color photo with a yellow player's name, and white team name. The NBA players are numbered by the number indicated; stickers of ABA players have the suffix "A" added to their numbers in order to differentiate them. The stickers were printed on a sheet of 77 (7 rows and 11 columns). There are a number of oddities with respect to the distribution on the sheet and hence also to the availability of respective cards in the set. The most difficult cards in the set (34, 37, 40, 43, 1A, 4A, 7A, 10A, 13A, 16A, 19A, 23A, and 24A) appeared on the sheet only twice; they are designated as short prints (SP) in the checklist below. Cards 1, 4, 7, 10, 13, 16, 19, 22, 25, 28, and 31 were all printed three times on the sheet and are hence 50 percent more available than the SP's. The rest of the sheet is comprised of 4 copies of card 22A and 14 copies of card 46; they are referenced as DP and QP respectively. The logo stickers are hard to find in good shape.

	NRMT	VG-E	GOOD
COMPLETE SET (26)	450.00	225.00	45.00
COMMON CARD	2.00	1.00	.20
☐ 1 Lou Hudson 2 Bob Rule 3 Calvin Murphy	6.00	3.00	.60
☐ 4 Walt Wesley 5 JoJo White 6 Bob Dandridge	2.50	1.25	.25
☐ 7 Nate Thurmond 8 Earl Monroe 9 Spencer Haywood	12.00	6.00	1.20
☐ 10 Dave DeBusschere 11 Bob Lanier 12 Tom Van Arsdale	12.00	6.00	1.20
☐ 13 Hal Greer 14 Johnny Green 15 Elvin Hayes	12.00	6.00	1.20
☐ 16 Jimmy Walker 17 Don May 18 Archie Clark	2.50	1.25	.25
☐ 19 Happy Hairston 20 Leroy Ellis 21 Jerry Sloan	2.50	1.25	.25
☐ 22 Pete Maravich 23 Bob Kauffman 24 John Havlicek	60.00	30.00	6.00
☐ 25 Walt Frazier 26 Dick Van Arsdale 27 Dave Bing	15.00	7.50	1.50
☐ 28 Bob Love 29 Ron Williams 30 Dave Cowens	10.00	5.00	1.00
☐ 31 Jerry West 32 Willis Reed 33 Chet Walker	60.00	30.00	6.00
☐ 34 Oscar Robertson SP 35 Wes Unseld 36 Bobby Smith	45.00	22.50	4.50
☐ 37 Connie Hawkins SP 38 Jeff Mullins 39 Lew Alcindor	100.00	50.00	10.00
☐ 40 Billy Cunningham SP 41 Walt Bellamy 42 Geoff Petrie	7.50	3.75	.75
☐ 43 Wilt Chamberlain SP 44 Gus Johnson 45 Norm Van Lier	60.00	30.00	6.00
☐ 46 NBA Team QP Logo Stickers	2.00	1.00	.20
☐ 1A James Jones SP 2A Willie Wise 3A Dan Issel	10.00	5.00	1.00
☐ 4A Mack Calvin SP 5A Roger Brown 6A Bob Verga	2.50	1.25	.25
☐ 7A Bill Melchionni SP 8A Mel Daniels 9A Donnie Freeman	2.50	1.25	.25
☐ 10A Joe Caldwell SP 11A Louie Dampier 12A Mike Lewis	2.00	1.00	.20
☐ 13A Rick Barry SP 14A Larry Jones 15A Julius Keye	15.00	7.50	1.50
☐ 16A Larry Cannon SP 17A Zelmo Beaty 18A Charlie Scott	2.00	1.00	.20
☐ 19A Steve Jones SP 20A George Carter 21A John Brisker	2.00	1.00	.20
☐ 22A ABA Team DP Logo Stickers	2.00	1.00	.20
☐ 23A ABA Team SP Logo Stickers	35.00	17.50	3.50
☐ 24A ABA Team SP Logo Stickers	35.00	17.50	3.50

1972-73 Topps

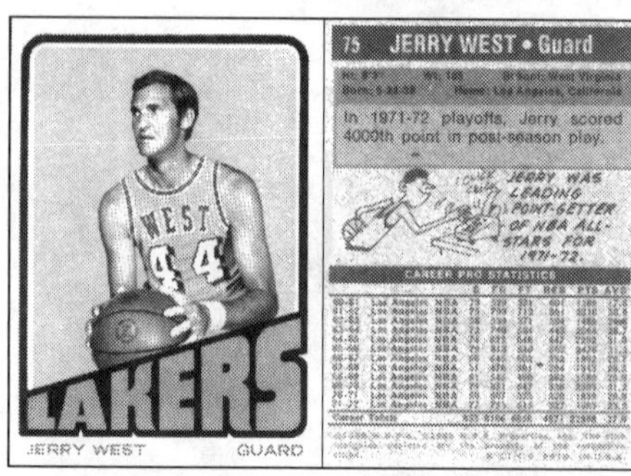

The 1972-73 Topps set of 264 cards contains NBA players (1-176) and ABA players (177-264). The cards in the set measure standard size, 2 1/2" by 3 1/2". All-Star selections are depicted for the NBA on cards numbered 161 to 170 and for the ABA on cards numbered 249 to 258. Special subseries within this set include NBA Playoffs (154-159), NBA Statistical Leaders (171-176), ABA Playoffs (241-247), and ABA Statistical Leaders (259-264). The key rookie cards in this set are Julius Erving, Artis Gilmore, and Phil Jackson.

	NRMT	VG-E	GOOD
COMPLETE SET (264)	825.00	375.00	95.00
COMMON PLAYER (1-132)	.80	.40	.08
COMMON PLAYER (133-264)	1.00	.50	.10
☐ 1 Wilt Chamberlain Los Angeles Lakers	75.00	20.00	4.00
☐ 2 Stan Love Baltimore Bullets	.80	.40	.08
☐ 3 Geoff Petrie Portland Trail Blazers	1.00	.50	.10
☐ 4 Curtis Perry Milwaukee Bucks	1.25	.60	.12
☐ 5 Pete Maravich Atlanta Hawks	25.00	12.50	2.50
☐ 6 Gus Johnson Phoenix Suns	1.75	.85	.17
☐ 7 Dave Cowens Boston Celtics	14.00	7.00	1.40
☐ 8 Randy Smith Buffalo Braves	2.00	1.00	.20
☐ 9 Matt Guokas Kansas City-Omaha Kings	1.25	.60	.12
☐ 10 Spencer Haywood Seattle Supersonics	3.00	1.50	.30
☐ 11 Jerry Sloan Chicago Bulls	2.25	1.10	.22
☐ 12 Dave Sorenson Cleveland Cavaliers	.80	.40	.08
☐ 13 Howie Komives Detroit Pistons	.80	.40	.08
☐ 14 Joe Ellis Golden State Warriors	.80	.40	.08
☐ 15 Jerry Lucas New York Knicks	7.00	3.50	.70
☐ 16 Stu Lantz Detroit Pistons	.80	.40	.08
☐ 17 Bill Bridges Philadelphia 76ers	1.00	.50	.10
☐ 18 Leroy Ellis Los Angeles Lakers	.80	.40	.08
☐ 19 Art Williams Boston Celtics	.80	.40	.08
☐ 20 Sidney Wicks Portland Trail Blazers	9.00	4.50	.90
☐ 21 Wes Unseld Baltimore Bullets	4.50	2.25	.45
☐ 22 Jim Washington Atlanta Hawks	.80	.40	.08
☐ 23 Fred Hilton Buffalo Braves	.80	.40	.08

☐ 24 Curtis Rowe, Detroit Pistons	3.00	1.50	.30
☐ 25 Oscar Robertson, Milwaukee Bucks	20.00	10.00	2.00
☐ 26 Larry Steele, Portland Trail Blazers	1.25	.60	.12
☐ 27 Charlie Davis, Cleveland Cavaliers	.80	.40	.08
☐ 28 Nate Thurmond, Golden State Warriors	4.00	2.00	.40
☐ 29 Fred Carter, Philadelphia 76ers	.80	.40	.08
☐ 30 Connie Hawkins, Phoenix Suns	4.00	2.00	.40
☐ 31 Calvin Murphy, Houston Rockets	3.50	1.75	.35
☐ 32 Phil Jackson, New York Knicks	18.00	9.00	1.80
☐ 33 Lee Winfield, Seattle Supersonics	.80	.40	.08
☐ 34 Jim Fox, Seattle Supersonics	.80	.40	.08
☐ 35 Dave Bing, Detroit Pistons	4.00	2.00	.40
☐ 36 Gary Gregor, Portland Trail Blazers	.80	.40	.08
☐ 37 Mike Riordan, Baltimore Bullets	1.00	.50	.10
☐ 38 George Trapp, Atlanta Hawks	.80	.40	.08
☐ 39 Mike Davis, Buffalo Braves	.80	.40	.08
☐ 40 Bob Rule, Philadelphia 76ers	.80	.40	.08
☐ 41 John Block, Philadelphia 76ers	.80	.40	.08
☐ 42 Bob Dandridge, Milwaukee Bucks	1.25	.60	.12
☐ 43 John Johnson, Cleveland Cavaliers	1.00	.50	.10
☐ 44 Rick Barry, Golden State Warriors	25.00	12.50	2.50
☐ 45 JoJo White, Boston Celtics	3.00	1.50	.30
☐ 46 Cliff Meely, Houston Rockets	.80	.40	.08
☐ 47 Charlie Scott, Phoenix Suns	1.50	.75	.15
☐ 48 Johnny Green, Kansas City-Omaha Kings	.80	.40	.08
☐ 49 Pete Cross, Kansas City-Omaha Kings	.80	.40	.08
☐ 50 Gail Goodrich, Los Angeles Lakers	3.00	1.50	.30
☐ 51 Jim Davis, Detroit Pistons	.80	.40	.08
☐ 52 Dick Barnett, New York Knicks	1.25	.60	.12
☐ 53 Bob Christian, Atlanta Hawks	.80	.40	.08
☐ 54 Jon McGlocklin, Milwaukee Bucks	1.00	.50	.10
☐ 55 Paul Silas, Boston Celtics	2.00	1.00	.20
☐ 56 Hal Greer, Philadelphia 76ers	3.00	1.50	.30
☐ 57 Barry Clemens, Seattle Supersonics	.80	.40	.08
☐ 58 Nick Jones, Golden State Warriors	.80	.40	.08
☐ 59 Cornell Warner, Buffalo Braves	.80	.40	.08
☐ 60 Walt Frazier, New York Knicks	10.00	5.00	1.00
☐ 61 Dorrie Murray, Baltimore Bullets	.80	.40	.08
☐ 62 Dick Cunningham, Houston Rockets	.80	.40	.08
☐ 63 Sam Lacey, Kansas City-Omaha Kings	1.00	.50	.10
☐ 64 John Warren, Cleveland Cavaliers	.80	.40	.08
☐ 65 Tom Boerwinkle, Chicago Bulls	.80	.40	.08
☐ 66 Fred Foster, Detroit Pistons	.80	.40	.08
☐ 67 Mel Counts, Phoenix Suns	.80	.40	.08
☐ 68 Toby Kimball, Milwaukee Bucks	.80	.40	.08
☐ 69 Dale Schlueter, Portland Trail Blazers	.80	.40	.08
☐ 70 Jack Marin, Houston Rockets	1.00	.50	.10
☐ 71 Jim Barnett, Golden State Warriors	.80	.40	.08
☐ 72 Clem Haskins, Phoenix Suns	1.00	.50	.10
☐ 73 Earl Monroe, New York Knicks	7.00	3.50	.70
☐ 74 Tom Sanders, Boston Celtics	1.00	.50	.10
☐ 75 Jerry West, Los Angeles Lakers	27.00	13.50	2.70
☐ 76 Elmore Smith, Buffalo Braves	1.25	.60	.12
☐ 77 Don Adams, Atlanta Hawks	.80	.40	.08
☐ 78 Wally Jones, Milwaukee Bucks	.80	.40	.08
☐ 79 Tom Van Arsdale, Kansas City-Omaha Kings	1.00	.50	.10
☐ 80 Bob Lanier, Detroit Pistons	8.50	4.25	.85
☐ 81 Len Wilkens, Seattle Supersonics	4.00	2.00	.40
☐ 82 Neal Walk, Phoenix Suns	.80	.40	.08
☐ 83 Kevin Loughery, Philadelphia 76ers	2.00	1.00	.20
☐ 84 Stan McKenzie, Portland Trail Blazers	.80	.40	.08
☐ 85 Jeff Mullins, Golden State Warriors	1.00	.50	.10
☐ 86 Otto Moore, Houston Rockets	.80	.40	.08
☐ 87 John Tresvant, Baltimore Bullets	.80	.40	.08
☐ 88 Dean Meminger, New York Knicks	1.50	.75	.15
☐ 89 Jim McMillian, Los Angeles Lakers	1.00	.50	.10
☐ 90 Austin Carr, Cleveland Cavaliers	5.50	2.75	.55
☐ 91 Clifford Ray, Chicago Bulls	2.00	1.00	.20
☐ 92 Don Nelson, Boston Celtics	4.00	2.00	.40
☐ 93 Mahdi Abdul-Rahman, Buffalo Braves (formerly Walt Hazzard)	2.00	1.00	.20
☐ 94 Willie Norwood, Detroit Pistons	.80	.40	.08
☐ 95 Dick Van Arsdale, Phoenix Suns	1.00	.50	.10
☐ 96 Don May, Atlanta Hawks	.80	.40	.08
☐ 97 Walt Bellamy, Atlanta Hawks	2.50	1.25	.25
☐ 98 Garfield Heard, Seattle Supersonics	2.00	1.00	.20
☐ 99 Dave Wohl, Philadelphia 76ers	.80	.40	.08
☐ 100 Kareem Abdul-Jabbar, Milwaukee Bucks	65.00	32.50	6.50
☐ 101 Ron Knight, Portland Trail Blazers	.80	.40	.08
☐ 102 Phil Chenier, Baltimore Bullets	3.00	1.50	.30
☐ 103 Rudy Tomjanovich, Houston Rockets	2.25	1.10	.22
☐ 104 Flynn Robinson, Los Angeles Lakers	.80	.40	.08
☐ 105 Dave DeBusschere, New York Knicks	7.00	3.50	.70
☐ 106 Dennis Layton, Phoenix Suns	1.00	.50	.10
☐ 107 Bill Hewitt, Detroit Pistons	.80	.40	.08
☐ 108 Dick Garrett, Buffalo Braves	.80	.40	.08
☐ 109 Walt Wesley, Cleveland Cavaliers	.80	.40	.08
☐ 110 John Havlicek, Boston Celtics	25.00	12.50	2.50
☐ 111 Norm Van Lier, Chicago Bulls	1.50	.75	.15
☐ 112 Cazzie Russell, Golden State Warriors	2.00	1.00	.20
☐ 113 Herm Gilliam, Atlanta Hawks	.80	.40	.08
☐ 114 Greg Smith, Houston Rockets	.80	.40	.08
☐ 115 Nate Archibald, Kansas City-Omaha Kings	8.50	4.25	.85
☐ 116 Don Kojis, Kansas City-Omaha Kings	.80	.40	.08
☐ 117 Rick Adelman	2.25	1.10	.22

Portland Trail Blazers
☐ 118 Luke Jackson .80 .40 .08
Philadelphia 76ers
☐ 119 Lamar Green .80 .40 .08
Phoenix Suns
☐ 120 Archie Clark 1.00 .50 .10
Baltimore Bullets
☐ 121 Happy Hairston 1.25 .60 .12
Los Angeles Lakers
☐ 122 Bill Bradley 35.00 17.50 3.50
New York Knicks
☐ 123 Ron Williams .80 .40 .08
Golden State Warriors
☐ 124 Jimmy Walker .80 .40 .08
Houston Rockets
☐ 125 Bob Kauffman .80 .40 .08
Buffalo Braves
☐ 126 Rick Roberson .80 .40 .08
Cleveland Cavaliers
☐ 127 Howard Porter 2.00 1.00 .20
Chicago Bulls
☐ 128 Mike Newlin 1.25 .60 .12
Houston Rockets
☐ 129 Willis Reed 7.00 3.50 .70
New York Knicks
☐ 130 Lou Hudson 1.75 .85 .17
Atlanta Hawks
☐ 131 Don Chaney 2.00 1.00 .20
Boston Celtics
☐ 132 Dave Stallworth 1.00 .50 .10
Baltimore Bullets
☐ 133 Charlie Yelverton 1.00 .50 .10
Portland Trail Blazers
☐ 134 Ken Durrett 1.00 .50 .10
Kansas City-Omaha Kings
☐ 135 John Brisker 1.25 .60 .12
Seattle Supersonics
☐ 136 Dick Snyder 1.00 .50 .10
Seattle Supersonics
☐ 137 Jim McDaniels 1.25 .60 .12
Seattle Supersonics
☐ 138 Clyde Lee 1.00 .50 .10
Golden State Warriors
☐ 139 Dennis Awtrey UER 1.00 .50 .10
Philadelphia 76ers
(Misspelled Awtry
on card front)
☐ 140 Keith Erickson 1.25 .60 .12
Los Angeles Lakers
☐ 141 Bob Weiss 1.25 .60 .12
Chicago Bulls
☐ 142 Butch Beard 1.75 .85 .17
Cleveland Cavaliers
☐ 143 Terry Dischinger 1.25 .60 .12
Portland Trail Blazers
☐ 144 Pat Riley 10.00 5.00 1.00
Los Angeles Lakers
☐ 145 Lucius Allen 1.25 .60 .12
Milwaukee Bucks
☐ 146 John Mengelt 1.50 .75 .15
Kansas City-Omaha Kings
☐ 147 John Hummer 1.00 .50 .10
Buffalo Braves
☐ 148 Bob Love 2.00 1.00 .20
Chicago Bulls
☐ 149 Bobby Smith 1.00 .50 .10
Cleveland Cavaliers
☐ 150 Elvin Hayes 12.50 6.25 1.25
Baltimore Bullets
☐ 151 Nate Williams 1.00 .50 .10
Kansas City-Omaha Kings
☐ 152 Chet Walker 2.00 1.00 .20
Chicago Bulls
☐ 153 Steve Kuberski 1.00 .50 .10
Boston Celtics
☐ 154 NBA Playoffs G1 2.50 1.25 .25
Knicks win Opener
(Earl Monroe)
☐ 155 NBA Playoffs G2 2.00 1.00 .20
Lakers Come Back
(under the basket)
☐ 156 NBA Playoffs G3 2.00 1.00 .20
Two in a Row
(under the basket)
☐ 157 NBA Playoffs G4 2.00 1.00 .20
Ellis provides
bench strength
☐ 158 NBA Playoffs G5 5.50 2.75 .55
Jerry drives in
(Jerry West)
☐ 159 NBA Champs-Lakers 6.00 3.00 .60
(Wilt rebounding)
☐ 160 NBA Checklist 1-176 12.50 1.50 .30
UER (135 Jim King)

☐ 161 John Havlicek AS 11.00 5.50 1.10
Boston Celtics
☐ 162 Spencer Haywood AS 2.00 1.00 .20
Seattle Supersonics
☐ 163 Kareem Abdul-Jabbar AS 25.00 12.50 2.50
Milwaukee Bucks
☐ 164 Jerry West AS 14.00 7.00 1.40
Los Angeles Lakers
☐ 165 Walt Frazier AS 5.50 2.75 .55
New York Knicks
☐ 166 Bob Love AS 1.50 .75 .15
Chicago Bulls
☐ 167 Billy Cunningham AS 3.00 1.50 .30
Philadelphia 76ers
☐ 168 Wilt Chamberlain AS 25.00 12.50 2.50
Los Angeles Lakers
☐ 169 Nate Archibald AS 4.00 2.00 .40
Kansas City-Omaha Kings
☐ 170 Archie Clark AS 1.50 .75 .15
Baltimore Bullets
☐ 171 NBA Scoring Leaders 9.00 4.50 .90
Kareem Abdul-Jabbar
John Havlicek
Nate Archibald
☐ 172 NBA Scoring Average 9.00 4.50 .90
Leaders
Kareem Abdul-Jabbar
Nate Archibald
John Havlicek
☐ 173 NBA FG Pct Leaders 9.00 4.50 .90
Wilt Chamberlain
Kareem Abdul-Jabbar
Walt Bellamy
☐ 174 NBA FT Pct Leaders 2.00 1.00 .20
Jack Marin
Calvin Murphy
Gail Goodrich
☐ 175 NBA Rebound Leaders 11.00 5.50 1.10
Wilt Chamberlain
Kareem Abdul-Jabbar
Wes Unseld
☐ 176 NBA Assist Leaders 5.00 2.50 .50
Len Wilkens
Jerry West
Nate Archibald
☐ 177 Roland Taylor 1.00 .50 .10
Virginia Squires
☐ 178 Art Becker 1.00 .50 .10
San Diego Conquistadors
☐ 179 Mack Calvin 1.75 .85 .17
Carolina Cougars
☐ 180 Artis Gilmore 27.00 13.50 2.70
Kentucky Colonels
☐ 181 Collis Jones 1.25 .60 .12
Dallas Chaparrals
☐ 182 John Roche 1.75 .85 .17
New York Nets
☐ 183 George McGinnis 9.00 4.50 .90
Indiana Pacers
☐ 184 Johnny Neumann 1.25 .60 .12
Memphis Tams
☐ 185 Willie Wise 1.25 .60 .12
Utah Stars
☐ 186 Bernie Williams 1.00 .50 .10
Virginia Squires
☐ 187 Byron Beck 1.00 .50 .10
Denver Rockets
☐ 188 Larry Miller 1.00 .50 .10
San Diego Conquistadors
☐ 189 Cincy Powell 1.00 .50 .10
Kentucky Colonels
☐ 190 Donnie Freeman 1.25 .60 .12
Dallas Chaparrals
☐ 191 John Baum 1.00 .50 .10
New York Nets
☐ 192 Billy Keller 1.25 .60 .12
Indiana Pacers
☐ 193 Wilbert Jones 1.00 .50 .10
Memphis Tams
☐ 194 Glen Combs 1.00 .50 .10
Utah Stars
☐ 195 Julius Erving 270.00 125.00 25.00
Virginia Squires
(Forward on front,
but Center on back)
☐ 196 Al Smith 1.00 .50 .10
Denver Rockets
☐ 197 George Carter 1.00 .50 .10
New York Nets
☐ 198 Louie Dampier 1.75 .85 .17
Kentucky Colonels
☐ 199 Rich Jones 1.00 .50 .10
Dallas Chaparrals
☐ 200 Mel Daniels 1.75 .85 .17

Indiana Pacers
☐ 201 Gene Moore .... 1.00 .50 .10
San Diego Conquistadors
☐ 202 Randy Denton .... 1.00 .50 .10
Memphis Tams
☐ 203 Larry Jones .... 1.00 .50 .10
Utah Stars
☐ 204 Jim Ligon .... 1.00 .50 .10
Virginia Squires
☐ 205 Warren Jabali .... 1.25 .60 .12
Denver Rockets
☐ 206 Joe Caldwell .... 1.25 .60 .12
Carolina Cougars
☐ 207 Darrell Carrier .... 1.25 .60 .12
Kentucky Colonels
☐ 208 Gene Kennedy .... 1.25 .60 .12
Dallas Chaparrals
☐ 209 Ollie Taylor .... 1.25 .60 .12
San Diego Conquistadors
☐ 210 Roger Brown .... 1.25 .60 .12
Indiana Pacers
☐ 211 George Lehmann .... 1.00 .50 .10
Memphis Tams
☐ 212 Red Robbins .... 1.00 .50 .10
San Diego Conquistadors
☐ 213 Jim Eakins .... 1.00 .50 .10
Virginia Squires
☐ 214 Willie Long .... 1.00 .50 .10
Denver Rockets
☐ 215 Billy Cunningham .... 6.00 3.00 .60
Carolina Cougars
☐ 216 Steve Jones .... 1.75 .85 .17
Dallas Chaparrals
☐ 217 Les Hunter .... 1.00 .50 .10
San Diego Conquistadors
☐ 218 Billy Paultz .... 1.50 .75 .15
New York Nets
☐ 219 Freddie Lewis .... 1.25 .60 .12
Indiana Pacers
☐ 220 Zelmo Beaty .... 1.75 .85 .17
Utah Stars
☐ 221 George Thompson .... 1.00 .50 .10
Memphis Tams
☐ 222 Neil Johnson .... 1.00 .50 .10
Virginia Squires
☐ 223 Dave Robisch .... 2.00 1.00 .20
Denver Rockets
☐ 224 Walt Simon .... 1.00 .50 .10
Kentucky Colonels
☐ 225 Bill Melchionni .... 1.25 .60 .12
New York Nets
☐ 226 Wendell Ladner .... 1.50 .75 .15
Memphis Tams
☐ 227 Joe Hamilton .... 1.00 .50 .10
Dallas Chaparrals
☐ 228 Bob Netolicky .... 1.25 .60 .12
Dallas Chaparrals
☐ 229 James Jones .... 1.25 .60 .12
Utah Stars
☐ 230 Dan Issel 10.00 5.00 1.00
Kentucky Colonels
☐ 231 Charlie Williams .... 1.00 .50 .10
San Diego Conquistadors
☐ 232 Willie Sojourner .... 1.00 .50 .10
Virginia Squires
☐ 233 Merv Jackson .... 1.00 .50 .10
Utah Stars
☐ 234 Mike Lewis .... 1.25 .60 .12
Carolina Cougars
☐ 235 Ralph Simpson .... 1.50 .75 .15
Denver Rockets
☐ 236 Darnell Hillman .... 1.25 .60 .12
Indiana Pacers
☐ 237 Rick Mount .... 2.00 1.00 .20
Kentucky Colonels
☐ 238 Gerald Govan .... 1.00 .50 .10
Memphis Tams
☐ 239 Ron Boone .... 1.25 .60 .12
Utah Stars
☐ 240 Tom Washington .... 1.00 .50 .10
New York Nets
☐ 241 ABA Playoffs G1 .... 1.75 .85 .17
Pacers take lead
(under the basket)
☐ 242 ABA Playoffs G2 .... 3.25 1.60 .32
Barry evens things
☐ 243 ABA Playoffs G3 .... 2.00 1.00 .20
McGinnis blocks
a jumper
☐ 244 ABA Playoffs G4 .... 3.25 1.60 .32
Rick (Barry) scores
on fast break
☐ 245 ABA Playoffs G5 .... 1.75 .85 .17
Keller becomes
Net killer
☐ 246 ABA Playoffs G6 .... 1.75 .85 .17
Tight Defense
☐ 247 ABA Champs: Pacers .... 1.75 .85 .17
☐ 248 ABA Checklist 177-264 .... 12.50 1.50 .30
UER (236 John Brisker)
☐ 249 Dan Issel AS .... 4.00 2.00 .40
Kentucky Colonels
☐ 250 Rick Barry AS 12.50 6.25 1.25
New York Nets
☐ 251 Artis Gilmore AS .... 5.00 2.50 .50
Kentucky Colonels
☐ 252 Donnie Freeman AS .... 1.25 .60 .12
Dallas Chaparrals
☐ 253 Bill Melchionni AS .... 1.25 .60 .12
New York Nets
☐ 254 Willie Wise AS .... 1.25 .60 .12
Utah Stars
☐ 255 Julius Erving AS 65.00 32.50 6.50
Virginia Squires
☐ 256 Zelmo Beaty AS .... 1.25 .60 .12
Utah Stars
☐ 257 Ralph Simpson AS .... 1.25 .60 .12
Denver Rockets
☐ 258 Charlie Scott AS .... 1.25 .60 .12
Virginia Squires
☐ 259 ABA Scoring Average .... 2.50 1.25 .25
Leaders
Charlie Scott
Rick Barry
Dan Issel
☐ 260 ABA 2pt FG Pct. .... 2.00 1.00 .20
Leaders
Artis Gilmore
Tom Washington
Larry Jones
☐ 261 ABA 3pt FG Pct. .... 1.75 .85 .17
Leaders
Glen Combs
Louie Dampier
Warren Jabali
☐ 262 ABA FT Pct Leaders .... 2.00 1.00 .20
Rick Barry
Mack Calvin
Steve Jones
☐ 263 ABA Rebound Leaders 11.00 5.50 1.10
Artis Gilmore
Julius Erving
Mel Daniels
☐ 264 ABA Assist Leaders .... 2.50 1.00 .20
Bill Melchionni
Larry Brown
Louie Dampier

1973-74 Topps

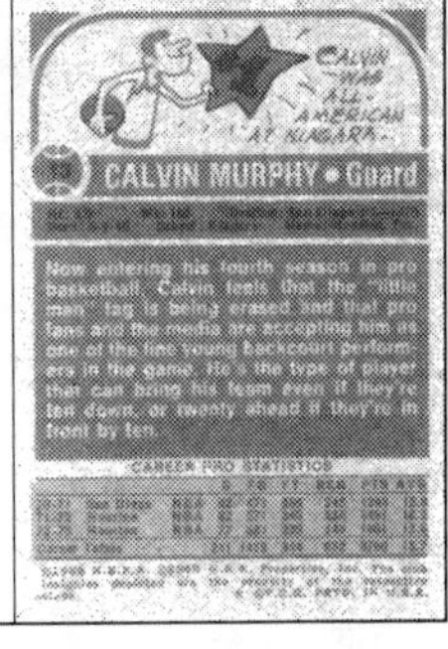

The 1973-74 Topps set of 264 contains NBA players on cards numbered 1 to 176 and ABA players on cards numbered 177 to 264. The cards in the set measure the standard 2 1/2" by 3 1/2". All-Star selections (first and second team) for both leagues are noted on the respective player's regular cards. Card backs are printed in red and green on gray card stock. The backs feature year-by-year ABA and NBA statistics. Subseries within the set include NBA Playoffs (62-68), NBA League Leaders (153-158), ABA Playoffs (202-208), and ABA League Leaders

(234-239). The only notable rookie cards in this set are Bob McAdoo and Paul Westphal.

	NRMT	VG-E	GOOD
COMPLETE SET (264)	360.00	165.00	45.00
COMMON PLAYER (1-132)	.50	.25	.05
COMMON PLAYER (133-264)	.50	.25	.05

	NRMT	VG-E	GOOD
☐ 1 Nate Archibald AS1 Kansas City-Omaha Kings	7.50	2.00	.40
☐ 2 Steve Kuberski Boston Celtics	.50	.25	.05
☐ 3 John Mengelt Detroit Pistons	.75	.35	.07
☐ 4 Jim McMillian Los Angeles Lakers	.75	.35	.07
☐ 5 Nate Thurmond Golden State Warriors	3.00	1.50	.30
☐ 6 Dave Wohl Buffalo Braves	.50	.25	.05
☐ 7 John Brisker Seattle Supersonics	.50	.25	.05
☐ 8 Charlie Davis Portland Trail Blazers	.50	.25	.05
☐ 9 Lamar Green Phoenix Suns	.50	.25	.05
☐ 10 Walt Frazier AS2 New York Knicks	8.00	4.00	.80
☐ 11 Bob Christian Atlanta Hawks	.50	.25	.05
☐ 12 Cornell Warner Cleveland Cavaliers	.50	.25	.05
☐ 13 Calvin Murphy Houston Rockets	2.50	1.25	.25
☐ 14 Dave Sorenson Philadelphia 76ers	.50	.25	.05
☐ 15 Archie Clark Capital Bullets	.75	.35	.07
☐ 16 Clifford Ray Chicago Bulls	.75	.35	.07
☐ 17 Terry Driscoll Milwaukee Bucks	.50	.25	.05
☐ 18 Matt Guokas Kansas City-Omaha Kings	.75	.35	.07
☐ 19 Elmore Smith Buffalo Braves	.75	.35	.07
☐ 20 John Havlicek AS1 Boston Celtics	14.00	7.00	1.40
☐ 21 Pat Riley Los Angeles Lakers	8.00	4.00	.80
☐ 22 George Trapp Detroit Pistons	.50	.25	.05
☐ 23 Ron Williams Golden State Warriors	.50	.25	.05
☐ 24 Jim Fox Seattle Supersonics	.50	.25	.05
☐ 25 Dick Van Arsdale Phoenix Suns	.75	.35	.07
☐ 26 John Tresvant Capital Bullets	.50	.25	.05
☐ 27 Rick Adelman Portland Trail Blazers	1.75	.85	.17
☐ 28 Eddie Mast Atlanta Hawks	.50	.25	.05
☐ 29 Jim Cleamons Cleveland Cavaliers	.75	.35	.07
☐ 30 Dave DeBusschere AS2 New York Knicks	6.00	3.00	.60
☐ 31 Norm Van Lier Chicago Bulls	.75	.35	.07
☐ 32 Stan McKenzie Houston Rockets	.50	.25	.05
☐ 33 Bob Dandridge Milwaukee Bucks	.75	.35	.07
☐ 34 Leroy Ellis Philadelphia 76ers	.50	.25	.05
☐ 35 Mike Riordan Capital Bullets	.75	.35	.07
☐ 36 Fred Hilton Buffalo Braves	.50	.25	.05
☐ 37 Toby Kimball Kansas City-Omaha Kings	.50	.25	.05
☐ 38 Jim Price Los Angeles Lakers	.50	.25	.05
☐ 39 Willie Norwood Detroit Pistons	.50	.25	.05
☐ 40 Dave Cowens AS2 Boston Celtics	6.00	3.00	.60
☐ 41 Cazzie Russell Golden State Warriors	1.25	.60	.12
☐ 42 Lee Winfield Seattle Supersonics	.50	.25	.05
☐ 43 Connie Hawkins Phoenix Suns	3.25	1.60	.32
☐ 44 Mike Newlin Houston Rockets	.75	.35	.07
☐ 45 Chet Walker Chicago Bulls	1.25	.60	.12
☐ 46 Walt Bellamy Atlanta Hawks	1.75	.85	.17
☐ 47 John Johnson Portland Trail Blazers	.75	.35	.07
☐ 48 Henry Bibby New York Knicks	1.75	.85	.17
☐ 49 Bobby Smith Cleveland Cavaliers	.50	.25	.05
☐ 50 Kareem Abdul-Jabbar AS1 Milwaukee Bucks	42.00	21.00	4.20
☐ 51 Mike Price Philadelphia 76ers	.50	.25	.05
☐ 52 John Hummer Buffalo Braves	.50	.25	.05
☐ 53 Kevin Porter Capital Bullets	4.00	2.00	.40
☐ 54 Nate Williams Kansas City-Omaha Kings	.50	.25	.05
☐ 55 Gail Goodrich Los Angeles Lakers	2.00	1.00	.20
☐ 56 Fred Foster Detroit Pistons	.50	.25	.05
☐ 57 Don Chaney Boston Celtics	1.25	.60	.12
☐ 58 Bud Stallworth Seattle Supersonics	.50	.25	.05
☐ 59 Clem Haskins Phoenix Suns	.75	.35	.07
☐ 60 Bob Love AS2 Chicago Bulls	1.25	.60	.12
☐ 61 Jimmy Walker Houston Rockets	.50	.25	.05
☐ 62 NBA Eastern Semis Knicks shoot down Bullets in 5	1.00	.50	.10
☐ 63 NBA Eastern Semis Celts oust Hawks 2nd Straight Year	1.00	.50	.10
☐ 64 NBA Western Semis Lakers outlast Bulls at Wire (W.Chamberlain)	5.00	2.50	.50
☐ 65 NBA Western Semis Warriors over- whelm Milwaukee	1.00	.50	.10
☐ 66 NBA Eastern Finals Knicks stun Celtics at Boston (W.Reed/Finkel)	2.50	1.25	.25
☐ 67 NBA Western Finals Lakers Breeze Past Golden State	1.00	.50	.10
☐ 68 NBA Championship Knicks Do It, Repeat '70 Miracle (W.Frazier/Erickson)	3.00	1.50	.30
☐ 69 Larry Steele Portland Trail Blazers	.50	.25	.05
☐ 70 Oscar Robertson Milwaukee Bucks	20.00	10.00	2.00
☐ 71 Phil Jackson New York Knicks	4.50	2.25	.45
☐ 72 John Wetzel Atlanta Hawks	.50	.25	.05
☐ 73 Steve Patterson Cleveland Cavaliers	1.00	.50	.10
☐ 74 Manny Leaks Philadelphia 76ers	.50	.25	.05
☐ 75 Jeff Mullins Golden State Warriors	.75	.35	.07
☐ 76 Stan Love Capital Bullets	.50	.25	.05
☐ 77 Dick Garrett Buffalo Braves	.50	.25	.05
☐ 78 Don Nelson Boston Celtics	2.50	1.25	.25
☐ 79 Chris Ford Detroit Pistons	6.00	3.00	.60
☐ 80 Wilt Chamberlain Los Angeles Lakers	45.00	22.50	4.50
☐ 81 Dennis Layton Phoenix Suns	.50	.25	.05
☐ 82 Bill Bradley New York Knicks	21.00	10.50	2.10
☐ 83 Jerry Sloan Chicago Bulls	1.50	.75	.15
☐ 84 Cliff Meely Houston Rockets	.50	.25	.05

☐ 85 Sam Lacey Kansas City-Omaha Kings	.75	.35	.07
☐ 86 Dick Snyder Seattle Supersonics	.50	.25	.05
☐ 87 Jim Washington Atlanta Hawks	.50	.25	.05
☐ 88 Lucius Allen Milwaukee Bucks	.75	.35	.07
☐ 89 LaRue Martin Portland Trail Blazers	.75	.35	.07
☐ 90 Rick Barry Golden State Warriors	15.00	7.50	1.50
☐ 91 Fred Boyd Philadelphia 76ers	.50	.25	.05
☐ 92 Barry Clemens Cleveland Cavaliers	.50	.25	.05
☐ 93 Dean Meminger New York Knicks	.75	.35	.07
☐ 94 Henry Finkel Boston Celtics	.50	.25	.05
☐ 95 Elvin Hayes Capital Bullets	8.00	4.00	.80
☐ 96 Stu Lantz Detroit Pistons	.50	.25	.05
☐ 97 Bill Hewitt Buffalo Braves	.50	.25	.05
☐ 98 Neal Walk Phoenix Suns	.50	.25	.05
☐ 99 Garfield Heard Chicago Bulls	.75	.35	.07
☐ 100 Jerry West AS1 Los Angeles Lakers	24.00	12.00	2.40
☐ 101 Otto Moore Houston Rockets	.50	.25	.05
☐ 102 Don Kojis Kansas City-Omaha Kings	.50	.25	.05
☐ 103 Fred Brown Seattle Supersonics	4.25	2.10	.42
☐ 104 Dwight Davis Cleveland Cavaliers	.75	.35	.07
☐ 105 Willis Reed New York Knicks	6.00	3.00	.60
☐ 106 Herm Gilliam Atlanta Hawks	.50	.25	.05
☐ 107 Mickey Davis Milwaukee Bucks	.75	.35	.07
☐ 108 Jim Barnett Golden State Warriors	.50	.25	.05
☐ 109 Ollie Johnson Portland Trail Blazers	.50	.25	.05
☐ 110 Bob Lanier Detroit Pistons	6.00	3.00	.60
☐ 111 Fred Carter Philadelphia 76ers	.50	.25	.05
☐ 112 Paul Silas Boston Celtics	1.25	.60	.12
☐ 113 Phil Chenier Capital Bullets	1.00	.50	.10
☐ 114 Dennis Awtrey Chicago Bulls	.50	.25	.05
☐ 115 Austin Carr Cleveland Cavaliers	1.00	.50	.10
☐ 116 Bob Kauffman Buffalo Braves	.50	.25	.05
☐ 117 Keith Erickson Los Angeles Lakers	.75	.35	.07
☐ 118 Walt Wesley Phoenix Suns	.50	.25	.05
☐ 119 Steve Bracey Atlanta Hawks	.50	.25	.05
☐ 120 Spencer Haywood AS1 Seattle Supersonics	1.75	.85	.17
☐ 121 NBA Checklist 1-176	9.00	.90	.18
☐ 122 Jack Marin Houston Rockets	.75	.35	.07
☐ 123 Jon McGlocklin Milwaukee Bucks	.75	.35	.07
☐ 124 Johnny Green Kansas City-Omaha Kings	.50	.25	.05
☐ 125 Jerry Lucas New York Knicks	5.50	2.75	.55
☐ 126 Paul Westphal Boston Celtics	10.00	5.00	1.00
☐ 127 Curtis Rowe Detroit Pistons	1.00	.50	.10
☐ 128 Mahdi Abdul-Rahman Seattle Supersonics (formerly Walt Hazzard)	1.25	.60	.12
☐ 129 Lloyd Neal Portland Trail Blazers	1.25	.60	.12
☐ 130 Pete Maravich AS1 Atlanta Hawks	15.00	7.50	1.50
☐ 131 Don May Philadelphia 76ers	.50	.25	.05
☐ 132 Bob Weiss Chicago Bulls	.75	.35	.07
☐ 133 Dave Stallworth Capital Bullets	.75	.35	.07
☐ 134 Dick Cunningham Milwaukee Bucks	.50	.25	.05
☐ 135 Bob McAdoo Buffalo Braves	15.00	7.50	1.50
☐ 136 Butch Beard Golden State Warriors	.75	.35	.07
☐ 137 Happy Hairston Los Angeles Lakers	.75	.35	.07
☐ 138 Bob Rule Cleveland Cavaliers	.50	.25	.05
☐ 139 Don Adams Detroit Pistons	.50	.25	.05
☐ 140 Charlie Scott Phoenix Suns	1.00	.50	.10
☐ 141 Ron Riley Kansas City-Omaha Kings	.50	.25	.05
☐ 142 Earl Monroe New York Knicks	6.00	3.00	.60
☐ 143 Clyde Lee Golden State Warriors	.50	.25	.05
☐ 144 Rick Roberson Portland Trail Blazers	.50	.25	.05
☐ 145 Rudy Tomjanovich Houston Rockets (Printed without Houston on basket)	1.25	.60	.12
☐ 146 Tom Van Arsdale Philadelphia 76ers	.75	.35	.07
☐ 147 Art Williams Boston Celtics	.50	.25	.05
☐ 148 Curtis Perry Milwaukee Bucks	.50	.25	.05
☐ 149 Rich Rinaldi Capital Bullets	.50	.25	.05
☐ 150 Lou Hudson Atlanta Hawks	1.25	.60	.12
☐ 151 Mel Counts Los Angeles Lakers	.50	.25	.05
☐ 152 Jim McDaniels Seattle Supersonics	.50	.25	.05
☐ 153 NBA Scoring Leaders Nate Archibald Kareem Abdul-Jabbar Spencer Haywood	5.00	2.50	.50
☐ 154 NBA Scoring Average Leaders Nate Archibald Kareem Abdul-Jabbar Spencer Haywood	5.00	2.50	.50
☐ 155 NBA FG Pct Leaders Wilt Chamberlain Matt Guokas Kareem Abdul-Jabbar	6.50	3.25	.65
☐ 156 NBA FT Pct Leaders Rick Barry Calvin Murphy Mike Newlin	2.00	1.00	.20
☐ 157 NBA Rebound Leaders Wilt Chamberlain Nate Thurmond Dave Cowens	5.00	2.50	.50
☐ 158 NBA Assist Leaders Nate Archibald Len Wilkens Dave Bing	2.50	1.25	.25
☐ 159 Don Smith Houston Rockets	.50	.25	.05
☐ 160 Sidney Wicks Portland Trail Blazers	2.00	1.00	.20
☐ 161 Howie Komives Buffalo Braves	.50	.25	.05
☐ 162 John Gianelli New York Knicks	.50	.25	.05
☐ 163 Jeff Halliburton Philadelphia 76ers	.50	.25	.05
☐ 164 Kennedy McIntosh Seattle Supersonics	.50	.25	.05
☐ 165 Len Wilkens Cleveland Cavaliers	2.50	1.25	.25
☐ 166 Corky Calhoun Phoenix Suns	.75	.35	.07
☐ 167 Howard Porter Chicago Bulls	.75	.35	.07
☐ 168 JoJo White Boston Celtics	2.00	1.00	.20
☐ 169 John Block Kansas City-Omaha Kings	.50	.25	.05
☐ 170 Dave Bing Detroit Pistons	3.25	1.60	.32
☐ 171 Joe Ellis	.50	.25	.05

	No.	Player			
		Golden State Warriors			
☐	172	Chuck Terry	.50	.25	.05
		Milwaukee Bucks			
☐	173	Randy Smith	.75	.35	.07
		Buffalo Braves			
☐	174	Bill Bridges	.75	.35	.07
		Los Angeles Lakers			
☐	175	Geoff Petrie	.75	.35	.07
		Portland Trail Blazers			
☐	176	Wes Unseld	4.50	2.25	.45
		Capital Bullets			
☐	177	Skeeter Swift	.50	.25	.05
		San Antonio Spurs			
☐	178	Jim Eakins	.50	.25	.05
		Virginia Squires			
☐	179	Steve Jones	.75	.35	.07
		Carolina Cougars			
☐	180	George McGinnis AS1	2.50	1.25	.25
		Indiana Pacers			
☐	181	Al Smith	.50	.25	.05
		Denver Rockets			
☐	182	Tom Washington	.50	.25	.05
		New York Nets			
☐	183	Louie Dampier	.75	.35	.07
		Kentucky Colonels			
☐	184	Simmie Hill	.50	.25	.05
		San Diego Conquistadors			
☐	185	George Thompson	.50	.25	.05
		Memphis Tams			
☐	186	Cincy Powell	.50	.25	.05
		Utah Stars			
☐	187	Larry Jones	.50	.25	.05
		San Antonio Spurs			
☐	188	Neil Johnson	.50	.25	.05
		Virginia Squires			
☐	189	Tom Owens	.75	.35	.07
		Carolina Cougars			
☐	190	Ralph Simpson AS2	.75	.35	.07
		Denver Rockets			
☐	191	George Carter	.50	.25	.05
		Virginia Squires			
☐	192	Rick Mount	1.00	.50	.10
		Kentucky Colonels			
☐	193	Red Robbins	.50	.25	.05
		San Diego Conquistadors			
☐	194	George Lehmann	.50	.25	.05
		Memphis Tams			
☐	195	Mel Daniels AS2	1.25	.60	.12
		Indiana Pacers			
☐	196	Bob Warren	.50	.25	.05
		Utah Stars			
☐	197	Gene Kennedy	.50	.25	.05
		San Antonio Spurs			
☐	198	Mike Barr	.50	.25	.05
		Virginia Squires			
☐	199	Dave Robisch	.75	.35	.07
		Denver Rockets			
☐	200	Billy Cunningham AS1	5.00	2.50	.50
		Carolina Cougars			
☐	201	John Roche	.75	.35	.07
		New York Nets			
☐	202	ABA Western Semis Pacers Oust Injured Rockets	1.00	.50	.10
☐	203	ABA Western Semis Stars sweep Q's in Four Straight	1.00	.50	.10
☐	204	ABA Eastern Semis Kentucky overcomes Squires and Dr. J. (Issel jump shot)	2.00	1.00	.20
☐	205	ABA Eastern Semis Cougars in strong finish over Nets	1.00	.50	.10
☐	206	ABA Western Finals Pacers nip bitter rival, Stars	1.00	.50	.10
☐	207	ABA Eastern Finals Colonels prevail in grueling Series (Gilmore shooting)	2.00	1.00	.20
☐	208	ABA Championship McGinnis leads Pacers to Title (center jump)	1.00	.50	.10
☐	209	Glen Combs	.50	.25	.05
		Utah Stars			
☐	210	Dan Issel AS2	6.00	3.00	.60
		Kentucky Colonels			
☐	211	Randy Denton	.50	.25	.05
		Memphis Tams			
☐	212	Freddie Lewis	.75	.35	.07
		Indiana Pacers			
☐	213	Stew Johnson	.50	.25	.05
		San Diego Conquistadors			
☐	214	Roland Taylor	.50	.25	.05
		Virginia Squires			
☐	215	Rich Jones	.50	.25	.05
		San Antonio Spurs			
☐	216	Billy Paultz	.75	.35	.07
		New York Nets			
☐	217	Ron Boone	.75	.35	.07
		Utah Stars			
☐	218	Walt Simon	.50	.25	.05
		Kentucky Colonels			
☐	219	Mike Lewis	.50	.25	.05
		Carolina Cougars			
☐	220	Warren Jabali AS1	.75	.35	.07
		Denver Rockets			
☐	221	Wilbert Jones	.50	.25	.05
		Memphis Tams			
☐	222	Don Buse	1.50	.75	.15
		Indiana Pacers			
☐	223	Gene Moore	.50	.25	.05
		San Diego Conquistadors			
☐	224	Joe Hamilton	.50	.25	.05
		San Antonio Spurs			
☐	225	Zelmo Beaty	.75	.35	.07
		Utah Stars			
☐	226	Brian Taylor	1.25	.60	.12
		New York Nets			
☐	227	Julius Keye	.50	.25	.05
		Denver Rockets			
☐	228	Mike Gale	1.00	.50	.10
		Kentucky Colonels			
☐	229	Warren Davis	.50	.25	.05
		Memphis Tams			
☐	230	Mack Calvin AS2	1.00	.50	.10
		Carolina Cougars			
☐	231	Roger Brown	.75	.35	.07
		Indiana Pacers			
☐	232	Chuck Williams	.50	.25	.05
		San Diego Conquistadors			
☐	233	Gerald Govan	.50	.25	.05
		Utah Stars			
☐	234	ABA Scoring Average Leaders Julius Erving George McGinnis Dan Issel	6.00	3.00	.60
☐	235	ABA 2 Pt. Pct. Leaders Artis Gilmore Gene Kennedy Tom Owens	1.00	.50	.10
☐	236	ABA 3 Pt. Pct. Leaders Glen Combs Roger Brown Louie Dampier	1.00	.50	.10
☐	237	ABA F.T. Pct. Leaders Billy Keller Ron Boone Bob Warren	1.00	.50	.10
☐	238	ABA Rebound Leaders Artis Gilmore Mel Daniels Bill Paultz	1.00	.50	.10
☐	239	ABA Assist Leaders Bill Melchionni Chuck Williams Warren Jabali	1.00	.50	.10
☐	240	Julius Erving AS2	75.00	37.50	7.50
		Virginia Squires			
☐	241	Jimmy O'Brien	.75	.35	.07
		Kentucky Colonels			
☐	242	ABA Checklist 177-264	9.00	.90	.18
☐	243	Johnny Neumann	.75	.35	.07
		Memphis Tams			
☐	244	Darnell Hillman	.75	.35	.07
		Indiana Pacers			
☐	245	Willie Wise	.75	.35	.07
		Utah Stars			
☐	246	Collis Jones	.50	.25	.05
		San Antonio Spurs			
☐	247	Ted McClain	.50	.25	.05
		Carolina Cougars			
☐	248	George Irvine	1.00	.50	.10
		Virginia Squires			
☐	249	Bill Melchionni	.75	.35	.07
		New York Nets			
☐	250	Artis Gilmore AS1	5.50	2.75	.55
		Kentucky Colonels			
☐	251	Willie Long	.50	.25	.05
		Denver Rockets			
☐	252	Larry Miller	.75	.35	.07
		San Diego Conquistadors			
☐	253	Lee Davis	.50	.25	.05

Memphis Tams			
☐ 254 Donnie Freeman .... Indiana Pacers	.75	.35	.07
☐ 255 Joe Caldwell .... Carolina Cougars	.75	.35	.07
☐ 256 Bob Netolicky .... San Antonio Spurs	.75	.35	.07
☐ 257 Bernie Williams .... Virginia Squires	.50	.25	.05
☐ 258 Byron Beck .... Denver Rockets	.50	.25	.05
☐ 259 Jim Chones .... New York Nets	1.25	.60	.12
☐ 260 James Jones AS1 .... Utah Stars	.75	.35	.07
☐ 261 Wendell Ladner .... Kentucky Colonels	.75	.35	.07
☐ 262 Ollie Taylor .... San Diego Conquistadors	.50	.25	.05
☐ 263 Les Hunter .... Memphis Tams	.50	.25	.05
☐ 264 Billy Keller .... Indiana Pacers	.75	.35	.07

1974-75 Topps

The 1974-75 Topps set of 264 cards contains NBA players on cards numbered 1 to 176 and ABA players on cards numbered 177 to 264. For the first time Team Leader (TL) cards are provided for each team. The cards in the set measure the standard 2 1/2" by 3 1/2". All-Star selections (first and second team) for both leagues are noted on the respective player's regular cards. The card backs are printed in blue and red on gray card stock. Subseries within the set include NBA Team Leaders (81-98), NBA Statistical Leaders (144-149), NBA Playoffs (161-164), ABA Statistical Leaders (207-212), ABA Team Leaders (221-230), and ABA Playoffs (246-249). The key rookie cards in this set are George Gervin and Bill Walton.

	NRMT	VG-E	GOOD
COMPLETE SET (264)	350.00	175.00	35.00
COMMON PLAYER (1-132)	.50	.25	.05
COMMON PLAYER (133-264)	.50	.25	.05
☐ 1 Kareem Abdul-Jabbar .... AS1 Milwaukee Bucks	40.00	12.50	2.50
☐ 2 Don May .... Philadelphia 76ers	.50	.25	.05
☐ 3 Bernie Fryer .... Portland Trail Blazers	.75	.35	.07
☐ 4 Don Adams .... Detroit Pistons	.50	.25	.05
☐ 5 Herm Gilliam .... Atlanta Hawks	.50	.25	.05
☐ 6 Jim Chones .... Cleveland Cavaliers	.75	.35	.07
☐ 7 Rick Adelman .... Chicago Bulls	1.50	.75	.15
☐ 8 Randy Smith .... Buffalo Braves	.75	.35	.07
☐ 9 Paul Silas .... Boston Celtics	1.25	.60	.12
☐ 10 Pete Maravich .... New Orleans Jazz	12.50	6.25	1.25
☐ 11 Ron Behagen .... Kansas City-Omaha Kings	.50	.25	.05
☐ 12 Kevin Porter .... Washington Bullets	1.00	.50	.10
☐ 13 Bill Bridges .... Los Angeles Lakers (On back team shown as Los And., should be Los Ang.)	.75	.35	.07
☐ 14 Charles Johnson .... Golden State Warriors	1.00	.50	.10
☐ 15 Bob Love .... Chicago Bulls	1.25	.60	.12
☐ 16 Henry Bibby .... New York Knicks	.75	.35	.07
☐ 17 Neal Walk .... Phoenix Suns	.50	.25	.05
☐ 18 John Brisker .... Seattle Supersonics	.50	.25	.05
☐ 19 Lucius Allen .... Milwaukee Bucks	.75	.35	.07
☐ 20 Tom Van Arsdale .... Philadelphia 76ers	.75	.35	.07
☐ 21 Larry Steele .... Portland Trail Blazers	.50	.25	.05
☐ 22 Curtis Rowe .... Detroit Pistons	.75	.35	.07
☐ 23 Dean Meminger .... Atlanta Hawks	.50	.25	.05
☐ 24 Steve Patterson .... Cleveland Cavaliers	.50	.25	.05
☐ 25 Earl Monroe .... New York Knicks	5.50	2.75	.55
☐ 26 Jack Marin .... Buffalo Braves	.50	.25	.05
☐ 27 JoJo White .... Boston Celtics	1.75	.85	.17
☐ 28 Rudy Tomjanovich .... Houston Rockets	1.00	.50	.10
☐ 29 Otto Moore .... Kansas City-Omaha Kings	.50	.25	.05
☐ 30 Elvin Hayes AS2 .... Washington Bullets	7.00	3.50	.70
☐ 31 Pat Riley .... Los Angeles Lakers	6.50	3.25	.65
☐ 32 Clyde Lee .... Golden State Warriors	.50	.25	.05
☐ 33 Bob Weiss .... Chicago Bulls	.75	.35	.07
☐ 34 Jim Fox .... Seattle Supersonics	.50	.25	.05
☐ 35 Charlie Scott .... Phoenix Suns	.75	.35	.07
☐ 36 Cliff Meely .... Houston Rockets	.50	.25	.05
☐ 37 Jon McGlocklin .... Milwaukee Bucks	.75	.35	.07
☐ 38 Jim McMillian .... Buffalo Braves	.50	.25	.05
☐ 39 Bill Walton .... Portland Trail Blazers	40.00	20.00	4.00
☐ 40 Dave Bing AS2 .... Detroit Pistons	3.00	1.50	.30
☐ 41 Jim Washington .... Atlanta Hawks	.50	.25	.05
☐ 42 Jim Cleamons .... Cleveland Cavaliers	.50	.25	.05
☐ 43 Mel Davis .... New York Knicks	.50	.25	.05
☐ 44 Garfield Heard .... Buffalo Braves	.50	.25	.05
☐ 45 Jimmy Walker .... Kansas City-Omaha Kings	.50	.25	.05
☐ 46 Don Nelson .... Boston Celtics	2.50	1.25	.25
☐ 47 Jim Barnett .... New Orleans Jazz	.50	.25	.05
☐ 48 Manny Leaks .... Washington Bullets	.50	.25	.05
☐ 49 Elmore Smith .... Los Angeles Lakers	.50	.25	.05
☐ 50 Rick Barry AS1 .... Golden State Warriors	0.00	5.00	1.00
☐ 51 Jerry Sloan .... Chicago Bulls	1.00	.50	.10
☐ 52 John Hummer .... Seattle Supersonics	.50	.25	.05
☐ 53 Keith Erickson .... Phoenix Suns	.75	.35	.07
☐ 54 George E. Johnson .... Houston Rockets	.50	.25	.05
☐ 55 Oscar Robertson .... Milwaukee Bucks	16.00	8.00	1.60

☐ 56 Steve Mix .... Philadelphia 76ers	1.00	.50	.10
☐ 57 Rick Roberson .... Portland Trail Blazers	.50	.25	.05
☐ 58 John Mengelt .... Detroit Pistons	.50	.25	.05
☐ 59 Dwight Jones .... Atlanta Hawks	.75	.35	.07
☐ 60 Austin Carr .... Cleveland Cavaliers	.75	.35	.07
☐ 61 Nick Weatherspoon .... Washington Bullets	1.00	.50	.10
☐ 62 Clem Haskins .... Phoenix Suns	.75	.35	.07
☐ 63 Don Kojis .... Kansas City-Omaha Kings	.50	.25	.05
☐ 64 Paul Westphal .... Boston Celtics	2.50	1.25	.25
☐ 65 Walt Bellamy .... New Orleans Jazz	1.50	.75	.15
☐ 66 John Johnson .... Portland Trail Blazers	.50	.25	.05
☐ 67 Butch Beard .... Golden State Warriors	.50	.25	.05
☐ 68 Happy Hairston .... Los Angeles Lakers	.75	.35	.07
☐ 69 Tom Boerwinkle .... Chicago Bulls	.50	.25	.05
☐ 70 Spencer Haywood AS2 .... Seattle Supersonics	1.50	.75	.15
☐ 71 Gary Melchionni .... Phoenix Suns	.50	.25	.05
☐ 72 Ed Ratleff .... Houston Rockets	1.00	.50	.10
☐ 73 Mickey Davis .... Milwaukee Bucks	.50	.25	.05
☐ 74 Dennis Awtrey .... New Orleans Jazz	.50	.25	.05
☐ 75 Fred Carter .... Philadelphia 76ers	.50	.25	.05
☐ 76 George Trapp .... Detroit Pistons	.50	.25	.05
☐ 77 John Wetzel .... Atlanta Hawks	.50	.25	.05
☐ 78 Bobby Smith .... Cleveland Cavaliers	.50	.25	.05
☐ 79 John Gianelli .... New York Knicks	.50	.25	.05
☐ 80 Bob McAdoo AS2 .... Buffalo Braves	4.00	2.00	.40
☐ 81 Atlanta Hawks TL .... Pete Maravich, Lou Hudson, Walt Bellamy, Pete Maravich	2.50	1.25	.25
☐ 82 Boston Celtics TL .... John Havlicek, JoJo White, Dave Cowens, JoJo White	4.00	2.00	.40
☐ 83 Buffalo Braves TL .... Bob McAdoo, Ernie DiGregorio, Bob McAdoo, Ernie DiGregorio	1.25	.60	.12
☐ 84 Chicago Bulls TL .... Bob Love, Chet Walker, Clifford Ray, Norm Van Lier	1.25	.60	.12
☐ 85 Cleveland Cavs TL .... Austin Carr, Austin Carr, Dwight Davis, Len Wilkens	1.25	.60	.12
☐ 86 Detroit Pistons TL .... Bob Lanier, Stu Lantz, Bob Lanier, Dave Bing	1.25	.60	.12
☐ 87 Golden State Warriors TL .... Rick Barry, Rick Barry, Nate Thurmond, Rick Barry	2.50	1.25	.25
☐ 88 Houston Rockets TL .... Rudy Tomjanovich, Calvin Murphy, Don Smith, Calvin Murphy	1.25	.60	.12
☐ 89 Kansas City Omaha TL .... Jimmy Walker, Jimmy Walker, Sam Lacey, Jimmy Walker	1.00	.50	.10
☐ 90 Los Angeles Lakers TL .... Gail Goodrich, Gail Goodrich, Happy Hairston, Gail Goodrich	1.25	.60	.12
☐ 91 Milwaukee Bucks TL .... Kareem Abdul-Jabbar, Oscar Robertson, Kareem Abdul-Jabbar, Oscar Robertson	7.00	3.50	.70
☐ 92 New Orleans Jazz .... Emblem; Expansion Draft Picks on Back	1.00	.50	.10
☐ 93 New York Knicks TL .... Walt Frazier, Bill Bradley, Dave DeBusschere, Walt Frazier	4.25	2.10	.42
☐ 94 Philadelphia 76ers TL .... Fred Carter, Tom Van Arsdale, Leroy Ellis, Fred Carter	1.00	.50	.10
☐ 95 Phoenix Suns TL .... Charlie Scott, Dick Van Arsdale, Neal Walk, Neal Walk	1.00	.50	.10
☐ 96 Portland Trail Blazers TL .... Geoff Petrie, Geoff Petrie, Rick Roberson, Sidney Wicks	1.00	.50	.10
☐ 97 Seattle Supersonics TL .... Spencer Haywood, Dick Snyder, Spencer Haywood, Fred Brown	1.00	.50	.10
☐ 98 Capitol Bullets TL .... Phil Chenier, Phil Chenier, Elvin Hayes, Kevin Porter	1.00	.50	.10
☐ 99 Sam Lacey .... Kansas City-Omaha Kings	.50	.25	.05
☐ 100 John Havlicek AS1 .... Boston Celtics	14.00	7.00	1.40
☐ 101 Stu Lantz .... New Orleans Jazz	.50	.25	.05
☐ 102 Mike Riordan .... Washington Bullets	.50	.25	.05
☐ 103 Larry Jones .... Philadelphia 76ers	.50	.25	.05
☐ 104 Connie Hawkins .... Los Angeles Lakers	3.00	1.50	.30
☐ 105 Nate Thurmond .... Golden State Warriors	3.00	1.50	.30
☐ 106 Dick Gibbs .... Seattle Supersonics	.50	.25	.05
☐ 107 Corky Calhoun .... Phoenix Suns	.50	.25	.05
☐ 108 Dave Wohl .... Houston Rockets	.50	.25	.05
☐ 109 Cornell Warner .... Milwaukee Bucks	.50	.25	.05
☐ 110 Geoff Petrie UER .... Portland Trail Blazers (Misspelled Patrie on card front)	.75	.35	.07
☐ 111 Leroy Ellis .... Philadelphia 76ers	.50	.25	.05
☐ 112 Chris Ford .... Detroit Pistons	2.00	1.00	.20
☐ 113 Bill Bradley .... New York Knicks	20.00	10.00	2.00
☐ 114 Clifford Ray .... Chicago Bulls	.75	.35	.07
☐ 115 Dick Snyder .... Cleveland Cavaliers	.50	.25	.05
☐ 116 Nate Williams .... Kansas City-Omaha Kings	.50	.25	.05
☐ 117 Matt Guokas .... Buffalo Braves	.75	.35	.07
☐ 118 Henry Finkel .... Boston Celtics	.50	.25	.05
☐ 119 Curtis Perry .... New Orleans Jazz	.50	.25	.05
☐ 120 Gail Goodrich AS1 .... Los Angeles Lakers	1.75	.85	.17
☐ 121 Wes Unseld .... Washington Bullets	3.50	1.75	.35

☐ 122	Howard Porter New York Knicks	.75	.35	.07
☐ 123	Jeff Mullins Golden State Warriors	.75	.35	.07
☐ 124	Mike Bantom Phoenix Suns	.75	.35	.07
☐ 125	Fred Brown Seattle Supersonics	1.25	.60	.12
☐ 126	Bob Dandridge Milwaukee Bucks	.75	.35	.07
☐ 127	Mike Newlin Houston Rockets	.50	.25	.05
☐ 128	Greg Smith Portland Trail Blazers	.50	.25	.05
☐ 129	Doug Collins Philadelphia 76ers	9.00	4.50	.90
☐ 130	Lou Hudson Atlanta Hawks	1.00	.50	.10
☐ 131	Bob Lanier Detroit Pistons	4.00	2.00	.40
☐ 132	Phil Jackson New York Knicks	3.50	1.75	.35
☐ 133	Don Chaney Boston Celtics	.75	.35	.07
☐ 134	Jim Brewer Cleveland Cavaliers	.75	.35	.07
☐ 135	Ernie DiGregorio Buffalo Braves	2.00	1.00	.20
☐ 136	Steve Kuberski New Orleans Jazz	.50	.25	.05
☐ 137	Jim Price Los Angeles Lakers	.50	.25	.05
☐ 138	Mike D'Antoni Kansas City-Omaha Kings	.50	.25	.05
☐ 139	John Brown Atlanta Hawks	.50	.25	.05
☐ 140	Norm Van Lier AS2 Chicago Bulls	.75	.35	.07
☐ 141	NBA Checklist 1-176	8.00	.80	.16
☐ 142	Don(Slick) Watts Seattle Supersonics	1.00	.50	.10
☐ 143	Walt Wesley Washington Bullets	.50	.25	.05
☐ 144	NBA Scoring Leaders Bob McAdoo Kareem Abdul-Jabbar Pete Maravich	4.50	2.25	.45
☐ 145	NBA Scoring Avg. Leaders Bob McAdoo Pete Maravich Kareem Abdul-Jabbar	4.50	2.25	.45
☐ 146	NBA F.G. Pct. Leaders Bob McAdoo Kareem Abdul-Jabbar Rudy Tomjanovich	3.50	1.75	.35
☐ 147	NBA F.T. Pct. Leaders Ernie DiGregorio Rick Barry Jeff Mullins	1.25	.60	.12
☐ 148	NBA Rebound Leaders Elvin Hayes Dave Cowens Bob McAdoo	1.75	.85	.17
☐ 149	NBA Assist Leaders Ernie DiGregorio Calvin Murphy Len Wilkens	1.25	.60	.12
☐ 150	Walt Frazier AS1 New York Knicks	7.00	3.50	.70
☐ 151	Cazzie Russell Golden State Warriors	1.00	.50	.10
☐ 152	Calvin Murphy Houston Rockets	1.75	.85	.17
☐ 153	Bob Kauffman Atlanta Hawks	.50	.25	.05
☐ 154	Fred Boyd Philadelphia 76ers	.50	.25	.05
☐ 155	Dave Cowens Boston Celtics	6.00	3.00	.60
☐ 156	Willie Norwood Detroit Pistons	.50	.25	.05
☐ 157	Lee Winfield Buffalo Braves	.50	.25	.05
☐ 158	Dwight Davis Cleveland Cavaliers	.50	.25	.05
☐ 159	George T. Johnson Golden State Warriors	.50	.25	.05
☐ 160	Dick Van Arsdale Phoenix Suns	.75	.35	.07
☐ 161	NBA Eastern Semis Celts over Braves Knicks edge Bullets	1.00	.50	.10
☐ 162	NBA Western Semis Bucks over Lakers Bulls edge Pistons	1.00	.50	.10
☐ 163	NBA Div. Finals Celts over Knicks Bucks sweep Bulls	1.00	.50	.10
☐ 164	NBA Championship Celtics over Bucks	1.00	.50	.10
☐ 165	Phil Chenier Washington Bullets	.75	.35	.07
☐ 166	Kermit Washington Los Angeles Lakers	1.00	.50	.10
☐ 167	Dale Schlueter Atlanta Hawks	.50	.25	.05
☐ 168	John Block New Orleans Jazz	.50	.25	.05
☐ 169	Don Smith Houston Rockets	.50	.25	.05
☐ 170	Nate Archibald Kansas City-Omaha Kings	4.50	2.25	.45
☐ 171	Chet Walker Chicago Bulls	1.25	.60	.12
☐ 172	Archie Clark Washington Bullets	.75	.35	.07
☐ 173	Kennedy McIntosh Seattle Supersonics	.50	.25	.05
☐ 174	George Thompson Milwaukee Bucks	.50	.25	.05
☐ 175	Sidney Wicks Portland Trail Blazers	1.25	.60	.12
☐ 176	Jerry West Los Angeles Lakers	20.00	10.00	2.00
☐ 177	Dwight Lamar San Diego Conquistadors	.75	.35	.07
☐ 178	George Carter Virginia Squires	.50	.25	.05
☐ 179	Wil Robinson Memphis Sounds	.50	.25	.05
☐ 180	Artis Gilmore AS1 Kentucky Colonels	3.75	1.85	.37
☐ 181	Brian Taylor New York Nets	.75	.35	.07
☐ 182	Darnell Hillman Indiana Pacers	.50	.25	.05
☐ 183	Dave Robisch Denver Nuggets	.75	.35	.07
☐ 184	Gene Littles St. Louis Spirits	1.00	.50	.10
☐ 185	Willie Wise AS2 Utah Stars	.75	.35	.07
☐ 186	James Silas San Antonio Spurs	1.50	.75	.15
☐ 187	Caldwell Jones San Diego Conquistadors	3.00	1.50	.30
☐ 188	Roland Taylor Virginia Squires	.50	.25	.05
☐ 189	Randy Denton Memphis Sounds	.50	.25	.05
☐ 190	Dan Issel AS2 Kentucky Colonels	4.50	2.25	.45
☐ 191	Mike Gale New York Nets	.50	.25	.05
☐ 192	Mel Daniels Memphis Sounds	1.00	.50	.10
☐ 193	Steve Jones Denver Nuggets	.75	.35	.07
☐ 194	Marv Roberts St. Louis Spirits	.50	.25	.05
☐ 195	Ron Boone AS2 Utah Stars	.75	.35	.07
☐ 196	George Gervin San Antonio Spurs	36.00	18.00	3.60
☐ 197	Flynn Robinson San Diego Conquistadors	.50	.25	.05
☐ 198	Cincy Powell Virginia Squires	.50	.25	.05
☐ 199	Glen Combs Memphis Sounds	.50	.25	.05
☐ 200	Julius Erving AS1 UER New York Nets (Misspelled Irving on card back)	42.00	21.00	4.20
☐ 201	Billy Keller Indiana Pacers	.75	.35	.07
☐ 202	Willie Long Denver Nuggets	.50	.25	.05
☐ 203	ABA Checklist 177-264	8.00	.80	.16
☐ 204	Joe Caldwell St. Louis Spirits	.75	.35	.07
☐ 205	Swen Nater AS2 San Antonio Spurs	2.00	1.00	.20
☐ 206	Rick Mount Utah Stars	.75	.35	.07
☐ 207	ABA Scoring Avg. Leaders	4.50	2.25	.45

Julius Erving
George McGinnis
Dan Issel
☐ 208 ABA Two-Point Field .... 1.00 .50 .10
Goal Percent Leaders
Swen Nater
James Jones
Tom Owens
☐ 209 ABA Three-Point Field .... 1.00 .50 .10
Goal Percent Leaders
Louie Dampier
Billy Keller
Roger Brown
☐ 210 ABA Free Throw .... 1.00 .50 .10
Percent Leaders
James Jones
Mack Calvin
Ron Boone
☐ 211 ABA Rebound Leaders .... 1.00 .50 .10
Artis Gilmore
George McGinnis
Caldwell Jones
☐ 212 ABA Assist Leaders .... 1.00 .50 .10
Al Smith
Chuck Williams
Louie Dampier
☐ 213 Larry Miller .... .75 .35 .07
Virginia Squires
☐ 214 Stew Johnson .... .50 .25 .05
San Diego Conquistadors
☐ 215 Larry Finch .... 2.00 1.00 .20
Memphis Sounds
☐ 216 Larry Kenon .... 2.00 1.00 .20
New York Nets
☐ 217 Joe Hamilton .... .50 .25 .05
Kentucky Colonels
☐ 218 Gerald Govan .... .50 .25 .05
Utah Stars
☐ 219 Ralph Simpson .... .75 .35 .07
Denver Nuggets
☐ 220 George McGinnis AS1 .... 1.50 .75 .15
Indiana Pacers
☐ 221 Carolina Cougars TL .... 1.25 .60 .12
Billy Cunningham
Mack Calvin
Tom Owens
Joe Caldwell
☐ 222 Denver Nuggets TL .... 1.00 .50 .10
Ralph Simpson
Byron Beck
Dave Robisch
Al Smith
☐ 223 Indiana Pacers TL .... 1.25 .60 .12
George McGinnis
Billy Keller
George McGinnis
Freddie Lewis
☐ 224 Kentucky Colonels TL .... 2.00 1.00 .20
Dan Issel
Louie Dampier
Artis Gilmore
Louie Dampier
☐ 225 Memphis Sounds TL .... 1.00 .50 .10
George Thompson
Larry Finch
Randy Denton
George Thompson
☐ 226 New York Nets TL .... 5.50 2.75 .55
Julius Erving
John Roche
Larry Kenon
Julius Erving
☐ 227 San Antonio Spurs TL .... 4.00 2.00 .40
George Gervin
George Gervin
Swen Nater
James Silas
☐ 228 San Diego Conq. TL .... 1.00 .50 .10
Dwight Lamar
Stew Johnson
Caldwell Jones
Chuck Williams
☐ 229 Utah Stars TL .... 1.00 .50 .10
Willie Wise
James Jones
Gerald Govan
James Jones
☐ 230 Virginia Squires TL .... 1.00 .50 .10
George Carter
George Irvine
Jim Eakins
Roland Taylor
☐ 231 Bird Averitt .... .75 .35 .07
Kentucky Colonels
☐ 232 John Roche .... .75 .35 .07
Kentucky Colonels
☐ 233 George Irvine .... .75 .35 .07
Virginia Squires
☐ 234 John Williamson .... 1.50 .75 .15
New York Nets
☐ 235 Billy Cunningham .... 4.00 2.00 .40
St. Louis Spirits
☐ 236 Jimmy O'Brien .... .50 .25 .05
San Diego Conquistadors
☐ 237 Wilbert Jones .... .50 .25 .05
Kentucky Colonels
☐ 238 Johnny Neumann .... .75 .35 .07
Utah Stars
☐ 239 Al Smith .... .50 .25 .05
Denver Nuggets
☐ 240 Roger Brown .... .75 .35 .07
Memphis Sounds
☐ 241 Chuck Williams .... .50 .25 .05
Kentucky Colonels
☐ 242 Rich Jones .... .50 .25 .05
San Antonio Spurs
☐ 243 Dave Twardzik .... 1.25 .60 .12
Virginia Squires
☐ 244 Wendell Ladner .... .50 .25 .05
New York Nets
☐ 245 Mack Calvin AS1 .... .75 .35 .07
St. Louis Spirits
☐ 246 ABA Eastern Semis .... 1.00 .50 .10
Nets over Squires
Colonels sweep Cougars
☐ 247 ABA Western Semis .... 1.00 .50 .10
Stars over Conquistadors
Pacers over Spurs
☐ 248 ABA Div. Finals .... 1.00 .50 .10
Nets sweep Colonels
Stars edge Pacers
☐ 249 ABA Championship .... 3.00 1.50 .30
Nets over Stars
(Julius Erving)
☐ 250 Wilt Chamberlain CO 45.00 22.50 4.50
San Diego Conquistadors
☐ 251 Ron Robinson .... .50 .25 .05
Memphis Sounds
☐ 252 Zelmo Beaty .... .75 .35 .07
Utah Stars
☐ 253 Donnie Freeman .... .75 .35 .07
Indiana Pacers
☐ 254 Mike Green .... .50 .25 .05
Denver Nuggets
☐ 255 Louie Dampier AS2 .... .75 .35 .07
Kentucky Colonels
☐ 256 Tom Owens .... .50 .25 .05
St. Louis Spirits
☐ 257 George Karl .... 3.00 1.50 .30
San Antonio Spurs
☐ 258 Jim Eakins .... .50 .25 .05
Virginia Squires
☐ 259 Travis Grant .... .75 .35 .07
San Diego Conquistadors
☐ 260 James Jones AS1 .... .75 .35 .07
Utah Stars
☐ 261 Mike Jackson .... .50 .25 .05
Memphis Sounds
☐ 262 Billy Paultz .... .75 .35 .07
New York Nets
☐ 263 Freddie Lewis .... .75 .35 .07
Memphis Sounds
☐ 264 Byron Beck .... .75 .35 .07
Denver Nuggets
(Back refers to ANA,
should be ABA)

1975-76 Topps

The 1975-76 Topps basketball card set of 330 was the largest basketball set ever produced to that time. NBA players are depicted on cards 1-220 and ABA players on cards 221-330. The cards in the set measure the standard 2 1/2" by 3 1/2". Team Leader (TL) cards are provided for each team on cards 116-133 and 278-287. Other subseries in this set include NBA Statistical Leaders (1-6), NBA Playoffs (188-189), NBA Team Checklists (203-220), ABA Statistical Leaders (221-226), ABA Playoffs (309-310), and ABA Team Checklists (321-330). All-Star selections (first and second team) for both leagues are noted on

the respective player's regular cards. Card backs are printed in blue and green on gray card stock. The set is particularly hard to sort numerically, as the small card number on the back is printed in blue on a dark green background. The set was printed on three large sheets each containing 110 different cards. Investigation of the second (series) sheet reveals that 22 of the cards were double printed; they are marked DP in the checklist below. The key rookie card in this set is Moses Malone.

	NRMT	VG-E	GOOD
COMPLETE SET (330)	475.00	225.00	47.00
COMMON PLAYER (1-110)	.50	.25	.05
COMMON PLAYER (111-220)	.50	.25	.05
COMMON PLAYER (221-330)	.75	.35	.07
☐ 1 NBA Scoring Average Leaders Bob McAdoo Rick Barry Kareem Abdul-Jabbar	9.00	2.50	.50
☐ 2 NBA Field Goal Percentage Leaders Don Nelson Butch Beard Rudy Tomjanovich	1.00	.50	.10
☐ 3 NBA Free Throw Percentage Leaders Rick Barry Calvin Murphy Bill Bradley	3.50	1.75	.35
☐ 4 NBA Rebounds Leaders Wes Unseld Dave Cowens Sam Lacey	1.25	.60	.12
☐ 5 NBA Assists Leaders Kevin Porter Dave Bing Nate Archibald	1.25	.60	.12
☐ 6 NBA Steals Leaders Rick Barry Walt Frazier Larry Steele	2.00	1.00	.20
☐ 7 Tom Van Arsdale Atlanta Hawks	.75	.35	.07
☐ 8 Paul Silas Boston Celtics	1.00	.50	.10
☐ 9 Jerry Sloan Chicago Bulls	1.00	.50	.10
☐ 10 Bob McAdoo AS1 Buffalo Braves	3.25	1.60	.32
☐ 11 Dwight Davis Golden State Warriors	.50	.25	.05
☐ 12 John Mengelt Detroit Pistons	.50	.25	.05
☐ 13 George Johnson Golden State Warriors	.50	.25	.05
☐ 14 Ed Ratleff Houston Rockets	.75	.35	.07
☐ 15 Nate Archibald AS1 Kansas City Kings	4.00	2.00	.40
☐ 16 Elmore Smith Milwaukee Bucks	.50	.25	.05
☐ 17 Bob Dandridge Milwaukee Bucks	.75	.35	.07
☐ 18 Louie Nelson New Orleans Jazz	.75	.35	.07
☐ 19 Neal Walk New York Knicks	.50	.25	.05
☐ 20 Billy Cunningham Philadelphia 76ers	4.00	2.00	.40
☐ 21 Gary Melchionni Phoenix Suns	.50	.25	.05
☐ 22 Barry Clemens Portland Trail Blazers	.50	.25	.05
☐ 23 Jimmy Jones Washington Bullets	.50	.25	.05
☐ 24 Tom Burleson Seattle Supersonics	2.00	1.00	.20
☐ 25 Lou Hudson Atlanta Hawks	1.00	.50	.10
☐ 26 Henry Finkel Boston Celtics	.50	.25	.05
☐ 27 Jim McMillian Buffalo Braves	.50	.25	.05
☐ 28 Matt Guokas Chicago Bulls	.75	.35	.07
☐ 29 Fred Foster DP Cleveland Cavaliers	.50	.25	.05
☐ 30 Bob Lanier Detroit Pistons	4.00	2.00	.40
☐ 31 Jimmy Walker Kansas City Kings	.50	.25	.05
☐ 32 Cliff Meely Houston Rockets	.50	.25	.05
☐ 33 Butch Beard Cleveland Cavaliers	.50	.25	.05
☐ 34 Cazzie Russell Los Angeles Lakers	1.00	.50	.10
☐ 35 Jon McGlocklin Milwaukee Bucks	.75	.35	.07
☐ 36 Bernie Fryer New Orleans Jazz	.50	.25	.05
☐ 37 Bill Bradley New York Knicks	18.00	9.00	1.80
☐ 38 Fred Carter Philadelphia 76ers	.50	.25	.05
☐ 39 Dennis Awtrey DP Phoenix Suns	.50	.25	.05
☐ 40 Sidney Wicks Portland Trail Blazers	1.25	.60	.12
☐ 41 Fred Brown Seattle Supersonics	1.00	.50	.10
☐ 42 Rowland Garrett Chicago Bulls	.50	.25	.05
☐ 43 Herm Gilliam Atlanta Hawks	.50	.25	.05
☐ 44 Don Nelson Boston Celtics	2.50	1.25	.25
☐ 45 Ernie DiGregorio Buffalo Braves	.75	.35	.07
☐ 46 Jim Brewer Cleveland Cavaliers	.50	.25	.05
☐ 47 Chris Ford Detroit Pistons	1.50	.75	.15
☐ 48 Nick Weatherspoon Washington Bullets	.50	.25	.05
☐ 49 Zaid Abdul-Aziz (formerly Don Smith) Houston Rockets	.50	.25	.05
☐ 50 Keith Wilkes Golden State Warriors	8.00	4.00	.80
☐ 51 Ollie Johnson DP Kansas City Kings	.50	.25	.05
☐ 52 Lucius Allen Los Angeles Lakers	.75	.35	.07
☐ 53 Mickey Davis Milwaukee Bucks	.50	.25	.05
☐ 54 Otto Moore New Orleans Jazz	.50	.25	.05
☐ 55 Walt Frazier AS1 New York Knicks	7.00	3.50	.70
☐ 56 Steve Mix Philadelphia 76ers	.50	.25	.05
☐ 57 Nate Hawthorne Phoenix Suns	.50	.25	.05
☐ 58 Lloyd Neal Portland Trail Blazers	.50	.25	.05
☐ 59 Don Watts Seattle Supersonics	.75	.35	.07
☐ 60 Elvin Hayes Washington Bullets	7.00	3.50	.70
☐ 61 Checklist 1-110	7.00	.70	.14
☐ 62 Mike Sojourner Atlanta Hawks	.50	.25	.05
☐ 63 Randy Smith Buffalo Braves	.75	.35	.07
☐ 64 John Block DP Chicago Bulls	.50	.25	.05
☐ 65 Charlie Scott Boston Celtics	.75	.35	.07
☐ 66 Jim Chones Cleveland Cavaliers	.50	.25	.05
☐ 67 Rick Adelman	1.25	.60	.12

Kansas City Kings
☐ 68 Curtis Rowe .... .75 .35 .07
Detroit Pistons
☐ 69 Derrek Dickey .... .75 .35 .07
Golden State Warriors
☐ 70 Rudy Tomjanovich .... 1.00 .50 .10
Houston Rockets
☐ 71 Pat Riley .... 6.50 3.25 .65
Los Angeles Lakers
☐ 72 Cornell Warner .... .50 .25 .05
Milwaukee Bucks
☐ 73 Earl Monroe .... 5.50 2.75 .55
New York Knicks
☐ 74 Allan Bristow .... 1.75 .85 .17
Philadelphia 76ers
☐ 75 Pete Maravich DP .... 9.00 4.50 .90
New Orleans Jazz
☐ 76 Curtis Perry .... .50 .25 .05
Phoenix Suns
☐ 77 Bill Walton 15.00 7.50 1.50
Portland Trail Blazers
☐ 78 Leonard Gray .... .50 .25 .05
Seattle Supersonics
☐ 79 Kevin Porter .... .75 .35 .07
Washington Bullets
☐ 80 John Havlicek AS2 .... 15.00 7.50 1.50
Boston Celtics
☐ 81 Dwight Jones .... .50 .25 .05
Atlanta Hawks
☐ 82 Jack Marin .... .50 .25 .05
Buffalo Braves
☐ 83 Dick Snyder .... .50 .25 .05
Cleveland Cavaliers
☐ 84 George Trapp .... .50 .25 .05
Detroit Pistons
☐ 85 Nate Thurmond .... 2.50 1.25 .25
Chicago Bulls
☐ 86 Charles Johnson .... .50 .25 .05
Golden State Warriors
☐ 87 Ron Riley .... .50 .25 .05
Houston Rockets
☐ 88 Stu Lantz .... .50 .25 .05
Los Angeles Lakers
☐ 89 Scott Wedman .... 1.75 .85 .17
Kansas City Kings
☐ 90 Kareem Abdul-Jabbar 40.00 20.00 4.00
Los Angeles Lakers
☐ 91 Aaron James .... .50 .25 .05
New Orleans Jazz
☐ 92 Jim Barnett .... .50 .25 .05
New York Knicks
☐ 93 Clyde Lee .... .50 .25 .05
Philadelphia 76ers
☐ 94 Larry Steele .... .50 .25 .05
Portland Trail Blazers
☐ 95 Mike Riordan .... .50 .25 .05
Washington Bullets
☐ 96 Archie Clark .... .75 .35 .07
Seattle Supersonics
☐ 97 Mike Bantom .... .50 .25 .05
Phoenix Suns
☐ 98 Bob Kauffman .... .50 .25 .05
Atlanta Hawks
☐ 99 Kevin Stacom .... .75 .35 .07
Boston Celtics
☐ 100 Rick Barry AS1 .... 10.00 5.00 1.00
Golden State Warriors
☐ 101 Ken Charles .... .50 .25 .05
Buffalo Braves
☐ 102 Tom Boerwinkle .... .50 .25 .05
Chicago Bulls
☐ 103 Mike Newlin .... .50 .25 .05
Houston Rockets
☐ 104 Leroy Ellis .... .50 .25 .05
Philadelphia 76ers
☐ 105 Austin Carr .... .75 .35 .07
Cleveland Cavaliers
☐ 106 Ron Behagen .... .50 .25 .05
New Orleans Jazz
☐ 107 Jim Price .... .50 .25 .05
Milwaukee Bucks
☐ 108 Bud Stallworth .... .50 .25 .05
New Orleans Jazz
☐ 109 Earl Williams .... .50 .25 .05
Detroit Pistons
☐ 110 Gail Goodrich .... 1.50 .75 .15
Los Angeles Lakers
☐ 111 Phil Jackson .... 3.50 1.75 .35
New York Knicks
☐ 112 Rod Derline .... .50 .25 .05
Seattle Supersonics
☐ 113 Keith Erickson .... .75 .35 .07
Phoenix Suns
☐ 114 Phil Lumpkin .... .50 .25 .05
Phoenix Suns
☐ 115 Wes Unseld .... 3.50 1.75 .35
Washington Bullets
☐ 116 Atlanta Hawks TL .... 1.00 .50 .10
Lou Hudson
Lou Hudson
John Drew
Dean Meminger
☐ 117 Boston Celtics TL .... 1.75 .85 .17
Dave Cowens
Kevin Stacom
Paul Silas
JoJo White
☐ 118 Buffalo Braves TL .... 1.00 .50 .10
Bob McAdoo
Jack Marin
Bob McAdoo
Randy Smith
☐ 119 Chicago Bulls TL .... 1.25 .60 .12
Bob Love
Chet Walker
Nate Thurmond
Norm Van Lier
☐ 120 Cleveland Cavs TL .... 1.00 .50 .10
Bobby Smith
Dick Snyder
Jim Chones
Jim Cleamons
☐ 121 Detroit Pistons TL .... 1.50 .75 .15
Bob Lanier
John Mengelt
Bob Lanier
Dave Bing
☐ 122 Golden State TL .... 2.00 1.00 .20
Rick Barry
Rick Barry
Clifford Ray
Rick Barry
☐ 123 Houston Rockets TL .... 1.00 .50 .10
Rudy Tomjanovich
Calvin Murphy
Kevin Kunnert
Mike Newlin
☐ 124 Kansas City Kings TL .... 1.25 .60 .12
Nate Archibald
Ollie Johnson
Sam Lacey UER
(Lacy on front)
Nate Archibald
☐ 125 Los Angeles Lakers TL .... 1.25 .60 .12
Gail Goodrich
Cazzie Russell
Happy Hairston
Gail Goodrich
☐ 126 Milwaukee Bucks TL .... 4.50 2.25 .45
Kareem Abdul-Jabbar
Mickey Davis
Kareem Abdul-Jabbar
Kareem Abdul-Jabbar
☐ 127 New Orleans Jazz TL .... 2.00 1.00 .20
Pete Maravich
Stu Lantz
E.C. Coleman
Pete Maravich
☐ 128 New York Knicks TL DP .... 2.50 1.25 .25
Walt Frazier
Bill Bradley
John Gianelli
Walt Frazier
☐ 129 Phila. 76ers TL DP .... 1.25 .60 .12
Fred Carter
Doug Collins
Billy Cunningham
Billy Cunningham
☐ 130 Phoenix Suns TL DP .... 1.00 .50 .10
Charlie Scott
Keith Erickson
Curtis Perry
Dennis Awtrey
☐ 131 Portland Blazers TL DP .... 1.00 .50 .10
Sidney Wicks
Geoff Petrie
Sidney Wicks
Geoff Petrie
☐ 132 Seattle Sonics TL .... 1.00 .50 .10
Spencer Haywood
Archie Clark
Spencer Haywood
Don Watts
☐ 133 Washington Bullets TL .... 1.50 .75 .15
Elvin Hayes
Clem Haskins
Wes Unseld
Kevin Porter

☐	134	John Drew Atlanta Hawks	1.50	.75	.15
☐	135	JoJo White AS2 Boston Celtics	1.75	.85	.17
☐	136	Garfield Heard Buffalo Braves	.50	.25	.05
☐	137	Jim Cleamons Cleveland Cavaliers	.50	.25	.05
☐	138	Howard Porter Detroit Pistons	.50	.25	.05
☐	139	Phil Smith Golden State Warriors	1.00	.50	.10
☐	140	Bob Love Chicago Bulls	1.00	.50	.10
☐	141	John Gianelli DP New York Knicks	.50	.25	.05
☐	142	Larry McNeill Kansas City Kings	.75	.35	.07
☐	143	Brian Winters Milwaukee Bucks	1.50	.75	.15
☐	144	George Thompson Milwaukee Bucks	.50	.25	.05
☐	145	Kevin Kunnert Houston Rockets	.50	.25	.05
☐	146	Henry Bibby New Orleans Jazz	.75	.35	.07
☐	147	John Johnson Portland Trail Blazers	.50	.25	.05
☐	148	Doug Collins Philadelphia 76ers	3.25	1.60	.32
☐	149	John Brisker Seattle Supersonics	.50	.25	.05
☐	150	Dick Van Arsdale Phoenix Suns	.75	.35	.07
☐	151	Leonard Robinson Washington Bullets	2.50	1.25	.25
☐	152	Dean Meminger Atlanta Hawks	.50	.25	.05
☐	153	Phil Hankinson Boston Celtics	.50	.25	.05
☐	154	Dale Schlueter Buffalo Braves	.50	.25	.05
☐	155	Norm Van Lier Chicago Bulls	.75	.35	.07
☐	156	Campy Russell Cleveland Cavaliers	2.00	1.00	.20
☐	157	Jeff Mullins Golden State Warriors	.75	.35	.07
☐	158	Sam Lacey Kansas City Kings	.75	.35	.07
☐	159	Happy Hairston Los Angeles Lakers	.75	.35	.07
☐	160	Dave Bing DP Detroit Pistons	2.00	1.00	.20
☐	161	Kevin Restani Milwaukee Bucks	.75	.35	.07
☐	162	Dave Wohl Houston Rockets	.50	.25	.05
☐	163	E.C. Coleman New Orleans Jazz	.50	.25	.05
☐	164	Jim Fox Seattle Supersonics	.50	.25	.05
☐	165	Geoff Petrie Portland Trail Blazers	.75	.35	.07
☐	166	Hawthorne Wingo DP UER New York Knicks (Misspelled Harthorne on card front)	.50	.25	.05
☐	167	Fred Boyd Philadelphia 76ers	.50	.25	.05
☐	168	Willie Norwood Phoenix Suns	.50	.25	.05
☐	169	Bob Wilson Chicago Bulls	.50	.25	.05
☐	170	Dave Cowens Boston Celtics	5.50	2.75	.55
☐	171	Tom Henderson Atlanta Hawks	.75	.35	.07
☐	172	Jim Washington Buffalo Braves	.50	.25	.05
☐	173	Clem Haskins Washington Bullets	.75	.35	.07
☐	174	Jim Davis Detroit Pistons	.50	.25	.05
☐	175	Bobby Smith DP Cleveland Cavaliers	.50	.25	.05
☐	176	Mike D'Antoni Kansas City Kings	.50	.25	.05
☐	177	Zelmo Beaty Los Angeles Lakers	.75	.35	.07
☐	178	Gary Brokaw Milwaukee Bucks	.75	.35	.07
☐	179	Mel Davis New York Knicks	.50	.25	.05
☐	180	Calvin Murphy Houston Rockets	1.50	.75	.15
☐	181	Checklist 111-220 DP	7.00	.70	.14
☐	182	Nate Williams New Orleans Jazz	.50	.25	.05
☐	183	LaRue Martin Portland Trail Blazers	.50	.25	.05
☐	184	George McGinnis Philadelphia 76ers	1.50	.75	.15
☐	185	Clifford Ray Golden State Warriors	.50	.25	.05
☐	186	Paul Westphal Phoenix Suns	2.00	1.00	.20
☐	187	Talvin Skinner Seattle Supersonics	.50	.25	.05
☐	188	NBA Playoff Semis DP Warriors edge Bulls Bullets over Celts	1.00	.50	.10
☐	189	NBA Playoff Finals Warriors sweep Bullets (C.Ray blocks shot)	1.00	.50	.10
☐	190	Phil Chenier AS2 DP Washington Bullets	.75	.35	.07
☐	191	John Brown Atlanta Hawks	.50	.25	.05
☐	192	Lee Winfield Buffalo Braves	.50	.25	.05
☐	193	Steve Patterson Cleveland Cavaliers	.50	.25	.05
☐	194	Charles Dudley Golden State Warriors	.50	.25	.05
☐	195	Connie Hawkins DP Los Angeles Lakers	2.00	1.00	.20
☐	196	Leon Benbow Chicago Bulls	.50	.25	.05
☐	197	Don Kojis Kansas City Kings	.50	.25	.05
☐	198	Ron Williams Milwaukee Bucks	.50	.25	.05
☐	199	Mel Counts New Orleans Jazz	.50	.25	.05
☐	200	Spencer Haywood AS2 Seattle Supersonics	1.50	.75	.15
☐	201	Greg Jackson Phoenix Suns	.50	.25	.05
☐	202	Tom Kozelko DP Washington Bullets	.50	.25	.05
☐	203	Atlanta Hawks Checklist	1.00	.35	.07
☐	204	Boston Celtics Checklist	1.00	.35	.07
☐	205	Buffalo Braves Checklist	1.00	.35	.07
☐	206	Chicago Bulls Checklist	1.00	.35	.07
☐	207	Cleveland Cavs Checklist	1.00	.35	.07
☐	208	Detroit Pistons Checklist	1.00	.35	.07
☐	209	Golden State Checklist	1.00	.35	.07
☐	210	Houston Rockets Checklist	1.00	.35	.07
☐	211	Kansas City Kings DP Checklist	1.00	.35	.07
☐	212	Los Angeles Lakers DP Checklist	1.00	.35	.07
☐	213	Milwaukee Bucks Checklist	1.00	.35	.07
☐	214	New Orleans Jazz Checklist	1.00	.35	.07
☐	215	New York Knicks Checklist	1.00	.35	.07
☐	216	Philadelphia 76ers Checklist	1.00	.35	.07
☐	217	Phoenix Suns DP Checklist	1.00	.35	.07
☐	218	Portland Blazers Checklist	1.00	.35	.07
☐	219	Seattle Sonics DP Checklist	1.50	.50	.10
☐	220	Washington Bullets Checklist	1.00	.35	.07
☐	221	ABA Scoring Average Leaders George McGinnis Julius Erving Ron Boone	3.50	1.75	.35
☐	222	ABA 2 Pt. Field Goal Percentage Leaders Bobby Jones Artis Gilmore Moses Malone	5.00	2.50	.50
☐	223	ABA 3 Pt. Field Goal	1.00	.50	.10

Percentage Leaders
Billy Shepherd
Louie Dampier
Al Smith
☐ 224 ABA Free Throw .... 1.00 .50 .10
Percentage Leaders
Mack Calvin
James Silas
Dave Robisch
☐ 225 ABA Rebounds Leaders ...... 1.00 .50 .10
Swen Nater
Artis Gilmore
Marvin Barnes
☐ 226 ABA Assists Leaders .... 1.00 .50 .10
Mack Calvin
Chuck Williams
George McGinnis
☐ 227 Mack Calvin AS1 .... .75 .35 .07
Virginia Squires
☐ 228 Billy Knight AS1 .... 1.75 .85 .17
Indiana Pacers
☐ 229 Bird Averitt .... .75 .35 .07
Kentucky Colonels
☐ 230 George Carter .... .75 .35 .07
Memphis Sounds
☐ 231 Swen Nater AS2 .... 1.00 .50 .10
New York Nets
☐ 232 Steve Jones .... 1.00 .50 .10
St. Louis Spirits
☐ 233 George Gervin .... 9.00 4.50 .90
San Antonio Spurs
☐ 234 Lee Davis .... .75 .35 .07
San Diego Sails
☐ 235 Ron Boone AS1 .... 1.00 .50 .10
Utah Stars
☐ 236 Mike Jackson .... .75 .35 .07
Virginia Squires
☐ 237 Kevin Joyce .... 1.00 .50 .10
Indiana Pacers
☐ 238 Marv Roberts .... .75 .35 .07
Kentucky Colonels
☐ 239 Tom Owens .... .75 .35 .07
Memphis Sounds
☐ 240 Ralph Simpson .... 1.00 .50 .10
Denver Nuggets
☐ 241 Gus Gerard .... .75 .35 .07
St. Louis Spirits
☐ 242 Brian Taylor AS2 .... 1.00 .50 .10
New York Nets
☐ 243 Rich Jones .... .75 .35 .07
San Antonio Spurs
☐ 244 John Roche .... 1.00 .50 .10
Utah Stars
☐ 245 Travis Grant .... .75 .35 .07
San Diego Sails
☐ 246 Dave Twardzik .... 1.00 .50 .10
Virginia Squires
☐ 247 Mike Green .... .75 .35 .07
Virginia Squires
☐ 248 Billy Keller .... 1.00 .50 .10
Indiana Pacers
☐ 249 Stew Johnson .... .75 .35 .07
Memphis Sounds
☐ 250 Artis Gilmore AS1 .... 3.50 1.75 .35
Kentucky Colonels
☐ 251 John Williamson .... 1.00 .50 .10
New York Nets
☐ 252 Marvin Barnes AS2 .... 4.25 2.10 .42
St. Louis Spirits
☐ 253 James Silas AS2 .... 1.00 .50 .10
San Antonio Spurs
☐ 254 Moses Malone 70.00 35.00 7.00
Utah Stars
☐ 255 Willie Wise .... 1.00 .50 .10
Virginia Squires
☐ 256 Dwight Lamar .... .75 .35 .07
San Diego Sails
☐ 257 Checklist 221-330 .... 7.00 .70 .14
☐ 258 Byron Beck .... .75 .35 .07
Denver Nuggets
☐ 259 Len Elmore .... 3.00 1.50 .30
Indiana Pacers
☐ 260 Dan Issel .... 4.50 2.25 .45
Kentucky Colonels
☐ 261 Rick Mount .... 1.25 .60 .12
Memphis Sounds
☐ 262 Billy Paultz .... 1.00 .50 .10
New York Nets
☐ 263 Donnie Freeman .... 1.00 .50 .10
San Antonio Spurs
☐ 264 George Adams .... .75 .35 .07
San Diego Sails
☐ 265 Don Chaney .... 1.00 .50 .10
St. Louis Spirits

☐ 266 Randy Denton .... .75 .35 .07
Utah Stars
☐ 267 Don Washington .... .75 .35 .07
Denver Nuggets
☐ 268 Roland Taylor .... .75 .35 .07
Denver Nuggets
☐ 269 Charlie Edge .... .75 .35 .07
Indiana Pacers
☐ 270 Louie Dampier .... 1.25 .60 .12
Kentucky Colonels
☐ 271 Collis Jones .... .75 .35 .07
Memphis Sounds
☐ 272 Al Skinner .... .75 .35 .07
New York Nets
☐ 273 Coby Dietrick .... .75 .35 .07
San Antonio Spurs
☐ 274 Tim Bassett .... .75 .35 .07
San Diego Sails
☐ 275 Freddie Lewis .... 1.00 .50 .10
St. Louis Spirits
☐ 276 Gerald Govan .... .75 .35 .07
Utah Stars
☐ 277 Ron Thomas .... .75 .35 .07
Kentucky Colonels
☐ 278 Denver Nuggets TL .... 1.25 .60 .12
Ralph Simpson
Mack Calvin
Mike Green
Mack Calvin
☐ 279 Indiana Pacers TL .... 1.25 .60 .12
George McGinnis
Billy Keller
George McGinnis
George McGinnis
☐ 280 Kentucky Colonels TL .... 1.50 .75 .15
Artis Gilmore
Louie Dampier
Artis Gilmore
Louie Dampier
☐ 281 Memphis Sounds TL .... 1.25 .60 .12
George Carter
Larry Finch
Tom Owens
Chuck Williams
☐ 282 New York Nets TL .... 4.50 2.25 .45
Julius Erving
John Williamson
Julius Erving
Julius Erving
☐ 283 St. Louis Spirits TL .... 1.25 .60 .12
Marvin Barnes
Freddie Lewis
Marvin Barnes
Freddie Lewis
☐ 284 San Antonio Spurs TL .... 2.50 1.25 .25
George Gervin
James Silas
Swen Nater
James Silas
☐ 285 San Diego Sails TL .... 1.25 .60 .12
Travis Grant
Jimmy O'Brien
Caldwell Jones
Jimmy O'Brien
☐ 286 Utah Stars TL .... 7.00 3.50 .70
Ron Boone
Ron Boone
Moses Malone
Al Smith
☐ 287 Virginia Squires TL .... 1.25 .60 .12
Willie Wise
Red Robbins
Dave Vaughn
Dave Twardzik
☐ 288 Claude Terry .... .75 .35 .07
Denver Nuggets
☐ 289 Wilbert Jones .... .75 .35 .07
Kentucky Colonels
☐ 290 Darnell Hillman .... .75 .35 .07
Indiana Pacers
☐ 291 Bill Melchionni .... 1.00 .50 .10
New York Nets
☐ 292 Mel Daniels .... 1.25 .60 .12
Memphis Sounds
☐ 293 Fly Williams .... 1.25 .60 .12
St. Louis Spirits
☐ 294 Larry Kenon .... 1.00 .50 .10
San Antonio Spurs
☐ 295 Red Robbins .... .75 .35 .07
Virginia Squires
☐ 296 Warren Jabali .... 1.00 .50 .10
San Diego Sails
☐ 297 Jim Eakins .... .75 .35 .07
Utah Stars

☐ 298	Bobby Jones Denver Nuggets	7.00	3.50	.70
☐ 299	Don Buse Indiana Pacers	.75	.35	.07
☐ 300	Julius Erving AS1 New York Nets	42.00	21.00	4.20
☐ 301	Billy Shepherd Memphis Sounds	.75	.35	.07
☐ 302	Maurice Lucas St. Louis Spirits	7.50	3.75	.75
☐ 303	George Karl San Antonio Spurs	1.25	.60	.12
☐ 304	Jim Bradley Kentucky Colonels	.75	.35	.07
☐ 305	Caldwell Jones San Diego Sails	1.25	.60	.12
☐ 306	Al Smith Utah Stars	.75	.35	.07
☐ 307	Jan Van Breda Kolff Virginia Squires	1.00	.50	.10
☐ 308	Darrell Elston Virginia Squires	.75	.35	.07
☐ 309	ABA Playoff Semifinals Colonels over Spirits; Pacers edge Nuggets	1.25	.60	.12
☐ 310	ABA Playoff Finals Colonels over Pacers (Gilmore hooking)	1.50	.75	.15
☐ 311	Ted McClain Kentucky Colonels	.75	.35	.07
☐ 312	Willie Sojourner New York Nets	.75	.35	.07
☐ 313	Bob Warren San Antonio Spurs	.75	.35	.07
☐ 314	Bob Netolicky Indiana Pacers	.75	.35	.07
☐ 315	Chuck Williams Memphis Sounds	.75	.35	.07
☐ 316	Gene Kennedy St. Louis Spirits	.75	.35	.07
☐ 317	Jimmy O'Brien San Diego Sails	.75	.35	.07
☐ 318	Dave Robisch Denver Nuggets	1.00	.50	.10
☐ 319	Wali Jones Utah Stars	.75	.35	.07
☐ 320	George Irvine Denver Nuggets	1.00	.50	.10
☐ 321	Denver Nuggets Checklist	1.25	.50	.10
☐ 322	Indiana Pacers Checklist	1.25	.50	.10
☐ 323	Kentucky Colonels Checklist	1.25	.50	.10
☐ 324	Memphis Sounds Checklist	1.25	.50	.10
☐ 325	New York Nets Checklist	1.25	.50	.10
☐ 326	St. Louis Spirits Checklist	1.25	.50	.10
☐ 327	San Antonio Spurs Checklist	1.25	.50	.10
☐ 328	San Diego Sails Checklist	1.25	.50	.10
☐ 329	Utah Stars Checklist	1.25	.50	.10
☐ 330	Virginia Squires Checklist	1.50	.50	.10

1975-76 Topps Team Checklist

These team checklists were issued in three panels, with nine teams per panel. Each panel measures approximately 7 1/2" by 10 1/2" and are joined together to form one continuous sheet. The checklists are printed in blue and green on white card stock and list all NBA and ABA teams. They are numbered on the front and listed alphabetically according to the city names. The backs are blank. Since there was only room for 27 teams on the three-part sheet, Topps apparently left off card 324 Memphis Sounds, which is in the regular set.

	NRMT	VG-E	GOOD
COMPLETE SET (27)	60.00	30.00	6.00

321 Denver Nuggets CHECKLIST

Card #	Player	Unif. #	Position
258	Beck, Byron	40	Forward
247	Irvine, George	22	Forward
298	Jones, Bobby	24	Forward
318	Robisch, Dave	25	Center
240	Simpson, Ralph	44	Guard
268	Taylor, Roland	14	Guard
288	Terry, Claude	21	Guard
278	TEAM CARD		

©1970 A.B.A.P.A. © 1971 A.B.A. • A.B.A. club insignias depicted are property of respective clubs. © 1975 TOPPS CHEWING GUM, INC. PRTD. IN U.S.A.

COMMON TEAM		2.50	1.25	.25
☐ 203	Atlanta Hawks	2.50	1.25	.25
☐ 204	Boston Celtics	2.50	1.25	.25
☐ 205	Buffalo Braves	2.50	1.25	.25
☐ 206	Chicago Bulls	2.50	1.25	.25
☐ 207	Cleveland Cavaliers	2.50	1.25	.25
☐ 208	Detroit Pistons	2.50	1.25	.25
☐ 209	Golden State Warriors	2.50	1.25	.25
☐ 210	Houston Rockets	2.50	1.25	.25
☐ 211	Kansas City Kings	2.50	1.25	.25
☐ 212	Los Angeles Lakers	2.50	1.25	.25
☐ 213	Milwaukee Bucks	2.50	1.25	.25
☐ 214	New Orleans Jazz	2.50	1.25	.25
☐ 215	New York Knicks	2.50	1.25	.25
☐ 216	Philadelphia 76ers	2.50	1.25	.25
☐ 217	Phoenix Suns	2.50	1.25	.25
☐ 218	Portland Trail Blazers	2.50	1.25	.25
☐ 219	Seattle SuperSonics	2.50	1.25	.25
☐ 220	Washington Bullets	2.50	1.25	.25
☐ 321	Denver Nuggets	2.50	1.25	.25
☐ 322	Indiana Pacers	2.50	1.25	.25
☐ 323	Kentucky Colonels	2.50	1.25	.25
☐ 325	New York Nets	2.50	1.25	.25
☐ 326	Spirits of St. Louis	2.50	1.25	.25
☐ 327	San Antonio Spurs	2.50	1.25	.25
☐ 328	San Diego Sails	2.50	1.25	.25
☐ 329	Utah Stars	2.50	1.25	.25
☐ 330	Virginia Squires	2.50	1.25	.25

1976-77 Topps

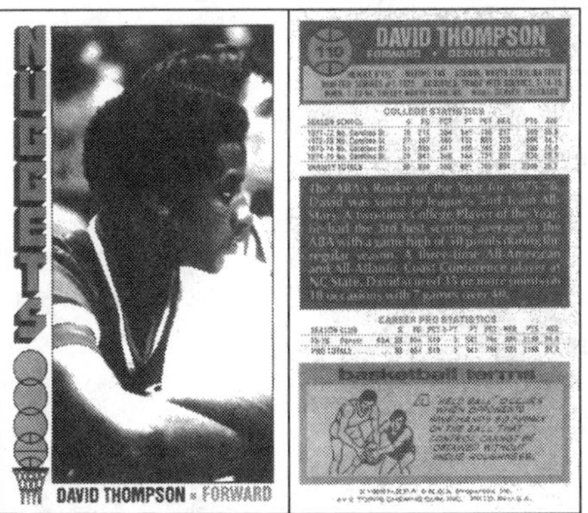

The 144-card 1976-77 Topps set witnesses a return to the larger-sized cards, with each card measuring approximately 3 1/8" by 5 1/4". Cards numbered 126-135 are the previous season's NBA All-Star selections. The cards were printed on two large sheets, each with eight rows and nine columns. The checklist card was located in the lower right corner of the second sheet. The key rookie card in this set is David Thompson.

	NRMT	VG-E	GOOD
COMPLETE SET (144)	200.00	100.00	20.00
COMMON PLAYER (1-144)	.60	.30	.06
☐ 1 Julius Erving New York Nets	40.00	12.50	2.50
☐ 2 Dick Snyder Cleveland Cavaliers	.60	.30	.06
☐ 3 Paul Silas Boston Celtics	1.00	.50	.10
☐ 4 Keith Erickson Phoenix Suns	.80	.40	.08
☐ 5 Wes Unseld Washington Bullets	3.50	1.75	.35
☐ 6 Butch Beard New York Knicks	.60	.30	.06
☐ 7 Lloyd Neal Portland Trail Blazers	.60	.30	.06
☐ 8 Tom Henderson Atlanta Hawks	.60	.30	.06
☐ 9 Jim McMillian Buffalo Braves	.60	.30	.06
☐ 10 Bob Lanier Detroit Pistons	3.50	1.75	.35
☐ 11 Junior Bridgeman Milwaukee Bucks	2.00	1.00	.20
☐ 12 Corky Calhoun Los Angeles Lakers	.60	.30	.06
☐ 13 Billy Keller Indiana Pacers	.60	.30	.06
☐ 14 Mickey Johnson Chicago Bulls	1.25	.60	.12
☐ 15 Fred Brown Seattle Supersonics	.80	.40	.08
☐ 16 Jamaal Wilkes Golden State Warriors	2.00	1.00	.20
☐ 17 Louie Nelson New Orleans Jazz	.60	.30	.06
☐ 18 Ed Ratleff Houston Rockets	.60	.30	.06
☐ 19 Billy Paultz San Antonio Spurs	.80	.40	.08
☐ 20 Nate Archibald Kansas City Kings	3.50	1.75	.35
☐ 21 Steve Mix Philadelphia 76ers	.60	.30	.06
☐ 22 Ralph Simpson Denver Nuggets	.60	.30	.06
☐ 23 Campy Russell Cleveland Cavaliers	.80	.40	.08
☐ 24 Charlie Scott Boston Celtics	.80	.40	.08
☐ 25 Artis Gilmore Chicago Bulls	3.00	1.50	.30
☐ 26 Dick Van Arsdale Phoenix Suns	.80	.40	.08
☐ 27 Phil Chenier Washington Bullets	.80	.40	.08
☐ 28 Spencer Haywood New York Knicks	1.25	.60	.12
☐ 29 Chris Ford Detroit Pistons	1.25	.60	.12
☐ 30 Dave Cowens Boston Celtics	5.00	2.50	.50
☐ 31 Sidney Wicks Portland Trail Blazers	1.25	.60	.12
☐ 32 Jim Price Milwaukee Bucks	.60	.30	.06
☐ 33 Dwight Jones Houston Rockets	.60	.30	.06
☐ 34 Lucius Allen Los Angeles Lakers	.80	.40	.08
☐ 35 Marvin Barnes Detroit Pistons	1.00	.50	.10
☐ 36 Henry Bibby New Orleans Jazz	.80	.40	.08
☐ 37 Joe Meriweather Atlanta Hawks	1.00	.50	.10
☐ 38 Doug Collins Philadelphia 76ers	2.50	1.25	.25
☐ 39 Garfield Heard Phoenix Suns	.60	.30	.06
☐ 40 Randy Smith Buffalo Braves	.80	.40	.08
☐ 41 Tom Burleson Seattle Supersonics	.80	.40	.08
☐ 42 Dave Twardzik Portland Trail Blazers	.80	.40	.08
☐ 43 Bill Bradley New York Knicks	20.00	10.00	2.00
☐ 44 Calvin Murphy Houston Rockets	1.50	.75	.15
☐ 45 Bob Love Chicago Bulls	1.00	.50	.10
☐ 46 Brian Winters Milwaukee Bucks	.80	.40	.08
☐ 47 Glenn McDonald Boston Celtics	.60	.30	.06
☐ 48 Checklist Card	9.00	.90	.18
☐ 49 Bird Averitt Buffalo Braves	.60	.30	.06
☐ 50 Rick Barry Golden State Warriors	8.50	4.25	.85
☐ 51 Ticky Burden New York Knicks	.60	.30	.06
☐ 52 Rich Jones New York Nets	.60	.30	.06
☐ 53 Austin Carr Cleveland Cavaliers	.80	.40	.08
☐ 54 Steve Kuberski Boston Celtics	.60	.30	.06
☐ 55 Paul Westphal Phoenix Suns	1.50	.75	.15
☐ 56 Mike Riordan Washington Bullets	.60	.30	.06
☐ 57 Bill Walton Portland Trail Blazers	11.00	5.50	1.10
☐ 58 Eric Money Detroit Pistons	.80	.40	.08
☐ 59 John Drew Atlanta Hawks	.80	.40	.08
☐ 60 Pete Maravich New Orleans Jazz	9.00	4.50	.90
☐ 61 John Shumate Buffalo Braves	2.50	1.25	.25
☐ 62 Mack Calvin Los Angeles Lakers	.80	.40	.08
☐ 63 Bruce Seals Seattle Supersonics	.60	.30	.06
☐ 64 Walt Frazier New York Knicks	6.00	3.00	.60
☐ 65 Elmore Smith Milwaukee Bucks	.60	.30	.06
☐ 66 Rudy Tomjanovich Houston Rockets	.80	.40	.08
☐ 67 Sam Lacey Kansas City Kings	.60	.30	.06
☐ 68 George Gervin San Antonio Spurs	8.50	4.25	.85
☐ 69 Gus Williams Golden State Warriors	6.00	3.00	.60
☐ 70 George McGinnis Philadelphia 76ers	1.00	.50	.10
☐ 71 Len Elmore Indiana Pacers	.80	.40	.08
☐ 72 Jack Marin Chicago Bulls	.60	.30	.06
☐ 73 Brian Taylor New York Nets	.80	.40	.08
☐ 74 Jim Brewer Cleveland Cavaliers	.60	.30	.06
☐ 75 Alvan Adams Phoenix Suns	3.00	1.50	.30
☐ 76 Dave Bing Washington Bullets	2.50	1.25	.25
☐ 77 Phil Jackson New York Knicks	3.00	1.50	.30
☐ 78 Geoff Petrie Portland Trail Blazers	.80	.40	.08
☐ 79 Mike Sojourner Atlanta Hawks	.60	.30	.06
☐ 80 James Silas San Antonio Spurs	.80	.40	.08
☐ 81 Bob Dandridge Milwaukee Bucks	.80	.40	.08
☐ 82 Ernie DiGregorio Buffalo Braves	.80	.40	.08
☐ 83 Cazzie Russell Los Angeles Lakers	1.00	.50	.10
☐ 84 Kevin Porter Detroit Pistons	.80	.40	.08
☐ 85 Tom Boerwinkle Chicago Bulls	.60	.30	.06
☐ 86 Darnell Hillman Indiana Pacers	.60	.30	.06
☐ 87 Herm Gilliam Seattle Supersonics	.60	.30	.06
☐ 88 Nate Williams New Orleans Jazz	.60	.30	.06
☐ 89 Phil Smith Golden State Warriors	.60	.30	.06
☐ 90 John Havlicek Boston Celtics	10.00	5.00	1.00
☐ 91 Kevin Kunnert Houston Rockets	.60	.30	.06
☐ 92 Jimmy Walker Kansas City Kings	.60	.30	.06
☐ 93 Billy Cunningham	4.00	2.00	.40

Philadelphia 76ers			
☐ 94 Dan Issel .... Denver Nuggets	3.50	1.75	.35
☐ 95 Ron Boone .... Kansas City Kings	.80	.40	.08
☐ 96 Lou Hudson .... Atlanta Hawks	1.00	.50	.10
☐ 97 Jim Chones .... Cleveland Cavaliers	.60	.30	.06
☐ 98 Earl Monroe .... New York Knicks	4.50	2.25	.45
☐ 99 Tom Van Arsdale .... Buffalo Braves	.80	.40	.08
☐ 100 Kareem Abdul-Jabbar .... Los Angeles Lakers	27.00	13.50	2.70
☐ 101 Moses Malone .... Portland Trail Blazers	25.00	12.50	2.50
☐ 102 Ricky Sobers .... Phoenix Suns	1.00	.50	.10
☐ 103 Swen Nater .... Milwaukee Bucks	.80	.40	.08
☐ 104 Leonard Robinson .... Washington Bullets	.80	.40	.08
☐ 105 Don Watts .... Seattle Supersonics	.60	.30	.06
☐ 106 Otto Moore .... New Orleans Jazz	.60	.30	.06
☐ 107 Maurice Lucas .... Portland Trail Blazers	1.50	.75	.15
☐ 108 Norm Van Lier .... Chicago Bulls	.80	.40	.08
☐ 109 Clifford Ray .... Golden State Warriors	.60	.30	.06
☐ 110 David Thompson .... Denver Nuggets	17.00	8.50	1.70
☐ 111 Fred Carter .... Philadelphia 76ers	.60	.30	.06
☐ 112 Caldwell Jones .... Philadelphia 76ers	.80	.40	.08
☐ 113 John Williamson .... New York Nets	.80	.40	.08
☐ 114 Bobby Smith .... Cleveland Cavaliers	.60	.30	.06
☐ 115 JoJo White .... Boston Celtics	1.25	.60	.12
☐ 116 Curtis Perry .... Phoenix Suns	.60	.30	.06
☐ 117 John Gianelli .... New York Knicks	.60	.30	.06
☐ 118 Curtis Rowe .... Detroit Pistons	.80	.40	.08
☐ 119 Lionel Hollins .... Portland Trail Blazers	1.75	.85	.17
☐ 120 Elvin Hayes .... Washington Bullets	6.00	3.00	.60
☐ 121 Ken Charles .... Atlanta Hawks	.60	.30	.06
☐ 122 Dave Meyers .... Milwaukee Bucks	2.50	1.25	.25
☐ 123 Jerry Sloan .... Chicago Bulls	.80	.40	.08
☐ 124 Billy Knight .... Indiana Pacers	.80	.40	.08
☐ 125 Gail Goodrich .... Los Angeles Lakers	1.50	.75	.15
☐ 126 Kareem Abdul-Jabbar AS .... Los Angeles Lakers	14.00	7.00	1.40
☐ 127 Julius Erving AS .... New York Nets	14.00	7.00	1.40
☐ 128 George McGinnis AS .... Philadelphia 76ers	.80	.40	.08
☐ 129 Nate Archibald AS .... Kansas City Kings	1.50	.75	.15
☐ 130 Pete Maravich AS .... New Orleans Jazz	4.00	2.00	.40
☐ 131 Dave Cowens AS .... Boston Celtics	2.25	1.10	.22
☐ 132 Rick Barry AS .... Golden State Warriors	4.00	2.00	.40
☐ 133 Elvin Hayes AS .... Washington Bullets	3.00	1.50	.30
☐ 134 James Silas AS .... San Antonio Spurs	.80	.40	.08
☐ 135 Randy Smith AS .... Buffalo Braves	.80	.40	.08
☐ 136 Leonard Gray .... Seattle Supersonics	.60	.30	.06
☐ 137 Charles Johnson .... Golden State Warriors	.60	.30	.06
☐ 138 Ron Behagen .... New Orleans Jazz	.60	.30	.06
☐ 139 Mike Newlin .... Houston Rockets	.60	.30	.06
☐ 140 Bob McAdoo .... Buffalo Braves	3.00	1.50	.30
☐ 141 Mike Gale .... San Antonio Spurs	.60	.30	.06
☐ 142 Scott Wedman .... Kansas City Kings	.80	.40	.08
☐ 143 Lloyd Free .... Philadelphia 76ers	3.50	1.75	.35
☐ 144 Bobby Jones .... Denver Nuggets	3.00	1.00	.20

1977-78 Topps

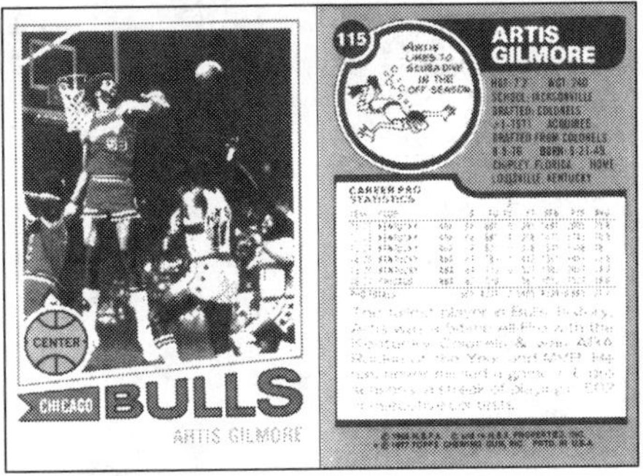

The 1977-78 Topps basketball card set consists of 132 standard-sized (2 1/2" by 3 1/2") cards. Card backs are printed in green and black on either white or gray card stock. The white card stock is considered more desirable by most collectors and may even be a little tougher to find. The key rookie cards in this set are Adrian Dantley and Robert Parish.

	NRMT	VG-E	GOOD
COMPLETE SET (132)	120.00	60.00	12.00
COMMON PLAYER (1-132)	.25	.12	.02
☐ 1 Kareem Abdul-Jabbar .... Los Angeles Lakers	20.00	9.00	1.75
☐ 2 Henry Bibby .... Philadelphia 76ers	.40	.20	.04
☐ 3 Curtis Rowe .... Boston Celtics	.40	.20	.04
☐ 4 Norm Van Lier .... Chicago Bulls	.40	.20	.04
☐ 5 Darnell Hillman .... New Jersey Nets	.25	.12	.02
☐ 6 Earl Monroe .... New York Knicks	3.00	1.50	.30
☐ 7 Leonard Gray .... Washington Bullets	.25	.12	.02
☐ 8 Bird Averitt .... Buffalo Braves	.25	.12	.02
☐ 9 Jim Brewer .... Cleveland Cavaliers	.25	.12	.02
☐ 10 Paul Westphal .... Phoenix Suns	.75	.35	.07
☐ 11 Bob Gross .... Portland Trail Blazers	.60	.30	.06
☐ 12 Phil Smith .... Golden State Warriors	.25	.12	.02
☐ 13 Dan Roundfield .... Indiana Pacers	1.00	.50	.10
☐ 14 Brian Taylor .... Denver Nuggets	.40	.20	.04
☐ 15 Rudy Tomjanovich .... Houston Rockets	.40	.20	.04
☐ 16 Kevin Porter .... Detroit Pistons	.40	.20	.04
☐ 17 Scott Wedman .... Kansas City Kings	.40	.20	.04
☐ 18 Lloyd Free .... Philadelphia 76ers	.75	.35	.07
☐ 19 Tom Boswell .... Boston Celtics	.40	.20	.04
☐ 20 Pete Maravich .... New Orleans Jazz	6.00	3.00	.60
☐ 21 Cliff Poindexter .... Chicago Bulls	.25	.12	.02

☐ 22 Bubbles Hawkins .40 .20 .04
New Jersey Nets
☐ 23 Kevin Grevey .75 .35 .07
Washington Bullets
☐ 24 Ken Charles .25 .12 .02
Atlanta Hawks
☐ 25 Bob Dandridge .40 .20 .04
Washington Bullets
☐ 26 Lonnie Shelton .60 .30 .06
New York Knicks
☐ 27 Don Chaney .40 .20 .04
Los Angeles Lakers
☐ 28 Larry Kenon .40 .20 .04
San Antonio Spurs
☐ 29 Checklist Card 3.00 .30 .06
☐ 30 Fred Brown .40 .20 .04
Seattle Supersonics
☐ 31 John Gianelli UER .25 .12 .02
Cleveland Cavaliers
(Listed as Cavaliers,
should be Buffalo Braves)
☐ 32 Austin Carr .40 .20 .04
Cleveland Cavaliers
☐ 33 Jamaal Wilkes 1.00 .50 .10
Los Angeles Lakers
☐ 34 Caldwell Jones .40 .20 .04
Philadelphia 76ers
☐ 35 JoJo White 1.00 .50 .10
Boston Celtics
☐ 36 Scott May 1.25 .60 .12
Chicago Bulls
☐ 37 Mike Newlin .25 .12 .02
Houston Rockets
☐ 38 Mel Davis .25 .12 .02
New Jersey Nets
☐ 39 Lionel Hollins .40 .20 .04
Portland Trail Blazers
☐ 40 Elvin Hayes 4.00 2.00 .40
Washington Bullets
☐ 41 Dan Issel 2.00 1.00 .20
Denver Nuggets
☐ 42 Ricky Sobers .25 .12 .02
Phoenix Suns
☐ 43 Don Ford .25 .12 .02
Los Angeles Lakers
☐ 44 John Williamson .40 .20 .04
Indiana Pacers
☐ 45 Bob McAdoo 1.50 .75 .15
New York Knicks
☐ 46 Geoff Petrie .40 .20 .04
Atlanta Hawks
☐ 47 M.L. Carr 1.75 .85 .17
Detroit Pistons
☐ 48 Brian Winters .40 .20 .04
Milwaukee Bucks
☐ 49 Sam Lacey .25 .12 .02
Kansas City Kings
☐ 50 George McGinnis .75 .35 .07
Philadelphia 76ers
☐ 51 Don Watts .25 .12 .02
Seattle Supersonics
☐ 52 Sidney Wicks .60 .30 .06
Boston Celtics
☐ 53 Wilbur Holland .25 .12 .02
Chicago Bulls
☐ 54 Tim Bassett .25 .12 .02
New Jersey Nets
☐ 55 Phil Chenier .40 .20 .04
Washington Bullets
☐ 56 Adrian Dantley 14.00 7.00 1.40
Buffalo Braves
☐ 57 Jim Chones .25 .12 .02
Cleveland Cavaliers
☐ 58 John Lucas 2.50 1.25 .25
Houston Rockets
☐ 59 Cazzie Russell .40 .20 .04
Los Angeles Lakers
☐ 60 David Thompson 2.50 1.25 .25
Denver Nuggets
☐ 61 Bob Lanier 2.00 1.00 .20
Detroit Pistons
☐ 62 Dave Twardzik .25 .12 .02
Portland Trail Blazers
☐ 63 Wilbert Jones .25 .12 .02
Indiana Pacers
☐ 64 Clifford Ray .25 .12 .02
Golden State Warriors
☐ 65 Doug Collins 1.25 .60 .12
Philadelphia 76ers
☐ 66 Tom McMillen 4.00 2.00 .40
New York Knicks
☐ 67 Rich Kelley .40 .20 .04
New Orleans Jazz
☐ 68 Mike Bantom .25 .12 .02
New Jersey Nets
☐ 69 Tom Boerwinkle .25 .12 .02
Chicago Bulls
☐ 70 John Havlicek 7.50 3.75 .75
Boston Celtics
☐ 71 Marvin Webster .60 .30 .06
Seattle Supersonics
☐ 72 Curtis Perry .25 .12 .02
Phoenix Suns
☐ 73 George Gervin 5.00 2.50 .50
San Antonio Spurs
☐ 74 Leonard Robinson .40 .20 .04
New Orleans Jazz
☐ 75 Wes Unseld 1.75 .85 .17
Washington Bullets
☐ 76 Dave Meyers .60 .30 .06
Milwaukee Bucks
☐ 77 Gail Goodrich 1.00 .50 .10
New Orleans Jazz
☐ 78 Richard Washington .75 .35 .07
Kansas City Kings
☐ 79 Mike Gale .25 .12 .02
San Antonio Spurs
☐ 80 Maurice Lucas .75 .35 .07
Portland Trail Blazers
☐ 81 Harvey Catchings .40 .20 .04
Philadelphia 76ers
☐ 82 Randy Smith .40 .20 .04
Buffalo Braves
☐ 83 Campy Russell .40 .20 .04
Cleveland Cavaliers
☐ 84 Kevin Kunnert .25 .12 .02
Houston Rockets
☐ 85 Lou Hudson .60 .30 .06
Atlanta Hawks
☐ 86 Mickey Johnson .40 .20 .04
Chicago Bulls
☐ 87 Lucius Allen .40 .20 .04
Kansas City Kings
☐ 88 Spencer Haywood .75 .35 .07
New York Knicks
☐ 89 Gus Williams 1.00 .50 .10
Golden State Warriors
☐ 90 Dave Cowens 3.25 1.60 .32
Boston Celtics
☐ 91 Al Skinner .25 .12 .02
New Jersey Nets
☐ 92 Swen Nater .40 .20 .04
Buffalo Braves
☐ 93 Tom Henderson .25 .12 .02
Washington Bullets
☐ 94 Don Buse .25 .12 .02
Indiana Pacers
☐ 95 Alvan Adams .60 .30 .06
Phoenix Suns
☐ 96 Mack Calvin .40 .20 .04
Denver Nuggets
☐ 97 Tom Burleson .25 .12 .02
Kansas City Kings
☐ 98 John Drew .40 .20 .04
Atlanta Hawks
☐ 99 Mike Green .25 .12 .02
Seattle Supersonics
☐ 100 Julius Erving 20.00 10.00 2.00
Philadelphia 76ers
☐ 101 John Mengelt .25 .12 .02
Chicago Bulls
☐ 102 Howard Porter .25 .12 .02
Detroit Pistons
☐ 103 Billy Paultz .40 .20 .04
San Antonio Spurs
☐ 104 John Shumate .75 .35 .07
Buffalo Braves
☐ 105 Calvin Murphy 1.00 .50 .10
Houston Rockets
☐ 106 Elmore Smith .25 .12 .02
Cleveland Cavaliers
☐ 107 Jim McMillian .25 .12 .02
New York Knicks
☐ 108 Kevin Stacom .25 .12 .02
Boston Celtics
☐ 109 Jan Van Breda Kolff .25 .12 .02
New Jersey Nets
☐ 110 Billy Knight .40 .20 .04
Indiana Pacers
☐ 111 Robert Parish 50.00 25.00 5.00
Golden State Warriors
☐ 112 Larry Wright .25 .12 .02
Washington Bullets
☐ 113 Bruce Seals .25 .12 .02
Seattle Supersonics
☐ 114 Junior Bridgeman .40 .20 .04
Milwaukee Bucks
☐ 115 Artis Gilmore 1.75 .85 .17

Card	Player / Team	NRMT	VG-E	GOOD
	Chicago Bulls			
☐ 116	Steve Mix Philadelphia 76ers	.25	.12	.02
☐ 117	Ron Lee Phoenix Suns	.25	.12	.02
☐ 118	Bobby Jones Denver Nuggets	1.00	.50	.10
☐ 119	Ron Boone Kansas City Kings	.25	.12	.02
☐ 120	Bill Walton Portland Trail Blazers	6.00	3.00	.60
☐ 121	Chris Ford Detroit Pistons	.75	.35	.07
☐ 122	Earl Tatum Los Angeles Lakers	.25	.12	.02
☐ 123	E.C. Coleman New Orleans Jazz	.25	.12	.02
☐ 124	Moses Malone Houston Rockets	10.00	5.00	1.00
☐ 125	Charlie Scott Boston Celtics	.40	.20	.04
☐ 126	Bobby Smith Cleveland Cavaliers	.25	.12	.02
☐ 127	Nate Archibald New Jersey Nets	2.00	1.00	.20
☐ 128	Mitch Kupchak Washington Bullets	2.25	1.10	.22
☐ 129	Walt Frazier New York Knicks	4.00	2.00	.40
☐ 130	Rick Barry Golden State Warriors	5.00	2.50	.50
☐ 131	Ernie DiGregorio Buffalo Braves	.40	.20	.04
☐ 132	Darryl Dawkins Philadelphia 76ers	5.00	1.25	.25

1978-79 Topps

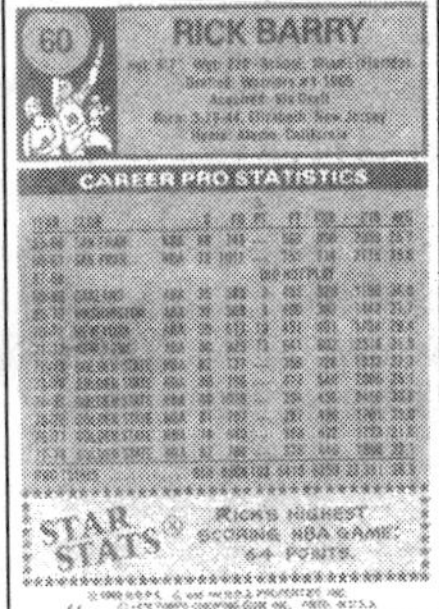

The 1978-79 Topps basketball card set contains 132 cards. The cards in the set measure the standard 2 1/2" by 3 1/2". Card backs are printed in orange and brown on gray card stock. The key rookie cards in this set are Walter Davis, Dennis Johnson, Marques Johnson, Bernard King, and Jack Sikma.

Card	Player / Team	NRMT	VG-E	GOOD
	COMPLETE SET (132)	80.00	40.00	8.00
	COMMON PLAYER (1-132)	.20	.10	.02
☐ 1	Bill Walton Portland Trail Blazers	9.00	2.50	.50
☐ 2	Doug Collins Philadelphia 76ers	.75	.35	.07
☐ 3	Jamaal Wilkes Los Angeles Lakers	.60	.30	.06
☐ 4	Wilbur Holland Chicago Bulls	.20	.10	.02
☐ 5	Bob McAdoo New York Knicks	1.00	.50	.10
☐ 6	Lucius Allen Kansas City Kings	.35	.17	.03
☐ 7	Wes Unseld Washington Bullets	1.25	.60	.12
☐ 8	Dave Meyers Milwaukee Bucks	.35	.17	.03
☐ 9	Austin Carr Cleveland Cavaliers	.35	.17	.03
☐ 10	Walter Davis Phoenix Suns	5.00	2.50	.50
☐ 11	John Williamson New Jersey Nets	.35	.17	.03
☐ 12	E.C. Coleman Golden State Warriors	.20	.10	.02
☐ 13	Calvin Murphy Houston Rockets	.75	.35	.07
☐ 14	Bobby Jones Denver Nuggets	.60	.30	.06
☐ 15	Chris Ford Detroit Pistons	.75	.35	.07
☐ 16	Kermit Washington Boston Celtics	.35	.17	.03
☐ 17	Butch Beard New York Knicks	.20	.10	.02
☐ 18	Steve Mix Philadelphia 76ers	.20	.10	.02
☐ 19	Marvin Webster Seattle Supersonics	.20	.10	.02
☐ 20	George Gervin San Antonio Spurs	3.00	1.50	.30
☐ 21	Steve Hawes Atlanta Hawks	.20	.10	.02
☐ 22	Johnny Davis Portland Trail Blazers	.20	.10	.02
☐ 23	Swen Nater San Diego Clippers	.35	.17	.03
☐ 24	Lou Hudson Los Angeles Lakers	.50	.25	.05
☐ 25	Elvin Hayes Washington Bullets	3.50	1.75	.35
☐ 26	Nate Archibald San Diego Clippers	1.50	.75	.15
☐ 27	James Edwards Indiana Pacers	3.00	1.50	.30
☐ 28	Howard Porter New Jersey Nets	.20	.10	.02
☐ 29	Quinn Buckner Milwaukee Bucks	2.00	1.00	.20
☐ 30	Leonard Robinson New Orleans Jazz	.35	.17	.03
☐ 31	Jim Cleamons New York Knicks	.20	.10	.02
☐ 32	Campy Russell Cleveland Cavaliers	.20	.10	.02
☐ 33	Phil Smith Golden State Warriors	.20	.10	.02
☐ 34	Darryl Dawkins Philadelphia 76ers	1.00	.50	.10
☐ 35	Don Buse Phoenix Suns	.20	.10	.02
☐ 36	Mickey Johnson Chicago Bulls	.20	.10	.02
☐ 37	Mike Gale San Antonio Spurs	.20	.10	.02
☐ 38	Moses Malone Houston Rockets	7.00	3.50	.70
☐ 39	Gus Williams Seattle Supersonics	.60	.30	.06
☐ 40	Dave Cowens Boston Celtics	2.50	1.25	.25
☐ 41	Bobby Wilkerson Denver Nuggets	.50	.25	.05
☐ 42	Wilbert Jones San Diego Clippers	.20	.10	.02
☐ 43	Charlie Scott Los Angeles Lakers	.35	.17	.03
☐ 44	John Drew Atlanta Hawks	.35	.17	.03
☐ 45	Earl Monroe New York Knicks	2.50	1.25	.25
☐ 46	John Shumate Detroit Pistons	.35	.17	.03
☐ 47	Earl Tatum Indiana Pacers	.20	.10	.02
☐ 48	Mitch Kupchak Washington Bullets	.35	.17	.03
☐ 49	Ron Boone Kansas City Kings	.20	.10	.02
☐ 50	Maurice Lucas Portland Trail Blazers	.35	.17	.03
☐ 51	Louie Dampier San Antonio Spurs	.35	.17	.03
☐ 52	Aaron James New Orleans Jazz	.20	.10	.02
☐ 53	John Mengelt Chicago Bulls	.20	.10	.02
☐ 54	Garfield Heard Phoenix Suns	.20	.10	.02
☐ 55	George Johnson New Jersey Nets	.20	.10	.02
☐ 56	Junior Bridgeman Milwaukee Bucks	.35	.17	.03
☐ 57	Elmore Smith	.20	.10	.02

	Cleveland Cavaliers			
□ 58	Rudy Tomjanovich	.35	.17	.03
	Houston Rockets			
□ 59	Fred Brown	.35	.17	.03
	Seattle Supersonics			
□ 60	Rick Barry UER	4.00	2.00	.40
	Golden State Warriors (reversed negative)			
□ 61	Dave Bing	1.50	.75	.15
	Boston Celtics			
□ 62	Anthony Roberts	.20	.10	.02
	Denver Nuggets			
□ 63	Norm Nixon	2.50	1.25	.25
	Los Angeles Lakers			
□ 64	Leon Douglas	.35	.17	.03
	Detroit Pistons			
□ 65	Henry Bibby	.35	.17	.03
	Philadelphia 76ers			
□ 66	Lonnie Shelton	.35	.17	.03
	New York Knicks			
□ 67	Checklist Card	2.00	.20	.04
□ 68	Tom Henderson	.20	.10	.02
	Washington Bullets			
□ 69	Dan Roundfield	.35	.17	.03
	Indiana Pacers			
□ 70	Armond Hill	.35	.17	.03
	Atlanta Hawks			
□ 71	Larry Kenon	.35	.17	.03
	San Antonio Spurs			
□ 72	Billy Knight	.20	.10	.02
	San Diego Clippers			
□ 73	Artis Gilmore	1.25	.60	.12
	Chicago Bulls			
□ 74	Lionel Hollins	.35	.17	.03
	Portland Trail Blazers			
□ 75	Bernard King	14.00	7.00	1.40
	New Jersey Nets			
□ 76	Brian Winters	.35	.17	.03
	Milwaukee Bucks			
□ 77	Alvan Adams	.35	.17	.03
	Phoenix Suns			
□ 78	Dennis Johnson	8.50	4.25	.85
	Seattle Supersonics			
□ 79	Scott Wedman	.35	.17	.03
	Kansas City Kings			
□ 80	Pete Maravich	4.50	2.25	.45
	New Orleans Jazz			
□ 81	Dan Issel	1.50	.75	.15
	Denver Nuggets			
□ 82	M.L. Carr	.35	.17	.03
	Detroit Pistons			
□ 83	Walt Frazier	3.50	1.75	.35
	Cleveland Cavaliers			
□ 84	Dwight Jones	.20	.10	.02
	Houston Rockets			
□ 85	JoJo White	.75	.35	.07
	Boston Celtics			
□ 86	Robert Parish	11.00	5.50	1.10
	Golden State Warriors			
□ 87	Charlie Criss	.35	.17	.03
	Atlanta Hawks			
□ 88	Jim McMillian	.20	.10	.02
	New York Knicks			
□ 89	Chuck Williams	.20	.10	.02
	San Diego Clippers			
□ 90	George McGinnis	.50	.25	.05
	Philadelphia 76ers			
□ 91	Billy Paultz	.20	.10	.02
	San Antonio Spurs			
□ 92	Bob Dandridge	.35	.17	.03
	Washington Bullets			
□ 93	Ricky Sobers	.20	.10	.02
	Indiana Pacers			
□ 94	Paul Silas	.50	.25	.05
	Seattle Supersonics			
□ 95	Gail Goodrich	.75	.35	.07
	New Orleans Jazz			
□ 96	Tim Bassett	.20	.10	.02
	New Jersey Nets			
□ 97	Ron Lee	.20	.10	.02
	Phoenix Suns			
□ 98	Bob Gross	.20	.10	.02
	Portland Trail Blazers			
□ 99	Sam Lacey	.20	.10	.02
	Kansas City Kings			
□ 100	David Thompson	2.00	1.00	.20
	Denver Nuggets (College North Carolina, should be NC State)			
□ 101	John Gianelli	.20	.10	.02
	Milwaukee Bucks			
□ 102	Norm Van Lier	.35	.17	.03
	Chicago Bulls			
□ 103	Caldwell Jones	.35	.17	.03
	Philadelphia 76ers			
□ 104	Eric Money	.20	.10	.02
	Detroit Pistons			
□ 105	Jim Chones	.20	.10	.02
	Cleveland Cavaliers			
□ 106	John Lucas	.50	.25	.05
	Houston Rockets			
□ 107	Spencer Haywood	.50	.25	.05
	New York Knicks			
□ 108	Eddie Johnson	.60	.30	.06
	Atlanta Hawks			
□ 109	Sidney Wicks	.50	.25	.05
	Boston Celtics			
□ 110	Kareem Abdul-Jabbar	14.00	7.00	1.40
	Los Angeles Lakers			
□ 111	Sonny Parker	.35	.17	.03
	Golden State Warriors			
□ 112	Randy Smith	.35	.17	.03
	San Diego Clippers			
□ 113	Kevin Grevey	.35	.17	.03
	Washington Bullets			
□ 114	Rich Kelley	.20	.10	.02
	New Orleans Jazz			
□ 115	Scott May	.35	.17	.03
	Chicago Bulls			
□ 116	Lloyd Free	.35	.17	.03
	Philadelphia 76ers			
□ 117	Jack Sikma	7.00	3.50	.70
	Seattle Supersonics			
□ 118	Kevin Porter	.35	.17	.03
	New Jersey Nets			
□ 119	Darnell Hillman	.20	.10	.02
	Denver Nuggets			
□ 120	Paul Westphal	.60	.30	.06
	Phoenix Suns			
□ 121	Richard Washington	.35	.17	.03
	Kansas City Kings			
□ 122	Dave Twardzik	.20	.10	.02
	Portland Trail Blazers			
□ 123	Mike Bantom	.20	.10	.02
	Indiana Pacers			
□ 124	Mike Newlin	.20	.10	.02
	Houston Rockets			
□ 125	Bob Lanier	1.50	.75	.15
	Detroit Pistons			
□ 126	Marques Johnson	3.50	1.75	.35
	Milwaukee Bucks			
□ 127	Foots Walker	.35	.17	.03
	Cleveland Cavaliers			
□ 128	Cedric Maxwell	1.50	.75	.15
	Boston Celtics			
□ 129	Ray Williams	.75	.35	.07
	New York Knicks			
□ 130	Julius Erving	14.00	7.00	1.40
	Philadelphia 76ers			
□ 131	Clifford Ray	.20	.10	.02
	Golden State Warriors			
□ 132	Adrian Dantley	3.00	1.00	.20
	Los Angeles Lakers			

1979-80 Topps

The 1979-80 Topps basketball card set contains 132 cards of NBA players. The cards in the set measure the standard 2 1/2" by 3 1/2". Card backs are printed in red and black on gray card stock. All-Star selections are designated as AS1 for first team selections and AS2 for second team selections and are denoted on the front of the player's regular card. Past U.S Olympic basketball team members are indicated in the checklist below by having the year of their participation followed by an "O" to signify that the player was an Olympic team member. Notable rookie cards in this set include Alex English and Reggie Theus.

	MINT	EXC	G-VG
COMPLETE SET (132)	75.00	37.50	7.50
COMMON PLAYER (1-132)	.15	.07	.01
☐ 1 George Gervin San Antonio Spurs	3.00	1.00	.20
☐ 2 Mitch Kupchak Washington Bullets	.25	.12	.02
☐ 3 Henry Bibby Philadelphia 76ers	.25	.12	.02
☐ 4 Bob Gross Portland Trail Blazers	.15	.07	.01
☐ 5 Dave Cowens Boston Celtics	2.00	1.00	.20
☐ 6 Dennis Johnson Seattle Supersonics	2.00	1.00	.20
☐ 7 Scott Wedman Kansas City Kings	.25	.12	.02
☐ 8 Earl Monroe New York Knicks	2.00	1.00	.20
☐ 9 Mike Bantom 720 Indiana Pacers	.15	.07	.01
☐ 10 Kareem Abdul-Jabbar AS Los Angeles Lakers	12.50	6.25	1.25
☐ 11 JoJo White 680 Golden State Warriors	.60	.30	.06
☐ 12 Spencer Haywood 680 Utah Jazz	.45	.22	.04
☐ 13 Kevin Porter Detroit Pistons	.25	.12	.02
☐ 14 Bernard King New Jersey Nets	4.00	2.00	.40
☐ 15 Mike Newlin Houston Rockets	.15	.07	.01
☐ 16 Sidney Wicks San Diego Clippers	.40	.20	.04
☐ 17 Dan Issel Denver Nuggets	1.25	.60	.12
☐ 18 Tom Henderson 720 Washington Bullets	.15	.07	.01
☐ 19 Jim Chones Cleveland Cavaliers	.15	.07	.01
☐ 20 Julius Erving Philadelphia 76ers	12.50	6.25	1.25
☐ 21 Brian Winters Milwaukee Bucks	.15	.07	.01
☐ 22 Billy Paultz San Antonio Spurs	.15	.07	.01
☐ 23 Cedric Maxwell Boston Celtics	.40	.20	.04
☐ 24 Eddie Johnson Atlanta Hawks	.25	.12	.02
☐ 25 Artis Gilmore Chicago Bulls	.75	.35	.07
☐ 26 Maurice Lucas Portland Trail Blazers	.35	.17	.03
☐ 27 Gus Williams Seattle Supersonics	.50	.25	.05
☐ 28 Sam Lacey Kansas City Kings	.15	.07	.01
☐ 29 Toby Knight New York Knicks	.15	.07	.01
☐ 30 Paul Westphal AS1 Phoenix Suns	.50	.25	.05
☐ 31 Alex English Indiana Pacers	18.00	9.00	1.80
☐ 32 Gail Goodrich Utah Jazz	.60	.30	.06
☐ 33 Caldwell Jones Philadelphia 76ers	.25	.12	.02
☐ 34 Kevin Grevey Washington Bullets	.15	.07	.01
☐ 35 Jamaal Wilkes Los Angeles Lakers	.50	.25	.05
☐ 36 Sonny Parker Golden State Warriors	.15	.07	.01
☐ 37 John Gianelli New Jersey Nets	.15	.07	.01
☐ 38 John Long Detroit Pistons	.75	.35	.07
☐ 39 George Johnson New Jersey Nets	.15	.07	.01
☐ 40 Lloyd Free AS2 San Diego Clippers	.25	.12	.02
☐ 41 Rudy Tomjanovich Houston Rockets	.35	.17	.03
☐ 42 Foots Walker Cleveland Cavaliers	.15	.07	.01
☐ 43 Dan Roundfield Atlanta Hawks	.25	.12	.02
☐ 44 Reggie Theus Chicago Bulls	4.00	2.00	.40
☐ 45 Bill Walton San Diego Clippers	3.50	1.75	.35
☐ 46 Fred Brown Seattle Supersonics	.35	.17	.03
☐ 47 Darnell Hillman Kansas City Kings	.15	.07	.01
☐ 48 Ray Williams New York Knicks	.25	.12	.02
☐ 49 Larry Kenon San Antonio Spurs	.25	.12	.02
☐ 50 David Thompson Denver Nuggets	1.50	.75	.15
☐ 51 Billy Knight Indiana Pacers	.15	.07	.01
☐ 52 Alvan Adams Phoenix Suns	.25	.12	.02
☐ 53 Phil Smith Golden State Warriors	.15	.07	.01
☐ 54 Adrian Dantley 760 Los Angeles Lakers	1.25	.60	.12
☐ 55 John Williamson New Jersey Nets	.25	.12	.02
☐ 56 Campy Russell Cleveland Cavaliers	.15	.07	.01
☐ 57 Armond Hill Atlanta Hawks	.15	.07	.01
☐ 58 Bob Lanier Detroit Pistons	1.25	.60	.12
☐ 59 Mickey Johnson Chicago Bulls	.15	.07	.01
☐ 60 Pete Maravich Utah Jazz	4.25	2.10	.42
☐ 61 Nick Weatherspoon San Diego Clippers	.15	.07	.01
☐ 62 Robert Reid Houston Rockets	.75	.35	.07
☐ 63 Mychal Thompson Portland Trail Blazers	3.00	1.50	.30
☐ 64 Doug Collins 720 Philadelphia 76ers	.50	.25	.05
☐ 65 Wes Unseld Washington Bullets	1.25	.60	.12
☐ 66 Jack Sikma Seattle Supersonics	1.50	.75	.15
☐ 67 Bobby Wilkerson Denver Nuggets	.25	.12	.02
☐ 68 Bill Robinzine Kansas City Kings	.25	.12	.02
☐ 69 Joe Meriweather New York Knicks	.15	.07	.01
☐ 70 Marques Johnson AS1 Milwaukee Bucks	.75	.35	.07
☐ 71 Ricky Sobers Indiana Pacers	.15	.07	.01
☐ 72 Clifford Ray Golden State Warriors	.15	.07	.01
☐ 73 Tim Bassett New Jersey Nets	.15	.07	.01
☐ 74 James Silas San Antonio Spurs	.15	.07	.01
☐ 75 Bob McAdoo Boston Celtics	.75	.35	.07
☐ 76 Austin Carr Cleveland Cavaliers	.35	.17	.03
☐ 77 Don Ford Los Angeles Lakers	.15	.07	.01
☐ 78 Steve Hawes Atlanta Hawks	.25	.12	.02
☐ 79 Ron Brewer Portland Trail Blazers	.35	.17	.03
☐ 80 Walter Davis Phoenix Suns	1.25	.60	.12
☐ 81 Calvin Murphy Houston Rockets	.75	.35	.07
☐ 82 Tom Boswell Denver Nuggets	.15	.07	.01
☐ 83 Lonnie Shelton Seattle Supersonics	.15	.07	.01
☐ 84 Terry Tyler Detroit Pistons	.35	.17	.03
☐ 85 Randy Smith San Diego Clippers	.25	.12	.02
☐ 86 Rich Kelley Utah Jazz	.15	.07	.01
☐ 87 Otis Birdsong Kansas City Kings	.60	.30	.06
☐ 88 Marvin Webster New York Knicks	.25	.12	.02

☐ 89 Eric Money .... .15 .07 .01
Philadelphia 76ers
☐ 90 Elvin Hayes AS1 .... 3.00 1.50 .30
Washington Bullets
☐ 91 Junior Bridgeman .... .25 .12 .02
Milwaukee Bucks
☐ 92 Johnny Davis .... .15 .07 .01
Indiana Pacers
☐ 93 Robert Parish .... 7.50 3.75 .75
Golden State Warriors
☐ 94 Eddie Jordan .... .15 .07 .01
New Jersey Nets
☐ 95 Leonard Robinson .... .25 .12 .02
Phoenix Suns
☐ 96 Rick Robey .... .35 .17 .03
Boston Celtics
☐ 97 Norm Nixon .... .60 .30 .06
Los Angeles Lakers
☐ 98 Mark Olberding .... .15 .07 .01
San Antonio Spurs
☐ 99 Wilbur Holland .... .15 .07 .01
Utah Jazz
☐ 100 Moses Malone AS1 .... 6.00 3.00 .60
Houston Rockets
☐ 101 Checklist Card .... 1.75 .15 .03
☐ 102 Tom Owens .... .15 .07 .01
Portland Trail Blazers
☐ 103 Phil Chenier .... .25 .12 .02
Washington Bullets
☐ 104 John Johnson .... .25 .12 .02
Seattle Supersonics
☐ 105 Darryl Dawkins .... .75 .35 .07
Philadelphia 76ers
☐ 106 Charlie Scott 680 .... .25 .12 .02
Denver Nuggets
☐ 107 M.L. Carr .... .25 .12 .02
Detroit Pistons
☐ 108 Phil Ford 760 .... 2.00 1.00 .20
Kansas City Kings
☐ 109 Swen Nater .... .25 .12 .02
San Diego Clippers
☐ 110 Nate Archibald .... 1.25 .60 .12
Boston Celtics
☐ 111 Aaron James .... .15 .07 .01
Utah Jazz
☐ 112 Jim Cleamons .... .15 .07 .01
New York Knicks
☐ 113 James Edwards .... .75 .35 .07
Indiana Pacers
☐ 114 Don Buse .... .15 .07 .01
Phoenix Suns
☐ 115 Steve Mix .... .15 .07 .01
Philadelphia 76ers
☐ 116 Charles Johnson .... .15 .07 .01
Washington Bullets
☐ 117 Elmore Smith .... .15 .07 .01
Cleveland Cavaliers
☐ 118 John Drew .... .25 .12 .02
Atlanta Hawks
☐ 119 Lou Hudson .... .40 .20 .04
Los Angeles Lakers
☐ 120 Rick Barry .... 3.50 1.75 .35
Houston Rockets
☐ 121 Kent Benson .... .50 .25 .05
Milwaukee Bucks
☐ 122 Mike Gale .... .15 .07 .01
San Antonio Spurs
☐ 123 Jan Van Breda Kolff .... .15 .07 .01
New Jersey Nets
☐ 124 Chris Ford .... .45 .22 .04
Boston Celtics
☐ 125 George McGinnis .... .40 .20 .04
Denver Nuggets
☐ 126 Leon Douglas .... .15 .07 .01
Detroit Pistons
☐ 127 John Lucas .... .25 .12 .02
Golden State Warriors
☐ 128 Kermit Washington .... .15 .07 .01
San Diego Clippers
☐ 129 Lionel Hollins .... .25 .12 .02
Portland Trail Blazers
☐ 130 Bob Dandridge AS2 .... .25 .12 .02
Washington Bullets
☐ 131 James McElroy .... .15 .07 .01
Utah Jazz
☐ 132 Bobby Jones 720 .... .50 .20 .04
Philadelphia 76ers

1980-81 Topps

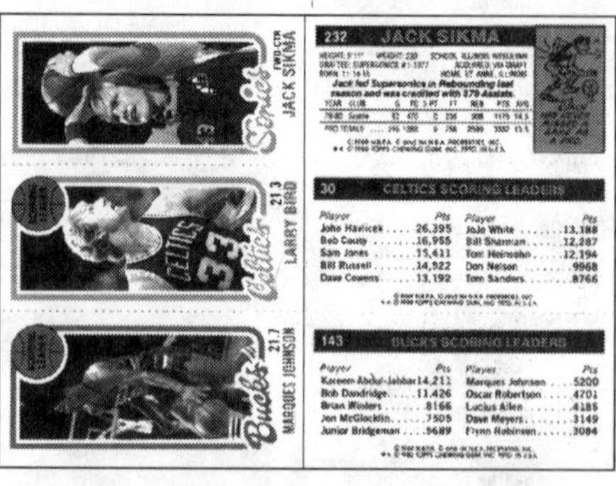

The 1980-81 Topps basketball card set contains 264 different individual players (1 1/6" by 2 1/2") on 176 different panels of three (2 1/2" by 3 1/2"). The cards come with three individual players per standard card. A perforation line segments each card into three players. In all, there are 176 different complete cards; however, the same player will be on more than one card. The variations stem from the fact that the cards in this set were printed on two separate sheets. In the checklist below, the first 88 cards comprise a complete set of all 264 players. The second 88 cards (89-176) provide a slight rearrangement of players within the card, but still contain the same 264 players. The cards are numbered within each series of 88 by any ordering of the left-hand player's number when the card is viewed from the back. In the checklist below, SD refers to a "Slam Dunk" star card. The letters AS in the checklist refer to an All-Star selection pictured on the front of the checklist card. There are a number of team leader (TL) cards which depict the team's leader in assists scoring or rebounds. Prices given below are for complete panels, as that is the typical way these cards are collected; cards which have been separated into the three parts are relatively valueless. The key card in this set is the combination of Larry Bird, Julius Erving, and Magic Johnson which features both rookie type cards of Bird and Johnson together on the same card. Since this confusing set was issued in three-player panels, there are no single-player rookie cards as the other basketball sets have. However the following players made their first card appearance in this set: James Bailey, Greg Ballard, Larry Bird, Dudley Bradley, Mike Bratz, Joe Bryant, Kenny Carr, Bill Cartwright, Maurice Cheeks, Michael Cooper, Wayne Cooper, David Greenwood, Phil Hubbard, Geoff Huston, Abdul Jeelani, Magic Johnson, Reggie King, Tom LaGarde, Mark Landsberger, Allen Leavell, Sidney Moncrief, Calvin Natt, Roger Phegley, Ben Poquette, Micheal Ray Richardson, Cliff Robinson, Purvis Short, Jerome Whitehead, and Freeman Williams.

	MINT	EXC	G-VG
COMPLETE SET (1-176)	750.00	375.00	75.00
COMMON PANEL	.20	.10	.02
☐ 1 3 Dan Roundfield AS .... 181 Julius Erving 258 Ron Brewer SD	5.00	2.50	.50
☐ 2 7 Moses Malone AS .... 185 Steve Mix 92 Robert Parish TL	2.00	1.00	.20
☐ 3 12 Gus Williams AS .... 67 Geoff Huston 5 John Drew AS	.20	.10	.02
☐ 4 24 Steve Hawes .... 32 Nate Archibald TL 248 Elvin Hayes	1.00	.50	.10
☐ 5 29 Dan Roundfield .... 73 Dan Issel TL 152 Brian Winters	.20	.10	.02
☐ 6 34 Larry Bird .... 174 Julius Erving TL 139 Magic Johnson	500.00	250.00	50.00
☐ 7 36 Dave Cowens	.75	.35	.07

186 Paul Westphal TL
142 Jamaal Wilkes
☐ 8 38 Pete Maravich .... 2.25 1.10 .22
264 Lloyd Free SD
194 Dennis Johnson
☐ 9 40 Rick Robey .... .30 .15 .03
234 Ad.Dantley TL
26 Eddie Johnson
☐ 10 47 Scott May .... .20 .10 .02
196 K.Washington TL
177 Henry Bibby
☐ 11 55 Don Ford .... .20 .10 .02
145 Quinn Buckner TL
138 Brad Holland
☐ 12 58 Campy Russell .... .20 .10 .02
247 Kevin Grevey
52 Dave Robisch TL
☐ 13 60 Foots Walker .... .20 .10 .02
113 Mick.Johnson TL
130 Bill Robinzine
☐ 14 61 Austin Carr .... 2.75 1.35 .27
8 Kareem Abdul-Jabbar AS
200 Calvin Natt
☐ 15 63 Jim Cleamons .... .20 .10 .02
256 Robert Reid SD
22 Charlie Criss
☐ 16 69 Tom LaGarde .... .20 .10 .02
215 Swen Nater TL
213 James Silas
☐ 17 71 Jerome Whitehead .... .30 .15 .03
259 Artis Gilmore SD
184 Caldwell Jones
☐ 18 74 John Roche TL .... .20 .10 .02
99 Clifford Ray
235 Ben Poquette TL
☐ 19 75 Alex English .... 2.00 1.00 .20
2 Marques Johnson AS
68 Jeff Judkins
☐ 20 82 Terry Tyler TL .... .20 .10 .02
21 Armond Hill TL
171 M.R. Richardson
☐ 21 84 Kent Benson .... .20 .10 .02
212 John Shumate
229 Paul Westphal
☐ 22 86 Phil Hubbard .... 1.50 .75 .15
93 Robert Parish TL
126 Tom Burleson
☐ 23 88 John Long .... 2.50 1.25 .25
1 Julius Erving AS
49 Ricky Sobers
☐ 24 90 Eric Money .... .20 .10 .02
57 Dave Robisch
254 Rick Robey SD
☐ 25 95 Wayne Cooper .... .20 .10 .02
226 John Johnson TL
45 David Greenwood
☐ 26 97 Robert Parish .... 3.50 1.75 .35
187 Leon.Robinson TL
46 Dwight Jones
☐ 27 98 Sonny Parker .... .30 .15 .03
197 Dave Twardzik TL
39 Cedric Maxwell
☐ 28 105 Rick Barry .... 1.00 .50 .10
122 Otis Birdsong TL
48 John Mengelt
☐ 29 106 Allen Leavell .... .20 .10 .02
53 Foots Walker TL
223 Freeman Williams
☐ 30 108 Calvin Murphy .... 1.00 .50 .10
176 Maur.Cheeks TL
87 Greg Kelser
☐ 31 110 Robert Reid .... .40 .20 .04
243 Wes Unseld TL
50 Reggie Theus
☐ 32 111 Rudy Tomjanovich .... .20 .10 .02
13 Eddie Johnson AS
179 Doug Collins
☐ 33 112 Mickey Johnson TL .... .30 .15 .03
28 Wayne Rollins
15 M.R.Richardson AS
☐ 34 115 Mike Bantom .... .30 .15 .03
6 Adrian Dantley AS
227 James Bailey
☐ 35 116 Dudley Bradley .... .20 .10 .02
155 Eddie Jordan TL
239 Allan Bristow
☐ 36 118 James Edwards .... .20 .10 .02
153 Mike Newlin TL
182 Lionel Hollins
☐ 37 119 Mickey Johnson .... .20 .10 .02
154 Geo.Johnson TL
193 Leonard Robinson
☐ 38 120 Billy Knight .... .20 .10 .02
16 Paul Westphal AS

59 Randy Smith
☐ 39 121 George McGinnis .... .20 .10 .02
83 Eric Money TL
65 Mike Bratz
☐ 40 124 Phil Ford TL .... .20 .10 .02
101 Phil Smith
224 Gus Williams TL
☐ 41 127 Phil Ford .... .20 .10 .02
19 John Drew TL
209 Larry Kenon
☐ 42 131 Scott Wedman .... .20 .10 .02
164 B.Cartwright TL
23 John Drew
☐ 43 132 K.Abdul-Jabbar TL .... 2.50 1.25 .25
56 Mike Mitchell
81 Terry Tyler TL
☐ 44 135 K.Abdul-Jabbar .... 5.00 2.50 .50
79 David Thompson
216 Brian Taylor TL
☐ 45 137 Michael Cooper .... 2.75 1.35 .27
103 Moses Malone TL
148 George Johnson
☐ 46 140 Mark Landsberger .... 1.25 .60 .12
10 Bob Lanier AS
222 Bill Walton
☐ 47 141 Norm Nixon .... .20 .10 .02
123 Sam Lacey TL
54 Kenny Carr
☐ 48 143 Marq.Johnson TL 27.00 13.50 2.70
30 Larry Bird TL
232 Jack Sikma
☐ 49 146 Junior Bridgeman 27.00 13.50 2.70
31 Larry Bird TL
198 Ron Brewer
☐ 50 147 Quinn Buckner .... 2.00 1.00 .20
133 K.Abdul-Jabbar TL
207 Mike Gale
☐ 51 149 Marques Johnson .... 2.00 1.00 .20
262 Julius Erving SD
62 Abdul Jeelani
☐ 52 151 Sidney Moncrief .... 3.50 1.75 .35
260 Lonnie Shelton SD
220 Paul Silas
☐ 53 156 George Johnson .... .20 .10 .02
9 Bill Cartwright AS
199 Bob Gross
☐ 54 158 Maurice Lucas .... .20 .10 .02
261 James Edwards SD
157 Eddie Jordan
☐ 55 159 Mike Newlin .... .20 .10 .02
134 Norm Nixon TL
180 Darryl Dawkins
☐ 56 160 Roger Phegley .... .20 .10 .02
206 James Silas TL
91 Terry Tyler
☐ 57 161 Cliff Robinson .... .20 .10 .02
51 Mike Mitchell TL
80 Bobby Wilkerson
☐ 58 162 Jan V.Breda Kolff .... .30 .15 .03
204 George Gervin TL
117 Johnny Davis
☐ 59 165 M.R.Richardson TL .... .50 .25 .05
214 Lloyd Free TL
44 Artis Gilmore
☐ 60 166 Bill Cartwright .... 3.00 1.50 .30
244 Kevin Porter TL
25 Armond Hill
☐ 61 168 Toby Knight .... .50 .25 .05
14 Lloyd Free AS
240 Adrian Dantley
☐ 62 169 Joe Meriweather .... .20 .10 .02
218 Lloyd Free
42 D.Greenwood TL
☐ 63 170 Earl Monroe .... .75 .35 .07
27 James McElroy
85 Leon Douglas
☐ 64 172 Marvin Webster .... .20 .10 .02
175 Caldwell Jones TL
129 Sam Lacey
☐ 65 173 Ray Williams .... .20 .10 .02
94 John Lucas TL
202 Dave Twardzik
☐ 66 178 Maurice Cheeks 45.00 22.50 4.50
18 Magic Johnson AS
237 Ron Boone
☐ 67 183 Bobby Jones .... .20 .10 .02
37 Chris Ford
66 Joe Hassett
☐ 68 189 Alvan Adams .... .60 .30 .06
163 B.Cartwright TL
76 Dan Issel
☐ 69 190 Don Buse .... .30 .15 .03
242 Elvin Hayes TL
35 M.L. Carr

☐ 70	191 Walter Davis 11 George Gervin AS 136 Jim Chones	.40	.20	.04
☐ 71	192 Rich Kelley 102 Moses Malone TL 64 Winford Boynes	1.00	.50	.10
☐ 72	201 Tom Owens 225 Jack Sikma TL 100 Purvis Short	.30	.15	.03
☐ 73	208 George Gervin 72 Dan Issel TL 249 Mitch Kupchak	1.00	.50	.10
☐ 74	217 Joe Bryant 263 Bobby Jones SD 107 Moses Malone	2.50	1.25	.25
☐ 75	219 Swen Nater 17 Calvin Murphy AS 70 Rich.Washington	.20	.10	.02
☐ 76	221 Brian Taylor 253 John Shumate SD 167 Larry Demic	.20	.10	.02
☐ 77	228 Fred Brown 205 Larry Kenon TL 203 Kerm.Washington	.20	.10	.02
☐ 78	230 John Johnson 4 Walter Davis AS 33 Nate Archibald	.60	.30	.06
☐ 79	231 Lonnie Shelton 104 Allen Leavell TL 96 John Lucas	.20	.10	.02
☐ 80	233 Gus Williams 20 Dan Roundfield TL 211 Kevin Restani	.20	.10	.02
☐ 81	236 Allan Bristow TL 210 Mark Olberding 255 James Bailey SD	.20	.10	.02
☐ 82	238 Tom Boswell 109 Billy Paultz 150 Bob Lanier	.50	.25	.05
☐ 83	241 Ben Poquette 188 Paul Westphal TL 77 Charlie Scott	.20	.10	.02
☐ 84	245 Greg Ballard 43 Reggie Theus TL 252 John Williamson	.20	.10	.02
☐ 85	246 Bob Dandridge 41 Reggie Theus TL 128 Reggie King	.20	.10	.02
☐ 86	250 Kevin Porter 114 Johnny Davis TL 125 Otis Birdsong	.20	.10	.02
☐ 87	251 Wes Unseld 195 Tom Owens TL 78 John Roche	.50	.25	.05
☐ 88	257 Elvin Hayes SD 144 Marq.Johnson TL 89 Bob McAdoo	.60	.30	.06
☐ 89	3 Dan Roundfield 218 Lloyd Free 42 D.Greenwood TL	.20	.10	.02
☐ 90	7 Moses Malone 247 Kevin Grevey 52 Dave Robisch TL	1.00	.50	.10
☐ 91	12 Gus Williams 210 Mark Olberding 255 James Bailey SD	.20	.10	.02
☐ 92	24 Steve Hawes 226 John Johnson TL 45 David Greenwood	.20	.10	.02
☐ 93	29 Dan Roundfield 113 Mick.Johnson TL 130 Bill Robinzine	.20	.10	.02
☐ 94	34 Larry Bird 164 B.Cartwright TL 23 John Drew	55.00	27.50	5.50
☐ 95	36 Dave Cowens 16 Paul Westphal AS 59 Randy Smith	.75	.35	.07
☐ 96	38 Pete Maravich 187 Leon.Robinson TL 46 Dwight Jones	1.50	.75	.15
☐ 97	40 Rick Robey 37 Chris Ford 66 Joe Hassett	.20	.10	.02
☐ 98	47 Scott May 30 Larry Bird TL 232 Jack Sikma	27.00	13.50	2.70
☐ 99	55 Don Ford 144 Marq.Johnson TL 89 Bob McAdoo	.30	.15	.03
☐ 100	58 Campy Russell 21 Armond Hill TL 171 M.R.Richardson	.20	.10	.02
☐ 101	60 Foots Walker 122 Otis Birdsong TL 48 John Mengelt	.20	.10	.02
☐ 102	61 Austin Carr 56 Mike Mitchell 81 Terry Tyler TL	.20	.10	.02
☐ 103	63 Jim Cleamons 261 James Edwards SD 157 Eddie Jordan	.20	.10	.02
☐ 104	69 Tom LaGarde 109 Billy Paultz 150 Bob Lanier	.50	.25	.05
☐ 105	71 Jerome Whitehead 17 Calvin Murphy AS 70 Rich.Washington	.20	.10	.02
☐ 106	74 John Roche TL 28 Wayne Rollins 15 M.R.Richardson AS	.30	.15	.03
☐ 107	75 Alex English 102 Moses Malone TL 64 Winford Boynes	2.50	1.25	.25
☐ 108	82 Terry Tyler TL 79 David Thompson 216 Brian Taylor TL	.40	.20	.04
☐ 109	84 Kent Benson 259 Artis Gilmore SD 184 Caldwell Jones	.30	.15	.03
☐ 110	86 Phil Hubbard 195 Tom Owens TL 78 John Roche	.20	.10	.02
☐ 111	88 John Long 18 Magic Johnson AS 237 Ron Boone	38.00	15.00	3.00
☐ 112	90 Eric Money 215 Swen Nater TL 213 James Silas	.20	.10	.02
☐ 113	95 Wayne Cooper 154 Geo.Johnson TL 193 Leon.Robinson	.20	.10	.02
☐ 114	97 Robert Parish 103 Moses Malone TL 148 George Johnson	4.00	2.00	.40
☐ 115	98 Sonny Parker 94 John Lucas TL 202 Dave Twardzik	.20	.10	.02
☐ 116	105 Rick Barry 123 Sam Lacey TL 54 Kenny Carr	1.00	.50	.10
☐ 117	106 Allen Leavell 197 Dave Twardzik TL 39 Cedric Maxwell	.30	.15	.03
☐ 118	108 Calvin Murphy 51 Mike Mitchell TL 80 Bobby Wilkerson	.30	.15	.03
☐ 119	110 Robert Reid 153 Mike Newlin TL 182 Lionel Hollins	.20	.10	.02
☐ 120	111 Rudy Tomjanovich 73 Dan Issel TL 152 Brian Winters	.30	.15	.03
☐ 121	112 Mick.Johnson TL 264 Lloyd Free SD 194 Dennis Johnson	.40	.20	.04
☐ 122	115 Mike Bantom 204 George Gervin TL 117 Johnny Davis	.30	.15	.03
☐ 123	116 Dudley Bradley 186 Paul Westphal TL 142 Jamaal Wilkes	.20	.10	.02
☐ 124	118 James Edwards 32 Nate Archibald TL 248 Elvin Hayes	1.00	.50	.10
☐ 125	119 Mickey Johnson 72 Dan Issel TL 249 Mitch Kupchak	.30	.15	.03
☐ 126	120 Billy Knight 104 Allen Leavell TL 96 John Lucas	.20	.10	.02
☐ 127	121 George McGinnis 10 Bob Lanier AS 222 Bill Walton	1.00	.50	.10
☐ 128	124 Phil Ford TL 234 Adr.Dantley TL 26 Eddie Johnson	.30	.15	.03
☐ 129	127 Phil Ford 43 Reggie Theus TL 252 John Williamson	.20	.10	.02
☐ 130	131 Scott Wedman 244 Kevin Porter TL 25 Armond Hill	.20	.10	.02
☐ 131	132 K.Abdul-Jabbar TL 93 Robert Parish TL 126 Tom Burleson	3.50	1.75	.35
☐ 132	135 K.Abdul-Jabbar 253 John Shumate SD	5.00	2.50	.50

	Card			
	167 Larry Demic			
☐ 133	137 Michael Cooper	1.50	.75	.15
	212 John Shumate			
	229 Paul Westphal			
☐ 134	140 Mark Landsberger	.50	.25	.05
	214 Lloyd Free TL			
	44 Artis Gilmore			
☐ 135	141 Norm Nixon	.35	.17	.03
	242 Elvin Hayes TL			
	35 M.L. Carr			
☐ 136	143 Marq.Johnson TL	.20	.10	.02
	57 Dave Robisch			
	254 Rick Robey SD			
☐ 137	146 Junior Bridgeman	2.50	1.25	.25
	1 Julius Erving AS			
	49 Ricky Sobers			
☐ 138	147 Quinn Buckner	.20	.10	.02
	2 Marques Johnson AS			
	68 Jeff Judkins			
☐ 139	149 Marques Johnson	.30	.15	.03
	83 Eric Money TL			
	65 Mike Bratz			
☐ 140	151 Sidney Moncrief	5.00	2.50	.50
	133 K.Abdul-Jabbar TL			
	207 Mike Gale			
☐ 141	156 George Johnson	.20	.10	.02
	175 Caldw.Jones TL			
	129 Sam Lacey			
☐ 142	158 Maurice Lucas	2.00	1.00	.20
	262 Julius Erving SD			
	62 Abdul Jeelani			
☐ 143	159 Mike Newlin	.40	.20	.04
	243 Wes Unseld TL			
	50 Reggie Theus			
☐ 144	160 Roger Phegley	.20	.10	.02
	145 Quinn Buckner TL			
	138 Brad Holland			
☐ 145	161 Cliff Robinson	.20	.10	.02
	114 Johnny Davis TL			
	125 Otis Birdsong			
☐ 146	162 Jan V.Breda Kolff	100.00	50.00	10.00
	174 Julius Erving TL			
	139 Magic Johnson			
☐ 147	165 M.R.Richardson TL	1.25	.60	.12
	185 Steve Mix			
	92 Robert Parish TL			
☐ 148	166 Bill Cartwright	3.00	1.50	.30
	13 Eddie Johnson AS			
	179 Doug Collins			
☐ 149	168 Toby Knight	.20	.10	.02
	188 Paul Westphal TL			
	77 Charlie Scott			
☐ 150	169 Joe Meriweather	.20	.10	.02
	196 K.Washington TL			
	177 Henry Bibby			
☐ 151	170 Earl Monroe	.75	.35	.07
	206 James Silas TL			
	91 Terry Tyler			
☐ 152	172 Marvin Webster	.20	.10	.02
	155 Eddie Jordan TL			
	239 Allan Bristow			
☐ 153	173 Ray Williams	.30	.15	.03
	225 Jack Sikma TL			
	100 Purvis Short			
☐ 154	178 Maurice Cheeks	4.00	2.00	.40
	11 George Gervin AS			
	136 Jim Chones			
☐ 155	183 Bobby Jones	.20	.10	.02
	99 Clifford Ray			
	235 Ben Poquette TL			
☐ 156	189 Alvan Adams	.50	.25	.05
	14 Lloyd Free AS			
	240 Adrian Dantley			
☐ 157	190 Don Buse	.30	.15	.03
	6 Adrian Dantley AS			
	227 James Bailey			
☐ 158	191 Walter Davis	.30	.15	.03
	9 Bill Cartwright AS			
	199 Bob Gross			
☐ 159	192 Rich Kelley	2.50	1.25	.25
	263 Bobby Jones SD			
	107 Moses Malone			
☐ 160	201 Tom Owens	.30	.15	.03
	134 Norm Nixon TL			
	180 Darryl Dawkins			
☐ 161	208 George Gervin	1.00	.50	.10
	53 Foots Walker TL			
	223 Freeman Williams			
☐ 162	217 Joe Bryant	2.50	1.25	.25
	8 K.Abdul-Jabbar AS			
	200 Calvin Natt			
☐ 163	219 Swen Nater	.20	.10	.02
	101 Phil Smith			
	224 Gus Williams TL			
☐ 164	221 Brian Taylor	.20	.10	.02
	256 Robert Reid SD			
	22 Charlie Criss			
☐ 165	228 Fred Brown	27.00	13.50	2.70
	31 Larry Bird TL			
	198 Ron Brewer			
☐ 166	230 John Johnson	.50	.25	.05
	163 B.Cartwright TL			
	76 Dan Issel			
☐ 167	231 Lonnie Shelton	.20	.10	.02
	205 Larry Kenon TL			
	203 Kermit Washington			
☐ 168	233 Gus Williams	.20	.10	.02
	41 Reggie Theus TL			
	128 Reggie King			
☐ 169	236 Allan Bristow TL	.20	.10	.02
	260 Lonnie Shelton SD			
	220 Paul Silas			
☐ 170	238 Tom Boswell	.20	.10	.02
	27 James McElroy			
	85 Leon Douglas			
☐ 171	241 Ben Poquette	1.00	.50	.10
	176 Maurice Cheeks TL			
	87 Greg Kelser			
☐ 172	245 Greg Ballard	.60	.30	.06
	4 Walter Davis AS			
	33 Nate Archibald			
☐ 173	246 Bob Dandridge	.20	.10	.02
	19 John Drew TL			
	209 Larry Kenon			
☐ 174	250 Kevin Porter	.20	.10	.02
	20 Dan Roundfield TL			
	211 Kevin Restani			
☐ 175	251 Wes Unseld	.50	.25	.05
	67 Geoff Huston			
	5 John Drew AS			
☐ 176	257 Elvin Hayes SD	5.00	2.50	.50
	181 Julius Erving			
	258 Ron Brewer SD			

1980-81 Topps Team Posters

This set of 16 numbered team mini-posters was issued in regular packs of 1980-81 Topps basketball cards. The small posters feature a full-color posed team picture, with the team name in the frame line. These posters are on thin, white paper stock and measure approximately 4 7/8" by 6 7/8" when unfolded.

	MINT	EXC	G-VG
COMPLETE SET (16)	7.50	3.75	.75
COMMON TEAM (1-16)	.50	.25	.05
☐ 1 Atlanta Hawks	.50	.25	.05
☐ 2 Boston Celtics	1.50	.75	.15
☐ 3 Chicago Bulls	.50	.25	.05
☐ 4 Cleveland Cavaliers	.50	.25	.05
☐ 5 Detroit Pistons	.50	.25	.05
☐ 6 Houston Rockets	.50	.25	.05
☐ 7 Indiana Pacers	.50	.25	.05
☐ 8 Los Angeles Lakers	2.00	1.00	.20
☐ 9 Milwaukee Bucks	.50	.25	.05
☐ 10 New Jersey Nets	.50	.25	.05
☐ 11 New York Knicks	.50	.25	.05
☐ 12 Philadelphia 76ers	.50	.25	.05
☐ 13 Phoenix Suns	.50	.25	.05

☐ 14 Portland Blazers	.50	.25	.05
☐ 15 Seattle Sonics	.50	.25	.05
☐ 16 Washington Bullets	.50	.25	.05

1981 Topps Thirst Break *

This 56-card set is actually a set of gum wrappers. These wrappers were issued in Thirst Break Orange Gum, which was reportedly only distributed in Pennsylvania and Ohio. Each of these small gum wrappers has a cartoon-type image of a particular great moment in sports. As the checklist below shows, many different sports are represented in this set. The wrappers each measure approximately 2 9/16" by 1 5/8". The wrappers are numbered in small print at the top. The backs of the wrappers are blank. The "1981 Topps" copyright is at the bottom of each card.

	MINT	EXC	G-VG
COMPLETE SET (56)	75.00	37.50	7.50
COMMON PLAYER (1-56)	.75	.35	.07
☐ 1 Shortest Baseball Game	.75	.35	.07
☐ 2 Lefty Gomez World Series Fact	1.50	.75	.15
☐ 3 Bob Gibson World Series Strikeout Record	2.50	1.25	.25
☐ 4 Hoyt Wilhelm 1070 Games	1.50	.75	.15
☐ 5 Babe Ruth Best Clutch Hitter	7.50	3.75	.75
☐ 6 Toby Harrah Fielding Fact	.75	.35	.07
☐ 7 Carl Hubbell 24 Consecutive Wins	1.25	.60	.12
☐ 8 Harvey Haddix 12 Perfect Innings	.75	.35	.07
☐ 9 Steve Carlton Strikeout Fact	2.50	1.25	.25
☐ 10 Nolan Ryan, Tom Seaver, and Steve Carlton	6.00	3.00	.60
☐ 11 Lou Brock Stolen Base Record	2.50	1.25	.25
☐ 12 Mickey Mantle 565 ft. Home Run	7.50	3.75	.75
☐ 13 Tom Seaver Strikeout Record	3.00	1.50	.30
☐ 14 Don Drysdale Scoreless Innings	1.50	.75	.15
☐ 15 Billy Williams Consecutive Games	1.50	.75	.15
☐ 16 Wilt Chamberlain 100 Points One Game	4.00	2.00	.40
☐ 17 Wilt Chamberlain 50.4 Avg/Game	4.00	2.00	.40
☐ 18 Wilt Chamberlain No Foulout Record	4.00	2.00	.40
☐ 19 Kevin Porter Assist Record	.75	.35	.07
☐ 20 Christy Mathewson World Series Shutout	1.50	.75	.15
☐ 21 Hank Aaron Home Run Record	3.50	1.75	.35
☐ 22 Ron Blomberg First DH in Majors	.75	.35	.07
☐ 23 Joe Nuxhall Youngest Player	.75	.35	.07
☐ 24 Reggie Jackson World Series Home Runs	3.00	1.50	.30
☐ 25 John Havlicek Most Games Played	3.00	1.50	.30
☐ 26 Oscar Robertson Free Throw Record	3.00	1.50	.30
☐ 27 Calvin Murphy Free Throw Fact	1.50	.75	.15
☐ 28 Clarence(Bevo) Francis Basketball Fact	1.00	.50	.10
☐ 29 Garo Yepremian 20 Consecutive Field Goals	.75	.35	.07
☐ 30 Bert Jones 17 Consecutive Passes	1.00	.50	.10
☐ 31 Norm Van Brocklin Yardage Record	1.50	.75	.15
☐ 32 Fran Tarkenton Touchdown Record	3.00	1.50	.30
☐ 33 Johnny Unitas Football Fact	3.50	1.75	.35
☐ 34 Bob Beamon Long Jump Record	1.00	.50	.10
☐ 35 Jesse Owens Track Records	1.50	.75	.15
☐ 36 Bart Starr Passing Fact	3.00	1.50	.30
☐ 37 O.J. Simpson Touchdown Record	3.50	1.75	.35
☐ 38 Jim Brown Football Fact	4.00	2.00	.40
☐ 39 Jim Marshall 256 Consecutive Games	1.25	.60	.12
☐ 40 George Blanda Extra Point Fact	2.50	1.25	.25
☐ 41 Jack Tatum Football Record	.75	.35	.07
☐ 42 Tim Brown Touchdown Record	.75	.35	.07
☐ 43 Gerry Cheevers Hockey Fact	2.00	1.00	.20
☐ 44 Dave Schultz Hockey Penalty Record	1.00	.50	.10
☐ 45 Mark Spitz 9 Olympic Gold Medals	1.00	.50	.10
☐ 46 Byron Nelson Golf Fact	1.00	.50	.10
☐ 47 Soccer Attendance Record, 1950 World Cup	.75	.35	.07
☐ 48 Tom Dempsey Field Goal Record	.75	.35	.07
☐ 49 Gale Sayers Football Fact	2.50	1.25	.25
☐ 50 Bobby Hull Hockey Fact	3.00	1.50	.30
☐ 51 Bobby Hull Hockey Fact	3.00	1.50	.30
☐ 52 Bobby Hull Assist Record	3.00	1.50	.30
☐ 53 Giorgio Chinaglia Soccer Fact	1.00	.50	.10
☐ 54 Muhammad Ali Boxing Record	3.00	1.50	.30
☐ 55 Gene Tunney and Rocky Marciano	1.50	.75	.15
☐ 56 Roger Bannister 4 Minute Mile	.75	.35	.07

1981-82 Topps

The 1981-82 Topps basketball card set contains a total of 198 cards. The cards in the set measure the standard 2 1/2" by 3 1/2". These cards, however, are numbered depending upon the regional distribution used in the issue. A 66-card national set was issued to all parts of the country; however, subsets of 44 cards each were issued in the east, mid-west, and west. Card numbers over 66 are prefaced on the card by the region in which they were distributed, e.g., East 96. The cards themselves feature the Topps logo in the frame line and a quarter-round sunburst in the lower left-hand corner which lists the name, position, and team of the player depicted. Cards 44-66 are Team Leader (TL) cards picturing each team's statistical leaders.

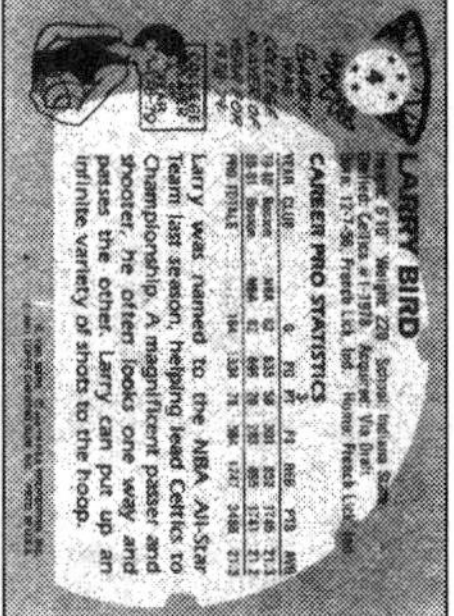

The back, printed in orange and brown on gray stock, features standard Topps biographical data and career statistics. There are a number of Super Action (SA) cards in the set. Rookie Cards included in this set are Joe Barry Carroll, Mike Dunleavy, Mike Gminski, Darrell Griffith, Vinnie Johnson, Bill Laimbeer, Rick Mahorn, Kevin McHale, and Larry Smith. The card numbering sequence is alphabetical within team within series.

	MINT	EXC	G-VG
COMPLETE SET (198)	110.00	55.00	11.00
COMMON CARD (1-43)	.10	.05	.01
COMMON CARD (44-66)	.15	.07	.01
COMMON CARD (67-110)	.15	.07	.01
☐ 1 John Drew Atlanta Hawks	.20	.10	.02
☐ 2 Dan Roundfield Atlanta Hawks	.10	.05	.01
☐ 3 Nate Archibald Boston Celtics	.75	.35	.07
☐ 4 Larry Bird Boston Celtics	30.00	15.00	3.00
☐ 5 Cedric Maxwell Boston Celtics	.20	.10	.02
☐ 6 Robert Parish Boston Celtics	3.00	1.50	.30
☐ 7 Artis Gilmore Chicago Bulls	.75	.35	.07
☐ 8 Ricky Sobers Chicago Bulls	.10	.05	.01
☐ 9 Mike Mitchell Cleveland Cavaliers	.10	.05	.01
☐ 10 Tom LaGarde Dallas Mavericks	.10	.05	.01
☐ 11 Dan Issel Denver Nuggets	.75	.35	.07
☐ 12 David Thompson Denver Nuggets	.50	.25	.05
☐ 13 Lloyd Free Golden State Warriors	.20	.10	.02
☐ 14 Moses Malone Houston Rockets	2.75	1.35	.27
☐ 15 Calvin Murphy Houston Rockets	.30	.15	.03
☐ 16 Johnny Davis Indiana Pacers	.10	.05	.01
☐ 17 Otis Birdsong Milwaukee Bucks	.10	.05	.01
☐ 18 Phil Ford Kansas City Kings	.25	.12	.02
☐ 19 Scott Wedman Cleveland Cavaliers	.20	.10	.02
☐ 20 Kareem Abdul-Jabbar Los Angeles Lakers	7.00	3.50	.70
☐ 21 Magic Johnson Los Angeles Lakers	45.00	22.50	4.50
☐ 22 Norm Nixon Los Angeles Lakers	.25	.12	.02
☐ 23 Jamaal Wilkes Los Angeles Lakers	.25	.12	.02
☐ 24 Marques Johnson Milwaukee Bucks	.25	.12	.02
☐ 25 Bob Lanier Milwaukee Bucks	.75	.35	.07
☐ 26 Bill Cartwright New York Knicks	1.00	.50	.10
☐ 27 M.R. Richardson New York Knicks	.20	.10	.02
☐ 28 Ray Williams New York Knicks	.10	.05	.01
☐ 29 Darryl Dawkins Philadelphia 76ers	.40	.20	.04
☐ 30 Julius Erving Philadelphia 76ers	7.00	3.50	.70
☐ 31 Lionel Hollins Philadelphia 76ers	.10	.05	.01
☐ 32 Bobby Jones Philadelphia 76ers	.20	.10	.02
☐ 33 Walter Davis Phoenix Suns	.30	.15	.03
☐ 34 Dennis Johnson Phoenix Suns	.60	.30	.06
☐ 35 Leonard Robinson Phoenix Suns	.10	.05	.01
☐ 36 Mychal Thompson Portland Trail Blazers	.35	.17	.03
☐ 37 George Gervin San Antonio Spurs	1.00	.50	.10
☐ 38 Swen Nater San Diego Clippers	.10	.05	.01
☐ 39 Jack Sikma Seattle Supersonics	.40	.20	.04
☐ 40 Adrian Dantley Utah Jazz	.75	.35	.07
☐ 41 Darrell Griffith Utah Jazz	1.50	.75	.15
☐ 42 Elvin Hayes Houston Rockets	1.25	.60	.12
☐ 43 Fred Brown Seattle Supersonics	.25	.12	.02
☐ 44 Atlanta Hawks TL John Drew Dan Roundfield Eddie Johnson	.15	.07	.01
☐ 45 Boston Celtics TL Larry Bird Larry Bird Nate Archibald	1.50	.75	.15
☐ 46 Chicago Bulls TL Reggie Theus Artis Gilmore Reggie Theus	.20	.10	.02
☐ 47 Cleveland Cavs TL Mike Mitchell Kenny Carr Mike Bratz	.15	.07	.01
☐ 48 Dallas Mavericks TL Jim Spanarkel Tom LaGarde Brad Davis	.15	.07	.01
☐ 49 Denver Nuggets TL David Thompson Dan Issel Kenny Higgs	.25	.12	.02
☐ 50 Detroit Pistons TL John Long Phil Hubbard Ron Lee	.15	.07	.01
☐ 51 Golden State TL Lloyd Free Larry Smith John Lucas	.15	.07	.01
☐ 52 Houston Rockets TL Moses Malone Moses Malone Allen Leavell	.45	.22	.04
☐ 53 Indiana Pacers TL Billy Knight James Edwards Johnny Davis	.15	.07	.01
☐ 54 Kansas City Kings TL Otis Birdsong Reggie King Phil Ford	.15	.07	.01
☐ 55 Los Angeles Lakers TL Kareem Abdul-Jabbar Kareem Abdul-Jabbar Norm Nixon	1.25	.60	.12
☐ 56 Milwaukee Bucks TL Marques Johnson Mickey Johnson Quinn Buckner	.20	.10	.02
☐ 57 New Jersey Nets TL Mike Newlin Maurice Lucas Mike Newlin	.15	.07	.01
☐ 58 New York Knicks TL Bill Cartwright Bill Cartwright M.R. Richardson	.20	.10	.02
☐ 59 Philadelphia 76ers TL Julius Erving Caldwell Jones	1.25	.60	.12

Card			
Maurice Cheeks			
☐ 60 Phoenix Suns TL	.20	.10	.02
Truck Robinson			
Truck Robinson			
Alvan Adams			
☐ 61 Portland Blazers TL	.25	.12	.02
Jim Paxson			
Mychal Thompson			
Kermit Washington			
Kelvin Ransey			
☐ 62 San Antonio Spurs TL	.25	.12	.02
George Gervin			
Dave Corzine			
Johnny Moore			
☐ 63 San Diego Clippers TL	.15	.07	.01
Freeman Williams			
Swen Nater			
Brian Taylor			
☐ 64 Seattle Sonics TL	.25	.12	.02
Jack Sikma			
Jack Sikma			
Vinnie Johnson			
☐ 65 Utah Jazz TL	.25	.12	.02
Adrian Dantley			
Ben Poquette			
Allan Bristow			
☐ 66 Washington Bullets TL	.30	.15	.03
Elvin Hayes			
Elvin Hayes			
Kevin Porter			
☐ E67 Charlie Criss	.15	.07	.01
Atlanta Hawks			
☐ E68 Eddie Johnson	.15	.07	.01
Atlanta Hawks			
☐ E69 Wes Matthews	.15	.07	.01
Atlanta Hawks			
☐ E70 Tom McMillen	.50	.25	.05
Atlanta Hawks			
☐ E71 Tree Rollins	.25	.12	.02
Atlanta Hawks			
☐ E72 M.L. Carr	.25	.12	.02
Boston Celtics			
☐ E73 Chris Ford	.40	.20	.04
Boston Celtics			
☐ E74 Gerald Henderson	.50	.25	.05
Boston Celtics			
☐ E75 Kevin McHale	14.00	7.00	1.40
Boston Celtics			
☐ E76 Rick Robey	.15	.07	.01
Boston Celtics			
☐ E77 Darwin Cook	.30	.15	.03
Milwaukee Bucks			
☐ E78 Mike Gminski	1.00	.50	.10
Milwaukee Bucks			
☐ E79 Maurice Lucas	.25	.12	.02
Milwaukee Bucks			
☐ E80 Mike Newlin	.15	.07	.01
New York Knicks			
☐ E81 Mike O'Koren	.35	.17	.03
Milwaukee Bucks			
☐ E82 Steve Hawes	.15	.07	.01
Atlanta Hawks			
☐ E83 Foots Walker	.15	.07	.01
Milwaukee Bucks			
☐ E84 Campy Russell	.15	.07	.01
New York Knicks			
☐ E85 DeWayne Scales	.15	.07	.01
New York Knicks			
☐ E86 Randy Smith	.15	.07	.01
New York Knicks			
☐ E87 Marvin Webster	.15	.07	.01
New York Knicks			
☐ E88 Sly Williams	.15	.07	.01
New York Knicks			
☐ E89 Mike Woodson	.40	.20	.04
Milwaukee Bucks			
☐ E90 Maurice Cheeks	2.00	1.00	.20
Philadelphia 76ers			
☐ E91 Caldwell Jones	.25	.12	.02
Philadelphia 76ers			
☐ E92 Steve Mix	.15	.07	.01
Philadelphia 76ers			
☐ E93A Checklist 1-110 ERR	2.00	.20	.04
(WEST above card number)			
☐ E93B Checklist 1-110 COR	1.00	.10	.02
☐ E94 Greg Ballard	.15	.07	.01
Washington Bullets			
☐ E95 Don Collins	.15	.07	.01
Washington Bullets			
☐ E96 Kevin Grevey	.15	.07	.01
Washington Bullets			
☐ E97 Mitch Kupchak	.15	.07	.01
Washington Bullets			
☐ E98 Rick Mahorn	1.00	.50	.10
Washington Bullets			
☐ E99 Kevin Porter	.15	.07	.01
Washington Bullets			
☐ E100 Nate Archibald SA	.40	.20	.04
Boston Celtics			
☐ E101 Larry Bird SA	9.00	4.50	.90
Boston Celtics			
☐ E102 Bill Cartwright SA	.40	.20	.04
New York Knicks			
☐ E103 Darryl Dawkins SA	.25	.12	.02
Philadelphia 76ers			
☐ E104 Julius Erving SA	4.00	2.00	.40
Philadelphia 76ers			
☐ E105 Kevin Porter SA	.15	.07	.01
Washington Bullets			
☐ E106 Bobby Jones SA	.25	.12	.02
Philadelphia 76ers			
☐ E107 Cedric Maxwell SA	.25	.12	.02
Boston Celtics			
☐ E108 Robert Parish SA	1.50	.75	.15
Boston Celtics			
☐ E109 M.R.Richardson SA	.25	.12	.02
New York Knicks			
☐ E110 Dan Roundfield SA	.25	.12	.02
Atlanta Hawks			
☐ MW67 David Greenwood	.25	.12	.02
Chicago Bulls			
☐ MW68 Dwight Jones	.15	.07	.01
Chicago Bulls			
☐ MW69 Reggie Theus	.25	.12	.02
Chicago Bulls			
☐ MW70 Bobby Wilkerson	.15	.07	.01
Cleveland Cavaliers			
☐ MW71 Mike Bratz	.15	.07	.01
Cleveland Cavaliers			
☐ MW72 Kenny Carr	.15	.07	.01
Cleveland Cavaliers			
☐ MW73 Geoff Huston	.15	.07	.01
Cleveland Cavaliers			
☐ MW74 Bill Laimbeer	6.00	3.00	.60
Cleveland Cavaliers			
☐ MW75 Roger Phegley	.15	.07	.01
Cleveland Cavaliers			
☐ MW76 Checklist 1-110	1.00	.10	.02
☐ MW77 Abdul Jeelani	.15	.07	.01
Dallas Mavericks			
☐ MW78 Bill Robinzine	.15	.07	.01
Dallas Mavericks			
☐ MW79 Jim Spanarkel	.15	.07	.01
Dallas Mavericks			
☐ MW80 Kent Benson	.25	.12	.02
Detroit Pistons			
☐ MW81 Keith Herron	.15	.07	.01
Detroit Pistons			
☐ MW82 Phil Hubbard	.25	.12	.02
Detroit Pistons			
☐ MW83 John Long	.15	.07	.01
Detroit Pistons			
☐ MW84 Terry Tyler	.15	.07	.01
Detroit Pistons			
☐ MW85 Mike Dunleavy	2.50	1.25	.25
Houston Rockets			
☐ MW86 Tom Henderson	.15	.07	.01
Houston Rockets			
☐ MW87 Billy Paultz	.15	.07	.01
Houston Rockets			
☐ MW88 Robert Reid	.15	.07	.01
Houston Rockets			
☐ MW89 Mike Bantom	.15	.07	.01
Indiana Pacers			
☐ MW90 James Edwards	.35	.17	.03
Cleveland Cavaliers			
☐ MW91 Billy Knight	.15	.07	.01
Indiana Pacers			
☐ MW92 George McGinnis	.30	.15	.03
Indiana Pacers			
☐ MW93 Louis Orr	.15	.07	.01
Indiana Pacers			
☐ MW94 Ernie Grunfeld	.60	.30	.06
Kansas City Kings			
☐ MW95 Reggie King	.15	.07	.01
Kansas City Kings			
☐ MW96 Sam Lacey	.15	.07	.01
Kansas City Kings			
☐ MW97 Junior Bridgeman	.25	.12	.02
Milwaukee Bucks			
☐ MW98 Mickey Johnson	.15	.07	.01
Milwaukee Bucks			
☐ MW99 Sidney Moncrief	1.50	.75	.15
Milwaukee Bucks			
☐ MW100 Brian Winters	.15	.07	.01
Milwaukee Bucks			
☐ MW101 Dave Corzine	.35	.17	.03
San Antonio Spurs			

☐ MW102 Paul Griffin San Antonio Spurs	.15	.07	.01
☐ MW103 Johnny Moore San Antonio Spurs	.30	.15	.03
☐ MW104 Mark Olberding San Antonio Spurs	.15	.07	.01
☐ MW105 James Silas Cleveland Cavaliers	.15	.07	.01
☐ MW106 George Gervin SA San Antonio Spurs	.50	.25	.05
☐ MW107 Artis Gilmore SA Chicago Bulls	.30	.15	.03
☐ MW108 Marq.Johnson SA Milwaukee Bucks	.20	.10	.02
☐ MW109 Bob Lanier SA Milwaukee Bucks	.35	.17	.03
☐ MW110 Moses Malone SA Houston Rockets	1.50	.75	.15
☐ W67 T.R. Dunn Denver Nuggets	.30	.15	.03
☐ W68 Alex English Denver Nuggets	1.75	.85	.17
☐ W69 Billy McKinney Denver Nuggets	.30	.15	.03
☐ W70 Dave Robisch Denver Nuggets	.15	.07	.01
☐ W71 Joe Barry Carroll Golden State Warriors	.60	.30	.06
☐ W72 Bernard King Golden State Warriors	1.50	.75	.15
☐ W73 Sonny Parker Golden State Warriors	.15	.07	.01
☐ W74 Purvis Short Golden State Warriors	.25	.12	.02
☐ W75 Larry Smith Golden State Warriors	.75	.35	.07
☐ W76 Jim Chones Los Angeles Lakers	.15	.07	.01
☐ W77 Michael Cooper Los Angeles Lakers	1.00	.50	.10
☐ W78 Mark Landsberger Los Angeles Lakers	.15	.07	.01
☐ W79 Alvan Adams Phoenix Suns	.25	.12	.02
☐ W80 Jeff Cook Phoenix Suns	.25	.12	.02
☐ W81 Rich Kelley Phoenix Suns	.15	.07	.01
☐ W82 Kyle Macy Phoenix Suns	.35	.17	.03
☐ W83 Billy Ray Bates Portland Trail Blazers	.35	.17	.03
☐ W84 Bob Gross Portland Trail Blazers	.15	.07	.01
☐ W85 Calvin Natt Portland Trail Blazers	.25	.12	.02
☐ W86 Lonnie Shelton Seattle Supersonics	.15	.07	.01
☐ W87 Jim Paxson Portland Trail Blazers	.75	.35	.07
☐ W88 Kelvin Ransey Portland Trail Blazers	.15	.07	.01
☐ W89 Kermit Washington Portland Trail Blazers	.15	.07	.01
☐ W90 Henry Bibby San Diego Clippers	.15	.07	.01
☐ W91 Michael Brooks San Diego Clippers	.25	.12	.02
☐ W92 Joe Bryant San Diego Clippers	.15	.07	.01
☐ W93 Phil Smith San Diego Clippers	.15	.07	.01
☐ W94 Brian Taylor San Diego Clippers	.15	.07	.01
☐ W95 Freeman Williams San Diego Clippers	.25	.12	.02
☐ W96 James Bailey Seattle Supersonics	.15	.07	.01
☐ W97 Checklist 1-110	1.00	.10	.02
☐ W98 John Johnson Seattle Supersonics	.15	.07	.01
☐ W99 Vinnie Johnson Seattle Supersonics	2.50	1.25	.25
☐ W100 Wally Walker Seattle Supersonics	.30	.15	.03
☐ W101 Paul Westphal Seattle Supersonics	.30	.15	.03
☐ W102 Allan Bristow Utah Jazz	.25	.12	.02
☐ W103 Wayne Cooper Utah Jazz	.25	.12	.02
☐ W104 Carl Nicks Utah Jazz	.25	.12	.02
☐ W105 Ben Poquette Utah Jazz	.15	.07	.01
☐ W106 Kareem Abdul-Jabbar SA Los Angeles Lakers	4.00	2.00	.40
☐ W107 Dan Issel SA Denver Nuggets	.40	.20	.04
☐ W108 Dennis Johnson SA Phoenix Suns	.40	.20	.04
☐ W109 Magic Johnson SA Los Angeles Lakers	15.00	7.50	1.50
☐ W110 Jack Sikma SA Seattle Supersonics	.35	.17	.03

1977-78 Trail Blazers Police

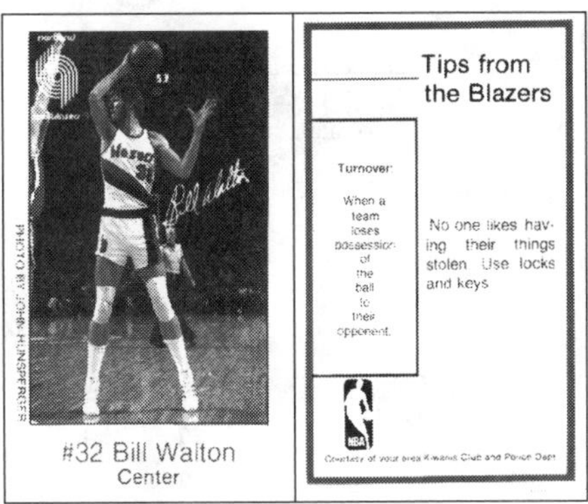

This set contains 14 cards measuring 2 5/8" by 4 1/8" featuring the Portland Trail Blazers. The cards are unnumbered except for uniform number. Backs contain safety tips ("Tips from the Blazers") and are written in black ink with red accent. The set was sponsored by the Kiwanis and the Police Department.

	NRMT	VG-E	GOOD
COMPLETE SET (14)	60.00	30.00	6.00
COMMON CARD	3.00	1.50	.30
☐ 10 Corky Calhoun	3.00	1.50	.30
☐ 13 Dave Twardzik	5.00	2.50	.50
☐ 14 Lionel Hollins	5.00	2.50	.50
☐ 15 Larry Steele	3.00	1.50	.30
☐ 16 Johnny Davis	3.00	1.50	.30
☐ 20 Maurice Lucas	6.00	3.00	.60
☐ 23 T.R. Dunn	4.00	2.00	.40
☐ 25 Tom Owens	3.00	1.50	.30
☐ 30 Bob Gross	4.00	2.00	.40
☐ 32 Bill Walton	20.00	10.00	2.00
☐ 36 Lloyd Neal	3.00	1.50	.30
☐ xx Jack Ramsay CO	4.00	2.00	.40
☐ xx Jack McKinney assistant coach	4.00	2.00	.40
☐ xx Ron Culp, trainer	3.00	1.50	.30

1979-80 Trail Blazers Police

This set contains 16 cards measuring 2 5/8" by 4 1/8" featuring the Portland Trail Blazers. Backs contain safety tips and are available with either light red or maroon printing on the backs. The year of issue and a facsimile autograph are printed on the front of the cards. The set was sponsored by 7-Up, Safeway, Kiwanis, KEX-1190AM, and the Police Departments. The cards are ordered below according to uniform number. The set features an early professional card of Mychal Thompson.

	MINT	EXC	G-VG
COMPLETE SET (16)	12.50	6.25	1.25

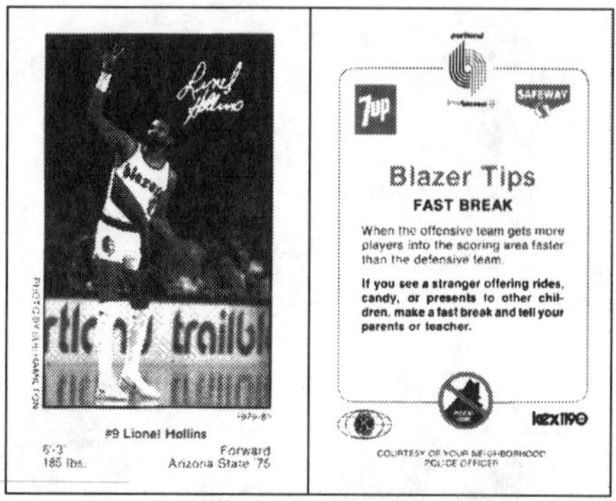

COMMON PLAYER (1-16)	.60	.30	.06
☐ 4 Jim Paxson	1.00	.50	.10
☐ 9 Lionel Hollins	1.00	.50	.10
☐ 10 Ron Brewer	.75	.35	.07
☐ 11 Abdul Jeelani	.60	.30	.06
☐ 13 Dave Twardzik	1.00	.50	.10
☐ 15 Larry Steele	.60	.30	.06
☐ 20 Maurice Lucas	1.50	.75	.15
☐ 23 T.R. Dunn	.60	.30	.06
☐ 25 Tom Owens	.60	.30	.06
☐ 30 Bob Gross	.75	.35	.07
☐ 42 Kermit Washington	.75	.35	.07
☐ 43 Mychal Thompson	1.50	.75	.15
☐ 44 Kevin Kunnert	.60	.30	.06
☐ xx Jack Ramsay CO	.75	.35	.07
☐ xx Morris "Bucky" Buckwalter, Assistant Coach	.60	.30	.06
☐ xx Bill Schonely, Voice of the Blazers	.60	.30	.06

1981-82 Trail Blazers Police

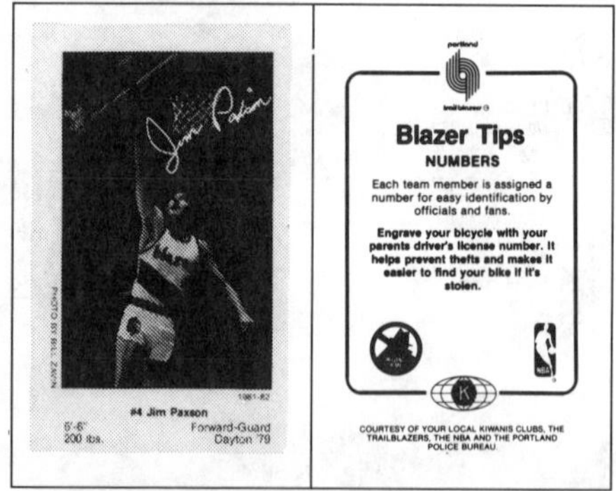

This set contains 16 cards measuring 2 5/8" by 4 1/8" featuring the Portland Trail Blazers. Backs contain safety tips and are written in black ink with red accent. Cards are unnumbered except for uniform number. The year of issue is indicated on the card front. The set was produced courtesy of Kiwanis, the Trail Blazers, the NBA, and the Portland Police Bureau.

	MINT	EXC	G-VG
COMPLETE SET (16)	10.00	5.00	1.00
COMMON PLAYER (1-16)	.50	.25	.05
☐ 3 Jeff Lamp	.60	.30	.06
☐ 4 Jim Paxson	.75	.35	.07
☐ 10 Darnell Valentine	.75	.35	.07
☐ 12 Billy Ray Bates	.75	.35	.07
☐ 14 Kelvin Ransey	.75	.35	.07
☐ 30 Bob Gross	.75	.35	.07
☐ 31 Peter Verhoeven	.50	.25	.05
☐ 32 Mike Harper	.50	.25	.05
☐ 33 Calvin Natt	.75	.35	.07
☐ 40 Petur Gudmundsson	.50	.25	.05
☐ 42 Kermit Washington	.75	.35	.07
☐ 43 Mychal Thompson	1.00	.50	.10
☐ 44 Kevin Kunnert	.50	.25	.05
☐ xx Jack Ramsay CO	.75	.35	.07
☐ xx Morris Buckwalter, Assistant Coach	.50	.25	.05
☐ xx Jimmy Lynam ACO	.75	.35	.07

1982-83 Trail Blazers Police

This set contains 16 cards measuring 2 5/8" by 4 1/8" featuring the Portland Trail Blazers. Backs contain safety tips and are written in black ink with red accent. The year of issue and a facsimile autograph are given on the front. The cards are ordered below according to uniform number. The set features the first professional card of Lafayette "Fat" Lever.

	MINT	EXC	G-VG
COMPLETE SET (16)	8.00	4.00	.80
COMMON PLAYER	.50	.25	.05
☐ 2 Linton Townes	.50	.25	.05
☐ 3 Jeff Lamp	.60	.30	.06
☐ 4 Jim Paxson	.75	.35	.07
☐ 12 Lafayette Lever	1.50	.75	.15
☐ 14 Darnell Valentine	.50	.25	.05
☐ 22 Jeff Judkins	.50	.25	.05
☐ 24 Audie Norris	.50	.25	.05
☐ 31 Peter Verhoeven	.50	.25	.05
☐ 33 Calvin Natt	.75	.35	.07
☐ 34 Kenny Carr	.75	.35	.07
☐ 42 Wayne Cooper	.75	.35	.07
☐ 43 Mychal Thompson	1.00	.50	.10
☐ xx Jack Ramsay CO	.75	.35	.07
☐ xx Morris Buckwalter, Assistant Coach	.50	.25	.05
☐ xx Jim Lynam ACO	.75	.35	.07

1983-84 Trail Blazers Police

This set contains 16 cards measuring 2 5/8" by 4 1/8" featuring the Portland Trail Blazers. Backs contain safety tips ("Blazer Tips") and are written in black ink with red accent. Drexler and the coaches are the only cards without small inset photo. The year of issue is indicated on the front of the card. A facsimile autograph is printed on the back of the card. The cards are ordered below according to uniform number. This set features one of Clyde Drexler's first cards.

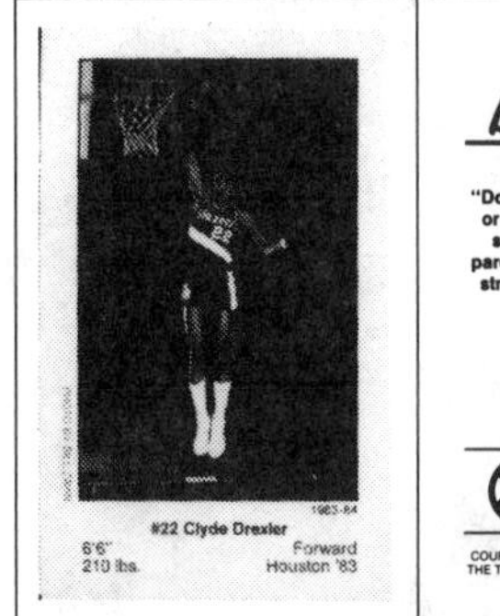

	MINT	EXC	G-VG
COMPLETE SET (16)	12.00	6.00	1.20
COMMON PLAYER	.35	.17	.03
□ 3 Jeff Lamp	.45	.22	.04
□ 4 Jim Paxson	.60	.30	.06
□ 12 Lafayette Lever	.75	.35	.07
□ 14 Darnell Valentine	.45	.22	.04
□ 22 Clyde Drexler	7.50	3.75	.75
□ 24 Audie Norris	.35	.17	.03
□ 31 Peter Verhoeven	.35	.17	.03
□ 33 Calvin Natt	.45	.22	.04
□ 34 Kenny Carr	.45	.22	.04
□ 42 Wayne Cooper	.45	.22	.04
□ 43 Mychal Thompson	.75	.35	.07
□ 54 Tom Piotrowski	.35	.17	.03
□ xx Jack Ramsay CO	.45	.22	.04
□ xx Morris Buckwalter, Assistant Coach	.35	.17	.03
□ xx Rick Adelman, Assistant Coach	.60	.30	.06
□ xx Ron Culp, Trainer	.35	.17	.03
□ xx Dave Twardzik and Bill Schonely, The Blazer Voices	.35	.17	.03

1984-85 Trail Blazers Franz/Star

This 13-card set was produced for the Franz Bakery in Portland, Oregon by the Star Company. One card was placed in each loaf of Franz Bread as a promotional giveaway. Cards were printed with FDA approved vegetable ink. Cards measure 2 1/2" by 3 1/2" and have a red border around the fronts of the cards and red printing on the backs. Cards feature the Franz logo on the fronts. These numbered cards were ordered alphabetically by player. The set features one of the first professional cards of Jerome Kersey.

	MINT	EXC	G-VG
COMPLETE SET (13)	70.00	35.00	7.00
COMMON PLAYER (1-13)	2.00	1.00	.20
□ 1 Jack Ramsay CO	2.50	1.25	.25
□ 2 Sam Bowie	7.50	3.75	.75
□ 3 Kenny Carr	2.50	1.25	.25
□ 4 Steve Colter	2.00	1.00	.20
□ 5 Clyde Drexler	45.00	22.50	4.50
□ 6 Jerome Kersey	25.00	12.50	2.50
□ 7 Audie Norris	2.00	1.00	.20
□ 8 Jim Paxson	2.50	1.25	.25
□ 9 Tom Scheffler	2.00	1.00	.20
□ 10 Bernard Thompson	2.00	1.00	.20
□ 11 Mychal Thompson	3.50	1.75	.35
□ 12 Darnell Valentine	2.50	1.25	.25
□ 13 Kiki Vandeweghe	4.50	2.25	.45

1984-85 Trail Blazers Police

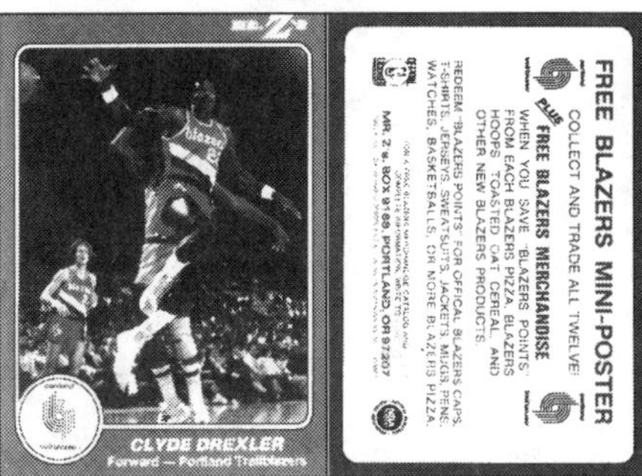

This set contains 16 cards measuring 2 5/8" by 4 1/8" featuring the Portland Trail Blazers. Backs contain safety tips ("Blazer Tips") and are written in black ink with red accent. The cards are numbered in the upper left corner of the obverse; the year of issue is indicated in the lower right corner. The set features one of the first professional cards of Jerome Kersey.

	MINT	EXC	G-VG
COMPLETE SET (16)	10.00	5.00	1.00
COMMON PLAYER (1-16)	.25	.12	.02
□ 1 Portland Team	.35	.17	.03
□ 2 Jim Paxson	.50	.25	.05
□ 3 Bernard Thompson	.35	.17	.03
□ 4 Darnell Valentine	.25	.12	.02
□ 5 Jack Ramsay CO, Rick Adelman, Asst. and Morris Buckwalter, Assistant Coach	.35	.17	.03
□ 6 Steve Colter	.25	.12	.02
□ 7 Clyde Drexler	4.50	2.25	.45
□ 8 Audie Norris	.25	.12	.02
□ 9 Jerome Kersey	3.00	1.50	.30
□ 10 Sam Bowie	1.25	.60	.12
□ 11 Kenny Carr	.35	.17	.03
□ 12 Lloyd Neal	.35	.17	.03
□ 13 Mychal Thompson	.50	.25	.05
□ 14 Geoff Petrie	.35	.17	.03
□ 15 Tom Scheffler	.25	.12	.02
□ 16 Kiki Vandeweghe	.50	.25	.05

1985-86 Trail Blazers Franz/Star

The 1985-86 Franz Portland Trail Blazers set was produced by The Star Company for Franz Bread. There are 12 player cards and one coach card. The front borders are reddish orange, and the backs feature statistics and biographical information. The cards measure standard size, 2 1/2" by 3 1/2". These numbered cards were ordered alphabetically by player. The set features the first professional card of Terry Porter.

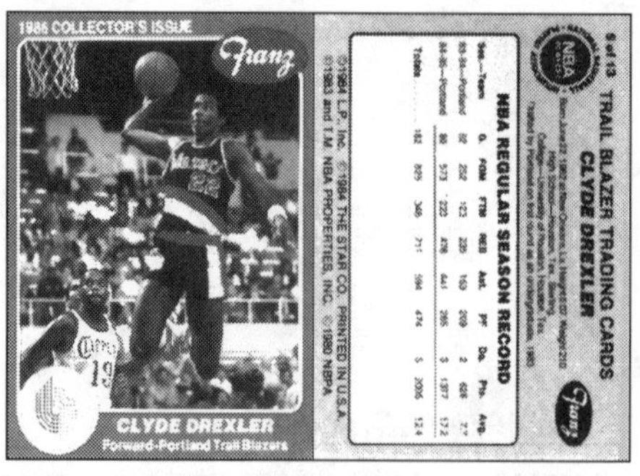

	MINT	EXC	G-VG
COMPLETE SET (13)	65.00	32.50	6.50
COMMON PLAYER (1-13)	2.00	1.00	.20
☐ 1 Jack Ramsay CO	2.50	1.25	.25
☐ 2 Sam Bowie	4.00	2.00	.40
☐ 3 Kenny Carr	2.50	1.25	.25
☐ 4 Steve Colter	2.00	1.00	.20
☐ 5 Clyde Drexler	30.00	15.00	3.00
☐ 6 Ken Johnson	2.00	1.00	.20
☐ 7 Caldwell Jones	2.50	1.25	.25
☐ 8 Jerome Kersey	12.00	6.00	1.20
☐ 9 Jim Paxson	2.50	1.25	.25
☐ 10 Terry Porter	25.00	12.50	2.50
☐ 11 Mychal Thompson	3.00	1.50	.30
☐ 12 Darnell Valentine	2.50	1.25	.25
☐ 13 Kiki Vandeweghe	3.00	1.50	.30

1986-87 Trail Blazers Franz/Star

The 1986-87 Franz Portland Trail Blazers set was produced by The Star Company for Franz Bread. There are 12 player cards and one coach card. The front borders are reddish-orange, and the backs feature statistics and biographical information. Card backs are printed in pink and red on white card stock. The cards measure standard size, 2 1/2" by 3 1/2". These numbered cards were ordered alphabetically by player.

	MINT	EXC	G-VG
COMPLETE SET (13)	45.00	22.50	4.50
COMMON PLAYER (1-13)	2.00	1.00	.20
☐ 1 Walter Berry	3.00	1.50	.30
☐ 2 Sam Bowie	3.00	1.50	.30
☐ 3 Kenny Carr	2.50	1.25	.25
☐ 4 Clyde Drexler	25.00	12.50	2.50
☐ 5 Michael Holton	2.50	1.25	.25
☐ 6 Steve Johnson	2.50	1.25	.25
☐ 7 Caldwell Jones	2.50	1.25	.25
☐ 8 Jerome Kersey	10.00	5.00	1.00
☐ 9 Fernando Martin	2.00	1.00	.20
☐ 10 Jim Paxson	2.50	1.25	.25
☐ 11 Terry Porter	12.00	6.00	1.20
☐ 12 Kiki Vandeweghe	3.00	1.50	.30
☐ 13 Mike Schuler CO	2.00	1.00	.20

1987-88 Trail Blazers Franz

This 13-card was produced by Fleer as a promotion for Franz Bread. The cards measure the standard size (2 1/2" by 3 1/2") and were distributed in loaves of Franz Bread. The backs have biographical and statistical information. The cards are numbered on the back and are ordered alphabetically by player.

	MINT	EXC	G-VG
COMPLETE SET (13)	50.00	25.00	5.00
COMMON PLAYER (1-13)	2.00	1.00	.20
☐ 1 Clyde Drexler	25.00	12.50	2.50
☐ 2 Kevin Duckworth	6.00	3.00	.60
☐ 3 Michael Holton	2.00	1.00	.20
☐ 4 Steve Johnson	2.00	1.00	.20
☐ 5 Caldwell Jones	2.50	1.25	.25
☐ 6 Jerome Kersey	10.00	5.00	1.00
☐ 7 Maurice Lucas	3.00	1.50	.30
☐ 8 Jim Paxson	2.50	1.25	.25
☐ 9 Terry Porter	12.00	6.00	1.20
☐ 10 Mike Schuler CO	2.00	1.00	.20
☐ 11 Kiki Vandeweghe	2.50	1.25	.25
☐ 12 Steve Johnson	2.00	1.00	.20
☐ 13 Kiki Vandeweghe	2.50	1.25	.25

1988-89 Trail Blazers Franz

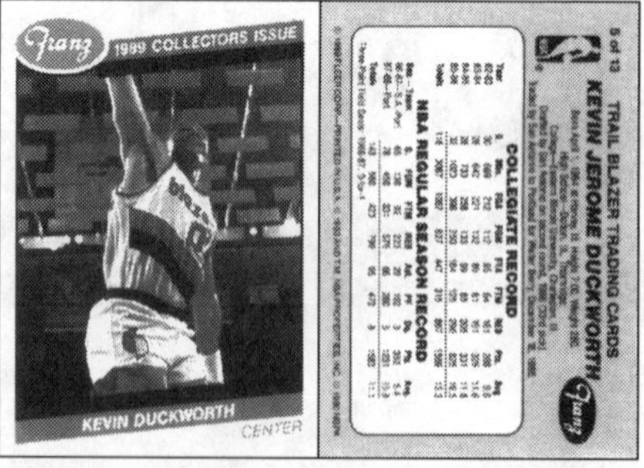

The 1988-89 Franz Portland Trail Blazers set was produced by The Fleer Corporation for Franz Bread. There are 12 player cards and one coach card. The front borders are white with red bars and the backs feature statistics and biographical information. Card backs are printed in pink and red on white card stock. The cards measure standard size, 2 1/2" by 3 1/2". These numbered cards were ordered alphabetically by player.

	MINT	EXC	G-VG
COMPLETE SET (13)	30.00	15.00	3.00
COMMON PLAYER (1-13)	1.50	.75	.15
☐ 1 Richard Anderson	1.50	.75	.15
☐ 2 Sam Bowie	2.50	1.25	.25
☐ 3 Mark Bryant	2.00	1.00	.20
☐ 4 Clyde Drexler	15.00	7.50	1.50
☐ 5 Kevin Duckworth	4.00	2.00	.40
☐ 6 Rolando Ferreira	2.00	1.00	.20
☐ 7 Steve Johnson	1.50	.75	.15
☐ 8 Caldwell Jones	2.00	1.00	.20
☐ 9 Jerome Kersey	5.00	2.50	.50
☐ 10 Terry Porter	6.00	3.00	.60
☐ 11 Mike Schuler CO	1.50	.75	.15
☐ 12 Jerry Sichting	2.00	1.00	.20
☐ 13 Kiki Vandeweghe	2.00	1.00	.20

1989-90 Trail Blazers Franz

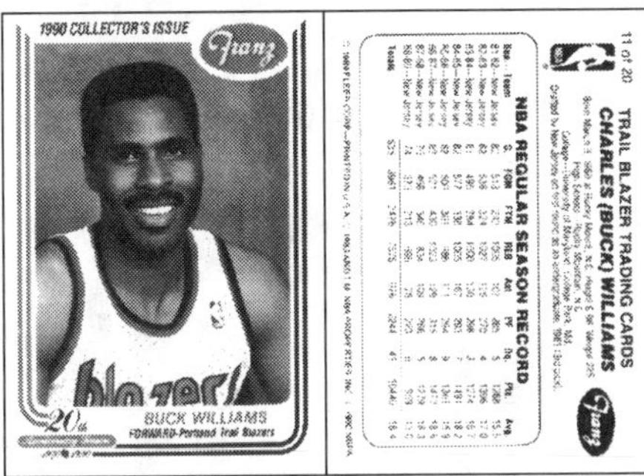

This 20-card set was produced by the Fleer Corporation for Franz Bread. The set commemorates the 20th anniversary season of the Trail Blazers and showcases current players as well as some "Blazer Greats" from past teams. The cards measure the standard size (2 1/2" by 3 1/2"). The front features color action photos on white card stock, with orange border stripes on the left side and black border stripes on the right side and bottom of the picture. The Franz Bread logo appears in the upper right corner. The horizontally oriented back has biographical and statistical information, printed in pink and red on white card stock. The cards are numbered on the back. The set ordering is alphabetical within each group of current (1-11) and past (12-20) Trail Blazers. The set features the first professional card of Drazen Petrovic.

	MINT	EXC	G-VG
COMPLETE SET (20)	25.00	12.50	2.50
COMMON PLAYER (1-11)	.75	.35	.07
COMMON PLAYER (12-20)	.75	.35	.07
☐ 1 Rick Adelman CO	1.00	.50	.10
☐ 2 Mark Bryant	.90	.45	.09
☐ 3 Wayne Cooper	.75	.35	.07
☐ 4 Kevin Duckworth	2.50	1.25	.25
☐ 5 Clyde Drexler	10.00	5.00	1.00
☐ 6 Byron Irvin	.90	.45	.09
☐ 7 Jerome Kersey	3.50	1.75	.35
☐ 8 Drazen Petrovic	2.50	1.25	.25
☐ 9 Terry Porter	4.50	2.25	.45
☐ 10 Cliff Robertson	3.00	1.50	.30
☐ 11 Buck Williams	2.50	1.25	.25
☐ 12 Lionel Hollins	.90	.45	.09
☐ 13 Maurice Lucas	1.25	.60	.12
☐ 14 Calvin Natt	.90	.45	.09
☐ 15 Lloyd Neal	.75	.35	.07
☐ 16 Jim Paxson	.90	.45	.09
☐ 17 Geoff Petrie	1.00	.50	.10
☐ 18 Larry Steele	.75	.35	.07
☐ 19 Mychal Thompson	.90	.45	.09
☐ 20 Bill Walton	2.00	1.00	.20

1990-91 Trail Blazers British Petroleum

These large (approximately 8 1/2" by 11") high-gloss action player photos were taken by Bryan Drake. The photos are printed on thin paper and have white, red, and white borders (in that order), on a black background. The player's name appears below the picture, between the team and the sponsor's logos. The backs are blank. The set features members of the Portland Trail Blazers. These unnumbered cards were ordered alphabetically by player in the checklist below.

	MINT	EXC	G-VG
COMPLETE SET (6)	12.00	6.00	1.20
COMMON PLAYER (1-6)	1.50	.75	.15
☐ 1 Danny Ainge	2.00	1.00	.20
☐ 2 Clyde Drexler	6.00	3.00	.60
☐ 3 Kevin Duckworth	1.50	.75	.15
☐ 4 Jerome Kersey	2.50	1.25	.25
☐ 5 Terry Porter	3.00	1.50	.30
☐ 6 Buck Williams	2.50	1.25	.25

1990-91 Trail Blazers Franz

This 20-card set was produced by the Fleer Corporation for Franz Bread for distribution in the Portland area. The cards measure the standard size (2 1/2" by 3 1/2"). The fronts feature color action player photos on a white card face, with black borders on the left side and red borders on the right. The Franz logo appears in a blue oval in the upper left corner, with the words "1991 Collector's Issue" to the right. The player's name, position, and team name appear below the picture. The back has biographical information and player statistics printed in pink and red on white. The cards are numbered on the back. The team card can be found with and without the notation, 1989-90 Western Conference Champions, at the bottom of the (horizontally oriented) obverse. The set features an early professional card of Cliff Robinson.

	MINT	EXC	G-VG
COMPLETE SET (20)	18.00	9.00	1.80
COMMON PLAYER (1-20)	.50	.25	.05

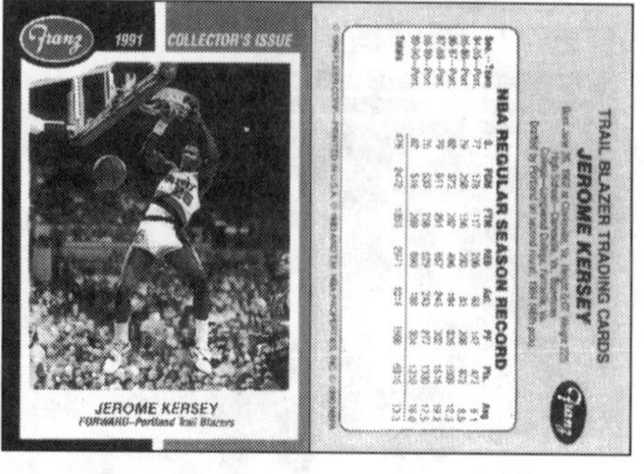

☐ 1 Team Card	1.00	.50	.10
☐ 2 '89-90 Playoffs	.50	.25	.05
☐ 3 '89-90 Playoffs	.50	.25	.05
☐ 4 '89-90 Playoffs	.50	.25	.05
☐ 5 '89-90 Playoffs	.50	.25	.05
☐ 6 Bill Walton	1.50	.75	.15
☐ 7 Rick Adelman CO	.75	.35	.07
☐ 8 John Schalow CO and John Wetzel CO	.50	.25	.05
☐ 9 Alaa Abdelnaby	1.00	.50	.10
☐ 10 Danny Ainge	1.00	.50	.10
☐ 11 Mark Bryant	.60	.30	.06
☐ 12 Wayne Cooper	.50	.25	.05
☐ 13 Clyde Drexler	5.00	2.50	.50
☐ 14 Kevin Duckworth	1.25	.60	.12
☐ 15 Jerome Kersey	1.75	.85	.17
☐ 16 Drazen Petrovic	1.25	.60	.12
☐ 17 Terry Porter	2.25	1.10	.22
☐ 18 Cliff Robinson	1.50	.75	.15
☐ 19 Buck Williams	1.50	.75	.15
☐ 20 Danny Young	.50	.25	.05

1991-92 Trail Blazers Franz

This 17-card standard size (2 1/2" by 3 1/2") set was produced by Hoops for Franz Bread. The print run was 150,000 of each card. Beginning in November, one card per week was issued in a plastic sleeve in loaves of Franz Premium White Bread and Franz 100 Percent Wheat Bread. Robert Pack made the roster in October, and his card (17) was added to the rotation for distribution in February. After the 17-week promotion, Franz repeated each card statewide for one day each to allow collectors who might have missed one or more cards to complete their sets. The front features a full-bleed gold border with a color action photo at a slight angle within a three-sided black border and a red border at the bottom. The player's name appears in a black border beneath the picture. The horizontally oriented backs display a head shot, biography, statistics (by season and career), and career highlights. The cards are numbered in a basketball icon at the upper right corner.

	MINT	EXC	G-VG
COMPLETE SET (17)	15.00	7.50	1.50
COMMON PLAYER (1-17)	.50	.25	.05
☐ 1 Team Photo	1.00	.50	.10
☐ 2 Blazers All-Star Weekend	.50	.25	.05
☐ 3 Buck Williams NBA All-Defensive 1st Team	1.00	.50	.10
☐ 4 Rick Adelman CO	.75	.35	.07
☐ 5 Alaa Abdelnaby	.75	.35	.07
☐ 6 Danny Ainge	1.00	.50	.10
☐ 7 Mark Bryant	.60	.30	.06
☐ 8 Wayne Cooper	.50	.25	.05
☐ 9 Walter Davis	1.00	.50	.10
☐ 10 Clyde Drexler	4.50	2.25	.45
☐ 11 Kevin Duckworth	1.00	.50	.10
☐ 12 Jerome Kersey	1.50	.75	.15
☐ 13 Terry Porter	2.00	1.00	.20
☐ 14 Cliff Robinson	1.00	.50	.10
☐ 15 Buck Williams	1.25	.60	.12
☐ 16 Danny Young	.50	.25	.05
☐ 17 Robert Pack	2.50	1.25	.25

1957-59 Union Oil Booklets *

These booklets were distributed by Union Oil. The front cover of each booklet features a drawing of the subject player. The booklets are numbered and were issued over several years beginning in 1957. These are 12-page pamphlets and are approximately 4" by 5 1/2". The set is subtitled "Family Sports Fun." This was apparently a primarily Southern California promotion.

	NRMT	VG-E	GOOD
COMPLETE SET (44)	150.00	75.00	15.00
COMMON PLAYER (1-44)	3.00	1.50	.30
☐ 1 Elroy Hirsch Football 57	7.50	3.75	.75
☐ 2 Les Richter Football 57	5.00	2.50	.50
☐ 3 Frankie Albert Football 57	5.00	2.50	.50
☐ 4 Y.A. Tittle Football 57	10.00	5.00	1.00
☐ 5 Bill Russell Basketball 57	20.00	10.00	2.00

☐ 6 Forrest Twogood Basketball 57	5.00	2.50	.50
☐ 7 Bob Richards Body Conditioning 57	5.00	2.50	.50
☐ 8 Phil Woolpert Basketball 58	5.00	2.50	.50
☐ 9 Bill Sharman Basketball 58	7.50	3.75	.75
☐ 10 Alf Engen Skiing 58	3.00	1.50	.30
☐ 11 Bob Mathias Track 58	5.00	2.50	.50
☐ 12 Duke Snider Baseball 58	10.00	5.00	1.00
☐ 13 Payton Jordan Track 58	3.00	1.50	.30
☐ 14 Bob Lemon Baseball 58	7.50	3.75	.75
☐ 15 Red Schoendienst Baseball 58	7.50	3.75	.75
☐ 16 Johnny Dieckman Fishing 58	3.00	1.50	.30
☐ 17 Pancho Gonzalez Tennis 58	3.00	1.50	.30
☐ 18 Mal Whitfield Track 58	3.00	1.50	.30
☐ 19 Mike Peppe Swimming 58	3.00	1.50	.30
☐ 20 Bill Rigney Baseball 58	3.00	1.50	.30
☐ 21 Nancy Chaffee Kiner Tennis 58	3.00	1.50	.30
☐ 22 Lloyd Mangrum Golf 58	3.00	1.50	.30
☐ 23 Pat McCormick Diving 58	3.00	1.50	.30
☐ 24 Perry T. Jones Tennis 58	3.00	1.50	.30
☐ 25 Howard Hill Archery 58	3.00	1.50	.30
☐ 26 Herb Parsons Hunting 58	3.00	1.50	.30
☐ 27 Bob Waterfield Football 58	9.00	4.50	.90
☐ 28 Pete Elliott Football 58	5.00	2.50	.50
☐ 29 Elroy Hirsch Football 58	7.50	3.75	.75
☐ 30 Frank Gifford Football 58	10.00	5.00	1.00
☐ 31 George Yardley Basketball 58	5.00	2.50	.50
☐ 32 John Wooden Basketball 58	9.00	4.50	.90
☐ 33 Ralph Borrelli Tumbling 58	3.00	1.50	.30
☐ 34 Bob Cousy Basketball 59	10.00	5.00	1.00
☐ 35 Yves Latreille Skiing 59	3.00	1.50	.30
☐ 36 Slats Gill Basketball 59	5.00	2.50	.50
☐ 37 Jess Mortensen Track 59	3.00	1.50	.30
☐ 38 Jackie Jensen Baseball 59	6.00	3.00	.60
☐ 39 Warren Spahn Baseball 59	9.00	4.50	.90
☐ 40 Jack Kramer Tennis 59	5.00	2.50	.50
☐ 41 Ernie Banks Baseball 59	9.00	4.50	.90
☐ 42 Cary Middlecoff Golf 59	3.00	1.50	.30
☐ 43 Greta Andersen Swimming 59	3.00	1.50	.30
☐ 44 Lon Garrison Camping 59	3.00	1.50	.30

1961 Union Oil

The 1961 Union Oil basketball card set contains 10 oversized (3" by 3 15/16"), attractive, brown-tinted cards. The cards feature players from the Hawaii Chiefs of the American Basketball League. The backs, printed in dark blue ink, feature a short biography of the player, an ad for KGU radio and the Union Oil

circle 76 logo. The catalog number for this set is UO-17. These unnumbered cards are ordered alphabetically by player in the checklist below.

	NRMT	VG-E	GOOD
COMPLETE SET (10)	125.00	60.00	12.50
COMMON PLAYER (1-10)	15.00	7.50	1.50
☐ 1 Frank Burgess	15.00	7.50	1.50
☐ 2 Jeff Cohen	15.00	7.50	1.50
☐ 3 Lee Harman	15.00	7.50	1.50
☐ 4 Rick Herrscher	15.00	7.50	1.50
☐ 5 Lowery Kirk	15.00	7.50	1.50
☐ 6 Dave Mills	15.00	7.50	1.50
☐ 7 Max Perry	15.00	7.50	1.50
☐ 8 George Price	15.00	7.50	1.50
☐ 9 Fred Sawyer	15.00	7.50	1.50
☐ 10 Dale Wise	15.00	7.50	1.50

1991-92 Upper Deck McDonald's

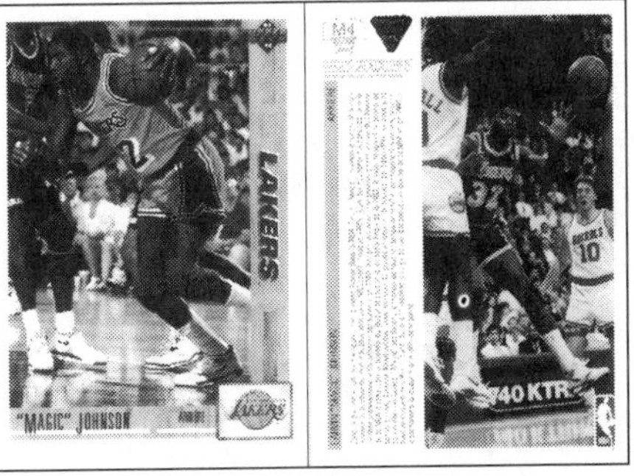

This 11-card set was issued by Upper Deck to highlight their involvement in the McDonald's Open held in Paris, France on October 18-19, 1991. The McDonald's Open features four leading international basketball teams, including the Los Angeles Lakers and three European teams. A special 11" by 8 1/2" commemorative sheet and card packs, containing five Laker player cards and a special hologram card, were distributed to fans attending the event. The front design was the same as the regular issue cards, featuring a full color player photo with a wooden basketball court border on the right and bottom of the picture. The backs have a different color action photo and brief biography of the player in French. The cards are numbered on the back.

	MINT	EXC	G-VG
COMPLETE SET (11)	20.00	10.00	2.00
COMMON PLAYER (1-10)	1.00	.50	.10
☐ M1 Elden Campbell	2.00	1.00	.20

Card	MINT	EXC	G-VG
☐ M2 Vlade Divac	2.00	1.00	.20
☐ M3 A.C. Green	1.50	.75	.15
☐ M4 Magic Johnson	10.00	5.00	1.00
☐ M5 Sam Perkins	2.00	1.00	.20
☐ M6 Byron Scott	1.50	.75	.15
☐ M7 Tony Smith	1.00	.50	.10
☐ M8 Terry Teagle	1.00	.50	.10
☐ M9 James Worthy	4.00	2.00	.40
☐ M10 Checklist	1.00	.50	.10
☐ xx Hologram card	7.50	3.75	.75

1991-92 Upper Deck

The 1991-92 Upper Deck low series basketball set contains 400 cards, measuring the standard size (2 1/2" by 3 1/2"). Six NBA Award Winner holograms were randomly inserted in high series foil packs. The fronts feature glossy color player photos, bordered below and on the right by a hardwood basketball floor design. The player's name appears beneath the picture, while the team name is printed vertically alongside the picture. The backs display a second color player photo as well as biographical and statistical information. Special subsets featured include Draft Choices (1-21), Classic Confrontations (30-34), All-Rookie Team (35-39), All-Stars (49-72), and Team Checklists (73-99). The key rookie cards in this series are Stacey Augmon, Larry Johnson, Dikembe Mutombo, Steve Smith, and John Starks.

	MINT	EXC	G-VG
COMPLETE SET (400)	23.00	10.00	2.00
COMMON PLAYER (1-400)	.03	.01	.00
☐ 1 Draft Checklist (Stacey Augmon and Rodney Monroe)	.30	.15	.03
☐ 2 Larry Johnson	9.00	4.50	.90
☐ 3 Dikembe Mutombo	5.00	2.50	.50
☐ 4 Steve Smith	2.00	1.00	.20
☐ 5 Stacey Augmon	1.75	.85	.17
☐ 6 Terrell Brandon	.75	.35	.07
☐ 7 Greg Anthony	.75	.35	.07
☐ 8 Rich King	.15	.07	.01
☐ 9 Chris Gatling	.40	.20	.04
☐ 10 Victor Alexander	.30	.15	.03
☐ 11 John Turner	.15	.07	.01
☐ 12 Eric Murdock	.35	.17	.03
☐ 13 Mark Randall	.15	.07	.01
☐ 14 Rodney Monroe	.30	.15	.03
☐ 15 Myron Brown	.10	.05	.01
☐ 16 Mike Iuzzolino	.30	.15	.03
☐ 17 Chris Corchiani	.20	.10	.02
☐ 18 Elliot Perry	.15	.07	.01
☐ 19 Jimmy Oliver	.12	.06	.01
☐ 20 Doug Overton	.10	.05	.01
☐ 21 Steve Hood UER (Card has NBA record, but he's a rookie)	.10	.05	.01
☐ 22 Michael Jordan Stay In School	.50	.25	.05
☐ 23 Kevin Johnson Stay In School	.10	.05	.01
☐ 24 Kurk Lee	.10	.05	.01
☐ 25 Sean Higgins	.15	.07	.01
☐ 26 Morlon Wiley	.03	.01	.00
☐ 27 Derek Smith	.03	.01	.00
☐ 28 Kenny Payne	.03	.01	.00
☐ 29 Magic Johnson Assist Record	1.00	.50	.10
☐ 30 Larry Bird CC and Chuck Person	.20	.10	.02
☐ 31 Karl Malone CC and Charles Barkley	.20	.10	.02
☐ 32 Kevin Johnson CC and John Stockton	.20	.10	.02
☐ 33 Hakeem Olajuwon CC and Patrick Ewing	.20	.10	.02
☐ 34 Magic Johnson CC and Michael Jordan	1.00	.50	.10
☐ 35 Derrick Coleman ART	.25	.12	.02
☐ 36 Lionel Simmons ART	.15	.07	.01
☐ 37 Dee Brown ART	.20	.10	.02
☐ 38 Dennis Scott ART	.10	.05	.01
☐ 39 Kendall Gill ART	.40	.20	.04
☐ 40 Winston Garland	.03	.01	.00
☐ 41 Danny Young	.03	.01	.00
☐ 42 Rick Mahorn	.06	.03	.00
☐ 43 Michael Adams	.08	.04	.01
☐ 44 Michael Jordan	1.50	.75	.15
☐ 45 Magic Johnson	1.00	.50	.10
☐ 46 Doc Rivers	.06	.03	.00
☐ 47 Moses Malone	.12	.06	.01
☐ 48 Michael Jordan All-Star Checklist	.60	.30	.06
☐ 49 James Worthy AS	.08	.04	.01
☐ 50 Tim Hardaway AS	.40	.20	.04
☐ 51 Karl Malone AS	.12	.06	.01
☐ 52 John Stockton AS	.12	.06	.01
☐ 53 Clyde Drexler AS	.15	.07	.01
☐ 54 Terry Porter AS	.08	.04	.01
☐ 55 Kevin Duckworth AS	.03	.01	.00
☐ 56 Tom Chambers AS	.06	.03	.00
☐ 57 Magic Johnson AS	.50	.25	.05
☐ 58 David Robinson AS	.50	.25	.05
☐ 59 Kevin Johnson AS	.12	.06	.01
☐ 60 Chris Mullin AS	.10	.05	.01
☐ 61 Joe Dumars AS	.08	.04	.01
☐ 62 Kevin McHale AS	.08	.04	.01
☐ 63 Brad Daugherty AS	.10	.05	.01
☐ 64 Alvin Robertson AS	.06	.03	.00
☐ 65 Bernard King AS	.06	.03	.00
☐ 66 Dominique Wilkins AS	.10	.05	.01
☐ 67 Ricky Pierce AS	.06	.03	.00
☐ 68 Patrick Ewing AS	.12	.06	.01
☐ 69 Michael Jordan AS	.75	.35	.07
☐ 70 Charles Barkley AS	.12	.06	.01
☐ 71 Hersey Hawkins AS	.06	.03	.00
☐ 72 Robert Parish AS	.08	.04	.01
☐ 73 Alvin Robertson TC	.06	.03	.00
☐ 74 Bernard King TC	.06	.03	.00
☐ 75 Michael Jordan TC	.50	.25	.05
☐ 76 Brad Daugherty TC	.08	.04	.01
☐ 77 Larry Bird TC	.20	.10	.02
☐ 78 Ron Harper TC	.06	.03	.00
☐ 79 Dominique Wilkins TC	.10	.05	.01
☐ 80 Rony Seikaly TC	.06	.03	.00
☐ 81 Rex Chapman TC	.06	.03	.00
☐ 82 Mark Eaton TC	.03	.01	.00
☐ 83 Lionel Simmons TC	.12	.06	.01
☐ 84 Gerald Wilkins TC	.06	.03	.00
☐ 85 James Worthy TC	.08	.04	.01
☐ 86 Scott Skiles TC	.03	.01	.00
☐ 87 Rolando Blackman TC	.06	.03	.00
☐ 88 Derrick Coleman TC	.20	.10	.02
☐ 89 Chris Jackson TC	.06	.03	.00
☐ 90 Reggie Miller TC	.08	.04	.01
☐ 91 Isiah Thomas TC	.10	.05	.01
☐ 92 Hakeem Olajuwon TC	.12	.06	.01
☐ 93 Hersey Hawkins TC	.06	.03	.00
☐ 94 David Robinson TC	.30	.15	.03
☐ 95 Tom Chambers TC	.06	.03	.00
☐ 96 Shawn Kemp TC	.30	.15	.03
☐ 97 Pooh Richardson TC	.08	.04	.01
☐ 98 Clyde Drexler TC	.15	.07	.01
☐ 99 Chris Mullin TC	.12	.06	.01
☐ 100 Checklist 1-100	.06	.01	.00
☐ 101 John Shasky	.03	.01	.00
☐ 102 Dana Barros	.03	.01	.00
☐ 103 Stojko Vrankovic	.15	.07	.01
☐ 104 Larry Drew	.03	.01	.00
☐ 105 Randy White	.03	.01	.00
☐ 106 Dave Corzine	.03	.01	.00
☐ 107 Joe Kleine	.03	.01	.00
☐ 108 Lance Blanks	.06	.03	.00
☐ 109 Rodney McCray	.03	.01	.00
☐ 110 Sedale Threatt	.06	.03	.00
☐ 111 Ken Norman	.06	.03	.00
☐ 112 Rickey Green	.03	.01	.00
☐ 113 Andy Toolson	.10	.05	.01
☐ 114 Bo Kimble	.06	.03	.00

☐ 115 Mark West .03 .01 .00
☐ 116 Mark Eaton .03 .01 .00
☐ 117 John Paxson .06 .03 .00
☐ 118 Mike Brown .03 .01 .00
☐ 119 Brian Oliver .06 .03 .00
☐ 120 Will Perdue .03 .01 .00
☐ 121 Michael Smith .03 .01 .00
☐ 122 Sherman Douglas .06 .03 .00
☐ 123 Reggie Lewis .20 .10 .02
☐ 124 James Donaldson .03 .01 .00
☐ 125 Scottie Pippen .50 .25 .05
☐ 126 Elden Campbell .15 .07 .01
☐ 127 Michael Cage .03 .01 .00
☐ 128 Tony Smith .06 .03 .00
☐ 129 Ed Pinckney .03 .01 .00
☐ 130 Keith Askins .10 .05 .01
☐ 131 Darrell Griffith .03 .01 .00
☐ 132 Vinnie Johnson .06 .03 .00
☐ 133 Ron Harper .06 .03 .00
☐ 134 Andre Turner .10 .05 .01
☐ 135 Jeff Hornacek .12 .06 .01
☐ 136 John Stockton .25 .12 .02
☐ 137 Derek Harper .06 .03 .00
☐ 138 Loy Vaught .12 .06 .01
☐ 139 Thurl Bailey .03 .01 .00
☐ 140 Olden Polynice .03 .01 .00
☐ 141 Kevin Edwards .03 .01 .00
☐ 142 Byron Scott .06 .03 .00
☐ 143 Dee Brown .40 .20 .04
☐ 144 Sam Perkins .08 .04 .01
☐ 145 Rony Seikaly .12 .06 .01
☐ 146 James Worthy .12 .06 .01
☐ 147 Glen Rice .50 .25 .05
☐ 148 Craig Hodges .03 .01 .00
☐ 149 Bimbo Coles .12 .06 .01
☐ 150 Mychal Thompson .03 .01 .00
☐ 151 Xavier McDaniel .08 .04 .01
☐ 152 Roy Tarpley .06 .03 .00
☐ 153 Gary Payton .20 .10 .02
☐ 154 Rolando Blackman .06 .03 .00
☐ 155 Hersey Hawkins .12 .06 .01
☐ 156 Ricky Pierce .06 .03 .00
☐ 157 Fat Lever .06 .03 .00
☐ 158 Andrew Lang .12 .06 .01
☐ 159 Benoit Benjamin .03 .01 .00
☐ 160 Cedric Ceballos .20 .10 .02
☐ 161 Charles Smith .10 .05 .01
☐ 162 Jeff Martin .03 .01 .00
☐ 163 Robert Parish .12 .06 .01
☐ 164 Danny Manning .15 .07 .01
☐ 165 Mark Aguirre .06 .03 .00
☐ 166 Jeff Malone .08 .04 .01
☐ 167 Bill Laimbeer .06 .03 .00
☐ 168 Willie Burton .12 .06 .01
☐ 169 Dennis Hopson .06 .03 .00
☐ 170 Kevin Gamble .06 .03 .00
☐ 171 Terry Teagle .03 .01 .00
☐ 172 Dan Majerle .12 .06 .01
☐ 173 Shawn Kemp 1.00 .50 .10
☐ 174 Tom Chambers .08 .04 .01
☐ 175 Vlade Divac .12 .06 .01
☐ 176 Johnny Dawkins .03 .01 .00
☐ 177 A.C. Green .06 .03 .00
☐ 178 Manute Bol .03 .01 .00
☐ 179 Terry Davis .06 .03 .00
☐ 180 Ron Anderson .03 .01 .00
☐ 181 Horace Grant .15 .07 .01
☐ 182 Stacey King .06 .03 .00
☐ 183 William Bedford .03 .01 .00
☐ 184 B.J. Armstrong .20 .10 .02
☐ 185 Dennis Rodman .15 .07 .01
☐ 186 Nate McMillan .03 .01 .00
☐ 187 Cliff Levingston .03 .01 .00
☐ 188 Quintin Dailey .03 .01 .00
☐ 189 Bill Cartwright .06 .03 .00
☐ 190 John Salley .06 .03 .00
☐ 191 Jayson Williams .06 .03 .00
☐ 192 Grant Long .03 .01 .00
☐ 193 Negele Knight .10 .05 .01
☐ 194 Alec Kessler .03 .01 .00
☐ 195 Gary Grant .03 .01 .00
☐ 196 Billy Thompson .03 .01 .00
☐ 197 Delaney Rudd .03 .01 .00
☐ 198 Alan Ogg .10 .05 .01
☐ 199 Blue Edwards .03 .01 .00
☐ 200 Checklist 101-200 .06 .01 .00
☐ 201 Mark Acres .03 .01 .00
☐ 202 Craig Ehlo .06 .03 .00
☐ 203 Anthony Cook .03 .01 .00
☐ 204 Eric Leckner .03 .01 .00
☐ 205 Terry Catledge .03 .01 .00
☐ 206 Reggie Williams .06 .03 .00
☐ 207 Greg Kite .03 .01 .00
☐ 208 Steve Kerr .03 .01 .00
☐ 209 Kenny Battle .03 .01 .00
☐ 210 John Morton .03 .01 .00
☐ 211 Kenny Williams .03 .01 .00
☐ 212 Mark Jackson .06 .03 .00
☐ 213 Alaa Abdelnaby .10 .05 .01
☐ 214 Rod Strickland .06 .03 .00
☐ 215 Micheal Williams .06 .03 .00
☐ 216 Kevin Duckworth .03 .01 .00
☐ 217 David Wingate .03 .01 .00
☐ 218 LaSalle Thompson .03 .01 .00
☐ 219 John Starks 1.00 .50 .10
☐ 220 Cliff Robinson .20 .10 .02
☐ 221 Jeff Grayer .06 .03 .00
☐ 222 Marcus Liberty .30 .15 .03
☐ 223 Larry Nance .08 .04 .01
☐ 224 Michael Ansley .06 .03 .00
☐ 225 Kevin McHale .10 .05 .01
☐ 226 Scott Skiles .06 .03 .00
☐ 227 Darnell Valentine .03 .01 .00
☐ 228 Nick Anderson .20 .10 .02
☐ 229 Brad Davis .03 .01 .00
☐ 230 Gerald Paddio .03 .01 .00
☐ 231 Sam Bowie .06 .03 .00
☐ 232 Sam Vincent .03 .01 .00
☐ 233 George McCloud .03 .01 .00
☐ 234 Gerald Wilkins .06 .03 .00
☐ 235 Mookie Blaylock .06 .03 .00
☐ 236 Jon Koncak .03 .01 .00
☐ 237 Danny Ferry .06 .03 .00
☐ 238 Vern Fleming .03 .01 .00
☐ 239 Mark Price .20 .10 .02
☐ 240 Sidney Moncrief .06 .03 .00
☐ 241 Jay Humphries .03 .01 .00
☐ 242 Muggsy Bogues .03 .01 .00
☐ 243 Tim Hardaway 1.00 .50 .10
☐ 244 Alvin Robertson .06 .03 .00
☐ 245 Chris Mullin .25 .12 .02
☐ 246 Pooh Richardson .20 .10 .02
☐ 247 Winston Bennett .03 .01 .00
☐ 248 Kelvin Upshaw .03 .01 .00
☐ 249 John Williams .06 .03 .00
☐ 250 Steve Alford .06 .03 .00
☐ 251 Spud Webb .06 .03 .00
☐ 252 Sleepy Floyd .03 .01 .00
☐ 253 Chuck Person .06 .03 .00
☐ 254 Hakeem Olajuwon .25 .12 .02
☐ 255 Dominique Wilkins .20 .10 .02
☐ 256 Reggie Miller .15 .07 .01
☐ 257 Dennis Scott .20 .10 .02
☐ 258 Charles Oakley .06 .03 .00
☐ 259 Sidney Green .03 .01 .00
☐ 260 Detlef Schrempf .06 .03 .00
☐ 261 Rod Higgins .03 .01 .00
☐ 262 J.R. Reid .06 .03 .00
☐ 263 Tyrone Hill .10 .05 .01
☐ 264 Reggie Theus .06 .03 .00
☐ 265 Mitch Richmond .15 .07 .01
☐ 266 Dale Ellis .06 .03 .00
☐ 267 Terry Cummings .08 .04 .01
☐ 268 Johnny Newman .06 .03 .00
☐ 269 Doug West .10 .05 .01
☐ 270 Jim Petersen .03 .01 .00
☐ 271 Otis Thorpe .06 .03 .00
☐ 272 John Williams .06 .03 .00
☐ 273 Kennard Winchester .08 .04 .01
☐ 274 Duane Ferrell .03 .01 .00
☐ 275 Vernon Maxwell .06 .03 .00
☐ 276 Kenny Smith .06 .03 .00
☐ 277 Jerome Kersey .10 .05 .01
☐ 278 Kevin Willis .08 .04 .01
☐ 279 Danny Ainge .06 .03 .00
☐ 280 Larry Smith .03 .01 .00
☐ 281 Maurice Cheeks .06 .03 .00
☐ 282 Willie Anderson .06 .03 .00
☐ 283 Tom Tolbert .03 .01 .00
☐ 284 Jerrod Mustaf .08 .04 .01
☐ 285 Randolph Keys .03 .01 .00
☐ 286 Jerry Reynolds .03 .01 .00
☐ 287 Sean Elliott .20 .10 .02
☐ 288 Otis Smith .03 .01 .00
☐ 289 Terry Mills .20 .10 .02
☐ 290 Kelly Tripucka .03 .01 .00
☐ 291 Jon Sundvold .03 .01 .00
☐ 292 Rumeal Robinson .06 .03 .00
☐ 293 Fred Roberts .03 .01 .00
☐ 294 Rik Smits .06 .03 .00
☐ 295 Jerome Lane .03 .01 .00
☐ 296 Dave Jamerson .06 .03 .00
☐ 297 Joe Wolf .03 .01 .00
☐ 298 David Wood .10 .05 .01
☐ 299 Todd Lichti .03 .01 .00
☐ 300 Checklist 201-300 .06 .01 .00
☐ 301 Randy Breuer .03 .01 .00
☐ 302 Buck Johnson .03 .01 .00

☐ 303 Scott Brooks	.03	.01	.00
☐ 304 Jeff Turner	.03	.01	.00
☐ 305 Felton Spencer	.08	.04	.01
☐ 306 Greg Dreiling	.03	.01	.00
☐ 307 Gerald Glass	.12	.06	.01
☐ 308 Tony Brown	.03	.01	.00
☐ 309 Sam Mitchell	.03	.01	.00
☐ 310 Adrian Caldwell	.03	.01	.00
☐ 311 Chris Dudley	.03	.01	.00
☐ 312 Blair Rasmussen	.03	.01	.00
☐ 313 Antoine Carr	.03	.01	.00
☐ 314 Greg Anderson	.03	.01	.00
☐ 315 Drazen Petrovic	.25	.12	.02
☐ 316 Alton Lister	.03	.01	.00
☐ 317 Jack Haley	.03	.01	.00
☐ 318 Bobby Hansen	.03	.01	.00
☐ 319 Chris Jackson	.12	.06	.01
☐ 320 Herb Williams	.03	.01	.00
☐ 321 Kendall Gill	1.00	.50	.10
☐ 322 Tyrone Corbin	.03	.01	.00
☐ 323 Kiki Vandeweghe	.06	.03	.00
☐ 324 David Robinson	1.25	.60	.12
☐ 325 Rex Chapman	.06	.03	.00
☐ 326 Tony Campbell	.03	.01	.00
☐ 327 Dell Curry	.03	.01	.00
☐ 328 Charles Jones	.03	.01	.00
☐ 329 Kenny Gattison	.06	.03	.00
☐ 330 Haywoode Workman	.10	.05	.01
☐ 331 Travis Mays	.06	.03	.00
☐ 332 Derrick Coleman	.60	.30	.06
☐ 333 Isiah Thomas	.15	.07	.01
☐ 334 Jud Buechler	.03	.01	.00
☐ 335 Joe Dumars	.12	.06	.01
☐ 336 Tate George	.06	.03	.00
☐ 337 Mike Sanders	.06	.03	.00
☐ 338 James Edwards	.03	.01	.00
☐ 339 Chris Morris	.06	.03	.00
☐ 340 Scott Hastings	.03	.01	.00
☐ 341 Trent Tucker	.03	.01	.00
☐ 342 Harvey Grant	.15	.07	.01
☐ 343 Patrick Ewing	.30	.15	.03
☐ 344 Larry Bird	.40	.20	.04
☐ 345 Charles Barkley	.25	.12	.02
☐ 346 Brian Shaw	.06	.03	.00
☐ 347 Kenny Walker	.03	.01	.00
☐ 348 Danny Schayes	.03	.01	.00
☐ 349 Tom Hammonds	.03	.01	.00
☐ 350 Frank Brickowski	.03	.01	.00
☐ 351 Terry Porter	.15	.07	.01
☐ 352 Orlando Woolridge	.06	.03	.00
☐ 353 Buck Williams	.08	.04	.01
☐ 354 Sarunas Marciulionis	.20	.10	.02
☐ 355 Karl Malone	.25	.12	.02
☐ 356 Kevin Johnson	.25	.12	.02
☐ 357 Clyde Drexler	.30	.15	.03
☐ 358 Duane Causwell	.08	.04	.01
☐ 359 Paul Pressey	.03	.01	.00
☐ 360 Jim Les	.10	.05	.01
☐ 361 Derrick McKey	.06	.03	.00
☐ 362 Scott Williams	.40	.20	.04
☐ 363 Mark Alarie	.03	.01	.00
☐ 364 Brad Daugherty	.20	.10	.02
☐ 365 Bernard King	.06	.03	.00
☐ 366 Steve Henson	.03	.01	.00
☐ 367 Darrell Walker	.03	.01	.00
☐ 368 Larry Krystkowiak	.03	.01	.00
☐ 369 Henry James UER (Scored 20 points versus Pistons, not Jazz)	.10	.05	.01
☐ 370 Jack Sikma	.06	.03	.00
☐ 371 Eddie Johnson	.06	.03	.00
☐ 372 Wayman Tisdale	.06	.03	.00
☐ 373 Joe Barry Carroll	.03	.01	.00
☐ 374 David Greenwood	.03	.01	.00
☐ 375 Lionel Simmons	.25	.12	.02
☐ 376 Dwayne Schintzius	.06	.03	.00
☐ 377 Tod Murphy	.03	.01	.00
☐ 378 Wayne Cooper	.03	.01	.00
☐ 379 Anthony Bonner	.08	.04	.01
☐ 380 Walter Davis	.06	.03	.00
☐ 381 Lester Conner	.03	.01	.00
☐ 382 Ledell Eackles	.03	.01	.00
☐ 383 Brad Lohaus	.03	.01	.00
☐ 384 Derrick Gervin	.03	.01	.00
☐ 385 Pervis Ellison	.30	.15	.03
☐ 386 Tim McCormick	.03	.01	.00
☐ 387 A.J. English	.12	.06	.01
☐ 388 John Battle	.03	.01	.00
☐ 389 Roy Hinson	.03	.01	.00
☐ 390 Armon Gilliam	.03	.01	.00
☐ 391 Kurt Rambis	.06	.03	.00
☐ 392 Mark Bryant	.03	.01	.00
☐ 393 Chucky Brown	.03	.01	.00
☐ 394 Avery Johnson	.03	.01	.00
☐ 395 Rory Sparrow	.03	.01	.00
☐ 396 Mario Elie	.25	.12	.02
☐ 397 Ralph Sampson	.06	.03	.00
☐ 398 Mike Gminski	.03	.01	.00
☐ 399 Bill Wennington	.03	.01	.00
☐ 400 Checklist 301-400	.06	.01	.00

1991-92 Upper Deck Award Winner Holograms

These holograms feature NBA statistical leaders in nine different categories. The first six holograms were random inserts in 1991-92 Upper Deck low series foil and jumbo packs, while the last three were inserted in high series foil and jumbo packs. The standard-size (2 1/2" by 3 1/2") holograms have the player's name and award received in the lower right corner on the front. The back has a color player photo and a summary of the player's performance. The cards are numbered on the back with an AW prefix before the number.

	MINT	EXC	G-VG
COMPLETE SET (9)	10.00	5.00	1.00
COMMON PLAYER (1-9)	.40	.20	.04
☐ 1 Michael Jordan Scoring Leader	3.50	1.75	.35
☐ 2 Alvin Robertson Steals Leader	.40	.20	.04
☐ 3 John Stockton Assists Leader	1.00	.50	.10
☐ 4 Michael Jordan MVP	3.50	1.75	.35
☐ 5 Detlef Schrempf Sixth Man	.40	.20	.04
☐ 6 David Robinson Rebounds Leader	2.50	1.25	.25
☐ 7 Derrick Coleman Rookie-of-the-Year	1.50	.75	.15
☐ 8 Hakeem Olajuwon Blocked Shots Leader	1.00	.50	.10
☐ 9 Dennis Rodman Defensive POY	.75	.35	.07

1991-92 Upper Deck Rookie Standouts

The first 20 cards of this subset were randomly inserted (one per pack) in 1991-92 Upper Deck series one jumbo packs and locker series boxes, while the second 20 cards were offered in the same packaging in the second series. The fronts of the standard-size (2 1/2" by 3 1/2") cards feature color action player photos, bordered on the right and below by a hardwood basketball court and with the "91-92 Rookie Standouts" emblem in the lower right corner. The back features a second color player photo and player profile. The cards are numbered on the back with an R prefix on the card number.

	MINT	EXC	G-VG
COMPLETE SET (40)	35.00	17.50	3.50
COMMON PLAYER (1-20)	.35	.17	.03
COMMON PLAYER (21-40)	.35	.17	.03
☐ 1 Gary Payton Seattle Supersonics	1.00	.50	.10
☐ 2 Dennis Scott Orlando Magic	1.00	.50	.10
☐ 3 Kendall Gill Charlotte Hornets	5.00	2.50	.50
☐ 4 Felton Spencer Minnesota Timberwolves	.35	.17	.03
☐ 5 Bo Kimble Los Angeles Clippers	.35	.17	.03
☐ 6 Willie Burton Miami Heat	.50	.25	.05
☐ 7 Tyrone Hill Golden State Warriors	.50	.25	.05
☐ 8 Loy Vaught Los Angeles Clippers	.35	.17	.03
☐ 9 Travis Mays Sacramento Kings	.35	.17	.03
☐ 10 Derrick Coleman New Jersey Nets	3.00	1.50	.30
☐ 11 Duane Causwell Sacramento Kings	.35	.17	.03
☐ 12 Dee Brown Boston Celtics	1.75	.85	.17
☐ 13 Gerald Glass Minnesota Timberwolves	.50	.25	.05
☐ 14 Jayson Williams Philadelphia 76ers	.35	.17	.03
☐ 15 Elden Campbell Los Angeles Lakers	.60	.30	.06
☐ 16 Negele Knight Phoenix Suns	.35	.17	.03
☐ 17 Chris Jackson Denver Nuggets	.60	.30	.06
☐ 18 Danny Ferry Cleveland Cavaliers	.35	.17	.03
☐ 19 Tony Smith Los Angeles Lakers	.35	.17	.03
☐ 20 Cedric Ceballos Phoenix Suns	.75	.35	.07
☐ 21 Victor Alexander Golden State Warriors	.35	.17	.03
☐ 22 Terrell Brandon Cleveland Cavaliers	.75	.35	.07
☐ 23 Rick Fox Boston Celtics	1.75	.85	.17
☐ 24 Stacey Augmon Atlanta Hawks	1.75	.85	.17
☐ 25 Mark Macon Denver Nuggets	.60	.30	.06
☐ 26 Larry Johnson Charlotte Hornets	9.00	4.50	.90
☐ 27 Paul Graham Atlanta Hawks	.35	.17	.03
☐ 28 Stanley Roberts UER Orlando Magic (Not the Magic's 1st pick in 1991)	1.25	.60	.12
☐ 29 Dikembe Mutombo Denver Nuggets	5.00	2.50	.50
☐ 30 Robert Pack Portland Trail Blazers	.90	.45	.09
☐ 31 Doug Smith Dallas Mavericks	.60	.30	.06
☐ 32 Steve Smith Miami Heat	2.00	1.00	.20
☐ 33 Billy Owens Golden State Warriors	5.00	2.50	.50
☐ 34 David Benoit Utah Jazz	.60	.30	.06
☐ 35 Brian Williams Orlando Magic	.60	.30	.06
☐ 36 Kenny Anderson New Jersey Nets	1.75	.85	.17
☐ 37 Greg Anthony New York Knicks	.75	.35	.07
☐ 38 Dale Davis Indiana Pacers	.50	.25	.05
☐ 39 Larry Stewart Washington Bullets	.50	.25	.05
☐ 40 Mike Iuzzolino Dallas Mavericks	.50	.25	.05

1991-92 Upper Deck Extended

The 1991-92 Upper Deck high series consists of 100 standard-size (2 1/2" by 3 1/2") cards. Three NBA Award Winner holograms were randomly inserted in high series foil packs. Also inserted in the high series are cards of HOFer Jerry West, who is highlighted in a nine-card Basketball Heroes subset. West has signed 2,500 of the set's checklist cards. High series lockers contained seven 12-card packs of cards 1-500 and a special "Rookie Standouts" card. Both low and high series were offered in a 500-card factory set. The fronts feature glossy color player photos, bordered below and on the right by a hardwood basketball floor design. The player's name appears beneath the picture, while the team name is printed vertically alongside the picture. The backs display a second color player photo as well as biographical and statistical information. In addition to rookie and traded players, the high series includes the following topical subsets: Top Prospects (438-448), All-Star Skills (476-484), capturing players who participated in the slam dunk competition as well as the three-point shootout winner, Eastern All-Star Team (449, 451-462), and Western All-Star Team (450, 463-475). The cards are numbered on the back and checklisted below accordingly. The key rookie cards in this series are Kenny Anderson, Rick Fox, and Billy Owens.

	MINT	EXC	G-VG
COMPLETE SET (100)	13.00	6.50	1.30
COMMON PLAYER (401-500)	.03	.01	.00
☐ 401 David Wingate Washington Bullets	.03	.01	.00
☐ 402 Moses Malone Milwaukee Bucks	.12	.06	.01
☐ 403 Darrell Walker Detroit Pistons	.03	.01	.00
☐ 404 Antoine Carr San Antonio Spurs	.03	.01	.00
☐ 405 Charles Shackleford Philadelphia 76ers	.03	.01	.00
☐ 406 Orlando Woolridge Detroit Pistons	.06	.03	.00
☐ 407 Robert Pack Portland Trail Blazers	.90	.45	.09
☐ 408 Bobby Hansen Chicago Bulls	.03	.01	.00

Card	Player	MINT	EXC	G-VG
☐ 409	Dale Davis, Indiana Pacers	.35	.17	.03
☐ 410	Vincent Askew, Golden State Warriors	.15	.07	.01
☐ 411	Alexander Volkov, Atlanta Hawks	.06	.03	.00
☐ 412	Dwayne Schintzius, Sacramento Kings	.06	.03	.00
☐ 413	Tim Perry, Phoenix Suns	.06	.03	.00
☐ 414	Tyrone Corbin, Utah Jazz	.03	.01	.00
☐ 415	Pete Chilcutt, Sacramento Kings	.15	.07	.01
☐ 416	James Edwards, Los Angeles Clippers	.03	.01	.00
☐ 417	Jerrod Mustaf, Phoenix Suns	.10	.05	.01
☐ 418	Thurl Bailey, Minnesota Timberwolves	.03	.01	.00
☐ 419	Spud Webb, Sacramento Kings	.06	.03	.00
☐ 420	Doc Rivers, Los Angeles Clippers	.06	.03	.00
☐ 421	Sean Green, Indiana Pacers	.12	.06	.01
☐ 422	Walter Davis, Denver Nuggets	.06	.03	.00
☐ 423	Terry Davis, Dallas Mavericks	.06	.03	.00
☐ 424	John Battle, Cleveland Cavaliers	.03	.01	.00
☐ 425	Vinnie Johnson, San Antonio Spurs	.06	.03	.00
☐ 426	Sherman Douglas, Boston Celtics	.06	.03	.00
☐ 427	Kevin Brooks, Denver Nuggets	.12	.06	.01
☐ 428	Greg Sutton, San Antonio Spurs	.10	.05	.01
☐ 429	Rafael Addison, New Jersey Nets	.15	.07	.01
☐ 430	Anthony Mason, New York Knicks	.40	.20	.04
☐ 431	Paul Graham, Atlanta Hawks	.35	.17	.03
☐ 432	Anthony Frederick, Charlotte Hornets	.15	.07	.01
☐ 433	Dennis Hopson, Sacramento Kings	.06	.03	.00
☐ 434	Rory Sparrow, Los Angeles Lakers	.03	.01	.00
☐ 435	Michael Adams, Washington Bullets	.08	.04	.01
☐ 436	Kevin Lynch, Charlotte Hornets	.15	.07	.01
☐ 437	Randy Brown, Sacramento Kings	.15	.07	.01
☐ 438	NBA Top Prospects Checklist (Larry Johnson and Billy Owens)	.75	.35	.07
☐ 439	Stacey Augmon TP, Atlanta Hawks	.50	.25	.05
☐ 440	Larry Stewart TP, Washington Bullets	.50	.25	.05
☐ 441	Terrell Brandon TP, Cleveland Cavaliers	.25	.12	.02
☐ 442	Billy Owens TP, Golden State Warriors	5.00	2.50	.50
☐ 443	Rick Fox TP, Boston Celtics	1.75	.85	.17
☐ 444	Kenny Anderson TP, New Jersey Nets	1.75	.85	.17
☐ 445	Larry Johnson TP, Charlotte Hornets	3.50	1.75	.35
☐ 446	Dikembe Mutombo TP, Denver Nuggets	1.25	.60	.12
☐ 447	Steve Smith TP, Miami Heat	.60	.30	.06
☐ 448	Greg Anthony TP, New York Knicks	.25	.12	.02
☐ 449	East All-Star Checklist	.12	.02	.00
☐ 450	West All-Star Checklist	.12	.02	.00
☐ 451	Isiah Thomas AS (Magic Johnson also shown)	.20	.10	.02
☐ 452	Michael Jordan AS	.75	.35	.07
☐ 453	Scottie Pippen AS	.30	.15	.03
☐ 454	Charles Barkley AS	.12	.06	.01
☐ 455	Patrick Ewing AS	.15	.07	.01
☐ 456	Michael Adams AS	.06	.03	.00
☐ 457	Dennis Rodman AS	.08	.04	.01
☐ 458	Reggie Lewis AS	.12	.06	.01
☐ 459	Joe Dumars AS	.08	.04	.01
☐ 460	Mark Price AS	.08	.04	.01
☐ 461	Brad Daugherty AS	.10	.05	.01
☐ 462	Kevin Willis AS	.06	.03	.00
☐ 463	Clyde Drexler AS	.15	.07	.01
☐ 464	Magic Johnson AS	.60	.30	.06
☐ 465	Chris Mullin AS	.10	.05	.01
☐ 466	Karl Malone AS	.12	.06	.01
☐ 467	David Robinson AS	.40	.20	.04
☐ 468	Tim Hardaway AS	.40	.20	.04
☐ 469	Jeff Hornacek AS	.08	.04	.01
☐ 470	John Stockton AS	.12	.06	.01
☐ 471	Dikembe Mutombo AS UER (Drafted in 1992, should be 1991)	.50	.25	.05
☐ 472	Hakeem Olajuwon AS	.10	.05	.01
☐ 473	James Worthy AS	.08	.04	.01
☐ 474	Otis Thorpe AS	.06	.03	.00
☐ 475	Dan Majerle AS	.06	.03	.00
☐ 476	Cedric Ceballos CL, All-Star Skills	.10	.05	.01
☐ 477	Nick Anderson SD, Orlando Magic	.10	.05	.01
☐ 478	Stacey Augmon SD, Atlanta Hawks	.25	.12	.02
☐ 479	Cedric Ceballos SD, Phoenix Suns	.10	.05	.01
☐ 480	Larry Johnson SD, Charlotte Hornets	1.25	.60	.12
☐ 481	Shawn Kemp SD, Seattle Supersonics	.40	.20	.04
☐ 482	John Starks SD, New York Knicks	.25	.12	.02
☐ 483	Doug West SD, Minnesota Timberwolves	.06	.03	.00
☐ 484	Craig Hodges, Long Distance Shoot Out	.03	.01	.00
☐ 485	LaBradford Smith, Washington Bullets	.20	.10	.02
☐ 486	Winston Garland, Denver Nuggets	.03	.01	.00
☐ 487	David Benoit, Utah Jazz	.60	.30	.06
☐ 488	John Bagley, Boston Celtics	.06	.03	.00
☐ 489	Mark Macon, Denver Nuggets	.60	.30	.06
☐ 490	Mitch Richmond, Sacramento Kings	.15	.07	.01
☐ 491	Luc Longley, Minnesota Timberwolves	.30	.15	.03
☐ 492	Sedale Threatt, Los Angeles Lakers	.06	.03	.00
☐ 493	Doug Smith, Dallas Mavericks	.60	.30	.06
☐ 494	Travis Mays, Atlanta Hawks	.06	.03	.00
☐ 495	Xavier McDaniel, New York Knicks	.08	.04	.01
☐ 496	Brian Shaw, Miami Heat	.06	.03	.00
☐ 497	Stanley Roberts, Orlando Magic	1.25	.60	.12
☐ 498	Blair Rasmussen, Atlanta Hawks	.03	.01	.00
☐ 499	Brian Williams, Orlando Magic	.60	.30	.06
☐ 500	Checklist Card	.06	.01	.00

1991-92 Upper Deck Heroes Jerry West

This ten-card insert set was randomly inserted in Upper Deck's high series basketball foil packs. Also included in the packs were 2,500 checklist cards autographed by West. The fronts of the standard-size (2 1/2" by 3 1/2") cards capture memorable moments from his college and professional career. The player photos are cut out and superimposed over a jump ball circle on a hardwood basketball floor design. The card backs present commentary. The cards are numbered on the back.

	MINT	EXC	G-VG
COMPLETE SET (10)	35.00	17.50	3.50
COMMON PLAYER (1-9)	3.00	1.50	.30

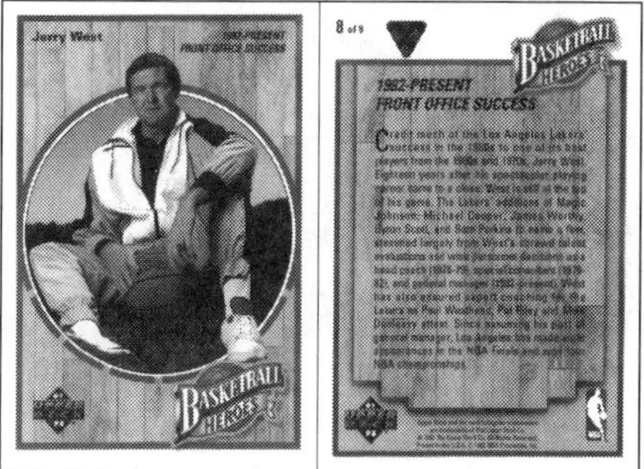

☐ 1 Jerry West ... 1959 NCAA Tournament MVP	3.00	1.50	.30
☐ 2 Jerry West ... 1960 U.S. Team	3.00	1.50	.30
☐ 3 Jerry West ... 1968-69 NBA Playoff MVP	3.00	1.50	.30
☐ 4 Jerry West ... 1969-70 NBA Scoring Leader	3.00	1.50	.30
☐ 5 Jerry West ... 1972 NBA World Championship	3.00	1.50	.30
☐ 6 Jerry West ... 1973-74 25,000 Points	3.00	1.50	.30
☐ 7 Jerry West ... 1979 Basketball Hall of Fame	3.00	1.50	.30
☐ 8 Jerry West ... 1982 to the present Front Office Success	3.00	1.50	.30
☐ 9 Jerry West ... Portrait Card	3.00	1.50	.30
☐ NNO Jerry West ... Cover/Title Card	15.00	7.50	1.50

1991-92 Upper Deck Heroes Jerry West Wax Box Bottoms

These oversized cards, measuring approximately 5" by 7", are actually the bottom panel of the 1991-92 Upper Deck hi number series basketball wax/foil boxes. Except for the size and the blank backs, these waxbox bottoms are identical to the first eight cards in the Jerry West Basketball Heroes insert set.

	MINT	EXC	G-VG
COMPLETE SET (8) ...	6.00	3.00	.60
COMMON PLAYER (1-8) ...	1.00	.50	.10
☐ 1 Jerry West ... 1959 NCAA Tournament MVP	1.00	.50	.10
☐ 2 Jerry West ... 1960 U.S. Team	1.00	.50	.10
☐ 3 Jerry West ... 1968-69 NBA Playoff MVP	1.00	.50	.10
☐ 4 Jerry West ... 1969-70 NBA Scoring Leader	1.00	.50	.10
☐ 5 Jerry West ... 1972 NBA World Championship	1.00	.50	.10
☐ 6 Jerry West ... 1973-74 25,000 Points	1.00	.50	.10
☐ 7 Jerry West ... 1979 Basketball Hall of Fame	1.00	.50	.10
☐ 8 Jerry West ... 1982 to the present Front Office Success	1.00	.50	.10

1988-89 Warriors Smokey

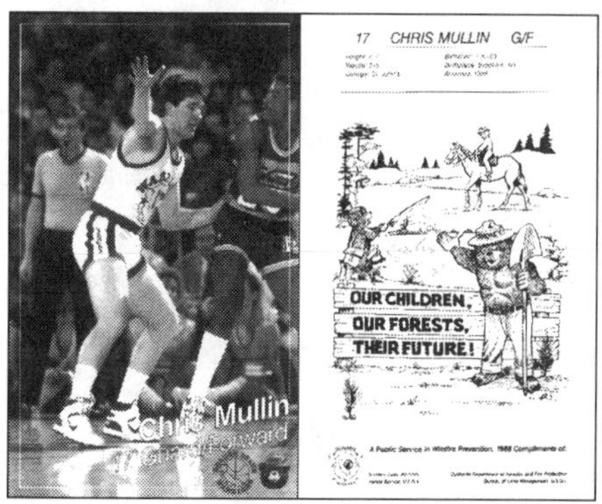

The 1988-89 Smokey Golden State Warriors set contains four 5" by 8" (approximately) cards featuring color action photos. The card backs feature a large fire safety cartoon and minimal player information. The cards are unnumbered and are ordered below alphabetically. The set was sponsored by the California Department of Forestry and Fire Protection and the Bureau of Land Management. The player's name, number, and position are overprinted in the lower right corner of each obverse.

	MINT	EXC	G-VG
COMPLETE SET (4) ...	20.00	10.00	2.00
COMMON PLAYER (1-4) ...	3.00	1.50	.30
☐ 1 Winston Garland 12 ... (Guard)	3.00	1.50	.30
☐ 2 Chris Mullin 17 ... (Guard/Forward)	12.00	6.00	1.20
☐ 3 Ralph Sampson 50 ... (Center)	4.50	2.25	.45
☐ 4 Larry Smith 13 ... (Forward)	3.00	1.50	.30

1991-92 Wild Card Collegiate

The Wild Card Collegiate Basketball set contains 120 cards measuring the standard size (2 1/2" by 3 1/2"). One out of every 100 cards is "Wild", with a numbered stripe to indicate how

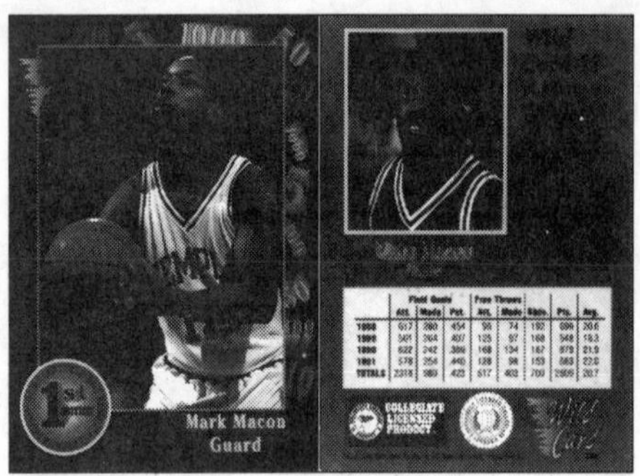

many cards it can be redeemed for. There are 5, 10, 20, 50, 100, and 1,000 denominations, with the highest numbers the scarcest. Whatever the number, the card can be redeemed for that number of regular cards of the same player, after paying a redemption fee of 4.95 per order. The front design features glossy color action player photos on a black card face, with an orange frame around the picture and different color numbers in the top and right borders. The backs have different shades of purple and a color head shot, biography, and statistics. The cards are numbered on the back. At the San Francisco Card Expo (Aug. 30 to Sept. 2, 1991), promo cards of Kenny Anderson and Larry Johnson were given away. These cards are identical to those inserted in 1991 Wild Card Collegiate football packs, except that they have the San Francisco Expo logo at the lower left corner on the back.

	MINT	EXC	G-VG
COMPLETE SET (120)	10.00	5.00	1.00
COMMON PLAYER (1-120)	.05	.02	.00
☐ 1 Larry Johnson First NBA Draft Pick	1.25	.60	.12
☐ 2 LeRon Ellis Syracuse	.12	.06	.01
☐ 3 Alvaro Teheran Houston	.05	.02	.00
☐ 4 Eric Murdock Providence	.30	.15	.03
☐ 5A Surprise Card 1	1.00	.50	.10
☐ 5B Dikembe Mutombo Georgetown	1.75	.85	.17
☐ 6 Anthony Avent Seton Hall	.20	.10	.02
☐ 7 Isiah Thomas Indiana	.15	.07	.01
☐ 8 Abdul Shamsid-Deen Providence	.05	.02	.00
☐ 9 Linton Townes James Madison	.05	.02	.00
☐ 10 Joe Wylie Miami	.08	.04	.01
☐ 11 Cozell McQueen North Carolina State	.08	.04	.01
☐ 12 David Benoit Alabama	.50	.25	.05
☐ 13 Chris Mullin St. John's	.20	.10	.02
☐ 14 Dale Davis Clemson	.35	.17	.03
☐ 15 Patrick Ewing Georgetown	.25	.12	.02
☐ 16 Greg Anthony UNLV	.40	.20	.04
☐ 17 Robert Pack USC	.75	.35	.07
☐ 18 Phil Zevenbergen Washington	.05	.02	.00
☐ 19 Rick Fox North Carolina	1.00	.50	.10
☐ 20 Chris Corchiani North Carolina State	.15	.07	.01
☐ 21 Elliot Perry Memphis State	.15	.07	.01
☐ 22 Kevin Brooks SW Louisiana	.15	.07	.01
☐ 23 Mark Macon Temple	.35	.17	.03
☐ 24 Larry Johnson UNLV	5.00	2.50	.50
☐ 25 George Ackles UNLV	.08	.04	.01
☐ 26A Surprise Card 5	.75	.35	.07
☐ 26B Christian Laettner (Promo) Duke	1.25	.60	.12
☐ 27 Andy Fields Cheyney State	.05	.02	.00
☐ 28 Kevin Lynch Minnesota	.15	.07	.01
☐ 29 Graylin Warner SW Louisiana	.05	.02	.00
☐ 30 James Bullock Purdue	.05	.02	.00
☐ 31 Steve Bucknall North Carolina	.08	.04	.01
☐ 32 Carl Thomas Eastern Michigan	.08	.04	.01
☐ 33 Doug Overton La Salle	.08	.04	.01
☐ 34 Brian Shorter Pittsburgh	.08	.04	.01
☐ 35 Chad Gallagher Creighton	.08	.04	.01
☐ 36 Antonio Davis Texas-El Paso	.05	.02	.00
☐ 37 Sean Green Iona	.15	.07	.01
☐ 38 Randy Brown New Mexico State	.15	.07	.01
☐ 39 Richard Dumas Oklahoma State	.08	.04	.01
☐ 40 Terrell Brandon Oregon	.40	.20	.04
☐ 41 Marty Embry DePaul	.05	.02	.00
☐ 42 Ronald Coleman USC	.08	.04	.01
☐ 43 King Rice North Carolina	.08	.04	.01
☐ 44 Perry Carter Ohio State	.08	.04	.01
☐ 45A Surprise Card 2	1.00	.50	.10
☐ 45B Billy Owens Syracuse	1.75	.85	.17
☐ 46A Surprise Card 3	.60	.30	.06
☐ 46B Stacey Augmon UNLV	1.00	.50	.10
☐ 47 Andrew Gaze Seton Hall	.05	.02	.00
☐ 48 Jimmy Oliver Purdue	.20	.10	.02
☐ 49 Treg Lee Ohio State	.08	.04	.01
☐ 50 Ricky Winslow Houston	.08	.04	.01
☐ 51 Danny Vranes Utah	.08	.04	.01
☐ 52 Jay Murphy Boston College	.08	.04	.01
☐ 53 Adrian Dantley Notre Dame	.08	.04	.01
☐ 54 Joe Arlauckas Niagara University	.05	.02	.00
☐ 55 Moses Scurry UNLV	.08	.04	.01
☐ 56 Andy Toolson Brigham Young	.08	.04	.01
☐ 57 Ramon Rivas Temple	.08	.04	.01
☐ 58 Charles Davis Vanderbilt	.05	.02	.00
☐ 59 Butch Wade Michigan	.05	.02	.00
☐ 60 John Pinone Villanova	.05	.02	.00
☐ 61 Bill Wennington St. John's	.08	.04	.01
☐ 62 Walter Berry St. John's	.08	.04	.01
☐ 63 Terry Dozier South Carolina	.05	.02	.00
☐ 64 Mitchell Anderson Bradley	.05	.02	.00
☐ 65 Pace Mannion Utah	.08	.04	.01
☐ 66 Pete Myers Little Rock	.05	.02	.00
☐ 67 Eddie Lee Wilkins Gardner Webb	.08	.04	.01
☐ 68 Mark Hughes	.05	.02	.00

	Michigan			
☐ 69	Darryl Dawkins (No College)	.08	.04	.01
☐ 70	Jay Vincent Michigan State	.05	.02	.00
☐ 71	Doug Lee Purdue	.12	.06	.01
☐ 72	Russ Schoene Tennessee-Chattanooga	.05	.02	.00
☐ 73	Tim Kempton Notre Dame	.05	.02	.00
☐ 74	Earl Cureton Detroit	.08	.04	.01
☐ 75	Terence Stansbury Temple	.08	.04	.01
☐ 76	Frank Kornet Vanderbilt	.05	.02	.00
☐ 77	Bob McAdoo North Carolina	.08	.04	.01
☐ 78	Haywoode Workman Oral Roberts	.08	.04	.01
☐ 79	Vinny Del Negro North Carolina State	.08	.04	.01
☐ 80	Harold Pressley Villanova	.08	.04	.01
☐ 81	Robert Smith UNLV	.05	.02	.00
☐ 82	Adrian Caldwell Lamar	.05	.02	.00
☐ 83	Scottie Pippen Central Arkansas	.30	.15	.03
☐ 84	John Stockton Gonzaga	.20	.10	.02
☐ 85	Elwayne Campbell Henderson State	.05	.02	.00
☐ 86	Chris Gatling Old Dominion	.40	.20	.04
☐ 87	Cedric Henderson Georgia	.05	.02	.00
☐ 88	Mike Iuzzolino St. Francis	.35	.17	.03
☐ 89	Fennis Dembo Wyoming	.08	.04	.01
☐ 90	Darnell Valentine Kansas	.05	.02	.00
☐ 91	Michael Brooks LaSalle	.05	.02	.00
☐ 92	Marty Conlon Providence	.12	.06	.01
☐ 93	Lamont Strothers Christopher Newport	.12	.06	.01
☐ 94	Donald Hodge Temple	.35	.17	.03
☐ 95	Pete Chilcutt North Carolina	.20	.10	.02
☐ 96	Kenny Anderson Georgia Tech	1.50	.75	.15
☐ 97	Ian Lockhart Tennessee	.05	.02	.00
☐ 98A	Surprise Card 4	.90	.45	.09
☐ 98B	Steve Smith Michigan State	1.50	.75	.15
☐ 99	Larry Lawrence Dartmouth	.05	.02	.00
☐ 100	Jerome Mincy Alabama-Birmingham	.08	.04	.01
☐ 101	Ben Coleman Maryland	.08	.04	.01
☐ 102	Tom Copa Marquette	.05	.02	.00
☐ 103	Demetrius Calip Michigan	.12	.06	.01
☐ 104	Myron Brown Slippery Rock	.10	.05	.01
☐ 105	Derrick Pope Montana	.05	.02	.00
☐ 106	Kelvin Upshaw Utah	.08	.04	.01
☐ 107	Andrew Moten Florida	.08	.04	.01
☐ 108	Terry Tyler Detroit	.05	.02	.00
☐ 109	Kevin Magee Cal-Irvine	.05	.02	.00
☐ 110	Tharon Mayes Florida State	.12	.06	.01
☐ 111	Perry McDonald Georgetown	.08	.04	.01
☐ 112	Jose Ortiz Oregon State	.08	.04	.01
☐ 113	Rick Mahorn Hampton	.08	.04	.01
☐ 114	David Butler UNLV	.08	.04	.01
☐ 115	Carl Herrera Houston	.20	.10	.02
☐ 116	Darrell Mickens Houston	.05	.02	.00
☐ 117	Steve Bardo Illinois	.08	.04	.01
☐ 118	Checklist 1	.05	.02	.00
☐ 119	Checklist 2	.05	.02	.00
☐ 120	Checklist 3	.05	.02	.00

1991-92 Wild Card Red Hot Rookies

These cards were randomly packed in the Collegiate Basketball foil cases, and they included denomination cards. The cards measure the standard size (2 1/2" by 3 1/2"). The front design features glossy color action player photos on a black card face, with an orange frame around the picture and different color numbers in the top and right borders. The "Red Hot Rookies" emblem in the lower left corner rounds out the card face. The backs have a color close-up photo, biography, and complete college statistics. The cards are numbered on the back.

		MINT	EXC	G-VG
COMPLETE SET (10)		45.00	22.50	4.50
COMMON PLAYER (1-10)		2.00	1.00	.20
☐ 1	Dikembe Mutombo Georgetown	8.00	4.00	.80
☐ 2	Larry Johnson UNLV	15.00	7.50	1.50
☐ 3	Steve Smith Michigan State	6.50	3.25	.65
☐ 4	Billy Owens Syracuse	9.00	4.50	.90
☐ 5	Mark Macon Temple	2.50	1.25	.25
☐ 6	Stacey Augmon UNLV	6.00	3.00	.60
☐ 7	Victor Alexander Iowa State	2.00	1.00	.20
☐ 8	Mike Iuzzolino St. Francis	2.00	1.00	.20
☐ 9	Rick Fox North Carolina	4.00	2.00	.40
☐ 10	Terrell Brandon UER Oregon (Name misspelled Terrel on card front)	3.00	1.50	.30

1991 Wooden Award Winners

This 21-card set was released by Little Sun of Monrovia, California, to commemorate the John R. Wooden Award. Only 28,000 sets were produced, and the set number is given on the certification card. The set is accompanied by a deluxe card album with two-up plastic sheets to house the cards. The cards

chronicle the career of John Wooden and feature all 14 winners (in their college uniforms) of college basketball's most prestigious award. The cards measure the standard size (2 1/2" by 3 1/2"). With the exception of some early black and white Wooden photos, the fronts feature borderless color player photos. Each picture is bordered on the left side by a gray stripe, with the Little Sun logo superimposed at the top. A lavender stripe traverses the bottom of the card face and gives a title for that card. The backs have biographical information and full close-ups of each player printed in a blue Mezzo-tint process. The cards are numbered on the back.

	MINT	EXC	G-VG
COMPLETE SET (21)	12.50	6.25	1.25
COMMON PLAYER (1-21)	.50	.25	.05
☐ 1 John Wooden 1991	.75	.35	.07
☐ 2 Wooden Trophy	.50	.25	.05
☐ 3 John Wooden Purdue	.50	.25	.05
☐ 4 John Wooden UCLA	.50	.25	.05
☐ 5 Wooden Summer Camp	.50	.25	.05
☐ 6 Duke Llewellyn	.50	.25	.05
☐ 7 Marques Johnson	.60	.30	.06
☐ 8 Phil Ford	.60	.30	.06
☐ 9 Larry Bird	2.50	1.25	.25
☐ 10 Darrell Griffith	.60	.30	.06
☐ 11 Danny Ainge	.75	.35	.07
☐ 12 Ralph Sampson	.60	.30	.06
☐ 13 Michael Jordan	3.50	1.75	.35
☐ 14 Chris Mullin	1.25	.60	.12
☐ 15 Walter Berry	.60	.30	.06
☐ 16 David Robinson	2.50	1.25	.25
☐ 17 Danny Manning	1.00	.50	.10
☐ 18 Sean Elliott	1.00	.50	.10
☐ 19 Lionel Simmons	1.00	.50	.10
☐ 20 Larry Johnson	2.50	1.25	.25
☐ 21 Press Conference 1991	.50	.25	.05
☐ xx Certification of Limited Edition	.50	.25	.05

1981-82 Arizona Police

This 20-card set measures 2 5/8" by 3 5/8". It is sponsored by Golden Eagle Distributors. A posed color photo appears on the front of the card, with the name and uniform number underneath the picture. The back of the card provides basic biographical information, a discussion or definition of an aspect of basketball, and a safety message. The cards have been arranged and numbered alphabetically in the checklist below.

	MINT	EXC	G-VG
COMPLETE SET (20)	30.00	15.00	3.00
COMMON PLAYER (1-20)	1.50	.75	.15
☐ 1 Ken Atkins CO	1.50	.75	.15
☐ 2 John Belobraydic 55	1.50	.75	.15
☐ 3 Brock Brunkhorst 10	1.50	.75	.15
☐ 4 Jeff Collins 24	1.50	.75	.15
☐ 5 Greg Cook 22	4.00	2.00	.40
☐ 6 Len Gordy CO	1.50	.75	.15
☐ 7 Gary J. Heintz CO	1.50	.75	.15
☐ 8 Keith Jackson 21	1.50	.75	.15
☐ 9 Mark Jung 33	1.50	.75	.15
☐ 10 Jack Magno 41	1.50	.75	.15
☐ 11 Donald Mellow 35	1.50	.75	.15
☐ 12 Charles Miller 52	1.50	.75	.15
☐ 13 Pete Murphy 15	1.50	.75	.15
☐ 14 Kevin Ronndfield 44	1.50	.75	.15
☐ 15 Frank Smith 31	1.50	.75	.15
☐ 16 Fred Snowden CO	2.00	1.00	.20
☐ 17 Ernest Taylor-Harris 32	1.50	.75	.15
☐ 18 Harvey Thompson 34	1.50	.75	.15
☐ 19 John Vlahogeorge 14	1.50	.75	.15
☐ 20 Ricky Walker 12	2.00	1.00	.20

1983-84 Arizona Police

This 18-card set was cosponsored by the Tucson Police Department and Golden Eagle Distributors. The cards measure approximately 2 1/4" by 3 3/4". The fronts feature borderless posed color player photos, with the player's name and uniform number in the white stripe beneath the picture. The Beard and Haskin cards differ from the others in having the 1983-84 basketball schedule printed on the front. The backs present player profile, a discussion or definition of some aspect of basketball, and a safety message. The cards are unnumbered and checklisted below in alphabetical order, with the uniform number after the player's name.

	MINT	EXC	G-VG
COMPLETE SET (18)	25.00	12.50	2.50
COMMON PLAYER (1-18)	1.25	.60	.12
☐ 1 Van Beard 54	1.25	.60	.12
☐ 2 Ricky Byrdsong Assistant CO	1.25	.60	.12
☐ 3 Brock Brunkhorst 10	1.25	.60	.12
☐ 4 Ken Burmeister	1.25	.60	.12

Assistant CO			
☐ 5 Troy Cooke 20	1.25	.60	.12
☐ 6 Ken Ensor 22	1.25	.60	.12
☐ 7 David Haskin 24	1.25	.60	.12
☐ 8 Keith Jackson 21	1.25	.60	.12
☐ 9 Steve Kerr 25	6.00	3.00	.60
☐ 10 Lute Olson CO	2.00	1.00	.20
☐ 11 Eddie Smith 14	1.25	.60	.12
☐ 12 Michael Tait 11	1.25	.60	.12
☐ 13 Greg Taylor 52	1.25	.60	.12
☐ 14 Harvey Thompson 34	1.25	.60	.12
☐ 15 Scott Thompson Assistant CO	1.25	.60	.12
☐ 16 Pete Williams 32	1.25	.60	.12
☐ 17 Andy Woodtli 44	1.25	.60	.12
☐ 18 The Brain Trust Scott Thompson ASST CO Lute Olson CO Ricky Byrdsong ASST CO Ken Burmeister ASST CO	1.75	.85	.17

1984-85 Arizona Police

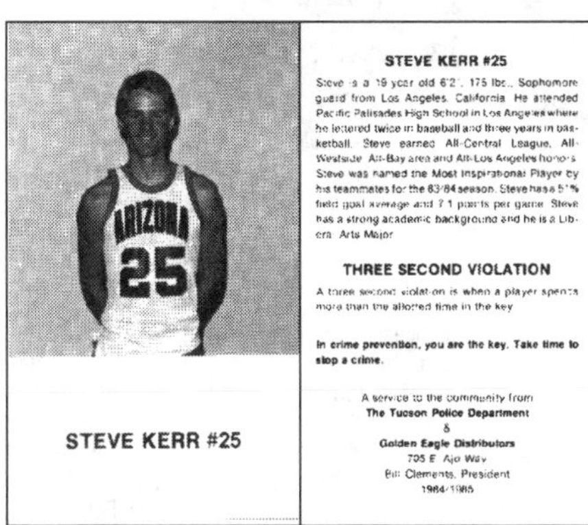

This 16-card set measures approximately 2 1/4" by 3 3/4". It is jointly sponsored by the Tucson Police Department and Golden Eagle Distributors. The front of the card features a posed color photo of the player on the top portion, and the name and uniform number underneath the picture. The back of the card gives basic biographical information (including the player's nickname where appropriate), a discussion or definition of an aspect of basketball, and a safety message. Among the players in the set is Steve Kerr, who would later go on to a career in the NBA.

	MINT	EXC	G-VG
COMPLETE SET (16)	15.00	7.50	1.50
COMMON PLAYER (1-16)	.80	.40	.08
☐ 1 Brock Brunkhorst 10	.80	.40	.08
☐ 2 Ken Burmeister CO	.80	.40	.08
☐ 3 Ricky Byrdsong CO	.80	.40	.08
☐ 4 John Edgar 50	.80	.40	.08
☐ 5 Bruce Fraser 22	.80	.40	.08
☐ 6 David Haskin 24	.80	.40	.08
☐ 7 Keith Jackson 21	.80	.40	.08
☐ 8 Rolf Jacobs 13	.80	.40	.08
☐ 9 Steve Kerr 25	5.00	2.50	.50
☐ 10 Craig McMillan 20	.80	.40	.08
☐ 11 Lute Olson CO	1.50	.75	.15
☐ 12 Eddie Smith 14	.80	.40	.08
☐ 13 Morgan Taylor 34	.80	.40	.08
☐ 14 Scott Thompson CO	.80	.40	.08
☐ 15 Joe Turner 33	.80	.40	.08
☐ 16 Pete Williams 32	.80	.40	.08

1985-86 Arizona Police

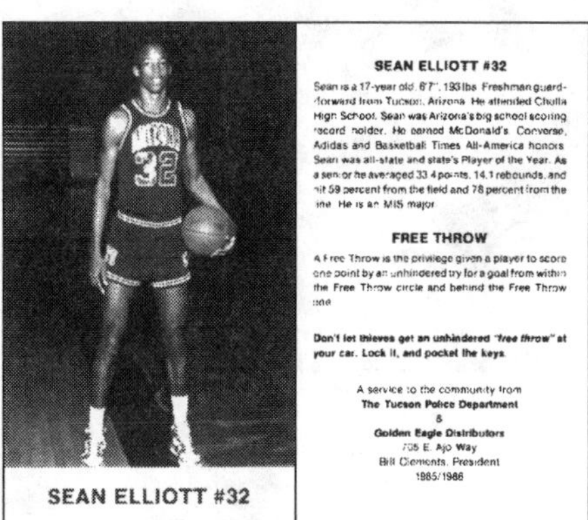

This 14-card set measures approximately 2 1/4" by 3 3/4". It is jointly sponsored by the Tucson Police Department and Golden Eagle Distributors. The front of the card features a posed color photo of the player on the top portion, and the name and uniform number underneath the picture. The back of the card gives basic biographical information, a discussion or definition of an aspect of basketball, and a safety message. This set includes future NBA players Sean Elliott and Steve Kerr as well as Major League baseball player Kenny Lofton.

	MINT	EXC	G-VG
COMPLETE SET (14)	25.00	12.50	2.50
COMMON PLAYER (1-14)	.80	.40	.08
☐ 1 Anthony Cook 00	3.50	1.75	.35
☐ 2 Eric Cooper 21	.80	.40	.08
☐ 3 Brian David 34	.80	.40	.08
☐ 4 John Edgar 50	.80	.40	.08
☐ 5 Sean Elliott 32	10.00	5.00	1.00
☐ 6 Bruce Fraser 22	.80	.40	.08
☐ 7 David Haskin 24	.80	.40	.08
☐ 8 Rolf Jacobs 13	.80	.40	.08
☐ 9 Steve Kerr 25	2.50	1.25	.25
☐ 10 Kenny Lofton 11	7.00	3.50	.70
☐ 11 Craig McMillan 20	.80	.40	.08
☐ 12 Lute Olson CO	1.50	.75	.15
☐ 13 Joe Turner 33	.80	.40	.08
☐ 14 Bruce Wheatley 45	.80	.40	.08

1986-87 Arizona Police

This 12-card set was cosponsored by The Tucson Police Department and Golden Eagle Distributors. The cards measure 2 1/4" by 3 3/4". The front features a borderless posed photo of the player. The player's name, number, and the Pacific-10 Conference logo appear in the white stripe below the picture. The back has brief biographical information, a definition of an aspect of the game of basketball, and an anti-crime or public service message. The cards are unnumbered and are checklisted below in alphabetical order, with the uniform number after the player's name. This set includes future NBA players Sean Elliott and Steve Kerr as well as Major League baseball player Kenny Lofton.

	MINT	EXC	G-VG
COMPLETE SET (12)	16.00	8.00	1.60
COMMON PLAYER (1-12)	.80	.40	.08
☐ 1 Jud Buechler 33	3.50	1.75	.35
☐ 2 Anthony Cook 00	1.75	.85	.17
☐ 3 Brian David 34	.80	.40	.08
☐ 4 Sean Elliott 32	5.00	2.50	.50
☐ 5 Bruce Fraser 22	.80	.40	.08

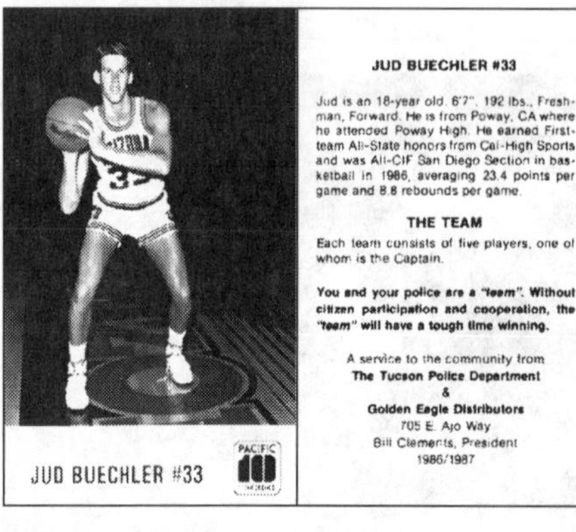

☐ 6 Steve Kerr 25	2.00	1.00	.20
☐ 7 Kenny Lofton 11	3.50	1.75	.35
☐ 8 Harvey Mason 44	.80	.40	.08
☐ 9 Craig McMillan 20	.80	.40	.08
☐ 10 Lute Olson CO	1.50	.75	.15
☐ 11 Tom Tolbert 31	3.50	1.75	.35
☐ 12 Joe Turner 33	.80	.40	.08

1987-88 Arizona Police

This 14-card set measures approximately 2 1/4" by 3 3/4". It is jointly sponsored by the Tucson Police Department and Golden Eagle Distributors. The front of the card features a posed color photo of the player on the top portion, and the name and uniform number underneath the picture. The back of the card gives basic biographical information, a discussion or definition of an aspect of basketball, and a safety message. On three cards the jersey number does not correspond to the number the player actually wears during games (Georgeson wears 45, Muehlebach 24, and Rooks 42). The cards are unnumbered and are checklisted below in alphabetical order, with the uniform number after the player's name. This set includes future NBA players Sean Elliott and Steve Kerr as well as Major League baseball player Kenny Lofton.

	MINT	EXC	G-VG
COMPLETE SET (14)	16.00	8.00	1.60
COMMON PLAYER (1-14)	.80	.40	.08
☐ 1 Jud Buechler 35	2.00	1.00	.20
☐ 2 Anthony Cook 00	1.25	.60	.12
☐ 3 Brian David 34	.80	.40	.08
☐ 4 Sean Elliott 32	3.50	1.75	.35
☐ 5 Mark Georgeson 34	.80	.40	.08
☐ 6 Steve Kerr 25	1.50	.75	.15
☐ 7 Kenny Lofton 11	3.00	1.50	.30
☐ 8 Harvey Mason 44	.80	.40	.08
☐ 9 Craig McMillan 20	.80	.40	.08
☐ 10 Matt Muehlebach 44	2.00	1.00	.20
☐ 11 Lute Olson CO	1.50	.75	.15
☐ 12 Sean Rooks 23	3.50	1.75	.35
☐ 13 Tom Tolbert 23	1.75	.85	.17
☐ 14 Joe Turner 33	.80	.40	.08

1988-89 Arizona Police

This 13-card set measures approximately 2 1/4" by 3 3/4". It is jointly sponsored by the Tucson Police Department and Golden Eagle Distributors. The front of the card features a posed color photo of the player on the top portion, and the name and uniform number underneath the picture. The back of the card gives basic biographical information, a discussion or definition of an aspect of basketball, and a safety message. Future NBA star Sean Elliott (misspelled Elliot) is included in this set as well as Major League baseball player Kenny Lofton. The cards are unnumbered and are checklisted below in alphabetical order, with the uniform number after the player's name.

	MINT	EXC	G-VG
COMPLETE SET (13)	15.00	7.50	1.50
COMMON PLAYER (1-13)	.80	.40	.08
☐ 1 Jud Buechler 35	1.50	.75	.15
☐ 2 Anthony Cook 00	1.25	.60	.12
☐ 3 Ron Curry 33	.80	.40	.08
☐ 4 Brian David 34	.80	.40	.08
☐ 5 Sean Elliott 32 (Misspelled Elliot)	3.00	1.50	.30
☐ 6 Mark Georgeson 45	.80	.40	.08
☐ 7 Ken Lofton 11	2.50	1.25	.25
☐ 8 Harvey Mason 44	.80	.40	.08
☐ 9 Matt Muehlebach 24	1.50	.75	.15
☐ 10 Lute Olson CO	1.50	.75	.15
☐ 11 Matt Othick 12	1.50	.75	.15
☐ 12 Sean Rooks 42	2.00	1.00	.20
☐ 13 Wayne Womack 30	1.50	.75	.15

1989-90 Arizona Police

This 14-card set was cosponsored by the Tucson Police Department and Golden Eagle Distributors. The cards measure approximately 2 1/4" by 3 3/4". The fronts feature borderless posed color player photos, with the player's name and uniform number in the white stripe beneath the picture. The backs present player profile, a discussion or definition of some aspect of basketball, and a safety message. The cards are unnumbered and checklisted below in alphabetical order, with the uniform

CHRIS MILLS #42

number after the player's name. The key cards in the set are Chris Mills and Brian Williams.

	MINT	EXC	G-VG
COMPLETE SET (14)	15.00	7.50	1.50
COMMON PLAYER (1-14)	.80	.40	.08
□ 1 Jud Buechler 35	1.25	.60	.12
□ 2 Brian David 34	.80	.40	.08
□ 3 Kevin Flanagan 51	.80	.40	.08
□ 4 Deron Johnson 23	.80	.40	.08
□ 5 Harvey Mason 44	.80	.40	.08
□ 6 Chris Mills 42	4.00	2.00	.40
□ 7 Matt Muehlebach 24	1.25	.60	.12
□ 8 Lute Olson CO	1.50	.75	.15
□ 9 Matt Othick 12	1.25	.60	.12
□ 10 Sean Rooks 45	1.50	.75	.15
□ 11 Casey Schmidt 11	.80	.40	.08
□ 12 Ed Stokes 41	2.00	1.00	.20
□ 13 Brian Williams 21	3.00	1.50	.30
□ 14 Wayne Womack 30	.80	.40	.08

1990-91 Arizona Promos *

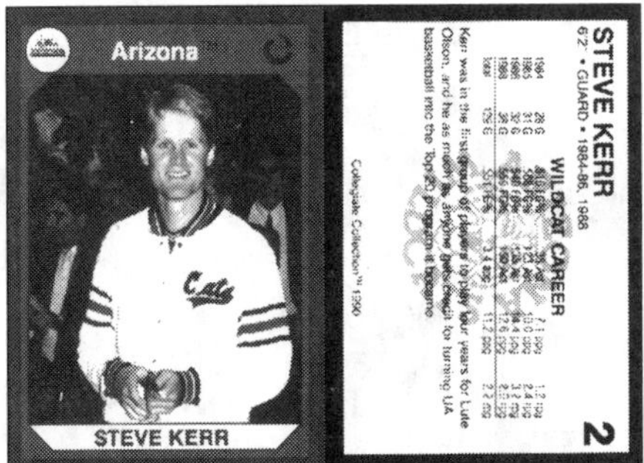

This 10-card standard size (2 1/2" by 3 1/2") set was produced by Collegiate Collection and features some of the great players of Arizona over the past few years. This set involves players of different sports and we have added a two-letter abbreviation next to the person's name to indicate what sport is pictured on the card. The back of the card either has statistical or biographical information about the player during their college career.

	MINT	EXC	G-VG
COMPLETE SET (10)	5.00	2.50	.50
COMMON PLAYER (1-10)	.50	.25	.05
□ 1 Chuck Cecil FB	.50	.25	.05
□ 2 Steve Kerr BK	.60	.30	.06
□ 3 Lute Olson CO BK	.50	.25	.05
(Watch Visible)			
□ 4 Chris Singleton FB	.75	.35	.07
□ 5 Lute Olson CO BK	.50	.25	.05
□ 6 Vance Johnson FB	.75	.35	.07
□ 7 Dick Tomey CO FB	.50	.25	.05
(Waist)			
□ 8 Robert Lee Thompson FB	.50	.25	.05
□ 9 Sean Elliott BK	1.00	.50	.10
□ 10 Dick Tomey CO FB	.50	.25	.05
(Head and Shoulders)			

1990-91 Arizona 125 *

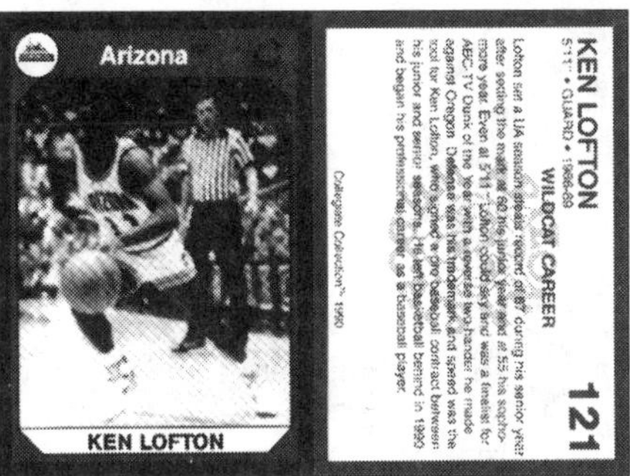

This 125-card set was produced by Collegiate Collection and measures the standard size (2 1/2" by 3 1/2"). The front features a mix of black and white or color player photos, with red and dark blue borders. All four corners of the picture are cut off. In white lettering the school name appears above the picture, with the player's name at the bottom of the card face. In a horizontal format the back presents biographical information and career summary, on a white background with dark blue lettering and borders. The cards are numbered on the back.

	MINT	EXC	G-VG
COMPLETE SET (125)	15.00	7.50	1.50
COMMON PLAYER (1-125)	.10	.05	.01
□ 1 Steve Kerr	.35	.17	.03
□ 2 Sean Elliott	.75	.35	.07
□ 3 Vance Johnson	.35	.17	.03
□ 4 Lute Olson CO	.20	.10	.02
□ 5 Chris Singleton	.35	.17	.03
□ 6 Robert Gamez	.35	.17	.03
□ 7 Ricky Hunley	.30	.15	.03
□ 8 Terry Francona	.20	.10	.02
□ 9 Chuck Cecil	.20	.10	.02
□ 10 Craig Lefferts	.25	.12	.02
□ 11 Warren Rustand	.10	.05	.01
□ 12 Tommy Tunnicliffe	.10	.05	.01
□ 13 Steve Strong	.10	.05	.01
□ 14 T. Bell	.20	.10	.02
□ 15 Jerry Kindall CO	.20	.10	.02
□ 16 Kevin Long	.10	.05	.01
□ 17 Fred Snowden CO	.10	.05	.01
□ 18 Anthony Smith	.20	.10	.02
□ 19 Laurie Brunet	.10	.05	.01
□ 20 Wes Clements	.10	.05	.01
□ 21 Larry Demic	.20	.10	.02
□ 22 Peter Evans	.10	.05	.01
□ 23 Gilbert Heredia	.20	.10	.02
□ 24 Chuck Cecil	.20	.10	.02
□ 25 Todd Trafton	.20	.10	.02
□ 26 Alan Durden	.10	.05	.01
□ 27 Eric Meeks	.10	.05	.01
□ 28 Steve Kerr	.35	.17	.03
□ 29 Rosie Wegrich	.10	.05	.01
□ 30 Danny Lockett	.10	.05	.01
□ 31 Dana Wells	.10	.05	.01
□ 32 Katrena Johnson	.10	.05	.01
□ 33 Anthony Cook	.20	.10	.02
□ 34 Anita Moss	.10	.05	.01
□ 35 David Adams	.10	.05	.01
□ 36 Eddie Leon	.10	.05	.01
□ 37 Vance Johnson	.35	.17	.03

☐ 38 Sean Elliott	.75	.35	.07
☐ 39 Alan Zinter	.35	.17	.03
☐ 40 Russell Brown	.10	.05	.01
☐ 41 Joe Magrane	.30	.15	.03
☐ 42 Derek Hill	.30	.15	.03
☐ 43 Hubie Oliver	.20	.10	.02
☐ 44 Scott Geyer	.10	.05	.01
☐ 45 Bill Wright	.10	.05	.01
☐ 46 Max Zendejas	.20	.10	.02
☐ 47 Jim Young CO	.20	.10	.02
☐ 48 Mark Arneson	.20	.10	.02
☐ 49 Doug Pfaff	.10	.05	.01
☐ 50 George DiCarlo	.10	.05	.01
☐ 51 Brad Henke	.10	.05	.01
☐ 52 Bruce Hill	.35	.17	.03
☐ 53 Ron Hassey	.25	.12	.02
☐ 54 Jim Gault	.10	.05	.01
☐ 55 Byron Evans	.35	.17	.03
☐ 56 Hoan Hansen	.10	.05	.01
☐ 57 Pete Williams	.10	.05	.01
☐ 58 Frank Busch	.10	.05	.01
☐ 59 David Wood	.20	.10	.02
☐ 60 Dave Murray	.10	.05	.01
☐ 61 Carla Garrett	.10	.05	.01
☐ 62 Ivan Lesnik	.10	.05	.01
☐ 63 J.T. Snow	.75	.35	.07
☐ 64 Al Fleming	.10	.05	.01
☐ 65 Don Lee	.10	.05	.01
☐ 66 Dave Towne	.10	.05	.01
☐ 67 Brad Anderson	.10	.05	.01
☐ 68 Chuck Cecil	.20	.10	.02
☐ 69 Mike Dawson	.20	.10	.02
☐ 70 Ed Vosberg	.20	.10	.02
☐ 71 Joe Tofflemire	.10	.05	.01
☐ 72 Rick LaRose	.10	.05	.01
☐ 73 Larry Silveria	.10	.05	.01
☐ 74 Lamonte Hunley	.10	.05	.01
☐ 75 June Olkowski	.10	.05	.01
☐ 76 Dave Stegman	.10	.05	.01
☐ 77 Melissa McLinden	.10	.05	.01
☐ 78 Chris Johnson	.10	.05	.01
☐ 79 Kenny Lofton	.75	.35	.07
☐ 80 Ken Erickson	.10	.05	.01
☐ 81 Martina Koch	.10	.05	.01
☐ 82 Joel Estes	.10	.05	.01
☐ 83 Diane Johnson	.10	.05	.01
☐ 84 Jon Abbott	.10	.05	.01
☐ 85 Sean Elliott	.75	.35	.07
☐ 86 Thom Hunt	.10	.05	.01
☐ 87 Jeff Kiewel	.10	.05	.01
☐ 88 Morris Udall	.35	.17	.03
☐ 89 Becky Bell	.10	.05	.01
☐ 90 Ruben Rodriguez	.15	.07	.01
☐ 91 Randy Robbins	.10	.05	.01
☐ 92 Eddie Smith	.10	.05	.01
☐ 93 Steve Kerr	.35	.17	.03
☐ 94 Dwight Taylor	.10	.05	.01
☐ 95 Mike Candrea	.10	.05	.01
☐ 96 Vance Johnson	.35	.17	.03
☐ 97 Bob Elliott	.10	.05	.01
☐ 98 Glenn Parker	.10	.05	.01
☐ 99 Joe Nehls	.10	.05	.01
☐ 100 Director Card 1-99	.10	.05	.01
☐ 101 Derek Huff	.10	.05	.01
☐ 102 Mark Roby	.10	.05	.01
☐ 103 Lute Olson CO	.20	.10	.02
☐ 104 Art Luppino	.10	.05	.01
☐ 105 Kevin Long	.10	.05	.01
☐ 106 Bob Elliott	.10	.05	.01
☐ 107 George Young	.10	.05	.01
☐ 108 Don Pooley	.10	.05	.01
☐ 109 Byron Evans	.35	.17	.03
☐ 110 Sean Elliott	.75	.35	.07
☐ 111 Kim Haddow	.10	.05	.01
☐ 112 David Adams	.10	.05	.01
☐ 113 Bobby Thompson	.15	.07	.01
☐ 114 Brad Anderson	.10	.05	.01
☐ 115 Eddie Wilson	.10	.05	.01
☐ 116 Dan Pohl	.20	.10	.02
☐ 117 Joe Hernandez	.10	.05	.01
☐ 118 J.F.(Pop) McKale	.10	.05	.01
☐ 119 Gayle Hopkins	.10	.05	.01
☐ 120 Carl Cooper	.10	.05	.01
☐ 121 Kenny Lofton	.75	.35	.07
☐ 122 Robert Lee Thompson	.15	.07	.01
☐ 123 Robert Ruman	.10	.05	.01
☐ 124 Meg Ritchie	.10	.05	.01
☐ 125 John Byrd Salmon	.10	.05	.01

1990 Arizona State Promos *

This ten-card standard size (2 1/2" by 3 1/2") set was issued by Collegiate Collection to honor some of the leading athletes in all sports played at Arizona State. The front features a full-color photo while the back of the card has information or statistical information about the player featured. To help identify the player there is a two-letter abbreviation of the athlete's sport next to the player's name.

	MINT	EXC	G-VG
COMPLETE SET (10)	5.00	2.50	.50
COMMON PLAYER (1-10)	.50	.25	.05
☐ 1 Reggie Jackson BB	1.00	.50	.10
☐ 2 Lafayette Lever BK	.60	.30	.06
☐ 3 Linty Ingram BB	.50	.25	.05
☐ 4 Luis Zendejas FB	.50	.25	.05
☐ 5 Byron Scott BK	.75	.35	.07
☐ 6 Sam Williams BK	.50	.25	.05
☐ 7 Lenny Randle BB	.50	.25	.05
☐ 8 Brian Noble FB	.60	.30	.06
☐ 9 Trace Armstrong FB	.60	.30	.06
☐ 10 Sun Devil Stadium	.50	.25	.05

1990 Arizona State 200 *

This 200-card set was produced by Collegiate Collection and measures the standard size (2 1/2" by 3 1/2"). The front features a mix of black and white or color player photos, with crimson and gold borders. All four corners of the picture give the appearance of being cut off in the design of the card. In gold lettering the school name appears above the picture, with the player's name at the bottom of the card face. In a horizontal format the back presents biographical information, career summary, and statistics, on a white background with gold lettering and borders. The cards are numbered on the back.

	MINT	EXC	G-VG
COMPLETE SET (200)	22.00	11.00	2.20
COMMON PLAYER (1-200)	.10	.05	.01
☐ 1 Reggie Jackson	.75	.35	.07
☐ 2 Gerald Riggs	.35	.17	.03
☐ 3 John Jefferson	.35	.17	.03
☐ 4 Sam Williams	.20	.10	.02
☐ 5 Charley Taylor	.40	.20	.04
☐ 6 Mike Davies	.10	.05	.01
☐ 7 Barry Bonds	.90	.45	.09
☐ 8 Byron Scott	.35	.17	.03
☐ 9 Lafayette(Fat) Lever	.35	.17	.03
☐ 10 Oddibe McDowell	.20	.10	.02
☐ 11 Dan Saleaumua	.20	.10	.02
☐ 12 Lionel Hollins	.25	.12	.02
☐ 13 Donnie Hill	.20	.10	.02
☐ 14 Doug Allen	.10	.05	.01
☐ 15 Kurt Nimphius	.15	.07	.01
☐ 16 Mike Benjamin	.10	.05	.01
☐ 17 Mark Malone	.20	.10	.02
☐ 18 Scott Lloyd	.20	.10	.02
☐ 19 Fair Hooker	.20	.10	.02
☐ 20 Jim Brock	.20	.10	.02
☐ 21 Linty Ingram	.10	.05	.01
☐ 22 Larry Gorden	.10	.05	.01
☐ 23 Chris Beasley	.10	.05	.01
☐ 24 Bruce Hill	.20	.10	.02
☐ 25 Elliot(Bump) Wills	.20	.10	.02
☐ 26 Steve Beck	.10	.05	.01
☐ 27 Scott Stephen	.10	.05	.01
☐ 28 Mike Haynes	.35	.17	.03
☐ 29 Packard Stadium West	.10	.05	.01
☐ 30 Vernon Maxwell	.25	.12	.02
☐ 31 Alton Lister	.25	.12	.02
☐ 32 Eric Allen	.20	.10	.02
☐ 33 Lafayette(Fat) Lever	.35	.17	.03
☐ 34 Al Bannister	.15	.07	.01
☐ 35 Skip McClendon	.15	.07	.01
☐ 36 David Fulcher	.30	.15	.03
☐ 37 Todd Kahs	.10	.05	.01
☐ 38 Larry Gura	.20	.10	.02
☐ 39 Aaron Cox	.35	.17	.03
☐ 40 Bob Kohrs	.20	.10	.02
☐ 41 Mark Landsberger	.20	.10	.02
☐ 42 Mike Richardson	.20	.10	.02
☐ 43 Shawn Patterson	.25	.12	.02
☐ 44 Paul Williams	.10	.05	.01
☐ 45 Danny Villa	.20	.10	.02
☐ 46 Eddie Bane	.20	.10	.02
☐ 47 Mike Pagel	.25	.12	.02
☐ 48 Jim Jeffcoat	.35	.17	.03
☐ 49 John Harris	.20	.10	.02
☐ 50 Lenny Randle	.20	.10	.02
☐ 51 Jeff Van Raaphorst	.20	.10	.02
☐ 52 Alvin Davis	.35	.17	.03
☐ 53 Freddie Williams	.10	.05	.01
☐ 54 Kevin Higgins	.10	.05	.01
☐ 55 Brian Noble	.25	.12	.02
☐ 56 Junior Ah You	.25	.12	.02
☐ 57 Kendall Carter	.10	.05	.01
☐ 58 Tony Novick	.10	.05	.01
☐ 59 Liz Aronshone	.10	.05	.01
☐ 60 Buzz Hayes	.10	.05	.01
☐ 61 Danny White	.30	.15	.03
☐ 62 Mistler	.10	.05	.01
☐ 63 Heather Farr	.35	.17	.03
☐ 64 Byron Scott	.35	.17	.03
☐ 65 Bill Mayfair	.10	.05	.01
☐ 66 Tammy Webb	.10	.05	.01
☐ 67 Curly Culp	.35	.17	.03
☐ 68 Mona Plummer Aquatic	.10	.05	.01
☐ 69 Norris Stevenson	.10	.05	.01
☐ 70 John Henry Johnson	.40	.20	.04
☐ 71 Roger Schmuck	.10	.05	.01
☐ 72 Al Harris	.25	.12	.02
☐ 73 Pearl Sinn	.10	.05	.01
☐ 74 John Finn	.10	.05	.01
☐ 75 Bruce Hardy	.15	.07	.01
☐ 76 Lisa Zeys	.10	.05	.01
☐ 77 Andrew Parker	.10	.05	.01
☐ 78 Ben Malone	.20	.10	.02
☐ 79 Brent McClanahan	.25	.12	.02
☐ 80 Sheri Rhodes	.10	.05	.01
☐ 81 Mike Black	.10	.05	.01
☐ 82 Floyd Bannister	.25	.12	.02
☐ 83 Danielle Ammaccapore	.30	.15	.03
☐ 84 Trace Armstrong	.25	.12	.02
☐ 85 Darryl Clack	.20	.10	.02
☐ 86 Steve Holden	.20	.10	.02
☐ 87 Pam Richmond	.10	.05	.01
☐ 88 Whiteman Tennis	.10	.05	.01
☐ 89 Art Malone	.20	.10	.02
☐ 90 Regina Stahl	.10	.05	.01
☐ 91 Darryl Harris	.10	.05	.01
☐ 92 Activity Center	.10	.05	.01
☐ 93 Randall McDaniel	.35	.17	.03
☐ 94 Sun Devil Stadium	.10	.05	.01
☐ 95 Luis Zendejas	.25	.12	.02
☐ 96 Sun Angel Track	.10	.05	.01
☐ 97 J.D. Hill	.25	.12	.02
☐ 98 Rod Severn	.10	.05	.01
☐ 99 Bobby Douglas	.25	.12	.02
☐ 100 Director Card 1-99	.10	.05	.01
☐ 101 1977 National Champs	.10	.05	.01
☐ 102 Bobby Winkles CO	.15	.07	.01
☐ 103 Zeke Jones	.10	.05	.01
☐ 104 Christy Nore	.10	.05	.01
☐ 105 Dan Devine	.20	.10	.02
☐ 106 Andy Astbury	.10	.05	.01
☐ 107 Lisa Stuck	.10	.05	.01
☐ 108 Dave Severn	.10	.05	.01
☐ 109 JoAnne Carner	.30	.15	.03
☐ 110 Doug Sachs	.10	.05	.01
☐ 111 Horner and Brooks (Bob and Hubie)	.25	.12	.02
☐ 112 Herman Finzier	.10	.05	.01
☐ 113 Team 1957	.10	.05	.01
☐ 114 Lynda Tolbert	.10	.05	.01
☐ 115 Team 1981	.10	.05	.01
☐ 116 Bob Gilder	.10	.05	.01
☐ 117 Ulis Williams	.10	.05	.01
☐ 118 Tracy Cox	.10	.05	.01
☐ 119 John Jefferson (The Catch)	.25	.12	.02
☐ 120 Mike Orn	.10	.05	.01
☐ 121 Team 1965	.10	.05	.01
☐ 122 Ron Brown	.25	.12	.02
☐ 123 1986 Team	.10	.05	.01
☐ 124 Jim Gressley	.10	.05	.01
☐ 125 Lucy Casazez	.10	.05	.01
☐ 126 Bwayne Evans	.10	.05	.01
☐ 127 Kathy Escarlega	.10	.05	.01
☐ 128 Ned Wulk	.20	.10	.02
☐ 129 Jim Carter	.20	.10	.02
☐ 130 Frank Covelli	.10	.05	.01
☐ 131 Dan St. John	.10	.05	.01
☐ 132 Jacinta Bartholomew	.10	.05	.01
☐ 133 Team 1967	.10	.05	.01
☐ 134 Jackie Brummer	.10	.05	.01
☐ 135 Danny White	.35	.17	.03
☐ 136 Alan Waldan	.10	.05	.01
☐ 137 Coleen Sommer	.10	.05	.01
☐ 138 1975 Team	.10	.05	.01
☐ 139 Eddie Urabano	.10	.05	.01
☐ 140 Jane Bastanchury	.10	.05	.01
☐ 141 Team 1969	.10	.05	.01
☐ 142 Leon Burton	.10	.05	.01
☐ 143 Mona Plummer	.10	.05	.01
☐ 144 Bob Mulgado	.10	.05	.01
☐ 145 Henry Carr	.20	.10	.02
☐ 146 Dan Severn	.10	.05	.01
☐ 147 Milissa Belose	.10	.05	.01
☐ 148 Ron Freeman	.10	.05	.01
☐ 149 Kim Neal	.10	.05	.01
☐ 150 Howard Twitty	.20	.10	.02
☐ 151 Reggie Jackson	.75	.35	.07
☐ 152 Lynn Nelson	.10	.05	.01
☐ 153 Ken Landacox	.10	.05	.01
☐ 154 Joe Caldwell	.20	.10	.02
☐ 155 Bob Breunig	.40	.20	.04
☐ 156 Larry Lawson	.10	.05	.01
☐ 157 Debbie Ochs	.10	.05	.01
☐ 158 Mike Devereaux	.40	.20	.04
☐ 159 Mike Sodders	.10	.05	.01
☐ 160 Keith Russell	.10	.05	.01
☐ 161 Art Becker	.20	.10	.02
☐ 162 Woody Green	.25	.12	.02
☐ 163 Ken Phelps	.20	.10	.02
☐ 164 Sherry Poole	.10	.05	.01
☐ 165 Rickey Peters	.15	.07	.01
☐ 166 Sherri Norris	.10	.05	.01
☐ 167 Paul Limne	.10	.05	.01
☐ 168 Whizzer White	.35	.17	.03
☐ 169 Maria Turjillo	.10	.05	.01
☐ 170 Karli Urban	.10	.05	.01
☐ 171 Sal Bando	.30	.15	.03
☐ 172 Bob Horner	.30	.15	.03
☐ 173 Hubie Brooks	.30	.15	.03
☐ 174 Mike Haynes	.35	.17	.03
☐ 175 Chris Jogis	.10	.05	.01
☐ 176 Charley Taylor	.40	.20	.04
☐ 177 Bernie Wrightson	.10	.05	.01
☐ 178 Kevin Romine	.20	.10	.02
☐ 179 Cassandra Lander	.10	.05	.01
☐ 180 1970 Football Team	.10	.05	.01
☐ 181 Sterling Slaughter	.15	.07	.01
☐ 182 Jerry Maddox	.10	.05	.01

		MINT	EXC	G-VG
☐ 183	Rick Monday	.25	.12	.02
☐ 184	Freddie Lewis	.20	.10	.02
☐ 185	Gary Gentry	.10	.05	.01
☐ 186	Tom Purtzer	.30	.15	.03
☐ 187	Jodi Rathburn	.10	.05	.01
☐ 188	Carl Donnelly	.10	.05	.01
☐ 189	Frank Kush CO	.15	.07	.01
☐ 190	Glenn McMinn	.10	.05	.01
☐ 191	Kym Hampton	.10	.05	.01
☐ 192	Marty Barrett	.20	.10	.02
☐ 193	Rick McKinney	.10	.05	.01
☐ 194	Michael Berlenheiter	.10	.05	.01
☐ 195	Duffy Dyer	.15	.07	.01
☐ 196	Mary Littlewood	.10	.05	.01
☐ 197	Ben Hawkins	.20	.10	.02
☐ 198	Dan Hayden	.10	.05	.01
☐ 199	Cheryl Gibson	.10	.05	.01
☐ 200	Director Card 101-200	.15	.07	.01

1982-83 Arkansas

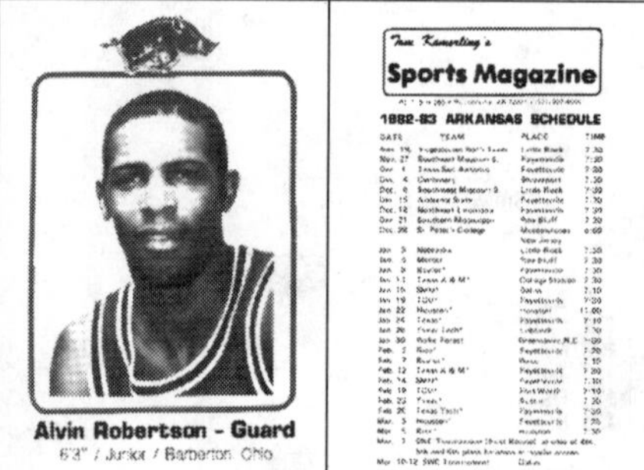

This 16-card set measures standard card size, 2 1/2" by 3 1/2". The card set was sponsored by Tom Kamerling's Sports Magazine. The black and white posed photo on the card's front is enclosed by a red border. The Arkansas Razorback logo appears above the photo, and the player's name, position, height, college classification, and hometown below the photo. The back of the card has the 1982-83 game schedule. Future NBA players included in this set are Joe Kleine, Alvin Robertson, and Darrell Walker. The cards are numbered for convenience in the checklist below alphabetically by subject.

		MINT	EXC	G-VG
COMPLETE SET (16)		100.00	50.00	10.00
COMMON PLAYER (1-16)		2.00	1.00	.20
☐ 1	Charles Balentine	5.00	2.50	.50
☐ 2	Darryl Bedford	2.00	1.00	.20
☐ 3	Robert Brannon	2.00	1.00	.20
☐ 4	Willie Cutts	2.00	1.00	.20
☐ 5	Keenan DeBose	3.00	1.50	.30
☐ 6	Carey Kelly	2.00	1.00	.20
☐ 7	Robert Kitchen	2.00	1.00	.20
☐ 8	Joe Kleine	15.00	7.50	1.50
☐ 9	Ricky Norton	5.00	2.50	.50
☐ 10	Eric Poerschke	2.00	1.00	.20
☐ 11	Mike Ratliff	2.00	1.00	.20
☐ 12	Alvin Robertson	40.00	20.00	4.00
☐ 13	John Snively	2.00	1.00	.20
☐ 14	Eddie Sutton CO	7.50	3.75	.75
☐ 15	Leroy Sutton	2.00	1.00	.20
☐ 16	Darrell Walker	15.00	7.50	1.50

1991 Arkansas 100 *

This 100-card multi-sport set was produced by Collegiate Collection for Arkansas Razorback fans and measures the standard size (2 1/2" by 3 1/2"). The fronts feature a mix of black and white or color player photos with the player's name in a red stripe below the picture. In a horizontal format the backs present biographical information, career summary, or statistics on a white background with black lettering and borders. The cards are numbered on the back. The cards were available in foil packs of seven cards per pack.

		MINT	EXC	G-VG
COMPLETE SET (100)		12.00	6.00	1.20
COMMON PLAYER (1-100)		.10	.05	.01
☐ 1	Frank Broyles CO	.25	.12	.02
☐ 2	Lance Alworth	.50	.25	.05
☐ 3	Sidney Moncrief	.50	.25	.05
☐ 4	Kevin McReynolds	.35	.17	.03
☐ 5	John Barnhill	.10	.05	.01
☐ 6	Dan Hampton	.50	.25	.05
☐ 7	Mike Conley	.35	.17	.03
☐ 8	John McDonnell	.10	.05	.01
☐ 9	Miller Barber	.25	.12	.02
☐ 10	Clyde Scott	.15	.07	.01
☐ 11	Kendall Trainor	.10	.05	.01
☐ 12	Les Lancaster	.20	.10	.02
☐ 13	Tom Pagnozzi	.35	.17	.03
☐ 14	Errick Floreal	.10	.05	.01
☐ 15	Tony Brown	.20	.10	.02
☐ 16	Derek Russell	.35	.17	.03
☐ 17	Niall O'Shaughnessy	.25	.12	.02
☐ 18	Jimmy Walker	.20	.10	.02
☐ 19	Ben Cowins	.15	.07	.01
☐ 20	Keith Wilson	.15	.07	.01
☐ 21	Tony Cherio	.10	.05	.01
☐ 22	Chip Hooper	.15	.07	.01
☐ 23	Tim Sherill	.15	.07	.01
☐ 24	Paul Donovan	.10	.05	.01
☐ 25	Billy Ray Smith	.25	.12	.02
☐ 26	Steve Little	.15	.07	.01
☐ 27	Steve Atwater	.35	.17	.03
☐ 28	Roddie Haley	.10	.05	.01
☐ 29	Ron Favrot	.10	.05	.01
☐ 30	Peter Doohan	.15	.07	.01
☐ 31	Darrell Akerfelds	.25	.12	.02
☐ 32	Dickey Morton	.15	.07	.01
☐ 33	Lon Farrell	.10	.05	.01
☐ 34	Jerry Spencer	.10	.05	.01
☐ 35	Scott Hastings	.25	.12	.02
☐ 36	Dick Bumpas	.10	.05	.01
☐ 37	Johnny Ray	.20	.10	.02
☐ 38	Joe Kleine	.30	.15	.03
☐ 39	George Cole	.10	.05	.01
☐ 40	Bruce Lahay	.10	.05	.01
☐ 41	Jim Benton	.10	.05	.01
☐ 42	Stanley Redwine	.10	.05	.01
☐ 43	Jim Kremers	.15	.07	.01
☐ 44	Marvin Delph	.15	.07	.01
☐ 45	Joe Falcon	.15	.07	.01
☐ 46	Bill Montgomery	.15	.07	.01
☐ 47	Lou Holtz CO	.25	.12	.02
☐ 48	John Daly (Golfer)	.60	.30	.06
☐ 49	Bill McClard	.10	.05	.01
☐ 50	Gary Anderson	.35	.17	.03
☐ 51	Alvin Robertson	.50	.25	.05
☐ 52	Glen Rose	.10	.05	.01
☐ 53	Ronnie Caveness	.15	.07	.01
☐ 54	Jeff King	.35	.17	.03
☐ 55	Bobby Joe Edmonds	.25	.12	.02
☐ 56	James Shibest	.10	.05	.01
☐ 57	Reuben Raina	.10	.05	.01
☐ 58	Martin Smith	.10	.05	.01
☐ 59	Wear Schoonover	.10	.05	.01
☐ 60	Bruce James	.10	.05	.01
☐ 61	Billy Moore	.10	.05	.01
☐ 62	Jim Mabay	.10	.05	.01
☐ 63	Ron Calcagni	.15	.07	.01
☐ 64	Wilson Matthews	.10	.05	.01
☐ 65	Martine Bercher	.10	.05	.01
☐ 66	Martin Terry	.10	.05	.01
☐ 67	Andrew Lang	.30	.15	.03
☐ 68	Mike Reppond	.10	.05	.01
☐ 69	Ron Brewer	.30	.15	.03
☐ 70	Ish Ordonez	.15	.07	.01
☐ 71	Steve Korte	.20	.10	.02
☐ 72	Jim Barnes	.20	.10	.02
☐ 73	Steve Cox	.20	.10	.02
☐ 74	Bud Brooks	.10	.05	.01
☐ 75	Roland Sales	.15	.07	.01
☐ 76	Chuck Dicus	.15	.07	.01
☐ 77	Rodney Brand	.10	.05	.01
☐ 78	Wayne Martin	.25	.12	.02
☐ 79	Greg Kolenda	.10	.05	.01

☐ 80 Ron Huery	.20	.10	.02
☐ 81 Brad Taylor	.15	.07	.01
☐ 82 Bill Burnett	.20	.10	.02
☐ 83 Glenn Ray Hines	.20	.10	.02
☐ 84 Leotis Harris	.10	.05	.01
☐ 85 Darrell Walker	.30	.15	.03
☐ 86 Joe Ferguson	.35	.17	.03
☐ 87 Grey Horne	.10	.05	.01
☐ 88 Lloyd Phillips	.20	.10	.02
☐ 89 James Rouse	.20	.10	.02
☐ 90 Ken Hatfield	.25	.12	.02
☐ 91 Bobby Crockett	.20	.10	.02
☐ 92 Quinn Grovey	.20	.10	.02
☐ 93 Wayne Harris	.25	.12	.02
☐ 94 Jim Mooty	.10	.05	.01
☐ 95 Barry Foster	.60	.30	.06
☐ 96 Mel McGaha	.15	.07	.01
☐ 97 Jim Lee Howell	.15	.07	.01
☐ 98 Jack Robbins	.10	.05	.01
☐ 99 Cliff Powell	.10	.05	.01
☐ 100 Director Card	.15	.07	.01

1991-92 Arkansas 25

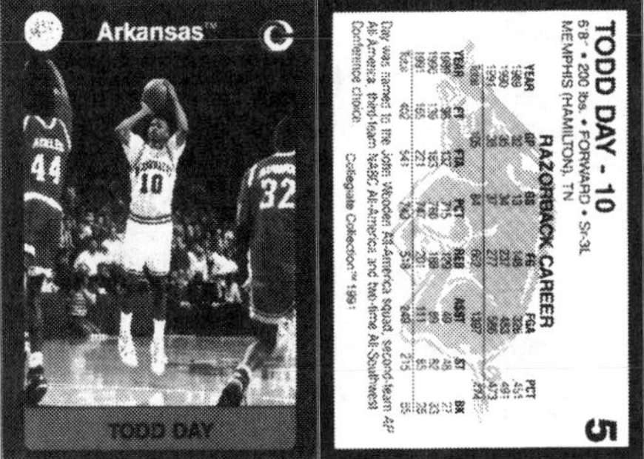

This 25-card standard-size (2 1/2" by 3 1/2") set was produced by Collegiate Collection. The fronts display either action or posed color player photos, with rounded corners and black borders. The player's name appears in a red stripe below the picture. The horizontally oriented backs have biography, statistics, and career summary, superimposed over a gray razorback. The cards are numbered on the back and generally arranged in alphabetical order. The key cards in the set are Todd Day, Lee Mayberry, and Oliver Miller.

	MINT	EXC	G-VG
COMPLETE SET (25)	30.00	15.00	3.00
COMMON PLAYER (1-25)	.75	.35	.07
☐ 1 Nolan Richardson CO	1.50	.75	.15
☐ 2 Ray Biggers	.75	.35	.07
☐ 3 Ken Biley	.75	.35	.07
☐ 4 Shawn Davis	.75	.35	.07
☐ 5 Todd Day	10.00	5.00	1.00
☐ 6 Clyde Fletcher	.75	.35	.07
☐ 7 Darrell Hawkins	.75	.35	.07
☐ 8 Warren Linn	.75	.35	.07
☐ 9 Elmer Martin	.75	.35	.07
☐ 10 Lee Mayberry	7.50	3.75	.75
☐ 11 Clint McDaniel	.75	.35	.07
☐ 12 Oliver Miller	7.50	3.75	.75
☐ 13 Isaiah Morris	4.00	2.00	.40
☐ 14 Davor Rimac	.75	.35	.07
☐ 15 Robert Shepherd	.75	.35	.07
☐ 16 Roosevelt Wallace	1.00	.50	.10
☐ 17 Alfred Warren	.75	.35	.07
☐ 18 Barnhill Arena	.75	.35	.07
☐ 19 Mike Anderson Assistant CO	.75	.35	.07
☐ 20 Brad Dunn Assistant CO	.75	.35	.07
☐ 21 Wayne Stehlik Assistant CO	.75	.35	.07
☐ 22 Nolan Richardson III Volunteer Assistant CO	1.00	.50	.10
☐ 23 Ernie Murry Graduate Assistant CO	.75	.35	.07
☐ 24 Team Photo	1.00	.50	.10
☐ 25 Director Card Checklist	.75	.35	.07

1987-88 Auburn Police

This 16-card set was issued by Auburn University and includes members from different sports programs. Supposedly only 5,000 sets were made by McDag Productions, and the cards were distributed by the Opelika, Alabama police department. The cards measure the standard size (2 1/2" by 3 1/2") and color player photos on white card stock. The backs present safety tips for children. The last three cards of the set feature "Tiger Greats," former Auburn athletes Bo Jackson, Rowdy Gaines, and Chuck Person. The sports represented in this set are football (1, 3, 5, 11-13, 16), basketball (4, 6, 9-10, 14), baseball (2), and swimming (15).

	MINT	EXC	G-VG
COMPLETE SET (16)	30.00	15.00	3.00
COMMON PLAYER (1-16)	.60	.30	.06
☐ 1 Pat Dye CO	.75	.35	.07
☐ 2 Frank Thomas	15.00	7.50	1.50
☐ 3 Jeff Burger	.75	.35	.07
☐ 4 Sonny Smith CO	.75	.35	.07
☐ 5 Kurt Crain	.60	.30	.06
☐ 6 Joe Ciampi	.60	.30	.06
☐ 7 Aubie (Mascot)	.60	.30	.06
☐ 8 Tiger (Mascot)	.60	.30	.06
☐ 9 Jeff Moore	.75	.35	.07
☐ 10 Vickie Orr	1.00	.50	.10
☐ 11 Tracy Rocker	1.00	.50	.10
☐ 12 Brian Shulman	.60	.30	.06
☐ 13 Lawyer Tillman	1.00	.50	.10
☐ 14 Chuck Person	5.00	2.50	.50
☐ 15 Rowdy Gaines	1.25	.60	.12
☐ 16 Bo Jackson	10.00	5.00	1.00

1987-88 Baylor Police *

This 17-card set was sponsored by the Hillcrest Baptist Medical Center, the Waco Police Department, and the Baylor University Department of Public Safety. The cards measure (not given in article) and the sports represented are baseball (1-3), basketball (4-6), track (7-10), and football (11-17). The front feature color action shots of the players on white card stock. At the top the words "Baylor Bears 1987-88" are printed between the Hillcrest and Baylor University logos. Player information is given below the picture. The back has more logos, brief career summaries, and "Bear Briefs," which consist of instructional sports information and an anti-drug or crime message.

	MINT	EXC	G-VG
COMPLETE SET (17)	24.00	12.00	2.40
COMMON PLAYER (1-17)	1.00	.50	.10
☐ 1 Nate Jones	1.00	.50	.10
☐ 2 Pat Combs	2.00	1.00	.20
☐ 3 Mickey Sullivan	1.00	.50	.10
☐ 4 Micheal Williams	4.00	2.00	.40
☐ 5 Darryl Middleton	2.00	1.00	.20
☐ 6 Gene Iba CO	2.00	1.00	.20
☐ 7 Victor Valen	1.00	.50	.10
☐ 8 Raymond Pierre	1.00	.50	.10
☐ 9 Darnell Chase	1.00	.50	.10
☐ 10 Clyde Hart CO	1.00	.50	.10
☐ 11 Ray Crockett	2.00	1.00	.20
☐ 12 Joel Porter	1.00	.50	.10
☐ 13 James Francis	3.50	1.75	.35
☐ 14 Russell Sheffield	1.00	.50	.10
☐ 15 Matt Clark	1.00	.50	.10
☐ 16 Eugene Hall	1.00	.50	.10
☐ 17 Grant Teaff CO	2.00	1.00	.20

1987-88 Brigham Young

This 25-card set was issued by Brigham Young University. Supposedly only 20,000 sets were produced, and each set was numbered from 1 to 20,000 on the back of every card. The cards measure the standard size (2 1/2" by 3 1/2"). The player cards feature color photos, while the team photo card is sepia-toned. The cards have a blue border, with the BYU logo in the lower right corner. Popular players on the team are featured on two cards, one action shot and one portrait. The backs have biographical and statistical information, as well as the card number.

	MINT	EXC	G-VG
COMPLETE SET (25)	18.00	9.00	1.80
COMMON PLAYER (1-25)	.60	.30	.06
☐ 1 Michael Smith	1.50	.75	.15
☐ 2 BYU Header card	1.00	.50	.10
☐ 3 Jim Usevitch	.60	.30	.06
☐ 4 Nathan Call	.60	.30	.06
☐ 5 Brian Taylor	.75	.35	.07
☐ 6 Ladell Anderson CO	1.00	.50	.10
☐ 7 Roger Reid	.60	.30	.06
☐ 8 Carl Ingersoll	.60	.30	.06
☐ 9 Jeff Chatman	1.00	.50	.10
☐ 10 Team Photo	1.00	.50	.10
☐ 11 Mike Herring	.60	.30	.06
☐ 12 Chris Lynch	.60	.30	.06
☐ 13 Steve Schreiner	.60	.30	.06
☐ 14 Gary Trost	.60	.30	.06
☐ 15 David Lynch	.60	.30	.06
☐ 16 Brian Taylor	.75	.35	.07
☐ 17 Andy Toolson	1.50	.75	.15
☐ 18 Jim Usevitch	.60	.30	.06
☐ 19 Vince Bryan	.60	.30	.06
☐ 20 Mark Clausen	.60	.30	.06
☐ 21 Alan Astle	.60	.30	.06
☐ 22 Nathan Call	.60	.30	.06
☐ 23 Jeff Chatman	1.00	.50	.10
☐ 24 Marty Haws	.60	.30	.06
☐ 25 Michael Smith	1.50	.75	.15

1989-90 Clemson

This 16-card set was sponsored by Carolina Pride, and its company logo appears in the lower left corner of the card face as well as on the back. The cards were issued on an unperforated sheet with four rows of four cards; after cutting, the cards measure the standard size (2 1/2" by 3 1/2"). The fronts feature color head and shoulders player photos on a white card face. Blue borders on the bottom and right of the picture form a shadow. The school and team names are printed in orange and blue above the picture, with an orange pawprint in the upper right corner. Player identification is given in the blue border below the picture. The backs have biographical information, player evaluation, and basketball advice in the form of "Tips from the Tigers." The cards are unnumbered and checklisted below in alphabetical order, with the uniform number after the player's name.

	MINT	EXC	G-VG
COMPLETE SET (16)	20.00	10.00	2.00
COMMON PLAYER (1-16)	.80	.40	.08
☐ 1 Colby Brown 44	.80	.40	.08
☐ 2 Donnell Bruce 14	.80	.40	.08
☐ 3 Wayne Buckingham 42	.80	.40	.08
☐ 4 Elden Campbell 41	9.00	4.50	.90
☐ 5 Marion Cash 12	.80	.40	.08
☐ 6 Dale Davis 34	6.00	3.00	.60
☐ 7 Cliff Ellis CO	1.25	.60	.12
☐ 8 Derrick Forrest 13	.80	.40	.08
☐ 9 Len Gordy CO	.80	.40	.08
☐ 10 Eugene Harris CO	.80	.40	.08
☐ 11 Kirkland Howling 4	.80	.40	.08
☐ 12 Ricky Jones 25	.80	.40	.08
☐ 13 Zlatko Josic 32	.80	.40	.08
☐ 14 Shawn Lastinger 15	.80	.40	.08
☐ 15 Sean Tyson 22	.80	.40	.08
☐ 16 David Young 11	.80	.40	.08

1990-91 Clemson

This 16-card set measures standard card size 2 1/2" by 3 1/2", and was issued by Carolina Pride. The orange color front of the card has an action color photo in the middle, with black text on each of its four sides. The back of each card includes basic biographical information and a basketball tip. The cards are numbered for convenience in the checklist below alphabetically by subject.

	MINT	EXC	G-VG
COMPLETE SET (16)	14.00	7.00	1.40
COMMON PLAYER (1-16)	.80	.40	.08

☐ 1 Andre Bovain 31	.80	.40	.08
☐ 2 Colby Brown 44	.80	.40	.08
☐ 3 Donnell Bruce 14	.80	.40	.08
☐ 4 Eric Burks 24	.80	.40	.08
☐ 5 Dale Davis 34	4.50	2.25	.45
☐ 6 Cliff Ellis CO	1.25	.60	.12
☐ 7 Len Gordy CO	.80	.40	.08
☐ 8 Eugene Harris CO	.80	.40	.08
☐ 9 Steve Harris 13	1.50	.75	.15
☐ 10 Ricky Jones 25	.80	.40	.08
☐ 11 Shawn Lastinger 15	.80	.40	.08
☐ 12 Jimmy Mason 10	.80	.40	.08
☐ 13 Tyrone Paul 32	.80	.40	.08
☐ 14 Sean Tyson 22	.80	.40	.08
☐ 15 Joey Watts 20	.80	.40	.08
☐ 16 David Young 11	.80	.40	.08

1990-91 Clemson Lady Tigers

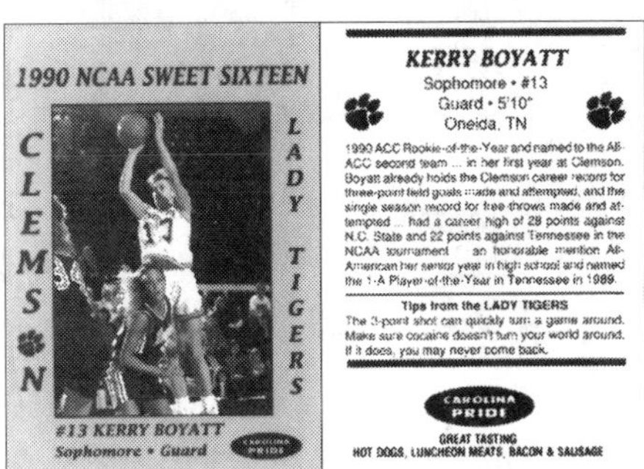

This 16-card set was sponsored by Carolina Pride and features Clemson's Lady Tigers basketball team, who made it to the round of sixteen in the 1990 NCAA tournament. The cards measure the standard size (2 1/2" by 3 1/2") and are printed on thin card stock. The fronts feature color action player photos enclosed by full-bleed orange borders. The top has 1990 NCAA Sweet Sixteen in black; the sides display the school and team names; and the bottom carries player information. The backs present biography, career summary, and "Tips from the Lady Tigers" which consist of anti-drug and alcohol messages. The cards are unnumbered and checklisted below in alphabetical order.

	MINT	EXC	G-VG
COMPLETE SET (16)	9.00	4.50	.90
COMMON PLAYER (1-16)	.60	.30	.06
☐ 1 Kerry Boyatt	.60	.30	.06
☐ 2 Shandy Bryan	.60	.30	.06
☐ 3 Jim Davis CO	.60	.30	.06
☐ 4 Jackie Farmer	.60	.30	.06
☐ 5 Donna Forrest	.60	.30	.06
☐ 6 Shanna Howard	.60	.30	.06
☐ 7 Courtney Johnson	.60	.30	.06
☐ 8 Jackie Mattress	.60	.30	.06
☐ 9 Melissa Miller	.60	.30	.06
☐ 10 Angie Peters	.60	.30	.06
☐ 11 Dana Puckett	.60	.30	.06
☐ 12 Peggy Sells	.60	.30	.06
☐ 13 Kim Stephens	.60	.30	.06
☐ 14 Cheron Wells	.60	.30	.06
☐ 15 Imani Wilson	.60	.30	.06
☐ 16 Title Card The Davis Era	.60	.30	.06

1990-91 Clemson Promos *

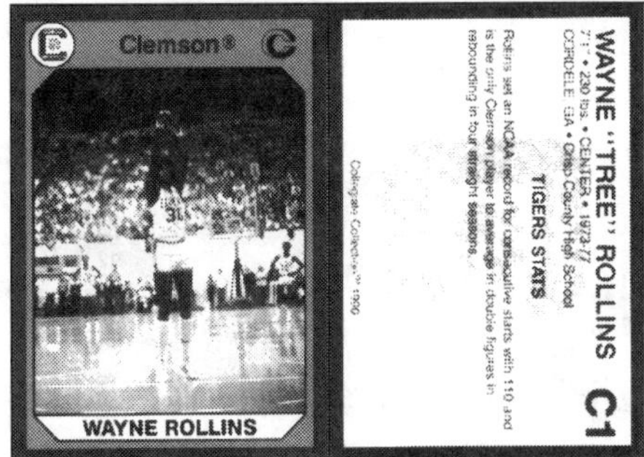

This ten-card set measures the standard card size of 2 1/2" by 3 1/2" and was issued by Collegiate Collection to honor some of the great athletes who played at Clemson. The front of the card features a full-color photo of the person featured while the back of the card has details about the person pictured. As this set is a multi-sport set we have used a two-letter identification of the sport next to the person's name.

	MINT	EXC	G-VG
COMPLETE SET (10)	5.00	2.50	.50
COMMON PLAYER (1-10)	.50	.25	.05
☐ C1 Wayne Rollins BK	.50	.25	.05
☐ C2 CU-USC Series FB	.50	.25	.05
☐ C3 William Perry FB Bio	.75	.35	.07
☐ C4 Michael Dean Perry FB	.75	.35	.07
☐ C5 Orange Bowl FB	.50	.25	.05
☐ C6 Ken Hatfield CO FB	.50	.25	.05
☐ C7 Tim Teufel BB	.50	.25	.05
☐ C8 Dwight Clark FB	.75	.35	.07
☐ C9 William Perry FB Stat	.75	.35	.07
☐ C10 Frank Howard CO FB	.60	.30	.06

1990-91 Clemson 200 *

This 200-card set was produced by Collegiate Collection and measures the standard size (2 1/2" by 3 1/2"). The front features a mix of black and white or color player photos, with dark blue and orange borders. All four corners of the picture are cut off. In dark blue lettering the school name appears above the picture, with the player's name at the bottom of the card face. In a horizontal format the back presents biographical information, career summary, and statistics, on a white background with dark blue lettering and borders. The cards are numbered on the back.

	MINT	EXC	G-VG
COMPLETE SET (200)	20.00	10.00	2.00
COMMON PLAYER (1-200)	.10	.05	.01
☐ 1 William Perry	.35	.17	.03
☐ 2 Kevin Mack	.30	.15	.03
☐ 3 Wayne(Tree) Rollins	.20	.10	.02
☐ 4 Donald Igwebuike	.15	.07	.01
☐ 5 Michael Dean Perry	.35	.17	.03
☐ 6 Larry Nance	.50	.25	.05
☐ 7 Steve Fuller	.20	.10	.02
☐ 8 Horace Grant	.75	.35	.07
☐ 9 Frank Howard CO	.15	.07	.01
☐ 10 Orange Bowl Champs '82	.10	.05	.01
☐ 11 Brian Barnes	.25	.12	.02
☐ 12 Bobby Joe Conrad	.25	.12	.02
☐ 13 John Phillips	.10	.05	.01
☐ 14 Kevin Johnson	.10	.05	.01
☐ 15 Terry Allen	.75	.35	.07
☐ 16 Chris Morocco	.10	.05	.01
☐ 17 Elden Campbell	.50	.25	.05
☐ 18 Jimmy Key	.35	.17	.03
☐ 19 Tracy Johnson	.10	.05	.01
☐ 20 Bill Spiers	.25	.12	.02
☐ 21 Lawson Duncan	.10	.05	.01
☐ 22 Eric Eichmann	.10	.05	.01
☐ 23 Tim Teufel	.20	.10	.02
☐ 24 Vincent Hamilton	.10	.05	.01
☐ 25 Mike Eppley	.10	.05	.01
☐ 26 Hans Koeleman	.10	.05	.01
☐ 27 Tennis Facilities	.10	.05	.01
☐ 28 Marvin Sim	.10	.05	.01
☐ 29 Tigers Win Classic	.10	.05	.01
☐ 30 Jim Riggs	.15	.07	.01
☐ 31 Adubarie Otorubio	.10	.05	.01
☐ 32 Mike Milchin	.20	.10	.02
☐ 33 Bruce Murray	.20	.10	.02
☐ 34 Banks McFadden	.10	.05	.01
☐ 35 Murray Jarman	.10	.05	.01
☐ 36 The Kick 1986	.10	.05	.01
☐ 37 Gary Conner	.10	.05	.01
☐ 38 Jason Griffith	.10	.05	.01
☐ 39 Terrance Flagler	.20	.10	.02
☐ 40 Grayson Marshall	.10	.05	.01
☐ 41 David Treadwell	.25	.12	.02
☐ 42 Perry Tuttle	.25	.12	.02
☐ 43 Billy Williams	.10	.05	.01
☐ 44 Homer Jordan	.15	.07	.01
☐ 45 Dale Hatcher	.20	.10	.02
☐ 46 Steve Reese	.10	.05	.01
☐ 47 Ray Williams	.20	.10	.02
☐ 48 Obed Ariri	.20	.10	.02
☐ 49 Soccer Team Wins '87	.10	.05	.01
☐ 50 Miquel Nido	.10	.05	.01
☐ 51 Cliff Austin	.20	.10	.02
☐ 52 Chris Sherman	.10	.05	.01
☐ 53 Jeff Nunamacher	.10	.05	.01
☐ 54 Steve Berlin	.10	.05	.01
☐ 55 Jess Neely	.20	.10	.02
☐ 56 Rick Rudeen	.10	.05	.01
☐ 57 Jeff Bryant	.20	.10	.02
☐ 58 Jerry Butler	.20	.10	.02
☐ 59 Randy Mazey	.10	.05	.01
☐ 60 Bob Paulling	.10	.05	.01
☐ 61 Matuszewski and Walters	.10	.05	.01
☐ 62 James Farr	.10	.05	.01
☐ 63 Bob Boettner	.10	.05	.01
☐ 64 Chuck McSwain	.20	.10	.02
☐ 65 Jim Stuckey	.20	.10	.02
☐ 66 Neil Simons	.10	.05	.01
☐ 67 Rodney Williams	.10	.05	.01
☐ 68 Butch Zatezalo	.10	.05	.01
☐ 69 Dr.I.M. Ibrahim	.10	.05	.01
☐ 70 Richard Matuszewski	.10	.05	.01
☐ 71 Dwight Clark	.50	.25	.05
☐ 72 Chuck Baldwin	.10	.05	.01
☐ 73 Kenny Flowers	.20	.10	.02
☐ 74 Michael Tait	.10	.05	.01
☐ 75 John Lee	.10	.05	.01
☐ 76 Horace Wyatt	.10	.05	.01
☐ 77 Terrence Herrington	.10	.05	.01
☐ 78 Gary Cooper	.20	.10	.02
☐ 79 Bert Hefferman	.20	.10	.02
☐ 80 Tigers with ACC Title	.10	.05	.01
☐ 81 Fred Cone	.15	.07	.01
☐ 82 Clarence Rose	.10	.05	.01
☐ 83 Jean Desdunes	.10	.05	.01
☐ 84 Donnell Woodford	.25	.12	.02
☐ 85 Ric Aronberg	.10	.05	.01
☐ 86 Mike Brown	.10	.05	.01
☐ 87 Howard Hall of Fame	.10	.05	.01
☐ 88 Swimming Pool	.10	.05	.01
☐ 89 Terry Kinard	.20	.10	.02
☐ 90 Chris Patton	.25	.12	.02
☐ 91 Baseball Stadium	.10	.05	.01
☐ 92 Cliff Ellis	.15	.07	.01
☐ 93 1989 Senior Football	.10	.05	.01
☐ 94 The Clemson Tiger	.10	.05	.01
☐ 95 Howard's Rock	.15	.07	.01
☐ 96 Jeff Davis	.20	.10	.02
☐ 97 Derrick Forrest	.10	.05	.01
☐ 98 Mack Dickson	.10	.05	.01
☐ 99 Clemson Wins Nebraska	.10	.05	.01
☐ 100 Director Card 1-99	.10	.05	.01
☐ 101 Hill shot from field	.10	.05	.01
☐ 102 Ray Williams	.20	.10	.02
☐ 103 Jim McCollom	.10	.05	.01
☐ 104 Charlie Waters	.25	.12	.02
☐ 105 Soccer and Tennis Area	.10	.05	.01
☐ 106 Bill Wilhelm	.10	.05	.01
☐ 107 Bubba Brown	.10	.05	.01
☐ 108 Ken Hatfield is hired	.10	.05	.01
☐ 109 Lester Brown	.10	.05	.01
☐ 110 James Robinson	.10	.05	.01
☐ 111 Perry and Perry	.25	.12	.02
☐ 112 Nuamoi Nwokocha	.10	.05	.01
☐ 113 Frank Howard CO	.15	.07	.01
☐ 114 Bill Foster CO	.10	.05	.01
☐ 115 Wesley McFadden	.10	.05	.01
☐ 116 Clemson 35, Penn State 10	.10	.05	.01
☐ 117 Jay Berger	.30	.15	.03
☐ 118 Andy Headen	.20	.10	.02
☐ 119 Hall of Famers	.10	.05	.01
☐ 120 Hill Shot from Board	.10	.05	.01
☐ 121 Harry Olszewski	.10	.05	.01
☐ 122 CU clinches season	.10	.05	.01
☐ 123 Super Bowl Rings	.10	.05	.01
☐ 124 Otis Moore	.10	.05	.01
☐ 125 Kirk Howling	.10	.05	.01
☐ 126 Defensive Rankings	.10	.05	.01
☐ 127 Bostic Brothers	.20	.10	.02
☐ 128 Bob Pollock	.10	.05	.01
☐ 129 Randy Scott	.10	.05	.01
☐ 130 Noel Loban	.10	.05	.01
☐ 131 Clemson and Stanford	.10	.05	.01
☐ 132 All Americans	.10	.05	.01
☐ 133 Danny Ford record	.15	.07	.01
☐ 134 Larry Penley	.10	.05	.01
☐ 135 Littlejohn Coliseum	.10	.05	.01
☐ 136 Clyde Browne	.10	.05	.01
☐ 137 Clemson 13, Okla. 6	.10	.05	.01
☐ 138 Clemson and West Virginia	.10	.05	.01
☐ 139 Clemson and Notre Dame	.10	.05	.01
☐ 140 Bush in jacket	.50	.25	.05
☐ 141 Fuller and Butler	.25	.12	.02
☐ 142 Safety Celebration	.10	.05	.01
☐ 143 Oswald Drawdy	.10	.05	.01
☐ 144 Phillips	.10	.05	.01
☐ 145 Chuck Kriese	.10	.05	.01
☐ 146 Balloon Launch	.10	.05	.01
☐ 147 Perry with poster	.25	.12	.02
☐ 148 Jim Davis	.15	.07	.01
☐ 149 Jim Brennan	.10	.05	.01
☐ 150 Death Valley	.10	.05	.01
☐ 151 Tina Krebs	.10	.05	.01
☐ 152 Andy Johnston	.10	.05	.01
☐ 153 Wayne Coffman	.10	.05	.01
☐ 154 Andy Tribble	.10	.05	.01
☐ 155 Mitzi Kremer	.10	.05	.01
☐ 156 Rusty Adkins	.10	.05	.01
☐ 157 Choppy Patterson	.10	.05	.01
☐ 158 Jill Bakehorn	.10	.05	.01
☐ 159 Baker vs. Tanner	.15	.07	.01
☐ 160 Jerry Butler	.25	.12	.02
☐ 161 Championship Rings	.10	.05	.01
☐ 162 Shawn Weatherly	.50	.25	.05
☐ 163 Homecoming	.10	.05	.01
☐ 164 Barbara Kennedy	.10	.05	.01
☐ 165 Sports Facilities	.10	.05	.01
☐ 166 Tommy Mahaffey	.10	.05	.01
☐ 167 Dillard Pruitt	.15	.07	.01
☐ 168 Bill Yarborough	.10	.05	.01
☐ 169 Billy O'Dell	.20	.10	.02
☐ 170 Joe Blalock	.10	.05	.01
☐ 171 Ute Jamrozy	.10	.05	.01
☐ 172 Jerry Pryor	.10	.05	.01
☐ 173 Susan Hill	.10	.05	.01
☐ 174 Eddie Griffin	.10	.05	.01
☐ 175 Jane Forman	.10	.05	.01
☐ 176 Obed Ariri	.15	.07	.01
☐ 177 Richie Mahaffey	.10	.05	.01
☐ 178 Bobby Gage	.10	.05	.01
☐ 179 John Heisman CO	.25	.12	.02
☐ 180 Joe Landrum	.10	.05	.01
☐ 181 Soccer and Tennis	.10	.05	.01
☐ 182 Clemson vs. USC	.10	.05	.01

		MINT	EXC	G-VG
☐	183 Linda White	.10	.05	.01
☐	184 Denise Murphy	.10	.05	.01
☐	185 Mary Ann Cubelic	.10	.05	.01
☐	186 Pam Hayden	.10	.05	.01
☐	187 Coy Cobb	.10	.05	.01
☐	188 Randy Mahaffey	.15	.07	.01
☐	189 Lou Cordileone	.10	.05	.01
☐	190 1949 Gator Bowl	.10	.05	.01
☐	191 Karen Ann Jenkins	.10	.05	.01
☐	192 Bobbie Mims	.10	.05	.01
☐	193 Janet Knight	.10	.05	.01
☐	194 Ray Matthews	.15	.07	.01
☐	195 Gigi Fernandez	.35	.17	.03
☐	196 Joey McKenna	.10	.05	.01
☐	197 Denny Walling	.15	.07	.01
☐	198 Janet Ellison	.10	.05	.01
☐	199 Donnie Mahaffey	.10	.05	.01
☐	200 Director Card 101-200	.10	.05	.01

1990-91 Connecticut Police

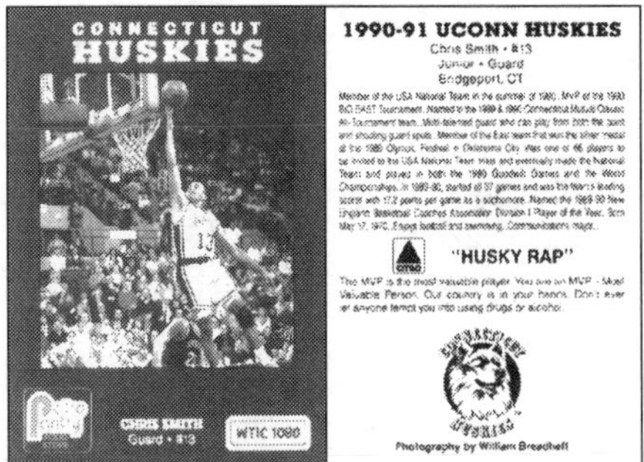

This 16-card set was sponsored by Petro Pantry food stores, WTIC 1080 radio, and Citgo. The cards were issued in four strips of four cards each; after perforation, they measure the standard size (2 1/2" by 3 1/2"). The front features a color action player photo on a dark blue background. In white lettering the team name appears above the picture. Player information is given below the picture, sandwiched between sponsors' logos. The back has biographical information, career summary, and "Husky Rap," which consists of an anti-drug or alcohol message. A Huskie's logo at the bottom completes the card back. The cards are unnumbered and are checklisted below in alphabetical order, with the uniform number after the player's name.

		MINT	EXC	G-VG
	COMPLETE SET (16)	15.00	7.50	1.50
	COMMON PLAYER (1-16)	.80	.40	.08
☐	1 Scott Burrell 24	3.00	1.50	.30
☐	2 Jim Calhoun CO	1.25	.60	.12
☐	3 Dan Cyrulik 55	.80	.40	.08
☐	4 Lyman DePriest 23	1.00	.50	.10
☐	5 Shawn Ellison 32	.80	.40	.08
☐	6 John Gwynn 15	.80	.40	.08
☐	7 Gilad Katz 10	.80	.40	.08
☐	8 Oliver Macklin 11	.80	.40	.08
☐	9 Steve Pikiell 21	.80	.40	.08
☐	10 Tim Pikiell 31	.80	.40	.08
☐	11 Rod Sellers 22	1.50	.75	.15
☐	12 Chris Smith 13	3.00	1.50	.30
☐	13 Marc Suhr 30	.80	.40	.08
☐	14 Torano Walker 42	1.00	.50	.10
☐	15 Murray Williams 20	.80	.40	.08
☐	16 Jonathan Mascot	.80	.40	.08

1991-92 Connecticut Legends

This 16-card standard-size (2 1/2" by 3 1/2") set was sponsored by Petro Pantry Food Stores and WTIC-1080. It was issued in four stripes with four cards each and features outstanding players and coaches from the University of Connecticut. The fronts feature a mix of black, white or color player photos. The pictures are bordered by white on the top and the sides, with the words "Connecticut Basketball Legends" printed in dark blue in these white borders. Sponsor logos and the player's name appear in the bottom dark blue border. In dark blue print on white, the backs present biography, career summary, and "Husky Rap," which consists of anti-drug and alcohol messages. The cards are unnumbered and checklisted below in alphabetical order. The key card in the set is Cliff Robinson.

		MINT	EXC	G-VG
	COMPLETE SET (16)	10.00	5.00	1.00
	COMMON PLAYER (1-16)	.50	.25	.05
☐	1 Wes Bialosuknia	.50	.25	.05
☐	2 Jim Calhoun CO	.75	.35	.07
☐	3 Walt Dropo	1.00	.50	.10
☐	4 Phil Gamble	.50	.25	.05
☐	5 Tate George	1.00	.50	.10
☐	6 Hugh Greer CO	.50	.25	.05
☐	7 Tony Hanson	.50	.25	.05
☐	8 Nadav Henefeld	1.00	.50	.10
☐	9 Toby Kimball	.75	.35	.07
☐	10 Mike McKay	.50	.25	.05
☐	11 Cliff Robinson	3.00	1.50	.30
☐	12 Dee Rowe CO	.50	.25	.05
☐	13 John Thomas	.50	.25	.05
☐	14 Corny Thompson	1.00	.50	.10
☐	15 Art Quimby	.50	.25	.05
☐	16 UConn Field House	.50	.25	.05

1991-92 Connecticut Police

This 16-card set was sponsored by Petro Pantry Food Stores and Citgo. The cards measure the standard size (2 1/2" by 3 1/2"). The fronts are accented in the team's colors (dark blue and white) and have color action player photos. The top of the pictures is curved to resemble an archway, and the school and team names follow the curve of the arch. In dark blue print on white, the backs have biography, career summary, and "Husky Rap," which consist of anti-drug and alcohol messages. The cards are unnumbered and checklisted below in alphabetical order. The key cards in the set are Scott Burrell and Chris Smith.

		MINT	EXC	G-VG
	COMPLETE SET (16)	12.00	6.00	1.20
	COMMON PLAYER (1-16)	.60	.30	.06
☐	1 Rich Ashmeade	.60	.30	.06
☐	2 Scott Burrell	2.00	1.00	.20
☐	3 Jeff Calhoun	.75	.35	.07
☐	4 Dan Cyrulik	.60	.30	.06

☐ 5 Brian Fair	.60	.30	.06
☐ 6 Rudy Johnson	.60	.30	.06
☐ 7 Gilad Katz	.60	.30	.06
☐ 8 Oliver Macklin	.60	.30	.06
☐ 9 Donny Marshall	.60	.30	.06
☐ 10 Donyell Marshall	.60	.30	.06
☐ 11 Kevin Ollie	.60	.30	.06
☐ 12 Tim Pikiell	.60	.30	.06
☐ 13 Rod Sellers	1.00	.50	.10
☐ 14 Chris Smith	2.00	1.00	.20
☐ 15 Toraino Walker	.75	.35	.07
☐ 16 Nantambu Willingham	.60	.30	.06

1983-84 Dayton Blue Shield

This 20-card set of Dayton Flyers was sponsored by Blue Shield and television Channel 7. The cards measure the standard size (2 1/2" by 3 1/2"). The front features borderless blue-tinted posed player photos, with the player's name above and team name below in red lettering on white card stock. The horizontally-oriented backs are printed in blue and provide biographical information and the sponsors' logos. The cards are unnumbered and are checklisted below in alphabetical order. There was a 21st card in the set which was pulled from the set just prior to mass distribution due to the fact that the player quit the team.

	MINT	EXC	G-VG
COMPLETE SET (20)	25.00	12.50	2.50
COMMON PLAYER (1-20)	1.00	.50	.10
☐ 1 Jack Butler and Dan Hipsher (Coaches)	1.50	.75	.15
☐ 2 Roosevelt Chapman	5.00	2.50	.50
☐ 3 Dan Christie	1.00	.50	.10
☐ 4 Dave Colbert	1.00	.50	.10
☐ 5 Rory Dahlinghaus	1.00	.50	.10
☐ 6 Don Donoher CO	2.50	1.25	.25
☐ 7 Damon Goodwin	1.00	.50	.10
☐ 8 Anthony Grant	1.00	.50	.10
☐ 9 Ted Harris	1.00	.50	.10
☐ 10 Mike Hartsock	1.00	.50	.10
☐ 11 Paul Hawkins	1.00	.50	.10
☐ 12 Mick Hubert	1.00	.50	.10
☐ 13 Don Hughes	1.00	.50	.10
☐ 14 Larry Schellenberg	1.00	.50	.10
☐ 15 Jim Shields	1.00	.50	.10
☐ 16 Sedric Toney	2.00	1.00	.20
☐ 17 Jeff Tressler	1.00	.50	.10
☐ 18 Ed Young	1.00	.50	.10
☐ 19 Jeff Zern	1.00	.50	.10
☐ 20 Flyer Fan Card	1.50	.75	.15

1986-87 DePaul Playing Cards

This set of playing cards was issued to honor Ray Meyer, who retired fifth on the all-time list of most career victories for Division I coaches. The cards measure the standard size (2 1/2" by 3 1/2"). The fronts feature posed or action black and white photos that span Meyer's career and his teams. The backs are turquoise with a white border and white lettering. At the top is a DePaul Blue Demons logo in white, then the school name, and in the lower half of the card is a head shot of Ray Meyer in a heart-shaped opening. At the bottom the coach's name is given along with the words "42 Memorable Years." Numerical values have been assigned to all the cards (ace 1; jack 11, etc.). The cards are listed according to suits as follows: hearts (H), clubs (C), diamonds (D), and spades (S). The two jokers are listed at the end.

	MINT	EXC	G-VG
COMPLETE SET (54)	35.00	17.50	3.50
COMMON PLAYER	.50	.25	.05
☐ H1 Ray Meyer	1.50	.75	.15
☐ H2 1st Team (1942)	.50	.25	.05
☐ H3 Dick Triptow	.50	.25	.05
☐ H4 1st NIT Championship 1945	.50	.25	.05
☐ H5 George Mikan	2.50	1.25	.25
☐ H6 NIT Starting Five 1945	.50	.25	.05
☐ H7 Ed Mikan and Whitey Kachan	1.00	.50	.10
☐ H8 Early Great Team	.50	.25	.05
☐ H9 George Mikan and Bill Donato	1.25	.60	.12
☐ H10 Bato Govedarica	.50	.25	.05
☐ H11 1948 Team	.50	.25	.05
☐ H12 Ray, Marge, and Family	.75	.35	.07
☐ H13 Dick Heise	.50	.25	.05
☐ C1 Coach of the Year 1944	.75	.35	.07
☐ C2 Frank Blum and Jim Lamkin	.50	.25	.05
☐ C3 Bill Robinzine and Ron Sobieszcyk	.75	.35	.07
☐ C4 Howie Carl	.75	.35	.07
☐ C5 McKinley Cowsen	.50	.25	.05
☐ C6 M.C. Thompson	.50	.25	.05
☐ C7 Emmette Bryant	.75	.35	.07
☐ C8 NIT Tournament 1963	.50	.25	.05
☐ C9 Tom Meyer	.50	.25	.05
☐ C10 Starting Five	.50	.25	.05

	1965-66			
☐ C11	Dave Mills	.50	.25	.05
☐ C12	400th Victory Celebration	.50	.25	.05
☐ C13	Joey Meyer	1.00	.50	.10
☐ D1	Basketball Hall of Fame	.50	.25	.05
☐ D2	Jim Mitchem	.50	.25	.05
☐ D3	Mark Aguirre	1.25	.60	.12
☐ D4	Gary Garland	.75	.35	.07
☐ D5	Final Four NCAA 1978-79	.50	.25	.05
☐ D6	Curtis Watkins	.50	.25	.05
☐ D7	Joe Ponsetto	.50	.25	.05
☐ D8	Ray and Digger Phelps	1.00	.50	.10
☐ D9	Ron Norwood	.50	.25	.05
☐ D10	Dave Corzine	.75	.35	.07
☐ D11	Ray and Al McGuire	1.00	.50	.10
☐ D12	Bill Robinzine Jr.	.50	.25	.05
☐ D13	500th Victory	.50	.25	.05
☐ S1	700th Victory	.50	.25	.05
☐ S2	Jerry McMillan	.50	.25	.05
☐ S3	Last Home Game	.50	.25	.05
☐ S4	Rosemont Horizon	.50	.25	.05
☐ S5	Ray and Joey	.75	.35	.07
☐ S6	Terry Cummings turns Pro	1.25	.60	.12
☐ S7	Terry Cummings	1.25	.60	.12
☐ S8	No. 1 Basketball Family	.50	.25	.05
☐ S9	Last Game at Alumni Hall	.50	.25	.05
☐ S10	Mark Aguirre and Clyde Bradshaw	.75	.35	.07
☐ S11	Mark Aguirre and Terry Cummings	1.50	.75	.15
☐ S12	1979-80 Team	.50	.25	.05
☐ S13	1970-80 Team Clowning	.50	.25	.05
☐ xx	Joker Card Year by year record	.50	.25	.05
☐ xx	Joker Card Milestones	.50	.25	.05

1987-88 Duke Police

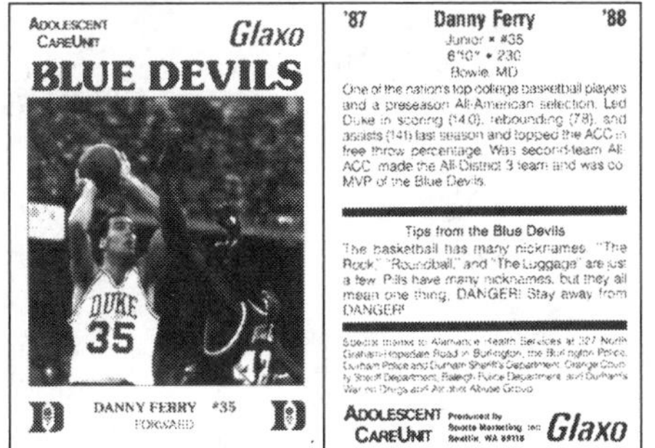

This 13-card set featuring the Duke Blue Devils basketball team measures the standard card size of 2 1/2" by 3 1/2". This set features members of the semi-finalists of the 1988 NCAA Tournament. The set is sponsored by Adolescent Care Unit and Glaxo and their company names are on the top of the card. Underneath their names is the Blue Devils' identification. The full-color players photo is in the middle of the card and on the bottom of the card is the players name, uniform number, and position. The back has basic biographical information about the players along with both a basketball and a anti-crime or drug message. Some of the key players in the set include future NBA players Danny Ferry and Alaa Abdelnaby. The set was produced by Sports Marketing of Seattle, Washington. The cards are numbered for convenience in the checklist below according to the player's uniform number.

		MINT	EXC	G-VG
COMPLETE SET (13)		40.00	20.00	4.00
COMMON PLAYER		2.00	1.00	.20
☐ 13	Joe Cook	2.00	1.00	.20
☐ 14	Quin Snyder	3.00	1.50	.30
☐ 21	Robert Brickey	5.00	2.50	.50
☐ 22	Greg Koubek	3.00	1.50	.30
☐ 30	Alaa Abdelnaby	8.00	4.00	.80
☐ 31	Kevin Strickland	3.00	1.50	.30
☐ 33	John Smith	2.00	1.00	.20
☐ 35	Danny Ferry	10.00	5.00	1.00
☐ 42	George Burgin	2.00	1.00	.20
☐ 44	Phil Henderson	5.00	2.50	.50
☐ 45	Clay Buckley	2.00	1.00	.20
☐ 55	Billy King	3.00	1.50	.30
☐ xx	Mike Krzyzewski CO	8.00	4.00	.80

1988-89 Duke Police/Glaxo

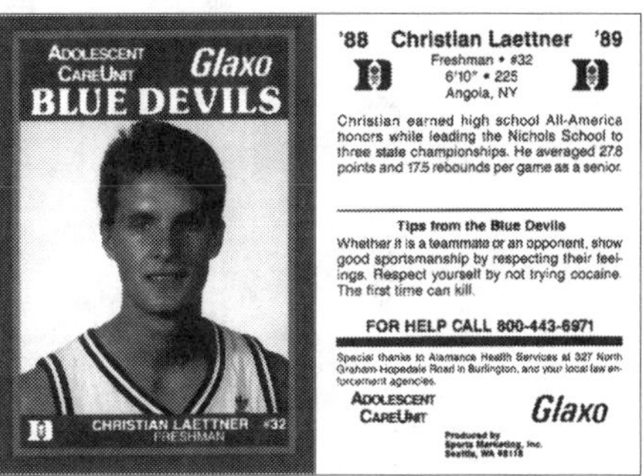

This 13-card set featuring the Duke Blue Devils was sponsored by Adolescent CareUnit, Glaxo, and local law enforcement agencies. The cards measure the standard size (2 1/2" by 3 1/2"). On a royal blue card face, the fronts show color action player photos enclosed by gray border stripes. Sponsor logos and the team name appear above the picture, while the player's name, jersey number, and position are given below it. In addition to sponsor acknowledgments, the backs carry player profile and "Tips from the Blue Devils," which consist of anti-drug and alcohol messages. The cards are unnumbered and checklisted below in alphabetical order.

		MINT	EXC	G-VG
COMPLETE SET (13)		45.00	22.50	4.50
COMMON PLAYER (1-13)		1.00	.50	.10
☐ 1	Alaa Abdelnaby	5.00	2.50	.50
☐ 2	Robert Brickey	3.00	1.50	.30
☐ 3	Clay Buckley	1.00	.50	.10
☐ 4	George Burgin	1.00	.50	.10
☐ 5	Brian Davis	7.50	3.75	.75
☐ 6	Danny Ferry	6.00	3.00	.60
☐ 7	Phil Henderson	3.00	1.50	.30
☐ 8	Greg Koubek	1.50	.75	.15
☐ 9	Mike Krzyzewski CO	5.00	2.50	.50
☐ 10	Christian Laettner	25.00	12.50	2.50
☐ 11	Crawford Palmer	1.00	.50	.10
☐ 12	John Smith	1.00	.50	.10
☐ 13	Quin Snyder	1.50	.75	.15

1982-83 Fairfield

This 18-card set for Fairfield University is numbered on the back and measures the standard, 2 1/2" by 3 1/2". The cards were produced by Big League Cards. The front features a posed color photo enframed by black and red borders, with the player's name, the university, and a basketball logo below the picture. The back gives biographical information.

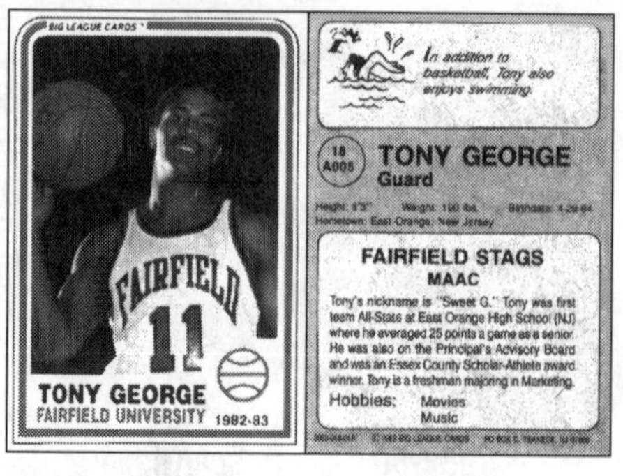

	MINT	EXC	G-VG
COMPLETE SET (18)	18.00	9.00	1.80
COMMON PLAYER (1-18)	1.00	.50	.10
☐ 1 Jay Byrne	1.00	.50	.10
☐ 2 Vin Cazzetta	1.00	.50	.10
☐ 3 Pete DeBisschop	1.00	.50	.10
☐ 4 Joe DeSantis CO	1.50	.75	.15
☐ 5 Tony George	1.00	.50	.10
☐ 6 Craig Golden	1.00	.50	.10
☐ 7 Bobby Hurt	1.00	.50	.10
☐ 8 Ed Janka CO	1.00	.50	.10
☐ 9 Jerry Johnson	1.00	.50	.10
☐ 10 John Leonard	1.00	.50	.10
☐ 11 Terry O'Connor	1.00	.50	.10
☐ 12 Tim O'Toole	1.00	.50	.10
☐ 13 Brendan Potter	1.00	.50	.10
☐ 14 Ron Ross CO	1.00	.50	.10
☐ 15 Greg Schwartz	1.00	.50	.10
☐ 16 Don Wilson	1.00	.50	.10
☐ 17 Pat Yerina	1.00	.50	.10
☐ 18 Fairfield Stags	1.00	.50	.10

1988-89 Florida Burger King *

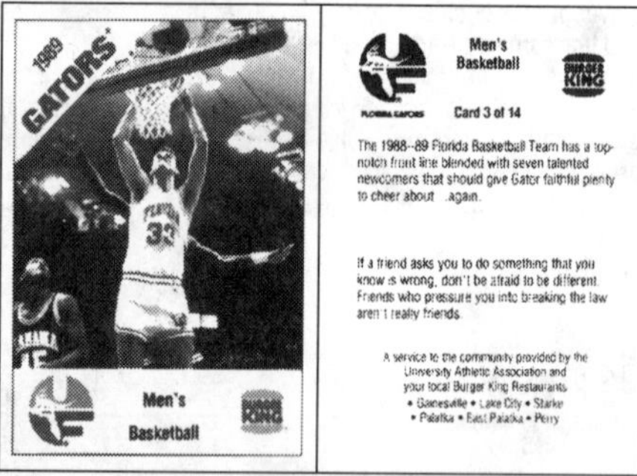

This 14-card set was sponsored by University Athletic Association in conjunction with Burger King. The cards measure the standard size (2 1/2" by 3 1/2"). The front features a color action shot of an athlete engaging in the particular sport highlighted on the card. The pictures are outlined by a thin black border on white card stock. The Burger King and the Gators' logo round out the card face. The back provides additional information on the sport as well as an anti-drug or crime message. The cards are numbered on the back.

	MINT	EXC	G-VG
COMPLETE SET (14)	10.00	5.00	1.00
COMMON PLAYER (1-14)	.75	.35	.07
☐ 1 Men's Swimming	.75	.35	.07
☐ 2 Baseball	1.00	.50	.10
☐ 3 Men's Basketball	2.50	1.25	.25
☐ 4 Women's Tennis	1.25	.60	.12
☐ 5 Women's Track and Field	.75	.35	.07
☐ 6 Gymnastics	.75	.35	.07
☐ 7 Cross Country	.75	.35	.07
☐ 8 Women's Volleyball	.75	.35	.07
☐ 9 Women's Swimming	.75	.35	.07
☐ 10 Women's Basketball	1.25	.60	.12
☐ 11 Men's Track and Field	.75	.35	.07
☐ 12 Men's Tennis	.75	.35	.07
☐ 13 Women's Golf	.75	.35	.07
☐ 14 Men's Golf	.75	.35	.07

1990-91 Florida State 200 *

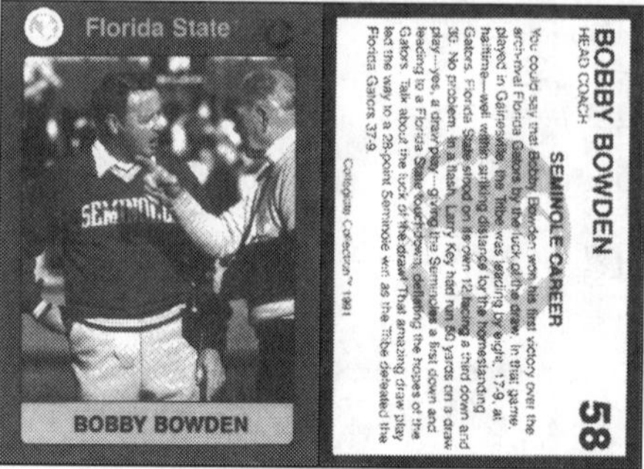

This 200-card set by Collegiate Collection features past and current athletes of Florida State University. The cards measure the standard size 2 1/2" by 3 1/2". The front has an action color photo of the player enclosed by a thin black border against a maroon background. The player's name appears in black print in a yellow box below the picture. The Florida State Seminoles logo is in the upper left hand corner. Biographical information is found on the back, with the card number located in the upper right hand corner.

	MINT	EXC	G-VG
COMPLETE SET (200)	20.00	10.00	2.00
COMMON PLAYER (1-200)	.10	.05	.01
☐ 1 Dick Howser	.25	.12	.02
☐ 2 Edwin Alicea	.15	.07	.01
☐ 3 Randy White	.10	.05	.01
☐ 4 Steve Gabbard	.10	.05	.01
☐ 5 Pat Tomberlin	.20	.10	.02
☐ 6 Herb Gainer	.10	.05	.01
☐ 7 Bobby Jackson	.15	.07	.01
☐ 8 Redus Coggin	.10	.05	.01
☐ 9 Pat Carter	.10	.05	.01
☐ 10 Kevin Grant	.10	.05	.01
☐ 11 Peter Tom Willis	.40	.20	.04
☐ 12 Phil Carollo	.10	.05	.01
☐ 13 Derek Schmidt	.10	.05	.01
☐ 14 Rick Stockstill	.15	.07	.01
☐ 15 Mike Martin	.10	.05	.01
☐ 16 Terry Anthony	.10	.05	.01
☐ 17 Darrin Holloman	.10	.05	.01
☐ 18 John McLean	.10	.05	.01
☐ 19 Rudy Maloy	.10	.05	.01
☐ 20 Gary Huff	.25	.12	.02
☐ 21 Jamey Shouppe	.10	.05	.01
☐ 22 Isaac Williams	.10	.05	.01
☐ 23 Weegie Thompson	.25	.12	.02
☐ 24 Jose Marzan	.10	.05	.01
☐ 25 Gerald Nichols	.10	.05	.01
☐ 26 John Brown	.10	.05	.01
☐ 27 Danny McManus	.25	.12	.02
☐ 28 Parrish Barwick	.10	.05	.01
☐ 29 Paul McGowan	.10	.05	.01
☐ 30 Keith Jones	.15	.07	.01
☐ 31 Alphonso Williams	.10	.05	.01
☐ 32 Luis Alicea	.30	.15	.03
☐ 33 Tony Yeomans	.10	.05	.01
☐ 34 Michael Tanks	.10	.05	.01
☐ 35 Stan Shiver	.10	.05	.01
☐ 36 Willie Jones	.10	.05	.01
☐ 37 Wally Woodham	.10	.05	.01
☐ 38 Chip Ferguson	.10	.05	.01

☐ 39 Sam Childers .10 .05 .01
☐ 40 Paul Piurowski .10 .05 .01
☐ 41 Joey Ionata .10 .05 .01
☐ 42 John Hadley .10 .05 .01
☐ 43 Tanner Holloman .10 .05 .01
☐ 44 Fred Jones .10 .05 .01
☐ 45 Terry Warren .10 .05 .01
☐ 46 John Merna .10 .05 .01
☐ 47 Jimmy Jordan .15 .07 .01
☐ 48 Dave Capellen .10 .05 .01
☐ 49 Martin Mayhew .20 .10 .02
☐ 50 Barry Barco .10 .05 .01
☐ 51 Ronald Lewis .10 .05 .01
☐ 52 Tom O'Malley .15 .07 .01
☐ 53 Rick Tuten .20 .10 .02
☐ 54 Ed Fulton .10 .05 .01
☐ 55 Marc Ronan .10 .05 .01
☐ 56 Bobby Bowden .20 .10 .02
☐ 57 Bobby Bowden .20 .10 .02
☐ 58 Bobby Bowden .20 .10 .02
☐ 59 Bobby Bowden .20 .10 .02
☐ 60 Bobby Bowden .20 .10 .02
☐ 61 John Grubb .20 .10 .02
☐ 62 Joe Wessel .10 .05 .01
☐ 63 Alphonso Carreker .20 .10 .02
☐ 64 Shelton Thompson .10 .05 .01
☐ 65 Tracy Sanders .10 .05 .01
☐ 66 Bobby Bowden .20 .10 .02
☐ 67 Bobby Bowden .20 .10 .02
☐ 68 Bobby Bowden .20 .10 .02
☐ 69 Bobby Bowden .20 .10 .02
☐ 70 Bobby Bowden .20 .10 .02
☐ 71 David Palmer .20 .10 .02
☐ 72 Jason Kuipers .10 .05 .01
☐ 73 Dayne Williams .10 .05 .01
☐ 74 Mark Salva .10 .05 .01
☐ 75 Bobby Butler .15 .07 .01
☐ 76 Bobby Bowden .20 .10 .02
☐ 77 Bobby Bowden .20 .10 .02
☐ 78 Bobby Bowden .20 .10 .02
☐ 79 Bobby Bowden .20 .10 .02
☐ 80 Bobby Bowden .20 .10 .02
☐ 81 Mike Loynd .20 .10 .02
☐ 82 Dexter Carter .40 .20 .04
☐ 83 Dedrick Dodge .10 .05 .01
☐ 84 Greg Allen .15 .07 .01
☐ 85 Barry Blackwell .10 .05 .01
☐ 86 Bobby Bowden .20 .10 .02
☐ 87 Bobby Bowden .20 .10 .02
☐ 88 Bobby Bowden .20 .10 .02
☐ 89 Bobby Bowden .20 .10 .02
☐ 90 Bobby Bowden .20 .10 .02
☐ 91 Bill Capece .15 .07 .01
☐ 92 Eric Hayes .10 .05 .01
☐ 93 Garth Jax .20 .10 .02
☐ 94 Odell Haggins .10 .05 .01
☐ 95 Leroy Butler .10 .05 .01
☐ 96 Monk Bonasorte .10 .05 .01
☐ 97 Richie Lewis .40 .20 .04
☐ 98 Terry Kennedy .20 .10 .02
☐ 99 Hubert Green .25 .12 .02
☐ 100 Director Card .10 .05 .01
☐ 101 Doc Hermann .10 .05 .01
☐ 102 Gary Futch .10 .05 .01
☐ 103 Tony Romeo .10 .05 .01
☐ 104 Lee Corso .20 .10 .02
☐ 105 Steve Bratton .10 .05 .01
☐ 106 Barry Rice .10 .05 .01
☐ 107 Jeff Hogan .10 .05 .01
☐ 108 John Wachtel .10 .05 .01
☐ 109 Dick Artmeier .10 .05 .01
☐ 110 Vic Szezepanik .10 .05 .01
☐ 111 Danny Litwhiler .15 .07 .01
☐ 112 Jack Fenwick .10 .05 .01
☐ 113 Nolan Henke .10 .05 .01
☐ 114 Mark Meseroll .10 .05 .01
☐ 115 Jimmy Everett .10 .05 .01
☐ 116 Gary Schull .10 .05 .01
☐ 117 Les Murdock .10 .05 .01
☐ 118 Ron Schomburger .10 .05 .01
☐ 119 Scott Warren .10 .05 .01
☐ 120 Eric Williams .10 .05 .01
☐ 121 Buddy Strauss .10 .05 .01
☐ 122 Juan Bonilla .10 .05 .01
☐ 123 Rowland Garrett .15 .07 .01
☐ 124 Kenny Knox .15 .07 .01
☐ 125 Bill Cappleman .15 .07 .01
☐ 126 Bill Kimber .10 .05 .01
☐ 127 Mike Fuentes .15 .07 .01
☐ 128 Bill Proctor .10 .05 .01
☐ 129 Kurt Unglaub .10 .05 .01
☐ 130 Woody Woodward .20 .10 .02
☐ 131 Dave Cowens .45 .22 .04
☐ 132 Lee Nelson .10 .05 .01
☐ 133 Robert Urich .50 .25 .05
☐ 134 Ron Fraser .15 .07 .01
☐ 135 Randy Coffield .10 .05 .01
☐ 136 Jimmy Lee Taylor .10 .05 .01
☐ 137 Max Wettstein .10 .05 .01
☐ 138 Brian Williams .15 .07 .01
☐ 139 T.K. Wetherell .10 .05 .01
☐ 140 Dale McCullers .10 .05 .01
☐ 141 Peter Tom Willis .40 .20 .04
☐ 142 Doug Little .10 .05 .01
☐ 143 J.T. Thomas .20 .10 .02
☐ 144 Hassan Jones .25 .12 .02
☐ 145 Deion Sanders .90 .45 .09
☐ 146 Barry Smith .10 .05 .01
☐ 147 Hugh Durham .20 .10 .02
☐ 148 Bill Moremen .10 .05 .01
☐ 149 Gary Henry .10 .05 .01
☐ 150 John Madden .50 .25 .05
☐ 151 J.T. Thomas .20 .10 .02
☐ 152 Tony Avitable .10 .05 .01
☐ 153 Keith Kinderman .10 .05 .01
☐ 154 Bill Dawson .10 .05 .01
☐ 155 Mike Good .10 .05 .01
☐ 156 Kim Hammond .10 .05 .01
☐ 157 Buddy Blankenship .10 .05 .01
☐ 158 Jimmy Black .10 .05 .01
☐ 159 Vic Prinzi .10 .05 .01
☐ 160 Bobby Renn .10 .05 .01
☐ 161 Mark Macek .20 .10 .02
☐ 162 Wayne McDuffie .10 .05 .01
☐ 163 Joe Avezzano .20 .10 .02
☐ 164 Hector Gray .10 .05 .01
☐ 165 Grant Guthrie .10 .05 .01
☐ 166 Tom Bailey .10 .05 .01
☐ 167 Ron Sellers .20 .10 .02
☐ 168 Dick Hermann .10 .05 .01
☐ 169 Bob Harbison .10 .05 .01
☐ 170 Winfred Bailey .10 .05 .01
☐ 171 James Harris .10 .05 .01
☐ 172 Jerry Jacobs .10 .05 .01
☐ 173 Mike Kincaid .10 .05 .01
☐ 174 Jimmy Heggins .10 .05 .01
☐ 175 Steve Kalenich .10 .05 .01
☐ 176 Del Williams .15 .07 .01
☐ 177 Fred Pickard .10 .05 .01
☐ 178 Walt Sumner .15 .07 .01
☐ 179 Bud Whitehead .10 .05 .01
☐ 180 Bobby Anderson .15 .07 .01
☐ 181 Paul Azinger .35 .17 .03
☐ 182 Burt Reynolds 1.00 .50 .10
☐ 183 Ron King .10 .05 .01
☐ 184 H. Donald Loucks .10 .05 .01
☐ 185 Jim Lyttle .15 .07 .01
☐ 186 Richard Amman .10 .05 .01
☐ 187 Bobby Crenshaw .10 .05 .01
☐ 188 Bill Dawkins .10 .05 .01
☐ 189 Ken Burnett .10 .05 .01
☐ 190 Duane Carrell .15 .07 .01
☐ 191 Gene McDowell .15 .07 .01
☐ 192 Paul Wernke .10 .05 .01
☐ 193 Beryl Rice .10 .05 .01
☐ 194 Dave Fedor .10 .05 .01
☐ 195 Brian Schmidt .10 .05 .01
☐ 196 Rhett Dawson .10 .05 .01
☐ 197 Greg Futch .10 .05 .01
☐ 198 Joe Majors .10 .05 .01
☐ 199 Stan Dobosz .10 .05 .01
☐ 200 Director Card .15 .07 .01

1985-86 Fort Hays State

As indicated on the bottom of the reverse, this 18-card set was sponsored by K-Bob's Steakhouse. Each set was accompanied by a coupon redeemable at K-Bob's. The cards measures the standard size (2 1/2" by 3 1/2") and are printed on thin card stock. The fronts feature black and white head shots framed by black borders on a white card face. A yellow diagonal bar in the upper right corner carries the college letters while the player's name appears beneath the photo in a yellow stripe. The backs have a Tiger pawprint in the upper left corner and present biography, statistics, and career summary. The cards are unnumbered and checklisted below in alphabetical order.

	MINT	EXC	G-VG
COMPLETE SET (18)	16.00	8.00	1.60

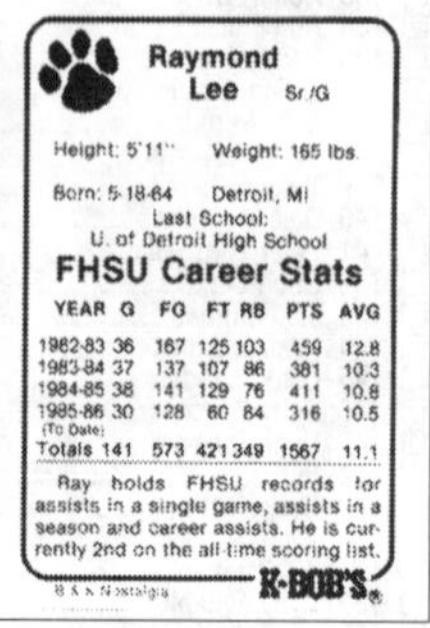

COMMON PLAYER (1-17)	1.00	.50	.10
☐ 1 Tyree Allen	1.00	.50	.10
☐ 2 Joe Anderson	1.00	.50	.10
☐ 3 Troy Applegate Student Coach	1.00	.50	.10
☐ 4 Kale Barton	1.00	.50	.10
☐ 5 Bruce Brawner	1.00	.50	.10
☐ 6 Fred Campbell	1.00	.50	.10
☐ 7 Craig Cox CO	1.00	.50	.10
☐ 8 Thomas Hardnett	1.00	.50	.10
☐ 9 Archie Johnson	1.00	.50	.10
☐ 10 David Lackey	1.00	.50	.10
☐ 11 Greg Lackey CO	1.00	.50	.10
☐ 12 Raymond Lee	1.00	.50	.10
☐ 13 Mike Miller	1.00	.50	.10
☐ 14 Bill Morse CO	1.00	.50	.10
☐ 15 Ron Morse	1.00	.50	.10
☐ 16 Cedric Williams	1.00	.50	.10
☐ 17 Team Photo	1.50	.75	.15
☐ xx Title Card	1.50	.75	.15

1989-90 Fresno State Smokey

This 16-card set was sponsored by the USDA Forest Service, several other federal agencies, and Grandy's restaurants. The cards measure the standard size (2 1/2" by 3 1/2"). The fronts feature either posed or action color player photos with a white card face background. The school name appears in red lettering above the picture, with the team name in the blue stripe just below it. Red and blue stripes appear below the picture, overlayed by the Smokey and Grandy's logos. The back has brief biographical information and a fire prevention cartoon starring Smokey the Bear. The cards are unnumbered and are checklisted below in alphabetical order, with the uniform number after the player's name.

	MINT	EXC	G-VG
COMPLETE SET (16)	10.00	5.00	1.00
COMMON PLAYER (1-16)	.75	.35	.07
☐ 1 Ron Adams CO	.75	.35	.07
☐ 2 Bijou Baly 15	.75	.35	.07
☐ 3 Dave Barnett 12	.75	.35	.07
☐ 4 Tod Bernard 33	.75	.35	.07
☐ 5 Chris Henderson 25	.75	.35	.07
☐ 6 Wilbert Hooker 30	.75	.35	.07
☐ 7 Pasi Lahtinen 3	.75	.35	.07
☐ 8 Dimitri Lambrecht 32	.75	.35	.07
☐ 9 Sammie Lindsey 50	.75	.35	.07
☐ 10 Joey Paglierani 00	.75	.35	.07
☐ 11 Todd Peebles 23	.75	.35	.07
☐ 12 Pat Riddlesprigger 34	.75	.35	.07
☐ 13 Sammy Taylor 22	.75	.35	.07
☐ 14 Carlo Williams 44	.75	.35	.07
☐ 15 Rey Young 54	.75	.35	.07
☐ 16 Greg Zuffelato 24	.75	.35	.07

1990-91 Fresno State Smokey

This 16-card set was sponsored by Grandy's and measures the standard, 2 1/2" by 3 1/2". The front features a color action photo enframed by a blue border on red background, with the player's name, position, and years below the photo, as well as a picture of Smokey the Bear in the left hand corner and a Grandy's logo in the right. The back has biographical information and a public service announcement (with cartoon) concerning wildfire prevention. Ron Anderson of the Philadelphia 76ers is included in this set. The cards are numbered for convenience in the checklist below according to alphabetical order of the player's name.

	MINT	EXC	G-VG
COMPLETE SET (16)	10.00	5.00	1.00
COMMON PLAYER (1-16)	.75	.35	.07
☐ 1 Ron Anderson	2.00	1.00	.20
☐ 2 Dave Barnett 12	.75	.35	.07
☐ 3 Tod Bernard 33	.75	.35	.07
☐ 4 Tyrone Bradley	.75	.35	.07
☐ 5 Gary Colson CO	.75	.35	.07
☐ 6 Carl Ray Harris 11	.75	.35	.07
☐ 7 Doug Harris 20	.75	.35	.07
☐ 8 Wilbert Hooker 30	.75	.35	.07
☐ 9 Dimitri Lambrecht 32	.75	.35	.07
☐ 10 Sammie Lindsey 50	.75	.35	.07
☐ 11 Michael Pearson 3	.75	.35	.07
☐ 12 Pat Riddlesprigger 34	.75	.35	.07
☐ 13 Sammy Taylor 22	.75	.35	.07
☐ 14 Rey Young 54	.75	.35	.07
☐ 15 Fresno State Mascot	.75	.35	.07
☐ 16 Selland Arena	.75	.35	.07

1981-82 Georgetown Police

This set contains 20 cards measuring approximately 2 5/8" by 4 1/8" featuring the Georgetown Hoyas. The fronts of the cards have a blue border. Backs contain safety tips with black print on

white card stock. The set was also sponsored by Safeway. The cards are numbered below by "Tip Number" as listed on the card back.

	MINT	EXC	G-VG
COMPLETE SET (20)	125.00	60.00	12.50
COMMON PLAYER (1-20)	1.00	.50	.10
☐ 1 Jack the Bulldog (Mascot)	1.00	.50	.10
☐ 2 Elvado Smith	1.00	.50	.10
☐ 3 Eric Smith	1.00	.50	.10
☐ 4 Pat Ewing	100.00	50.00	10.00
☐ 5 Anthony Jones	4.00	2.00	.40
☐ 6 Bill Martin	3.00	1.50	.30
☐ 7 Bill Stein, Assistant Coach	1.00	.50	.10
☐ 8 Norman Washington, Grad. Asst. Coach	1.00	.50	.10
☐ 9 Ed Spriggs	2.00	1.00	.20
☐ 10 Eric(Sleepy) Floyd	10.00	5.00	1.00
☐ 11 Gene Smith	2.00	1.00	.20
☐ 12 Fred Brown	2.50	1.25	.25
☐ 13 Mike Hancock	1.00	.50	.10
☐ 14 Kurt Kaull	1.00	.50	.10
☐ 15 Ed Meyers	1.00	.50	.10
☐ 16 Ron Blaylock	1.00	.50	.10
☐ 17 David Blue	1.00	.50	.10
☐ 18 John Thompson CO	8.00	4.00	.80
☐ 19 Ralph Dalton	2.00	1.00	.20
☐ 20 Hoyas Team 1981-1982	4.00	2.00	.40

1982-83 Georgetown Police

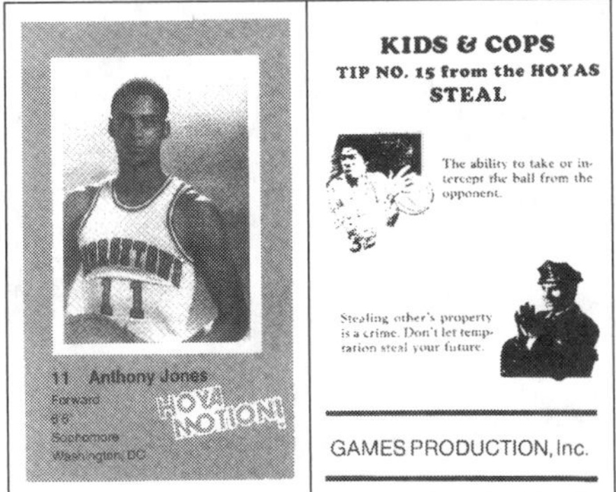

This set contains 15 cards measuring approximately 2 5/8" by 4 1/8" featuring the Georgetown Hoyas. The fronts of the cards have a blue border. Backs contain safety tips with black print on white card stock. The cards are numbered below by "Tip Number" as listed on the card back. The set was also sponsored by Games Production, Inc.

	MINT	EXC	G-VG
COMPLETE SET (15)	75.00	37.50	7.50
COMMON PLAYER (1-15)	1.00	.50	.10
☐ 1 John Thompson CO	6.00	3.00	.60
☐ 2 Patrick Ewing	45.00	22.50	4.50
☐ 3 David Dunn	1.00	.50	.10
☐ 4 Ralph Dalton	2.00	1.00	.20
☐ 5 Fred Brown	2.00	1.00	.20
☐ 6 Horace Broadnax	2.00	1.00	.20
☐ 7 David Blue	1.00	.50	.10
☐ 8 Michael Jackson (listed as Center on card front)	4.00	2.00	.40
☐ 9 David Wingate	6.00	3.00	.60
☐ 10 Vadi Smith	1.00	.50	.10
☐ 11 Gene Smith	2.00	1.00	.20
☐ 12 Victor Morris	2.00	1.00	.20
☐ 13 Bill Martin	3.00	1.50	.30
☐ 14 Kurt Kaull	1.00	.50	.10
☐ 15 Anthony Jones	2.00	1.00	.20

1983-84 Georgetown Police

This set contains 15 cards measuring approximately 2 5/8" by 4 1/8" featuring the Georgetown Hoyas. Backs contain safety tips. The set was also sponsored by Coca Cola. This set features the Hoya team that won the 1983-84 NCAA Championship.

	MINT	EXC	G-VG
COMPLETE SET (15)	50.00	25.00	5.00
COMMON PLAYER (1-15)	1.00	.50	.10
☐ 1 John Thompson CO	5.00	2.50	.50
☐ 2 Hoya 1983-84 Team	3.00	1.50	.30
☐ 3 Michael Jackson	3.00	1.50	.30
☐ 4 Bill Martin	2.00	1.00	.20
☐ 5 Jack the Bulldog, Hoya Mascot	1.00	.50	.10
☐ 6 Gene Smith	2.00	1.00	.20
☐ 7 Fred Brown	2.00	1.00	.20
☐ 8 Horace Broadnax	2.00	1.00	.20
☐ 9 Victor Morris	1.00	.50	.10
☐ 10 Patrick Ewing	30.00	15.00	3.00
☐ 11 Ralph Dalton	2.00	1.00	.20
☐ 12 Michael Graham	2.50	1.25	.25
☐ 13 Clifton Dairsow	1.00	.50	.10
☐ 14 David Wingate	3.00	1.50	.30
☐ 15 Reggie Williams	7.50	3.75	.75

1984-85 Georgetown Police

This set contains 14 cards each measuring approximately 2 5/8" by 4 1/8" featuring the Georgetown Hoyas. Fronts of the cards make reference to Georgetown's National Championship the year before. This set was also sponsored by Coca Cola. Backs

contain safety tips and are written in black ink with a red accent. The cards are numbered for convenience in the checklist below according to alphabetical order of the player's name.

	MINT	EXC	G-VG
COMPLETE SET (14)	40.00	20.00	4.00
COMMON PLAYER (1-14)	1.00	.50	.10
☐ 1 John Thompson CO	4.00	2.00	.40
☐ 2 Horace Broadnax	2.00	1.00	.20
☐ 3 Ralph Dalton	2.00	1.00	.20
☐ 4 Patrick Ewing	25.00	12.50	2.50
☐ 5 Kevin Floyd	1.00	.50	.10
☐ 6 Ron Highsmith	1.00	.50	.10
☐ 7 Michael Jackson	3.00	1.50	.30
☐ 8 Bill Martin	2.00	1.00	.20
☐ 9 Grady Mateen	1.00	.50	.10
☐ 10 Perry McDonald	2.00	1.00	.20
☐ 11 Reggie Williams	5.00	2.50	.50
☐ 12 David Wingate	3.50	1.75	.35
☐ 13 NCAA Championship Trophy	1.00	.50	.10
☐ 14 Team Photo	3.00	1.50	.30

1985-86 Georgetown Police

The 1985-86 Police Georgetown Hoyas set contains 16 cards measuring approximately 2 1/2" by 4". There are 13 player cards, plus one coach card, one team picture card, and one mascot card. The card fronts feature color photos and fascimile signatures. Each card back has one basketball tip and one safety tip. The cards are numbered for convenience in the checklist below according to alphabetical order of the player's name.

	MINT	EXC	G-VG
COMPLETE SET (16)	12.00	6.00	1.20
COMMON PLAYER (1-16)	.50	.25	.05
☐ 1 1985-86 Hoyas Team Photo	1.25	.60	.12
☐ 2 John Thompson CO	2.00	1.00	.20
☐ 3 Horace Broadnax	.75	.35	.07
☐ 4 Ralph Dalton	.75	.35	.07
☐ 5 Johnathan Edwards	.75	.35	.07
☐ 6 Hoyas Mascot	.50	.25	.05
☐ 7 Ronnie Highsmith	.50	.25	.05
☐ 8 Jaren Jackson	.75	.35	.07
☐ 9 Michael Jackson	1.50	.75	.15
☐ 10 Grady Mateen	.50	.25	.05
☐ 11 Perry McDonald	1.00	.50	.10
☐ 12 Victor Morris	.50	.25	.05
☐ 13 Charles Smith	3.00	1.50	.30
☐ 14 Reggie Williams	3.00	1.50	.30
☐ 15 David Wingate	2.00	1.00	.20
☐ 16 Bobby Winston	.50	.25	.05

1986-87 Georgetown Police

1986-87 HOYAS

21 Jaren Jackson
Guard/Forward
6'4"
Sophomore
New Orleans, LA

KIDS & COPS
TIP NO. 8 from the HOYAS
PURSUIT DEFENSE

Pursue 100% attendance in school. Arm yourself with the skills necessary for the pursuit of a career.

Deliberately allowing your man to drive by you and then attempting to tip the ball from behind is called pursuit defense.

The 1986-87 Police Georgetown Hoyas set contains 14 cards measuring approximately 2 1/2" by 4". There are 12 player cards, plus one coach card and one team picture card. The card fronts have color photos, and each card back has one basketball tip and one safety tip. The cards are numbered for convenience in the checklist below according to alphabetical order of the player's name.

	MINT	EXC	G-VG
COMPLETE SET (14)	8.00	4.00	.80
COMMON PLAYER (1-14)	.50	.25	.05
☐ 1 1986-87 Hoyas	1.00	.50	.10
☐ 2 John Thompson CO	1.50	.75	.15
☐ 3 Anthony Allen	.50	.25	.05
☐ 4 Dwayne Bryant	.75	.35	.07
☐ 5 Johnathan Edwards	.50	.25	.05
☐ 6 Ben Gillery	.50	.25	.05
☐ 7 Ronnie Highsmith	.50	.25	.05
☐ 8 Jaren Jackson	.75	.35	.07
☐ 9 Sam Jefferson	.75	.35	.07
☐ 10 Perry McDonald	.75	.35	.07
☐ 11 Charles Smith	1.50	.75	.15
☐ 12 Mark Tillmon	.75	.35	.07
☐ 13 Reggie Williams	1.50	.75	.15
☐ 14 Bobby Winston	.50	.25	.05

1987-88 Georgetown Police

The 1987-88 Police Georgetown Hoyas set contains 16 cards measuring approximately 2 1/2" by 4". There are 14 player cards, plus one coach card and one team picture card. The card fronts have color photos, and each card back has one basketball tip and one safety tip. The cards are numbered for convenience in the checklist below according to alphabetical order of the player's name.

	MINT	EXC	G-VG
COMPLETE SET (16)	8.00	4.00	.80
COMMON PLAYER (1-16)	.50	.25	.05
☐ 1 1987-88 Hoyas	1.00	.50	.10
☐ 2 John Thompson CO	1.25	.60	.12
☐ 3 Anthony Allen	.50	.25	.05
☐ 4 Dwayne Bryant	.75	.35	.07
☐ 5 Johnathan Edwards	.50	.25	.05
☐ 6 Ben Gillery	.50	.25	.05
☐ 7 Ronnie Highsmith	.50	.25	.05
☐ 8 Jaren Jackson	.75	.35	.07
☐ 9 Sam Jefferson	.50	.25	.05
☐ 10 Johnny Jones	.50	.25	.05
☐ 11 Tom Lang	.50	.25	.05
☐ 12 Perry McDonald	.75	.35	.07
☐ 13 Charles Smith	1.50	.75	.15
☐ 14 Mark Tillmon	1.00	.50	.10
☐ 15 Anthony Tucker	.50	.25	.05
☐ 16 Bobby Winston	.50	.25	.05

1988-89 Georgetown Police

The 1988-89 Police Georgetown Hoyas set contains 17 cards measuring approximately 2 1/2" by 4". There are 14 player cards, plus one coach card, one team picture card and one mascot card. The card fronts have color photos, and each card back has one safety tip. The cards are numbered for convenience in the checklist below according to alphabetical order of the player's name. The set features the first cards of future NBA Lottery picks Alonzo Mourning and Dikembe Mutombo.

	MINT	EXC	G-VG
COMPLETE SET (17)	24.00	12.00	2.40
COMMON PLAYER (1-17)	.50	.25	.05
☐ 1 1988-89 Hoyas	1.50	.75	.15
☐ 2 John Thompson CO	1.25	.60	.12
☐ 3 Anthony Allen	.50	.25	.05
☐ 4 Dwayne Bryant	.50	.25	.05
☐ 5 Johnathan Edwards	.50	.25	.05
☐ 6 Ronnie Thompson	.75	.35	.07
☐ 7 Milton Bell	.50	.25	.05
☐ 8 Jaren Jackson	.75	.35	.07
☐ 9 Sam Jefferson	.50	.25	.05
☐ 10 Johnny Jones	.50	.25	.05
☐ 11 Alonzo Mourning	10.00	5.00	1.00
☐ 12 John Turner	1.50	.75	.15
☐ 13 Charles Smith	1.00	.50	.10
☐ 14 Mark Tillmon	.75	.35	.07
☐ 15 Dikembe Mutombo	10.00	5.00	1.00
☐ 16 Bobby Winston	.50	.25	.05
☐ 17 McGruff The Crime Dog and Jack The Bulldog	.50	.25	.05

1989-90 Georgetown Police

The 1989-90 Police Georgetown Hoyas set contains 17 cards measuring approximately 2 1/2" by 4". The front has a posed color photo of the player, enclosed by a blue border on the top and a gray one below. The back is printed in blue and red ink and has a safety tip from McGruff the Crime Dog. The cards are numbered below by "Tip Number" as listed on the card back.

	MINT	EXC	G-VG
COMPLETE SET (17)	10.00	5.00	1.00
COMMON PLAYER (1-17)	.40	.20	.04
☐ 1 1989-90 Hoyas	.75	.35	.07
☐ 2 John Thompson CO	.75	.35	.07
☐ 3 Anthony Allen	.40	.20	.04
☐ 4 Dwayne Bryant	.40	.20	.04
☐ 5 David Edwards	.40	.20	.04
☐ 6 Ronny Thompson	.60	.30	.06
☐ 7 Milton Bell	.40	.20	.04
☐ 8 Kayode Vann	.40	.20	.04
☐ 9 Sam Jefferson	.40	.20	.04
☐ 10 Johnny Jones	.40	.20	.04
☐ 11 Alonzo Mourning	5.00	2.50	.50
☐ 12 Mike Sabol	.40	.20	.04
☐ 13 Michael Tate	.60	.30	.06
☐ 14 Mark Tillmon	.60	.30	.06
☐ 15 Dikembe Mutombo	5.00	2.50	.50
☐ 16 Antoine Stoudamire	.40	.20	.04
☐ 17 McGruff The Crime Dog and Jack the Bulldog	.40	.20	.04

1990-91 Georgetown Police

The 1990-91 Police Georgetown Hoyas set contains 15 cards measuring approximately 2 1/2" by 4". The front has a posed color photo of the player, enclosed by gray borders above and below. The back is printed in blue and red ink and has a safety tip from McGruff the Crime Dog. The cards are numbered below by "Tip Number" as listed on the card back.

	MINT	EXC	G-VG
COMPLETE SET (15)	7.00	3.50	.70
COMMON PLAYER (1-15)	.30	.15	.03
☐ 1 1990-91 Hoyas Team Photo	.75	.35	.07
☐ 2 Kayode Vann	.30	.15	.03
☐ 3 Mike Sabol	.30	.15	.03
☐ 4 Antoine Stoudamire	.30	.15	.03
☐ 5 Alonzo Mourning	3.00	1.50	.30
☐ 6 Ronny Thompson	.50	.25	.05
☐ 7 Dikembe Mutombo	3.00	1.50	.30
☐ 8 Charles Harrison	.30	.15	.03
☐ 9 Brian Kelly	.30	.15	.03
☐ 10 Robert Churchwell	.30	.15	.03
☐ 11 Joey Brown	.30	.15	.03
☐ 12 Vladimir Bosanac	.30	.15	.03
☐ 13 Lamont Morgan	.30	.15	.03
☐ 14 John Thompson CO	.75	.35	.07
☐ 15 McGruff The Crime Dog and Jack The Bulldog	.30	.15	.03

1991 Georgetown 100

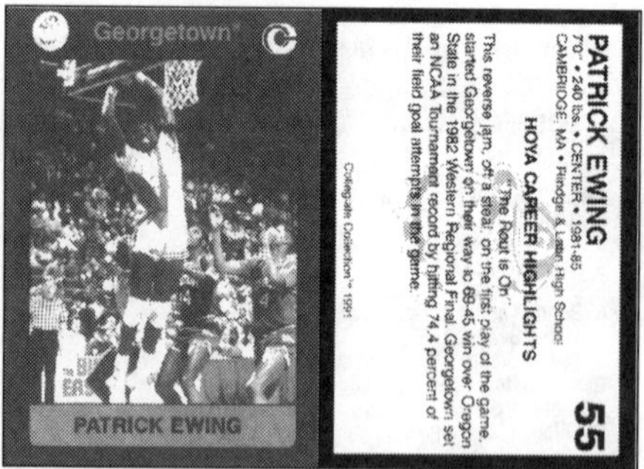

This 100-card set was produced by Collegiate Collection and measures the standard size (2 1/2" by 3 1/2"). The fronts feature color player photos, with dark blue borders and the player's name in the gray stripe below the picture. The horizontally oriented backs present biographical information, career summary, or statistics on a white background with dark blue lettering and borders. The cards are numbered on the back.

	MINT	EXC	G-VG
COMPLETE SET (100)	12.00	6.00	1.20
COMMON PLAYER (1-100)	.10	.05	.01
☐ 1 John Thompson CO	.35	.17	.03
☐ 2 Patrick Ewing	.75	.35	.07
☐ 3 Eric(Sleepy) Floyd	.35	.17	.03
☐ 4 Reggie Williams	.35	.17	.03
☐ 5 John Duren	.20	.10	.02
☐ 6 Craig Shelton	.25	.12	.02
☐ 7 Charles Smith	.30	.15	.03
☐ 8 Michael Jackson	.20	.10	.02
☐ 9 Jaren Jackson	.15	.07	.01
☐ 10 David Wingate	.25	.12	.02
☐ 11 Mark Tillmon	.20	.10	.02
☐ 12 Fred Brown	.15	.07	.01
☐ 13 Kurt Kaull	.10	.05	.01
☐ 14 Ron Highsmith	.10	.05	.01
☐ 15 Dwayne Bryant	.10	.05	.01
☐ 16 Michael Jackson	.20	.10	.02
☐ 17 Al Dutch	.10	.05	.01
☐ 18 Ben Gillery	.10	.05	.01
☐ 19 Ralph Dalton	.10	.05	.01
☐ 20 1984 NCAA Champs	.10	.05	.01
☐ 21 Craig Esherick	.10	.05	.01
☐ 22 Bobby Winston	.10	.05	.01
☐ 23 Bill Martin	.15	.07	.01
☐ 24 Horace Broadnax	.10	.05	.01
☐ 25 John Thompson CO	.35	.17	.03
☐ 26 Dwayne Bryant	.10	.05	.01
☐ 28 Perry McDonald	.10	.05	.01
☐ 29 Reggie Williams	.35	.17	.03
☐ 30 Patrick Ewing	.75	.35	.07
☐ 31 Patrick Ewing	.75	.35	.07
☐ 32 Peter McDonald	.10	.05	.01
☐ 33 Sam Jefferson	.10	.05	.01
☐ 34 Michael Jackson	.20	.10	.02
☐ 35 Anthony Allen	.10	.05	.01
☐ 36 Mike Riley	.10	.05	.01
☐ 37 John Duren	.20	.10	.02
☐ 38 Mark Tillmon	.20	.10	.02
☐ 39 Mike Frazier	.10	.05	.01
☐ 40 Eric Smith	.10	.05	.01
☐ 41 Ed Spriggs	.15	.07	.01
☐ 42 Johnathan Edwards	.10	.05	.01
☐ 43 Derrick Jackson	.10	.05	.01
☐ 44 Mike Hancock	.10	.05	.01
☐ 45 Tom Scales	.10	.05	.01
☐ 46 David Blue	.10	.05	.01
☐ 47 Charles Smith	.30	.15	.03
☐ 48 John Thompson CO	.35	.17	.03
☐ 49 Patrick Ewing	.75	.35	.07
☐ 50 Al Dutch	.10	.05	.01
☐ 51 Eric(Sleepy) Floyd	.35	.17	.03
☐ 52 Craig Shelton	.25	.12	.02
☐ 53 Reggie Williams	.35	.17	.03
☐ 53 Tom Lang	.10	.05	.01
☐ 54 Michael Jackson	.20	.10	.02
☐ 55 Patrick Ewing	.75	.35	.07
☐ 56 Bill Thomas	.10	.05	.01
☐ 57 Ed Hopkins	.10	.05	.01
☐ 58 John Thompson CO	.35	.17	.03
☐ 59 Jon Smith	.10	.05	.01
☐ 60 Merlin Wilson	.10	.05	.01
☐ 61 Gene Smith	.15	.07	.01
☐ 62 Johnny Jones	.10	.05	.01
☐ 63 Senior Night	.10	.05	.01
☐ 64 Eric(Sleepy) Floyd	.35	.17	.03
☐ 65 Reggie Williams	.35	.17	.03
☐ 66 Steve Martin	.10	.05	.01
☐ 67 Mark Gallagher	.10	.05	.01
☐ 68 Mike McDermont	.10	.05	.01
☐ 69 Greg Brooks	.10	.05	.01
☐ 70 Larry Long	.10	.05	.01
☐ 71 Felix Yeoman	.10	.05	.01
☐ 72 Lonnie Duren	.10	.05	.01
☐ 73 Terry Fenlon	.10	.05	.01
☐ 74 Steve Martin	.10	.05	.01
☐ 75 Fred Brown	.15	.07	.01
☐ 76 Bill Lynn	.10	.05	.01
☐ 77 Patrick Ewing	.75	.35	.07
☐ 78 Mike Laska	.10	.05	.01
☐ 79 Paul Tagliabue	.75	.35	.07
☐ 80 Don Weber	.10	.05	.01
☐ 81 Jaren Jackson	.10	.05	.01
☐ 82 1982 NCAA Finalists	.10	.05	.01
☐ 83 1985 NCAA Finalists	.10	.05	.01
☐ 84 Jim Brown	.10	.05	.01
☐ 85 Jim Christy	.10	.05	.01
☐ 86 Tim Mercier	.10	.05	.01
☐ 87 Joe Missett	.10	.05	.01
☐ 88 Charlie Adrian	.10	.05	.01
☐ 89 John Thompson CO	.35	.17	.03
☐ 90 Craig Esherick	.10	.05	.01
☐ 91 Dennis Cesar	.10	.05	.01
☐ 92 Ken Pichette	.10	.05	.01
☐ 93 Charlie Adrian	.10	.05	.01
☐ 94 Mike Laughna	.10	.05	.01
☐ 95 Tommy O'Keefe	.10	.05	.01
☐ 96 Merlin Wilson	.10	.05	.01
☐ 97 Craig Shelton	.25	.12	.02
☐ 98 Derrick Jackson	.10	.05	.01
☐ 99 Mike Riley	.10	.05	.01
☐ 100 Director Card	.15	.07	.01

1991-92 Georgetown Police

The 1991-92 Georgetown Hoyas police set contains 18 cards measuring approximately 2 1/2" by 4". The fronts carry a posed player photo enclosed by a white border. The year and team name appear in a purple stripe above the picture, while player information is printed in a gray stripe beneath the picture. In blue and red ink, the backs carry "Kids and Cops" safety tips (from McGruff the Crime Dog), a list of sponsor names, the McGruff logo, and the Coke logo. The cards are numbered by the safety tips on the back.

	MINT	EXC	G-VG
COMPLETE SET (18)	6.00	3.00	.60
COMMON PLAYER (1-18)	.30	.15	.03
☐ 1 Team Photo	.60	.30	.06
☐ 2 Robert Churchwell	.30	.15	.03
☐ 3 Charles Harrison	.30	.15	.03
☐ 4 Joey Brown	.30	.15	.03
☐ 5 Alonzo Mourning	2.00	1.00	.20
☐ 6 Ronny Thompson	.30	.15	.03
☐ 7 Vladimir Bosanac	.30	.15	.03
☐ 8 Pascal Fleury	.30	.15	.03
☐ 9 Brian Kelly	.30	.15	.03
☐ 10 Lamont Morgan	.30	.15	.03
☐ 11 Kevin Millen	.30	.15	.03
☐ 12 Don Reid	.30	.15	.03
☐ 13 Derrick Patterson	.30	.15	.03
☐ 14 Lonnie Harrell	.30	.15	.03
☐ 15 Irvin Church	.30	.15	.03
☐ 16 John Jacques	.30	.15	.03
☐ 17 McGruff The Crime Dog Jack The Bulldog	.30	.15	.03
☐ 18 John Thompson CO	.60	.30	.06

1990-91 Georgia Smokey

This 16-card set was sponsored by the USDA Forest Service in conjunction with several other federal agencies. The cards measure the standard size (2 1/2" by 3 1/2") and feature on fronts color action photos bordered in red. Inside the border the school name and player identification are given in gray stripes above and below the picture, with the Smokey icon in the lower left corner. The background color outside the red border varies from card to card, ranging from black to gray. The back presents either career statistics or summary, as well as a fire prevention cartoon starring Smokey. The cards are unnumbered and are checklisted below in alphabetical order, with the uniform number after the player's name.

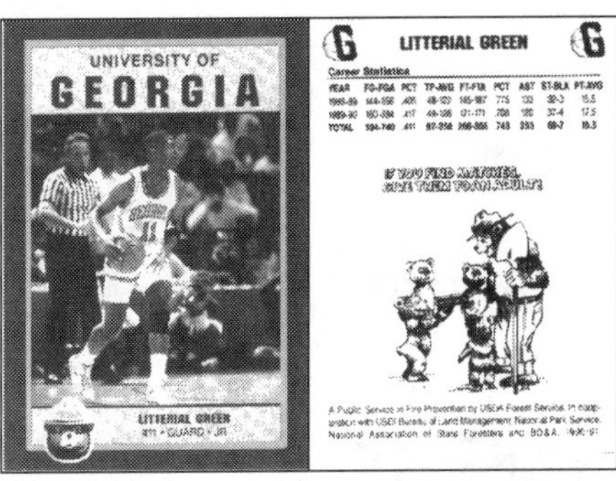

	MINT	EXC	G-VG
COMPLETE SET (16)	16.00	8.00	1.60
COMMON PLAYER (1-16)	1.00	.50	.10
☐ 1 Arlando Bennett 32	1.00	.50	.10
☐ 2 Charles Claxton 33	1.00	.50	.10
☐ 3 Rod Cole 22	1.00	.50	.10
☐ 4 Bernard Davis 23	1.00	.50	.10
☐ 5 Hugh Durham CO	1.50	.75	.15
☐ 6 Shaun Golden 10	1.00	.50	.10
☐ 7 Litterial Green 11	5.00	2.50	.50
☐ 8 Antonio Harvey 34	1.00	.50	.10
☐ 9 Neville Austin 35	1.00	.50	.10
☐ 10 Lem Howard 25	1.00	.50	.10
☐ 11 Marcel Kon 51	1.00	.50	.10
☐ 12 Jody Patton 12	1.00	.50	.10
☐ 13 Kendall Rhine 15	2.50	1.25	.25
☐ 14 Reggie Tinch 24	1.00	.50	.10
☐ 15 Marshall Wilson 44	1.00	.50	.10
☐ 16 1990-91 Bulldogs Team Photo	1.50	.75	.15

1988-89 Georgia Tech Nike

This 12-card set was sponsored by Nike, whose company name appears on both sides of the card. The cards measure the standard size, 2 1/2" by 3 1/2". The fronts feature either posed or action color photos, with a gold border on the left and dark blue borders on the bottom and right of the picture. The backs have biographical information and a tip from the Yellow Jackets consisting of an anti-drug message. The key cards are the first appearances of Brian Oliver and Dennis Scott on a basketball card of any type. Sets were given out to fans attending a certain Georgia Tech home game during the 1988-89 season. The cards are numbered for convenience alphabetically by player's name in the checklist below.

	MINT	EXC	G-VG
COMPLETE SET (12)	30.00	15.00	3.00
COMMON PLAYER (1-12)	1.00	.50	.10
☐ 1 Maurice Brittain 52	1.00	.50	.10
☐ 2 Karl Brown 5	1.00	.50	.10
☐ 3 Bobby Cremins CO	3.00	1.50	.30
☐ 4 Brian Domalik 12	1.00	.50	.10
☐ 5 Tom Hammonds 20	5.00	2.50	.50

☐ 6 Johnny McNeil 44	1.00	.50	.10
☐ 7 James Munlyn 24	1.00	.50	.10
☐ 8 Brian Oliver 13	4.00	2.00	.40
☐ 9 Willie Reese 31	1.00	.50	.10
☐ 10 Dennis Scott 4	12.00	6.00	1.20
☐ 11 Anthony Sherrod 42	2.00	1.00	.20
☐ 12 David Whitmore 23	1.00	.50	.10

1989-90 Georgia Tech Police/Coke

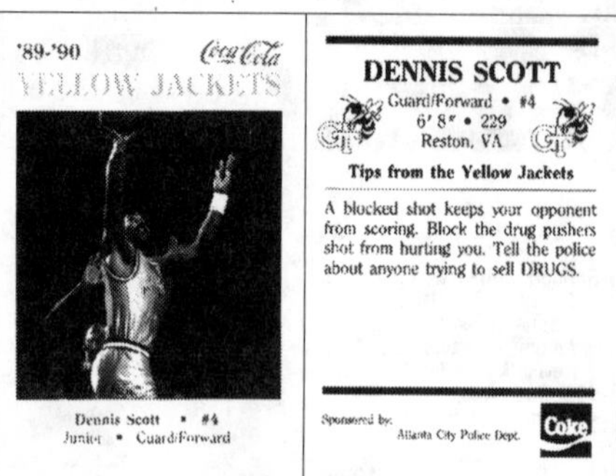

This 20-card set was sponsored by the Atlanta City Police Department and produced by Coca-Cola. The cards measure the standard size, 2 1/2" by 3 1/2". The cards were distributed in the Atlanta area by the Police Athletic League; reportedly 10,000 sets were distributed. The fronts feature either posed or action color photos on a white card stock. The backs have biographical information and a tip from the Yellow Jackets consisting of an anti-drug message. The cards are numbered for convenience alphabetically by player's name in the checklist below.

	MINT	EXC	G-VG
COMPLETE SET (20)	20.00	10.00	2.00
COMMON PLAYER (1-20)	.50	.25	.05
☐ 1 Kenny Anderson 12 (Portrait)	5.00	2.50	.50
☐ 2 Kenny Anderson 12 (Free Throw)	3.50	1.75	.35
☐ 3 Kenny Anderson 12 (Jump Shot)	3.50	1.75	.35
☐ 4 Rod Balanis 34	.50	.25	.05
☐ 5 Darryl Barnes 15	.50	.25	.05
☐ 6 Brian Black 23	.50	.25	.05
☐ 7 Karl Brown 5	.50	.25	.05
☐ 8 Bobby Cremins CO	1.00	.50	.10
☐ 9 Brian Domalik 3	.50	.25	.05
☐ 10 Matt Geiger 52	1.25	.60	.12
☐ 11 Malcolm Mackey 32	2.00	1.00	.20
☐ 12 Johnny McNeil 44	.50	.25	.05
☐ 13 James Munlyn 24	.50	.25	.05
☐ 14 Ivano Newbill 33	.50	.25	.05
☐ 15 Brian Oliver 13	1.00	.50	.10
☐ 16 Dennis Scott 4 (Free Throw)	2.50	1.25	.25
☐ 17 Dennis Scott 4 (Shooting)	2.50	1.25	.25
☐ 18 Greg White 14	.50	.25	.05
☐ 19 Team Photo	1.00	.50	.10
☐ 20 Lethal Weapon 3 Brian Oliver, Dennis Scott, and Kenny Anderson	3.50	1.75	.35

1990-91 Georgia Tech Police/Coke

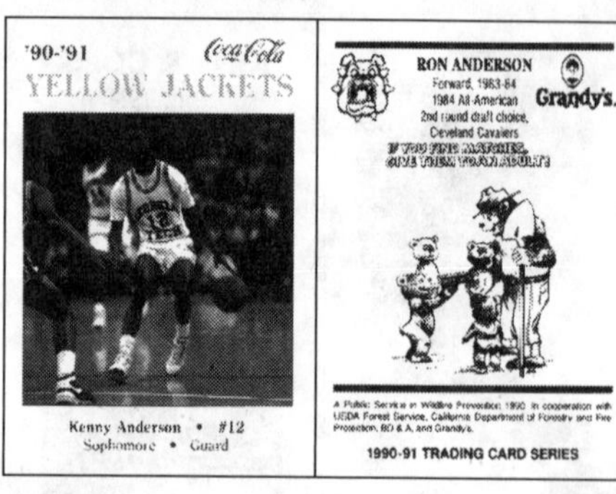

This 20-card set was sponsored by the Atlanta City Police Department and Coca-Cola, and the latter sponsor's logos appear in the upper right corner of the card face as well as at the bottom of the back. It is reported that 10,000 sets were issued in two lots: the first 5,000 went out to the housing projects and kids in the Atlanta Police Athletic Program, and the second lot was offered to the general public. The cards measure the standard size (2 1/2" by 3 1/2"). The front features a borderless color action photo of the player on white card stock. The team name appears in gold lettering above the picture, with player information in black lettering below the picture. The back has brief biographical information and "Tips from the Yellow Jackets," which consist of various public service announcements. The cards are unnumbered and are checklisted below in alphabetical order.

	MINT	EXC	G-VG
COMPLETE SET (20)	15.00	7.50	1.50
COMMON PLAYER (1-20)	.40	.20	.04
☐ 1 Kenny Anderson 12 (Shooting lay-up)	2.50	1.25	.25
☐ 2 Kenny Anderson 12 (Driving past defender)	2.50	1.25	.25
☐ 3 Kenny Anderson 12 (Dribbling)	2.50	1.25	.25
☐ 4 Ron Balanis 34	.40	.20	.04
☐ 5 Darryl Barnes 15	.40	.20	.04
☐ 6 Jon Barry 14	2.50	1.25	.25
☐ 7 Brian Black 23	.40	.20	.04
☐ 8 Bobby Cremins CO	1.00	.50	.10
☐ 9 Brian Domalik 3	.40	.20	.04
☐ 10 James Gaddy 10	.40	.20	.04
☐ 11 Todd Harlicka 30	.40	.20	.04
☐ 12 Bryan Hill 11	.40	.20	.04
☐ 13 Matt Geiger 52	1.00	.50	.10
☐ 14 Brian Gemberling 41	.40	.20	.04
☐ 15 Malcolm Mackey 32	1.50	.75	.15
☐ 16 Malcolm Mackey 32	1.50	.75	.15
☐ 17 James Munlyn 24	.40	.20	.04
☐ 18 Ivano Newbill 33	.40	.20	.04
☐ 19 Greg White 31	.40	.20	.04
☐ 20 Team Photo	.75	.35	.07

1991 Georgia Tech *

This 200-card set was produced by Collegiate Collection to honor some of the great athletes in Georgia Tech's history and measures the standard size (2 1/2" by 3 1/2"). The fronts feature color photos with blue borders and the player's name appearing in a gold stripe. The backs present statistics or career summary on a white background with blue lettering. The set's emphasis is on basketball and football players.

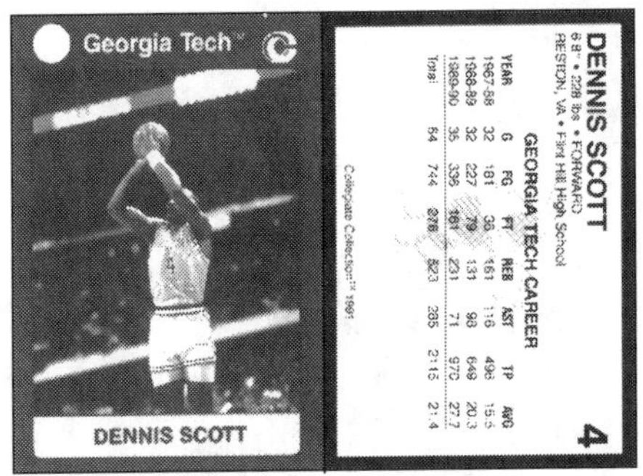

	MINT	EXC	G-VG
COMPLETE SET (200)	20.00	10.00	2.00
COMMON PLAYER (1-200)	.10	.05	.01
☐ 1 John Dewberry	.10	.05	.01
☐ 2 Ida Neal	.10	.05	.01
☐ 3 Lenny Horton	.10	.05	.01
☐ 4 Dennis Scott	.50	.25	.05
☐ 5 Steve Davenport	.10	.05	.01
☐ 6 Dolores Bootz	.10	.05	.01
☐ 7 Dante Jones	.20	.10	.02
☐ 8 Cory Collier	.10	.05	.01
☐ 9 Lee Ann Woodhull	.15	.07	.01
☐ 10 John Ivemeyer	.10	.05	.01
☐ 11 Ronny Cone	.10	.05	.01
☐ 12 George Malone	.10	.05	.01
☐ 13 Darrell Norton	.10	.05	.01
☐ 14 Bug Isom	.10	.05	.01
☐ 15 Tom Hammonds	.25	.12	.02
☐ 16 Bobby Dodd	.15	.07	.01
☐ 17 Cindy Cockran	.10	.05	.01
☐ 18 Andre Thomas	.10	.05	.01
☐ 19 Chuck Easley	.10	.05	.01
☐ 20 Willie Burns	.10	.05	.01
☐ 21 Eric Thomas	.15	.07	.01
☐ 22 Jerry Mays	.15	.07	.01
☐ 23 Sammy Drummer	.10	.05	.01
☐ 24 Tory Ehle	.10	.05	.01
☐ 25 Rob Healy	.10	.05	.01
☐ 26 Brook Steppe	.20	.10	.02
☐ 27 Darrell Gast	.10	.05	.01
☐ 28 David Bell	.10	.05	.01
☐ 29 Keith Glanton	.10	.05	.01
☐ 30 Brian Oliver	.30	.15	.03
☐ 31 Sean Smith	.10	.05	.01
☐ 32 Cedric Stallworth	.10	.05	.01
☐ 33 Craig Neal	.15	.07	.01
☐ 34 Danny Harrison	.10	.05	.01
☐ 35 Duane Ferrell	.20	.10	.02
☐ 36 Eric Bearden	.10	.05	.01
☐ 37 Andy Hearn	.10	.05	.01
☐ 38 Jim Anderson	.10	.05	.01
☐ 39 Anthony Harrison	.10	.05	.01
☐ 40 Marielle Walker	.10	.05	.01
☐ 41 Dean Weaver	.10	.05	.01
☐ 42 Yvon Joseph	.10	.05	.01
☐ 43 Mike Kelley	.10	.05	.01
☐ 44 John Davis	.10	.05	.01
☐ 45 Mark Hogan	.10	.05	.01
☐ 46 Karl Brown	.15	.07	.01
☐ 47 Kyle Ambrose	.10	.05	.01
☐ 48 Steve Mullen	.10	.05	.01
☐ 49 Willis Crockett	.20	.10	.02
☐ 50 Jeff Mathis	.10	.05	.01
☐ 51 Ellis Gardner	.10	.05	.01
☐ 52 Larry Good	.10	.05	.01
☐ 53 Billy Lothridge	.15	.07	.01
☐ 54 Bill Kinard	.15	.07	.01
☐ 55 Brent Cunningham	.10	.05	.01
☐ 56 Teddy Peeples	.10	.05	.01
☐ 57 Pat Swilling	.50	.25	.05
☐ 58 John Salley	.40	.20	.04
☐ 59 Lawrence Lowe	.10	.05	.01
☐ 60 Sheila Wagner	.30	.15	.03
☐ 61 Cam Bonifay	.10	.05	.01
☐ 62 George Brodnax	.10	.05	.01
☐ 63 Fred Braselton	.10	.05	.01
☐ 64 Joe Auer	.10	.05	.01
☐ 65 Franklin Brooks	.10	.05	.01
☐ 66 Rod Stephens	.10	.05	.01
☐ 67 Bill Curry	.25	.12	.02
☐ 68 Tim Manion	.10	.05	.01
☐ 69 Rick Strom	.20	.10	.02
☐ 70 Toby Pearson	.10	.05	.01
☐ 71 Jim Breland	.10	.05	.01
☐ 72 Don Bessillieu	.10	.05	.01
☐ 73 Craig Baynham	.15	.07	.01
☐ 74 Maxie Baughan	.25	.12	.02
☐ 75 Wade Mitchell	.10	.05	.01
☐ 76 Sammy Lilly	.15	.07	.01
☐ 77 Gary Lee	.10	.05	.01
☐ 78 Paul Jurgensen	.10	.05	.01
☐ 79 Robert Lavette	.15	.07	.01
☐ 80 Robert Jaracz	.10	.05	.01
☐ 81 Mike Oven	.10	.05	.01
☐ 82 Paul Menegazz	.10	.05	.01
☐ 83 Billy Martin	.10	.05	.01
☐ 84 Bobby Moorhead	.10	.05	.01
☐ 85 Wade Martin	.10	.05	.01
☐ 86 Buzz	.10	.05	.01
☐ 87 Malcolm King	.10	.05	.01
☐ 88 Bobby Ross	.35	.17	.03
☐ 89 Gary Lanier	.10	.05	.01
☐ 90 Bill Curry	.25	.12	.02
☐ 91 Bonnie Tale	.10	.05	.01
☐ 92 William Alexander	.10	.05	.01
☐ 93 Rick Lantz	.10	.05	.01
☐ 94 Eddie McAshen	.10	.05	.01
☐ 95 Kim King	.10	.05	.01
☐ 96 Cleve Pounds	.10	.05	.01
☐ 97 Rambling Wreck	.10	.05	.01
☐ 98 Bud(Coach) Carson	.20	.10	.02
☐ 99 Bobby Dodd Stadium	.10	.05	.01
☐ 100 Director Card	.10	.05	.01
☐ 101 Willie Burks	.10	.05	.01
☐ 102 Sheldon Fox	.10	.05	.01
☐ 103 Scott Erwin	.20	.10	.02
☐ 104 Danny Harrison	.10	.05	.01
☐ 105 Eric Thomas	.15	.07	.01
☐ 106 Kent Hill	.20	.10	.02
☐ 107 Ray Blemker	.10	.05	.01
☐ 108 Terry Randell	.10	.05	.01
☐ 109 Pete Silas	.10	.05	.01
☐ 110 Bob McDonnell	.10	.05	.01
☐ 111 Kevin Brown	.50	.25	.05
☐ 112 Ralph Malone	.10	.05	.01
☐ 113 Jerry Mays	.15	.07	.01
☐ 114 Mark Bradley	.10	.05	.01
☐ 115 Thomas Palmer	.10	.05	.01
☐ 116 Calvin Tiggle	.15	.07	.01
☐ 117 Roger Kinard	.10	.05	.01
☐ 118 Thomas Balkcom	.10	.05	.01
☐ 119 Steve Newbern	.10	.05	.01
☐ 120 Tripp Isenhour	.10	.05	.01
☐ 121 Rod Stephens	.10	.05	.01
☐ 122 Mark Price	.50	.25	.05
☐ 123 Keith Fleming	.10	.05	.01
☐ 124 Bobby Cremins CO	.20	.10	.02
☐ 125 Eddie Lee Ivery	.20	.10	.02
☐ 126 Darryl Jenkins	.10	.05	.01
☐ 127 Jeremiah McClary	.10	.05	.01
☐ 128 Dirk Morris	.10	.05	.01
☐ 129 Riccardo Ingram	.20	.10	.02
☐ 130 Lisa Neal	.10	.05	.01
☐ 131 Robert Massey	.25	.12	.02
☐ 132 Cedric Stallworth	.10	.05	.01
☐ 133 Ty Griffin	.25	.12	.02
☐ 134 Bruce Dalrymple	.20	.10	.02
☐ 135 Johnny McNeil	.10	.05	.01
☐ 136 Stefen Scotton	.10	.05	.01
☐ 137 Jim Lavin	.10	.05	.01
☐ 138 Joe Siffri	.10	.05	.01
☐ 139 Gary Newson	.10	.05	.01
☐ 140 Cristy Guardao	.10	.05	.01
☐ 141 Scott Petway	.10	.05	.01
☐ 142 Jim Poole	.20	.10	.02
☐ 143 Kenneth Wilson	.10	.05	.01
☐ 144 Bridget Koster	.10	.05	.01
☐ 145 James Purvis	.10	.05	.01
☐ 146 Walt McConnell	.10	.05	.01
☐ 147 Jay Martin	.15	.07	.01
☐ 148 T.J. Edwards	.10	.05	.01
☐ 149 Chris Simmons	.10	.05	.01
☐ 150 Jennifer Beemstebuer	.10	.05	.01
☐ 151 Eric Smith	.10	.05	.01
☐ 152 George Paulson	.10	.05	.01
☐ 153 Nacho Gervas	.10	.05	.01
☐ 154 Mark White	.10	.05	.01
☐ 155 Antonio McKay	.15	.07	.01
☐ 156 Taz Anderson	.15	.07	.01
☐ 157 Sam Bracken	.10	.05	.01
☐ 158 Kate Brandt	.10	.05	.01
☐ 159 Melvin Dole	.10	.05	.01
☐ 160 Tico Brown	.15	.07	.01
☐ 161 Lisa Kofskey	.10	.05	.01
☐ 162 Charlie Rymer	.10	.05	.01

☐ 163 Leigh Roberts	.10	.05	.01
☐ 164 Scott Jordan	.25	.12	.02
☐ 165 Bill McDonald	.10	.05	.01
☐ 166 Harper Brown	.10	.05	.01
☐ 167 Jim Caldwell	.10	.05	.01
☐ 168 Bud Blemker	.10	.05	.01
☐ 169 Bill Flowers	.10	.05	.01
☐ 170 Roger Kasier	.10	.05	.01
☐ 171 Margaret Gales	.10	.05	.01
☐ 172 Kathy Harrison	.10	.05	.01
☐ 173 Kenny Thorne	.10	.05	.01
☐ 174 Kim Lash	.10	.05	.01
☐ 175 Jens Skjoedt	.10	.05	.01
☐ 176 Bobby Kimmel	.10	.05	.01
☐ 177 Phil Wagner	.10	.05	.01
☐ 178 Jim Wood	.10	.05	.01
☐ 179 Rick Yunkus	.15	.07	.01
☐ 180 Unknown	.10	.05	.01
☐ 181 Rick Lockhood	.10	.05	.01
☐ 182 Jay Nichols	.10	.05	.01
☐ 183 Paige Lord	.10	.05	.01
☐ 184 Bryan Shelton	.25	.12	.02
☐ 185 Carrie Ollar	.10	.05	.01
☐ 186 Donnie Chisolm	.10	.05	.01
☐ 187 Floyd Faucette	.10	.05	.01
☐ 188 Jeff Ford	.10	.05	.01
☐ 189 Drew Hill	.35	.17	.03
☐ 190 Leon Hardman	.10	.05	.01
☐ 191 Ricky Gilbert	.10	.05	.01
☐ 192 Roger Kinard	.10	.05	.01
☐ 193 K.G. Whittle	.10	.05	.01
☐ 194 Andre Simm	.10	.05	.01
☐ 195 Franz Sydow	.10	.05	.01
☐ 196 Mackel Harris	.10	.05	.01
☐ 197 Eddie Lee Ivery	.35	.17	.03
☐ 198 Kris Krentra	.10	.05	.01
☐ 199 Lenny Snow	.10	.05	.01
☐ 200 Director Card	.15	.07	.01

1991-92 Georgia Tech Police

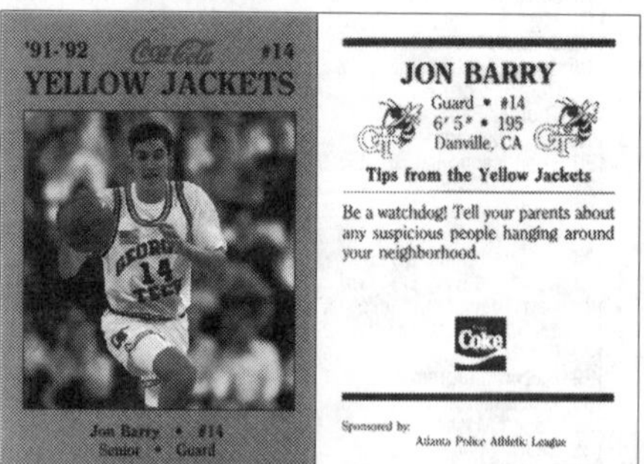

This 15-card standard-size (2 1/2" by 3 1/2") set was sponsored by Coca-Cola in conjunction with Atlanta Police Athletic League. The fronts feature glossy color player photos on a gold card face. The year, Coke logo, jersey number, and team name appear above the picture, while player information is given below it. The backs carry biographical information and "Tips from the Yellow Jackets," which consist of safety tips. The cards are unnumbered and checklisted below in alphabetical order.

	MINT	EXC	G-VG
COMPLETE SET (15)	10.00	5.00	1.00
COMMON PLAYER (1-15)	.50	.25	.05
☐ 1 Rod Balanis	.50	.25	.05
☐ 2 Darryl Barnes	.50	.25	.05
☐ 3 Drew Barry	.75	.35	.07
☐ 4 Jon Barry	1.50	.75	.15
☐ 5 Travis Best	2.50	1.25	.25
☐ 6 Bobby Cremins CO	1.00	.50	.10
☐ 7 James Forrest	2.00	1.00	.20
☐ 8 James Gaddy	.50	.25	.05
☐ 9 Matt Geiger	.75	.35	.07
☐ 10 Todd Harlicka	.50	.25	.05
☐ 11 Bryan Hill	.50	.25	.05
☐ 12 Malcolm Mackey	1.00	.50	.10
☐ 13 Ivano Newbill	.50	.25	.05
☐ 14 Fred Vinson	.50	.25	.05
☐ 15 Greg White	.50	.25	.05

1980-81 Illinois Arby's

This 15-card set was sponsored by Arby's Restaurants and features players of the 1980-81 Fighting Illini squad. The cards measure the standard 2 1/2" by 3 1/2". The player's signature and an Arby's advertisement appear below a color posed photo of the player. The horizontally oriented back provides biographical and statistical information. The cards are numbered for convenience alphabetically in the checklist below.

	MINT	EXC	G-VG
COMPLETE SET (15)	30.00	15.00	3.00
COMMON PLAYER (1-15)	1.00	.50	.10
☐ 1 Kevin Bontemps	1.00	.50	.10
☐ 2 James Griffin	1.00	.50	.10
☐ 3 Derek Harper	12.00	6.00	1.20
☐ 4 Lou Henson CO	2.50	1.25	.25
☐ 5 Derek Holcomb	1.50	.75	.15
☐ 6 Eddie Johnson	10.00	5.00	1.00
☐ 7 Bryan Leonard	1.00	.50	.10
☐ 8 Dick Nagy CO	1.00	.50	.10
☐ 9 Perry Range	1.00	.50	.10
☐ 10 Quinn Richardson	1.00	.50	.10
☐ 11 Mark Smith	1.00	.50	.10
☐ 12 Neale Stoner	1.00	.50	.10
☐ 13 Craig Tucker	1.00	.50	.10
☐ 14 Tony Yates CO	1.50	.75	.15
☐ 15 Team Photo	2.00	1.00	.20

1981-82 Illinois Arby's

This 16-card set was sponsored by Arby's Restaurants and features players of the 1981-82 Fighting Illini squad. The cards measure the standard 2 1/2" by 3 1/2". The player's signature and an Arby's advertisement appear below a color posed photo of the player. The horizontally oriented back provides biographical and statistical information. Lou Henson's last name is misspelled on the back of his card (Hensen). The cards are numbered for convenience alphabetically in the checklist below.

	MINT	EXC	G-VG
COMPLETE SET (16)	16.00	8.00	1.60
COMMON PLAYER (1-16)	.75	.35	.07
☐ 1 Kevin Bontemps	.75	.35	.07
☐ 2 Jay Daniels	.75	.35	.07
☐ 3 James Griffin	.75	.35	.07
☐ 4 Derek Harper	6.00	3.00	.60
☐ 5 Lou Henson CO UER	1.25	.60	.12

(Misspelled Hensen
on card back)

Card	MINT	EXC	G-VG
☐ 6 Dan Klier	.75	.35	.07
☐ 7 Bryan Leonard	.75	.35	.07
☐ 8 Dee Maras	.75	.35	.07
☐ 9 George Montgomery	.75	.35	.07
☐ 10 Dick Nagy CO	.75	.35	.07
☐ 11 Perry Range	.75	.35	.07
☐ 12 Quinn Richardson	.75	.35	.07
☐ 13 Craig Tucker	.75	.35	.07
☐ 14 Anthony Welch	1.50	.75	.15
☐ 15 Tony Yates CO	1.00	.50	.10
☐ 16 Team Photo	1.50	.75	.15

1986-87 Indiana Greats I

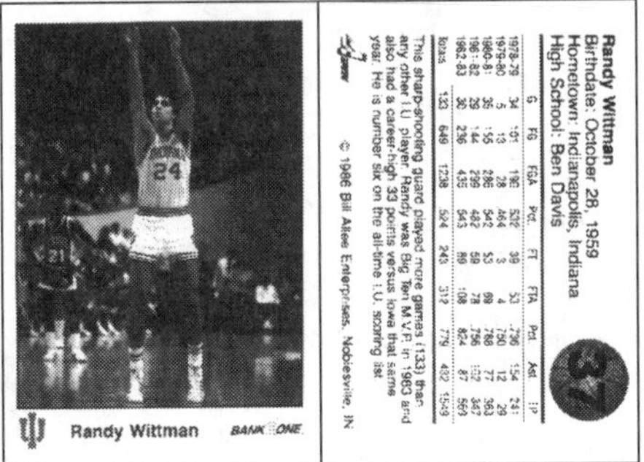

This 42-card set is the first series of the All-Time Greats of Indiana University. The cards measure the standard size, 2 1/2" by 3 1/2", and were sponsored by Bank One of Indiana. The fronts present a mixture of black and white or color photos, posed and action. The horizontally-oriented backs have biographical and statistical information on the player, with the card number in the upper right hand corner.

	MINT	EXC	G-VG
COMPLETE SET (42)	24.00	12.00	2.40
COMMON PLAYER (1-42)	.50	.25	.05

Card	MINT	EXC	G-VG
☐ 1 Bobby Knight CO	3.50	1.75	.35
☐ 2 Walt Bellamy	1.00	.50	.10
☐ 3 Pete Obremskey	.50	.25	.05
☐ 4 Jim Wisman	.50	.25	.05
☐ 5 Frank Radovich	.50	.25	.05
☐ 6 Ted Kitchel	.50	.25	.05
☐ 7 Don Schlundt	.75	.35	.07
☐ 8 Uwe Blab	.60	.30	.06
☐ 9 Lou Watson	.50	.25	.05
☐ 10 Bobby Masters	.50	.25	.05
☐ 11 Steve Redenbaugh	.50	.25	.05
☐ 12 Bob Wilkinson	.75	.35	.07
☐ 13 Kent Benson	1.00	.50	.10
☐ 14 Everett Dean	.75	.35	.07
☐ 15 Rick Ford	.50	.25	.05
☐ 16 Hallie Bryant	.50	.25	.05
☐ 17 Dan Dakich	.60	.30	.06
☐ 18 Sam Gee	.50	.25	.05
☐ 19 George McGinnis	1.25	.60	.12
☐ 20 John Ritter	.50	.25	.05
☐ 21 Jon McGlocklin	.75	.35	.07
☐ 22 Landon Turner	1.25	.60	.12
☐ 23 Gary Long	.50	.25	.05
☐ 24 Jim Crews	.75	.35	.07
☐ 25 Steve Downing	.75	.35	.07
☐ 26 Vern Huffman	.50	.25	.05
☐ 27 Ernie Andres	.50	.25	.05
☐ 28 Charles Hodson	.50	.25	.05
☐ 29 Jerry Thompson	.50	.25	.05
☐ 30 Tom Abernethy	.60	.30	.06
☐ 31 Tom Bolyard	.50	.25	.05
☐ 32 Jimmy Rayl	.75	.35	.07
☐ 33 John Laskowski	.75	.35	.07
☐ 34 Archie Dees	.60	.30	.06
☐ 35 Joby Wright	.75	.35	.07
☐ 36 Gary Greiger	.50	.25	.05
☐ 37 Randy Wittman	1.00	.50	.10
☐ 38 Steve Green	.50	.25	.05
☐ 39 Erv Inniger	.50	.25	.05
☐ 40 Steve Risley	.50	.25	.05
☐ 41 Bill DeHeer	.50	.25	.05
☐ 42 Checklist Card	.75	.35	.07

1987-88 Indiana Greats II

This 42-card set is the second series of the All-Time Greats of Indiana University. The cards measure the standard size, 2 1/2" by 3 1/2", and were sponsored by Bank One of Indiana. The fronts present a mixture of black and white or color photos, posed and action. The horizontally oriented backs have biographical and statistical information on the player, with the card number in the upper right hand corner. The back of the checklist card contains an offer to buy either Series I or II for $10.00 from the Big Red Gift Center.

	MINT	EXC	G-VG
COMPLETE SET (42)	25.00	12.50	2.50
COMMON PLAYER (1-42)	.50	.25	.05

Card	MINT	EXC	G-VG
☐ 1 Steve Alford's Farewell	1.50	.75	.15
☐ 2 Bob Dro	.50	.25	.05
☐ 3 Butch Joyner	.50	.25	.05
☐ 4 Bobby Leonard	.75	.35	.07
☐ 5 Branch McCracken	.75	.35	.07
☐ 6 Roy Tolbert	1.00	.50	.10
☐ 7 Wayne Radford	.60	.30	.06
☐ 8 Earl Schneider	.50	.25	.05
☐ 9 Jim Strickland	.50	.25	.05
☐ 10 Al Harden	.50	.25	.05
☐ 11 Bob Menke	.50	.25	.05
☐ 12 Steve Alford	1.50	.75	.15
☐ 13 Mike Woodson	1.00	.50	.10
☐ 14 Tom/Dick Van Arsdale	1.00	.50	.10
☐ 15 Wally Choice	.50	.25	.05
☐ 16 Charlie Hall	.50	.25	.05
☐ 17 Indiana Coach Legend	.75	.35	.07
☐ 18 Stew Robinson	.60	.30	.06
☐ 19 Dynamic Duo	.75	.35	.07

☐ 20 Steve Alford	1.50	.75	.15
☐ 21 Quinn Buckner	1.25	.60	.12
☐ 22 Indiana Coach Legends	.75	.35	.07
☐ 23 Winston Morgan	.50	.25	.05
☐ 24 1975-76 Seniors	.50	.25	.05
☐ 25 Jim Thomas	.60	.30	.06
☐ 26 Vern Payne	.50	.25	.05
☐ 27 Scott May	1.00	.50	.10
☐ 28 Dave Porter	.50	.25	.05
☐ 29 Dick Farley	.50	.25	.05
☐ 30 Isiah Thomas	7.50	3.75	.75
☐ 31 Butch Carter	.75	.35	.07
☐ 32 Burke Scott	.50	.25	.05
☐ 33 Jack Johnson	.50	.25	.05
☐ 34 Charley Kraak	.50	.25	.05
☐ 35 Marv Huffman	.50	.25	.05
☐ 36 Steve Bouchie	.60	.30	.06
☐ 37 Bobby Knight's Record	1.50	.75	.15
☐ 38 Bill Garrett	.50	.25	.05
☐ 39 Jerry Bass	.50	.25	.05
☐ 40 Jay McCreary	.50	.25	.05
☐ 41 Ken Johnson	.50	.25	.05
☐ 42 Checklist Card (Send-in offer on back)	.75	.35	.07

1982-83 Indiana State Police *

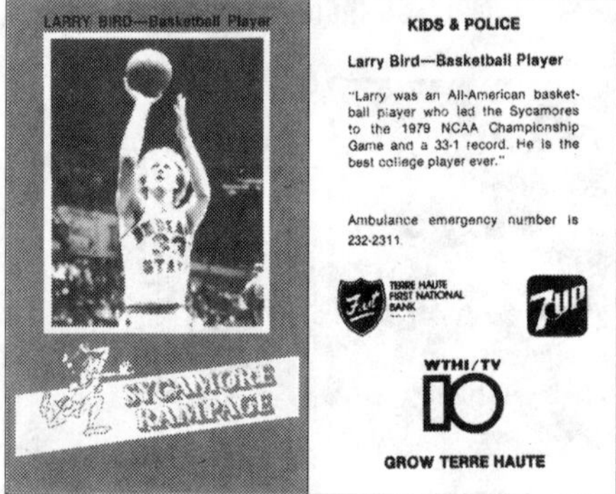

This 15-card multi-sport set was sponsored by the First National Bank of Terre Haute, 7-Up, and WTHI/TV Channel 10. The cards measure 2 5/8" by 4 1/8". On a bright blue card face, the fronts feature black and white player photos enclosed by a white border. A white diagonal stripe appears beneath the picture, with a drawing of the Sycamores' mascot and the words "Sycamore Rampage." The backs have brief biographical information, a quote about the player, a safety tip, and sponsor logos. Sports represented in this set include wrestling (1), basketball (2-3, 4-10, 12), football (11), and gymnastics (13). Olympic athletes included in the set are Bruce Baumgartner and Kurt Thomas. The cards are unnumbered and checklisted below in alphabetical order.

	MINT	EXC	G-VG
COMPLETE SET (15)	175.00	85.00	18.00
COMMON PLAYER (1-15)	2.50	1.25	.25
☐ 1 Bruce Baumgartner (Wrestling)	2.50	1.25	.25
☐ 2 Larry Bird	135.00	60.00	12.00
☐ 3 Terry Braun	2.50	1.25	.25
☐ 4 Myron Christian	2.50	1.25	.25
☐ 5 Al Cole	2.50	1.25	.25
☐ 6 Rick Fields	2.50	1.25	.25
☐ 7 Mark Golden	2.50	1.25	.25
☐ 8 Jeff McComb	2.50	1.25	.25
☐ 9 Scott Mugg	2.50	1.25	.25
☐ 10 Dave Schellhase CO	5.00	2.50	.50
☐ 11 Craig Shaffer (Football)	2.50	1.25	.25
☐ 12 James Smith	2.50	1.25	.25
☐ 13 Kurt Thomas (Gymnastics)	10.00	5.00	1.00

☐ 14 Chief Ouibachi and The Indian Princess	2.50	1.25	.25
☐ 15 Cheerleaders	2.50	1.25	.25

1991-92 Iowa

This 15-card set measures the standard size (2 1/2" by 3 1/2") and is printed on thin card stock. The fronts feature color player photos, with a gold and black parquet floor border. Player information appears in the black stripe at the bottom of the card face, while the school logo appears in an orange basketball at the lower left corner. In a horizontal format, the backs carry a black and white head shot and a player profile. The cards are unnumbered and checklisted below in alphabetical order. The key card in the set is Acie Earl.

	MINT	EXC	G-VG
COMPLETE SET (15)	10.00	5.00	1.00
COMMON PLAYER (1-15)	.60	.30	.06
☐ 1 Val Barnes	.60	.30	.06
☐ 2 Jim Bartels	.60	.30	.06
☐ 3 Phil Chime	.60	.30	.06
☐ 4 Rodell Davis	.75	.35	.07
☐ 5 Acie Earl	3.00	1.50	.30
☐ 6 Wade Lookingbill	.60	.30	.06
☐ 7 Paul Lusk	.60	.30	.06
☐ 8 Russ Millard	.60	.30	.06
☐ 9 James Moses	.75	.35	.07
☐ 10 Troy Skinner	.60	.30	.06
☐ 11 Kevin Smith	.60	.30	.06
☐ 12 Chris Street	.60	.30	.06
☐ 13 Brig Tubbs	.60	.30	.06
☐ 14 Jay Webb	.60	.30	.06
☐ 15 James Winters	.60	.30	.06

1991-92 James Madison Smokey

The 1991-92 James Madison basketball set was sponsored by the USDA Forest Service, the state forestry service, and James Madison University. The standard-size (2 1/2" by 3 1/2") cards are printed on thin card stock. The fronts display a mix of color posed and action player photos, enclosed by purple borders and accented by mustard stripes above and below. The school name, player's name, number, and position appear in the mustard stripes. In black print on white card stock, the backs have brief biographical information, a fire prevention cartoon starring Smokey, and sponsor acknowledgments. The cards are unnumbered and checklisted below alphabetically by player's last name.

	MINT	EXC	G-VG
COMPLETE SET (12)	12.00	6.00	1.20
COMMON PLAYER (1-12)	1.00	.50	.10
☐ 1 Troy Bostic	1.00	.50	.10
☐ 2 Paul Carter	1.00	.50	.10

	MINT	EXC	G-VG
☐ 3 Jeff Chambers	1.00	.50	.10
☐ 4 Vladimir Cuk	1.00	.50	.10
☐ 5 Kent Culuko	1.00	.50	.10
☐ 6 William Davis	1.00	.50	.10
☐ 7 Lefty Driesell CO	3.00	1.50	.30
☐ 8 Bryan Edwards	1.00	.50	.10
☐ 9 Gerry Lancaster	1.00	.50	.10
☐ 10 Keith Peoples	1.00	.50	.10
☐ 11 Clayton Ritter	1.00	.50	.10
☐ 12 Michael Venson	1.50	.75	.15

1987-88 Kansas Nike

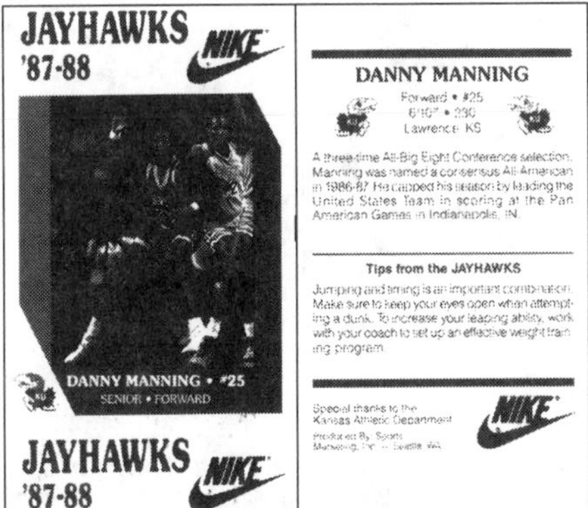

This 16-card set was sponsored by Nike and issued on an unperforated sheet with four rows of four cards. After cutting, they measure the standard size (2 1/2" by 3 1/2"). The fronts feature a mix of posed and action color player photos on a white card face. Above the picture appears the team name, year, and the Nike logo. The picture is bordered by red on the left and by dark blue on the right and bottom. The Jayhawk logo appears in the lower left corner, with player identification in the blue border below the picture. The backs have biographical information, player evaluation, and basketball advice in the form of "Tips from the Jayhawks." The cards are unnumbered and checklisted below in alphabetical order, with the uniform number after the player's name. This set features the team that won the 1987-88 NCAA Championship.

	MINT	EXC	G-VG
COMPLETE SET (16)	30.00	15.00	3.00
COMMON PLAYER (1-16)	1.00	.50	.10
☐ 1 Sean Alvarado 52	1.00	.50	.10
☐ 2 Scooter Barry 10	3.00	1.50	.30
☐ 3 Marvin Branch 54	1.25	.60	.12
☐ 4 Larry Brown CO	2.50	1.25	.25
☐ 5 Jeff Gueldner 33	1.50	.75	.15
☐ 6 Keith Harris 45	1.00	.50	.10
☐ 7 Otis Livingston 12	1.00	.50	.10
☐ 8 Mike Maddox 32	1.00	.50	.10
☐ 9 Danny Manning 25	15.00	7.50	1.50
☐ 10 Archie Marshall 23	1.25	.60	.12
☐ 11 Mike Masucci 44	1.00	.50	.10
☐ 12 Lincoln Minor 11	1.25	.60	.12
☐ 13 Milt Newton 21	3.00	1.50	.30
☐ 14 Chris Piper 24	1.00	.50	.10
☐ 15 Kevin Pritchard 14	3.00	1.50	.30
☐ 16 Mark Randall 42	4.00	2.00	.40

1989-90 Kansas Leesley

This 16-card set was licensed to Leesley by the University of Kansas. The cards measure the standard size (2 1/2" by 3 1/2") and feature on the fronts color action player shots, with white and black borders on dark blue background. The player's name is given below the picture, with the Jayhawk team logo on an orange basketball in the lower right corner. The backs present biographical information and a player profile. The cards are numbered on the back in continuation of the Kansas Football card set.

	MINT	EXC	G-VG
COMPLETE SET (16)	12.00	6.00	1.20
COMMON PLAYER (41-56)	.60	.30	.06
☐ 41 Frequent Flyers Poster Poster Card	.75	.35	.07
☐ 42 Jeff Gueldner	.75	.35	.07
☐ 43 Freeman West	.60	.30	.06
☐ 44 Rick Calloway	1.00	.50	.10
☐ 45 Mark Randall	1.25	.60	.12
☐ 46 Mike Maddox	1.00	.50	.10
☐ 47 Alonzo Jamison	2.00	1.00	.20
☐ 48 Kevin Pritchard	1.25	.60	.12
☐ 49 Terry Brown	1.00	.50	.10
☐ 50 Kirk Wagner	.60	.30	.06
☐ 51 Pekka Markkanen	.60	.30	.06
☐ 52 Sean Tunstall	.75	.35	.07
☐ 53 Macolm Nash	.60	.30	.06
☐ 54 Todd Alexander	.60	.30	.06
☐ 55 Adonis Jordan	2.50	1.25	.25
☐ 56 Roy Williams CO	1.25	.60	.12
☐ xx Title Card (unnumbered)	.75	.35	.07

1991-92 Kansas

This 18-card standard-size (2 1/2" by 3 1/2") set features on the fronts either posed or action color photos, enclosed by red and blue borders.The player's position appears in a gray stripe on the right side of the picture, while his name is printed in gray stripe beneath the picture. The horizontally oriented backs

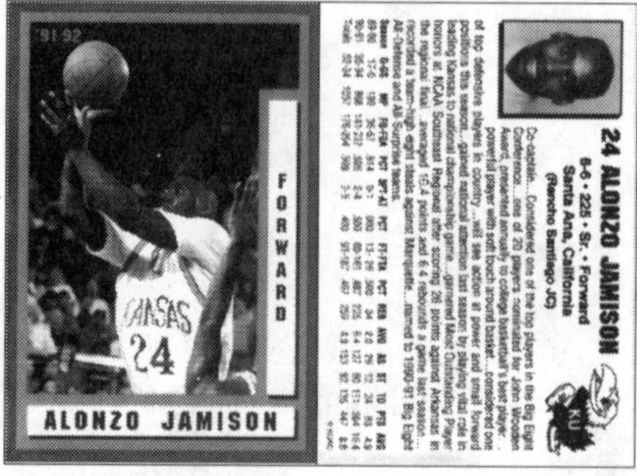

carry a black and white head shot, biography, and player profile. The cards are unnumbered and checklisted below in alphabetical order. The key cards in the set are Alonzo Jamison and Adonis Jordan.

	MINT	EXC	G-VG
COMPLETE SET (18)	10.00	5.00	1.00
COMMON PLAYER (1-18)	.50	.25	.05
☐ 1 Lane Czaplinski	.50	.25	.05
☐ 2 Ben Davis	.50	.25	.05
☐ 3 Greg Gurley	.50	.25	.05
☐ 4 Alonzo Jamison	1.25	.60	.12
☐ 5 David Johanning	.50	.25	.05
☐ 6 Adonis Jordan	1.50	.75	.15
☐ 7 Macolm Nash	.50	.25	.05
☐ 8 Greg Ostertag	.75	.35	.07
☐ 9 Eric Pauley	.75	.35	.07
☐ 10 Sean Pearson	.50	.25	.05
☐ 11 Calvin Rayford	.50	.25	.05
☐ 12 Patrick Richey	.50	.25	.05
☐ 13 Richard Scott	.50	.25	.05
☐ 14 Rex Walters	.75	.35	.07
☐ 15 Roy Williams CO	1.00	.50	.10
☐ 16 Steve Woodberry	.50	.25	.05
☐ 17 The O-Zone Alonzo Jamison	1.00	.50	.10
☐ 18 Team Photo Checklist	.75	.35	.07

1977-78 Kentucky Wildcat News

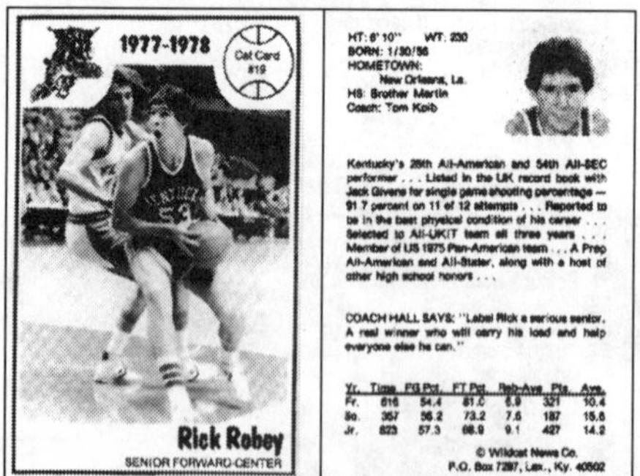

This 22-card set measures 2 1/2" by 3 3/4" and was produced by Wildcat News. The front features a black and white action photo with a royal blue border on white card stock. The player cards have the Wildcat logo, year, and the card number (in a basketball) across the top of the card face. The player's name and position appear below the picture. The back has a black and white head shot of the player in the upper right corner, with biographical and statistical information filling in the remainder of the space. This set features early cards of Kyle Macy and Rick Robey, who later played with different NBA teams. This set features the team that won the 1977-78 NCAA Championship.

	NRMT	VG-E	GOOD
COMPLETE SET (22)	40.00	20.00	4.00
COMMON PLAYER (1-22)	1.00	.50	.10
☐ 1 The Fabulous Five	4.00	2.00	.40
☐ 2 Joe Hall's First UK Team	2.00	1.00	.20
☐ 3 1975 NCAA Runners-Up	1.00	.50	.10
☐ 4 1977-78 Wildcats	1.00	.50	.10
☐ 5 Leonard Hamilton CO	2.00	1.00	.20
☐ 6 Joe Dean CO	1.00	.50	.10
☐ 7 Joe B. Hall CO	2.00	1.00	.20
☐ 8 Dick Parsons CO	1.00	.50	.10
☐ 9 Scott Courts	1.00	.50	.10
☐ 10 Chuck Aleksinas	2.00	1.00	.20
☐ 11 LaVon Williams	1.50	.75	.15
☐ 13 Dwane Casey	4.00	2.00	.40
☐ 14 Fred Cowan	1.50	.75	.15
☐ 15 Kyle Macy	7.50	3.75	.75
☐ 16 Tim Stephens	1.00	.50	.10
☐ 17 James Lee	3.00	1.50	.30
☐ 18 Jay Shidler	2.50	1.25	.25
☐ 19 Rick Robey	6.00	3.00	.60
☐ 20 Truman Claytor	2.00	1.00	.20
☐ 22 Mike Phillips	2.00	1.00	.20

1978-79 Kentucky Foodtown

This 22-card set was produced by Wildcat News and sponsored by Foodtown. The cards were originally given out one per week at the participating grocary stores. The cards measure approximately 2 1/2" by 3 3/4". The front features a black and white action photo, with the Wildcat logo, year, and the card number (in a basketball) to the left of the picture. The player's name and position appear below the picture, and a royal blue border outlines the card face. The back has a black and white head shot of the player in the upper right corner, with biographical and statistical information filling in the remainder of the space. This set features an early card of Kyle Macy, who later played in the NBA.

	NRMT	VG-E	GOOD
COMPLETE SET (22)	25.00	12.50	2.50
COMMON PLAYER (1-22)	.80	.40	.08
☐ 1 Homeward Bound (Joe B. Hall and wife)	1.25	.60	.12
☐ 2 Celebratin' Seniors	.80	.40	.08
☐ 3 Moment of Glory (Jack Givens)	1.25	.60	.12
☐ 4 Hagan's Hall of Fame Induction	1.25	.60	.12
☐ 5 1978-79 Wildcats	.80	.40	.08
☐ 6 1978 NCAA Champions	.80	.40	.08
☐ 7 Dwight Anderson	2.50	1.25	.25
☐ 8 Clarence Tillman	.80	.40	.08
☐ 9 Chuck Verderber	1.25	.60	.12
☐ 10 Dwane Casey	3.00	1.50	.30

☐ 11 Truman Claytor	1.50	.75	.15
☐ 12 Tim Stephens	.80	.40	.08
☐ 13 Kyle Macy	3.50	1.75	.35
☐ 14 LaVon Williams	1.25	.60	.12
☐ 15 Jay Shidler	1.50	.75	.15
☐ 16 Freddie Cowan	1.25	.60	.12
☐ 17 Chuck Aleksinas	1.50	.75	.15
☐ 18 Chris Gettelfinger	.80	.40	.08
☐ 19 Joe B. Hall CO	1.25	.60	.12
☐ 20 Dick Parsons CO	.80	.40	.08
☐ 21 Leonard Hamilton CO	1.00	.50	.10
☐ 22 Joe Dean CO	.80	.40	.08

1979-80 Kentucky Foodtown

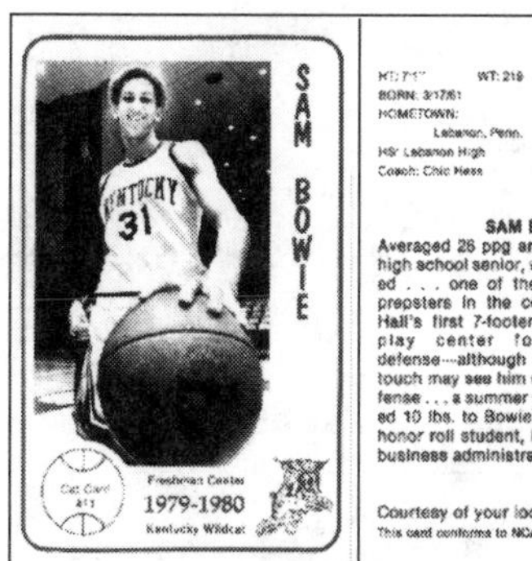

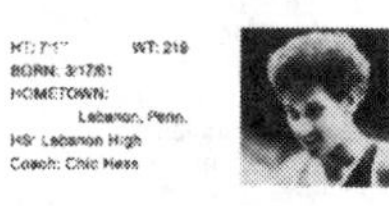

This 22-card set was sponsored by Foodtown. The cards measures 2 1/2" by 3 3/4". The front features a black and white action photo, with the player's name printed vertically to the right of the picture. The card number (in a basketball), the year, and the Wildcat logo appear at the bottom of the card face. A royal blue border outlines the card face. The back has a black and white head shot of the player in the upper right corner, with biographical information filling in the remainder of the space. This set features cards of Kyle Macy, Sam Bowie, and Dirk Minnifield, who later played with different NBA teams.

	NRMT	VG-E	GOOD
COMPLETE SET (22)	20.00	10.00	2.00
COMMON PLAYER (1-22)	.60	.30	.06
☐ 1 1979-1980 Wildcats	1.00	.50	.10
☐ 2 Kyle Macy	2.00	1.00	.20
☐ 3 Jay Shidler	1.25	.60	.12
☐ 4 LaVon Williams	1.00	.50	.10
☐ 5 Chris Gettelfinger	.60	.30	.06
☐ 6 Fred Cowan	1.00	.50	.10
☐ 7 Dwight Anderson	1.75	.85	.17
☐ 8 Bo Lanter	.60	.30	.06
☐ 9 Chuck Verderber	1.00	.50	.10
☐ 10 Dirk Minniefield	3.00	1.50	.30
☐ 11 Sam Bowie	6.00	3.00	.60
☐ 12 Charles Hurt	2.00	1.00	.20
☐ 13 Derrick Hord	1.50	.75	.15
☐ 14 Tom Heitz	.60	.30	.06
☐ 15 Joe Dean CO	.60	.30	.06
☐ 16 Leonard Hamilton CO	.75	.35	.07
☐ 17 Dick Parsons CO	.60	.30	.06
☐ 18 Joe B. Hall CO	1.00	.50	.10
☐ 19 Rupp Arena	.60	.30	.06
☐ 20 Kyle Macy	2.00	1.00	.20
☐ 21 The Freshman Five	1.00	.50	.10
☐ 22 The Seniors	.75	.35	.07

1981-82 Kentucky Schedules

This 14-card set features schedule cards each measuring approximately 2 1/4" by 3 1/4". The card fronts feature a borderless black and white player photo with a dark blue tint. Player information is given in the white stripe below the picture. In dark blue lettering the back has the 1981-82 basketball schedule. These unnumbered cards are ordered below alphabetically by player's name.

	MINT	EXC	G-VG
COMPLETE SET (14)	50.00	25.00	5.00
COMMON PLAYER (1-14)	3.00	1.50	.30
☐ 1 M. Ballenger	3.00	1.50	.30
☐ 2 Sam Bowie	10.00	5.00	1.00
☐ 3 Bob Chambers ACO	3.00	1.50	.30
☐ 4 Joe Dean ACO	3.00	1.50	.30
☐ 5 Joe B. Hall CO	4.00	2.00	.40
☐ 6 Leonard Hamilton ACO	4.00	2.00	.40
☐ 7 Tom Heitz	3.00	1.50	.30
☐ 8 Derrick Hord	5.00	2.50	.50
☐ 9 Charles Hurt	5.00	2.50	.50
☐ 10 Bo Lanter	3.00	1.50	.30
☐ 11 Jim Master	5.00	2.50	.50
☐ 12 Troy McKinley	3.00	1.50	.30
☐ 13 Dirk Minniefield	7.50	3.75	.75
☐ 14 Melvin Turpin	7.50	3.75	.75

1982-83 Kentucky Schedules

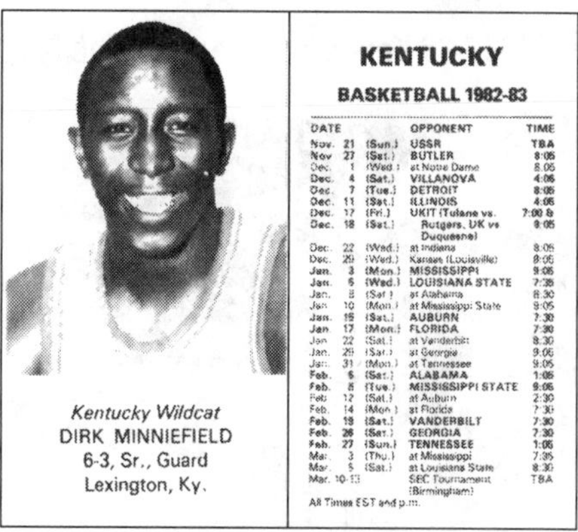

KENTUCKY

BASKETBALL 1982-83

DATE			OPPONENT	TIME
Nov.	21	(Sun.)	USSR	TBA
Nov	27	(Sat.)	BUTLER	8:05
Dec.	1	(Wed.)	at Notre Dame	8:05
Dec.	4	(Sat.)	VILLANOVA	4:05
Dec.	7	(Tue.)	DETROIT	8:05
Dec.	11	(Sat.)	ILLINOIS	4:05
Dec.	17	(Fri.)	UKIT (Tulane vs.	7:00 &
Dec.	18	(Sat.)	Rutgers, UK vs Duquesne)	9:05
Dec.	22	(Wed.)	at Indiana	8:05
Dec.	29	(Wed.)	Kansas (Louisville)	8:05
Jan.	3	(Mon.)	MISSISSIPPI	9:05
Jan.	5	(Wed.)	LOUISIANA STATE	7:35
Jan.	8	(Sat.)	at Alabama	8:30
Jan.	10	(Mon.)	at Mississippi State	9:05
Jan.	15	(Sat.)	AUBURN	7:30
Jan.	17	(Mon.)	FLORIDA	7:30
Jan.	22	(Sat.)	at Vanderbilt	8:30
Jan.	29	(Sat.)	at Georgia	9:05
Jan.	31	(Mon.)	at Tennessee	9:05
Feb.	5	(Sat.)	ALABAMA	1:05
Feb.	8	(Tue.)	MISSISSIPPI STATE	9:05
Feb.	12	(Sat.)	at Auburn	2:30
Feb.	14	(Mon.)	at Florida	7:30
Feb.	19	(Sat.)	VANDERBILT	7:30
Feb.	26	(Sat.)	GEORGIA	7:30
Feb.	27	(Sun.)	TENNESSEE	1:05
Mar.	3	(Thu.)	at Mississippi	7:35
Mar.	5	(Sat.)	at Louisiana State	8:30
Mar. 10-13			SEC Tournament (Birmingham)	TBA

All Times EST and p.m.

This 14-card set features schedule cards each measuring approximately 2 1/4" by 3 1/4". The card fronts feature a borderless black and white player photo with a dark blue tint. Player information is given in the white stripe below the picture. In dark blue lettering the back has the 1982-83 basketball schedule. These unnumbered cards are ordered below alphabetically by player's name.

	MINT	EXC	G-VG
COMPLETE SET (14)	50.00	25.00	5.00
COMMON PLAYER (1-14)	3.00	1.50	.30
☐ 1 Dicky Beal	3.00	1.50	.30
☐ 2 Bret Bearup	3.00	1.50	.30
☐ 3 Sam Bowie	10.00	5.00	1.00
☐ 4 Bob Chambers ACO	3.00	1.50	.30
☐ 5 Joe Dean ACO	3.00	1.50	.30
☐ 6 Joe B. Hall CO	4.00	2.00	.40
☐ 7 Leonard Hamilton ACO	4.00	2.00	.40
☐ 8 Tom Heitz	3.00	1.50	.30
☐ 9 Derrick Hord	4.00	2.00	.40
☐ 10 Charles Hurt	4.00	2.00	.40
☐ 11 Jim Master	4.00	2.00	.40
☐ 12 Troy McKinley	3.00	1.50	.30
☐ 13 Dirk Minniefield	6.00	3.00	.60
☐ 14 Melvin Turpin	6.00	3.00	.60

1983-84 Kentucky Schedules

This 17-card set features schedule cards each measuring approximately 2 1/4" by 3 1/4". The card fronts feature a borderless black and white player photo with a dark blue tint. Player information is given in the white stripe below the picture. In dark blue lettering the back has the 1983-84 basketball schedule. These unnumbered cards are ordered below alphabetically by player's name.

	MINT	EXC	G-VG
COMPLETE SET (17)	50.00	25.00	5.00
COMMON PLAYER (1-17)	3.00	1.50	.30
☐ 1 Paul Andrews	3.00	1.50	.30
☐ 2 Dicky Beal	3.00	1.50	.30
☐ 3 Bret Bearup	3.00	1.50	.30
☐ 4 Winston Bennett	5.00	2.50	.50
☐ 5 James Blackmon	4.00	2.00	.40
☐ 6 Sam Bowie	8.00	4.00	.80
☐ 7 Joe B. Hall CO	4.00	2.00	.40
☐ 8 Leonard Hamilton ACO	4.00	2.00	.40
☐ 9 Hatfield	3.00	1.50	.30
☐ 10 Tom Heitz	3.00	1.50	.30
☐ 11 John Kelly	3.00	1.50	.30
☐ 12 Jim Master	4.00	2.00	.40
☐ 13 T. May	3.00	1.50	.30
☐ 14 Troy McKinley	3.00	1.50	.30
☐ 15 Melvin Turpin	6.00	3.00	.60
☐ 16 Kenny Walker	8.00	4.00	.80
☐ 17 Todd Ziegler	3.00	1.50	.30

1987-88 Kentucky Coke/Valvoline *

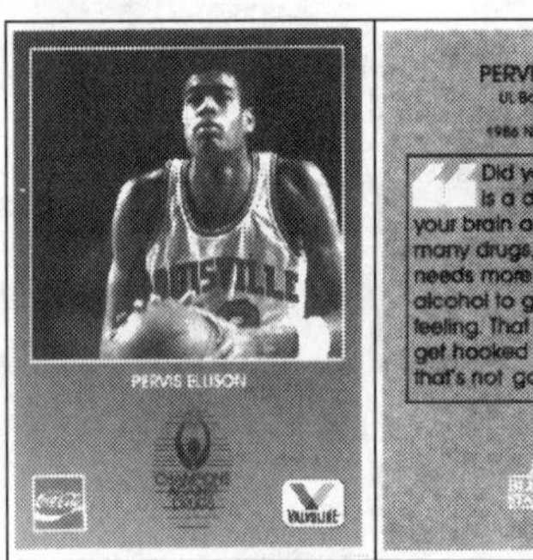

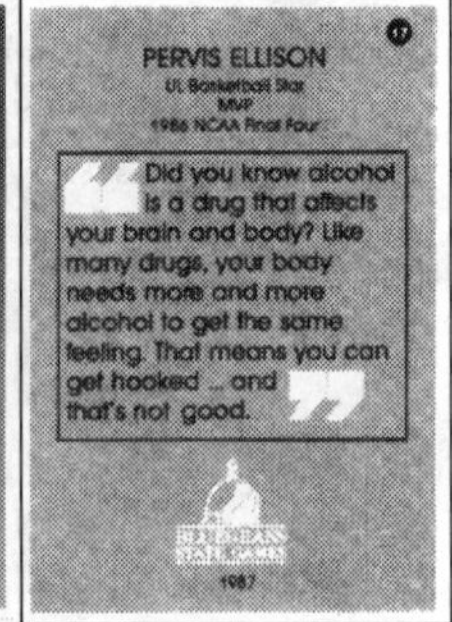

This 24-card set of standard size (2 1/2" by 3 1/2") cards was co-sponsored by Coca-Cola and Valvoline, and their company logos appear on the bottom of the card face. The card sets were originally given out by the Kentucky county sheriff's departments and the Kentucky Highway Patrol to kids 17 and under. Supposedly about 350 sets were given to the approximately 120 counties in the state of Kentucky. One card per week was given out from May 25 to October 19, 1987. Once all 22 of the numbered cards were collected, they could be turned in to a local sheriff's department for prizes. The front features a color action player photo, on a blue card face with a white outer border. The player's name and the "Champions Against Drugs" insignia appear below the picture. The back has a anti-drug or alcohol tip on a gray background, with white border. The cards are numbered on the back. The set commemorates Kentucky's hosting of the 1987 Bluegrass State Games and was endorsed by Governor Martha Layne Collins in Kentucky's Champions Against Drugs Crusade for Youth. The set features stars from a variety of sports as well as public figures. The two cards in the set numbered "SC" for special card were not distributed with the factory sets; they were in fact produced in smaller quantities than the 22 numbered cards.

	MINT	EXC	G-VG
COMPLETE SET (24)	65.00	32.50	6.50
COMMON PLAYER (1-22)	.60	.30	.06
☐ 1 Martha Layne Collins Governor of Kentucky	.60	.30	.06
☐ 2 Kenny Walker	1.00	.50	.10
☐ 3 Dr. William DeVries	.60	.30	.06
☐ 4 Dan Issel	2.00	1.00	.20
☐ 5 Doug Flynn	.75	.35	.07
☐ 6 Melinda Cumberledge	.60	.30	.06
☐ 7 Melvin Turpin and Sam Bowie	1.50	.75	.15
☐ 8 Darrell Griffith	1.50	.75	.15
☐ 9 Winston Bennett	1.00	.50	.10
☐ 10 Ricky Skaggs	1.00	.50	.10
☐ 11 Wildcat Mascot	.60	.30	.06
☐ 12 Cardinal Mascot	.60	.30	.06
☐ 13 Pee Wee Reese	2.00	1.00	.20
☐ 14 Mary T. Meagher	.75	.35	.07
☐ 15 Jim Master	.75	.35	.07
☐ 16 Kyle Macy	1.25	.60	.12
☐ 17 Pervis Ellison	3.00	1.50	.30
☐ 18 Dale Baldwin	.60	.30	.06
☐ 19 Frank Minniefield	1.25	.60	.12
☐ 20 Mark Higgs	3.00	1.50	.30
☐ 21 Rex Chapman	3.00	1.50	.30
☐ 22 A.B.(Happy) Chandler	1.25	.60	.12
☐ SC Billy Packer SP	3.50	1.75	.35
☐ SC David Robinson SP	45.00	22.50	4.50

1988 Kentucky Soviets

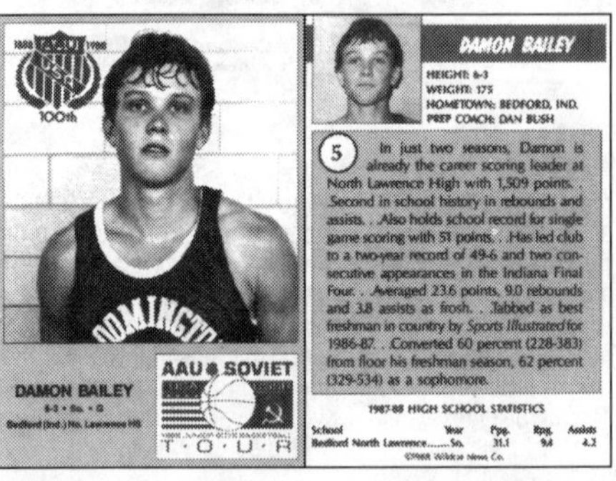

This 18-card set was issued as an insert in the U.S. AAU All-Stars vs. Soviet Junior Nationals official program for the game played at Memorial Coliseum in Lexington, KY, May 14, 1988. The set is the only one printed during the Russian Junior team's U.S. tour. The cards were issued in two panels; after perforation, the cards measure approximately 2 1/2" by 3 1/2". The front features a mix of posed or action, black and white player photos, with a light blue background and thin black border on white card stock. A 1888-1988 AAU/USA 100th anniversary emblem is superimposed at the left corner of the photo. Player information appears below the picture in the lower left corner. An AAU/Soviet tour emblem in the lower right corner rounds out the card face. The back has a black and white head shot of the player in the upper left corner. Biographical information appears in a light blue-tinted box, with high school statistics at the bottom. The cards are numbered on the back. The set features the first cards of Damon Bailey and several future college standouts.

	MINT	EXC	G-VG
COMPLETE SET (18)	75.00	37.50	7.50
COMMON PLAYER (1-18)	1.00	.50	.10
☐ 1 Checklist	1.50	.75	.15
☐ 2 Scott Davenport CO	1.00	.50	.10
☐ 3 Keith Adkins	1.00	.50	.10
☐ 4 Mike Allen	1.00	.50	.10
☐ 5 Damon Bailey	20.00	10.00	2.00
☐ 6 Scott Boley	1.00	.50	.10

	MINT	EXC	G-VG
7 David DeMarcus	1.00	.50	.10
8 Richie Farmer	4.00	2.00	.40
9 Travis Ford	2.00	1.00	.20
10 Pat Graham	4.00	2.00	.40
11 Robbie Graham	1.00	.50	.10
12 Allan Houston	12.00	6.00	1.20
13 Shawn Kemp	30.00	15.00	3.00
14 Don MacLean	10.00	5.00	1.00
15 Kenneth Martin	1.00	.50	.10
16 Chris Mills	10.00	5.00	1.00
17 Derek Miller	1.00	.50	.10
18 Sean Woods	6.00	3.00	.60

1988-89 Kentucky 269

The 1988-89 University of Kentucky Wildcats set contains 269 standard-sized (2 1/2" by 3 1/2") cards featuring "Kentucky's Finest" basketball players. The fronts have deep blue and white borders. The backs have various statistical and biographical information. This set was issued in eight-card cello packs.

	MINT	EXC	G-VG
COMPLETE SET (269)	30.00	15.00	3.00
COMMON PLAYER (1-269)	.10	.05	.01
1 Adolph Rupp CO	.50	.25	.05
2 Cliff Hagan	.45	.22	.04
3 Frank Ramsey	.35	.17	.03
4 Ralph Beard	.25	.12	.02
5 Alex Groza	.25	.12	.02
6 Wallace Jones	.10	.05	.01
7 Dan Issel	.45	.22	.04
8 Cotton Nash	.20	.10	.02
9 Kevin Grevey	.20	.10	.02
10 Kyle Macy	.25	.12	.02
11 Kenny Walker	.20	.10	.02
12 Louie Dampier	.20	.10	.02
13 Vernon Hatton	.10	.05	.01
14 Johnny Cox	.10	.05	.01
15 Jack Givens	.20	.10	.02
16 Bill Spivey	.10	.05	.01
17 Pat Riley	.45	.22	.04
18 Ellis Johnson	.10	.05	.01
19 Forest Sale	.10	.05	.01
20 Kenny Rollins	.10	.05	.01
21 Sam Bowie	.30	.15	.03
22 John DeMoisey	.10	.05	.01
23 Leroy Edwards	.10	.05	.01
24 Lee Huber	.10	.05	.01
25 Rick Robey	.20	.10	.02
26 Bob Burrow	.10	.05	.01
27 Cliff Barker	.10	.05	.01
28 Bernie Opper	.10	.05	.01
29 Ralph Carlisle	.10	.05	.01
30 Joe B. Hall CO	.15	.07	.01
31 Bob Brannum	.10	.05	.01
32 Jack Parkinson	.10	.05	.01
33 Jack Tingle	.10	.05	.01
34 Joe Holland	.10	.05	.01
35 Jim Line	.10	.05	.01
36 Bobby Watson	.10	.05	.01
37 Bill Evans	.10	.05	.01
38 Bill Lickert	.10	.05	.01
39 Larry Conley	.25	.12	.02
40 Eddie Sutton	.20	.10	.02
41 Larry Steele	.20	.10	.02
42 Tom Parker	.10	.05	.01
43 Shelby Linville	.10	.05	.01
44 Lou Tsioropoulos	.15	.07	.01
45 Gayle Rose	.15	.07	.01
46 Jim Andrews	.10	.05	.01
47 Ed Davender	.15	.07	.01
48 Winston Bennett	.20	.10	.02
49 Willie Rouse	.10	.05	.01
50 Mike Pratt	.15	.07	.01
51 Harry C. Lancaster	.10	.05	.01
52 Dirk Minniefield	.20	.10	.02
53 Russell Rice	.10	.05	.01
54 Carey Spicer	.10	.05	.01
55 Paul McBrayer	.10	.05	.01
56 Burgess Carey	.10	.05	.01
57 Ermal Allen	.20	.10	.02
58 Dale Barnstable	.10	.05	.01
59 Kenton Campbell	.10	.05	.01
60 Guy Strong	.10	.05	.01
61 Lucian Whitaker	.10	.05	.01
62 Bennie Coffman	.10	.05	.01
63 C.M. Newton	.25	.12	.02
64 Walt Hirsch	.10	.05	.01
65 John Brewer	.15	.07	.01
66 Phil Grawemeyer	.10	.05	.01
67 John Crigler	.10	.05	.01
68 Gerry Calvert	.10	.05	.01
69 Ed Beck	.10	.05	.01
70 Jerry Bird	.10	.05	.01
71 Harold Ross	.10	.05	.01
72 Adrian Smith	.20	.10	.02
73 Don Mills	.10	.05	.01
74 Ned Jennings	.10	.05	.01
75 Sid Cohen	.10	.05	.01
76 Dickie Parsons	.10	.05	.01
77 Larry Pursiful	.10	.05	.01
78 Herky Rupp	.15	.07	.01
79 Charles Ishmael	.10	.05	.01
80 Jim McDonald	.10	.05	.01
81 Terry Mobley	.10	.05	.01
82 Tommy Kron	.15	.07	.01
83 Randy Embry	.10	.05	.01
84 Steve Clevenger	.10	.05	.01
85 Jim LeMaster	.10	.05	.01
86 Basil Hayden	.10	.05	.01
87 Cliff Berger	.10	.05	.01
88 Jim Dinwiddie	.10	.05	.01
89 Randy Pool	.10	.05	.01
90 Terry Mills	.15	.07	.01
91 Bob McCowan	.10	.05	.01
92 Mike Casey	.15	.07	.01
93 Kent Hollenbeck	.10	.05	.01
94 Scotty Baesler	.10	.05	.01
95 Phil Argento	.10	.05	.01
96 John R. Adams	.10	.05	.01
97 Larry Stamper	.10	.05	.01
98 Ray Edelman	.10	.05	.01
99 Ronnie Lyons	.10	.05	.01
100 G.J. Smith	.10	.05	.01
101 Jerry Hale	.10	.05	.01
102 Bob Guyette	.10	.05	.01
103 Mike Flynn	.10	.05	.01
104 Jimmy Dan Connor	.20	.10	.02
105 Larry Johnson	.10	.05	.01
106 Joey Holland	.10	.05	.01
107 Reggie Warford	.10	.05	.01
108 Merion Haskins	.10	.05	.01
109 James Lee	.20	.10	.02
110 Dwane Casey	.30	.15	.03
111 Truman Claytor	.20	.10	.02
112 LaVon Williams	.20	.10	.02
113 Jay Shidler	.25	.12	.02
114 Fred Cowan	.15	.07	.01
115 Dwight Anderson	.30	.15	.03
116 Chuck Verderber	.15	.07	.01
117 Bo Lanter	.10	.05	.01
118 Charles Hurt	.20	.10	.02
119 Derrick Hord	.20	.10	.02
120 Tom Heitz	.10	.05	.01
121 Dicky Beal	.15	.07	.01
122 Bret Bearup	.15	.07	.01
123 Melvin Turpin	.20	.10	.02
124 Jim Master	.15	.07	.01
125 Troy McKinley	.10	.05	.01
126 Roger Harden	.15	.07	.01
127 James Blackmon	.25	.12	.02
128 Leroy Byrd	.10	.05	.01
129 Cedric Jenkins	.15	.07	.01
130 Rob Lock	.15	.07	.01
131 Richard Madison	.15	.07	.01
132 Cawood Ledford	.15	.07	.01
133 '47-'48 Team	.10	.05	.01
134 '48-'49 Team	.10	.05	.01

	No.	Player	MINT	EXC	G-VG
☐	135	'50-'51 Team	.10	.05	.01
☐	136	'57-'58 Team	.10	.05	.01
☐	137	'77-'78 Team	.10	.05	.01
☐	138	Stan Key	.10	.05	.01
☐	139	Mike Phillips	.15	.07	.01
☐	140	Joe B. Hall CO	.15	.07	.01
☐	141	Mike Flynn	.15	.07	.01
☐	142	Thad Jaracz	.20	.10	.02
☐	143	Larry Conley	.20	.10	.02
☐	144	Rex Chapman	.35	.17	.03
☐	145	Pat Riley	.45	.22	.04
☐	146	Melvin Turpin	.20	.10	.02
☐	147	Kenny Walker	.20	.10	.02
☐	148	Wallace Jones	.10	.05	.01
☐	149	Alex Groza	.25	.12	.02
☐	150	Mike Pratt	.15	.07	.01
☐	151	Cliff Barker	.10	.05	.01
☐	152	Jim Andrews	.10	.05	.01
☐	153	Kenny Walker	.20	.10	.02
☐	154	Kevin Grevey	.20	.10	.02
☐	155	Kyle Macy	.30	.15	.03
☐	156	Jim Line	.10	.05	.01
☐	157	Pat Riley	.45	.22	.04
☐	158	Larry Steele	.20	.10	.02
☐	159	Jack Givens	.20	.10	.02
☐	160	Ed Davender	.15	.07	.01
☐	161	Ralph Beard	.20	.10	.02
☐	162	Vernon Hatton	.10	.05	.01
☐	163	Frank Ramsey	.30	.15	.03
☐	164	Bob Burrow	.10	.05	.01
☐	165	Sam Bowie	.35	.17	.03
☐	166	Dan Issel	.50	.25	.05
☐	167	Rick Robey	.25	.12	.02
☐	168	Winston Bennett	.20	.10	.02
☐	169	Louie Dampier	.20	.10	.02
☐	170	Gayle Rose	.20	.10	.02
☐	171	Cliff Hagan	.40	.20	.04
☐	172	Cotton Nash	.20	.10	.02
☐	173	Mike Pratt	.15	.07	.01
☐	174	Richard Madison	.15	.07	.01
☐	175	Kyle Macy	.25	.12	.02
☐	176	Rob Lock	.15	.07	.01
☐	177	Larry Johnson	.10	.05	.01
☐	178	Cedric Jenkins	.15	.07	.01
☐	179	Dan Issel	.45	.22	.04
☐	180	Charles Hurt	.20	.10	.02
☐	181	Cliff Hagan	.40	.20	.04
☐	182	Wallace Jones	.10	.05	.01
☐	183	Roger Harden	.15	.07	.01
☐	184	Bob Guyette	.10	.05	.01
☐	185	Kevin Grevey	.20	.10	.02
☐	186	Jack Givens	.20	.10	.02
☐	187	Ed Davender	.15	.07	.01
☐	188	Jimmy Dan Connor	.15	.07	.01
☐	189	Fred Cowan	.15	.07	.01
☐	190	Larry Conley	.20	.10	.02
☐	191	Leroy Byrd	.10	.05	.01
☐	192	Sam Bowie	.35	.17	.03
☐	193	James Blackmon	.25	.12	.02
☐	194	Winston Bennett	.20	.10	.02
☐	195	Dicky Beal	.15	.07	.01
☐	196	Jim Andrews	.10	.05	.01
☐	197	Kenny Walker	.20	.10	.02
☐	198	Pat Riley	.45	.22	.04
☐	199	Frank Ramsey	.30	.15	.03
☐	200	Truman Claytor	.15	.07	.01
☐	201	Dwane Casey	.25	.12	.02
☐	202	Rex Chapman	.35	.17	.03
☐	203	Jim Master	.15	.07	.01
☐	204	Mike Phillips	.15	.07	.01
☐	205	Dirk Minniefield	.20	.10	.02
☐	206	Jimmy Dan Connor	.15	.07	.01
☐	207	Bill Lickert	.10	.05	.01
☐	208	Leroy Byrd	.10	.05	.01
☐	209	Mike Pratt	.15	.07	.01
☐	210	Rob Lock	.15	.07	.01
☐	211	Dickie Parsons	.10	.05	.01
☐	212	Frank Ramsey	.30	.15	.03
☐	213	Adolph Rupp CO	.40	.20	.04
☐	214	G.J. Smith	.10	.05	.01
☐	215	Rick Robey	.20	.10	.02
☐	216	James Blackmon	.25	.12	.02
☐	217	Mike Casey	.15	.07	.01
☐	218	LaVon Williams	.15	.07	.01
☐	219	Larry Pursiful	.10	.05	.01
☐	220	Terry Mobley	.10	.05	.01
☐	221	Kyle Macy	.30	.15	.03
☐	222	Larry Conley	.20	.10	.02
☐	223	Dirk Minniefield	.20	.10	.02
☐	224	Jim Master	.15	.07	.01
☐	225	Jerry Bird	.10	.05	.01
☐	226	Dan Issel	.45	.22	.04
☐	227	Larry Johnson	.10	.05	.01
☐	228	Bret Bearup	.15	.07	.01
☐	229	Ronnie Lyons	.10	.05	.01
☐	230	James Lee	.20	.10	.02
☐	231	Don Mills	.10	.05	.01
☐	232	Truman Claytor	.15	.07	.01
☐	233	Rex Chapman	.35	.17	.03
☐	234	Fred Cowan	.15	.07	.01
☐	235	Truman Claytor	.15	.07	.01
☐	236	Dicky Beal	.15	.07	.01
☐	237	Larry Johnson	.10	.05	.01
☐	238	John R. Adams	.10	.05	.01
☐	239	Sam Bowie	.30	.15	.03
☐	240	Thad Jaracz	.15	.07	.01
☐	241	Phil Argento	.10	.05	.01
☐	242	Cedric Jenkins	.15	.07	.01
☐	243	Charles Hurt	.20	.10	.02
☐	244	Charles Hurt	.20	.10	.02
☐	245	Cliff Hagan	.35	.17	.03
☐	246	Kent Hollenbeck	.10	.05	.01
☐	247	Wallace Jones	.10	.05	.01
☐	248	Roger Harden	.15	.07	.01
☐	249	Bob Guyette	.10	.05	.01
☐	250	Richard Madison	.15	.07	.01
☐	251	Kevin Grevey	.20	.10	.02
☐	252	Jack Givens	.20	.10	.02
☐	253	Tommy Kron	.20	.10	.02
☐	254	Derrick Hord	.20	.10	.02
☐	255	Tom Heitz	.15	.07	.01
☐	256	Cliff Hagan	.30	.15	.03
☐	257	Louie Dampier	.20	.10	.02
☐	258	Jimmy Dan Connor	.15	.07	.01
☐	259	Dwane Casey	.25	.12	.02
☐	260	Cliff Hagan	.30	.15	.03
☐	261	Walt Hirsch	.10	.05	.01
☐	262	Merion Haskins	.10	.05	.01
☐	263	Roger Harden	.15	.07	.01
☐	264	Bob Guyette	.10	.05	.01
☐	265	Phil Grawemeyer	.10	.05	.01
☐	266	Jay Shidler	.15	.07	.01
☐	267	Jim Dinwiddie	.10	.05	.01
☐	268	Fred Cowan	.15	.07	.01
☐	269	Leroy Byrd	.15	.07	.01

1988-89 Kentucky Big Blue Awards

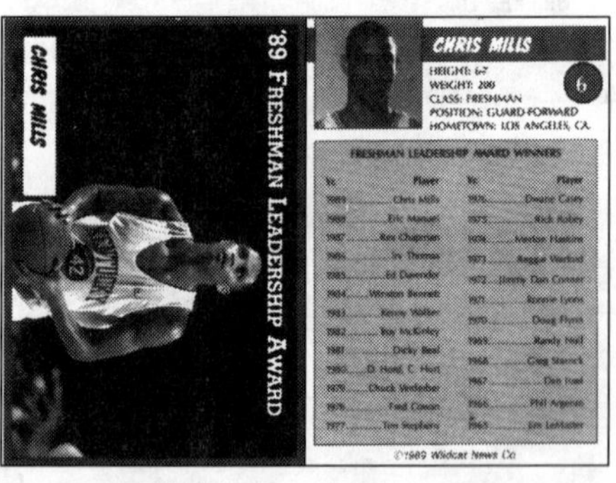

This 18-card set was issued as an insert in the Summer 1989 Volume 3, Number 2 issue of Oscar Combs' Big Blue Basketball magazine. The cards honor Kentucky players for various outstanding achievements. The cards were issued in two panels; after perforation, the cards measure approximately 2 1/2" by 3 1/2". In a horizontal format, the front features a color action player photo, with blue and black borders on white card stock. The name of the award appears in white lettering in the upper left corner of the photo, with the player's name in a white box in the lower left corner. The back has a black and white head shot of the player in the upper left corner. Biographical information appears in a light blue-tinted box. The cards are numbered on the back, and we have listed the award below after the player's name.

	MINT	EXC	G-VG
COMPLETE SET (18)	20.00	10.00	2.00
COMMON PLAYER (1-18)	.50	.25	.05

☐ 1 Sean Sutton Leadership	1.50	.75	.15
☐ 2 Chris Mills Most Valuable Player	6.00	3.00	.60
☐ 3 Mike Scott Outstanding Senior	.50	.25	.05
☐ 4 Richie Farmer Best Free Throw Percentage	2.00	1.00	.20
☐ 5 Derrick Miller Fewest Turnovers	.75	.35	.07
☐ 6 Chris Mills Freshman Leadership	5.00	2.50	.50
☐ 7 Mike Scott Scholastic	.50	.25	.05
☐ 8 Sean Sutton Most Assists	1.00	.50	.10
☐ 9 Chris Mills Most Rebounds	3.50	1.75	.35
☐ 10 LeRon Ellis Leading Scorer	3.00	1.50	.30
☐ 11 Reggie Hanson Best Defender	1.50	.75	.15
☐ 12 Deron Feldhaus 110 Percent Award	1.00	.50	.10
☐ 13 Sean Sutton and Leron Ellis Sacrifice Award	1.50	.75	.15
☐ 14 LeRon Ellis Best Field Goal Percentage	3.00	1.50	.30
☐ 15 Sean Sutton Best Three-pt. Field Goal Percentage	1.00	.50	.10
☐ 16 Reggie Hanson Most Steals	1.50	.75	.15
☐ 17 Eddie Sutton CO	.75	.35	.07
☐ 18 Checklist Card UER (Misspelled sacrifice as sacrafice)	.50	.25	.05
☐ 19 Checklist Card	.50	.25	.05
☐ 20 Richie Farmer Best FT Shooter	2.00	1.00	.20
☐ 21 Reggie Hanson Most Rebounds	1.50	.75	.15
☐ 22 Deron Feldhaus Fewest Turnovers	1.00	.50	.10
☐ 23 UK Assistants Best Defense Billy Donovan Herb Sendek Tubby Smith Ralph Willard	.50	.25	.05
☐ 24 Deron Feldhaus Mr. Hustle Award	1.00	.50	.10
☐ 25 Reggie Hanson Leadership	1.50	.75	.15
☐ 26 John Pelphrey Student Athlete	1.00	.50	.10
☐ 27 Derrick Miller Outstanding Senior	.50	.25	.05
☐ 28 Deron Feldhaus Most Improved	1.00	.50	.10
☐ 29 Happy Chandler Fan of the Year	1.50	.75	.15
☐ 30 John Pelphrey Best Playmaker	1.00	.50	.10
☐ 31 Hanson/Pelphrey Mr. Deflection	1.00	.50	.10
☐ 32 Reggie Hanson Most Valuable	1.50	.75	.15
☐ 33 Deron Feldhaus Best FG Shooter	1.00	.50	.10
☐ 34 Sean Woods Most Assists	1.00	.50	.10
☐ 35 Derrick Miller Leading Scorer	1.00	.50	.10
☐ 36 Rick Pitino Coach of the Year	2.50	1.25	.25

1989-90 Kentucky Big Blue Awards

This perforated 18-card set was issued as an insert in the Winter 1990 Volume 3,, Number 4 issue of Oscar Combs' Big Blue Basketball magazine. The cards honor Kentucky players for various outstanding achievements. The cards were issued in two panels; after perforation, the cards measure approximately 2 1/2" by 3 1/2". The front features a color action player photo, with dark blue and black borders on white card stock. The name of the award is written vertically in an orange bar to the left of the picture, while the player's name appears in a gray bar above the picture. The back has a black and white head shot of the player in the upper left corner. Biographical information appears in a blue-tinted box. The cards are numbered on the back, beginning with 19 in continuation of the numbering of the previous year's issue. The award is listed below after the player's name.

	MINT	EXC	G-VG
COMPLETE SET (18)	16.00	8.00	1.60
COMMON PLAYER (19-36)	.50	.25	.05

1989-90 Kentucky Big Blue Team of the 80's

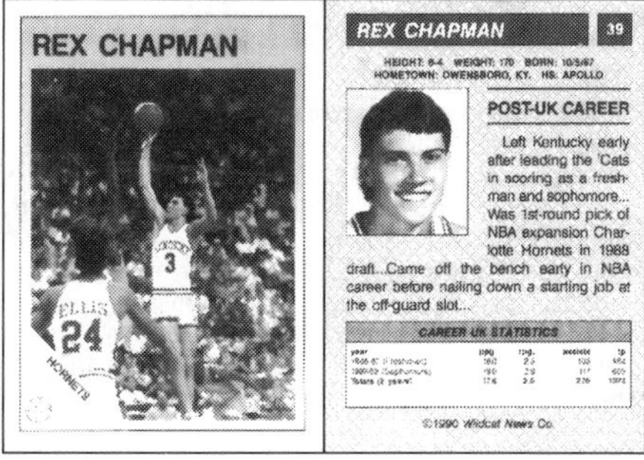

This perforated 18-card set was issued as an insert in the Spring 1990 Volume 4, Number 1 issue of Oscar Combs' Big Blue Basketball magazine. The cards honor outstanding Kentucky players for the decade of the 1980's. The cards were issued in two panels; after perforation, the cards measure approximately 2 1/2" by 3 1/2". The front features a color action player photo, on a light blue background that washes out as one moves from top to bottom. A thin black border outlines this blue background. The player's name appears in black lettering above the picture. The left lower corner of the photo is cut out, and in the triangular-shaped area appears a basketball icon and the pro team(s) played for. The back is blue tinted, and it has a black and white head shot of the player on the left side, with biographical information around the picture and career college statistics on the bottom. The cards are numbered on the back, beginning with 37 in continuation of the numbering of the previous year's issue.

	MINT	EXC	G-VG
COMPLETE SET (18)	18.00	9.00	1.80
COMMON PLAYER (37-54)	.50	.25	.05
☐ 37 Checklist Card	.75	.35	.07
☐ 38 Kyle Macy	1.50	.75	.15
☐ 39 Rex Chapman	2.50	1.25	.25
☐ 40 Kenny Walker	1.50	.75	.15
☐ 41 Winston Bennett	1.25	.60	.12
☐ 42 Melvin Turpin	1.25	.60	.12
☐ 43 Sam Bowie	2.50	1.25	.25
☐ 44 Dicky Beal	.75	.35	.07
☐ 45 Dirk Minniefield	1.25	.60	.12
☐ 46 Jim Master	.75	.35	.07
☐ 47 Rob Lock	.50	.25	.05
☐ 48 Chris Mills	3.50	1.75	.35
☐ 49 Roger Harden	.50	.25	.05
☐ 50 Jay Shidler	.75	.35	.07
☐ 51 LeRon Ellis	1.50	.75	.15
☐ 52 Fred Cowan	.75	.35	.07
☐ 53 Derrick Hord	1.00	.50	.10
☐ 54 Coaches Joe Hall Eddie Sutton Rick Pitino	1.25	.60	.12

1989-90 Kentucky 300 *

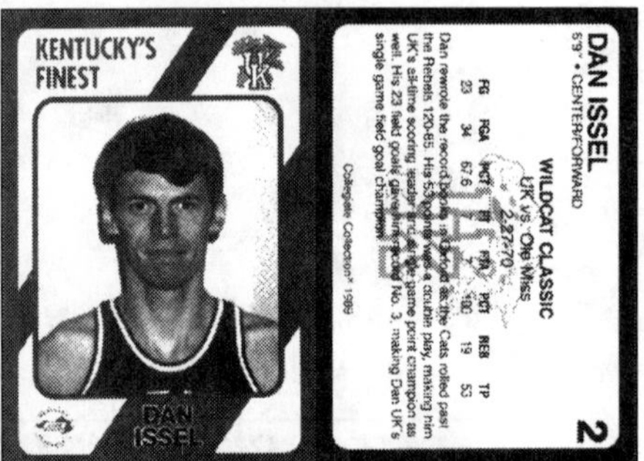

The 1989 University of Kentucky Basketball/Football set contains 300 cards, each measuring standard size (2 1/2" by 3 1/2"). The fronts feature a mix of black and white photos for earlier players and color for later ones, with rounded corners and blue borders. The pictures are superimposed over a blue and white diagonally striped card face, with a blue border. The top reads "Kentucky's Finest," and the school logo appears in the upper right corner. The horizontally oriented backs are printed in blue on white and present biographical information, career summaries, or statistics. The cards are numbered on the back.

	MINT	EXC	G-VG
COMPLETE SET (300)	25.00	12.50	2.50
COMMON PLAYER (1-300)	.07	.03	.01
☐ 1 C.M. Newton	.10	.05	.01
☐ 2 Dan Issel	.35	.17	.03
☐ 3 Alex Groza	.15	.07	.01
☐ 4 Jack Givens	.15	.07	.01
☐ 5 Kenny Walker	.15	.07	.01
☐ 6 Cliff Hagan	.25	.12	.02
☐ 7 Ralph Beard	.15	.07	.01
☐ 8 Dirk Minniefield	.15	.07	.01
☐ 9 Louie Dampier	.15	.07	.01
☐ 10 Dicky Beal	.10	.05	.01
☐ 11 Larry Pursiful	.07	.03	.01
☐ 12 Rex Chapman	.25	.12	.02
☐ 13 Rick Pitino CO	.25	.12	.02
☐ 14 Marvin Akers	.07	.03	.01
☐ 15 Allen Feldhaus	.10	.05	.01
☐ 16 Carroll Burchett	.07	.03	.01
☐ 17 Sam Potter	.07	.03	.01
☐ 18 Ted Deeken	.07	.03	.01
☐ 19 Dwight Anderson	.15	.07	.01
☐ 20 Charles Schrader	.07	.03	.01
☐ 21 Bill Trott	.07	.03	.01
☐ 22 Henry Besuden	.07	.03	.01
☐ 23 Edwin Knadler	.07	.03	.01
☐ 24 Vince Del Negro	.10	.05	.01
☐ 25 James Durham	.07	.03	.01
☐ 26 Mickey Gibson	.07	.03	.01
☐ 27 John Mauer	.07	.03	.01
☐ 28 John McIntosh	.07	.03	.01
☐ 29 Van Buren Ropke	.07	.03	.01
☐ 30 B.G. Marsh	.07	.03	.01
☐ 31 Tom Zerfoss	.07	.03	.01
☐ 32 George Zerfoss	.07	.03	.01
☐ 33 Harry Denham	.07	.03	.01
☐ 34 Mike Scott	.07	.03	.01
☐ 35 Adolph Rupp CO	.30	.15	.03
☐ 36 Jack Parkinson	.07	.03	.01
☐ 37 1953-54 Team	.07	.03	.01
☐ 38 Pat Riley	.30	.15	.03
☐ 39 Joe B. Hall	.10	.05	.01
☐ 40 Memorial Coliseum	.07	.03	.01
☐ 41 Sam Bowie	.30	.15	.03
☐ 42 Bob Burrow	.07	.03	.01
☐ 43 Melvin Turpin	.15	.07	.01
☐ 44 Frank Ramsey	.20	.10	.02
☐ 45 Pat Riley	.30	.15	.03
☐ 46 Mascot	.07	.03	.01
☐ 47 Charles Hurt	.15	.07	.01
☐ 48 Cliff Barker	.07	.03	.01
☐ 49 Kevin Grevey	.15	.07	.01
☐ 50 Bill Spivey	.07	.03	.01
☐ 51 George C. Buchheit	.07	.03	.01
☐ 52 Ray Mills	.07	.03	.01
☐ 53 Irving Thomas	.10	.05	.01
☐ 54 Chuck Aleksinas	.10	.05	.01
☐ 55 Paul Andrews	.07	.03	.01
☐ 56 Brad Bounds	.07	.03	.01
☐ 57 Clyde Parker	.10	.05	.01
☐ 58 Bill Busey	.07	.03	.01
☐ 59 Billy Ray Cassady	.07	.03	.01
☐ 60 George Critz	.07	.03	.01
☐ 61 Paul Noel	.07	.03	.01
☐ 62 Pat Doyle	.07	.03	.01
☐ 63 Rick Drewitz	.07	.03	.01
☐ 64 Fred Curtis	.07	.03	.01
☐ 65 Darrell Darby	.07	.03	.01
☐ 66 Humzey Yessin	.07	.03	.01
☐ 67 Chris Gettelfinger	.07	.03	.01
☐ 68 Sam Harper	.07	.03	.01
☐ 69 Bill Davis	.07	.03	.01
☐ 70 Lincoln Collinsworth	.07	.03	.01
☐ 71 Keith Farnsley	.07	.03	.01
☐ 72 Foster Helm	.07	.03	.01
☐ 73 Dick Howe	.07	.03	.01
☐ 74 Phil Johnson	.07	.03	.01
☐ 75 Roger Layne	.07	.03	.01
☐ 76 Art Laib	.07	.03	.01
☐ 77 Dave Lawrence	.07	.03	.01
☐ 78 Larry Lentz	.07	.03	.01
☐ 79 Steve Lochmueller	.07	.03	.01
☐ 80 Louis McGinnis	.07	.03	.01
☐ 81 Doug Pendygraft	.07	.03	.01
☐ 82 Tommy Porter	.07	.03	.01
☐ 83 Linville Puckett	.15	.07	.01
☐ 84 Don Rolfes	.07	.03	.01
☐ 85 Mark Soderberg	.07	.03	.01
☐ 86 Tim Stephens	.07	.03	.01
☐ 87 Gene Stewart	.07	.03	.01
☐ 88 George Yates	.07	.03	.01
☐ 89 Randy Noll	.07	.03	.01
☐ 90 Earl Adkins	.07	.03	.01
☐ 91 Truitt Demoisey	.07	.03	.01
☐ 92 Todd Ziegler	.07	.03	.01
☐ 93 Clint Wheeler	.07	.03	.01
☐ 94 Patrick Campbell	.07	.03	.01
☐ 95 Charles Alberts	.07	.03	.01
☐ 96 Brinkley Barnett	.07	.03	.01
☐ 97 Cecil Bell	.07	.03	.01
☐ 98 Mel Brewer	.07	.03	.01
☐ 99 Jake Bronston	.07	.03	.01
☐ 100 Albert Cummins	.07	.03	.01
☐ 101 Jerry D. Claiborne	.15	.07	.01
☐ 102 Bill Leskovar	.07	.03	.01
☐ 103 Sam Ball	.07	.03	.01
☐ 104 Sonny Collins	.25	.12	.02
☐ 105 Bob Hardy	.07	.03	.01
☐ 106 Mike Siganos	.07	.03	.01
☐ 107 Al Bruno	.07	.03	.01
☐ 108 Rick Norton	.07	.03	.01
☐ 109 Ray Correll	.07	.03	.01
☐ 110 Irvin Goode	.07	.03	.01
☐ 111 Bob Gain	.15	.07	.01
☐ 112 Paul Bryant	.35	.17	.03
☐ 113 Rick Kestner	.07	.03	.01
☐ 114 Larry Seiple	.10	.05	.01
☐ 115 George Blanda	.35	.17	.03
☐ 116 Calvin Bird	.07	.03	.01

☐	117 Don Phelps	.07	.03	.01
☐	118 Herschel Turner	.07	.03	.01
☐	119 Harry Jones	.07	.03	.01
☐	120 Larry Jones	.07	.03	.01
☐	121 Doug Moseley	.07	.03	.01
☐	122 Rodger Bird	.07	.03	.01
☐	123 Howard Schnellenberger	.30	.15	.03
☐	124 Vito(Babe) Parilli	.25	.12	.02
☐	125 Jim Kovach	.15	.07	.01
☐	126 Randy Jenkins	.07	.03	.01
☐	127 Emery Clark	.07	.03	.01
☐	128 David Hardt	.07	.03	.01
☐	129 Andy Molls	.07	.03	.01
☐	130 Tom Dornbrook	.07	.03	.01
☐	131 George Adams	.15	.07	.01
☐	132 Lou Michaels	.10	.05	.01
☐	133 Paul Calhoun	.07	.03	.01
☐	134 Joey Worley	.07	.03	.01
☐	135 Doug Kotar	.15	.07	.01
☐	136 Dicky Lyons	.10	.05	.01
☐	137 Art Still	.20	.10	.02
☐	138 Warren Bryant	.10	.05	.01
☐	139 Joe Federspiel	.10	.05	.01
☐	140 Mark Higgs	.30	.15	.03
☐	141 Steve Meilinger	.10	.05	.01
☐	142 Wilbur Hackett	.07	.03	.01
☐	143 Marc Logan	.10	.05	.01
☐	144 Rick Nuzum	.07	.03	.01
☐	145 Wilbur Jamerson	.07	.03	.01
☐	146 Felix Wilson	.07	.03	.01
☐	147 Rod Stewart	.07	.03	.01
☐	148 Tom Hutchinson	.07	.03	.01
☐	149 Greg Long	.07	.03	.01
☐	150 Mike Fanuzzi	.07	.03	.01
☐	151 Richard S. Webb Jr.	.07	.03	.01
☐	152 John S. Kelly	.07	.03	.01
☐	153 Eger V. Murphree	.07	.03	.01
☐	154 Ermal Allen	.15	.07	.01
☐	155 John G. Heber	.07	.03	.01
☐	156 Howard Kinne	.07	.03	.01
☐	157 Albert D. Kirwan	.07	.03	.01
☐	158 Price McLean	.07	.03	.01
☐	159 Curtis M. Sanders	.07	.03	.01
☐	160 Bob Davis	.07	.03	.01
☐	161 Bert Johnson	.07	.03	.01
☐	162 Ralph Kercheval	.10	.05	.01
☐	163 Charles Hughes	.07	.03	.01
☐	164 Clyde Johnson	.07	.03	.01
☐	165 Blanton Collier	.15	.07	.01
☐	166 Charlie Bradshaw	.10	.05	.01
☐	167 John Ray	.07	.03	.01
☐	168 Fran Curci	.15	.07	.01
☐	169 James Park	.07	.03	.01
☐	170 Ivy Joe Hunter	.10	.05	.01
☐	171 Chris Chenault	.07	.03	.01
☐	172 Jeff Van Note	.20	.10	.02
☐	173 Dick Barbee	.07	.03	.01
☐	174 Darryl Bishop	.07	.03	.01
☐	175 Jay Rhodemyre	.10	.05	.01
☐	176 William Rodes	.07	.03	.01
☐	177 Noah Mullins	.07	.03	.01
☐	178 Gene Myers	.07	.03	.01
☐	179 Darrell Cox	.07	.03	.01
☐	180 Jerry Eisaman	.07	.03	.01
☐	181 Ben Zaranka	.07	.03	.01
☐	182 Wash Serini	.07	.03	.01
☐	183 Dallas Owens	.07	.03	.01
☐	184 Bernie Scruggs	.07	.03	.01
☐	185 Wallace Jones	.07	.03	.01
☐	186 Walt Yowarsky	.10	.05	.01
☐	187 Clarkie Mayfield	.07	.03	.01
☐	188 John Grimsley	.15	.07	.01
☐	189 Jerry Woolum	.07	.03	.01
☐	190 John Tatterson	.07	.03	.01
☐	191 Delmar Hughes	.07	.03	.01
☐	192 Lowell Hughes	.07	.03	.01
☐	193 Frank Lemaster	.07	.03	.01
☐	194 Bill Ransdell	.07	.03	.01
☐	195 Tony Mayes	.07	.03	.01
☐	196 Dominic Fucci	.07	.03	.01
☐	197 David Roller	.07	.03	.01
☐	198 Bernie A. Shively	.07	.03	.01
☐	199 William Tuttle	.10	.05	.01
☐	200 Jerry Claiborne	.15	.07	.01
☐	201 Warfield Donohue	.07	.03	.01
☐	202 Russell Ellington	.07	.03	.01
☐	203 Kenny England	.07	.03	.01
☐	204 J.C. Everett	.07	.03	.01
☐	205 Jake Gaiser	.07	.03	.01
☐	206 Elmer Gilb	.07	.03	.01
☐	207 Jim Goforth	.07	.03	.01
☐	208 James Goodman	.07	.03	.01
☐	209 George Gumbert	.07	.03	.01
☐	210 Joseph Hagan	.07	.03	.01
☐	211 W.C. Harrison	.07	.03	.01
☐	212 D.W. Hart	.07	.03	.01
☐	213 Elmo Head	.07	.03	.01
☐	214 Walter Hodge	.07	.03	.01
☐	215 Charles T. Hughes	.07	.03	.01
☐	216 Lowell Hughes	.07	.03	.01
☐	217 R.Y. Ireland	.07	.03	.01
☐	218 Irvine Jeffries	.07	.03	.01
☐	219 Jim King	.07	.03	.01
☐	220 Bill Kleiser	.07	.03	.01
☐	221 Gary Gamble	.07	.03	.01
☐	222 Lawrence McGinnis	.07	.03	.01
☐	223 Ralph Morgan	.07	.03	.01
☐	224 Hays Owens	.07	.03	.01
☐	225 James Park	.07	.03	.01
☐	226 Buddy Parker	.07	.03	.01
☐	227 Sam Ridgeway	.07	.03	.01
☐	228 R.C. Preston	.07	.03	.01
☐	229 Roy Roberts	.07	.03	.01
☐	230 Wilber Schu	.07	.03	.01
☐	231 Evan Settle	.07	.03	.01
☐	232 Bobby Slusher	.07	.03	.01
☐	233 Bill Smith	.07	.03	.01
☐	234 Vince Splane	.07	.03	.01
☐	235 Carl Staker	.07	.03	.01
☐	236 John Stough	.07	.03	.01
☐	237 Milt Ticco	.07	.03	.01
☐	238 Homer Thompson	.07	.03	.01
☐	239 Clarence Tillman	.07	.03	.01
☐	240 Garland Townes	.07	.03	.01
☐	241 Charles Worthington	.07	.03	.01
☐	242 Rudy Yessin	.07	.03	.01
☐	243 Kark Zerfoss	.07	.03	.01
☐	244 Bob Lavin	.07	.03	.01
☐	245 J.A. Dishman	.07	.03	.01
☐	246 Jim Server	.07	.03	.01
☐	247 Fred Fest	.07	.03	.01
☐	248 Ralph Boren	.07	.03	.01
☐	249 James McFarland	.07	.03	.01
☐	250 A.T. Rice	.07	.03	.01
☐	251 Walter White	.07	.03	.01
☐	252 Tom Moseley	.07	.03	.01
☐	253 Paul Jenkins	.07	.03	.01
☐	254 Lovell Underwood	.07	.03	.01
☐	255 William Tuttle	.10	.05	.01
☐	256 Bob Tallent	.07	.03	.01
☐	257 Jack Tucker	.07	.03	.01
☐	258 Roger Newman	.07	.03	.01
☐	259 Stanley Milward	.07	.03	.01
☐	260 Bill Sturgill	.07	.03	.01
☐	261 Gayle Mohney	.07	.03	.01
☐	262 Will Milward	.07	.03	.01
☐	263 Ercel Little	.07	.03	.01
☐	264 Garland Lewis	.07	.03	.01
☐	265 Ron Kennett	.07	.03	.01
☐	266 Howard Kreuter	.07	.03	.01
☐	267 William King	.07	.03	.01
☐	268 Walter Johnson	.10	.05	.01
☐	269 Jim Jordan	.07	.03	.01
☐	270 Mulford Davis	.07	.03	.01
☐	271 Berkley Davis	.07	.03	.01
☐	272 Cecil Combs	.07	.03	.01
☐	273 Carl Combs	.07	.03	.01
☐	274 Milerd Anderson	.07	.03	.01
☐	275 George Vulich	.07	.03	.01
☐	276 Paul Adkins	.07	.03	.01
☐	277 Hugh Coy	.07	.03	.01
☐	278 J. Rice Walker	.07	.03	.01
☐	279 Adrian Back	.07	.03	.01
☐	280 Charley Combs	.07	.03	.01
☐	281 Harry Hurd	.07	.03	.01
☐	282 Tom Harper	.07	.03	.01
☐	283 Dan Hall	.07	.03	.01
☐	284 Ed Lander	.07	.03	.01
☐	285 Bill Barlow	.07	.03	.01
☐	286 James Sharp	.07	.03	.01
☐	287 Al Robinson	.07	.03	.01
☐	288 Frank Phipps	.07	.03	.01
☐	289 Bob Fowler	.07	.03	.01
☐	290 George Skinner	.07	.03	.01
☐	291 Harry Bliss	.07	.03	.01
☐	292 Bill Bibb	.07	.03	.01
☐	293 Herschel Scott	.07	.03	.01
☐	294 Clair Dees	.07	.03	.01
☐	295 Lawrence Burnham	.07	.03	.01
☐	296 Lloyd Ramsey	.07	.03	.01
☐	297 Bruce Davis	.07	.03	.01
☐	298 Bob Taylor	.07	.03	.01
☐	299 Alonzo Nelson	.07	.03	.01
☐	300 Herbert Jerome	.07	.03	.01

1990 Kentucky Class A

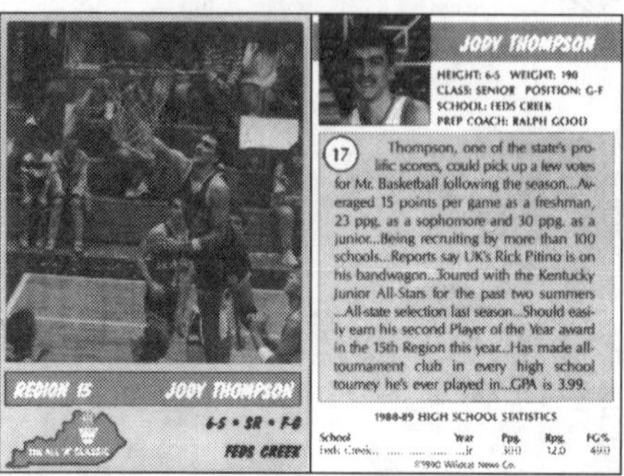

This 18-card set was issued as an insert in the Kentucky All "A" Classic official program (produced by Wildcat News) for the state tournament played at Memorial Coliseum in Lexington, KY, February 7-10, 1990. The set consists of a checklist card, a special card honoring current Lexington mayor Scotty Baesler as a "Class A Great" player of the past, and 16 cards honoring the coaches' preseason choices for best players in each of the sixteen regions. The cards were issued in two panels; after perforation, the cards measure approximately 2 1/2" by 3 1/2". The front features a mix of posed or action, black and white player photos, with a peach color background and thin blue border on white card stock. Below the picture, the region number and player's name appears in a gray stripe, with player information further below in the right corner. A Kentucky shaped emblem in the lower left corner rounds out the card face. The back has a black and white head shot of the player in the upper left corner. Biographical information appears in a peach-tinted box, with high school statistics on the bottom. The cards are numbered on the back.

	MINT	EXC	G-VG
COMPLETE SET (18)	10.00	5.00	1.00
COMMON PLAYER (1-18)	.60	.30	.06
☐ 1 Checklist Card	.60	.30	.06
☐ 2 Scott Baesler	1.00	.50	.10
☐ 3 Eugene Alexander	.60	.30	.06
☐ 4 Sergio Luyk	.60	.30	.06
☐ 5 Chris Knight	.60	.30	.06
☐ 6 Chris Huffman	1.00	.50	.10
☐ 7 Shannon Phillips	.60	.30	.06
☐ 8 Glen Wathen	.60	.30	.06
☐ 9 Jason Hagan	.60	.30	.06
☐ 10 Bryan Milburn	.60	.30	.06
☐ 11 Andre McClendon	.60	.30	.06
☐ 12 Chris Harrison	.60	.30	.06
☐ 13 Daniel Swintosky	.60	.30	.06
☐ 14 Jamie Cromer	.60	.30	.06
☐ 15 Mo Hollingsworth	.60	.30	.06
☐ 16 Jeff Moore	.60	.30	.06
☐ 17 Jody Thompson	.60	.30	.06
☐ 18 Mike Helton	.60	.30	.06

1990 Kentucky Soviets

This 18-card set was issued in two panels inside the AAU/Soviet Tour program (produced by Wildcat News) for the game played in Memorial Coliseum at Lexington, Kentucky, on May 15, 1990. After perforation, the cards measure approximately 2 1/2" by 3 1/2" and showcase the Kentucky AAU All-Stars. The fronts feature a mix of action or posed, black and white player photos, with red borders on a white and blue diagonally-striped background. The words "Ky. AAU All-Stars" appear in blue lettering in white stripe above the picture; the player's name is presented in the same format below the picture. The backs have black and white head shots of the player in the upper left corners. In a lavender colored box, they present career summaries, with high school statistics appearing at the bottom of the card. The cards are numbered on the back in the upper right corners.

	MINT	EXC	G-VG
COMPLETE SET (18)	15.00	7.50	1.50
COMMON PLAYER (1-18)	.60	.30	.06
☐ 1 Checklist Card	.75	.35	.07
☐ 2 Kentucky/USSR rosters	.60	.30	.06
☐ 3 Jim Lankster	.60	.30	.06
☐ 4 Paul Bingham	.60	.30	.06
☐ 5 James Crutcher	.60	.30	.06
☐ 6 Jason Eitutis	.60	.30	.06
☐ 7 Greg Glass	.60	.30	.06
☐ 8 Arlando Johnson	.60	.30	.06
☐ 9 Gimel Martinez	.60	.30	.06
☐ 10 Jamal Mashburn	6.00	3.00	.60
☐ 11 Jeff Moore	.60	.30	.06
☐ 12 Dwayne Morton	2.00	1.00	.20
☐ 13 Keith Peel	.60	.30	.06
☐ 14 Andy Penick	.60	.30	.06
☐ 15 Daniel Swintosky	.60	.30	.06
☐ 16 Jody Thompson	.60	.30	.06
☐ 17 Carlos Toomer	.60	.30	.06
☐ 18 Kelly Wells	.60	.30	.06

1990-91 Kentucky Big Blue Dream Team/Award Winners

This perforated 18-card set was issued as an insert in the Spring 1991 Volume 5, Number 1 issue of Oscar Combs' Big Blue Basketball magazine. The cards were issued in two panels of nine cards each. After perforation, the cards measure approximately 2 9/16" by 3 5/8". The cards are numbered 19-36, in continuation of an 18-card insert set of 1990-91 Kentucky players in an earlier issue of Big Blue Basketball. The fronts feature a color action photo enclosed by a white border. A blue box in the upper left corner indicates whether the player belongs to the Dream Team (19-26), which consists the most impressive opponents faced during the season as voted by the captains on the Kentucky squad, or is an Award Winner (28-36). The player's name appears in a color stripe at the bottom of the picture. Within a light blue border, the backs show a black and white head shot and a career summmary presented in the format of a newspaper article. The cards are numbered on the back. Supposedly only 7,500 sets were produced.

	MINT	EXC	G-VG
COMPLETE SET (18)	45.00	22.50	4.50
COMMON PLAYER (19-36)	.50	.25	.05
☐ 19 Shaquille O'Neal LSU	25.00	12.50	2.50
☐ 20 Allan Houston Tennessee	5.00	2.50	.50
☐ 21 Calbert Cheaney Indiana	8.00	4.00	.80
☐ 22 Rick Fox North Carolina	3.50	1.75	.35
☐ 23 Litterial Green Georgia	2.00	1.00	.20
☐ 24 Bobby Knight CO Indiana	2.00	1.00	.20
☐ 25 Dean Smith CO North Carolina	2.00	1.00	.20
☐ 26 Freedom Hall	.50	.25	.05
☐ 27 Checklist	.50	.25	.05
☐ 28 Richie Farmer	1.00	.50	.10
☐ 29 Jamal Mashburn	5.00	2.50	.50
☐ 30 Jeff Brassow	.50	.25	.05
☐ 31 Todd Bearup	.50	.25	.05
☐ 32 Sean Woods	.75	.35	.07
☐ 33 Deron Feldhaus	.75	.35	.07
☐ 34 John Pelphrey	.75	.35	.07
☐ 35 Reggie Hanson	.75	.35	.07
☐ 36 Rick Pitino CO	.75	.35	.07

1991-92 Kentucky Big Blue Double

This 20-card set was issued as inserts in the Summer 1991 Volume 5, Number 2, and Fall 1991 Volume 5, Number 3 issues of Oscar Combs' Big Blue Basketball magazine. Each issue had two insert sheets: an 8 1/2" by 11" photo and a sheet of player cards. After perforation, the player cards measure 2 9/16" by 3 5/8." The horizontally oriented fronts feature a color head shot to the left of the Wildcats' logo. A blue stripe traverses the top of the card face, while the player's name appears in a short red stripe at the lower right corner. The backs are vertically oriented and display black and white action photos. The cards are numbered on the back.

	MINT	EXC	G-VG
COMPLETE SET (20)	12.00	6.00	1.20
COMMON PLAYER (1-18)	.50	.25	.05
☐ 1 John Pelphrey	.75	.35	.07
☐ 2 Deron Feldhaus	.75	.35	.07
☐ 3 Richie Farmer	.75	.35	.07
☐ 4 Jeff Brassow	.50	.25	.05
☐ 5 Junior Braddy	.50	.25	.05
☐ 6 Sean Woods	.75	.35	.07
☐ 7 Gimel Martinez	.50	.25	.05
☐ 8 Travis Ford	.50	.25	.05
☐ 9 Dale Brown	.75	.35	.07
☐ 10 Chris Harrison	.50	.25	.05
☐ 11 Carlos Toomer	.50	.25	.05
☐ 12 Jamal Mashburn	3.00	1.50	.30
☐ 13 Rick Pitino CO	.75	.35	.07
☐ 14 Aminu Timberlake	.50	.25	.05
☐ 15 Andre Riddick	.50	.25	.05
☐ 16 Bernadette Locke-Mattox Asst. CO	.50	.25	.05
☐ 17 Billy Donovan Asst. CO	.50	.25	.05
☐ 18 Herb Sendek Asst. CO	.50	.25	.05
☐ xx '91-92 Wildcat Seniors (Volume 5, Number 2)	.50	.25	.05
☐ xx Team Photo (Volume 5, Number 3)	1.00	.50	.10

1991-92 Kentucky Big Blue

This perforated 18-card set was issued as an insert in Oscar Combs' Big Blue Basketball magazine. After perforation, the cards measure 2 5/8" by 3 5/8." The fronts display a mix of action and posed color head shots enclosed by a white border. The player's name appears in black lettering in a yellow bar at the top flanked by a basketball to the left. In a horizontal format, the backs have blue and white reverse lettering and carry a black and white head shot, a Fun Fact, and a "Coach Pitino Sez" feature. The cards are numbered on the back.

	MINT	EXC	G-VG
COMPLETE SET (18)	12.00	6.00	1.20
COMMON PLAYER (1-18)	.50	.25	.05
☐ 1 Johnathon Davis	1.50	.75	.15
☐ 2 Reggie Hanson	.75	.35	.07
☐ 3 Richie Farmer	.75	.35	.07
☐ 4 Deron Feldhaus	.75	.35	.07
☐ 5 John Pelphrey	.75	.35	.07
☐ 6 Sean Woods	.75	.35	.07
☐ 7 Todd Bearup	.50	.25	.05
☐ 8 Junior Braddy	.50	.25	.05
☐ 9 Jeff Brassow	.50	.25	.05
☐ 10 Gimel Martinez	.50	.25	.05
☐ 11 Jamal Mashburn	3.00	1.50	.30
☐ 12 Henry Thomas	.50	.25	.05
☐ 13 Carlos Toomer	.50	.25	.05
☐ 14 Travis Ford	.50	.25	.05
☐ 15 Rick Pitino CO	.75	.35	.07
☐ 16 UK Cracks Top 10	.50	.25	.05
☐ 17 UK 93, U of L 85	.50	.25	.05
☐ 18 Checklist	.75	.35	.07

1981-82 Louisville Police

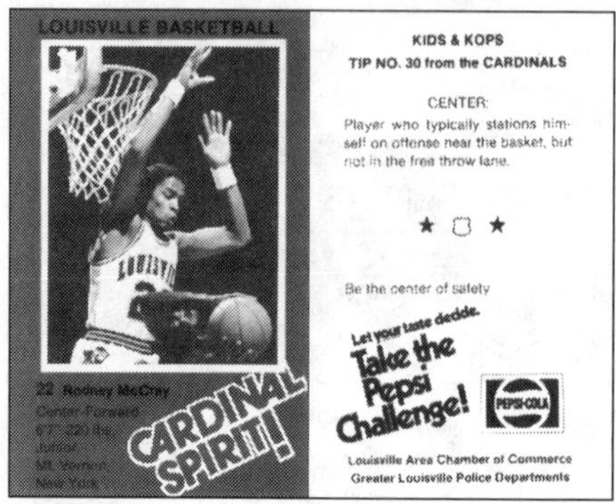

This 30-card set was sponsored by Pepsi, the Louisville Area Chamber of Commerce, and Greater Louisville Police Departments. The cards measure 2 5/8" by 4 1/8" and are printed in thin card stock. On a red card face, the fronts show black and white player photos enclosed by a white border. Player information and the words "Cardinal Spirit" appear beneath the picture. The backs include a safety tip, a definition or discussion of an aspect of basketball, and sponsor logos. The cards are numbered on the back by the tip number.

	MINT	EXC	G-VG
COMPLETE SET (30)	75.00	37.50	7.50
COMMON PLAYER (1-30)	2.00	1.00	.20
☐ 1 Charles Jones	4.00	2.00	.40
☐ 2 Rodin's The Thinker	2.00	1.00	.20
☐ 3 1981-82 Schedule	2.00	1.00	.20
☐ 4 Bill Olsen ATH DIR and family	2.00	1.00	.20
☐ 5 Coaching Staff	2.00	1.00	.20
☐ 6 Lancaster Gordon	7.50	3.75	.75
☐ 7 Donald C. Swain PRES	2.00	1.00	.20
☐ 8 Scooter McCray	6.00	3.00	.60
☐ 9 Cheerleaders	3.00	1.50	.30
☐ 10 Marty Pulliam	2.00	1.00	.20
☐ 11 Derek Smith	6.00	3.00	.60
☐ 12 Jack Tennant ANN Van Vance ANN	2.00	1.00	.20
☐ 13 Jerry Eaves	3.00	1.50	.30
☐ 14 Greg Deuser	2.00	1.00	.20
☐ 15 Manuel Forrest	3.00	1.50	.30
☐ 16 Danny Mitchell	2.00	1.00	.20
☐ 17 Team Photo Men's team	4.00	2.00	.40
☐ 18 Jerry May TR Rudy Ellis Dir. Sports Medicine	2.00	1.00	.20
☐ 19 Poncho Wright	3.00	1.50	.30
☐ 20 James Jeter	2.00	1.00	.20
☐ 21 Cardinal Bird Mascot	2.00	1.00	.20
☐ 22 Milt Wagner	7.50	3.75	.75
☐ 23 Denny Crum CO and 1981-82 Freshman	3.00	1.50	.30
☐ 24 Team Photo Women's Team	2.00	1.00	.20
☐ 25 Wiley Brown	4.00	2.00	.40
☐ 26 Kent Jones	2.00	1.00	.20
☐ 27 Denny Crum CO and Returning Starters	4.00	2.00	.40
☐ 28 Darrell Griffith U of L Professional Basketball Players	9.00	4.50	.90
☐ 29 Denny Crum CO	3.00	1.50	.30
☐ 30 Rodney McCray	9.00	4.50	.90

1983-84 Louisville 5x7

This 20-card set consists of oversized cards measuring approximately 7" by 5". On the left portion the front features a borderless color action photo, measuring 4" by 5". On the remaining portion, a head shot of the player, player information (in white lettering), and a Cardinal logo appear on a red background. The back of the cards presents biographical information, career summary, and statistics in a two-column format, along with the player's autograph. The cards are ordered and numbered below by uniform number.

	MINT	EXC	G-VG
COMPLETE SET (20)	60.00	30.00	6.00
COMMON PLAYER	2.00	1.00	.20
☐ 00 Robbie Valentine	2.00	1.00	.20
☐ 4 Lancaster Gordon	6.00	3.00	.60
☐ 12 Kent Jones	2.00	1.00	.20
☐ 20 Milt Wagner	6.00	3.00	.60
☐ 23 Chris West	2.00	1.00	.20
☐ 24 Will Olliges	2.00	1.00	.20
☐ 25 James Jeter	2.00	1.00	.20
☐ 30 Manuel Forrest	3.00	1.50	.30
☐ 32 Mark McSwain	3.00	1.50	.30
☐ 33 Charles Jones	3.00	1.50	.30
☐ 35 Darrell Griffith	6.00	3.00	.60
☐ 40 Barry Sumpter	3.00	1.50	.30
☐ 42 Jeff Hall	3.00	1.50	.30
☐ 45 Danny Mitchell	2.00	1.00	.20
☐ 55 Billy Thompson	6.00	3.00	.60
☐ xx Denny Crum (Head Coach)	5.00	2.50	.50
☐ xx Assistant Coaches Bobby Dotson Wade Houston Jerry Jones	3.00	1.50	.30
☐ xx Cheerleaders	3.00	1.50	.30
☐ xx Pep Band	2.00	1.00	.20
☐ xx Freedom Hall Home of the Cardinals	2.00	1.00	.20

1988-89 Louisville 194

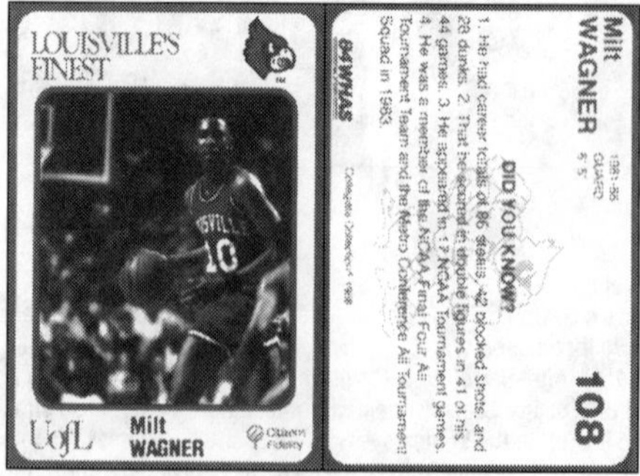

The 1988-89 University of Louisville Cardinals basketball set contains 194 standard-sized (2 1/2" by 3 1/2") cards featuring "Louisville's Finest" basketball players. The fronts have red and white borders. The backs have various statistical and biographical information. This set was issued in eight-card cello packs.

	MINT	EXC	G-VG
COMPLETE SET (194)	24.00	12.00	2.40
COMMON PLAYER (1-194)	.10	.05	.01
☐ 1 Denny Crum CO	.20	.10	.02
☐ 2 Wesley Unseld	.50	.25	.05
☐ 3 Darrell Griffith	.30	.15	.03
☐ 4 John Dromo	.20	.10	.02
☐ 5 Bernard(Peck) Hickman	.20	.10	.02
☐ 6 Butch Beard	.20	.10	.02
☐ 7 Herbert Crook	.20	.10	.02
☐ 8 Milt Wagner	.20	.10	.02
☐ 9 Lancaster Gordon	.20	.10	.02
☐ 10 Billy Thompson	.20	.10	.02
☐ 11 Rodney McCray	.25	.12	.02
☐ 12 Scooter McCray	.15	.07	.01
☐ 13 Wade Houston	.20	.10	.02
☐ 14 Jerry Jones	.10	.05	.01
☐ 15 Derek Smith	.20	.10	.02
☐ 16 Tony Branch	.15	.07	.01
☐ 17 Wesley Cox	.15	.07	.01
☐ 18 Manuel Forrest	.15	.07	.01
☐ 19 Jerry Eaves	.15	.07	.01
☐ 20 1980 NCAA Champs	.10	.05	.01
☐ 21 Junior Bridgeman	.20	.10	.02
☐ 22 Jeff Hall	.15	.07	.01
☐ 23 Charles Jones	.15	.07	.01
☐ 24 Rick Wilson	.10	.05	.01
☐ 25 The Cardinal Bird	.10	.05	.01
☐ 26 Wiley Brown	.15	.07	.01
☐ 27 Charlie Tyra	.15	.07	.01
☐ 28 Phil Rollins	.10	.05	.01
☐ 29 James Jeter	.10	.05	.01
☐ 30 Poncho Wright	.15	.07	.01
☐ 31 Vladmir Gastevich	.10	.05	.01
☐ 32 Terry Howard	.10	.05	.01
☐ 33 Mark McSwain	.15	.07	.01
☐ 34 Ricky Gallon	.15	.07	.01
☐ 35 1975 NCAA Final Four	.10	.05	.01
☐ 36 1972 NCAA Final Four	.10	.05	.01
☐ 37 Mike Lawhon	.10	.05	.01
☐ 38 Bill Bunton	.15	.07	.01
☐ 39 Roger Burkman	.15	.07	.01
☐ 40 Henry Bacon	.10	.05	.01
☐ 41 Larry Williams	.10	.05	.01
☐ 42 Phil Bond	.15	.07	.01
☐ 43 Bobby Brown	.10	.05	.01
☐ 44 Charles Jones	.15	.07	.01
☐ 45 Mike Grosso	.10	.05	.01
☐ 46 Freedom Hall	.10	.05	.01
☐ 47 Fred Holden	.10	.05	.01
☐ 48 1948 NAIB Champs	.10	.05	.01
☐ 49 Glen Combs	.20	.10	.02
☐ 50 Jadie Frazier	.10	.05	.01
☐ 51 Marty Pulliam	.10	.05	.01
☐ 52 Eddie Whitehead	.10	.05	.01
☐ 53 Bobby Turner	.10	.05	.01
☐ 54 Will Olliges	.10	.05	.01
☐ 55 Eddie Creamer	.10	.05	.01
☐ 56 Corky Cox	.10	.05	.01
☐ 57 Bob Lochmueller	.10	.05	.01
☐ 58 Jeff Hall	.15	.07	.01
☐ 59 Al Vilcheck	.10	.05	.01
☐ 60 Jim Morgan	.10	.05	.01
☐ 61 Jim Price	.20	.10	.02
☐ 62 Ron Thomas	.20	.10	.02
☐ 63 Bobby Dotson	.10	.05	.01
☐ 64 Jerry Eaves	.15	.07	.01
☐ 65 1956 NIT Champs	.10	.05	.01
☐ 66 John Reuther	.10	.05	.01
☐ 67 Ron Hawley	.10	.05	.01
☐ 68 Kent Jones	.10	.05	.01
☐ 69 1983 NCAA Final Four	.10	.05	.01
☐ 70 1982 NCAA Final Four	.10	.05	.01
☐ 71 1959 Louisville Cardinals	.10	.05	.01
☐ 72 Fred Sawyer	.10	.05	.01
☐ 73 Kenny Reeves	.10	.05	.01
☐ 74 Chris West	.10	.05	.01
☐ 75 Dick Peloff	.10	.05	.01
☐ 76 Allen Murphy	.10	.05	.01
☐ 77 John Prudhoe	.10	.05	.01
☐ 78 Mike Abram	.10	.05	.01
☐ 79 Bud Olsen	.15	.07	.01
☐ 80 Ron Rubenstein	.10	.05	.01
☐ 81 Gerald Moreman	.10	.05	.01
☐ 82 Chuck Noble	.15	.07	.01
☐ 83 Bill Darragh	.15	.07	.01
☐ 84 Jerry Dupont	.10	.05	.01
☐ 85 Danny Mitchell	.10	.05	.01
☐ 86 John Turner	.10	.05	.01
☐ 87 Daryl Cleveland	.10	.05	.01
☐ 88 Greg Deuser	.10	.05	.01
☐ 89 Don Goldstein	.10	.05	.01
☐ 90 Marv Selvy	.10	.05	.01
☐ 91 Dave Gilbert	.10	.05	.01
☐ 92 Tommy Finnegan	.10	.05	.01
☐ 93 Joe Liedtke	.10	.05	.01
☐ 94 Jack Coleman	.10	.05	.01
☐ 95 Dennis Clifford	.10	.05	.01
☐ 96 Robbie Valentine	.10	.05	.01
☐ 97 Ron Rooks	.10	.05	.01
☐ 98 The Coaching Staff	.10	.05	.01
☐ 99 Denny Crum CO	.20	.10	.02
☐ 100 Manuel Forrest	.15	.07	.01
☐ 101 Darrell Griffith	.30	.15	.03
☐ 102 Wesley Cox	.15	.07	.01
☐ 103 Wes Unseld	.35	.17	.03
☐ 104 John Dromo	.20	.10	.02
☐ 105 Peck Hickman	.20	.10	.02
☐ 106 Butch Beard	.20	.10	.02
☐ 107 Herbert Crook	.20	.10	.02
☐ 108 Milt Wagner	.20	.10	.02
☐ 109 Lancaster Gordon	.20	.10	.02
☐ 110 Billy Thompson	.20	.10	.02
☐ 111 Rodney McCray	.20	.10	.02
☐ 112 Scooter McCray	.15	.07	.01
☐ 113 Derek Smith	.15	.07	.01
☐ 114 Tony Branch	.15	.07	.01
☐ 115 Manuel Forrest	.15	.07	.01
☐ 116 Jerry Eaves	.15	.07	.01
☐ 117 Jeff Hall	.15	.07	.01
☐ 118 Charles Jones	.15	.07	.01
☐ 119 Rick Wilson	.10	.05	.01
☐ 120 Wiley Brown	.15	.07	.01
☐ 121 Charlie Tyra	.15	.07	.01
☐ 122 Phil Rollins	.10	.05	.01
☐ 123 Poncho Wright	.15	.07	.01
☐ 124 Terry Howard	.10	.05	.01
☐ 125 Mark McSwain	.15	.07	.01
☐ 126 Ricky Gallon	.10	.05	.01
☐ 127 Mike Lawhon	.10	.05	.01
☐ 128 Roger Burkman	.15	.07	.01
☐ 129 Henry Bacon	.10	.05	.01
☐ 130 Larry Williams	.10	.05	.01
☐ 131 Phil Bond	.15	.07	.01
☐ 132 Stanley Bunton	.10	.05	.01
☐ 133 Fred Holden	.10	.05	.01
☐ 134 Marty Pulliam	.10	.05	.01
☐ 135 Bobby Turner	.10	.05	.01
☐ 136 Will Olliges	.10	.05	.01
☐ 137 Al Vilcheck	.10	.05	.01
☐ 138 Jim Price	.20	.10	.02
☐ 139 Chris West	.10	.05	.01
☐ 140 Allen Murphy	.10	.05	.01
☐ 141 Mike Abram	.10	.05	.01
☐ 142 Danny Mitchell	.10	.05	.01
☐ 143 John Turner	.10	.05	.01
☐ 144 Daryl Cleveland	.10	.05	.01
☐ 145 Don Goldstein	.10	.05	.01
☐ 146 Marv Selvy	.10	.05	.01
☐ 147 Dave Gilbert	.10	.05	.01
☐ 148 Joe Liedtke	.10	.05	.01
☐ 149 Robbie Valentine	.10	.05	.01
☐ 150 Tony Branch	.15	.07	.01
☐ 151 Manuel Forrest	.15	.07	.01
☐ 152 Jerry Eaves	.15	.07	.01
☐ 153 Rick Wilson	.10	.05	.01
☐ 154 Jeff Hall	.15	.07	.01
☐ 155 Charles Jones	.15	.07	.01
☐ 156 Derek Smith	.15	.07	.01
☐ 157 Scooter McCray	.15	.07	.01
☐ 158 Robbie Valentine	.10	.05	.01
☐ 159 Mike Abram	.10	.05	.01
☐ 160 Rodney McCray	.25	.12	.02
☐ 161 Roger Burkman	.15	.07	.01
☐ 162 Henry Bacon	.10	.05	.01
☐ 163 Mike Lawhon	.10	.05	.01
☐ 164 Ricky Gallon	.10	.05	.01
☐ 165 Billy Thompson	.20	.10	.02
☐ 166 Milt Wagner	.20	.10	.02
☐ 167 Lancaster Gordon	.20	.10	.02
☐ 168 Butch Beard	.20	.10	.02
☐ 169 Herbert Crook	.20	.10	.02
☐ 170 Wes Unseld	.35	.17	.03
☐ 171 Wesley Cox	.15	.07	.01
☐ 172 Darrell Griffith	.30	.15	.03
☐ 173 Denny Crum CO	.20	.10	.02
☐ 174 Mark McSwain	.15	.07	.01
☐ 175 Wiley Brown	.15	.07	.01
☐ 176 Will Olliges	.10	.05	.01
☐ 177 Phil Bond	.15	.07	.01
☐ 178 Phil Bond	.15	.07	.01
☐ 179 Wiley Brown	.15	.07	.01

		MINT	EXC	G-VG
☐ 180	Mark McSwain	.15	.07	.01
☐ 181	Denny Crum CO	.20	.10	.02
☐ 182	Darrell Griffith	.30	.15	.03
☐ 183	Wesley Cox	.15	.07	.01
☐ 184	Peck Hickman CO	.20	.10	.02
☐ 185	Lancaster Gordon	.20	.10	.02
☐ 186	Billy Thompson	.20	.10	.02
☐ 187	Rodney McCray	.20	.10	.02
☐ 188	Stanley Bunton	.10	.05	.01
☐ 189	Henry Bacon	.10	.05	.01
☐ 190	Scooter McCray	.15	.07	.01
☐ 191	Derek Smith	.20	.10	.02
☐ 192	Jerry King	.10	.05	.01
☐ 193	Van Vance and Jock Sutherland	.10	.05	.01
☐ 194	Bill Olsen	.10	.05	.01

1989-90 Louisville 300 *

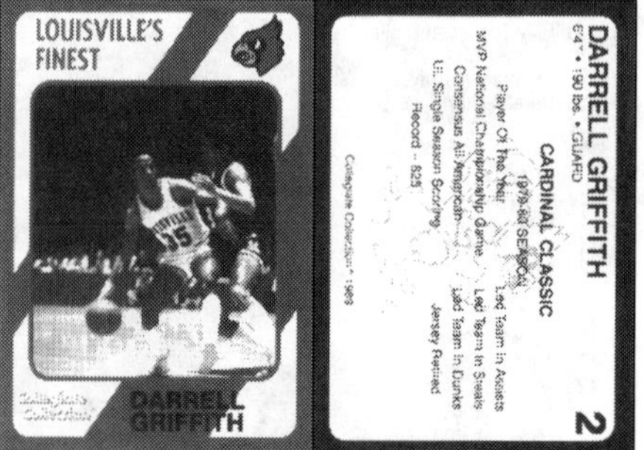

This 300-card set was produced by Collegiate Collection and measures the standard size (2 1/2" by 3 1/2"). The fronts feature a mix of black and white photos for earlier players and color for later ones, with rounded corners and red borders. The pictures are superimposed over a red and white diagonally-striped card face, with a red outer border. The top reads "Louisville's Finest," and the school logo appears in the upper right corner. The horizontally oriented backs are printed in red on white and present biographical information, career summaries, or statistics. The cards are numbered on the back.

		MINT	EXC	G-VG
COMPLETE SET (300)		25.00	12.50	2.50
COMMON PLAYER (1-300)		.07	.03	.01
☐ 1	Denny Crum CO	.20	.10	.02
☐ 2	Darrell Griffith	.25	.12	.02
☐ 3	Wes Unseld	.30	.15	.03
☐ 4	Pervis Ellison	.35	.17	.03
☐ 5	Charlie Tyra	.10	.05	.01
☐ 6	Phil Bond	.10	.05	.01
☐ 7	Butch Beard	.15	.07	.01
☐ 8	Jim Price	.15	.07	.01
☐ 9	Jerry Eaves	.10	.05	.01
☐ 10	Manuel Forrest	.10	.05	.01
☐ 11	Butch Beard	.15	.07	.01
☐ 12	Herbert Crook	.15	.07	.01
☐ 13	John Turner	.07	.03	.01
☐ 14	Wes Unseld	.30	.15	.03
☐ 15	Fred Holden	.07	.03	.01
☐ 16	Bill Bunton	.15	.07	.01
☐ 17	Milt Wagner	.15	.07	.01
☐ 18	Ricky Gallon	.10	.05	.01
☐ 19	Jerry King	.07	.03	.01
☐ 20	Don Goldstein	.07	.03	.01
☐ 21	Rick Wilson	.10	.05	.01
☐ 22	John Reuther	.07	.03	.01
☐ 23	Charles Jones	.10	.05	.01
☐ 24	Bobby Turner	.07	.03	.01
☐ 25	Darrell Griffith	.25	.12	.02
☐ 26	Scooter McCray	.10	.05	.01
☐ 27	George Hauptfuhrer	.07	.03	.01
☐ 28	Frank Epley	.07	.03	.01
☐ 29	Ed Kupper	.07	.03	.01
☐ 30	Don Kinker	.07	.03	.01
☐ 31	Roger Burkman	.10	.05	.01
☐ 32	Jerry Eaves	.10	.05	.01
☐ 33	Derek Smith	.10	.05	.01
☐ 34	Jeff Hall	.10	.05	.01
☐ 35	Billy Thompson	.15	.07	.01
☐ 36	Mike Abram	.07	.03	.01
☐ 37	Mark McSwain	.10	.05	.01
☐ 38	Herbert Crook	.15	.07	.01
☐ 39	Kenny Payne	.15	.07	.01
☐ 40	Johnny Knopf	.07	.03	.01
☐ 41	Pervis Ellison	.30	.15	.03
☐ 42	Deward Compton	.07	.03	.01
☐ 43	Poncho Wright	.10	.05	.01
☐ 44	Scooter McCray	.10	.05	.01
☐ 45	Rodney McCray	.20	.10	.02
☐ 46	Milt Wagner	.15	.07	.01
☐ 47	Lancaster Gordon	.15	.07	.01
☐ 48	Manuel Forrest	.15	.07	.01
☐ 49	Charles Jones	.15	.07	.01
☐ 50	Cal Johnson	.07	.03	.01
☐ 51	Forrest Able	.07	.03	.01
☐ 52	Bob Peterson	.07	.03	.01
☐ 53	Clyde(Ace) Parker	.10	.05	.01
☐ 54	Roy Rubin	.07	.03	.01
☐ 55	Al Russak	.07	.03	.01
☐ 56	Roy Combs	.07	.03	.01
☐ 57	Robert Davis	.07	.03	.01
☐ 58	Randall Ford	.07	.03	.01
☐ 59	Clyde Bryant	.07	.03	.01
☐ 60	Frank Lentz	.07	.03	.01
☐ 61	Bob Dunbar	.07	.03	.01
☐ 62	William Powell	.07	.03	.01
☐ 63	Bob Manion	.07	.03	.01
☐ 64	Al Glaza	.07	.03	.01
☐ 65	Harold Andrews	.07	.03	.01
☐ 66	Wade Houston	.10	.05	.01
☐ 67	Joe Reuther	.07	.03	.01
☐ 68	Judd Rothman	.07	.03	.01
☐ 69	Tony Kinnaird	.07	.03	.01
☐ 70	Danny Brown	.07	.03	.01
☐ 71	Ike Whitfield	.07	.03	.01
☐ 72	Billy Harmon	.07	.03	.01
☐ 73	Joe Meiman	.07	.03	.01
☐ 74	Ed Linonis	.07	.03	.01
☐ 75	Larry Carter	.07	.03	.01
☐ 76	Ken Bradley	.07	.03	.01
☐ 77	Ken Butters	.07	.03	.01
☐ 78	John Studer	.07	.03	.01
☐ 79	Dennis Deeken	.07	.03	.01
☐ 80	Bob Gorius	.07	.03	.01
☐ 81	Paul Pry	.07	.03	.01
☐ 82	Ron Stallings	.07	.03	.01
☐ 83	John Varoscak	.07	.03	.01
☐ 84	Bob Naber	.07	.03	.01
☐ 85	Howard Stacey	.07	.03	.01
☐ 86	Buddy Leathers	.07	.03	.01
☐ 87	Joe Kitchen	.07	.03	.01
☐ 88	Alex Mantel	.07	.03	.01
☐ 89	Rodger Tieman	.07	.03	.01
☐ 90	Dick Keffer	.07	.03	.01
☐ 91	Dick Robison	.07	.03	.01
☐ 92	Barry Sumpter	.10	.05	.01
☐ 93	Herb Harah	.07	.03	.01
☐ 94	Bill Sullivan	.07	.03	.01
☐ 95	Chet Beam	.07	.03	.01
☐ 96	Roscoe Shackelford	.07	.03	.01
☐ 97	David Smith	.07	.03	.01
☐ 98	Jerry Armstrong	.07	.03	.01
☐ 99	James"Lum" Edwards	.07	.03	.01
☐ 100	Jesse"Oz" Johnson	.07	.03	.01
☐ 101	Howard Schnellenberger	.20	.10	.02
☐ 102	Johnny Unitas	.75	.35	.07
☐ 103	Lenny Lyles	.10	.05	.01
☐ 104	Ken Porco	.07	.03	.01
☐ 105	Jay Gruden	.07	.03	.01
☐ 106	Tom Lucia	.07	.03	.01
☐ 107	Ken Kortas	.10	.05	.01
☐ 108	Howard Stevens	.15	.07	.01
☐ 109	Doug Buffone	.15	.07	.01
☐ 110	Lenny Lyles	.10	.05	.01
☐ 111	Wilbur Summers	.07	.03	.01
☐ 112	Dean May	.07	.03	.01
☐ 113	Deon Booker	.07	.03	.01
☐ 114	Walter Peacock	.07	.03	.01
☐ 115	Ernest Givens	.35	.17	.03
☐ 116	Otis Wilson	.15	.07	.01
☐ 117	Mark Clayton	.40	.20	.04
☐ 118	Dwayne Woodruff	.15	.07	.01
☐ 119	Frank Minnifield	.20	.10	.02
☐ 120	Ernie Green	.20	.10	.02
☐ 121	Wally Oyler	.07	.03	.01
☐ 122	Nathan Poole	.07	.03	.01
☐ 123	Ron Davenport	.10	.05	.01
☐ 124	Tom Laframboise	.07	.03	.01
☐ 125	Ed Rubbert	.07	.03	.01

☐ 126 Jon Cade	.07	.03	.01
☐ 127 Howard Schnellenberger	.20	.10	.02
☐ 128 Rick Lantz	.07	.03	.01
☐ 129 Brad Bradford	.07	.03	.01
☐ 130 Danny Hope	.07	.03	.01
☐ 131 Bob Maddox	.07	.03	.01
☐ 132 Gary Nord	.07	.03	.01
☐ 133 Ty Smith	.07	.03	.01
☐ 134 Christ Vagotis	.07	.03	.01
☐ 135 Trent Walters	.07	.03	.01
☐ 136 Jeff Morrow	.07	.03	.01
☐ 137 Vince Gibson	.07	.03	.01
☐ 138 Lee Corso	.15	.07	.01
☐ 139 Frank Camp	.07	.03	.01
☐ 140 Benny Russell	.07	.03	.01
☐ 141 Paul Mattingly	.07	.03	.01
☐ 142 Joe Jacoby	.15	.07	.01
☐ 143 Jay Gruden	.07	.03	.01
☐ 144 Chris Thieneman	.07	.03	.01
☐ 145 Matt Battaglia	.07	.03	.01
☐ 146 Eddie Johnson	.07	.03	.01
☐ 147 Stu Stramm	.07	.03	.01
☐ 148 Donald Craft	.07	.03	.01
☐ 149 Pete Compise	.07	.03	.01
☐ 150 Jim Zamberlan	.07	.03	.01
☐ 151 Marc Mitchell	.07	.03	.01
☐ 152 Tom Abood	.07	.03	.01
☐ 153 Lee Calland	.07	.03	.01
☐ 154 Larry Ball	.07	.03	.01
☐ 155 Phil Ellis	.07	.03	.01
☐ 156 Greg Pianko	.07	.03	.01
☐ 157 Bruce Armstrong	.10	.05	.01
☐ 158 Calvin Prince	.07	.03	.01
☐ 159 Marty Smith	.07	.03	.01
☐ 160 Joe Trabue	.07	.03	.01
☐ 161 Gene Sartini	.07	.03	.01
☐ 162 Rodney Knighton	.07	.03	.01
☐ 163 George Cain	.07	.03	.01
☐ 164 Stu Gibson	.07	.03	.01
☐ 165 Larry Compton	.07	.03	.01
☐ 166 Charlie Mudd	.07	.03	.01
☐ 167 Al MacFarlane	.07	.03	.01
☐ 168 Willie Shelby	.07	.03	.01
☐ 169 Herbie Phelps	.07	.03	.01
☐ 170 Dale Orem	.07	.03	.01
☐ 171 Lee Bouggess	.10	.05	.01
☐ 172 John Neidert	.07	.03	.01
☐ 173 Amos Martin	.10	.05	.01
☐ 174 Norman Heard	.07	.03	.01
☐ 175 Charlie Johnson	.07	.03	.01
☐ 176 Len Depaola	.10	.05	.01
☐ 177 Dave Nuss	.07	.03	.01
☐ 178 Tom Lucia	.07	.03	.01
☐ 179 Bill Gatti	.07	.03	.01
☐ 180 Greg Hickman	.07	.03	.01
☐ 181 Wayne Patrick	.07	.03	.01
☐ 182 Otto Knop Sr.	.07	.03	.01
☐ 183 John Giles	.07	.03	.01
☐ 184 Doug Hockensmith	.07	.03	.01
☐ 185 A.J.Jacobs	.07	.03	.01
☐ 186 Pat Patterson	.07	.03	.01
☐ 187 David Hatfield	.07	.03	.01
☐ 188 Eric Vaughn	.07	.03	.01
☐ 189 Brian Miller	.07	.03	.01
☐ 190 Leon Williams	.07	.03	.01
☐ 191 Kenny Robinson	.07	.03	.01
☐ 192 John Madeya	.07	.03	.01
☐ 193 Zarko Ellis	.07	.03	.01
☐ 194 Cookie Brinkman	.07	.03	.01
☐ 195 Kevin Miller	.07	.03	.01
☐ 196 Ricky Skiles	.07	.03	.01
☐ 197 John Adams	.07	.03	.01
☐ 198 Dave Betz	.07	.03	.01
☐ 199 Jeff Henry	.07	.03	.01
☐ 200 Tom Jackson	.25	.12	.02
☐ 201 Louisville Cardinals	.07	.03	.01
☐ 202 Louisville Cardinals	.07	.03	.01
☐ 203 Louisville Cardinals	.07	.03	.01
☐ 204 Louisville Cardinals	.07	.03	.01
☐ 205 Louisville Cardinals	.07	.03	.01
☐ 206 Pervis Ellison	.30	.15	.03
☐ 207 Wes Unseld	.30	.15	.03
☐ 208 Charlie Tyra	.10	.05	.01
☐ 209 Darrell Griffith	.20	.10	.02
☐ 210 Steve Clark	.07	.03	.01
☐ 211 Ellis Bryant	.07	.03	.01
☐ 212 Gil Waggoner	.07	.03	.01
☐ 213 Bob Borah	.07	.03	.01
☐ 214 Bill Akridge	.07	.03	.01
☐ 215 Cliff York	.07	.03	.01
☐ 216 Harry Hinton	.07	.03	.01
☐ 217 Ray Potts	.07	.03	.01
☐ 218 Bob Wellman	.07	.03	.01
☐ 219 Truett Demoisey	.07	.03	.01

☐ 220 John Prudhoe	.07	.03	.01
☐ 221 Dale Hall	.07	.03	.01
☐ 222 Phil Rollins	.07	.03	.01
☐ 223 Ron Thomas	.10	.05	.01
☐ 224 John Turner	.07	.03	.01
☐ 225 Charles Tyra	.10	.05	.01
☐ 226 Henry Bacon	.07	.03	.01
☐ 227 Butch Beard	.15	.07	.01
☐ 228 Phillip Bond	.10	.05	.01
☐ 229 Junior Bridgeman	.20	.10	.02
☐ 230 Jim Price	.15	.07	.01
☐ 231 Jack Coleman	.07	.03	.01
☐ 232 Wesley Cox	.15	.07	.01
☐ 233 Jerry Eaves	.10	.05	.01
☐ 234 Lancaster Gordon	.15	.07	.01
☐ 235 Milt Wagner	.15	.07	.01
☐ 236 Mike Grosso	.10	.05	.01
☐ 237 Rick Wilson	.10	.05	.01
☐ 238 Wes Unseld	.30	.15	.03
☐ 239 Scooter McCray	.10	.05	.01
☐ 240 Allen Murphy	.07	.03	.01
☐ 241 Chuck Noble	.10	.05	.01
☐ 242 Bud Olsen	.10	.05	.01
☐ 243 Roger Burkman	.10	.05	.01
☐ 244 Henry Bacon	.07	.03	.01
☐ 245 Jim Price	.15	.07	.01
☐ 246 Al Vilcheck	.07	.03	.01
☐ 247 Ron Thomas	.10	.05	.01
☐ 248 Mike Lawhon	.07	.03	.01
☐ 249 Don Goldstein	.07	.03	.01
☐ 250 John Turner	.07	.03	.01
☐ 251 Fred Sawyer	.07	.03	.01
☐ 252 Wiley Brown	.10	.05	.01
☐ 253 Pervis Ellison	.30	.15	.03
☐ 254 Herbert Crook	.15	.07	.01
☐ 255 Mark McSwain	.10	.05	.01
☐ 256 Jeff Hall	.10	.05	.01
☐ 257 Billy Thompson	.15	.07	.01
☐ 258 Milt Wagner	.15	.07	.01
☐ 259 Charles Jones	.10	.05	.01
☐ 260 Lancaster Gordon	.15	.07	.01
☐ 261 Poncho Wright	.10	.05	.01
☐ 262 Jerry Eaves	.10	.05	.01
☐ 263 Scooter McCray	.10	.05	.01
☐ 264 Rodney McCray	.20	.10	.02
☐ 265 Derek Smith	.15	.07	.01
☐ 266 Darrell Griffith	.20	.10	.02
☐ 267 Roger Burkman	.10	.05	.01
☐ 268 Kevin Walls	.15	.07	.01
☐ 269 Allen Murphy	.07	.03	.01
☐ 270 Junior Bridgeman	.20	.10	.02
☐ 271 Wesley Cox	.15	.07	.01
☐ 272 Bill Bunton	.15	.07	.01
☐ 273 Phillip Bond	.10	.05	.01
☐ 274 Ricky Gallon	.10	.05	.01
☐ 275 Manuel Forrest	.10	.05	.01
☐ 276 Jerry Jones	.07	.03	.01
☐ 277 Scooter McCray	.10	.05	.01
☐ 278 Larry Williams	.10	.05	.01
☐ 279 Peck Hickman	.15	.07	.01
☐ 280 John Dromo	.15	.07	.01
☐ 281 Darrell Griffith	.20	.10	.02
☐ 282 Derek Smith	.15	.07	.01
☐ 283 Paul Pry	.07	.03	.01
☐ 284 Henry Bacon	.07	.03	.01
☐ 285 Charles Jones	.10	.05	.01
☐ 286 Butch Beard	.15	.07	.01
☐ 287 Herbert Crook	.15	.07	.01
☐ 288 Denny Crum CO	.15	.07	.01
☐ 289 Mike Abram	.07	.03	.01
☐ 290 Pervis Ellison	.30	.15	.03
☐ 291 Billy Thompson	.15	.07	.01
☐ 292 Rodney McCray	.20	.10	.02
☐ 293 Terry Howard	.07	.03	.01
☐ 294 Mike Grosso	.10	.05	.01
☐ 295 Kenny Payne	.10	.05	.01
☐ 296 Chris West	.07	.03	.01
☐ 297 Darrell Griffith	.20	.10	.02
☐ 298 Denny Crum CO	.15	.07	.01
☐ 299 Jeff Hall	.10	.05	.01
☐ 300 Billy Thompson	.20	.10	.02

1986 LSU Police *

This 16-card set was sponsored by LSU, Baton Rouge General Medical Center, Chemical Dependency Unit of Baton Rouge, and various law enforcement agencies and produced by McDag

Productions. The General and the Chemical Dependency Unit logos adorn the top of the observe and the bottom of the reverse. The cards measure 2 1/2" by 3 1/2". The fronts feature a mix of borderless posed and action color photos of the players on white card stock. Player information appears below the pictures between two Tiger logos. The back has additional player information with two more Tiger logos at the top. The card backs provide "Tips from the Tigers" in the form of an anti-crime or drug message. The cards are unnumbered and we have checklisted them below in alphabetical order. Since this set includes athletes from two different sports, we have indicated the sport after the player's name (B for baseball; BK for basketball). The set features future Major Leaguers Joey (Albert) Belle, Mark Guthrie, and Jeff Reboulet.

	MINT	EXC	G-VG
COMPLETE SET (16)	12.00	6.00	1.20
COMMON PLAYER (1-16)	.50	.25	.05
☐ 1 Joey Belle B	6.00	3.00	.60
☐ 2 Skip Bertman B CO	.50	.25	.05
☐ 3 Ricky Blanton BK	1.00	.50	.10
☐ 4 Dale Brown BK CO	1.00	.50	.10
☐ 5 Ollie Brown BK	.50	.25	.05
☐ 6 Mark Guthrie B	.75	.35	.07
☐ 7 Rob Leary B	.50	.25	.05
☐ 8 Stan Loewer B	.50	.25	.05
☐ 9 Greg Patterson B	.50	.25	.05
☐ 10 Jeff Reboulet B	1.00	.50	.10
☐ 11 Don Redden BK	.75	.35	.07
☐ 12 Derrick Taylor BK	.75	.35	.07
☐ 13 Jose Vargas BK	1.00	.50	.10
☐ 14 John Williams BK	2.00	1.00	.20
☐ 15 Nikita Wilson BK	1.00	.50	.10
☐ 16 Anthony Wilson BK	.50	.25	.05

1987-88 LSU Police *

This 16-card set was sponsored by LSU, Baton Rouge General Medical Center, Chemical Dependency Unit of Baton Rouge, and various law enforcement agencies and was produced by McDag Productions. The General and the Chemical Dependency Unit logos adorn the bottom of both sides of the card. Six thousand sets were printed, and they were distributed by participating police agencies in the Baton Rouge area. The cards measure 2 1/2" by 3 1/2" and are numbered on the back. The fronts feature borderless action or posed color photos of the players on white card stock. The upper left and right corners give the school name and player information. The backs have additional player information and "Tips from the Tigers", which consist of anti-drug or alcohol messages. This set includes athletes from basketball (1-7, 16) and baseball (8-15). Of special interest is card number 16, issued in memory of the late Pete Maravich, the all-time leading scorer in college basketball history. The set features the first card of Ben McDonald.

	MINT	EXC	G-VG
COMPLETE SET (16)	12.00	6.00	1.20
COMMON PLAYER (1-16)	.50	.25	.05
☐ 1 Dale Brown BK CO	1.00	.50	.10
☐ 2 Ricky Blanton BK	.75	.35	.07
☐ 3 Jose Vargas BK	.75	.35	.07
☐ 4 Fess Irvin BK	.75	.35	.07
☐ 5 Darryl Joe BK	.75	.35	.07
☐ 6 Bernard Woodside BK	.50	.25	.05
☐ 7 Neboisha Bukumirovich BK	.50	.25	.05
☐ 8 Parker Griffin B	.50	.25	.05
☐ 9 Skip Bertman B CO	.50	.25	.05
☐ 10 Dan Kite B	.50	.25	.05
☐ 11 Russ Springer B	1.25	.60	.12
☐ 12 Ben McDonald B	5.00	2.50	.50
☐ 13 Richie Vasquez B	.50	.25	.05
☐ 14 Andy Galy B	.50	.25	.05
☐ 15 Pete Bush B	.50	.25	.05
☐ 16 Pete Maravich BK	5.00	2.50	.50

1988-89 LSU Police *

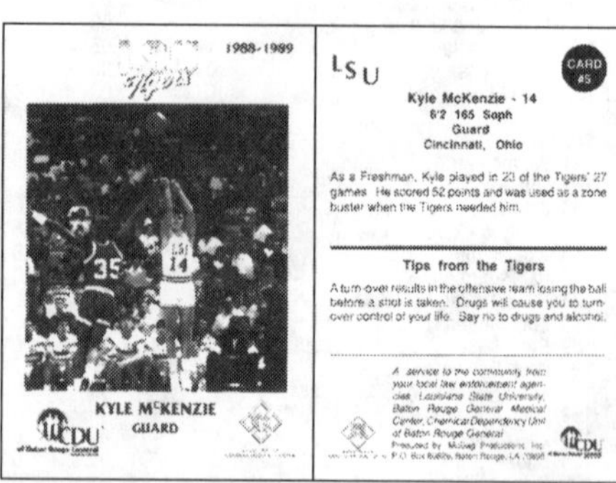

This 16-card set was sponsored by LSU, Baton Rouge General Medical Center, Chemical Dependency Unit of Baton Rouge, and various law enforcement agencies and was produced by McDag Productions. The General Medical Center and Chemical Dependency Unit logos adorn the bottom of both sides of the card. The cards were distributed in the Baton Rouge area by participating law enforcement agencies, the Medical Center, and the Chemical Dependency Unit. The cards measure 2 1/2" by 3 1/2" and are numbered on the back. The fronts feature borderless action or posed color photos of the players on white card stock. The title "LSU Tigers" is centered at the top of the card face, with player information below the picture. The back has additional player information and "Tips from the Tigers", which consist of an anti-drug or alcohol message. This set features athletes from basketball (1-8) and baseball (9-16). This set includes early cards of Chris Jackson, who plays in the

NBA, and of Ben McDonald, who pitched for the USA Olympic Baseball Team and the Baltimore Orioles.

	MINT	EXC	G-VG
COMPLETE SET (16)	12.00	6.00	1.20
COMMON PLAYER (1-16)	.50	.25	.05

	MINT	EXC	G-VG
☐ 1 Ricky Blanton	.75	.35	.07
☐ 2 Dale Brown CO	1.00	.50	.10
☐ 3 Wayne Simms	.50	.25	.05
☐ 4 Chris Jackson	3.00	1.50	.30
☐ 5 Kyle McKenzie	.50	.25	.05
☐ 6 Lyle Mouton	1.00	.50	.10
☐ 7 Vernel Singleton	1.00	.50	.10
☐ 8 Russell Grant	.50	.25	.05
☐ 9 Skip Bertman CO	.50	.25	.05
☐ 10 Ben McDonald	3.00	1.50	.30
☐ 11 Pete Bush	.50	.25	.05
☐ 12 Mike Bianco	.50	.25	.05
☐ 13 Craig Cala	.50	.25	.05
☐ 14 Mat Gruver	.50	.25	.05
☐ 15 Keith Osik	.50	.25	.05
☐ 16 Russell Springer	1.00	.50	.10

1990 LSU Promos *

This ten-card standard size (2 1/2" by 3 1/2") set features some of the best athletes of LSU's history. Since this set features athletes from different sports we have placed a two-letter abbreviation of the sport next to the player's name.

	MINT	EXC	G-VG
COMPLETE SET (10)	5.00	2.50	.50
COMMON PLAYER (1-10)	.50	.25	.05

	MINT	EXC	G-VG
☐ 1 Billy Cannon FB	.75	.35	.07
☐ 2 Chris Jackson BK	.75	.35	.07
☐ 3 Tiger Stadium	.50	.25	.05
☐ 4 Wendell Harris FB	.50	.25	.05
☐ 5 Bob Pettit BK	.75	.35	.07
☐ 6 Pete Maravich BK	1.00	.50	.10
☐ 7 Pete Maravich Center	.50	.25	.05
☐ 8 Dale Brown CO BK	.50	.25	.05
☐ 9 Mike V Mascot FB	.50	.25	.05
☐ 10 Joe Dean BK	.50	.25	.05

1990 LSU 200 *

This 200-card set was produced by Collegiate Collection and measures the standard size (2 1/2" by 3 1/2"). Although a few color photos are included, the front features mostly black and white player photos, with borders in the team's colors of gold and purple. All four corners of the picture are cut off. In purple lettering the school name appears above the picture, with the player's name at the bottom of the card face. In a horizontal format the back presents biographical information, career

summary, and statistics, on a white background with purple lettering and borders. The cards are numbered on the back.

	MINT	EXC	G-VG
COMPLETE SET (200)	20.00	10.00	2.00
COMMON PLAYER (1-200)	.10	.05	.01

	MINT	EXC	G-VG
☐ 1 Pete Maravich	.50	.25	.05
☐ 2 Chris Jackson	.30	.15	.03
☐ 3 Y.A. Tittle	.50	.25	.05
☐ 4 Ricky Blanton	.20	.10	.02
☐ 5 Charles Alexander	.15	.07	.01
☐ 6 Joe Dean	.10	.05	.01
☐ 7 Billy Cannon	.25	.12	.02
☐ 8 Dalton Hilliard	.25	.12	.02
☐ 9 Bert Jones	.25	.12	.02
☐ 10 Tommy Hodson	.30	.15	.03
☐ 11 Dale Brown CO	.20	.10	.02
☐ 12 Mike Archer	.15	.07	.01
☐ 13 Jimmy Taylor	.30	.15	.03
☐ 14 John Williams	.20	.10	.02
☐ 15 Brian Kinchen	.15	.07	.01
☐ 16 Chris Carrier	.10	.05	.01
☐ 17 Jess Fatheree	.10	.05	.01
☐ 18 Chris Jackson	.30	.15	.03
☐ 19 Orlando McDaniel	.10	.05	.01
☐ 20 Billy Hendrix	.10	.05	.01
☐ 21 Eddie Ray	.15	.07	.01
☐ 22 Glenn Hansen	.10	.05	.01
☐ 23 Bo Strange	.15	.07	.01
☐ 24 Eric Hill	.15	.07	.01
☐ 25 Leonard Mitchell	.15	.07	.01
☐ 26 Larry Shipp	.10	.05	.01
☐ 27 Malcolm Scott	.10	.05	.01
☐ 28 A.J. Duhe	.15	.07	.01
☐ 29 George Brancato	.10	.05	.01
☐ 30 Jim Roshso	.10	.05	.01
☐ 31 Karl Wilson	.10	.05	.01
☐ 32 Ethan Martin	.10	.05	.01
☐ 33 Julie Gross	.10	.05	.01
☐ 34 Lyman White	.10	.05	.01
☐ 35 Eddie Palubinskas	.15	.07	.01
☐ 36 Michael Brooks	.15	.07	.01
☐ 37 Frank Brian	.15	.07	.01
☐ 38 Gaynell Tinsley	.15	.07	.01
☐ 39 Mike Anderson	.10	.05	.01
☐ 40 Howard Carter	.15	.07	.01
☐ 41 Jerry Stovall	.25	.12	.02
☐ 42 Nikita Wilson	.15	.07	.01
☐ 43 Bill Fortier	.10	.05	.01
☐ 44 Mike V	.10	.05	.01
☐ 45 Richard Granier	.10	.05	.01
☐ 46 DeWayne Scales	.15	.07	.01
☐ 47 Pinky Rohm	.10	.05	.01
☐ 48 Bernie Moore Stadium	.10	.05	.01
☐ 49 Toby Caston	.15	.07	.01
☐ 50 Durand Macklin	.20	.10	.02
☐ 51 John Ed Bradley	.10	.05	.01
☐ 52 Mark Lumpkin	.10	.05	.01
☐ 53 Joyce Walker	.10	.05	.01
☐ 54 Bobby Lowther	.10	.05	.01
☐ 55 Al Sanders	.10	.05	.01
☐ 56 Curt Gore	.10	.05	.01
☐ 57 Eric Martin	.25	.12	.02
☐ 58 George Nattin	.10	.05	.01
☐ 59 Roland Barray	.10	.05	.01
☐ 60 Craig Duhe	.10	.05	.01
☐ 61 Maree Jackson	.10	.05	.01
☐ 62 Sparky Wade	.10	.05	.01
☐ 63 Karl Dunbar	.10	.05	.01
☐ 64 Mike Williams	.10	.05	.01
☐ 65 Al Green	.10	.05	.01

No.	Card			
☐ 66	Lew Sibley	.10	.05	.01
☐ 67	John Sage	.10	.05	.01
☐ 68	Craig Burns	.10	.05	.01
☐ 69	Schwoonda Williams	.10	.05	.01
☐ 70	Wendell Davis	.30	.15	.03
☐ 71	Dick Maile	.10	.05	.01
☐ 72	Kenny Bordelon	.15	.07	.01
☐ 73	Rusty Jackson	.10	.05	.01
☐ 74	Pete Maravich	.60	.30	.06
☐ 75	Garry James	.20	.10	.02
☐ 76	Lance Smith	.10	.05	.01
☐ 77	Willie Teal	.15	.07	.01
☐ 78	John Wood	.10	.05	.01
☐ 79	Mike Robichaux	.15	.07	.01
☐ 80	Earl Leggett	.15	.07	.01
☐ 81	Alex Box Stadium	.10	.05	.01
☐ 82	Steve Cassidy	.10	.05	.01
☐ 83	Kenny Konz	.15	.07	.01
☐ 84	Wendell Harris	.15	.07	.01
☐ 85	Alan Risher	.15	.07	.01
☐ 86	Gerald Keigley	.10	.05	.01
☐ 87	Robert Dugas	.10	.05	.01
☐ 88	Chris Williams	.10	.05	.01
☐ 89	John DeMarie	.15	.07	.01
☐ 90	Eddie Fuller	.15	.07	.01
☐ 91	Chris Jackson	.30	.15	.03
☐ 92	Bo Harris	.15	.07	.01
☐ 93	Mel Lyle	.10	.05	.01
☐ 94	Greg Jackson	.15	.07	.01
☐ 95	Liffort Hobley	.20	.10	.02
☐ 96	Shawn Burks	.10	.05	.01
☐ 97	David Browndyke	.15	.07	.01
☐ 98	Jerry Reynolds	.20	.10	.02
☐ 99	Eric Andolsek	.20	.10	.02
☐ 100	Director Card 1-99	.10	.05	.01
☐ 101	Jon Streete	.10	.05	.01
☐ 102	Barry Wilson	.10	.05	.01
☐ 103	Remi Prudhomme	.15	.07	.01
☐ 104	Abe Mickal	.15	.07	.01
☐ 105	Henry Thomas	.15	.07	.01
☐ 106	George Tarasovic	.15	.07	.01
☐ 107	Tiger Stadium	.10	.05	.01
☐ 108	Benjy Thibodeaux	.10	.05	.01
☐ 109	Jeffery Dale	.15	.07	.01
☐ 110	Sid Fournet	.15	.07	.01
☐ 111	John Adams	.10	.05	.01
☐ 112	Dennis Gaubatz	.15	.07	.01
☐ 113	Ben McDonald	.50	.25	.05
☐ 114	Joe Tuminello	.10	.05	.01
☐ 115	Billy Truax	.15	.07	.01
☐ 116	Warren Rabb	.15	.07	.01
☐ 117	Albert Richardson	.10	.05	.01
☐ 118	Jay Whitey	.10	.05	.01
☐ 119	Clinton Burrell	.15	.07	.01
☐ 120	Mike Miley	.15	.07	.01
☐ 121	Tommy Casanova	.20	.10	.02
☐ 122	George Bevan	.10	.05	.01
☐ 123	Binks Miciotto	.10	.05	.01
☐ 124	Joe Michaelson	.10	.05	.01
☐ 125	Mickey Mangham	.15	.07	.01
☐ 126	Ronnie Estay	.10	.05	.01
☐ 127	John Hazard	.10	.05	.01
☐ 128	Darrell Phillips	.10	.05	.01
☐ 129	Nacho Ablergamo	.10	.05	.01
☐ 130	John Garlington	.15	.07	.01
☐ 131	Arthur Cantrelle	.10	.05	.01
☐ 132	Monk Guillot	.10	.05	.01
☐ 133	Gene Knight	.10	.05	.01
☐ 134	Gerry Kent	.10	.05	.01
☐ 135	Ron Sancho	.15	.07	.01
☐ 136	Kenny Higgs	.20	.10	.02
☐ 137	Rip Collins	.10	.05	.01
☐ 138	Bob Pettit	.40	.20	.04
☐ 139	Mike Vincent	.10	.05	.01
☐ 140	Tyler LaFauci	.10	.05	.01
☐ 141	Richard Broks	.10	.05	.01
☐ 142	Billy Booth	.10	.05	.01
☐ 143	Brad Davis	.10	.05	.01
☐ 144	Roy Winston	.20	.10	.02
☐ 145	Andy Hamilton	.20	.10	.02
☐ 146	Rene Bourgeois	.10	.05	.01
☐ 147	Terry Robiskie	.15	.07	.01
☐ 148	Godfrey Zaunbrecher	.10	.05	.01
☐ 149	George Atiyeh	.10	.05	.01
☐ 150	Billy Hardin	.10	.05	.01
☐ 151	Jeff Wickersham	.20	.10	.02
☐ 152	Charlie McClendon	.15	.07	.01
☐ 153	Hokie Gajan	.20	.10	.02
☐ 154	Pete Maravich Center	.10	.05	.01
☐ 155	Bill Arnsparger	.15	.07	.01
☐ 156	Max Fuglar	.20	.10	.02
☐ 157	Greg Lafleur	.10	.05	.01
☐ 158	George Rice	.10	.05	.01
☐ 159	Dave McCormick	.10	.05	.01
☐ 160	Fred Miller	.10	.05	.01
☐ 161	Steve Van Buren	.25	.12	.02
☐ 162	Sid Bowman	.10	.05	.01
☐ 163	Wes Grisham	.10	.05	.01
☐ 164	Jeff Torrance	.10	.05	.01
☐ 165	Buddy Blair	.10	.05	.01
☐ 166	Doug Moreau	.15	.07	.01
☐ 167	Mike DeMarie	.10	.05	.01
☐ 168	James Britt	.10	.05	.01
☐ 169	Matt DeFrank	.10	.05	.01
☐ 170	Al Moreau	.10	.05	.01
☐ 171	Joe Bill Padcock	.10	.05	.01
☐ 172	Pat Screen	.10	.05	.01
☐ 173	Ralph Norwood	.10	.05	.01
☐ 174	Marcus Quinn	.10	.05	.01
☐ 175	Johnny Robinson	.20	.10	.02
☐ 176	Tony Moss	.10	.05	.01
☐ 177	Dan Alexander	.15	.07	.01
☐ 178	Norman Jefferson	.10	.05	.01
☐ 179	Bert Jones	.25	.12	.02
☐ 180	Joe LaBruzzo	.15	.07	.01
☐ 181	Jimmy Field	.10	.05	.01
☐ 182	David Woodley	.20	.10	.02
☐ 183	Paul Dietzel	.20	.10	.02
☐ 184	Abner Wimbley	.10	.05	.01
☐ 185	Steve Ensminger	.10	.05	.01
☐ 186	Carlos Carson	.20	.10	.02
☐ 187	Ken Kanauna Sr.	.10	.05	.01
☐ 188	Paul Ziegler	.10	.05	.01
☐ 189	Chris Jackson	.30	.15	.03
☐ 190	Chris Jackson	.30	.15	.03
☐ 191	W.T. Robinson Tennis	.10	.05	.01
☐ 192	Donnie Leaycraft	.10	.05	.01
☐ 193	Fernando Perez	.10	.05	.01
☐ 194	Steve Faulk	.10	.05	.01
☐ 195	Warren Capone	.15	.07	.01
☐ 196	Howard Carter	.15	.07	.01
☐ 197	Glenn Hansen	.10	.05	.01
☐ 198	Durand Macklin	.15	.07	.01
☐ 199	Sam Grezaffi	.15	.07	.01
☐ 200	Director Card	.15	.07	.01

1987-88 Maine Police *

Basketball

KIDS & KOPS
Tip *No. 13* from the
BLACK BEARS

DUMB FOULS

Going along with the crowd is dumb. Drug use & vandalism are crimes that hurt you and other people.

Dumb fouls are those caused by playing defense with the hands instead of the mind.

Bangor Daily News Charities

This 14-card set of Maine Black Bears is part of a "Kids and Kops" promotion, and one card was printed each Saturday in the Bangor Daily News. The cards measure approximately 2 1/2" by 4". The fronts feature posed color player photos, outlined by a black border on white card stock. Player information is given below the picture in the lower left corner, with a facsimile autograph in turquoise in the lower right corner. The cards were to be collected from any participating police officer. Once five cards had been collected (including card number 1), they could be turned in at a police station for a University of Maine ID card, which permitted free admission to selected university activities. When all 14 cards had been collected, they could be turned in at a police station to register for the Grand Prize drawing (bicycle) and to pick up a free "Kids and Kops" tee-shirt. The backs have tips in the form of an anti-drug or alcohol message and logos of Burger King, University of Maine, and Pepsi across the bottom. With the exception of the rules card, the cards are numbered on the back. Sports represented in this set include hockey (2), basketball (3, 9, 13), tennis (4), baseball (5), swimming (6), soccer (7), track (8), football (10), field hockey (11), and softball (12).

	MINT	EXC	G-VG
COMPLETE SET (14)	15.00	7.50	1.50
COMMON PLAYER (1-14)	1.00	.50	.10
☐ 1 Bananas (Mascot) and K.C. Jones	5.00	2.50	.50
☐ 2 Mike McHugh	1.00	.50	.10
☐ 3 Matt Rossignol	1.00	.50	.10
☐ 4 Cindy Sprague	1.00	.50	.10
☐ 5 Gary LaPierre	1.00	.50	.10
☐ 6 Dana Billington	1.00	.50	.10
☐ 7 Scott Atherley	1.00	.50	.10
☐ 8 Elke Brutsaert	1.00	.50	.10
☐ 9 Elizabeth(Liz) Coffin	1.00	.50	.10
☐ 10 David Ingalls	1.00	.50	.10
☐ 11 Wendy J. Nadeau	1.00	.50	.10
☐ 12 Stacy Caron	1.00	.50	.10
☐ 13 Amadou Coco Barry	1.00	.50	.10
☐ xx Kids and Kops Rules	1.00	.50	.10

1982-83 Marquette Lite Beer

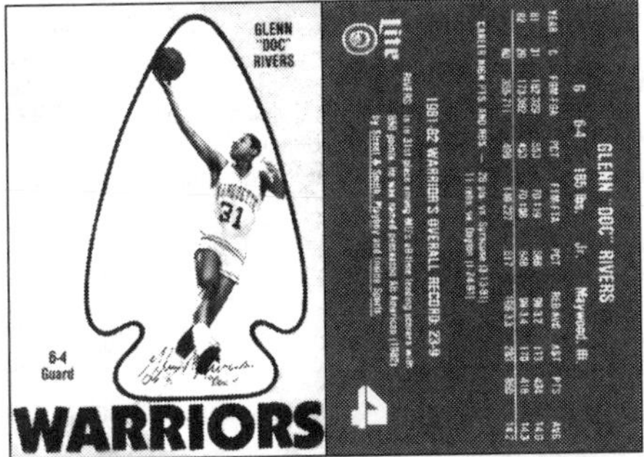

This 16-card set measures the standard card size, 2 1/2" by 3 1/2", and was issued in conjunction with Lite Beer. The front of the card features a black and white action photo inside an "arrowhead" against a pale yellow background, surrounded by the player's name, height, and position, with the team name ("Warriors") emblazoned across the bottom. The back has biographical and statistical information. The set also features an early card of Glenn "Doc" Rivers.

	MINT	EXC	G-VG
COMPLETE SET (16)	18.00	9.00	1.80
COMMON PLAYER (1-16)	1.00	.50	.10
☐ 1 Ric Cobb CO	2.00	1.00	.20
☐ 2 Dwayne"DJ" Johnson	1.00	.50	.10
☐ 3 Mandy Johnson	1.00	.50	.10
☐ 4 Vic Lazzaretti	1.00	.50	.10
☐ 5 Rick Majerus CO	4.00	2.00	.40
☐ 6 Marc Marotta	1.00	.50	.10
☐ 7 Lloyd Moore	1.00	.50	.10
☐ 8 Paul Newman	1.00	.50	.10
☐ 9 Tom Pipines	1.00	.50	.10
☐ 10 Hank Raymonds CO	1.50	.75	.15
☐ 11 Terry Reason	1.00	.50	.10
☐ 12 Glenn"Doc" Rivers	8.00	4.00	.80
☐ 13 Terrell Schlundt	2.00	1.00	.20
☐ 14 Don Smolinski	1.00	.50	.10
☐ 15 Kerry Trotter	1.00	.50	.10
☐ xx Title Card	1.50	.75	.15

1988-89 Maryland Police

This set consists of 12 cards, measuring the standard card size 2 1/2" by 3 1/2". The company name of the sponsor, Group Health Association, appears in the right corner on the front of the card. The action color photo on the front is bordered on three sides by Maryland's colors (red and yellow), with the player's name, uniform number, classification, and position listed below the photo. The Terrapin logo in the lower left hand corner completes the front of the card. The back includes biographical information and a basketball tip. For convenience the cards are ordered and numbered below in alphabetical order. The set features first cards of future NBA players Tony Massenburg, Jerrod Mustaf, and Walt Williams.

	MINT	EXC	G-VG
COMPLETE SET (12)	14.00	7.00	1.40
COMMON PLAYER (1-12)	.60	.30	.06
☐ 1 Vincent Broadnax 40	.60	.30	.06
☐ 2 Dave Dickerson 23	.60	.30	.06
☐ 3 John Johnson 21	.60	.30	.06
☐ 4 Matt Kaluzienski 13	.60	.30	.06
☐ 5 Mitch Kasoff 5	.60	.30	.06
☐ 6 Cedric Lewis 43	1.00	.50	.10
☐ 7 Jesse Martin 14	.60	.30	.06
☐ 8 Tony Massenburg 25	2.00	1.00	.20
☐ 9 Jerrod Mustaf 32	3.00	1.50	.30
☐ 10 Greg Nared 22	.60	.30	.06
☐ 11 Bob Wade CO	.75	.35	.07
☐ 12 Walt Williams 42	6.00	3.00	.60

1989 McNeese State *

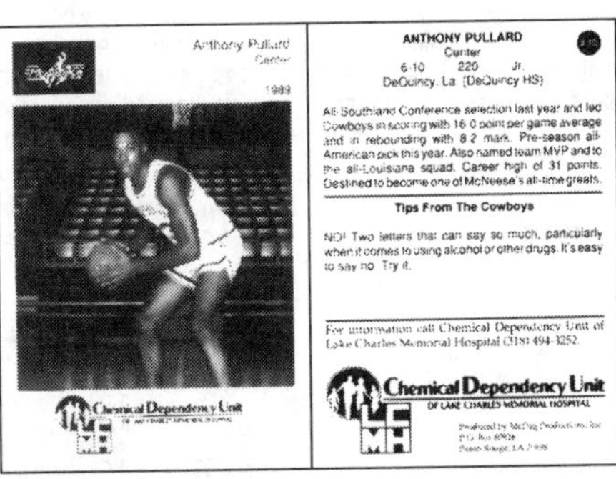

This 16-card set was sponsored by the Behavioral Health Unit of Lake Charles Memorial Hospital, and the sponsor's logo appears at the bottom of both sides of the card. The cards measure the standard size (2 1/2" by 3 1/2"); they were produced by McDag Productions. The front features a color posed player photo, with the McNeese logo and player information in the upper corners. The back presents biographical information and "Tips from The Cowboys," which consist of mental health tips. The cards are numbered on the back. Sports represented in this set include basketball (1-6, 9-12), softball (7), golf (8), and baseball (13-15).

	MINT	EXC	G-VG
COMPLETE SET (16)	8.00	4.00	.80
COMMON PLAYER (1-16)	.50	.25	.05
☐ 1 Kevin Williams	1.00	.50	.10
☐ 2 Terry Griggley	.50	.25	.05
☐ 3 Tab Harris	.50	.25	.05
☐ 4 Chandra Davis	.75	.35	.07
☐ 5 Tom McGrath	.50	.25	.05
☐ 6 Angie Perry	.75	.35	.07
☐ 7 Christine Lee	.50	.25	.05
☐ 8 Lawrence David	.50	.25	.05
☐ 9 Michael Cutright	1.00	.50	.10
☐ 10 Anthony Pullard	1.50	.75	.15
☐ 11 Mark Thompson	.50	.25	.05
☐ 12 Kim Turner	.50	.25	.05
☐ 13 Steve Boulet	.50	.25	.05
☐ 14 Charlie Phillips	.50	.25	.05
☐ 15 Mark Bowling	.50	.25	.05
☐ 16 David J. Drez Team Physician	.50	.25	.05

1988-89 Michigan Nike

This 16-card set was sponsored by Nike and distributed at Michigan Wolverine games during the 1988-89 season. The cards measure 2 1/2" by 3 1/2". The front features a color action photo, with a yellow border on the left side and purple borders on the right and below. The sponsor logo appears in the upper right corner, and player information is given in the bottom border. The back has biographical information and an anti-drug tip. The cards are unnumbered and are checklisted below in alphabetical order.

	MINT	EXC	G-VG
COMPLETE SET (16)	50.00	25.00	5.00
COMMON PLAYER (1-16)	2.00	1.00	.20
☐ 1 Demetrius Calip	4.00	2.00	.40
☐ 2 Bill Frieder CO	3.00	1.50	.30
☐ 3 Mike Griffin	2.00	1.00	.20
☐ 4 Sean Higgins	6.00	3.00	.60
☐ 5 Mark Hughes	2.00	1.00	.20
☐ 6 Marc Koenig	2.00	1.00	.20
☐ 7 Terry Mills	9.00	4.50	.90
☐ 8 J.P. Oosterbaan	2.00	1.00	.20
☐ 9 Rob Pelinka	2.00	1.00	.20
☐ 10 Glen Rice	25.00	12.50	2.50
☐ 11 Eric Riley	3.00	1.50	.30
☐ 12 Rumeal Robinson	10.00	5.00	1.00
☐ 13 Chris Seter	2.00	1.00	.20
☐ 14 Kirk Taylor	2.00	1.00	.20
☐ 15 Loy Vaught	8.00	4.00	.80
☐ 16 James Voskuil	2.00	1.00	.20

1989 Michigan Wolverines

This 17-card set measures approximately 2 3/8" by 4" and is numbered on the back. The set features members of the 1989 Michigan Wolverines NCAA Championship basketball team. The front features a color photo, and the school and team name are printed in the school's colors (purple and yellow) on the top of the card. Below the photo appears the team logo (lower left hand corner) and the player's name. The back has biographical information (black lettering on white card stock). Future NBA players Demetrius Calip, Sean Higgins, Terry Mills, Glen Rice, Rumeal Robinson, and Loy Vaught are featured in this set.

	MINT	EXC	G-VG
COMPLETE SET (17)	18.00	9.00	1.80
COMMON PLAYER (1-17)	1.00	.50	.10
☐ 1 Steve Fisher CO	1.50	.75	.15
☐ 2 Brian Dutcher	1.00	.50	.10
☐ 3 Kirk Taylor	1.00	.50	.10
☐ 4 Chris Seter	1.00	.50	.10
☐ 5 Glen Rice	8.00	4.00	.80
☐ 6 Rob Pelinka	1.00	.50	.10
☐ 7 Rumeal Robinson	3.00	1.50	.30
☐ 8 Terry Mills	3.00	1.50	.30
☐ 9 Demetrius Calip	1.50	.75	.15
☐ 10 James Voskull	1.00	.50	.10
☐ 11 Loy Vaught	2.50	1.25	.25
☐ 12 J.P. Oosterbaan	1.00	.50	.10
☐ 13 Sean Higgins	2.50	1.25	.25
☐ 14 Marc Koenig	1.00	.50	.10
☐ 15 Mark Hughes	1.00	.50	.10
☐ 16 Eric Riley	1.00	.50	.10
☐ 17 Mike Griffin	1.00	.50	.10

1991 Michigan 56 *

This 56-card multi-sport set was issued by College Classics and measures the standard size 2 1/2" by 3 1/2". The fronts feature a mix of color or black and white player photos. The yellow borders (on white card stock) and blue lettering reflect the team's colors. In the cut-out corners appear a Michigan Wolverine football helmet (on the football cards) or an "M" (for other sports). The backs have a career summary in a light blue box with orange borders, with an "M" in the upper left corner. This set features a card of Gerald Ford, center for the Wolverine football squad from 1932-34. Ford autographed 200 of his cards, one of which was to be included in each of the 200 cases of 50 sets. A letter of authenticity on Gerald Ford stationery accompanies each Ford autographed card. All 200 cases were reportedly purchased by American Card Investors. The cards are unnumbered and we have checklisted them below according to alphabetical order.

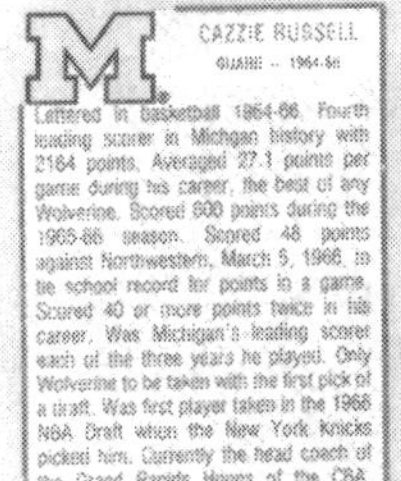

	MINT	EXC	G-VG
COMPLETE SET (56)	15.00	7.50	1.50
COMMON PLAYER (1-56)	.30	.15	.03
☐ 1 Jim Abbott	1.25	.60	.12
☐ 2 Moby Benedict	.30	.15	.03
☐ 3 Red Berenson	.50	.25	.05
☐ 4 John Blum	.30	.15	.03
☐ 5 Marty Bodnar	.30	.15	.03
☐ 6 Dave Brown	.50	.25	.05
☐ 7 M.C. Burton	.30	.15	.03
☐ 8 Andy Cannavino	.30	.15	.03
☐ 9 Anthony Carter	.90	.45	.09
☐ 10 Gil Chapman	.30	.15	.03
☐ 11 Bob Chappuis	.30	.15	.03
☐ 12 Casey Close	.50	.25	.05
☐ 13 Evan Cooper	.30	.15	.03
☐ 14 Tom Curtis	.30	.15	.03
☐ 15 Diane Dietz	.30	.15	.03
☐ 16 Dean Dingman	.30	.15	.03
☐ 17 Mark Donahue	.30	.15	.03
☐ 18 Donald Dufek	.50	.25	.05
☐ 19 Bump Elliott	.50	.25	.05
☐ 20 Greg Everson	.30	.15	.03
☐ 21 Gerald Ford	1.00	.50	.10
☐ 22 Wally Grant	.30	.15	.03
☐ 23 Curtis Greer	.50	.25	.05
☐ 24 Ali Haji-Sheikh	.50	.25	.05
☐ 25 Elroy Hirsch	.75	.35	.07
☐ 26 Stefan Humphries	.30	.15	.03
☐ 27 Phil Hubbard	.50	.25	.05
☐ 28 Ron Johnson	.50	.25	.05
☐ 29 Brad Jones	.30	.15	.03
☐ 30 Eric Kattus	.50	.25	.05
☐ 31 Ron Kramer	.50	.25	.05
☐ 32 Barry Larkin	1.50	.75	.15
☐ 33 Michael Leach	.30	.15	.03
☐ 34 Jim Mandich	.50	.25	.05
☐ 35 Wilf Martin	.30	.15	.03
☐ 36 Tim McCormick	.50	.25	.05
☐ 37 Hal Morris	1.00	.50	.10
☐ 38 Jeff Norton	.30	.15	.03
☐ 39 Frank Nunley	.30	.15	.03
☐ 40 Calvin O'Neal	.50	.25	.05
☐ 41 Steve Ontiveros	.50	.25	.05
☐ 42 Bennie Oosterbaan	.30	.15	.03
☐ 43 Richard Rellford	.30	.15	.03
☐ 44 Steve Richmond	.30	.15	.03
☐ 45 Cazzie Russell	.75	.35	.07
☐ 46 Chris Sabo	1.00	.50	.10
☐ 47 Alicia Seegert	.30	.15	.03
☐ 48 Warren Sharples	.30	.15	.03
☐ 49 Ted Sizemore	.50	.25	.05
☐ 50 Lary Sorensen	.50	.25	.05
☐ 51 Bob Timberlake	.50	.25	.05
☐ 52 Rudy Tomjanovich	.75	.35	.07
☐ 53 John Wangler	.50	.25	.05
☐ 54 Gary Wayne	.30	.15	.03
☐ 55 Tripp Welborne	.50	.25	.05
☐ 56 Wistert Brothers	.30	.15	.03

1990-91 Michigan State Promos *

This ten-card standard size (2 1/2" by 3 1/2") set features some of the great athletes from Michigan State History. Most of the

cards in the set feature an action photograph on the front of the card along with either statistical or biographical information on the back of the card. Since this set involves more than one sport we have put a two-letter abbreviation to indicate the sport played.

	MINT	EXC	G-VG
COMPLETE SET (10)	5.00	2.50	.50
COMMON PLAYER (1-10)	.50	.25	.05
☐ 1 Ron Scott HK	.50	.25	.05
☐ 2 Steve Garvey BB	.75	.35	.07
☐ 3 Percy Snow FB	.60	.30	.06
☐ 4 Magic Johnson BK	1.50	.75	.15
☐ 5 Andre Rison FB	1.00	.50	.10
☐ 6 Lorenzo White FB	.60	.30	.06
☐ 7 Kirk Gibson FB/BB	.75	.35	.07
☐ 8 Tony Mandarich FB	.60	.30	.06
☐ 9 Gregory Kelser BK	.50	.25	.05
☐ 10 Kip Miller HK	.60	.30	.06

1990-91 Michigan State 200 *

This 200-card set was produced by Collegiate Collection and measures the standard size (2 1/2" by 3 1/2"). The fronts feature black and white shots for earlier players or color shots for later players, with borders in the team's colors white and green. The card design gives the impression that all four corners of the pictures are cut off. In green lettering the school name appears above the picture, with the player's name at the bottom of the card face. In a horizontal format the back presents biographical information and career summary, on a white background with green lettering and borders. The cards are numbered on the back.

	MINT	EXC	G-VG
COMPLETE SET (200)	20.00	10.00	2.00
COMMON PLAYER (1-200)	.10	.05	.01

☐ 1 Ray Stachowicvz	.10	.05	.01
☐ 2 Larry Fowler	.10	.05	.01
☐ 3 Allen Brenner	.10	.05	.01
☐ 4 Greg Montgomery	.10	.05	.01
☐ 5 Ron Goovert	.10	.05	.01
☐ 6 Ed Bagdon	.10	.05	.01
☐ 7 Carl(Buck) Nystrom	.10	.05	.01
☐ 8 Earl Lattimer	.10	.05	.01
☐ 9 Bob Kula	.10	.05	.01
☐ 10 James Ellis	.10	.05	.01
☐ 11 Brad Van Pelt	.20	.10	.02
☐ 12 Andre Rison	.40	.20	.04
☐ 13 Sherman Lewis	.20	.10	.02
☐ 14 Eric Allen	.20	.10	.02
☐ 15 Robert Apisa	.20	.10	.02
☐ 16 Earl Morrall	.30	.15	.03
☐ 17 Danny Litwhiler	.15	.07	.01
☐ 18 Harold Lucas	.10	.05	.01
☐ 19 Lorenzo White	.30	.15	.03
☐ 20 Dorne Dibble	.15	.07	.01
☐ 21 Ronald Saul	.15	.07	.01
☐ 22 Ed Budde	.20	.10	.02
☐ 23 Gene Washington	.20	.10	.02
☐ 24 John S. Pingel	.10	.05	.01
☐ 25 Morten Andersen	.25	.12	.02
☐ 26 Lynn Chandnois	.15	.07	.01
☐ 27 Don Coleman	.10	.05	.01
☐ 28 Dave Behrman	.15	.07	.01
☐ 29 Bill Simpson	.15	.07	.01
☐ 30 LeRoy Bolden	.10	.05	.01
☐ 31 Lorenzo White	.30	.15	.03
☐ 32 Sidney P. Wagner	.10	.05	.01
☐ 33 Ellis Duckett	.10	.05	.01
☐ 34 Dick Tamburo	.15	.07	.01
☐ 35 Gerald Planutis	.10	.05	.01
☐ 36 Steve Juday	.20	.10	.02
☐ 37 Everett Grandelius	.15	.07	.01
☐ 38 Spartans All American	.15	.07	.01
☐ 39 Ray Stachowicz	.10	.05	.01
☐ 40 Mark Brammer	.15	.07	.01
☐ 41 James Burroughs	.15	.07	.01
☐ 42 Harlon Barnett	.20	.10	.02
☐ 43 Charles(Bubba) Smith	.50	.25	.05
☐ 44 Percy Snow	.30	.15	.03
☐ 45 Norman Masters	.10	.05	.01
☐ 46 Jerry West	.10	.05	.01
☐ 47 Williams and Daugherty	.15	.07	.01
☐ 48 Tom Yewcic	.15	.07	.01
☐ 49 Kirk Gibson	.25	.12	.02
☐ 50 Clinton Jones	.20	.10	.02
☐ 51 Frank E. Pellerin	.10	.05	.01
☐ 52 Don(Zippy) Thompson	.10	.05	.01
☐ 53 Kirk Gibson	.25	.12	.02
☐ 54 Edward Erickson	.10	.05	.01
☐ 55 Doug Roberts	.10	.05	.01
☐ 56 Percy Snow	.30	.15	.03
☐ 57 Dick Idzkowski	.10	.05	.01
☐ 58 Robert W.(Bob) Carey	.15	.07	.01
☐ 59 Clarence Munn	.15	.07	.01
☐ 60 Dan Currie	.15	.07	.01
☐ 61 Al Dorow	.15	.07	.01
☐ 62 Amo Bessone	.10	.05	.01
☐ 63 Joseph DeLamielleure	.20	.10	.02
☐ 64 Tom Ross	.10	.05	.01
☐ 65 Steve Preston	.10	.05	.01
☐ 66 Gibson and Garvey	.25	.12	.02
☐ 67 Eric Allen	.15	.07	.01
☐ 68 George Smith	.10	.05	.01
☐ 69 John Chandik	.10	.05	.01
☐ 70 Cordell Ross	.10	.05	.01
☐ 71 George Saimes	.20	.10	.02
☐ 72 Walt Kowalczyk	.15	.07	.01
☐ 73 Billy Joe Dupree	.25	.12	.02
☐ 74 Phil Fulton	.10	.05	.01
☐ 75 Weldon Olson	.10	.05	.01
☐ 76 Kirk Gibson	.25	.12	.02
☐ 77 Andre Rison	.40	.20	.04
☐ 78 Dean Look	.10	.05	.01
☐ 79 Hugh(Duffy) Daugherty	.15	.07	.01
☐ 80 Don McAuliffe	.20	.10	.02
☐ 81 Ronald Curl	.10	.05	.01
☐ 82 Percy Snow	.30	.15	.03
☐ 83 Carl Banks	.35	.17	.03
☐ 84 Joe Selinger	.10	.05	.01
☐ 85 Mel Behney	.15	.07	.01
☐ 86 Lorenzo White	.30	.15	.03
☐ 87 Ron Pruitt	.10	.05	.01
☐ 88 George Webster	.20	.10	.02
☐ 89 Tony Mandarich	.20	.10	.02
☐ 90 Ray Stachowicz	.10	.05	.01
☐ 91 Blake Miller	.10	.05	.01
☐ 92 Dupree, Van Pelt, and Daugherty	.20	.10	.02
☐ 93 Morten Andersen	.25	.12	.02
☐ 94 Kevin Dalson	.10	.05	.01
☐ 95 Norm Barnes	.10	.05	.01
☐ 96 Andre Rison	.40	.20	.04
☐ 97 Craig Simpson	.20	.10	.02
☐ 98 Kirk Gibson	.25	.12	.02
☐ 99 Ralph Mojsiejenko	.15	.07	.01
☐ 100 Director Card 1-99	.10	.05	.01
☐ 101 Michael Robinson	.10	.05	.01
☐ 102 Jack Quiggle	.10	.05	.01
☐ 103 Robert Anderegg	.10	.05	.01
☐ 104 Rick Miller	.15	.07	.01
☐ 105 Steve Garvey	.30	.15	.03
☐ 106 John Herman Kobs	.10	.05	.01
☐ 107 Steve Garvey	.30	.15	.03
☐ 108 Vernon Carr	.10	.05	.01
☐ 109 Albert R. Ferrari	.10	.05	.01
☐ 110 Lance Olson	.10	.05	.01
☐ 111 Lee Lafayette	.10	.05	.01
☐ 112 Gregory Kelser	.15	.07	.01
☐ 113 Stan Washington	.10	.05	.01
☐ 114 Ron Perranoski	.20	.10	.02
☐ 115 Doug Volmar	.10	.05	.01
☐ 116 Robert Clancy	.10	.05	.01
☐ 117 Bob Boyd	.15	.07	.01
☐ 118 Lindsay Hairston	.15	.07	.01
☐ 119 Kevin Willis	.35	.17	.03
☐ 120 Bill Rapchak	.10	.05	.01
☐ 121 Marcus Sanders	.10	.05	.01
☐ 122 Mike Brkovich	.15	.07	.01
☐ 123 Jay Vincent	.15	.07	.01
☐ 124 Ron Scott	.15	.07	.01
☐ 125 Craig Simpson	.15	.07	.01
☐ 126 Mike Davidson	.10	.05	.01
☐ 127 Jim Watt	.10	.05	.01
☐ 128 Johnny Green	.15	.07	.01
☐ 129 Robert Chapman	.10	.05	.01
☐ 130 Pete Gent	.20	.10	.02
☐ 131 Magic Johnson	.75	.35	.07
☐ 132 Gregory Kelser	.20	.10	.02
☐ 133 Magic Johnson	.75	.35	.07
☐ 134 Bobby Reynolds	.10	.05	.01
☐ 135 Joe Murphy	.35	.17	.03
☐ 136 Mike Donnelly	.15	.07	.01
☐ 137 Bob Essensa	.25	.12	.02
☐ 138 Kevin Smith	.10	.05	.01
☐ 139 Kirk Manns	.10	.05	.01
☐ 140 Scott Skiles	.25	.12	.02
☐ 141 Matthew Aitch	.10	.05	.01
☐ 142 Rudy Benjamin	.10	.05	.01
☐ 143 Michael Robinson	.10	.05	.01
☐ 144 Kip Miller	.25	.12	.02
☐ 145 Kelly Miller	.25	.12	.02
☐ 146 Ron Mason	.15	.07	.01
☐ 147 Dan McFall	.10	.05	.01
☐ 148 Sam Vincent	.15	.07	.01
☐ 149 Carlton Valentine	.10	.05	.01
☐ 150 Ron Charles	.15	.07	.01
☐ 151 John Bennington	.10	.05	.01
☐ 152 Scott Skiles	.25	.12	.02
☐ 153 William Kilgore	.10	.05	.01
☐ 154 Dick Holmes	.10	.05	.01
☐ 155 Steven Colp	.10	.05	.01
☐ 156 Robert Ellis	.10	.05	.01
☐ 157 Brian Wolcott	.10	.05	.01
☐ 158 Ken Redfield	.10	.05	.01
☐ 159 Jud Heathcote	.15	.07	.01
☐ 160 Dave Fahs	.10	.05	.01
☐ 161 Pete Newell	.25	.12	.02
☐ 162 Larry Polec	.10	.05	.01
☐ 163 Kevin Willis	.25	.12	.02
☐ 164 Gaye Cooley	.10	.05	.01
☐ 165 Richard Vary	.10	.05	.01
☐ 166 Al Weston	.10	.05	.01
☐ 167 Scott Makarewicz	.10	.05	.01
☐ 168 Darryl Johnson	.15	.07	.01
☐ 169 Derek Perry	.10	.05	.01
☐ 170 Ralph Simpson	.20	.10	.02
☐ 171 Terry Furlow	.15	.07	.01
☐ 172 Forrest Anderson	.10	.05	.01
☐ 173 Ted Williams	.15	.07	.01
☐ 174 Dan Masteller	.10	.05	.01
☐ 175 Brad Lamont Jr.	.10	.05	.01
☐ 176 Steve Garvey	.30	.15	.03
☐ 177 Mike Eddington	.10	.05	.01
☐ 178 Jud Heathcote	.15	.07	.01
☐ 179 Kevin Willis	.25	.12	.02
☐ 180 Ben Van Alstyne	.10	.05	.01
☐ 181 Chet Aubuchon	.15	.07	.01
☐ 182 Magic Johnson	.75	.35	.07
☐ 183 Larry Hedden	.10	.05	.01
☐ 184 Larry Ike	.10	.05	.01
☐ 185 Frank Kush	.15	.07	.01
☐ 186 Magic Johnson	.75	.35	.07
☐ 187 Mitch Messier	.15	.07	.01

☐ 188 Julius McCoy	.10	.05	.01
☐ 189 Magic Johnson	.75	.35	.07
☐ 190 Forrest Anderson	.15	.07	.01
☐ 191 Gus Ganakas	.15	.07	.01
☐ 192 Jay Vincent	.15	.07	.01
☐ 193 Horace Walker	.10	.05	.01
☐ 194 Magic Johnson	.75	.35	.07
☐ 195 Tom Smith	.10	.05	.01
☐ 196 Don McSween	.10	.05	.01
☐ 197 Rod Brind'Amour	.35	.17	.03
☐ 198 Sam Vincent	.15	.07	.01
☐ 199 Terry Donnelly	.10	.05	.01
☐ 200 Director Card 101-199	.15	.07	.01

1991 Michigan State

This 20-card set was produced by Collegiate Collection and features the 1990-91 Michigan State Spartan basketball team. The cards measure the standard size (2 1/2" by 3 1/2"). The fronts display color action player photos, bordered in white and green, and with the corners of the pictures cut off. In green print on a white background, the backs have biography, statistics, and player profile. The cards are numbered on the back. This set features a card of All-American Steve Smith.

	MINT	EXC	G-VG
COMPLETE SET (20)	20.00	10.00	2.00
COMMON PLAYER (1-20)	.75	.35	.07
☐ 1 Jud Heathcote CO	1.00	.50	.10
☐ 2 Matt Hofkamp	.75	.35	.07
☐ 3 Parish Hickman	1.00	.50	.10
☐ 4 Matt Steigenga	2.50	1.25	.25
☐ 5 Dwayne Stephens	.75	.35	.07
☐ 6 Jon Zulauf	.75	.35	.07
☐ 7 Shawn Respert	.75	.35	.07
☐ 8 Jeff Casler	.75	.35	.07
☐ 9 Steve Smith	10.00	5.00	1.00
☐ 10 Andy Penick	.75	.35	.07
☐ 11 Mark Montgomery	1.00	.50	.10
☐ 12 Kris Weshinskey	.75	.35	.07
☐ 13 Jack Breslin Center	.75	.35	.07
☐ 14 Spartan Captains Steve Smith Matt Steigenga	2.50	1.25	.25
☐ 15 Brian Gregory CO	.75	.35	.07
☐ 16 Jim Boylen CO	.75	.35	.07
☐ 17 Stan Joplin CO	.75	.35	.07
☐ 18 Tom Izzo CO	.75	.35	.07
☐ 19 Mike Peplowski	1.00	.50	.10
☐ 20 Team Photo	1.00	.50	.10

1988-89 Missouri

This 16-card set of Missouri Tigers was sponsored by Kodak, KMIZ-17 TV, and Columbia Photo. The cards measure the standard, 2 1/2" by 3 1/2". The cards were originally issued in four-card sheets. The front features a color photo, with borders above and below in the school's colors (black and yellow). The player's name, uniform number, classification, and position appear below the picture, with a tiger pawprint in the lower left hand corner. Biographical information and "tips for better sports pictures" are provided on the card backs. The first three panels of cards were given out at games between Missouri and Oklahoma State (January 21), Nebraska (February 19), and Colorado. The final panel was available at Columbia Photo and Video sometime after March 4. For convenience the cards are ordered and numbered alphabetically by player's name.

	MINT	EXC	G-VG
COMPLETE SET (16)	40.00	20.00	4.00
COMMON PLAYER (1-16)	1.00	.50	.10
☐ 1 Nathan Buntin	2.00	1.00	.20
☐ 2 Derrick Chievous PRO	3.00	1.50	.30
☐ 3 Greg Church	1.00	.50	.10
☐ 4 Jamal Coleman	1.00	.50	.10
☐ 5 Jim Horton	1.00	.50	.10
☐ 6 Byron Irvin	4.00	2.00	.40
☐ 7 Gary Leonard	3.00	1.50	.30
☐ 8 John McIntyre	1.00	.50	.10
☐ 9 Anthony Peeler	10.00	5.00	1.00
☐ 10 Mike Sandbothe	1.00	.50	.10
☐ 11 Doug Smith	12.00	6.00	1.20
☐ 12 Norm Stewart CO	2.00	1.00	.20
☐ 13 Steve Stipanovich	3.00	1.50	.30
☐ 14 Jon Sundvold PRO	2.00	1.00	.20
☐ 15 Bradd Sutton	1.00	.50	.10
☐ 16 Mike Wawrzyniak	1.00	.50	.10

1989-90 Missouri

This 16-card set was originally issued on three four-card sheets and sponsored by Kodak, Jiffy Lube, and Columbia Photo and Video. The cards measure the standard 2 1/2" by 3 1/2". The front has an action color photo, with borders in the school's colors (yellow and black). The player's name, classification, and position appear below the card, with a tiger pawprint in the lower left hand corner. The back has biographical information and a tip for better sports pictures. For convenience the cards are ordered and numbered alphabetically by player's name.

	MINT	EXC	G-VG
COMPLETE SET (16)	25.00	12.50	2.50
COMMON PLAYER (1-16)	1.00	.50	.10
☐ 1 Nathan Buntin 22	1.50	.75	.15
☐ 2 John Burns 33	1.00	.50	.10
☐ 3 Jamal Coleman 32	1.50	.75	.15
☐ 4 Lee Coward 4	1.50	.75	.15
☐ 5 Larry Drew	2.00	1.00	.20
☐ 6 Travis Ford 5	2.00	1.00	.20
☐ 7 Chris Heller 41	1.00	.50	.10
☐ 8 Jim Horton 13	1.00	.50	.10
☐ 9 John McIntyre 23	1.00	.50	.10
☐ 10 Anthony Peeler 44	5.00	2.50	.50
☐ 11 Todd Satalowich 54	1.00	.50	.10
☐ 12 Doug Smith 34	7.00	3.50	.70
☐ 13 Norm Stewart CO	1.50	.75	.15
☐ 14 Steve Stipanovich	2.00	1.00	.20
☐ 15 Bradd Sutton 35	1.00	.50	.10
☐ 16 Jeff Warren 45	1.00	.50	.10

1990-91 Missouri

This 16-card set was issued in four four-card strips and given away at four non-conference games last season. The standard-size (2 1/2" by 3 1/2") cards are similar in design to the previous year's issue, with color action photos bordered in the school's colors (yellow and black). One difference is that "Missouri Tigers" appears in white rather than yellow lettering. The backs contain biographical information and Missouri Basketball Fun Facts. The cards are unnumbered and checklisted below in alphabetical order.

	MINT	EXC	G-VG
COMPLETE SET (16)	20.00	10.00	2.00
COMMON PLAYER (1-16)	.75	.35	.07
☐ 1 Melvin Booker	.75	.35	.07
☐ 2 John Brown Tiger of the Past	1.50	.75	.15
☐ 3 John Burns	.75	.35	.07
☐ 4 Jamal Coleman	1.25	.60	.12
☐ 5 Jevon Crudup	1.25	.60	.12
☐ 6 Derek Dunham	.75	.35	.07
☐ 7 Lamont Frazier	.75	.35	.07
☐ 8 Jed Frost	.75	.35	.07
☐ 9 Chris Heller	.75	.35	.07
☐ 10 Jim Horton	.75	.35	.07
☐ 11 Anthony Peeler	4.00	2.00	.40
☐ 12 Doug Smith	5.00	2.50	.50
☐ 13 Reggie Smith	.75	.35	.07
☐ 14 Willie Smith Tiger of the Past	1.50	.75	.15
☐ 15 Norm Stewart CO	1.00	.50	.10
☐ 16 Jeff Warren	.75	.35	.07

1991-92 Missouri

This 16-card set was sponsored by Coca-Cola, Farm Bureau Insurance, and Columbia Photo. The production run was limited to 9,000 sets, with eight cards per perforated sheet. One sheet was given away at the February 23 home game against Oklahoma State, while the second sheet was given out at the March 4 game against Oklahoma. In total, 7,000 sets were distributed at home games; the rest of the sets were given to the sponsors. The standard size (2 1/2" by 3 1/2") cards have on the fronts color action photos enclosed by white and black borders, with the words "Mizzou Tigers" inscribed above the picture. The player's name appears beneath the picture, with his jersey number in a basketball at the lower right corner. The backs have biographical information, player profile, and "Tips for Better Sports Pictures." The cards are unnumbered and checklisted below in alphabetical order.

	MINT	EXC	G-VG
COMPLETE SET (16)	15.00	7.50	1.50
COMMON PLAYER (1-16)	.75	.35	.07
☐ 1 Kim Anderson Tiger of the Past	1.25	.60	.12
☐ 2 Melvin Booker	.75	.35	.07
☐ 3 John Burns	.75	.35	.07
☐ 4 Jamal Coleman	1.00	.50	.10
☐ 5 Jevon Crudup	1.00	.50	.10
☐ 6 Derek Dunham	.75	.35	.07
☐ 7 Lamont Frazier	.75	.35	.07
☐ 8 Ricky Frazier Tiger of the Past	1.25	.60	.12
☐ 9 Jed Frost	.75	.35	.07
☐ 10 Chris Heller	.75	.35	.07
☐ 11 Steve Horton	.75	.35	.07
☐ 12 Anthony Peeler	3.00	1.50	.30
☐ 13 Chris Smith	.75	.35	.07
☐ 14 Reggie Smith	.75	.35	.07
☐ 15 Norm Stewart CO	1.00	.50	.10
☐ 16 Jeff Warren	.75	.35	.07

1990-91 Murray State

This 16-card set was sponsored by The Pro Image, a sporting goods store in Paducah, Kentucky. The production run was limited to 2,000 sets, with only 1,000 of these being distributed as sets. The other 1,000 sets were given away as singles. Moreover, 45 uncut and numbered sheets were produced. The cards measure approximately 2 1/4" by 3 1/4" and are printed on thin card stock. The fronts feature black and white action or posed photos enclosed by full-bleed canary yellow borders. "Murray State Basketball," the player's name, and the sponsor logo appear on the front in blue ink. The horizontally oriented backs have biography, statistics, and player profile. The cards are numbered in the upper right corner.

	MINT	EXC	G-VG
COMPLETE SET (16)	10.00	5.00	1.00
COMMON PLAYER (1-16)	.50	.25	.05
□ 1 Paul King	.50	.25	.05
□ 2 Doug Gold	.50	.25	.05
□ 3 Donald Overstreet	.50	.25	.05
□ 4 Greg Coble	.50	.25	.05
□ 5 John Jackson	.50	.25	.05
□ 6 Popeye Jones	3.00	1.50	.30
□ 7 Donnie Langhi	.50	.25	.05
□ 8 Terry Birdsong	.50	.25	.05
□ 9 Scott Adams	.50	.25	.05
□ 10 Frank Allen	.50	.25	.05
□ 11 Scott Sivills	.50	.25	.05
□ 12 Cedric Gumm	.50	.25	.05
□ 13 Jerry Wilson	.50	.25	.05
□ 14 Jason Karem	.50	.25	.05
□ 15 The Coaching Staff Steve Newton CO Craig Morris ACO James Holland ACO	.50	.25	.05
□ 16 Team Photo	1.00	.50	.10

1991-92 Murray State

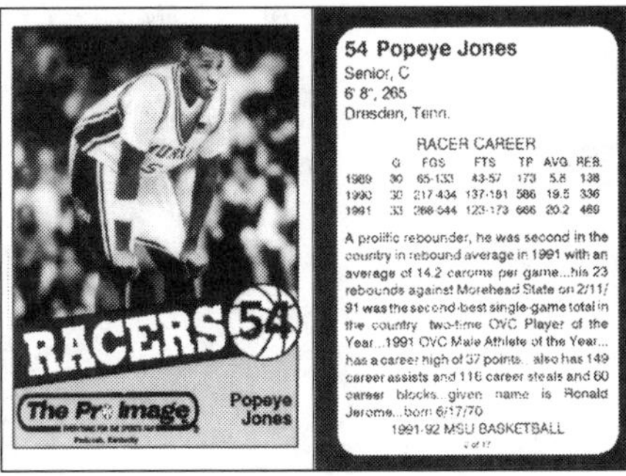

This 17-card set was sponsored by The Pro Image, a sporting goods store in Paducah, Kentucky. The production run was limited to 1,500 sets, with 1,000 of these being distributed as sets and the rest as singles. Moreover, 35 uncut sheets were produced. The cards measure 2 1/2" by 3 1/2" and are printed on thin card stock. The fronts feature black and white action photos enclosed by white borders. The team name "Racers" appears in a blue diagonal toward the bottom of the card; the stripe intersects a basketball icon, which has the player's uniform number. The sponsor logo and player's name round out the card face and are printed on a yellow background immediately below the stripe. The backs have biography and player profile on a white background enclosed by blue borders. The cards are numbered on the back.

	MINT	EXC	G-VG
COMPLETE SET (17)	9.00	4.50	.90
COMMON PLAYER (1-17)	.50	.25	.05
□ 1 Scott Adams	.50	.25	.05
□ 2 Popeye Jones	2.00	1.00	.20
□ 3 Frank Allen	.50	.25	.05
□ 4 Maurice Cannon	.50	.25	.05
□ 5 Jamal Evans	.50	.25	.05
□ 6 Darren Hill	.50	.25	.05
□ 7 Michael Hunt	.50	.25	.05
□ 8 Rafeal Peterson	.50	.25	.05
□ 9 Scott Sivills	.50	.25	.05
□ 10 Bo Walden	.50	.25	.05
□ 11 Craig Gray	.50	.25	.05
□ 12 Cedric Gumm	.50	.25	.05
□ 13 Jerry Wilson	.50	.25	.05
□ 14 Scott Edgar CO	.50	.25	.05
□ 15 Ken Roth ACO	.50	.25	.05
□ 16 Eddie Fields ACO	.50	.25	.05
□ 17 Team Photo	.75	.35	.07

1984-85 Nebraska Police *

This 31-card multi-sport set was distributed by the Lincoln Police Department. The cards measure 2 1/4" by 3 5/8" and are printed on thin card stock. The fronts feature color player photos enclosed by a red border. The team name and year are printed at the top in reversed-out white lettering, while the player's jersey number, name, and other personal information appear in black beneath the picture. The backs present a "Husker Tip", which consists of sport rules or advice and a "Crime Prevention Tip". Sponsor names and logos round out the back. The sports represented are football (1-10), volleyball (11-12), gymnastics (13-15), basketball (16-19), baseball (20-24, 26, 28, 30), and track (25, 27, 29, 31). The cards are numbered on the back.

	MINT	EXC	G-VG
COMPLETE SET (31)	35.00	17.50	3.50
COMMON PLAYER (1-31)	1.00	.50	.10
□ 1 Mark Traynowicz	2.00	1.00	.20
□ 2 Tom Osborne CO	4.00	2.00	.40
□ 3 Jeff Smith	3.00	1.50	.30
□ 4 Scott Strasburger	2.00	1.00	.20
□ 5 Craig Sundberg	1.00	.50	.10
□ 6 Bill Weber	1.00	.50	.10
□ 7 Shane Swanson	1.00	.50	.10
□ 8 Neil Harris	1.00	.50	.10
□ 9 Mark Behning	1.50	.75	.15
□ 10 Dave Burke	1.00	.50	.10
□ 11 Mary Buysee	1.00	.50	.10
□ 12 Cathy Noth	1.00	.50	.10
□ 13 Terri Furman	1.00	.50	.10
□ 14 Char Hagamann	1.00	.50	.10
□ 15 Wes Suter	1.00	.50	.10
□ 16 Dave Hoppen	4.00	2.00	.40
□ 17 Debra Powell	1.00	.50	.10
□ 18 Ronnie Smith	1.00	.50	.10
□ 19 Angie Miller	1.00	.50	.10

☐ 20 Bill McGuire	1.00	.50	.10
☐ 21 Paul Meyers	1.00	.50	.10
☐ 22 Jeff Carter	1.50	.75	.15
☐ 23 Kurt Eubanks	1.00	.50	.10
☐ 24 Mori Emmons	1.00	.50	.10
☐ 25 Glen Cunningham	1.00	.50	.10
☐ 26 Denise Eckert	1.00	.50	.10
☐ 27 Angele Thacker	1.00	.50	.10
☐ 28 Ann Schroeder	1.00	.50	.10
☐ 29 Darren Burton	1.00	.50	.10
☐ 30 Lori Sippel	1.00	.50	.10
☐ 31 Rhonda Blanford	1.00	.50	.10
☐ 29 Von Sheppard	1.00	.50	.10
☐ 30 Laura Wight	1.00	.50	.10
☐ 31 Lori Sippel	1.00	.50	.10
☐ 32 Paul Meyers	1.00	.50	.10
☐ 33 Donna Deardorff	1.00	.50	.10
☐ 34 Larry Mimms	1.00	.50	.10
☐ 35 Lori Richins	1.00	.50	.10
☐ 36 Rich King	5.00	2.50	.50
☐ 37 Amy Love	1.00	.50	.10

1985-86 Nebraska Police *

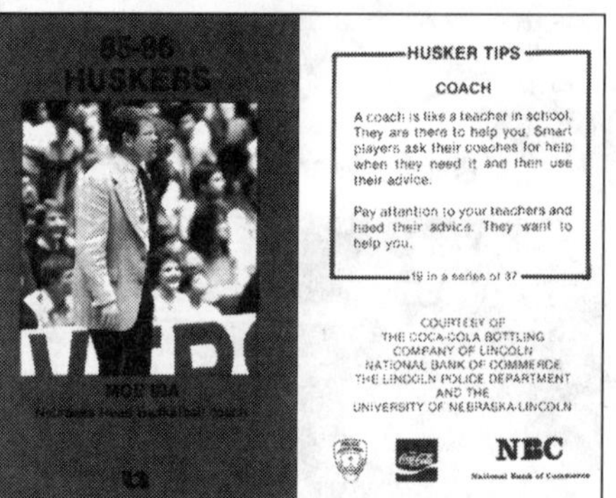

This 37-card multi-sport set measuring 2 1/2" by 4" has on the fronts color action and posed player photos enclosed by a red border. The team name and year is at the top in reversed-out white lettering while the player's jersey number, name, and other personal information appears beneath the picture. The backs feature "Husker Tips," which consist of sport rules or advice and a crime prevention tip. Sponsor names and logos round out the back. The sports represented are football (2-11), volleyball (12, 14), gymnastics (13, 15-17), track (18, 20, 29-30), basketball (19, 21, 23, 26), baseball (20-24, 31-37), and swimming (22, 24, 27-28). The cards are numbered on the back. Some of the key cards in the set are Rich King and Tom Rathman.

	MINT	EXC	G-VG
COMPLETE SET (37)	40.00	20.00	4.00
COMMON PLAYER (1-37)	1.00	.50	.10
☐ 1 Title Card	2.00	1.00	.20
☐ 2 Doug DuBose	2.00	1.00	.20
☐ 3 Marc Munford	1.00	.50	.10
☐ 4 Travis Turner	1.00	.50	.10
☐ 5 Mike Knox	1.00	.50	.10
☐ 6 Todd Frain	1.00	.50	.10
☐ 7 Danny Noonan	4.00	2.00	.40
☐ 8 Tom Rathman	7.50	3.75	.75
☐ 9 Jim Skow	3.00	1.50	.30
☐ 10 Stan Parker	1.00	.50	.10
☐ 11 Bill Lewis	2.00	1.00	.20
☐ 12 Michelle Smith	1.00	.50	.10
☐ 13 Wes Suter	1.00	.50	.10
☐ 14 Karen Dahlgren	1.00	.50	.10
☐ 15 Renee Gould	1.00	.50	.10
☐ 16 Neil Palmer	1.00	.50	.10
☐ 17 Racine Smith	1.00	.50	.10
☐ 18 Gerard O'Callaghan	1.00	.50	.10
☐ 19 Moe Iba CO	2.00	1.00	.20
☐ 20 Angela Thacker	1.00	.50	.10
☐ 21 Stacy Imming	1.00	.50	.10
☐ 22 Ernie Duran	1.00	.50	.10
☐ 23 Dave Hoppen	3.00	1.50	.30
☐ 24 Emily Ricketts	1.00	.50	.10
☐ 25 Missing	0.00	.00	.00
☐ 26 Brian Carr	1.00	.50	.10
☐ 27 Ed Jowdy	1.00	.50	.10
☐ 28 Erin Hurley	1.00	.50	.10

1990-91 Nebraska Police *

This 28-card set was sponsored by the National Bank of Commerce, the University of Nebraska-Lincoln, and the Lincoln Police Department. The cards measure approximately 2 1/2 by 4" and are printed on thin cardboard stock. The front features color action player photos against a red background. In black lettering the words "90-91 Huskers" appear over the picture, with the player's name and hometown given below. The back has "Husker Tips," which consists of a comment about the player and a crime prevention tip. Sponsors' logos at the bottom round out the back. The cards are numbered on the back. The sports represented in this set are football (2-13), volleyball (14-15), wrestling (16), gymnastics (17-20), basketball (21-24), softball (25, 27), and baseball (26, 28). The key cards in the set are Kenny Walker and Mike Croel.

	MINT	EXC	G-VG
COMPLETE SET (28)	20.00	10.00	2.00
COMMON PLAYER (1-28)	.50	.25	.05
☐ 1 Bob Devaney ATH DIR	.75	.35	.07
☐ 2 Reggie Cooper	.50	.25	.05
☐ 3 Terry Rodgers	.50	.25	.05
☐ 4 Kenny Walker	4.00	2.00	.40
☐ 5 Gregg Barrios	.50	.25	.05
☐ 6 Mike Croel	6.00	3.00	.60
☐ 7 Tom Punt	.50	.25	.05
☐ 8 Mike Grant	.50	.25	.05
☐ 9 Joe Sims	.50	.25	.05
☐ 10 Mickey Joseph	1.00	.50	.10
☐ 11 Lance Lewis	.50	.25	.05
☐ 12 Bruce Pickens	2.50	1.25	.25
☐ 13 Nate Turner	.50	.25	.05
☐ 14 Linda Barsness	.50	.25	.05
☐ 15 Becky Bolli	.50	.25	.05
☐ 16 Jason Kelber	.50	.25	.05
☐ 17 Brad Bryan	.50	.25	.05
☐ 18 Ted Dimas	.50	.25	.05
☐ 19 Nita Lichtenstein	.50	.25	.05
☐ 20 Lisa McCrady	.50	.25	.05
☐ 21 Clifford Scales	.75	.35	.07
☐ 22 Ann Halsne	.50	.25	.05
☐ 23 Carl Hayes	.50	.25	.05
☐ 24 Kelly Hubert	.50	.25	.05
☐ 25 Deanna Mays	.50	.25	.05
☐ 26 Shawn Buchanan	.50	.25	.05
☐ 27 Michelle Cuddeford	.50	.25	.05
☐ 28 Eddie Anderson	.75	.35	.07

1991-92 Nebraska Police *

This 22-card multi-sport set was sponsored by the National Bank of Commerce, University of Nebraska, and the Lincoln Police Department. The cards measure approximately 2 1/2" by 4" and are printed on thin card stock. The fronts feature color player photos enclosed by a red border. The year and team name are printed at the top in reversed-out black lettering, while the player's name, jersey number, and other personal information appear beneath the picture. The backs present "Husker Tips", which consist of sports rules or advice and a "Crime Prevention Tip". Sponsor names and logos round out the back. The sports represented are football (1-8), wrestling (9-10), volleyball (11-12), men's basketball (13-14, 16, 18), women's basketball (15, 17, 19), and baseball (20-22). The cards are numbered on the back.

	MINT	EXC	G-VG
COMPLETE SET (22)	12.00	6.00	1.20
COMMON PLAYER (1-22)	.50	.25	.05

	MINT	EXC	G-VG
☐ 1 Mickey Joseph	1.00	.50	.10
☐ 2 Pat Engelbert	.50	.25	.05
☐ 3 Jon Bostick	.50	.25	.05
☐ 4 Scott Baldwin	1.00	.50	.10
☐ 5 Tim Johnk	.50	.25	.05
☐ 6 Tom Haase	.50	.25	.05
☐ 7 Erik Wiegert	.50	.25	.05
☐ 8 Chris Garrett	.50	.25	.05
☐ 9 John Buxton	.50	.25	.05
☐ 10 Chris Nelson	.50	.25	.05
☐ 11 Janet Kruse	.50	.25	.05
☐ 12 Cris Hall	.50	.25	.05
☐ 13 Danny Lee CO	.50	.25	.05
☐ 14 Carl Hayes	.50	.25	.05
☐ 15 Carol Russell	.50	.25	.05
☐ 16 Eric Piatkowski	.75	.35	.07
☐ 17 Karen Jennings	.50	.25	.05
☐ 18 DaPreis Owens	.50	.25	.05
☐ 19 Sue Hesch	.50	.25	.05
☐ 20 Ann Halsne	.50	.25	.05
☐ 21 Misty Guenther	.50	.25	.05
☐ 22 Kris Vucurevic	.50	.25	.05

1990-91 New Mexico

This 17-card set was sponsored by Arby's restaurants and KGGM-TV (Channel 13). The cards measure the standard size (2 1/2" by 3 1/2"). The fronts feature color posed player photos enclosed by white borders. Sponsor logos and the words "Lobos 90-91" appear above the picture, while player information is given below the picture. The cards are unnumbered and checklisted below in alphabetical order.

	MINT	EXC	G-VG
COMPLETE SET (17)	12.50	6.25	1.25
COMMON PLAYER (1-17)	.60	.30	.06

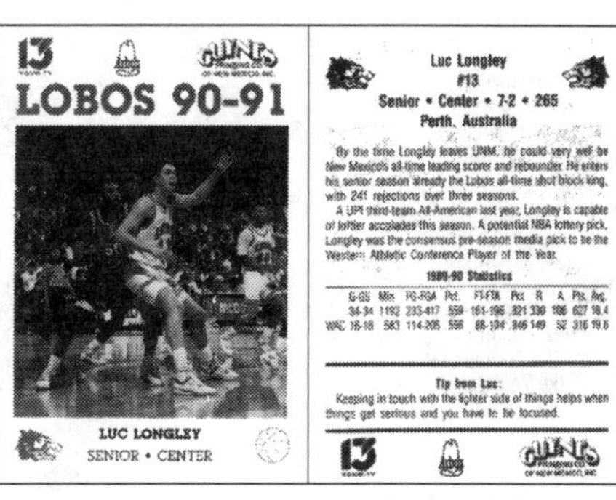

	MINT	EXC	G-VG
☐ 1 Doug Ash Assistant CO	.60	.30	.06
☐ 2 Willie Banks	.60	.30	.06
☐ 3 Dave Bliss CO	1.00	.50	.10
☐ 4 Paul Graham Assistant CO	.60	.30	.06
☐ 5 Khari Jaxon	.60	.30	.06
☐ 6 Luc Longley	4.00	2.00	.40
☐ 7 Marvin McBurrows	.60	.30	.06
☐ 8 Vladimir McCrary	.60	.30	.06
☐ 9 John McCullough Assistant CO	.60	.30	.06
☐ 10 Lance Milford	.60	.30	.06
☐ 11 Kurt Miller	.60	.30	.06
☐ 12 Rob Newton	.60	.30	.06
☐ 13 George Powdrill	.60	.30	.06
☐ 14 Rob Robbins	.60	.30	.06
☐ 15 Jimmy Taylor	.60	.30	.06
☐ 16 Ike Williams	.60	.30	.06
☐ 17 The Pit University Arena	.60	.30	.06

1991-92 New Mexico

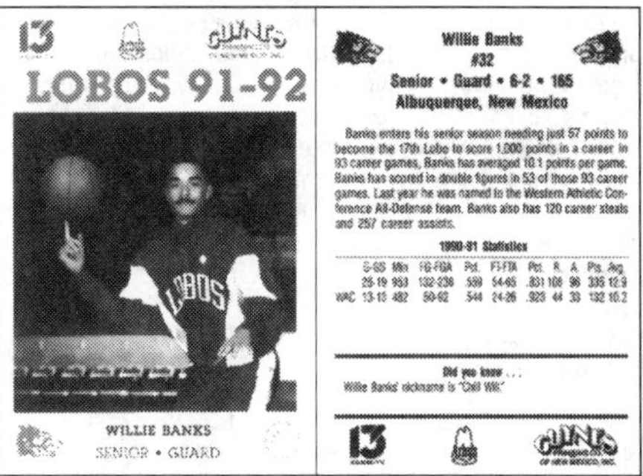

This 18-card set was sponsored by Arby's restaurants and KGGM-TV (Channel 13). It is reported that 10,000 sets were printed, and two to four cards per week were given away at Arby's restaurants in the Albuquerque area. The cards measure the standard size (2 1/2" by 3 1/2"). The fronts feature color posed player photos enclosed by white borders. Sponsor logos and the words "Lobos 91-92" appear above the picture, while player information is given below the picture. The cards are unnumbered and checklisted below in alphabetical order.

	MINT	EXC	G-VG
COMPLETE SET (18)	10.00	5.00	1.00
COMMON PLAYER (1-18)	.60	.30	.06

	MINT	EXC	G-VG
☐ 1 Doug Ash Assistant CO	.60	.30	.06
☐ 2 Willie Banks	.60	.30	.06
☐ 3 Dave Bliss CO	1.00	.50	.10
☐ 4 Paul Graham	.60	.30	.06

	MINT	EXC	G-VG
Assistant CO			
☐ 5 J.J. Griego	.60	.30	.06
☐ 6 Brian Hayden	.60	.30	.06
☐ 7 Trent Heffner	.60	.30	.06
☐ 8 Khari Jaxon	.60	.30	.06
☐ 9 Lewis Lamar	.60	.30	.06
☐ 10 Steve Logan	.60	.30	.06
☐ 11 Vladimir McCrary	.60	.30	.06
☐ 12 John McCullough Assistant CO	.60	.30	.06
☐ 13 Andre McGee	.60	.30	.06
☐ 14 Lance Milford	.60	.30	.06
☐ 15 Scott Pritchett	.60	.30	.06
☐ 16 Will Scott	.60	.30	.06
☐ 17 Eric Thomas	.60	.30	.06
☐ 18 Ike Williams	.60	.30	.06

1986-87 North Carolina Police

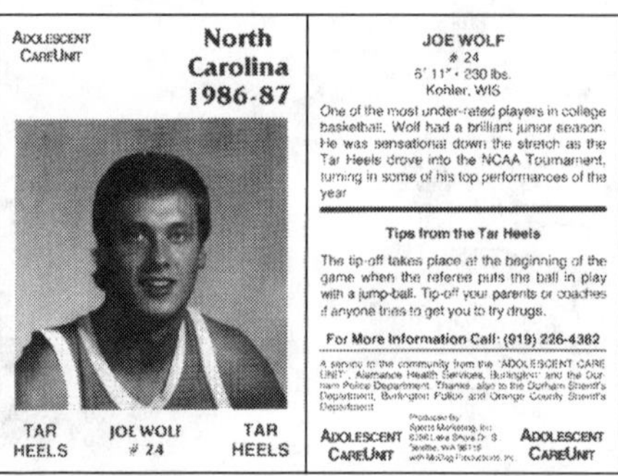

This 13-card set was sponsored by Adolescent CareUnit, Alamance Health Services, and various police departments. The cards measure the standard size (2 1/2" by 3 1/2"). The front features a posed color head-and-shoulders shot of the player on a white card face. In black lettering, the Adolescent Care Unit logo, the school name, and year appear above the picture. The player's name and number are given below, sandwiched between the team name. The back is printed in black on white card stock and presents biographical information and "Tips from the Tar Heels," which consist of anti-drug and alcohol messages. The cards are unnumbered and checklisted below by uniform number.

	MINT	EXC	G-VG
COMPLETE SET (13)	25.00	12.50	2.50
COMMON PLAYER	1.00	.50	.10
☐ 3 Jeff Denny	1.00	.50	.10
☐ 14 Jeff Lebo	2.50	1.25	.25
☐ 20 Steve Bucknall	2.50	1.25	.25
☐ 21 Michael Norwood	1.00	.50	.10
☐ 24 Joe Wolf	2.50	1.25	.25
☐ 30 Kenny Smith	6.00	3.00	.60
☐ 32 Pete Chilcutt	3.00	1.50	.30
☐ 33 Ranzino Smith	1.50	.75	.15
☐ 34 J.R. Reid	4.00	2.00	.40
☐ 35 Dave Popson	2.50	1.25	.25
☐ 42 Scott Williams	5.00	2.50	.50
☐ 43 Curtis Hunter	1.50	.75	.15
☐ 45 Marty Hensley	1.00	.50	.10

1987-88 North Carolina Police

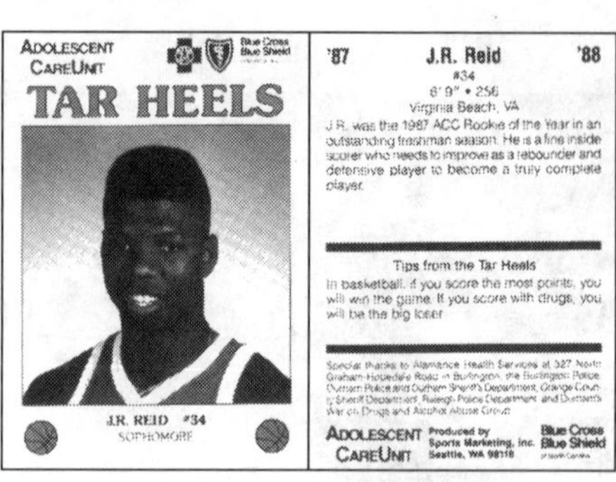

This 12-card set was sponsored by Adolescent CareUnit, Alamance Health Services, and various police departments. The cards measure the standard size (2 1/2" by 3 1/2"). The front features a posed color head-and-shoulders shot of the player on a white card face. In black lettering, the Adolescent CareUnit and Blue Cross/Blue Shield logos appear above the picture. In contrast to the previous year's issue, these cards have "Tar Heels" printed in large blue type above the picture. The player's name and number are given below, sandwiched between two blue basketballs. The back is printed in black on white card stock and presents biographical information and "Tips from the Tar Heels," which consist of anti-drug and alcohol messages. The cards are unnumbered and checklisted below by uniform number.

	MINT	EXC	G-VG
COMPLETE SET (12)	20.00	10.00	2.00
COMMON PLAYER	1.00	.50	.10
☐ 3 Jeff Denny	1.00	.50	.10
☐ 11 Rodney Hyatt	1.00	.50	.10
☐ 14 Jeff Lebo	2.00	1.00	.20
☐ 20 Steve Bucknall	2.00	1.00	.20
☐ 21 King Rice	2.00	1.00	.20
☐ 22 Kevin Madden	2.00	1.00	.20
☐ 32 Pete Chilcutt	2.50	1.25	.25
☐ 33 Ranzino Smith	1.50	.75	.15
☐ 34 J.R. Reid	3.00	1.50	.30
☐ 42 Scott Williams	3.50	1.75	.35
☐ 44 Rick Fox	8.00	4.00	.80
☐ 45 Marty Hensley	1.00	.50	.10

1988-89 North Carolina Police

This 13-card set was sponsored by Adolescent CareUnit, Alamance Health Services, and local law enforcement agencies. The cards measure the standard size (2 1/2" by 3 1/2"). The front features a color action photo of the player, with black borders on a medium blue card face. In black lettering, the Adolescent CareUnit and Blue Cross/Blue Shield logos appear within the border above the picture. These cards have "Tar Heels" printed in large white type above the picture. The player's name and number are given below, with the letters "NC" superimposed over one another in the lower left corner. The back is printed in black on white card stock and presents biographical information and "Tips from the Tar Heels," which consist of anti-drug and alcohol messages. The cards are unnumbered and checklisted below by uniform number. The Defense card is mysteriously listed on the back as '87 and '88 in the upper corners.

	MINT	EXC	G-VG
COMPLETE SET (13)	15.00	7.50	1.50
COMMON PLAYER	1.00	.50	.10
☐ 3 Jeff Denny	1.00	.50	.10
☐ 14 Jeff Lebo	1.50	.75	.15
☐ 20 Steve Bucknall	1.50	.75	.15
☐ 21 King Rice	1.50	.75	.15
☐ 22 Kevin Madden	1.50	.75	.15
☐ 32 Pete Chilcutt	2.00	1.00	.20
☐ 42 Scott Williams	3.00	1.50	.30
☐ 44 Rick Fox	4.50	2.25	.45
☐ 45 Marty Hensley	1.00	.50	.10
☐ xx Dean Smith CO	2.50	1.25	.25
☐ xx Defense (Scott Williams and Jeff Lebo defending)	1.00	.50	.10
☐ xx The Fast Break (King Rice dribbling)	1.00	.50	.10
☐ xx A Fun Game (bench scene with Rick Fox and Scott Williams)	2.50	1.25	.25

1989-90 North Carolina Coke

This 200-card set was produced by Collegiate Collection and sponsored by Coca-Cola, and the Coke logo appears in the lower left corner on the card face. The cards measure the standard size (2 1/2" by 3 1/2"). The fronts feature a mix of black and white photos for earlier players and color for later ones, with rounded corners and powder blue borders. The pictures are superimposed over a powder blue and white diagonally striped card face, with a powder blue outer border. The top reads "North Carolina's Finest," and the school logo appears in the upper right corner. The horizontally oriented backs are printed in powder blue on white and present biographical information, career summaries, or statistics. The cards are numbered on the back. The following numbers are found without the trademark notation, 18, 23, 25, 26, 46, 50-54, 59, 66, 67, 74, 75, 79, 109, 111, 142, 163, 166, 167, 170, 171, 174, 176, 177, 185-190, 192, 194, 195, and 197.

	MINT	EXC	G-VG
COMPLETE SET (200)	20.00	10.00	2.00
COMMON PLAYER (1-200)	.07	.03	.01
☐ 1 Dean Smith	.20	.10	.02
☐ 2 Dean Smith	.20	.10	.02
☐ 3 Dean Smith	.20	.10	.02
☐ 4 Dean Smith	.20	.10	.02
☐ 5 Dean Smith	.20	.10	.02
☐ 6 Dean Smith	.20	.10	.02
☐ 7 Phil Ford	.15	.07	.01
☐ 8 Phil Ford	.15	.07	.01
☐ 9 Phil Ford	.15	.07	.01
☐ 10 Phil Ford	.15	.07	.01
☐ 11 Phil Ford	.15	.07	.01
☐ 12 Phil Ford	.15	.07	.01
☐ 13 Michael Jordan	1.00	.50	.10
☐ 14 Michael Jordan	1.00	.50	.10
☐ 15 Michael Jordan	1.00	.50	.10
☐ 16 Michael Jordan	1.00	.50	.10
☐ 17 Michael Jordan	1.00	.50	.10
☐ 18 Michael Jordan	1.00	.50	.10
☐ 19 James Worthy	.25	.12	.02
☐ 20 James Worthy	.25	.12	.02
☐ 21 James Worthy	.25	.12	.02
☐ 22 James Worthy	.25	.12	.02
☐ 23 James Worthy	.25	.12	.02
☐ 24 Larry Miller	.10	.05	.01
☐ 25 Larry Miller	.10	.05	.01
☐ 26 Larry Miller	.10	.05	.01
☐ 27 Larry Miller	.10	.05	.01
☐ 28 Charlie Scott	.15	.07	.01
☐ 29 Charlie Scott	.15	.07	.01
☐ 30 Charlie Scott	.15	.07	.01
☐ 31 Charlie Scott	.15	.07	.01
☐ 32 Sam Perkins	.20	.10	.02
☐ 33 Sam Perkins	.20	.10	.02
☐ 34 Sam Perkins	.20	.10	.02
☐ 35 Sam Perkins	.20	.10	.02
☐ 36 Sam Perkins	.20	.10	.02
☐ 37 Billy Cunningham	.15	.07	.01
☐ 38 Billy Cunningham	.15	.07	.01
☐ 39 Billy Cunningham	.15	.07	.01
☐ 40 Billy Cunningham	.15	.07	.01
☐ 41 Lennie Rosenbluth	.10	.05	.01
☐ 42 Lennie Rosenbluth	.10	.05	.01
☐ 43 Lennie Rosenbluth	.10	.05	.01
☐ 44 Bobby Jones	.15	.07	.01
☐ 45 Bobby Jones	.15	.07	.01
☐ 46 Bobby Jones	.15	.07	.01
☐ 47 Mitch Kupchak	.10	.05	.01
☐ 48 Mitch Kupchak	.10	.05	.01
☐ 49 Mitch Kupchak	.10	.05	.01
☐ 50 1980-81 Tar Heels	.07	.03	.01
☐ 51 Walter Davis	.15	.07	.01
☐ 52 Walter Davis	.15	.07	.01
☐ 53 Walter Davis	.15	.07	.01
☐ 54 Walter Davis	.15	.07	.01
☐ 55 Mike O'Koren	.10	.05	.01
☐ 56 Mike O'Koren	.10	.05	.01
☐ 57 Mike O'Koren	.10	.05	.01
☐ 58 Mike O'Koren	.10	.05	.01
☐ 59 The Huddle	.07	.03	.01
☐ 60 Larry Brown	.15	.07	.01
☐ 61 Billy Cunningham	.15	.07	.01
☐ 62 Matt Doherty	.10	.05	.01
☐ 63 Phil Ford	.15	.07	.01
☐ 64 Doug Moe	.20	.10	.02
☐ 65 Michael Jordan	1.00	.50	.10
☐ 66 Kenny Smith	.15	.07	.01
☐ 67 Kenny Smith	.15	.07	.01
☐ 68 Kenny Smith	.15	.07	.01
☐ 69 Bob Lewis	.07	.03	.01
☐ 70 Bob Lewis	.07	.03	.01
☐ 71 Bob Lewis	.07	.03	.01
☐ 72 Charlie Scott	.15	.07	.01
☐ 73 Sam Perkins	.20	.10	.02
☐ 74 Doug Moe	.20	.10	.02
☐ 75 Doug Moe	.20	.10	.02
☐ 76 Robert McAdoo	.20	.10	.02
☐ 77 Robert McAdoo	.20	.10	.02
☐ 78A Pete Brennan ERR (No trademark on back)	.07	.03	.01
☐ 78B Pete Brennan COR	.07	.03	.01
☐ 79 Pete Brennan	.07	.03	.01
☐ 80 J.R. Reid	.15	.07	.01
☐ 81 J.R. Reid	.15	.07	.01
☐ 82 J.R. Reid	.15	.07	.01
☐ 83 Tommy Kearns	.07	.03	.01
☐ 84 Tommy Kearns	.07	.03	.01
☐ 85 John Dillon	.07	.03	.01
☐ 86 The Smith Center	.07	.03	.01
☐ 87 Dick Grubar	.07	.03	.01
☐ 88 Dick Grubar	.07	.03	.01
☐ 89 Rusty Clark	.10	.05	.01
☐ 90 Rusty Clark	.10	.05	.01
☐ 91 Bill Bunting	.10	.05	.01
☐ 92 Bill Bunting	.10	.05	.01
☐ 93 Jimmy Black	.10	.05	.01
☐ 94 Jimmy Black	.10	.05	.01
☐ 95 5 Tournament Titles	.07	.03	.01
☐ 96 UNC Cheerleaders	.07	.03	.01
☐ 97 Bobby Jones	.15	.07	.01
☐ 98 J.R. Reid	.15	.07	.01
☐ 99 Frank McGuire	.10	.05	.01

☐ 100 1957 NCAA Champions	.07	.03	.01
☐ 101 Bill Guthridge	.07	.03	.01
☐ 102 York Larese	.15	.07	.01
☐ 103 York Larese	.15	.07	.01
☐ 104 Frank McGuire	.15	.07	.01
☐ 105 Bones McKinney	.10	.05	.01
☐ 106 Larry Miller	.10	.05	.01
☐ 107 Kenny Smith	.15	.07	.01
☐ 108 Steve Previs	.07	.03	.01
☐ 109 Steve Previs	.07	.03	.01
☐ 110 Larry Brown	.20	.10	.02
☐ 111 Larry Brown	.20	.10	.02
☐ 112 Eddie Fogler	.15	.07	.01
☐ 113 Eddie Fogler	.15	.07	.01
☐ 114 James Worthy	.25	.12	.02
☐ 115 Robert McAdoo	.20	.10	.02
☐ 116 UNC Basketball	.07	.03	.01
☐ 117 UNC Basketball	.07	.03	.01
☐ 118 Cartwright Carmichael	.07	.03	.01
☐ 119 Steve Hale	.07	.03	.01
☐ 120 Steve Hale	.07	.03	.01
☐ 121 Joe Quigg	.07	.03	.01
☐ 122 Joe Quigg	.07	.03	.01
☐ 123 Bob Cunningham	.07	.03	.01
☐ 124 Bob Cunningham	.07	.03	.01
☐ 125 Jim Delany	.07	.03	.01
☐ 126 Bones McKinney	.10	.05	.01
☐ 127 Jerry Vayda	.07	.03	.01
☐ 128 Matt Doherty	.10	.05	.01
☐ 129 Matt Doherty	.10	.05	.01
☐ 130 Bob Paxton	.07	.03	.01
☐ 131 Dave Chadwick	.07	.03	.01
☐ 132 Dave Hanners	.07	.03	.01
☐ 133 Jim Jordan	.07	.03	.01
☐ 134 Jeff Lebo	.10	.05	.01
☐ 135 Jeff Lebo	.10	.05	.01
☐ 136 Lee Shaffer	.07	.03	.01
☐ 137 Lee Shaffer	.07	.03	.01
☐ 138 Joe Wolf	.10	.05	.01
☐ 139 Joe Wolf	.10	.05	.01
☐ 140 Warren Martin	.07	.03	.01
☐ 141 Warren Martin	.07	.03	.01
☐ 142 Carmichael Aud.	.07	.03	.01
☐ 143 Jim Hudock	.07	.03	.01
☐ 144 Darrell Elston	.07	.03	.01
☐ 145 Brad Hoffman	.07	.03	.01
☐ 146 Harvey Salz	.07	.03	.01
☐ 147 Dave Colescott	.07	.03	.01
☐ 148 Ed Stahl	.07	.03	.01
☐ 149 Joe Brown	.07	.03	.01
☐ 150 Gerald Tuttle	.07	.03	.01
☐ 151 Richard Tuttle	.07	.03	.01
☐ 152 Tony Radovich	.07	.03	.01
☐ 153 Dave Popson	.10	.05	.01
☐ 154 Donnie Walsh	.07	.03	.01
☐ 155 Rich Yonakor	.10	.05	.01
☐ 156 Jeff Wolf	.10	.05	.01
☐ 157 Pete Budko	.10	.05	.01
☐ 158 Randy Wiel	.07	.03	.01
☐ 159 Tom Gauntlett	.07	.03	.01
☐ 160 Mike Pepper	.07	.03	.01
☐ 161 Jim Braddock	.07	.03	.01
☐ 162 Yogi Poteet	.10	.05	.01
☐ 163 Charlie Shaffer	.07	.03	.01
☐ 164 Lee Dedmon	.07	.03	.01
☐ 165 Bob Bennett	.07	.03	.01
☐ 166 Ray Hite	.07	.03	.01
☐ 167 Tom Zaliagiris UER (Tim on front)	.07	.03	.01
☐ 168 Kim Huband	.07	.03	.01
☐ 169 Ranzino Smith	.10	.05	.01
☐ 170 Donn Johnson	.07	.03	.01
☐ 171 Dale Gipple	.07	.03	.01
☐ 172 Curtis Hunter	.10	.05	.01
☐ 173 John Yokley	.07	.03	.01
☐ 174 Bryan McSweeney	.07	.03	.01
☐ 175 John O'Donnell	.07	.03	.01
☐ 176 Hugh Donahue	.07	.03	.01
☐ 177 1968-69 Tar Heels	.07	.03	.01
☐ 178 Bruce Buckley	.07	.03	.01
☐ 179 Ray Respess	.07	.03	.01
☐ 180 Buzz Peterson	.10	.05	.01
☐ 181 Mike Cooke	.07	.03	.01
☐ 182 Mickey Bell	.07	.03	.01
☐ 183 John Virgil	.07	.03	.01
☐ 184 Charles Waddell	.07	.03	.01
☐ 185 Mark Mirken	.07	.03	.01
☐ 186 Ralph Fletcher	.07	.03	.01
☐ 187 1971-72 ACC Champs	.07	.03	.01
☐ 188 Ged Doughton	.07	.03	.01
☐ 189 Bill Chambers	.07	.03	.01
☐ 190 Billy Chambers	.07	.03	.01
☐ 191 James Daye	.07	.03	.01
☐ 192 Jeb Barlow	.07	.03	.01
☐ 193 Chris Brust	.07	.03	.01
☐ 194 Eric Kenny	.07	.03	.01
☐ 195 1970-71 NIT Champs	.07	.03	.01
☐ 196 Don Eggleston	.07	.03	.01
☐ 197 Ricky Webb	.07	.03	.01
☐ 198 Jim Frye	.07	.03	.01
☐ 199 Timo Makkonen	.07	.03	.01
☐ 200 1982 NCAA Champions	.10	.05	.01

1990-91 North Carolina Promos *

This ten-card set features various sports stars of North Carolina from recent years. Since this set features athletes from more than one sport we have put a two letter abbreviation next to the player's name which identifies the sport he plays. This set includes a Michael Jordan card. All the cards in the set feature full-color photos of the athletes on the front along with either a biography or statistics of the players pictured on the card.

	MINT	EXC	G-VG
COMPLETE SET (10)	5.00	2.50	.50
COMMON PLAYER (1-10)	.50	.25	.05
☐ NC1 Michael Jordan BK	2.00	1.00	.20
☐ NC2 Ethan Horton FB	.60	.30	.06
☐ NC3 Steve Hale BK	.50	.25	.05
☐ NC4 Mark Maye FB	.50	.25	.05
☐ NC5 Matt Doherty BK	.50	.25	.05
☐ NC6 Tyrone Anthony FB	.50	.25	.05
☐ NC7 Sam Perkins BK	.75	.35	.07
☐ NC8 Kelvin Bryant FB	.60	.30	.06
☐ NC9 Kenny Smith BK	.75	.35	.07
☐ NC10 Kenan Stadium	.50	.25	.05

1990-91 North Carolina 200 *

This 200-card set was produced by Collegiate Collection and measures the standard size (2 1/2" by 3 1/2"). The front features a mix of black and white or color player photos, on a light blue background with a powder blue outer border. All four corners of the picture are cut off. In black lettering the school name appears above the picture, with the player's name at the bottom of the card face. In a horizontal format the back presents biographical information, career summary, and statistics, on a white background with powder blue borders. The cards are numbered on the back.

	MINT	EXC	G-VG
COMPLETE SET (200)	20.00	10.00	2.00
COMMON PLAYER (1-200)	.07	.03	.01
☐ 1 Dean Smith CO	.20	.10	.02
☐ 2 John Swofford	.07	.03	.01
☐ 3 Michael Jordan	1.00	.50	.10
☐ 4 Lawrence Taylor	.50	.25	.05
☐ 5 James Worthy	.25	.12	.02

☐ 6 Kelvin Bryant	.15	.07	.01
☐ 7 Phil Ford	.15	.07	.01
☐ 8 Chris Hanburger	.20	.10	.02
☐ 9 Walter Davis	.15	.07	.01
☐ 10 Ethan Horton	.15	.07	.01
☐ 11 J.R. Reid	.15	.07	.01
☐ 12 Rod Elkins	.10	.05	.01
☐ 13 Buzz Peterson	.10	.05	.01
☐ 14 Darrell Nicholson	.07	.03	.01
☐ 15 Mark Maye	.10	.05	.01
☐ 16 Kenny Smith	.15	.07	.01
☐ 17 Matt Kupec	.10	.05	.01
☐ 18 Dave Popson	.10	.05	.01
☐ 19 Matt Doherty	.10	.05	.01
☐ 20 Buddy Curry	.07	.03	.01
☐ 21 Donnell Thompson	.10	.05	.01
☐ 22 Sam Perkins	.15	.07	.01
☐ 23 Mack Brown	.15	.07	.01
☐ 24 Ranzino Smith	.10	.05	.01
☐ 25 Curtis Hunter	.10	.05	.01
☐ 26 Doug Paschal	.07	.03	.01
☐ 27 Dean Smith	.20	.10	.02
☐ 28 Steve Streater	.10	.05	.01
☐ 29 David Drechsler	.07	.03	.01
☐ 30 Jimmy Black	.07	.03	.01
☐ 31 Kelvin Bryant	.10	.05	.01
☐ 32 Steve Hale	.07	.03	.01
☐ 33 Kenny Smith	.15	.07	.01
☐ 34 Tim Goad	.07	.03	.01
☐ 35 Harris Barton	.15	.07	.01
☐ 36 Jeff Lebo	.10	.05	.01
☐ 37 Rick Donnalley	.10	.05	.01
☐ 38 Don McCauley	.10	.05	.01
☐ 39 Sam Perkins	.15	.07	.01
☐ 40 Bill Paschall	.07	.03	.01
☐ 41 Scott Stankavage	.10	.05	.01
☐ 42 Joe Wolf	.10	.05	.01
☐ 43 Rueben Davis	.10	.05	.01
☐ 44 Michael Jordan	1.00	.50	.10
☐ 45 Jeff Garnica	.07	.03	.01
☐ 46 Kevin Anthony	.07	.03	.01
☐ 47 Eddie Fogler CO	.10	.05	.01
☐ 48 Warren Martin	.07	.03	.01
☐ 49 Buddy Curry	.07	.03	.01
☐ 50 Jim Braddock	.07	.03	.01
☐ 51 Matt Kupec	.07	.03	.01
☐ 52 Dean Smith CO	.20	.10	.02
☐ 53 Danny Talbott	.07	.03	.01
☐ 54 Sam Perkins	.15	.07	.01
☐ 55 Randy Weil	.07	.03	.01
☐ 56 Mike Chatham	.07	.03	.01
☐ 57 Jimmy Black	.07	.03	.01
☐ 58 Harris Barton	.10	.05	.01
☐ 59 David Popson	.10	.05	.01
☐ 60 Tom Biddle	.07	.03	.01
☐ 61 Michael Jordan	1.00	.50	.10
☐ 62 Ron Wooten	.07	.03	.01
☐ 63 J.R. Reid	.15	.07	.01
☐ 64 Lawrence Taylor	.50	.25	.05
☐ 65 Matt Doherty	.10	.05	.01
☐ 66 Alan Caldwell	.07	.03	.01
☐ 67 Warren Martin	.07	.03	.01
☐ 68 Tyrone Anthony	.07	.03	.01
☐ 69 Brook Barwick	.07	.03	.01
☐ 70 Steve Hale	.07	.03	.01
☐ 71 Mike Salzano	.07	.03	.01
☐ 72 Kelvin Bryant	.15	.07	.01
☐ 73 Ken Willard	.15	.07	.01
☐ 74 Jeff Lebo	.10	.05	.01
☐ 75 Kenny Smith	.20	.10	.02
☐ 76 Ramses (Mascot)	.07	.03	.01
☐ 77 Mike Voight	.07	.03	.01
☐ 78 James Worthy	.25	.12	.02
☐ 79 Joe Wolf	.10	.05	.01
☐ 80 Ethan Horton	.10	.05	.01
☐ 81 Ricky Barden	.10	.05	.01
☐ 82 Steve Hale	.07	.03	.01
☐ 83 Joe Wolf	.10	.05	.01
☐ 84 Bob Loomis	.07	.03	.01
☐ 85 Kenan Stadium	.07	.03	.01
☐ 86 Lawrence Taylor	.50	.25	.05
☐ 87 Sam Perkins	.20	.10	.02
☐ 88 Ron Wooten	.07	.03	.01
☐ 89 Michael Jordan	1.00	.50	.10
☐ 90 Tom Guanlett	.07	.03	.01
☐ 91 Tyrone Anthony	.07	.03	.01
☐ 92 Mark Maye	.07	.03	.01
☐ 93 Michael Jordan	1.00	.50	.10
☐ 94 Kenny Smith	.15	.07	.01
☐ 95 David Drechsler	.07	.03	.01
☐ 96 York Larese	.15	.07	.01
☐ 97 Joe Quigg	.07	.03	.01
☐ 98 Lennie Rosenbluth	.10	.05	.01
☐ 99 Pete Brennan	.07	.03	.01
☐ 100 Director Card 1-99	.10	.05	.01
☐ 101 Chris Kupec	.07	.03	.01
☐ 102 Moyer Smith	.07	.03	.01
☐ 103 Brad Hoffman	.07	.03	.01
☐ 104 James Worthy	.25	.12	.02
☐ 105 Hosea Rodgers	.07	.03	.01
☐ 106 Johnny Swofford	.07	.03	.01
☐ 107 Charlie Justice	.20	.10	.02
☐ 108 Mitch Kupchak	.15	.07	.01
☐ 109 Steve Previs	.07	.03	.01
☐ 110 Jimmy DeRatt	.07	.03	.01
☐ 111 Phil Ford	.15	.07	.01
☐ 112 Chris Kupec	.07	.03	.01
☐ 113 Lou Angelo	.07	.03	.01
☐ 114 John Bunting	.07	.03	.01
☐ 115 Dick Grubar	.07	.03	.01
☐ 116 Gerald Tuttle	.07	.03	.01
☐ 117 Bill Guthridge CO	.07	.03	.01
☐ 118 Junior Edge	.07	.03	.01
☐ 119 Art Weiner	.07	.03	.01
☐ 120 Dave Hanners CO	.07	.03	.01
☐ 121 George Barclay	.07	.03	.01
☐ 122 Joe Brown	.07	.03	.01
☐ 123 Mitch Kupchak	.15	.07	.01
☐ 124 Ken Powell	.07	.03	.01
☐ 125 Larry Miller	.10	.05	.01
☐ 126 Jerry Sain	.07	.03	.01
☐ 127 Don McCauley	.10	.05	.01
☐ 128 Bobby Jones	.15	.07	.01
☐ 129 Jimmy Jerome	.07	.03	.01
☐ 130 Larry Miller	.10	.05	.01
☐ 131 Ronny Johnson	.07	.03	.01
☐ 132 Ron Rusnak	.07	.03	.01
☐ 133 Charlie Scott	.15	.07	.01
☐ 134 Pete Budko	.10	.05	.01
☐ 135 Robert Pratt	.07	.03	.01
☐ 136 Bill Bunting	.10	.05	.01
☐ 137 Al Goldstein	.07	.03	.01
☐ 138 Charlie Carr	.07	.03	.01
☐ 139 Charlie Scott	.15	.07	.01
☐ 140 Ken Huff	.10	.05	.01
☐ 141 Don McCauley	.10	.05	.01
☐ 142 Dave Colescott	.07	.03	.01
☐ 143 Charlie Justice	.20	.10	.02
☐ 144 Ernie Williamson	.07	.03	.01
☐ 145 Dave Chadwick	.07	.03	.01
☐ 146 Rick Yonakor	.10	.05	.01
☐ 147 George Karl	.15	.07	.01
☐ 148 Ken Willard	.15	.07	.01
☐ 149 Phil Blazer	.07	.03	.01
☐ 150 Dean Smith CO	.20	.10	.02
☐ 151 Carl Snavely	.07	.03	.01
☐ 152 James Worthy	.25	.12	.02
☐ 153 Ron Rusnak	.07	.03	.01
☐ 154 Mike O'Koren	.10	.05	.01
☐ 155 Lewis and Miller	.10	.05	.01
☐ 156 Gene Brown	.07	.03	.01
☐ 157 Ed Stahl	.07	.03	.01
☐ 158 Rusty Clark	.10	.05	.01
☐ 159 Joe Robinson	.07	.03	.01
☐ 160 Gayle Bomar	.07	.03	.01
☐ 161 Bob Lewis	.07	.03	.01
☐ 162 Jim Delaney	.07	.03	.01
☐ 163 Paul Hoolahan	.07	.03	.01
☐ 164 Rod Broadway	.07	.03	.01
☐ 165 Darrell Elston	.07	.03	.01
☐ 166 Mickey Bell	.07	.03	.01
☐ 167 Ray Farris	.07	.03	.01
☐ 168 Charlie Justice	.20	.10	.02
☐ 169 Buddy Payne	.07	.03	.01
☐ 170 Lee Shaffer	.07	.03	.01
☐ 171 Mike Voight	.07	.03	.01

☐ 172 Kim Hubano	.07	.03	.01
☐ 173 Dean Smith CO	.15	.07	.01
☐ 174 Charlie Justice	.20	.10	.02
☐ 175 George Karl	.15	.07	.01
☐ 176 Ed Sutton	.10	.05	.01
☐ 177 Ken Craven	.07	.03	.01
☐ 178 Jeff Wolf	.07	.03	.01
☐ 179 Tom Zaliagiris	.07	.03	.01
☐ 180 Charles Waddell	.07	.03	.01
☐ 181 Lee Demond	.07	.03	.01
☐ 182 Irv Holdash	.07	.03	.01
☐ 183 Jack Cummings	.07	.03	.01
☐ 184 Bob Lewis	.07	.03	.01
☐ 185 Phil Ford	.15	.07	.01
☐ 186 Bobby Lacey	.07	.03	.01
☐ 187 Larry Brown	.15	.07	.01
☐ 188 Larry Voight	.07	.03	.01
☐ 189 Mike O'Koren	.10	.05	.01
☐ 190 Crowell Little	.07	.03	.01
☐ 191 Paul Miller	.07	.03	.01
☐ 192 Tommy Kearns	.07	.03	.01
☐ 193 Frank McGuire CO	.10	.05	.01
☐ 194 Sammy Johnson	.07	.03	.01
☐ 195 Carmichael Auditorium	.07	.03	.01
☐ 196 Nick Vidnovic	.07	.03	.01
☐ 197 Paul Severin	.07	.03	.01
☐ 198 Don Walsh	.07	.03	.01
☐ 199 Smith Center	.07	.03	.01
☐ 200 Director Card 101-199	.10	.05	.01

1987-88 North Carolina State Police

This 15-card standard size (2 1/2" by 3 1/2") set commemorates the Wolfpack's 1987 ACC title. It was sponsored by Adolescent CareUnit, IBM, and local police agencies. The sets were distributed at a home game and by police officers. Most fans in attendance at the home game only received 14 cards, because Sean Green transferred after the cards were printed and his cards were removed from the set. A small number of his cards still made their way to the general public. The fronts feature either posed or action color photos on a white card face, with a drop border in red on the bottom and right side of picture. The school name in red and ACC Champions in black appear above the picture, while the player's name is printed in white in the bottom red drop border. The backs carry biography, career summary, and "Tips from the Wolfpack," which consist of anti-drug or alcohol messages. The cards are unnumbered and checklisted below in alphabetical order.

	MINT	EXC	G-VG
COMPLETE SET (15)	20.00	10.00	2.00
COMMON PLAYER (1-15)	.75	.35	.07
☐ 1 Chucky Brown	2.00	1.00	.20
☐ 2 Chris Corchiani	3.50	1.75	.35
☐ 3 Brian D'Amico	.75	.35	.07
☐ 4 Vinny Del Negro	2.50	1.25	.25
☐ 5 Sean Green SP	3.50	1.75	.35
☐ 6 Brian Howard	1.25	.60	.12
☐ 7 Quentin Jackson	.75	.35	.07
☐ 8 Avie Lester	1.25	.60	.12
☐ 9 Rodney Monroe	5.00	2.50	.50
☐ 10 Kenny Poston	1.00	.50	.10
☐ 11 Charles Shackleford	2.00	1.00	.20
☐ 12 Bryon Tucker	.75	.35	.07
☐ 13 Jim Valvano CO	2.00	1.00	.20
☐ 14 Kelsey Weems	1.00	.50	.10
☐ 15 Team Photo	1.00	.50	.10

1988-89 North Carolina State Police

This 16-card standard size (2 1/2" by 3 1/2") set was sponsored by Adolescent CareUnit, IBM, and local police agencies. The sets were given away at a home game and by local police officers. On a white card face, the fronts feature action or posed color photos enclosed by a black drop border on the left and red drop borders on the right and bottom of the picture. A Wolfpack logo appears in the lower left corner while player information appears in the bottom red drop border. The backs carry biography, player profile, and "Tips from the Wolfpack," which consist of anti-drug or alcohol messages. The cards are unnumbered and checklisted below in alphabetical order.

	MINT	EXC	G-VG
COMPLETE SET (16)	18.00	9.00	1.80
COMMON PLAYER (1-16)	.75	.35	.07
☐ 1 Chucky Brown 52	1.25	.60	.12
☐ 2 Chris Corchiani 13	2.00	1.00	.20
☐ 3 Brian D'Amico 54	.75	.35	.07
☐ 4 Tom Gugliotta 24	6.00	3.00	.60
☐ 5 Mickey Hinnant 3	.75	.35	.07
☐ 6 Brian Howard 22	1.00	.50	.10
☐ 7 James Knox 23	.75	.35	.07
☐ 8 David Lee 25	.75	.35	.07
☐ 9 Avie Lester 32	1.00	.50	.10
☐ 10 Rodney Monroe	3.00	1.50	.30
☐ 11 Kenny Poston 30	1.00	.50	.10
☐ 12 Jim Valvano CO	1.50	.75	.15
☐ 13 Kelsey Weems 11	1.00	.50	.10
☐ 14 Mr. and Mrs. Wuf Mascots	.75	.35	.07
☐ 15 Kay Yow CO Women's Basketball	.75	.35	.07
☐ 16 Women's Team Basketball Schedule	.75	.35	.07

1989 North Carolina State Coke

This 200-card set was produced by Collegiate Collection and sponsored by Coca-Cola, and the Coke logo appears in the lower left corner on the card face. The cards measure the standard size (2 1/2" by 3 1/2"). The fronts feature a mix of black and white photos for earlier players and color for later ones, with rounded corners and red borders. The pictures are superimposed over a red and white diagonally-striped card face, with a red outer border. The top reads "N.C. State's Finest," and the school logo appears in the upper right corner. The horizontally oriented backs are printed in red on white and

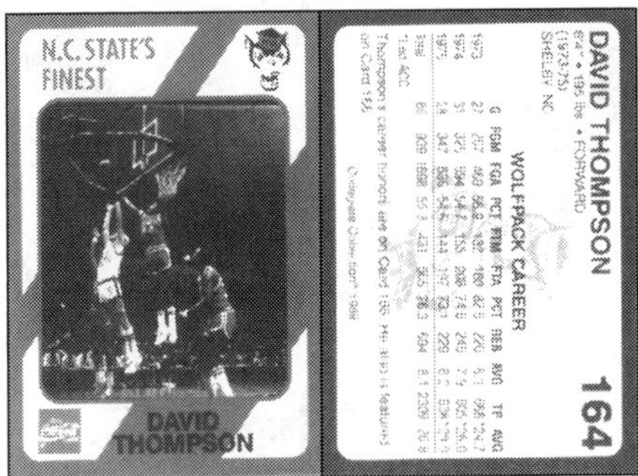

present biographical information, career summaries, or statistics. The cards are numbered on the back.

	MINT	EXC	G-VG
COMPLETE SET (200)	16.00	8.00	1.60
COMMON PLAYER (1-200)	.07	.03	.01
□ 1 Rick Anheuser	.07	.03	.01
□ 2 Rick Anheuser	.07	.03	.01
□ 3 Rick Anheuser	.07	.03	.01
□ 4 Pete Auksel	.07	.03	.01
□ 5 Pete Auksel	.07	.03	.01
□ 6 Pete Auksel	.07	.03	.01
□ 7 Clyde Austin	.10	.05	.01
□ 8 Clyde Austin	.10	.05	.01
□ 9 Clyde Austin	.10	.05	.01
□ 10 Thurl Bailey	.15	.07	.01
□ 11 Thurl Bailey	.15	.07	.01
□ 12 Thurl Bailey	.15	.07	.01
□ 13 Eddie Bartels	.07	.03	.01
□ 14 Eddie Bartels	.07	.03	.01
□ 15 Eddie Bartels	.07	.03	.01
□ 16 Alvin Battle	.07	.03	.01
□ 17 Alvin Battle	.07	.03	.01
□ 18 Alvin Battle	.07	.03	.01
□ 19 William Bell	.07	.03	.01
□ 20 William Bell	.07	.03	.01
□ 21 Eddie Bierderbach	.07	.03	.01
□ 22 Eddie Bierderbach	.07	.03	.01
□ 23 Eddie Bierderbach	.07	.03	.01
□ 24 Dick Braucher	.07	.03	.01
□ 25 Dick Braucher	.07	.03	.01
□ 26 Dick Braucher	.07	.03	.01
□ 27 Chuck Brown	.10	.05	.01
□ 28 Chuck Brown	.10	.05	.01
□ 29 Chuck Brown	.10	.05	.01
□ 30 Vic Bubas	.10	.05	.01
□ 31 Vic Bubas	.10	.05	.01
□ 32 Tom Burleson	.15	.07	.01
□ 33 Tom Burleson	.15	.07	.01
□ 34 Tom Burleson	.15	.07	.01
□ 35 Charles Shackleford	.10	.05	.01
□ 36 Charles Shackleford	.10	.05	.01
□ 37 Charles Shackleford	.10	.05	.01
□ 38 Terry Shackleford	.07	.03	.01
□ 39 Ronnie Shavik	.07	.03	.01
□ 40 Ronnie Shavik	.07	.03	.01
□ 41 Ronnie Shavik	.07	.03	.01
□ 42 Jon Garwood Speaks	.07	.03	.01
□ 43 Jon Garwood Speaks	.07	.03	.01
□ 44 Jon Garwood Speaks	.07	.03	.01
□ 45 Craig Watts	.07	.03	.01
□ 46 Phil Spence	.07	.03	.01
□ 47 Phil Spence	.07	.03	.01
□ 48 Phil Spence	.07	.03	.01
□ 49 Tim Stoddard	.10	.05	.01
□ 50 Tim Stoddard	.10	.05	.01
□ 51 Tim Stoddard	.10	.05	.01
□ 52 Glenn Joseph Sudhop	.07	.03	.01
□ 53 Glenn Joseph Sudhop	.07	.03	.01
□ 54 Glenn Joseph Sudhop	.07	.03	.01
□ 55 Joe Cafferky	.07	.03	.01
□ 56 Joe Cafferky	.07	.03	.01
□ 57 Larry Wosley	.07	.03	.01
□ 58 Kenny Carr	.10	.05	.01
□ 59 Kenny Carr	.10	.05	.01
□ 60 Kenny Carr	.10	.05	.01
□ 61 Horace McKinney	.10	.05	.01
□ 62 John Richter	.07	.03	.01
□ 63 Warren Cartier	.07	.03	.01
□ 64 Paul Coder	.07	.03	.01
□ 65 Paul Coder	.07	.03	.01
□ 66 Paul Coder	.07	.03	.01
□ 67 Bill Kretzer	.07	.03	.01
□ 68 Darnell Adell	.07	.03	.01
□ 69 Gary Stokan	.07	.03	.01
□ 70 Pete Coker	.07	.03	.01
□ 71 Dereck Whittenburg	.10	.05	.01
□ 72 Pete Coker	.07	.03	.01
□ 73 Craig Davis	.07	.03	.01
□ 74 Smedes York	.07	.03	.01
□ 75 Craig Davis	.07	.03	.01
□ 76 Dick Dickey	.07	.03	.01
□ 77 Dick Dickey	.07	.03	.01
□ 78 Dick Dickey	.07	.03	.01
□ 79 Tommy Dinardo	.07	.03	.01
□ 80 Tommy Dinardo	.07	.03	.01
□ 81 Van Williford	.07	.03	.01
□ 82 Bob Distefano	.07	.03	.01
□ 83 Dan Englehardt	.07	.03	.01
□ 84 Dan Englehardt	.07	.03	.01
□ 85 Gary Stokan	.07	.03	.01
□ 86 Smedes York	.07	.03	.01
□ 87 Van Williford	.07	.03	.01
□ 88 Vinny Del Negro	.10	.05	.01
□ 89 Vinny Del Negro	.10	.05	.01
□ 90 Vinny Del Negro	.10	.05	.01
□ 91 Larry Larkins	.07	.03	.01
□ 92 Larry Larkins	.07	.03	.01
□ 93 Larry Larkins	.07	.03	.01
□ 94 Larry Larkins	.07	.03	.01
□ 95 Sidney Lowe	.10	.05	.01
□ 96 Sidney Lowe	.10	.05	.01
□ 97 Ernest Myers	.07	.03	.01
□ 98 Ernest Myers	.07	.03	.01
□ 99 Ernest Myers	.07	.03	.01
□ 100 Checklist 1-100	.10	.05	.01
□ 101 Hal Blondeau	.07	.03	.01
□ 102 Les Robinson	.15	.07	.01
□ 103 Nate McMillan	.15	.07	.01
□ 104 Nate McMillan	.15	.07	.01
□ 105 Nate McMillan	.15	.07	.01
□ 106 Charles G. Nevitt	.10	.05	.01
□ 107 Charles G. Nevitt	.10	.05	.01
□ 108 Charles G. Nevitt	.10	.05	.01
□ 109 Quinton Leonard	.07	.03	.01
□ 110 Bruce Hoadley	.07	.03	.01
□ 111 Les Robinson	.15	.07	.01
□ 112 Bruce Hoadley	.07	.03	.01
□ 113 Emmett Lay	.07	.03	.01
□ 114 Emmett Lay	.07	.03	.01
□ 115 Larry Worsley	.07	.03	.01
□ 116 Harold Thompson	.07	.03	.01
□ 117 Harold Thompson	.07	.03	.01
□ 118 Harold Thompson	.07	.03	.01
□ 119 Howard Turner	.07	.03	.01
□ 120 Mike O'Neal Warren	.07	.03	.01
□ 121 Mike O'Neal Warren	.07	.03	.01
□ 122 Kenny Matthews	.07	.03	.01
□ 123 Anthony Warren	.07	.03	.01
□ 124 Anthony Warren	.07	.03	.01
□ 125 Vann Williford	.07	.03	.01
□ 126 Raymond Walters	.07	.03	.01
□ 127 Raymond Walters	.07	.03	.01
□ 128 Raymond Walters	.07	.03	.01
□ 129 Craig T. Watts	.07	.03	.01
□ 130 Larry Worsley	.07	.03	.01
□ 131 Craig T. Watts	.07	.03	.01
□ 132 Spud Webb	.15	.07	.01
□ 133 Spud Webb	.15	.07	.01
□ 134 Spud Webb	.15	.07	.01
□ 135 Ray Hodgdon	.07	.03	.01
□ 136 Herb Applebaum	.07	.03	.01
□ 137 Bill Kretzer	.07	.03	.01
□ 138 Charles Whitney	.10	.05	.01
□ 139 Charles Whitney	.10	.05	.01
□ 140 Charles Whitney	.10	.05	.01
□ 141 Dereck Whittenburg	.10	.05	.01
□ 142 Dereck Whittenburg	.10	.05	.01
□ 143 Tom Mattocks	.07	.03	.01
□ 144 Tom Mattocks	.07	.03	.01
□ 145 Tom Mattocks	.07	.03	.01
□ 146 Mark Moeller	.07	.03	.01
□ 147 Mark Moeller	.07	.03	.01
□ 148 Mark Moeller	.07	.03	.01
□ 149 Cheerleader/Mascot	.07	.03	.01
□ 150 Quinton Jackson	.07	.03	.01
□ 151 Quinton Jackson	.07	.03	.01
□ 152 Steve Nuce	.07	.03	.01
□ 153 Steve Nuce	.07	.03	.01
□ 154 Steve Nuce	.07	.03	.01
□ 155 Scott Parzych	.07	.03	.01
□ 156 Scott Parzych	.07	.03	.01
□ 157 Scott Parzych	.07	.03	.01
□ 158 Dan Wherry	.07	.03	.01

☐ 159 Hal Blondeau	.07	.03	.01
☐ 160 Dan Wherry	.07	.03	.01
☐ 161 Mascots	.07	.03	.01
☐ 162 Max Perry	.07	.03	.01
☐ 163 Max Perry	.07	.03	.01
☐ 164 David Thompson	.30	.15	.03
☐ 165 David Thompson	.30	.15	.03
☐ 166 David Thompson	.30	.15	.03
☐ 167 Monte Towe	.10	.05	.01
☐ 168 Monte Towe	.10	.05	.01
☐ 169 Monte Towe	.10	.05	.01
☐ 170 Press Maravich	.10	.05	.01
☐ 171 Terry Gannon	.07	.03	.01
☐ 172 Nick Pond	.07	.03	.01
☐ 173 Lou Pucillo	.07	.03	.01
☐ 174 Ray Hodgdon	.07	.03	.01
☐ 175 Darnell Adell	.07	.03	.01
☐ 176 Herb Applebaum	.07	.03	.01
☐ 177 Max Perry	.07	.03	.01
☐ 178 John Richter	.07	.03	.01
☐ 179 Kenny Polston	.07	.03	.01
☐ 180 Terry Gannon	.07	.03	.01
☐ 181 Pete Coker	.07	.03	.01
☐ 182 Quinton Jackson	.07	.03	.01
☐ 183 Jim Rezinger	.07	.03	.01
☐ 184 Kenny Poston	.07	.03	.01
☐ 185 Rick Hoot	.07	.03	.01
☐ 186 Everett Case	.10	.05	.01
☐ 187 Everett Case	.10	.05	.01
☐ 188 Everett Case	.10	.05	.01
☐ 189 Kenny Mathews	.07	.03	.01
☐ 190 Reynold Stadium	.07	.03	.01
☐ 191 James T. Valvano CO	.25	.12	.02
☐ 192 James T. Valvano CO	.25	.12	.02
☐ 193 James T. Valvano CO	.25	.12	.02
☐ 194 Cheerleaders	.07	.03	.01
☐ 195 Ray Hodgdon	.07	.03	.01
☐ 196 Lou Pucillo	.07	.03	.01
☐ 197 Kenny Poston	.07	.03	.01
☐ 198 Everett Case	.10	.05	.01
☐ 199 Reynolds Coliseum	.07	.03	.01
☐ 200 Checklist 101-200	.10	.05	.01

1989-90 North Carolina State Police

This 16-card set of standard size (2 1/2" by 3 1/2") cards was sponsored by Hardee's WPTF/680 AM radio, and IBM; these company logos adorn the top of observe and the bottom of the reverse. The front features a color action player photo, with red borders on the top, right, and for most of the bottom. The school name and player identification is given in the top and bottom borders, with the year "1989-90" in the lower left corner. The back has biographical information and "Tips from the Wolfpack," which consist of anti-drug messages. The cards are unnumbered and are checklisted below in alphabetical order, with the uniform number after the player's name.

	MINT	EXC	G-VG
COMPLETE SET (16)	16.00	8.00	1.60
COMMON PLAYER (1-16)	.75	.35	.07
☐ 1 Chris Corchiani 13	1.50	.75	.15
☐ 2 Brian D'Amico 54	.75	.35	.07
☐ 3 Bryant Feggins 34	.75	.35	.07
☐ 4 Tom Gugliotta 24	3.50	1.75	.35
☐ 5 Mickey Hinnant 3	.75	.35	.07
☐ 6 Brian Howard 22	1.00	.50	.10
☐ 7 Jamie Knox 23	.75	.35	.07
☐ 8 David Lee 25	.75	.35	.07
☐ 9 Avie Lester 32	1.00	.50	.10
☐ 10 Rodney Monroe 21	2.50	1.25	.25
☐ 11 Andrea Stinson 32	1.25	.60	.12
☐ 12 Kevin Thompson 42	.75	.35	.07
☐ 13 Jim Valvano CO	1.50	.75	.15
☐ 14 Roland Whitley 15	.75	.35	.07
☐ 15 "Wuf" Mascot	.75	.35	.07
☐ 16 Kay Yow Women's Coach	.75	.35	.07

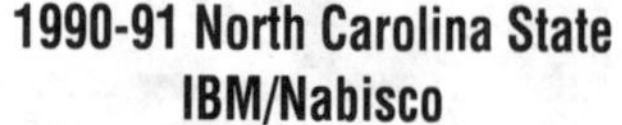

1990-91 North Carolina State IBM/Nabisco

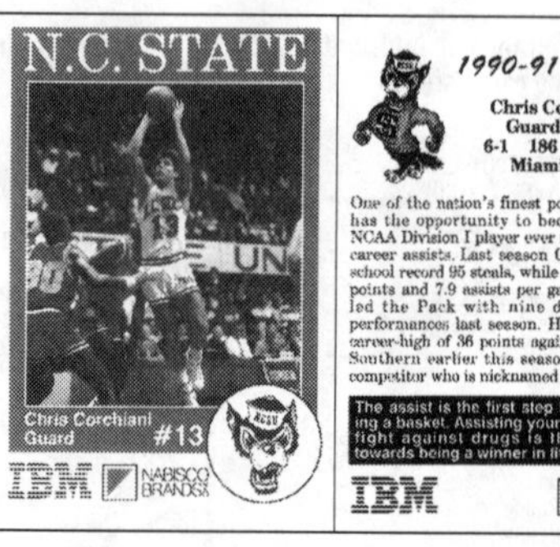

This 15-card standard size (2 1/2" by 3 1/2") set was cosponsored by IBM and Nabisco Brands. Two thousand five hundred sets were given away at Youth Night before a home game, and an equal number of sets were distributed by local police officers. On a white card face, the fronts feature action or posed color photos enclosed by a red border. The school name appears above the picture, while player information is provided beneath the picture. A Wolfpack logo appears in the lower right corner in a circle. The backs carry biography and player profile, with anti-drug and alcohol messages in a black box. The cards are unnumbered and checklisted below in alphabetical order. This set includes a card of Andrea Stinson, dubbed the "Female Michael Jordan" for her scoring ability and dynamic flair.

	MINT	EXC	G-VG
COMPLETE SET (15)	12.00	6.00	1.20
COMMON PLAYER (1-15)	.75	.35	.07
☐ 1 Migjen Bakalli	.75	.35	.07
☐ 2 Chris Corchiani	1.50	.75	.15
☐ 3 Bryant Feggins	.75	.35	.07
☐ 4 Adam Fletcher	.75	.35	.07
☐ 5 Jamie Knox	.75	.35	.07
☐ 6 David Lee	.75	.35	.07
☐ 7 Marc Lewis	.75	.35	.07
☐ 8 Rodney Monroe	2.50	1.25	.25
☐ 9 Anthony Robinson	1.00	.50	.10
☐ 10 Les Robinson CO	1.00	.50	.10
☐ 11 Andrea Stinson	1.25	.60	.12
☐ 12 Kevin Thompson	.75	.35	.07
☐ 13 Kay Yow CO Women's Basketball	.75	.35	.07
☐ 14 Celebrating a Victory Paul Campion Chris Ritter Tim Thompson	.75	.35	.07
☐ 15 Mr. Wuf Mascot	.75	.35	.07

1991-92 North Carolina State IBM/Nabisco

This 16-card standard size (2 1/2" by 3 1/2") set was cosponsored by IBM and Nabisco Biscuit Company. The print run was limited to 5,000 sets, and the sets were given away at Youth Night and distributed by the local police department. The fronts feature action color player photos enclosed by a red border. The team name is superimposed in white lettering at the top of the picture, while the player's name, Wolfpack logo, and sponsor names appear at the bottom of the card face. In a horizontal format, the backs carry a black and white mug shot, biography, career highlights, and anti-drug messages in a black box. The cards are unnumbered and checklisted below in alphabetical order.

	MINT	EXC	G-VG
COMPLETE SET (16)	12.00	6.00	1.20
COMMON PLAYER (1-16)	.75	.35	.07
☐ 1 Migjen Bakalli	.75	.35	.07
☐ 2 Mark Davis	.75	.35	.07
☐ 3 Bryant Feggins	.75	.35	.07
☐ 4 Adam Fletcher	.75	.35	.07
☐ 5 Tom Gugliotta	2.50	1.25	.25
☐ 6 Jamie Knox	.75	.35	.07
☐ 7 Marc Lewis	.75	.35	.07
☐ 8 Curtis Marshall	.75	.35	.07
☐ 9 Lakista McCuller	.75	.35	.07
☐ 10 Victor Newman	.75	.35	.07
☐ 11 Anthony Robinson	1.00	.50	.10
☐ 12 Les Robinson CO	1.00	.50	.10
☐ 13 Donnie Seale	.75	.35	.07
☐ 14 Kevin Thompson	.75	.35	.07
☐ 15 Mr. Wuf Mascot	.75	.35	.07
☐ 16 Reynolds Coliseum	.75	.35	.07

1991-92 North Dakota *

This 20-card multi-sport set features the 1991-92 Fighting Sioux hockey team, and the 1989-90 and 1990-91 men's and women's basketball championship teams. The cards measure the standard size (2 1/2" by 3 1/2"), and the production run was limited to 500 sets. On white card stock, the fronts have a multi-player format, displaying three color player photos per card. The cards presenting basketball players have green and black borders, while the cards presenting hockey players have orange and black borders. The team logo appears in a white circle at the lower right corner. The horizontally oriented backs present biographical and statistical information enclosed by black borders. The cards are unnumbered and listed below according to the checklist card.

	MINT	EXC	G-VG
COMPLETE SET (20)	12.00	6.00	1.20
COMMON PLAYER (1-20)	.60	.30	.06
☐ 1 Whitney Meier Greg Johnson David Vonesh	1.00	.50	.10
☐ 2 Marty McDermott Chris Gardner Scott Guldseth	.60	.30	.06
☐ 3 Ben Jacobson Steve McAndrew David Robertson	.60	.30	.06
☐ 4 Jonathon Marshall Mike Wiskus Broderick Powell	.60	.30	.06
☐ 5 Todd Johnson Mark Sipple James Baird	.60	.30	.06
☐ 6 Team Photo Men's Basketball Team	.75	.35	.07
☐ 7 Team Photo Women's Basketball Team	.60	.30	.06
☐ 8 Darcy Deutsch Tracey Pudenz Jenny Walter	.60	.30	.06
☐ 9 Heidi Kasprowicz Misty Langseth Shea Smirl	.60	.30	.06
☐ 10 Maria Oistad Heidi Meyer Emily Shilhanek	.60	.30	.06
☐ 11 Team Photo Football Team	.75	.35	.07
☐ 12 Shanon Burnell Kory Wahl Bill Riviere	.60	.30	.06
☐ 13 Team Photo Hockey Team	.75	.35	.07
☐ 14 Dixon Ward Marty Schriner Greg Johnson	1.00	.50	.10
☐ 15 Russ Romaniuk Jeff McLean Jason Herter	2.00	1.00	.20
☐ 16 Donny Riendeau Chad Johnson Dane Jackson	.60	.30	.06
☐ 17 The Roseau Connection Chris Gotziaman Corey Howe Jon Larson	.60	.30	.06
☐ 18 Darren Bear Jamie Burt Brad Bombardir	1.00	.50	.10
☐ 19 Brad Pascall Dave Hakstol Justin Duberman	.60	.30	.06
☐ 20 Jeff Lembke Todd Jones Corey Cadden Checklist	.60	.30	.06

1990-91 Notre Dame

This set is a retrospective on famous and outstanding players at Notre Dame, consisting of 59 cards measuring the standard

size, 2 1/2" by 3 1/2". The cards are numbered up to "58 of 58"; the Anson card is unnumbered and is the only baseball player in the set. On the front, older players appear in black and white photos while newer players appear in color. The photos are enframed by a black line on a white background, with the school name and the Notre Dame logo (upper right hand corner) above the photo, and the player's name below. The card backs provide biographical information, including the player's position and the team they played on. Past and present NBA players included are Gary Brokaw, Austin Carr, Adrian Dantley, Bill Hanzlik, Tom Hawkins, Toby Knight, Bill Laimbeer, John Paxson, David Rivers, John Shumate, Kelly Tripucka, and Orlando Woolridge.

	MINT	EXC	G-VG
COMPLETE SET (59)	15.00	7.50	1.50
COMMON PLAYER (1-59)	.20	.10	.02
☐ 1 Richard(Digger) Phelps	.30	.15	.03
☐ 2 Collis Jones	.30	.15	.03
☐ 3 Dick Rosenthal	.20	.10	.02
☐ 4 Tim Singleton	.30	.15	.03
☐ 5 Austin Carr	.50	.25	.05
☐ 6 Kevin O'Shea	.20	.10	.02
☐ 7 Keith Tower	.20	.10	.02
☐ 8 Tom Hawkins	.30	.15	.03
☐ 9 Leo Barnhorst	.30	.15	.03
☐ 10 John Shumate	.50	.25	.05
☐ 11 Donald Royal	.40	.20	.04
☐ 12 Edward(Moose) Krause	.30	.15	.03
☐ 13 Bill Laimbeer	1.00	.50	.10
☐ 14 Adrian Dantley	1.25	.60	.12
☐ 15 Keith Robinson	.50	.25	.05
☐ 16 Edward(Monk) Malloy	.30	.15	.03
☐ 17 Leo Klier	.30	.15	.03
☐ 18 Rich Branning	.30	.15	.03
☐ 19 Don(Duck) Williams	.30	.15	.03
☐ 20 Kevin Ellery	.20	.10	.02
☐ 21 Eddie Smith	.20	.10	.02
☐ 22 Ken Barlow	.30	.15	.03
☐ 23 LaPhonso Ellis	.60	.30	.06
☐ 24 John Nyikos	.20	.10	.02
☐ 25 Daimon Sweet	.30	.15	.03
☐ 26 Jack Stephens	.20	.10	.02
☐ 27 Orlando Woolridge	.60	.30	.06
☐ 28 Noble Kizer	.20	.10	.02
☐ 29 John Smyth	.20	.10	.02
☐ 30 John Paxson	1.25	.60	.12
☐ 31 Paul Nowak	.20	.10	.02
☐ 32 Elmer Bennett	.40	.20	.04
☐ 33 Toby Knight	.30	.15	.03
☐ 34 Dave Batton	.30	.15	.03
☐ 35 Bob Whitmore	.20	.10	.02
☐ 36 David Rivers	.50	.25	.05
☐ 37 Gary Brokaw	.50	.25	.05
☐ 38 Gary Novak	.20	.10	.02
☐ 39 Lloyd Aubrey	.20	.10	.02
☐ 40 Robert Faught	.20	.10	.02
☐ 41 Raymond Scanlan	.20	.10	.02
☐ 42 Bill Hanzlik	.40	.20	.04
☐ 43 Vince Boryla	.30	.15	.03
☐ 44 Eddie Riska	.20	.10	.02
☐ 45 Dwight Clay	.20	.10	.02
☐ 46 Bruce Flowers	.30	.15	.03
☐ 47 Ray Meyer	.30	.15	.03
☐ 48 Monty Williams	.20	.10	.02
☐ 49 John Moir	.20	.10	.02
☐ 50 Bill Hassett	.20	.10	.02
☐ 51 Bob Arnzen	.30	.15	.03
☐ 52 Robert Rensberger	.20	.10	.02
☐ 53 Larry Sheffield	.20	.10	.02
☐ 54 Kelly Tripucka	.50	.25	.05
☐ 55 Ron Reed	.30	.15	.03
☐ 56 George Ireland	.30	.15	.03
☐ 57 Tracy Jackson	.50	.25	.05
☐ 58 Walt Sahm	.20	.10	.02
☐ xx Adrian(Cap) Anson (unnumbered)	.75	.35	.07

1991-92 Ohio State

This 15-card standard-size (2 1/2" by 3 1/2") set was produced by College Classics of Columbus, Ohio. The cards were sold in the university bookstore and at a souvenir shop in St. John Arena. The cards were sold through April 30, and the print run was limited by the number of sets requested by the bookstore. It is reported that more than 10,000 sets were sold in the first four weeks. The fronts features either action or posed color player photos enclosed by red and gray borders. The player's name is printed in a gray stripe beneath the picture, while his position appears in a gray stripe along the right side of the picture. The school logo appears at the top right of the photo. In a horizontal format, the backs carry a color head shot, school logo, biography, career summary, and statistics. The cards are unnumbered and checklisted below in alphabetical order. The key card in the set is Jim Jackson, 1992 NBA Draft lottery pick.

	MINT	EXC	G-VG
COMPLETE SET (15)	12.00	6.00	1.20
COMMON PLAYER (1-15)	.50	.25	.05
☐ 1 Randy Ayers CO	1.00	.50	.10
☐ 2 Mark Baker	1.00	.50	.10
☐ 3 Tom Brandewie	.50	.25	.05
☐ 4 Jamaal Brown	1.00	.50	.10
☐ 5 Alex Davis	.50	.25	.05
☐ 6 Rickey Dudley	.50	.25	.05
☐ 7 Doug Etzler	.50	.25	.05
☐ 8 Lawrence Funderburke	2.50	1.25	.25
☐ 9 Steve Hall	.50	.25	.05
☐ 10 Jim Jackson	6.00	3.00	.60
☐ 11 Chris Jent	1.00	.50	.10
☐ 12 Jimmy Ratliff	.50	.25	.05
☐ 13 Joe Reid	.50	.25	.05
☐ 14 Bill Robinson	.50	.25	.05
☐ 15 Jamie Skelton	.50	.25	.05

1991 Oklahoma State 100 *

This 100-card multi-sport set was produced by Collegiate Collection and measures the standard size (2 1/2" by 3 1/2"). The fronts features a mix of black and white or color player photos with orange borders, with the player's name in a black stripe below the picture. In a horizontal format the backs

present biographical information, career summary, or statistics on a white background. The cards are numbered on the back.

	MINT	EXC	G-VG
COMPLETE SET (100)	12.50	6.25	1.25
COMMON PLAYER (1-100)	.10	.05	.01

	MINT	EXC	G-VG
☐ 1 Henry Iba	.30	.15	.03
☐ 2 Barry Sanders	1.00	.50	.10
☐ 3 Thurman Thomas	.75	.35	.07
☐ 4 Robin Ventura	.75	.35	.07
☐ 5 Bob Kurland	.30	.15	.03
☐ 6 Athletic Tradition	.10	.05	.01
☐ 7 1959 NCAA Baseball Champions	.10	.05	.01
☐ 8 1945 NCAA Basketball Champions	.10	.05	.01
☐ 9 Bob Tway	.25	.12	.02
☐ 10 Allie Reynolds	.20	.10	.02
☐ 11 Rodney Harling	.10	.05	.01
☐ 12 Ed Gallagher	.10	.05	.01
☐ 13 Walt Garrison	.25	.12	.02
☐ 14 Terry Miller	.15	.07	.01
☐ 15 Bob Fenimore	.10	.05	.01
☐ 16 Gerald Hudson	.10	.05	.01
☐ 17 Hart Lee Dykes	.20	.10	.02
☐ 18 1976 Big 8 Conference	.10	.05	.01
☐ 19 Jimmy Johnson	.30	.15	.03
☐ 20 Terry Brown	.15	.07	.01
☐ 21 Derrel Gofourth	.10	.05	.01
☐ 22 Paul Blair	.20	.10	.02
☐ 23 John Little	.10	.05	.01
☐ 24 1983 Bluebonnet Bowl	.10	.05	.01
☐ 25 John Smith	.10	.05	.01
☐ 26 1976 Tangerine Bowl	.10	.05	.01
☐ 27 Gary Cutsinger	.10	.05	.01
☐ 28 Rusty Hilger	.15	.07	.01
☐ 29 Ron Baker	.10	.05	.01
☐ 30 Pat Jones	.15	.07	.01
☐ 31 Phillip Dokes	.10	.05	.01
☐ 32 Neil Armstrong	.15	.07	.01
☐ 33 Joel Horlen	.20	.10	.02
☐ 34 Jon Kolb	.15	.07	.01
☐ 35 1958 NCAA Wrestling Champs	.10	.05	.01
☐ 36 Doug Tewell	.15	.07	.01
☐ 37 1984 Gator Bowl Catch	.10	.05	.01
☐ 38 Scott Verplank	.30	.15	.03
☐ 39 1946 Sugar Bowl	.10	.05	.01
☐ 40 John Starks	.35	.17	.03
☐ 41 Liz Brown	.10	.05	.01
☐ 42 1984 Gator Bowl	.10	.05	.01
☐ 43 Yojiro Uetake	.10	.05	.01
☐ 44 1988 Holiday Bowl	.10	.05	.01
☐ 45 Ernest Anderson	.10	.05	.01
☐ 46 Leslie O'Neal	.20	.10	.02
☐ 47 Ken Monday	.10	.05	.01
☐ 48 Leonard Thompson	.15	.07	.01
☐ 49 Jess(Cob) Rennick	.10	.05	.01
☐ 50 Mike Gundy	.20	.10	.02
☐ 51 Mark Moore	.10	.05	.01
☐ 52 Clinette Jordan	.10	.05	.01
☐ 53 O.A.(Bum) Phillips	.25	.12	.02
☐ 54 John Ward	.10	.05	.01
☐ 55 Larry Roach	.15	.07	.01
☐ 56 Jerry Sherk	.15	.07	.01
☐ 57 Matt Monger	.10	.05	.01
☐ 58 Dick Soergel	.10	.05	.01
☐ 59 Ricky Young	.15	.07	.01
☐ 60 Labron Harris and 1963 NCAA Championship Team	.10	.05	.01
☐ 61 Barry Sanders	1.00	.50	.10
☐ 62 Gary Green	.15	.07	.01
☐ 63 Henry Iba	.25	.12	.02
☐ 64 David Edwards	.20	.10	.02
☐ 65 Tom Chesbro	.10	.05	.01
☐ 66 Chris Rockins	.10	.05	.01
☐ 67 Buddy Ryan	.30	.15	.03
☐ 68 Thurman Thomas	.75	.35	.07
☐ 69 Frank Lewis	.20	.10	.02
☐ 70 Doug Dascenzo	.20	.10	.02
☐ 71 Pete Incaviglia	.30	.15	.03
☐ 72 Willie Wood	.25	.12	.02
☐ 73 James Butler	.10	.05	.01
☐ 74 Lori McNeil	.25	.12	.02
☐ 75 Monty Farris	.25	.12	.02
☐ 76 Barry Sanders	1.00	.50	.10
☐ 77 Mickey Tettleton	.35	.17	.03
☐ 78 Barry and Thurman	1.00	.50	.10
☐ 80 Gale McArthur	.10	.05	.01
☐ 81 Thurman Thomas	.75	.35	.07
☐ 82 Danny Edwards	.10	.05	.01
☐ 83 Barry Sanders	1.00	.50	.10
☐ 84 Mike Sheets	.10	.05	.01
☐ 85 Jerry Adair	.15	.07	.01
☐ 86 Thurman Thomas	.75	.35	.07
☐ 87 Garth Brooks	3.00	1.50	.30
☐ 88 John Farrell	.15	.07	.01
☐ 89 Mike Holder and 1987 NCAA Championship Team	.10	.05	.01
☐ 90 Jim Traber	.15	.07	.01
☐ 91 Lindy Miller	.15	.07	.01
☐ 92 Mike Henneman	.30	.15	.03
☐ 93 Thurman Thomas	.75	.35	.07
☐ 94 John Washington	.10	.05	.01
☐ 95 Michael Daniel	.10	.05	.01
☐ 96 Ralph Higgins	.10	.05	.01
☐ 97 1987 Sun Bowl	.10	.05	.01
☐ 98 Garrett Limbrick	.10	.05	.01
☐ 99 Eddie Sutton	.15	.07	.01
☐ 100 Director Card	.10	.05	.01

1991-92 Oklahoma State Motion Sports

Produced by Motion Sports, this 54-card set features the Oklahoma State Cowboys basketball team. Two sets were available: 1) a team-issued set (no more than 5,000 sets produced); and 2) a set of 8" by 10" photos autographed by all players and coaches, and encased in an 8" by 10" leather binder. The regular set was sold to the public at all home games and through the Student Union Bookstore. The cards measure the standard size (2 1/2" by 3 1/2"). The fronts of card numbers 1-25 display a full-color head shot of the player on a screened red background enframed by a black border. The player's name appears in a gray-to-red screened band at the top of the photo while the school name and sponsor's name (Johnsons) appear in a red band at the bottom. Card numbers 28-32 have on the fronts action photos of seniors on the squad. The last major section of the set consists of card numbers 37-54. These cards are similar to SkyBox in design, with color action player photos cut out and superimposed over a background of computer-generated graphics and geometric shapes. The player information on the backs of all cards is superimposed over ghosted OSU campus scenes. The cards are numbered on the back.

	MINT	EXC	G-VG
COMPLETE SET (57)	22.00	11.00	2.20
COMMON PLAYER (1-54)	.40	.20	.04
☐ 1 Earl Jones	.50	.25	.05
☐ 2 Corey Williams	.75	.35	.07
☐ 3 Jason Turk	.40	.20	.04
☐ 4 Binky Triplett	.40	.20	.04
☐ 5 Sean Sutton	.60	.30	.06
☐ 6 Darwyn Alexander	.40	.20	.04
☐ 7 Sean Walker	.40	.20	.04
☐ 8 Terry Collins	.40	.20	.04
☐ 9 Byron Houston	2.00	1.00	.20
☐ 10 Randy Davis	.40	.20	.04
☐ 11 Scott Sutton	.50	.25	.05
☐ 12 Brooks Thompson	.40	.20	.04
☐ 13 Mike Philpott	.40	.20	.04
☐ 14 Cornell Hatcher	.40	.20	.04
☐ 15 Milton Brown	.40	.20	.04
☐ 16 Sean Pell	.40	.20	.04
☐ 17 Von Bennett	.40	.20	.04
☐ 18 Bryant Reeves	.40	.20	.04
☐ 19 Steve Anthis	.40	.20	.04
Assistant CO			
☐ 20 Scott Streller	.40	.20	.04
Assistant CO			
☐ 21 Russ Pennell	.40	.20	.04
Assistant CO			
☐ 22 Eddie Sutton CO	.60	.30	.06
☐ 23 Rob Evans	.40	.20	.04
Assistant CO			
☐ 24 Bill Self	.40	.20	.04
Assistant CO			
☐ 25 Pistol Pete	.50	.25	.05
Mascot			
☐ 26 Eddie Sutton CO	.60	.30	.06
☐ 27 Trophies	.40	.20	.04
☐ 28 Cornell Hatcher	.40	.20	.04
☐ 29 Byron Houston	2.00	1.00	.20
☐ 30 Corey Williams	.40	.20	.04
☐ 31 Sean Sutton	.75	.35	.07
☐ 32 Darwyn Alexander	.40	.20	.04
☐ 33 Eddie Sutton CO	.60	.30	.06
Henry Iba			
☐ 34 Team Photo	.60	.30	.06
☐ 35 Mike Johnson	.40	.20	.04
John Johnson			
Basketball Sponsors			
☐ 36 Scott Sutton	.75	.35	.07
Sean Sutton			
Eddie Sutton CO			
☐ 37 Milton Brown	.40	.20	.04
☐ 38 Earl Jones	.40	.20	.04
☐ 39 Terry Collins	.40	.20	.04
☐ 40 Von Bennett	.40	.20	.04
☐ 41 Byron Houston	2.00	1.00	.20
☐ 42 Darwyn Alexander	.40	.20	.04
☐ 43 Mike Philpott	.40	.20	.04
☐ 44 Sean Pell	.40	.20	.04
☐ 45 Bryant Reeves	.40	.20	.04
☐ 46 Randy Davis	.40	.20	.04
☐ 47 Cornell Hatcher	.40	.20	.04
☐ 48 Jason Turk	.40	.20	.04
☐ 49 Sean Sutton	.75	.35	.07
☐ 50 Sean Walker	.40	.20	.04
☐ 51 Sean Walker	.40	.20	.04
☐ 52 Binky Triplett	.40	.20	.04
☐ 53 Corey Williams	.40	.20	.04
☐ 54 Brooks Thompson	.40	.20	.04
☐ xx Title Card	.40	.20	.04
☐ xx Card Directory	.40	.20	.04
Checklist			
☐ xx Ad Card	.40	.20	.04
Motion Sports			

1989-90 Oregon State

This 16-card set was printed on thin cardboard stock and issued in one sheet; after perforation, the cards measure approximately 3" by 4 1/16". The set may also have been issued as single unperforated cards. It is reported that some autographed sets were available in limited quantities. The front

features a black and white action player photo, with white borders. The player's name appears in an orange and black basketball superimposed in the upper left corner. The player's name and position appear below the picture in a black stripe. In orange lettering, the team name "Beavers" is printed, with an oversized "B". The backs are printed in orange and black, and present a black and white head shot as well as biographical and statistical information. The cards are unnumbered and are checklisted below in alphabetical order, with the uniform number after the player's name. This set includes an early card of Gary Payton, who was chosen as the second pick by Seattle in the 1990 NBA draft.

	MINT	EXC	G-VG
COMPLETE SET (16)	20.00	10.00	2.00
COMMON PLAYER (1-16)	1.00	.50	.10
☐ 1 Teo Alibegovic 12	1.00	.50	.10
☐ 2 Karl Anderson 22	1.50	.75	.15
☐ 3 Jim Anderson CO	1.50	.75	.15
☐ 4 Will Brantley 25	1.00	.50	.10
☐ 5 Bob Cavell 4	1.00	.50	.10
☐ 6 Allan Celestine 40	1.00	.50	.10
☐ 7 Kevin Grant 11	1.00	.50	.10
☐ 8 Kevin Harris 14	1.00	.50	.10
☐ 9 Scott Haskin 44	1.00	.50	.10
☐ 10 Earl Martin 24	1.00	.50	.10
☐ 11 Lamont McIntosh 33	1.00	.50	.10
☐ 12 Charles McKinney 23	1.00	.50	.10
☐ 13 Gary Payton 20	10.00	5.00	1.00
☐ 14 Chris Rueppell 21	1.00	.50	.10
☐ 15 Travis Stel 13	1.00	.50	.10
☐ 16 Jim Anderson CO	1.50	.75	.15

1990-91 Oregon State

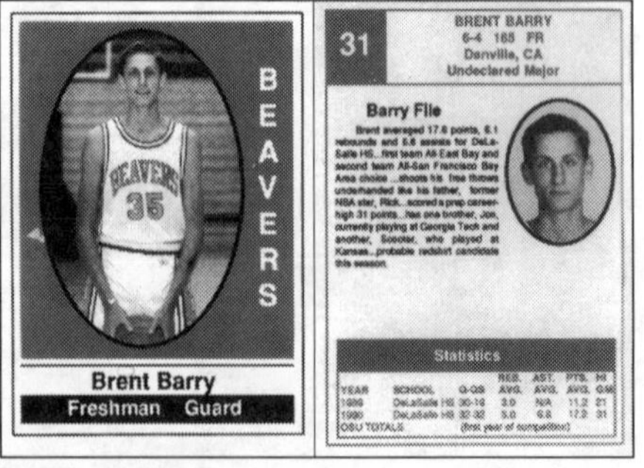

The 1990-91 Oregon State basketball set was issued on a perforated sheet, with three rows of six cards each. After perforation, the cards measure approximately 2 1/2" by 3 1/2". Supposedly 2,000 perforated sheets were produced. This set includes a card of Brent Barry, son of HOFer Rick Barry. On an orange background enclosed by white and black borders, the fronts feature black and white player photos inside an oval design. Player information appears beneath the picture. In orange and black print, the backs carry biography, career summary, and statistics. The cards are unnumbered and checklisted below in alphabetical order.

	MINT	EXC	G-VG
COMPLETE SET (18)	10.00	5.00	1.00
COMMON PLAYER (1-18)	.60	.30	.06
☐ 1 Teo Alibegovic	.60	.30	.06
☐ 2 Jim Anderson CO	.75	.35	.07
☐ 3 Karl Anderson	.75	.35	.07
☐ 4 Brent Barry	1.00	.50	.10
☐ 5 Will Brantley	.60	.30	.06
☐ 6 Bob Cavell	.60	.30	.06
☐ 7 Allan Celestine	.60	.30	.06
☐ 8 Canaan Chatman	.60	.30	.06
☐ 9 Kevin Harris	.60	.30	.06
☐ 10 Scott Haskin	.60	.30	.06
☐ 11 Mario Jackson	.60	.30	.06
☐ 12 Charles McKinney	.60	.30	.06
☐ 13 Henrik Ringmar	.60	.30	.06
☐ 14 Tony Ross	.60	.30	.06
☐ 15 Chris Rueppell	.60	.30	.06
☐ 16 Chad Scott	.60	.30	.06
☐ 17 Travis Stel	.60	.30	.06
☐ 18 Assistant Coaches Fred Boyd Andy McClouskey Jim Shaw Brent Wilder	.60	.30	.06

1991-92 Oregon State

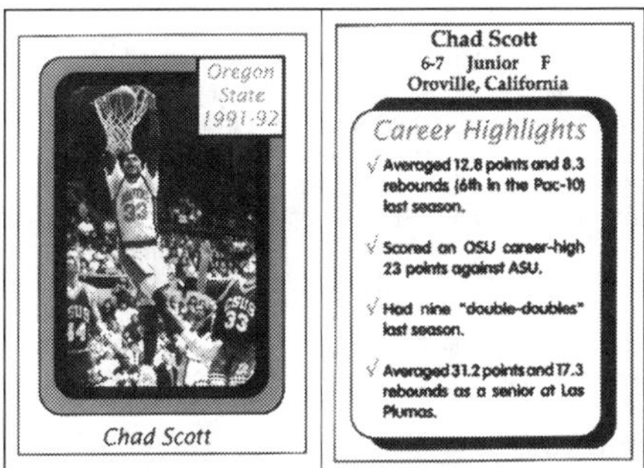

The 1991-92 Oregon State basketball set was issued on a perforated sheet, with three rows of six cards each. After perforation, the cards measure approximately 2 1/2" by 3 1/2". On a white card face, the fronts feature black and white player photos enclosed by black and orange borders. The player's name appears beneath the picture, while the words "Oregon State 1991-92" are printed in a box at the upper right corner of the picture. The backs present biography and career highlights. The cards are unnumbered and checklisted below in alphabetical order. Supposedly 2,000 perforated sheets were produced. No complete autographed sheets exist; Earl Killum died two days before the sets were complete.

	MINT	EXC	G-VG
COMPLETE SET (18)	9.00	4.50	.90
COMMON PLAYER (1-18)	.60	.30	.06
☐ 1 Jim Anderson CO	.75	.35	.07
☐ 2 Kareem Anderson	.75	.35	.07
☐ 3 Karl Anderson	.75	.35	.07
☐ 4 Brent Barry	1.25	.60	.12
☐ 5 Freddie Boyd CO	.75	.35	.07
☐ 6 David Brown	.60	.30	.06
☐ 7 Canaan Chatman	.60	.30	.06
☐ 8 Kevin Harris	.60	.30	.06
☐ 9 Scott Haskin	.60	.30	.06
☐ 10 Mario Jackson	.60	.30	.06
☐ 11 Earnest Killum	.75	.35	.07
☐ 12 David Lawson	.60	.30	.06
☐ 13 Andy McClouskey CO	.60	.30	.06
☐ 14 Charles McKinney	.60	.30	.06
☐ 15 Ray Ross	.60	.30	.06
☐ 16 Chad Scott	.60	.30	.06
☐ 17 Pat Strickland	.60	.30	.06
☐ 18 Brent Wilder CO	.60	.30	.06

1992 Penn State *

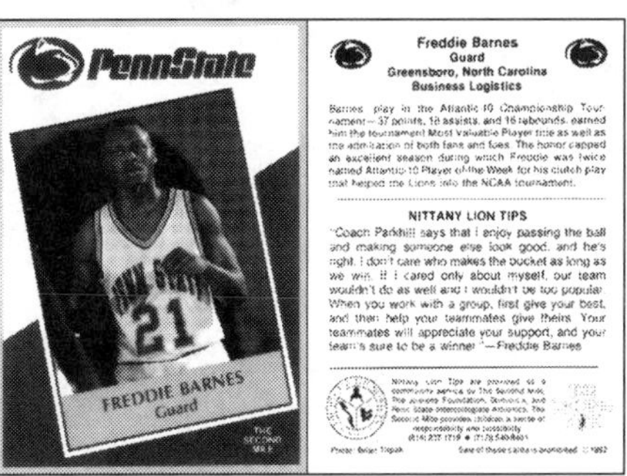

This 16-card set was sponsored by The Second Mile, the Jostens Foundation, Kmart, and Penn State Intercollegiate Athletics. The cards measure the standard size (2 1/2" by 3 1/2") and are printed on thin card stock. A diagonal cuts across the card face, separating the top white portion from the bottom blue portion. The color player photos are superimposed on this background and are tilted slightly to the left. The backs have career summary, Nittany Lion Tips in the form of player quotes, and sponsor logos. The cards are unnumbered and checklisted below in alphabetical order within sports. The sports represented in this set are men's basketball (1-3), women's basketball (4-7), gymnastics (8-13), and wrestling (14-16).

	MINT	EXC	G-VG
COMPLETE SET (16)	8.00	4.00	.80
COMMON PLAYER (1-16)	.50	.25	.05
☐ 1 Freddie Barnes	2.00	1.00	.20
☐ 2 Monroe Brown	.60	.30	.06
☐ 3 Dave Degitz	.60	.30	.06
☐ 4 Lynn Dougherty	.50	.25	.05
☐ 5 Dana Eikenberg	.50	.25	.05
☐ 6 Kathy Phillips	.50	.25	.05
☐ 7 Susan Robinson	.50	.25	.05
☐ 8 Adam Carton	.50	.25	.05
☐ 9 Wayne Cowden	.50	.25	.05
☐ 10 Jada Hiltabrand	.50	.25	.05
☐ 11 Mike Reichenbach	.50	.25	.05
☐ 12 Janice Rogers	.50	.25	.05
☐ 13 Laurie Russo	.50	.25	.05
☐ 14 Jeff Prescott	.50	.25	.05
☐ 15 Troy Sunderland	.50	.25	.05
☐ 16 Tim Wittman	.50	.25	.05

1989-90 Pitt Foodland

This 12-card set featuring members of the Pittsburgh Panthers basketball team was sponsored by Foodland; each card measures the standard size 2 1/2" by 3 1/2". The front features an action color photo enframed by orange border on blue background. Above the photo appears the school's name "Panthers" (in orange print), player's name, jersey number,

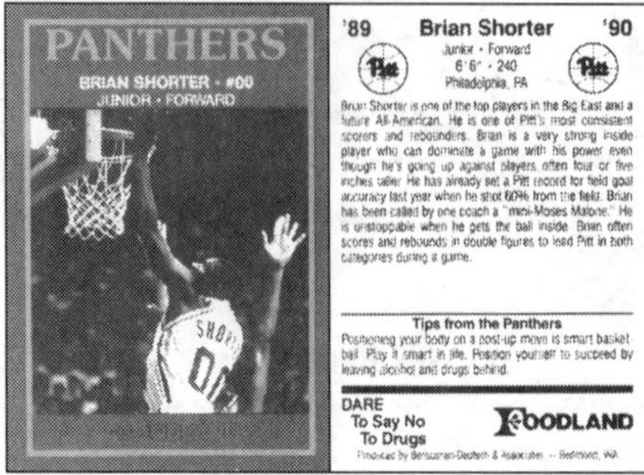

classification, and position. The sponsor's name is found below the photo. The back is filled with biographical information, a basketball tip from the Panthers, and an anti-drug message. The set is ordered below by uniform number.

	MINT	EXC	G-VG
COMPLETE SET (12)	10.00	5.00	1.00
COMMON PLAYER	.50	.25	.05
☐ 00 Brian Shorter	2.00	1.00	.20
☐ 3 Sean Miller	1.50	.75	.15
☐ 12 Pat Cavanaugh	.50	.25	.05
☐ 20 Darelle Porter	.60	.30	.06
☐ 21 Rod Brookin	1.25	.60	.12
☐ 22 Jason Matthews	1.25	.60	.12
☐ 23 Travis Ziegler	.50	.25	.05
☐ 33 Darren Morningstar	2.00	1.00	.20
☐ 42 Gilbert Johnson	.50	.25	.05
☐ 55 Bobby Martin	1.25	.60	.12
☐ xx Pitt Panther (team mascot)	.50	.25	.05
☐ xx Paul Evans CO	.75	.35	.07

1990-91 Pitt Foodland

This 12-card was sponsored by Foodland and measures the standard size (2 1/2" by 3 1/2"). The front features a borderless color action photo of the player, with "Panthers" written in blue letter on white above the picture. Two color stripes appear below the picture; in the blue one appears the player's name and number, while in the thicker orange one appears the sponsor's logo. A basketball icon superimposed over these two bars at the left completes the card face. The back has biographical information, a tip from the Pittsburgh Panthers in the form of an anti-drug or alcohol message, and the sponsor's logo. The cards are unnumbered and are checklisted them below in alphabetical order, with uniform number after the player's name.

	MINT	EXC	G-VG
COMPLETE SET (12)	9.00	4.50	.90
COMMON PLAYER (1-12)	.50	.25	.05
☐ 1 Antoine Jones 21	.50	.25	.05
☐ 2 Gandhi Jordan 4	.50	.25	.05
☐ 3 Bobby Martin 55	1.25	.60	.12
☐ 4 Jason Matthews 22	1.25	.60	.12
☐ 5 Chris McNeal 24	.75	.35	.07
☐ 6 Jermaine Morgan 42	.50	.25	.05
☐ 7 Sean Miller 3	1.50	.75	.15
☐ 8 Darren Morningstar 33	2.00	1.00	.20
☐ 9 Omo Moses 44	.50	.25	.05
☐ 10 Darelle Porter 20	.60	.30	.06
☐ 11 Ahmad Shareef 13	.50	.25	.05
☐ 12 Brian Shorter 00	2.00	1.00	.20

1991-92 Providence

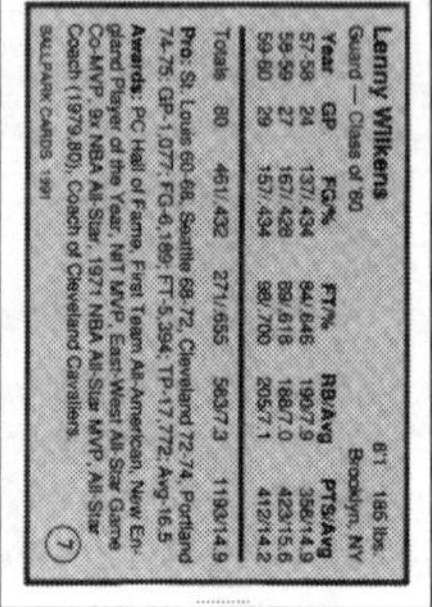

This 24-card retrospective set features the all-time great basketball players of Providence. The set was produced by Ballpark Cards, and each card measures the standard size (2 1/2" by 3 1/2"). The fronts feature a mix of black and white action or posed player photos enclosed by an orange border. The words "Providence Friars" appear at the top superimposed over an orange basketball. In black lettering on a gray background, the horizontally oriented backs have collegiate statistics, pro stints, and awards received. The card numbers appear in a circle at the bottom right. The sets were originally available direct from the school for 7.00 postpaid.

	MINT	EXC	G-VG
COMPLETE SET (24)	10.00	5.00	1.00
COMMON PLAYER (1-24)	.50	.25	.05
☐ 1 Joseph Mullaney CO 1955-1969, 1981-1985	.60	.30	.06
☐ 2 Dave Gavitt CO 1969-1979	1.00	.50	.10
☐ 3 Rick Pitino CO 1985-1987	.75	.35	.07
☐ 4 Rick Barnes CO 1988-Present	.60	.30	.06
☐ 5 Team Photo 1973 Friars	.60	.30	.06
☐ 6 Team Photo 1987 Friars	.60	.30	.06
☐ 7 Lenny Wilkens	1.00	.50	.10
☐ 8 John Egan	.60	.30	.06
☐ 9 Jim Hadnot	.60	.30	.06
☐ 10 Vinny Ernst	.50	.25	.05
☐ 11 Ray Flynn	.60	.30	.06
☐ 12 John Thompson	1.00	.50	.10
☐ 13 Mike Riordan	.75	.35	.07
☐ 14 Jimmy Walker	.75	.35	.07
☐ 15 Jim Larranaga	.60	.30	.06
☐ 16 Ernie DiGregorio	.75	.35	.07
☐ 17 Marvin Barnes	1.00	.50	.10
☐ 18 Kevin Stacom	.60	.30	.06
☐ 19 Joe Hassett	.60	.30	.06
☐ 20 Bruce Campbell	.50	.25	.05
☐ 21 Otis Thorpe	1.00	.50	.10
☐ 22 Billy Donovan	.75	.35	.07
☐ 23 Eric Murdock	1.00	.50	.10
☐ 24 Checklist	.50	.25	.05

1979-80 St. Bonaventure

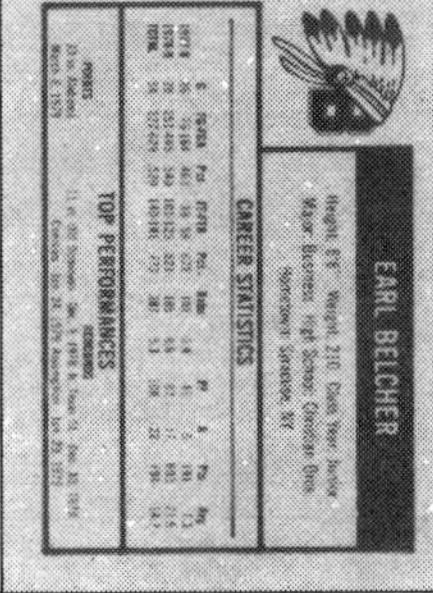

This 18-card set measures the standard size, 2 1/2" by 3 1/2". The front features a sepia-toned photo with the player's name above and jersey number in a basketball logo at upper right hand corner; the team name "Bonnies" appears below the photo. The photo is also enframed by a thin brown border on white card stock. The back is filled with biographical and statistical information. The set is ordered below alphabetically for convenience.

	NRMT	VG-E	GOOD
COMPLETE SET (18)	60.00	30.00	6.00
COMMON PLAYER (1-18)	3.00	1.50	.30
☐ 1 Earl Belcher 25	5.00	2.50	.50
☐ 2 Dan Burns 41	3.00	1.50	.30
☐ 3 Bruno DeGiglio 24	3.00	1.50	.30
☐ 4 Jim Elenz 10	3.00	1.50	.30
☐ 5 Lacey Fulmer 20	3.00	1.50	.30
☐ 6 Delmar Harrod 52	3.00	1.50	.30
☐ 7 Alfonza Jones 12	3.00	1.50	.30
☐ 8 Mark Jones 11	3.00	1.50	.30
☐ 9 Bill Kalbaugh CO	3.00	1.50	.30
☐ 10 Lloyd Praedel 44	3.00	1.50	.30
☐ 11 Pat Rodgers 35	3.00	1.50	.30
☐ 12 Bob Sassone CO	3.00	1.50	.30
☐ 13 Jim Satalin CO	3.00	1.50	.30
☐ 14 Mark Spencer 15	3.00	1.50	.30
☐ 15 Eric Stover 40	3.00	1.50	.30
☐ 16 Shawn Waterman 33	3.00	1.50	.30
☐ 17 Brian West 30	3.00	1.50	.30
☐ 18 Title Card	7.50	3.75	.75

1990-91 San Jose State Smokey

This nine-card set was printed in the same style as the 1990 San Jose football set. The cards measure 2 1/2" by 3 1/2" and are printed on thin white stock. The fronts feature color action player photos. The picture is enframed by an orange border on a blue background. The backs provide player information and have public service announcements. The cards are unnumbered and are checklisted below in alphabetical order, with the player's jersey number after the name and non-player cards listed at the end.

	MINT	EXC	G-VG
COMPLETE SET (9)	8.00	4.00	.80
COMMON PLAYER (1-9)	1.00	.50	.10
☐ 1 Troy Batiste 23	1.00	.50	.10
☐ 2 Terry Cannon 10	1.00	.50	.10
☐ 3 Robert Dunlap 50	1.00	.50	.10
☐ 4 Kevin Logan 31	1.00	.50	.10
☐ 5 Stan Morrison CO	1.00	.50	.10
☐ 6 Daryl Scott 32	1.00	.50	.10
☐ 7 Charles Terrell 4	1.50	.75	.15
☐ 8 Event Center	1.00	.50	.10
☐ 9 Smokey Bear	1.00	.50	.10

1991 South Carolina 200 *

This 200-card multi-sport set was produced by Collegiate Collection and measures the standard size (2 1/2" by 3 1/2"). The fronts features a mix of black and white or color player photos, with black borders and the player's name in the maroon stripe below the picture. In a horizontal format the backs present biographical information, career summary, or statistics on a white background with black lettering and borders. The cards are numbered on the back.

	MINT	EXC	G-VG
COMPLETE SET (200)	20.00	10.00	2.00
COMMON PLAYER (1-200)	.10	.05	.01
☐ 1 Frank McGuire CO	.25	.12	.02
☐ 2 Todd Ellis	.20	.10	.02
☐ 3 Alex English	.30	.15	.03
☐ 4 Cocky (Mascot)	.10	.05	.01
☐ 5 Kevin Darmody	.10	.05	.01
☐ 6 Kent Hagood	.10	.05	.01
☐ 7 Duane Kendall	.10	.05	.01
☐ 8 Harold Green	.60	.30	.06
☐ 9 Linwood Moye	.10	.05	.01
☐ 10 George Rogers	.30	.15	.03
☐ 11 Hardin Brown	.10	.05	.01
☐ 12 Kent Demars	.10	.05	.01
☐ 13 Bonnie Kenny	.10	.05	.01
☐ 14 Adrian Adkins	.10	.05	.01
☐ 15 George Felton	.15	.07	.01
☐ 16 Marty Baltzegar	.10	.05	.01
☐ 17 Chris Wade	.10	.05	.01
☐ 18 Nancy Wilson	.10	.05	.01
☐ 19 James Seawright	.10	.05	.01
☐ 20 Lisa Dias	.10	.05	.01
☐ 21 Kevin White	.10	.05	.01
☐ 22 June Raines	.10	.05	.01
☐ 23 Gretchen Koenig	.10	.05	.01
☐ 24 Carton Hilton	.10	.05	.01
☐ 25 Derrick Little	.10	.05	.01
☐ 26 Zam Fredrick	.10	.05	.01
☐ 27 Karen Sanchelli	.10	.05	.01
☐ 28 Ron Rabune	.10	.05	.01
☐ 29 Carolina Culik	.10	.05	.01
☐ 30 Greg Kraft	.10	.05	.01

☐	31 Warren Lipka	.10	.05	.01
☐	32 Martha Parker	.10	.05	.01
☐	33 Vic McConnell	.10	.05	.01
☐	34 Stephane Simian	.10	.05	.01
☐	35 Alex English	.30	.15	.03
☐	36 Doug Allison	.10	.05	.01
☐	37 Randy Harwell	.10	.05	.01
☐	38 Jimmy Hawthorne	.10	.05	.01
☐	39 Fritgerald Davis	.10	.05	.01
☐	40 Linda Mescan	.10	.05	.01
☐	41 Rita Winebarger	.10	.05	.01
☐	42 Bill Hency	.10	.05	.01
☐	43 Mark Berson	.10	.05	.01
☐	44 Todd Ellis	.20	.10	.02
☐	45 Joyce Compton	.10	.05	.01
☐	46 Darlene Lowery	.10	.05	.01
☐	47 David Poinsett	.10	.05	.01
☐	48 Shonna Banner	.10	.05	.01
☐	49 Joe Cardwell	.15	.07	.01
☐	50 Arlo Elkins	.10	.05	.01
☐	51 Greg Morhardt	.10	.05	.01
☐	52 Sparky Woods	.15	.07	.01
☐	53 Charles Arndt	.10	.05	.01
☐	54 Joe Morrison	.25	.12	.02
☐	55 Jeff Grantz	.10	.05	.01
☐	56 Fritz Von Kolnitz	.10	.05	.01
☐	57 Mike Caskey	.10	.05	.01
☐	58 John Roche	.20	.10	.02
☐	59 Alex Hawkins	.20	.10	.02
☐	60 Phil Lavole	.10	.05	.01
☐	61 Lee Collins	.10	.05	.01
☐	62 Jack Thompson	.10	.05	.01
☐	63 Andrew Provence	.10	.05	.01
☐	64 Kevin Joyce	.20	.10	.02
☐	65 Brian Winstead	.10	.05	.01
☐	66 J. McIver Riley	.10	.05	.01
☐	67 Bobby Heald	.15	.07	.01
☐	68 Cerrick Hordges	.10	.05	.01
☐	69 Leon Cunningham	.10	.05	.01
☐	70 Randy Martz	.15	.07	.01
☐	71 Rex Enright	.10	.05	.01
☐	72 Chris Boyle	.10	.05	.01
☐	73 Grady Wallace	.10	.05	.01
☐	74 Paul Hollins	.10	.05	.01
☐	75 Norman Rucks	.10	.05	.01
☐	76 Dan Reeves	.50	.25	.05
☐	77 Tim Lewis	.10	.05	.01
☐	78 Tom Riker	.10	.05	.01
☐	79 King Dixon	.15	.07	.01
☐	80 Bobby Cremins	.25	.12	.02
☐	81 Billy Gambrell	.15	.07	.01
☐	82 Bob Rinehart	.15	.07	.01
☐	83 Max Runager	.15	.07	.01
☐	84 Mike Cook	.10	.05	.01
☐	85 Gary Gregor	.15	.07	.01
☐	86 Bill Landrum	.20	.10	.02
☐	87 Mark Van Bever	.10	.05	.01
☐	88 Pat Dufficy	.10	.05	.01
☐	89 Joe Datin	.10	.05	.01
☐	90 Ronnie Collins	.10	.05	.01
☐	91 Del Wilkes	.10	.05	.01
☐	92 Earl Bass	.10	.05	.01
☐	93 Johnny Gregory	.10	.05	.01
☐	94 Lou Sossamon	.10	.05	.01
☐	95 Lindy James	.10	.05	.01
☐	96 Sam Daniel	.10	.05	.01
☐	97 Sharon Gilmore	.10	.05	.01
☐	98 Steve Wadiak	.10	.05	.01
☐	99 Joe Smith	.10	.05	.01
☐	100 Director Card	.10	.05	.01
☐	101 James Sumpter	.15	.07	.01
☐	102 Mark Nelson	.10	.05	.01
☐	103 Terry Dozier	.15	.07	.01
☐	104 Scott Hagler	.10	.05	.01
☐	105 Todd Berry	.10	.05	.01
☐	106 Jack Gillon	.10	.05	.01
☐	107 Carl Hill	.10	.05	.01
☐	108 Steve Liebler	.10	.05	.01
☐	109 Earl Johnson	.10	.05	.01
☐	110 Dominique Blasingame	.10	.05	.01
☐	111 Jim Desmond	.10	.05	.01
☐	112 Keith Bing	.10	.05	.01
☐	113 Garret Carter	.10	.05	.01
☐	114 Ken Diller	.10	.05	.01
☐	115 Chris Corley	.10	.05	.01
☐	116 Jay Sandberry	.10	.05	.01
☐	117 Ron Bass	.10	.05	.01
☐	118 Charlie Gowan	.10	.05	.01
☐	119 Ray Carpenter	.10	.05	.01
☐	120 Glen Thompson	.10	.05	.01
☐	121 Pat Mihn	.10	.05	.01
☐	122 Bryant Gillard	.10	.05	.01
☐	123 Darryl Martin	.10	.05	.01
☐	124 Matt McKernan	.10	.05	.01
☐	125 Mike Doyle	.10	.05	.01
☐	126 Brad Jergenson	.10	.05	.01
☐	127 Mark Fryer	.10	.05	.01
☐	128 Michael Foster	.10	.05	.01
☐	129 Anthony Smith	.10	.05	.01
☐	130 Robert Robinson	.10	.05	.01
☐	131 Mark Fleetwood	.10	.05	.01
☐	132 Skeets Thomas	.10	.05	.01
☐	133 Bobby Richardson CO	.25	.12	.02
☐	134 Rodney Price	.10	.05	.01
☐	135 Willie McIntee	.10	.05	.01
☐	136 Kenny Haynes	.10	.05	.01
☐	137 Arn Thorsson	.10	.05	.01
☐	138 Willie Scott	.10	.05	.01
☐	139 Ricky Daniels	.10	.05	.01
☐	140 Bill Barnhill	.10	.05	.01
☐	141 Gordon Beckham	.10	.05	.01
☐	142 Tim Dyches	.10	.05	.01
☐	143 John Hudson	.10	.05	.01
☐	144 Brian Williams	.15	.07	.01
☐	145 Jim Walsh	.10	.05	.01
☐	146 Keith Switer	.10	.05	.01
☐	147 Thomas Dendy	.15	.07	.01
☐	148 Gerald Peacock	.10	.05	.01
☐	149 Bill Bradshaw	.10	.05	.01
☐	150 Mike Brittain	.10	.05	.01
☐	151 Tim Berra	.20	.10	.02
☐	152 Eric Poole	.10	.05	.01
☐	153 Leonard Burton	.15	.07	.01
☐	154 Danny Smith	.10	.05	.01
☐	155 Scott Windsor	.10	.05	.01
☐	156 Art Whisnant	.10	.05	.01
☐	157 Jim Slaughter	.10	.05	.01
☐	158 Skip Harlicka	.10	.05	.01
☐	159 Bishop Strickland	.15	.07	.01
☐	160 Brian Winters	.20	.10	.02
☐	161 Rod Carroway	.10	.05	.01
☐	162 Allen Mitchell	.10	.05	.01
☐	163 Kenneth Robinson	.10	.05	.01
☐	164 Paul Vogel	.10	.05	.01
☐	165 Norman Floyd	.10	.05	.01
☐	166 Carl Brazell	.10	.05	.01
☐	167 Rod Carroway	.10	.05	.01
☐	168 Fred Ziegler	.10	.05	.01
☐	169 Frank Mincevich	.10	.05	.01
☐	170 Bobby Bryant	.15	.07	.01
☐	171 J.D. Fuller	.10	.05	.01
☐	172 Harry South	.10	.05	.01
☐	173 Tom O'Conner	.10	.05	.01
☐	174 Kevin Hendrix	.10	.05	.01
☐	175 Greg Philpot	.10	.05	.01
☐	176 Warren Muier	.10	.05	.01
☐	177 Chris Mayotte	.10	.05	.01
☐	178 Cookie Pericola	.10	.05	.01
☐	179 Tommy Suggs	.10	.05	.01
☐	180 Don Bailey	.10	.05	.01
☐	181 Zam Fredrick	.10	.05	.01
☐	182 Chris Major	.20	.10	.02
☐	183 Mike Hold	.15	.07	.01
☐	184 Brendan McCormach	.10	.05	.01
☐	185 David Taylor	.10	.05	.01
☐	186 Hank Small	.10	.05	.01
☐	187 Bryant Meeks	.10	.05	.01
☐	188 Brantley Southers	.10	.05	.01
☐	189 John Sullivan	.10	.05	.01
☐	190 Elylen Johnson	.10	.05	.01
☐	191 Harry Skipper	.15	.07	.01
☐	192 Derrick Frazier	.10	.05	.01
☐	193 Raynard Brown	.10	.05	.01
☐	194 Quinton Lewis	.10	.05	.01
☐	195 Tony Gyton	.10	.05	.01
☐	196 John Leheup	.15	.07	.01
☐	197 Dick Harris	.15	.07	.01
☐	198 Shelia Foster	.10	.05	.01
☐	199 Johnny Gramling	.10	.05	.01
☐	200 Director Card	.15	.07	.01

1987-88 Southern Police *

This 16-card set of standard size (2 1/2" by 3 1/2") cards was sponsored by McDonald's, Southern University, and local law enforcement agenciesand was produced by McDag Productions. The McDonald's logo appears at the bottom of both sides of the card. The front features a mix of action or posed, black and white player photos. The pictures are bordered in turquoise on the sides, yellow above, and white below. The school name and

AVERY JOHNSON
Guard • Senior • #15
5'11 • New Orleans, LA

Card #7

JAG FACTS

Avery was MVP of the SU Basketball team, first team ALL-SWAC, and the MVP of the SWAC Tourney. He led the nation in assists in 1987.

Tips From The Jaguars

Each player must follow the rules of the game or face a penalty. Using drugs is against the law; the penalty could cost you your freedom or worse — your life.

A service to the community from Southern University, Sam Williams, owner, McDonalds Hamburgers, Harding Blvd., and your local law enforcement agencies.

Produced by McDag Productions, Inc. P.O. Box 14686 Baton Rouge, LA 70898

player information appear in black lettering in the yellow border. A picture of the school mascot in the lower right corner rounds out the card face. The back presents biographical information, Jag Facts, and "Tips from The Jaguars" in the form of an anti-drug message. The cards are numbered on the back. The sports represented in this set are football (1-3, 14-16) and basketball (4-13).

	MINT	EXC	G-VG
COMPLETE SET (16)	10.00	5.00	1.00
COMMON PLAYER (1-16)	.60	.30	.06
□ 1 Marino Casem CO	.60	.30	.06
□ 2 Gerald Perry	2.50	1.25	.25
□ 3 Michael Ball and Toren Robinson	.60	.30	.06
□ 4 Ben Jobe CO	.60	.30	.06
□ 5 Daryl Battles	.60	.30	.06
□ 6 Patrick Garner	.60	.30	.06
□ 7 Avery Johnson	2.00	1.00	.20
□ 8 Rodney Washington	.60	.30	.06
□ 9 Kevin Florent	.60	.30	.06
□ 10 Dervynn Johnson	.60	.30	.06
□ 11 Claudene Stovall	.60	.30	.06
□ 12 Michelle Currie	.60	.30	.06
□ 13 Gibbie Phillips	.60	.30	.06
□ 14 Allan Ratliff	.60	.30	.06
□ 15 Eric Foxworth	.60	.30	.06
□ 16 Jeff Swain	.60	.30	.06

1990-91 Southern Cal Smokey *

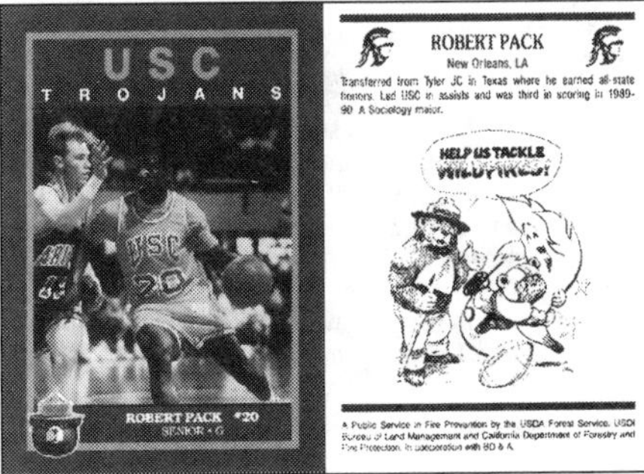

This 20-card set was sponsored by the USDA Forest Service in conjunction with several other agencies. The standard size (2 1/2" by 3 1/2") cards have color action shots, with orange borders on a maroon card face with the words "USC Trojans" above the player's picture and his name, uniform number, school year, and position underneath his picture. The back has two Trojan logos at the top and features a player profile and a fire prevention cartoon starring Smokey. The cards are unnumbered and checklisted below in alphabetical order, with the uniform number after the name. Cards 1-2 and 12 feature basketball rather than football players. The checklist card in the set lists the football players but not the basketball players. The set features the first card of Ricky Ervins.

	MINT	EXC	G-VG
COMPLETE SET (20)	12.50	6.25	1.25
COMMON PLAYER (1-20)	.50	.25	.05
□ 1 Calvin Banks 34 (Basketball)	.75	.35	.07
□ 2 Ronnie Coleman 24 (Basketball)	1.00	.50	.10
□ 3 Ricky Ervins 34	6.00	3.00	.60
□ 4 Shane Foley 10	.50	.25	.05
□ 5 Gene Fruge 91	.50	.25	.05
□ 6 Don Gibson 92	.50	.25	.05
□ 7 Frank Griffin 87	.50	.25	.05
□ 8 Pat Harlow 77	1.50	.75	.15
□ 9 Craig Hartsuyker 40	.50	.25	.05
□ 10 Marcus Hopkins 2	.50	.25	.05
□ 11 Pat O'Hara 4	1.00	.50	.10
□ 12 Robert Pack 20 (Basketball)	3.00	1.50	.30
□ 13 Marc Preston 22	.50	.25	.05
□ 14 Quin Rodriguez 11	.50	.25	.05
□ 15 Scott Ross 35	.75	.35	.07
□ 16 Grant Runnerstrum 23	.50	.25	.05
□ 17 Mark Tucker 75	.50	.25	.05
□ 18 Brian Tuliau 56	.50	.25	.05
□ 19 Gary Wellman 83	1.00	.50	.10
□ 20 Checklist Card Smokey Bear	.50	.25	.05

1987-88 Southern Mississippi

This 14-card set, measuring 2 3/8" by 3 1/2", was co-sponsored by Deposit Guaranty National Bank and Coca-Cola, and their company names appear at the bottom corners on the front. The front has a posed action photo on a yellow background; two cards of the set feature two players. Player's names and team logo surmount the photo. The back presents biographical information and the card number.

	MINT	EXC	G-VG
COMPLETE SET (14)	14.00	7.00	1.40
COMMON PLAYER (1-14)	1.00	.50	.10
□ 1 The Freshmen	1.00	.50	.10
□ 2 The Coaches	1.00	.50	.10
□ 3 Casey Fisher	1.00	.50	.10
□ 4 Derrek Hamilton	1.00	.50	.10
□ 5 Randolph Keys	4.00	2.00	.40
□ 6 John White	1.00	.50	.10
□ 7 D.J. and Allen D.J. Bowe and Allen Chapman	1.00	.50	.10
□ 8 The Browns John Brown and Willie Brown	1.00	.50	.10
□ 9 Jurado Hinton	1.00	.50	.10
□ 10 Jay Ladner	1.00	.50	.10

	MINT	EXC	G-VG
☐ 11 Randy Pettus	1.00	.50	.10
☐ 12 Jimmy Smith	1.00	.50	.10
☐ 13 Roger Boyd	1.00	.50	.10
☐ 14 The Team	1.50	.75	.15

1986-87 Southwestern Louisiana Police *

This 16-card set was sponsored by the Chemical Dependency Unit of Acadiana in Lafayette, the University of Southwest Louisiana, and local law enforcement agencies and was produced by McDag Productions. Only 3,500 sets were produced. The cards were distributed by the CDU adolescent program and by law enforcement officers, and they measure the standard size (2 1/2" by 3 1/2"). The front features borderless color action player photos, on white card stock with black lettering. The CDU logo and the words "USL Ragin' Cajuns" appear on the top of the card, with player information below the picture. The back has biographical information and "Tips from the Ragin' Cajuns" which encourage children to avoid drug use. Sports represented in the set include basketball (1, 4, 9, 11, 15), baseball (2, 5, 8, 16), softball (7, 14), track (3), and tennis (6, 10, 12-13). The cards are unnumbered and we have checklisted them below in alphabetical order.

	MINT	EXC	G-VG
COMPLETE SET (16)	8.00	4.00	.80
COMMON PLAYER (1-16)	.60	.30	.06
☐ 1 Stephen Beene	.60	.30	.06
☐ 2 Eddie Citronnelli	.60	.30	.06
☐ 3 Hollis Conway	1.25	.60	.12
☐ 4 Teena Cooper	.60	.30	.06
☐ 5 Herb Erhardt	.60	.30	.06
☐ 6 Bret Garnett	.60	.30	.06
☐ 7 Allison Gray	.60	.30	.06
☐ 8 Bobby Hobbs	.60	.30	.06
☐ 9 Brian Jolivette	.60	.30	.06
☐ 10 Dianne Lowings	.60	.30	.06
☐ 11 Rodney McNeil	.60	.30	.06
☐ 12 Cathy O'Donovan	.60	.30	.06
☐ 13 Ashley Rhoney	.60	.30	.06
☐ 14 Alisa Smith	.60	.30	.06
☐ 15 Randal Smith	.60	.30	.06
☐ 16 Merv Waukau	.60	.30	.06

1987-88 Southwestern Louisiana McDag *

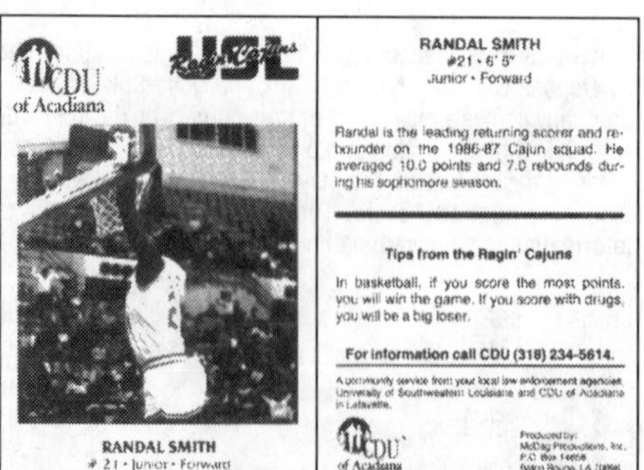

This 16-card standard-size (2 1/2" by 3 1/2") set was sponsored by CDU of Acadiana in Lafayette, University of Southwestern Louisiana, and local law enforcement agencies. The fronts display color action player photos on a white card face. The CDU logo, school logo, and year appear above the picture, while player information is given below the picture. The backs carry player profile, advertisements, and "Tips From the Ragin' Cajuns," which consist of anti-drug and alcohol messages. Sports represented in this set include men's basketball (1-4), women's basketball (5-6), tennis (7-8), men's baseball (9-12), women's softball (14-16), and track (13). The set includes a card of high jumper Hollis Conway, who competed for the 1992 United States Olympic team at Barcelona. The cards are numbered on the back in the upper right corner.

	MINT	EXC	G-VG
COMPLETE SET (16)	8.00	4.00	.80
COMMON PLAYER (1-16)	.60	.30	.06
☐ 1 Randal Smith	.60	.30	.06
☐ 2 Earl Watkins	.60	.30	.06
☐ 3 Kevin Brooks	.60	.30	.06
☐ 4 Stephen Beene	.60	.30	.06
☐ 5 Kim Perrot	.60	.30	.06
☐ 6 Teena Cooper	.60	.30	.06
☐ 7 Bret Garnett	.60	.30	.06
☐ 8 Ashley Rhoney	.60	.30	.06
☐ 9 Terry Fitzpatrick	.60	.30	.06
☐ 10 Joe Turk	.60	.30	.06
☐ 11 Brad Hebets	.60	.30	.06
☐ 12 Ron Vincent	.60	.30	.06
☐ 13 Hollis Conway	1.25	.60	.12
☐ 14 Marria Blackwell	.60	.30	.06
☐ 15 Stefni Whitton	.60	.30	.06
☐ 16 Janine Johnson	.60	.30	.06

1988-89 Syracuse Louis Rich

This 12-card set was sponsored by Louis Rich; their company logo appears on the bottom of the reverse. The cards measure the standard size (2 1/2" by 3 1/2"). The front features a posed color photo of the player, shot from waist up on a blue background. The lettering and border on the card face are orange on white card stock. The back has biographical information and career summary, and "The Orangemen Say" feature, which consists of an anti-drug or alcohol message. The cards are unnumbered and are checklisted below in alphabetical order. Future NBA stars showcased in this set are Sherman Douglas, Derrick Coleman, and Billy Owens.

	MINT	EXC	G-VG
COMPLETE SET (12)	90.00	45.00	9.00
COMMON PLAYER (1-12)	3.00	1.50	.30
☐ 1 Jim Boeheim CO	6.00	3.00	.60
☐ 2 Derrick Coleman	30.00	15.00	3.00
☐ 3 Sherman Douglas	15.00	7.50	1.50
☐ 4 Herman Harried	3.00	1.50	.30
☐ 5 David Johnson	15.00	7.50	1.50
☐ 6 Rich Manning	5.00	2.50	.50
☐ 7 Billy Owens	40.00	20.00	4.00
☐ 8 Matt Roe	5.00	2.50	.50
☐ 9 Erik Rogers	3.00	1.50	.30
☐ 10 Anthony Scott	3.00	1.50	.30
☐ 11 Dave Siock	3.00	1.50	.30
☐ 12 Stephen Thompson	8.00	4.00	.80

1989-90 Syracuse Pepsi/Burger King

This 15-card set was sponsored by Pepsi, Y94FM radio, and Burger King. The cards measure approximately 2 5/8" by 3 1/2" and are numbered on the back. The action color photo on the front is outlined by orange border on white background. Below the photo in an orange bar appears the school's name, year, and the player's name in white lettering. The back has biographical information and a brief anti-drug message. Several players have two cards in this set: Derrick Coleman, Stephen Thompson, and Billy Owens.

	MINT	EXC	G-VG
COMPLETE SET (15)	15.00	7.50	1.50
COMMON PLAYER (1-15)	.40	.20	.04
☐ 1 Derrick Coleman 44	3.00	1.50	.30
☐ 2 LeRon Ellis 25	.90	.45	.09
☐ 3 Rich Manning 34	.40	.20	.04
☐ 4 Stephen Thompson 32	1.25	.60	.12
☐ 5 Michael Edwards 5	.40	.20	.04
☐ 6 David Johnson 23	2.00	1.00	.20
☐ 7 Billy Owens 30	4.00	2.00	.40
☐ 8 Conrad McRae 13	.75	.35	.07
☐ 9 Jim Boeheim CO	.75	.35	.07
☐ 10 Stephen Thompson 32	1.25	.60	.12
☐ 11 Mike Hopkins 33	.40	.20	.04
☐ 12 Tony Scott 40	.40	.20	.04
☐ 13 Billy Owens 30	4.00	2.00	.40
☐ 14 Erik Rogers 41	.40	.20	.04
☐ 15 Derrick Coleman 44	3.00	1.50	.30

1988-89 Tennessee Smokey

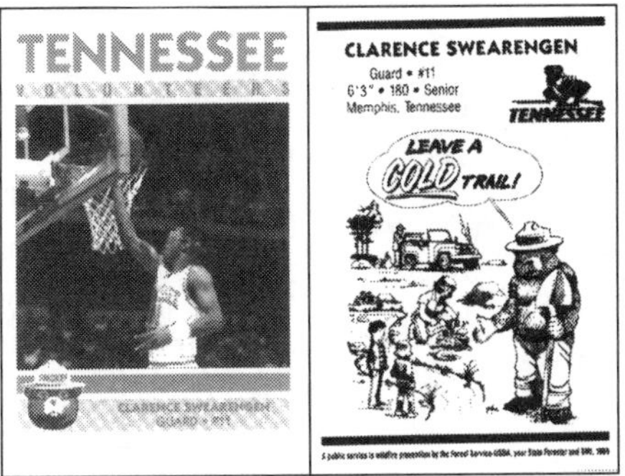

This 12-card set features members of the Tenessee Volunteers basketball team and measures the standard card size, 2 1/2" by 3 1/2". The front features a color action photo; above and below appear orange and gray lettering and borders. The Smokey the Bear logo in the lower left hand corner completes the front. The back gives brief biographical information and a public service announcement (illustrated with cartoon) concerning wildfire prevention. The set is checklisted below according to uniform number.

	MINT	EXC	G-VG
COMPLETE SET (12)	20.00	10.00	2.00
COMMON PLAYER	1.25	.60	.12
☐ 11 Clarence Swearengen	2.00	1.00	.20
☐ 23 Greg Bell	1.25	.60	.12
☐ 24 Rickey Clark	1.25	.60	.12
☐ 25 Travis Henry	1.25	.60	.12
☐ 31 Dyron Nix	6.00	3.00	.60
☐ 33 Mark Griffin	1.25	.60	.12
☐ 34 Ronnie Reese	1.25	.60	.12
☐ 50 Doug Roth	1.25	.60	.12
☐ 51 Ian Lockhart	1.25	.60	.12
☐ xx Don Devoe CO	2.00	1.00	.20
☐ xx Smokey The Hound (mascot)	1.25	.60	.12
☐ xx Thompson-Boling Arena	1.25	.60	.12

1991 Texas A and M 100 *

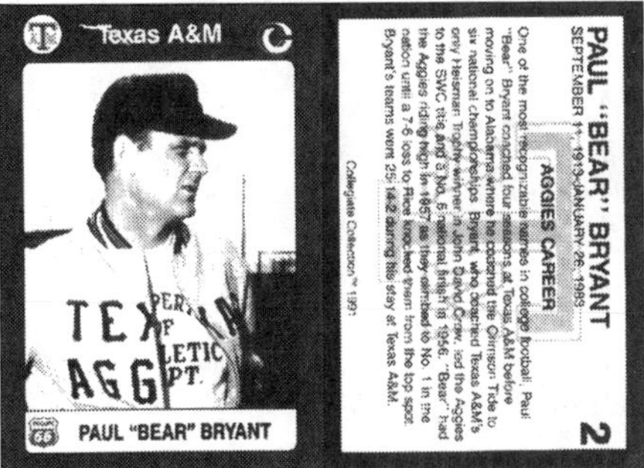

This 100-card multi-sport set was produced by Collegiate Collection and measures the standard size (2 1/2" by 3 1/2"). The fronts feature a mix of black and white or color player photos with maroon borders, with the player's name in a white stripe below the picture. In a horizontal format the backs present biographical information, career summary, or statistics on a white background with black lettering and borders. The cards are numbered on the back.

	MINT	EXC	G-VG
COMPLETE SET (100)	12.00	6.00	1.20
COMMON PLAYER (1-100)	.10	.05	.01
☐ 1 Rod Bernstine	.30	.15	.03
☐ 2 Paul(Bear) Bryant	.30	.15	.03
☐ 3 Shirley Furlong	.10	.05	.01
☐ 4 R.C. Slocum	.20	.10	.02
☐ 5 Gary Kubiak	.20	.10	.02
☐ 6 Gary Horton	.10	.05	.01
☐ 7 Billy Cannon	.20	.10	.02
☐ 8 John Beasley	.15	.07	.01
☐ 9 Ray Childress	.25	.12	.02
☐ 10 John David Crow	.25	.12	.02
☐ 11 Bob Ellis	.15	.07	.01
☐ 12 Billy Hodge	.10	.05	.01
☐ 13 Layne Talbot	.10	.05	.01
☐ 14 Larry Stegent	.15	.07	.01
☐ 15 Lisa Langston	.10	.05	.01
☐ 16 Tom Chandler	.10	.05	.01
☐ 17 Scott Livingstone	.30	.15	.03
☐ 18 Jimmy Teal	.10	.05	.01
☐ 19 Ted Nelson	.10	.05	.01
☐ 20 Lance Pavlas	.15	.07	.01
☐ 21 James(Hoot) Gibson	.10	.05	.01
☐ 22 Mickey Washington	.10	.05	.01
☐ 23 Rodney Hodde	.10	.05	.01
☐ 24 Rob Swain	.10	.05	.01
☐ 25 Thomas Sanders	.15	.07	.01

☐ 26 Loyd Taylor	.10	.05	.01
☐ 27 Danny Roberts	.10	.05	.01
☐ 28 Bob Brock	.10	.05	.01
☐ 29 Curtis Dickey	.20	.10	.02
☐ 30 John Thornton	.10	.05	.01
☐ 31 Matt McCall	.10	.05	.01
☐ 32 David Kent	.10	.05	.01
☐ 33 Melinda Clark	.10	.05	.01
☐ 34 Brad Dusek	.15	.07	.01
☐ 35 Mark Ross	.10	.05	.01
☐ 36 Gary Oliver	.10	.05	.01
☐ 37 Charley Milstead	.10	.05	.01
☐ 38 Mark Johnson	.10	.05	.01
☐ 39 Ever Magallanes	.15	.07	.01
☐ 40 Mark Thurmond	.15	.07	.01
☐ 41 Keith Langston	.10	.05	.01
☐ 42 Phillip Taylor	.10	.05	.01
☐ 43 Jacob Green	.20	.10	.02
☐ 44 Randy Matson	.20	.10	.02
☐ 45 Shawn Andaya	.10	.05	.01
☐ 46 Kevin Monk	.10	.05	.01
☐ 47 Larry Kelm	.15	.07	.01
☐ 48 Tory Parks	.10	.05	.01
☐ 49 Barry Davis	.10	.05	.01
☐ 50 Kitty Holley	.10	.05	.01
☐ 51 Kent Adams	.10	.05	.01
☐ 52 Randy Hall	.10	.05	.01
☐ 53 Dave Goff	.10	.05	.01
☐ 54 Rolf Krueger	.15	.07	.01
☐ 55 Lynn Hickey	.10	.05	.01
☐ 56 Sylvester Morgan	.10	.05	.01
☐ 57 Bucky Sams	.15	.07	.01
☐ 58 Jeff Nelson	.15	.07	.01
☐ 59 Gary Jones	.10	.05	.01
☐ 60 John Byington	.10	.05	.01
☐ 61 Pat Thomas	.15	.07	.01
☐ 62 Mark Dennard	.15	.07	.01
☐ 63 James(Mike) Heitmann	.10	.05	.01
☐ 64 Kyle Field	.10	.05	.01
☐ 65 Edd Hargett	.20	.10	.02
☐ 66 Robert Slavens	.10	.05	.01
☐ 67 Scott Slater	.10	.05	.01
☐ 68 Louis Cheek	.15	.07	.01
☐ 69 Ken Ford	.10	.05	.01
☐ 70 Bill Hobbs	.10	.05	.01
☐ 71 Bob Long	.10	.05	.01
☐ 72 Jeff Paine	.10	.05	.01
☐ 73 Garth Tennaper	.10	.05	.01
☐ 74 David Bandy	.10	.05	.01
☐ 75 Dennis Swilley	.15	.07	.01
☐ 76 Mike Whitewell	.10	.05	.01
☐ 77 Jim Cashion	.10	.05	.01
☐ 78 Lisa Jordon	.10	.05	.01
☐ 79 Yvonne Van Brandt	.10	.05	.01
☐ 80 A-M Marching Band	.10	.05	.01
☐ 81 Bobby Joe Conrad	.15	.07	.01
☐ 82 Mike Mosley	.20	.10	.02
☐ 83 Olsen Field	.10	.05	.01
☐ 84 Jeff Schow	.10	.05	.01
☐ 85 Al Givens	.10	.05	.01
☐ 86 Steve Hughes	.10	.05	.01
☐ 87 Lisa Herner	.10	.05	.01
☐ 88 Traci Thomas	.10	.05	.01
☐ 89 Karen Guerrero	.10	.05	.01
☐ 90 Billy Pickard	.10	.05	.01
☐ 91 David Ogrin	.10	.05	.01
☐ 92 Kim Bauer	.10	.05	.01
☐ 93 Warren Trahan	.10	.05	.01
☐ 94 Bobby Kleinecke	.10	.05	.01
☐ 95 Dave Elmendorf	.20	.10	.02
☐ 96 Vicki Brown	.10	.05	.01
☐ 97 Yvonne Hill	.10	.05	.01
☐ 98 David Rollen	.10	.05	.01
☐ 99 David Hardy	.10	.05	.01
☐ 100 Director Card	.15	.07	.01

1990-91 UCLA

This 40-card set was produced by Collegiate Collection and features the men's and women's basketball teams. The standard size (2 1/2" by 3 1/2") cards feature on the fronts a mix of posed or action color player photos (with rounded corners), with a thin black border on royal blue background. While the school name appears above the picture in yellow lettering, the player's name appears in black lettering in a yellow stripe below the picture. The UCLA and Collegiate Collection logos at the top

complete the card face. The horizontally oriented backs provide brief biography, statistics, and the card number, all within a royal blue border. Due to a production error, the Keith Owens card incorrectly depicts Destah Owens. A coupon was included in the set to exchange for a free replacement card. Note that the back of the corrected card differs from the regular issue in format and color. Men's basketball is represented by cards 1-15 and 35-39; women's basketball by cards 16-34.

	MINT	EXC	G-VG
COMPLETE SET (40)	18.00	9.00	1.80
COMMON PLAYER (1-40)	.30	.15	.03
☐ 1 Team Photo	1.00	.50	.10
☐ 2 Tracy Murray	5.00	2.50	.50
☐ 3 Ed O'Bannon	2.50	1.25	.25
☐ 4 Darrick Martin	1.50	.75	.15
☐ 5 Mitchell Butler	1.50	.75	.15
☐ 6 Mike Lanier	.75	.35	.07
☐ 7 Chris Kenny	.50	.25	.05
☐ 8A Keith Owens ERR (Photo actually Destah Owens)	2.00	1.00	.20
☐ 8B Keith Owens COR	2.00	1.00	.20
☐ 9 Dave Paulsell	.30	.15	.03
☐ 10 Shon Tarver	2.50	1.25	.25
☐ 11 Rodney Zimmerman	.30	.15	.03
☐ 12 Zan Mason	.30	.15	.03
☐ 13 Gerald Madkins	2.00	1.00	.20
☐ 14 Don MacLean	5.00	2.50	.50
☐ 15 Lou Richie	.30	.15	.03
☐ 16 Billie Moore CO	.30	.15	.03
☐ 17 Rehema Stephens	.30	.15	.03
☐ 18 Nicole Anderson	.30	.15	.03
☐ 19 Amy Jalewalia	.30	.15	.03
☐ 20 Pam Walker CO	.30	.15	.03
☐ 21 Lynn Kamrath	.30	.15	.03
☐ 22 Detra Lockhart	.30	.15	.03
☐ 23 Stacie Gravely	.30	.15	.03
☐ 24 Laura Collins	.30	.15	.03
☐ 25 Genevieve Vanoostveen	.30	.15	.03
☐ 26 Dede Mosman	.30	.15	.03
☐ 27 Nicole Young	.30	.15	.03
☐ 28 Dawn Baker	.30	.15	.03
☐ 29 Melissa Gische	.30	.15	.03
☐ 30 Rachelle Roulier	.30	.15	.03
☐ 31 Marcy Tarabochia	.30	.15	.03
☐ 32 Natalie Williams	.30	.15	.03
☐ 33 Kathy Olivier CO	.30	.15	.03
☐ 34 Mary Hegarty CO	.30	.15	.03
☐ 35 Jim Harrick CO	.50	.25	.05
☐ 36 Brad Holland CO	.50	.25	.05
☐ 37 Tony Fuller CO	.30	.15	.03
☐ 38 Ken Barone CO	.30	.15	.03
☐ 39 Mark Gottfried CO	.30	.15	.03
☐ 40 Checklist Card	.30	.15	.03

1991 UCLA 144

This 144-card set was produced by Collegiate Collection and measures the standard size (2 1/2" by 3 1/2"). The fronts feature a mix of black and white or color player photos, with royal blue

borders and the player's name in the yellow stripe below the picture. The horizontally oriented backs present biographical information, career summary, or statistics on a white background with blue lettering and borders. The cards are numbered on the back.

	MINT	EXC	G-VG
COMPLETE SET (144)	16.00	8.00	1.60
COMMON PLAYER (1-144)	.10	.05	.01
☐ 1 John Wooden CO	.30	.15	.03
☐ 2 Kareem Abdul-Jabbar	.50	.25	.05
☐ 3 Bill Walton	.35	.17	.03
☐ 4 Larry Farmer	.20	.10	.02
☐ 5 Marques Johnson	.25	.12	.02
☐ 6 Walt Hazzard	.20	.10	.02
☐ 7 Henry Bibby	.15	.07	.01
☐ 8 Gail Goodrich	.20	.10	.02
☐ 9 Jim Harrick	.15	.07	.01
☐ 10 Kareem Abdul-Jabbar	.50	.25	.05
☐ 11 Mike Warren	.20	.10	.02
☐ 12 Gary Maloncon	.10	.05	.01
☐ 13 James Wilkes	.10	.05	.01
☐ 14 Kiki Vandeweghe	.20	.10	.02
☐ 15 1969 NCAA Champs	.10	.05	.01
☐ 16 Sidney Wicks	.20	.10	.02
☐ 17 Andre McCarter	.15	.07	.01
☐ 18 Michael Holton	.10	.05	.01
☐ 19 Greg Lee	.10	.05	.01
☐ 20 John Wooden CO	.25	.12	.02
☐ 21 Gene Bartow CO	.10	.05	.01
☐ 22 Richard Washington	.15	.07	.01
☐ 23 Brad Wright	.10	.05	.01
☐ 24 Pooh Richardson	.25	.12	.02
☐ 25 Terry Shofield	.10	.05	.01
☐ 26 Gig Sims	.10	.05	.01
☐ 27 Darren Daye	.15	.07	.01
☐ 28 Dave Immel	.10	.05	.01
☐ 29 Tommy Curtis	.10	.05	.01
☐ 30 Bill Walton	.35	.17	.03
☐ 31 Larry Brown	.15	.07	.01
☐ 32 Kevin Walker	.10	.05	.01
☐ 33 Kareem Abdul-Jabbar	.50	.25	.05
☐ 34 Kenny Heitz	.15	.07	.01
☐ 35 Gary Cunningham	.10	.05	.01
☐ 36 Lynn Shackelford	.20	.10	.02
☐ 37 Keith Wilkes	.20	.10	.02
☐ 38 1975 NCAA Champs	.10	.05	.01
☐ 39 Raymond Townsend	.15	.07	.01
☐ 40 Pete Trgovich	.15	.07	.01
☐ 41 Kelvin Butler	.10	.05	.01
☐ 42 Ed Sheldrake	.10	.05	.01
☐ 43 Larry Hollyfield	.20	.10	.02
☐ 44 Montel Hatcher	.15	.07	.01
☐ 45 Denise Curry	.20	.10	.02
☐ 46 Curtis Rowe	.20	.10	.02
☐ 47 David Meyers	.20	.10	.02
☐ 48 Lucius Allen	.20	.10	.02
☐ 49 Kenny Fields	.15	.07	.01
☐ 50 John Vallely	.20	.10	.02
☐ 51 Wooden and Nell	.20	.10	.02
☐ 52 Sidney Wicks	.20	.10	.02
☐ 53 1973 NCAA Champs	.10	.05	.01
☐ 54 Jack Haley	.15	.07	.01
☐ 55 Ralph Drollinger	.15	.07	.01
☐ 56 Don Johnson	.10	.05	.01
☐ 57 Bill Ellis	.10	.05	.01
☐ 58 Willie Naulls	.15	.07	.01
☐ 59 Ron Livingston	.10	.05	.01
☐ 60 Bill Putnam	.10	.05	.01
☐ 61 Rod Foster	.15	.07	.01
☐ 62 Bill Walton	.35	.17	.03
☐ 63 Roy Hamilton	.15	.07	.01
☐ 64 Jim Spillane	.10	.05	.01
☐ 65 Ralph Jackson	.15	.07	.01
☐ 66 Morris Taft	.10	.05	.01
☐ 67 Dick Ridgeway	.10	.05	.01
☐ 68 Dave Minor	.10	.05	.01
☐ 69 1965 Champs	.10	.05	.01
☐ 70 Karl Kraushaar	.10	.05	.01
☐ 71 Craig Jackson	.15	.07	.01
☐ 72 Kenny Washington	.20	.10	.02
☐ 73 Keith Wilkes	.20	.10	.02
☐ 74 Stuart Gray	.20	.10	.02
☐ 75 John Green	.10	.05	.01
☐ 76 Doug McIntosh	.15	.07	.01
☐ 77 Walt Hazzard	.20	.10	.02
☐ 78 Frank Lubin	.10	.05	.01
☐ 79 Don Piper	.10	.05	.01
☐ 80 1967 Champs	.10	.05	.01
☐ 81 Kenny Booker	.15	.07	.01
☐ 82 Marques Johnson	.20	.10	.02
☐ 83 Bill Walton	.35	.17	.03
☐ 84 1972 Champs	.10	.05	.01
☐ 85 Steve Patterson	.15	.07	.01
☐ 86 1964 NCAA Champs	.10	.05	.01
☐ 87 Alan Sawyer	.10	.05	.01
☐ 88 Walt Torrence	.10	.05	.01
☐ 89 Gail Goodrich	.20	.10	.02
☐ 90 Ralph Bunche	.15	.07	.01
☐ 91 Swen Nater	.20	.10	.02
☐ 92 Larry Farmer	.15	.07	.01
☐ 93 Kareem Abdul-Jabbar	.50	.25	.05
☐ 94 Mike Sanders	.20	.10	.02
☐ 95 Niguel Miguel	.15	.07	.01
☐ 96 Jackie Robinson	.35	.17	.03
☐ 97 Dick West	.10	.05	.01
☐ 98 Rafer Johnson	.30	.15	.03
☐ 99 John Berberich	.10	.05	.01
☐ 100 Director Card	.10	.05	.01
☐ 101 Richard Linthicum	.10	.05	.01
☐ 102 Chuck Clustka	.10	.05	.01
☐ 103 Wooden, Crum, and Cunningham	.15	.07	.01
☐ 104 Jerry Norman	.10	.05	.01
☐ 105 John Moore	.10	.05	.01
☐ 106 Trevor Wilson	.25	.12	.02
☐ 107 David Greenwood	.20	.10	.02
☐ 108 Wooden and Morgan	.20	.10	.02
☐ 109 Kareem Abdul-Jabbar	.50	.25	.05
☐ 110 Ann Meyers	.25	.12	.02
☐ 111 Denny Crum	.15	.07	.01
☐ 112 Pierce Works	.10	.05	.01
☐ 113 Carl Cozens	.10	.05	.01
☐ 114 George Stanich	.10	.05	.01
☐ 115 Don Ashen	.10	.05	.01
☐ 116 David Greenwood	.15	.07	.01
☐ 117 1971 Team Photo	.15	.07	.01
☐ 118 Johns Barksdale	.10	.05	.01
☐ 119 1978 Champion	.15	.07	.01
☐ 120 John Stanich	.10	.05	.01
☐ 121 Don Barksdale	.10	.05	.01
☐ 122 1968 Champs	.15	.07	.01
☐ 123 Carl Knowles	.10	.05	.01
☐ 124 Don Bragg	.15	.07	.01
☐ 125 Ducky Drake	.15	.07	.01
☐ 126 John Ball	.10	.05	.01
☐ 127 Pauley Pavilion	.10	.05	.01
☐ 128 Sam Balter	.10	.05	.01
☐ 129 A Caddy Works Team	.10	.05	.01
☐ 130 John Wooden CO	.25	.12	.02
☐ 131 Fred Goss	.15	.07	.01
☐ 132 Keith Erickson	.20	.10	.02
☐ 133 Pete Blackman	.10	.05	.01
☐ 134 Gail Goodrich	.20	.10	.02
☐ 135 Kent Miller	.10	.05	.01
☐ 136 Jack Ketchum	.10	.05	.01
☐ 137 1970 Team Photo	.15	.07	.01
☐ 138 Jim Milhorn	.10	.05	.01
☐ 139 Bill Rankin	.10	.05	.01
☐ 140 Kenny Heitz	.15	.07	.01
☐ 141 Bob(Ace) Caikins	.10	.05	.01
☐ 142 J.D. Morgan AD	.10	.05	.01
☐ 143 Fred Slaughter	.15	.07	.01
☐ 144 Director Card	.15	.07	.01

1991-92 UCLA

This 21-card set was produced by Collegiate Collection and measures the standard size (2 1/2" by 3 1/2"). The fronts feature color action player photos, with royal blue borders and the player's name in a yellow stripe beneath the picture. The horizontally oriented backs present biographical information, statistics, and career summary on a white background with blue lettering and borders. The cards are numbered on the back in the upper right corner.

	MINT	EXC	G-VG
COMPLETE SET (21)	11.00	5.50	1.10
COMMON PLAYER (1-21)	.40	.20	.04
☐ 1 Mike Lanier	.60	.30	.06
☐ 2 Don MacLean	2.00	1.00	.20
☐ 3 Rodney Zimmerman	.40	.20	.04
☐ 4 Pauley Pavilion	.40	.20	.04
☐ 5 Tyus Edney	.40	.20	.04
☐ 6 Jiri Zidek	.40	.20	.04
☐ 7 Brad Holland CO	.60	.30	.06
☐ 8 Ed O'Bannon	1.00	.50	.10
☐ 9 Richard Petruska	.40	.20	.04
☐ 10 Darrick Martin	.60	.30	.06
☐ 11 Tony Fuller	.40	.20	.04
☐ 12 Tracy Murray	2.00	1.00	.20
☐ 13 Gerald Madkins	.75	.35	.07
☐ 14 Mitchell Butler	.60	.30	.06
☐ 15 Mark Gottfried	.40	.20	.04
☐ 16 Jim Harrick CO	.60	.30	.06
☐ 17 Jonah Naulls	.40	.20	.04
☐ 18 Steve Lavin CO	.40	.20	.04
☐ 19 Steve Elkind	.40	.20	.04
☐ 20 Shon Tarver	1.00	.50	.10
☐ 21 Checklist	.40	.20	.04

1988-89 UNLV HOF/Police

This 12-card set was produced by Hall of Fame Cards, Inc. The cards measure the standard size (2 1/2" by 3 1/2"). The front features a color action shot of the player, trimmed in red borders on a gray card face. The words "Runnin' Rebels" appears in red lettering above the picture, while the school name, player's name, and his position appear below. The back is printed in red and includes biographical information, career statistics at UNLV, and an anti-drug message titled "Rebel Rap." The cards are numbered on the back and checklisted below accordingly. Supposedly there were only 10,000 sets produced.

	MINT	EXC	G-VG
COMPLETE SET (12)	40.00	20.00	4.00
COMMON PLAYER (1-12)	1.50	.75	.15
☐ 1 Stacey Augmon	12.00	6.00	1.20
☐ 2 Greg Anthony	8.00	4.00	.80
☐ 3 Anderson Hunt	4.00	2.00	.40
☐ 4 George Ackles	3.50	1.75	.35
☐ 5 David Butler	2.50	1.25	.25
☐ 6 Clint Rossum	1.50	.75	.15
☐ 7 Moses Scurry	2.50	1.25	.25
☐ 8 Barry Young	1.50	.75	.15
☐ 9 James Jones	1.50	.75	.15
☐ 10 Stacey Cvijanovich	1.50	.75	.15
☐ 11 Chris Jeter	1.50	.75	.15
☐ 12 Bryan Emerzian	1.50	.75	.15

1989-90 UNLV HOF/Police

This 14-card set was produced by Hall of Fame Cards, Inc. and measures the standard size (2 1/2" by 3 1/2"). The front features a color action player photo outlined by a thin black border. The school name is superimposed at the right upper corner of the picture. The background is red for the top half of the card face and gray for the bottom half. The player's name is printed in red lettering below the picture. In a horizontal format the back has biographical information and the slogan "Say No to Drugs." The cards are numbered on the back. Supposedly less than 6000 sets were produced.

	MINT	EXC	G-VG
COMPLETE SET (14)	30.00	15.00	3.00
COMMON PLAYER (1-14)	1.00	.50	.10
☐ 1 Stacey Augmon	7.50	3.75	.75
☐ 2 Greg Anthony	5.00	2.50	.50
☐ 3 Larry Johnson	15.00	7.50	1.50
☐ 4 George Ackles	2.50	1.25	.25
☐ 5 Moses Scurry	2.00	1.00	.20
☐ 6 Anderson Hunt (Hank Gathers visible in background)	5.00	2.50	.50
☐ 7 Travis Bice	1.50	.75	.15
☐ 8 David Butler	2.00	1.00	.20
☐ 9 Stacey Cvijanovich	1.00	.50	.10
☐ 10 Chris Jeter	1.00	.50	.10
☐ 11 Bryan Emerzian	1.00	.50	.10
☐ 12 James Jones (Hank Gathers vis-	3.00	1.50	.30

ible in background)			
☐ 13 Barry Young	1.00	.50	.10
☐ 14 Dave Rice	1.00	.50	.10

1989-90 UNLV 7-Eleven

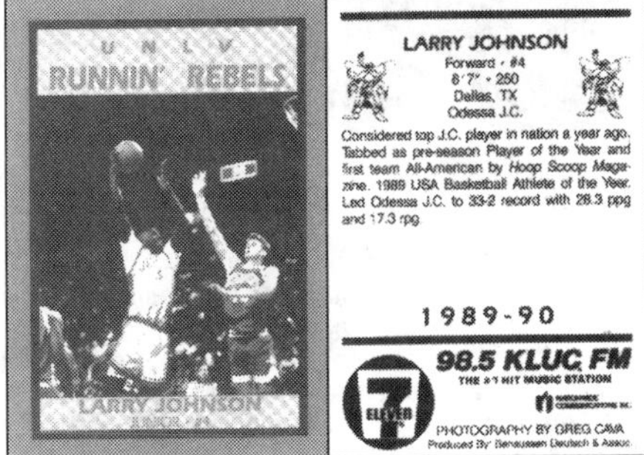

This 13-card set was sponsored by 7-Eleven, 98.5 KLUC-FM radio, and Nationwide Communications Inc. The cards measure the standard size (2 1/2" by 3 1/2") and are printed on very thin card stock. The fronts feature color action player photos, with black borders on red card face. The team and player's names appear in red lettering in gray boxes above and below the picture respectively. The backs are printed in black on white card stock and provide biographical information and player profile. The cards are unnumbered and are checklisted below in alphabetical order, with the uniform number after the player's name.

	MINT	EXC	G-VG
COMPLETE SET (13)	25.00	12.50	2.50
COMMON PLAYER (1-13)	.75	.35	.07
☐ 1 Greg Anthony 50	3.00	1.50	.30
☐ 2 Stacey Augmon 32	5.00	2.50	.50
☐ 3 Travis Bice 13	1.00	.50	.10
☐ 4 David Butler 00	1.25	.60	.12
☐ 5 Stacey Cvijanovich 05	.75	.35	.07
☐ 6 Bryan Emerzian 15	.75	.35	.07
☐ 7 Anderson Hunt 12	1.50	.75	.15
☐ 8 Chris Jeter 53	.75	.35	.07
☐ 9 Larry Johnson 04	10.00	5.00	1.00
☐ 10 James Jones 34	.75	.35	.07
☐ 11 Moses Scurry 35	1.25	.60	.12
☐ 12 Barry Young 33	.75	.35	.07
☐ 13 Jerry Tarkanian CO	2.00	1.00	.20

1990-91 UNLV HOF/Police

This 15-card set was produced by Hall of Fame Cards, Inc. and features the UNLV Runnin' Rebels, the 1990 NCAA national champions. The cards measure the standard size (2 1/2" by 3 1/2"). The fronts feature color action player photos; cards numbered 11-13 feature "Future Rebels" and have posed color photos. All cards have red borders on the top and bottom and white borders on the sides. A red diagonal cuts across the lower right corner of the picture, with the words "1990 Nat'l Champions" in white lettering. The player's name and position are given in white lettering in the bottom red border. The backs have statistical information and the slogan "Say No to Drugs" in either horizontal or vertical formats. The cards are numbered on the back. Supposedly only 15,000 sets were produced; each set is individually numbered on card number 4 Anderson Hunt.

	MINT	EXC	G-VG
COMPLETE SET (15)	20.00	10.00	2.00
COMMON PLAYER (1-15)	.75	.35	.07
☐ 1 Larry Johnson	8.00	4.00	.80
☐ 2 Stacey Augmon	4.00	2.00	.40
☐ 3 Greg Anthony	2.50	1.25	.25
☐ 4 Anderson Hunt	1.25	.60	.12
☐ 5 Travis Bice	1.00	.50	.10
☐ 6 George Ackles	1.25	.60	.12
☐ 7 Bryan Emerzian	.75	.35	.07
☐ 8 Dave Rice	.75	.35	.07
☐ 9 Chris Jeter	.75	.35	.07
☐ 10 Anderson Hunt	1.25	.60	.12
☐ 11 Evric Gray	1.00	.50	.10
☐ 12 Bobby Joyce	.75	.35	.07
☐ 13 H. Waldman	.75	.35	.07
☐ 14 Larry Johnson	8.00	4.00	.80
☐ 15 Runnin' Rebels (Card lists records broken by UNLV)	.75	.35	.07

1990-91 UNLV Smokey

This 15-card set was sponsored by the USDA Forest Service in cooperation with other federal agencies. The standard size (2 1/2" by 3 1/2") cards were issued as a set of single cards or as a sheet consisting of four rows of four cards (the 16th slot is blank). The front features a color action player photo, with gray border on dark red background. In black lettering the words "1990-91 UNLV Runnin' Rebels" are printed above the picture, with the player's name and number below. The Smokey the Bear logo in the lower left corner completes the card face. The back presents biographical information and a fire prevention cartoon starring Smokey. The cards unnumbered and we have checklisted them below in alphabetical order, with the jersey number to the right of the name.

	MINT	EXC	G-VG
COMPLETE SET (15)	25.00	12.50	2.50
COMMON PLAYER (1-15)	.75	.35	.07

		MINT	EXC	G-VG
☐ 1	George Ackles 44	1.25	.60	.12
☐ 2	Greg Anthony 50	2.50	1.25	.25
☐ 3	Stacey Augmon 32	4.00	2.00	.40
☐ 4	Travis Bice 3	1.00	.50	.10
☐ 5	Bryan Emerzian 15	.75	.35	.07
☐ 6	Evric Gray 23	1.00	.50	.10
☐ 7	Anderson Hunt 12	1.25	.60	.12
☐ 8	Chris Jeter 53	.75	.35	.07
☐ 9	Larry Johnson 4	8.00	4.00	.80
☐ 10	Bobby Joyce 42	.75	.35	.07
☐ 11	Melvin Love 40	.75	.35	.07
☐ 12	Dave Rice 30	.75	.35	.07
☐ 13	Elmore Spencer 24	2.50	1.25	.25
☐ 14	Jerry Tarkanian CO	2.00	1.00	.20
☐ 15	H. Waldman 31	.75	.35	.07

1990-91 UNLV Season to Remember

This 15-card set features the UNLV Runnin' Rebels, who were runner-ups for the 1991 NCAA championship. The cards measure the standard size (2 1/2" by 3 1/2"). The front features a color action photo of the player, with a thin black border on dark red background. The school name is superimposed at the right upper corner of the picture, and the player's name is inscribed across the bottom of the picture. In black lettering the words "A Season to Remember" appear below the photo. The back gives biographical and statistical information in a horizontal format, and repeats the words "A Season to Remember," with the team record "34-1." The cards are numbered on the back.

		MINT	EXC	G-VG
COMPLETE SET (15)		10.00	5.00	1.00
COMMON PLAYER (1-15)		.50	.25	.05
☐ 1	Larry Johnson	5.00	2.50	.50
☐ 2	Stacey Augmon	2.50	1.25	.25
☐ 3	Greg Anthony	1.50	.75	.15
☐ 4	Anderson Hunt	.90	.45	.09
☐ 5	Travis Bice	.60	.30	.06
☐ 6	George Ackles	.90	.45	.09
☐ 7	Bryan Emerzian	.50	.25	.05
☐ 8	Dave Rice	.50	.25	.05
☐ 9	Chris Jeter	.50	.25	.05
☐ 10	Elmore Spencer	1.25	.60	.12
☐ 11	Evric Gray	.60	.30	.06
☐ 12	Bobby Joyce	.50	.25	.05
☐ 13	H. Waldman	.50	.25	.05
☐ 14	Melvin Love	.50	.25	.05
☐ 15	Rebel All-Americans (Hunt, Anthony, Ackles, Johnson, and Augmon)	1.50	.75	.15

1989-90 UTEP Drug Emporium

This 24-card set was sponsored by 7-Together and Drug Emporium and their names are on the top of the card. The cards measure (the standard) 2 1/2" by 3 1/2". The team name/subtitle ("Star Miners") is given above the photo, and the player's name

and position below it, with black and white photos for older players and color for newer players. Biographical information is on the back. Current and past NBA Stars featured in this set are Nate Archibald and Tim Hardaway; also note the presence of a card of Nolan Richardson, who went on to coach the Arkansas Razorbacks. The set is not numbered so the subjects are listed below in alphabetical order by name.

		MINT	EXC	G-VG
COMPLETE SET (24)		12.00	6.00	1.20
COMMON PLAYER (1-24)		.25	.12	.02
☐ 1	Nate Archibald	1.25	.60	.12
☐ 2	Jim Barnes	.50	.25	.05
☐ 3	Rus Bradburd	.25	.12	.02
☐ 4	Dallas David	.25	.12	.02
☐ 5	Antonio Davis	.50	.25	.05
☐ 6	Ralph Davis	.35	.17	.03
☐ 7	Norm Ellenberger CO	.35	.17	.03
☐ 8	Francis Ezenwa	.25	.12	.02
☐ 9	Greg Foster	.50	.25	.05
☐ 10	Joe Griffin	.25	.12	.02
☐ 11	Henry Hall	.25	.12	.02
☐ 12	Tim Hardaway	6.00	3.00	.60
☐ 13	Don Haskins CO	.35	.17	.03
☐ 14	Merle Heimer	.25	.12	.02
☐ 15	Bobby Joe Hill	.50	.25	.05
☐ 16	Greg Lackey	.25	.12	.02
☐ 17	David Lattin	.50	.25	.05
☐ 18	Marlon Maxey	.50	.25	.05
☐ 19	Mark McCall	.25	.12	.02
☐ 20	Chris Perez	.25	.12	.02
☐ 21	Nolan Richardson	.75	.35	.07
☐ 22	Arlandis Rush	.25	.12	.02
☐ 23	Alprentice Stewart	.25	.12	.02
☐ 24	David Van Dyke	.25	.12	.02

1987-88 Vanderbilt Police

This 14-card set was sponsored by Vanderbilt University Police and Security. The cards measure 2 1/2" by 4". On a white card face, the fronts feature black and white player photos enclosed by black and yellow borders. Player information and the school logo appear in a box below the picture. The backs have biography, a safety tip, and a list of phone numbers to call for a police response. The cards are numbered on the back.

		MINT	EXC	G-VG
COMPLETE SET (14)		25.00	12.50	2.50
COMMON PLAYER (1-14)		1.50	.75	.15
☐ 1	Team Photo	3.00	1.50	.30
☐ 2	C.M. Newton CO	2.00	1.00	.20
☐ 3	Fred Benjamin	1.50	.75	.15
☐ 4	Barry Booker	1.50	.75	.15
☐ 5	Missing	1.50	.75	.15
☐ 6	Scott Laughinghouse	1.50	.75	.15
☐ 7	Eric Reid	1.50	.75	.15
☐ 8	Steve Grant	1.50	.75	.15
☐ 9	Derrick Wilcox	1.50	.75	.15
☐ 10	Will Perdue	6.00	3.00	.60

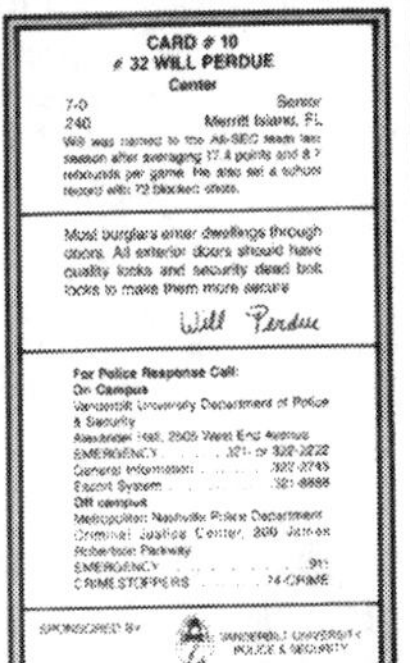

☐ 11 Frank Kornet	2.00	1.00	.20
☐ 12 Charles Mayes	1.50	.75	.15
☐ 13 Barry Goheen	2.00	1.00	.20
☐ 14 Scott Draud	2.00	1.00	.20

1983-84 Victoria Police

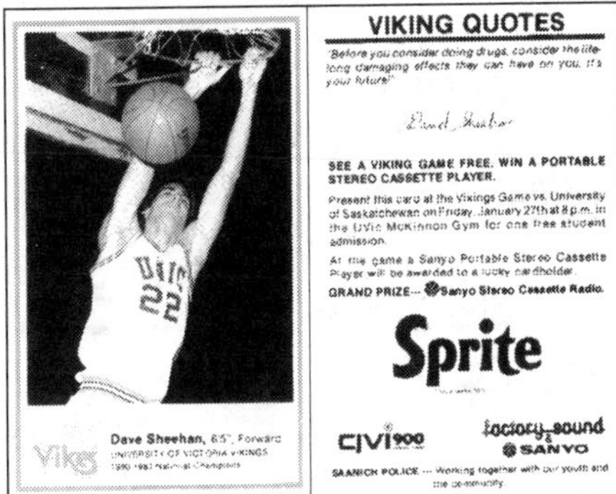

This 15-card set was sponsored by Sprite, CJVI900 (a radio station), Factory Sound , Sanyo, and the Saanich Police. The cards measure approximately 2 5/8" by 4". On a white card face, the fronts feature posed action photos. The pictures and the player information below them are enclosed by a blue border. The backs have player quotes ("Viking Quotes"), a facsimile autograph, an offer to see a game free and win a stereo cassette walkman, and sponsor logos. The game at which the card holder will be admitted free is noted on the back. The safety slogan "Working together with our youth and the community" rounds out the back. The cards are unnumbered and checklisted below in alphabetical order.

	MINT	EXC	G-VG
COMPLETE SET (15)	12.00	6.00	1.20
COMMON PLAYER (1-15)	1.00	.50	.10
☐ 1 Cord Clemens	1.00	.50	.10
☐ 2 Quinn Groenhyde	1.00	.50	.10
☐ 3 Ian Hyde-Lay Assistant CO	1.00	.50	.10
☐ 4 Sean Kalinovich	1.00	.50	.10
☐ 5 Ken Larson	1.00	.50	.10
☐ 6 John Munro	1.00	.50	.10
☐ 7 Jamie Newman	1.00	.50	.10
☐ 8 Phil Ohl	1.00	.50	.10
☐ 9 Eli Pasquale	1.00	.50	.10
☐ 10 Dave Sheehan	1.00	.50	.10
☐ 11 Ken Shields CO	1.00	.50	.10
☐ 12 Randy Steel	1.00	.50	.10
☐ 13 Graham Taylor	1.00	.50	.10
☐ 14 Greg Wiltjer	1.00	.50	.10
☐ 15 Logo Card Saanich Police	1.00	.50	.10

1984-85 Victoria Police

This 16-card set was sponsored by Westcoast Savings Credit Union, CJVI-900 (a radio station), Factory Sound and Sanyo, and the Saanich Police. The cards measure approximately 2 5/8" by 4". On a white card face, the fronts feature posed action photos. The pictures and the player information below them are enclosed by a blue border. The backs have player quotes ("Viking Quotes"), a facsimile autograph, an offer to see a game free and win a stereo cassette walkman, and sponsor logos. The game at which the card holder will be admitted free is noted on the back. The safety slogan "Working together with our youth and the community" rounds out the back. The cards are unnumbered and checklisted below in alphabetical order.

	MINT	EXC	G-VG
COMPLETE SET (16)	12.00	6.00	1.20
COMMON PLAYER (1-16)	1.00	.50	.10
☐ 1 Cord Clemens	1.00	.50	.10
☐ 2 Jerry Divoky	1.00	.50	.10
☐ 3 Quinn Groenhyde Assistant CO	1.00	.50	.10
☐ 4 Shawn Kalinovich	1.00	.50	.10
☐ 5 Robert Kreke	1.00	.50	.10
☐ 6 Wade Loukes	1.00	.50	.10
☐ 7 James Newman	1.00	.50	.10
☐ 8 Phil Ohl	1.00	.50	.10
☐ 9 Vito Pasquale	1.00	.50	.10
☐ 10 Lloyd Scrubb UER (Name misspelled Llyod on front)	1.00	.50	.10
☐ 11 David Sheehan	1.00	.50	.10
☐ 12 Ken Shields CO	1.00	.50	.10
☐ 13 Randy Steel	1.00	.50	.10
☐ 14 Graham Taylor	1.00	.50	.10
☐ 15 Ellis Whalen	1.00	.50	.10
☐ 16 Logo Card Saanich Police	1.00	.50	.10

1985-86 Victoria Police

This 17-card set was sponsored by Pacific Coast Savings Credit Union, Converse, 1200-CKDA, and the Saanich Police. The cards measure approximately 2 5/8" by 4". On a white card face, the fronts feature posed action photos. The pictures and the player information below them are enclosed by a blue border. The backs have player quotes ("Viking Quotes"), a facsimile autograph, an offer to see a game free and win a stereo cassette

walkman, and sponsor logos. The game at which the card holder will be admitted free is noted on the back. The safety slogan "Crime prevention is everyone's business" rounds out the back. The cards are unnumbered and checklisted below in alphabetical order.

	MINT	EXC	G-VG
COMPLETE SET (17)	10.00	5.00	1.00
COMMON PLAYER (1-17)	.75	.35	.07
☐ 1 Maurice Basso	.75	.35	.07
☐ 2 Clint Hamilton	.75	.35	.07
☐ 3 Fraser Jefferson	.75	.35	.07
☐ 4 Tom Johnson	.75	.35	.07
☐ 5 Jim Knox	.75	.35	.07
☐ 6 David Lescheid	.75	.35	.07
☐ 7 Vesa Linnamo	.75	.35	.07
☐ 8 David McIntosh	.75	.35	.07
☐ 9 Geoff McKay	.75	.35	.07
☐ 10 Spencer McKay	.75	.35	.07
☐ 11 Rick Mesich	.75	.35	.07
☐ 12 Kevin Ottewell	.75	.35	.07
☐ 13 Roger Rai	.75	.35	.07
☐ 14 Chris Schriek	.75	.35	.07
☐ 15 Scott Stinson Assistant CO	.75	.35	.07
☐ 16 Guy Vetrie CO	.75	.35	.07
☐ 17 Logo Card Saanich Police	.75	.35	.07

1988-89 Victoria Police

This 16-card set was sponsored by Pacific Coast Savings Credit Union, Converse, 1200-CKDA, and the Saanich Police. The cards were issued on an unperforated sheet; if cut, they would measure approximately 2 5/8" by 4". On a white card face, the fronts feature posed action photos. The pictures and the player information below them are enclosed by a blue border. The backs have player quotes ("Viking Quotes"), a facsimile autograph, an offer to see a game free and win a stereo cassette walkman, and sponsor logos. The game at which the card holder will be admitted free is noted on the back. The safety slogan "Crime prevention is everyone's business" rounds out the back. The cards are unnumbered and checklisted below in alphabetical order.

	MINT	EXC	G-VG
COMPLETE SET (16)	9.00	4.50	.90
COMMON PLAYER (1-16)	.60	.30	.06
☐ 1 Maurice Basso	.60	.30	.06
☐ 2 Colin Brousson	.60	.30	.06
☐ 3 Jerry Divoky	.60	.30	.06
☐ 4 Kevin Harrington	.60	.30	.06
☐ 5 Tom Johnson	.60	.30	.06
☐ 6 Daryn Lansdell	.60	.30	.06
☐ 7 Wade Loukes	.60	.30	.06
☐ 8 Geoff McKay	.60	.30	.06
☐ 9 Spencer McKay	.60	.30	.06
☐ 10 Rick Mesich	.60	.30	.06
☐ 11 Dale Olson	.60	.30	.06
☐ 12 Ken Olynyk CO	.60	.30	.06
☐ 13 Kevin Ottewell	.60	.30	.06
☐ 14 Tug Rados	.60	.30	.06
☐ 15 Ken Shields CO	.60	.30	.06
☐ 16 Guy Vetrie CO	.60	.30	.06

1988-89 Virginia Hardee's

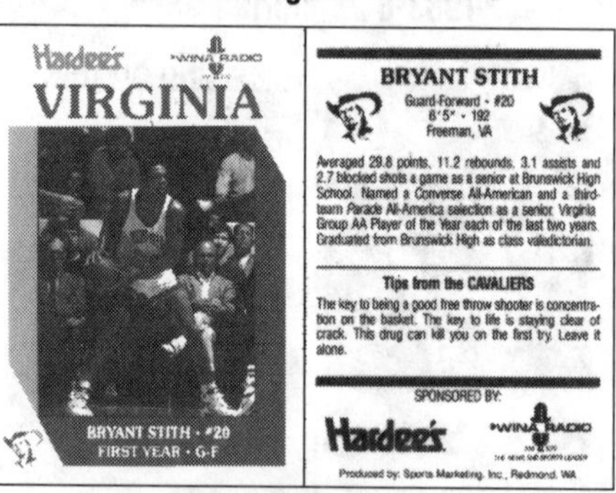

This 16-card set was sponsored by Hardee's Restaurants in conjunction with WINA Radio AM 1070, and their company names appear on the top of the card. The cards measure (the standard) 2 1/2" by 3 1/2". The action color photos are surrounded on their sides and bottom by blue and orange thick borders (the school's colors), with the Cavalier logo in the lower left hand corner. The player's name, jersey number, year, and position appear below the photo. The back gives biographical information and Tips from the Cavaliers. The cards are ordered and numbered below according to the alphabetical order of the player's name. The set features a card of Matt Blundin, drafted by the NFL as a quarterback and NBA first-rounder Bryant Stith.

	MINT	EXC	G-VG
COMPLETE SET (16)	50.00	25.00	5.00
COMMON PLAYER (1-16)	2.00	1.00	.20
☐ 1 Brent Bair 42	2.00	1.00	.20
☐ 2 Matt Blundin 30	10.00	5.00	1.00
☐ 3 Mark Cooke 31	2.00	1.00	.20
☐ 4 John Crotty 22	6.00	3.00	.60
☐ 5 Brent Dabbs 32	3.00	1.50	.30
☐ 6 Jeff Daniel 44	2.00	1.00	.20
☐ 7 Terry Holland CO	5.00	2.50	.50
☐ 8 Dirk Katstra 24	2.00	1.00	.20
☐ 9 Richard Morgan 11	3.00	1.50	.30
☐ 10 Anthony Oliver 10	3.00	1.50	.30
☐ 11 Bryant Stith 20	12.00	6.00	1.20
☐ 12 Kenny Turner 12	2.00	1.00	.20
☐ 13 Curtis Williams 21	2.00	1.00	.20
☐ 14 Cheerleaders	2.00	1.00	.20
☐ 15 Coaching Staff	2.00	1.00	.20
☐ 16 Title Card	3.00	1.50	.30

1991-92 Virginia

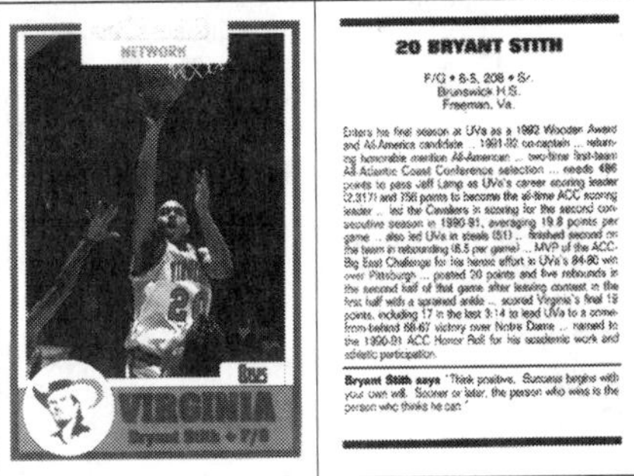

This 16-card set was sponsored by Capitol Sports Network, whose logo appears at the top of each card front. The cards are perforated and measure the standard size, 2 1/2" by 3 1/2". The fronts feature posed head and shoulders shots enclosed by white and purple borders. Player identification appears in an orange stripe beneath the picture, and the team logo at the lower left corner rounds out the card face. The backs carry biographical information, career summary, and a player quote. The cards are unnumbered and checklisted below in alphabetical order.

	MINT	EXC	G-VG
COMPLETE SET (16)	15.00	7.50	1.50
COMMON PLAYER (1-16)	1.00	.50	.10
☐ 1 Chris Alexander	1.00	.50	.10
☐ 2 Cory Alexander	1.00	.50	.10
☐ 3 Yuri Barnes	1.00	.50	.10
☐ 4 Junior Burrough	1.00	.50	.10
☐ 5 Chris Havlicek	2.00	1.00	.20
☐ 6 Ted Jeffries	1.50	.75	.15
☐ 7 Derrick Johnson	1.00	.50	.10
☐ 8 Jeff Jones CO	2.00	1.00	.20
☐ 9 Terry Kirby	4.00	2.00	.40
☐ 10 Anthony Oliver	1.50	.75	.15
☐ 11 Cornel Parker	1.00	.50	.10
☐ 12 Doug Smith	1.00	.50	.10
☐ 13 Corey Stewart	1.00	.50	.10
☐ 14 Bryant Stith	5.00	2.50	.50
☐ 15 Jason Williford	1.00	.50	.10
☐ 16 Shawn Wilson	1.00	.50	.10

1991-92 Virginia Lady Cavaliers

This 16-card set was issued as a perforated sheet and sponsored by McDonald's. After perforation, the cards measure the standard size (2 1/2" by 3 1/2"). On a white card face, the fronts feature a mix of posed or action color player photos enclosed by blue borders. A McDonald's logo with the words "Food Folks and Fun" appears in a bar above the picture, while school logo and player information appear in an orange stripe at the bottom. In black print on white, the backs carry biography, player profile, and an inspirational quote. This set includes a card of Dawn Staley, nicknamed by her Lady Cavalier fans as the female "Michael Jordan." The cards are unnumbered and checklisted below in alphabetical order.

	MINT	EXC	G-VG
COMPLETE SET (16)	15.00	7.50	1.50
COMMON PLAYER (1-16)	.75	.35	.07
☐ 1 Charleata Beale	.75	.35	.07
☐ 2 Heather Burge	2.00	1.00	.20
☐ 3 Heidi Burge	2.00	1.00	.20
☐ 4 Dena Evans	.75	.35	.07
☐ 5 Chris Lesoravage	.75	.35	.07
☐ 6 Amy Lofstedt	.75	.35	.07
☐ 7 Allison Moore	.75	.35	.07
☐ 8 Tammi Reiss	2.00	1.00	.20
☐ 9 Debbie Ryan CO	1.00	.50	.10
☐ 10 Felicia Santelli	.75	.35	.07
☐ 11 Audra Smith	.75	.35	.07
☐ 12 Dawn Staley	5.00	2.50	.50
☐ 13 Wendy Toussaint	.75	.35	.07
☐ 14 Melanee Wagener	.75	.35	.07
☐ 15 NCAA Midwest Regional Tournament Champions March 17-21, 1991	.75	.35	.07
☐ 16 Virginia vs NC State February 23, 1991	.75	.35	.07

1988-89 Wake Forest Police

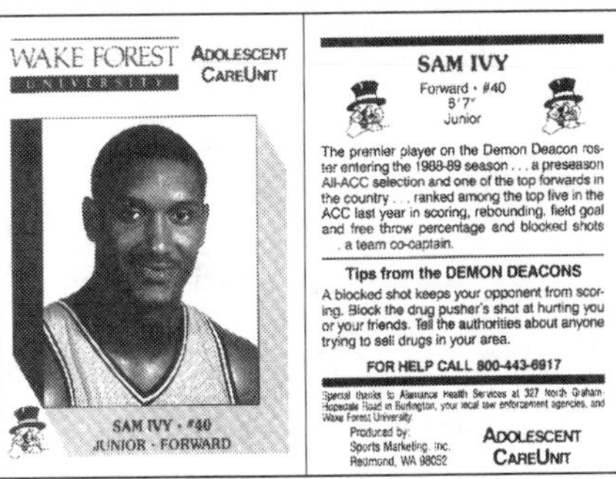

This 16-card set was sponsored by the Adolescent CareUnit of Almanac Health Services, local law enforcement agencies, and Wake Forest University. The standard-size (2 1/2" by 3 1/2") cards feature on the front posed color head and shoulders shots, bordered in black on the left and in yellow on the right and below. Player information appears in the bottom yellow border, while the school logo in the lower left corner rounds out the front. The backs present biography, player profile, and "Tips from the Demon Deacons," which consist of anti-drug and alcohol messages. The cards are unnumbered and checklisted below in alphabetical order.

	MINT	EXC	G-VG
COMPLETE SET (16)	20.00	10.00	2.00
COMMON PLAYER (1-16)	1.50	.75	.15
☐ 1 Tony Black	1.50	.75	.15
☐ 2 Cal Boyd	1.50	.75	.15
☐ 3 David Carlyle	1.50	.75	.15
☐ 4 Darryl Cheeley	1.50	.75	.15
☐ 5 Sam Ivy	2.00	1.00	.20
☐ 6 Antonio Johnson	1.50	.75	.15
☐ 7 Daric Keys	1.50	.75	.15
☐ 8 Chris King	4.00	2.00	.40
☐ 9 Ralph Kitley	1.50	.75	.15
☐ 10 Derrick McQueen	2.00	1.00	.20
☐ 11 Phil Medlin	1.50	.75	.15

		MINT	EXC	G-VG
☐ 12	Steve Ray	1.50	.75	.15
☐ 13	Todd Sanders	1.50	.75	.15
☐ 14	Robert Siler	1.50	.75	.15
☐ 15	Bob Staak CO	1.50	.75	.15
☐ 16	Tom Wise	1.50	.75	.15

1991-92 Washington TCI

This nine-card standard-size (2 1/2" by 3 1/2") set was sponsored by Prime Sports Northwest and TCI Cablevision of Washington. The fronts display color action player photos enframed by purple borders. The school and team name appear above the pictures, while player information is printed in a gold stripe beneath them. The backs have career statistics, an announcement of the Husky KidSports Program, and sponsor logos. The cards are unnumbered and checklisted below in alphabetical order.

	MINT	EXC	G-VG
COMPLETE SET (9)	9.00	4.50	.90
COMMON PLAYER (1-9)	1.00	.50	.10
☐ 1 Dion Brown	1.00	.50	.10
☐ 2 Tim Caviezel	1.00	.50	.10
☐ 3 James French	1.00	.50	.10
☐ 4 Mike Hayward	1.00	.50	.10
☐ 5 Todd Lautenbach	1.00	.50	.10
☐ 6 Doug Meekins	1.00	.50	.10
☐ 7 Brent Merritt	1.00	.50	.10
☐ 8 Lynn Nance CO	1.50	.75	.15
☐ 9 Quentin Youngblood	1.00	.50	.10

1991-92 Washington Viacom

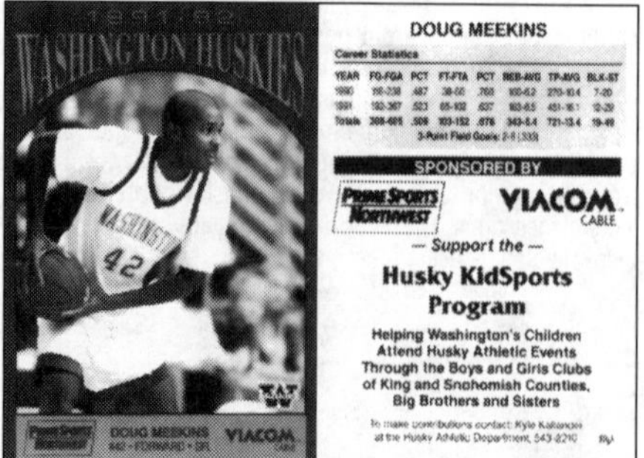

This 17-card standard-size (2 1/2" by 3 1/2") basketball set was sponsored by Prime Sports Northwest and Viacom Cable. The fronts are accented in the team's colors (purple and gold) and have color action player photos. The top of the pictures is curved to resemble an archway, and the team name follows the curve of the arch. Sponsor logos and player identification appear in the gold stripe below the picture. The backs carry statistics (or career summary), an announcement of the Husky KidSports Program, and sponsor logos. The cards are unnumbered and checklisted below in alphabetical order as follows: men's basketball (1-9) and women's basketball (10-17).

	MINT	EXC	G-VG
COMPLETE SET (17)	12.00	6.00	1.20
COMMON PLAYER (1-9)	1.00	.50	.10
COMMON PLAYER (10-17)	.75	.35	.07
☐ 1 Bryant Boston	1.00	.50	.10
☐ 2 Tim Caviezel	1.00	.50	.10
☐ 3 Rich Manning	1.50	.75	.15
☐ 4 Doug Meekins	1.00	.50	.10
☐ 5 Chandler Nairn	1.00	.50	.10
☐ 6 Lynn Nance CO	1.50	.75	.15
☐ 7 Mark Pope	1.00	.50	.10
☐ 8 Andy Woods	1.00	.50	.10
☐ 9 Quentin Youngblood	1.00	.50	.10
☐ 10 Tara Davis	.75	.35	.07
☐ 11 Katia Foucade	.75	.35	.07
☐ 12 Shaunda Greene	.75	.35	.07
☐ 13 Chris Gobrecht CO	.75	.35	.07
☐ 14 Erika Hardwick	.75	.35	.07
☐ 15 Laura Moore	.75	.35	.07
☐ 16 Joe Shafer	.75	.35	.07
☐ 17 Dianne Williams	.75	.35	.07

1991-92 Washington State

This 12-card standard-size (2 1/2" by 3 1/2") basketball set was sponsored by Prime Sports Northwest and CableVision. The set was issued as an perforated sheet with three rows of four cards each; the first six cards feature the women's basketball team, while the last six cards present the men's team. The fronts are accented in the team's colors (maroon and gray) and have posed and action player photos. The top of the pictures is curved to resemble an archway, and the team name follows the curve of the arch. Sponsor logos and player identification appear in the gray stripe below the picture. The backs carry statistics, player profile, and sponsor advertisements. The cards are unnumbered and checklisted below in alphabetical order as follows: men's basketball (1-6) and women's basketball (7-12).

	MINT	EXC	G-VG
COMPLETE SET (12)	10.00	5.00	1.00
COMMON PLAYER (1-6)	1.00	.50	.10
COMMON PLAYER (7-12)	.75	.35	.07
☐ 1 Rob Corkrum	1.00	.50	.10
☐ 2 Ken Critton	1.00	.50	.10
☐ 3 Eddie Hill	1.00	.50	.10
☐ 4 Tyrone Maxey	1.00	.50	.10
☐ 5 Sean Tresvant	1.00	.50	.10
☐ 6 Joey Warmenhoven	1.00	.50	.10

☐ 7 Janel Benton Erika Wheeler	.75	.35	.07
☐ 8 Lori Lollis	.75	.35	.07
☐ 9 Heather Norman	.75	.35	.07
☐ 10 Camille Thompson Kathy Weber	.75	.35	.07
☐ 11 Darla Williamson	.75	.35	.07
☐ 12 Team Photo Women's Basketball	1.00	.50	.10

1980-81 Wichita State Police

This 15-card standard size (2 1/2" by 3 1/2") set was sponsored by Service Auto Glass and the Wichita Police Department. The cards were given away at the Wichita State athletic banquet and also by police officers. The fronts feature a close-up of the player enclosed by a border. The slogan "Love 'Ya Shockers" appears in the upper right corner, while player information is printed beneath the picture. Each card back carries a different safety message and a reminder to call 911. The cards are unnumbered and checklisted below in alphabetical order. Key cards in the set include Antoine Carr and Cliff Levingston.

	MINT	EXC	G-VG
COMPLETE SET (15)	125.00	60.00	12.50
COMMON PLAYER (1-15)	3.50	1.75	.35
☐ 1 Antoine Carr	50.00	25.00	5.00
☐ 2 Mike Denny	3.50	1.75	.35
☐ 3 Zarko Djuricic	3.50	1.75	.35
☐ 4 James Gibbs	3.50	1.75	.35
☐ 5 Jay Jackson	3.50	1.75	.35
☐ 6 Mike Jones	3.50	1.75	.35
☐ 7 Ozell Jones	5.00	2.50	.50
☐ 8 Eric Kuhn	3.50	1.75	.35
☐ 9 Cliff Levingston	50.00	25.00	5.00
☐ 10 Tony Martin	3.50	1.75	.35
☐ 11 Karl Papke	3.50	1.75	.35
☐ 12 Zoran Rdovic	3.50	1.75	.35
☐ 13 Gene Smithson CO	5.00	2.50	.50
☐ 14 Randy Smithson	5.00	2.50	.50
☐ 15 Team Photo	7.50	3.75	.75

1989-90 Wisconsin Smokey

This 14-card set was sponsored by the USDA Forest Service in cooperation with the National Association of State Foresters and BD and A, Inc. The cards were issued on an unperforated sheet with four rows of four cards; two of the cards slots are blacked out where the photo should appear and feature a fire cartoon on their backs. After cutting, the cards measure the standard size (2 1/2" by 3 1/2"). The fronts feature a mix of posed and action color player photos on a white card face. Above the picture appears the school name (in red lettering) and a black stripe. Red and black stripes traverse the card below the picture, with the Smokey logo in the lower left corner and player identification to the right. The backs have biographical information, player evaluation, and a fire prevention cartoon starring Smokey. The cards are unnumbered and checklisted below in alphabetical order, with the uniform number after the player's name.

	MINT	EXC	G-VG
COMPLETE SET (14)	10.00	5.00	1.00
COMMON PLAYER (1-14)	.75	.35	.07
☐ 1 Bobby Douglass 10	1.00	.50	.10
☐ 2 John Ellenson 40	.75	.35	.07
☐ 3 Brian Good 12	.75	.35	.07
☐ 4 Damon Harrell 41	.75	.35	.07
☐ 5 Larry Hisle Jr. 4	1.25	.60	.12
☐ 6 Danny Jones 50	.75	.35	.07
☐ 7 Jason Johnsen 5	.75	.35	.07
☐ 8 Grant Johnson 52	.75	.35	.07
☐ 9 Tim Locum 44	.75	.35	.07
☐ 10 Carlton McGee 32	.75	.35	.07
☐ 11 Kurt Portmann 53	.75	.35	.07
☐ 12 Willie Simms 23	.75	.35	.07
☐ 13 Patrick Tompkins 43	.75	.35	.07
☐ 14 Steve Yoder CO	1.00	.50	.10

LATE-BREAKING 1992 SETS

1992-93 Fleer

The 1992-93 Fleer basketball set contains 264 standard-size (2 1/2" by 3 1/2") cards. Larry Johnson is spotlighted on a 12-card signature series, and he autographed more than 2,000 of these cards, which were randomly inserted in wax packs. Collectors were also able to receive three additional Johnson cards and the premiere edition of NBA Inside Stuff magazine by sending in ten wrappers and 1.00 in a mail-in offer. The fronts display color action player photos, enclosed by metallic bronze borders and accented on the right by two pebble-grain colored stripes. On a tan pebble-grain background, the horizontally oriented backs have a color close-up photo framed by an archway as well as biography, career statistics, and player profile. The cards are numbered on the back and checklisted below alphabetically according to teams as follows: Atlanta Hawks (1-9), Boston Celtics (10-19), Charlotte Hornets (20-27), Chicago Bulls (28-37), Cleveland Cavaliers (38-46), Dallas Mavericks (47-53), Denver Nuggets (54-61), Detroit Pistons (62-71), Golden State Warriors (72-79), Houston Rockets (80-87), Indiana Pacers (88-96), Los Angeles Clippers (97-105), Los Angeles Lakers (106-114), Miami Heat (115-123), Milwaukee Bucks (124-130), Minnesota Timberwolves (131-139), New Jersey Nets (140-147), New York Knicks (148-157), Orlando Magic (158-165), Philadelphia 76ers (166-176), Phoenix Suns (177-184), Portland Trail Blazers (185-193), Sacramento Kings (194-200), San Antonio Spurs (201-208), Seattle Supersonics (209-217), Utah Jazz (218-227), and Washington Bullets (228-237). The set closes with the following special subsets: League Leaders (238-245), Award Winners (246-249), Pro-Visions (250-255), and Schoolyard Stars (256-264).

	MINT	EXC	G-VG
COMPLETE SET (264)	15.00	7.50	1.50
COMMON PLAYER (1-264)	.03	.01	.00
☐ 1 Stacey Augmon	.15	.07	.01
☐ 2 Duane Ferrell	.03	.01	.00
☐ 3 Paul Graham	.03	.01	.00
☐ 4 Jon Koncak	.03	.01	.00
☐ 5 Blair Rasmussen	.03	.01	.00
☐ 6 Rumeal Robinson	.03	.01	.00
☐ 7 Bob Weiss CO	.03	.01	.00
☐ 8 Dominique Wilkins	.10	.05	.01
☐ 9 Kevin Willis	.06	.03	.00
☐ 10 John Bagley	.03	.01	.00
☐ 11 Larry Bird	.25	.12	.02
☐ 12 Dee Brown	.15	.07	.01
☐ 13 Chris Ford CO	.03	.01	.00
☐ 14 Rick Fox	.15	.07	.01
☐ 15 Kevin Gamble	.03	.01	.00
☐ 16 Reggie Lewis	.12	.06	.01
☐ 17 Kevin McHale	.08	.04	.01
☐ 18 Robert Parish	.10	.05	.01
☐ 19 Ed Pinckney	.03	.01	.00
☐ 20 Muggsy Bogues	.03	.01	.00
☐ 21 Allan Bristow CO	.03	.01	.00
☐ 22 Dell Curry	.03	.01	.00
☐ 23 Kenny Gattison	.03	.01	.00
☐ 24 Kendall Gill	.35	.17	.03
☐ 25 Larry Johnson	1.00	.50	.10
☐ 26 Johnny Newman	.03	.01	.00
☐ 27 J.R. Reid	.03	.01	.00
☐ 28 B.J. Armstrong	.06	.03	.00
☐ 29 Bill Cartwright	.03	.01	.00
☐ 30 Horace Grant	.08	.04	.01
☐ 31 Phil Jackson CO	.03	.01	.00
☐ 32 Michael Jordan	.90	.45	.09
☐ 33 Stacey King	.03	.01	.00
☐ 34 Cliff Levingston	.03	.01	.00
☐ 35 John Paxson	.06	.03	.00
☐ 36 Scottie Pippen	.25	.12	.02
☐ 37 Scott Williams	.06	.03	.00
☐ 38 John Battle	.03	.01	.00
☐ 39 Terrell Brandon	.10	.05	.01
☐ 40 Brad Daugherty	.12	.06	.01
☐ 41 Craig Ehlo	.03	.01	.00
☐ 42 Larry Nance	.08	.04	.01
☐ 43 Mark Price	.10	.05	.01
☐ 44 Mike Sanders	.03	.01	.00
☐ 45 Lenny Wilkens CO	.06	.03	.00
☐ 46 Hot Rod Williams	.06	.03	.00
☐ 47 Richie Adubato CO	.03	.01	.00
☐ 48 Terry Davis	.03	.01	.00
☐ 49 Derek Harper	.06	.03	.00
☐ 50 Donald Hodge	.08	.04	.01
☐ 51 Mike Iuzzolino	.06	.03	.00
☐ 52 Rodney McCray	.03	.01	.00
☐ 53 Doug Smith	.10	.05	.01
☐ 54 Greg Anderson	.03	.01	.00
☐ 55 Winston Garland	.03	.01	.00
☐ 56 Dan Issel CO	.06	.03	.00
☐ 57 Chris Jackson	.06	.03	.00
☐ 58 Marcus Liberty	.06	.03	.00
☐ 59 Mark Macon	.10	.05	.01
☐ 60 Dikembe Mutombo	.50	.25	.05
☐ 61 Reggie Williams	.03	.01	.00
☐ 62 Mark Aguirre	.06	.03	.00
☐ 63 Joe Dumars	.10	.05	.01
☐ 64 Bill Laimbeer	.06	.03	.00
☐ 65 Olden Polynice	.03	.01	.00
☐ 66 Dennis Rodman	.08	.04	.01
☐ 67 Ron Rothstein CO	.03	.01	.00
☐ 68 John Salley	.03	.01	.00
☐ 69 Isiah Thomas	.12	.06	.01
☐ 70 Darrell Walker	.03	.01	.00
☐ 71 Orlando Woolridge	.03	.01	.00
☐ 72 Victor Alexander	.06	.03	.00
☐ 73 Mario Elie	.03	.01	.00
☐ 74 Tim Hardaway	.30	.15	.03
☐ 75 Tyrone Hill	.06	.03	.00
☐ 76 Sarunas Marciulionis	.10	.05	.01
☐ 77 Chris Mullin	.15	.07	.01
☐ 78 Don Nelson CO	.03	.01	.00
☐ 79 Billy Owens	.50	.25	.05
☐ 80 Sleepy Floyd	.03	.01	.00
☐ 81 Avery Johnson	.03	.01	.00
☐ 82 Buck Johnson	.03	.01	.00
☐ 83 Vernon Maxwell	.03	.01	.00
☐ 84 Hakeem Olajuwon	.12	.06	.01
☐ 85 Kenny Smith	.03	.01	.00
☐ 86 Otis Thorpe	.06	.03	.00
☐ 87 Rudy Tomjanovich CO	.03	.01	.00
☐ 88 Dale Davis	.06	.03	.00
☐ 89 Vern Fleming	.03	.01	.00
☐ 90 Bob Hill CO	.03	.01	.00
☐ 91 Reggie Miller	.08	.04	.01
☐ 92 Chuck Person	.06	.03	.00
☐ 93 Detlef Schrempf	.06	.03	.00
☐ 94 Rik Smits	.03	.01	.00
☐ 95 LaSalle Thompson	.03	.01	.00
☐ 96 Micheal Williams	.06	.03	.00
☐ 97 Larry Brown CO	.03	.01	.00
☐ 98 James Edwards	.03	.01	.00
☐ 99 Gary Grant	.03	.01	.00
☐ 100 Ron Harper	.06	.03	.00
☐ 101 Danny Manning	.10	.05	.01
☐ 102 Ken Norman	.06	.03	.00
☐ 103 Doc Rivers	.06	.03	.00
☐ 104 Charles Smith	.06	.03	.00
☐ 105 Loy Vaught	.06	.03	.00
☐ 106 Elden Campbell	.06	.03	.00
☐ 107 Vlade Divac	.06	.03	.00
☐ 108 A.C. Green	.06	.03	.00
☐ 109 Sam Perkins	.06	.03	.00
☐ 110 Randy Pfund CO	.06	.03	.00
☐ 111 Byron Scott	.06	.03	.00
☐ 112 Terry Teagle	.03	.01	.00
☐ 113 Sedale Threatt	.06	.03	.00
☐ 114 James Worthy	.10	.05	.01
☐ 115 Willie Burton	.06	.03	.00

☐ 116 Bimbo Coles	.06	.03	.00
☐ 117 Kevin Edwards	.03	.01	.00
☐ 118 Grant Long	.06	.03	.00
☐ 119 Kevin Loughery CO	.03	.01	.00
☐ 120 Glen Rice	.20	.10	.02
☐ 121 Rony Seikaly	.08	.04	.01
☐ 122 Brian Shaw	.03	.01	.00
☐ 123 Steve Smith	.15	.07	.01
☐ 124 Frank Brickowski	.03	.01	.00
☐ 125 Mike Dunleavy CO	.03	.01	.00
☐ 126 Blue Edwards	.03	.01	.00
☐ 127 Moses Malone	.10	.05	.01
☐ 128 Eric Murdock	.06	.03	.00
☐ 129 Fred Roberts	.03	.01	.00
☐ 130 Alvin Robertson	.03	.01	.00
☐ 131 Thurl Bailey	.03	.01	.00
☐ 132 Tony Campbell	.03	.01	.00
☐ 133 Gerald Glass	.03	.01	.00
☐ 134 Luc Longley	.06	.03	.00
☐ 135 Sam Mitchell	.03	.01	.00
☐ 136 Pooh Richardson	.10	.05	.01
☐ 137 Jimmy Rodgers CO	.03	.01	.00
☐ 138 Felton Spencer	.06	.03	.00
☐ 139 Doug West	.06	.03	.00
☐ 140 Kenny Anderson	.15	.07	.01
☐ 141 Mookie Blaylock	.06	.03	.00
☐ 142 Sam Bowie	.06	.03	.00
☐ 143 Derrick Coleman	.20	.10	.02
☐ 144 Chuck Daly CO	.06	.03	.00
☐ 145 Terry Mills	.06	.03	.00
☐ 146 Chris Morris	.03	.01	.00
☐ 147 Drazen Petrovic	.10	.05	.01
☐ 148 Greg Anthony	.12	.06	.01
☐ 149 Rolando Blackman	.06	.03	.00
☐ 150 Patrick Ewing	.15	.07	.01
☐ 151 Mark Jackson	.06	.03	.00
☐ 152 Anthony Mason	.03	.01	.00
☐ 153 Xavier McDaniel	.08	.04	.01
☐ 154 Charles Oakley	.06	.03	.00
☐ 155 Pat Riley CO	.06	.03	.00
☐ 156 John Starks	.10	.05	.01
☐ 157 Gerald Wilkins	.06	.03	.00
☐ 158 Nick Anderson	.10	.05	.01
☐ 159 Anthony Bowie	.03	.01	.00
☐ 160 Terry Catledge	.03	.01	.00
☐ 161 Matt Guokas CO	.03	.01	.00
☐ 162 Stanley Roberts	.12	.06	.01
☐ 163 Dennis Scott	.08	.04	.01
☐ 164 Scott Skiles	.03	.01	.00
☐ 165 Brian Williams	.06	.03	.00
☐ 166 Ron Anderson	.03	.01	.00
☐ 167 Manute Bol	.03	.01	.00
☐ 168 Johnny Dawkins	.03	.01	.00
☐ 169 Armon Gilliam	.06	.03	.00
☐ 170 Hersey Hawkins	.08	.04	.01
☐ 171 Jeff Hornacek	.08	.04	.01
☐ 172 Andrew Lang	.03	.01	.00
☐ 173 Doug Moe CO	.03	.01	.00
☐ 174 Tim Perry	.03	.01	.00
☐ 175 Jeff Ruland	.03	.01	.00
☐ 176 Charles Shackleford	.03	.01	.00
☐ 177 Danny Ainge	.06	.03	.00
☐ 178 Charles Barkley	.15	.07	.01
☐ 179 Cedric Ceballos	.06	.03	.00
☐ 180 Tom Chambers	.08	.04	.01
☐ 181 Kevin Johnson	.15	.07	.01
☐ 182 Dan Majerle	.08	.04	.01
☐ 183 Mark West	.03	.01	.00
☐ 184 Paul Westphal CO	.03	.01	.00
☐ 185 Rick Adelman CO	.06	.03	.00
☐ 186 Clyde Drexler	.20	.10	.02
☐ 187 Kevin Duckworth	.03	.01	.00
☐ 188 Jerome Kersey	.08	.04	.01
☐ 189 Robert Pack	.12	.06	.01
☐ 190 Terry Porter	.10	.05	.01
☐ 191 Cliff Robinson	.10	.05	.01
☐ 192 Rod Strickland	.06	.03	.00
☐ 193 Buck Williams	.06	.03	.00
☐ 194 Anthony Bonner	.03	.01	.00
☐ 195 Duane Causwell	.03	.01	.00
☐ 196 Mitch Richmond	.10	.05	.01
☐ 197 Garry St. Jean CO	.06	.03	.00
☐ 198 Lionel Simmons	.15	.07	.01
☐ 199 Wayman Tisdale	.06	.03	.00
☐ 200 Spud Webb	.06	.03	.00
☐ 201 Willie Anderson	.06	.03	.00
☐ 202 Antoine Carr	.06	.03	.00
☐ 203 Terry Cummings	.06	.03	.00
☐ 204 Sean Elliott	.08	.04	.01
☐ 205 Dale Ellis	.06	.03	.00
☐ 206 Vinnie Johnson	.06	.03	.00
☐ 207 David Robinson	.50	.25	.05
☐ 208 Jerry Tarkanian CO	.15	.07	.01
☐ 209 Benoit Benjamin	.06	.03	.00
☐ 210 Michael Cage	.03	.01	.00
☐ 211 Eddie Johnson	.06	.03	.00
☐ 212 George Karl CO	.03	.01	.00
☐ 213 Shawn Kemp	.35	.17	.03
☐ 214 Derrick McKey	.06	.03	.00
☐ 215 Nate McMillan	.03	.01	.00
☐ 216 Gary Payton	.08	.04	.01
☐ 217 Ricky Pierce	.06	.03	.00
☐ 218 David Benoit	.10	.05	.01
☐ 219 Mike Brown	.03	.01	.00
☐ 220 Tyrone Corbin	.03	.01	.00
☐ 221 Mark Eaton	.03	.01	.00
☐ 222 Jay Humphries	.03	.01	.00
☐ 223 Larry Krystkowiak	.03	.01	.00
☐ 224 Jeff Malone	.08	.04	.01
☐ 225 Karl Malone	.15	.07	.01
☐ 226 Jerry Sloan CO	.03	.01	.00
☐ 227 John Stockton	.15	.07	.01
☐ 228 Michael Adams	.08	.04	.01
☐ 229 Rex Chapman	.06	.03	.00
☐ 230 Ledell Eackles	.03	.01	.00
☐ 231 Pervis Ellison	.12	.06	.01
☐ 232 A.J. English	.06	.03	.00
☐ 233 Harvey Grant	.06	.03	.00
☐ 234 LaBradford Smith	.08	.04	.01
☐ 235 Larry Stewart	.06	.03	.00
☐ 236 Wes Unseld CO	.06	.03	.00
☐ 237 David Wingate	.03	.01	.00
☐ 238 Michael Jordan LL Scoring	.40	.20	.04
☐ 239 Dennis Rodman LL Rebounding	.08	.04	.01
☐ 240 John Stockton LL Assists/Steals	.10	.05	.01
☐ 241 Buck Williams LL Field Goal Percentage	.06	.03	.00
☐ 242 Mark Price LL Free Throw Percentage	.08	.04	.01
☐ 243 Dana Barros LL Three Point Percentage	.06	.03	.00
☐ 244 David Robinson LL Shots Blocked	.25	.12	.02
☐ 245 Chris Mullin LL Minutes Played	.10	.05	.01
☐ 246 Michael Jordan MVP	.40	.20	.04
☐ 247 Larry Johnson ROY	.50	.25	.05
☐ 248 David Robinson Defensive Player of the Year	.25	.12	.02
☐ 249 Detlef Schrempf Sixth Man of the Year	.06	.03	.00
☐ 250 Clyde Drexler PV	.20	.10	.02
☐ 251 Tim Hardaway PV	.20	.10	.02
☐ 252 Kevin Johnson PV	.15	.07	.01
☐ 253 Larry Johnson PV	1.00	.50	.10
☐ 254 Scottie Pippen PV	.25	.12	.02
☐ 255 Isiah Thomas PV	.12	.06	.01
☐ 256 Larry Bird SY	.15	.07	.01
☐ 257 Brad Daugherty SY	.08	.04	.01
☐ 258 Kevin Johnson SY	.10	.05	.01
☐ 259 Larry Johnson SY	.50	.25	.05
☐ 260 Scottie Pippen SY	.15	.07	.01
☐ 261 Dennis Rodman SY	.06	.03	.00
☐ 262 Checklist 1	.06	.01	.00
☐ 263 Checklist 2	.06	.01	.00
☐ 264 Checklist 3	.06	.01	.00

1992-93 Fleer All-Stars

These 24 All-Star cards were inserted exclusively in wax packs and feature outstanding players from the Eastern Conference (1-12) and Western (13-24) Conference. The cards measure the standard size (2 1/2" by 3 1/2") and are highlighted by gold-foil stamping. The cards are numbered on the back.

	MINT	EXC	G-VG
COMPLETE SET (24)	27.00	13.50	2.70
COMMON PLAYER (1-24)	1.00	.50	.10
☐ 1 Michael Adams Washington Bullets	1.00	.50	.10
☐ 2 Charles Barkley Phoenix Suns	2.50	1.25	.25
☐ 3 Brad Daugherty Cleveland Cavaliers	1.50	.75	.15
☐ 4 Joe Dumars Detroit Pistons	1.25	.60	.12

☐ 5 Patrick Ewing New York Knicks	2.50	1.25	.25
☐ 6 Michael Jordan Chicago Bulls	6.00	3.00	.60
☐ 7 Reggie Lewis Boston Celtics	2.00	1.00	.20
☐ 8 Scottie Pippen Chicago Bulls	2.50	1.25	.25
☐ 9 Mark Price Cleveland Cavaliers	1.50	.75	.15
☐ 10 Dennis Rodman Detroit Pistons	1.25	.60	.12
☐ 11 Isiah Thomas Detroit Pistons	1.50	.75	.15
☐ 12 Kevin Willis Atlanta Hawks	1.00	.50	.10
☐ 13 Clyde Drexler Portland Trail Blazers	3.00	1.50	.30
☐ 14 Tim Hardaway Golden State Warriors	3.00	1.50	.30
☐ 15 Jeff Hornacek Philadelphia 76ers	1.00	.50	.10
☐ 16 Dan Majerle Phoenix Suns	1.00	.50	.10
☐ 17 Karl Malone Utah Jazz	2.50	1.25	.25
☐ 18 Chris Mullin Golden State Warriors	2.50	1.25	.25
☐ 19 Dikembe Mutombo Denver Nuggets	2.50	1.25	.25
☐ 20 Hakeem Olajuwon Houston Rockets	2.00	1.00	.20
☐ 21 David Robinson San Antonio Spurs	3.00	1.50	.30
☐ 22 John Stockton Utah Jazz	2.50	1.25	.25
☐ 23 Otis Thorpe Houston Rockets	1.00	.50	.10
☐ 24 James Worthy Los Angeles Lakers	1.25	.60	.12

1992-93 Hoops I

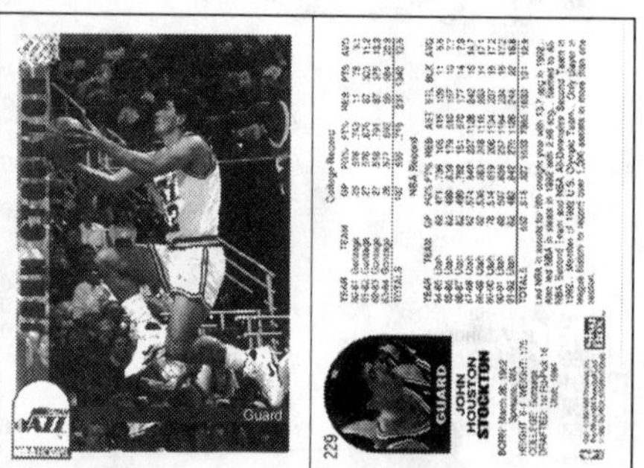

The 1992-93 Hoops I basketball set contains 350 cards measuring the standard size (2 1/2" by 3 1/2"). A Magic Johnson "Commemorative Card" and a Patrick Ewing "Ultimate Game" card were randomly inserted in the foil packs, and a limited number of these have been personally autographed. Also randomly inserted were a USA Basketball Team card and a NBA Draft Lottery Exchange card. The latter card can be redeemed for a pack of up to 11 cards of lottery picks. The fronts display color action player photos enclosed by white borders. A color stripe reflecting one of the team's colors cuts across the picture, and the player's name is printed vertically in a transparent stripe bordering the left side of the picture. The horizontally oriented backs carry a color head shot, biography, career highlights, and complete statistics (college and pro). The cards are checklisted below alphabetically according to teams as follows: Atlanta Hawks (1-9), Boston Celtics (10-18), Charlotte Hornets (19-26), Chicago Bulls (27-35), Cleveland Cavaliers (36-44), Dallas Mavericks (45-53), Denver Nuggets (54-61), Detroit Pistons (62-70), Golden State Warriors (71-79), Houston Rockets (80-88), Indiana Pacers (89-97), Los Angeles Clippers (98-106), Los Angeles Lakers (107-115), Miami Heat (116-124), Milwaukee Bucks (125-133), Minnesota Timberwolves (134-142), New Jersey Nets (143-151), New York Knicks (152-159), Orlando Magic (160-168), Philadelphia 76ers (169-177), Phoenix Suns (178-186), Portland Trail Blazers (187-195), Sacramento Kings (196-203), San Antonio Spurs (204-211), Seattle Supersonics (212-220), Utah Jazz (221-229), and Washington Bullets (230-238). Topical subsets featured include coaches (239-265), team cards (266-292), NBA All-Stars East (293-305), NBA All-Stars West (306-319), League Leaders (320-327), Magic Moments (328-331), NBA Inside Stuff (332-333), NBA Stay in School (334-335), and Basketball Tournament of the Americas (336-347). The set concludes with checklists (348-350).

	MINT	EXC	G-VG
COMPLETE SET (350)	15.00	7.50	1.50
COMMON PLAYER (1-350)	.03	.01	.00
☐ 1 Stacey Augmon	.15	.07	.01
☐ 2 Maurice Cheeks	.06	.03	.00
☐ 3 Duane Ferrell	.03	.01	.00
☐ 4 Paul Graham	.03	.01	.00
☐ 5 Jon Koncak	.03	.01	.00
☐ 6 Blair Rasmussen	.03	.01	.00
☐ 7 Rumeal Robinson	.03	.01	.00
☐ 8 Dominique Wilkins	.12	.06	.01
☐ 9 Kevin Willis	.06	.03	.00
☐ 10 Larry Bird	.25	.12	.02
☐ 11 Dee Brown	.15	.07	.01
☐ 12 Sherman Douglas	.06	.03	.00
☐ 13 Rick Fox	.15	.07	.01
☐ 14 Kevin Gamble	.03	.01	.00
☐ 15 Reggie Lewis	.12	.06	.01
☐ 16 Kevin McHale	.08	.04	.01
☐ 17 Robert Parish	.10	.05	.01
☐ 18 Ed Pinckney	.03	.01	.00
☐ 19 Muggsy Bogues	.03	.01	.00
☐ 20 Dell Curry	.03	.01	.00
☐ 21 Kenny Gattison	.03	.01	.00
☐ 22 Kendall Gill	.35	.17	.03
☐ 23 Mike Gminski	.03	.01	.00
☐ 24 Larry Johnson	1.00	.50	.10
☐ 25 Johnny Newman	.03	.01	.00
☐ 26 J.R. Reid	.03	.01	.00
☐ 27 B.J. Armstrong	.06	.03	.00
☐ 28 Bill Cartwright	.03	.01	.00
☐ 29 Horace Grant	.08	.04	.01
☐ 30 Michael Jordan	.90	.45	.09
☐ 31 Stacey King	.03	.01	.00
☐ 32 John Paxson	.06	.03	.00
☐ 33 Will Perdue	.03	.01	.00
☐ 34 Scottie Pippen	.25	.12	.02
☐ 35 Scott Williams	.06	.03	.00
☐ 36 John Battle	.03	.01	.00
☐ 37 Terrell Brandon	.10	.05	.01
☐ 38 Brad Daugherty	.12	.06	.01
☐ 39 Craig Ehlo	.03	.01	.00
☐ 40 Danny Ferry	.06	.03	.00
☐ 41 Henry James	.03	.01	.00
☐ 42 Larry Nance	.08	.04	.01
☐ 43 Mark Price	.10	.05	.01
☐ 44 Hot Rod Williams	.06	.03	.00
☐ 45 Rolando Blackman	.06	.03	.00
☐ 46 Terry Davis	.03	.01	.00
☐ 47 Derek Harper	.06	.03	.00
☐ 48 Mike Iuzzolino	.06	.03	.00
☐ 49 Fat Lever	.06	.03	.00
☐ 50 Rodney McCray	.03	.01	.00
☐ 51 Doug Smith	.10	.05	.01
☐ 52 Randy White	.03	.01	.00
☐ 53 Herb Williams	.03	.01	.00
☐ 54 Greg Anderson	.03	.01	.00
☐ 55 Winston Garland	.03	.01	.00
☐ 56 Chris Jackson	.06	.03	.00
☐ 57 Marcus Liberty	.06	.03	.00
☐ 58 Todd Lichti	.03	.01	.00
☐ 59 Mark Macon	.10	.05	.01
☐ 60 Dikembe Mutombo	.50	.25	.05
☐ 61 Reggie Williams	.03	.01	.00
☐ 62 Mark Aguirre	.06	.03	.00
☐ 63 William Bedford	.03	.01	.00
☐ 64 Joe Dumars	.08	.04	.01
☐ 65 Bill Laimbeer	.06	.03	.00
☐ 66 Dennis Rodman	.08	.04	.01
☐ 67 John Salley	.03	.01	.00
☐ 68 Isiah Thomas	.12	.06	.01
☐ 69 Darrell Walker	.03	.01	.00
☐ 70 Orlando Woolridge	.06	.03	.00

☐ 71 Victor Alexander	.06	.03	.00
☐ 72 Mario Elie	.03	.01	.00
☐ 73 Chris Gatling	.08	.04	.01
☐ 74 Tim Hardaway	.30	.15	.03
☐ 75 Tyrone Hill	.06	.03	.00
☐ 76 Alton Lister	.03	.01	.00
☐ 77 Sarunas Marciulionis	.08	.04	.01
☐ 78 Chris Mullin	.15	.07	.01
☐ 79 Billy Owens	.50	.25	.05
☐ 80 Matt Bullard	.03	.01	.00
☐ 81 Eric Floyd	.03	.01	.00
☐ 82 Avery Johnson	.03	.01	.00
☐ 83 Buck Johnson	.03	.01	.00
☐ 84 Vernon Maxwell	.03	.01	.00
☐ 85 Hakeem Olajuwon	.12	.06	.01
☐ 86 Kenny Smith	.03	.01	.00
☐ 87 Larry Smith	.03	.01	.00
☐ 88 Otis Thorpe	.03	.01	.00
☐ 89 Dale Davis	.03	.01	.00
☐ 90 Vern Fleming	.03	.01	.00
☐ 91 George McCloud	.03	.01	.00
☐ 92 Reggie Miller	.08	.04	.01
☐ 93 Chuck Person	.06	.03	.00
☐ 94 Detlef Schrempf	.06	.03	.00
☐ 95 Rik Smits	.03	.01	.00
☐ 96 LaSalle Thompson	.03	.01	.00
☐ 97 Micheal Williams	.06	.03	.00
☐ 98 James Edwards	.03	.01	.00
☐ 99 Gary Grant	.03	.01	.00
☐ 100 Ron Harper	.06	.03	.00
☐ 101 Danny Manning	.10	.05	.01
☐ 102 Ken Norman	.06	.03	.00
☐ 103 Olden Polynice	.03	.01	.00
☐ 104 Doc Rivers	.06	.03	.00
☐ 105 Charles Smith	.06	.03	.00
☐ 106 Loy Vaught	.06	.03	.00
☐ 107 Elden Campbell	.06	.03	.00
☐ 108 Vlade Divac	.06	.03	.00
☐ 109 A.C. Green	.06	.03	.00
☐ 110 Sam Perkins	.06	.03	.00
☐ 111 Byron Scott	.06	.03	.00
☐ 112 Tony Smith	.03	.01	.00
☐ 113 Terry Teagle	.03	.01	.00
☐ 114 Sedale Threatt	.06	.03	.00
☐ 115 James Worthy	.10	.05	.01
☐ 116 Willie Burton	.06	.03	.00
☐ 117 Bimbo Coles	.06	.03	.00
☐ 118 Kevin Edwards	.03	.01	.00
☐ 119 Alec Kessler	.03	.01	.00
☐ 120 Grant Long	.06	.03	.00
☐ 121 Glen Rice	.20	.10	.02
☐ 122 Rony Seikaly	.08	.04	.01
☐ 123 Brian Shaw	.03	.01	.00
☐ 124 Steve Smith	.15	.07	.01
☐ 125 Frank Brickowski	.03	.01	.00
☐ 126 Dale Ellis	.06	.03	.00
☐ 127 Jeff Grayer	.03	.01	.00
☐ 128 Jay Humphries	.03	.01	.00
☐ 129 Larry Krystkowiak	.03	.01	.00
☐ 130 Moses Malone	.10	.05	.01
☐ 131 Fred Roberts	.03	.01	.00
☐ 132 Alvin Robertson	.03	.01	.00
☐ 133 Dan Schayes	.03	.01	.00
☐ 134 Thurl Bailey	.03	.01	.00
☐ 135 Scott Brooks	.03	.01	.00
☐ 136 Tony Campbell	.03	.01	.00
☐ 137 Gerald Glass	.03	.01	.00
☐ 138 Luc Longley	.06	.03	.00
☐ 139 Sam Mitchell	.06	.03	.00
☐ 140 Pooh Richardson	.10	.05	.01
☐ 141 Felton Spencer	.06	.03	.00
☐ 142 Doug West	.03	.01	.00
☐ 143 Rafael Addison	.03	.01	.00
☐ 144 Kenny Anderson	.15	.07	.01
☐ 145 Mookie Blaylock	.06	.03	.00
☐ 146 Sam Bowie	.06	.03	.00
☐ 147 Derrick Coleman	.20	.10	.02
☐ 148 Chris Dudley	.03	.01	.00
☐ 149 Terry Mills	.06	.03	.00
☐ 150 Chris Morris	.03	.01	.00
☐ 151 Drazen Petrovic	.10	.05	.01
☐ 152 Greg Anthony	.12	.06	.01
☐ 153 Patrick Ewing	.15	.07	.01
☐ 154 Mark Jackson	.06	.03	.00
☐ 155 Anthony Mason	.03	.01	.00
☐ 156 Xavier McDaniel	.08	.04	.01
☐ 157 Charles Oakley	.06	.03	.00
☐ 158 John Starks	.10	.05	.01
☐ 159 Gerald Wilkins	.06	.03	.00
☐ 160 Nick Anderson	.10	.05	.01
☐ 161 Terry Catledge	.06	.03	.00
☐ 162 Jerry Reynolds	.03	.01	.00
☐ 163 Stanley Roberts	.12	.06	.01
☐ 164 Dennis Scott	.08	.04	.01
☐ 165 Scott Skiles	.03	.01	.00
☐ 166 Jeff Turner	.03	.01	.00
☐ 167 Sam Vincent	.03	.01	.00
☐ 168 Brian Williams	.06	.03	.00
☐ 169 Ron Anderson	.03	.01	.00
☐ 170 Charles Barkley	.15	.07	.01
☐ 171 Manute Bol	.03	.01	.00
☐ 172 Johnny Dawkins	.03	.01	.00
☐ 173 Armon Gilliam	.06	.03	.00
☐ 174 Hersey Hawkins	.08	.04	.01
☐ 175 Brian Oliver	.03	.01	.00
☐ 176 Charles Shackleford	.03	.01	.00
☐ 177 Jayson Williams	.03	.01	.00
☐ 178 Cedric Ceballos	.06	.03	.00
☐ 179 Tom Chambers	.08	.04	.01
☐ 180 Jeff Hornacek	.08	.04	.01
☐ 181 Kevin Johnson	.15	.07	.01
☐ 182 Negele Knight	.06	.03	.00
☐ 183 Andrew Lang	.03	.01	.00
☐ 184 Dan Majerle	.08	.04	.01
☐ 185 Tim Perry	.03	.01	.00
☐ 186 Mark West	.03	.01	.00
☐ 187 Alaa Abdelnaby	.06	.03	.00
☐ 188 Danny Ainge	.06	.03	.00
☐ 189 Clyde Drexler	.20	.10	.02
☐ 190 Kevin Duckworth	.03	.01	.00
☐ 191 Jerome Kersey	.08	.04	.01
☐ 192 Robert Pack	.12	.06	.01
☐ 193 Terry Porter	.10	.05	.01
☐ 194 Cliff Robinson	.08	.04	.01
☐ 195 Buck Williams	.06	.03	.00
☐ 196 Anthony Bonner	.03	.01	.00
☐ 197 Duane Causwell	.03	.01	.00
☐ 198 Pete Chilcutt	.03	.01	.00
☐ 199 Dennis Hopson	.03	.01	.00
☐ 200 Mitch Richmond	.10	.05	.01
☐ 201 Lionel Simmons	.15	.07	.01
☐ 202 Wayman Tisdale	.06	.03	.00
☐ 203 Spud Webb	.06	.03	.00
☐ 204 Willie Anderson	.06	.03	.00
☐ 205 Antoine Carr	.06	.03	.00
☐ 206 Terry Cummings	.06	.03	.00
☐ 207 Sean Elliott	.08	.04	.01
☐ 208 Sidney Green	.03	.01	.00
☐ 209 David Robinson	.50	.25	.05
☐ 210 Rod Strickland	.06	.03	.00
☐ 211 Greg Sutton	.03	.01	.00
☐ 212 Dana Barros	.03	.01	.00
☐ 213 Benoit Benjamin	.06	.03	.00
☐ 214 Michael Cage	.03	.01	.00
☐ 215 Eddie Johnson	.06	.03	.00
☐ 216 Shawn Kemp	.35	.17	.03
☐ 217 Derrick McKey	.06	.03	.00
☐ 218 Nate McMillan	.03	.01	.00
☐ 219 Gary Payton	.08	.04	.01
☐ 220 Ricky Pierce	.06	.03	.00
☐ 221 David Benoit	.10	.05	.01
☐ 222 Mike Brown	.03	.01	.00
☐ 223 Tyrone Corbin	.03	.01	.00
☐ 224 Mark Eaton	.03	.01	.00
☐ 225 Blue Edwards	.03	.01	.00
☐ 226 Jeff Malone	.08	.04	.01
☐ 227 Karl Malone	.15	.07	.01
☐ 228 Eric Murdock	.06	.03	.00
☐ 229 John Stockton	.15	.07	.01
☐ 230 Michael Adams	.08	.04	.01
☐ 231 Rex Chapman	.06	.03	.00
☐ 232 Ledell Eackles	.03	.01	.00
☐ 233 Pervis Ellison	.12	.06	.01
☐ 234 A.J. English	.06	.03	.00
☐ 235 Harvey Grant	.06	.03	.00
☐ 236 Charles Jones	.03	.01	.00
☐ 237 LaBradford Smith	.08	.04	.01
☐ 238 Larry Stewart	.06	.03	.00
☐ 239 Bob Weiss CO	.03	.01	.00
☐ 240 Chris Ford CO	.03	.01	.00
☐ 241 Allan Bristow CO	.03	.01	.00
☐ 242 Phil Jackson CO	.03	.01	.00
☐ 243 Lenny Wilkens CO	.06	.03	.00
☐ 244 Richie Adubato CO	.03	.01	.00
☐ 245 Dan Issel CO	.06	.03	.00
☐ 246 Ron Rothstein CO	.03	.01	.00
☐ 247 Don Nelson CO	.03	.01	.00
☐ 248 Rudy Tomjanovich CO	.03	.01	.00
☐ 249 Bob Hill CO	.03	.01	.00
☐ 250 Larry Brown CO	.03	.01	.00
☐ 251 Randy Pfund CO	.06	.03	.00
☐ 252 Kevin Loughery CO	.03	.01	.00
☐ 253 Mike Dunleavy CO	.03	.01	.00
☐ 254 Jimmy Rodgers CO	.03	.01	.00
☐ 255 Chuck Daly CO	.06	.03	.00
☐ 256 Pat Riley CO	.06	.03	.00
☐ 257 Matt Guokas CO	.03	.01	.00
☐ 258 Doug Moe CO	.03	.01	.00

☐ 259 Paul Westphal CO	.03	.01	.00
☐ 260 Rick Adelman CO	.03	.01	.00
☐ 261 Garry St. Jean CO	.06	.03	.00
☐ 262 Jerry Tarkanian CO	.15	.07	.01
☐ 263 George Karl CO	.03	.01	.00
☐ 264 Jerry Sloan CO	.03	.01	.00
☐ 265 Wes Unseld CO	.06	.03	.00
☐ 266 Atlanta Hawks Team Card	.06	.03	.00
☐ 267 Boston Celtics Team Card	.06	.03	.00
☐ 268 Charlotte Hornets Team Card	.06	.03	.00
☐ 269 Chicago Bulls Team Card	.06	.03	.00
☐ 270 Cleveland Cavaliers Team Card	.06	.03	.00
☐ 271 Dallas Mavericks Team Card	.06	.03	.00
☐ 272 Denver Nuggets Team Card	.06	.03	.00
☐ 273 Detroit Pistons Team Card	.06	.03	.00
☐ 274 Golden State Warriors Team Card	.06	.03	.00
☐ 275 Houston Rockets Team Card	.06	.03	.00
☐ 276 Indiana Pacers Team Card	.06	.03	.00
☐ 277 Los Angeles Clippers Team Card	.06	.03	.00
☐ 278 Los Angeles Lakers Team Card	.06	.03	.00
☐ 279 Miami Heat Team Card	.06	.03	.00
☐ 280 Milwaukee Bucks Team Card	.06	.03	.00
☐ 281 Minnesota Timberwolves Team Card	.06	.03	.00
☐ 282 New Jersey Nets Team Card	.06	.03	.00
☐ 283 New York Knicks Team Card	.06	.03	.00
☐ 284 Orlando Magic Team Card	.06	.03	.00
☐ 285 Philadelphia 76ers Team Card	.06	.03	.00
☐ 286 Phoenix Suns Team Card	.06	.03	.00
☐ 287 Portland Trail Blazers Team Card	.06	.03	.00
☐ 288 Sacramento Kings Team Card	.06	.03	.00
☐ 289 San Antonio Spurs Team Card	.06	.03	.00
☐ 290 Seattle Supersonics Team Card	.06	.03	.00
☐ 291 Utah Jazz Team Card	.06	.03	.00
☐ 292 Washington Bullets Team Card	.06	.03	.00
☐ 293 Michael Adams AS	.06	.03	.00
☐ 294 Charles Barkley AS	.10	.05	.01
☐ 295 Brad Daugherty AS	.08	.04	.01
☐ 296 Joe Dumars AS	.06	.03	.00
☐ 297 Patrick Ewing AS	.10	.05	.01
☐ 298 Michael Jordan AS	.40	.20	.04
☐ 299 Reggie Lewis AS	.08	.04	.01
☐ 300 Scottie Pippen AS	.15	.07	.01
☐ 301 Mark Price AS	.08	.04	.01
☐ 302 Dennis Rodman AS	.06	.03	.00
☐ 303 Isiah Thomas AS	.08	.04	.01
☐ 304 Kevin Willis AS	.06	.03	.00
☐ 305 Phil Jackson CO AS	.03	.01	.00
☐ 306 Clyde Drexler AS	.12	.06	.01
☐ 307 Tim Hardaway AS	.20	.10	.02
☐ 308 Jeff Hornacek AS	.06	.03	.00
☐ 309 Magic Johnson AS	.30	.15	.03
☐ 310 Dan Majerle AS	.06	.03	.00
☐ 311 Karl Malone AS	.10	.05	.01
☐ 312 Chris Mullin AS	.10	.05	.01
☐ 313 Dikembe Mutombo AS	.25	.12	.02
☐ 314 Hakeem Olajuwon AS	.08	.04	.01
☐ 315 David Robinson AS	.25	.12	.02
☐ 316 John Stockton AS	.10	.05	.01
☐ 317 Otis Thorpe AS	.06	.03	.00
☐ 318 James Worthy AS	.08	.04	.01
☐ 319 Don Nelson CO AS	.03	.01	.00
☐ 320 Scoring League Leaders Michael Jordan Karl Malone	.40	.20	.04
☐ 321 Three-Point Field Goal Percent League Leaders Dana Barros Drazen Petrovic	.03	.01	.00
☐ 322 Free Throw Percent League Leaders Mark Price Larry Bird	.20	.10	.02
☐ 323 Blocks League Leaders David Robinson Hakeem Olajuwon	.20	.10	.02
☐ 324 Steals League Leaders John Stockton Micheal Williams	.10	.05	.01
☐ 325 Rebounds League Leaders Dennis Rodman Kevin Willis	.06	.03	.00
☐ 326 Assists League Leaders John Stockton Kevin Johnson	.15	.07	.01
☐ 327 Field Goal Percent League Leaders Buck Williams Otis Thorpe	.03	.01	.00
☐ 328 Magic Moments 1980	.30	.15	.03
☐ 329 Magic Moments 1985	.30	.15	.03
☐ 330 Magic Moments 1987, 1988	.30	.15	.03
☐ 331 Magic Numbers	.30	.15	.03
☐ 332 Drazen Petrovic Inside Stuff	.06	.03	.00
☐ 333 Patrick Ewing Inside Stuff	.10	.05	.01
☐ 334 David Robinson Stay in School	.25	.12	.02
☐ 335 Kevin Johnson Stay in School	.10	.05	.01
☐ 336 Charles Barkley Tournament of The Americas	.15	.07	.01
☐ 337 Larry Bird Tournament of The Americas	.25	.12	.02
☐ 338 Clyde Drexler Tournament of The Americas	.20	.10	.02
☐ 339 Patrick Ewing Tournament of The Americas	.15	.07	.01
☐ 340 Magic Johnson Tournament of The Americas	.50	.25	.05
☐ 341 Michael Jordan Tournament of The Americas	.90	.45	.09
☐ 342 Christian Laettner Tournament of The Americas	1.50	.75	.15
☐ 343 Karl Malone Tournament of The Americas	.15	.07	.01
☐ 344 Chris Mullin Tournament of The Americas	.15	.07	.01
☐ 345 Scottie Pippen Tournament of The Americas	.25	.12	.02
☐ 346 David Robinson Tournament of The Americas	.50	.25	.05
☐ 347 John Stockton Tournament of The Americas	.15	.07	.01
☐ 348 Checklist 1	.06	.01	.00
☐ 349 Checklist 2	.06	.01	.00
☐ 350 Checklist 3	.06	.01	.00

1992-93 SkyBox I

The 1992-93 SkyBox I basketball set contains 327 cards, measuring the standard size (2 1/2" by 3 1/2"). Special gold-foil stamped cards of Magic Johnson and David Robinson, some personally autographed, were randomly inserted in foil packs. The new front design features computer-generated screens of color blended with full-bleed color action photos. The backs carry full-bleed nonaction close-up photos, overlayed by a column displaying complete statistics and a color stripe with a

personal "bio-bit." The cards are checklisted below alphabetically according to and within teams as follows: Atlanta Hawks (1-9), Boston Celtics (10-18), Charlotte Hornets (19-27), Chicago Bulls (28-36), Cleveland Cavaliers (37-46), Dallas Mavericks (47-56), Denver Nuggets (57-65), Detroit Pistons (66-75), Golden State Warriors (76-84), Houston Rockets (85-93), Indiana Pacers (94-102), Los Angeles Clippers (103-112), Los Angeles Lakers (113-121), Miami Heat (122-131), Milwaukee Bucks (132-140), Minnesota Timberwolves (141-149), New Jersey Nets (150-159), New York Knicks (160-168), Orlando Magic (169-177), Philadelphia 76ers (178-187), Phoenix Suns (188-197), Portland Trail Blazers (198-207), Sacramento Kings (208-217), San Antonio Spurs (218-226), Seattle Supersonics (227-235), Utah Jazz (236-244), and Washington Bullets (245-254). Other cards featured include Coaches (255-281), Team Tix (282-308), 1992 NBA All-Star Weekend Highlights (309-313), 1992 NBA Finals (314-318), 1992 NBA All-Rookie Team (319), and Public Service (230-321). The set concludes with checklist cards (322-327). The cards are numbered on the back.

	MINT	EXC	G-VG
COMPLETE SET (327)	20.00	10.00	2.00
COMMON PLAYER (1-327)	.05	.02	.00
☐ 1 Stacey Augmon	.20	.10	.02
☐ 2 Maurice Cheeks	.08	.04	.01
☐ 3 Duane Ferrell	.05	.02	.00
☐ 4 Paul Graham	.05	.02	.00
☐ 5 Jon Koncak	.05	.02	.00
☐ 6 Blair Rasmussen	.05	.02	.00
☐ 7 Rumeal Robinson	.05	.02	.00
☐ 8 Dominique Wilkins	.15	.07	.01
☐ 9 Kevin Willis	.08	.04	.01
☐ 10 Larry Bird	.35	.17	.03
☐ 11 Dee Brown	.20	.10	.02
☐ 12 Sherman Douglas	.08	.04	.01
☐ 13 Rick Fox	.20	.10	.02
☐ 14 Kevin Gamble	.05	.02	.00
☐ 15 Reggie Lewis	.15	.07	.01
☐ 16 Kevin McHale	.10	.05	.01
☐ 17 Robert Parish	.12	.06	.01
☐ 18 Ed Pinckney	.05	.02	.00
☐ 19 Muggsy Bogues	.05	.02	.00
☐ 20 Dell Curry	.05	.02	.00
☐ 21 Kenny Gattison	.08	.04	.01
☐ 22 Kendall Gill	.60	.30	.06
☐ 23 Mike Gminski	.05	.02	.00
☐ 24 Tom Hammonds	.05	.02	.00
☐ 25 Larry Johnson	1.50	.75	.15
☐ 26 Johnny Newman	.05	.02	.00
☐ 27 J.R. Reid	.05	.02	.00
☐ 28 B.J. Armstrong	.08	.04	.01
☐ 29 Bill Cartwright	.05	.02	.00
☐ 30 Horace Grant	.10	.05	.01
☐ 31 Michael Jordan	1.25	.60	.12
☐ 32 Stacey King	.05	.02	.00
☐ 33 John Paxson	.08	.04	.01
☐ 34 Will Perdue	.05	.02	.00
☐ 35 Scottie Pippen	.35	.17	.03
☐ 36 Scott Williams	.08	.04	.01
☐ 37 John Battle	.05	.02	.00
☐ 38 Terrell Brandon	.15	.07	.01
☐ 39 Brad Daugherty	.15	.07	.01
☐ 40 Craig Ehlo	.05	.02	.00
☐ 41 Danny Ferry	.08	.04	.01
☐ 42 Henry James	.05	.02	.00
☐ 43 Larry Nance	.10	.05	.01
☐ 44 Mark Price	.12	.06	.01
☐ 45 Mike Sanders	.05	.02	.00
☐ 46 Hot Rod Williams	.08	.04	.01
☐ 47 Rolando Blackmon	.08	.04	.01
☐ 48 Terry Davis	.05	.02	.00
☐ 49 Derek Harper	.08	.04	.01
☐ 50 Donald Hodge	.10	.05	.01
☐ 51 Mike Iuzzolino	.08	.04	.01
☐ 52 Fat Lever	.08	.04	.01
☐ 53 Rodney McCray	.05	.02	.00
☐ 54 Doug Smith	.15	.07	.01
☐ 55 Randy White	.05	.02	.00
☐ 56 Herb Williams	.05	.02	.00
☐ 57 Greg Anderson	.05	.02	.00
☐ 58 Walter Davis	.08	.04	.01
☐ 59 Winston Garland	.05	.02	.00
☐ 60 Chris Jackson	.08	.04	.01
☐ 61 Marcus Liberty	.08	.04	.01
☐ 62 Todd Lichti	.05	.02	.00
☐ 63 Mark Macon	.15	.07	.01
☐ 64 Dikembe Mutombo	.75	.35	.07
☐ 65 Reggie Williams	.05	.02	.00
☐ 66 Mark Aguirre	.08	.04	.01
☐ 67 William Bedford	.05	.02	.00
☐ 68 Lance Blanks	.05	.02	.00
☐ 69 Joe Dumars	.10	.05	.01
☐ 70 Bill Laimbeer	.08	.04	.01
☐ 71 Dennis Rodman	.10	.05	.01
☐ 72 John Salley	.05	.02	.00
☐ 73 Isiah Thomas	.15	.07	.01
☐ 74 Darrell Walker	.05	.02	.00
☐ 75 Orlando Woolridge	.08	.04	.01
☐ 76 Victor Alexander	.08	.04	.01
☐ 77 Mario Elie	.05	.02	.00
☐ 78 Chris Gatling	.12	.06	.01
☐ 79 Tim Hardaway	.50	.25	.05
☐ 80 Tyrone Hill	.08	.04	.01
☐ 81 Alton Lister	.05	.02	.00
☐ 82 Sarunas Marciulionis	.12	.06	.01
☐ 83 Chris Mullin	.20	.10	.02
☐ 84 Billy Owens	.75	.35	.07
☐ 85 Matt Bullard	.05	.02	.00
☐ 86 Eric Floyd	.05	.02	.00
☐ 87 Avery Johnson	.05	.02	.00
☐ 88 Buck Johnson	.05	.02	.00
☐ 89 Vernon Maxwell	.05	.02	.00
☐ 90 Hakeem Olajuwon	.15	.07	.01
☐ 91 Kenny Smith	.05	.02	.00
☐ 92 Larry Smith	.05	.02	.00
☐ 93 Otis Thorpe	.08	.04	.01
☐ 94 Dale Davis	.08	.04	.01
☐ 95 Vern Fleming	.05	.02	.00
☐ 96 George McCloud	.05	.02	.00
☐ 97 Reggie Miller	.10	.05	.01
☐ 98 Chuck Person	.08	.04	.01
☐ 99 Detlef Schrempf	.08	.04	.01
☐ 100 Rik Smits	.05	.02	.00
☐ 101 LaSalle Thompson	.05	.02	.00
☐ 102 Micheal Williams	.08	.04	.01
☐ 103 James Edwards	.05	.02	.00
☐ 104 Gary Grant	.05	.02	.00
☐ 105 Ron Harper	.08	.04	.01
☐ 106 Bo Kimble	.05	.02	.00
☐ 107 Danny Manning	.15	.07	.01
☐ 108 Ken Norman	.08	.04	.01
☐ 109 Olden Polynice	.05	.02	.00
☐ 110 Doc Rivers	.08	.04	.01
☐ 111 Charles Smith	.08	.04	.01
☐ 112 Loy Vaught	.08	.04	.01
☐ 113 Elden Campbell	.08	.04	.01
☐ 114 Vlade Divac	.08	.04	.01
☐ 115 A.C. Green	.08	.04	.01
☐ 116 Jack Haley	.05	.02	.00
☐ 117 Sam Perkins	.08	.04	.01
☐ 118 Byron Scott	.08	.04	.01
☐ 119 Tony Smith	.05	.02	.00
☐ 120 Sedale Threatt	.08	.04	.01
☐ 121 James Worthy	.12	.06	.01
☐ 122 Keith Askins	.05	.02	.00
☐ 123 Willie Burton	.08	.04	.01
☐ 124 Bimbo Coles	.08	.04	.01
☐ 125 Kevin Edwards	.05	.02	.00
☐ 126 Alec Kessler	.05	.02	.00
☐ 127 Grant Long	.08	.04	.01
☐ 128 Glen Rice	.30	.15	.03
☐ 129 Rony Seikaly	.10	.05	.01
☐ 130 Brian Shaw	.05	.02	.00
☐ 131 Steve Smith	.20	.10	.02
☐ 132 Frank Brickowski	.05	.02	.00
☐ 133 Dale Ellis	.08	.04	.01
☐ 134 Jeff Grayer	.05	.02	.00

☐ 135 Jay Humphries	.05	.02	.00
☐ 136 Larry Krystkowiak	.05	.02	.00
☐ 137 Moses Malone	.12	.06	.01
☐ 138 Fred Roberts	.05	.02	.00
☐ 139 Alvin Robertson	.05	.02	.00
☐ 140 Dan Schayes	.05	.02	.00
☐ 141 Thurl Bailey	.05	.02	.00
☐ 142 Scott Brooks	.05	.02	.00
☐ 143 Tony Campbell	.05	.02	.00
☐ 144 Gerald Glass	.05	.02	.00
☐ 145 Luc Longley	.08	.04	.01
☐ 146 Sam Mitchell	.08	.04	.01
☐ 147 Pooh Richardson	.15	.07	.01
☐ 148 Felton Spencer	.08	.04	.01
☐ 149 Doug West	.05	.02	.00
☐ 150 Rafael Addison	.05	.02	.00
☐ 151 Kenny Anderson	.20	.10	.02
☐ 152 Mookie Blaylock	.08	.04	.01
☐ 153 Sam Bowie	.08	.04	.01
☐ 154 Derrick Coleman	.30	.15	.03
☐ 155 Chris Dudley	.05	.02	.00
☐ 156 Tate George	.05	.02	.00
☐ 157 Terry Mills	.08	.04	.01
☐ 158 Chris Morris	.05	.02	.00
☐ 159 Drazen Petrovic	.15	.07	.01
☐ 160 Greg Anthony	.15	.07	.01
☐ 161 Patrick Ewing	.20	.10	.02
☐ 162 Mark Jackson	.08	.04	.01
☐ 163 Anthony Mason	.05	.02	.00
☐ 164 Tim McCormick	.05	.02	.00
☐ 165 Xavier McDaniel	.10	.05	.01
☐ 166 Charles Oakley	.08	.04	.01
☐ 167 John Starks	.15	.07	.01
☐ 168 Gerald Wilkins	.08	.04	.01
☐ 169 Nick Anderson	.15	.07	.01
☐ 170 Terry Catledge	.08	.04	.01
☐ 171 Jerry Reynolds	.05	.02	.00
☐ 172 Stanley Roberts	.15	.07	.01
☐ 173 Dennis Scott	.12	.06	.01
☐ 174 Scott Skiles	.05	.02	.00
☐ 175 Jeff Turner	.05	.02	.00
☐ 176 Sam Vincent	.05	.02	.00
☐ 177 Brian Williams	.08	.04	.01
☐ 178 Ron Anderson	.05	.02	.00
☐ 179 Charles Barkley	.20	.10	.02
☐ 180 Manute Bol	.05	.02	.00
☐ 181 Johnny Dawkins	.05	.02	.00
☐ 182 Armon Gilliam	.08	.04	.01
☐ 183 Greg Grant	.05	.02	.00
☐ 184 Hersey Hawkins	.10	.05	.01
☐ 185 Brian Oliver	.05	.02	.00
☐ 186 Charles Shackleford	.05	.02	.00
☐ 187 Jayson Williams	.05	.02	.00
☐ 188 Cedric Ceballos	.08	.04	.01
☐ 189 Tom Chambers	.10	.05	.01
☐ 190 Jeff Hornacek	.10	.05	.01
☐ 191 Kevin Johnson	.20	.10	.02
☐ 192 Negele Knight	.08	.04	.01
☐ 193 Andrew Lang	.05	.02	.00
☐ 194 Dan Majerle	.10	.05	.01
☐ 195 Jerrod Mustaf	.05	.02	.00
☐ 196 Tim Perry	.05	.02	.00
☐ 197 Mark West	.05	.02	.00
☐ 198 Alaa Abdelnaby	.08	.04	.01
☐ 199 Danny Ainge	.08	.04	.01
☐ 200 Mark Bryant	.05	.02	.00
☐ 201 Clyde Drexler	.30	.15	.03
☐ 202 Kevin Duckworth	.05	.02	.00
☐ 203 Jerome Kersey	.10	.05	.01
☐ 204 Robert Pack	.20	.10	.02
☐ 205 Terry Porter	.12	.06	.01
☐ 206 Cliff Robinson	.12	.06	.01
☐ 207 Buck Williams	.08	.04	.01
☐ 208 Anthony Bonner	.05	.02	.00
☐ 209 Randy Brown	.05	.02	.00
☐ 210 Duane Causwell	.05	.02	.00
☐ 211 Pete Chilcutt	.05	.02	.00
☐ 212 Dennis Hopson	.05	.02	.00
☐ 213 Jim Les	.05	.02	.00
☐ 214 Mitch Richmond	.12	.06	.01
☐ 215 Lionel Simmons	.20	.10	.02
☐ 216 Wayman Tisdale	.08	.04	.01
☐ 217 Spud Webb	.08	.04	.01
☐ 218 Willie Anderson	.08	.04	.01
☐ 219 Antoine Carr	.08	.04	.01
☐ 220 Terry Cummings	.08	.04	.01
☐ 221 Sean Elliott	.10	.05	.01
☐ 222 Sidney Green	.05	.02	.00
☐ 223 Vinnie Johnson	.08	.04	.01
☐ 224 David Robinson	.75	.35	.07
☐ 225 Rod Strickland	.08	.04	.01
☐ 226 Greg Sutton	.05	.02	.00
☐ 227 Dana Barros	.05	.02	.00
☐ 228 Benoit Benjamin	.08	.04	.01
☐ 229 Michael Cage	.05	.02	.00
☐ 230 Eddie Johnson	.08	.04	.01
☐ 231 Shawn Kemp	.60	.30	.06
☐ 232 Derrick McKey	.08	.04	.01
☐ 233 Nate McMillan	.05	.02	.00
☐ 234 Gary Payton	.12	.06	.01
☐ 235 Ricky Pierce	.08	.04	.01
☐ 236 David Benoit	.15	.07	.01
☐ 237 Mike Brown	.05	.02	.00
☐ 238 Tyrone Corbin	.05	.02	.00
☐ 239 Mark Eaton	.05	.02	.00
☐ 240 Blue Edwards	.05	.02	.00
☐ 241 Jeff Malone	.10	.05	.01
☐ 242 Karl Malone	.20	.10	.02
☐ 243 Eric Murdock	.08	.04	.01
☐ 244 John Stockton	.20	.10	.02
☐ 245 Michael Adams	.10	.05	.01
☐ 246 Rex Chapman	.08	.04	.01
☐ 247 Ledell Eackles	.05	.02	.00
☐ 248 Pervis Ellison	.20	.10	.02
☐ 249 A.J. English	.08	.04	.01
☐ 250 Harvey Grant	.08	.04	.01
☐ 251 Charles Jones	.05	.02	.00
☐ 252 Bernard King	.08	.04	.01
☐ 253 LaBradford Smith	.10	.05	.01
☐ 254 Larry Stewart	.08	.04	.01
☐ 255 Bob Weiss CO Atlanta Hawks	.05	.02	.00
☐ 256 Chris Ford CO Boston Celtics	.05	.02	.00
☐ 257 Allan Bristow CO Charlotte Hornets	.05	.02	.00
☐ 258 Phil Jackson CO Chicago Bulls	.05	.02	.00
☐ 259 Lenny Wilkens CO Cleveland Cavaliers	.08	.04	.01
☐ 260 Richie Adubato CO Dallas Mavericks	.05	.02	.00
☐ 261 Dan Issel CO Denver Nuggets	.08	.04	.01
☐ 262 Ron Rothstein CO Detroit Pistons	.05	.02	.00
☐ 263 Don Nelson CO Golden State Warriors	.05	.02	.00
☐ 264 Rudy Tomjanovich CO Houston Rockets	.05	.02	.00
☐ 265 Bob Hill CO Indiana Pacers	.05	.02	.00
☐ 266 Larry Brown CO Los Angeles Clippers	.05	.02	.00
☐ 267 Randy Pfund CO Los Angeles Lakers	.08	.04	.01
☐ 268 Kevin Loughery CO Miami Heat	.05	.02	.00
☐ 269 Mike Dunleavy CO Milwaukee Bucks	.05	.02	.00
☐ 270 Jimmy Rodgers CO Minnesota Timberwolves	.05	.02	.00
☐ 271 Chuck Daly CO New Jersey Nets	.08	.04	.01
☐ 272 Pat Riley CO New York Knicks	.08	.04	.01
☐ 273 Matt Guokas CO Orlando Magic	.05	.02	.00
☐ 274 Doug Moe CO Philadelphia 76ers	.05	.02	.00
☐ 275 Paul Westphal CO Phoenix Suns	.05	.02	.00
☐ 276 Rick Adelman CO Portland Trail Blazers	.05	.02	.00
☐ 277 Garry St. Jean CO Sacramento Kings	.08	.04	.01
☐ 278 Jerry Tarkanian CO San Antonio Spurs	.20	.10	.02
☐ 279 George Karl CO Seattle Supersonics	.05	.02	.00
☐ 280 Jerry Sloan CO Utah Jazz	.05	.02	.00
☐ 281 Wes Unseld CO Washington Bullets	.08	.04	.01
☐ 282 Dominique Wilkins TT Atlanta Hawks	.10	.05	.01
☐ 283 Reggie Lewis TT Boston Celtics	.10	.05	.01
☐ 284 Kendall Gill TT Charlotte Hornets	.30	.15	.03
☐ 285 Horace Grant TT Chicago Bulls	.08	.04	.01
☐ 286 Brad Daugherty TT Cleveland Cavaliers	.10	.05	.01
☐ 287 Derek Harper TT Dallas Mavericks	.05	.02	.00
☐ 288 Chris Jackson TT Denver Nuggets	.08	.04	.01

☐ 289 Isiah Thomas TT Detroit Pistons	.10	.05	.01
☐ 290 Chris Mullin TT Golden State Warriors	.12	.06	.01
☐ 291 Kenny Smith TT Houston Rockets	.05	.02	.00
☐ 292 Reggie Miller TT Indiana Pacers	.08	.04	.01
☐ 293 Ron Harper TT Los Angeles Clippers	.05	.02	.00
☐ 294 Vlade Divac TT Los Angeles Lakers	.08	.04	.01
☐ 295 Glen Rice TT Miami Heat	.15	.07	.01
☐ 296 Moses Malone TT Milwaukee Bucks	.08	.04	.01
☐ 297 Doug West TT Minnesota Timberwolves	.05	.02	.00
☐ 298 Derrick Coleman TT New Jersey Nets	.15	.07	.01
☐ 299 Patrick Ewing TT New York Knicks	.12	.06	.01
☐ 300 Scott Skiles TT Orlando Magic	.05	.02	.00
☐ 301 Hersey Hawkins TT Philadelphia 76ers	.08	.04	.01
☐ 302 Kevin Johnson TT Phoenix Suns	.12	.06	.01
☐ 303 Cliff Robinson TT Portland Trail Blazers	.08	.04	.01
☐ 304 Anthony Webb TT Sacramento Kings	.05	.02	.00
☐ 305 David Robinson TT San Antonio Spurs	.40	.20	.04
☐ 306 Shawn Kemp TT Seattle Supersonics	.30	.15	.03
☐ 307 John Stockton TT Utah Jazz	.12	.06	.01
☐ 308 Pervis Ellison TT Washington Bullets	.10	.05	.01
☐ 309 Craig Hodges	.05	.02	.00
☐ 310 Magic Johnson A-S MVP	.40	.20	.04
☐ 311 Cedric Ceballos Slam Dunk Champ	.05	.02	.00
☐ 312 West in Action	.05	.02	.00
☐ 313 East in Action	.05	.02	.00
☐ 314 Michael Jordan MVP	.60	.30	.06
☐ 315 Clyde Drexler NBA Finals	.20	.10	.02
☐ 316 Western Conference Danny Ainge	.08	.04	.01
☐ 317 Eastern Conference Scottie Pippen	.20	.10	.02
☐ 318 NBA Champs Chicago Bulls	.08	.04	.01
☐ 319 NBA Rookie of the Year All-Rookie Team Larry Johnson Dikembe Mutombo	.50	.25	.05
☐ 320 NBA Stay in School	.05	.02	.00
☐ 321 Boys and Girls Clubs of America	.05	.02	.00
☐ 322 Checklist 1	.06	.01	.00
☐ 323 Checklist 2	.06	.01	.00
☐ 324 Checklist 3	.06	.01	.00
☐ 325 Checklist 4	.06	.01	.00
☐ 326 Checklist 5	.06	.01	.00
☐ 327 Checklist 6	.06	.01	.00

1992-93 SkyBox David Robinson Flagship

This five-card subset captures moments in Robinson's life, beginning with his childhood and ending with his present day super stardom. The standard-size (2 1/2" by 3 1/2") feature a different design than the regular issue cards.

	MINT	EXC	G-VG
COMPLETE SET (5)	10.00	5.00	1.00
COMMON PLAYER (1-5)	2.00	1.00	.20
☐ R1 David Robinson Childhood	2.00	1.00	.20
☐ R2 David Robinson At Ease	2.00	1.00	.20
☐ R3 David Robinson College	2.00	1.00	.20
☐ R4 David Robinson College	2.00	1.00	.20
☐ R5 David Robinson At Ease	2.00	1.00	.20

BASKETBALL ALPHABETICAL INDEX

This alphabetical index presents all the cards issued for any particular player (or person) included in the card sets listed in this Sport Americana Basketball Card Price Guide. It will prove to be an invaluable tool for seasoned and novice collectors alike. Although this book was carefully compiled and proofread, it is inevitable that errors, misspellings, and inconsistencies may occur. Please keep a record of any errors that come to your attention and send them to the author, so that these corrections may be incorporated into future editions of the basketball alphabetical checklist.

How to Use the Alphabetical Checklist

This alphabetical checklist has been designed to be user friendly. The set code abbreviations used throughout are easily memorized. The format adopted for card identification is explained below. However, the large number of card sets contained in this volume require that the reader become familiar first with the abbreviations and format used in card identification. **PLEASE READ THE FOLLOWING SECTION CAREFULLY BEFORE ATTEMPTING TO USE THE CHECKLIST.**

The player cards are listed alphabetically by the player's current last name. Nicknames (e.g., "Fat" Lever) and former names (e.g., Lew Alcindor) are given in parentheses on the second line of each entry. Different players with otherwise identical names are sometimes distinguished by additional information (e.g., school [Adams, John Louisville versus Adams, John LSU] or sport [Anthony, Greg BB]). The codes following the players' names are indented and give the card sets and card numbers in the sets in which the players appeared. The set code abbreviations are designed so that each code is distinctive for a particular card set.

Depending on the particular card set, the set code abbreviations consist of from three to five distinctive elements:

a) Year of issue (listed in ascending chronological order);
b) Maker (producer or manufacturer);
c) Set code suffixes (always after a slash);
d) Number on card (always separated from the maker or set code suffix by a dash);
e) Individual card descriptive suffixes.

When two different makers issued cards for a player in the same year, the cards are listed alphabetically according to the maker's name (e.g., 1991 Courtside precedes 1991 Star Pics). Note that postal abbreviations have often been used for college sets (e.g., VA for Virginia).

Many cards can be distinguished by three parameters. For some cards, however, it is necessary to have four parameters for unambiguous identification. For example, there are two 1988-89 Dallas Maverick Bud Light card sets. Note in the following sample entry the use of set code suffixes to distinguish different cards from each of these sets:

Davis, Brad
88Mavs/BLC-15 =1988-89 Dallas Mavericks Bud Light Big League Cards #15
88Mavs/CardN-15 =1988-89 Dallas Mavericks Bud Light Card Night #15

The card number typically corresponds to the particular number on the card itself; in some instances, the card number also involves letter prefixes. For example, the 1990-91 North Carolina Promo cards are numbered "NC1-NC10." For the most part, cards in unnumbered sets are usually entered alphabetically according to the player's last name and assigned a number arbitrarily. In a few instances unnumbered cards are simply identified as if their card number were "x" or "xx."

Although individual card suffixes are not necessary for unambiguous card identification, they do provide the reader with additional information about the card. These abbreviations were added by the author and always follow the card number. In rare cases involving numbers with letter prefixes or the "x/xx" designations, the individual card suffixes were omitted to avoid a cumbersome designation. The individual card suffix codes are listed below at the end of the set code list.

Lastly, the user of this checklist will notice that the cards of players from sports other than basketball (as well as subjects not even from the world of sports) are contained in this checklist. This circumstance arose because of the decision to include multi-sport sets containing basketball cards in this checklist. In the price guide, these multi-sport card sets are typically indicated by an asterisk (*), which is placed after the set code suffix in the alphabetical checklist.

T .... Topps
TCMA .... TCMA
Test .... Test Issue
TexAM .... Texas A & M
Thirst .... Thirst Break
Tm .... Team
TmLeader ...... Team Leader
TN .... Tennessee
Trio .... Trio Stickers
TWolv .... Timberwolves
Union .... Union Oil
Up .... Update
VA .... Virginia
Warr .... Warriors
WASt .... Washington State
West .... Jerry West
WestWax .... Jerry West Wax Box Bottoms
WhHen .... White Hen Pantry
WI .... Wisconsin
WichSt........... Wichita State
Wilkins .... Dominique Wilkins Inserts
WildCard .... Wild Card
Wildct .... Wildcat News
Wooden .... Wooden Award
100 .... Italian/English 100

Individual Card Suffix Codes

Code Explanation

ACC .... Accomplishment
ACO .... Assistant Coach
ANN .... Announcer
ART .... All-Rookie Team
AS .... All-Star
AW .... Award Winner
BC .... Bonus card
CC .... Classic Confrontations
CL .... Checklist
CO .... Coach
DIR .... Director
FB .... Flashback
GF .... Game Frame
HC .... Head of the Class (Hoops)
HL .... Highlight
IS .... Inside Stuff
KC .... Kid card
LL .... League Leader
LP .... Lottery Pick
M .... multi-player or miscellaneous card
MS .... Milestone
PRES .... President
PV .... Pro Vision
RS .... Rising Star
SC .... Supreme Court
SD .... Slam Dunk
SiS .... Stay in School
SM .... Sixth Man
SPON .... Sponsor
SS .... Shooting Star
SY .... Schoolyard Star
TC .... Team checklist
TP .... Top Prospect
TR .... Trainer
TT .... Team Tix
TW .... Teamwork
USA .... USA Olympic team
YB .... (NBA) Yearbook

Aaron, Hank
81T/Thirst-21
Abbott, Jim
91MI/56*-1
Abbott, Jon
90AZ/125*-84
Abdelnaby, Alaa
87Duke/Pol-30
88Duke/Pol-1
90Blaz/Franz-9
90F/Up-U78
90StarPic-6
91Blaz/Franz-5
91F/Up-344
91Hoops/II-423
91SkyBox/I-232
91UD-213
92Hoops/I-187
92SkyBox/I-198
Abdul-Aziz, Zaid
(Don Smith)
69T-52
70T-39
71Sonic/Sunb-8
71T-109
73T-159
74T-169
74T-88M
75T-49
Abdul-Jabbar, Kareem
(Lew Alcindor)
69T-25
69T/Ins-10
70T-1LL
70T-2LL
70T-5LL
70T-75
70T/Ins-13
71Bucks/Linn-1
71T-100
71T-133M
71T-138LL
71T-139LL
71T-140LL
71T-142LL
71T/Ins-39
72Icee-10
72T-100
72T-163AS
72T-171LL
72T-172LL
72T-173LL
72T-175LL
73T-153LL
73T-154LL
73T-155LL
73T-50AS
74Nab-25
74T-1
74T-144LL
74T-145LL
74T-146LL
74T-91M
75Carv-15
75Nab-25
75T-126M
75T-1LL
75T-90
76Buck-12
76T-100
76T-126AS
77Dell-1
77Pep/AS-4
77T-1
78RCCola-1
78T-110
79Lakers/Alta-3
79T-10AS
80T-131
80T-132
80T-14
80T-140
80T-162
80T-43
80T-44
80T-50
81T-20
81T-55M
81T-W106
82Lakers/BASF-1
83Lakers/BASF-1
83Star/ASG-14
83Star/ASG-x
83Star/NBA-14
83Star/Sixers-3M
84Lakers/BASF-1
84Star/Arena-D1
84Star/Arena-D10
84Star/ASG-14
84Star/Award-21LL
84Star/Celt-16
84Star/Celt-18
84Star/Celt-20
84Star/Celt-2M
84Star/Celt-8M
84Star/CrtKg-1
84Star/NBA-173
84Star/NBA-282
84Star/PolASG-14
85JMS-20
85Prism-4M
85Star/Crunch-7
85Star/Kareem-1
85Star/Kareem-10
85Star/Kareem-11
85Star/Kareem-12
85Star/Kareem-13
85Star/Kareem-14
85Star/Kareem-15
85Star/Kareem-16
85Star/Kareem-17
85Star/Kareem-18
85Star/Kareem-2
85Star/Kareem-3
85Star/Kareem-4
85Star/Kareem-5
85Star/Kareem-6
85Star/Kareem-7
85Star/Kareem-8
85Star/Kareem-9
85Star/Lakers-10
85Star/Lakers-1M
85Star/Lakers-8
85Star/LiteAS-8
85Star/NBA-26
85Star/TmSuper-LA1
86F-1
86F/Ins-1
86Star/Best-5
86Star/CrtKg-2
87F-1
87F/Ins-8
88Bucks/Green-1
88F-64
88Fourn-5
88Fourn/St-1
91UCLA/144-10
91UCLA/144-109
91UCLA/144-2
91UCLA/144-33
91UCLA/144-93
92Crtside/ColFB-18
Abdul-Rahman, Mahdi
(Walt Hazzard)
69T-27
70T-134
71T-24
72T-93
73T-128
91UCLA/144-6
91UCLA/144-77
92Crtside/ColFB-17
Abernethy, Tom
86IN/GreatI-30
Able, Forrest
55Ash-73
89Louville/300*-51
Ablergamo, Nacho
90LSU/200*-129
Abood, Tom
89Louville/300*-152
Abram, Mike
88Louville/194-141
88Louville/194-159
88Louville/194-78
89Louville/300*-289
89Louville/300*-36
Abrams, Wayne
80TCMA/CBA-24
81TCMA/CBA-2
82TCMA/CBA-73
Ackles, George
88UNLV/HOF-4
89UNLV/HOF-4
90UNLV/HOF-6
90UNLV/Season-15M
90UNLV/Season-6
90UNLV/Smok-1
91Classic-19
91Classic/DPColl*-167
91Crtside-2
91FrRow/100-5
91FrRow/50-5
91FrRow/Premier-108
91StarPic-16
91WildCard/Coll-25
Acres, Mark
89Hoops-73
89Hoops/II-307
90Hoops-213
90SkyBox-198
91Hoops/II-407
91SkyBox/I-199
91UD-201
Adair, Jerry
91OKSt*-85
Adams, Alvan
75Suns-1
76Suns-1
76T-75
77Suns/Discs-33
77T-95
78T-77
79T-52
80Suns/Pep-5
80T-156
80T-68
81T-60M
81T-W79
83Star/NBA-110
84Star/NBA-38
84Suns/Pol-33
85Star/NBA-35
85Star/ROY-10
86F-2
87F-2
87Suns/Circ-1
Adams, David
90AZ/125*-112
90AZ/125*-35
Adams, Don
72T-77
73T-139
74T-4
Adams, George
75T-264
89KY/300*-131
Adams, Jack
55Ash-1
Adams, Jerry
89ProC/CBA-71
Adams, John
89Louville/300*-197
Adams, John LSU
90LSU/200*-111
Adams, John R.
88KY/269-238
88KY/269-96
Adams, Kent
91TexAM-51
Adams, Michael
85Kings/Smok-5
88F-33
88Nugget/Pol-14
89F-38
89Hoops-52
89Nugget/Pol-1
90F-46
90Hoops-91
90Hoops/CollB-25
90Hoops/II-361TC
90Hoops/Super-24
90Panini-61
90SkyBox-71
91F/Up-367
91F/Up-398TL
91Hoops/I-51
91Hoops/II-443
91Hoops/II-530
91Hoops/Super-25
91SkyBox/I-300
91SkyBox/I-308
91SkyBox/I-67
91SkyBox/II-431GF
91SkyBox/II-589SS
91SkyBox/II-650
91UD-43
91UD/Ext-435
91UD/Ext-456AS
92F-228
92F/AS-1
92Hoops/I-230
92Hoops/I-293AS
92SkyBox/I-245
Adams, Ron
89Fresno/Smok-1CO
Adams, Scott
90MurraySt-9
91MurraySt-1
Adams, Tommy
91Classic/DPColl*-99
Addison, Rafael
91Hoops/II-398
91SkyBox/II-636
91UD/Ext-429
92Hoops/I-143
92SkyBox/I-150
Adell, Darnell
89NCSt/Coke-175
89NCSt/Coke-68
Adelman, Rick
68Rocket/Jack-1
69T-23
70T-118
71T-11
72T-117
73T-27
74T-7
75T-67
83Blaz/Pol-x
84Blaz/Pol-5M
89Blaz/Franz-1CO
89Hoops-291CO
90Blaz/Franz-7CO
90Hoops-326CO
90Hoops/II-353CO
90SkyBox/II-322CO
91Blaz/Franz-4CO
91F-166CO
91Hoops/I-242CO
91Hoops/I-273AS
91SkyBox/II-399CO
92F-185CO
92Hoops/I-260CO
92SkyBox/I-276CO
Adkins, Adrian
91SC/200*-14
Adkins, Earl
55Ash-13
89KY/300*-90
Adkins, Keith
88KY/Sov-3
Adkins, Paul
89KY/300*-276
Adkins, Rusty
90Clemson/200*-156
Adrian, Charlie
91George/100-88
91George/100-93
Adubato, Richie
88Mavs/BLC-x
90Hoops-310CO
90SkyBox/II-306CO
91F-42CO
91Hoops/I-226CO
91SkyBox/II-383CO
92F-47CO
92Hoops/I-244CO
92SkyBox/I-260CO
Aguirre, Mark
83Star/NBA-49
84Star/Arena-B1
84Star/ASG-15
84Star/CrtKg-3
84Star/NBA-250
84Star/PolASG-15
85Star/NBA-160
86DePaul-10
86DePaul-11
86DePaul-D3
86F-3
86Star/CrtKg-1
87F-3
87F/Ins-9
88F-27
88F/Ins-1
88Fourn-13
88Fourn/St-2
88Mavs/BLC-24
89Conv-1
89F-44
89Hoops-95
90F-54
90Hoops-101
90Piston/Star-1
90Piston/Unocal-1
90SkyBox-82
91F-57
91Hoops/I-59
91Piston/Unocal-1
91Piston/Unocal-15M
91SkyBox/I-78
91SkyBox/II-439SM
91UD-165
92F-62
92Hoops/I-62
92SkyBox/I-66
Ah You, Junior
90AZSt/200*-56
Aherne, Brian
48T/Magic*-J16
Ainge, Danny
83Star/NBA-27
84Star/Arena-A2
84Star/Celt-12
84Star/Celt-6M
84Star/NBA-2
85JMS-11
85Star/Lakers-11M
85Star/Lakers-4
85Star/NBA-96
85Star/TmSuper-BC5
86F-4
87F-4
88F-8

88Kings/Carl-7
89F-133
89Hoops-215
89Kings/Carl-7
90Blaz/BP-1
90Blaz/Franz-10
90F-162
90F/Up-U79
90Hoops-253
90Hoops/II-427
90Hoops/Super-83
90Panini-39
90SkyBox-242
90SkyBox/II-407
91Blaz/Franz-6
91F-167
91Hoops/I-171
91Panini-32
91SkyBox/I-233
91SkyBox/II-453SM
91SkyBox/II-590SS
91UD-279
91Wooden-11
92F-177
92Hoops/I-188
92SkyBox/I-199
92SkyBox/I-316
Aitch, Matthew
90MISt/200*-141
Akerfelds, Darrell
91AR/100*-31
Akers, Marvin
89KY/300*-14
Akridge, Bill
89Louville/300*-214
Alarie, Mark
89F-157
89Hoops-94
90F-190
90Hoops-295
90Panini-145
90SkyBox-285
91Hoops/II-444
91SkyBox/I-287
91UD-363
Albeck, Stan
84Nets/Getty-1CO
Albert, Eddie
48T/Magic*-J34
Albert, Frankie
57Union-3
Alberts, Charles
89KY/300*-95
Alcindor, Lew
(See Kareem Abdul-Jabbar
Aleksinas, Chuck
77KY/Wildct-10
78KY/Food-17
84Star/NBA-150
89KY/300*-54
Alexander, Charles
90LSU/200*-5
Alexander, Cory
91VA-2
Alexander, Dan
90LSU/200*-177
Alexander, Darwyn
91OKSt-32
91OKSt-42
91OKSt-6
Alexander, Eugene
90KY/ClassA-3
Alexander, Grover
48T/Magic*-K12
Alexander, Rex
55Ash-61
Alexander, Todd
89KS/Leesley-54
89ProC/CBA-159
Alexander, Victor
91Classic-11
91Classic/DPColl*-159
91F/Up-284
91FrRow/Premier-61
91FrRow/Up-62
91UD-10
91UD/Rook-21
91WildCard/RHRook-7
92F-72
92Hoops/I-71
92SkyBox/I-76
Alexander, William
91GATech*-92
Alford, Steve
87IN/GreatII-1
87IN/GreatII-12
87IN/GreatII-20
89Hoops-143
90Hoops-81
90SkyBox-59
91SkyBox/I-56
91UD-250
Ali, Muhammed
81PhilM-5
81T/Thirst-54
Alibegovic, Teo
89ORSt-1
90ORSt-1
91ProC/CBA-89
Alicea, Edwin
90FLSt/200*-2
Alicea, Luis
90FLSt/200*-32
Allen, Anthony
86George/Pol-3
87George/Pol-3
88George/Pol-3
89George/Pol-3
91George/100-35
Allen, Doug
90AZSt/200*-14
Allen, Eric
90AZSt/200*-32
Allen, Eric MSU
90MISt/200*-14
90MISt/200*-67
Allen, Ermal
88KY/269-57
89KY/300*-154
Allen, Forrest C.
(Phog)
68HOF-1
92CenterCrt-13CO
Allen, Frank
90MurraySt-10
91MurraySt-3
Allen, Greg
90FLSt/200*-84
Allen, Lucius
69Sonic/Sunb-1
69T-6
70T-31
71T-27
72T-145
73NBAPA-1
73T-88
74T-19
75T-52
76T-34
77T-87
78T-6
91UCLA/144-48
Allen, Mike
88KY/Sov-4
Allen, Randy
89Kings/Carl-40
90Hoops-254
90SkyBox-243
Allen, Sonny
89ProC/CBA-126
Allen, Ted
48ExhSC-1
Allen, Terry
90Clemson/200*-15
Allen, Tyree
85FortHaysSt-1
Allison, Doug
91SC/200*-36
Allyson, June
48T/Magic*-F9
Alvarado, Sean
87KS/Nike-1
Alworth, Lance
91AR/100*-2
Amaker, Tommy
92Crtside/ColFB-1
Ambrose, Kyle
91GATech*-47
Ammaccapore, Danielle
90AZSt/200*-83
Amman, Richard
90FLSt/200*-186
Andaya, Shawn
91TexAM-45
Anderegg, Robert
90MISt/200*-103
Andersen, Greta
57Union-43
Andersen, Morten
90MISt/200*-25
90MISt/200*-93
Anderson, Bobby
90FLSt/200*-180
Anderson, Brad
90AZ/125*-114
90AZ/125*-67
Anderson, Dwight
78KY/Food-7
79KY/Food-7
82TCMA/CBA-11
88KY/269-115
89KY/300*-19
Anderson, Eddie
90NE/Pol*-28
Anderson, Eric
92Classic/DP-52
92StarPic-21
Anderson, Ernest
91OKSt*-45
Anderson, Forrest
90MISt/200*-172
90MISt/200*-190
Anderson, Gary
91AR/100*-50
Anderson, Greg
88F-101
88Spurs/Pol-1
89F-85
89Hoops-7
89Hoops/II-342
90F/Up-U51
90Hoops-173
90Panini-100
90SkyBox-155
91F/Up-272
91Hoops/II-354
91SkyBox/I-68
91UD-314
92F-54
92Hoops/I-54
92SkyBox/I-57
Anderson, Jim OSU
89ORSt-16CO
89ORSt-3CO
90ORSt-2CO
91ORSt-1CO
Anderson, Jim
91GATech*-38
Anderson, Joe
85FortHaysSt-2
Anderson, Jorgen
55Ash-62
Anderson, Kareem
91ORSt-2
Anderson, Karl
89ORSt-2
90ORSt-3
91ORSt-3
Anderson, Kenny
89GATech/Pol-1
89GATech/Pol-2
89GATech/Pol-20M
89GATech/Pol-3
90GATech/Pol-1
90GATech/Pol-2
90GATech/Pol-3
91Crtside-3
91F/Up-322
91FrRow/100-2
91FrRow/50-2
91FrRow/Premier-2
91Hoops/II-547
91Hoops/II-HC
91Hoops/McDon-50
91Kell/ColGrt-1
91SkyBox/II-514LP
91StarPic-5
91StarPic-70
91UD/Ext-444TP
91UD/Rook-36
91WildCard/Coll-96
92F-140
92Hoops/I-144
92SkyBox/I-151
Anderson, Kim
91MO-1
Anderson, Ladell
87BYU-6
Anderson, Michael
91ProC/CBA-68
Anderson, Mike
90LSU/200*-39
91AR25-19ACO
Anderson, Milerd
89KY/300*-274
Anderson, Mitchell
83Star/NBA-134
84Star/NBA-226
85Star/NBA-139
91WildCard/Coll-64
Anderson, Nick
89Magic/Pep-1
90F-132
90F/Rook-7
90Hoops-214
90Hoops/II-373TC
90Panini-123
90SkyBox-199
91Hoops/I-147
91Hoops/Super-68
91Panini-70
91SkyBox/I-200
91UD-228
91UD/Ext-477SD
92F-158
92Hoops/I-160
92SkyBox/I-169
Anderson, Nicole
90UCLA-18
Anderson, Richard
83Nugget/Pol-35
83Star/NBA-182
88Blaz/Franz-1
89F-126
89Hoops-182
90Hoops-49
90SkyBox-25
Anderson, Ron
84Star/NBA-214
89F-112
89Hoops-32
89Sixers/Kodak-1
90F-138
90Fresno/Smok-1
90Hoops-224
90Panini-128
90SkyBox-210
91F-150
91Hoops/I-155
91Panini-171
91SkyBox/I-210
91SkyBox/II-451SM
91UD-180
92F-166
92Hoops/I-169
92SkyBox/I-178
Anderson, Taz
91GATech*-156
Anderson, Tim
90ProC/CBA-141
91ProC/CBA-38
Anderson, Willie
88Spurs/Pol-2
89F-140
89Hoops-235
90F-168
90Hoops-263
90Hoops/Super-86
90Panini-46
90SkyBox-252
91F-182
91Hoops/I-188
91Hoops/II-565
91Hoops/Super-86
91Panini-78
91SkyBox/I-254
91SkyBox/II-547US
91UD-282
92F-201
92Hoops/I-204
92SkyBox/I-218
Anderzunas, Wally
70T-21
Andolsek, Eric
90LSU/200*-99
Andres, Ernie
86IN/GreatI-27
Andrews, Harold
89Louville/300*-65
Andrews, Jim
88KY/269-152
88KY/269-196
88KY/269-46
Andrews, Paul
83KY/Sched-1
89KY/300*-55
Angelo, Lou
90NC/200*-113
Anheuser, Rick
89NCSt/Coke-1
89NCSt/Coke-2
89NCSt/Coke-3
Ansley, Michael
89Magic/Pep-2
90F/Up-U66
90Hoops-215
90SkyBox-200
91Hoops/I-148
91ProC/CBA-201
91SkyBox/I-201
91UD-224
Anson, Adrian
(Cap)
90NotreDame-xx
Anthis, Steve
91OKSt-19ACO
Anthony, Greg BB
91Classic/DPColl*-77
Anthony, Greg
88UNLV/HOF-2
89UNLV/HOF-2
89UNLV/Seven-1
90UNLV/HOF-3
90UNLV/Season-15M

90UNLV/Season-3
90UNLV/Smok-2
91Classic-7
91Classic/DPColl*-155
91Crtside-4
91Crtside/Holo-1
91F/Up-325
91FrRow/100-42
91FrRow/100-7
91FrRow/50-42
91FrRow/50-7
91FrRow/Premier-51
91StarPic-15
91UD-7
91UD/Ext-448TP
91UD/Rook-37
91WildCard/Coll-16
92F-148
92F/Rook-1
92Hoops/I-152
92SkyBox/I-160
Anthony, Kevin
90NC/200*-46
Anthony, Terry
90FLSt/200*-16
Anthony, Tyrone
90NC/200*-68
90NC/200*-91
90NC/Promos*-NC6
Apisa, Robert
90MISt/200*-15
Applebaum, Herb
89NCSt/Coke-136
89NCSt/Coke-176
Applegate, Troy
85FortHaysSt-3ACO
Archer, Mike
90LSU/200*-12
Archbold, Darin
92Classic/DP-14
Archibald, Nate
71T-29
72T-115
72T-169AS
72T-171LL
72T-172LL
72T-176LL
73T-153LL
73T-154LL
73T-158LL
73T-1AS
74T-170
75Carv-1
75T-124M
75T-15AS
75T-5LL
76Buck-1
76T-129AS
76T-20
77T-127
78RCCola-2
78T-26
79T-110
80T-124
80T-172
80T-4
80T-78
81T-3
81T-45M
81T-E100
83Star/NBA-39
84Star/Arena-C1
89UTEP/Drug-1
Ard, Jim
71T-191
Arden, Eve
48T/Magic*-F16
Argento, Phil
88KY/269-241
88KY/269-95
Ariri, Obed
90Clemson/200*-176
90Clemson/200*-48
Arizin, Paul
57T-10
61F-2
61F-45IA
92CenterCrt-12
Arlauckas, Joe
91WildCard/Coll-54
Armstrong, B.J.
89Bulls/Eq-1
90F-22
90Hoops-60
90SkyBox-37
91F-25
91Hoops/I-26
91Hoops/McDon-63
91Panini-118
91SkyBox/I-34
91SkyBox/II-435SM
91SkyBox/II-489RS
91UD-184
92F-28
92Hoops/I-27
92SkyBox/I-28
Armstrong, Bruce
89Louville/300*-157
Armstrong, Jack
91Foot*-4
Armstrong, Jerry
89Louville/300*-98
Armstrong, Neill
91OKSt*-32
Armstrong, Paul
48Bowman-13
52Bread-1
Armstrong, Trace
90AZSt/200*-84
90AZSt/Promos*-9
Armstrong, Warren
(See Warren Jabali)
Arndt, Charles
91SC/200*-53
Arneson, Mark
90AZ/125*-48
Arnette, Jay
63Kahn's-1
64Kahn's-4
Arnsparger, Bill
90LSU/200*-155
Arnzen, Bob
71T-94
90NotreDame-51
Aronberg, Ric
90Clemson/200*-85
Aronshone, Liz
90AZSt/200*-59
Arthur, Jean
48T/Magic*-F19
Artmeier, Dick
90FLSt/200*-109
Ash, Doug
90NM-1ACO
91NM-1ACO
Ashen, Don
91UCLA/144-115
Ashley, Robert
55Ash-37
Ashmeade, Rich
91CT/Pol-1
Askew, Vincent
89ProC/CBA-103
90ProC/CBA-155
91F/Up-285
91Hoops/II-365
91UD/Ext-410
Askins, Keith
90Heat/Publix-1
91F/Up-305
91Hoops/II-386
91UD-130
92SkyBox/I-122
Astbury, Andy
90AZSt/200*-106
Astle, Alan
87BYU-21
Atha, Dick
57T-14
Atherley, Scott
87ME/Pol*-7
Atiyeh, George
90LSU/200*-149
Atkins, Ken
81AZ/Pol-1CO
Atkinson, Kenny
90ProC/CBA-123
Attles, Al
61F-1
69T-24
70T-59
Atwater, Steve
91AR/100*-27
Aubrey, Lloyd
90NotreDame-39
Aubuchon, Chet
90MISt/200*-181
90NC/200*-195
Auerbach, Arnold
(Red)
68HOF-2
84Star/Celt-1M
84Star/Celt-23
Augmon, Stacey
88UNLV/HOF-1
89UNLV/HOF-1
89UNLV/Seven-2
90UNLV/HOF-2
90UNLV/Season-15M
90UNLV/Season-2
90UNLV/Smok-3
91F/Up-241
91FrRow/Augmon-Set
91FrRow/Premier-47ACC
91FrRow/Premier-82
91FrRow/Premier-99HL
91FrRow/Up-56
91Hoops/II-554
91Hoops/II-566
91SkyBox/II-521LP
91SkyBox/II-548US
91StarPic-17
91UD-1CL
91UD-5
91UD/Ext-439TP
91UD/Ext-478SD
91UD/Rook-24
91WildCard/Coll-46B
91WildCard/RHRook-6
92Classic/DP-95FB
92F-1
92F/Rook-2
92FrRow/DreamPk-11
92FrRow/DreamPk-12
92FrRow/DreamPk-13
92FrRow/DreamPk-14
92FrRow/DreamPk-15
92Hoops/I-1
92SkyBox/I-1
Augustine, Jerry
79Bucks/OpenP-1
Auksel, Pete
89NCSt/Coke-4
89NCSt/Coke-5
89NCSt/Coke-6
Ausbie, Hubert
(Geese)
71Globe-21
71Globe-22
71Globe-23
71Globe-24
71Globe-25
71Globe-26M
71Globe-64M
71Globe-66M
71Globe-69M
71Globe/Cocoa-18
71Globe/Cocoa-19
71Globe/Cocoa-1M
71Globe/Cocoa-4M
71Globe/Cocoa-6M
71Globe/Cocoa-7M
71Globe/Cocoa-9M
Austefjord, Haakon
90ProC/CBA-49
Austin, Alex
90ProC/CBA-166
91ProC/CBA-92
Austin, Cliff
90Clemson/200*-51
Austin, Clyde
89NCSt/Coke-7
89NCSt/Coke-8
89NCSt/Coke-9
Austin, Isaac
91Classic-38
91Classic/DPColl*-186
91FrRow/Premier-53
91FrRow/Up-60
Austin, Neville
90GA/Smok-9
Avent, Anthony
91Classic-9
91Classic/DPColl*-157
91Crtside-5
91FrRow/100-9
91FrRow/50-9
91FrRow/Premier-105
91StarPic-24
91WildCard/Coll-6
Aver, Joe
91GATech*-64
Averitt, Bird
74T-231
75T-229
76T-49
77T-8
Avezzano, Joe
90FLSt/200*-163
Avitable, Tony
90FLSt/200*-152
Awrey, Don
75Nab-22
Awtrey, Dennis
71T-124
72Icee-1
72T-139
73T-114
74T-74
75Suns-2
75T-130M
75T-39
76Suns-2
77Suns/Discs-21
79Bulls/Pol-20
Ayers, Randy
91OhioSt-1CO
91StarPic-59CO
Azinger, Paul
90FLSt/200*-181
Bach, John
85Star/CO-1
Back, Adrian
89KY/300*-279
Bacon, Henry
88Louville/194-129
88Louville/194-162
88Louville/194-189
88Louville/194-40
89Louville/300*-226
89Louville/300*-244
89Louville/300*-284
Baer, Buddy
48T/Magic*-A24
Baer, Max
48T/Magic*-A13
Baesler, Scott
88KY/269-94
90KY/ClassA-2
Bagdon, Ed
90MISt/200*-6
Bagley, John
83Star/NBA-229
84Star/NBA-215
85Star/NBA-153
86F-5
87F-5
88F-77
89Hoops-163
90Hoops-38
90SkyBox-13
91F/Up-247
91Hoops/II-338
91UD/Ext-488
92F-10
Bailey, Carl
80TCMA/CBA-18
81TCMA/CBA-31
Bailey, Damon
88KY/Sov-5
Bailey, Don
91SC/200*-180
Bailey, James
79Sonic/Pol-2
80T-157
80T-34
80T-81
80T-91
81T-W96
83Star/NBA-74
84Star/NBA-26
Bailey, Thurl
83Star/NBA-135
84Star/NBA-227
85Star/NBA-140
86F-6
87F-6
88F-111
88Jazz/Smok-1
89F-151
89Hoops-251
89Jazz/OldH-1
89NCSt/Coke-10
89NCSt/Coke-11
89NCSt/Coke-12
90F-182
90Hoops-285
90Hoops/Super-95
90Jazz/Star-5
90Panini-54
90SkyBox-274
91F-197
91F/Up-316
91Hoops/I-205
91Hoops/Super-94
91Panini-84
91SkyBox/I-276
91SkyBox/II-635
91UD-139
91UD/Ext-418
92F-131
92Hoops/I-134
92SkyBox/I-141
Bailey, Tom
90FLSt/200*-166
Bailey, Winfred
90FLSt/200*-170
Bair, Brent
88VA/Hardee-1
Baird, James
91ND*-5M
Bakalli, Migjen
90NCSt/IBM-1
91NCSt/IBM-1
Bakehorn, Jill

89Louville/300*-145
Battle, Alvin
89NCSt/Coke-16
89NCSt/Coke-17
89NCSt/Coke-18
Battle, John
87Hawks/Pizza-6
89F-1
89Hoops-154
90F-1
90Hoops-27
90SkyBox-1
91F-1
91F/Up-260
91Hoops/I-1
91Hoops/II-347
91Panini-103
91SkyBox/I-1
91SkyBox/II-621
91UD-388
91UD/Ext-424
92F-38
92Hoops/I-36
92SkyBox/I-37
Battle, Kenny
90F/Up-U74
90Hoops-233
90SkyBox/II-405
91ProC/CBA-153
91UD-209
Battles, Daryl
87South/Pol*-5
Batton, Dave
90NotreDame-34
Bauer, Kim
91TexAM-92
Baugh, Sammy
48ExhSC-2
Baughan, Maxie
91GATech*-74
Baum, John
72T-191
Baumgartner, Bruce
82INSt/Pol*-1
Baxter, Ron
82TCMA/CBA-31
Baxter, William
55Ash-2
Baylor, Elgin
61F-3
61F-46IA
61Lakers/Bell-1
68T/Test-18
69T-35
70T-113AS
70T-65
71T-10
81TCMA-19
92CenterCrt-20
Baynham, Craig
91GATech*-73
Beal, Dicky
82KY/Sched-1
83KY/Sched-2
88KY/269-121
88KY/269-195
88KY/269-236
89KY/300*-10
89KY/Tm80-44
Beale, Charleata
91VA/Lady-1
Beam, Chet
89Louville/300*-95
Beamon, Bob
81T/Thirst-34
Bear, Darren
91ND*-18M
Beard, Butch
72T-142
73T-136
74T-67
75T-2LL
75T-33
76T-6
78T-17
88Louville/194-106
88Louville/194-168
88Louville/194-6
89Louville/300*-11
89Louville/300*-227
89Louville/300*-286
89Louville/300*-7
Beard, Ralph
48T/Magic*-B1
88KY/269-161
88KY/269-4
89KY/300*-7
Beard, Van
83AZ/Pol-1
Bearden, Eric
91GATech*-36
Bearup, Bret
82KY/Sched-2
83KY/Sched-3
88KY/269-122
88KY/269-228
Bearup, Todd
90KY/BB/DT/AW-31
91KY/BB-7
Beasley, Chris
90AZSt/200*-23
Beasley, Corey
91ProC/CBA-31
Beasley, John
71T-211
91TexAM-8
Beaty, Zelmo
68T/Test-17
71T-148LL
71T-165
71T/Ins-17A
72T-220
72T-256AS
73T-225
74T-252
75T-177
85Star/Schick-3
Beck, Byron
71T-210
72T-187
73T-258
74T-222M
74T-264
75T-258
Beck, Ed
88KY/269-69
Beck, Ernie
57T-36
Beck, Steve
90AZSt/200*-26
Becker, Art
72T-178
90AZSt/200*-161
Becker, George
48T/Magic*-D7
Becker, Mark
90ProC/CBA-127
Beckham, Gordon
91SC/200*-141
Bedell, Bob
71T-153
Bedford, Darryl
82AR-2
Bedford, William
90F/Up-U28
90Hoops-102
90Piston/Star-2
90SkyBox-83
91F/Up-278
91Hoops/II-360
91Piston/Unocal-16M
91SkyBox/I-79
91UD-183
92Hoops/I-63
92SkyBox/I-67
Bednarik, Charles P.
(Chuck)
48T/Magic*-C7
Bee, Clair F.
54Bullet/Gunth-2CO
68HOF-3
Beene, Stephen
86SWLou/Pol*-1
87SWLou/McDag*-4
Behagen, Ron
74T-11
75T-106
76T-138
Behney, Mel
90MISt/200*-85
Behning, Mark
84NE/Pol*-9
Behrman, Dave
90MISt/200*-28
Belcher, Earl
79StBon-1
Bell, Alexander Graham
48T/Magic*-N8
Bell, Becky
90AZ/125*-89
Bell, Cecil
89KY/300*-97
Bell, David
91GATech*-28
Bell, Greg
88TN/Smok-23
Bell, Mickey
89NC/Coke-182
90NC/200*-166
Bell, Milton
88George/Pol-7
89George/Pol-7
Bell, Nick
91Classic/DPColl*-139
Bell, T.
90AZ/125*-14
Bell, William
89NCSt/Coke-19
89NCSt/Coke-20
Bellamy, Walt
61F-4
69T-95
69T/Ins-1
70T-18
71T-116
71T/Ins-41
72T-173LL
72T-97
73T-46
74T-65
74T-81M
81TCMA-42
85Star/Schick-4
86IN/GreatI-2
Belle, Joey/Albert
86LSU/Pol*-1
Belobraydic, John
81AZ/Pol-2
Belose, Milissa
90AZSt/200*-147
Benbow, Leon
75T-196
Benbrook, Tom
55Ash-74
Bench, Johnny
68PartM-1
71Keds*-2M
Bendix, William
48T/Magic*-J17
Benedict, Billy
48T/Magic*-J28
Benedict, Moby
91MI/56*-2
Benjamin, Benoit
86F-8
87F-10
88F-61
89F-69
89Hoops-114
90F-84
90Hoops-142
90Hoops/Super-43
90Panini-33
90SkyBox-124
90Sonic/Kayo-5
91F-189
91Hoops/I-197
91Panini-39
91SkyBox/I-266
91UD-159
92F-209
92Hoops/I-213
92SkyBox/I-228
Benjamin, Fred
87Vanderbilt/Pol-3
Benjamin, Mike
90AZSt/200*-16
Benjamin, Rudy
90MISt/200*-142
Bennett, Arlando
90GA/Smok-1
Bennett, Bob
89NC/Coke-165
Bennett, Constance
48T/Magic*-J38
Bennett, Elmer
90NotreDame-32
92Classic/DP-74
92StarPic-55
Bennett, Mel
80TCMA/CBA-40
Bennett, Tony
92Classic/DP-4
92StarPic-11
Bennett, Von
91OKSt-17
91OKSt-40
Bennett, Winston
83KY/Sched-4
87KY/Coke-9
88KY/269-168
88KY/269-194
88KY/269-48
89KY/Tm80-41
90Hoops-70
90Panini-104
90SkyBox-48
91F/Up-261
91Hoops/II-348
91SkyBox/I-45
91UD-247
Bennington, John
90MISt/200*-151
Benoit, David
91F/Up-362
91FrRow/100-66
91FrRow/Premier-30
91FrRow/Up-70
91UD/Ext-487
91UD/Rook-34
91WildCard/Coll-12
92F-218
92Hoops/I-221
92SkyBox/I-236
Benson, Kent
77Bucks/ActPh-1
79Bucks/OpenP-6
79Bucks/Pol-54
79T-121
80T-109
80T-21
81T-MW80
83Star/NBA-86
84Star/NBA-262
85Star/NBA-12
86IN/GreatI-13
Bentley, Doug
48ExhSC-3M
Bentley, Max
48ExhSC-3M
Benton, Janel
91WASt-7M
Benton, Jim
91AR/100*-41
Berberich, John
91UCLA/144-99
Bercher, Martine
91AR/100*-65
Berenson, Gordon
(Red)
91MI/56*-3
Berger, Cliff
88KY/269-87
Berger, Jay
90Clemson/200*-117
Berger, Steve
91ProC/CBA-30
Bergines, William
55Ash-85
Bergman, Ingrid
48T/Magic*-F4
Berlenheiter, Michael
90AZSt/200*-194
Berlin, Steve
90Clemson/200*-54
Bernard, Tod
89Fresno/Smok-4
90Fresno/Smok-3
Bernstine, Rod
91TexAM-1
Berra, Tim
91SC/200*-151
Berry, Curtis
81TCMA/CBA-41
82TCMA/Lanc-11
82TCMA/Lanc-12IA
Berry, Ricky
88Kings/Carl-34
89F-134
89Hoops-186
Berry, Todd
91SC/200*-105
Berry, Walter
86Blaz/Franz-1
88F-102
89Hoops-44
91WildCard/Coll-62
91Wooden-15
Berson, Mark
91SC/200*-43
Bertman, Skip
86LSU/Pol*-2CO
87LSU/Pol*-9CO
88LSU/Pol*-9CO
Beshore, Delmer
79Bulls/Pol-1
Bessillieu, Don
91GATech*-72
Bessone, Amo
90MISt/200*-62
Best, Travis
91GATech/Pol-5
Besuden, Henry
89KY/300*-22
Betz, Dave
89Louville/300*-198
Bevan, George
90LSU/200*-122
Bianchi, Al
57T-59
75Suns-3
84Suns/Pol-x
Bianco, Mike
88LSU/Pol*-12
Bibb, William

55Ash-14
89KY/300*-292
Bibby, Henry
73T-48
74T-16
75T-146
76T-36
77T-2
78T-65
79T-3
80T-10
80T-150
81T-W90
81TCMA/CBA-5
82TCMA/Lanc-8IA
89ProC/CBA-147
90ProC/CBA-117
91ProC/CBA-59CO
91UCLA/144-7
Bice, Travis
89UNLV/HOF-7
89UNLV/Seven-3
90UNLV/HOF-5
90UNLV/Season-5
90UNLV/Smok-4
Bickerstaff, Bernie
89Hoops-269CO
Bickford, Charles
48T/Magic*-J43
Biddle, Tom
90NC/200*-60
Bieniemy, Eric
91Classic/DPColl*-135
Bierderbach, Eddie
89NCSt/Coke-21
89NCSt/Coke-22
89NCSt/Coke-23
Biggers, Ray
91AR25-2
Biley, Ken
91AR25-3
Billington, Dana
87ME/Pol*-6
Bilodeau, Brent
91Classic/DPColl*-14
Bing, Dave
68T/Test-10
69T-55
69T/Ins-16
70T-125
70T/Ins-7
71Keds*-1M
71T-78
71T/Ins-27
72T-35
73NBAPA-2
73T-158LL
73T-170
74T-40AS
74T-86M
75T-121M
75T-160
75T-5LL
76T-76
78T-61
81TCMA-22
85Star/Schick-5
91Piston/Unocal-2
92CenterCrt-21
Bing, Keith
91SC/200*-112
Bingham, Paul
90KY/Sov-4
Biondi, Matt
89Foot*-6
91Foot*-25
Bird, Calvin
89KY/300*-116
Bird, Jerry
55Ash-15
88KY/269-225
88KY/269-70
Bird, Larry
80T-165
80T-48
80T-49
80T-6
80T-94
80T-98
81T-45M
81T-E101
82INSt/Pol*-2
83Star/ASG-2
83Star/ASG-29M
83Star/NBA-26
84Star/Arena-A1
84Star/ASG-2
84Star/Award-15LL
84Star/Award-8
84Star/Bird-1
84Star/Bird-10
84Star/Bird-11
84Star/Bird-12
84Star/Bird-13
84Star/Bird-14
84Star/Bird-15
84Star/Bird-16
84Star/Bird-17
84Star/Bird-18
84Star/Bird-2
84Star/Bird-3
84Star/Bird-4
84Star/Bird-5
84Star/Bird-6
84Star/Bird-7
84Star/Bird-8
84Star/Bird-9
84Star/Celt-11M
84Star/Celt-14
84Star/Celt-24
84Star/Celt-4
84Star/Celt-7
84Star/CrtKg-18
84Star/NBA-1
84Star/NBA-12
84Star/PolASG-2
85JMS-14
85Prism-1M
85Star/Crunch-2
85Star/Lakers-2
85Star/Lakers-9
85Star/LiteAS-2
85Star/NBA-95
85Star/ROY-6
85Star/TmSuper-BC1
86F-9
86F/Ins-2
86Star/CrtKg-4
87F-11
87F/Ins-4
88F-124AS
88F-9
88F/Ins-2
88Fourn-1
88Fourn/St-3
89Conv-2
89F-8
89F/AS-10
89Hoops-150
90F-8
90F/AS-2
90Hoops-2AS
90Hoops-39
90Hoops/CollB-37
90Hoops/II-356TC
90Hoops/Super-6
90Panini-135
90Panini-HAS
90Panini-L
90SkyBox-14
91F-8
91F/Up-373TL
91Hoops/Bird-NNO
91Hoops/I-314MS
91Hoops/I-319YB
91Hoops/I-9
91Hoops/II-451SC
91Hoops/II-532
91Hoops/II-576
91Hoops/McDon-2
91Hoops/McDon-52USA
91Hoops/Proto-9
91Hoops/Super-5
91Kell/ColGrt-7
91Panini-100AS
91Panini-146
91SkyBox/Canada-2
91SkyBox/I-12
91SkyBox/II-460TW
91SkyBox/II-531US
91SkyBox/II-591SS
91UD-344
91UD-77TC
91Wooden-9
92Crtside/ColFB-4
92F-11
92F-256SY
92Hoops/I-10
92Hoops/I-322LL
92Hoops/I-337
92LimeRock/Bird-Set
92SkyBox/I-10
92SkyBox/Olympic-USA6
92SkyBox/USA-10
92SkyBox/USA-102
92SkyBox/USA-11
92SkyBox/USA-12
92SkyBox/USA-13
92SkyBox/USA-14
92SkyBox/USA-15
92SkyBox/USA-16
92SkyBox/USA-17
92SkyBox/USA-18
81T-4
Bird, Rodger
89KY/300*-122
Birdsong, Otis
79T-87
80T-101
80T-145
80T-28
80T-86
81T-17
81T-54M
83Star/NBA-146
84Nets/Getty-2
84Star/ASG-3
84Star/CrtKg-43
84Star/NBA-89
84Star/PolASG-3
85Star/NBA-59
86F-10
86Star/LifeNets-2
Birdsong, Terry
90MurraySt-8
Bishop, Darryl
89KY/300*-174
Bishop, Gale
48Bowman-3
Blab, Uwe
86IN/GreatI-8
88Mavs/BLC-33
88Mavs/CardN-33
89Hoops-104
90Hoops-264
90SkyBox-253
Black, Brian
89GATech/Pol-6
90GATech/Pol-7
Black, Charles
(Hawk)
48Bowman-50
Black, Jimmy
89NC/Coke-93
89NC/Coke-94
90FLSt/200*-158
90NC/200*-30
90NC/200*-57
Black, Mike
90AZSt/200*-81
Black, Norman
81TCMA/CBA-57
Black, Tom
70Sonic/Sunb-1
Black, Tony
88WakeForest/Pol-1
Blackburn, Bob
83Sonic/Pol-10
Blackman, Pete
91UCLA/144-133
Blackman, Rolando
83Star/NBA-50
84Star/Arena-B2
84Star/CrtKg-27
84Star/NBA-251
85Star/NBA-159
86F-11
86Star/CrtKg-5
87F-12
88F-28
88Mavs/BLC-22
88Mavs/CardN-22
89Conv-3
89F-32
89Hoops-20
90F-38
90Hoops-14AS
90Hoops-82
90Hoops/CollB-38
90Hoops/II-360TC
90Hoops/Super-21
90Panini-55
90SkyBox-60
91F-43
91Hoops/I-43
91Hoops/II-459SC
91Hoops/McDon-10
91Hoops/Super-20
91Panini-50
91SkyBox/Canada-11
91SkyBox/I-57
91SkyBox/II-464TW
91UD-154
91UD-87TC
92F-149
92Hoops/I-45
92SkyBox/I-47
Blackmon, James
83KY/Sched-5
88KY/269-127
88KY/269-193
88KY/269-216
Blackwell, Alex
92Classic/DP-80
92StarPic-34
Blackwell, Barry
90FLSt/200*-85
Blackwell, Cory
84Star/NBA-114
Blackwell, Marria
87SWLou/McDag*-14
Blade, Freeman
80TCMA/CBA-32
81TCMA/CBA-42
Blair, Buddy
90LSU/200*-165
Blair, Curtis
92Classic/DP-10
Blair, Paul
91OKSt*-22
Blake, Rodney
90ProC/CBA-128
Blakley, Anthony
89ProC/CBA-191
91FrRow/100-59
91FrRow/Premier-39
91ProC/CBA-181
Blalock, Joe
90Clemson/200*-170
Blanda, George
81T/Thirst-40
89KY/300*-115
Blanford, Rhonda
84NE/Pol*-31
Blankenship, Buddy
90FLSt/200*-157
Blanks, Lance
90F/Up-U29
90StarPic-69
91F/Up-279
91Hoops/II-361
91Piston/Unocal-16M
91SkyBox/I-80
91SkyBox/II-493RS
91UD-108
92SkyBox/I-68
Blanton, Ricky
86LSU/Pol*-3
87LSU/Pol*-2
88LSU/Pol*-1
90LSU/200*-4
90ProC/CBA-168
Blasingame, Dominique
91SC/200*-110
Blaylock, Mookie
90F-117
90Hoops-193
90Nets/Kayo-1
90Panini-162
90SkyBox-176
91F-128
91Hoops/I-131
91Panini-159
91SkyBox/I-177
91UD-235
92F-141
92Hoops/I-145
92SkyBox/I-152
Blaylock, Ron
81George/Pol-16
Blazer, Phil
90NC/200*-149
Blears, Lord Jan
48T/Magic*-D21
Blemker, Bud
91GATech*-168
Bliss, Dave
90NM-3CO
91NM-3CO
Bliss, Harry
89KY/300*-291
Block, John
68Rocket/Jack-4
69T-9
70T-58
71T-16
72T-41
73T-169
74T-168
75T-64
Blomberg, Ron
81T/Thirst-22
Blondeau, Hal
89NCSt/Coke-101
89NCSt/Coke-159
Blue, David
81George/Pol-17
82George/Pol-7
91George/100-46
Blum, Frank
86DePaul-C2
Blum, John
91MI/56*-4
Blundin, Matt
88VA/Hardee-2

Brand, Rodney
91AR/100*-77

Brandewie, Tom
91OhioSt-3

Brandon, Terrell
91Classic-6
91Classic/DPColl*-154
91Crtside-6
91F/Up-262
91FrRow/100-10
91FrRow/100-41
91FrRow/50-10
91FrRow/50-41
91FrRow/Premier-114
91FrRow/Premier-73HL
91Hoops/II-556
91SkyBox/II-523LP
91StarPic-39
91UD-6
91UD/Ext-441TP
91UD/Rook-22
91WildCard/Coll-40
91WildCard/RHRook-10
92F-39
92F/Rook-3
92FrRow/DreamPk-100
92FrRow/DreamPk-96
92FrRow/DreamPk-97
92FrRow/DreamPk-98
92FrRow/DreamPk-99
92Hoops/I-37
92SkyBox/I-38

Brandt, Kate
91GATech*-158

Branning, Rich
90NotreDame-18

Brannon, Robert
82AR-3

Brannum, Bob
88KY/269-31

Branson, Brad
81TCMA/CBA-65

Brantley, Will
89ORSt-4
90ORSt-5

Braselton, Fred
91GATech*-63

Brassow, Jeff
90KY/BB/DT/AW-30
91KY/BB-9
91KY/BB/Double-4

Bratton, Steve
90FLSt/200*-105

Bratz, Mike
77Suns/Discs-23
80T-139
80T-39
81T-47M
81T-MW71
83Star/NBA-253
84Star/NBA-151

Braucher, Dick
89NCSt/Coke-24
89NCSt/Coke-25
89NCSt/Coke-26

Braun, Carl
48Bowman-72
57T-4
61F-7
81TCMA-23
81TCMA-40M

Braun, Terry
82INSt/Pol*-3

Brawner, Bruce
85FortHaysSt-5

Braxton, Mel
89ProC/CBA-185

Brazell, Carl
91SC/200*-166

Breaker, Bubby
89ProC/CBA-153

Breeze, David
55Ash-49

Breland, Jim
91GATech*-71

Brennan, James
55Ash-86

Brennan, Jim
90Clemson/200*-149

Brennan, Pete
89NC/Coke-78
89NC/Coke-79
90NC/200*-99

Brenner, Allen
90MISt/200*-3

Breuer, Randy
83Star/NBA-40
84Star/NBA-126
85Star/Bucks-2
86Star/LifeBucks-2
87Bucks/Polar-45
88Bucks/Green-2
88F-73
89Hoops-153
89TWolv/BK-45
90F-111
90Hoops-184
90Panini-77
90SkyBox-167
91F/Up-317
91Hoops/I-123
91SkyBox/I-166
91UD-301

Breunig, Bob
90AZSt/200*-155

Brewer, Jim
74T-134
75T-46
76T-74
77T-9

Brewer, John
55Ash-16
88KY/269-65

Brewer, Mel
89KY/300*-98

Brewer, Ron
79Blaz/Pol-10
79T-79
80T-1
80T-165
80T-176
80T-49
83Star/NBA-243
84Star/NBA-66
91AR/100*-69

Brian, Frank
52Royal-4
90LSU/200*-37

Brickey, Robert
87Duke/Pol-21
88Duke/Pol-2
90ProC/CBA-167

Brickowski, Frank
84Star/NBA-115
88F-103
88Spurs/Pol-3
89F-141
89Hoops-206
90F-169
90F/Up-U52
90Hoops-265
90Hoops/II-417
90Panini-48
90SkyBox-254
90SkyBox/II-394
91F-113
91Hoops/I-115
91Panini-138
91SkyBox/I-155
91UD-350
92F-124
92Hoops/I-125
92SkyBox/I-132

Bridgeman, Junior
76T-11
77Bucks/ActPh-2
77T-114
78T-56
79Bucks/OpenP-7
79Bucks/Pol-2
79T-91
80T-137
80T-49
81T-MW97
83Star/NBA-41
84Star/Arena-C2
84Star/NBA-14
87Bucks/Polar-2
88Louville/194-21
89Louville/300*-229
89Louville/300*-270

Bridges, Bill
68T/Test-16
69T-86
70T-71
71T-132
72T-17
73T-174
74T-13

Brind'Amour, Rod
90MISt/200*-197

Brinkman, Cookie
89Louville/300*-194

Brisker, John
71T-146LL
71T-147LL
71T-180
71T/Ins-21A
72T-236
73Sonic/Shur-1
73T-7
74T-18
75T-149

Bristow, Allan
75T-74
80T-152
80T-169
80T-35
80T-81
81T-65M
81T-W102
91F/Up-252CO
91SkyBox/II-380CO
92F-21CO
92Hoops/I-241CO
92SkyBox/I-257CO

Britt, James
90LSU/200*-168

Brittain, Mike
91SC/200*-150

Brittain, Maurice
88GATech/Nike-1

Britton, Dave
81TCMA/CBA-52

Brkovich, Mike
90MISt/200*-122

Broadnax, Horace
82George/Pol-6
83George/Pol-8
84George/Pol-2
85George/Pol-3
91George/100-24

Broadnax, Vincent
88MD/Pol-1

Broadway, Rod
90NC/200*-164

Brock, Bob
91TexAM-28

Brock, Jeffrey
55Ash-3

Brock, Jim
90AZSt/200*-20CO

Brock, Lou
81T/Thirst-11

Brockington, John
74Nab-8
75Nab-8

Brodnax, George
91GATech*-62

Brogan, Jim
80TCMA/CBA-8
81TCMA/CBA-75

Brokaw, Gary
71Bucks/Linn-2
75T-178
90NotreDame-37

Broks, Richard
90LSU/200*-141

Bronston, Jake
89KY/300*-99

Brookfield, Price
48Bowman-26

Brookin, Rod
89Pitt/Food-21

Brooks, Bud
91AR/100*-74

Brooks, Franklin
91GATech*-65

Brooks, Garth
91OKSt*-87

Brooks, Greg
91George/100-69

Brooks, Hazel
48T/Magic*-F20

Brooks, Hubie
90AZSt/200*-111M
90AZSt/200*-173

Brooks, Kevin
87SWLou/McDag*-3
91Classic-12
91Classic/DPColl*-160
91Crtside-7
91F/Up-273
91FrRow/100-11
91FrRow/50-11
91FrRow/Premier-104
91StarPic-8
91UD/Ext-427
91WildCard/Coll-22

Brooks, Michael
81T-W91
83Star/NBA-122
90LSU/200*-36
91WildCard/Coll-91

Brooks, Scott
89F-114
89Hoops-34
89Sixers/Kodak-3
90F-140
90Hoops-226
90Hoops/II-419
90SkyBox-212
90SkyBox/II-396
91F/Up-318
91Hoops/II-395
91SkyBox/I-167
91UD-303
92Hoops/I-135
92SkyBox/I-142

Brousson, Colin
88Victoria/Pol-2

Brown, Bobby
88Louville/194-43

Brown, Boyd
48T/Magic*-E10

Brown, Bubba
90Clemson/200*-107

Brown, Carl
90ProC/CBA-80

Brown, Chucky
87NCSt/Pol-1
88NCSt/Pol-1
89NCSt/Coke-27
89NCSt/Coke-28
89NCSt/Coke-29
90F/Up-U16
90Hoops-71
90SkyBox-49
91Hoops/I-35
91SkyBox/I-46
91UD-393

Brown, Colby
89Clemson-1
90Clemson-2

Brown, Dale
86LSU/Pol*-4CO
87LSU/Pol*-1CO
88LSU/Pol*-2CO
90LSU/200*-11
90LSU/Promos*-8CO
91KY/BB/Double-9

Brown, Danny
89Louville/300*-70

Brown, Dave
91MI/56*-6

Brown, David
91ORSt-6

Brown, Dee
90F/Up-U6
90StarPic-8
91F-228
91F-9
91F/Rook-10
91Hoops/I-10
91Hoops/SlamD-6
91Panini-180AR
91SkyBox/I-13
91SkyBox/I-315
91SkyBox/I-322AR
91SkyBox/II-406GF
91SkyBox/II-487RS
91SkyBox/II-577
91StarPic-40
91UD-143
91UD-37ART
91UD/Rook-12
92F-12
92Hoops/I-11
92SkyBox/I-11

Brown, Dion
91WA/TCI-1

Brown, Eric
89ProC/CBA-7

Brown, Fred
73Sonic/Shur-2
73T-103
74T-125
74T-97M
75T-41
76T-15
77T-30
78Sonic/Pol-1
78T-59
79Sonic/Pol-13
79T-46
80T-165
80T-77
81George/Pol-12
81T-43
82George/Pol-5
83George/Pol-7
83Sonic/Pol-15
83Star/NBA-194
91George/100-12
91George/100-75

Brown, Gary
91Classic/DPColl*-203

Brown, Gene
90NC/200*-156

Brown, Hardin
91SC/200*-11

Brown, Harper
91GATech*-166

Brown, Herb
87Suns/Circ-2CO

Brown, Hubie
78Hawks/Coke-1CO
79Hawks/Majik-x
85Star/CO-2
Brown, Jamaal
91OhioSt-4
Brown, Jim
91George/100-84
Brown, Jimmy
81T/Thirst-38
Brown, Joe
89NC/Coke-149
90NC/200*-122
Brown, Joey
90George/Pol-11
91George/Pol-4
Brown, John FSU
90FLSt/200*-26
Brown, John MO
74T-139
75T-191
79Hawks/Majik-50
90MO-2
Brown, John SM
87SoMiss-8M
Brown, Johnny Mack
48T/Magic*-J1
Brown, Karl
88GATech/Nike-2
89GATech/Pol-7
91GATech*-46
Brown, Larry
71T-152
72T-264LL
87KS/Nike-4CO
88Spurs/Pol-4CO
89Hoops-102CO
89NC/Coke-110
89NC/Coke-111
89NC/Coke-60
90Hoops-328CO
90NC/200*-187
90SkyBox/II-324CO
91F-183CO
91Hoops/I-244CO
91SkyBox/II-401CO
91UCLA/144-31
92Crtside/ColFB-5CO
92F-97CO
92Hoops/I-250CO
92SkyBox/I-266CO
Brown, Lester
90Clemson/200*-109
Brown, Liz
91OKSt*-41
Brown, Mack
90NC/200*-23
Brown, Marc
91Crtside-8
91FrRow/100-76
91FrRow/Premier-19
91ProC/CBA-162
Brown, Mike
87Bulls/Ent-5
89Hoops/II-336
89Jazz/OldH-2
90Clemson/200*-86
90F-183
90Hoops-286
90Jazz/Star-6
90SkyBox-275
91F/Up-363
91Hoops/I-206
91SkyBox/I-277
91SkyBox/II-457SM
91UD-118
92F-219
92Hoops/I-222
92SkyBox/I-237
Brown, Milton
91OKSt-15
91OKSt-37
Brown, Monroe
92PennSt*-2
Brown, Myron
91Classic-24
91Classic/DPColl*-172
91Crtside-9
91FrRow/100-12
91FrRow/50-12
91FrRow/Premier-103
91StarPic-43
91UD-15
91WildCard/Coll-104
Brown, Ollie
86LSU/Pol*-5
Brown, P.J.
92Classic/DP-51
92StarPic-77
Brown, Randy
91Classic-21
91Classic/DPColl*-169
91Crtside-10
91FrRow/100-25
91FrRow/50-25
91FrRow/Premier-68
91StarPic-45
91UD/Ext-437
91WildCard/Coll-38
92SkyBox/I-209
Brown, Raymond
89ProC/CBA-35
Brown, Raynard
91SC/200*-193
Brown, Rickey
83Star/NBA-264
84Star/NBA-77
Brown, Roger
71Pacer/Mara-1
71T-148LL
71T-225
71T/Ins-5A
72T-210
73T-231
73T-236LL
74T-209LL
74T-240
85Star/Schick-6
Brown, Ron
90AZSt/200*-122
Brown, Russell
90AZ/125*-40
Brown, Terry
(Kansas)
89KS/Leesley-49
Brown, Terry
(Oklahoma State)
91OKSt*-20
Brown, Tico
80TCMA/CBA-31
81TCMA/CBA-32
82TCMA/CBA-33
91GATech*-160
Brown, Tim
91Foot*-8
Brown, Timmy
81T/Thirst-42
Brown, Tony
82TCMA/CBA-71
84Star/NBA-53
87F-14
89ProC/CBA-134
91AR/100*-15
91Hoops/II-376
91SkyBox/I-278
91SkyBox/II-629
91UD-308
Brown, Vicki
91TexAM-96
Brown, Walter A.
68HOF-5
Brown, Wiley
81Louville/Pol-25
88Louville/194-120
88Louville/194-175
88Louville/194-179
88Louville/194-26
89Louville/300*-252
89ProC/CBA-42
Brown, Willie
87SoMiss-8M
Browndyke, David
90LSU/200*-97
Browne, Clyde
90Clemson/200*-136
Browning, Jim
48T/Magic*-D4
Broyles, Frank
91AR/100*-1
Bruce, Donnell
89Clemson-2
90Clemson-3
Brummer, Jackie
90AZSt/200*-134
Brundy, Stanley
91ProC/CBA-64
Brunet, Laurie
90AZ/125*-19
Brunkhorst, Brock
81AZ/Pol-3
83AZ/Pol-3
84AZ/Pol-1
Bruno, Al
89KY/300*-107
Brust, Chris
89NC/Coke-193
Brutsaert, Elke
87ME/Pol*-8
Bryan, Brad
90NE/Pol*-17
Bryan, Fred
90ProC/CBA-42
Bryan, Shandy
90Clemson/Lady-2
Bryan, Vince
87BYU-19
Bryant, Bobby
91SC/200*-170
Bryant, Clyde
89Louville/300*-59
Bryant, Dwayne
86George/Pol-4
87George/Pol-4
88George/Pol-4
89George/Pol-4
91George/100-15
91George/100-26
Bryant, Ellis
89Louville/300*-211
Bryant, Emmette
69T-47
70T-116
70T/Ins-11
71T-48
73Sonic/Shur-3
86DePaul-C7
Bryant, Hallie
86IN/GreatI-16
Bryant, Jeff
90Clemson/200*-57
Bryant, Joe
80T-162
80T-74
81T-W92
Bryant, Kelvin
90NC/200*-31
90NC/200*-6
90NC/200*-72
90NC/Promos*-NC8
Bryant, Mark
88Blaz/Franz-3
89Blaz/Franz-2
89F-127
89Hoops-36
90Blaz/Franz-11
90F/Up-U80
90Hoops-243
90SkyBox-231
91Blaz/Franz-7
91Hoops/I-172
91SkyBox/I-234
91UD-392
92SkyBox/I-200
Bryant, Paul
(Bear)
89KY/300*-112
91TexAM-2
Bryant, Wallace
83Star/NBA-170
84Star/NBA-252
Bryant, Warren
89KY/300*-138
Bubas, Vic
89NCSt/Coke-30
89NCSt/Coke-31
Buchanan, Shawn
90NE/Pol*-26
Buchheit, George C.
89KY/300*-51
Buckhalter, Joe
61Kahn's-3
Buckingham, Wayne
89Clemson-3
Buckley, Bruce
89NC/Coke-178
Buckley, Clay
87Duke/Pol-45
88Duke/Pol-3
Bucknall, Steve
86NC/Pol-20
87NC/Pol-20
88NC/Pol-20
91WildCard/Coll-31
Buckner, Quinn
77Bucks/ActPh-3
78T-29
79Bucks/OpenP-8
79Bucks/Pol-21
80T-11
80T-138
80T-144
80T-50
81T-56M
83Star/NBA-28
84Star/NBA-3
85Star/NBA-82
87IN/GreatII-21
92Crtside/ColFB-6
Buckwalter, Morris
(Bucky)
79Blaz/Pol-x
81Blaz/Pol-x
82Blaz/Pol-x
83Blaz/Pol-x
84Blaz/Pol-5M
Budde, Ed
90MISt/200*-22
Budge, Donald
48Kell*-11
Budko, Pete
89NC/Coke-157
90NC/200*-134
Budko, Walter
48Bowman-70
52Bread-4
Buechler, Jud
86AZ/Pol-1
87AZ/Pol-1
88AZ/Pol-1
89AZ/Pol-1
90F/Up-U59
90Nets/Kayo-3
90StarPic-36
91Hoops/I-133
91Hoops/II-432
91SkyBox/I-179
91SkyBox/II-647
91UD-334
Buffone, Doug
89Louville/300*-109
Bukumirovich, Neboisha
87LSU/Pol*-7
Bull, Sitting
48T/Magic*-S3
Bullard, Matt
90StarPic-51
91F/Up-289
91Hoops/II-368
92Hoops/I-80
92SkyBox/I-85
Bullock, James
91WildCard/Coll-30
Bumpas, Dick
91AR/100*-36
Bunche, Ralph
91UCLA/144-90
Bunn, John W.
68HOF-6
Buntin, Nathan
88MO-1
89MO-1
Bunting, Bill
89NC/Coke-91
89NC/Coke-92
90NC/200*-136
Bunting, John
90NC/200*-114
Bunton, Bill
88Louville/194-38
89Louville/300*-16
89Louville/300*-272
Bunton, Stanley
88Louville/194-132
88Louville/194-188
Burchett, Carroll
89KY/300*-16
Burden, Ticky
76T-51
Burge, Heather
91VA/Lady-2
Burge, Heidi
91VA/Lady-3
Burger, Jeff
87Auburn/Pol*-3
Burgess, Frank
61Union-1
Burgin, George
87Duke/Pol-42
88Duke/Pol-4
Burke, Dave
84NE/Pol*-10
Burkhamer, Jeff
91ProC/CBA-108AC
Burkman, Roger
88Louville/194-128
88Louville/194-161
88Louville/194-39
89Louville/300*-243
89Louville/300*-267
89Louville/300*-31
Burks, Luther
89ProC/CBA-116
90ProC/CBA-184
Burks, Shawn
90LSU/200*-96
Burks, Steve
82TCMA/CBA-56
Burks, Eric
90Clemson-4
Burleson, Tom
75T-24
76T-41
77T-97
80T-131
80T-22

90AZSt/200*-109
Carnera, Primo
48T/Magic*-A12
48T/Magic*-D19
Carnesecca, Lou
92CenterCrt-25CO
Carnevale, Bernard
68HOF-47
Carollo, Phil
90FLSt/200*-12
Caron, Stacy
87ME/Pol*-12
Carpenter, Leonard
55Ash-50
Carpenter, Ray
91SC/200*-119
Carpenter, Rob
91Classic/DPColl*-204
Carr, Antoine
80WichSt/Pol-1
84Star/NBA-78
87Hawks/Pizza-7
88F-1
89Hoops-278
90F-163
90Hoops-255
90Kings/Safe-2
90Panini-38
90SkyBox-244A
90SkyBox-244B
91F-174
91F/Up-353
91Hoops/I-181
91Hoops/II-433
91Hoops/Super-84
91Panini-34
91SkyBox/I-244
91SkyBox/II-648
91UD-313
91UD/Ext-404
92F-202
92Hoops/I-205
92SkyBox/I-219
Carr, Austin
72Icee-3
72T-90
73NBAPA-5
73T-115
74T-60
74T-85M
75T-105
76T-53
77T-32
78T-9
79T-76
80T-102
80T-14
90NotreDame-5
92Crtside/ColFB-8
Carr, Brian
85NE/Pol*-26
Carr, Charlie
90NC/200*-138
Carr, Henry
90AZSt/200*-145
Carr, Kenny
80T-116
80T-47
81T-47M
81T-MW72
82Blaz/Pol-34
83Blaz/Pol-34
83Star/NBA-98
84Blaz/Franz-3
84Blaz/Pol-11
84Star/Blaz-1
84Star/NBA-163
85Blaz/Franz-3
85Star/NBA-105
86Blaz/Franz-3
89NCSt/Coke-58
89NCSt/Coke-59
89NCSt/Coke-60
Carr, M.L.
77T-47
78T-82
79T-107
80T-135
80T-69
81T-E72
83Star/NBA-29
84Star/Celt-13M
84Star/Celt-22
84Star/NBA-5
Carr, Vernon
90MISt/200*-108
Carreker, Alphonso
90FLSt/200*-63
Carrell, Duane
90FLSt/200*-190
Carrier, Chris
90LSU/200*-16
Carrier, Darrell
71Col/Mara-1
71T-149LL
71T-177
72T-207
Carrington, Dave
91ProC/CBA-84ACO
Carroll, Joe Barry
81T-W71
83Star/NBA-252
85Star/NBA-132
86F-14
87F-16
88F-50
89F-95
89Hoops-198
90Hoops-92
90Panini-66
90SkyBox-72
91SkyBox/I-221
91UD-373
Carroll, Wesley
91Classic/DPColl*-138
Carroway, Rod
91SC/200*-161
91SC/200*-167
Carson, Bud
91GATech*-98CO
Carson, Carlos
90LSU/200*-186
Carter, Anthony
91MI/56*-9
Carter, Butch
83Star/NBA-158
84Star/NBA-28
87IN/GreatII-31
Carter, Dexter
90FLSt/200*-82
Carter, Fred
70T-129
71T-14
72T-29
73NBAPA-4
73T-111
74T-75
74T-94M
75Sixers/McDon-1
75T-129M
75T-38
76T-111
89Sixers/Kodak-15CO
Carter, Garret
91SC/200*-113
Carter, Gary
82TCMA/CBA-62
Carter, George
71T-205
71T/Ins-20A
72T-197
73T-191
74T-178
74T-230M
75T-230
75T-281M
Carter, Howard
83Nugget/Pol-32
83Star/NBA-183
90LSU/200*-196
90LSU/200*-40
Carter, James
90ProC/CBA-109
Carter, Jeff
84NE/Pol*-22
Carter, Jim
90AZSt/200*-129
Carter, Kendall
90AZSt/200*-57
Carter, Larry
89Louville/300*-75
Carter, Pat
90FLSt/200*-9
91Classic/DPColl*-211
91WildCard/Coll-44
Carter, Paul
91JMadison/Smok-2
Carter, Perry
91StarPic-55
Cartier, Warren
89NCSt/Coke-63
Carton, Adam
92PennSt*-8
Cartwright, Bill
80T-148
80T-158
80T-166
80T-42
80T-53
80T-60
80T-68
80T-94
81T-26
81T-58M
81T-E102
83Star/NBA-62
84Star/NBA-29
85Star/NBA-167
87F-17
88Bulls/Ent-24
89Bulls/Eq-2
89F-19
89Hoops-255
90Bulls/Eq-4
90F-23A
90F-23B
90Hoops-61
90Hoops/Super-15
90SkyBox-38
91F-26
91Hoops/I-27
91Hoops/McDon-64
91Panini-114
91SkyBox/I-35
91UD-189
92F-29
92Hoops/I-28
92SkyBox/I-29
Carver, A.C.
91ProC/CBA-178
Casanova, Tommy
90LSU/200*-121
Casazez, Lucy
90AZSt/200*-125
Case, Everett
89NCSt/Coke-186
89NCSt/Coke-187
89NCSt/Coke-188
89NCSt/Coke-198
Casem, Marino
87South/Pol*-1CO
Casey, Dwane
77KY/Wildct-13
78KY/Food-10
88KY/269-110
88KY/269-201
88KY/269-259
Casey, Mike
88KY/269-217
88KY/269-92
Casey, Don
89Hoops-107CO
Cash, Marion
89Clemson-5
Cashion, Jim
91TexAM-77
Caskey, Mike
91SC/200*-57
Casler, Jeff
90MISt-8
Cassady, Billy Ray
89KY/300*-59
Cassidy, Steve
90LSU/200*-82
Caston, Tob
90LSU/200*-49
Catchings, Harvey
75Sixers/McDon-2
77T-81
79Bucks/Pol-42
83Star/NBA-42
84Star/NBA-16
Catledge, Terry
87F-18
89F-108
89Hoops-239
89Hoops/II-308
89Magic/Pep-3
90F-133
90Hoops-216
90Hoops/Super-70
90Panini-126
90SkyBox-201
91F-144
91Hoops/I-149
91Hoops/Super-69
91Panini-71
91SkyBox/I-202
91UD-205
92F-160
92Hoops/I-161
92SkyBox/I-170
Cattage, Bobby
82TCMA/CBA-22
86Star/LifeNets-3
Causwell, Duane
90F/Up-U83
90Kings/Safe-3
90StarPic-47
91F-175
91Hoops/I-182
91Panini-38
91SkyBox/I-245
91UD-358
91UD/Rook-11
92F-195
92Hoops/I-197
92SkyBox/I-210
Cavanaugh, Pat
89Pitt/Food-12
Cavarretta, Phil
48Kell*-1
Cavell, Bob
89ORSt-5
90ORSt-6
Cavenall, Ron
90ProC/CBA-170
Caveness, Ronnie
91AR/100*-53
Caviezel, Tim
91WA/TCI-2
91WA/Viacom-2
Cazzetta, Vin
82Fairf-2
Ceballos, Cedric
90F/Up-U75
90StarPic-23
91F/Up-339
91Hoops/II-417
91SkyBox/I-222
91UD-160
91UD/Ext-476CL
91UD/Ext-479SD
91UD/Rook-20
92F-179
92Hoops/I-178
92SkyBox/I-188
92SkyBox/I-311SD
Cecil, Chuck
90AZ/125*-24
90AZ/125*-68
90AZ/125*-9
90AZ/Promos*-1
Celestine, Allan
89ORSt-6
90ORSt-7
Cerdan, Marcel
48T/Magic*-A23
Cervi, Al
52Bread-5
Cesar, Dennis
91George/100-91
Chadwick, Dave
89NC/Coke-131
90NC/200*-145
Chaffee-Kiner, Nancy
57Union-21
Chamberlain, Wilt
61F-47
61F-8
68T/Test-1
69T-1
69T/Ins-11
70T-50
70T/Ins-17
71T-140LL
71T-142LL
71T-70
71T/Ins-43
72Icee-4
72T-1
72T-159
72T-168AS
72T-173LL
72T-175LL
73T-155LL
73T-157LL
73T-64M
73T-80
74T-250
81T/Thirst-16
81T/Thirst-17
81T/Thirst-18
81TCMA-44
91Foot*-11
91Foot*-29
Chambers, Bill
89NC/Coke-189
89NC/Coke-190
Chambers, Bob
81KY/Sched-3ACO
82KY/Sched-4ACO
Chambers, Jeff
91JMadison/Smok-3
Chambers, Jerry
69Suns/Carn-1
70T-62
71T-13
91Hoops/ASMVP-8
91Hoops/II-489SC
91Hoops/II-523Ar
91Hoops/McDon-32
91Hoops/Super-75
91Panini-26
91SkyBox/I-223

91SkyBox/II-479TW
91SkyBox/Proto-223
91UD-174
91UD-56AS
91UD-95TC
92F-180
92Hoops/I-179
Chambers, Tom
83Sonic/Pol-3
83Star/NBA-195
84Star/CrtKg-39
84Star/NBA-113
85Star/NBA-66
86F-15
86Star/CrtKg-6
87F-19
88F-106
88Fourn-28
89F-119
89F/AS-11
89Hoops-170
89Hoops-197AS
90F-146
90F/AS-8
90Hoops-15AS
90Hoops-234A
90Hoops-234B
90Hoops/CollB-2
90Hoops/Super-77
90Panini-13
90SkyBox-220
90Suns/Smok-1
91F-158
91Hoops/I-163
91Hoops/I-261AS
92SkyBox/I-189
Chambers, Wally
75Nab-5
Chancellor, Darrin
91Classic-47
91Classic/DPColl*-195
91Crtside-11
91FrRow/100-21
91FrRow/50-21
91FrRow/Premier-74
91StarPic-67
Chandik, John
90MISt/200*-69
Chandler, A.B.
(Happy)
87KY/Coke-22
89KY/Award-29
Chandler, Tom
91TexAM-16
Chandnois, Lynn
90MISt/200*-26
Chaney, Don
70T-47
71T-82
72T-131
73T-57
74T-133
75Carv-3
75T-265
77T-27
87Hawks/Pizza-4CO
89Hoops-123ACO
89Hoops-123BCO
90Hoops-314CO
90Hoops/II-350CO
90SkyBox/II-310CO
91F-73CO
91Hoops/I-230CO
91SkyBox/II-387CO
Chaney, Lon
48T/Magic*-J26
Chapman, Allen
87SoMiss-7M
Chapman, Gil
91MI/56*-10
Chapman, Rex
87KY/Coke-21
88KY/269-144
88KY/269-202
88KY/269-233
89Conv-5
89F-15
89Hoops-54
89KY/300*-12
89KY/Tm80-39
90F-17
90Hoops-51
90Hoops/II-357TC
90Hoops/Super-10
90Panini-79
90SkyBox-27
91F-18
91F-229
91F/Up-374TL
91Hoops/I-19
91Hoops/II-453SC
91Hoops/McDon-5
91Panini-109
91SkyBox/I-24
91SkyBox/II-407GF
91SkyBox/II-461TW
91SkyBox/II-578
91SkyBox/Proto-24
91UD-325
91UD-81TC
92F-229
92SkyBox/I-246
92Hoops/I-231
Chapman, Robert
90MISt/200*-129
Chapman, Roosevelt
83Dayton/Blue-2
Chappell, Len
69T-68
70T-146
70T/Ins-24
Chappins, Bob
48T/Magic*-C11
Chappuis, Bob
91MI/56*-11
Charles, Ken
75T-101
76T-121
77T-24
Charles, Ron
82TCMA/CBA-3
90MISt/200*-150
Charlesworth, Charles
91ProC/CBA-11TR
Chase, Darnell
87Baylor/Pol*-9
Chatham, Mike
90NC/200*-56
Chatman, Canaan
90ORSt-8
91ORSt-7
Chatman, Jeff
87BYU-23
87BYU-9
Cheaney, Calbert
90KY/BB/DT/AW-21
Cheatum, Melvin
91Classic/DPColl*-212
91StarPic-12
Cheek, Louis
91TexAM-68
Cheeks, Maurice
80T-154
80T-171
80T-30
80T-66
81T-59M
81T-E90
83Star/ASG-3
83Star/NBA-2
83Star/Sixers-16
83Star/Sixers-9
84Star/Arena-E2
84Star/CrtKg-29
84Star/NBA-203
85JMS-1
85Star/NBA-1
85Star/TmSuper-PS2
86F-16
86Star/CrtKg-7
87F-20
88F-86
89F-115
89Hoops-65
89Hoops/II-320
90F-124
90Hoops-202
90Panini-139
90SkyBox-186
91F-135
91F/Up-242
91Hoops/I-139
91Hoops/I-320YB
91Hoops/II-331
91Hoops/II-533
91Hoops/Super-64
91Panini-165
91SkyBox/I-188
91SkyBox/II-405GF
91SkyBox/II-615
91UD-281
92Hoops/I-2
92SkyBox/I-2
Cheeley, Darryl
88WakeForest/Pol-4
Cheevers, Gerry
81T/Thirst-43
Chenault, Chris
89KY/300*-171
Chenier, Phil
72T-102
73Bullet/Stand-1
73T-113
74T-165
74T-98M
75T-190AS
76T-27
77T-55
79T-103
Cherio, Tony
91AR/100*-21
Chesbro, Tom
91OKSt*-65
Chickerella, Vincent
91ProC/CBA-146CO
Chievous, Derrick
88MO-2
89F-58
89Hoops-16
90Hoops-72
90SkyBox/II-373
91ProC/CBA-160
Chilcutt, Pete
86NC/Pol-32
87NC/Pol-32
88NC/Pol-32
91Classic-17
91Classic/DPColl*-165
91Crtside-12
91F/Up-348
91FrRow/100-4
91FrRow/50-4
91FrRow/Premier-119
91StarPic-13
91UD/Ext-415
91WildCard/Coll-95
92Hoops/I-198
92SkyBox/I-211
Childers, Sam
90FLSt/200*-39
Childress, Ray
91TexAM-9
Childs, Chris
89ProC/CBA-32
90ProC/CBA-181
90ProC/CBA-51
91ProC/CBA-1
Chime, Phil
91Iowa-3
Chinaglia, Giorgio
81T/Thirst-53
Chisolm, Donnie
91GATech*-186
Choice, Wally
87IN/GreatII-15
Cholowsky, Dan
91Classic/DPColl*-85
Chones, Jim
73T-259
74T-6
75T-120M
75T-66
76T-97
77T-57
78RCCola-4
78T-105
79T-19
80T-154
80T-70
81T-W76
Christensen, Brian
89ProC/CBA-117
90ProC/CBA-90
Christian, Bob
72T-53
73T-11
Christian, Jerry
80TCMA/CBA-25
Christian, Myron
82INSt/Pol*-4
Christie, Dan
83Dayton/Blue-3
Christie, Doug
92Classic/DP-20
92StarPic-73
Christy, Jim
91George/100-85
Church, Greg
88MO-3
Church, Irvin
91George/Pol-15
Churchwell, Robert
90George/Pol-10
91George/Pol-2
Ciampi, Joe
87Auburn/Pol*-6
Citronnelli, Eddie
86SWLou/Pol*-2
Clack, Darryl
90AZSt/200*-85
Claiborne, Jerry
89KY/300*-101
89KY/300*-200
Clancy, Robert
90MISt/200*-116
Clancy, Sam
81TCMA/CBA-61
Clarida, Riley
82TCMA/CBA-7
Clark, Archie
69T-32
70T-105
71T-106
71T/Ins-18
72Icee-5
72T-120
72T-170AS
73Bullet/Stand-2
73T-15
74T-172
75T-132M
75T-96
Clark, Carlos
83Star/NBA-30
89ProC/CBA-163
Clark, Dwight
90Clemson/200*-71
90Clemson/Promos*-C8
Clark, Emery
89KY/300*-127
Clark, Matt
87Baylor/Pol*-15
Clark, Melinda
91TexAM-33
Clark, Rickey
88TN/Smok-24
Clark, Ronald
55Ash-75
Clark, Rusty
89NC/Coke-89
89NC/Coke-90
90NC/200*-158
Clark, Steve
89Louville/300*-210
Clark, Vinnie
91Classic/DPColl*-117
Clausen, Mark
87BYU-20
Claxton, Charles
90GA/Smok-2
Clay, Dwight
90NotreDame-45
Clayton, Mark
89Louville/300*-117
Claytor, Truman
77KY/Wildct-20
78KY/Food-11
88KY/269-111
88KY/269-200
88KY/269-232
88KY/269-235
Cleamons, Jim
73T-29
74T-42
75T-120M
75T-137
78T-31
79T-112
80T-103
80T-15
Clem, Glen
89ProC/CBA-169
Clemens, Barry
69Sonic/Sunb-3
70Sonic/Sunb-2
70T-119
71T-119
72T-57
73T-92
75T-22
Clemens, Cord
83Victoria/Pol-1
Clements, Wes
90AZ/125*-20
Cleveland, Daryl
88Louville/194-144
88Louville/194-87
Clevenger, Steve
88KY/269-84
Clifford, Dennis
88Louville/194-95
Clifton, Nat
57T-1
Close, Casey
91MI/56*-12
Clustka, Chuck
91UCLA/144-102
Clutter, Jack
55Ash-63
Clyde, Andy
48T/Magic*-J2
Cobb, Coy
90Clemson/200*-187
Cobb, John
48ExhSC-7

Cobb, Ric
82Marq/Lite-1CO
Cobb, Ty
48T/Magic*-K13
Coble, Greg
90MurraySt-4
Cockran, Cindy
91GATech*-17
Coder, Paul
89NCSt/Coke-64
89NCSt/Coke-65
89NCSt/Coke-66
Cody, Buffalo Bill
48T/Magic*-S2
Coffield, Randy
90FLSt/200*-135
Coffin, Elizabeth
(Liz)
87ME/Pol*-9
Coffman, Bennie
88KY/269-62
Coffman, Wayne
90Clemson/200*-153
Cofield, Fred
89ProC/CBA-92
Coggin, Redus
90FLSt/200*-8
Cohen, Jeff
61Union-2
Cohen, Sid
88KY/269-75
Coker, Pete
89NCSt/Coke-181
89NCSt/Coke-70
89NCSt/Coke-72
Colangelo, Jerry
75Suns-4
Colbert, Claudette
48T/Magic*-F15
Colbert, Dave
83Dayton/Blue-4
Cole, Al
82INSt/Pol*-5
Cole, Gary
(See Abdul Jeelani)
Cole, George
91AR/100*-39
Cole, Jervis
89ProC/CBA-202
90ProC/CBA-198
Cole, Lynn
55Ash-76
Cole, Rod
90GA/Smok-3
Coleman, Ben
90SkyBox-156
91WildCard/Coll-101
Coleman, Derrick
88Syr/Rich-2
89Syr/Pep-1
89Syr/Pep-15
90F/Up-U60
90Hoops/II-390LS
90Nets/Kayo-4
90SkyBox/II-362LP
90StarPic-43
91F-130
91F/Rook-3
91F/Up-388TL
91Hoops/I-134
91Hoops/II-482SC
91Hoops/II-519Ar
91Hoops/McDon-25
91Panini-157
91Panini-179AR
91SkyBox/Canada-31
91SkyBox/I-180
91SkyBox/I-318AR
91SkyBox/II-475TW
91SkyBox/II-502RS
91StarPic-2
91UD-332
91UD-35ART
91UD-88TC
91UD/AWHolo-7
91UD/Rook-10
92F-143
92F/TmLeader-17
92Hoops/I-147
92SkyBox/I-154
92SkyBox/I-298TT
Coleman, Don
90MISt/200*-27
Coleman, E.C.
75T-127M
75T-163
77T-123
78T-12
Coleman, Jack
57T-70
88Louville/194-94
89Louville/300*-231
Coleman, Jamal
88MO-4
89MO-3
90MO-4
91MO-4
Coleman, Ronald
91WildCard/Coll-42
Coleman, Ronnie
90SoCal/Smok*-2
Coleman, Vince
89Foot*-3
Coles, Vernell
(Bimbo)
90F/Up-U48
90Heat/Publix-3
90StarPic-25
91F-106
91Hoops/I-108
91Hoops/II-567
91SkyBox/I-145
91SkyBox/II-418GF
91SkyBox/II-549US
91UD-149
92F-116
92Hoops/I-117
92SkyBox/I-124
Colescott, Dave
89NC/Coke-147
90NC/200*-142
Collier, Blanton
89KY/300*-165
Collier, Chris
91ProC/CBA-196
Collier, Cory
91GATech*-8
Collins, Don
81T-E95
83Star/NBA-254
Collins, Doug
74T-129
75Sixers/McDon-3
75T-129M
75T-148
76T-38
77T-65
78RCCola-5
78T-2
79T-64
80T-148
80T-32
87Bulls/Ent-12CO
Collins, Jeff
81AZ/Pol-4
Collins, Jimmy
70T-157
Collins, Laura
90UCLA-24
Collins, Lee
91SC/200*-61
Collins, Martha Layne
87KY/Coke-1
Collins, Paul
55Ash-4
Collins, Rip
90LSU/200*-137
Collins, Ronnie
91SC/200*-90
Collins, Sonny
89KY/300*-104
Collins, Tank
91ProC/CBA-7
Collins, Terry
91OKSt-39
91OKSt-8
Collinsworth, Lincoln
89KY/300*-70
Colp, Steven
90MISt/200*-155
Colson, Gary
90Fresno/Smok-5CO
Colter, Steve
84Blaz/Franz-4
84Blaz/Pol-6
84Star/NBA-164
85Blaz/Franz-4
89Hoops-214
90Kings/Safe-4
90SkyBox-286
90SkyBox/II-408
Combs, Carl
89KY/300*-273
Combs, Cecil
89KY/300*-272
Combs, Charley
89KY/300*-280
Combs, Edwin Leroy
83Star/NBA-159
90ProC/CBA-113
Combs, Glen
71T-215
72T-194
72T-261LL
73T-209
73T-236LL
74T-199
Combs, Glenn
88Louville/194-49
Combs, Pat
87Baylor/Pol*-2
Combs, Roy
89Louville/300*-56
Comegys, Dallas
88Spurs/Pol-5
Compise, Pete
89Louville/300*-149
Compton, Deward
89Louville/300*-42
Compton, Joyce
91SC/200*-45
Compton, Larry
89Louville/300*-165
Conacher, Roy
48ExhSC-8
Cone, Fred
90Clemson/200*-81
Cone, Ronny
91GATech*-11
Conley, Larry
88KY/269-143
88KY/269-190
88KY/269-222
88KY/269-39
Conley, Mike
88Foot*-2
89Foot*-1
91AR/100*-7
91Foot*-9
Conlin, Ed
57T-58
Conlon, Marty
90ProC/CBA-53
91F/Up-359
91FrRow/100-50B
91FrRow/50-50B
91FrRow/Premier-49
91WildCard/Coll-92
Connelly, Jeffty
91ProC/CBA-126
Conner, Gary
90Clemson/200*-37
Conner, Lester
83Star/NBA-255
84Star/NBA-153
85Star/NBA-133
89F-96
89Hoops-222
90F-119
90Hoops-195
90Nets/Kayo-5
90Panini-159
90SkyBox-178
91F/Up-310
91Hoops/II-390
91SkyBox/I-156
91SkyBox/I-299
91UD-381
Connor, George
48T/Magic*-C9
Connor, Jimmy Dan
88KY/269-104
88KY/269-188
88KY/269-206
88KY/269-258
Conrad, Bobby Joe
90Clemson/200*-12
91TexAM-81
Constantine, Marc
55Ash-87
Conway, Hollis
86SWLou/Pol*-3
87SWLou/McDag*-13
Coogan, Jackie
48T/Magic*-J5
Cook, Anthony
85AZ/Pol-1
86AZ/Pol-2
87AZ/Pol-2
88AZ/Pol-2
90AZ/125*-33
90F/Up-U24
91Hoops/II-355
91SkyBox/I-69
91UD-203
Cook, Bob
(Tarmac)
48ExhSC-9
Cook, Darwin
81T-E77
83Star/NBA-147
84Nets/Getty-3
84Star/NBA-90
85Star/NBA-60
86Star/LifeNets-4
Cook, Greg
81AZ/Pol-5
Cook, Jeff
80Suns/Pep-9
81T-W80
83Star/NBA-230
87Suns/Circ-3
Cook, Joe
87Duke/Pol-13
Cook, Mike
91SC/200*-84
Cooke, Joe
71T-62
Cooke, Mark
88VA/Hardee-3
Cooke, Mike
89NC/Coke-181
Cooke, Troy
83AZ/Pol-5
Cooley, Gaye
90MISt/200*-164
Cooper, Carl
90AZ/125*-120
Cooper, Cecil
79Bucks/OpenP-3
Cooper, Duane
92Classic/DP-72
92StarPic-24
Cooper, Eric
85AZ/Pol-2
Cooper, Evan
91MI/56*-13
Cooper, Gary
90Clemson/200*-78
Cooper, Jackie
48T/Magic*-J7
Cooper, Joe
81TCMA/CBA-16
82TCMA/CBA-70
82TCMA/Lanc-10IA
Cooper, John
91ProC/CBA-80
Cooper, Michael
80T-133
80T-45
81T-W77
82Lakers/BASF-2
83Lakers/BASF-2
83Star/NBA-15
84Lakers/BASF-2
84Star/Arena-D2
84Star/NBA-174
84Star/PolASG-26
84Star/SlamD-2
85JMS-19
85Star/Lakers-11M
85Star/NBA-27
86F-17
87F-21
88F-65
89F-75
89Hoops-187
90F-90
90Hoops-153
90SkyBox-134
Cooper, Reggie
90NE/Pol*-2
Cooper, Teena
86SWLou/Pol*-4
87SWLou/McDag*-6
Cooper, Wayne
80T-113
80T-25
81T-W103
82Blaz/Pol-42
83Blaz/Pol-42
83Star/NBA-99
84Star/NBA-138
85Nugget/Pol-6
85Star/NBA-51
86F-18
88Nugget/Pol-42
89Blaz/Franz-3
89Hoops-122
89Hoops/II-335
90Blaz/Franz-12
90Hoops-244
90SkyBox-232
91Blaz/Franz-8
91Hoops/II-424
91SkyBox/I-235
91UD-378
Copa, Tom
91FrRow/100-86
91FrRow/Premier-7
91FrRow/Up-77
91WildCard/Coll-102
Copeland, Lanard
89Sixers/Kodak-4
90ProC/CBA-79

90SkyBox-213
91Hoops/II-377
Corbet, Rene
91Classic/DPColl*-21
Corbett, James J.
48T/Magic*-A3
Corbin, Tyrone
89Hoops-263
89Hoops/II-319
89TWolv/BK-23
90F-113
90Hoops-186
90Hoops/Super-58
90Panini-75
90SkyBox-169
91F-122
91F/Up-364
91Hoops/I-125
91Hoops/II-479SC
91Hoops/Super-59
91Panini-66
91SkyBox/I-169
91SkyBox/II-649
91UD-322
91UD/Ext-414
92F-220
92Hoops/I-223
92SkyBox/I-238
Corbitt, Anthony
91ProC/CBA-75
Corchiani, Chris
87NCSt/Pol-2
88NCSt/Pol-2
89NCSt/Pol-1
90NCSt/IBM-2
91Classic-26
91Classic/DPColl*-174
91Crtside-13
91FrRow/100-13
91FrRow/50-13
91FrRow/Premier-102
91StarPic-46
91UD-17
91WildCard/Coll-20
Cordileone, Lou
90Clemson/200*-189
Corkrum, Rob
91WASt-1
Corley, Chris
91SC/200*-115
Cornelius, Greg
81TCMA/CBA-47
Correll, Ray
89KY/300*-109
Corrigan, Doug
48T/Magic*-L7
Corso, Lee
89Louville/300*-138
90FLSt/200*-104
Corzine, Dave
81T-62
81T-MW101
83Star/NBA-169
84Star/CrtKg-24
84Star/NBA-102
85Star/NBA-119
85Star/TmSuper-CB4
86DePaul-10
87Bulls/Ent-10
87F-22
88Bulls/Ent-40
88F-15
89F-109
89Hoops-93
89Hoops/II-343
89Magic/Pep-4
90Hoops-217
90Hoops/II-436
90SkyBox-202
90SkyBox/II-417
90Sonic/Kayo-6
90Sonic/Smok-3
91UD-106
Costello, Larry
57T-33
61F-48IA
61F-9
Costner, Tony
90ProC/CBA-54
Couch, Sean
89ProC/CBA-47
Coughran, John
82TCMA/CBA-12
Counts, Mel
69T-49
70Suns/A1-1A
70Suns/A1-1B
70Suns/Carn-1
70T-103
71T-127
72T-67
73T-151
75T-199
Courts, Scott
77KY/Wildct-9
Cousineau, Marcel
91Classic/DPColl*-50
Cousy, Robert J.
(Bob)
57T-17
57Union-34
61F-10
61F-49IA
68HOF-49
81TCMA-41
85Star/Schick-7
91Cousy/Coll-Set
91Cousy/CollPrev-Set
Covelli, Frank
90AZSt/200*-130
Cowan, Fred
77KY/Wildct-14
78KY/Food-16
79KY/Food-6
88KY/269-114
88KY/269-189
88KY/269-234
88KY/269-268
89KY/Tm80-52
Coward, Lee
89MO-4
Cowden, Wayne
92PennSt*-9
Cowens, Dave
71T-47
71T/Ins-30
72T-7
73NBAPA-6
73T-157LL
73T-40AS
74T-148LL
74T-155
74T-82M
75Carv-4
75T-117M
75T-170
75T-4LL
76Buck-5
76T-131AS
76T-30
77Dell-2
77Pep/AS-2
77T-90
78RCCola-6
78T-40
79T-5
80T-7
80T-95
90FLSt/200*-131
Cowins, Ben
91AR/100*-19
Cowsen, McKinley
86DePaul-C5
Cox, Aaron
90AZSt/200*-39
Cox, Chubby
80TCMA/CBA-1
Cox, Corky
88Louville/194-56
Cox, Craig
85FortHaysSt-7CO
Cox, Darrell
89KY/300*-179
Cox, Johnny
88KY/269-14
Cox, Steve
91AR/100*-73
Cox, Tracy
90AZSt/200*-118
Cox, Wesley
88Louville/194-102
88Louville/194-17
88Louville/194-171
88Louville/194-183
89Louville/300*-232
89Louville/300*-271
Coy, Hugh
89KY/300*-277
Cozens, Carl
91UCLA/144-113
Craft, Donald
89Louville/300*-148
Craig, Steve
81TCMA/CBA-83
Crain, Kurt
87Auburn/Pol*-5
Craven, Ken
90NC/200*-177
Crawford, Fred
70T-162
Crawford, Laurent
89ProC/CBA-4
Creamer, Eddie
88Louville/194-55
Cremins, Bobby
88GATech/Nike-3CO
89GATech/Pol-8CO
90GATech/Pol-8CO
91GATech/Pol-6CO
91SC/200*-80
Crenshaw, Bobby
90FLSt/200*-187
Crews, Jim
86IN/GreatI-24
Crigler, John
88KY/269-67
Criss, Charlie
78Hawks/Coke-2
78T-87
79Hawks/Majik-14
80T-15
80T-164
81T-E67
Crite, Winston
89ProC/CBA-132
Crittenden, Howard
55Ash-64
Critton, Ken
91WASt-2
Critz, George
89KY/300*-60
Crockett, Bobby
91AR/100*-91
Crockett, Ray
87Baylor/Pol*-11
Crockett, Willis
91GATech*-49
Croel, Mike
90NE/Pol*-6
91Classic/DPColl*-106
Croft, Bobby
71Col/Mara-2
Cromer, Jamie
90KY/ClassA-14
Crompton, Geoff
80TCMA/CBA-12
83Star/NBA-231
Crook, Herbert
88Louville/194-107
88Louville/194-169
88Louville/194-7
89Louville/300*-12
89Louville/300*-254
89Louville/300*-287
89Louville/300*-38
89ProC/CBA-138
Cross, Pete
70Sonic/Sunb-3
71Sonic/Sunb-2
71T-33
72T-49
Crotty, John
88VA/Hardee-4
91Crtside-14
91FrRow/100-92
91FrRow/Premier-113
91FrRow/Up-80
91StarPic-6
Crow, John David
91TexAM-10
Crowder, Corey
91FrRow/100-68
91FrRow/ItalPromo-2
91FrRow/Premier-28
91FrRow/Up-71
Crudup, Jevon
90MO-5
91MO-5
Crum, Denny
81Louville/Pol-23CO
81Louville/Pol-27CO
81Louville/Pol-29CO
83Louville-x
88Louville/194-1
88Louville/194-173
88Louville/194-181
88Louville/194-99
89Louville/300*-1
89Louville/300*-288
89Louville/300*-298
91UCLA/144-103M
91UCLA/144-111
Crum, Francis
55Ash-39
Crutcher, James
90KY/Sov-5
Cubelic, Mary Ann
90Clemson/200*-185
Cuddeford, Michelle
90NE/Pol*-27
Cueto, Al
71T-223
Cuk, Vladimir
91JMadison/Smok-4
Culbertson, Richard
55Ash-5
Culik, Carolina
91SC/200*-29
Culp, Curley
90AZSt/200*-67
Culp, Ron
77Blaz/Pol-TR
83Blaz/Pol-TR
Cullimore, Jassen
91Classic/DPColl*-26
Culuko, Kent
91JMadison/Smok-5
Cumberledge, Melinda
87KY/Coke-6
Cummings, Jack
90NC/200*-183
Cummings, Pat
79Bucks/Pol-6
83Star/NBA-51
84Star/NBA-30
85Star/NBA-168
86F-19
89Hoops-158
Cummings, Robert
48T/Magic*-J15
Cummings, Terry
83Star/All-R-1
83Star/NBA-123
84Star/CrtKg-37
84Star/NBA-125
85Star/Bucks-3
85Star/NBA-124
85Star/ROY-3
85Star/TmSuper-MB1
86DePaul-11
86DePaul-S6
86DePaul-S7
86F-20
86Star/CrtKg-8
86Star/LifeBucks-3
87Bucks/Polar-34
87F-23
88Bucks/Green-3
88F-74
89F-142
89Hoops-100
89Hoops-256AS
89Hoops/II-312
90F-170
90Hoops-266
90Hoops/CollB-14
90Hoops/Super-87
90Panini-45
90SkyBox-255
91F-184
91Hoops/I-189
91Hoops/II-495SC
91Hoops/McDon-39
91Hoops/Super-87
91Panini-75
91SkyBox/Canada-42
91SkyBox/I-255
91SkyBox/II-482TW
91UD-267
92F-203
92Hoops/I-206
92SkyBox/I-220
Cummins, Albert
89KY/300*-100
Cunningham, Billy
69T-40
69T/Ins-21
70T-108AS
70T-140
70T/Ins-16
71T-79
71T/Ins-40
72T-167AS
72T-215
73T-200AS
74T-221M
74T-235
75Sixers/McDon-4
75T-129M
75T-20
76T-93
81TCMA-43
83Star/Sixers-2
89NC/Coke-37
89NC/Coke-38
89NC/Coke-39
89NC/Coke-40
89NC/Coke-61
Cunningham, Bob
89NC/Coke-123
89NC/Coke-124
Cunningham, Brent
91GATech*-55
Cunningham, Dick
70T-49

Davis, Craig
89NCSt/Coke-73
89NCSt/Coke-75
Davis, Dale
89Clemson-6
90Clemson-5
91Classic-8
91Classic/DPColl*-156
91Crtside-15
91F/Up-293
91FrRow/100-31
91FrRow/100-39
91FrRow/50-31
91FrRow/50-39
91FrRow/Premier-52
91StarPic-63
91UD/Ext-409
91UD/Rook-38
91WildCard/Coll-14
92F-88
92Hoops/I-89
92SkyBox/I-94
Davis, Dexter
91Classic/DPColl*-216
Davis, Dwight
73T-104
74T-158
74T-85M
75T-11
Davis, Emanuel
91FrRow/100-78
91FrRow/Premier-17
91FrRow/Up-91
Davis, Fritgerald
91SC/200*-39
Davis, Harry
80TCMA/CBA-3
81TCMA/CBA-84
Davis, Hubert
92Classic/DP-22
92StarPic-51
Davis, Jeff
90Clemson/200*-96
Davis, Jim
69T-53
70T-54
71T-97
72T-51
75T-174
90Clemson/200*-148
90Clemson/Lady-3CO
Davis, John
91GATech*-44
Davis, Johnathon
91KY/BB-1
Davis, Johnny
77Blaz/Pol-16
78T-22
79T-92
80T-122
80T-145
80T-58
80T-86
81T-16
81T-53M
83Star/NBA-265
84Star/NBA-216
85Star/NBA-154
Davis, Lee
71T-212
73T-253
75T-234
Davis, Lucius
92Classic/DP-36
92StarPic-25
Davis, Mark
91NCSt/IBM-2
91ProC/CBA-156
Davis, Melvin
(Mel)
71Globe-18M
71Globe-30M
71Globe-33
71Globe-34
71Globe-35
71Globe-36
71Globe-37M
71Globe-38
71Globe/Cocoa-10M
71Globe/Cocoa-27
71Globe/Cocoa-5M
71Globe/Cocoa-8M
74T-43
75T-179
77T-38
80TCMA/CBA-34
Davis, Mickey
71Bucks/Linn-4
73T-107
74T-73
75T-126M
75T-53
Davis, Mike
70T-29
71T-99
72T-39
82TCMA/CBA-61
90ProC/CBA-133
91ProC/CBA-22ACO
Davis, Mulford
89KY/300*-270
Davis, Percy
81TCMA/CBA-33
Davis, Ralph
89UTEP/Drug-6
Davis, Ralph E.
60Kahn's-3
Davis, Randy
91OKSt-10
91OKSt-46
Davis, Robert
89Louville/300*-57
Davis, Rodell
91Iowa-4
Davis, Ron
80TCMA/CBA-30
81TCMA/CBA-80
Davis, Rueben
90NC/200*-43
Davis, Shawn
91AR25-4
Davis, Tara
91WA/Viacom-10
Davis, Terry
89Heat/Publix-1
90F/Up-U49
90Heat/Publix-4
90SkyBox-144
91F/Up-267
91Hoops/I-109
91Hoops/II-352
91SkyBox/I-146
91SkyBox/II-622
91UD-179
91UD/Ext-423
92F-48
92F/TmLeader-6
92Hoops/I-46
92SkyBox/I-48
Davis, Walt
57T-49
Davis, Walter
77Suns/Discs-6
78RCCola-8
78T-10
79T-80
80Suns/Pep-1
80T-158
80T-172
80T-70
80T-78
81T-33
82Suns/Giant-1
83Star/NBA-109
84Star/ASG-17
84Star/NBA-39
84Star/PolASG-17
84Suns/Pol-6
85Star/NBA-36
85Star/ROY-8
86F-23
87F-26
87Suns/Circ-4
88Nugget/Pol-6
89F-39
89Hoops-61
89NC/Coke-51
89NC/Coke-52
89NC/Coke-53
89NC/Coke-54
89Nugget/Pol-2
90F-47
90Hoops-93
90NC/200*-9
90Panini-64
90SkyBox-73
91Blaz/Franz-9
91F/Up-274
91Hoops/I-173
91Hoops/II-356
91Hoops/II-557
91SkyBox/I-236
91SkyBox/II-623
91UD-380
91UD/Ext-422
92SkyBox/I-58
Davis, Warren
71T-219
73T-229
Davis, Wendell
90LSU/200*-70
Davis, William
91JMadison/Smok-6
Dawe, Jason
91Classic/DPColl*-31
Dawkins, Bill
90FLSt/200*-188
Dawkins, Darryl
77T-132
78T-34
79T-105
80T-160
80T-55
81T-29
81T-E103
83Star/NBA-148
84Nets/Getty-4
84Star/NBA-88
85Star/NBA-61
86F-24
86Star/CrtKg-10
86Star/LifeNets-5
91WildCard/Coll-69
Dawkins, Johnny
87F-27
88F-104
88Spurs/Pol-6
89F-143
89Hoops-78
89Hoops/II-311
89Sixers/Kodak-5
90F-141
90Hoops-227
90Hoops/Super-72
90Panini-131
90SkyBox-214
91F-152
91Hoops/I-158
91Hoops/Super-72
91SkyBox/I-213
91UD-176
92F-168
92Hoops/I-172
92SkyBox/I-181
Dawsey, Lawrence
91Classic/DPColl*-222
Dawson, Bill
90FLSt/200*-154
Dawson, Mike
90AZ/125*-69
Dawson, Rhett
90FLSt/200*-196
Dawson, Tony
89ProC/CBA-56
90ProC/CBA-37
Day, Ned
48ExhSC-11
Day, Todd
91AR25-5
92Classic/DP-12
92Classic/DPLP-LP8
92FrRow/DreamPk-71
92FrRow/DreamPk-72
92FrRow/DreamPk-73
92FrRow/DreamPk-74
92FrRow/DreamPk-75
92StarPic-4
92StarPic-83KC
Daye, Darren
83Star/NBA-207
84Star/NBA-188
85Star/NBA-111
91UCLA/144-27
Daye, James
89NC/Coke-191
Dean, Everett S.
54Quaker-24
68HOF-9
86IN/GreatI-14
Dean, Joe
77KY/Wildct-6CO
78KY/Food-22CO
79KY/Food-15CO
81KY/Sched-4ACO
90LSU/200*-6
90LSU/Promos*-10
Deardorff, Donna
85NE/Pol*-33
DeBernardi, Forrest S.
68HOF-10
DeBisschop, Pete
82Fairf-3
DeBortoli, Joel
90ProC/CBA-140
DeBose, Keenan
82AR-5
DeBusschere, Dave
68T/Test-11
69T-85
70T-135
71T-107
71T/Ins-10
72Icee-6
72T-105
73NBAPA-7
73T-30AS
74T-93M
81TCMA-39
85Star/Schick-10
Dedmon, Lee
89NC/Coke-164
Deeken, Dennis
89Louville/300*-79
Deeken, Ted
89KY/300*-18
Dees, Archie
58Kahn's-2
86IN/GreatI-34
Dees, Clair
89KY/300*-294
DeFrank, Matt
90LSU/200*-169
DeGiglio, Bruno
79StBon-3
Degitz, Dave
92PennSt*-3
DeHavilland, Olivia
48T/Magic*-F7
DeHeer, Bill
86IN/GreatI-41
Dehnert, Henry G.
68HOF-11
DeLamielleure, Joe
90MISt/200*-63
Delany, Jim
89NC/Coke-125
90NC/200*-162
DelNegro, Vinnie
87NCSt/Pol-4
88Kings/Carl-15
89Hoops-6
89Kings/Carl-15
89KY/300*-24
89NCSt/Coke-88
89NCSt/Coke-89
89NCSt/Coke-90
90Hoops-256
90Panini-42
90SkyBox-245
91WildCard/Coll-79
Delph, Marvin
91AR/100*-44
DeMarcus, David
88KY/Sov-7
DeMarie, John
90LSU/200*-89
DeMarie, Mike
90LSU/200*-167
Demars, Kent
91SC/200*-12
Dembo, Fennis
89Hoops-72
90ProC/CBA-77
91WildCard/Coll-89
Demic, Larry
80T-132
80T-76
90AZ/125*-21
DeMoisey, John
88KY/269-22
DeMoisey, Truett
89Louville/300*-219
DeMoisey, Truitt
89KY/300*-91
Demond, Lee
90NC/200*-181
Dempsey, George
57T-60
Dempsey, Jack
48ExhSC-12
48T/Magic*-A8
Dempsey, Tom
81T/Thirst-48
Dendy, Thomas
91SC/200*-147
Denham, Harry
89KY/300*-33
Dennard, Ken
81TCMA/CBA-35
83Nugget/Pol-33
Dennard, Mark
91TexAM-62
Dennis, Greg
92Classic/DP-85
92StarPic-66
Denny, Jeff
86NC/Pol-3
87NC/Pol-3
88NC/Pol-3
Denny, Mike
80WichSt/Pol-2
Denton, Randy
72T-202
73T-211
74T-189

74T-225M
75T-266
Depaola, Len
89Louville/300*-176
DePre, Joe
71T-226
DePriest, Lyman
90CT/Pol-4
DeRatt, Jimmy
90NC/200*-110
Derline, Rod
75T-112
Derouillere, Jean
91ProC/CBA-5
91StarPic-32
DeSantis, Joe
82Fairf-4CO
Desdunes, Jean
90Clemson/200*-83
DeShields, Delino
91Foot*-2
Desmond, Jim
91SC/200*-111
Detton, Dean
48T/Magic*-D10
Deuser, Greg
81Louville/Pol-14
88Louville/194-88
Deutsch, Darcy
91ND*-8M
Devaney, Bob
90NE/Pol*-1
Deveaux, Drexel
91FrRow/100-52
91FrRow/Premier-46
Devereaux, Mike
90AZSt/200*-158
Devine, Dan
90AZSt/200*-105
Devoe, Don
88TN/Smok-x
Devries, William
87KY/Coke-3
Dewberry, John
91GATech*-1
Dewey, George
48T/Magic*-O9
Dias, Lisa
91SC/200*-20
Dibble, Dorne
90MISt/200*-20
DiCarlo, George
90AZ/125*-50
Dickerson, Dave
88MD/Pol-2
Dickerson, Eric
89Foot*-4
91Foot*-27
Dickey, Curtis
91TexAM-29
Dickey, Derrek
75T-69
Dickey, Dick
89NCSt/Coke-76
89NCSt/Coke-77
89NCSt/Coke-78
Dickson, Mack
90Clemson/200*-98
Dicus, Chuck
91AR/100*-76
Diddle, Ed
55Ash-78
Dieckman, Johnny
57Union-16
Dierking, Connie
69T-28
70T-66
Dietrick, Coby
75T-273
79Bulls/Pol-26
Dietz, Diane
91MI/56*-15
Dietzel, Paul
90LSU/200*-183
DiGregorio, Ernie
73NBAPA-8
74T-135
74T-147LL
74T-149LL
74T-83M
75Carv-6
75T-45
76T-82
77T-131
91Providence-16
Dillard, Harrison
48ExhSC-13
48T/Magic*-E4
Dillard, Skip
82TCMA/CBA-46
Diller, Ken
91SC/200*-114
Dillon, John
89NC/Coke-85
Dillon, Tim
89ProC/CBA-98
91ProC/CBA-25
Dimas, Ted
90NE/Pol*-18
Dinardo, Tommy
89NCSt/Coke-79
89NCSt/Coke-80
Dingman, Dean
91MI/56*-16
Dinkins, Byron
90Hoops-123
91ProC/CBA-139
Dinwiddie, Jim
88KY/269-267
88KY/269-88
Dionne, Marcel
79Lakers/Alta-5
Dischinger, Terry
69T-33
70T-96
71T-8
72T-143
Dishman, J.A.
89KY/300*-245
Distefano, Bob
89NCSt/Coke-82
Divac, Vlade
90F-91
90F/Rook-9
90Hoops-154
90Panini-3
90SkyBox-135
91F-97
91Hoops/I-99
91Hoops/II-540
91Hoops/II-542M
91Hoops/McDon-21
91Hoops/Super-46
91Panini-16
91SkyBox/I-134
91SkyBox/I-335
91SkyBox/II-498RS
91UD-175
91UD/McDon-M2
92F-107
92Hoops/I-108
92SkyBox/I-114
92SkyBox/I-294TT
92StarPic-30FB
Divoky, Jerry
84Victoria/Pol-2
88Victoria/Pol-3
Dixon, Herb
90ProC/CBA-67
Dixon, King
91SC/200*-79
Djuricic, Zarko
80WichSt/Pol-3
Dobbs, Glenn
48ExhSC-14
Dobosz, Stan
90FLSt/200*-199
Dobras, Radenko
92Classic/DP-9
92StarPic-37
Dodd, Bobby
91GATech*-16
Dodds, Gil
48ExhSC-15
Dodge, Dedrick
90FLSt/200*-83
Doherty, Matt
89NC/Coke-128
89NC/Coke-129
89NC/Coke-62
90NC/200*-19
90NC/200*-65
90NC/Promos*-NC5
Dokes, Phillip
91OKSt*-31
Doktorczyk, Mike
89ProC/CBA-197
Dole, Melvin
91GATech*-159
Doll, Bob
48Bowman-45
Domako, Tom
89ProC/CBA-182
Domalik, Brian
88GATech/Nike-4
89GATech/Pol-9
90GATech/Pol-9
Donahue, Hugh
89NC/Coke-176
Donahue, Mark
91MI/56*-17
Donaldson, James
83Star/NBA-124
84Star/NBA-17
87F-28
88F-29
88Mavs/BLC-40
88Mavs/CardN-40
89F-34
89Hoops-189
90F-41
90Hoops-85
90Hoops/Super-23
90Panini-57
90SkyBox-63
91F-44
91Hoops/I-45
91Hoops/Super-21
91Panini-46
91SkyBox/I-59
91SkyBox/II-410GF
91UD-124
Donaldson, Mario
90ProC/CBA-47
91ProC/CBA-29
Donato, Bill
86DePaul-H9
Donnalley, Rick
90NC/200*-37
Donnelly, Carl
90AZSt/200*-188
Donnelly, Mike
90MISt/200*-136
Donnelly, Terry
90MISt/200*-199
Donoher, Don
83Dayton/Blue-6CO
Donohue, Warfield
89KY/300*-201
Donovan, Billy
91KY/BB/Double-17ACO
91Providence-22
Donovan, Paul
91AR/100*-24
Doohan, Peter
91AR/100*-30
Doolittle, James
48T/Magic*-L2
Dornbrook, Tom
89KY/300*-130
Dorow, Al
90MISt/200*-61
Dorsey, Jacky
81TCMA/CBA-85
Dossey, Bernice
48T/Magic*-H2
Dotson, Bobby
83Louville-x
88Louville/194-63
Dougherty, Lynn
92PennSt*-4
Doughton, Ged
89NC/Coke-188
Douglas, John
82TCMA/CBA-66
Douglas, Leon
78T-64
79T-126
80T-170
80T-63
Douglas, Sherman
88Syr/Rich-3
89Heat/Publix-2
90F-98
90F/Rook-10
90Heat/Publix-5
90Hoops-164
90Panini-156
90SkyBox-145
91F-107
91Hoops/I-110
91Hoops/II-475SC
91Hoops/II-516Ar
91Hoops/Super-53
91Panini-149
91SkyBox/Canada-27
91SkyBox/I-147
91UD-122
91UD/Ext-426
92Hoops/I-12
92SkyBox/I-12
Douglass, Bobby
74Nab-5
90AZSt/200*-99
Douglass, Bobby
89WI/Smok-1
Douglass, Monroe
89ProC/CBA-199
Dove, Sonny
71T-209
Dow, Marty
91Crtside-16
91StarPic-35
Downing, Steve
86IN/GreatI-25
Doyle, Mike
91SC/200*-125
Doyle, Pat
89KY/300*-62
Dozier, Terry
91SC/200*-103
91WildCard/Coll-63
Drake, Ducky
91UCLA/144-125
Draper, Ron
90ProC/CBA-142
90ProC/CBA-164
Draud, Scott
87Vanderbilt/Pol-14
Drawdy, Oswald
90Clemson/200*-143
Drechsler, David
90NC/200*-29
90NC/200*-95
Dreiling, Greg
90F/Up-U37
90Hoops-132
90SkyBox/II-387
91Hoops/II-372
91SkyBox/I-111
91UD-306
Drew, John
75T-116M
75T-134
76T-59
77T-98
78Hawks/Coke-3
78RCCola-9
78T-44
79Hawks/Majik-22
79T-118
80T-173
80T-175
80T-3
80T-41
80T-42
80T-94
81T-1
81T-44M
83Star/NBA-137
Drew, Larry
83Star/NBA-218
84Star/NBA-272
85Kings/Smok-6
85Star/NBA-75
86F-25
87F-29
89Hoops/II-329
89MO-5
90Hoops-155
90SkyBox-136
91SkyBox/I-135
91UD-104
Drewitz, Rick
89KY/300*-63
Drexler, Clyde
83Blaz/Pol-22
83Star/NBA-100
84Blaz/Franz-5
84Blaz/Pol-7
84Star/Blaz-2
84Star/NBA-165
84Star/PolASG-27
84Star/SlamD-3
85Blaz/Franz-5
85Star/Gator-4
85Star/NBA-106
85Star/SlamD-2
86Blaz/Franz-4
86F-26
87Blaz/Franz-1
87F-30
88Blaz/Franz-4
88F-92
88F/Ins-3
88Fourn-11
89Blaz/Franz-5
89F-128
89F-164M
89Hoops-190
89Hoops-69AS
90Blaz/BP-2
90Blaz/Franz-13
90F-154
90F/AS-11
90Hoops-16AS
90Hoops-245
90Hoops/CollB-3
90Hoops/II-376TC
90Hoops/Super-80
90Panini-8
90SkyBox-233
90SkyBox/Proto-233
91Blaz/Franz-10
91F-168

91F/Up-393TL
91Hoops/I-174
91Hoops/I-262AS
91Hoops/II-491SC
91Hoops/McDon-34
91Hoops/Proto/00-001
91Hoops/Super-80
91Kell/ColGrt-3
91Panini-29
91SkyBox/Canada-39
91SkyBox/I-237
91SkyBox/II-480TW
91SkyBox/II-579
91SkyBox/II-NNO
91SkyBox/Proto-237
91UD-357
91UD-53AS
91UD-98TC
91UD/Ext-463AS
92F-186
92F-250PV
92F/AS-13
92F/TmLeader-22
92Hoops/I-189
92Hoops/I-306AS
92Hoops/I-338
92SkyBox/I-201
92SkyBox/I-315
92SkyBox/Olympic-USA1

Drez, David J.
89McNees*-16

Driesell, Lefty
91JMadison/Smok-7CO

Driscoll, Terry
73T-17

Dro, Bob
87IN/GreatII-2

Drollinger, Ralph
91UCLA/144-55

Dromo, John
88Louville/194-104
88Louville/194-4
89Louville/300*-280

Dropo, Walt
91CT/Legend-3

Drucker, Jim
81TCMA/CBA-88

Drummer, Sammy
91GATech*-23

Drummond, Kenny
89ProC/CBA-189

Drysdale, Don
81T/Thirst-14

DuBose, Doug
85NE/Pol*-2

Duberman, Justin
91ND*-19M

Duckett, Ellis
90MISt/200*-33

Duckett, Richard
57Kahn's-1

Duckworth, Kevin
87Blaz/Franz-2
88Blaz/Franz-5
88F-93
89Blaz/Franz-4
89F-129
89Hoops-103
89Hoops-193AS
90Blaz/BP-3
90Blaz/Franz-14
90F-155
90Hoops-246
90Hoops/Super-82
90Panini-10
90SkyBox-234
91Blaz/Franz-11
91F-169
91Hoops/I-175
91Hoops/I-263AS
91Panini-28
91SkyBox/I-238
91UD-216
91UD-55AS
92F-187
92Hoops/I-190
92SkyBox/I-202

Dude, Little
90ProC/CBA-95

Dudley, Charles
75T-194

Dudley, Chris
90Nets/Kayo-6
90SkyBox/II-398
91F-131
91Hoops/I-135
91SkyBox/I-181
91SkyBox/II-448SM
91UD-311
92Hoops/I-148
92SkyBox/I-155

Dudley, Rickey
91OhioSt-6

Dufek, Donald
91MI/56*-18

Dufficy, Pat
91SC/200*-88

Dugas, Robert
90LSU/200*-87

Duhe, Adam
90LSU/200*-28

Duhe, Craig
90LSU/200*-60

Dukes, Walter
57T-30
61F-11
61F-50IA

Dumars, Joe
86F-27
87F-31
88F-40
89F-45
89Hoops-1
90F-55
90Hoops-103
90Hoops-3AS
90Hoops/CollB-27
90Hoops/II-362TC
90Hoops/Super-28
90Panini-86
90Piston/Star-3
90Piston/Unocal-3
90SkyBox-84
91F-59
91F/Up-379TL
91Hoops/I-250AS
91Hoops/I-60
91Hoops/II-463SC
91Hoops/McDon-12
91Hoops/Super-27
91Panini-129
91Piston/Unocal-15M
91Piston/Unocal-4
91Piston/Unocal-5
91SkyBox/Blister-6M
91SkyBox/Canada-15
91SkyBox/I-317M
91SkyBox/I-81
91SkyBox/II-565
91UD-335
91UD-61AS
91UD/Ext-459AS
92F-63
92F/AS-4
92Hoops/I-296AS
92Hoops/I-64
92SkyBox/I-69

Dumas, Mike
91Classic/DPColl*-124

Dumas, Richard
91Classic-36
91Classic/DPColl*-184
91Crtside-17
91FrRow/100-30
91FrRow/50-30
91FrRow/Premier-62
91StarPic-71
91WildCard/Coll-39

Dunbar, Bob
89Louville/300*-61

Dunbar, Karl
90LSU/200*-63

Duncan, Calvin
90ProC/CBA-17
91ProC/CBA-133AC

Duncan, Lawson
90Clemson/200*-21

Dunham, Derek
90MO-6
91MO-6

Dunlap, Robert
90SanJ/Smok-3

Dunleavy, Mike
81T-MW85
84Star/Arena-C3
84Star/NBA-128
85Star/Bucks-5
85Star/TmSuper-MB4
87Bucks/Polar-x
88Bucks/Green-16M
90Hoops/II-351CO
90Hoops/II-410CO
90SkyBox/II-313CO
91F-98CO
91Hoops/I-233CO
91SkyBox/II-390CO
92F-125CO
92Hoops/I-253CO
92SkyBox/I-269CO

Dunn, Brad
91AR25-20ACO

Dunn, David
82George/Pol-3

Dunn, Eric
91ProC/CBA-125

Dunn, T.R.
77Blaz/Pol-23
79Blaz/Pol-23
81T-W67
82Nugget/Pol-23
83Nugget/Pol-23
83Star/NBA-184
84Star/NBA-139
85Nugget/Pol-10
85Star/NBA-52
89Nugget/Pol-3
90SkyBox/II-378

Dupont, Jerry
88Louville/194-84

Dupre, Yanick
91Classic/DPColl*-41

Dupree, Billy Joe
90MISt/200*-73
90MISt/200*-92M

Duran, Ernie
85NE/Pol*-22

Durant, Mike
91Classic/DPColl*-92

Durden, Alan
90AZ/125*-26

Duren, John
91George/100-37
91George/100-5

Duren, Lonnie
91George/100-72

Durham, Hugh
90FLSt/200*-147CO
90GA/Smok-5CO

Durham, James
89KY/300*-25

Durham, Pat
90ProC/CBA-18

Durnan, Bill
48ExhSC-16

Durrant, Devin
84Star/NBA-54

Durrett, Ken
72T-134

Duryea, C.E.
48T/Magic*-N3

Dusek, Brad
91TexAM-34

Dusek, Ernie
48T/Magic*-D8

Dusek, Rudy
48T/Magic*-D9

Dutch, Al
91George/100-17
91George/100-50

Dutcher, Brian
89MI-2

Dwan, Jack
48Bowman-51

Dwyer, Richard
54Quaker-22

Dyches, Tim
91SC/200*-142

Dye, Pat
87Auburn/Pol*-1CO

Dyer, Duffy
90AZSt/200*-195

Dykes, Hart Lee
91OKSt*-17

Eackles, Ledell
89F-158
89Hoops-194
90F-191
90Hoops-296
90Panini-150
90SkyBox-287
91F-204
91Hoops/I-213
91Panini-174
91SkyBox/I-288
91SkyBox/II-458SM
91UD-382
92F-230
92Hoops/I-232
92SkyBox/I-247

Eakins, Jim
71T-197
72T-213
73T-178
74T-230M
74T-258
75T-297

Earhart, Amelia
48T/Magic*-L5

Earl, Acie
91Iowa-5

Easley, Chuck
91GATech*-19

Eastman, Ben
48T/Magic*-E3

Eaton, Mark
83Star/NBA-138
84Star/Award-19LL
84Star/CrtKg-32
84Star/NBA-225
84Star/NBA-286
85Star/NBA-141
86F-28
86Star/CrtKg-11
87F-32
88F-112
88F-131AS
88Jazz/Smok-2
89F-152
89Hoops-155
89Hoops-174AS
89Jazz/OldH-3
90F-184
90Hoops-287
90Hoops/CollB-39
90Hoops/Super-96
90Jazz/Star-3
90Panini-53
90SkyBox-276
91F-198
91Hoops/I-207
91Hoops/II-534
91Panini-83
91SkyBox/I-279
91SkyBox/II-421GF
91UD-116
91UD-82TC
92F-221
92Hoops/I-224
92SkyBox/I-239

Eaves, Jerry
81Louville/Pol-13
83Star/NBA-139
88Louville/194-116
88Louville/194-152
88Louville/194-19
88Louville/194-64
89Louville/300*-233
89Louville/300*-262
89Louville/300*-32
89Louville/300*-9

Eckert, Denise
84NE/Pol*-26

Eckwood, Stan
80TCMA/CBA-41

Eddie, Patrick
91FrRow/100-35
91FrRow/50-35
91FrRow/Premier-57

Eddleman, Dwight
52Bread-7

Eddington, Mike
90MISt/200*-177

Edelman, Ray
88KY/269-98

Edgar, John
84AZ/Pol-4
85AZ/Pol-4

Edgar, Scott
91MurraySt-14CO

Edge, Charlie
75T-269

Edge, Junior
90NC/200*-118

Edison, Thomas A.
48T/Magic*-N2

Edmonds, Bobby Joe
91AR/100*-55

Edmonson, Keith
83Star/NBA-185

Edney, Tyus
91UCLA-5

Edwards, Bryan
91JMadison/Smok-8

Edwards, Danny
91OKSt*-82

Edwards, David
89George/Pol-5
91OKSt*-64

Edwards, Dixon
91Classic/DPColl*-133

Edwards, Franklin
83Star/NBA-3
84Star/Arena-E3
85Star/NBA-90
86Kings/Smok-2

Edwards, James
78T-27
79T-113
80T-103
80T-124
80T-36
80T-54
81T-53M
81T-MW90
83Star/NBA-111

84Star/NBA-40
84Suns/Pol-53
85Star/NBA-37
86F-29
87Suns/Circ-5
89F-46
89Hoops-284A
89Hoops-284B
90F-56
90Hoops-104
90Panini-90
90Piston/Star-4
90Piston/Unocal-4
90SkyBox-85
91F-60
91F/Up-296
91Hoops/I-61
91Hoops/II-378
91Panini-126
91SkyBox/I-82
91SkyBox/II-630
91UD-338
91UD/Ext-416
92F-98
92Hoops/I-98
92SkyBox/I-103

Edwards, James
(Lum)
89Louville/300*-99

Edwards, Johnathan
85George/Pol-5
86George/Pol-5
87George/Pol-5
88George/Pol-5
89ProC/CBA-57
91George/100-42

Edwards, Kevin
89F-81
89Heat/Publix-3
89Hoops-41
90F-99
90Heat/Publix-6
90Hoops-165
90Hoops/Super-51
90Panini-152
90SkyBox-146
91F-108
91Hoops/I-111
91SkyBox/I-148
91SkyBox/II-445SM
91UD-141
92F-117
92Hoops/I-118
92SkyBox/I-125

Edwards, Leroy
88KY/269-23

Edwards, Michael
89Syr/Pep-5

Edwards, Theodore
(Blue)
90F-185
90Hoops-288
90Jazz/Star-4
90Panini-52
90SkyBox-277
91F-199
91F-227
91Hoops/I-208
91Panini-86
91SkyBox/I-280
91SkyBox/II-511RS
91SkyBox/II-580
91UD-199
92F-126
92Hoops/I-225
92SkyBox/I-240

Egan, Johnny
69T-16
70T-34
81TCMA-33
91Providence-8

Eggleston, Don
89NC/Coke-196

Eggleston, Marty
89ProC/CBA-48

Ehle, Tory
91GATech*-24

Ehlers, Eddie
48Bowman-19

Ehlo, Craig
84Star/NBA-238
89F-26
89Hoops-106
90F-32
90Hoops-74
90Panini-106
90SkyBox-51
91F-35
91Hoops/I-37
91Hoops/Super-16
91Panini-122
91SkyBox/I-48
91SkyBox/II-463TW
91UD-202
92F-41
92Hoops/I-39
92SkyBox/I-40

Eichmann, Eric
90Clemson/200*-22

Eikenberg, Dana
92PennSt*-5

Eisaman, Jerry
89KY/300*-180

Eisenhower, Dwight
48T/Magic*-O10

Eitutis, Jason
90KY/Sov-6

Ekker, Ron
89ProC/CBA-12

Elenz, Jim
79StBon-4

Elie, Mario
89ProC/CBA-109
90ProC/CBA-151
91F/Up-286
91Hoops/II-366
91SkyBox/I-89
91UD-396
92F-73
92Hoops/I-72
92SkyBox/I-77

Elkind, Steve
91UCLA-19

Elkins, Arlo
91SC/200*-50

Elkins, Rod
90NC/200*-12

Ellenberger, Norm
89UTEP/Drug-7

Ellenson, John
89WI/Smok-2

Ellery, Kevin
90NotreDame-20

Ellington, Russell
89KY/300*-202

Elliott, Bob
48T/Magic*-K3
90AZ/125*-106
90AZ/125*-97

Elliott, Chalmers
(Bump)
48ExhSC-17
91MI/56*-19

Elliott, Pete
48T/Magic*-C2
57Union-28

Elliott, Sean
85AZ/Pol-5
86AZ/Pol-4
87AZ/Pol-4
88AZ/Pol-5
90AZ/125*-110
90AZ/125*-2
90AZ/125*-38
90AZ/125*-85
90AZ/Promos*-9
90F-171
90F/Rook-2
90Hoops-267
90Panini-44
90SkyBox-256
91F-185
91Hoops/I-190
91Hoops/II-526Ar
91Hoops/McDon-40
91Panini-79
91SkyBox/I-256
91SkyBox/II-482TW
91UD-287
91Wooden-18
92F-204
92Hoops/I-207
92SkyBox/I-221

Ellis, Bill
91UCLA/144-57

Ellis, Bo
81TCMA/CBA-25

Ellis, Bob
91TexAM-11

Ellis, Cliff
89Clemson-7CO
90Clemson/200*-92
90Clemson-6CO

Ellis, Dale
83Star/NBA-53
84Star/Arena-B4
84Star/NBA-254
85Star/NBA-162
87F-33
88F-107
89F-146
89F/AS-8
89Hoops-10
89Hoops-43AS
90F-177
90Hoops-277
90Hoops/Super-89
90Panini-21
90SkyBox-266
90Sonic/Smok-5
91F-114
91Hoops/I-116
91Hoops/II-517Ar
91Panini-137
91SkyBox/I-161
91SkyBox/II-446SM
91SkyBox/II-592SS
91UD-266
92F-205
92Hoops/I-126
92SkyBox/I-133

Ellis, Harold
92StarPic-88

Ellis, James
90MISt/200*-10

Ellis, Jim
89ProC/CBA-195

Ellis, Joe
69T-57
70T-28
71T-51
72T-14
73T-171

Ellis, LaPhonso
90NotreDame-23
92Classic/DP-47
92Classic/DPLP-LP5
92FrRow/DreamPk-91
92FrRow/DreamPk-92
92FrRow/DreamPk-93
92FrRow/DreamPk-94
92FrRow/DreamPk-95
92StarPic-33KC
92StarPic-69
92StarPic-89

Ellis, LeRon
88KY/Award-10
88KY/Award-14
89KY/Tm80-51
89Syr/Pep-2
91Classic-14
91Classic/DPColl*-162
91Crtside-18
91F/Up-297
91FrRow/100-27
91FrRow/50-27
91FrRow/Premier-66
91StarPic-54
91WildCard/Coll-2

Ellis, Leroy
69T-42
70T-35
70T/Ins-9
71T-111
71T/Ins-20
72T-157
72T-18
73T-34
74T-111
74T-94M
75T-104
81TCMA-27

Ellis, Phil
89Louville/300*-155

Ellis, Robert
90MISt/200*-156

Ellis, Ron
92Classic/DP-92

Ellis, Rudy
81Louville/Pol-18DIR

Ellis, Todd
91SC/200*-2
91SC/200*-44

Ellis, Zarko
89Louville/300*-193

Ellison, Janet
90Clemson/200*-198

Ellison, Pervis
87KY/Coke-17
89Kings/Carl-42
89Louville/300*-206
89Louville/300*-253
89Louville/300*-290
89Louville/300*-4
89Louville/300*-41
90F-164
90F/Up-U97
90Hoops-257
90Hoops/II-438
90SkyBox-246
90SkyBox/II-419
90StarPic-50
91F-205
91Hoops/I-214
91SkyBox/I-289
91UD-385
92F-231
92F/TmLeader-27
92Hoops/I-233
92SkyBox/I-248
92SkyBox/I-308TT

Ellison, Shawn
90CT/Pol-5

Elmendorf, Dave
91TexAM-95

Elmore, Len
75T-259
76T-71
83Star/NBA-63

Elston, Darrell
75T-308
89NC/Coke-144
90NC/200*-165

Embry, Marty
91WildCard/Coll-41

Embry, Randy
88KY/269-83

Embry, Wayne
59Kahn's-2
60Kahn's-4
61F-12
61Kahn's-4
62Kahn's-3
63Kahn's-4
64Kahn's-6
65Kahn's-1

Emerzian, Bryan
88UNLV/HOF-12
89UNLV/HOF-11
89UNLV/Seven-6
90UNLV/HOF-7
90UNLV/Season-7
90UNLV/Smok-5

Emmons, Mori
84NE/Pol*-24

Engelbert, Pat
91NE/Pol*-2

Engelland, Chip
89ProC/CBA-78
91ProC/CBA-188

Engen, Alf
57Union-10

England, Kenny
89KY/300*-203

Englehardt, Dan
89NCSt/Coke-83
89NCSt/Coke-84

Engler, Chris
83Star/NBA-256

English, A.J.
90F/Up-U98
90StarPic-46
91F-206
91Hoops/I-215
91SkyBox/I-290
91UD-387
92F-232
92Hoops/I-234
92SkyBox/I-249

English, Alex
77Bucks/ActPh-4
79T-31
80T-107
80T-19
81T-W68
82Nugget/Pol-2
83Nugget/Pol-2
83Star/ASG-15
83Star/ASG-x
83Star/NBA-186
84Star/ASG-18
84Star/CrtKg-22
84Star/NBA-137
84Star/PolASG-18
85Nugget/Pol-1
85Star/NBA-50
86F-30
86F/Ins-4
86Star/CrtKg-12
87F-34
87F/Ins-11
88F-34
88F/Ins-4
88Fourn-19
88Nugget/Pol-2A
88Nugget/Pol-2B
89F-40
89Hoops-120
89Hoops-133AS
89Nugget/Pol-4
90F-48
90F/Up-U19
90Hoops-94
90Hoops/II-407
90Hoops/Super-26

90SkyBox-74
90SkyBox/II-375
91Hoops/I-315MS
91Panini-49
91SC/200*-3
91SC/200*-35
English, Claude
71T-46
English, Jo Jo
92Classic/DP-79
Enright, Rex
91SC/200*-71
Ensminger, Steve
90LSU/200*-185
Ensor, Ken
83AZ/Pol-6
Epley, Frank
89Louville/300*-28
Eppley, Mike
90Clemson/200*-25
Erhardt, Herb
86SWLou/Pol*-5
Erickson, Edward
90MISt/200*-54
Erickson, Keith
69T-29
70T-38
71T-61
72T-140
73T-117
73T-68M
74T-53
75Suns-5
75T-113
75T-130M
76Suns-3
76T-4
91UCLA/144-132
Erickson, Ken
90AZ/125*-80
Ernst, Vinny
91Providence-10
Errol, Leon
48T/Magic*-J25
Erving, Julius
72T-195
72T-255AS
72T-263LL
73T-204M
73T-234LL
73T-240AS
74T-200AS
74T-207LL
74T-226M
75T-221LL
75T-282M
75T-300AS
76T-1
76T-127AS
77Dell-3
77Pep/AS-3
77T-100
78RCCola-10
78T-130
79T-20
80T-1
80T-137
80T-142
80T-146
80T-176
80T-23
80T-51
80T-6
81T-30
81T-59M
81T-E104
83Star/ASG-1
83Star/ASG-26
83Star/ASG-4
83Star/NBA-1
83Star/Sixers-10
83Star/Sixers-18
83Star/Sixers-22
83Star/Sixers-24
83Star/Sixers-4
84Star/Arena-E1
84Star/ASG-4
84Star/CrtKg-4
84Star/Erving-1
84Star/Erving-10
84Star/Erving-11
84Star/Erving-12
84Star/Erving-13
84Star/Erving-14
84Star/Erving-15
84Star/Erving-16
84Star/Erving-17
84Star/Erving-18
84Star/Erving-2
84Star/Erving-3
84Star/Erving-4
84Star/Erving-5
84Star/Erving-6
84Star/Erving-7
84Star/Erving-8
84Star/Erving-9
84Star/NBA-204
84Star/NBA-281
84Star/PolASG-28
84Star/PolASG-4
84Star/SlamD-4
85JMS-5
85Star/Crunch-3
85Star/Gator-5
85Star/LiteAS-3
85Star/NBA-3
85Star/SlamD-3
85Star/TmSuper-PS1
86F-31
86F/Ins-5
86Star/Best-6
86Star/CrtKg-13
87F-35
Ervins, Ricky
90SoCal/Smok*-3
91Classic/DPColl*-205
Escarlega, Kathy
90AZSt/200*-127
Esherick, Craig
91George/100-21
91George/100-90
Espeland, Gene
89ProC/CBA-113
Esposito, Phil
74Nab-11
75Nab-11
Essensa, Bob
90MISt/200*-137
Estay, Ronnie
90LSU/200*-126
Estes, Joel
90AZ/125*-82
Estes, Shawn
91Classic/DPColl*-58
Etzler, Doug
91OhioSt-7
Eubanks, Kurt
84NE/Pol*-23
Evans, Bill
88KY/269-37
Evans, Bryon
90AZ/125*-109
90AZ/125*-55
Evans, Dena
91VA/Lady-4
Evans, Dwayne
90AZSt/200*-126
Evans, Jamal
91MurraySt-5
Evans, Mike
79Spurs/Pol-1
82TCMA/CBA-13
83Nugget/Pol-5
83Star/NBA-187
84Star/NBA-140
85Nugget/Pol-2
85Star/NBA-53
87F-36
Evans, Paul
89Pitt/Food-x
Evans, Peter
90AZ/125*-22
Evans, Rob
91OKSt-23ACO
Evans, William
55Ash-19
Everett, J.C.
89KY/300*-204
Everett, Jimmy
90FLSt/200*-115
Evers, Johnny
48T/Magic*-K18
Everson, Greg
91MI/56*-20
Ewing, Patrick
81George/Pol-4
82George/Pol-2
83George/Pol-10
84George/Pol-4
85Prism-2
85Star/NBA-166
86F-32
86F/Ins-6
86Star/Best-1
86Star/CrtKg-14
87F-37
88F-130AS
88F-80
88F/Ins-5
88Fourn-15
88Knick/FrLay-2
89F-100
89F-167M
89F/AS-7
89Hoops-159AS
89Hoops-80
89Knicks/Marine-2
90F-125
90F/AS-12
90Hoops-203
90Hoops-4AS
90Hoops/CollB-15
90Hoops/II-372TC
90Hoops/II-388
90Hoops/Super-67
90Panini-140
90Panini-IAS
90SkyBox-187
91F-136
91F-215
91F/ProV-4
91F/Up-389TL
91George/100-2
91George/100-30
91George/100-31
91George/100-49
91George/100-55
91George/100-77
91Hoops/I-140
91Hoops/I-251AS
91Hoops/II-483SC
91Hoops/II-577
91Hoops/McDon-26
91Hoops/McDon-53USA
91Hoops/Proto/00-002
91Hoops/Super-65
91Panini-163
91Panini-189AS
91Panini-99AS
91SkyBox/I-189
91SkyBox/II-476TW
91SkyBox/II-532US
91UD-343
91UD-68AS
91UD/Ext-455AS
91WildCard/Coll-15
92F-150
92F/AS-5
92F/TmLeader-18
92Hoops/I-153
92Hoops/I-297AS
92Hoops/I-333
92Hoops/I-339
92SkyBox/I-161
92SkyBox/I-299TT
92SkyBox/Olympic-USA8
92SkyBox/USA-103
92SkyBox/USA-19
92SkyBox/USA-20
92SkyBox/USA-21
92SkyBox/USA-22
92SkyBox/USA-23
92SkyBox/USA-24
92SkyBox/USA-25
92SkyBox/USA-26
92SkyBox/USA-27
Ezenwa, Francis
89UTEP/Drug-8
Fabregas, Jorge
91Classic/DPColl*-80
Faggins, Terry
89ProC/CBA-142
Fahs, Dave
90MISt/200*-160
Fair, Brian
91CT/Pol-5
Falcon, Joe
91AR/100*-45
Falloon, Pat
91Classic/DPColl*-2
Fannin, Omar
55Ash-51
Fanuzzi, Mike
89KY/300*-150
Farley, Dick
87IN/GreatII-29
Farmer, Jackie
90Clemson/Lady-4
Farmer, Jim
89Hoops-227
89Hoops/II-334
89ProC/CBA-58
Farmer, Larry
91UCLA/144-4
91UCLA/144-92
Farmer, Mike
60Kahn's-5
Farmer, Richie
88KY/Award-4
88KY/Sov-8
89KY/Award-20
90KY/BB/DT/AW-28
91KY/BB-3
91KY/BB/Double-3
Farmer, Tony
91Classic-50
91Classic/DPColl*-198
91Crtside-19
91FrRow/100-17
91FrRow/50-17
91FrRow/Premier-78
91ProC/CBA-113
91StarPic-36
Farnsley, Keith
89KY/300*-71
Farr, Heather
90AZSt/200*-63
Farr, James
90Clemson/200*-62
Farragut, David
48T/Magic*-O5
Farrell, John
91OKSt*-88
Farrell, Jon
91Classic/DPColl*-70
Farrell, Lon
91AR/100*-33
Farris, Monty
91OKSt*-75
Farris, Ray
90NC/200*-167
Fatheree, Jess
90LSU/200*-17
Faucette, Floyd
91GATech*-187
Faught, Robert
90NotreDame-40
Faulk, Steve
90LSU/200*-194
Favre, Brett
91Classic/DPColl*-129
Favrot, Ron
91AR/100*-29
Federspiel, Joe
89KY/300*-139
Fedor, Dave
90FLSt/200*-194
Feerick, Bob
48Bowman-6
Feggins, Bryant
89NCSt/Pol-3
90NCSt/IBM-3
91NCSt/IBM-3
Feher, Butch
76Suns-4
Feitl, Dave
91Hoops/II-399
Feldhaus, Allen
89KY/300*-15
Feldhaus, Deron
88KY/Award-12
89KY/Award-22
89KY/Award-24
89KY/Award-28
89KY/Award-33
90KY/BB/DT/AW-33
91KY/BB-4
91KY/BB/Double-2
Felix, Ray
54Bullet/Gunth-4
57T-35
61Lakers/Bell-2
81TCMA-12
Fellmuth, Catherine
54Quaker-8
Felton, George
91SC/200*-15
Fenimore, Bob
91OKSt*-15
Fenlon, Terry
91George/100-73
Fenwick, Jack
90FLSt/200*-112
Ferguson, Chip
90FLSt/200*-38
Ferguson, Joe
91AR/100*-86
Fernandez, Gigi
90Clemson/200*-195
Fernsten, Eric
83Star/NBA-64
Ferrari, Albert R.
61Hawks/Essex-2
90MISt/200*-109
Ferreira, Rolando
88Blaz/Franz-6
Ferrell, Duane
90SkyBox-2
91GATech*-35
91Hoops/II-332
91SkyBox/I-2
91SkyBox/II-432SM
91UD-274
92F-2
92Hoops/I-3

92SkyBox/I-3
Ferrer, Jim
89ProC/CBA-106
Ferrier, James
48Kell*-12
Ferrin, Arnold
52Bread-8
Ferry, Danny
87Duke/Pol-35
88Duke/Pol-6
90F-33
90Hoops-336
90Hoops/II-406
90SkyBox-300
90SkyBox/II-374
90StarPic-10
91F-36
91FrRow/100-97
91FrRow/ItalPromo-3
91FrRow/Premier-92FB
91Hoops/I-38
91Panini-124
91SkyBox/I-49
91SkyBox/II-490RS
91UD-237
91UD/Rook-18
92Hoops/I-40
92SkyBox/I-41
Fest, Fred
89KY/300*-247
Ficke, Bill
82Nugget/Pol-x
83Nugget/Pol-x
Field, Jimmy
90LSU/200*-181
Fields, Andy
91WildCard/Coll-27
Fields, Eddie
91MurraySt-16ACO
Fields, Kenny
84Star/NBA-129
85Star/Bucks-6
86Star/LifeBucks-5
89ProC/CBA-131
91UCLA/144-49
Fields, Rick
82INSt/Pol*-6
Figaro, Kevin
82TCMA/CBA-68
Finch, Larry
74T-215
74T-225M
75T-281M
Finkel, Henry
68Rocket/Jack-5
69T-34
70T-27
71T-18
73T-66M
73T-94
74T-118
75T-26
Finn, John
90AZSt/200*-74
Finnegan, Tommy
88Louville/194-92
Finzier, Herman
90AZSt/200*-112
Fiorentino, Tony
89Heat/Publix-4CO
90Heat/Publix-16CO
Fischer, Bill
48T/Magic*-C5
Fish, Matt
92Classic/DP-82
92StarPic-17
Fisher, Casey
87SoMiss-3
Fisher, Roy
91Crtside-20
91ProC/CBA-98
91StarPic-68
Fisher, Scott
89ProC/CBA-200
Fisher, Steve
89MI-1CO
Fitch, Bill
89Hoops/II-327CO
90Hoops-321CO
90Nets/Kayo-13CO
90SkyBox/II-317CO
91F-132CO
91Hoops/I-237CO
91SkyBox/II-394CO
Fitzpatrick, Terry
87SWLou/McDag*-9
Fitzsimmons, Bob
48T/Magic*-A4
Fitzsimmons, Cotton
85Star/CO-3
89Hoops-14CO
90Hoops-325CO
90SkyBox/II-321CO
91F-159CO
91Hoops/I-241CO
91SkyBox/II-398CO
Flagler, Terrance
90Clemson/200*-39
Flanagan, Kevin
89AZ/Pol-3
Flannery, John
91Classic/DPColl*-140
Fleetwood, Mark
91SC/200*-131
Fleisher, Larry
91StarPic-30
Fleming, Al
90AZ/125*-64
Fleming, Ed
57T-79
Fleming, Reg
74Nab-13
Fleming, Vern
84Star/NBA-196
84Star/NBA-55
85Star/NBA-83
85Star/RTm-6
86F-33
87F-38
88F-55
89F-64
89Hoops-231
90F-76
90Hoops-133
90Hoops/Super-39
90Panini-114
90SkyBox-114
91F-81
91Hoops/I-83
91Hoops/II-558
91Panini-135
91SkyBox/I-112
91SkyBox/II-557US
91UD-238
92F-89
92Hoops/I-90
92SkyBox/I-95
Fletcher, Adam
90NCSt/IBM-4
91NCSt/IBM-4
Fletcher, Clyde
91AR25-6
Fletcher, Ralph
89NC/Coke-186
Fleury, Pascal
91George/Pol-8
Floreal, Errick
91AR/100*-14
Florent, Kevin
87South/Pol*-9
Flowers, Bill
91GATech*-169
Flowers, Bruce
90NotreDame-46
Flowers, Kenny
90Clemson/200*-73
Floyd, Charlie
81TCMA/CBA-46
82TCMA/CBA-45
82TCMA/Lanc-16
82TCMA/Lanc-17
Floyd, Cliff
91Classic/DPColl*-61
Floyd, Eric
(Sleepy)
81George/Pol-10
83Star/NBA-257
84Star/NBA-154
85Star/NBA-134
86F-34
87F-39
88F-51
89F-59
89Hoops-117
90F-70
90Hoops-124
90Hoops/Super-35
90Panini-71
90SkyBox-107
91F-74
91George/100-3
91George/100-51
91George/100-64
91Hoops/I-75
91Hoops/Super-35
91SkyBox/I-101
91SkyBox/II-441SM
91UD-252
92F-80
92Hoops/I-81
92SkyBox/I-86
Floyd, James
55Ash-6
Floyd, Kevin
84George/Pol-5
Floyd, Norman
91SC/200*-165
Flynn, Doug
87KY/Coke-5
Flynn, Mike
88KY/269-103
88KY/269-141
Flynn, Ray
91Providence-11
Fogle, Larry
80TCMA/CBA-23
81TCMA/CBA-81
Fogler, Eddie
89NC/Coke-112
89NC/Coke-113
90NC/200*-47CO
Foley, Shane
90SoCal/Smok*-4
Fontaine, Joan
48T/Magic*-F8
Fontaine, Levi
71T-92
Fontenet, B.B.
82TCMA/CBA-26
Fonville, Charlie
48T/Magic*-E12
Ford, Chris
73T-79
74T-112
75T-47
76T-29
77T-121
78T-15
79T-124
80T-67
80T-97
81T-E73
90Hoops-306CO
90Hoops/II-347CO
90SkyBox/II-302CO
91F-10CO
91Hoops/I-222CO
91Hoops/I-260AS
91SkyBox/II-379CO
92F-13CO
92Hoops/I-240CO
92SkyBox/I-256CO
Ford, Danny
90Clemson/200*-133
Ford, Don
77T-43
79Lakers/Alta-2
79T-77
80T-11
80T-99
89ProC/CBA-127
91ProC/CBA-10ACO
Ford, Gerald
91MI/56*-21
Ford, Jake
70Sonic/Sunb-4
71Sonic/Sunb-3
Ford, Jeff
91GATech*-188
Ford, Ken
91TexAM-69
Ford, Phil
79T-108
80T-128
80T-129
80T-40
80T-41
81T-18
81T-54M
83Star/NBA-75
85Star/ROY-7
89NC/Coke-10
89NC/Coke-11
89NC/Coke-12
89NC/Coke-63
89NC/Coke-7
89NC/Coke-8
89NC/Coke-9
90NC/200*-111
90NC/200*-185CO
90NC/200*-7
91Wooden-8
92Crtside/ColFB-9
Ford, Randall
89Louville/300*-58
Ford, Rick
86IN/GreatI-15
Ford, Travis
88KY/Sov-9
89MO-6
91KY/BB-14
91KY/BB/Double-8
Forman, Jane
90Clemson/200*-175
Forrest, Bayard
77Suns/Discs-35
Forrest, Derrick
89Clemson-8
90Clemson/200*-97
Forrest, Donna
90Clemson/Lady-5
Forrest, James
91GATech/Pol-7
Forrest, Manuel
81Louville/Pol-15
83Louville-30
88Louville/194-100
88Louville/194-115
88Louville/194-151
88Louville/194-18
89Louville/300*-10
89Louville/300*-275
89Louville/300*-48
Forsberg, Peter
91Classic/DPColl*-5
Fortier, Bill
90LSU/200*-43
Foster, Barry
91AR/100*-95
Foster, Bill
90Clemson/200*-114
Foster, Fred
70T-53
72T-66
73T-56
75T-29
Foster, Greg
89UTEP/Drug-9
90F/Up-U99
90StarPic-57
91Hoops/II-445
Foster, Harold E.
68HOF-12
Foster, Michael
91SC/200*-128
Foster, Rod
83Star/NBA-112
84Star/NBA-41
84Suns/Pol-10
91UCLA/144-61
Foster, Shelia
91SC/200*-198
Foucade, Katia
91WA/Viacom-11
Fournet, Sid
90LSU/200*-110
Foust, Larry
57T-18
61Hawks/Essex-3
81TCMA-2
Fowler, Bob
89KY/300*-289
Fowler, Larry
90MISt/200*-2
Fox, Jim
68Suns/Carn-1
69Suns/Carn-2
69T-88
70T-98
71T-3
72T-34
73Sonic/Shur-4
73T-24
74T-34
75T-164
Fox, Reggie
90ProC/CBA-163
Fox, Rick
87NC/Pol-44
88NC/Pol-44
88NC/Pol-x
90KY/BB/DT/AW-22
91Classic-16
91Classic/DPColl*-164
91Crtside-21
91F/Up-248
91FrRow/100-3
91FrRow/100-40
91FrRow/50-3
91FrRow/50-40
91FrRow/Premier-65
91FrRow/Premier-8HL
91StarPic-69
91UD/Ext-443TP
91UD/Rook-23
91WildCard/Coll-19
91WildCard/RHRook-9
92F-14
92F/Rook-4
92FrRow/DreamPk-36
92FrRow/DreamPk-37
92FrRow/DreamPk-38
92FrRow/DreamPk-39
92FrRow/DreamPk-40
92Hoops/I-13

92SkyBox/I-13
Foxworth, Eric
87South/Pol*-15
Frain, Todd
85NE/Pol*-6
Fraler, Harold
55Ash-7
Francewar, Kevin
89ProC/CBA-118
Francis, Clarence
(Bevo)
81T/Thirst-28
Francis, George Jr.
55Ash-8
Francis, James
87Baylor/Pol*-13
Francona, Terry
90AZ/125*-8
Frank, Tellis
89Heat/Publix-5
90Hoops-166
90Panini-153
90SkyBox-147
91Hoops/II-396
Franklin, Benjamin
48T/Magic*-N4
Franz, Ron
71Flor/McDon-3
71T-172
Fraser, Bruce
84AZ/Pol-5
85AZ/Pol-6
86AZ/Pol-5
Fraser, Ron
90FLSt/200*-134
Fratello, Mike
78Hawks/Coke-4CO
79Hawks/Majik-x
87Hawks/Pizza-1CO
89Hoops-179CO
Frawley, William
48T/Magic*-J27
Frazier, Derrick
91SC/200*-192
Frazier, Jadie
88Louville/194-50
Frazier, Lamont
90MO-7
91MO-7
Frazier, Mike
91George/100-39
Frazier, Raymond
55Ash-40
Frazier, Ricky
91MO-8
Frazier, Walt
69T-98
69T/Ins-17
70T-106AS
70T-120
70T-6LL
70T/Ins-1
71T-65
71T/Ins-25
72Icee-7
72T-165AS
72T-60
73T-10AS
73T-68M
74T-150AS
74T-93M
75Carv-7
75T-128M
75T-55AS
75T-6M
76Buck-7
76T-64
77T-129
78RCCola-11
78T-83
81TCMA-30
85Star/Schick-11
92CenterCrt-10
Frederick, Anthony
90ProC/CBA-102
91Hoops/II-342
91UD/Ext-432
Fredrick, Joe
90ProC/CBA-45
Fredrick, Zam
91SC/200*-181
91SC/200*-26
Free, Lloyd
76T-143
77T-18
78Clipp/Handy-5
78T-116
79T-40AS
80T-121
80T-134
80T-156
80T-59
80T-61
80T-62
80T-8
80T-89
81T-13
81T-51M
83Star/NBA-228
84Star/CrtKg-8
84Star/NBA-217
85Star/NBA-152
86F-35
Freeman, Donnie
71T-220
71T/Ins-9A
72T-190
72T-252AS
73T-254
74T-253
75T-263
Freeman, Ron
90AZSt/200*-148
French, James
91WA/TCI-3
Frieder, Bill
88MI/Nike-2CO
Friend, Larry
57T-47
Fritsche, Jim
54Bullet/Gunth-5
Frost, Jed
90MO-8
91MO-9
Fruge, Gene
90SoCal/Smok*-5
Frye, Jim
89NC/Coke-198
Fryer, Bernie
74T-3
75T-36
Fryer, Jeff
90ProC/CBA-153
91ProC/CBA-177
Fryer, Mark
91SC/200*-127
Fucci, Dominic
89KY/300*-196
Fuentes, Mike
90FLSt/200*-127
Fuglar, Max
90LSU/200*-156
Fulcher, David
90AZSt/200*-36
Fulks, Joe
48Bowman-34
48ExhSC-18
52Bread-9
52Royal-5
Fuller, Eddie
90LSU/200*-90
Fuller, J.D.
91SC/200*-171
Fuller, Steve
90Clemson/200*-141M
90Clemson/200*-7
Fuller, Tony
81TCMA/CBA-14
90UCLA-37CO
91UCLA-11CO
Fulmer, Lacey
79StBon-5
Fulton, Ed
90FLSt/200*-54
Fulton, Phil
90MISt/200*-74
Fulton, Robert
48T/Magic*-N6
Funchess, Carlos
91FrRow/100-62
91FrRow/Premier-35
Funderburke, Lawrence
91OhioSt-8
Furlong, Shirley
91TexAM-3
Furlow, Terry
90MISt/200*-171
Furman, Terri
84NE/Pol*-13
Furtado, Frank
78Sonic/Pol-14
79Sonic/Pol-12
83Sonic/Pol-2
Futch, Gary
90FLSt/200*-102
Futch, Greg
90FLSt/200*-197
Gabbard, Steve
90FLSt/200*-4
Gable, Clark
48T/Magic*-F1
Gabriel, Roman
74Nab-4
Gaddy, James
90GATech/Pol-10
91GATech/Pol-8
Gage, Bobby
90Clemson/200*-178
Gain, Bob
89KY/300*-111
Gainer, Herb
90FLSt/200*-6
Gaines, Corey
89ProC/CBA-74
90ProC/CBA-186
90SkyBox/II-379
91ProC/CBA-116
Gaines, Reginald
82TCMA/Lanc-24
Gaines, Rowdy
87Auburn/Pol*-15
Gainey, James
55Ash-65
Gaiser, Jake
89KY/300*-205
Gajan, Hokie
90LSU/200*-153
Gale, Mike
73T-220
74T-191
76T-141
77T-79
78T-37
79Spurs/Pol-12
79T-122
80T-140
80T-50
Galento, Tony
48T/Magic*-D14
Gallagher, Chad
91Classic-22
91Classic/DPColl*-170
91Crtside-22
91FrRow/100-20
91FrRow/50-20
91FrRow/Premier-75
91StarPic-34
91WildCard/Coll-35
Gallagher, Ed
91OKSt*-12
Gallagher, Mark
91George/100-67
Gallatin, Harry
52Bread-10
57T-62
92CenterCrt-5
Gallon, Ricky
88Louville/194-126
88Louville/194-164
88Louville/194-34
89Louville/300*-18
89Louville/300*-274
Galy, Andy
87LSU/Pol*-14
Gambee, Dave
61F-13
70T-154
Gamble, Gary
89KY/300*-221
Gamble, Kevin
89Hoops/II-338
90F/Up-U8
90Hoops-40
90SkyBox-15
91F-11
91Hoops/I-11
91Panini-145
91SkyBox/I-14
91UD-170
92F-15
92Hoops/I-14
92SkyBox/I-14
Gamble, Phil
91CT/Legend-4
Gambrell, Billy
91SC/200*-81
Gamez, Robert
90AZ/125*-6
Ganakas, Gus
90MISt/200*-191
Gannon, Terry
89NCSt/Coke-171
89NCSt/Coke-180
Garabaldi, Gino
48T/Magic*-D20
Gardner, Chris
91ND*-2M
Gardner, Ellis
91GATech*-51
Gardner, Moe
91Classic/DPColl*-220
Garfinkel, Jack
48Bowman-30
Garland, Gary
86DePaul-D4
Garland, Winston
88F-46
88Warr/Smok-1
89F-53
89Hoops-294
90Clip/Star-2
90F-85
90Hoops-143
90SkyBox-125
91F/Up-275
91Hoops/I-91
91Hoops/II-357
91SkyBox/I-123
91SkyBox/II-624
91UD-40
91UD/Ext-486
92F-55
92Hoops/I-55
92SkyBox/I-59
Garlington, John
90LSU/200*-130
Garmaker, Dick
57T-23
Garner, Patrick
87South/Pol*-6
Garnett, Bill
83Star/NBA-54
84Star/Arena-B5
84Star/NBA-56
85Star/NBA-84
Garnett, Bret
86SWLou/Pol*-6
87SWLou/McDag*-7
Garnica, Jeff
90NC/200*-45
Garrett, Bill
87IN/GreatII-38
Garrett, Calvin
82TCMA/CBA-5
83Lakers/BASF-3
83Star/NBA-16
Garrett, Carla
90AZ/125*-61
Garrett, Chris
91NE/Pol*-8
Garrett, Dick
70T-85
71T-67
72T-108
73T-77
Garrett, Lionel
82TCMA/CBA-89
Garrett, Rowland
75T-42
90FLSt/200*-123
Garrick, Tom
89Hoops-91
90Clip/Star-3
90Hoops-144
90SkyBox-126
91Hoops/II-434
Garris, John
83Star/NBA-232
Garrison, Lon
57Union-44
Garrison, Walt
91OKSt*-13
Garvey, Steve
90MISt/200*-105
90MISt/200*-107
90MISt/200*-176
90MISt/200*-66M
90MISt/Promos*-2
Gast, Darrell
91GATech*-27
Gastevich, Vladimir
55Ash-26
88Louville/194-31
Gates, Brent
91Classic/DPColl*-72
Gates, William
(Pop)
92CenterCrt-6
Gathers, Hank
89UNLV/HOF-12M
89UNLV/HOF-6M
Gatling, Chris
91Classic-10
91Classic/DPColl*-158
91Crtside-23
91FrRow/100-14
91FrRow/50-14
91FrRow/Premier-101
91StarPic-25
91UD-9
91WildCard/Coll-86
92Hoops/I-73
92SkyBox/I-78
Gatti, Bill
89Louville/300*-179

Gattison, Kenny
89ProC/CBA-39
90Hoops-53
90SkyBox/II-368
91F/Up-253
91Hoops/II-343
91SkyBox/I-26
91UD-329
92F-23
92Hoops/I-21
92SkyBox/I-21
Gaubatz, Dennis
90LSU/200*-112
Gauden, Edward
48ExhSC-19
Gault, Jim
90AZ/125*-54
Gaunce, Donnie
55Ash-52
Gauntlett, Tom
89NC/Coke-159
Gavitt, Dave
91Providence-2CO
Gaze, Andrew
91WildCard/Coll-47
92Crtside/ColFB-10
Gee, Sam
86IN/GreatI-18
Gehrig, Lou
48T/Magic*-K14
Geiger, Matt
89GATech/Pol-10
90GATech/Pol-13
91GATech/Pol-9
92Classic/DP-30
92StarPic-8
Gemberling, Brian
90GATech/Pol-14
Gent, Pete
90MISt/200*-130
Gentry, Gary
90AZSt/200*-185
George, John
(Jack)
57T-67
81TCMA-40M
George, Tate
90F/Up-U61
90Nets/Kayo-7
90StarPic-28
91CT/Legend-5
91F/Up-323
91Hoops/II-400
91SkyBox/I-182
91UD-336
92SkyBox/I-156
George, Tony
82Fairf-5
Georgeson, Mark
87AZ/Pol-5
88AZ/Pol-6
Gerard, Gus
75T-241
Geronimo
48T/Magic*-S6
Gervin, Derrick
89ProC/CBA-120
90Hoops-196
90Nets/Kayo-8
90SkyBox-179
91UD-384
Gervin, George
74T-196
74T-227M
75T-233
75T-284M
76T-68
77T-73
78RCCola-12
78T-20
79Spurs/Pol-44
79T-1
80T-122
80T-154
80T-161
80T-58
80T-70
80T-73
81T-37
81T-62
81T-MW106
83Star/ASG-16
83Star/NBA-241
84Star/ASG-19
84Star/CrtKg-25
84Star/NBA-67
84Star/PolASG-19
85Star/Crunch-9
85Star/LiteAS-10
85Star/NBA-121
86F-36
86Star/Best-7
86Star/CrtKg-15
Gettelfinger, Chris
78KY/Food-18
79KY/Food-5
89KY/300*-67
Geyer, Scott
90AZ/125*-44
Gianelli, John
73T-162
74T-79
75Carv-8
75T-128M
75T-141
76T-117
77Bucks/ActPh-5
77T-31
78T-101
79T-37
Gibbs, Dick
73Sonic/Shur-5
74T-106
Gibbs, James
80WichSt/Pol-4
Gibson, Bob
81T/Thirst-3
Gibson, Cheryl
90AZSt/200*-199
Gibson, Cheyenne
90ProC/CBA-34
Gibson, Don
90SoCal/Smok*-6
Gibson, James
(Hoot)
91TexAM-21
Gibson, Kirk
90MISt/200*-49
90MISt/200*-53
90MISt/200*-66M
90MISt/200*-76
90MISt/200*-98
90MISt/Promos*-7
Gibson, Michael
83Star/NBA-208
Gibson, Mickey
89KY/300*-26
Gibson, Stu
89Louville/300*-164
Gibson, Vince
89Louville/300*-137
Giddings, Erv
81TCMA/CBA-73
82TCMA/CBA-85
Gifford, Frank
57Union-30
Gil, Benji
91Classic/DPColl*-65
Gilb, Elmer
89KY/300*-206
Gilbert, Dave
88Louville/194-147
88Louville/194-91
Gilder, Bob
90AZSt/200*-116
Giles, Chris
82TCMA/CBA-27
Giles, John
89Louville/300*-183
Gill, Amory T.
68HOF-13
Gill, Kendall
90F/Up-U11
90Hoops/II-394LS
90SkyBox/II-356LP
90StarPic-45
91F-20
91F-232
91F/Rook-4
91Hoops/I-21
91Hoops/II-454SC
91Panini-112
91Panini-186AR
91SkyBox/Canada-5
91SkyBox/I-27
91SkyBox/I-321AR
91SkyBox/II-461TW
91SkyBox/II-488RS
91UD-321
91UD-39ART
91UD/Rook-3
92F-24
92Hoops/I-22
92SkyBox/I-22
92SkyBox/I-284TT
92StarPic-50FB
Gill, Slats
57Union-36
Gillard, Bryant
91SC/200*-122
Gillery, Ben
86George/Pol-6
87George/Pol-6
88Kings/Carl-50
91George/100-18
Gilliam, Armon
88F-89
89F-120
89Hoops-64
90F-19
90F/Up-U70
90Hoops-54
90Panini-83
90SkyBox-29
91F-153
91Hoops/I-159
91Hoops/Proto-159
91Panini-172
91SkyBox/I-214
91UD-390
92F-169
92Hoops/I-173
92SkyBox/I-182
Gilliam, Herm
69T-87
70T-73
71T-123
72T-113
73T-106
74T-5
75T-43
76T-87
Gilliam, John
74Nab-6
75Nab-6
Gillon, Jack
91SC/200*-106
Gilmore, Artis
72T-180
72T-251AS
72T-260LL
72T-263LL
73T-207M
73T-235LL
73T-238LL
73T-250AS
74T-180AS
74T-211LL
74T-224M
75T-222LL
75T-225LL
75T-250AS
75T-280M
75T-310
76T-25
77Bulls/WhHen-2
77T-115
78RCCola-13
78T-73
79Bulls/Pol-53
79T-25
80T-109
80T-134
80T-17
80T-59
81T-46M
81T-7
81T-MW107
83Star/ASG-17
83Star/ASG-x
83Star/NBA-244
84Star/Award-14LL
84Star/CrtKg-34
84Star/NBA-64
85Star/NBA-145
86F-37
87F-40
90Bulls/Eq-5
92Crtside/ColFB-11
Gilmore, George
92StarPic-57
Gilmore, Sharon
91SC/200*-97
Gilmur, Charles
48Bowman-31
52Bread-11
Gipple, Dale
89NC/Coke-171
Gipson, Al
89ProC/CBA-148
Gische, Melissa
90UCLA-29
Givens, Al
91TexAM-85
Givens, Jack
78Hawks/Coke-5
78KY/Food-3
79Hawks/Majik-21
88KY/269-15
88KY/269-159
88KY/269-186
88KY/269-252
89KY/300*-4
92Crtside/ColFB-12
Givins, Ernest
89Louville/300*-115
Gladden, Darryl
81TCMA/CBA-56
82TCMA/CBA-43
82TCMA/Lanc-18
82TCMA/Lanc-19
Glanton, Keith
91GATech*-29
Glanville, Doug
91Classic/DPColl*-59
Glanzer, Barry
89ProC/CBA-66
Glass, Gerald
90F/Up-U56
90StarPic-67
91F/Up-319
91Hoops/I-126
91SkyBox/I-170
91UD-307
91UD/Rook-13
92F-133
92Hoops/I-137
92SkyBox/I-144
Glass, Greg
90KY/Sov-7
Glass, Willie
89ProC/CBA-107
Glaza, Allan
55Ash-27
89Louville/300*-64
Gleason, James
48T/Magic*-J30
Glenn, Mike
83Star/NBA-266
84Star/NBA-79
Gminski, Mike
81T-E78
83Star/NBA-149
84Nets/Getty-5
84Star/NBA-91
85Star/NBA-62
86F-38
86Star/LifeNets-6
87F-41
88F-87
89F-116
89Hoops-33
89Sixers/Kodak-6
90F-142
90Hoops-228
90Hoops/Super-74
90Panini-130
90SkyBox-215
91F/Up-254
91Hoops/I-22
91Panini-111
91SkyBox/I-28
91UD-398
92Hoops/I-23
92SkyBox/I-23
Goad, Tim
90NC/200*-34
Gobrecht, Chris
91WA/Viacom-13CO
Godfread, Dan
90ProC/CBA-48
90StarPic-42
91ProC/CBA-28
Goff, Dave
91TexAM-53
Goforth, Jim
89KY/300*-207
Gofourth, Derrel
91OKSt*-21
Goheen, Barry
87Vanderbilt/Pol-13
Gola, Tom
57T-44
61F-14
61F-51IA
Gold, Doug
90MurraySt-2
Golden, Craig
82Fairf-6
Golden, Mark
82INSt/Pol*-7
Golden, Shaun
90GA/Smok-6
Goldstein, Al
90NC/200*-137
Goldstein, Don
88Louville/194-145
88Louville/194-89
89Louville/300*-20
89Louville/300*-249
Gomez, Lefty
81T/Thirst-2
Gondrezick, Glen
82Nugget/Pol-22
Gonzalez, Jimmy

91Classic/DPColl*-86
Gonzalez, Pancho
57Union-17
Good, Brian
89WI/Smok-3
Good, Larry
91GATech*-52
Good, Mike
90FLSt/200*-155
Goode, Irvin
89KY/300*-110
Goodman, Jim
89KY/300*-208
90ProC/CBA-43
Goodrich, Gail
68Suns/Carn-2
69Suns/Carn-3
69T-2
69T/Ins-7
70T-93
71T-121
72T-174LL
72T-50
73NBAPA-9
73T-55
74T-120AS
74T-90M
75Carv-9
75T-110
75T-125M
76Buck-8
76T-125
77T-77
78T-95
79T-32
91UCLA/144-134
91UCLA/144-8
91UCLA/144-89
92Crtside/ColFB-13
Goodson, Mike
91FrRow/100-51
91FrRow/Premier-48
91FrRow/Up-79
91ProC/CBA-138
Goodwin, Damon
83Dayton/Blue-7
Goovert, Ron
90MISt/200*-5
Gorcey, Leo
48T/Magic*-J24
Gorden, Larry
90AZSt/200*-22
Gordon, Lancaster
81Louville/Pol-6
83Louville-4
84Star/NBA-18
88Louville/194-109
88Louville/194-167
88Louville/194-185
88Louville/194-9
89Louville/300*-234
89Louville/300*-260
89Louville/300*-47
Gordy, Len
81AZ/Pol-6CO
89Clemson-9ACO
90Clemson-7CO
Gore, Curt
90LSU/200*-56
Goring, Butch
79Lakers/Alta-6
Gorius, Bob
89Louville/300*-80
Goss, Fred
91UCLA/144-131
Gotch, Frank
48T/Magic*-D1
Gottfried, Mark
90UCLA-39CO
91UCLA-15
Gotziaman, Chris
91ND*-17M
Goudin, Lucien
48ExhSC-20
Gould, Renee
85NE/Pol*-15
Gould, Terry
89ProC/CBA-13
Govan, Gerald
71T-176
72T-238
73T-233
74T-218
74T-229M
75T-276
Govedarica, Bato
86DePaul-H10
Gowan, Charlie
91SC/200*-118
Grable, Betty
48T/Magic*-F5
Graboski, Joe
57T-41
Graebner, Clark
71Keds*-1M
Graham, Ernie
81TCMA/CBA-21
Graham, Jeff
91Classic/DPColl*-142
Graham, Kevin
81TCMA/CBA-22
Graham, Michael
83George/Pol-12
Graham, Orlando
90ProC/CBA-186
91ProC/CBA-145
Graham, Otto
48ExhSC-21
Graham, Pat
88KY/Sov-10
Graham, Paul
90NM-4ACO
90ProC/CBA-156
91F/Up-243
91FrRow/100-93
91FrRow/Premier-115
91NM-4ACO
91UD/Ext-431
91UD/Rook-27
92F-3
92Hoops/I-4
92SkyBox/I-4
Graham, Robbie
88KY/Sov-11
Gramling, Johnny
91SC/200*-199
Grandelius, Everett
90MISt/200*-37
Grandison, Ronnie
89Hoops-248
91ProC/CBA-185
Granger, Stewart
83Star/NBA-233
Granier, Richard
90LSU/200*-45
Grant, Anthony
83Dayton/Blue-8
Grant, Gary
89F-70
89Hoops-274
90Clip/Star-4
90F/Up-U40
90Hoops-145
90Hoops/Super-45
90Panini-31
90SkyBox-127
91F-89
91Hoops/I-92
91Panini-13
91SkyBox/I-124
91UD-195
92F-99
92Hoops/I-99
92SkyBox/I-104
Grant, Greg
90F/Up-U63
90Hoops-235
90Hoops/II-421
90SkyBox-221
90SkyBox/II-400
92SkyBox/I-183
Grant, Harvey
89Hoops-67
90F-192A
90F-192B
90Hoops-297
90Panini-149
90SkyBox-288
91F-207
91Hoops/I-216
91Hoops/II-501SC
91Hoops/II-529Ar
91Hoops/Super-98
91Panini-178
91SkyBox/Canada-48
91SkyBox/I-291
91SkyBox/II-485TW
91SkyBox/II-512RS
91UD-342
92F-233
92Hoops/I-235
92SkyBox/I-250
Grant, Horace
87Bulls/Ent-11
88Bulls/Ent-54
88F-16
89Bulls/Eq-4
89F-20
89Hoops-242
90Bulls/Eq-6
90Clemson/200*-8
90F-24
90Hoops-63
90Panini-95
90SkyBox-39
91F-27
91Hoops/I-28
91Hoops/McDon-65
91Hoops/Super-12
91Kell/ColGrt-4
91Panini-117
91SkyBox/I-36
91SkyBox/II-566
91UD-181
92F-30
92Hoops/I-29
92SkyBox/I-285TT
92SkyBox/I-30
92StarPic-40FB
Grant, Kevin
89ORSt-7
90FLSt/200*-10
Grant, Mike
90NE/Pol*-8
Grant, Russell
88LSU/Pol*-8
Grant, Steve
87Vanderbilt/Pol-8
Grant, Travis
74T-259
75T-245
75T-285M
Grant, Wally
91MI/56*-22
Grantz, Jeff
91SC/200*-55
Gravely, Stacie
90UCLA-23
Grawemeyer, Phil
55Ash-20
88KY/269-265
88KY/269-66
Gray, Allison
86SWLou/Pol*-7
Gray, Craig
91MurraySt-11
Gray, Evric
90UNLV/HOF-11
90UNLV/Season-11
90UNLV/Smok-6
Gray, Hector
90FLSt/200*-164
Gray, Herb
81TCMA/CBA-86
Gray, Leonard
75T-78
76T-136
77T-7
Gray, Roland
89ProC/CBA-72
91ProC/CBA-192
Gray, Stuart
84Star/NBA-57
89Hoops-253
89Hoops/II-352
90Hoops-204
90SkyBox-188
91UCLA/144-74
Gray, Sylvester
89Hoops-204
89ProC/CBA-36
Grayer, Jeff
88Bucks/Green-4
90F-104
90Hoops-174
90SkyBox-157
91F/Up-311
91Hoops/II-391
91Hoops/II-568
91SkyBox/I-157
91SkyBox/II-500RS
91SkyBox/II-550US
91UD-221
92Hoops/I-127
92SkyBox/I-134
Grayer, Steve
89ProC/CBA-5
90ProC/CBA-19
Green, A.C.
87F-42
88F-66
89F-76
89Hoops-124
90F-92
90Hoops-156
90Hoops-17AS
90Hoops/Super-49
90Panini-6
90Panini-C
90SkyBox-137
91F-99
91Hoops/I-100
91Hoops/Super-47
91Panini-19
91SkyBox/I-136
91UD-177
91UD/McDon-M3
92F-108
92Hoops/I-109
92SkyBox/I-115
Green, Al
80TCMA/CBA-6
90LSU/200*-65
Green, Carlton
80TCMA/CBA-45
Green, Ernie
89Louville/300*-120
Green, Gary
91OKSt*-62
Green, Harold
91SC/200*-8
Green, Hubert
90FLSt/200*-99
Green, Jacob
91TexAM-43
Green, John
91UCLA/144-75
Green, Johnny
70T-3LL
70T-81
71T-140LL
71T-86
71T/Ins-14
72T-48
73T-124
81TCMA-40M
90MISt/200*-128
Green, Ken
81TCMA/CBA-53
Green, Lamar
70Suns/A1-2
70Suns/Carn-2
71T-39
72T-119
73T-9
Green, Litterial
90GA/Smok-7
90KY/BB/DT/AW-23
92Classic/DP-5
92StarPic-45
Green, Mike
74T-254
75T-247
75T-278M
77T-99
Green, Rickey
81TCMA/CBA-70
83Star/NBA-140
84Star/ASG-20
84Star/Award-18LL
84Star/CrtKg-11
84Star/NBA-229
84Star/PolASG-20
85Star/NBA-142
86F-39
87F-43
89Hoops-56
90Hoops-134
90Hoops/II-425
90SkyBox-115
90SkyBox/II-404
91F/Up-249
91Hoops/I-160
91Hoops/II-339
91Panini-170
91SkyBox/I-215
91SkyBox/II-619
91UD-112
Green, Sean
87NCSt/Pol-5
91Classic-31
91Classic/DPColl*-179
91Crtside-24
91F/Up-294
91FrRow/100-28
91FrRow/50-28
91FrRow/Premier-64
91StarPic-22
91UD/Ext-421
91WildCard/Coll-37
Green, Shawn
91Classic/DPColl*-225
Green, Sidney
83Star/NBA-172
84Star/NBA-104
86F-40
87F-44
88F-81
88Knick/FrLay-3
89Hoops-97
89Hoops/II-305
89Magic/Pep-5
90F-134
90F/Up-U88
90Hoops-218

90Hoops/II-435
90Panini-122
90SkyBox-203
90SkyBox/II-413
91F/Up-354
91Hoops/I-191
91SkyBox/I-257
91UD-259
92Hoops/I-208
92SkyBox/I-222
Green, Sihugo
58Kahn's-3
61F-15
Green, Steve
86IN/GreatI-38
Green, Tyler
91Classic/DPColl*-57
Green, Woody
90AZSt/200*-162
Greenberg, Fran
81TCMA/CBA-79
Greene, Gerald
89ProC/CBA-44
Greene, Shaunda
91WA/Viacom-12
Greenwood, David
79Bulls/Pol-34
80T-25
80T-62
80T-89
80T-92
81T-MW67
83Star/NBA-173
84Star/NBA-105
86F-41
87F-45
90Hoops/II-433
90Piston/Star-5
90SkyBox-86
90SkyBox/II-414
91Hoops/I-192
91SkyBox/I-258
91UCLA/144-107
91UCLA/144-116
91UD-374
Greer, Curtis
91MI/56*-23
Greer, Hal
61F-16
68T/Test-2
69T-84
69T/Ins-13
70T-155
70T/Ins-10
71T-60
71T/Ins-13
72T-56
73NBAPA-10
Greer, Hugh
91CT/Legend-6CO
Gregor, Gary
68Suns/Carn-3
69T-11
70T-89
71T-56
72T-36
91SC/200*-85
Gregory, Brian
90MISt-15ACO
Gregory, Johnny
91SC/200*-93
Greiger, Gary
86IN/GreatI-36
Gressley, Jim
90AZSt/200*-124
Gretzky, Wayne
91Arena/Holo*-2
Grevey, Kevin
77T-23
78T-113
79T-34
80T-12
80T-90
81T-E96
83Star/NBA-43
84Star/Arena-C4
84Star/NBA-130
85Star/Bucks-7
88KY/269-154
88KY/269-185
88KY/269-251
88KY/269-9
89KY/300*-49
92Crtside/ColFB-14
Grezaffi, Sam
90LSU/200*-199
Grider, Sydney
91FrRow/100-69
91FrRow/Premier-27
Griego, J.J.
91NM-5
Griffey, Ken Jr.
91Foot*-1
Griffin, Andra
81TCMA/CBA-17
Griffin, Eddie
90Clemson/200*-174
Griffin, Frank
90SoCal/Smok*-7
Griffin, James
80IL/Arby's-2
81IL/Arby's-3
Griffin, Joe
89UTEP/Drug-10
Griffin, Mark
88TN/Smok-33
Griffin, Mike
88MI/Nike-3
89MI-17
Griffin, Paul
79Spurs/Pol-30
81T-MW102
Griffin, Parker
87LSU/Pol*-8
Griffith, Darrell
81Louville/Pol-28
81T-41
83Louville-35
83Star/NBA-141
84Star/Award-16LL
84Star/CrtKg-45
84Star/NBA-230
84Star/PolASG-29
84Star/SlamD-5
85Star/Gator-6
85Star/NBA-143
85Star/ROY-5
85Star/SlamD-4
86F-42
86Star/CrtKg-16
87F-46
87KY/Coke-8
88Louville/194-101
88Louville/194-172
88Louville/194-182
88Louville/194-3
89F-153
89Hoops-241
89Jazz/OldH-4
89Louville/300*-2
89Louville/300*-209
89Louville/300*-25
89Louville/300*-266
89Louville/300*-281
89Louville/300*-297
90Hoops-289
90Jazz/Star-9
90Panini-50
90SkyBox-278
91Hoops/I-209
91SkyBox/I-281
91UD-131
91Wooden-10
Griffith, Jason
90Clemson/200*-38
Griggley, Terry
89McNees*-2
Grimsley, John
89KY/300*-188
Grisham, Wes
90LSU/200*-163
Grissom, Greg
89ProC/CBA-100
Groenhyde, Quinn
83Victoria/Pol-2
84Victoria/Pol-3ACO
Groleau, Francois
91Classic/DPColl*-35
Groppuso, Mike
91Classic/DPColl*-89
Gross, Bob
77Blaz/Pol-30
77T-11
78T-98
79Blaz/Pol-30
79T-4
80T-158
80T-53
81Blaz/Pol-30
81T-W84
Gross, Julie
90LSU/200*-33
Grosso, Mike
88Louville/194-45
89Louville/300*-236
89Louville/300*-294
Grove, Orval
48Kell*-2
Grovey, Quinn
91AR/100*-92
Groza, Alex
52Bread-12
88KY/269-149
88KY/269-5
89KY/300*-3
Groza, Lou
48Kell*-6
Grubar, Dick
89NC/Coke-87
89NC/Coke-88
90NC/200*-115
Grubb, John
90FLSt/200*-61
Gruden, Jay
89Louville/300*-105
89Louville/300*-143
Grunfeld, Ernie
77Bucks/ActPh-6
81T-MW94
83Star/NBA-65
84Star/NBA-31
85Star/NBA-169
92Crtside/ColFB-15
Gruver, Mat
88LSU/Pol*-14
Guanlett, Tom
90NC/200*-90
Gudmondsson, Peter
81Blaz/Pol-40
Gueldner, Jeff
87KS/Nike-5
89KS/Leesley-42
Guenther, Misty
91NE/Pol*-21
Guerin, Richie
61F-17
61F-52IA
81TCMA-40M
Guerrero, Karen
91TexAM-89
Guest, Darren
89ProC/CBA-93
Gugliotta, Tom
88NCSt/Pol-4
89NCSt/Pol-4
91NCSt/IBM-5
92Classic/DP-46
92Classic/DPLP-LP6
92FrRow/DreamPk-66
92FrRow/DreamPk-67
92FrRow/DreamPk-68
92FrRow/DreamPk-69
92FrRow/DreamPk-70
92StarPic-13
92StarPic-78
Guillot, Monk
90LSU/200*-132
Guldseth, Scott
91ND*-2M
Gumbert, George
89KY/300*-209
Gumm, Cedric
90MurraySt-12
91MurraySt-12
Gundmundsson, Petur
91ProC/CBA-110
Gundy, Mike
91OKSt*-50
Guokas, Matt
70T-124
71T-113
72T-9
73T-155LL
73T-18
74T-117
75T-28
89Hoops/II-321CO
90Hoops-323CO
90Hoops/II-352CO
90SkyBox/II-319CO
91F-145CO
91Hoops/I-239CO
91SkyBox/II-396CO
92F-161CO
92Hoops/I-257CO
92SkyBox/I-273CO
Gura, Larry
90AZSt/200*-38
Gurley, Greg
91KS-3
Guthridge, Bill
89NC/Coke-101
90NC/200*-117CO
Guthrie, Grant
90FLSt/200*-165
Guthrie, Mark
86LSU/Pol*-6
Guy, Tony
82TCMA/CBA-79
Guyette, Bob
88KY/269-102
88KY/269-184
88KY/269-249
88KY/269-264
Gwynn, John
90CT/Pol-6
Gyton, Tony
91SC/200*-195
Haase, Tom
91NE/Pol*-6
Habegger, Les
78Sonic/Pol-13CO
79Sonic/Pol-11
Hackenschmidt, George
48T/Magic*-D2
Hackett, Wilbur
89KY/300*-142
Haddix, Harvey
81T/Thirst-8
Haddow, Kim
90AZ/125*-111
Hadley, John
90FLSt/200*-42
Hadnot, Jim
91Providence-9
Haffner, Scott
89Heat/Publix-6
90SkyBox-148
Hagamann, Char
84NE/Pol*-14
Hagan, Cliff
56Busch-1
57T-37
61F-18
61F-53
61Hawks/Essex-4
78KY/Food-4
88KY/269-171
88KY/269-181
88KY/269-2
88KY/269-245
88KY/269-256
88KY/269-260
89KY/300*-6
Hagan, Glenn
80TCMA/CBA-22
81TCMA/CBA-20
Hagan, Jason
90KY/ClassA-9
Hagan, Joseph
89KY/300*-210
Hagg, Gunner
48T/Magic*-E7
Haggins, Odell
90FLSt/200*-94
Hagler, Scott
91SC/200*-104
Hagood, Kent
91SC/200*-6
Hairston, Harold
(Happy)
64Kahn's-1
69T-83
70T-77
71T-25
71T/Ins-19
72T-121
73T-137
74T-68
74T-90M
75Carv-10
75T-125M
75T-159
Hairston, Lindsay
90MISt/200*-118
Haji-Sheikh, Ali
91MI/56*-24
Hakstol, Dave
91ND*-19M
Halas, George
54Quaker-19
Halbert, Chuck
48Bowman-43
Hale, Bruce
48Bowman-15
52Bread-13
Hale, Jerry
88KY/269-101
Hale, Steve
89NC/Coke-119
89NC/Coke-120
90NC/200*-32
90NC/200*-70
90NC/200*-82
90NC/Promos*-NC3
Haley, Jack
88Bulls/Ent-15
90Hoops-197
90Nets/Kayo-9
90SkyBox-180
91F/Up-301
91Hoops/II-383
91SkyBox/I-183
91SkyBox/II-632
91UCLA/144-54

91UD-317
92SkyBox/I-116
Haley, Roddie
91AR/100*-28
Halimon, Shaler
70T-127
71T-89
Hall, Bob
(Showboat)
71Globe-1
71Globe-2
71Globe-3
71Globe-63M
Hall, Charlie
87IN/GreatII-16
Hall, Cris
91NE/Pol*-12
Hall, Dale
89Louville/300*-221
Hall, Dan
89KY/300*-283
Hall, Eugene
87Baylor/Pol*-16
Hall, Henry
89UTEP/Drug-11
Hall, Jeff
83Louville-42
88Louville/194-117
88Louville/194-154
88Louville/194-22
88Louville/194-58
89Louville/300*-256
89Louville/300*-299
89Louville/300*-34
Hall, Joe B.
77KY/Wildct-2M
77KY/Wildct-7CO
78KY/Food-19CO
79KY/Food-18CO
81KY/Sched-5CO
83KY/Sched-7CO
88KY/269-140
88KY/269-30
89KY/300*-39
89KY/Tm80-54
Hall, Randy
91TexAM-52
Hall, Ray
89ProC/CBA-80
Hall, Ricky
91ProC/CBA-79
Hall, Steve
91OhioSt-9
Hall, Terrill
91ProC/CBA-132
Halliburton, Jeff
73T-163
Halsne, Ann
90NE/Pol*-22
91NE/Pol*-20
Halverson, Trevor
91Classic/DPColl*-18
Hamblen, Frank
85Kings/Smok-3M
87Bucks/Polar-x
88Bucks/Green-16M
91F/Up-312CO
Hamilton, Andy
90LSU/200*-145
Hamilton, Clint
85Victoria/Pol-2
Hamilton, Derrek
87SoMiss-4
Hamilton, Joe
71T-164
72T-227
73T-224
74T-217
Hamilton, Joey
91Classic/DPColl*-218
Hamilton, Leonard
77KY/Wildct-5CO
78KY/Food-21CO
79KY/Food-16CO
81KY/Sched-6ACO
83KY/Sched-8ACO
Hamilton, Ralph
48Bowman-2
Hamilton, Roy
91UCLA/144-63
Hamilton, Steve
55Ash-53
Hamilton, Vince
89ProC/CBA-156
90Clemson/200*-24
90ProC/CBA-63
91ProC/CBA-157
Hammond, Julian
71T-174
Hammond, Kim
90FLSt/200*-156
Hammonds, Kerry
90ProC/CBA-177
Hammonds, Tom
88GATech/Nike-5
90F-193
92SkyBox/I-24
Hammonds, Tom
90Hoops-298A
90Hoops-298B
90SkyBox-289
91F/Up-368
91GATech*-15
91Hoops/II-446
91SkyBox/I-292
91UD-349
Hampton, Dan
91AR/100*-6
Hampton, Kym
90AZSt/200*-191
Hamrlik, Martin
91Classic/DPColl*-27
Hanburger, Chris
90NC/200*-8
Hancock, Mike
81George/Pol-13
91George/100-44
Hankinson, Phil
75T-153
Hanners, Dave
89NC/Coke-132
90NC/200*-120CO
Hannum, Alex
81TCMA-1
Hans, Rollen
54Bullet/Gunth-6
Hansen, Bobby
83Star/NBA-142
88F-113
88Jazz/Smok-8
89Hoops-27
89Jazz/OldH-5
90F-186
90F/Up-U84
90Hoops-290
90Hoops/II-428
90Kings/Safe-5
90SkyBox-279
90SkyBox/II-409
91F/Up-256
91Hoops/I-183
91SkyBox/I-246
91SkyBox/II-620
91UD-318
91UD/Ext-408
Hansen, Glenn
90LSU/200*-197
90LSU/200*-22
Hansen, Hoan
90AZ/125*-56
Hansen, Phil
91Classic/DPColl*-147
Hanson, Reggie
88KY/Award-11
88KY/Award-16
89KY/Award-21
89KY/Award-25
89KY/Award-31
89KY/Award-32
90KY/BB/DT/AW-35
91Crtside-25
91KY/BB-2
91StarPic-38
Hanson, Tony
91CT/Legend-7
Hanson, Victor A.
68HOF-14
Hanzlik, Bill
82Nugget/Pol-24
83Nugget/Pol-24
83Star/NBA-188
84Star/NBA-141
85Nugget/Pol-3
86F-43
87F-47
88Nugget/Pol-24
89Hoops-129
89Nugget/Pol-5
90F-49
90Hoops-95
90NotreDame-42
90SkyBox-75
Harbison, Bob
90FLSt/200*-169
Hardaway, Tim
89UTEP/Drug-12
90F-63
90F/Rook-8
90Hoops-113
90Panini-28
90SkyBox-95
91F-216
91F-65
91Hoops/I-264AS
91Hoops/I-67
91Hoops/II-465SC
91Hoops/II-511Ar
91Hoops/McDon-15
91Hoops/Super-33
91Kell/ColGrt-14
91Panini-6
91SkyBox/Canada-17
91SkyBox/I-303M
91SkyBox/I-90
91SkyBox/II-413GF
91SkyBox/II-467TW
91SkyBox/II-494RS
91StarPic-10
91UD-243
91UD-50AS
91UD/Ext-468AS
92F-251PV
92F-74
92F/AS-14
92Hoops/I-307AS
92Hoops/I-74
92SkyBox/I-79
Harden, Al
87IN/GreatII-10
Harden, Roger
88KY/269-126
88KY/269-183
88KY/269-248
88KY/269-263
89KY/Tm80-49
Harder, Pat
48ExhSC-22
Hardin, Billy
90LSU/200*-150
Hardman, Leon
91GATech*-190
Hardnett, Thomas
85FortHaysSt-8
Hardt, David
89KY/300*-128
Hardwick, Erika
91WA/Viacom-14
Hardwick, Mary
48Kell*-13
Hardy, Alan
82TCMA/CBA-14
Hardy, Bob
89KY/300*-105
Hardy, Bruce
90AZSt/200*-75
Hardy, David
91TexAM-99
Hardy, James
80TCMA/CBA-35
Harge, Ira
71Flor/McDon-4
71T-193
Hargett, Edd
91TexAM-65
Harlicka, Skip
91SC/200*-158
Harlicka, Todd
90GATech/Pol-11
91GATech/Pol-10
Harling, Rodney
91OKSt*-11
Harlow, Pat
90SoCal/Smok*-8
91Classic/DPColl*-111
Harman, Lee
61Union-3
Harmon, Billy
89Louville/300*-72
Harmon, Jerome
91Classic/DPColl*-213
91StarPic-66
Harned, Victor
55Ash-79
Harper, Alvin
91Classic/DPColl*-112
Harper, Derek
80IL/Arby's-3
81IL/Arby's-4
83Star/NBA-55
84Star/Arena-B6
84Star/NBA-255
85Star/NBA-163
86F-44
87F-48
88F-30
88Mavs/BLC-12
88Mavs/CardN-12
89F-35
89Hoops-184
90F-42
90Hoops-86
90Hoops/Super-20
90Panini-60
90SkyBox-64
91F-45
91F/Up-377TL
91Hoops/I-46
91Hoops/II-460SC
91Hoops/II-508Ar
91Hoops/McDon-11
91Hoops/Super-22
91Panini-45
91SkyBox/Canada-12
91SkyBox/I-60
91SkyBox/II-464TW
91UD-137
92F-49
92Hoops/I-47
92SkyBox/I-287TT
92SkyBox/I-49
Harper, Mike
81Blaz/Pol-32
Harper, Ron
87F-49
88F-23
88Fourn-18
89F-27
89Hoops-205
90Clip/Star-5
90F-86
90Hoops-146
90Panini-34
90SkyBox-128
91F-90
91Hoops/I-93
91Hoops/II-471SC
91Hoops/II-514Ar
91Hoops/Super-44
91Panini-10
91SkyBox/I-125
91SkyBox/II-581
91UD-133
91UD-78TC
92F-100
92Hoops/I-100
92SkyBox/I-105
92SkyBox/I-293TT
Harper, Sam
89KY/300*-68
Harper, Tom
89KY/300*-282
Harrah, Herbert
55Ash-28
89Louville/300*-93
Harrah, Toby
81T/Thirst-6
Harrell, Damon
89WI/Smok-4
Harrell, Lonnie
91George/Pol-14
Harrick, Jim
90UCLA-35CO
91UCLA-16CO
91UCLA/144-9
Harried, Herman
88Syr/Rich-4
Harrington, Kevin
88Victoria/Pol-4
Harris, Al
90AZSt/200*-72
Harris, Art
69Sonic/Sunb-4
69T-76
70Suns/Carn-3
70T-149
71T-32
Harris, Bo
90LSU/200*-92
Harris, Carl Ray
90Fresno/Smok-6
Harris, Chris
91FrRow/100-91
91FrRow/Premier-11
91FrRow/Up-98
91ProC/CBA-56
Harris, Darryl
90AZSt/200*-91
Harris, Del
87Bucks/Polar-x
88Bucks/Green-16M
88Bucks/Green-5CO
89Hoops-126CO
90Hoops-319CO
90SkyBox/II-315CO
91F-115CO
91Hoops/I-235CO
91SkyBox/II-392CO
Harris, Dick
91SC/200*-197
Harris, Doug
90Fresno/Smok-7
Harris, Eugene
89Clemson-10ACO
90Clemson-8CO
Harris, James

90FLSt/200*-171
Harris, John
89ProC/CBA-157
90AZSt/200*-49
Harris, Keith
87KS/Nike-6
Harris, Kevin
89ORSt-8
90ORSt-9
91ORSt-8
Harris, Labron
91OKSt*-60
Harris, Leonard
89ProC/CBA-3
90ProC/CBA-83
91ProC/CBA-140
Harris, Leotis
91AR/100*-84
Harris, Mackel
91GATech*-196
Harris, Neil
84NE/Pol*-8
Harris, Pete
81TCMA/CBA-58
Harris, Rufus
81TCMA/CBA-6
82TCMA/Lanc-30
Harris, Steve
89ProC/CBA-85
90Clemson-9
Harris, Tab
89McNees*-3
Harris, Ted
83Dayton/Blue-9
Harris, Tony
90ProC/CBA-137
90StarPic-68
91ProC/CBA-43
Harris, Wayne
91AR/100*-93
Harris, Wendell
90LSU/200*-84
90LSU/Promos*-4
Harrison, Anthony
91GATech*-39
Harrison, Bob
57T-63
Harrison, Charles
90George/Pol-8
91George/Pol-3
Harrison, Chris
90KY/ClassA-12
91KY/BB/Double-10
Harrison, Danny
91GATech*-34
Harrison, Lester
92CenterCrt-22
Harrison, W.C.
89KY/300*-211
Harrod, Delmar
79StBon-6
Harshman, Dave
82TCMA/CBA-80
83Sonic/Pol-4
Hart, Clyde
87Baylor/Pol*-10CO
Hart, D.W.
89KY/300*-212
Hart, Tom
89ProC/CBA-89
90ProC/CBA-56
Harter, Dick
89Hoops-127CO
Hartsock, Mike
83Dayton/Blue-10
Hartsuyker, Craig
90SoCal/Smok*-9
Harvey, Antonio
90GA/Smok-8
Harvey, Boo
90StarPic-34
Harwell, Randy
91SC/200*-37
Haskin, David
83AZ/Pol-7
84AZ/Pol-6
85AZ/Pol-7
Haskin, Scott
89ORSt-9
90ORSt-10
91ORSt-9
Haskins, Clem
70Suns/A1-3
70Suns/Carn-4
70T-165
70T-6LL
71T-96
72T-72
73T-59
74T-62
75T-133M
75T-173
Haskins, Don
89UTEP/Drug-13CO
Haskins, Merion
88KY/269-108
88KY/269-262
Hassett, Bill
90NotreDame-50
Hassett, Joe
78Sonic/Pol-2
80T-67
80T-97
91Providence-19
Hassey, Ron
90AZ/125*-53
Hastings, Scott
83Star/NBA-267
84Star/NBA-80
85Star/NBA-43
87Hawks/Pizza-8
89Hoops-176
89Hoops/II-317
90F/Up-U30
90Hoops-105
90Piston/Star-6
90SkyBox-87
91AR/100*-35
91Hoops/II-358
91SkyBox/I-83
91SkyBox/II-625
91UD-340
Hatcher, Dale
90Clemson/200*-45
Hatcher, Cornell
91OKSt-14
91OKSt-28
91OKSt-47
Hatcher, Montel
91UCLA/144-44
Hatfield
83KY/Sched-9
Hatfield, David
89Louville/300*-187
Hatfield, Ken
90Clemson/200*-108
90Clemson/Promos*-C6
91AR/100*-90
Hatteberg, Scott
91Classic/DPColl*-88
Hatton, Raymond
48T/Magic*-J32
Hatton, Vern
58Kahn's-4
61Hawks/Essex-5
88KY/269-13
88KY/269-162
Hauptfuhrer, George
89Louville/300*-27
Havlicek, Chris
91VA-5
Havlicek, John
68T/Test-5
69T-20
69T/Ins-9
70T-10
70T-112AS
70T/Ins-18
71T-138LL
71T-139LL
71T-35
71T/Ins-24
72Icee-8
72T-110
72T-161AS
72T-171LL
72T-172LL
73NBAPA-11
73T-20AS
74T-100AS
74T-82M
75Carv-11
75T-80AS
76Buck-9
76T-90
77T-70
81T/Thirst-25
85Star/Schick-12
91Foot*-14
91Foot*-17
Hawes, Steve
78Hawks/Coke-6
78T-21
79Hawks/Majik-10
79T-78
80T-4
80T-92
81T-E82
83Sonic/Pol-13
83Star/NBA-196
Hawkins, Alex
91SC/200*-59
Hawkins, Ben
90AZSt/200*-197
Hawkins, Bubbles
77T-22
Hawkins, Connie
69Suns/Carn-4
69T-15
70Suns/A1-4
70Suns/Carn-5
70T-109AS
70T-130
70T/Ins-22
71T-105
71T/Ins-37
72Icee-9
72T-30
73NBAPA-12
73T-43
74Nab-20
74T-104
75Nab-20
75T-195
76Buck-10
85Star/Schick-13
Hawkins, Darrell
91AR25-7
Hawkins, Hersey
89F-117
89Hoops-137
89Sixers/Kodak-7
90F-143
90Hoops-229
90Hoops/CollB-28
90Hoops/Super-71
90Panini-129
90SkyBox-216
91F-154
91Hoops/I-161
91Hoops/I-252AS
91Hoops/II-488SC
91Hoops/II-569
91Hoops/McDon-31
91Hoops/Super-73
91Panini-167
91SkyBox/Canada-36
91SkyBox/I-216
91SkyBox/II-478TW
91SkyBox/II-505RS
91SkyBox/II-551US
91SkyBox/II-593SS
91SkyBox/Proto-216
91UD-155
91UD-71AS
91UD-93TC
92F-170
92F/TmLeader-20
92Hoops/I-174
92SkyBox/I-184
92SkyBox/I-301TT
Hawkins, Paul
83Dayton/Blue-11
Hawkins, Tom
61Lakers/Bell-3
62Kahn's-4
63Kahn's-5
64Kahn's-7
90NotreDame-8
Hawley, Ron
88Louville/194-67
Haws, Marty
87BYU-24
Hawthorne, Jimmy
91SC/200*-38
Hawthorne, Nate
75Suns-6
75T-57
Hayden, Basil
88KY/269-86
Hayden, Brian
91NM-6
Hayden, Dan
90AZSt/200*-198
Hayden, Pam
90Clemson/200*-186
Hayes, Buzz
90AZSt/200*-60
Hayes, Carl
90NE/Pol*-23
91NE/Pol*-14
Hayes, Elvin
68Rocket/Jack-6
69T-75
69T/Ins-4
70T-1LL
70T-2LL
70T-5LL
70T-70
70T/Ins-4
71T-120
71T-138LL
71T-139LL
71T-142LL
71T/Ins-15
72T-150
73Bullet/Stand-3
73T-95
74T-148LL
74T-30AS
74T-98M
75T-133M
75T-60
76T-120
76T-133AS
77T-40
78RCCola-14
78T-25
79T-90AS
80T-124
80T-135
80T-176
80T-4
80T-69
80T-88
81T-42
81T-66M
83Star/NBA-76
91Foot*-23
92CenterCrt-11
92Crtside/ColFB-16
Hayes, Eric
90FLSt/200*-92
Hayes, Steve
81TCMA/CBA-30
83Star/NBA-197
90ProC/CBA-55
91ProC/CBA-134CO
Haynes, Kenny
91SC/200*-136
Haynes, Mike
90AZSt/200*-174
90AZSt/200*-28
Hays, Butch
89ProC/CBA-196
Hayward, Mike
91WA/TCI-4
Haywood, Spencer
71Sonic/Sunb-4
71T-20
71T/Ins-9
72T-10
72T-162AS
73NBAPA-13
73Sonic/Shur-6
73T-120AS
73T-153LL
73T-154LL
74Nab-18
74T-70AS
74T-97M
75Carv-12
75Nab-18
75T-132M
75T-200AS
76T-28
77T-88
78T-107
79T-12
Hazard, John
90LSU/200*-127
Hazzard, Walt
(See Mahdi Abdul-Rahman)
Head, Elmo
89KY/300*-213
Headen, Andy
90Clemson/200*-118
Heald, Bobby
91SC/200*-67
Healy, Rob
91GATech*-25
Heard, Garfield
70Sonic/Sunb-5
71Sonic/Sunb-5
72T-98
73T-99
74T-44
75Carv-13
75Suns-7
75T-136
76Suns-5
76T-39
77Suns/Discs-24
78T-54
88Mavs/BLC-x
Heard, Norman
89Louville/300*-174
Hearn, Andy
91GATech*-37
Hearns, Thomas
88Foot*-3
91Foot*-24
Heathcote, Jud
90MISt-1CO

90MISt/200*-159
90MISt/200*-178
Heber, John G.
89KY/300*-155
Hebets, Brad
87SWLou/McDag*-11
Hedden, Larry
90MISt/200*-183
Hefferman, Bert
90Clemson/200*-79
Heffner, Trent
91NM-7
Hegarty, Mary
90UCLA-34CO
Heggins, Jimmy
90FLSt/200*-174
Heggs, Alvin
90ProC/CBA-100
Heimer, Merle
89UTEP/Drug-14
Heine, Sonja
48ExhSC-23
Heineken, Harry
81TCMA/CBA-39
Heinsohn, Tom
57T-19
61F-19
61F-54IA
85Star/Schick-14
Heintz, Gary J.
81AZ/Pol-7
Heise, Dick
86DePaul-H13
Heisman, John
90Clemson/200*-179
Heitmann, James
(Mike)
91TexAM-63
Heitz, Kenny
91UCLA/144-140
91UCLA/144-34
Heitz, Tom
79KY/Food-14
81KY/Sched-7
83KY/Sched-10
88KY/269-120
88KY/269-255
Heller, Chris
89MO-7
90MO-9
91MO-10
Helm, Foster
89KY/300*-72
Helms, Tommy
68PartM-3
Helton, Mike
90KY/ClassA-18
Hency, Bill
91SC/200*-42
Henderson, Cam
55Ash-41
Henderson, Cedric
91WildCard/Coll-87
Henderson, Chris
89Fresno/Smok-5
Henderson, Gerald
81T-E74
83Star/NBA-31
84Star/NBA-116
85Star/NBA-67
86F-45
87F-50
89Hoops-208
90Hoops-106
90Piston/Star-7
90SkyBox-88
91Hoops/II-369
Henderson, Hubert
89ProC/CBA-174
Henderson, Jerome
81TCMA/CBA-67
90ProC/CBA-179
91Classic/DPColl*-137
Henderson, Phil
87Duke/Pol-44
88Duke/Pol-7
90ProC/CBA-136
90StarPic-18
Henderson, Tom
75T-171
76T-8
77T-93
78T-68
79T-18
81T-MW86
Hendrix, Billy
90LSU/200*-20
Hendrix, Kevin
91SC/200*-174
Henefeld, Nadav
91CT/Legend-8
Henke, Brad
90AZ/125*-51
Henke, Nolan
90FLSt/200*-113
Henneman, Mike
91OKSt*-92
Henrie, Darren
90ProC/CBA-172
91FrRow/100-90
91FrRow/Premier-111
Henry, Carl
85Kings/Smok-7
Henry, Conner
87Bucks/Polar-21
Henry, Gary
90FLSt/200*-149
Henry, Jeff
89Louville/300*-199
Henry, Randy
89ProC/CBA-20
Henry, Skeeter
90ProC/CBA-30
91ProC/CBA-197
Henry, Travis
88TN/Smok-25
Hensley, Marty
86NC/Pol-45
87NC/Pol-45
88NC/Pol-45
Henson, Lou
80IL/Arby's-4CO
81IL/Arby's-5CO
Henson, Steve
90F/Up-U53
90StarPic-56
91F/Up-313
91Hoops/II-392
91UD-366
Heredia, Gilbert
90AZ/125*-23
Hermann, Dick
90FLSt/200*-168
Hermann, Doc
90FLSt/200*-101
Hernandez, Joe
90AZ/125*-117
Herner, Lisa
91TexAM-87
Herrera, Carl
91F/Up-290
91WildCard/Coll-115
Herring, Mike
87BYU-11
Herrington, Terrence
90Clemson/200*-77
Herron, Keith
81T-MW81
Herrscher, Rick
61Union-4
Herter, Jason
91ND*-15M
Hertzberg, Sid
48Bowman-16
Hesch, Sue
91NE/Pol*-19
Hester, Dan
71T-166
Hetzel, Fred
70T-79
Hewitt, Bill
70T-56
71T-23
72T-107
73T-97
Hextall, Donevan
91Classic/DPColl*-29
Hickey, Lynn
91TexAM-55
Hickman, Bernard
(Peck)
55Ash-29
88Louville/194-105
88Louville/194-184
88Louville/194-5
89Louville/300*-279
Hickman, Greg
89Louville/300*-180
Hickman, Parish
90MISt-3
Hickox, Edward J.
68HOF-15
Higgins, Earle
71Pacer/Mara-3
Higgins, Kevin
90AZSt/200*-54
Higgins, Mike
90ProC/CBA-187
Higgins, Ralph
91OKSt*-96
Higgins, Roderick
(Rod)
83Star/All-R-3
83Star/NBA-174
84Star/NBA-106
88F-47
89F-54
89Hoops-209
90F-64
90Hoops-114
90Hoops/Super-34
90SkyBox-96
91F-66
91Hoops/I-68
91Panini-8
91SkyBox/I-91
91SkyBox/II-440SM
91UD-261
Higgins, Sean
88MI/Nike-4
89MI-13
90StarPic-14
91Hoops/II-435
91UD-25
Higgs, Kenny
81T-49M
90LSU/200*-136
Higgs, Mark
87KY/Coke-20
89KY/300*-140
High, Johnny
80Suns/Pep-3
Highsmith, Ronnie
84George/Pol-6
85George/Pol-7
86George/Pol-7
87George/Pol-7
91George/100-14
Hightower, Wayne
71T-187
Hilger, Rusty
91OKSt*-28
Hill, Armond
78Hawks/Coke-7
78T-70
79Hawks/Majik-24
79T-57
80T-100
80T-130
80T-20
80T-60
Hill, Bob
91F-82CO
91Hoops/I-231CO
91SkyBox/II-388CO
92F-90CO
92Hoops/I-249CO
92SkyBox/I-265CO
Hill, Bobby Joe
89UTEP/Drug-15
Hill, Brian
87Hawks/Pizza-3CO
Hill, Bruce
90AZ/125*-52
90AZSt/200*-24
Hill, Bryan
90GATech/Pol-12
91GATech/Pol-11
Hill, Carl
91SC/200*-107
Hill, Cleo
61Hawks/Essex-6
Hill, Darren
91MurraySt-6
Hill, Derek
90AZ/125*-42
Hill, Donnie
90AZSt/200*-13
Hill, Drew
91GATech*-189
Hill, Eddie
91WASt-3
Hill, Eric
90LSU/200*-24
Hill, Howard
57Union-25
Hill, J.D.
90AZSt/200*-97
Hill, Keith
91ProC/CBA-4
Hill, Randal
91Classic/DPColl*-121
Hill, Simmie
73T-184
Hill, Susan
90Clemson/200*-173
Hill, Tyrone
90F/Up-U31
90Hoops/II-400LS
90SkyBox/II-358LP
90StarPic-38
91Classic/DPColl*-62
91F-67
91Hoops/I-69
91SkyBox/I-92
91UD-263
91UD/Rook-7
92F-75
92Hoops/I-75
92SkyBox/I-80
Hill, Yvonne
91TexAM-97
Hilliad, Johnnie
91ProC/CBA-163
Hilliard, Dalton
90LSU/200*-8
Hilliard, Keith
82TCMA/Lanc-27
82TCMA/Lanc-28
Hillman, Darnell
73T-244
74T-182
75T-290
76T-86
77T-5
78T-119
79T-47
Hiltabrand, Jada
92PennSt*-10
Hilton, Carton
91SC/200*-24
Hilton, Fred
72T-23
73T-36
Himes, Doug
71Globe-57
71Globe-58
Hines, Glenn Ray
91AR/100*-83
Hinkle, Paul D.
68HOF-16
Hinnant, Mickey
88NCSt/Pol-5
89NCSt/Pol-5
Hinson, Roy
83Star/NBA-234
84Star/NBA-218
85Star/NBA-155
86F-46
87F-51
88F-78
89F-97
89Hoops-276
90Hoops-198
90Hoops/Super-63
90Panini-157
90SkyBox-181
91Hoops/Super-61
91UD-389
Hinton, Harry
89Louville/300*-216
Hinton, Jurado
87SoMiss-9
Hinz, Gib
82TCMA/CBA-48
Hipsher, Dan
83Dayton/Blue-1M
Hirsch, Elroy
57Union-1
57Union-29
91MI/56*-25
Hirsch, Walt
88KY/269-261
88KY/269-64
Hisle, Larry
79Bucks/OpenP-4
Hisle, Larry Jr.
89WI/Smok-5
Hite, Ray
89NC/Coke-166
Hoadley, Bruce
89NCSt/Coke-110
89NCSt/Coke-112
Hobbs, Bill
91TexAM-70
Hobbs, Bobby
86SWLou/Pol*-8
Hobson, Howard A.
68HOF-17
Hockensmith, Doug
89Louville/300*-184
Hodde, Rodney
91TexAM-23
Hodgdon, Ray
89NCSt/Coke-135
89NCSt/Coke-174
89NCSt/Coke-195
Hodge, Billy
91TexAM-12
Hodge, Donald
91Classic-23
91Classic/DPColl*-171
91Crtside-26
91F/Up-268
91FrRow/100-24

91FrRow/50-24
91FrRow/Premier-69
91StarPic-48
91WildCard/Coll-94
92F-50
92SkyBox/I-50
Hodge, Jeff
89ProC/CBA-23
91ProC/CBA-57
Hodge, Walter
89KY/300*-214
Hodges, Craig
83Star/NBA-125
84Star/NBA-131
85Star/Bucks-8
85Star/NBA-125
86F-47
86Star/LifeBucks-6
87Bucks/Polar-15
87F-52
88Bulls/Ent-14
89Bulls/Eq-5
89Hoops-113
90F-25
90Hoops-64
90Panini-96
90SkyBox-40
91F/Up-257
91Hoops/I-29
91Hoops/McDon-66
91SkyBox/I-314
91SkyBox/I-37
91UD-148
91UD/Ext-484
92SkyBox/I-309
Hodson, Charles
86IN/GreatI-28
Hodson, Tommy
90LSU/200*-10
Hoffman, Brad
89NC/Coke-145
90NC/200*-103
Hoffman, Paul
52Bread-14
54Bullet/Gunth-7
Hofkamp, Matt
90MISt-2
Hogan, Ben
48ExhSC-24
Hogan, Jeff
90FLSt/200*-107
Hogan, Mark
91GATech*-45
Hoges, Daron
91ProC/CBA-148
Holcomb, Derek
80IL/Arby's-5
Hold, Mike
91SC/200*-183
Holdash, Irv
90NC/200*-182
Holden, Fred
88Louville/194-133
88Louville/194-47
89Louville/300*-15
Holden, Steve
90AZSt/200*-86
Holder, Mike
91OKSt*-89
Holland, Brad
80T-11
80T-144
90UCLA-36CO
91UCLA-7ACO
Holland, James
90MurraySt-15ACO
Holland, Joe
88KY/269-106
88KY/269-34
Holland, Terry
88VA/Hardee-7CO
Holland, Wilbur
77Bulls/WhHen-3
77T-53
78T-4
79T-99
Hollas, Donald
91Classic/DPColl*-206
Hollenbeck, Kent
88KY/269-246
88KY/269-93
Holley, Kitty
91TexAM-50
Hollingsworth, Mo
90KY/ClassA-15
Hollins, Lionel
76T-119
77Blaz/Pol-14
77T-39
78T-74
79Blaz/Pol-9
79T-129
80T-119
80T-36
81T-31
83Star/NBA-88
84Star/NBA-239
85Star/TmSuper-HR5
89Blaz/Franz-12
90AZSt/200*-12
Hollins, Paul
91SC/200*-74
Hollis, Richard
90ProC/CBA-38
Holloman, Darrin
90FLSt/200*-17
Holloman, Tanner
90FLSt/200*-43
Hollyfield, Larry
91UCLA/144-43
Holman, Nat
68HOF-18
Holmes, Dick
90MISt/200*-154
Holmes, Kermit
91ProC/CBA-137
Holmes, Larry
81TCMA/CBA-29
Holt, Michael
55Ash-88
Holton, Michael
84Star/NBA-42
86Blaz/Franz-5
87Blaz/Franz-3
89Hoops-119
90SkyBox-30
91ProC/CBA-131
91UCLA/144-18
Holtz, Lou
91AR/100*-47
Holup, Joe
57T-76
Holzman, Red
92CenterCrt-16CO
Holzman, William
(Red)
48Bowman-32
85Star/Schick-15
Hood, Steve
91Classic-32
91Classic/DPColl*-180
91Crtside-27
91FrRow/100-33
91FrRow/50-33
91FrRow/Premier-59
91StarPic-44
91UD-21
Hooker, Fair
90AZSt/200*-19
Hooker, Wilbert
89Fresno/Smok-6
90Fresno/Smok-8
Hooks, Jasper
91ProC/CBA-172
Hoolahan, Paul
90NC/200*-163
Hooper, Chip
91AR/100*-22
Hoot, Rick
89NCSt/Coke-185
Hope, Danny
89Louville/300*-130
Hopkins, Bob
57T-53
Hopkins, Ed
91George/100-57
Hopkins, Gayle
90AZ/125*-119
Hopkins, Marcus
90SoCal/Smok*-10
Hopkins, Mike
89Syr/Pep-11
Hoppe, Willie
48ExhSC-25
Hoppen, Dave
84NE/Pol*-16
85NE/Pol*-23
89Hoops-99
90Hoops-55
90SkyBox-31
91Hoops/II-411
Hopson, Dennis
89Hoops-199
90F-120
90F/Up-U14
90Hoops-199
90Hoops/II-404
90Hoops/Super-61
90SkyBox-182
90SkyBox/II-371
91Hoops/II-426
91SkyBox/I-38
91SkyBox/II-642
91UD-169
91UD/Ext-433
92Hoops/I-199
92SkyBox/I-212
Hord, Derrick
79KY/Food-13
81KY/Sched-8
82KY/Sched-3
88KY/269-119
88KY/269-254
89KY/Tm80-53
Hordges, Cerrick
91SC/200*-68
Horford, Tito
88Bucks/Green-6
Horlen, Joel
91OKSt*-33
Horn, Terry
91Classic/DPColl*-96
Hornacek, Jeff
87Suns/Circ-6
89F-121
89Hoops-229
90F-147
90Hoops-236
90Hoops/Super-76
90Panini-17
90SkyBox-222
90Suns/Smok-2
91F-160
91Hoops/I-164
91Hoops/Super-76
91Panini-24
91SkyBox/Canada-37
91SkyBox/I-224
91SkyBox/II-594SS
91UD-135
91UD/Ext-469AS
92F-171
92F/AS-15
92Hoops/I-180
92Hoops/I-308AS
92SkyBox/I-190
Horne, Grey
91AR/100*-87
Horner, Bob
90AZSt/200*-111M
90AZSt/200*-172
Hornsby, Rogers
48T/Magic*-K8
Horry, Robert
92Classic/DP-33
92SkyBox/NBADP-DP11
92StarPic-27
Horton, Ed
91ProC/CBA-62
Horton, Ethan
90NC/200*-10
90NC/200*-80
90NC/Promos*-NC2
Horton, Gary
91TexAM-6
Horton, Jim
88MO-5
89MO-8
90MO-10
Horton, Lenny
80TCMA/CBA-17
81TCMA/CBA-66
91GATech*-3
Horton, Steve
91MO-11
Hosket, Bill
70T-104
Houbregs, Bob
54Bullet/Gunth-8
57T-56
Houston, Allan
88KY/Sov-12
90KY/BB/DT/AW-20
Houston, Anthony
91FrRow/100-74
91FrRow/Premier-22
91ProC/CBA-199
Houston, Byron
91OKSt-29
91OKSt-41
91OKSt-9
92Classic/DP-48
92StarPic-53
Houston, Wade
83Louville-x
88Louville/194-13
89Louville/300*-66
Houzer, Larry
89ProC/CBA-54
90ProC/CBA-36
Howard, Brian
87NCSt/Pol-6
88NCSt/Pol-6
89NCSt/Pol-6
90ProC/CBA-5
91ProC/CBA-189
Howard, Frank
90Clemson/200*-113
90Clemson/200*-9
90Clemson/Promos*-C10
Howard, Greg
70Suns/A1-5
70T-117
Howard, Lem
90GA/Smok-10
Howard, Shanna
90Clemson/Lady-6
Howard, Stephen
92Classic/DP-55
Howard, Terry
88Louville/194-124
88Louville/194-32
89Louville/300*-293
Howe, Corey
91ND*-17M
Howe, Dick
89KY/300*-73
Howell, Bailey
61F-20
61F-55IA
69T-5
69T/Ins-3CO
Howell, Jim Lee
91AR/100*-97
Howling, Kirkland
(Kirk)
89Clemson-11
90Clemson/200*-125
Howser, Dick
90FLSt/200*-1
Huband, Kim
89NC/Coke-168
90NC/200*-172
Hubbard, Phil
80T-110
80T-22
81T-50M
81T-MW82
83Star/NBA-235
84Star/NBA-219
85Star/NBA-156
86F-48
87F-53
91MI/56*-27
Hubbell, Carl
81T/Thirst-7
Huber, Lee
88KY/269-24
Hubert, Kelly
90NE/Pol*-24
Hubert, Mick
83Dayton/Blue-12
Hubley, Liffort
90LSU/200*-95
Hudock, Jim
89NC/Coke-143
Hudson, Gerald
91OKSt*-16
Hudson, John
91SC/200*-143
Hudson, Lou
69T-65
69T/Ins-14
70T-115AS
70T-30
70T-3LL
70T/Ins-19
71T-110
71T/Ins-1
72T-130
73NBAPA-14
73T-150
74T-130
74T-81M
75Carv-14
75T-116M
75T-25
76Buck-11
76T-96
77T-85
78T-24
79T-119
Huery, Ron
91AR/100*-80
Huff, Derek
90AZ/125*-101
Huff, Gary
90FLSt/200*-20
Huff, Ken
90NC/200*-140
Huffman, Chris
90KY/ClassA-6
Huffman, Marv
87IN/GreatII-35
Huffman, Vern

86IN/Greatl-26
Hughes, Charles T.
89KY/300*-163
89KY/300*-215
Hughes, Delmar
89KY/300*-191
Hughes, Don
83Dayton/Blue-13
Hughes, Eddie
89Nugget/Pol-6
Hughes, Keith
91Classic-37
91Classic/DPColl*-185
91Crtside-28
91FrRow/100-18
91FrRow/50-18
91FrRow/Premier-77
91StarPic-56
Hughes, Lowell
89KY/300*-192
89KY/300*-216
Hughes, Mark
88MI/Nike-5
89MI-15
91WildCard/Coll-68
Hughes, Rex
91F/Up-349
Hughes, Steve
91TexAM-86
Hull, Bobby
81PhilM-7
81T/Thirst-50
81T/Thirst-51
81T/Thirst-52
Hull, Dennis
74Nab-12
Hummer, John
71T-125
72T-147
73T-52
74T-52
Humphries, Jay
84Star/NBA-43
85Star/NBA-38
86F-49
88Bucks/Green-7
89F-86
89Hoops-298
90F-105
90Hoops-175
90Hoops/Super-54
90Panini-102
90SkyBox-158
91F-116
91Hoops/I-117
91Hoops/II-477SC
91Hoops/Super-55
91Panini-139
91SkyBox/I-158
91SkyBox/II-473TW
91UD-241
92F-222
92Hoops/I-128
92SkyBox/I-135
Humphries, Stefan
91MI/56*-26
Hundley, Rod
55Ash-89
57T-43
61F-21
61Lakers/Bell-4
Hunley, Lamonte
90AZ/125*-74
Hunley, Ricky
90AZ/125*-7
Hunnicutt, Joseph
55Ash-42
Hunt, Anderson
88UNLV/HOF-3
89UNLV/HOF-6M
89UNLV/Seven-7
90UNLV/HOF-10
90UNLV/HOF-4
90UNLV/Season-15M
90UNLV/Season-4
90UNLV/Smok-7
91Classic-46
91Classic/DPColl*-194
Hunt, Michael
91MurraySt-7
Hunt, Thom
90AZ/125*-86
Hunter, Bobby Joe
71Globe-73
71Globe-74
71Globe-75
71Globe-76
71Globe-77
71Globe/Cocoa-20
71Globe/Cocoa-21
Hunter, Cedric
89ProC/CBA-167
90ProC/CBA-9
91ProC/CBA-184
Hunter, Curtis
86NC/Pol-43
89NC/Coke-172
90NC/200*-25
Hunter, Deon
89ProC/CBA-19
Hunter, Ivy Joe
89KY/300*-170
Hunter, Jo Jo
82TCMA/CBA-86
Hunter, Les
71Col/Mara-4
71T-157
72T-217
73T-263
Hunter, Tat
89ProC/CBA-69
91ProC/CBA-193
Hurd, Harry
89KY/300*-281
Hurley, Erin
85NE/Pol*-28
Hurt, Bobby
82Fairf-7
Hurt, Charles
79KY/Food-12
81KY/Sched-9
82KY/Sched-4
88KY/269-118
88KY/269-180
88KY/269-243
88KY/269-244
89KY/300*-47
Huston, Geoff
80T-175
80T-3
81T-MW73
83Star/NBA-236
85Star/NBA-135
Hutchins, Mel
(Hutch)
57T-46
81TCMA-4
Hutchinson, Tom
89KY/300*-148
Hyatt, Charles D.
68HOF-19
Hyatt, Rodney
87NC/Pol-11
Iavaroni, Marc
83Star/NBA-4
84Star/Arena-E4
85Star/NBA-146
88Jazz/Smok-5
89Hoops-142
89Jazz/OldH-6
Iba, Henry P.
68HOF-20
91OKSt*-1
91OKSt*-63
91OKSt-33CO
Iba, Gene
87Baylor/Pol*-6CO
Iba, Moe
85NE/Pol*-19CO
Ibrahim, I.M.
90Clemson/200*-69
Idelman
90ProC/CBA-12
Idzkowski, Dick
90MISt/200*-57
Igwebuike, Donald
90Clemson/200*-4
Ike, Larry
90MISt/200*-184
Imhoff, Darrall
69T-4
70T-3LL
70T-57
Immel, Dave
91UCLA/144-28
Imming, Stacy
85NE/Pol*-21
Incaviglia, Pete
91OKSt*-71
Ingalls, David
87ME/Pol*-10
Ingersoll, Carl
87BYU-8
Ingram, Linty
90AZSt/200*-21
90AZSt/Promos*-3
Inniger, Erv
86IN/Greatl-39
Ionata, Joey
90FLSt/200*-41
Ireland, George
90NotreDame-56
Ireland, R.Y.
89KY/300*-217
Irish, Edward S.
68HOF-21
Irvin, Byron
88MO-6
89Blaz/Franz-6
90F-156
90SkyBox-235
90SkyBox/II-420
91ProC/CBA-150
Irvin, Fess
87LSU/Pol*-4
Irvine, George
73T-248
74T-230M
74T-233
75T-320
Isaac, Reggie
91ProC/CBA-99
Ishmael, Charles
88KY/269-79
Ismail, Raghib
(Rocket)
91Classic/DPColl*-102
91Classic/DPCollLP*-LP1
91Classic/DPCollLP*-LP2
91Classic/DPCollLP*-LP3
91Classic/DPCollLP*-LP4
91Classic/DPCollLP*-LP5
Isom, Bud
91GATech*-14
Issel, Dan
71Col/Mara-5
71T-146LL
71T-147LL
71T-200
71T/Ins-3A
72T-230
72T-249AS
72T-259LL
73T-204M
73T-210AS
73T-234LL
74T-190AS
74T-207LL
74T-224M
75T-260
76T-94
77T-41
78RCCola-15
78T-81
79T-17
80T-120
80T-125
80T-166
80T-5
80T-68
80T-73
81T-11
81T-49M
81T-W107
82Nugget/Pol-44
83Nugget/Pol-44
83Star/NBA-189
84Star/CrtKg-28
84Star/NBA-142
84Star/NBA-283
87KY/Coke-4
88KY/269-166
88KY/269-179
88KY/269-226
88KY/269-7
89KY/300*-2
92F-56CO
92Hoops/I-245CO
92SkyBox/I-261CO
Iuzzolino, Mike
91Classic-25
91Classic/DPColl*-173
91Crtside-29
91F/Up-269
91FrRow/100-8
91FrRow/50-8
91FrRow/Premier-107
91StarPic-53
91UD-16
91UD/Rook-40
91WildCard/Coll-88
91WildCard/RHRook-8
92F-51
92Hoops/I-48
92SkyBox/I-51
Ivemeyer, John
91GATech*-10
Ivery, Eddie Lee
91GATech*-197
Ivy, Sam
88WakeForest/Pol-5
Izzo, Tom
90MISt-18ACO
Jabali, Warren
(Warren Armstrong)
71Flor/McDon-1
71T-188
72T-205
72T-261LL
73T-220AS
73T-239LL
75T-296
Jackson, Bo
87Auburn/Pol*-16
88Foot*-4
91Foot*-22
Jackson, Bobby
90FLSt/200*-7
Jackson, Chris
88LSU/Pol*-4
90F/Up-U25
90Hoops/II-392LS
90LSU/200*-18
90LSU/200*-189
90LSU/200*-190
90LSU/200*-2
90LSU/200*-91
90LSU/Promos*-2
90SkyBox/II-357LP
90StarPic-62
91F-49
91F/Rook-8
91Hoops/I-52
91Hoops/II-461SC
91Hoops/II-509Ar
91Panini-53
91SkyBox/Canada-13
91SkyBox/I-70
91SkyBox/II-465TW
91SkyBox/II-492RS
91UD-319
91UD-89TC
91UD/Rook-17
92F-57
92Hoops/I-56
92SkyBox/I-288TT
92SkyBox/I-60
Jackson, Craig
89ProC/CBA-172
91UCLA/144-71
Jackson, Dane
91ND*-16M
Jackson, Derrick
91George/100-43
91George/100-98
Jackson, Elfrem
89ProC/CBA-168
Jackson, Greg
75T-201
80TCMA/CBA-28
90LSU/200*-94
Jackson, Jackie
71Globe-78
71Globe-79
71Globe-80
71Globe-81
Jackson, Jaren
85George/Pol-8
86George/Pol-8
87George/Pol-8
88George/Pol-8
90ProC/CBA-124
91George/100-81
91George/100-9
91ProC/CBA-154
Jackson, Jay
80WichSt/Pol-5
Jackson, Jimmy
91OhioSt-10
92Classic/DP-31
92Classic/DPLP-LP4
Jackson, John
90MurraySt-5
Jackson, Keith OK
88Foot*-5
89Foot*-2
Jackson, Keith
81AZ/Pol-8
83AZ/Pol-8
84AZ/Pol-7
Jackson, Luke
69T-67
70T-33
71T-5
72T-118
Jackson, Maree
90LSU/200*-61
Jackson, Mario
90ORSt-11
91ORSt-10
Jackson, Mark
88F-121AS
88F-82
88Knick/FrLay-4
89F-101

88Fourn-4
88Fourn/St-4
89Conv-6
89F-77
89F/AS-5
89Hoops-166AS
89Hoops-270
90F-93
90F/AS-4
90Hoops-157
90Hoops-18AS
90Hoops/CollB-29
90Hoops/II-367TC
90Hoops/Super-47
90MISt/200*-131
90MISt/200*-133
90MISt/200*-182
90MISt/200*-186
90MISt/200*-189
90MISt/200*-194
90MISt/Promos*-4
90Panini-1
90Panini-B
90SkyBox-138
90SkyBox/Proto-138
91F-100
91F/ProV-6
91Hoops/ASMVP-11
91Hoops/I-101
91Hoops/I-266AS
91Hoops/I-312M
91Hoops/I-316MS
91Hoops/I-321YB
91Hoops/II-473SC
91Hoops/II-535
91Hoops/II-578
91Hoops/McDon-54USA
91Hoops/Proto/00-003
91Hoops/Super-48
91Panini-18
91Panini-192AS
91Panini-90AS
91SkyBox/Blister-5M
91SkyBox/Canada-25
91SkyBox/I-137
91SkyBox/I-323
91SkyBox/I-333M
91SkyBox/II-413GF
91SkyBox/II-417GF
91SkyBox/II-471TW
91SkyBox/II-533US
91SkyBox/Johnson-NNO
91SkyBox/Proto-137
91UD-29
91UD-45
91UD-57AS
91UD/Ext-451M
91UD/Ext-464AS
91UD/McDon-M4
92Hoops/I-309AS
92Hoops/I-328
92Hoops/I-329
92Hoops/I-330
92Hoops/I-331
92Hoops/I-340
92SkyBox/I-310MV
92SkyBox/Olympic-USA12
92SkyBox/USA-104
92SkyBox/USA-28
92SkyBox/USA-29
92SkyBox/USA-30
92SkyBox/USA-31
92SkyBox/USA-32
92SkyBox/USA-33
92SkyBox/USA-34
92SkyBox/USA-35
92SkyBox/USA-36
Johnson, Eddie
(Fast Eddie/Auburn)
78Hawks/Coke-8
78T-108
79Hawks/Majik-3
79T-24
80IL/Arby's-6
80T-128
80T-148
80T-152
80T-32
80T-9
81T-44M
81T-E68
83Star/NBA-268
84Star/NBA-81
85Star/NBA-44
Johnson, Eddie
(Illinois)
83Star/NBA-219
84Star/NBA-273
85Kings/Smok-8
85Star/NBA-76
86F-51
86Kings/Smok-3
87F-55
88F-90
89F-122
89Hoops-195
90F-148
90Hoops-237
90Hoops/Super-78
90SkyBox-223
90Sonic/Kayo-10
90Suns/Smok-3
91F-190
91Hoops/I-199
91SkyBox/I-270
91SkyBox/II-483TW
91UD-371
92F-211
92Hoops/I-215
92SkyBox/I-230
Johnson, Eddie
(Louisville)
89Louville/300*-146
Johnson, Ellis
88KY/269-18
Johnson, Elylen
91SC/200*-190
Johnson, Eric
90SkyBox-280
91ProC/CBA-203
Johnson, Frank
83Star/NBA-209
84Star/NBA-189
86F-52
89Hoops-57
89Hoops/II-333
Johnson, Gary
(Cat)
82TCMA/CBA-39
82TCMA/Lanc-25
82TCMA/Lanc-26
Johnson, George
71T-21
75T-13
78T-55
79T-39
80T-113
80T-114
80T-141
80T-37
80T-45
80T-53
84Star/NBA-206
Johnson, George E.
74T-54
Johnson, George L.
83Star/NBA-160
84Star/NBA-92
Johnson, George T.
74T-159
Johnson, Gilbert
89Pitt/Food-42
Johnson, Grant
89WI/Smok-8
Johnson, Greg
91ND*-14M
91ND*-1M
Johnson, Gus
69T-12
69T/Ins-18
70Suns/Carn-6
70T-92
71T-77
71T/Ins-44
72T-6
Johnson, J.J.
91Classic/DPColl*-83
Johnson, Jack
48T/Magic*-A6
87IN/GreatII-33
Johnson, Janine
87SWLou/McDag*-16
Johnson, Jerry
82Fairf-9
91ProC/CBA-164
Johnson, Jesse
(Oz)
89Louville/300*-100
Johnson, Jimmy
91OKSt*-19
Johnson, Joey
91ProC/CBA-90
Johnson, John
71T-4
72T-43
73T-47
74T-66
75T-147
78Sonic/Pol-4
79Sonic/Pol-14
79T-104
80T-166
80T-25
80T-78
80T-92
81T-W98
Johnson, John Henry
90AZSt/200*-70
Johnson, John MD
88MD/Pol-3
Johnson, John OK
91OKSt-35SPON
Johnson, Katrena
90AZ/125*-32
Johnson, Ken
85Blaz/Franz-6
87IN/GreatII-41
Johnson, Kevin
89F-123
89Hoops-35
90Clemson/200*-14
90F-149
90Hoops-19AS
90Hoops-238A
90Hoops-238B
90Hoops/CollB-40
90Hoops/II-375TC
90Hoops/Super-75
90Panini-16
90SkyBox-224A
90SkyBox-224B
90SkyBox/Proto-224
90Suns/Smok-4
91F-161
91F-210
91F/School-4
91F/Up-392TL
91Hoops/I-165
91Hoops/I-265AS
91Hoops/I-302IS
91Hoops/II-490SC
91Hoops/McDon-33
91Hoops/Super-77
91Kell/ColGrt-5
91Panini-21
91Panini-87
91SkyBox/Canada-38
91SkyBox/I-225
91SkyBox/II-479TW
91SkyBox/II-582
91UD-23
91UD-356
91UD-59AS
92F-181
92F-252PV
92F-258SY
92F/TmLeader-21
92Hoops/I-181
92Hoops/I-326LL
92Hoops/I-335
92SkyBox/I-191
92SkyBox/I-302TT
Johnson, Larry
88KY/269-105
88KY/269-177
88KY/269-227
88KY/269-237
Johnson, Larry UNLV
89UNLV/HOF-3
89UNLV/Seven-9
90UNLV/HOF-1
90UNLV/HOF-14
90UNLV/Season-1
90UNLV/Season-15M
90UNLV/Smok-9
91Classic-1
91Classic-44
91Classic-45M
91Classic/DPColl*-149
91Classic/DPColl*-192
91Classic/DPColl*-199M
91Classic/DPColl*-1M
91Classic/DPColl*-200M
91Classic/DPColl*-201M
91Classic/DPColl*-202M
91Classic/DPCollLP*-LP6
91Classic/DPCollLP*-LP9M
91Crtside-1
91Crtside-31
91Crtside-45
91Crtside/Holo-2
91F/Up-255
91FrRow/100-1
91FrRow/100-44
91FrRow/100-45
91FrRow/100-46
91FrRow/100-47
91FrRow/100-48
91FrRow/100-49
91FrRow/50-1
91FrRow/50-44
91FrRow/50-45
91FrRow/50-46
91FrRow/50-47
91FrRow/50-48
91FrRow/50-49
91FrRow/Johnson-Set
91FrRow/Premier-100HL
91FrRow/Premier-31ACC
91FrRow/Premier-81
91Hoops/II-546
91Hoops/II-HC
91Hoops/McDon-47
91SkyBox/II-513LP
91Smokey/Johnson-Set
91StarPic-18
91UD-2
91UD/Ext-438CL
91UD/Ext-445TP
91UD/Ext-480SD
91UD/Rook-26
91WildCard/Coll-1
91WildCard/Coll-24
91WildCard/RHRook-2
91Wooden-20
92F-247AW
92F-25
92F-253PV
92F-259SY
92F/Johnson-Set
92F/Rook-5
92F/TmLeader-3
92FrRow/DreamPk-1
92FrRow/DreamPk-2
92FrRow/DreamPk-3
92FrRow/DreamPk-4
92FrRow/DreamPk-5
92Hoops/I-24
92SkyBox/I-25
92SkyBox/I-319RO
Johnson, Lynbert
(Cheese)
81TCMA/CBA-89
Johnson, Mandy
82Marq/Lite-3
Johnson, Mark
91TexAM-38
Johnson, Marques
77Bucks/ActPh-7
78RCCola-16
78T-126
79Bucks/OpenP-9
79Bucks/Pol-8
79T-70AS
80T-136
80T-138
80T-139
80T-19
80T-48
80T-51
80T-88
80T-99
81T-24
81T-56M
81T-MW108
83Star/ASG-5
83Star/NBA-44
84Star/Arena-C5
84Star/CrtKg-48
84Star/NBA-13
85Star/NBA-88
86F-54
91UCLA/144-5
91UCLA/144-82
91Wooden-7
92Crtside/ColFB-19
Johnson, Mickey
76T-14
77Bulls/WhHen-4
77T-86
78T-36
79T-59
80T-121
80T-125
80T-13
80T-33
80T-37
80T-93
81T-56M
81T-MW98
84Star/NBA-155
85Star/NBA-63
86Star/LifeNets-7
Johnson, Mike
91OKSt-35SPO
Johnson, Nate
91ProC/CBA-65
Johnson, Neil
68Suns/Carn-4
70T-17
71T-216
72T-222
73T-188
Johnson, Ollie
73T-109

75T-124M
75T-51
79Bulls/Pol-27
Johnson, Phil
79Bulls/Pol-x
85Kings/Smok-2CO
89KY/300*-74
Johnson, Rafer
91UCLA/144-98
Johnson, Randy
81TCMA/CBA-87
Johnson, Reggie
83Star/NBA-150
Johnson, Reggie
91Classic/DPColl*-126
Johnson, Rich
70T-102
Johnson, Richard
81TCMA/CBA-76
89ProC/CBA-160
Johnson, Ron
91MI/56*-28
Johnson, Ronny
90NC/200*-131
Johnson, Rudy
91CT/Pol-6
Johnson, Sam
91ProC/CBA-176
Johnson, Sammy
90NC/200*-194
Johnson, Steffond
89ProC/CBA-124
Johnson, Steve
84Star/NBA-107
85Star/NBA-147
85Star/TmSuper-CB5
86Blaz/Franz-6
86F-55
87Blaz/Franz-12
87Blaz/Franz-4
87F-57
88Blaz/Franz-7
88F-94
89F-92
89Hoops-132
89Hoops/II-324
90F/Up-U33
90Hoops-278
90Hoops/Super-60
90SkyBox-267
90SkyBox/II-384
Johnson, Stew
71T-159
73T-213
74T-214
74T-228M
75T-249
Johnson, Todd
91ND*-5M
Johnson, Tom
85Victoria/Pol-4
88Victoria/Pol-5
Johnson, Tracy
90Clemson/200*-19
Johnson, Van
48T/Magic*-F13
Johnson, Vance
90AZ/125*-3
90AZ/125*-37
90AZ/125*-96
90AZ/Promos*-6
Johnson, Vinnie
79Sonic/Pol-8
81T-64M
81T-W99
83Star/NBA-89
84Star/NBA-264
85Star/NBA-14
85Star/TmSuper-DP3
86F-56
87F-58
88F-41
89F-47
89Hoops-188
90F-57
90Hoops-107
90Panini-89
90Piston/Star-8
90Piston/Unocal-5
90Piston/Unocal-6
90SkyBox-89
91F-61
91F/Up-355
91Hoops/I-62
91Hoops/Super-29
91Panini-128
91SkyBox/I-84
91UD-132
91UD/Ext-425
92F-206
92SkyBox/I-223
Johnson, Wallace
83Star/NBA-258
Johnson, Walter
48T/Magic*-K15
89KY/300*-268
Johnston, Andy
90Clemson/200*-152
Johnston, Neil
57T-3
Johnstone, Jim
82TCMA/CBA-8
Joliff, Howard
61Lakers/Bell-5
Jolivette, Brian
86SWLou/Pol*-9
Jones, Alfonza
79StBon-7
Jones, Anthony
81George/Pol-5
82George/Pol-15
88Mavs/CardN-21
90SkyBox-65
91Classic-41
91Classic/DPColl*-189
Jones, Antoine
90Pitt/Food-1
Jones, Bert
81T/Thirst-30
90LSU/200*-179
90LSU/200*-9
Jones, Bill TR
85Kings/Smok-3TR
86Kings/Smok-4TR
Jones, Bill
89Hoops/II-341
89ProC/CBA-46
Jones, Bobby
75T-222LL
75T-298
76T-144
77T-118
78T-14
79T-132
80T-155
80T-159
80T-67
80T-74
81T-32
81T-E106
83Star/NBA-6
83Star/Sixers-19
83Star/Sixers-8
84Star/Arena-E6
84Star/NBA-207
85JMS-3
85Star/NBA-5
85Star/TmSuper-PS3
89NC/Coke-44
89NC/Coke-45
89NC/Coke-46
89NC/Coke-97
90NC/200*-128
91Foot*-13
Jones, Bobby BB
91Classic/DPColl*-82
Jones, Brad
91MI/56*-29
Jones, Caldwell
74T-187
74T-211LL
74T-228M
75T-285M
75T-305
76T-112
77T-34
78T-103
79T-33
80T-109
80T-141
80T-17
80T-64
81T-59M
81T-E91
83Star/NBA-77
84Star/NBA-108
85Blaz/Franz-7
86Blaz/Franz-7
87Blaz/Franz-5
88Blaz/Franz-8
89Hoops/II-347
90Hoops-268
90SkyBox-257
Jones, Charles
(Louisville)
81Louville/Pol-1
83Louville-33
84Star/NBA-44
88Louville/194-118
88Louville/194-155
88Louville/194-23
88Louville/194-44
89Louville/300*-23
89Louville/300*-259
89Louville/300*-285
89Louville/300*-49
Jones, Charles
(Albany State)
84Star/NBA-190
90Hoops-299
90SkyBox-290
91Hoops/I-217
91SkyBox/I-293
91UD-328
92Hoops/I-236
92SkyBox/I-251
Jones, Charlie
82TCMA/CBA-32
Jones, Clinton
90MISt/200*-50
Jones, Collis
72T-181
73T-246
75T-271
90NotreDame-2
Jones, Danny
89WI/Smok-6
91ProC/CBA-32
Jones, Dante
91GATech*-7
Jones, Dwight
74T-59
75T-81
76T-33
78T-84
79Bulls/Pol-13
80T-26
80T-96
81T-MW68
Jones, Earl
84Star/NBA-175
Jones, Earl
91OKSt-1
91OKSt-38
Jones, Edgar
80TCMA/CBA-26
83Star/NBA-245
84Star/NBA-220
84Star/NBA-68
84Star/PolASG-30
84Star/SlamD-6
Jones, Fred
90FLSt/200*-44
Jones, Gary
91TexAM-59
Jones, Greg
89ProC/CBA-149
Jones, Harry
89KY/300*-119
Jones, Hassan
90FLSt/200*-144
Jones, Henry
91Classic/DPColl*-123
Jones, Herb
92Classic/DP-64
92StarPic-64
Jones, Jackie
91FrRow/100-80
91FrRow/Premier-14
91FrRow/Up-92
91StarPic-61
Jones, James
71T-185
71T/Ins-1A
72T-229
73T-260AS
74T-208LL
74T-210LL
74T-229M
74T-260AS
75T-23
Jones, James UNLV
88UNLV/HOF-9
89UNLV/HOF-12M
89UNLV/Seven-10
Jones, Jeff
91VA-8CO
Jones, Jerry
83Louville-x
88Louville/194-14
89Louville/300*-276
Jones, Johnny
87George/Pol-10
88George/Pol-10
89George/Pol-10
91George/100-62
Jones, K.C.
61F-22
84Star/Celt-21
84Star/Celt-6M
85Star/Lakers-13
85Star/LiteAS-7CO
87ME/Pol*-1M
90Hoops-329CO
90Hoops/II-343CO
90SkyBox/II-325CO
90Sonic/Kayo-7CO
90Sonic/Smok-6CO
91F-191
91Hoops/I-245CO
91SkyBox/II-402CO
Jones, Keith
90FLSt/200*-30
Jones, Ken
80TCMA/CBA-19
Jones, Kent
81Louville/Pol-26
83Louville-12
88Louville/194-68
Jones, Larry
71Flor/McDon-5
71T-230
71T/Ins-14A
72T-203
72T-260LL
73T-187
74T-103
89KY/300*-120
Jones, Lyndon
91ProC/CBA-73
Jones, Major
83Star/NBA-78
Jones, Mark
79StBon-8
Jones, Mike
80WichSt/Pol-6
91Classic/DPColl*-128
Jones, Nate
87Baylor/Pol*-1
Jones, Nick
72T-58
Jones, Ozell
80WichSt/Pol-7
84Star/NBA-69
89ProC/CBA-143
90ProC/CBA-98
Jones, Pat
91OKSt*-30
Jones, Perry T.
57Union-24
Jones, Rich
71T-198
72T-199
73T-215
74T-242
75T-243
76T-52
Jones, Ricky
89Clemson-12
90Clemson-10
91ProC/CBA-186
Jones, Ron
(Popeye)
90MurraySt-6
91MurraySt-2
92Classic/DP-50
92StarPic-35
Jones, Sam
61F-23
Jones, Shelton
89Hoops-51
89Hoops/II-306
Jones, Steve
71T-175
71T/Ins-19A
72T-216
72T-262LL
73T-179
74T-193
75T-232
Jones, Todd
91ND*-20CL
Jones, Wallace
(WahWah)
88KY/269-148
88KY/269-182
88KY/269-247
88KY/269-6
89KY/300*-185
Jones, Wally
(Wali)
69T-54
70T-83
71T-42
72T-78
75T-319
Jones, Wilbert
71T-168
72T-193
73T-221
74T-237
75T-289
77T-63
78T-42
Jones, Willie

82TCMA/CBA-6
90FLSt/200*-36
Jones, Zeke
90AZSt/200*-103
Joplin, Stan
90MISt-17ACO
Jordan, Adonis
89KS/Leesley-55
91KS-6
Jordan, Clinette
91OKSt*-52
Jordan, Eddie
79T-94
80T-103
80T-35
80T-54
82Lakers/BASF-5
Jordan, Gandhi
90Pitt/Food-2
Jordan, Homer
90Clemson/200*-44
Jordan, Jim
89KY/300*-269
Jordan, Jim NC
89NC/Coke-133
Jordan, Jimmy
90FLSt/200*-47
Jordon, Lisa
91TexAM-78
Jordan, Michael
84Star/CrtKg-26
84Star/NBA-101
84Star/NBA-195
84Star/NBA-288
85Bull/Interlake-1
85Star/Crunch-4
85Star/Gator-7
85Star/LiteAS-4
85Star/NBA-117
85Star/ROY-1
85Star/RTm-2
85Star/SlamD-5
85Star/TmSuper-CB1
86F-57
86F/Ins-8
86Star/Best-2
86Star/CrtKg-18
86Star/Jordan-1
86Star/Jordan-10
86Star/Jordan-2
86Star/Jordan-3
86Star/Jordan-4
86Star/Jordan-5
86Star/Jordan-6
86Star/Jordan-7
86Star/Jordan-8
86Star/Jordan-9
87Bulls/Ent-6
87F-59
87F/Ins-2
88Bulls/Ent-23
88F-120AS
88F-17
88F/Ins-7
88Fourn-22
88Fourn-x
88Fourn/St-5
89Bulls/Eq-6
89F-21
89F/AS-3
89Hoops-200
89Hoops-21AS
89NC/Coke-13
89NC/Coke-14
89NC/Coke-15
89NC/Coke-16
89NC/Coke-17
89NC/Coke-18
89NC/Coke-65
90Bulls/Eq-1
90F-26
90F/AS-5
90Hoops-5AS
90Hoops-65
90Hoops/CollB-4
90Hoops/II-358TC
90Hoops/II-382
90Hoops/Super-12
90McDon/Jordan-1-8
90NC/200*-3
90NC/200*-44
90NC/200*-61
90NC/200*-89
90NC/200*-93
90NC/Promos*-NC1
90Panini-91
90Panini-GAS
90Panini-K
90SkyBox-41
90SkyBox/Proto-41
91Arena/Holo*-3
91F-211
91F-220
91F-29
91F/ProV-2
91F/Up-375TL
91Hoops/ASMVP-9
91Hoops/I-253AS
91Hoops/I-30
91Hoops/I-306M
91Hoops/I-317MS
91Hoops/II-455SC
91Hoops/II-536
91Hoops/II-542M
91Hoops/II-543
91Hoops/II-579
91Hoops/McDon-55USA
91Hoops/McDon-6
91Hoops/Proto/00-004
91Hoops/SlamD-4
91Hoops/Super-13
91Nike/Jordan-Set
91Panini-116
91Panini-190AS
91Panini-96AS
91SkyBox/Canada-7
91SkyBox/I-307
91SkyBox/I-333M
91SkyBox/I-334
91SkyBox/I-39
91SkyBox/II-408GF
91SkyBox/II-462TW
91SkyBox/II-534US
91SkyBox/II-572
91SkyBox/II-583
91UD-22
91UD-44
91UD-48CL
91UD-69AS
91UD-75TC
91UD/AWHolo-1
91UD/AWHolo-4
91UD/Ext-452AS
91Wooden-13
92F-238LL
92F-246AW
92F-32
92F/AS-6
92F/TmLeader-4
92Hoops/I-298AS
92Hoops/I-30
92Hoops/I-320LL
92Hoops/I-341
92SkyBox/I-31
92SkyBox/I-314MV
92SkyBox/Olympic-USA11
92SkyBox/USA-105
92SkyBox/USA-37
92SkyBox/USA-38
92SkyBox/USA-39
92SkyBox/USA-40
92SkyBox/USA-41
92SkyBox/USA-42
92SkyBox/USA-43
92SkyBox/USA-44
92SkyBox/USA-45
Jordan, Payton
57Union-13
Jordan, Phil
57T-55
60Kahn's-6
61F-24
Jordan, Reggie
91ProC/CBA-100
Jordan, Thomas
91Classic-49
91Classic/DPColl*-197
Jordan, Walter
91ProC/CBA-84ACO
Joseph, Mickey
90NE/Pol*-10
91NE/Pol*-1
Joseph, Yvon
91GATech*-42
Josic, Zlatko
89Clemson-13
Jowdy, Ed
85NE/Pol*-27
Joyce, Bobby
90UNLV/HOF-12
90UNLV/Season-12
90UNLV/Smok-10
Joyce, Kevin
75T-237
91SC/200*-64
Joyner, Butch
87IN/GreatII-3
Joyner-Kersee, Jackie
90McDon/Jordan-JK1-8
Juday, Steve
90MISt/200*-36
Judkins, Jeff
80T-138
80T-19
82Blaz/Pol-22
Julian, Alvin F.
68HOF-22
Jung, Mark
81AZ/Pol-9
Jurgensen, Paul
91GATech*-78
Jurgensen, Sonny
76Nab-4M
Justice, Charlie
90NC/200*-107
90NC/200*-143
90NC/200*-168
90NC/200*-174
Justice, Dave
91Foot*-5
Kacer, Kevin
91ProC/CBA-84TR
Kachan, Whitey
86DePaul-H7
Kahl, Steve
90ProC/CBA-27
Kahs, Todd
90AZSt/200*-37
Kalbaugh, Bill
79StBon-9CO
Kalenich, Steve
90FLSt/200*-175
Kalinovich, Shawn
(Sean)
83Victoria/Pol-4
84Victoria/Pol-4
Kaluzienski, Matt
88MD/Pol-4
Kamrath, Lynn
90UCLA-21
Kanauna, Ken Sr.
90LSU/200*-187
Karasek, Tony
91ProC/CBA-76
Karem, Jason
90MurraySt-14
Karl, George
74T-257
75T-303
79Spurs/Pol-x
80TCMA/CBA-14
81TCMA/CBA-77
90NC/200*-147
90NC/200*-175
90ProC/CBA-159
92F-212CO
92Hoops/I-263CO
92SkyBox/I-279CO
Kasier, Roger
91GATech*-170
Kasoff, Mitch
88MD/Pol-5
Kasprowicz, Heidi
91ND*-9M
Katstra, Dirk
88VA/Hardee-8
Kattus, Eric
91MI/56*-30
Katz, Gilad
90CT/Pol-7
91CT/Pol-7
Kauffman, Bob
69T-48
71T-84
71T/Ins-23
72T-125
73NBAPA-15
73T-116
74T-153
75T-98
Kaull, Kurt
81George/Pol-14
82George/Pol-14
91George/100-13
Kea, Clarence
81TCMA/CBA-82
82TCMA/CBA-44
Kearns, Tommy
89NC/Coke-83
89NC/Coke-84
90NC/200*-192
Keefe, Adam
92Classic/DP-45
92Classic/DPLP-LP10
92FrRow/DreamPk-61
92FrRow/DreamPk-62
92FrRow/DreamPk-63
92FrRow/DreamPk-64
92FrRow/DreamPk-65
92SkyBox/NBADP-DP10
92StarPic-31
92StarPic-75
Keffer, Richard
(Dick)
55Ash-30
89Louville/300*-90
Keigley, Gerald
90LSU/200*-86
Kelber, Jason
90NE/Pol*-16
Keller, Billy
71Pacer/Mara-4
71T-149LL
71T-171
72T-192
72T-245
73T-237LL
73T-264
74T-201
74T-209LL
74T-223M
75T-248
75T-279M
76T-13
Kelley, Mike
91GATech*-43
Kelley, Rich
77T-67
78T-114
79T-86
80Suns/Pep-6
80T-159
80T-71
81T-W81
82Nugget/Pol-53
83Star/NBA-143
84Star/NBA-231
85Kings/Smok-9
Kellogg, Clark
83Star/All-R-4
83Star/NBA-161
84Star/CrtKg-20
84Star/NBA-52
85Star/NBA-81
86F-58
86Star/CrtKg-19
Kellogg, Ron
89ProC/CBA-68
90ProC/CBA-188
Kelly, Arvesta
71T-228
Kelly, Brian
90George/Pol-9
91George/Pol-9
Kelly, Carey
82AR-6
Kelly, John S.
83KY/Sched-11
89KY/300*-152
Kelly, Mike
91Classic/DPColl*-52
Kelm, Larry
91TexAM-47
Kelmmer, Grover
48T/Magic*-E9
Kelser, Greg
80T-171
80T-30
83Star/NBA-126
90MISt/200*-112
90MISt/200*-132
90MISt/Promos*-9
Kemp, Shawn
88KY/Sov-13
90F-178
90Hoops-279
90Panini-20
90SkyBox-268
90Sonic/Kayo-1
90Sonic/Smok-7
91F-192
91F-231
91Hoops/I-200
91Hoops/II-497SC
91Hoops/II-527Ar
91Hoops/McDon-42
91Hoops/Super-92
91Panini-42
91SkyBox/Canada-44
91SkyBox/I-271
91SkyBox/II-584
91StarPic-50
91UD-173
91UD-96TC
91UD/Ext-481SD
92F-213
92Hoops/I-216
92SkyBox/I-231
92SkyBox/I-306TT
Kempton, Tim
89Hoops-288
89Nugget/Pol-7
90SkyBox-76
91WildCard/Coll-73
Kendall, Duane

91SC/200*-7
Kennedy, Andy
91FrRow/100-64
91FrRow/Premier-33
91FrRow/Up-86
Kennedy, Barbara
90Clemson/200*-164
Kennedy, Darryl
91ProC/CBA-51
Kennedy, Gene
72T-208
73T-197
73T-235LL
75T-316
Kennedy, Marcus
91Classic-43
91Classic/DPColl*-191
91FrRow/100-15
91FrRow/50-15
91FrRow/Premier-80
91StarPic-58
Kennedy, Matthew P.
68HOF-23
Kennedy, Terry
90FLSt/200*-98
Kennett, Ron
89KY/300*-265
Kenny, Bonnie
91SC/200*-13
Kenny, Chris
90UCLA-7
Kenny, Eric
89NC/Coke-194
Kenon, Larry
74T-216
74T-226M
75T-294
77T-28
78T-71
79Spurs/Pol-35
79T-49
80T-167
80T-173
80T-41
80T-77
Kent, David
91TexAM-32
Kent, Gerry
90LSU/200*-134
Kercheval, Ralph
89KY/300*-162
Kerr, Johnny
(Red)
57T-32
61F-25
61F-56
68Suns/Carn-5CO
81TCMA-31
85Star/Schick-16
90Bulls/Eq-8
Kerr, Steve
83AZ/Pol-9
84AZ/Pol-9
85AZ/Pol-9
86AZ/Pol-6
87AZ/Pol-6
89Hoops/II-351
90AZ/125*-1
90AZ/125*-28
90AZ/125*-93
90AZ/Promos*-2
90F-34
90Hoops-75
90SkyBox-52
91F/Up-264
91Hoops/II-350
91SkyBox/I-50
91UD-208
Kersey, Jerome
84Blaz/Franz-6
84Blaz/Pol-9
85Blaz/Franz-8
85Star/NBA-107
86Blaz/Franz-8
87Blaz/Franz-6
87F-60
88Blaz/Franz-9
88F-95
89Blaz/Franz-7
89F-130
89Hoops-285
90Blaz/BP-4
90Blaz/Franz-15
90F-157
90Hoops-247
90Hoops/Super-81
90Panini-7
90SkyBox-236
91Blaz/Franz-12
91F-170
91Hoops/I-176
91Hoops/Super-82
91Panini-30
91SkyBox/I-239
91SkyBox/II-604
91UD-277
92F-188
92Hoops/I-191
92SkyBox/I-203
Kessler, Alec
90F/Up-U50
90Heat/Publix-7
90StarPic-32
91F/Up-306
91Hoops/I-112
91SkyBox/I-149
91UD-194
92Hoops/I-119
92SkyBox/I-126
Kestner, Rick
89KY/300*-113
Ketchum, Jack
91UCLA/144-136
Key, Jimmy
90Clemson/200*-18
Key, Stan
88KY/269-138
Keye, Julius
71T-150LL
71T-186
71T/Ins-15A
73T-227
Keys, Daric
88WakeForest/Pol-7
Keys, Randolph
87SoMiss-5
89Hoops-181
90Hoops-56
90SkyBox/II-369
91SkyBox/I-29
91UD-285
Khing, Tony
90ProC/CBA-94
Kiefer, Adolph
48Kell*-14
Kiewel, Jeff
90AZ/125*-87
Kiffin, Irv
79Spurs/Pol-21
Kilgore, Mik
92Classic/DP-65
Kilgore, William
90MISt/200*-153
Killilea, John
79Bucks/Pol-x
Killum, Earnest
91ORSt-11
Kilstein, Seymour
82TCMA/Lanc-3
Kimball, Toby
68Rocket/Jack-7
69T-39
70T-32
72T-68
73T-37
91CT/Legend-9
Kimber, Bill
90FLSt/200*-126
Kimble, Bo
90Clip/Star-6
90F/Up-U41
90Hoops/II-397LS
90SkyBox/II-359LP
90StarPic-15
91F-91
91Hoops/II-379
91SkyBox/I-126
91UD-114
91UD/Rook-5
92SkyBox/I-106
Kimbrough, Stan
90ProC/CBA-169
Kimmel, Bobby
91GATech*-176
Kinard, Bill
91GATech*-54
Kinard, Terry
90Clemson/200*-89
Kincaid, Mike
90FLSt/200*-173
Kinchen, Brian
90LSU/200*-15
Kindall, Jerry
90AZ/125*-15
Kinder, Richard
55Ash-66
Kinderman, Keith
90FLSt/200*-153
King, Albert
83Star/NBA-151
84Nets/Getty-6
84Star/NBA-93
86F-59
86Star/LifeNets-8
90ProC/CBA-149
King, Bernard
78RCCola-17
78T-75
79T-14
81T-W72
83Star/NBA-61
84Star/ASG-5
84Star/CrtKg-23
84Star/NBA-25
84Star/NBA-284
84Star/PolASG-5
86F-60
86Star/CrtKg-20
88F-116
89Conv-7
89F-159
89Hoops-240
90F-194
90Hoops-300
90Hoops/CollB-30
90Hoops/II-381TC
90Hoops/Super-99
90Panini-148
90SkyBox-291
91F-208
91Hoops/I-218
91Hoops/I-254AS
91Hoops/I-322YB
91Hoops/II-502SC
91Hoops/McDon-46
91Hoops/Super-99
91Kell/ColGrt-13
91Panini-173
91SkyBox/Canada-49
91SkyBox/I-294
91SkyBox/II-485TW
91SkyBox/II-573
91SkyBox/Proto-294
91UD-365
91UD-65AS
91UD-74TC
92SkyBox/I-252
King, Billy
87Duke/Pol-55
King, Chris
88WakeForest/Pol-8
92Classic/DP-37
92StarPic-14
King, Ed
91Classic/DPColl*-125
King, George
57T-6
King, Jeff
91ProC/CBA-143
King, Jeff BB
91AR/100*-54
King, Jerry
88Louville/194-192
89Louville/300*-19
King, Jim
57Kahn's-2
68T/Test-14
69T-66
70T-131
71T-72
72T-135
89KY/300*-219
King, Kim
91GATech*-95
King, Malcolm
91GATech*-87
King, Paul
90MurraySt-1
King, Reggie
80T-168
80T-85
81T-54M
81T-MW95
83Sonic/Pol-1
83Star/NBA-198
84Star/NBA-117
King, Rich
85NE/Pol*-36
91F/Up-360
91FrRow/Premier-1
91FrRow/Up-61
91StarPic-4
91UD-8
King, Ron
90FLSt/200*-183
King, Stacey
89Bulls/Eq-7
90F-27
90F/Rook-5
90Hoops-66
90Panini-92
90SkyBox-42
91F/Up-258
91Hoops/I-31
91Hoops/McDon-67
91SkyBox/I-40
91UD-182
92F-33
92Hoops/I-31
92SkyBox/I-32
King, William
89KY/300*-267
Kinker, Don
89Louville/300*-30
Kinnaird, Tony
89Louville/300*-69
Kinne, Howard
89KY/300*-156
Kinney, Bob
48Bowman-49
52Bread-16
Kiraly, Karch
88Foot*-6
Kirby, Terry
91VA-9
Kirk, Lowery
61Union-5
Kirkwood, Joe Jr.
48T/Magic*-J6
Kirwan, Albert D.
89KY/300*-157
Kishbaugh, Clayce
55Ash-90
Kitchel, Ted
86IN/GreatI-6
Kitchen, Joe
89Louville/300*-87
Kitchen, Robert
82AR-7
Kite, Dan
87LSU/Pol*-10
Kite, Greg
83Star/NBA-37
84Star/NBA-7
85JMS-18
89Hoops-202
89Kings/Carl-32
90Hoops-258
90Hoops/II-423
90SkyBox-247
90SkyBox/II-401
91Hoops/II-408
91Panini-74
91SkyBox/I-203
91UD-207
Kitley, Ralph
88WakeForest/Pol-9
Kizer, Noble
90NotreDame-28
Kleine, Joe
82AR-8
85Kings/Smok-10
86Kings/Smok-5
88F-97
89Hoops-47
90F-10
90Hoops-42
90Panini-137
90SkyBox-17
91AR/100*-38
91F/Up-250
91Hoops/I-12
91Hoops/II-559
91SkyBox/I-15
91SkyBox/II-558US
91UD-107
Kleinecke, Bobby
91TexAM-94
Kleiser, Bill
89KY/300*-220
Klier, Dan
81IL/Arby's-6
Klier, Leo
(Crystal)
48Bowman-24
90NotreDame-17
Kloppenburg, Bob
90Sonic/Smok-8CO
Klucas, Bill
80TCMA/CBA-33
81TCMA/CBA-49
82TCMA/CBA-24
91ProC/CBA-95CO
Knadler, Edwin
89KY/300*-23
Knight, Billy
75T-228AS
76T-124
77T-110
78T-72
79T-51
80T-126
80T-38
81T-53M
81T-MW91

83Star/NBA-216
84Star/NBA-274
Knight, Bobby
86IN/GreatI-1CO
87IN/GreatII-37
90KY/BB/DT/AW-24CO
92CenterCrt-7CO
92StarPic-5CO
Knight, Chris
90KY/ClassA-5
Knight, Gene
90LSU/200*-133
Knight, Janet
90Clemson/200*-193
Knight, Larry
80TCMA/CBA-39
Knight, Negele
90F/Up-U76
90StarPic-55
91F-162
91Hoops/II-418
91SkyBox/I-226
91SkyBox/II-506RS
91UD-193
91UD/Rook-16
92Hoops/I-182
92SkyBox/I-192
Knight, Ron
72T-101
Knight, Toby
79T-29
80T-149
80T-61
90NotreDame-33
Knighton, Rodney
89Louville/300*-162
Knop, Otto Sr.
89Louville/300*-182
Knopf, Johnny
89Louville/300*-40
Knorek, Lee
48Bowman-68
Knowles, Carl
91UCLA/144-123
Knox, Elyse
48T/Magic*-J40
Knox, James
(Jamie)
88NCSt/Pol-7
89NCSt/Pol-7
90NCSt/IBM-5
91NCSt/IBM-6
Knox, Jim
85Victoria/Pol-5
Knox, Kenny
90FLSt/200*-124
Knox, Mike
85NE/Pol*-5
Kobs, John Herman
90MISt/200*-106
Koback, Ed
82TCMA/Lanc-6
Koch, Martina
90AZ/125*-81
Koeleman, Hans
90Clemson/200*-26
Koenig, Gretchen
91SC/200*-23
Koenig, Marc
88MI/Nike-6
89MI-14
Koenigsmark, Theo.
55Ash-67
Kofoed, Bart
90ProC/CBA-189
90ProC/CBA-65
91Hoops/II-440
Kohrs, Bob
90AZSt/200*-40
Kojis, Don
68Rocket/Jack-8
69T-64
70Sonic/Sunb-6
70T-136
71Sonic/Sunb-6
71T-64
72T-116
73T-102
74T-63
75T-197
Kolb, Jon
91OKSt*-34
Kolehmainen, Duke
48T/Magic*-E6
Kolenda, Greg
91AR/100*-79
Komives, Howie
69T-71
70T-42
71T-53
72T-13
73T-161
Kon, Marcel
90GA/Smok-11
Koncak, Jon
87Hawks/Pizza-9
89F-2
89Hoops-151
90F/Up-U1
90Hoops-28
90SkyBox-3
91F-2
91Hoops/II-333
91Hoops/II-560
91SkyBox/I-3
91SkyBox/II-559US
91UD-236
92F-4
92Hoops/I-5
92SkyBox/I-5
Konowalchuk, Steve
91Classic/DPColl*-46
Konz, Kenny
90LSU/200*-83
Koonce, Donnie
81TCMA/CBA-7
Kopicki, Joe
82TCMA/CBA-76
83Star/NBA-210
84Star/NBA-143
Korab, Jerry
74Nab-16
Kornet, Frank
87Vanderbilt/Pol-11
90Hoops-176
90SkyBox-159
91WildCard/Coll-76
Kortas, Ken
89Louville/300*-107
Korte, Steve
91AR/100*-71
Kotar, Doug
89KY/300*-135
Koubek, Greg
87Duke/Pol-22
88Duke/Pol-8
Koufax, Sandy
81PhilM-2
Kovach, Jim
89KY/300*-125
Kowalczyk, Walt
90MISt/200*-72
Kozelko, Tom
73Bullet/Stand-4
75T-202
Kraak, Charley
87IN/GreatII-34
Kraft, Greg
91SC/200*-30
Kramer, Jack
48ExhSC-27
57Union-40
Kramer, Joel
80Suns/Pep-8
Kramer, Ron
91MI/56*-31
Krause, Edward
(Moose)
90NotreDame-12
Kraushaar, Karl
91UCLA/144-70
Krebs, Jim
57T-25
Krebs, Tina
90Clemson/200*-151
Kreke, Robert
84Victoria/Pol-5
Kreklow, Wayne
82TCMA/CBA-78
Kremer, Mitzi
90Clemson/200*-155
Kremers, Jim
91AR/100*-43
Krentra, Kris
91GATech*-198
Kretzer, Bill
89NCSt/Coke-137
89NCSt/Coke-67
Kreuter, Howard
89KY/300*-266
Kriese, Chuck
90Clemson/200*-145
Kron, Tommy
88KY/269-253
88KY/269-82
Kroon, Marc
91Classic/DPColl*-219
Krueger, Rolf
91TexAM-54
Kruse, Janet
91NE/Pol*-11
Krystkowiak, Larry
87Bucks/Polar-42
88Bucks/Green-8
89F-87
89Hoops-258
90Hoops-177
90SkyBox-160
91F/Up-314
91Hoops/II-393
91SkyBox/I-159
91UD-368
92F-223
92Hoops/I-129
92SkyBox/I-136
Krzyzewski, Mike
87Duke/Pol-x
88Duke/Pol-9CO
91Hoops/II-588CO
91SkyBox/II-542US
92SkyBox/USA-95CO
92SkyBox/USA-96CO
92StarPic-15CO
Kuberski, Steve
70T-67
71Bucks/Linn-5
71T-98
72T-153
73T-2
74T-136
76T-54
Kubiak, Gary
91TexAM-5
Kuhn, Eric
80WichSt/Pol-8
Kuipers, Jason
90FLSt/200*-72
Kuka, Ray
48Bowman-39
Kukoc, Toni
90StarPic-39
Kula, Bob
90MISt/200*-9
Kulick, Paul
90ProC/CBA-57
Kull, Herman
91ProC/CBA-9CO
Kunnert, Kevin
75T-123M
75T-145
76T-91
77T-84
78Clipp/Handy-9
79Blaz/Pol-44
81Blaz/Pol-44
Kupchak, Mitch
77T-128
78T-48
79T-2
80T-125
80T-73
81T-E97
83Lakers/BASF-5
83Star/NBA-17
84Lakers/BASF-4
84Star/NBA-176
85Star/NBA-29
89NC/Coke-47
89NC/Coke-48
89NC/Coke-49
90NC/200*-108
90NC/200*-123
Kupec, Chris
90NC/200*-101
90NC/200*-112
Kupec, Matt
90NC/200*-17
90NC/200*-51
Kupper, Ed
89Louville/300*-29
Kurland, Robert A.
(Bob)
68HOF-24
91OKSt*-5
Kush, Frank
90AZSt/200*-189
90MISt/200*-185
LaBruzzo, Joe
90LSU/200*-180
Lacey, Bobby
90NC/200*-186
Lacey, Sam
71T-57
72T-63
73T-85
74T-89M
74T-99
75Carv-17
75T-124M
75T-158
75T-4LL
76Buck-13
76T-67
77T-49
78T-99
79T-28
80T-116
80T-141
80T-47
80T-64
81T-MW96
Lachance, Scott
91Classic/DPColl*-4
Lackey, David
85FortHaysSt-10
Lackey, Greg
85FortHaysSt-11CO
89UTEP/Drug-16
LaCour, Fred
61Hawks/Essex-7
Ladner, Jay
87SoMiss-10
Ladner, Wendell
72T-226
73T-261
74T-244
Laettner, Christian
88Duke/Pol-10
91WildCard/Coll-26B
92Classic/BKPrev-BK5
92Classic/DP-43
92Classic/DP-BC
92Classic/DPLP-LP3
92FrRow/DreamPk-41
92FrRow/DreamPk-42
92FrRow/DreamPk-43
92FrRow/DreamPk-44
92FrRow/DreamPk-45
92Hoops/I-342
92SkyBox/Olympic-USA9
92StarPic-10
92StarPic-32
LaFauci, Tyloer
90LSU/200*-140
Lafayette, Lee
90MISt/200*-111
Lafleur, Greg
90LSU/200*-157
Laframboise, Tom
89Louville/300*-124
LaGarde, Tom
78Sonic/Pol-5
79Sonic/Pol-4
80T-104
80T-16
81T-10
81T-48M
Lahay, Bruce
91AR/100*-40
Lahtinen, Pasi
89Fresno/Smok-7
Laib, Art
89KY/300*-76
Laimbeer, Bill
81T-MW74
83Star/ASG-6
83Star/NBA-90
84Star/ASG-6
84Star/NBA-265
84Star/PolASG-6
85Star/NBA-10
85Star/TmSuper-DP4
86F-61
87F-61
88F-42
89Conv-8
89F-48
89Hoops-135
90F-58
90Hoops-108
90Hoops/Super-29
90NotreDame-13
90Panini-88
90Piston/Star-9
90Piston/Unocal-7
90SkyBox-90
91F-62
91Hoops/I-63
91Hoops/McDon-13
91Hoops/Super-28
91Panini-127
91Piston/Unocal-15M
91Piston/Unocal-6
91Piston/Unocal-7
91SkyBox/I-85
91SkyBox/II-466TW
91UD-167
92F-64
92Hoops/I-65
92SkyBox/I-70
Lake, Arthur
48T/Magic*-J8
Lamar, Dwight
74T-177
74T-228M

75T-256
Lamar, Lewis
91NM-9
Lamarr, Hedy
48T/Magic*-J14
Lambert, Ward L.
68HOF-25
Lambrecht, Dimitri
89Fresno/Smok-8
90Fresno/Smok-9
Lamkin, Jim
86DePaul-C2
Lamont, Brad Jr.
90MISt/200*-175
Lamour, Dorothy
48T/Magic*-F10
Lamp, Jeff
81Blaz/Pol-3
82Blaz/Pol-3
83Blaz/Pol-3
83Star/NBA-101
86Star/LifeBucks-7
89Hoops-144
Lampley, Jim
89ProC/CBA-6
90ProC/CBA-116
Lancaster, Gerry
91JMadison/Smok-9
Lancaster, Harry C.
88KY/269-51
Lancaster, Les
91AR/100*-12
Landacox, Ken
90AZSt/200*-153
Lander, Cassandra
90AZSt/200*-179
Lander, Ed
89KY/300*-284
Landrum, Bill
91SC/200*-86
Landrum, Joe
90Clemson/200*-180
Landry, Greg
74Nab-10
Landsberger, Mark
79Bulls/Pol-54
80T-134
80T-46
81T-W78
82Lakers/BASF-6
83Star/NBA-269
90AZSt/200*-41
Lane, Jerome
88Nugget/Pol-35
89Hoops-201
89Nugget/Pol-8
90Hoops-96
90Panini-63
90SkyBox-77
91Hoops/I-53
91SkyBox/Canada-14
91SkyBox/I-305
91SkyBox/I-309M
91SkyBox/I-71
91UD-295
LaNeve, Ronald
55Ash-91
Lang, Andrew
90SkyBox-225
91AR/100*-67
91F/Up-340
91Hoops/I-166
91Hoops/II-419
91SkyBox/I-227
91UD-158
92F-172
92Hoops/I-183
92SkyBox/I-193
Lang, Tom
87George/Pol-11
91George/100-53
Langhi, Donnie
90MurraySt-7
Langseth, Misty
91ND*-9M
Langston, Keith
91TexAM-41
Langston, Lisa
91TexAM-15
Lanier, Bob
71T-63
71T/Ins-11
72T-80
73NBAPA-16
73T-110
74T-131
74T-86M
75Carv-18
75Nab-19
75T-121M
75T-30
76Buck-14
76T-10
77T-61
78RCCola-18
78T-125
79T-58
80T-104
80T-127
80T-46
80T-82
81T-25
81T-MW109
83Star/NBA-45
Lanier, Gary
91GATech*-89
Lanier, Mike
90UCLA-6
91UCLA-1
Lanier, Willie
75Nab-10
Lankster, Jim
90KY/Sov-3
Lansdell, Daryn
88Victoria/Pol-6
Lanter, Bo
79KY/Food-8
81KY/Sched-10
88KY/269-117
Lantz, Rick
89Louville/300*-128
91GATech*-93
Lantz, Stu
68Rocket/Jack-9
70T-44
71T-108
72T-16
73T-96
74T-101
74T-86M
75T-127M
75T-88
Lapchick, Joe
68HOF-26
92CenterCrt-23
LaPierre, Gary
87ME/Pol*-5
Lapointe, Martin
91Classic/DPColl*-9
LaReau, Bernie
79Spurs/Pol-x
Larese, York
89NC/Coke-102
89NC/Coke-103
90NC/200*-96
Larkin, Barry
91MI/56*-32
Larkins, Larry
89NCSt/Coke-91
89NCSt/Coke-92
89NCSt/Coke-93
89NCSt/Coke-94
LaRose, Rick
90AZ/125*-72
Larranaga, Jim
91Providence-15
Larson, Jon
91ND*-17M
Larson, Ken
83Victoria/Pol-5
LaRusso, Rudy
61F-26
61F-57IA
61Lakers/Bell-6
Laska, Mike
91George/100-78
Laskowski, John
86IN/GreatI-33
Lastinger, Shawn
89Clemson-14
90Clemson-11
Latreille, Yves
57Union-35
Lattimer, Earl
90MISt/200*-8
Lattin, Dave
68Suns/Carn-6
89UTEP/Drug-17
Laughinghouse, Scott
87Vanderbilt/Pol-6
Laughlin, Bobby
55Ash-54
Laughna, Mike
91George/100-94
Lautenbach, Todd
91WA/TCI-5
Lavelli, Dante
52Bread-17
Lavette, Robert
91GATech*-79
Lavigne, Eric
91Classic/DPColl*-22
Lavin, Bob
89KY/300*-244
Lavin, Steve
91UCLA-18ACO
LaVine, Jackie
54Quaker-15
Lavole, Phil
91SC/200*-60
Law, Billy
92Classic/DP-88
Lawhon, Mike
88Louville/194-127
88Louville/194-163
88Louville/194-37
89Louville/300*-248
Lawrence, Dave
89KY/300*-77
Lawrence, Larry
81TCMA/CBA-43
91WildCard/Coll-99
Lawson, David
91ORSt-12
Lawson, Larry
90AZSt/200*-156
Lay, Emmett
89NCSt/Coke-113
89NCSt/Coke-114
Lay, Ian Hyde
83Victoria/Pol-3ACO
Layden, Frank
78Hawks/Coke-9CO
84Star/Award-2
88Jazz/Smok-3CO
89Jazz/OldH-7CO
Layne, Roger
89KY/300*-75
Layton, Dennis
(Moe)
72T-106
73T-81
Lazzaretti, Vic
82Marq/Lite-4
Leach, Michael
91MI/56*-33
Leaks, Manny
71T-217
73Bullet/Stand-5
73T-74
74T-48
Lear, Geoff
92Classic/DP-89
Leary, Rob
86LSU/Pol*-7
Leathers, Buddy
89Louville/300*-86
Leavell, Allen
80T-117
80T-126
80T-29
80T-79
81T-52M
83Star/NBA-79
84Star/NBA-240
85Star/NBA-19
86F-62
89Hoops-77
Leaycraft, Donnie
90LSU/200*-192
Lebo, Jeff
86NC/Pol-14
87NC/Pol-14
88NC/Pol-14
88NC/Pol-x
89NC/Coke-134
89NC/Coke-135
90NC/200*-36
90NC/200*-74
Leckner, Eric
89F-154
89Hoops-12
89Jazz/OldH-8
90F-187
90F/Up-U85
90Hoops-291
90Hoops/II-429
90Kings/Safe-6
90SkyBox-281
90SkyBox/II-410
91F-21
91Hoops/II-344
91SkyBox/I-30
91UD-204
Ledford, Cawood
88KY/269-132
Lee, Butch
78Hawks/Coke-10
Lee, Christine
89McNees*-7
Lee, Clyde
69T-93
70T-144
71T-12
72T-138
73T-143
74T-32
75T-93
Lee, Danny
91NE/Pol*-13CO
Lee, David
88NCSt/Pol-8
89NCSt/Pol-8
90NCSt/IBM-6
Lee, Don
90AZ/125*-65
Lee, Doug
91FrRow/100-84
91FrRow/ItalPromo-4
91FrRow/Premier-10
91FrRow/Up-76
91WildCard/Coll-71
Lee, Gary
91GATech*-77
Lee, George
61F-27
Lee, Greg
91UCLA/144-19
Lee, James
77KY/Wildct-17
81TCMA/CBA-11
82TCMA/CBA-19
82TCMA/Lanc-13
82TCMA/Lanc-14
88KY/269-109
88KY/269-230
Lee, John
90Clemson/200*-75
Lee, Keith
89Hoops-236
Lee, Kirk
90Nets/Kayo-10
Lee, Kurk
91UD-24
Lee, Raymond
85FortHaysSt-12
Lee, Ron
76Suns-6
77Suns/Discs-30
77T-117
78T-97
81T-50M
Lee, Spike
91Nike/Jordan-Set
Lee, Theodis Ray
71Globe-54
71Globe-55
Lee, Treg
91Crtside-32
91StarPic-3
91WildCard/Coll-49
Leeks, Ken
92Classic/DP-66
Lefferts, Craig
90AZ/125*-10
Leggett, Earl
90LSU/200*-80
Legler, Tim
89ProC/CBA-73
90ProC/CBA-8
91ProC/CBA-187
Leheup, John
91SC/200*-196
Lehmann, George
71T-192
72T-211
73T-194
Lemaster, Frank
89KY/300*-193
LeMaster, Jim
88KY/269-85
Lembke, Jeff
91ND*-20CL
Lemon, Bob
57Union-14
Lemon, Meadowlark
71Globe-10
71Globe-11
71Globe-12
71Globe-13
71Globe-14
71Globe-15
71Globe-16
71Globe-17
71Globe-18M
71Globe-19M
71Globe-20
71Globe-64M
71Globe-66M
71Globe-67M
71Globe-69M
71Globe-70
71Globe-72M
71Globe-9
71Globe/Cocoa-10M

71Globe/Cocoa-22
71Globe/Cocoa-23
71Globe/Cocoa-26
71Globe/Cocoa-2M
71Globe/Cocoa-3
71Globe/Cocoa-4M
71Globe/Cocoa-6M
71Globe/Cocoa-7M
71Globe/Cocoa-9M
Lentz, Frank
89Louville/300*-60
Lentz, Larry
89KY/300*-78
Leon, Eddie
90AZ/125*-36
Leonard, Bob
57T-74
61F-28
71Pacer/Mara-5
81TCMA-35
85Star/Schick-17
87IN/GreatII-4
Leonard, Bryan
80IL/Arby's-7
81IL/Arby's-7
Leonard, Ed
90ProC/CBA-39
Leonard, Gary
88MO-7
91Hoops/II-334
Leonard, John
82Fairf-10
82TCMA/CBA-36
Leonard, Quinton
89NCSt/Coke-109
Les, Jim
89Jazz/OldH-9
90ProC/CBA-1
91F-176
91Hoops/I-307M
91Hoops/II-428
91SkyBox/I-247
91SkyBox/II-454SM
91UD-360
92SkyBox/I-213
Lescheid, David
85Victoria/Pol-6
Leskovar, Bill
89KY/300*-102
Leslie, Al
81TCMA/CBA-34
Lesnevich, Gus
48T/Magic*-A16
Lesnik, Ivan
90AZ/125*-62
Lesoravage, Chris
91VA/Lady-5
Lester, Avie
87NCSt/Pol-8
88NCSt/Pol-9
89NCSt/Pol-9
Lester, Ronnie
83Star/NBA-176
84Lakers/BASF-5
84Star/NBA-177
Lett, Clifford
89ProC/CBA-55
90ProC/CBA-35
Levane, Andrew
(Fuzzy)
48Bowman-21
61Hawks/Essex-8
Leveque, Guy
91Classic/DPColl*-36
Lever, Lafayette
(Fat)
82Blaz/Pol-12
83Blaz/Pol-12
83Star/All-R-5
83Star/NBA-102
84Star/NBA-144
85Nugget/Pol-9
85Star/NBA-54
86F-63
87F-62
88F-35
88Nugget/Pol-12A
88Nugget/Pol-12B
89F-41
89Hoops-220
89Nugget/Pol-9
90AZSt/200*-33
90AZSt/200*-9
90AZSt/Promos*-2
90F-50
90F/Up-U20
90Hoops-20AS
90Hoops-97
90Hoops/II-408
90Hoops/Super-25
90SkyBox-78
90SkyBox/II-376
91F/Up-270
91Hoops/I-47
91Hoops/Super-23
91SkyBox/I-61
91UD-157
92Hoops/I-49
92SkyBox/I-52
Levine, Chas. A.
48T/Magic*-L8
Levine, Sam
48T/Magic*-J9
Levingston, Cliff
80WichSt/Pol-9
83Star/NBA-91
84Star/NBA-82
85Star/NBA-45
87F-63
87Hawks/Pizza-10
88F-2
89F-3
89Hoops-22
90F-2
90F/Up-U15
90Hoops-29
90Hoops/II-405
90SkyBox-4
90SkyBox/II-372
91F-30
91Hoops/I-32
91Hoops/McDon-68
91SkyBox/I-41
91UD-187
92F-34
Levitt, Harold
(Bunny)
54Quaker-5
Lewis, Bill
85NE/Pol*-11
Lewis, Bob
71T-22
89NC/Coke-69
89NC/Coke-70
89NC/Coke-71
90NC/200*-155M
90NC/200*-161
90NC/200*-184
Lewis, Carl
89Foot*-7
91Foot*-28
Lewis, Cedric
88MD/Pol-6
91Crtside-33
91FrRow/100-73
91FrRow/Premier-23
91FrRow/Up-90
91ProC/CBA-101
Lewis, Darren
91Classic/DPColl*-208
Lewis, Darryl
91Classic/DPColl*-134
Lewis, Frank
91OKSt*-69
Lewis, Fred
48Bowman-4CO
Lewis, Freddie
71Pacer/Mara-6
71T-204
72T-219
73T-212
74T-223M
74T-263
75T-275
75T-283M
90AZSt/200*-184
Lewis, Garland
89KY/300*-264
Lewis, Greg
91Classic/DPColl*-207
Lewis, Gus
48ExhSC-28
Lewis, Jimmy
91Classic/DPColl*-94
Lewis, Junie
91ProC/CBA-55
Lewis, Lance
90NE/Pol*-11
Lewis, Marc
90NCSt/IBM-7
91NCSt/IBM-7
Lewis, Mike
71T-150LL
71T-189
71T/Ins-12A
72T-234
73T-219
Lewis, Quinton
91SC/200*-194
Lewis, Ralph
89ProC/CBA-9
91ProC/CBA-111
Lewis, Reggie
89F-10
89Hoops-17
90F-11
90Hoops-43
90Hoops/Super-5
90Panini-134
90SkyBox-18
91F-12
91Hoops/I-13
91Hoops/Super-6
91Panini-147
91SkyBox/I-16
91SkyBox/II-408GF
91SkyBox/II-567
91UD-123
91UD/Ext-458AS
92F-16
92F/AS-7
92F/TmLeader-2
92Hoops/I-15
92Hoops/I-299AS
92SkyBox/I-15
92SkyBox/I-283TT
Lewis, Richie
90FLSt/200*-97
Lewis, Ronald
90FLSt/200*-51
Lewis, Sherman
90MISt/200*-13
Lewis, Strangler
48T/Magic*-D6
Lewis, Terrence
92Classic/DP-16
Lewis, Tim
91SC/200*-77
Liberty, Marcus
90F/Up-U26
90StarPic-53
91F-50
91Hoops/II-359
91Panini-56
91SkyBox/I-72
91SkyBox/II-438SM
91UD-222
92F-58
92Hoops/I-57
92SkyBox/I-61
Lichtenstein, Nita
90NE/Pol*-19
Lichti, Todd
89Nugget/Pol-10
90F-51
90Hoops-98
90Panini-65
90SkyBox-79
91F-51
91Hoops/I-54
91Hoops/II-462SC
91Panini-52
91SkyBox/I-73
91UD-299
92Hoops/I-58
92SkyBox/I-62
Lickert, Bill
88KY/269-207
88KY/269-38
Lidman, Haaken
48T/Magic*-E15
Liebler, Steve
91SC/200*-108
Liedtke, Joe
88Louville/194-148
88Louville/194-93
Ligon, Jim
71Col/Mara-6
72T-204
Lilly, Bob
74Nab-7
75Nab-7
Lilly, Sammy
91GATech*-76
Limbrick, Garrett
91OKSt*-98
Limne, Paul
90AZSt/200*-167
Lindbergh, Charles
48T/Magic*-L6
Lindquist, Fredrik
91Classic/DPColl*-44
Lindros, Eric
91Classic/DPColl*-1M
Lindsey, Sammie
89Fresno/Smok-9
90Fresno/Smok-10
Line, Jim
88KY/269-156
88KY/269-35
Linn, Warren
91AR25-8
Linnamo, Vesa
85Victoria/Pol-7
Linonis, Ed
89Louville/300*-74
Linthicum, Richard
91UCLA/144-101
Linville, Shelby
88KY/269-43
Lipka, Warren
91SC/200*-31
Lister, Alton
83Star/NBA-46
84Star/Arena-C7
84Star/NBA-132
85Star/Bucks-9
85Star/NBA-126
85Star/TmSuper-MB5
86F-64
86Star/LifeBucks-8
87F-64
89F-147
89Hoops-293
89Hoops/II-325
90AZSt/200*-31
91F/Up-287
91Hoops/I-70
91Panini-5
91SkyBox/I-94
91UD-316
92Hoops/I-76
92SkyBox/I-81
Little, Crowell
90NC/200*-190
Little, Derrick
91SC/200*-25
Little, Doug
90FLSt/200*-142
Little, Ercel
89KY/300*-263
Little, Floyd
74Nab-2
75Nab-2
Little, John
91OKSt*-23
Little, Steve
91AR/100*-26
Littles, Gene
74T-184
90Hoops-307CO
90SkyBox/II-303CO
91F-22CO
91Hoops/I-223CO
Littlewood, Mary
90AZSt/200*-196
Litwhiler, Danny
90FLSt/200*-111
90MISt/200*-17
Livingston, Otis
87KS/Nike-7
Livingston, Ron
91UCLA/144-59
Livingstone, Ron
52Bread-18
Livingstone, Scott
91TexAM-17
Livsey, Shawn
91Classic/DPColl*-75
Llewellyn, Duke
91Wooden-6
Lloyd, Earl
57T-54
Lloyd, Lewis
83Star/NBA-80
84Star/NBA-241
85Star/NBA-20
85Star/TmSuper-HR3
86F-65
Lloyd, Scott
90AZSt/200*-18
Loban, Noel
90Clemson/200*-130
Lochmueller, Bob
88Louville/194-57
Lochmueller, Steve
89KY/300*-79
Lock, Rob
88KY/269-130
88KY/269-176
88KY/269-210
89KY/Tm80-47
Locke-Mattox, Bernadette
91KY/BB/Double-16ACO
Lockett, Danny
90AZ/125*-30
Lockhart, Detra
90UCLA-22
Lockhart, Ian
88TN/Smok-51
91WildCard/Coll-97
Lockhart, June
48T/Magic*-J13
Locum, Tim
89WI/Smok-9

Loeffler, Kenneth D.
68HOF-27
Loescher, Doug
91FrRow/100-98
Loewer, Stan
86LSU/Pol*-8
Lofstedt, Amy
91VA/Lady-6
Lofton, Kenny
85AZ/Pol-10
86AZ/Pol-7
87AZ/Pol-7
88AZ/Pol-7
90AZ/125*-121
90AZ/125*-79
Logan, John
48Bowman-7
Logan, Kevin
90SanJ/Smok-4
Logan, Marc
89KY/300*-143
Logan, Steve
91NM-10
Lohaus, Brad
88Kings/Carl-54
89Hoops-74
89Hoops/II-332
89TWolv/BK-54
90F/Up-U54
90Hoops-178
90Panini-97
90SkyBox-161
91Hoops/I-118
91SkyBox/I-160
91UD-383
Lollis, Lori
91WASt-8
Lombardo, Guy
48ExhSC-29
Londos, Jim
48T/Magic*-D5
Long, Bob
91TexAM-71
Long, Gary
86IN/GreatI-23
Long, Grant
89F-82
89Heat/Publix-7
89Hoops-141
90F-100
90Heat/Publix-8
90Hoops-167
90SkyBox-149
91F-109
91Hoops/II-387
91Panini-152
91SkyBox/I-150
91UD-192
92F-118
92Hoops/I-120
92SkyBox/I-127
Long, Greg
89KY/300*-149
Long, John
79T-38
80T-111
80T-23
81T-50M
81T-MW83
83Star/NBA-92
84Star/NBA-266
85Star/NBA-15
85Star/TmSuper-DP5
87F-65
88F-56
89Hoops-167
90Hoops-30
90SkyBox-5
Long, Kevin
90AZ/125*-105
90AZ/125*-16
Long, Larry
91George/100-70
Long, Ryan
91Classic/DPColl*-90
Long, Willie
71Flor/McDon-6
72T-214
73T-251
74T-202
Longley, Luc
90NM-6
91F/Up-320
91FrRow/Premier-37
91FrRow/Premier-95HL
91FrRow/Up-54
91Hoops/II-552
91SkyBox/II-519LP
91StarPic-31
91UD/Ext-491
92F-134
92Hoops/I-138
92SkyBox/I-145
Look, Dean
90MISt/200*-78
Lookingbill, Wade
91Iowa-6
Loomis, Bob
90NC/200*-84
Lopez, Damon
91Classic-48
91Classic/DPColl*-196
Lorenzen, Al
89ProC/CBA-183
Loscutoff, Jim
57T-39
81TCMA-34
Lothridge, Billy
91GATech*-53
Loucks, H. Donald
90FLSt/200*-184
Loughery, Kevin
69T-94
70T-51
71T-7
72T-83
85Star/CO-4
91F-110CO
91Hoops/I-234CO
91SkyBox/II-391CO
92F-119CO
92Hoops/I-252CO
92SkyBox/I-268CO
Louis, Joe
48ExhSC-30
48T/Magic*-A15
81PhilM-9
Loukes, Wade
84Victoria/Pol-6
88Victoria/Pol-7
Love, Amy
85NE/Pol*-37
Love, Bob
69T-78
70Bulls/Hawth-1
70T-84
71T-45
71T/Ins-28
72Icee-11
72T-148
72T-166AS
73NBAPA-17
73T-60AS
74T-15
74T-84M
75Carv-19
75T-119M
75T-140
76Buck-15
76T-45
90Bulls/Eq-9
Love, Melvin
90UNLV/Season-14
90UNLV/Smok-11
Love, Stan
72T-2
73T-76
Lovellette, Clyde
56Busch-2
57Kahn's-3
57T-78
61F-29
61F-58
61Hawks/Essex-9
81TCMA-14
Lowe, Lawrence
91GATech*-59
Lowe, Sidney
83Star/NBA-162
89Hoops-31
89Hoops/II-313
89NCSt/Coke-95
89NCSt/Coke-96
89TWolv/BK-35
90Hoops-187
90Hoops/Super-59
90SkyBox-170
Lowery, Darlene
91SC/200*-46
Lowery, Terrell
92Classic/DP-8
92StarPic-79
Lowings, Dianne
86SWLou/Pol*-10
Lowther, Bobby
90LSU/200*-54
Loynd, Mike
90FLSt/200*-81
Lubin, Frank
91UCLA/144-78
Lucas, Harold
90MISt/200*-18
Lucas, Jerry
63Kahn's-6
64Kahn's-8A
64Kahn's-8B
65Kahn's-2
68T/Test-21
69T-45
69T/Ins-15
70T-46
71T-81
72Icee-12
72T-15
73T-125
81TCMA-38
91Foot*-21
Lucas, John
77T-58
78T-106
79T-127
80T-115
80T-126
80T-65
80T-79
81T-51M
83Star/NBA-246
84Star/NBA-242
85Star/NBA-21
87Bucks/Polar-10
87F-66
92Crtside/ColFB-20
Lucas, Maurice
75T-302
76T-107
77Blaz/Pol-20
77T-80
78RCCola-19
78T-50
79Blaz/Pol-20
79T-26
80T-142
80T-54
81T-57M
81T-E79
82Suns/Giant-2
83Star/ASG-19
83Star/NBA-113
84Star/NBA-45
84Suns/Pol-21
85Star/NBA-30
86F-66
87Blaz/Franz-7
89Blaz/Franz-13
Lucia, Tom
89Louville/300*-106
89Louville/300*-178
Luckman, Sid
48ExhSC-31
Luisetti, Angelo
68HOF-28
Lujack, Johnny
48ExhSC-32
48T/Magic*-C6
Luke, Keye
48T/Magic*-J4
Lumpkin, Mark
90LSU/200*-52
Lumpkin, Phil
75Suns-8
75T-114
Luppino, Art
90AZ/125*-104
Lusk, Paul
91Iowa-7
Luyk, Sergio
90KY/ClassA-4
Lyght, Todd
91Classic/DPColl*-107
Lyle, Mel
90LSU/200*-93
Lyles, Lenny
89Louville/300*-103
89Louville/300*-110
Lynam, Jim
81Blaz/Pol-CO
82Blaz/Pol-x
89Hoops-68CO
89Sixers/Kodak-14CO
90Hoops-324CO
90SkyBox/II-320CO
91F-155CO
91Hoops/I-240CO
91SkyBox/II-397CO
Lynch, Chris
87BYU-12
Lynch, David
87BYU-15
Lynch, Kevin
91Classic-18
91Classic/DPColl*-166
91Crtside-34
91FrRow/100-19
91FrRow/50-19
91FrRow/Premier-76
91StarPic-47
91UD/Ext-436
91WildCard/Coll-28
Lynn, Bill
91George/100-76
Lyons, Dicky
89KY/300*-136
Lyons, Ronnie
88KY/269-229
88KY/269-99
Lysiak, Tom
75Nab-14
Lyttle, Jim
90FLSt/200*-185
Mabay, Jim
91AR/100*-62
MacArthur, Douglas
48T/Magic*-O7
Macauley, Edward C.
(Easy Ed)
48T/Magic*-B3
57T-27
68HOF-29
81TCMA-13
92CenterCrt-4
Macek, Mark
90FLSt/200*-161
MacFarlane, Al
89Louville/300*-167
Mack, Connie
48T/Magic*-K9
Mack, Kevin
90Clemson/200*-2
Mack, Oliver
82TCMA/CBA-16
Mack, Sam
92Classic/DP-67
92StarPic-16
Mack, Tony
89ProC/CBA-173
Mackey, Malcolm
89GATech/Pol-11
90GATech/Pol-15
90GATech/Pol-16
91GATech/Pol-12
Macklin, Durand
90LSU/200*-198
90LSU/200*-50
Macklin, Oliver
90CT/Pol-8
91CT/Pol-8
MacLane, Barton
48T/Magic*-J45
MacLean, Don
88KY/Sov-14
90UCLA-14
91UCLA-2
92Classic/DP-44
MacLeod, John
75Suns-9CO
80Suns/Pep-12CO
84Suns/Pol-x
85Star/CO-5
88Mavs/BLC-x
88Mavs/CardN-x
89Hoops-171
Macon, Mark
91Classic-4
91Classic/DPColl*-152
91Crtside-35
91Crtside/Holo-3
91F/Up-276
91FrRow/100-43
91FrRow/100-6
91FrRow/50-43
91FrRow/50-6
91FrRow/Premier-50
91Hoops/II-553
91Kell/ColGrt-16
91SkyBox/II-520LP
91StarPic-26
91UD/Ext-489
91UD/Rook-25
91WildCard/Coll-23
91WildCard/RHRook-5
92F-59
92F/Rook-6
92FrRow/DreamPk-56
92FrRow/DreamPk-57
92FrRow/DreamPk-58
92FrRow/DreamPk-59
92FrRow/DreamPk-60
92Hoops/I-59
92SkyBox/I-63
Macy, Kyle
77KY/Wildct-15
78KY/Food-13
79KY/Food-2
79KY/Food-20
80Suns/Pep-11

81T-W82
83Star/NBA-114
84Star/NBA-46
84Suns/Pol-4
87KY/Coke-16
88KY/269-10
88KY/269-155
88KY/269-175
88KY/269-221
89KY/Tm80-38
92Crtside/ColFB-21
Madden, John
90FLSt/200*-150
Madden, Kevin
87NC/Pol-22
88NC/Pol-22
Maddox, Bob
89Louville/300*-131
Maddox, Jerry
90AZSt/200*-182
Maddox, Mike
87KS/Nike-8
89KS/Leesley-46
Madeya, John
89Louville/300*-192
Madison, Guy
48T/Magic*-J44
Madison, Richard
88KY/269-131
88KY/269-174
88KY/269-250
Madkins, Gerald
90UCLA-13
91UCLA-13
92Classic/DP-78
Magallanes, Ever
91TexAM-39
Magee, Kevin
91WildCard/Coll-109
Magno, Jack
81AZ/Pol-10
Magrane, Joe
90AZ/125*-41
Mahaffey, Donnie
90Clemson/200*-199
Mahaffey, Randy
71T-221
90Clemson/200*-188
Mahaffey, Richie
90Clemson/200*-177
Mahaffey, Tommy
90Clemson/200*-166
Mahnken, John
48Bowman-63
Mahorn, Rick
81T-E98
83Star/NBA-211
84Star/NBA-191
85Star/NBA-16
89F-93
89Hoops-46
89Hoops/II-330
89Sixers/Kodak-8
90F-144
90Hoops-230
90Panini-132
90SkyBox-217
91F-156
91Hoops/I-162
91Hoops/Super-74
91Panini-168
91SkyBox/I-217
91UD-42
91WildCard/Coll-113
Maile, Dick
90LSU/200*-71
Majerle, Dan
89F-124
89Hoops-183
90F-150A
90F-150B
90Hoops-239
90Panini-14
90SkyBox-226
90Suns/Smok-5
91F-163
91Hoops/I-167
91Hoops/II-570
91Hoops/Super-78
91Panini-23
91SkyBox/I-228
91SkyBox/II-425GF
91SkyBox/II-452SM
91SkyBox/II-552US
91UD-172
91UD/Ext-475AS
92F-182
92F/AS-16
92Hoops/I-184
92Hoops/I-310AS
92SkyBox/I-194
92StarPic-60FB
Majerle, Jeff
91ProC/CBA-17
Majerus, Rick
82Marq/Lite-5CO
Major, Chris
91SC/200*-182
Majors, Joe
90FLSt/200*-198
Makarewicz, Scott
90MISt/200*-167
Makkonen, Timo
89NC/Coke-199
Mallory, Trevor
91Classic/DPColl*-100
Malloy, Edward
(Monk)
90NotreDame-16
Maloncon, Gary
91UCLA/144-12
Malone, Art
90AZSt/200*-89
Malone, Ben
90AZSt/200*-78
Malone, George
91GATech*-12
Malone, Jeff
83Star/NBA-212
84Star/NBA-192
85Star/NBA-112
86F-67
87F-67
88F-117
88Fourn-21
89F-160
89Hoops-85
90F-195
90F/Up-U94
90Hoops-301
90Hoops/II-437
90Hoops/Super-97
90Jazz/Star-7
90SkyBox-292
90SkyBox/II-418
91F-200
91Hoops/I-210
91Hoops/I-308M
91Hoops/Super-95
91Panini-82
91SkyBox/I-282
91SkyBox/II-595SS
91UD-166
92F-224
92Hoops/I-226
92SkyBox/I-241
Malone, Karl
86F-68
87F-68
88F-114
88F/Ins-8
88Fourn-16
88Jazz/Smok-4
89Conv-9
89F-155
89F-163M
89F/AS-1
89Hoops-116AS
89Hoops-30
89Jazz/OldH-10
90F-188
90F/AS-7
90Hoops-21AS
90Hoops-292
90Hoops/CollB-5
90Hoops/II-380TC
90Hoops/Super-94
90Jazz/Star-1
90Panini-49
90SkyBox-282
90SkyBox/Proto-282
91F-201
91F-219
91F/ProV-5
91F/School-5
91Hoops/ASMVP-10
91Hoops/I-211
91Hoops/I-267AS
91Hoops/I-306M
91Hoops/II-499SC
91Hoops/II-580
91Hoops/McDon-44
91Hoops/McDon-56USA
91Hoops/Proto/00-005
91Hoops/Super-96
91Kell/ColGrt-6
91Panini-191AS
91Panini-85
91Panini-91AS
91SkyBox/Canada-46
91SkyBox/I-283
91SkyBox/II-430GF
91SkyBox/II-484TW
91SkyBox/II-535US
91UD-355
91UD-51AS
91UD/Ext-466AS
92F-225
92F/AS-17
92F/TmLeader-26
92Hoops/I-227
92Hoops/I-311AS
92Hoops/I-320LL
92Hoops/I-343
92SkyBox/I-242
92SkyBox/Olympic-USA4
92SkyBox/USA-106
92SkyBox/USA-46
92SkyBox/USA-47
92SkyBox/USA-48
92SkyBox/USA-49
92SkyBox/USA-50
92SkyBox/USA-51
92SkyBox/USA-52
92SkyBox/USA-53
92SkyBox/USA-54
Malone, Mark
90AZSt/200*-17
Malone, Moses
75T-222LL
75T-254
75T-286M
76T-101
77T-124
78T-38
79T-100AS
80T-107
80T-114
80T-159
80T-2
80T-45
80T-71
80T-74
80T-90
81T-14
81T-52M
81T-MW110
83Star/ASG-27M
83Star/ASG-7
83Star/NBA-7
83Star/Sixers-14
83Star/Sixers-20
83Star/Sixers-25
83Star/Sixers-3M
84Star/Arena-E7
84Star/Award-20LL
84Star/CrtKg-17
84Star/NBA-201
84Star/NBA-285
85JMS-2
85Prism-3
85Prism-4M
85Star/Crunch-5
85Star/LiteAS-5
85Star/NBA-6
85Star/TmSuper-PS6
86F-69
86Star/CrtKg-21
87F-69
88F-118
88Fourn/St-6
89F-165M
89F-4
89Hoops-290
89Hoops-84AS
90F-3
90Hoops-31
90Hoops/Super-4
90Panini-115
90SkyBox-6
91F/Up-315
91Hoops/I-2
91Hoops/I-315MS
91Hoops/I-318MS
91Hoops/I-323YB
91Hoops/II-394
91Hoops/II-537
91Hoops/Super-1
91Panini-106
91SkyBox/I-4
91SkyBox/II-574
91SkyBox/II-634
91UD-47
91UD/Ext-402
92F-127
92Hoops/I-130
92SkyBox/I-137
92SkyBox/I-296TT
Maloney, Jim
71Keds*-1M
Maloy, Rudy
90FLSt/200*-19
Mandarich, Tony
90MISt/200*-89
90MISt/Promos*-8
Mandich, Jim
91MI/56*-34
Mangham, Mickey
90LSU/200*-125
Mangrum, Lloyd
48Kell*-15
57Union-22
Manion, Bob
89Louville/300*-63
Manion, Tim
91GATech*-68
Mann, Cyrus
82TCMA/CBA-21
Manning, Danny
87KS/Nike-9
88Fourn-30
89F-71
89Hoops-40
90Clip/Star-7
90F-87
90Hoops-147
90Hoops/CollB-17
90Hoops/II-366TC
90Hoops/Super-46
90Panini-32
90SkyBox-129
91F-92
91Hoops/I-94
91Hoops/II-571
91Hoops/Super-42
91Panini-14
91SkyBox/Canada-23
91SkyBox/I-127
91SkyBox/II-416GF
91SkyBox/II-470TW
91SkyBox/II-553US
91UD-164
91Wooden-17
92F-101
92F/TmLeader-12
92Hoops/I-101
92SkyBox/I-107
Manning, Ed
70T-132
71T-122
Manning, Rich
88Syr/Rich-6
89Syr/Pep-3
91WA/Viacom-3
Mannion, Pace
83Star/NBA-259
84Star/NBA-232
87Bucks/Polar-3
91WildCard/Coll-65
Manns, Kirk
90MISt/200*-139
Mantel, Alex
89Louville/300*-88
Mantle, Mickey
81T/Thirst-12
Manuel, Eric
92StarPic-49
Maras, Dee
81IL/Arby's-8
Maravich, Pete
70T-123
71T-55
71T/Ins-22
72Icee-13
72T-5
73T-130AS
74T-10
74T-144LL
74T-145LL
74T-81M
75T-127M
75T-75
76T-130AS
76T-60
77Dell-4
77Pep/AS-5
77T-20
78RCCola-20
78T-80
79T-60
80T-8
80T-96
85Star/Schick-18
87LSU/Pol*-16
90LSU/200*-1
90LSU/200*-74
90LSU/Promos*-6
Maravich, Press
89NCSt/Coke-170
Marble, Roy
90ProC/CBA-20
Marciano, Rocky
81T/Thirst-55M
Marciulionis, Sarunas
90F-65

90Hoops-115
90Panini-29
90SkyBox-97
91F-68
91Hoops/I-71
91SkyBox/I-95
91UD-354
92F-76
92Hoops/I-77
92SkyBox/I-82
92StarPic-70FB
Marin, Jack
69T-26
70T-36
71T-112
72T-174LL
72T-70
73NBAPA-18
73T-122
74T-26
75T-118M
75T-82
76T-72
Marinovich, Todd
91Classic/DPColl*-122
Markkanen, Pekka
89KS/Leesley-51
Marotta, Marc
82Marq/Lite-6
Marsh, B.G.
89KY/300*-30
Marshall, Archie
87KS/Nike-10
Marshall, Curtis
91NCSt/IBM-8
Marshall, Donny
91CT/Pol-9
Marshall, Donyell
91CT/Pol-10
Marshall, Grayson
90Clemson/200*-40
Marshall, Jim
81T/Thirst-39
Marshall, Jonathon
91ND*-4M
Marshall, Tom
57Kahn's-4
57T-22
58Kahn's-5
59Kahn's-3
Martin, Amos
89Louville/300*-173
Martin, Anthony
82TCMA/CBA-57
Martin, Bill
81George/Pol-6
82George/Pol-13
83George/Pol-4
84George/Pol-8
90ProC/CBA-62
90ProC/CBA-82
91George/100-23
Martin, Billy
91GATech*-83
Martin, Bobby
89Pitt/Food-55
90Pitt/Food-3
91ProC/CBA-36
Martin, Brian
89ProC/CBA-79
90ProC/CBA-178
Martin, Clifford
91FrRow/100-95
91FrRow/Premier-117
91FrRow/Up-85
Martin, Darrick
90UCLA-4
91UCLA-10
92Classic/DP-77
Martin, Darryl
91SC/200*-123
Martin, Earl
89ORSt-10
Martin, Elmer
91AR25-9
Martin, Eric
90LSU/200*-57
Martin, Ethan
90LSU/200*-32
Martin, Fernando
86Blaz/Franz-9
Martin, Jeff
90Clip/Star-8
90Hoops-148
90SkyBox-130
91Hoops/I-95
91ProC/CBA-102
91SkyBox/I-128
91UD-162
Martin, Jesse
88MD/Pol-7
Martin, Kenneth
88KY/Sov-15
Martin, LaRue
73T-89
75T-183
Martin, Mike
90FLSt/200*-15
Martin, Slater
(Dugie)
57T-12
81TCMA-15
Martin, Steve
91George/100-66
91George/100-74
Martin, Tony CRSB
90ProC/CBA-21
Martin, Tony RCT
90ProC/CBA-75
Martin, Tony WS
80WichSt/Pol-10
Martin, T.X.
82TCMA/CBA-74
Martin, Vada
89ProC/CBA-164
Martin, Wade
91GATech*-85
Martin, Warren
89NC/Coke-140
89NC/Coke-141
90NC/200*-48
90NC/200*-67
Martin, Wayne
91AR/100*-78
Martin, Wilf
91MI/56*-35
Martinez, Gimel
90KY/Sov-9
91KY/BB-10
91KY/BB/Double-7
Martz, Randy
91SC/200*-70
Maryland, Russell
91Classic/DPColl*-103
91Classic/DPColl*-1M
91Classic/DPCollLP*-LP10
Marzan, Jose
90FLSt/200*-24
Mashak, Mike
89ProC/CBA-139
91ProC/CBA-47ACO
Mashburn, Jamal
90KY/BB/DT/AW-29
90KY/Sov-10
91KY/BB-11
91KY/BB/Double-12
Mason, Anthony
90ProC/CBA-114
91F/Up-326
91Hoops/II-404
91UD/Ext-430
92F-152
92Hoops/I-155
92SkyBox/I-163
Mason, Bobby Joe
71Globe-39
71Globe-40
71Globe-41
71Globe-42M
71Globe-43
71Globe-44
71Globe/Cocoa-14
Mason, Harvey
86AZ/Pol-8
87AZ/Pol-8
88AZ/Pol-8
89AZ/Pol-5
Mason, Jimmy
90Clemson-12
Mason, Rod
90ProC/CBA-3
91ProC/CBA-191
Mason, Ron
90MISt/200*-146
Mason, Zan
90UCLA-12
Massenburg, Todd
88MD/Pol-8
Massenburg, Tony
90F/Up-U89
90StarPic-22
91Hoops/II-437
Massey, Gary
89ProC/CBA-97
90ProC/CBA-50
Massimino, Rollie
92Crtside/ColFB-22CO
Mast, Eddie
73T-28
80TCMA/CBA-29
Masteller, Dan
90MISt/200*-174
Master, Jim
81KY/Sched-11
82KY/Sched-5
83KY/Sched-12
87KY/Coke-15
88KY/269-124
88KY/269-203
88KY/269-224
89KY/Tm80-46
Masters, Bobby
86IN/GreatI-10
Masters, Norman
90MISt/200*-45
Masucci, Mike
87KS/Nike-11
Mateen, Grady
84George/Pol-9
85George/Pol-10
Mathewson, Christy
48T/Magic*-K10
81T/Thirst-20
Mathias, Bob
48ExhSC-34
57Union-11
Mathis, Jeff
91GATech*-50
Matson, Ollie
81TCMA/CBA-26
Matson, Randy
91TexAM-44
Matthews, Jamie
91Classic/DPColl*-37
Matthews, Jason
89Pitt/Food-22
90Pitt/Food-4
91Crtside-36
Matthews, Kenny
89NCSt/Coke-122
89NCSt/Coke-189
Matthews, Ray
90Clemson/200*-194
Matthews, Wes
81T-E69
84Star/NBA-109
Matthews, Wilson
91AR/100*-64
Mattingly, Paul
89Louville/300*-141
Mattocks, Tom
89NCSt/Coke-143
89NCSt/Coke-144
89NCSt/Coke-145
Mattress, Jackie
90Clemson/Lady-8
Matuszewski, Richard
90Clemson/200*-61M
90Clemson/200*-70
Matvichuk, Richard
91Classic/DPColl*-7
Mauer, John
89KY/300*-27
Maughan, Ariel
48Bowman-60
Maxey, Marlon
89UTEP/Drug-18
92Classic/DP-34
92StarPic-9
Maxey, Tyrone
91WASt-4
Maxwell, Cedric
78T-128
79T-23
80T-117
80T-27
81T-5
81T-E107
83Star/NBA-33
84Star/Arena-A5
84Star/Celt-13M
84Star/Celt-1M
84Star/NBA-8
85Star/NBA-91
86F-70
87F-70
92Crtside/ColFB-23
Maxwell, Vernon
89F-144
89Hoops-271
90AZSt/200*-30
90F-72
90Hoops-126
90Panini-67
90SkyBox-109
91F-76
91Hoops/I-77
91Panini-59
91SkyBox/I-104
91SkyBox/II-468TW
91SkyBox/II-495RS
91UD-275
92F-83
92Hoops/I-84
92SkyBox/I-89
May, Dean
89Louville/300*-112
May, Don
70T-152
71T-6
71T/Ins-17
72T-96
73T-131
74T-2
May, Jerry
81Louville/Pol-18TR
May, Scott
77Bulls/WhHen-5
77T-36
78T-115
79Bulls/Pol-17
80T-10
80T-98
87IN/GreatII-27
May, T.
83KY/Sched-13
Mayabb, Jesse
55Ash-55
Mayberry, Lee
91AR25-10
92Classic/DP-3
92StarPic-72
Maye, Mark
90NC/200*-15
90NC/200*-92
90NC/Promos*-NC4
Mayes, Charles
87Vanderbilt/Pol-12
Mayes, Tharon
90ProC/CBA-84
91FrRow/100-63
91FrRow/ItalPromo-5
91FrRow/Premier-34
91FrRow/Up-69
91WildCard/Coll-110
Mayes, Tony
89KY/300*-195
Mayfair, Bill
90AZSt/200*-65
Mayfield, Clarkie
89KY/300*-187
Mayhew, Martin
90FLSt/200*-49
Mayo, Virginia
48T/Magic*-F14
Mayotte, Chris
91SC/200*-177
Maypole, John B.
54Quaker-4
Mays, Deanna
90NE/Pol*-25
Mays, Jerry
91GATech*-22
Mays, Travis
90F/Up-U86
90Kings/Safe-7
90StarPic-59
91F-177
91F/Rook-5
91Hoops/I-184
91Hoops/II-335
91Hoops/II-503Ar
91Panini-185AR
91Panini-36
91SkyBox/I-248
91SkyBox/II-616
91UD-331
91UD/Ext-494
91UD/Rook-9
Mays, Willie
81PhilM-3
Mazey, Randy
90Clemson/200*-59
Mazza, Gary
81TCMA/CBA-13
82TCMA/CBA-82
McAdoo, Bob
73T-135
74T-144LL
74T-145LL
74T-146LL
74T-148LL
74T-80AS
74T-83M
75Carv-20
75Nab-24
75T-10AS
75T-118M
75T-1LL
76Buck-16
76T-140
77Pep/AS-6
77T-45
78RCCola-21
78T-5

79T-75
80T-88
80T-99
82Lakers/BASF-7
83Lakers/BASF-6
83Star/NBA-18
84Lakers/BASF-6
84Star/NBA-178
85JMS-22
85Star/TmSuper-LA5
89NC/Coke-115
89NC/Coke-76
89NC/Coke-77
91WildCard/Coll-77
92Crtside/ColFB-24
McAfee, George
48Kell*-7
McAmmond, Dean
91Classic/DPColl*-19
McAndrew, Steve
91ND*-3M
McArthur, Gale
91OKSt*-80
McAshen, Eddie
91GATech*-94
McAuliffe, Don
90MISt/200*-80
McBrayer, Paul
55Ash-9
88KY/269-55
McBurrows, Marvin
90NM-7
McCaffrey, Ed
91Classic/DPColl*-217
McCall, Mark
89UTEP/Drug-19
McCall, Matt
91TexAM-31
McCann, Bob
89ProC/CBA-60
91Piston/Unocal-16M
McCants, Melvin
90ProC/CBA-85
McCarter, Andre
80TCMA/CBA-9
81TCMA/CBA-62
91UCLA/144-17
McCarter, Willie
69T-63
70T-141
71T-101
McCarthy, John
56Busch-3
61F-30
61Hawks/Essex-10
McCarthy, Sandy
91Classic/DPColl*-42
McCarty, David
91Classic/DPColl*-53
McCauley, Don
90NC/200*-127
90NC/200*-141
90NC/200*-38
McClain, Dwayne
89ProC/CBA-162
90ProC/CBA-64
McClain, Ted
73T-247
75T-311
McClanahan, Brent
90AZSt/200*-79
McClard, Bill
91AR/100*-49
McClary, Kenny
89ProC/CBA-21
90ProC/CBA-199
McClendon, Andre
90KY/ClassA-11
McClendon, Charlie
90LSU/200*-152
McClendon, Skip
90AZSt/200*-35
McCloud, George
90F-77
90SkyBox-116
91Hoops/II-373
91SkyBox/I-113
91UD-233
92Hoops/I-91
92SkyBox/I-96
McClouskey, Andy
90ORSt-18ACO
91ORSt-13ACO
McCollom, Jim
90Clemson/200*-103
McCollow, Mike
91ProC/CBA-158AC
McComb, Jeff
82INSt/Pol*-8
McConnell, Vic
91SC/200*-33
McCormach, Brendan
91SC/200*-184
McCormick, Dave
90LSU/200*-159
McCormick, Pat
57Union-23
McCormick, Tim
84Star/NBA-118
85Star/NBA-68
85Star/RTm-10
87F-71
89F-60
89Hoops-272
90F/Up-U2
90Hoops/II-401
90SkyBox/II-366
91F/Up-327
91Hoops/II-402
91MI/56*-36
91SkyBox/I-5
91SkyBox/II-637
91UD-386
92SkyBox/I-164
McCovery, Smokey
92StarPic-56
McCowan, Bob
88KY/269-91
McCoy, James
92Classic/DP-17
92StarPic-67
McCoy, Julius
90MISt/200*-188
McCracken, Branch
68HOF-30
87IN/GreatII-5
McCrady, Lisa
90NE/Pol*-20
McCrary, Vladimir
90NM-8
91NM-11
McCray, Rodney
81Louville/Pol-30
83Star/NBA-81
84Star/NBA-243
85Star/NBA-22
85Star/TmSuper-HR4
86F-71
87F-72
88F-52
88Kings/Carl-22
88Louville/194-11
88Louville/194-111
88Louville/194-160
88Louville/194-187
89F-135
89Hoops-257
89Kings/Carl-22
89Louville/300*-264
89Louville/300*-292
89Louville/300*-45
90F-165
90F/Up-U21
90Hoops-259
90Hoops/II-409
90Hoops/Super-84
90SkyBox-248
90SkyBox/II-377
91F-46
91Hoops/I-48
91Panini-48
91SkyBox/I-62
91UD-109
92F-52
92Hoops/I-50
92SkyBox/I-53
McCray, Scooter
81Louville/Pol-8
83Sonic/Pol-7
83Star/NBA-199
88Louville/194-112
88Louville/194-12
88Louville/194-157
88Louville/194-190
89Louville/300*-239
89Louville/300*-26
89Louville/300*-263
89Louville/300*-277
89Louville/300*-44
McCreary, Jay
87IN/GreatII-40
McCuller, Lakista
91NCSt/IBM-9
McCullers, Dale
90FLSt/200*-140
McCullough, John
82TCMA/CBA-34
90NM-9ACO
91NM-12ACO
McCurdy, Paris
91FrRow/100-79
91FrRow/Premier-15
91FrRow/Up-74
McDade, Von
91Classic-42
91Classic/DPColl*-190
91FrRow/100-23
91FrRow/50-23
91FrRow/Premier-70
91ProC/CBA-149
91StarPic-28
McDaniel, Clint
91AR25-11
McDaniel, Orlando
90LSU/200*-19
McDaniel, Randall
90AZSt/200*-93
McDaniel, Shawn
(LaShun)
89ProC/CBA-10
90ProC/CBA-22
91ProC/CBA-175
McDaniel, Xavier
86F-72
87F-73
88F-108
88Fourn-20
89F-148
89Hoops-70
90F-179
90F/Up-U77
90Hoops-280
90Hoops/CollB-42
90Hoops/II-379TC
90Hoops/Super-91
90Panini-23
90SkyBox-269
90Sonic/Smok-9
91F-164
91F/Up-328
91Hoops/I-168
91Hoops/II-403
91Hoops/McDon-27
91Panini-25
91SkyBox/I-229
91SkyBox/II-585
91SkyBox/II-638
91UD-151
91UD/Ext-495
92F-153
92Hoops/I-156
92SkyBox/I-165
McDaniels, Jim
72T-137
73Sonic/Shur-8
73T-152
McDermont, Mike
91George/100-68
McDermott, Bob
48ExhSC-35
McDermott, Marty
91ND*-2M
McDonald, Ben
87LSU/Pol*-12
88LSU/Pol*-10
90LSU/200*-113
90ProC/CBA-157
McDonald, Darryl
90ProC/CBA-104
91ProC/CBA-115
McDonald, Glenn
76T-47
McDonald, Jim
88KY/269-80
McDonald, Perry
84George/Pol-10
85George/Pol-11
86George/Pol-10
87George/Pol-12
91George/100-28
91WildCard/Coll-111
McDonald, Peter
91George/100-32
McDonnell, John
91AR/100*-8
McDowall, Roddy
48T/Magic*-J3
McDowell, Eugene
90FLSt/200*-191
90ProC/CBA-31
91ProC/CBA-202
McDowell, Hank
83Star/NBA-127
84Star/NBA-244
McDowell, Oddibe
90AZSt/200*-10
McDuffie, Wayne
90FLSt/200*-162
McDuffie, Willie
90ProC/CBA-158
McElroy, James
(Jimmy)
79Hawks/Majik-33
79T-131
80T-170
80T-63
McFadden, Banks
90Clemson/200*-34
McFadden, Wesley
90Clemson/200*-115
McFall, Dan
90MISt/200*-147
McFarland, James
89KY/300*-249
McGaha, Mel
91AR/100*-96
McGee, Andre
91NM-13
McGee, Carlton
89WI/Smok-10
McGee, Michael
(Mike)
82Lakers/BASF-8
83Lakers/BASF-7
83Star/NBA-19
84Lakers/BASF-7
84Star/Arena-D4
84Star/NBA-179
85JMS-25
89F-98
90SkyBox-227
McGeorge, Rich
79Bucks/OpenP-11
McGinnis, George
72T-183
72T-243
73T-180AS
73T-208
73T-234LL
74T-207LL
74T-211LL
74T-220AS
74T-223M
74T-223M
75Sixers/McDon-5
75T-184
75T-221LL
75T-226LL
75T-279M
76T-128AS
76T-70
77T-50
78RCCola-22
78T-90
79T-125
80T-127
80T-39
81T-MW92
86IN/GreatI-19
McGinnis, Lawrence
89KY/300*-222
McGinnis, Louis
89KY/300*-80
McGlocklin, Jon
69T-14
70T-139
71Bucks/Linn-6
71T-74
72T-54
73T-123
74T-37
75T-35
79Bucks/OpenP-10
86IN/GreatI-21
McGowan, Paul
90FLSt/200*-29
McGrath, Tom
89McNees*-5
McGuire, Al
86DePaul-11
92Crtside/ColFB-25CO
McGuire, Bill
84NE/Pol*-20
McGwire, Dan
91Classic/DPColl*-115
McGuire, Dick
52Royal-2
57T-16
81TCMA-26
McGuire, Frank
89NC/Coke-104
89NC/Coke-99
90NC/200*-193
91SC/200*-1CO
McHale, Kevin
81T-E75
83Star/NBA-34
84Star/Arena-A6
84Star/ASG-7
84Star/Award-5
84Star/Celt-3
84Star/Celt-8M
84Star/CrtKg-42
84Star/NBA-9
84Star/PolASG-7

85JMS-13
85Star/Lakers-6
85Star/NBA-98
85Star/TmSuper-BC3
86F-73
86Star/CrtKg-22
87F-74
87F/Ins-5
88F-11
88F/Ins-9
88Fourn-3
88Fourn/St-7
89Conv-10
89F-11
89Hoops-156AS
89Hoops-280
90F-12
90Hoops-44
90Hoops-6AS
90Hoops/CollB-6
90Hoops/Super-7
90Panini-136
90SkyBox-19
91F-13
91F/School-3
91Hoops/I-14
91Hoops/I-255AS
91Hoops/II-504Ar
91Hoops/McDon-3
91Hoops/Super-7
91Panini-144
91SkyBox/Canada-3
91SkyBox/I-17
91SkyBox/I-317M
91SkyBox/II-433SM
91UD-225
91UD-62AS
92F-17
92Hoops/I-16
92SkyBox/I-16
McHone, Moe
91ProC/CBA-204CO
McHugh, Mike
87ME/Pol*-2
McIntee, Willie
91SC/200*-135
McIntosh, David
85Victoria/Pol-8
McIntosh, Doug
91UCLA/144-76
McIntosh, John
89KY/300*-28
McIntosh, Kennedy
73Sonic/Shur-9
73T-164
74T-173
McIntosh, Lamont
89ORSt-11
McIntyre, Jim
48T/Magic*-B5
McIntyre, John
88MO-8
89MO-9
90ProC/CBA-180
McKale, J.F.
(Pop)
90AZ/125*-118
McKay, Geoff
85Victoria/Pol-9
88Victoria/Pol-8
McKay, Mike
91CT/Legend-10
McKay, Spencer
85Victoria/Pol-10
88Victoria/Pol-9
McKenna, Joey
90Clemson/200*-196
McKenna, Kevin
83Star/NBA-163
90ProC/CBA-91
91ProC/CBA-120CO
McKenzie, Kyle
88LSU/Pol*-5
McKenzie, Stan
68Suns/Carn-7
69Suns/Carn-5
70T-52
72T-84
73T-32
McKernan, Matt
91SC/200*-124
McKey, Derrick
88F-109
89F-149
89Hoops-233
90F-180
90Hoops-281
90Hoops/Super-90
90Panini-24
90SkyBox-270
90Sonic/Kayo-3
90Sonic/Smok-10
91F-193
91Hoops/I-201
91Hoops/Super-93
91Panini-41
91SkyBox/I-272
91UD-361
92F-214
92Hoops/I-217
92SkyBox/I-232
McKinley, Troy
81KY/Sched-12
83KY/Sched-14
88KY/269-125
McKinney, Billy
81T-W69
82Nugget/Pol-7
83Star/NBA-128
McKinney, Charles
89ORSt-12
90ORSt-12
91ORSt-14
McKinney, Horace
(Bones)
48Bowman-46
52Bread-19
89NC/Coke-105
89NC/Coke-126
89NCSt/Coke-61
McKinney, Jack
77Blaz/Pol-x
McKinney, Rick
90AZSt/200*-193
McKinnon, Adrian
89ProC/CBA-96
McKinnon, Tom
91Classic/DPColl*-74
McLaughlin, Eric
89ProC/CBA-133
McLean, Don
92Classic/BKPrev-BK3
McLean, Jeff
91ND*-15M
McLean, John
90FLSt/200*-18
McLean, Price
89KY/300*-158
McLemore, McCoy
68Suns/Carn-8
70T-19
71T-83
McLennan, Jamie
91Classic/DPColl*-40
McLinden, Melissa
90AZ/125*-77
McMahon, Jack
57T-66
63Kahn's-7CO
64Kahn's-2CO
McMahon, Ronn
91ProC/CBA-86
McManus, Danny
90FLSt/200*-27
McMillan, Craig
84AZ/Pol-10
85AZ/Pol-11
86AZ/Pol-9
87AZ/Pol-9
McMillan, Jerry
86DePaul-S2
McMillan, Nate
87F-75
88F-110
89F-150
89Hoops-192
89NCSt/Coke-103
89NCSt/Coke-104
89NCSt/Coke-105
90F-181
90Hoops-282
90Panini-19
90SkyBox-271A
90SkyBox-271B
90Sonic/Kayo-11
90Sonic/Smok-11
91F/Up-361
91Hoops/II-441
91SkyBox/I-273
91SkyBox/II-429GF
91UD-186
92F-215
92Hoops/I-218
92SkyBox/I-233
McMillen, Tom
77T-66
78Hawks/Coke-11
79Hawks/Majik-54
81T-E70
83Star/NBA-213
84Star/NBA-193
85Star/NBA-113
McMillian, Jim
71T-41
72T-89
73NBAPA-19
73T-4
74T-38
75Carv-21
75T-27
76T-9
77T-107
78T-88
McMillon, Shellie
61Hawks/Essex-11
McMinn, Glenn
90AZSt/200*-190
McMullen, Mitch
89ProC/CBA-125
McNabb, Buck
91Classic/DPColl*-93
McNamara, Mark
83Star/NBA-248
84Star/NBA-70
89Hoops-289
90Hoops-158
90Hoops/II-434
90SkyBox-139
90SkyBox/II-402
McNeal, Chris
90Pitt/Food-5
McNeil, Johnny
88GATech/Nike-6
89GATech/Pol-12
McNeil, Lori
91OKSt*-74
McNeil, Rodney
86SWLou/Pol*-11
McNeill, Larry
75T-142
McQueen, Cozell
91WildCard/Coll-11
McQueen, Derrick
88WakeForest/Pol-10
McRae, Conrad
89Syr/Pep-8
McReynolds, Kevin
91AR/100*-4
McSwain, Chuck
90Clemson/200*-64
McSwain, Mark
83Louville-32
88Louville/194-125
88Louville/194-174
88Louville/194-180
88Louville/194-33
89Louville/300*-255
89Louville/300*-37
McSween, Don
90MISt/200*-196
McSweeney, Bryan
89NC/Coke-174
Meagher, Mary T.
87KY/Coke-14
Medlin, Phil
88WakeForest/Pol-11
Meekins, Doug
91WA/TCI-6
91WA/Viacom-4
Meeks, Bryant
91SC/200*-187
Meeks, Eric
90AZ/125*-27
Meely, Cliff
72T-46
73T-84
74T-36
75T-32
Meents, Scott
90Sonic/Kayo-2
90Sonic/Smok-12
Meggett, Bill
71Globe-37M
71Globe-59
71Globe-60
71Globe/Cocoa-5M
Meier, Whitney
91ND*-1M
Meilinger, Steve
89KY/300*-141
Meiman, Joe
89Louville/300*-73
Meineke, Don
57T-21
Melchionni, Bill
71T-151LL
71T-199
71T/Ins-7A
72T-225
72T-253AS
72T-264LL
73T-239LL
73T-249
75T-291
Melchionni, Gary
74T-71
75T-21
Mellow, Donald
81AZ/Pol-11
Meminger, Dean
72T-88
73T-93
74T-23
75Carv-22
75T-116M
75T-152
82TCMA/CBA-40
Menegazz, Paul
91GATech*-82
Mengelt, John
72T-146
73T-3
74T-58
75T-12
75T-121M
77Bulls/WhHen-6
77T-101
78T-53
79Bulls/Pol-15
80T-101
80T-28
Menke, Bob
87IN/GreatII-11
Mercier, Tim
91George/100-86
Meriweather, Joe
76T-37
79T-69
80T-150
80T-62
83Star/NBA-220
84Star/NBA-275
Merna, John
90FLSt/200*-46
Merrill, Gretchen
48ExhSC-36
Merritt, Brent
91WA/TCI-7
Merten, Joe
81TCMA/CBA-63
82TCMA/CBA-75
Mescan, Linda
91SC/200*-40
Meschery, Tom
61F-31
69Sonic/Sunb-5
69T-19
70Sonic/Sunb-7
70T-99
Meseroll, Mark
90FLSt/200*-114
Mesich, Rick
85Victoria/Pol-11
88Victoria/Pol-10
Messier, Mitch
90MISt/200*-187
Meyer, Heidi
91ND*-10M
Meyer, Joey
86DePaul-C13
86DePaul-S5
Meyer, Marge
86DePaul-H12
Meyer, Ray
86DePaul-11
86DePaul-C1
86DePaul-D8
86DePaul-H1
86DePaul-H12
86DePaul-S5
90NotreDame-47
Meyer, Tom
86DePaul-C9
Meyers, Ann
91UCLA/144-110
Meyers, Dave
76T-122
77Bucks/ActPh-8
77T-76
78T-8
79Bucks/Pol-7
91UCLA/144-47
Meyers, Ed
81George/Pol-15
Meyers, Paul
84NE/Pol*-21
85NE/Pol*-32
Miasek, Stan
48Bowman-40
52Bread-20
Michaels, Lou
89KY/300*-132
Michaelson, Joe
90LSU/200*-124
Micheaux, Larry

83Star/NBA-221
84Star/NBA-133
84Star/NBA-245
85Star/Bucks-10
Miciotto, Binks
90LSU/200*-123
Mickal, Abe
90LSU/200*-104
Mickens, Darrell
91WildCard/Coll-116
Middlebrooks, Levy
91ProC/CBA-6
Middlecoff, Cary
57Union-42
Middleton, Darryl
87Baylor/Pol*-5
Miguel, Niguel
91UCLA/144-95
Mihn, Pat
91SC/200*-121
Mikan, Ed
86DePaul-H7
Mikan, George L.
48Bowman-69
48ExhSC-37
48Kell*-16
52Bread-21
52Royal-6
68HOF-31
81TCMA-3
86DePaul-H5
86DePaul-H9
92CenterCrt-1
92Crtside/ColFB-26
Mikez, Joseph
55Ash-68
Mikkelsen, Vern
52Bread-22
57T-28
81TCMA-8
Milburn, Bryan
90KY/ClassA-10
Milchin, Mike
90Clemson/200*-32
Miles, Dick
48ExhSC-38
Miles, Eddie
69T-21
70T-159
71T-44
Miley, Mike
90LSU/200*-120
Milford, Lance
90NM-10
91NM-14
Milhorn, Jim
91UCLA/144-138
Millard, Russ
91Iowa-8
Millen, Kevin
91George/Pol-11
Miller, Angie
84NE/Pol*-19
Miller, Blake
90MISt/200*-91
Miller, Brian
89Louville/300*-189
Miller, Charles
81AZ/Pol-12
Miller, Dencil
55Ash-80
Miller, Derek
88KY/Sov-17
Miller, Derrick
88KY/Award-5
89KY/Award-27
89KY/Award-35
Miller, Ed
54Bullet/Gunth-9
Miller, Ferrel
55Ash-81
Miller, Fred
90LSU/200*-160
Miller, Jack
91ProC/CBA-96ACO
Miller, Johnny
54Quaker-1
Miller, Kelly
90MISt/200*-145
Miller, Kenny
91ProC/CBA-26
Miller, Kent
91UCLA/144-135
Miller, Kevin
89Louville/300*-195
Miller, Kip
90MISt/200*-144
90MISt/Promos*-10
Miller, Kurt
90NM-11
Miller, Larry
71T-208
72T-188
73T-252
74T-213
89NC/Coke-106
89NC/Coke-24
89NC/Coke-25
89NC/Coke-26
89NC/Coke-27
90NC/200*-125
90NC/200*-130
90NC/200*-155M
Miller, Lindy
91OKSt*-91
Miller, Melissa
90Clemson/Lady-9
Miller, Mike
85FortHaysSt-13
Miller, Oliver
91AR25-12
92Classic/DP-49
92StarPic-19
Miller, Paul
90NC/200*-191
Miller, Purvis
81TCMA/CBA-44
82TCMA/CBA-58
Miller, Reggie
88F-57
89F-65
89Hoops-29
90F-78
90Hoops-135
90Hoops-7AS
90Hoops/CollB-7
90Hoops/II-365TC
90Hoops/Super-40
90Panini-111
90SkyBox-117
91F-226
91F-83
91Hoops/I-303IS
91Hoops/I-308M
91Hoops/I-84
91Hoops/II-469SC
91Hoops/McDon-18
91Hoops/Super-39
91Panini-131
91SkyBox/Canada-21
91SkyBox/I-114
91SkyBox/II-469TW
91SkyBox/II-596SS
91SkyBox/Proto-114
91StarPic-20
91UD-256
91UD-90TC
92F-91
92F/TmLeader-11
92Hoops/I-92
92SkyBox/I-292TT
92SkyBox/I-97
Miller, Rick
90MISt/200*-104
Miller, Sean
89Pitt/Food-3
90Pitt/Food-7
92Classic/DP-68
Miller, Terry
91OKSt*-14
Miller, Trever
91Classic/DPColl*-87
Mills, Chris
88KY/Award-2
88KY/Award-6
88KY/Award-9
88KY/Sov-16
89AZ/Pol-6
89KY/Tm80-48
Mills, Dave
61Union-6
86DePaul-C11
Mills, Don
88KY/269-231
88KY/269-73
Mills, Ray
55Ash-21
89KY/300*-52
Mills, Terry
88KY/269-90
88MI/Nike-7
89MI-8
90StarPic-44
91F/Up-324
91Hoops/II-401
91SkyBox/I-184
91UD-289
92F-145
92Hoops/I-149
92SkyBox/I-157
Milstead, Charley
91TexAM-37
Milward, Stanley
89KY/300*-259
Milward, Will
89KY/300*-262
Mimms, Larry
85NE/Pol*-34
Mims, Bobbie
90Clemson/200*-192
Mincevich, Frank
91SC/200*-169
Mincy, Jerome
91WildCard/Coll-100
Miner, Harold
92Classic/DP-84
92FrRow/DreamPk-51
92FrRow/DreamPk-52
92FrRow/DreamPk-53
92FrRow/DreamPk-54
92FrRow/DreamPk-55
92StarPic-84
Minniefield, Dirk
79KY/Food-10
81KY/Sched-13
82KY/Sched-6
88KY/269-205
88KY/269-223
88KY/269-52
89KY/300*-8
89KY/Tm80-45
Minnifield, Frank
87KY/Coke-19
89Louville/300*-119
Minor, Dave
91UCLA/144-68
Minor, Lincoln
87KS/Nike-12
Mirken, Mark
89NC/Coke-185
Missett, Joe
91George/100-87
Mistler
90AZSt/200*-62
Mitchell, Allen
91SC/200*-162
Mitchell, Barry
91ProC/CBA-44
Mitchell, Ben
90ProC/CBA-69
Mitchell, Danny
81Louville/Pol-16
83Louville-45
88Louville/194-142
88Louville/194-85
Mitchell, James
55Ash-10
Mitchell, Leonard
90LSU/200*-25
Mitchell, Marc
89Louville/300*-151
Mitchell, Mike
(Auburn)
80T-102
80T-118
80T-43
80T-57
81T-47M
81T-9
83Star/NBA-247
84Star/NBA-71
85Star/NBA-148
86F-74
Mitchell, Mike
(Colorado State)
90ProC/CBA-121
90StarPic-19
Mitchell, Sam
89TWolv/BK-42
90F-114
90Hoops-188
90Panini-76
90SkyBox-171
91F-123
91Hoops/I-127
91Panini-68
91SkyBox/I-171
91SkyBox/II-420GF
91UD-309
92F-135
92Hoops/I-139
92SkyBox/I-146
Mitchell, Todd
90ProC/CBA-68
Mitchell, Tracy
90ProC/CBA-86
Mitchell, Wade
91GATech*-75
Mitchem, Jim
86DePaul-D2
Mix, Steve
74T-56
75Sixers/McDon-6
75T-56
76T-21
77T-116
78T-18
79T-115
80T-147
80T-2
81T-E92
Mobley, Terry
88KY/269-220
88KY/269-81
Moe, Doug
71T-181
79Spurs/Pol-x
82Nugget/Pol-x
83Nugget/Pol-CO
85Star/CO-6
89Hoops-283CO
89NC/Coke-64
89NC/Coke-74
89NC/Coke-75
90Hoops-311CO
92F-173CO
92Hoops/I-258CO
92SkyBox/I-274CO
Moeller, Mark
89NCSt/Coke-146
89NCSt/Coke-147
89NCSt/Coke-148
Mogus, Lee
48Bowman-67
Mohney, Gayle
89KY/300*-261
Moir, John
90NotreDame-49
Mojsiejenko, Ralf
90MISt/200*-99
Mokeski, Paul
83Star/NBA-47
84Star/NBA-134
85Star/Bucks-11
85Star/NBA-127
86Star/LifeBucks-9
87Bucks/Polar-44
88Bucks/Green-9
89Hoops-42
90Hoops-76
90SkyBox-53
Mokray, William G.
68HOF-32
Molls, Andy
89KY/300*-129
Monaghan, Rinty
48T/Magic*-A21
Moncrief, Sidney
79Bucks/Pol-4
80T-140
80T-52
81T-MW99
83Star/ASG-30
83Star/ASG-8
83Star/NBA-38
84Star/Arena-C8
84Star/ASG-8
84Star/Award-7
84Star/CrtKg-7
84Star/NBA-135
84Star/PolASG-8
85Prism-5
85Star/Bucks-12
85Star/NBA-128
85Star/TmSuper-MB2
86F-75
86Star/CrtKg-23
86Star/LifeBucks-10
87Bucks/Polar-4
87F-76
88Bucks/Green-10
89Hoops-275
90Hoops/II-402
90SkyBox/II-367
91AR/100*-3
91Hoops/I-3
91SkyBox/I-6
91UD-240
92Crtside/ColFB-27
Monday, Ken
91OKSt*-47
Monday, Rick
90AZSt/200*-183
Money, Eric
76T-58
78RCCola-23
78T-104
79T-89
80T-112
80T-139
80T-24
80T-39
Monger, Matt
91OKSt*-57
Monk, Kevin

91TexAM-46
Monroe, Earl
68T/Test-12
69T-80
69T/Ins-20
70T-20
70T/Ins-20
71T-130
71T/Ins-8
72T-154
72T-73
73T-142
74T-25
75Carv-23
75T-73
76Buck-17
76T-98
77T-6
78RCCola-24
78T-45
79T-8
80T-151
80T-63
85Star/Schick-19
91Foot*-26
Monroe, Rodney
87NCSt/Pol-9
88NCSt/Pol-10
89NCSt/Pol-10
90NCSt/IBM-8
91Classic-20
91Classic/DPColl*-168
91F/Up-244
91FrRow/Premier-88BC
91FrRow/Up-59
91UD-14
91UD-1CL
Montana, Joe
91Arena/Holo*-1
Montgomery, Bill
91AR/100*-46
Montgomery, George
81IL/Arby's-9
Montgomery, Greg
90MISt/200*-4
Montgomery, Mark
90MISt-11
Moody, Dwight
91ProC/CBA-37
Moore, Allison
91VA/Lady-7
Moore, Andre
89ProC/CBA-150
Moore, Billie
90UCLA-16CO
Moore, Billy
91AR/100*-61
Moore, Gene
71T-231
72T-201
73T-223
Moore, Jeff
87Auburn/Pol*-9
90KY/ClassA-16
90KY/Sov-11
Moore, John
91UCLA/144-105
Moore, Johnny
81T-62
81T-MW103
83Star/NBA-249
84Star/NBA-72
85Star/NBA-149
86F-76
90Hoops-269
90SkyBox-258
Moore, Laura
91WA/Viacom-15
Moore, Lefty
91ProC/CBA-180
Moore, Lloyd
82Marq/Lite-7
Moore, Lowes
81TCMA/CBA-40
82TCMA/CBA-10
91ProC/CBA-170AC
Moore, Mark
91OKSt*-51
Moore, Otis
90Clemson/200*-124
Moore, Otto
70Suns/Carn-7
70T-9
72T-86
73T-101
74T-29
75T-54
76T-106
Moore, Ron
90ProC/CBA-2
Moore, Shawn
91Classic/DPColl*-224
Moore, Tracy
89ProC/CBA-151
90ProC/CBA-110
91ProC/CBA-173
Moorhead, Bobby
91GATech*-84
Moota, Kip
90Sonic/Smok-13CO
Mooty, Jim
91AR/100*-94
Moreau, Al
90LSU/200*-170
Moreau, Doug
90LSU/200*-166
Moreman, Gerald
55Ash-31
88Louville/194-81
Moremen, Bill
90FLSt/200*-148
Morgan, Anthony
91Classic/DPColl*-209
Morgan, James
55Ash-32
Morgan, J.D.
91UCLA/144-108
91UCLA/144-142
Morgan, Jermaine
90Pitt/Food-6
Morgan, Jim
88Louville/194-60
Morgan, Lamont
90George/Pol-13
91George/Pol-10
Morgan, Ralph
89KY/300*-223
Morgan, Richard
88VA/Hardee-9
Morgan, Sylvester
91TexAM-56
Morgan, Winston
87IN/GreatII-23
Morhardt, Greg
91SC/200*-51
Morningstar, Darren
89Pitt/Food-33
90Pitt/Food-8
92Classic/DP-53
92StarPic-6
Morocco, Chris
90Clemson/200*-16
Morocco, Tony
91ProC/CBA-34ACO
Morrall, Earl
90MISt/200*-16
Morris, Chris
89F-99
89Hoops-26
90F-121
90Hoops-200
90Hoops/II-371TC
90Hoops/Super-62
90Nets/Kayo-11
90Panini-158
90SkyBox-183
91F-133
91Hoops/I-136
91Hoops/Super-62
91Panini-160
91SkyBox/I-185
91UD-339
92F-146
92Hoops/I-150
92SkyBox/I-158
Morris, Craig
90MurraySt-15ACO
Morris, Hal
91MI/56*-37
Morris, Isaiah
91AR25-13
92Classic/DP-54
92StarPic-39
Morris, Victor
82George/Pol-12
83George/Pol-9
85George/Pol-12
Morrison, Joe
91SC/200*-54
Morrison, Stan
90SanJ/Smok-5CO
Morrow, Jeff
89Louville/300*-136
Morse, Bill
85FortHaysSt-14CO
Morse, Ron
85FortHaysSt-15
Morse, Samuel
48T/Magic*-N7
Mortensen, Jess
57Union-37
Morton, Dickey
91AR/100*-32
Morton, Dwayne
90KY/Sov-12
Morton, John
90F/Up-U17
90Hoops-77
90SkyBox-54
91F/Up-307
91Hoops/II-351
91SkyBox/I-51
91UD-210
Morton, Richard
89ProC/CBA-204
90ProC/CBA-196
Moseley, Doug
89KY/300*-121
Moseley, Tom
89KY/300*-252
Moser, Clay
90ProC/CBA-93
91ProC/CBA-121AC
Moses, James
91Iowa-9
Moses, Omo
90Pitt/Food-9
Mosley, Mike
91TexAM-82
Mosman, Dede
90UCLA-26
Moss, Anita
90AZ/125*-34
Moss, Eddie
81TCMA/CBA-64
Moss, Perry
82TCMA/CBA-51
Moss, Tony
90LSU/200*-176
Moten, Andrew
91WildCard/Coll-107
Mcten, Eric
91Classic/DPColl*-143
Motley, Marion
48ExhSC-39
Motta, Dick
90Bulls/Eq-10CO
90Hoops-327CO
90Kings/Safe-8CO
90SkyBox/II-323CO
91F-178CO
91Hoops/I-243CO
91SkyBox/II-400CO
Mount, Rick
71Pacer/Mara-7
71T-213
72T-237
73T-192
74T-206
75T-261
Mourning, Alonzo
88George/Pol-11
89George/Pol-11
90George/Pol-5
91George/Pol-5
92Classic/BKPrev-BK2
92Classic/DP-60
92Classic/DPLP-LP2
92SkyBox/NBADP-DP2
Mouton, Lyle
88LSU/Pol*-6
Moye, Linwood
91SC/200*-9
Mudd, Charlie
89Louville/300*-166
Mudd, Eric
89ProC/CBA-83
Muehlebach, Matt
87AZ/Pol-10
88AZ/Pol-9
89AZ/Pol-7
Mueller, Erwin
69Sonic/Sunb-6
70T-82
71T-31
Mugg, Scott
82INSt/Pol*-9
Muier, Warren
91SC/200*-176
Mulgado, Bob
90AZSt/200*-144
Mullaney, Joe
89ProC/CBA-52
91Providence-1CO
Mullen, Steve
91GATech*-48
Mullin, Chris
86F-77
87F-77
88F-48
88Warr/Smok-2
89F-55
89F/AS-9
89Hoops-230AS
89Hoops-90
90F-66
90Hoops-116
90Hoops-22AS
90Hoops/CollB-31
90Hoops/II-363TC
90Hoops/Super-32
90Panini-26
90SkyBox-98
91F-218
91F-69
91F/School-1
91F/Up-380TL
91Hoops/I-268AS
91Hoops/I-72
91Hoops/II-466SC
91Hoops/II-581
91Hoops/McDon-16
91Hoops/McDon-57USA
91Hoops/Super-32
91Panini-3
91Panini-93AS
91SkyBox/Canada-18
91SkyBox/I-301
91SkyBox/I-303M
91SkyBox/I-96
91SkyBox/II-467TW
91SkyBox/II-536US
91SkyBox/II-597SS
91SkyBox/Proto-95
91UD-245
91UD-60AS
91UD-99TC
91UD/Ext-465AS
91WildCard/Coll-13
91Wooden-14
92Crtside/ColFB-28
92F-245LL
92F-77
92F/AS-18
92F/TmLeader-9
92Hoops/I-312AS
92Hoops/I-344
92Hoops/I-78
92SkyBox/I-290TT
92SkyBox/I-83
92SkyBox/Olympic-USA2
92SkyBox/USA-107
92SkyBox/USA-55
92SkyBox/USA-56
92SkyBox/USA-57
92SkyBox/USA-58
92SkyBox/USA-59
92SkyBox/USA-60
92SkyBox/USA-61
92SkyBox/USA-62
92SkyBox/USA-63
Mullins, Gary
55Ash-92
Mullins, Jeff
69T-70
69T/Ins-8
70T-4LL
70T-76
70T/Ins-5
71T-115
71T/Ins-38
72T-85
73T-75
74T-123
74T-147LL
75T-157
Mullins, Noah
89KY/300*-177
Munford, Marc
85NE/Pol*-3
Munk, Chris
90ProC/CBA-126
Munlyn, James
88GATech/Nike-7
89GATech/Pol-13
90GATech/Pol-17
Munn, Clarence
90MISt/200*-59
Munro, John
83Victoria/Pol-6
Murcer, Bobby
76Nab-25M
Murdock, Eric
91Classic-13
91Classic/DPColl*-161
91Crtside-37
91F/Up-365
91FrRow/100-16
91FrRow/50-16
91FrRow/Premier-79
91Providence-23
91StarPic-11
91UD-12
91WildCard/Coll-4
92F-128

92Hoops/I-228
92SkyBox/I-243
Murdock, Les
90FLSt/200*-117
Murphree, Eger V.
89KY/300*-153
Murphy, Allen
88Louville/194-140
88Louville/194-76
89Louville/300*-240
89Louville/300*-269
Murphy, Audie
48T/Magic*-J23
Murphy, Calvin
70T-137
71T-58
71T/Ins-3
72Icee-14
72T-174LL
72T-31
73NBAPA-20
73T-13
73T-156LL
74Nab-24
74T-149LL
74T-152
74T-88M
75T-123M
75T-180
75T-3LL
76T-44
77T-105
78RCCola-25
78T-13
79T-81
80T-105
80T-118
80T-30
80T-75
81T-15
81T/Thirst-27
91Foot*-15
92Crtside/ColFB-29
Murphy, Charles C.
68HOF-33
Murphy, Denise
90Clemson/200*-184
Murphy, Jay
84Star/NBA-19
91WildCard/Coll-52
Murphy, Joe
90MISt/200*-135
Murphy, Mike
79Lakers/Alta-7
Murphy, Pete
81AZ/Pol-13
Murphy, Tod
89Hoops/II-304
90F-115
90Hoops-189
90Panini-74
90SkyBox-172
91F-124
91Hoops/I-128
91Panini-65
91SkyBox/I-172
91SkyBox/II-447SM
91UD-377
Murray, Bruce
90Clemson/200*-33
Murray, Dave
90AZ/125*-60
Murray, Dorrie
72T-61
Murray, Glen
91Classic/DPColl*-15
Murray, Tracy
90UCLA-2
91UCLA-12
92Classic/DP-41
92SkyBox/NBADP-DP18
92StarPic-80
Murrey, Dorrie
69Sonic/Sunb-7
70T-94
Murry, Ernie
91AR25-23ACO
Musselman, Bill
89Hoops/II-314CO
90Hoops-320CO
90SkyBox/II-316CO
Musselman, Eric
89ProC/CBA-37
91ProC/CBA-69CO
Mustaf, Jerrod
88MD/Pol-9
90F/Up-U64
90StarPic-48
91F/Up-341
91Hoops/II-420
91SkyBox/I-191
91SkyBox/II-641
91UD-284
91UD/Ext-417
92SkyBox/I-195
Muto, Sean
91FrRow/100-53
91FrRow/Premier-45
91FrRow/Up-81
Mutombo, Dikembe
88George/Pol-15
89George/Pol-15
90George/Pol-7
91Classic-3
91Classic/DPColl*-151
91F/Mutombo-Set
91F/Up-277A
91F/Up-277A
91F/Up-378TL
91FrRow/Mutombo-Set
91FrRow/Premier-16ACC
91FrRow/Premier-83
91FrRow/Premier-98HL
91FrRow/Up-52
91Hoops/II-549
91Hoops/II-HC
91Hoops/McDon-48
91SkyBox/II-411GF
91SkyBox/II-516LP
91UD-3
91UD/Ext-446TP
91UD/Ext-471AS
91UD/Rook-29
91WildCard/Coll-5B
91WildCard/RHRook-1
92Classic/DP-98FB
92F-60
92F/AS-19
92F/Rook-7
92F/TmLeader-7
92FrRow/DreamPk-10
92FrRow/DreamPk-6
92FrRow/DreamPk-7
92FrRow/DreamPk-8
92FrRow/DreamPk-9
92Hoops/I-313AS
92Hoops/I-60
92SkyBox/I-319AR
92SkyBox/I-64
Myers, Ernest
89NCSt/Coke-97
89NCSt/Coke-98
89NCSt/Coke-99
Myers, Gene
89KY/300*-178
Myers, Pete
88Knick/FrLay-5
89Knicks/Marine-6
90SkyBox-184
91WildCard/Coll-66
Naber, Bob
89Louville/300*-84
Nadeau, Wendy J.
87ME/Pol*-11
Nagle, Browning
91Classic/DPColl*-130
Nagurski, Bronko
54Quaker-26
Nagy, Dick
80IL/Arby's-8CO
81IL/Arby's-10CO
Nairn, Chandler
91WA/Viacom-5
Naismith, James A.
68HOF-34
91Hoops/I-301
91Hoops/I-CC1
91SkyBox/I-332
Namath, Joe
81PhilM-6
Nance, Larry
82Suns/Giant-3
83Star/NBA-115
84Star/Award-9
84Star/CrtKg-19
84Star/NBA-47
84Star/PolASG-31
84Star/SlamD-11
84Star/SlamD-7
84Suns/Pol-22
85Star/Gator-2
85Star/NBA-34
85Star/SlamD-6
86F-78
86Star/CrtKg-24
87F-78
87Suns/Circ-7
88F-24
89F-28
89Hoops-217AS
89Hoops-25
90Clemson/200*-6
90F-35
90Hoops-78
90Hoops/CollB-18
90Hoops/Super-17
90Panini-107
90SkyBox-55
91F-37
91Hoops/I-39
91Hoops/II-458SC
91Hoops/SlamD-1
91Hoops/Super-17
91Panini-120
91SkyBox/Canada-10
91SkyBox/I-52
91UD-223
92F-42
92Hoops/I-42
92SkyBox/I-43
Nance, Lynn
91WA/TCI-8CO
91WA/Viacom-6CO
Nared, Greg
88MD/Pol-10
Nash, Cotton
88KY/269-172
88KY/269-8
Nash, Macolm
89KS/Leesley-53
91KS-7
Nash, Noreen
48T/Magic*-F22
Naslund, Markus
91Classic/DPColl*-13
Nater, Swen
74T-205AS
74T-208LL
74T-227M
75T-225LL
75T-231AS
75T-284M
76T-103
77T-92
78Clipp/Handy-6
78T-23
79T-109
80T-112
80T-16
80T-163
80T-75
81T-38
81T-63M
83Lakers/BASF-8
83Star/NBA-20
84Star/Arena-D5
91UCLA/144-91
Natt, Calvin
80T-14
80T-162
81Blaz/Pol-33
81T-W85
82Blaz/Pol-33
83Blaz/Pol-33
83Star/NBA-103
84Star/NBA-145
85Nugget/Pol-12
85Star/NBA-55
86F-79
89Blaz/Franz-14
Natt, Kenny
81TCMA/CBA-38
82TCMA/CBA-20
Nattin, George
90LSU/200*-58
Naulls, Jonah
91UCLA-17
Naulls, Willie
57T-29
61F-32
91UCLA/144-58
Neal, Craig
90ProC/CBA-175
91GATech*-33
Neal, Freddie
(Curly)
71Globe-18M
71Globe-26M
71Globe-27
71Globe-28
71Globe-29
71Globe-30M
71Globe-31
71Globe-32
71Globe-64M
71Globe-65
71Globe-66M
71Globe-67M
71Globe-69M
71Globe-72M
71Globe/Cocoa-10M
71Globe/Cocoa-24
71Globe/Cocoa-25
71Globe/Cocoa-28
71Globe/Cocoa-2M
71Globe/Cocoa-4M
71Globe/Cocoa-6M
71Globe/Cocoa-7M
71Globe/Cocoa-8M
71Globe/Cocoa-9M
Neal, Ida
91GATech*-2
Neal, Kim
90AZSt/200*-149
Neal, Lloyd
73T-129
75T-58
76T-7
77Blaz/Pol-36
84Blaz/Pol-12
89Blaz/Franz-15
Nealy, Ed
83Star/NBA-222
89Bulls/Eq-8
90Hoops/II-426
90SkyBox-43
90SkyBox/II-406
91Hoops/II-421
Neely, Jess
90Clemson/200*-55
Nehls, Joe
90AZ/125*-99
Neidert, John
89Louville/300*-172
Nelson, Alonzo
89KY/300*-299
Nelson, Byron
81T/Thirst-46
Nelson, Chris
91NE/Pol*-10
Nelson, Don
69T-82
70T-86
71T-114
72T-92
73T-78
74T-46
75Carv-24
75T-2LL
75T-44
79Bucks/Pol-x
85Star/Bucks-1
85Star/CO-7
86Star/LifeBucks-1CO
89Hoops-273CO
90Hoops-313CO
90Hoops/II-345CO
90SkyBox/II-309CO
91F-70CO
91Hoops/I-229CO
91SkyBox/II-386CO
92F-78CO
92Hoops/I-247CO
92Hoops/I-319CO
92SkyBox/I-263CO
Nelson, Jeff
91TexAM-58
Nelson, Jeff HOCK
91Classic/DPColl*-32
Nelson, Korky
80TCMA/CBA-13
Nelson, Lee
90FLSt/200*-132
Nelson, Louie
73Bullet/Stand-6
75T-18
76T-17
Nelson, Lynn
90AZSt/200*-152
Nelson, Mark
91SC/200*-102
Nelson, Ted
91TexAM-19
Nessley, Martin
89ProC/CBA-24
Netolicky, Bob
71Pacer/Mara-8
71T-183
72T-228
73T-256
75T-314
Neumann, Johnny
72T-184
73T-243
74T-238
82TCMA/CBA-60
Nevitt, Charles G.
89NCSt/Coke-106
89NCSt/Coke-107
89NCSt/Coke-108
Newbern, Melvin
90StarPic-52
91FrRow/100-89
91FrRow/Premier-109
91FrRow/Up-97

Newbill, Ivano
89GATech/Pol-14
90GATech/Pol-18
91GATech/Pol-13
Newell, Pete
90MISt/200*-161
Newlin, Mike
72T-128
73T-156LL
73T-44
74T-127
75T-103
75T-123M
76T-139
77T-37
78T-124
79T-15
80T-119
80T-143
80T-36
80T-55
81T-57M
81T-E80
Newman, Don
81TCMA/CBA-71
Newman, James
(Jamie)
83Victoria/Pol-7
84Victoria/Pol-7
Newman, Johnny
88Knick/FrLay-6
89F-102
89Hoops-58
89Knicks/Marine-7
90F-127A
90F-127B
90F/Up-U12
90Hoops-206
90Hoops/II-386
90Hoops/II-403
90SkyBox-190
90SkyBox/II-370
91F-23
91Hoops/I-23
91Hoops/Super-11
91Panini-108
91SkyBox/I-31
91UD-268
92F-26
92Hoops/I-25
92SkyBox/I-26
Newman, Paul
82Marq/Lite-8
Newman, Roger
89KY/300*-258
Newman, Victor
91NCSt/IBM-10
Newmark, Dave
70T-156
Newsome, Eric
89ProC/CBA-86
Newton, C.M.
87Vanderbilt/Pol-2CO
88KY/269-63
89KY/300*-1
Newton, Milt
87KS/Nike-13
89ProC/CBA-136
Newton, Rob
90NM-12
Newton, Steve
90MurraySt-15CO
Nichols, Chancellor
91FrRow/100-56
91FrRow/Premier-42
91FrRow/Up-82
Nichols, Gerald
90FLSt/200*-25
Nichols, Jack
52Royal-3
57T-9
Nicholson, Darrell
90NC/200*-14
Nicks, Carl
81T-W104
82TCMA/CBA-77
Nido, Miquel
90Clemson/200*-50
Niedermayer, Scott
91Classic/DPColl*-3
Niesen, Gertrude
48T/Magic*-J11
Niles, Mike
80Suns/Pep-10
Nillen, John
82TCMA/CBA-55
Nimitz, Chester
48T/Magic*-O2
Nimphius, Kurt
81TCMA/CBA-9
83Star/NBA-56
84Star/Arena-B7
84Star/NBA-256
89Sixers/Kodak-9
90AZSt/200*-15
Nix, Dyron
88TN/Smok-31
90SkyBox-118A
90SkyBox-118B
91ProC/CBA-103
Nixon, Kevin
89ProC/CBA-175
Nixon, Norm
78T-63
79Lakers/Alta-4
79T-97
80T-135
80T-160
80T-47
80T-55
81T-22
81T-55M
82Lakers/BASF-9
83Star/NBA-129
84Star/NBA-20
86F-80
Noble, Brian
90AZSt/200*-55
90AZSt/Promos*-8
Noble, Chuck
57T-11
88Louville/194-82
89Louville/300*-241
Noel, Paul
89KY/300*-61
Nolan, Gary
68PartM-4
Noll, Randy
89KY/300*-89
Noonan, Danny
85NE/Pol*-7
Nord, Gary
89Louville/300*-132
Nordmann, Bob
61Kahn's-5
Nore, Christy
90AZSt/200*-104
Norlander, John
48Bowman-27
Norman, Heather
91WASt-9
Norman, Jerry
91UCLA/144-104
Norman, Ken
89F-72
89Hoops-162
90Clip/Star-9
90F-88
90Hoops-149
90Panini-35
90SkyBox-131
91F-93
91Hoops/I-96
91Hoops/Super-43
91Panini-12
91SkyBox/I-129
91UD-111
92F-102
92Hoops/I-102
92SkyBox/I-108
Norris, Audie
82Blaz/Pol-24
83Blaz/Pol-24
83Star/NBA-104
84Blaz/Franz-7
84Blaz/Pol-8
84Star/Blaz-3
84Star/NBA-166
Norris, Sherri
90AZSt/200*-166
Norton, Darrell
91GATech*-13
Norton, Jeff
91MI/56*-38
Norton, Rick
89KY/300*-108
Norton, Ricky
82AR-9
Norwood, Michael
86NC/Pol-21
Norwood, Ralph
90LSU/200*-173
Norwood, Ron
86DePaul-D9
Norwood, Willie
72T-94
73T-39
74T-156
75T-168
Nostrand, George
48Bowman-42
Noth, Cathy
84NE/Pol*-12
Novak, Gary
90NotreDame-38
Novick, Tony
90AZSt/200*-58
Nowak, Paul
90NotreDame-31
Nucatola, John
92CenterCrt-19
Nuce, Steve
89NCSt/Coke-152
89NCSt/Coke-153
89NCSt/Coke-154
Nunamacher, Jeff
90Clemson/200*-53
Nunley, Frank
91MI/56*-39
Nunnally, Doc
89ProC/CBA-112
90ProC/CBA-161
Nuss, Dave
89Louville/300*-177
Nutt, Dennis
89ProC/CBA-8
90ProC/CBA-82
Nuxhall, Joe
81T/Thirst-23
Nuzum, Rick
89KY/300*-144
Nwokocha, Nuamoi
90Clemson/200*-112
Nyikos, John
90NotreDame-24
91Classic/DPColl*-47
Nystrom, Carl
(Buck)
90MISt/200*-7
O'Bannon, Ed
90UCLA-3
31UCLA-8
O'Brien, Jimmy
73T-241
74T-236
75T-285M
75T-317
O'Brien, Lawrence
90Piston/Unocal-8M
O'Callaghan, Gerard
85NE/Pol*-18
O'Conner, Tom
91SC/200*-173
O'Connor, Terry
82Fairf-11
O'Dell, Billy
90Clemson/200*-169
O'Donnell, John
89NC/Coke-175
O'Donovan, Cathy
86SWLou/Pol*-12
O'Hara, Maureen
48T/Magic*-F18
O'Hara, Pat
90SoCal/Smok*-11
O'Keefe, Dick
48Bowman-61
O'Keefe, Tommy
91George/100-95
O'Koren, Mike
81T-E81
83Star/NBA-152
84Nets/Getty-7
84Star/NBA-94
85Star/NBA-64
86Star/LifeNets-9
89NC/Coke-55
89NC/Coke-56
89NC/Coke-57
89NC/Coke-58
90NC/200*-154
90NC/200*-189
O'Malley, Tom
90FLSt/200*-52
O'Neal, Calvin
91MI/56*-40
O'Neal, Leslie
91OKSt*-46
O'Neal, Shaquille
90KY/BB/DT/AW-19
92Classic/BKPrev-BK1
92Classic/DP-1
92Classic/DPLP-LP1
O'Neal-Warren, Mike
89NCSt/Coke-120
89NCSt/Coke-121
O'Shaughnessy, Niall
91AR/100*-17
O'Shea, Kevin
48T/Magic*-B4
90NotreDame-6
O'Shea, Michael
48T/Magic*-J19
O'Toole, Joe
87Hawks/Pizza-5TR
O'Toole, Tim
82Fairf-12
Oakley, Annie
48T/Magic*-S4
Oakley, Charles
86F-81
87Bulls/Ent-9
87F-79
88F-18
88Knick/FrLay-7
89F-103
89Hoops-213
89Knicks/Marine-5
90F-128
90Hoops-207
90Hoops/CollB-32
90Hoops/Super-66
90Panini-141
90SkyBox-191
91F-138
91Hoops/I-142
91Hoops/II-484SC
91Hoops/Proto-142
91Hoops/Super-67
91Panini-162
91SkyBox/Canada-32
91SkyBox/I-192
91SkyBox/II-476TW
91SkyBox/II-605
91UD-258
92F-154
92Hoops/I-157
92SkyBox/I-166
Obremskey, Pete
86IN/GreatI-3
Ochs, Debbie
90AZSt/200*-157
Ogg, Alan
90Heat/Publix-9
90StarPic-49
91F/Up-308
91Hoops/II-388
91UD-198
Ogrin, David
91TexAM-91
Ohl, Don
61F-33
69T-77
70T-128
Ohl, Phil
83Victoria/Pol-8
84Victoria/Pol-8
Olajuwon, Hakeem
(Akeem)
84Star/CrtKg-47
84Star/NBA-237
85Star/NBA-18
85Star/RTm-1
85Star/TmSuper-HR2
86F-82
86F/Ins-9
86Star/Best-3
86Star/CrtKg-25
87F-80
87F/Ins-3
88F-126AS
88F-53
88Fourn-23
89F-164M
89F-61
89F/AS-2
89Hoops-178AS
89Hoops-180
90F-73
90F/AS-3
90Hoops-127
90Hoops-23AS
90Hoops/CollB-43
90Hoops/II-364TC
90Hoops/Super-38
90Panini-69
90Panini-DAS
90Panini-M
90SkyBox-110
91F-214
91F-223
91F-77
91F/Up-381TL
91Hoops/I-304IS
91Hoops/I-309M
91Hoops/I-78
91Hoops/II-467SC
91Hoops/McDon-17
91Hoops/Proto/00-006
91Hoops/Super-36
91Kell/ColGrt-11
91Panini-57
91SkyBox/Canada-19
91SkyBox/I-105
91SkyBox/I-311M

91SkyBox/I-324
91SkyBox/II-414GF
91SkyBox/II-568
91UD-254
91UD-92TC
91UD/AWHolo-8
91UD/Ext-472AS
92F-84
92F/AS-20
92F/TmLeader-10
92Hoops/I-314AS
92Hoops/I-323LL
92Hoops/I-85
92SkyBox/I-90
Oistad, Maria
91ND*-10M
Olberding, Mark
79Spurs/Pol-53
79T-98
80T-81
80T-91
81T-MW104
83Star/NBA-223
84Star/NBA-276
85Kings/Smok-11
85Star/NBA-77
86Kings/Smok-6
Oldham, Calvin
91ProC/CBA-12
Oldham, Jawann
81TCMA/CBA-60
83Star/NBA-177
84Star/NBA-110
85Star/NBA-122
91ProC/CBA-179
Oliver, Anthony
88VA/Hardee-10
91VA-10
Oliver, Brian
88GATech/Nike-8
89GATech/Pol-15
89GATech/Pol-20M
90F/Up-U71
90StarPic-58
91F-157
91GATech*-30
91Hoops/II-412
91SkyBox/I-218
91UD-119
92Hoops/I-175
92SkyBox/I-185
Oliver, Gary
91TexAM-36
Oliver, Gerald
89ProC/CBA-114
91ProC/CBA-83CO
Oliver, Hubie
90AZ/125*-43
Oliver, Jimmy
91Classic-29
91Classic/DPColl*-177
91Crtside-38
91F/Up-265
91FrRow/100-22
91FrRow/50-22
91FrRow/Premier-72
91StarPic-64
91UD-19
91WildCard/Coll-48
Olivier, Kathy
90UCLA-33CO
Olkowski, June
90AZ/125*-75
Ollie, Kevin
91CT/Pol-11
Olliges, Will
83Louville-24
88Louville/194-136
88Louville/194-176
88Louville/194-54
Olsen, Bill
81Louville/Pol-4DIR
88Louville/194-194
Olsen, Bud
62Kahn's-5
63Kahn's-8
64Kahn's-9
88Louville/194-79
89Louville/300*-242
Olson, Dale
88Victoria/Pol-11
Olson, Lance
90MISt/200*-110
Olson, Lute
83AZ/Pol-10CO
83AZ/Pol-18CO
84AZ/Pol-11CO
85AZ/Pol-12CO
86AZ/Pol-10CO
87AZ/Pol-11CO
88AZ/Pol-10CO
89AZ/Pol-8CO
90AZ/125*-103
90AZ/125*-4
90AZ/Promos*-3
90AZ/Promos*-5
Olson, Merlin
75Nab-4
Olson, Weldon
90MISt/200*-75
Olszewski, Harry
90Clemson/200*-121
Olynyk, Ken
88Victoria/Pol-12CO
Ontiveros, Steve
91MI/56*-41
Oosterbaan, Bennie
91MI/56*-42
Oosterbaan, J.P.
88MI/Nike-8
89MI-12
Opper, Bernie
88KY/269-28
Ordonez, Ish
91AR/100*-70
Orem, Dale
89Louville/300*-170
Orn, Mike
90AZSt/200*-120
Orr, George
55Ash-82
Orr, Louis
81T-MW93
83Star/NBA-66
84Star/NBA-32
86F-83
Orr, Vickie
87Auburn/Pol*-10
Ortiz, Jose
89Hoops-223
89Jazz/OldH-11
91WildCard/Coll-112
Ortiz, Manuel
48T/Magic*-A22
Osborne, Tom
84NE/Pol*-2CO
Osgood, Chris
91Classic/DPColl*-43
Osik, Keith
88LSU/Pol*-15
Ostertag, Greg
91KS-8
Othick, Matt
88AZ/Pol-11
89AZ/Pol-9
Otorubio, Adubarie
90Clemson/200*-31
Ottewell, Kevin
85Victoria/Pol-12
88Victoria/Pol-13
Oven, Mike
91GATech*-81
Overstreet, Donald
90MurraySt-3
Overton, Doug
91Classic-30
91Classic/DPColl*-178
91Crtside-39
91FrRow/100-26
91FrRow/50-26
91FrRow/Premier-67
91StarPic-41
91UD-20
91WildCard/Coll-33
Owen, Steve
74Nab-3
Owens, Billy
88Syr/Rich-7
89Syr/Pep-13
89Syr/Pep-7
91Classic-2
91Classic-45M
91Classic/DPColl*-150
91Classic/DPColl*-199M
91Classic/DPColl*-200M
91Classic/DPColl*-201M
91Classic/DPColl*-202M
91Classic/DPCollLP*-LP9M
91F/Up-288
91FrRow/Owens-Set
91FrRow/Premier-3ACC
91FrRow/Premier-85
91FrRow/Premier-96HL
91FrRow/Up-51
91Hoops/II-548
91Hoops/II-HC
91Hoops/McDon-49
91SkyBox/II-515LP
91UD/Ext-438CL
91UD/Ext-442TP
91UD/Rook-33
91WildCard/Coll-45B
91WildCard/RHRook-4
92Classic/DP-97FB
92F-79
92F/Rook-8
92FrRow/DreamPk-16
92FrRow/DreamPk-17
92FrRow/DreamPk-18
92FrRow/DreamPk-19
92FrRow/DreamPk-20
92Hoops/I-79
92SkyBox/I-84
Owens, Dallas
89KY/300*-183
Owens, DaPreis
91NE/Pol*-18
Owens, Destah
90UCLA-8A
Owens, Hays
89KY/300*-224
Owens, Jesse
48T/Magic*-E1
81T/Thirst-35
Owens, Keith
90UCLA-8A
90UCLA-8B
91F/Up-302
91FrRow/100-54
91FrRow/Premier-44
91FrRow/Up-78
Owens, Randy
81TCMA/CBA-72
82TCMA/CBA-83
Owens, Reggie
89ProC/CBA-187
Owens, Tom
73T-189
73T-235LL
74T-208LL
74T-221M
74T-256
75T-239
75T-281M
77Blaz/Pol-25
79Blaz/Pol-25
79T-102
80T-110
80T-160
80T-72
80T-87
Oyler, Wally
89Louville/300*-121
Paar, Jack
58Kahn's-6
Pack, Robert
90SoCal/Smok*-12
91Blaz/Franz-17
91F/Up-345
91FrRow/100-83
91FrRow/ItalPromo-6
91FrRow/Premier-110HL
91FrRow/Premier-5
91FrRow/Up-75
91SkyBox/II-426GF
91UD/Ext-407
91UD/Rook-30
91WildCard/Coll-17
92F-189
92Hoops/I-192
92SkyBox/I-204
Packer, Billy
87KY/Coke-SC
Padcock, Joe Bill
90LSU/200*-171
Paddio, Gerald
90F/Up-U18
91ProC/CBA-106
91UD-230
Page, Alan
75Nab-3
Pagel, Mike
90AZSt/200*-47
Paglierani, Joey
89Fresno/Smok-10
Pagnozzi, Tom
91AR/100*-13
Paine, Jeff
91TexAM-72
Palffy, Zigmund
91Classic/DPColl*-23
Palmer, Bud
48Bowman-54
Palmer, Crawford
88Duke/Pol-11
Palmer, David
90FLSt/200*-71
Palmer, George
58Kahn's-7
Palmer, Jim
58Kahn's-8
Palmer, Neil
85NE/Pol*-16
Palmer, Walter
90F/Up-U95
90Jazz/Star-11
90StarPic-54
Palombizio, Dan
91ProC/CBA-78
Palubinskas, Edde
90LSU/200*-35
Panaggio, Dan
89ProC/CBA-50
90ProC/CBA-147
91ProC/CBA-46CO
Panaggio, Mauro
80TCMA/CBA-21
81TCMA/CBA-24
89ProC/CBA-49
90ProC/CBA-146
Papile, Leo
81TCMA/CBA-28
Papke, Karl
80WichSt/Pol-11
Parent, Bernie
75Nab-15
Parent, Leo
89ProC/CBA-11
Parilli, Vito
(Babe)
89KY/300*-124
Parish, Robert
77T-111
78RCCola-26
78T-86
79T-93
80T-114
80T-131
80T-147
80T-2
80T-22
80T-26
81T-6
81T-E108
83Star/ASG-29M
83Star/ASG-9
83Star/NBA-35
84Star/Arena-A7
84Star/ASG-9
84Star/Celt-17
84Star/Celt-2M
84Star/CrtKg-31
84Star/NBA-10
84Star/PolASG-9
85JMS-12
85Star/NBA-99
85Star/TmSuper-BC2
86F-84
86Star/CrtKg-26
87F-81
88F-12
88Fourn-2
88Fourn/St-8
89F-12
89Hoops-185
90F-13
90Hoops-45
90Hoops-8AS
90Hoops/CollB-19
90Hoops/Super-8
90Panini-138
90SkyBox-20
91F-14
91Hoops/I-15
91Hoops/I-256AS
91Hoops/I-305IS
91Hoops/I-313M
91Hoops/I-324YB
91Hoops/II-452SC
91Hoops/McDon-4
91Hoops/Super-8
91Panini-143
91SkyBox/Canada-4
91SkyBox/I-18
91SkyBox/II-460TW
91SkyBox/II-575
91UD-163
91UD-72AS
92F-18
92Hoops/I-17
92SkyBox/I-17
Park, Brad
75Nab-13
Park, James
89KY/300*-169
89KY/300*-225
Park, Med
57T-45
59Kahn's-4
Parker, Andrew
80TCMA/CBA-42
90AZSt/200*-77
Parker, Buddy
89KY/300*-226
Parker, Clyde KY

91Hoops/II-422
91UD/Ext-413
92F-174
92Hoops/I-185
92SkyBox/I-196
Perry, William
(Refrigerator)
90Clemson/200*-1
90Clemson/200*-111
90Clemson/200*-147
90Clemson/Promos*-C3
90Clemson/Promos*-C9
Pershing, John
48T/Magic*-04
Person, Chuck
87Auburn/Pol*-14
87F-85
87F/Ins-10
88F-58
88Fourn-26
89F-66
89Hoops-45
90F-79
90Hoops-136
90Hoops/CollB-20
90Hoops/Super-41
90Panini-110
90SkyBox-119
91F-84
91F/Up-382TL
91Hoops/I-85
91Hoops/II-513Ar
91Hoops/McDon-19
91Hoops/Super-40
91Panini-133
91SkyBox/I-115
91SkyBox/II-570
91UD-253
92F-92
92Hoops/I-93
92SkyBox/I-98
Peters, Angie
90Clemson/Lady-10
Peters, Rickey
90AZSt/200*-165
Petersen, Jim
84Star/NBA-246
87F-86
88Kings/Carl-43
89F-136
89Hoops-147
90Hoops-117
90SkyBox-99
91Hoops/II-367
91SkyBox/I-97
91UD-270
Petersen, Loy
69T-37
70T-153
Peterson, Bob
89Louville/300*-52
Peterson, Buzz
89NC/Coke-180
90NC/200*-13
Peterson, Mark
89ProC/CBA-15
90ProC/CBA-10
91FrRow/100-81
91FrRow/Premier-13
91ProC/CBA-77
Peterson, Rafeal
91MurraySt-8
Petrie, Geoff
71T-34
71T/Ins-42
72T-3
73NBAPA-21
73T-175
74T-110
74T-96M
75Nab-21
75T-131M
75T-165
76T-78
77T-46
84Blaz/Pol-14
89Blaz/Franz-17
Petrovic, Drazen
89Blaz/Franz-8
90Blaz/Franz-16
90F/Up-U81
90Hoops-248
90SkyBox-237
91F-134
91Hoops/I-137
91Panini-158
91SkyBox/I-186
91SkyBox/II-599SS
91UD-315
92F-147
92Hoops/I-151
92Hoops/I-321LL
92Hoops/I-332
92SkyBox/I-159
Petruska, Richard
91UCLA-9
Pettit, Robert C.
(Bob)
56Busch-4
57T-24
61F-34
61F-59
61Hawks/Essex-12
68HOF-50
81TCMA-5
85Star/Schick-20
90LSU/200*-138
90LSU/Promos*-5
92CenterCrt-9
92F-110CO
92Hoops/I-251CO
Pettus, Randy
87SoMiss-11
Pfaff, Doug
90AZ/125*-49
Pfund, Randy
92SkyBox/I-267CO
Phegley, Roger
80T-144
80T-56
81T-MW75
Phelps, Don
89KY/300*-117
Phelps, Herbie
89Louville/300*-169
Phelps, Ken
90AZSt/200*-163
Phelps, Michael
89ProC/CBA-122
90ProC/CBA-89
Phelps, Richard
(Digger)
86DePaul-D8
90NotreDame-1
Phifer, Roman
91Classic/DPColl*-127
Phillip, Andy
48Bowman-9
48ExhSC-40
52Bread-23
57T-75
68HOF-35
Phillips, O.A.
(Bum)
91OKSt*-53
Phillips, Charlie
89McNees*-14
Phillips, Darrell
90LSU/200*-128
Phillips, Gibbie
87South/Pol*-13
Phillips, John
90Clemson/200*-13
90Clemson/200*-144M
Phillips, Kathy
92PennSt*-6
Phillips, Lloyd
91AR/100*-88
Phillips, Mike
77KY/Wildct-22
88KY/269-139
88KY/269-204
Phillips, Shannon
90KY/ClassA-7
Phills, Bobby
91Classic-35
91Classic/DPColl*-183
91FrRow/100-37
91FrRow/50-37
91FrRow/Premier-55
91StarPic-29
Philpot, Greg
91SC/200*-175
Philpott, Mike
91OKSt-13
91OKSt-43
Phipps, Frank
89KY/300*-288
Pianko, Greg
89Louville/300*-156
Piatkowski, Eric
91NE/Pol*-16
Pichette, Ken
91George/100-92
Pickard, Billy
91TexAM-90
Pickard, Fred
90FLSt/200*-177
Pickens, Bruce
91Classic/DPColl*-105
Pickins, Bruce
90NE/Pol*-12
Pierce, Ricky
83Star/NBA-130
85Star/NBA-129
86F-87
86Star/LifeBucks-11
87F-87
88Bucks/Green-11
89F-88
89Hoops-212
90F-106
90Hoops-179
90Hoops/CollB-21
90Hoops/Super-56
90Panini-99
90SkyBox-162
90SkyBox/Proto-162
90Sonic/Kayo-9
91F-195
91F/Up-396TL
91Hoops/I-203
91Hoops/I-257AS
91Hoops/II-498SC
91Hoops/McDon-43
91Panini-44
91SkyBox/Canada-45
91SkyBox/I-269
91SkyBox/II-456SM
91SkyBox/II-483TW
91SkyBox/II-600SS
91SkyBox/Proto-269
91UD-156
91UD-67AS
92F-217
92F/TmLeader-25
92Hoops/I-220
92SkyBox/I-235
Pierre, Raymond
87Baylor/Pol*-8
Pierson, Jerry
55Ash-44
Pietkiewicz, Stan
80TCMA/CBA-15
Pikiell, Steve
90CT/Pol-9
Pikiell, Tim
90CT/Pol-10
91CT/Pol-12
Pinckney, Ed
87F-88
89F-13
89Hoops-9
90F-15
90Hoops-47
90SkyBox-22
91F-15
91Hoops/I-16
91SkyBox/I-19
91UD-129
92F-19
92Hoops/I-18
92SkyBox/I-18
Pingel, John S.
90MISt/200*-24
Pinone, John
91WildCard/Coll-60
Piontek, Dave
57Kahn's-6
57T-31
58Kahn's-9
59Kahn's-5
Piotrowski, Tom
83Blaz/Pol-54
83Star/NBA-105
Piper, Chris
87KS/Nike-14
Piper, Don
91UCLA/144-79
Pipines, Tom
82Marq/Lite-9
Pippen, Scottie
87Bulls/Ent-8
88Bulls/Ent-33
88F-20
89Bulls/Eq-11
89F-23
89Hoops-244
90Bulls/Eq-12
90F-30
90Hoops-69
90Hoops-9AS
90Hoops/CollB-44
90Hoops/Super-13
90Panini-93
90SkyBox-46
91F-33
91Hoops/I-34
91Hoops/II-456SC
91Hoops/II-506Ar
91Hoops/II-539M
91Hoops/II-582
91Hoops/McDon-58USA
91Hoops/McDon-8
91Hoops/Super-14
91Kell/ColGrt-17
91Panini-113
91SkyBox/Canada-8
91SkyBox/I-44
91SkyBox/II-462TW
91SkyBox/II-537US
91SkyBox/II-586
91SkyBox/II-606
91UD-125
91UD/Ext-453AS
91WildCard/Coll-83
92F-254PV
92F-260SY
92F-36
92F/AS-8
92Hoops/I-300AS
92Hoops/I-34
92Hoops/I-345
92SkyBox/I-317
92SkyBox/I-35
92SkyBox/Olympic-USA5
92SkyBox/USA-108
92SkyBox/USA-64
92SkyBox/USA-65
92SkyBox/USA-66
92SkyBox/USA-67
92SkyBox/USA-68
92SkyBox/USA-69
92SkyBox/USA-70
92SkyBox/USA-71
92SkyBox/USA-72
Pisciotta, Scott
91Classic/DPColl*-226
Pitino, Rick
88Knick/FrLay-8CO
89KY/300*-13
89KY/Award-36
89KY/Tm80-54
90KY/BB/DT/AW-36CO
91KY/BB-15CO
91KY/BB/Double-13CO
91Providence-3CO
Pittman, Charles
82TCMA/CBA-4
83Star/NBA-116
84Star/NBA-48
84Suns/Pol-32
85Star/NBA-39
Pittman, Johnny
91StarPic-23
Piurowski, Paul
90FLSt/200*-40
Plansky, Mark
89ProC/CBA-190
90ProC/CBA-111
Planutis, Gerald
90MISt/200*-35
Plummer, Gary
84Star/NBA-156
Plummer, Mona
90AZSt/200*-143
Plunkett, Jim
74Nab-9
75Nab-9
Poerschke, Eric
82AR-10
Pohl, Dan
90AZ/125*-116
Poindexter, Cliff
77T-21
Poinsett, David
91SC/200*-47
Polec, Larry
90MISt/200*-162
Pollard, Alan
91ProC/CBA-127
Pollard, Jim
48Bowman-66
52Royal-7
Pollock, Bob
90Clemson/200*-128
Polston, Kenny
89NCSt/Coke-179
Polynice, Olden
89Hoops-152
90F/Up-U93
90Hoops-283
90SkyBox-272
90Sonic/Smok-15
91F-94
91Hoops/I-97
91Panini-11
91SkyBox/I-130
91UD-140
92F-65
92Hoops/I-103
92SkyBox/I-109
Pond, Nick
89NCSt/Coke-172
Ponsetto, Joe

86DePaul-D7
Pool, Randy
88KY/269-89
Poole, Barney
48T/Magic*-C1
Poole, Eric
91SC/200*-152
Poole, Nathan
89Louville/300*-122
Poole, Sherry
90AZSt/200*-164
Pooley, Don
90AZ/125*-108
Pope, Derrick
91WildCard/Coll-105
Pope, Mark
91WA/Viacom-7
Popson, Dave
86NC/Pol-35
89NC/Coke-153
89ProC/CBA-110
90F/Up-U7
90NC/200*-18
90NC/200*-59
91ProC/CBA-165
Poquette, Ben
80T-155
80T-171
80T-18
80T-83
81T-65M
81T-W105
83Star/NBA-237
84Star/NBA-221
85Star/NBA-157
Porche, Maia A.
90Piston/Star-14
Porco, Ken
89Louville/300*-104
Pores, Chas.
48T/Magic*-E8
Porter, Darelle
89Pitt/Food-20
90Pitt/Food-10
Porter, Dave
87IN/GreatII-28
Porter, Howard
72T-127
73T-167
74T-122
75T-138
77T-102
78T-28
Porter, Joel
87Baylor/Pol*-12
Porter, Kevin
73Bullet/Stand-7
73T-53
74T-12
74T-98M
75T-133M
75T-5LL
75T-79
76T-84
77T-16
78T-118
79T-13
80T-130
80T-174
80T-60
80T-86
81T-66M
81T-E105
81T-E99
81T/Thirst-19
Porter, Terry
85Blaz/Franz-10
86Blaz/Franz-11
87Blaz/Franz-9
87F-89
88Blaz/Franz-10
88F-96
88Fourn-12
89Blaz/Franz-9
89F-131
89Hoops-105
90Blaz/BP-5
90Blaz/Franz-17
90F-158
90Hoops-249A
90Hoops-249B
90Hoops/CollB-16
90Hoops/Super-79
90Panini-11
90SkyBox-238
91Blaz/Franz-13
91F-171
91Hoops/I-177
91Hoops/I-269AS
91Hoops/II-492SC
91Hoops/II-524Ar
91Hoops/McDon-35
91Hoops/Super-81
91Panini-27
91SkyBox/Canada-40
91SkyBox/I-240
91SkyBox/II-480TW
91SkyBox/II-607
91SkyBox/Proto-240
91UD-351
91UD-54AS
92F-190
92Hoops/I-193
92SkyBox/I-205
Porter, Tommy
89KY/300*-82
Portman, Kurt
91ProC/CBA-19
Portmann, Kurt
89WI/Smok-11
90ProC/CBA-129
Post, Wiley
48T/Magic*-L3
Poston, Kenny
87NCSt/Pol-10
88NCSt/Pol-11
89NCSt/Coke-184
89NCSt/Coke-197
Poteet, Yogi
89NC/Coke-162
Potter, Brendan
82Fairf-13
Potter, Sam
89KY/300*-17
Potts, Bobby
82TCMA/CBA-9
Potts, Ray
89Louville/300*-217
Poulin, Patrick
91Classic/DPColl*-8
Pounds, Cleve
91GATech*-96
Powdrill, George
90NM-13
Powell, Broderick
91ND*-4M
Powell, Cincy
71Col/Mara-7
71T-207
72T-189
73T-186
74T-198
Powell, Cliff
91AR/100*-99
Powell, Debra
84NE/Pol*-17
Powell, Ken
90NC/200*-124
Powell, Mike
89Foot*-9
91Foot*-10
Powell, William
48T/Magic*-F11
89Louville/300*-62
Power, Tyrone
48T/Magic*-F6
Powless, John
55Ash-69
Praedel, Lloyd
79StBon-10
Pratt, Mike
71Col/Mara-8
88KY/269-150
88KY/269-173
88KY/269-209
88KY/269-50
Pratt, Robert
90NC/200*-135
Prescott, Jeff
92PennSt*-14
Pressey, Paul
83Star/All-R-6
83Star/NBA-48
84Star/Arena-C9
84Star/NBA-136
85Star/Bucks-13
85Star/NBA-130
85Star/TmSuper-MB3
86F-88
86Star/LifeBucks-12
87Bucks/Polar-25
87F-90
88Bucks/Green-12
88F-75
88Fourn-29
89F-89
89Hoops-79
90F-107
90F/Up-U90
90Hoops-180
90Hoops/II-432
90SkyBox-163
90SkyBox/II-415
91F-186
91Hoops/I-193
91Hoops/Super-88
91Panini-80
91SkyBox/I-260
91SkyBox/II-455SM
91UD-359
Pressley, Dominic
90ProC/CBA-66
Pressley, Harold
86Kings/Smok-7
88Kings/Carl-21
89F-137
89Hoops-24
89Kings/Carl-21
90F-166
90Hoops-260
90Panini-37
90SkyBox-249
91WildCard/Coll-80
Preston, Marc
90SoCal/Smok*-13
Preston, R.C.
89KY/300*-228
Preston, Steve
90MISt/200*-65
Previs, Steve
89NC/Coke-108
89NC/Coke-109
90NC/200*-109
Price, Brent
92Classic/DP-75
92StarPic-28
Price, Cebert
55Ash-47
Price, George
61Union-8
Price, Jim
71Bucks/Linn-7
73T-38
74T-137
75Carv-25
75T-107
76T-32
88Louville/194-138
88Louville/194-61
89Louville/300*-230
89Louville/300*-245
89Louville/300*-8
Price, Mark
88F-25
89Conv-11
89F-166M
89F-29
89Hoops-160
89Hoops-28AS
90F-36
90Hoops-79
90Hoops/CollB-8
90Hoops/II-359TC
90Hoops/Super-16
90Panini-103
90SkyBox-56
91F-38
91Hoops/I-40
91Hoops/Super-18
91Kell/ColGrt-10
91SkyBox/I-53
91SkyBox/II-463TW
91SkyBox/II-601SS
91UD-239
91UD/Ext-460AS
92F-242LL
92F-43
92F/AS-9
92F/TmLeader-5
92Hoops/I-301AS
92Hoops/I-322LL
92Hoops/I-43
92SkyBox/I-44
Price, Mike
73T-51
Price, Rodney
91SC/200*-134
Price, Tim
89ProC/CBA-65
Prince, Calvin
89Louville/300*-158
Prinzi, Vic
90FLSt/200*-159
Pritchard, Kevin
87KS/Nike-15
89KS/Leesley-48
90F/Up-U34
90StarPic-65
Pritchard, Mike
91Classic/DPColl*-113
Pritchett, Kelvin
91Classic/DPColl*-118
Pritchett, Scott
91NM-15
Proctor, Bill
90FLSt/200*-128
Proski, Joe
75Suns-11
84Suns/Pol-x
Provence, Andrew
91SC/200*-63
Prudhoe, John
55Ash-33
88Louville/194-77
89Louville/300*-220
Prudhomme, Remi
90LSU/200*-103
Pruitt, Dillard
90Clemson/200*-167
Pruitt, Jason
91Classic/DPColl*-76
Pruitt, Ron
90MISt/200*-87
Pry, Paul
89Louville/300*-283
89Louville/300*-81
Pryor, Jerry
90Clemson/200*-172
Pucillo, Lou
89NCSt/Coke-173
89NCSt/Coke-196
Puckett, Dana
90Clemson/Lady-11
Puckett, Linville
55Ash-22
89KY/300*-83
Pudenz, Tracey
91ND*-8M
Puddy, Glenn
90ProC/CBA-78
Pullard, Anthony
89McNees*-10
90StarPic-17
Pulliam, Marty
81Louville/Pol-10
88Louville/194-134
88Louville/194-51
Punt, Tom
90NE/Pol*-7
Pursiful, Larry
88KY/269-219
88KY/269-77
89KY/300*-11
Purtzer, Tom
90AZSt/200*-186
Pushor, Jamie
91Classic/DPColl*-28
Putnam, Bill
91UCLA/144-60
Putman, Don
48Bowman-28
Quam, George
54Quaker-3
Queen, Mel
68PartM-6
Queenan, Daren
89ProC/CBA-27
Quick, Bob
70T-161
71T-117
Quick, Mike
89Foot*-8
Quigg, Joe
89NC/Coke-121
89NC/Coke-122
90NC/200*-97
Quiggle, Jack
90MISt/200*-102
Quimby, Art
91CT/Legend-15
Quinn, Marcus
90LSU/200*-174
Quinnett, Brian
89Knicks/Marine-8
90SkyBox-192
91F/Up-329
91Hoops/II-405
91SkyBox/I-193
Raab, Steve
90ProC/CBA-92
Rabb, Warren
90LSU/200*-116
Rabune, Ron
91SC/200*-28
Rackley, Luther
69T-13
70T-61
71T-88
Radford, Wayne
87IN/GreatII-7
Radocha, Jerry
80TCMA/CBA-27
Rados, Tug
88Victoria/Pol-14
Radovich, Frank

86IN/Greatl-5
Radovich, Tony
89NC/Coke-152
Rahilly, Brian
89ProC/CBA-144
90ProC/CBA-61
91ProC/CBA-152
Rai, Roger
85Victoria/Pol-13
Raina, Reuben
91AR/100*-57
Raines, June
91SC/200*-22
Rambis, Kurt
82Lakers/BASF-10
83Lakers/BASF-9
83Star/NBA-21
84Lakers/BASF-8
84Star/Arena-D6
84Star/NBA-180
85JMS-26
85Star/NBA-31
86F-89
89F-16
89Hoops-246
90F-152
90Hoops-241
90Panini-18
90SkyBox-229
91F/Up-343
91Hoops/I-169
91SkyBox/I-230
91UD-391
Ramirez, Manny
91Classic/DPColl*-60
Ramos, Eddie
91Classic/DPColl*-95
Ramsey, Cal
91Foot*-12
Ramsey, Frank
57T-15
61F-35
61F-60IA
88KY/269-163
88KY/269-199
88KY/269-212
88KY/269-3
89KY/300*-44
Ramsey, Jack
77Blaz/Pol-x
79Blaz/Pol-x
81Blaz/Pol-x
82Blaz/Pol-x
83Blaz/Pol-x
84Blaz/Franz-1CO
84Blaz/Pol-5M
85Blaz/Franz-1CO
85Star/CO-8
Ramsey, Lloyd
89KY/300*-296
Randall, Mark
87KS/Nike-16
89KS/Leesley-45
91FrRow/Premier-90BC
91StarPic-7
91UD-13
Randle, Lenny
90AZSt/200*-50
90AZSt/Promos*-7
Range, Perry
80IL/Arby's-9
81IL/Arby's-11
Rankin, Bill
91UCLA/144-139
Ransdell, Bill
89KY/300*-194
Ransey, Kelvin
81Blaz/Pol-14
81T-61M
81T-W88
83Star/NBA-153
84Nets/Getty-8
84Star/NBA-95
86Star/LifeNets-10
89ProC/CBA-77
Rapchak, Bill
90MISt/200*-120
Rasmussen, Blair
85Nugget/Pol-7
88F-36
88Nugget/Pol-41
89F-42
89Hoops-261
89Nugget/Pol-11
90F-52
90Hoops-99
90Panini-62
90SkyBox-80
91F-52
91F/Up-245
91Hoops/I-55
91Hoops/II-336
91Panini-54
91SkyBox/I-74
91SkyBox/II-617
91UD-312
91UD/Ext-498
92F-5
92Hoops/I-6
92SkyBox/I-6
Rathburn, Jodi
90AZSt/200*-187
Rathman, Tom
85NE/Pol*-8
Ratleff, Ed
74T-72
75T-14
76T-18
Ratliff, Allan
87South/Pol*-14
Ratliff, Jimmy
91OhioSt-12
Ratliff, Mike
82AR-11
89ProC/CBA-123
Rautins, Leo
83Star/NBA-8
84Star/NBA-83
89ProC/CBA-161
Ray, Clifford
72T-91
73T-16
74T-114
74T-84M
75Carv-26
75T-122M
75T-185
75T-189
76T-109
77T-64
78T-131
79T-72
80T-155
80T-18
Ray, Eddie
90LSU/200*-21
Ray, James
82Nugget/Pol-43
Ray, John
89KY/300*-167
Ray, Johnny
91AR/100*-37
Ray, Steve
88WakeForest/Pol-12
Rayford, Calvin
91KS-11
Rayl, Jimmy
86IN/Greatl-32
Raymond, Craig
71T-203
Raymonds, Hank
82Marq/Lite-10
Rdovic, Zoran
80WichSt/Pol-12
Reagan, Ronald
85Star/Lakers-18M
Reason, Terry
82Marq/Lite-11
Reboulet, Jeff
86LSU/Pol*-10
Redden, Don
86LSU/Pol*-11
Redden, Willie
82TCMA/Lanc-23
Redenbaugh, Steve
86IN/Greatl-11
Redfield, Ken
90MISt/200*-158
90ProC/CBA-87
91FrRow/100-88
91FrRow/Premier-4
91FrRow/Up-96
91ProC/CBA-118
Redmond, Marlon
81TCMA/CBA-12
Redmond, Mickey
74Nab-22
75Nab-16
Redwine, Stanley
91AR/100*-42
Reed, Hub
59Kahn's-6
60Kahn's-7
61Kahn's-6
62Kahn's-6
Reed, Ron
90NotreDame-55
Reed, U.S.
81TCMA/CBA-78
Reed, Willis
68T/Test-7
69T-60
69T/Ins-19
70T-110AS
70T-150
70T/Ins-3
71Keds*-2M
71T-30
71T/Ins-32
72T-129
73NBAPA-22
73T-105
73T-66M
81TCMA-6
89Hoops-92CO
Reese, Calvin
91Classic/DPColl*-66
Reese, Pee Wee
87KY/Coke-13
Reese, Ronnie
88TN/Smok-34
Reese, Steve
90Clemson/200*-46
Reese, Willie
88GATech/Nike-9
Reeves, Bryant
91OKSt-18
91OKSt-45
Reeves, Dan
91SC/200*-76
Reeves, Kenny
88Louville/194-73
Regan, Richard
57Kahn's-7
57T-50
Regelsky, Dolph
55Ash-70
Reichenbach, Mike
92PennSt*-11
Reid, Billy
81TCMA/CBA-23
Reid, Don
91George/Pol-12
Reid, Eric
87Vanderbilt/Pol-7
Reid, J.R.
86NC/Pol-34
87NC/Pol-34
89NC/Coke-80
89NC/Coke-81
89NC/Coke-82
89NC/Coke-98
90F-20
90F/Rook-4
90Hoops-57
90Hoops/CollB-41
90NC/200*-11
90NC/200*-63
90Panini-82
90SkyBox-32
91F-24
91Hoops/I-24
91Hoops/II-572
91Panini-107
91SkyBox/Canada-6
91SkyBox/I-32
91SkyBox/II-554US
91UD-262
92F-27
92Hoops/I-26
92SkyBox/I-27
Reid, Joe
91OhioSt-13
Reid, Robert
79T-62
80T-119
80T-15
80T-164
80T-31
81T-MW88
83Star/NBA-82
84Star/NBA-247
85Star/NBA-23
86F-90
87F-91
89F-17
89Hoops-88
90Hoops-58
90SkyBox-33
Reid, Roger
87BYU-7
Reiss, Tammi
91VA/Lady-8
Rellford, Richard
91MI/56*-43
91ProC/CBA-117
Remington, George
48T/Magic*-H1M
Remington, Mrs. George
48T/Magic*-H1M
Renn, Bobby
90FLSt/200*-160
Rennick, Jess
(Cob)
91OKSt*-49
Rensberger, Robert
90NotreDame-52
Reppond, Mike
91AR/100*-68
Respert, Shawn
90MISt-7
Respess, Ray
89NC/Coke-179
Restani, Kevin
71Bucks/Linn-8
75T-161
79Spurs/Pol-31
80T-174
80T-80
Reuther, Joe
89Louville/300*-67
Reuther, John
88Louville/194-66
89Louville/300*-22
Reynolds, Allie
91OKSt*-10
Reynolds, Bobby
90MISt/200*-134
Reynolds, Burt
90FLSt/200*-182
Reynolds, Jerry
(Ice)
86Star/LifeBucks-13
87Bucks/Polar-35
89Hoops/II-339
90F/Up-U67
90Hoops-219
90LSU/200*-98
90Panini-125
90SkyBox-204
91F-146
91Hoops/I-150
91SkyBox/I-204
91SkyBox/II-450SM
91UD-286
92Hoops/I-162
92SkyBox/I-171
Reynolds, Jerry CO
85Kings/Smok-3M
86Kings/Smok-8CO
88Kings/Carl-x
89Hoops-161CO
89Kings/Carl-x
Rezinger, Jim
89NCSt/Coke-183
Rhine, Kendall
90GA/Smok-13
Rhodemyre, Jay
89KY/300*-175
Rhodes, Lafester
89ProC/CBA-40
Rhodes, Sheri
90AZSt/200*-80
Rhoney, Ashley
86SWLou/Pol*-13
87SWLou/McDag*-8
Riano, Renie
48T/Magic*-J21
Rice, A.T.
89KY/300*-250
Rice, Barry
90FLSt/200*-106
Rice, Beryl
90FLSt/200*-193
Rice, Dave
89UNLV/HOF-14
90UNLV/HOF-8
90UNLV/Season-8
90UNLV/Smok-12
Rice, George
90LSU/200*-158
Rice, Glen
88MI/Nike-10
89Heat/Publix-9
89MI-5
90F-101
90F/Rook-3
90Heat/Publix-10
90Hoops-168
90Panini-151
90SkyBox-150
91F-111
91F/Up-385TL
91Hoops/I-113
91Hoops/Super-54
91Panini-151
91SkyBox/I-151
91SkyBox/II-472TW
91UD-147
92F-120
92F/TmLeader-14
92Hoops/I-121
92SkyBox/I-128
92SkyBox/I-295TT
Rice, Greg

48T/Magic*-E5
Rice, King
87NC/Pol-21
88NC/Pol-21
88NC/Pol-x
91WildCard/Coll-43
Rice, Russell
88KY/269-53
Richard, Stanley
91Classic/DPColl*-110
Richards, Bob
57Union-7
Richardson, Albert
90LSU/200*-117
Richardson, Bobby
91SC/200*-133CO
Richardson, Clint
83Star/NBA-9
83Star/Sixers-5
84Star/Arena-E8
84Star/NBA-208
85JMS-6
85Star/TmSuper-PS9
Richardson, Dave
82TCMA/CBA-88
Richardson, Jerome
(Pooh)
89TWolv/BK-24
90F-116
90F/Rook-6
90Hoops-190
90Hoops/CollB-45
90Hoops/II-370TC
90Panini-78
90SkyBox-173
90SkyBox/Proto-173
91F-125
91Hoops/I-129
91Hoops/II-480SC
91Hoops/McDon-24
91Hoops/Super-60
91Panini-63
91SkyBox/I-173
91SkyBox/II-474TW
91SkyBox/II-501RS
91SkyBox/Proto-173
91UCLA/144-24
91UD-246
91UD-97TC
92F-136
92Hoops/I-140
92SkyBox/I-147
Richardson, Micheal Ray
80T-100
80T-106
80T-147
80T-20
80T-33
80T-59
81T-27
81T-58M
81T-E109
83Star/NBA-154
84Nets/Getty-9
84Star/NBA-96
85Star/NBA-65
86Star/LifeNets-11
Richardson, Mike
90AZSt/200*-42
Richardson, Nolan
89UTEP/Drug-21
91AR25-1CO
Richardson, Nolan III
91AR25-22ACO
Richardson, Quinn
80IL/Arby's-10
81IL/Arby's-12
Richey, Patrick
91KS-12
Richie, Lou
90UCLA-15
Richins, Lori
85NE/Pol*-35
Richmond, Mike
89ProC/CBA-170
Richmond, Mitch
89F-56
89Hoops-260
90F-67
90Hoops-118
90Hoops/CollB-9
90Hoops/Super-31
90Panini-30
90SkyBox-100
91F-71
91F/Up-350
91Hoops/I-73
91Hoops/II-429
91Hoops/II-573
91Hoops/McDon-37
91Hoops/Super-34
91Panini-4
91SkyBox/I-303M
91SkyBox/I-98
91SkyBox/II-555US
91SkyBox/II-644
91SkyBox/Proto-97
91UD-265
91UD/Ext-490
92F-196
92F/TmLeader-23
92Hoops/I-200
92SkyBox/I-214
Richmond, Pam
90AZSt/200*-87
Richmond, Steve
91MI/56*-44
Richter, John
89NCSt/Coke-178
89NCSt/Coke-62
Richter, Les
57Union-2
Rickenbacker, Eddie
48T/Magic*-L4
54Quaker-14
Ricketts, Emily
85NE/Pol*-24
Ricketts, Richard
(Dick)
57Kahn's-8
57T-8
Riddick, Andre
91KY/BB/Double-15
Riddle, Jerry
55Ash-56
Riddlesprigger, Pat
89Fresno/Smok-12
90Fresno/Smok-12
Ridgeway, Dick
91UCLA/144-67
Ridgeway, Sam
89KY/300*-227
Riebe, Mel
48Bowman-8
Riendeau, Donny
91ND*-16M
Rigby, Cathy
76Nab-23M
Riggs, Bobby
48ExhSC-41
Riggs, Gerald
90AZSt/200*-2
Riggs, Jim
90Clemson/200*-30
Rigney, Bill
57Union-20
Riker, Tom
91SC/200*-78
Riley, Eric
88MI/Nike-11
89MI-16
Riley, Jackie
54Quaker-16
Riley, J. McIver
91SC/200*-66
Riley, Mike
89ProC/CBA-178
91George/100-36
91George/100-99
Riley, Pat
68Rocket/Jack-10
70T-13
72T-144
73T-21
74T-31
75Suns-12
75T-71
84Star/Celt-15
85Star/CO-9
85Star/Lakers-12
85Star/LiteAS-13CO
88KY/269-145
88KY/269-157
88KY/269-17
88KY/269-198
89Hoops-108CO
89KY/300*-38
89KY/300*-45
90Hoops-317CO
91F-139CO
91Hoops/I-238CO
91SkyBox/II-395CO
91SkyBox/II-576CO
92F-155CO
92Hoops/I-256CO
92SkyBox/I-272CO
Riley, Ron
73T-141
75T-87
Rimac, Davor
91AR25-14
Rinaldi, Rich
73NBAPA-23
73T-149
Rinehart, Bob
91SC/200*-82
Ringmar, Henrik
90ORSt-13
Riordan, Mike
70T-26
71T-126
72T-37
73Bullet/Stand-8
73NBAPA-24
73T-35
74T-102
75T-95
76T-56
91Providence-13
Risen, Arnie
48Bowman-58
52Bread-24
57T-40
Risher, Alan
90LSU/200*-85
Riska, Eddie
90NotreDame-44
Risley, Steve
86IN/GreatI-40
Rison, Andre
90MISt/200*-12
90MISt/200*-77
90MISt/200*-96
90MISt/Promos*-5
Ritchie, Meg
90AZ/125*-124
Ritter, Chris
90NCSt/IBM-14M
Ritter, Clayton
91JMadison/Smok-11
Ritter, John
86IN/GreatI-20
Rivas, Ramon
91WildCard/Coll-57
Rivers, David
89F-94
89Hoops-203
89Hoops/II-346
90Hoops-150
90NotreDame-36
Rivers, Glenn
(Doc)
82Marq/Lite-12
83Star/NBA-271
84Star/NBA-84
85Star/NBA-47
86F-91
87F-92
87Hawks/Pizza-11
88F-3
89F-5
89Hoops-252
90F/Up-U3
90Hoops-32
90Hoops/CollB-10
90Hoops/Super-1
90Panini-116
90SkyBox-7
91F/Up-298
91Hoops/I-4
91Hoops/II-380
91Hoops/Super-2
91Panini-104
91SkyBox/I-7
91SkyBox/II-631
91UD-46
91UD/Ext-420
92F-103
92Hoops/I-104
92SkyBox/I-110
Riviere, Bill
91ND*-12M
Roach, Larry
91OKSt*-55
Robbins, Austin
(Red)
71T-233
72T-212
73T-193
75T-287M
75T-295
Robbins, Jack
91AR/100*-98
Robbins, Lee Roy
48Bowman-56
Robbins, Randy
90AZ/125*-91
Robbins, Rob
90NM-14
Roberson, Rick
70T-23
72T-126
73T-144
74T-57
74T-96M
Roberts, Anthony
78T-62
81TCMA/CBA-59
83Star/NBA-190
Roberts, Brett
92Classic/DP-73
Roberts, Danny
91TexAM-27
Roberts, Doug
90MISt/200*-55
Roberts, Fred
83Star/NBA-251
84Star/NBA-234
84Star/NBA-74
88Bucks/Green-13
89Hoops-136
90F-108
90Hoops-181
90SkyBox-164
91F-117
91Hoops/I-119
91Panini-141
91SkyBox/I-162
91UD-293
92F-129
92Hoops/I-131
92SkyBox/I-138
Roberts, Marv
74T-194
75T-238
Roberts, Roy
89KY/300*-229
Roberts, Stanley
91Classic-15
91Classic/DPColl*-163
91F/Up-331
91FrRow/Premier-86BC
91FrRow/Up-58
91UD/Ext-497
91UD/Rook-28
92F-162
92F/Rook-9
92FrRow/DreamPk-86
92FrRow/DreamPk-87
92FrRow/DreamPk-88
92FrRow/DreamPk-89
92FrRow/DreamPk-90
92Hoops/I-163
92SkyBox/I-172
Robertson, Alvin
82AR-12
84Star/NBA-198
84Star/NBA-75
85Star/NBA-150
85Star/RTm-11
86F-92
87F-93
88F-105
88F-128AS
88Fourn-27
88Spurs/Pol-7
89F-90
89Hoops-5
89Hoops/II-350
90F-109
90Hoops-182
90Hoops/CollB-33
90Hoops/II-369TC
90Hoops/Super-55
90Panini-101
90SkyBox-165
91AR/100*-51
91F-118
91F-222
91F/School-6
91F/Up-386TL
91Hoops/I-120
91Hoops/I-258AS
91Hoops/I-310M
91Hoops/II-478SC
91Hoops/II-562
91Hoops/Super-56
91Panini-142
91SkyBox/Canada-29
91SkyBox/I-163
91SkyBox/I-312
91SkyBox/II-419GF
91SkyBox/II-473TW
91SkyBox/II-561US
91UD-244
91UD-64AS
91UD-73TC
91UD/AWHolo-2
92F-130
92F/TmLeader-15
92Hoops/I-132
92SkyBox/I-139
Robertson, Cliff
89Blaz/Franz-10
Robertson, David

91ND*-3M
Robertson, Oscar
60Kahn's-8
61F-36
61F-61
61Kahn's-7
62Kahn's-7
63Kahn's-9
64Kahn's-10A
64Kahn's-10B
65Kahn's-3
68T/Test-22
69T-50
69T/Ins-24
70T-100
70T-114AS
70T/Ins-6
71T-1
71T-136M
71T-141LL
71T-143LL
71T/Ins-34
72Icee-15
72T-25
73T-70
74Nab-17
74T-55
74T-91M
81T/Thirst-26
81TCMA-17
85Star/Schick-21
92CenterCrt-14
Robertson, Pablo
(Pabs)
71Globe-4
71Globe-5
71Globe-6
71Globe-63M
71Globe-7
71Globe-8
71Globe/Cocoa-13
71Globe/Cocoa-15
Robey, Rick
77KY/Wildct-19
79T-96
80T-136
80T-24
80T-9
80T-97
81T-E76
83Star/NBA-117
84Star/NBA-49
84Suns/Pol-8
85Star/NBA-40
88KY/269-167
88KY/269-215
88KY/269-25
Robichaux, Mike
90LSU/200*-79
Robinson, Al
89KY/300*-287
Robinson, Anthony
90NCSt/IBM-9
91NCSt/IBM-11
Robinson, Betty
54Quaker-11
Robinson, Bill
91OhioSt-14
Robinson, Cliff USC
80T-145
80T-57
83Star/NBA-238
85Star/NBA-114
86F-93
88F-88
91Hoops/I-178
92SkyBox/I-206
92SkyBox/I-303TT
Robinson, Cliff UConn
90Blaz/Franz-18
90F-159
90Hoops-250
90Panini-12
90SkyBox-239
91Blaz/Franz-14
91CT/Legend-11
91F-172
91SkyBox/I-241
91SkyBox/II-507RS
91UD-220
92F-191
92Hoops/I-194
Robinson, Dave
55Ash-45
Robinson, David
87KY/Coke-SC
88Spurs/Pol-8
89Hoops-138
89Hoops/II-310
90F-172
90F/AS-10
90F/Rook-1
90Hoops-24AS
90Hoops-270
90Hoops-NO
90Hoops/CollB-34
90Hoops/II-378ATC
90Hoops/II-378ATC
90Hoops/Super-88
90Panini-43
90SkyBox-260
90SkyBox/Proto-260
90StarPic-2
91F-187
91F-225
91F/ProV-1
91F/Up-395TL
91Hoops/I-194
91Hoops/I-270AS
91Hoops/I-309M
91Hoops/I-311M
91Hoops/I-327
91Hoops/II-496SC
91Hoops/II-583
91Hoops/McDon-41
91Hoops/McDon-59USA
91Hoops/Super-89
91Panini-77
91Panini-92AS
91SkyBox/Canada-43
91SkyBox/I-261
91SkyBox/I-311M
91SkyBox/II-428GF
91SkyBox/II-509RS
91SkyBox/II-538US
91UD-324
91UD-58AS
91UD-94TC
91UD/AWHolo-6
91UD/Ext-467AS
91Wooden-16
92Crtside/ColFB-31
92F-207
92F-244LL
92F-248AW
92F/AS-21
92F/TmLeader-24
92Hoops/I-209
92Hoops/I-315AS
92Hoops/I-323LL
92Hoops/I-334
92Hoops/I-346
92SkyBox/I-224
92SkyBox/I-305TT
92SkyBox/Olympic-
USA10
92SkyBox/Robinson-Set
92SkyBox/USA-109
92SkyBox/USA-73
92SkyBox/USA-74
92SkyBox/USA-75
92SkyBox/USA-76
92SkyBox/USA-77
92SkyBox/USA-78
92SkyBox/USA-79
92SkyBox/USA-80
92SkyBox/USA-81
Robinson, Flynn
69T-92
70T-40
70T-4LL
72T-104
74T-197
Robinson, Jackie
91UCLA/144-96
Robinson, James
90Clemson/200*-110
Robinson, Joe
90NC/200*-159
Robinson, Johnny
90LSU/200*-175
Robinson, Keith
90NotreDame-15
90StarPic-13
91ProC/CBA-40
Robinson, Kenneth
91SC/200*-163
Robinson, Kenny
89Louville/300*-191
Robinson, Larry
91ProC/CBA-67
Robinson, Leonard
(Truck)
75T-151
76T-104
77T-74
78T-30
79T-95
80Suns/Pep-7
80T-113
80T-26
80T-37
80T-96
81T-35
81T-60M
83Star/NBA-67
84Star/NBA-33
Robinson, Les
89NCSt/Coke-102
89NCSt/Coke-111
90NCSt/IBM-10CO
91NCSt/IBM-12CO
Robinson, Melvin
92StarPic-82
Robinson, Michael
90MISt/200*-101
90MISt/200*-143
Robinson, Paul
68PartM-10
Robinson, Ray
48T/Magic*-A19
Robinson, Robert
91SC/200*-130
Robinson, Ron
74T-251
Robinson, Rumeal
88MI/Nike-12
89MI-7
90F/Up-U4
90Hoops/II-399LS
90SkyBox/II-355LP
91F-3
91Hoops/I-5
91SkyBox/I-8
91UD-292
92F-6
92Hoops/I-7
92SkyBox/I-7
Robinson, Sam
71Flor/McDon-7
71T-184
Robinson, Stew
87IN/GreatII-18
Robinson, Susan
92PennSt*-7
Robinson, Toren
87South/Pol*-3M
Robinson, Wil
74T-179
Robinson, W.T.
90LSU/200*-191
Robinzine, Bill Jr.
79T-68
80T-13
80T-93
81T-MW78
86DePaul-12
86DePaul-C3
Robisch, Dave
72T-223
73T-199
74T-183
74T-222M
75T-224LL
75T-318
80T-12
80T-136
80T-24
80T-90
81T-W70
82Nugget/Pol-25
83Star/NBA-224
Robiskie, Terry
90LSU/200*-147
Robison, Dick
89Louville/300*-91
Roby, Mark
90AZ/125*-102
Rocha, Red
48Bowman-18
Roche, John
72T-182
73T-201
74T-226M
74T-232
75T-244
80T-106
80T-110
80T-18
80T-87
91SC/200*-58
Rocker, Tracy
87Auburn/Pol*-11
Rockins, Chris
91OKSt*-66
Rockne, Knute
81PhilM-10
Rodes, William
89KY/300*-176
Rodgers, Guy
61F-37
69T-38
70T-22
90Bulls/Eq-13
Rodgers, Hosea
90NC/200*-105
Rodgers, Jimmy
89Hoops-277CO
91F-126CO
91Hoops/I-236CO
91SkyBox/II-393CO
92F-137CO
92Hoops/I-254CO
92SkyBox/I-270CO
Rodgers, Pat
79StBon-11
Rodgers, Terry
90NE/Pol*-3
Rodman, Dennis
88F-43
89F-49
89Hoops-211
90F-59
90Hoops-109
90Hoops-10AS
90Hoops/CollB-46
90Hoops/Super-30
90Panini-85
90Piston/Star-10
90Piston/Unocal-9
90SkyBox-91A
90SkyBox-91B
90SkyBox/Proto-91
91F-63
91Hoops/I-311M
91Hoops/I-64
91Hoops/Super-30
91Panini-130
91Piston/Unocal-15M
91Piston/Unocal-8
91SkyBox/Canada-16
91SkyBox/I-86
91SkyBox/II-608
91SkyBox/Proto-86
91UD-185
91UD/AWHolo-9
91UD/Ext-457AS
92F-239LL
92F-261SY
92F-66
92F/AS-10
92Hoops/I-302AS
92Hoops/I-325LL
92Hoops/I-66
92SkyBox/I-71
Rodriguez, Frankie
91Classic/DPColl*-101
Rodriguez, Quin
90SoCal/Smok*-14
Rodriguez, Ruben
90AZ/125*-90
Roe, Matt
88Syr/Rich-8
91FrRow/100-72
91FrRow/Premier-24
91FrRow/Up-89
91ProC/CBA-114
Rogers, Elbert
92Classic/DP-91
Rogers, Erik
88Syr/Rich-9
89Syr/Pep-14
Rogers, George
91SC/200*-10
Rogers, Janice
92PennSt*-12
Rogers, Johnny
86Kings/Smok-9
Rogers, Keir
92Classic/DP-87
Rogers, Steve
92Classic/DP-61
92StarPic-52
Roges, Al
54Bullet/Gunth-10
Rohm, Pinky
90LSU/200*-47
Roland, Gilbert
48T/Magic*-J31
Rolfes, Don
89KY/300*-84
Rollen, David
91TexAM-98
Roller, David
89KY/300*-197
Rollins, Kenny
88KY/269-20
Rollins, Phil
55Ash-34
59Kahn's-7
88Louville/194-122
88Louville/194-28
89Louville/300*-222
Rollins, Wayne
(Tree)

78Hawks/Coke-12
79Hawks/Majik-30
80T-106
80T-33
81T-E71
83Star/NBA-272
84Star/NBA-85
85Star/NBA-46
86F-94
87F-94
87Hawks/Pizza-12
89Hoops-2
90Clemson/200*-3
90Clemson/Promos*-C1
90Hoops/II-413
90SkyBox-57
90SkyBox/II-383
91F/Up-291
91Hoops/II-371
Romaniuk, Russ
91ND*-15M
Romeo, Tony
90FLSt/200*-103
Romine, Kevin
90AZSt/200*-178
Ronan, Marc
90FLSt/200*-55
Ronndfield, Kevin
81AZ/Pol-14
Rooks, Ron
88Louville/194-97
Rooks, Sean
87AZ/Pol-12
88AZ/Pol-12
89AZ/Pol-10
92Classic/DP-58
92StarPic-12
Ropke, Van Buren
89KY/300*-29
Rose, Clarence
90Clemson/200*-82
Rose, Gayle
55Ash-23
88KY/269-170
88KY/269-45
Rose, Glen
91AR/100*-52
Rose, Pete
68PartM-7
Rose, Rob
91ProC/CBA-15
Rosen, Charley
89ProC/CBA-88
90ProC/CBA-106
91ProC/CBA-169CO
Rosenblom, Joyce
54Quaker-20
Rosenbluth, Lennie
57T-48
89NC/Coke-41
89NC/Coke-42
89NC/Coke-43
90NC/200*-98
Rosenthal, Dick
90NotreDame-3
Roshso, Jim
90LSU/200*-30
Ross, Bobby
91GATech*-88
Ross, Cordell
90MISt/200*-70
Ross, Frank
90ProC/CBA-88
Ross, Harold
88KY/269-71
Ross, Mark
91TexAM-35
Ross, Ray
91ORSt-15
Ross, Ron
82Fairf-14CO
Ross, Scott
90SoCal/Smok*-15
Ross, Tom
90MISt/200*-64
Ross, Tony
90ORSt-14
Rossignol, Matt
87ME/Pol*-3
Roosma, John S.
68HOF-36
Rossiter, Mike
91Classic/DPColl*-84
Rossum, Clint
88UNLV/HOF-6
Roth, Doug
88TN/Smok-50
Roth, Ken
91MurraySt-15ACO
Roth, Scott
89Hoops/II-349
89Jazz/OldH-12
90Hoops-191
Rothman, Judd
89Louville/300*-68
Rothstein, Ron
89Heat/Publix-10CO
89Hoops-172CO
90Heat/Publix-14CO
90Hoops-318CO
90SkyBox/II-314CO
92F-67CO
92Hoops/I-246CO
92SkyBox/I-262CO
Roulier, Rachelle
90UCLA-30
Roulston, Jeff
92Classic/DP-86
Roundfield, Dan
77T-13
78Hawks/Coke-13
78T-69
79Hawks/Majik-32
79T-43
80T-1
80T-174
80T-5
80T-80
80T-89
80T-93
81T-2
81T-44M
81T-E110
83Star/NBA-273
84Star/NBA-267
85Star/NBA-115
86F-95
Rouse, James
91AR/100*-89
Rouse, Willie
88KY/269-49
Rowe, Curtis
72T-24
73T-127
74T-22
75T-68
76T-118
77T-3
91UCLA/144-46
92Crtside/ColFB-32
Rowe, Dee
91CT/Legend-12CO
Rowinski, Jim
89ProC/CBA-171
90ProC/CBA-190
Rowland, Derrick
91ProC/CBA-166
Rowsom, Brian
90ProC/CBA-74
90SkyBox-34
Royal, Donald
90NotreDame-11
90SkyBox-174
91ProC/CBA-122
Rubbert, Ed
89Louville/300*-125
Rubenstein, Ron
88Louville/194-80
Rubin, Roy
89Louville/300*-54
Rucinsky, Martin
91Classic/DPColl*-17
Rucks, Norman
91SC/200*-75
Rudd, Delaney
90F/Up-U96
90Hoops-293
90Jazz/Star-10
90SkyBox-283
91F/Up-366
91Hoops/II-442
91SkyBox/I-284
91UD-197
Rudeen, Rick
90Clemson/200*-56
Rueppell, Chris
89ORSt-14
90ORSt-15
Ruffcorn, Scott
91Classic/DPColl*-71
Ruland, Jeff
83Star/NBA-204
84Star/ASG-10
84Star/CrtKg-2
84Star/NBA-194
84Star/PolASG-10
85Star/NBA-116
86F-96
92F-175
Rule, Bob
69Sonic/Sunb-8
69T-30
69T/Ins-6
70T-15
70T/Ins-12
71Sonic/Sunb-7
71T-40
71T/Ins-2
72T-40
73T-138
Ruman, Robert
90AZ/125*-123
Runager, Max
91SC/200*-83
Runnerstrum, Grant
90SoCal/Smok*-16
Rupp, Adolph
55Ash-24
68HOF-37
88KY/269-1
88KY/269-213
89KY/300*-35
Rupp, Herky
88KY/269-78
Rush, Arlandis
89UTEP/Drug-22
Rusnak, Ron
90NC/200*-132
90NC/200*-153
Russak, Al
89Louville/300*-55
Russell, Benny
89Louville/300*-140
Russell, Bill
57T-77
57Union-5
61F-38
61F-62
68T/Test-4
73Sonic/Shur-7CO
81PhilM-4
81TCMA-16
Russell, Campy
75T-156
76T-23
77T-83
78T-32
79T-56
80T-100
80T-12
81T-E84
Russell, Carol
91NE/Pol*-15
Russell, Cazzie
68T/Test-6
69T-3
70T-95
71T-73
72T-112
73NBAPA-25
73T-41
74T-151
75T-125M
75T-34
76T-83
77T-59
80TCMA/CBA-5
81TCMA-9
81TCMA/CBA-50
82TCMA/CBA-1
82TCMA/Lanc-4
82TCMA/Lanc-5
91MI/56*-45
92Crtside/ColFB-33
Russell, Cory
89ProC/CBA-194
Russell, Derek
91AR/100*-16
Russell, John D.
68HOF-38
Russell, Keith
90AZSt/200*-160
Russell, Leonard
91Classic/DPColl*-114
Russo, Laurie
92PennSt*-13
Rustand, Warren
90AZ/125*-11
Ruth, Babe
48T/Magic*-K6
81T/Thirst-5
Ryan, Buddy
91OKSt*-67
Ryan, Debbie
91VA/Lady-9CO
Ryan, Nolan
81T/Thirst-10M
91Arena/Holo*-4
Ryan, Pat
48T/Magic*-E11
Sabo, Chris
91MI/56*-46
Sabol, Mike
89George/Pol-12
90George/Pol-3
Sachs, Doug
90AZSt/200*-110
Sadowski, Ed
48Bowman-48
Sage, John
90LSU/200*-67
Sahm, Walt
90NotreDame-58
Sailors, Kenny
48Bowman-12
Saimes, George
90MISt/200*-71
Sain, Jerry
90NC/200*-126
Sale, Forest
88KY/269-19
Saleaumua, Dan
90AZSt/200*-11
Sales, Roland
91AR/100*-75
Salisbury, Danny
80TCMA/CBA-4
Salley, John
88F-44
89F-51
89Hoops-109
90F-60
90Hoops-110
90Piston/Star-11
90Piston/Unocal-10
90SkyBox-92
91F/Up-280
91GATech*-58
91Hoops/I-65
91Piston/Unocal-9
91SkyBox/I-87
91UD-190
92F-68
92Hoops/I-67
92SkyBox/I-72
Salmon, John Byrd
90AZ/125*-125
Salva, Mark
90FLSt/200*-74
Salz, Harvey
89NC/Coke-146
Salzano, Mike
90NC/200*-71
Sampson, Ralph
83Star/NBA-73
84Star/ASG-23
84Star/Award-3
84Star/CrtKg-14
84Star/NBA-248
84Star/PolASG-23
84Star/PolASG-32
84Star/SlamD-8
85Star/Crunch-11
85Star/LiteAS-12
85Star/NBA-24
85Star/ROY-2
85Star/TmSuper-HR1
86F-97
86Star/Best-4
86Star/CrtKg-27
87F-95
88F-49
88Fourn-24
88Warr/Smok-3
89Hoops-39
89Kings/Carl-50
90Hoops-261
90Panini-41
90SkyBox-250
91SkyBox/I-249
91SkyBox/II-651
91UD-397
91Wooden-12
Sams, Bucky
91TexAM-57
Sanchelli, Karen
91SC/200*-27
Sancho, Ron
90LSU/200*-135
Sandberry, Jay
91SC/200*-116
Sandbothe, Mike
88MO-10
Sanders, Al
90LSU/200*-55
Sanders, Barry
91OKSt*-2
91OKSt*-61
91OKSt*-76
91OKSt*-78
91OKSt*-83
Sanders, Curtis M.
89KY/300*-159
Sanders, Deion
90FLSt/200*-145

Scurry, Carey
89ProC/CBA-28
Scurry, Moses
88UNLV/HOF-7
89UNLV/HOF-5
89UNLV/Seven-11
91WildCard/Coll-55
Seale, Donnie
91NCSt/IBM-13
Seals, Bruce
76T-63
77T-113
Seals, Donald
82TCMA/Lanc-29
Sealy, Malik
92Classic/DP-29
92FrRow/DreamPk-81
92FrRow/DreamPk-82
92FrRow/DreamPk-83
92FrRow/DreamPk-84
92FrRow/DreamPk-85
92StarPic-46
Sealyham, White
48T/Magic*-G4
Sears, Kenny
57T-7
Seaver, Tom
81T/Thirst-10M
81T/Thirst-13
Seawright, James
91SC/200*-19
Seegert, Alicia
91MI/56*-47
Seikaly, Rony
89F-83
89Heat/Publix-11
89Hoops-243
90F-102
90Heat/Publix-11
90Hoops-169
90Hoops/CollB-11
90Hoops/II-368TC
90Hoops/Super-53
90Panini-154
90SkyBox-151
90SkyBox/Proto-151
91F-112
91Hoops/I-114
91Hoops/II-476SC
91Hoops/McDon-23
91Hoops/Super-52
91Panini-150
91SkyBox/Canada-28
91SkyBox/I-152
91SkyBox/II-472TW
91UD-145
91UD-80TC
92F-121
92Hoops/I-122
92SkyBox/I-129
Seiple, Larry
89KY/300*-114
Sele, Aaron
91Classic/DPColl*-69
Self, Bill
91OKSt-24ACO
Selinger, Joe
90MISt/200*-84
Sellers, Brad
87Bulls/Ent-4
88Bulls/Ent-2
88F-21
89F-24
89Hoops-139
89Hoops/II-348
90Hoops-192
90SkyBox-175
91Hoops/II-362
91Piston/Unocal-16M
91SkyBox/II-626
Sellers, Ron
90FLSt/200*-167
Sellers, Rod
90CT/Pol-11
91CT/Pol-13
Sells, Peggy
90Clemson/Lady-12
Selvin, Maurice
89ProC/CBA-17
Selvy, Frank
57T-51
61F-40
61Lakers/Bell-8
81TCMA-24
Selvy, Marv
88Louville/194-146
88Louville/194-90
Sendek, Herb
91KY/BB/Double-18ACO
Senesky, George
48Bowman-25
52Bread-27
Serini, Wash
89KY/300*-182
Server, Jim
89KY/300*-246
Seter, Chris
88MI/Nike-13
89MI-4
Settle, Evan
89KY/300*-231
Severin, Paul
90NC/200*-197
Severn, Dan
90AZSt/200*-146
Severn, Dave
90AZSt/200*-108
Severn, Rod
90AZSt/200*-98
Sexton, Frank
48T/Magic*-D15
Seymour, Paul
52Bread-28
57T-72
Shackleford, Charles
87NCSt/Pol-11
89Hoops-169
89NCSt/Coke-35
89NCSt/Coke-36
89NCSt/Coke-37
90F-122
91F/Up-337
91Hoops/II-414
91SkyBox/II-639
91UD/Ext-405
92F-176
92Hoops/I-176
92SkyBox/I-186
Shackelford, Lynn
91UCLA/144-36
Shackelford, Roscoe
55Ash-35
89Louville/300*-96
Shackleford, Terry
89NCSt/Coke-38
Shafer, Joe
91WA/Viacom-16
Shaffer, Charlie
89NC/Coke-163
Shaffer, Craig
82INSt/Pol*-11
Shaffer, Lee
89NC/Coke-136
89NC/Coke-137
90NC/200*-170
Shamsid-Deen, Abdul
91WildCard/Coll-8
Shannon, Earl
48Bowman-22
Share, Chuck
57T-61
Shareef, Ahmad
90Pitt/Food-11
Sharkey, Jack
48T/Magic*-A11
Sharman, Bill
57T-5
57Union-9
81TCMA-20
Sharp, James
89KY/300*-286
Sharples, Warren
91MI/56*-48
Shasky, John
89Hoops-268
91UD-101
Shavik, Ronnie
89NCSt/Coke-39
89NCSt/Coke-40
89NCSt/Coke-41
Shaw, Brian
89F-14
89Hoops-62
90F/Up-U9
90Hoops-48
90SkyBox-23
91F-16
91FrRow/100-96
91FrRow/ItalPromo-7
91FrRow/Premier-87
91Hoops/I-17
91Hoops/Super-9
91Panini-148
91SkyBox/I-20
91UD-346
91UD/Ext-496
92F-122
92Hoops/I-123
92SkyBox/I-130
Shaw, Jim
90ORSt-18ACO
Sheehan, David
(Dave)
83Victoria/Pol-10
84Victoria/Pol-11
Sheehey, Tom
91ProC/CBA-45
Sheets, Mike
91OKSt*-84
Sheffield, Larry
90NotreDame-53
Sheffield, Russell
87Baylor/Pol*-14
Shelby, Willie
89Louville/300*-168
Sheldrake, Ed
91UCLA/144-42
Shell, Lambert
92Classic/DP-90
Shelton, Craig
81TCMA/CBA-51
91George/100-52
91George/100-6
91George/100-97
Shelton, Lonnie
77T-26
78Sonic/Pol-6
78T-66
79Sonic/Pol-6
79T-83
80T-167
80T-169
80T-52
80T-79
81T-W86
83Star/NBA-239
84Star/NBA-222
Shepherd, Billy
75T-223LL
75T-301
Shepherd, Robert
91AR25-15
Sheppard, Von
85NE/Pol*-29
Sherill, Tim
91AR/100*-23
Sherk, Jerry
91OKSt*-56
Sherman, Chris
90Clemson/200*-52
Sherod, Ed
82TCMA/Lanc-15
Sherrod, Anthony
88GATech/Nike-11
Shibest, James
91AR/100*-56
Shidler, Jay
77KY/Wildct-18
78KY/Food-15
79KY/Food-3
88KY/269-113
88KY/269-266
89KY/Tm80-50
Shields, Jim
83Dayton/Blue-15
Shields, Ken
83Victoria/Pol-11CO
84Victoria/Pol-12CO
88Victoria/Pol-15CO
Shikat, Dick
48T/Magic*-D23
Shilhanek, Emily
91ND*-10M
Shipp, Larry
90LSU/200*-26
Shirley, Al
91Classic/DPColl*-64
Shively, Bernie A.
89KY/300*-198
Shiver, Stan
90FLSt/200*-35
Shofield, Terry
91UCLA/144-25
Short, Purvis
80T-153
80T-72
81T-W74
83Star/NBA-260
84Star/CrtKg-10
84Star/NBA-149
85Star/NBA-131
86F-100
88F-54
89Hoops-76
90F-123
90Hoops-201
90Panini-161
90SkyBox-185
Shorter, Brian
89Pitt/Food-00
90Pitt/Food-12
91Classic/DPColl*-215
91Crtside-41
91StarPic-51
91WildCard/Coll-34
Shouppe, Jamey
90FLSt/200*-21
Shue, Gene
57T-26
61F-41
61F-64IA
81TCMA-37
Shulman, Brian
87Auburn/Pol*-12
Shumate, Howard
55Ash-57
Shumate, John
76T-61
77T-104
78T-46
80T-132
80T-133
80T-21
80T-76
90NotreDame-10
Sibley, Lew
90LSU/200*-66
Sichting, Jerry
83Star/NBA-164
84Star/NBA-58
85Star/NBA-100
86F-101
87F-99
88Blaz/Franz-12
89Hoops-157
Sidle, Don
71T-161
Sidney, Sylvia
48T/Magic*-F12
Siegfried, Larry
69T-59
70T-88
71T-36
Sienkiewicz, Tom
82TCMA/CBA-49
82TCMA/Lanc-20
82TCMA/Lanc-21
Siganos, Mike
89KY/300*-106
Sikma, Jack
78RCCola-28
78Sonic/Pol-7
78T-117
79Sonic/Pol-3
79T-66
80T-153
80T-48
80T-72
80T-98
81T-39
81T-64M
81T-W110
83Sonic/Pol-8
83Star/ASG-21
83Star/NBA-193
84Star/ASG-24
84Star/CrtKg-21
84Star/NBA-120
84Star/PolASG-24
85Star/NBA-69
86F-102
87Bucks/Polar-43
87F-100
88Bucks/Green-14
88F-76
89Conv-12
89F-91
89Hoops-66
90F-110
90Hoops-183
90Hoops/Super-57
90Panini-98
90SkyBox-166
91F-120
91Hoops/I-122
91Hoops/Super-57
91Panini-140
91SkyBox/I-165
91UD-370
Silas, James
74T-186
74T-227M
75T-224LL
75T-253AS
75T-284M
76T-134AS
76T-80
79Spurs/Pol-13
79T-74
80T-112
80T-151
80T-16
80T-56
81T-MW105
Silas, Paul

69Suns/Carn-6
69T-61
70Suns/A1-6
70Suns/Carn-8
70T-69
71T-54
72T-55
73T-112
74T-9
75Carv-28
75T-117M
75T-8
76T-3
78Sonic/Pol-8
78T-94
79Sonic/Pol-5
80T-169
80T-52
Siler, Robert
88WakeForest/Pol-14
Silveria, Larry
90AZ/125*-73
Sim, Marvin
90Clemson/200*-28
Simian, Stephane
91SC/200*-34
Simmons, Cornelius
48Bowman-52
52Bread-29
Simmons, Lionel
90F/Up-U87
90Hoops/II-396LS
90Kings/Safe-9
90SkyBox/II-364LP
90StarPic-66
91F-179
91F/Rook-1
91F/Up-394TL
91Hoops/I-185
91Hoops/II-493SC
91Hoops/II-525Ar
91Hoops/McDon-38
91Panini-181AR
91Panini-35
91SkyBox/I-250
91SkyBox/I-319AR
91SkyBox/II-481TW
91SkyBox/II-508RS
91UD-36ART
91UD-375
91UD-83TC
91Wooden-19
92F-198
92Hoops/I-201
92SkyBox/I-215
Simmons, Willie
89ProC/CBA-130
90ProC/CBA-99
Simms, Wayne
88LSU/Pol*-3
Simms, Willie
89WI/Smok-12
91ProC/CBA-130
Simon, Walt
71Col/Mara-9
71T-214
72T-224
73T-218
Simons, Neil
90Clemson/200*-66
Simpson, Bill
90MISt/200*-29
Simpson, Craig
90MISt/200*-125
90MISt/200*-97
Simpson, O.J.
81T/Thirst-37
Simpson, Ralph
71T-232
72T-235
72T-257AS
73T-190AS
74T-219
74T-222M
75T-240
75T-278M
76T-22
90MISt/200*-170
Sims, Bobby
61Hawks/Essex-13
Sims, Gerald
82TCMA/CBA-52
Sims, Gig
91UCLA/144-26
Sims, Joe
90NE/Pol*-9
Singleton, Chris
90AZ/125*-5
90AZ/Promos*-4
Singleton, McKinley
91ProC/CBA-88
Singleton, Tim
90NotreDame-4
Singleton, Vernel
88LSU/Pol*-7
92Classic/DP-42
Sinn, Pearl
90AZSt/200*-73
Siock, Dave
88Syr/Rich-11
Sippel, Lori
84NE/Pol*-30
85NE/Pol*-31
Sipple, Mark
91ND*-5M
Sisler, George
48T/Magic*-K17
Sitton, Charlie
84Star/NBA-258
Sivills, Scott
90MurraySt-11
91MurraySt-9
Sizemore, Ted
91MI/56*-49
Skaggs, Ricky
87KY/Coke-10
Skelton, Jamie
91OhioSt-15
Skiles, Ricky
89Louville/300*-196
Skiles, Scott
89F-110
89Hoops-249
89Hoops/II-318
90Hoops-220
90MISt/200*-140
90MISt/200*-152
90Panini-124
90SkyBox-205
91F-148
91F/Up-390TL
91Hoops/I-152
91Hoops/II-486SC
91Hoops/II-521Ar
91Hoops/McDon-29
91Hoops/Super-70
91Panini-72
91SkyBox/Canada-34
91SkyBox/I-206
91SkyBox/I-310
91SkyBox/II-477TW
91UD-226
91UD-86TC
92F-164
92F/TmLeader-19
92Hoops/I-165
92SkyBox/I-174
92SkyBox/I-300TT
Skinner, Al
75T-272
77T-91
Skinner, George
89KY/300*-290
Skinner, Talvin
75T-187
Skinner, Troy
91Iowa-10
Skipper, Harry
91SC/200*-191
Sklar, Ben
48ExhSC-43
Skow, Jim
85NE/Pol*-9
Slack, Charles
55Ash-48
Slater, Reggie
92Classic/DP-35
Slater, Scott
91TexAM-67
Slaughter, Fred
91UCLA/144-143
Slaughter, Jim
91SC/200*-157
Slaughter, Jose
89ProC/CBA-43
91ProC/CBA-167
Slaughter, Sterling
90AZSt/200*-181
Slavens, Robert
91TexAM-66
Sleeper, Jim
89ProC/CBA-140
Sloan, Jerry
68T/Test-20
70Bulls/Hawth-2
70T-148
70T/Ins-8
71T-87
71T/Ins-21
72Icee-16
72T-11
73NBAPA-26
73T-83
74T-51
75Carv-29
75Nab-17
75T-9
76Buck-18
76T-123
79Bulls/Pol-x
89Hoops-267CO
90Bulls/Eq-14
90Hoops-330CO
90Hoops/II-354CO
90Jazz/Star-12CO
90SkyBox/II-326CO
91F-202CO
91Hoops/I-246CO
91SkyBox/II-403CO
92F-226CO
92Hoops/I-264CO
92SkyBox/I-280CO
Slocum, R.C.
91TexAM-4
Sluby, Tom
84Star/NBA-259
Slusher, Bobby
89KY/300*-232
Small, Hank
91SC/200*-186
Smart, Keith
89ProC/CBA-29
90ProC/CBA-72
91ProC/CBA-66
Smiley, Jack
48Bowman-33
Smilgoff, Jimmy
54Quaker-18
Smirl, Shea
91ND*-9M
Smith, Adrian
(Odie)
61Kahn's-8
62Kahn's-8
63Kahn's-10
64Kahn's-11
68PartM-13
68T/Test-9
69T-97
70T-133
88KY/269-72
Smith, Al
72T-196
73T-181
74T-212LL
74T-222M
74T-239
75T-223LL
75T-286M
75T-306
82TCMA/CBA-25
Smith, Alisa
86SWLou/Pol*-14
Smith, Anthony
90AZ/125*-18
91SC/200*-129
Smith, Audra
91VA/Lady-11
Smith, Barry
90FLSt/200*-146
Smith, Bill
89KY/300*-233
Smith, Billy Ray
91AR/100*-25
Smith, Bobby
(Bingo)
68Rocket/Jack-11
70T-74
71T-93
71T/Ins-36
72T-149
73T-49
74T-78
75T-120M
75T-175
76T-114
77T-126
Smith, Bubba
71Keds*-1M
71Keds*-2M
90MISt/200*-43
Smith, Charles
85George/Pol-13
87George/Pol-13
88George/Pol-13
91George/100-47
91George/100-7
91Hoops/I-98
92SkyBox/I-111
Smith, Charles PITT
89F-73
89Hoops-262
90Clip/Star-11
90F-89
90Hoops-151
90Hoops/CollB-47
90Hoops/Super-44
90Panini-36
90SkyBox-132
91F-96
91F/Up-383TL
91Hoops/II-472SC
91Hoops/II-574
91Hoops/McDon-20
91Hoops/Super-45
91Kell/ColGrt-12
91Panini-9
91SkyBox/Canada-24
91SkyBox/I-131
91SkyBox/II-470TW
91SkyBox/II-497RS
91SkyBox/II-556US
91SkyBox/Proto-130
91UD-161
92F-104
92Hoops/I-105
Smith, Chris
90CT/Pol-12
91Classic/DPColl*-210
91CT/Pol-14
91MO-13
92Classic/DP-6
92StarPic-29
Smith, Clarence
71Globe-45
71Globe-46
71Globe-47
71Globe-48
71Globe/Cocoa-16
71Globe/Cocoa-17
Smith, Clinton
89ProC/CBA-104
90ProC/CBA-154
Smith, Danny
91SC/200*-154
Smith, David
89Louville/300*-97
Smith, Dean
88NC/Pol-x
89NC/Coke-1
89NC/Coke-2
89NC/Coke-3
89NC/Coke-4
89NC/Coke-5
89NC/Coke-6
90KY/BB/DT/AW-25CO
90NC/200*-1
90NC/200*-150
90NC/200*-173
90NC/200*-27
90NC/200*-52
92CenterCrt-18CO
92Crtside/ColFB-35CO
Smith, Derek
81Louville/Pol-11
83Star/NBA-131
84Star/NBA-21
85Star/NBA-92
86F-103
86Kings/Smok-10
88Louville/194-113
88Louville/194-15
88Louville/194-156
88Louville/194-191
89Hoops-83
89Louville/300*-265
89Louville/300*-282
89Louville/300*-33
89Sixers/Kodak-11
90F-145
90Hoops-231
90SkyBox-218
91Hoops/II-340
91UD-27
Smith, Don
(See Zaid Abdul-Aziz)
Smith, Doug
88MO-11
89MO-12
90MO-12
91F/Up-271
91FrRow/Premier-118
91FrRow/Premier-94HL
91FrRow/Up-55
91Hoops/II-551
91Hoops/II-HC
91Kell/ColGrt-9
91SkyBox/II-518LP
91StarPic-33
91UD/Ext-493
91UD/Rook-31
91VA-12
92F-53
92F/Rook-10
92Hoops/I-51

92SkyBox/I-54
Smith, Eddie
90NotreDame-21
Smith, Eddie AZ
83AZ/Pol-11
84AZ/Pol-12
90AZ/125*-92
Smith, Elmore
72T-76
73NBAPA-27
73T-19
74T-49
75T-16
76T-65
77T-106
78T-57
79T-117
Smith, Elvado
81George/Pol-2
Smith, Emmitt
91ProC/CBA-198
Smith, Eric
81George/Pol-3
91George/100-40
Smith, Frank
81AZ/Pol-15
Smith, Gene
81George/Pol-11
82George/Pol-11
83George/Pol-6
91George/100-61
Smith, George
90MISt/200*-68
Smith, Greg
69T-81
70T-166
71T-129
72T-114
74T-128
Smith, J.
88KY/269-100
88KY/269-214
Smith, James
82INSt/Pol*-12
Smith, Jeff
84NE/Pol*-3
Smith, Jimmy
87SoMiss-12
Smith, Joe
91SC/200*-99
Smith, John
81TCMA/CBA-37
82TCMA/CBA-69
Smith, John DUKE
87Duke/Pol-33
88Duke/Pol-12
91ProC/CBA-112
Smith, John OK
91OKSt*-25
Smith, Jon
91George/100-59
Smith, Keith
90ProC/CBA-150
Smith, Kenny
86NC/Pol-30
88F-100
88Kings/Carl-30
89F-138
89Hoops-232
89Kings/Carl-30
89NC/Coke-107
89NC/Coke-66
89NC/Coke-67
89NC/Coke-68
90F-4
90F/Up-U36
90Hoops/II-414
90NC/200*-16
90NC/200*-33
90NC/200*-75
90NC/200*-94
90Panini-120
90SkyBox/II-385
91F-230
91F-78
91Hoops/I-79
91Hoops/Super-37
91Panini-58
91SkyBox/I-106
91SkyBox/II-411GF
91SkyBox/II-468TW
91SkyBox/II-587
91UD-276
92F-85
92Hoops/I-86
92SkyBox/I-291TT
92SkyBox/I-91
Smith, Kevin
82TCMA/CBA-59
90MISt/200*-138
Smith, Kevin
91Iowa-11
Smith, LaBradford
91FrRow/Premier-11
91FrRow/Premier-89HL
91FrRow/Up-63
91StarPic-49
91UD/Ext-485
92F-234
92Hoops/I-237
92SkyBox/I-253
Smith, Lance
90LSU/200*-76
Smith, Larry
81T-51M
81T-W75
83Star/NBA-261
84Star/NBA-157
85Star/NBA-136
86F-104
87F-101
88Warr/Smok-4
89Hoops-168
89Hoops/II-309
90Hoops-128
90SkyBox-111
91F-79
91Hoops/I-80
91Panini-62
91ProC/CBA-13
91SkyBox/I-107
91SkyBox/I-309M
91UD-280
92Hoops/I-87
92SkyBox/I-92
Smith, Mark
80IL/Arby's-11
Smith, Mark BB
91Classic/DPColl*-56
Smith, Martin
91AR/100*-58
Smith, Marty
89Louville/300*-159
Smith, Michael
87BYU-1
87BYU-25
90F/Up-U10
90Panini-133
90SkyBox-24
91SkyBox/I-21
91UD-121
Smith, Michelle
85NE/Pol*-12
Smith, Moyer
90NC/200*-102
Smith, Otis
89Hoops-86
89Hoops/II-303
89Magic/Pep-6
90F-135
90Hoops-221
90Panini-121
90SkyBox-206
91F-149
91Hoops/I-153
91Hoops/II-544Si
91Panini-73
91SkyBox/I-207
91UD-288
Smith, Phil
75T-139
76T-89
77T-12
78T-33
79T-53
80T-163
80T-40
81T-W93
Smith, Racine
85NE/Pol*-17
Smith, Randal
86SWLou/Pol*-15
87SWLou/McDag*-1
Smith, Randy
72T-8
73T-173
74T-8
75Carv-30
75T-118M
75T-63
76T-135AS
76T-40
77T-82
78Clipp/Handy-1
78T-112
79T-85
80T-38
80T-95
81T-E86
Smith, Ranzino
86NC/Pol-33
87NC/Pol-33
89NC/Coke-169
90NC/200*-24
Smith, Reggie
90MO-13
91MO-14
92Classic/DP-56
92StarPic-3
Smith, Riley
90ProC/CBA-191
91ProC/CBA-91
Smith, Robert
82TCMA/CBA-30
Smith, Robert UNLV
(Slick)
91WildCard/Coll-81
Smith, Ronnie
84NE/Pol*-18
Smith, Sam
71Col/Mara-10
79Bulls/Pol-28
Smith, Sean
91GATech*-31
Smith, Sonny
87Auburn/Pol*-4
Smith, Stan
71Keds*-2M
Smith, Steve
90MISt-14M
90MISt-9
91F/Up-309
91FrRow/Premier-106AC
91FrRow/Premier-84
91FrRow/Premier-97HL
91FrRow/Smith-Set
91FrRow/Up-53
91Hoops/II-550
91Hoops/II-HC
91SkyBox/II-517LP
91StarPic-21
91UD-4
91UD/Ext-447TP
91UD/Rook-32
91WildCard/Coll-98B
91WildCard/RHRook-3
92Classic/DP-96FB
92F-123
92F/Rook-11
92FrRow/DreamPk-26
92FrRow/DreamPk-27
92FrRow/DreamPk-28
92FrRow/DreamPk-29
92FrRow/DreamPk-30
92Hoops/I-124
92SkyBox/I-131
Smith, Tom
90MISt/200*-195
Smith, Tony
90F/Up-U45
91F/Up-303
91Hoops/II-384
91SkyBox/I-140
91UD-128
91UD/McDon-M7
91UD/Rook-19
92Hoops/I-112
92SkyBox/I-119
Smith, Ty
89Louville/300*-133
Smith, Vadi
82George/Pol-10
Smith, Will
91Hoops/I-325
91Hoops/I-326
Smith, Willie
82TCMA/CBA-15
90NC/Promos*-NC9
Smith, Willie MO
90MO-14
Smithson, Gene
80WichSt/Pol-13CO
Smithson, Randy
80WichSt/Pol-14
Smits, Rik
89F-68
89Hoops-37
90F-82
90Hoops-139
90Hoops/Super-42
90Panini-109
90SkyBox-122
91F-86
91Hoops/I-88
91Panini-136
91SkyBox/I-118
91UD-294
92F-94
92Hoops/I-95
92SkyBox/I-100
Smolinski, Don
82Marq/Lite-14
Smrek, Mike
90Hoops-119
90SkyBox-101
Smyth, John
90NotreDame-29
Snavely, Carl
90NC/200*-151
Snead, Samuel J.
48Kell*-17
Snedeker, Jeff
87Bucks/Polar-TR
88Bucks/Green-16TR
Snider, Duke
57Union-12
Snite, Fred Sr.
54Quaker-2
Snively, John
82AR-13
Snow, J.T.
90AZ/125*-63
Snow, Lenny
91GATech*-199
Snow, Percy
90MISt/200*-44
90MISt/200*-56
90MISt/200*-82
90MISt/Promos*-3
Snowden, Fred
81AZ/Pol-16CO
90AZ/125*-17
Snyder, Dick
68Suns/Carn-9
69Suns/Carn-7
69T-73
70Sonic/Sunb-8
70T-64
71Sonic/Sunb-9
72T-136
73NBAPA-28
73Sonic/Shur-10
73T-86
74T-115
74T-97M
75T-120M
75T-83
76T-2
78Sonic/Pol-9
Snyder, Quin
87Duke/Pol-14
88Duke/Pol-13
Sobers, Ricky
75Suns-13
76Suns-8
76T-102
77T-42
78RCCola-29
78T-93
79Bulls/Pol-40
79T-71
80T-137
80T-23
81T-8
83Star/NBA-214
84Star/NBA-121
85Star/NBA-70
Sobie, Ron
57T-69
Sobieszcyk, Ron
86DePaul-C3
Sodders, Mike
90AZSt/200*-159
Soderberg, Mark
89KY/300*-85
Soergel, Dick
91OKSt*-58
Sojourner, Mike
75T-62
76T-79
Sojourner, Willie
72T-232
75T-312
Sommer, Coleen
90AZSt/200*-137
Sorensen, Lary
79Bucks/OpenP-5
91MI/56*-50
Sorenson, Dave
71T-71
72T-12
73T-14
Sossamon, Lou
91SC/200*-94
South, Harry
91SC/200*-172
Southers, Brantley
91SC/200*-188
Spadafore, Frank
55Ash-94
Spahn, Warren
57Union-39
Spanarkel, Jim
81T-48M
81T-MW79

83Star/NBA-57
84Star/Arena-B8
Sparrow, Guy
57T-38
Sparrow, Rory
80TCMA/CBA-20
83Star/NBA-68
84Star/NBA-34
85Star/NBA-170
86F-105
87Bulls/Ent-1
87F-102
89F-84
89Heat/Publix-12
89Hoops-207
90Hoops-170
90Hoops/II-430
90Hoops/Super-52
90Kings/Safe-10
90SkyBox-152
90SkyBox/II-411
91F-180
91Hoops/I-186
91Panini-37
91SkyBox/I-251
91UD-395
91UD/Ext-434
Speaker, Tris
48T/Magic*-K7
Speaks, Jon Garwood
89NCSt/Coke-42
89NCSt/Coke-43
89NCSt/Coke-44
Spector, Arthur
48Bowman-57
Spence, Phil
89NCSt/Coke-46
89NCSt/Coke-47
89NCSt/Coke-48
Spencer, Elmore
90UNLV/Season-10
90UNLV/Smok-13
92Classic/DP-57
92StarPic-61
Spencer, Felton
90F/Up-U57
90Hoops/II-395LS
90SkyBox/II-361LP
90StarPic-41
91F-127
91F/Rook-6
91Hoops/I-130
91Panini-182AR
91Panini-64
91SkyBox/I-174
91UD-305
91UD/Rook-4
92F-138
92Hoops/I-141
92SkyBox/I-148
Spencer, Jerry
91AR/100*-34
Spencer, Mark
79StBon-14
Spicer, Carey
88KY/269-54
Spiers, Bill
90Clemson/200*-20
Spillane, Jim
91UCLA/144-64
Spitz, Mark
81T/Thirst-45
Spivey, Bill
88KY/269-16
89KY/300*-50
Spivey, Ron
89ProC/CBA-146
90ProC/CBA-176
91ProC/CBA-144
Splane, Vince
89KY/300*-234
Spoelstra, Art
57T-52
Sprague, Cindy
87ME/Pol*-4
Sprewell, Latrell
92Classic/DP-21
92StarPic-38
Spriggs, Ed
81George/Pol-9
91George/100-41
Spriggs, Larry
81TCMA/CBA-36
82TCMA/CBA-50
83Lakers/BASF-11
83Star/NBA-23
84Lakers/BASF-10
84Star/NBA-182
89ProC/CBA-121
Springer, Russell
87LSU/Pol*-11
88LSU/Pol*-16
Springs, Albert
89ProC/CBA-137
90ProC/CBA-152
St.Jean, Garry
92F-197CO
92Hoops/I-261CO
92SkyBox/I-277CO
St.John, Dan
90AZSt/200*-131
Staak, Bob
88WakeForest/Pol-15CO
Stacey, Howard
89Louville/300*-85
Stachowicz, Ray
90MISt/200*-1
90MISt/200*-39
90MISt/200*-90
Stacom, Kevin
75T-117M
75T-99
77T-108
91Providence-18
Stagg, Amos Alonzo
54Quaker-7
68HOF-40
Stahl, Ed
89NC/Coke-148
90NC/200*-157
Stahl, Regina
90AZSt/200*-90
Stahoviak, Scott
91Classic/DPColl*-73
Staios, Steve
91Classic/DPColl*-24
Staker, Carl
89KY/300*-235
Staley, Dawn
91VA/Lady-12
Stallings, Ron
89Louville/300*-82
Stallworth, Bud
73Sonic/Shur-11
73T-58
75T-108
Stallworth, Cedric
91GATech*-32
Stallworth, Dave
69T-74
70T-78
71T-49
72T-132
73Bullet/Stand-9
73T-133
Stamper, Larry
88KY/269-97
Standlee, Norm
48Kell*-8
Stanich, George
91UCLA/144-114
Stanich, John
91UCLA/144-120
Stankavage, Scott
90NC/200*-41
Stansbury, Terence
84Star/NBA-59
85Star/Gator-3
85Star/NBA-85
85Star/SlamD-7
91WildCard/Coll-75
Stanwyck, Barbara
48T/Magic*-F2
Starks, John
89ProC/CBA-188
91F/Up-330
91Hoops/II-406
91OKSt*-40
91Panini-166
91SkyBox/I-194
91SkyBox/II-503RS
91UD-219
91UD/Ext-482SD
92F-156
92Hoops/I-158
92SkyBox/I-167
Starr, Bart
81T/Thirst-36
Staubach, Roger
74Nab-1
75Nab-1
Staverman, Larry
59Kahn's-8
60Kahn's-9
Steel, Randy
83Victoria/Pol-12
84Victoria/Pol-13
Steele, Larry
72T-26
73T-69
74T-21
75T-6M
75T-94
77Blaz/Pol-15
79Blaz/Pol-15
88KY/269-158
88KY/269-41
89Blaz/Franz-18
Steers, Leo
48T/Magic*-E2
Steffy, Joe
48T/Magic*-C8
Stegent, Larry
91TexAM-14
Stegman, Dave
90AZ/125*-76
Stehlik, Wayne
91AR25-21ACO
Steigenga, Matt
90MISt-14M
90MISt-4
92Classic/DP-32
92StarPic-26
Stein, Bill
81George/Pol-7
Steinke
48T/Magic*-D25
Stel, Travis
89ORSt-15
90ORSt-17
Stengel, Casey
81PhilM-1
Stephen, Scott
90AZSt/200*-27
Stephens, Dwayne
90MISt-5
Stephens, Everette
89ProC/CBA-192
90ProC/CBA-46
Stephens, Frank
71Globe-42M
71Globe-50
71Globe-51
71Globe-52
71Globe-53
Stephens, Jack
90NotreDame-26
Stephens, Kim
90Clemson/Lady-13
Stephens, Rehema
90UCLA-17
Stephens, Rod
91GATech*-66
Stephens, Tim
77KY/Wildct-16
78KY/Food-12
89KY/300*-86
Steppe, Brook
83Star/NBA-165
91GATech*-26
Stevens, Barry
90ProC/CBA-174
Stevens, Howard
89Louville/300*-108
Stevenson, Gil
48T/Magic*-R2
Stevenson, Mark
90StarPic-29
Stevenson, Norris
90AZSt/200*-69
Stewart, Alprentice
89UTEP/Drug-23
Stewart, Bruce
91ProC/CBA-107CO
Stewart, Corey
91VA-13
Stewart, Gene
89KY/300*-87
Stewart, Jim
68PartM-8
Stewart, Larry
91F/Up-369
91FrRow/100-71
91FrRow/ItalPromo-8
91FrRow/Premier-25
91FrRow/Up-72
91UD/Ext-440TP
91UD/Rook-39
92F-235
92F/Rook-12
92FrRow/DreamPk-31
92FrRow/DreamPk-32
92FrRow/DreamPk-33
92FrRow/DreamPk-34
92FrRow/DreamPk-35
92Hoops/I-238
92SkyBox/I-254
Stewart, Rod
89KY/300*-147
Stewart, Norm
88MO-12CO
89MO-13CO
90MO-15CO
91MO-15CO
Still, Art
89KY/300*-137
Stillwell, Joseph
48T/Magic*-O1
Stinson, Andrea
89NCSt/Pol-11
90NCSt/IBM-11
Stinson, Scott
85Victoria/Pol-15ACO
Stipanovich, Steve
83Star/NBA-157
84Star/NBA-60
85Star/NBA-86
86F-106
87F-103
88F-59
88MO-13
89Hoops-148
89MO-14
Stith, Bryant
88VA/Hardee-11
91VA-14
92Classic/DP-19
92FrRow/DreamPk-46
92FrRow/DreamPk-47
92FrRow/DreamPk-48
92FrRow/DreamPk-49
92FrRow/DreamPk-50
92StarPic-2
92StarPic-43
Stockstill, Rick
90FLSt/200*-14
Stockton, John
84Star/NBA-235
85Star/NBA-144
85Star/RTm-8
88F-115
88F-127AS
88Fourn-32
88Jazz/Smok-6
89F-156
89F-163M
89Hoops-140
89Hoops-297AS
89Jazz/OldH-13
90F-189
90F/AS-9
90Hoops-25AS
90Hoops-294
90Hoops/CollB-22
90Hoops/Super-93
90Jazz/Star-2
90Panini-51
90Panini-AAS
90SkyBox-284
91F-203
91F-217
91F-221
91F/Up-397TL
91Hoops/I-212
91Hoops/I-271AS
91Hoops/I-310M
91Hoops/I-312M
91Hoops/II-500SC
91Hoops/II-528Ar
91Hoops/II-584
91Hoops/McDon-45
91Hoops/McDon-60USA
91Hoops/Super-97
91Kell/ColGrt-8
91Panini-81
91SkyBox/Canada-47
91SkyBox/I-285
91SkyBox/I-306
91SkyBox/II-484TW
91SkyBox/II-539US
91UD-136
91UD-52AS
91UD/AWHolo-3
91UD/Ext-470AS
91WildCard/Coll-84
92F-227
92F-240LL
92F/AS-22
92Hoops/I-229
92Hoops/I-316AS
92Hoops/I-324LL
92Hoops/I-326LL
92Hoops/I-347
92SkyBox/I-244
92SkyBox/I-307TT
92SkyBox/Olympic-USA3
92SkyBox/USA-110
92SkyBox/USA-82
92SkyBox/USA-83
92SkyBox/USA-84
92SkyBox/USA-85
92SkyBox/USA-86
92SkyBox/USA-87
92SkyBox/USA-88
92SkyBox/USA-89

73T-214
74T-188
74T-230M
75T-268
Taylor, Sammy
89Fresno/Smok-13
90Fresno/Smok-13
Taylor-Harris, Ernest
81AZ/Pol-17
Teaff, Grant
87Baylor/Pol*-17CO
Teagle, Terry
83Star/NBA-83
86F-107
89F-57
89Hoops-196
90F-68
90F/Up-U46
90Hoops-120
90Hoops/II-416
90Panini-27
90SkyBox-102
90SkyBox/II-392
91F-103
91Hoops/I-104
91SkyBox/I-141
91SkyBox/II-444SM
91UD-171
91UD/McDon-M8
92F-112
92Hoops/I-113
Teahan, Matt
80TCMA/CBA-44
Teal, Jimmy
91TexAM-18
Teal, Willie
90LSU/200*-77
Teheran, Alvaro
91Classic-34
91Classic/DPColl*-182
91Crtside-42
91FrRow/100-38
91FrRow/50-38
91FrRow/Premier-54
91StarPic-19
91WildCard/Coll-3
Tennant, Jack
81Louville/Pol-12ANN
Tennaper, Garth
91TexAM-73
Terrell, Charles
90SanJ/Smok-7
Terrell, Ira
76Suns-9
77Suns/Discs-32
Terry, Chuck
73T-172
Terry, Claude
75T-288
Terry, James
82TCMA/CBA-54
Terry, Lloyd
82TCMA/CBA-41
Terry, Martin
91AR/100*-66
Tettleton, Mickey
91OKSt*-77
Teufel, Tim
90Clemson/200*-23
90Clemson/Promos*-C7
Tewell, Doug
91OKSt*-36
Thacker, Angela
84NE/Pol*-27
85NE/Pol*-20
Thacker, Tab
90Clemson/200*-159M
Thacker, Tom
63Kahn's-11
Theus, Reggie
79Bulls/Pol-24
79T-44
80T-129
80T-143
80T-168
80T-31
80T-84
80T-85
81T-46M
81T-MW69
83Star/ASG-10
83Star/ASG-27M
83Star/NBA-225
84Star/CrtKg-16
84Star/NBA-270
85Kings/Smok-12
85Star/NBA-74
86F-108
86Kings/Smok-11
87F-105
88F-98
89Conv-13
89F-111
89Hoops-165
89Hoops/II-302
90F-136
90F/Up-U62
90Hoops-222
90Hoops/II-420
90Hoops/Super-68
90Nets/Kayo-12
90SkyBox-207
90SkyBox/II-399
91Hoops/I-138
91Hoops/Super-63
91Panini-155
91SkyBox/I-187
91UD-264
Thibault, Mike
89ProC/CBA-206CO
90ProC/CBA-7
91ProC/CBA-194CO
Thibeaux, Peter
84Star/NBA-158
90ProC/CBA-23
Thibodeaux, Benjy
90LSU/200*-108
Thieben, Bill
57T-20
Thieneman, Chris
89Louville/300*-144
Thirdkill, David
83Star/NBA-93
Thomas, Andre
91GATech*-18
Thomas, Bill
91George/100-56
Thomas, Carl
91FrRow/100-58
91FrRow/ItalPromo-9
91FrRow/Premier-40
91FrRow/Up-68
91ProC/CBA-81
91WildCard/Coll-32
Thomas, Charles
91F/Up-281
91FrRow/100-57
91FrRow/ItalPromo-10
91FrRow/Premier-41
91FrRow/Up-67
91Piston/Unocal-16M
Thomas, Doug
91Classic/DPColl*-146
Thomas, Eric
91GATech*-21
Thomas, Eric
91NM-17
Thomas, Frank
87Auburn/Pol*-2
Thomas, Henry
90LSU/200*-105
Thomas, Henry
91KY/BB-12
Thomas, Irving
89KY/300*-53
91ProC/CBA-63
Thomas, Isiah
83Star/ASG-11
83Star/NBA-94
84Star/ASG-11
84Star/Award-12
84Star/CrtKg-30
84Star/NBA-261
84Star/NBA-287
84Star/PolASG-11
85Prism-6
85Star/Crunch-6
85Star/LiteAS-6
85Star/NBA-11
85Star/TmSuper-DP1
86F-109
86F/Ins-10
86Star/CrtKg-28
87F-106
87IN/GreatII-30
88F-45
88F/Ins-10
88Fourn-7
88Fourn/St-9
89F-50
89F/AS-6
89Hoops-177AS
89Hoops-250
90F-61
90F/AS-6
90Hoops-111
90Hoops-11AS
90Hoops/CollB-23
90Hoops/II-389
90Hoops/Super-27
90Panini-87
90Panini-FAS
90Piston/Star-12
90Piston/Unocal-11
90Piston/Unocal-12
90SkyBox-93
91F-64
91F/School-2
91Hoops/ASMVP-7
91Hoops/I-66
91Hoops/II-464SC
91Hoops/II-510Ar
91Hoops/McDon-14
91Hoops/Super-31
91Panini-125
91Panini-97AS
91Piston/Unocal-10
91Piston/Unocal-11
91Piston/Unocal-15M
91SkyBox/Blister-6M
91SkyBox/I-88
91SkyBox/II-412GF
91SkyBox/II-466TW
91UD-333
91UD-91TC
91UD/Ext-451AS
91WildCard/Coll-7
92F-255PV
92F-69
92F/AS-11
92F/TmLeader-8
92Hoops/I-303AS
92Hoops/I-68
92SkyBox/I-289TT
92SkyBox/I-73
Thomas, J.T.
90FLSt/200*-143
90FLSt/200*-151
Thomas, Jimmy
83Star/NBA-166
84Star/NBA-61
87IN/GreatII-25
89ProC/CBA-30
Thomas, John
91CT/Legend-13
Thomas, Kurt
82INSt/Pol*-13
Thomas, Pat
91TexAM-61
Thomas, Ron
75T-277
88Louville/194-62
89Louville/300*-223
89Louville/300*-247
Thomas, Skeets
91SC/200*-132
Thomas, Stan
91Classic/DPColl*-120
Thomas, Thurman
91OKSt*-3
91OKSt*-68
91OKSt*-78
91OKSt*-81
91OKSt*-86
91OKSt*-93
Thomas, Traci
91TexAM-88
Thompson, Bernard
84Blaz/Franz-10
84Blaz/Pol-3
84Star/NBA-169
87Suns/Circ-9
91ProC/CBA-49
Thompson, Billy
83Louville-55
88Louville/194-10
88Louville/194-110
88Louville/194-165
88Louville/194-186
89Heat/Publix-14
89Hoops-59
89Louville/300*-257
89Louville/300*-291
89Louville/300*-300
89Louville/300*-35
90F-103
90Heat/Publix-13
90Hoops-171B
90Hoops-172A
90Panini-155
90SkyBox-154
91Panini-153
91SkyBox/I-154
91UD-196
Thompson, Brooks
91OKSt-12
91OKSt-54
Thompson, Camille
91WASt-10M
Thompson, Charles
82TCMA/CBA-65
Thompson, Clarence
90ProC/CBA-24
Thompson, Corny
91CT/Legend-14
Thompson, David
76T-110
77Dell-5
77Pep/AS-7
77T-60
78RCCola-30
78T-100
79T-50
80T-108
80T-44
81T-12
81T-49M
83Star/ASG-22
89NCSt/Coke-164
89NCSt/Coke-165
89NCSt/Coke-166
92Crtside/ColFB-37
Thompson, Don
(Zippy)
90MISt/200*-52
Thompson, Donnell
90NC/200*-21
Thompson, George
71Bucks/Linn-9
71T-202
72T-221
73T-185
74T-174
74T-225M
75T-144
Thompson, Glen
91SC/200*-120
Thompson, Harold
89NCSt/Coke-116
89NCSt/Coke-117
89NCSt/Coke-118
Thompson, Harvey
81AZ/Pol-18
83AZ/Pol-14
Thompson, Homer
89KY/300*-238
Thompson, Jack
91SC/200*-62
Thompson, Jerry
86IN/GreatI-29
Thompson, Jody
90KY/ClassA-17
Thompson, John
90KY/Sov-16
Thompson, John A.
68HOF-42CO
Thompson, John R.
81George/Pol-18
82George/Pol-1CO
83George/Pol-1CO
84George/Pol-1CO
85George/Pol-2CO
86George/Pol-2CO
87George/Pol-2CO
88George/Pol-2CO
89George/Pol-2CO
90George/Pol-14CO
91George/100-1CO
91George/100-25
91George/100-48
91George/100-58
91George/100-89
91George/Pol-18CO
91Providence-12
Thompson, Justin
91Classic/DPColl*-78
Thompson, Kevin
89NCSt/Pol-12
90NCSt/IBM-12
91NCSt/IBM-14
Thompson, LaSalle
83Star/NBA-226
84Star/NBA-277
85Kings/Smok-13
85Star/NBA-78
86F-110
86Kings/Smok-12
87F-107
88Fourn-31
89Hoops-281
90F-83
90Hoops-140
90Panini-112
90SkyBox-123
91F-87
91Hoops/I-89
91Panini-134
91SkyBox/I-119
91UD-218
92F-95
92Hoops/I-96
92SkyBox/I-101
Thompson, Leonard
91OKSt*-48
Thompson, Mark

89McNees*-11
Thompson, M.C.
86DePaul-C6
Thompson, Mychal
79Blaz/Pol-43
79T-63
81Blaz/Pol-43
81T-36
81T-61M
82Blaz/Pol-43
83Blaz/Pol-43
83Star/NBA-106
84Blaz/Franz-11
84Blaz/Pol-13
84Star/Blaz-4
84Star/NBA-170
85Blaz/Franz-11
85Star/NBA-109
86F-111
87F-108
88F-69
89Blaz/Franz-19
89F-79
89Hoops-4
90F-95
90Hoops-160
90Panini-2
90SkyBox-141
91Hoops/I-105
91SkyBox/I-142
91UD-150
Thompson, Paul
83Star/NBA-240
Thompson, Robert Lee
(Bobby)
90AZ/125*-113
90AZ/125*-122
90AZ/Promos*-8
Thompson, Ronny
88George/Pol-6
89George/Pol-6
90George/Pol-6
91George/Pol-6
Thompson, Scott
83AZ/Pol-15ACO
83AZ/Pol-18ACO
84AZ/Pol-14CO
Thompson, Shelton
90FLSt/200*-64
Thompson, Stephen
(Stevie)
88Syr/Rich-12
89Syr/Pep-10
89Syr/Pep-4
90ProC/CBA-73
90StarPic-11
91FrRow/100-94
91FrRow/Premier-116
91FrRow/Up-83
91ProC/CBA-52
Thompson, Tim
90NCSt/IBM-14M
Thompson, Weegie
90FLSt/200*-23
Thorn, Rod
70T-167
Thornton, Bob
89Sixers/Kodak-12
90Hoops-232
90SkyBox-219
91SkyBox/I-175
Thornton, Dallas
71Globe-84
Thornton, George
91Classic/DPColl*-132
Thornton, John
91TexAM-30
Thorpe, Otis
84Star/NBA-278
85Kings/Smok-14
85Star/NBA-79
85Star/RTm-7
86Kings/Smok-13
87F-109
88F-99
89F-62
89Hoops-265
90F-74
90Hoops-129
90Hoops/Super-36
90Panini-68
90SkyBox-112A
90SkyBox-112B
91F-80
91Hoops/I-81
91Hoops/II-468SC
91Hoops/II-512Ar
91Hoops/Super-38
91Panini-60
91Providence-21
91SkyBox/Canada-20
91SkyBox/I-108
91SkyBox/I-302
91UD-271
91UD/Ext-474AS
92F-86
92F/AS-23
92Hoops/I-317AS
92Hoops/I-327LL
92Hoops/I-88
92SkyBox/I-93
Thorsson, Arn
91SC/200*-137
Threatt, Sedale
83Star/NBA-10
84Star/NBA-209
85JMS-8
85Star/NBA-7
85Star/TmSuper-PS10
86F-112
87Bulls/Ent-2
87F-110
89Hoops-287
90Hoops-284
90SkyBox-273
90Sonic/Kayo-13
90Sonic/Smok-16
91F-196
91F/Up-304
91Hoops/I-204
91Hoops/II-385
91SkyBox/I-275
91SkyBox/II-609
91SkyBox/II-633
91UD-110
91UD/Ext-492
92F-113
92Hoops/I-114
92SkyBox/I-120
Thurmond, Mark
91TexAM-40
Thurmond, Nate
68T/Test-13
69T-10
69T/Ins-12
70T-111AS
70T-90
71T-131
71T/Ins-7
72T-28
73NBAPA-29
73T-157LL
73T-5
74Nab-21
74T-105
74T-87M
75T-119M
75T-85
81TCMA-29
85Star/Schick-22
91Foot*-16
92Crtside/ColFB-38
Ticco, Milt
89KY/300*-237
Ticknor, Duane
91ProC/CBA-70ACO
Tidrick, Hal
48Bowman-36
Tieman, Rodger
89Louville/300*-89
Tillet, Maurice
48T/Magic*-D12
Tillis, Darren
83Star/NBA-262
Tillman, Clarence
78KY/Food-8
89KY/300*-239
Tillman, Lawyer
87Auburn/Pol*-13
Tillmon, Mark
87George/Pol-14
88George/Pol-14
89George/Pol-14
90ProC/CBA-201
91George/100-11
91George/100-38
91ProC/CBA-2
Timberlake, Aminu
91KY/BB/Double-14
Timberlake, Bob
91MI/56*-51
Timmons, Steve
89Foot*-5
Tinch, Reggie
90GA/Smok-14
Tingle, Jack
88KY/269-33
Tinker, Joe
48T/Magic*-K18
Tinkle, Wayne
91ProC/CBA-123
Tinsley, Gaynell
90LSU/200*-38
Tinsley, George
71Flor/McDon-8
Tisdale, Wayman
86F-113
87F-111
88F-60
88Kings/Carl-23
89F-139
89Hoops-225
89Kings/Carl-23
90F-167
90Hoops-262
90Hoops/CollB-12
90Hoops/II-377TC
90Hoops/Super-85
90Kings/Safe-11
90Panini-40
90SkyBox-251
91F-181
91Hoops/I-187
91Hoops/II-494SC
91Hoops/II-563
91Hoops/Super-85
91Kell/ColGrt-2
91Panini-33
91SkyBox/Canada-41
91SkyBox/I-252
91SkyBox/II-427GF
91SkyBox/II-481TW
91SkyBox/II-562US
91UD-372
92F-199
92Hoops/I-202
92SkyBox/I-216
Tittle, Y.A.
57Union-4
90LSU/200*-3
Tobey, David
68HOF-43
Tofflemire, Joe
90AZ/125*-71
Tolbert, Lynda
90AZSt/200*-114
Tolbert, Ray
83Star/NBA-95
87IN/GreatII-6
Tolbert, Tom
86AZ/Pol-11
87AZ/Pol-13
90Hoops-121
90SkyBox-103
91F-72
91Hoops/I-74
91Panini-7
91SkyBox/I-99
91UD-283
Tolle, Harlan
55Ash-59
Tomberlin, Pat
90FLSt/200*-5
Tomey, Dick
90AZ/Promos*-10CO
90AZ/Promos*-7CO
Tomjanovich, Rudy
71T-91
72T-103
73NBAPA-30
73T-145
74T-146LL
74T-28
74T-88M
75T-123M
75T-2LL
75T-70
76T-66
77T-15
78RCCola-31
78T-58
79T-41
80T-120
80T-32
91MI/56*-52
92F-87CO
92Hoops/I-248CO
92SkyBox/I-264CO
Tompkins, Patrick
89WI/Smok-13
91ProC/CBA-151
Toney, Andrew
83Star/ASG-12
83Star/NBA-11
83Star/Sixers-11
83Star/Sixers-6
84Star/Arena-E9
84Star/ASG-12
84Star/CrtKg-35
84Star/NBA-210
84Star/PolASG-12
85JMS-7
85Star/NBA-8
85Star/TmSuper-PS7
86F-114
86Star/CrtKg-29
Toney, Sedric
83Dayton/Blue-16
90ProC/CBA-165
Toolson, Andy
87BYU-17
90Jazz/Star-8
91SkyBox/I-286
91UD-113
91WildCard/Coll-56
Toomer, Carlos
90KY/Sov-17
91KY/BB-13
91KY/BB/Double-11
Torrance, Jeff
90LSU/200*-164
Torrence, Walt
91UCLA/144-88
Torres, George
81TCMA/CBA-4
Toussaint, Wendy
91VA/Lady-13
Towe, Monte
89NCSt/Coke-167
89NCSt/Coke-168
89NCSt/Coke-169
92Crtside/ColFB-39
Tower, Keith
90NotreDame-7
Tower, Oswald
68HOF-44
Towne, Dave
90AZ/125*-66
Townes, Garland
89KY/300*-240
Townes, Linton
82Blaz/Pol-2
91WildCard/Coll-9
Townsend, Raymond
80TCMA/CBA-16
91UCLA/144-39
Traber, Jim
91OKSt*-90
Trabue, Joe
89Louville/300*-160
Trafton, Todd
90AZ/125*-25
Trahan, Warren
91TexAM-93
Trainor, Kendall
91AR/100*-11
Trapp, George
72T-38
73T-22
74T-76
75T-84
Trapp, John Q.
68Rocket/Jack-12
70T-12
71T-68
Travaglini, Bob
82Nugget/Pol-x
Traynowicz, Mark
84NE/Pol*-1
Treadwell, David
90Clemson/200*-41
Treloar, John
90ProC/CBA-131
91ProC/CBA-21CO
Tresh, Mike
48Kell*-3
Tressler, Jeff
83Dayton/Blue-17
Tresvant, John
69Sonic/Sunb-9
69T-58
70T-126
71T-37
72T-87
73T-26
Tresvant, Sean
91WASt-5
Trevor, Claire
48T/Magic*-J37
Trgovich, Pete
91UCLA/144-40
Tribble, Andy
90Clemson/200*-154
Triplett, Binky
91OKSt-4
91OKSt-52
Triplett, Wally
48T/Magic*-R1
Trippi, Charlie
48Kell*-9A
48Kell*-9B
Triptow, Dick
86DePaul-H3
Tripucka, Kelly
83Star/NBA-85

84Star/ASG-13
84Star/CrtKg-5
84Star/NBA-268
84Star/PolASG-13
85Prism-7
85Star/NBA-17
85Star/TmSuper-DP2
86F-115
86Star/CrtKg-30
87F-112
89F-18
89Hoops-55
90F-21
90Hoops-59
90Hoops/Super-11
90NotreDame-54
90Panini-84
90SkyBox-35
91Hoops/I-25
91SkyBox/I-33
91UD-290
Trost, Gary
87BYU-14
Trott, Bill
89KY/300*-21
Trotter, Kerry
82Marq/Lite-15
Trout, Paul
(Dizzy)
48Kell*-4
Truax, Billy
90LSU/200*-115
Trumpy, Bob
68PartM-12
Truvillion, Troy
91ProC/CBA-155
Tsioropoulos, Lou
57T-57
88KY/269-44
Tuaolo, Esera
91Classic/DPColl*-131
Tubbs, Brig
91Iowa-13
Tucker, Anthony
87George/Pol-15
92Classic/DP-40
Tucker, Bryon
87NCSt/Pol-12
Tucker, Byron (GMason)
92Classic/DP-83
Tucker, Craig
80IL/Arby's-13
81IL/Arby's-13
82TCMA/CBA-47
Tucker, Jack
89KY/300*-257
Tucker, Mark
90SoCal/Smok*-17
Tucker, Trent
83Star/All-R-7
83Star/NBA-69
84Star/NBA-35
85Star/NBA-171
87F-113
88Knick/FrLay-10
89F-105
89Hoops-87
89Knicks/Marine-10
90F-129
90Hoops-208
90SkyBox-193
91F-140
91Hoops/I-143
91Hoops/I-307M
91SkyBox/I-195
91UD-341
Tuliau, Brian
90SoCal/Smok*-18
Tuminello, Joe
90LSU/200*-114
Tunney, Gene
48T/Magic*-A9
81T/Thirst-55M
Tunnicliffe, Tommy
90AZ/125*-12
Tunstall, Sean
89KS/Leesley-52
Turjillo, Maria
90AZSt/200*-169
Turk, Jason
91OKSt-3
91OKSt-48
Turk, Joe
87SWLou/McDag*-10
Turner, Andre
91F/Up-370
91Hoops/II-447
91SkyBox/I-219
91SkyBox/II-652
91UD-134
Turner, Bill
70T-158
Turner, Bobby
88Louville/194-135
88Louville/194-53
89Louville/300*-24
Turner, Clyde
(Bulldog)
48ExhSC-44
Turner, Elston
83Star/NBA-58
84Star/Arena-B9
84Star/NBA-147
85Nugget/Pol-8
85Star/NBA-57
88Nugget/Pol-20
89ProC/CBA-95
Turner, Eric
91Classic/DPColl*-104
Turner, Herschel
89KY/300*-118
Turner, Howard
89NCSt/Coke-119
Turner, Jeff
84Nets/Getty-10
84Star/NBA-199
84Star/NBA-98
86Star/LifeNets-12
89Hoops/II-322
90SkyBox-208
91F/Up-332
91Hoops/II-409
91Hoops/II-545Si
91Hoops/II-564
91SkyBox/I-208
91SkyBox/II-563US
91UD-304
92Hoops/I-166
92SkyBox/I-175
Turner, Joe
84AZ/Pol-15
85AZ/Pol-13
86AZ/Pol-12
87AZ/Pol-14
Turner, John
88George/Pol-12
91F/Up-292
91FrRow/Premier-21
91FrRow/Up-65
91StarPic-57
91UD-11
Turner, John Louisville
88Louville/194-143
88Louville/194-86
89Louville/300*-13
89Louville/300*-224
89Louville/300*-250
Turner, Kenny
88VA/Hardee-12
Turner, Kim
89McNees*-12
Turner, Lana
48T/Magic*-F3
Turner, Landon
86IN/GreatI-22
Turner, Nate
90NE/Pol*-13
Turner, Reginald
89ProC/CBA-70
Turner, Tony
81TCMA/CBA-27
Turner, Travis
85NE/Pol*-4
Turnquist, Dale
91FrRow/100-61
91FrRow/Premier-36
Turpin, Mel
81KY/Sched-14
82KY/Sched-7
83KY/Sched-15
84Star/CrtKg-50
84Star/NBA-213
85Star/NBA-158
86F-116
87KY/Coke-7M
88KY/269-123
88KY/269-146
89Hoops/II-316
89KY/300*-43
89KY/Tm80-42
90Hoops-302
Tuten, Rick
90FLSt/200*-53
Tuttle, Gerald
89NC/Coke-150
90NC/200*-116
Tuttle, Perry
90Clemson/200*-42
Tuttle, Richard
89NC/Coke-151
Tuttle, William
89KY/300*-199
89KY/300*-255
Twardzik, Dave
74T-243
75T-246
75T-287M
76T-42
77Blaz/Pol-13
77T-62
78T-122
79Blaz/Pol-13
80T-115
80T-117
80T-27
80T-65
83Blaz/Pol-x
Tway, Bob
91OKSt*-9
Twitty, Howard
90AZSt/200*-150
Twogood, Forrest
57Union-6
Twyman, Jack
57Kahn's-10
57T-71
58Kahn's-10
59Kahn's-9
60Kahn's-10
61F-42
61F-65
61Kahn's-9
62Kahn's-9
63Kahn's-12
64Kahn's-12
65Kahn's-4
81TCMA-28
92CenterCrt-17
Tyler, Terry
79T-84
80T-102
80T-108
80T-151
80T-20
80T-43
80T-56
81T-MW84
83Star/NBA-96
84Star/NBA-269
85Kings/Smok-15
86Kings/Smok-14
87F-114
88Mavs/BLC-41
88Mavs/CardN-41
91WildCard/Coll-108
Tyra, Charles
55Ash-36
57T-68
81TCMA-40M
88Louville/194-121
88Louville/194-27
89Louville/300*-208
89Louville/300*-225
89Louville/300*-5
Tyson, Sean
89Clemson-15
90Clemson-14
91ProC/CBA-87
Udall, Morris
90AZ/125*-88
Uetake, Yojiro
91OKSt*-43
Underwood, Lovell
89KY/300*-254
Underwood, Paul
55Ash-46
Unger, Garry
74Nab-14
Unglaub, Kurt
90FLSt/200*-129
Unitas, Johnny
81PhilM-8
81T/Thirst-33
89Louville/300*-102
Unseld, Wes
69T-56
69T/Ins-22
70T-5LL
70T-72
70T/Ins-21
71T-95
71T/Ins-35
72Icee-17
72T-175LL
72T-21
73Bullet/Stand-10
73NBAPA-31
73T-176
74T-121
75T-115
75T-133M
75T-4LL
76T-5
77T-75
78RCCola-32
78T-7
79T-65
80T-143
80T-175
80T-31
80T-87
88Louville/194-103
88Louville/194-170
88Louville/194-2
89Hoops-53
89Louville/300*-14
89Louville/300*-207
89Louville/300*-238
89Louville/300*-3
90Hoops-331CO
90Hoops/II-344CO
90SkyBox/II-327CO
91F-209CO
91Hoops/I-247CO
91SkyBox/II-404CO
92F-236CO
92Hoops/I-265CO
92SkyBox/I-281CO
Upchurch, Craig
92Classic/DP-69
92StarPic-41
Uplinger, Harold
54Bullet/Gunth-11
Upshaw, Kelvin
89Hoops-264
90SkyBox-104
91SkyBox/I-64
91UD-248
91WildCard/Coll-106
Urabano, Eddie
90AZSt/200*-139
Urban, Karli
90AZSt/200*-170
Urich, Robert
90FLSt/200*-133
Usevitch, Jim
87BYU-18
87BYU-3
91ProC/CBA-124
Usher, Van
92Classic/DP-70
Vagotis, Christ
89Louville/300*-134
Valen, Victor
87Baylor/Pol*-7
Valentine, Carlton
90MISt/200*-149
Valentine, Darnell
81Blaz/Pol-10
82Blaz/Pol-14
83Blaz/Pol-14
83Star/NBA-107
84Blaz/Franz-12
84Blaz/Pol-4
84Star/Blaz-5
84Star/NBA-171
85Blaz/Franz-12
87F-115
91F-39
91Hoops/I-41
91Panini-123
91SkyBox/I-54
91UD-227
91WildCard/Coll-90
Valentine, Robbie
83Louville-00
88Louville/194-149
88Louville/194-158
88Louville/194-96
Valentine, Ron
81TCMA/CBA-45
Vallely, John
91UCLA/144-50
Valvano, James T.
(Jim)
87NCSt/Pol-13CO
88NCSt/Pol-12CO
89NCSt/Coke-191CO
89NCSt/Coke-192CO
89NCSt/Coke-193CO
89NCSt/Pol-13CO
92Crtside/ColFB-40CO
Van Alstyne, Ben
90MISt/200*-180
Van Arsdale, Dick
68Suns/Carn-10
69Suns/Carn-8
69T-31
70Suns/A1-8A
70Suns/A1-8B
70Suns/Carn-9
70T-45
71T-85
71T/Ins-26
72Icee-18

72T-95
73NBAPA-32
73T-25
74T-160
74T-95M
75Carv-31
75Suns-14
75T-150
76Suns-10
76T-26
81TCMA-10
85Star/Schick-23
87IN/GreatII-14M

Van Arsdale, Tom
68PartM-14
69T-79
70T-145
70T/Ins-23
71T-75
71T/Ins-12
72T-79
73NBAPA-33
73T-146
74T-20
74T-94M
75T-7
76Suns-11
76T-99
85Star/Schick-24
87IN/GreatII-14M

Van Bever, Mark
91SC/200*-87

Van Brandt, Yvonne
91TexAM-79

Van Breda Kolff, Bill
70Suns/Carn-10CO

Van Breda Kolff, Jan
75T-307
77T-109
79T-123
80T-146
80T-58

Van Brocklin, Norm
81T/Thirst-31

Van Buren, Steve
48ExhSC-45
90LSU/200*-161

Van Dyke, David
89UTEP/Drug-24

Van Eman, Lanny
91ProC/CBA-33CO

Van Lier, Norm
70T-97
71T-143LL
71T-19
71T/Ins-45
72T-111
73T-31
74T-140AS
74T-84M
75Carv-32
75T-119M
75T-155
76Buck-19
76T-108
77Bulls/WhHen-7
77T-4
78RCCola-33
78T-102
90Bulls/Eq-15

Van Note, Jeff
89KY/300*-172

Van Pelt, Brad
90MISt/200*-11
90MISt/200*-92M

Van Raaphorst, Jeff
90AZSt/200*-51

Van Soelen, Greg
89ProC/CBA-16

Vance, Ellis
(Gene)
48Bowman-20
52Bread-30

Vance, Van
81Louville/Pol-12ANN
88Louville/194-193M

Vandeweghe, Kiki
82Nugget/Pol-55
83Nugget/Pol-55
83Star/ASG-23
83Star/NBA-181
84Blaz/Franz-13
84Blaz/Pol-16
84Star/ASG-25
84Star/CrtKg-46
84Star/NBA-161
84Star/PolASG-25
85Blaz/Franz-13
85Star/NBA-103
86Blaz/Franz-12
86F-117
86Star/CrtKg-31
87Blaz/Franz-11
87Blaz/Franz-13
87F-116
88Blaz/Franz-13
88Knick/FrLay-11
89F-106
89Hoops-295
89Knicks/Marine-11
90Hoops-209
90SkyBox-194
91F-141
91Hoops/I-144
91Panini-164
91SkyBox/I-196
91UCLA/144-14
91UD-323

Vandiver, Shaun
91FrRow/Premier-93BC
91StarPic-62

Vann, Kayode
89George/Pol-8
90George/Pol-2

Vanoostveen, Genevieve
90UCLA-25

Vargas, Jose
86LSU/Pol*-13
87LSU/Pol*-3

Varoscak, John
89Louville/300*-83

Vary, Richard
90MISt/200*-165

Vasquez, Richie
87LSU/Pol*-13

Vaughn, Dave
75T-287M

Vaughn, Eric
89Louville/300*-188

Vaughn, Jon
91Classic/DPColl*-221

Vaught, Loy
88MI/Nike-15
89MI-11
90Clip/Star-12
90F/Up-U42
90StarPic-37
91F/Up-299
91Hoops/II-381
91SkyBox/I-132
91SkyBox/II-443SM
91UD-138
91UD/Rook-8
92F-105
92Hoops/I-106
92SkyBox/I-112

Vayda, Jerry
89NC/Coke-127

Venable, Clinton
91FrRow/100-87
91FrRow/Premier-6
91FrRow/Up-95

Venable, Jerry
71Globe-49
71Globe-56

Venson, Michael
91JMadison/Smok-12

Ventura, Robin
91OKSt*-4

Verderber, Chuck
78KY/Food-9
79KY/Food-9
88KY/269-116

Verga, Bob
71T-167
71T/Ins-6A

Verhoeven, Peter
81Blaz/Pol-31
82Blaz/Pol-31
83Blaz/Pol-31
83Star/NBA-108
84Star/NBA-279

Veripapa, Andy
48ExhSC-46

Verner, Andrew
91Classic/DPColl*-30

Verplank, Scott
91OKSt*-38

Versace, Dick
89Hoops-292CO
90Hoops-315CO
90SkyBox/II-311CO

Vetrie, Guy
85Victoria/Pol-16CO
88Victoria/Pol-16CO

Viana, Joao
91FrRow/100-55
91FrRow/Premier-43
91FrRow/Up-66

Vickers, Martha
48T/Magic*-F21

Vidnovic, Nick
90NC/200*-196

Vilcheck, Al
88Louville/194-137
88Louville/194-59
89Louville/300*-246

Villa, Danny
90AZSt/200*-45

Vincent, Jay
83Star/NBA-59
84Star/Arena-B10
84Star/NBA-260
85Star/NBA-165
86F-118
88F-38
89Hoops-191
89Hoops/II-345
90Hoops-161
90MISt/200*-123
90MISt/200*-192
91WildCard/Coll-70

Vincent, Mike
90LSU/200*-139

Vincent, Ron
87SWLou/McDag*-12

Vincent, Sam
88Bulls/Ent-11
89Hoops-149
89Hoops/II-328
89Magic/Pep-7
90F-137
90Hoops-223A
90Hoops-223B
90Hoops/Super-69
90MISt/200*-148
90MISt/200*-198
90SkyBox-209
91F/Up-333
91Hoops/I-154
91SkyBox/I-209
91UD-232
92Hoops/I-167
92SkyBox/I-176

Vinson, Fred
91GATech/Pol-14

Virgil, John
89NC/Coke-183

Vitiello, Joe
91Classic/DPColl*-55

Vlahogeorge, John
81AZ/Pol-19

Voce, Gary
90ProC/CBA-115

Vogel, Paul
91SC/200*-164

Voight, Larry
90NC/200*-188

Voight, Mike
90NC/200*-171
90NC/200*-77

Volkov, Alexander
90Hoops-34
90SkyBox-9
91F/Up-246
91Hoops/II-337
91SkyBox/II-618
91UD/Ext-411

Volmar, Doug
90MISt/200*-115

Vonesh, David
91ND*-1M

Von Kolnitz, Fritz
91SC/200*-56

Vosberg, Ed
90AZ/125*-70

Voskuil, James
88MI/Nike-16
89MI-10

Vranes, Danny
83Sonic/Pol-11
83Star/NBA-201
84Star/NBA-123
85Star/NBA-71
91WildCard/Coll-51

Vrankovic, Stojko
91F/Up-251
91Hoops/II-341
91SkyBox/I-22
91UD-103

Vroman, Brett
80TCMA/CBA-38

Vucurevic, Kris
91NE/Pol*-22

Vulich, George
89KY/300*-275

Wachtel, John
90FLSt/200*-108

Waddell, Charles
89NC/Coke-184
90NC/200*-180

Wade, Bob
88MD/Pol-11CO

Wade, Butch
91WildCard/Coll-59

Wade, Chris
91SC/200*-17

Wade, Mark
89ProC/CBA-53
90ProC/CBA-33

Wade, Sparky
90LSU/200*-62

Wadiak, Steve
91SC/200*-98

Wadleslaw
48T/Magic*-D24

Wagener, Melanee
91VA/Lady-14

Waggoner, Gil
89Louville/300*-212

Wagner, Hans
48T/Magic*-K11

Wagner, Kirk
89KS/Leesley-50

Wagner, Milt
81Louville/Pol-22
83Louville-20
88Louville/194-108
88Louville/194-166
88Louville/194-8
89Louville/300*-17
89Louville/300*-235
89Louville/300*-258
89Louville/300*-46
90ProC/CBA-135
90SkyBox/II-393

Wagner, Phil
91GATech*-177

Wagner, Sheila
91GATech*-60

Wagner, Sidney P.
90MISt/200*-32

Wagner, Steve
79Bucks/OpenP-12

Wahl, Kory
91ND*-12M

Wainwright, Jonathan
48T/Magic*-O6

Waiters, Granville
83Star/NBA-167
84Star/NBA-62
87Bulls/Ent-7

Waites, Gary
91FrRow/100-67
91FrRow/Premier-29
91FrRow/Up-88
91ProC/CBA-105
91StarPic-52

Wakefield, Andre
80TCMA/CBA-37

Wakefield, Dick
48Kell*-5

Wakely, Jimmy
48T/Magic*-J22

Waldan, Alan
90AZSt/200*-136

Walden, Bo
91MurraySt-10

Waldman, H.
90UNLV/HOF-13
90UNLV/Season-13
90UNLV/Smok-15

Walk, Neal
69Suns/Carn-9
69T-46
70Suns/A1-9A
70Suns/A1-9B
70Suns/Carn-11
70T-87
71T-9
72T-82
73T-98
74T-17
74T-95M
75T-19

Walker, Brady
52Bread-31

Walker, Chet
68T/Test-3
69T-91
70Bulls/Hawth-3
70T-4LL
70T-60
70T/Ins-14
71T-141LL
71T-66
71T/Ins-33
72T-152
73NBAPA-34
73T-45
74Nab-23
74T-171
74T-84M
75Carv-33
75Nab-23

75T-119M
90Bulls/Eq-16
Walker, Clarence
(Foots)
78T-127
79T-42
80T-101
80T-13
80T-161
80T-29
81T-E83
83Star/NBA-155
Walker, Darrell
82AR-16
83Star/NBA-70
84Star/NBA-36
85Star/NBA-172
87F-117
89F-161
89Hoops-134
90F-196
90Hoops-303
90Hoops/Super-98
90Panini-147
90SkyBox-293
91AR/100*-85
91F/Up-282
91Hoops/I-219
91Hoops/II-363
91Hoops/Super-100
91Panini-176
91Piston/Unocal-12
91SkyBox/I-295
91SkyBox/I-304
91SkyBox/II-627
91UD-367
91UD/Ext-403
92F-70
92Hoops/I-69
92SkyBox/I-74
Walker, Daryll
91ProC/CBA-50
Walker, Doak
48T/Magic*-C3
Walker, Earl
89ProC/CBA-22
Walker, Horace
90MISt/200*-193
Walker, Jimmy
69T-8
70T-25
71T-90
71T/Ins-16
72T-124
73T-61
74T-45
74T-89M
75T-31
76T-92
91AR/100*-18
91Providence-14
Walker, Joyce
90LSU/200*-53
Walker, J. Rice
89KY/300*-278
Walker, Kenny
83KY/Sched-16
87KY/Coke-2
88F-83
88Knick/FrLay-12
88KY/269-11
88KY/269-147
88KY/269-153
88KY/269-197
89Hoops-3
89Knicks/Marine-12
89KY/300*-5
89KY/Tm80-40
90F-130
90Hoops-210
90NE/Pol*-4
90Panini-143
90SkyBox-195
91Hoops/I-145
91Hoops/SlamD-5
91SkyBox/I-197
91UD-347
Walker, Kevin
91UCLA/144-32
Walker, Marielle
91GATech*-40
Walker, Pam
90UCLA-20CO
Walker, Ricky
81AZ/Pol-20
Walker, Sean
91OKSt-50
91OKSt-51
91OKSt-7
Walker, Toraino
90CT/Pol-14
91CT/Pol-15
Walker, Wally
78Sonic/Pol-10
79Sonic/Pol-10
81T-W100
83Star/NBA-84
Wallace, Grady
91SC/200*-73
Wallace, Joe
90ProC/CBA-200
Wallace, Roosevelt
91AR25-16
Walling, Denny
90Clemson/200*-197
Walls, Kevin
89Louville/300*-268
Walsh, David H.
68HOF-45
Walsh, Donnie
89NC/Coke-154
90NC/200*-198
Walsh, Jim
91SC/200*-145
Walter, Jenny
91ND*-8M
Walters
90Clemson/200*-61M
Walters, Raymond
89NCSt/Coke-126
89NCSt/Coke-127
89NCSt/Coke-128
Walters, Rex
91KS-14
Walters, Trent
89Louville/300*-135
Walton, Bill
74T-39
75T-77
76T-57
77Blaz/Pol-32
77Dell-6
77Pep/AS-8
77T-120
78RCCola-34
78T-1
79T-45
80T-127
80T-46
83Star/NBA-121
84Star/CrtKg-9
84Star/NBA-22
85JMS-10
85Star/NBA-101
86F-119
86Star/Best-8
89Blaz/Franz-20
90Blaz/Franz-6
91UCLA/144-3
91UCLA/144-30
91UCLA/144-62
91UCLA/144-83
92Crtside/ColFB-41
Walton, Lloyd
77Bucks/ActPh-9
79Bucks/Pol-11
Wangler, John
91MI/56*-53
Wanzer, Bobby
57Kahn's-11
92CenterCrt-3
Ward, Dixon
91ND*-14M
Ward, Joe
90ProC/CBA-76
Ward, John
91OKSt*-54
Ware, Jeff
91Classic/DPColl*-81
Warford, Reggie
88KY/269-107
Warlick, Bob
68Suns/Carn-11
Warmenhoven, Joey
91WASt-6
Warmerdam, Cornelius
48T/Magic*-E13
Warner, Cornell
71Bucks/Linn-10
72T-59
73T-12
74T-109
75T-72
Warner, Graylin
91WildCard/Coll-29
Warren, Alfred
91AR25-17
Warren, Anthony
89NCSt/Coke-123
89NCSt/Coke-124
Warren, Bob
73T-196
73T-237LL
75T-313
Warren, Jeff
89MO-16
90MO-16
91MO-16
Warren, John
70T-91
71T-118
72T-64
Warren, Mike
91UCLA/144-11
Warren, Scott
90FLSt/200*-119
Warren, Terry
90FLSt/200*-45
Warrick, Bryan
83Star/NBA-215
84Star/NBA-23
Washburn, Chris
87Hawks/Pizza-13
Washington, Don
75T-267
Washington, Duane
(Pearl)
88F-71
89Hoops-101
89ProC/CBA-145
89ProC/CBA-31
90ProC/CBA-173
91ProC/CBA-136
Washington, Eugene
90MISt/200*-23
Washington, Jim
69T-17
70T-14
71T-28
72T-22
73T-87
74T-41
75T-172
Washington, John
91OKSt*-94
Washington, Kenny
91UCLA/144-72
Washington, Kermit
74T-166
78Clipp/Handy-8
78T-16
79Blaz/Pol-42
79T-128
80T-10
80T-150
80T-167
80T-77
81Blaz/Pol-42
81T-61M
81T-W89
Washington, Mickey
91TexAM-22
Washington, Norman
81George/Pol-8
Washington, Richard
77T-78
78T-121
79Bucks/Pol-31
80T-105
80T-75
91UCLA/144-22
Washington, Rodney
87South/Pol*-8
Washington, Stan
90MISt/200*-113
Washington, Tom
72T-240
72T-260LL
73T-182
Waterfield, Bob
48ExhSC-47
48Kell*-10
57Union-27
Waterman, Shawn
79StBon-16
Waters, Charlie
90Clemson/200*-104
Wathen, Glen
90KY/ClassA-8
Watkins, Curtis
86DePaul-D6
Watkins, Earl
87SWLou/McDag*-2
Watrous, Francis
55Ash-72
Watson, Allen
91Classic/DPColl*-67
Watson, Bobby
88KY/269-36
Watson, Lou
86IN/GreatI-9
Watt, Jim
90MISt/200*-127
Watters, Ricky
91Classic/DPColl*-141
Watts, Craig T.
89NCSt/Coke-129
89NCSt/Coke-131
89NCSt/Coke-45
Watts, Don
(Slick)
74T-142
75T-132M
75T-59
76T-105
77T-51
Watts, Joey
90Clemson-15
Watts, Walter
91ProC/CBA-104
Waukau, Merv
86SWLou/Pol*-16
Wawrzyniak, Mike
88MO-16
Wayne, Gary
91MI/56*-54
Weakly, Paul
90ProC/CBA-4
Weatherly, Shawn
90Clemson/200*-162
Weatherspoon, Clarence
92Classic/DP-28
92Classic/DPLP-LP9
92FrRow/DreamPk-21
92FrRow/DreamPk-22
92FrRow/DreamPk-23
92FrRow/DreamPk-24
92FrRow/DreamPk-25
92StarPic-68KC
92StarPic-7
92StarPic-81
Weatherspoon, Nick
73Bullet/Stand-11
74T-61
75T-48
78Clipp/Handy-2
79T-61
Weaver, Dean
91GATech*-41
Webb, Anthony
(Spud)
86F-120
87Hawks/Pizza-14
88F-4
88Fourn-10
89F-6
89Hoops-115A
89Hoops-115B
89NCSt/Coke-132
89NCSt/Coke-133
89NCSt/Coke-134
90F-5
90Hoops-35
90Hoops/CollB-24
90Hoops/Super-3
90Panini-118
90SkyBox-10
91F-4
91F/Up-352
91Hoops/I-6
91Hoops/II-431
91Hoops/SlamD-3
91Hoops/Super-3
91Kell/ColGrt-15
91Panini-105
91SkyBox/I-9
91SkyBox/II-646
91UD-251
91UD/Ext-419
92F-200
92Hoops/I-203
92SkyBox/I-217
92SkyBox/I-304TT
Webb, Jay
91Iowa-14
Webb, Ricky
89NC/Coke-197
Webb, Richard S. Jr.
89KY/300*-151
Webb, Tammy
90AZSt/200*-66
Weber, Bill
84NE/Pol*-6
Weber, Don
91George/100-80
Weber, Jerry
55Ash-83
Weber, Kathy
91WASt-10M
Webster, Demone
90ProC/CBA-144
90ProC/CBA-25
91ProC/CBA-58
Webster, George
90MISt/200*-88

Webster, Marvin
77T-71
78RCCola-35
78T-19
79T-88
80T-152
80T-64
81T-E87
83Star/NBA-71
Wedman, Scott
75T-89
76T-142
77T-17
78RCCola-36
78T-79
79T-7
80T-130
80T-42
81T-19
83Star/NBA-36
84Star/Arena-A8
84Star/NBA-11
85JMS-17
85Star/NBA-102
Weems, Kelsey
87NCSt/Pol-14
88NCSt/Pol-13
90ProC/CBA-101
91ProC/CBA-53
Wegrich, Rosie
90AZ/125*-29
Weil, Randy
90NC/200*-55
Weiner, Art
90NC/200*-119
Weir, Murray
48ExhSC-48
48T/Magic*-B2
Weiss, Bob
69T-62
70Bulls/Hawth-4
70Bulls/Hawth-5
70T-16
71T-128
72T-141
73T-132
74T-33
90Hoops-305CO
90Hoops/II-346CO
90SkyBox/II-301CO
91F-5CO
91Hoops/I-221CO
91SkyBox/II-378CO
92F-7CO
92Hoops/I-239CO
92SkyBox/I-255CO
Welborne, Tripp
91MI/56*-55
Welch, Anthony
81IL/Arby's-14
Wellman, Bob
89Louville/300*-218
Wellman, Gary
90SoCal/Smok*-19
Wells, Cheron
90Clemson/Lady-14
Wells, Dana
90AZ/125*-31
Wells, Kelly
90KY/Sov-18
Wells, Tony
81TCMA/CBA-69
Welp, Christian
89F-118
89Hoops-164
89Hoops/II-331
90Hoops-122
Wennington, Bill
88Mavs/BLC-23
88Mavs/CardN-23
89Hoops-81
90Hoops-89
90Hoops/II-431
90Kings/Safe-12
90SkyBox-68
90SkyBox/II-412
91SkyBox/I-253
91UD-399
91WildCard/Coll-61
Werdann, Robert
92Classic/DP-59
92StarPic-76
Werenka, Darcy
91Classic/DPColl*-33
Wernke, Paul
90FLSt/200*-192
Wesenhahn, Bob
61Kahn's-10
Weshinskey, Kris
90MISt-12
Wesley, Walt
69T-22
70T-55
71T-52
71T/Ins-4
72T-109
73Bullet/Stand-12
73T-118
74T-143
Wessel, Joe
90FLSt/200*-62
West, Brian
79StBon-17
West, Chris
83Louville-23
88Louville/194-139
88Louville/194-74
89Louville/300*-296
West, Dick
91UCLA/144-97
West, Doug
90F/Up-U58
90SkyBox/II-397
91F/Up-321
91Hoops/II-397
91SkyBox/I-176
91UD-269
91UD/Ext-483SD
92F-139
92Hoops/I-142
92SkyBox/I-149
92SkyBox/I-297TT
West, Freeman
89KS/Leesley-43
West, Jerry
60Kahn's-11
61F-43
61F-66IA
61Kahn's-11
61Lakers/Bell-9
62Kahn's-10
63Kahn's-13
68T/Test-19
69T-90
69T/Ins-2
70T-107AS
70T-160
70T-1LL
70T-2LL
70T/Ins-15
71T-143LL
71T-50
71T/Ins-31
72Icee-19
72T-158
72T-164AS
72T-176LL
72T-75
73T-100AS
74T-176
81TCMA-32
90MISt/200*-46
91UD/Hero/West-Set
91UD/Hero/WestWax-Set
West, Mark
83Star/NBA-60
84Star/Arena-B11
84Star/NBA-223
88F-91
89F-125
89Hoops-228
90F-153
90Hoops-242
90Panini-15
90SkyBox-230
91F-165
91Hoops/I-170
91Hoops/Super-79
91Panini-22
91SkyBox/I-231
91UD-115
92F-183
92Hoops/I-186
92SkyBox/I-197
Westhead, Paul
90Hoops/II-422CO
90SkyBox/II-307CO
91F-53CO
91Hoops/I-227CO
91SkyBox/II-384CO
Weston, Al
90MISt/200*-166
Westphal, Paul
73T-126
74T-64
75Carv-34
75Suns-15
75T-186
76Suns-12
76T-55
77Suns/Discs-44
77T-10
78RCCola-37
78T-120
79T-30AS
80T-123
80T-133
80T-149
80T-21
80T-38
80T-7
80T-83
80T-95
81T-W101
83Star/NBA-120
84Suns/Pol-44
92Crtside/ColFB-42
92F-184CO
92Hoops/I-259CO
92SkyBox/I-275CO
Wetherell, T.K.
90FLSt/200*-139
Wettstein, Max
90FLSt/200*-137
Wetzel, John
70Suns/A1-10
73T-72
74T-77
75Suns-16
87Suns/Circ-10CO
90Blaz/Franz-8M
Whalen, Ellis
84Victoria/Pol-15
Whatley, Ennis
83Star/NBA-178
84Star/NBA-111
90ProC/CBA-120
Wheatley, Bruce
85AZ/Pol-14
90ProC/CBA-32
Wheeler, Clint
89KY/300*-93
Wheeler, Erika
91WASt-7M
Wherry, Dan
89NCSt/Coke-158
89NCSt/Coke-160
Whisnant, Art
91SC/200*-156
Whitaker, Lucian
88KY/269-61
Whitaker, Steve
91Classic/DPColl*-79
White, Chuckie
91ProC/CBA-119
White, Danny
90AZSt/200*-135
90AZSt/200*-61
White, Devon
88Foot*-9
White, Greg
89GATech/Pol-18
90GATech/Pol-19
91GATech/Pol-15
White, Jo Jo
70T-143
71T-69
71T/Ins-5
72T-45
73NBAPA-35
73T-168
74Nab-19
74T-27
74T-82M
75Carv-35
75T-117M
75T-135AS
76Buck-20
76T-115
77T-35
78RCCola-38
78T-85
79T-11
White, John
87SoMiss-6
White, Kevin
91SC/200*-21
White, Linda
90Clemson/200*-183
White, Lorenzo
90MISt/200*-19
90MISt/200*-31
90MISt/200*-86
90MISt/Promos*-6
White, Lyman
90LSU/200*-34
White, Peter
55Ash-95
White, Randy
90F-44
90F/Up-U23
90FLSt/200*-3
90SkyBox-69
91F-47
91Hoops/II-353
91Panini-47
91SkyBox/I-65
91SkyBox/II-491RS
91UD-105
92Hoops/I-52
92SkyBox/I-55
White, Rory
84Star/NBA-24
85Star/NBA-93
White, Rudy
81TCMA/CBA-18
White, Tony
89ProC/CBA-158
White, Vincent
71Globe-61
71Globe-62
White, Walter
89KY/300*-251
White, Whizzer
90AZSt/200*-168
White, Willie
84Star/NBA-148
85Nugget/Pol-11
Whitehead, Bud
90FLSt/200*-179
Whitehead, Eddie
88Louville/194-52
Whitehead, Jerome
78Clipp/Handy-7
80T-105
80T-17
83Star/NBA-132
84Star/NBA-159
85Star/NBA-137
Whitehouse, Donald
55Ash-60
Whitewell, Mike
91TexAM-76
Whitey, Jay
90LSU/200*-118
Whitfield, Ike
89Louville/300*-71
Whitfield, Mal
57Union-18
Whitley, Roland
89NCSt/Pol-14
Whitmore, Bob
90NotreDame-35
Whitmore, David
88GATech/Nike-12
Whitney, Charles
89NCSt/Coke-138
89NCSt/Coke-139
89NCSt/Coke-140
Whitney, Dave
90ProC/CBA-132
91ProC/CBA-23ACO
Whitney, Eli
48T/Magic*-N1
Whitney, Ray
91Classic/DPColl*-20
Whitsell, Jerry
55Ash-84
Whittaker, George
89ProC/CBA-181
Whittenburg, Dereck
89NCSt/Coke-141
89NCSt/Coke-142
89NCSt/Coke-71
92Crtside/ColFB-43
Whitton, Stefni
87SWLou/McDag*-15
Wickersham, Jeff
90LSU/200*-151
Wicks, Sidney
72Icee-20
72T-20
73T-160
74T-175
74T-96M
75T-131M
75T-40
76T-31
77T-52
78Clipp/Handy-4
78T-109
79T-16
91UCLA/144-16
91UCLA/144-52
92Crtside/ColFB-44
Wiegert, Erik
91NE/Pol*-7
Wiel, Randy
89NC/Coke-158
Wiggins, Mitchell
83Star/NBA-179
84Star/NBA-249
85Star/NBA-25
90F-75
90Hoops-130

90Panini-72
90SkyBox-113
91Hoops/II-415
91SkyBox/II-640
Wight, Laura
85NE/Pol*-30
Wilcox, Derrick
87Vanderbilt/Pol-9
Wilder, Brent
90ORSt-18ACO
91ORSt-18ACO
Wiley, Morlon
88Mavs/BLC-20
88Mavs/CardN-20
89Hoops-247
89Hoops/II-301
91Hoops/II-410
91UD-26
Wilfong, Win
57T-65
59Kahn's-10
60Kahn's-12
Wilhelm, Bill
90Clemson/200*-106
Wilhelm, Hoyt
81T/Thirst-4
Wilkens, Len
61F-44
68T/Test-15
69Sonic/Sunb-10
69T-44
70Sonic/Sunb-9
70T-6LL
70T-80
71Sonic/Sunb-10
71T-80
72T-176LL
72T-81
73NBAPA-36
73T-158LL
73T-165
74T-149LL
74T-85M
78Sonic/Pol-12CO
79Sonic/Pol-16CO
81TCMA-11
83Sonic/Pol-16
85Star/CO-10
89Hoops-216CO
90Hoops-309CO
90Hoops/II-349CO
90SkyBox/II-305CO
91F-41CO
91Hoops/I-225CO
91Hoops/II-586CO
91Providence-7
91SkyBox/II-382CO
91SkyBox/II-543US
92F-45CO
92Hoops/I-243CO
92SkyBox/I-259CO
92SkyBox/USA-97CO
92SkyBox/USA-98CO
Wilkerson, Bobby
78T-41
79T-67
80T-118
80T-57
81T-MW70
86IN/GreatI-12
Wilkes, Del
91SC/200*-91
Wilkes, Keith
(Jamaal)
75T-50
76T-16
77T-33
78T-3
79T-35
80T-123
80T-7
81T-23
82Lakers/BASF-11
83Lakers/BASF-12
83Star/ASG-24
83Star/NBA-24
84Star/NBA-183
85JMS-21
85Star/NBA-94
85Star/ROY-11
91UCLA/144-37
91UCLA/144-73
Wilkes, James
91UCLA/144-13
Wilkins, Dominique
83Star/All-R-8
83Star/NBA-263
84Star/CrtKg-12
84Star/NBA-76
84Star/PolASG-33
84Star/SlamD-9
85Star/Gator-8
85Star/NBA-42
85Star/SlamD-10
85Star/SlamD-8
86F-121
86F/Ins-11
86Star/CrtKg-32
87F-118
87F/Ins-7
87Hawks/Pizza-15
88F-125AS
88F-5
88F/Ins-11
88Fourn-9
89F-165M
89F-7
89Hoops-130
89Hoops-234AS
90F-6
90Hoops-12AS
90Hoops-36
90Hoops/CollB-35
90Hoops/II-355TC
90Hoops/Super-2
90Panini-117
90SkyBox-11
91F-212
91F-6
91F/Up-372TL
91F/Wilkins-Set
91Hoops/I-259AS
91Hoops/I-7
91Hoops/II-449SC
91Hoops/McDon-1
91Hoops/SlamD-2
91Hoops/Super-4
91Panini-101
91SkyBox/I-10
91SkyBox/II-459TW
91SkyBox/II-588
91UD-255
91UD-66AS
91UD-79TC
92F-8
92F/TmLeader-1
92Hoops/I-8
92SkyBox/I-282TT
92SkyBox/I-8
Wilkins, Eddie Lee
84Star/NBA-37
88Knick/FrLay-13
89Knicks/Marine-14
90Hoops-211
90SkyBox-196
91SkyBox/II-409GF
91WildCard/Coll-67
90F/Up-U65
Wilkins, Gerald
86F-122
87F-119
88F-84
88Knick/FrLay-14
89F-107A
89F-107B
89Hoops-63
89Knicks/Marine-13
90F-131
90Hoops-212
90Hoops/Super-65
90Panini-142
90SkyBox-197
91F-142
91Hoops/I-146
91Hoops/II-520Ar
91Panini-161
91SkyBox/I-198
91SkyBox/I-327
91UD-234
91UD-84TC
92F-157
92Hoops/I-159
92SkyBox/I-168
Wilkins, Jeff
81TCMA/CBA-8
83Star/NBA-144
84Star/NBA-236
Wilkinson, Dale
82TCMA/CBA-38
Willard, Jess
48T/Magic*-A7
Willard, Ken
90NC/200*-148
90NC/200*-73
Williams, Alphonso
90FLSt/200*-31
Williams, Art
68Rocket/Jack-13
69T-96
70T-151
72T-19
73T-147
Williams, Benford
92Classic/DP-15
92StarPic-65
Williams, Bernie
68Rocket/Jack-14
70T-122
72T-186
73T-257
Williams, Billy BB
81T/Thirst-15
Williams, Billy
90Clemson/200*-43
Williams, Brian
90FLSt/200*-138
Williams, Brian
89AZ/Pol-13
91Classic-5
91Classic/DPColl*-153
91F/Up-334
91FrRow/Premier-91BC
91FrRow/Up-57
91Hoops/II-555
91SkyBox/II-522LP
91UD/Ext-499
91UD/Rook-35
92F-165
92Hoops/I-168
92SkyBox/I-177
Williams, Brian BB
91SC/200*-144
Williams, Buck
83Star/ASG-13
83Star/NBA-145
84Nets/Getty-11
84Star/CrtKg-6
84Star/NBA-99
85Prism-8
85Star/NBA-58
85Star/ROY-4
86F-123
86Star/LifeNets-13
87F-120
88F-79
88Fourn-25
89Blaz/Franz-11
89F-132
89Hoops-145
89Hoops/II-315
90Blaz/BP-6
90Blaz/Franz-19
90F-160
90Hoops-251
90Hoops/CollB-36
90Panini-9
90SkyBox-240
91Blaz/Franz-15
91Blaz/Franz-3
91F-173
91F-224
91Hoops/I-179
91Hoops/I-313M
91Hoops/McDon-36
91Hoops/Super-83
91Panini-31
91SkyBox/I-242
91SkyBox/II-571
91SkyBox/Proto-242
91UD-353
92F-193
92F-241LL
92Hoops/I-195
92Hoops/I-327LL
92SkyBox/I-207
Williams, Carlo
89Fresno/Smok-14
Williams, Cedric
85FortHaysSt-16
Williams, Charlie
71T-158
72T-231
Williams, Chris
90LSU/200*-88
Williams, Chuck
71T-218
73T-232
73T-239LL
74T-212LL
74T-228M
74T-241
75T-226LL
75T-281M
75T-315
78T-89
Williams, Corey
91OKSt-2
91OKSt-30
91OKSt-53
92Classic/DP-71
92StarPic-87
Williams, Curtis
88VA/Hardee-13
Williams, Dan
89ProC/CBA-205
Williams, Dayne
90FLSt/200*-73
Williams, Del
90FLSt/200*-176
Williams, Dennis
91ProC/CBA-93
Williams, Dianne
91WA/Viacom-17
Williams, Don
(Duck)
90NotreDame-19
Williams, Earl
75T-109
Williams, Eddie
91Classic/DPColl*-91
Williams, Eric
90FLSt/200*-120
Williams, Fly
75T-293
Williams, Freddie
90AZSt/200*-53
Williams, Freeman
78Clipp/Handy-3
80T-161
80T-29
81T-63M
81T-W95
Williams, Gene
69Suns/Carn-10
Williams, Gus
76T-69
77T-89
78Sonic/Pol-11
78T-39
79Sonic/Pol-1
79T-27
80T-163
80T-168
80T-3
80T-40
80T-80
80T-91
83Sonic/Pol-5
83Star/ASG-25
83Star/NBA-202
84Star/CrtKg-40
84Star/NBA-185
85Star/NBA-110
86F-124
Williams, Harvey
91Classic/DPColl*-119
Williams, Henry
92Classic/DP-7
92StarPic-22
Williams, Herb
83Star/NBA-168
84Star/NBA-63
85Star/NBA-87
86F-125
87F-121
88Mavs/CardN-32
89F-37
89Hoops-131
90F-45
90Hoops-90
90Panini-58
90SkyBox-70
91F-48
91Hoops/I-50
91SkyBox/I-66
91UD-320
92Hoops/I-53
92SkyBox/I-56
Williams, Ike
48T/Magic*-A18
90NM-16
91NM-18
Williams, Isaac
90FLSt/200*-22
Williams, Jayson
90F/Up-U73
90StarPic-5
91F/Up-338
91Hoops/II-416
91SkyBox/I-220
91UD-191
91UD/Rook-14
92Hoops/I-177
92SkyBox/I-187
Williams, John
(Hot Rod)
87F-123
88F-26
89F-31
89Hoops-118
90F-37
90Hoops-80
90Hoops/Super-18
90Panini-108
90SkyBox-58

91F-40
91Hoops/I-42
91Hoops/Super-19
91Panini-121
91SkyBox/I-55
91SkyBox/II-409GF
91SkyBox/II-436SM
91UD-249
92F-46
92Hoops/I-44
92SkyBox/I-46

Williams, John S.
86LSU/Pol*-14
87F-122
88F-119
89F-162
89Hoops-254
90Hoops-304
90Hoops/Super-100
90LSU/200*-14
90Panini-146
90SkyBox-294
91Hoops/I-220
91Panini-175
91SkyBox/I-296
91UD-272

Williams, Kenny
90F/Up-U38
91F/Up-295
91Hoops/II-374
91SkyBox/I-120
91UD-211

Williams, Kevin
84Star/NBA-224
88F-72
89McNees*-1

Williams, LaVon
77KY/Wildct-11
78KY/Food-14
79KY/Food-4
88KY/269-112
88KY/269-218

Williams, Larry
88Louville/194-130
88Louville/194-41
89Louville/300*-278

Williams, Leon
89Louville/300*-190

Williams, Micheal
87Baylor/Pol*-4
89Hoops-224
89Hoops/II-344
90F/Up-U39
90SkyBox-36
90SkyBox/II-388
91F-88
91Hoops/I-90
91SkyBox/I-121
91SkyBox/II-496RS
91UD-215
92F-96
92Hoops/I-324LL
92Hoops/I-97
92SkyBox/I-102

Williams, Mike
89ProC/CBA-155
90LSU/200*-64
90ProC/CBA-60

Williams, Monty
90NotreDame-48

Williams, Murray
90CT/Pol-15

Williams, Natalie
90UCLA-32

Williams, Nate
72T-151
73T-54
74T-116
75T-182
76T-88

Williams, Paul
90AZSt/200*-44

Williams, Pete
83AZ/Pol-16
84AZ/Pol-16
85Nugget/Pol-4
90AZ/125*-57

Williams, Ray
78T-129
79T-48
80T-153
80T-65
81T-28
83Star/NBA-72
85JMS-16

Williams, Ray CLEM
90Clemson/200*-102
90Clemson/200*-47

Williams, Reggie
83George/Pol-15
84George/Pol-11
85George/Pol-14
86George/Pol-13
89F-74
89Hoops-128
90Hoops-272
90SkyBox/II-416
91F-54
91George/100-29
91George/100-4
91George/100-53
91George/100-65
91Hoops/I-56
91Panini-55
91SkyBox/I-75
91SkyBox/II-465TW
91UD-206
92F-61
92Hoops/I-61
92SkyBox/I-65

Williams, Ricky
81TCMA/CBA-19

Williams, Rob
82Nugget/Pol-21
83Nugget/Pol-21
83Star/All-R-9
83Star/NBA-192

Williams, Rodney
90Clemson/200*-67

Williams, Ron
(Fritz)
69T-36
70T-8
71T-141LL
71T-38
71T/Ins-29
72T-123
73T-23
75T-198

Williams, Roy
89KS/Leesley-56CO
91KS-15CO

Williams, Sam
83Star/NBA-12
84Star/Arena-E10
84Star/NBA-211
90AZSt/200*-4
90AZSt/Promos*-6
91ProC/CBA-8

Williams, Schwoonda
90LSU/200*-69

Williams, Scott
86NC/Pol-42
87NC/Pol-42
88NC/Pol-42
88NC/Pol-x
88NC/Pol-x
90StarPic-26
91F/Up-259
91Hoops/II-346
91Hoops/McDon-70
91UD-362
92F-37
92Hoops/I-35
92SkyBox/I-36

Williams, Sly
81T-E88
83Star/NBA-274
84Star/NBA-87

Williams, Stan
82TCMA/Lanc-22

Williams, Ted
90MISt/200*-173
90MISt/200*-47M

Williams, Travis
91ProC/CBA-82

Williams, Ulis
90AZSt/200*-117

Williams, Walt
88MD/Pol-12
92Classic/BKPrev-BK4
92Classic/DP-2
92Classic/DPLP-LP7
92FrRow/DreamPk-76
92FrRow/DreamPk-77
92FrRow/DreamPk-78
92FrRow/DreamPk-79
92FrRow/DreamPk-80
92StarPic-36
92StarPic-71

Williamson, Darla
91WASt-11

Williamson, Ernie
90NC/200*-144

Williamson, John
74T-234
75T-251
75T-282M
76T-113
77T-44
78RCCola-39
78T-11
79T-55
80T-129
80T-84

Williford, Jason
91VA-15

Williford, Vann
71T-229
89NCSt/Coke-125
89NCSt/Coke-81
89NCSt/Coke-87

Willingham, Nantambu
91CT/Pol-16

Willis, Kevin
85Star/NBA-48
85Star/RTm-9
86F-126
87F-124
87Hawks/Pizza-16
88F-6
89Hoops-98
90F-7
90Hoops-37
90MISt/200*-119
90MISt/200*-163
90MISt/200*-179
90Panini-119
90SkyBox-12
91F-7
91Hoops/I-8
91Hoops/II-450SC
91Panini-102
91SkyBox/Canada-1
91SkyBox/I-11
91SkyBox/I-325
91SkyBox/I-326
91SkyBox/II-459TW
91UD-278
91UD/Ext-462AS
92F-9
92F/AS-12
92Hoops/I-304AS
92Hoops/I-325LL
92Hoops/I-9
92SkyBox/I-9

Willis, Peter Tom
90FLSt/200*-11
90FLSt/200*-141

Willoughby, Bill
83Star/NBA-156

Wills, Elliott
(Bump)
90AZSt/200*-25

Wilson, Anthony
86LSU/Pol*-16

Wilson, Barry
90LSU/200*-102

Wilson, Ben
89ProC/CBA-2

Wilson, Bill
54Quaker-9

Wilson, Bob
75T-169

Wilson, Bobby
91Classic/DPColl*-116

Wilson, Don
82Fairf-16

Wilson, Eddie
90AZ/125*-115

Wilson, Felix
89KY/300*-146

Wilson, George
(Jif)
64Kahn's-3
68Suns/Carn-12
70T-11
71T-26

Wilson, Imani
90Clemson/Lady-15

Wilson, Jerry
90MurraySt-13
91MurraySt-13

Wilson, Karl
90LSU/200*-31

Wilson, Keith
90ProC/CBA-108
91AR/100*-20
91ProC/CBA-174

Wilson, Marshall
90GA/Smok-15

Wilson, Merlin
91George/100-60
91George/100-96

Wilson, Michael
82TCMA/CBA-72
84Star/NBA-100

Wilson, Nancy
91SC/200*-18

Wilson, Nikita
86LSU/Pol*-15
90LSU/200*-42

Wilson, Othell
84Star/NBA-160
86Kings/Smok-15

Wilson, Otis
89Louville/300*-116

Wilson, Rick
78Hawks/Coke-14
80TCMA/CBA-7
88Louville/194-119
88Louville/194-153
88Louville/194-24
89Louville/300*-21

Wilson, Ricky
89ProC/CBA-135

Wilson, Shawn
91VA-16

Wilson, Trevor
90F/Up-U5
90StarPic-7
91UCLA/144-106

Wilson, Whip
48T/Magic*-J42

Wiltjer, Greg
83Victoria/Pol-14
89ProC/CBA-67
90ProC/CBA-11
91ProC/CBA-190

Wimbley, Abner
90LSU/200*-184

Winchester, Kennard
91SkyBox/I-109
91UD-273

Windsor, Scott
91SC/200*-155

Winebarger, Rita
91SC/200*-41

Winfield, Lee
70Sonic/Sunb-10
70T-147
71Sonic/Sunb-11
71T-103
72T-33
73Sonic/Shur-12
73T-42
74T-157
75T-192

Wingate, David
82George/Pol-9
83George/Pol-14
84George/Pol-12
85George/Pol-15
87F-125
89Hoops/II-323
90F-174
90Hoops-273
90SkyBox-262
91F/Up-371
91George/100-10
91Hoops/II-448
91SkyBox/I-264
91SkyBox/II-653
91UD-217
91UD/Ext-401
92F-237

Wingo, Hawthorne
75Carv-36
75T-166

Winkles, Bob
90AZSt/200*-102

Winslow, Ricky
91WildCard/Coll-50

Winstead, Brian
91SC/200*-65

Winston, Bobby
85George/Pol-16
86George/Pol-14
87George/Pol-16
88George/Pol-16
91George/100-22

Winston, Roy
90LSU/200*-144

Winters, Brian
75T-143
76T-46
77Bucks/ActPh-10
77T-48
78RCCola-40
78T-76
79Bucks/Pol-32
79T-21
80T-120
80T-5
81T-MW100
91SC/200*-160

Winters, James
91Iowa-15

Winters, Roland
48T/Magic*-J18

Wise, Dale
61Union-10

Wise, Earl
90StarPic-31

Wise, Stevie

91ProC/CBA-27
Wise, Tom
88WakeForest/Pol-16
Wise, Willie
71T-194
71T/Ins-2A
72T-185
72T-254AS
73T-245
74T-185AS
74T-229M
75T-255
75T-287M
Wiskus, Mike
91ND*-4M
Wisman, Jim
86IN/GreatI-4
Wistert, Albert
91MI/56*-56M
Wistert, Alvin
91MI/56*-56M
Wistert, Francis
91MI/56*-56M
Witherspoon, Leroy
89ProC/CBA-102
Witting, Paul
55Ash-96
Wittman, Randy
83Star/NBA-275
84Star/NBA-86
85Star/NBA-49
86F-127
86IN/GreatI-37
87F-126
87Hawks/Pizza-17
88F-7
89Hoops-238
90Hoops-141
90SkyBox/II-389
91Hoops/II-375
Wittman, Tim
92PennSt*-16
Witts, Garry
82TCMA/CBA-23
Wohl, Dave
72T-99
73T-6
74T-108
75T-162
86Star/LifeNets-1CO
89Heat/Publix-15CO
90Heat/Publix-15CO
Wolcott, Brian
90MISt/200*-157
Wolf, Charley
61Kahn's-12CO
62Kahn's-11CO
Wolf, Jeff
89NC/Coke-156
90NC/200*-178
Wolf, Joe
86NC/Pol-24
89Hoops-173
89NC/Coke-138
89NC/Coke-139
90Hoops-152
90Hoops/II-412
90NC/200*-42
90NC/200*-79
90NC/200*-83
90SkyBox-133
90SkyBox/II-381
91F-55
91Hoops/I-57
91SkyBox/I-76
91UD-297
Womack, Wayne
88AZ/Pol-13
Womack, Wayne
89AZ/Pol-14
Wood, Al
83Sonic/Pol-9
83Star/NBA-203
84Star/NBA-124
85Star/NBA-72
86F-128
Wood, David
91Hoops/I-82
91SkyBox/I-110
91UD-298
Wood, David AZ
90AZ/125*-59
Wood, Dody
91Classic/DPColl*-38
Wood, Jim
91GATech*-178
Wood, John
90LSU/200*-78
Wood, Leon
84Star/NBA-200
84Star/NBA-212
85Star/NBA-9
85Star/TmSuper-PS5
87F-127
89ProC/CBA-119
Wood, Willie
91OKSt*-72
Woodberry, Steve
91KS-16
Wooden, John R.
57Union-32
68HOF-46
91UCLA/144-1
91UCLA/144-103M
91UCLA/144-108
91UCLA/144-130
91UCLA/144-20
91Wooden-1
91Wooden-3
91Wooden-4
92CenterCrt-15CO
92Crtside/ColFB-45CO
Wooden, Nell
91UCLA/144-51M
Woodham, Wally
90FLSt/200*-37
Woodhull, Lee Ann
91GATech*-9
Woodley, David
90LSU/200*-182
Woodruff, Dwayne
89Louville/300*-118
Woods, Andy
91WA/Viacom-8
Woods, James
80TCMA/CBA-11
Woods, Randy
92Classic/DP-11
92SkyBox/NBADP-DP16
92StarPic-54
Woods, Sean
88KY/Sov-18
89KY/Award-34
90KY/BB/DT/AW-32
91KY/BB-6
91KY/BB/Double-6
Woods, Sparky
91SC/200*-52
Woodside, Bernard
87LSU/Pol*-6
Woodson, Mike
81T-E89
83Star/NBA-227
84Star/NBA-280
85Kings/Smok-16
85Star/NBA-80
86F-129
87F-128
87IN/GreatII-13
88F-63
89F-63
89Hoops-49
90Hoops-131
90SkyBox/II-386
Woodtli, Andy
83AZ/Pol-17
Woodward, Woody
90FLSt/200*-130
Woolford, Donnell
90Clemson/200*-84
Woolpert, Phil
57Union-8
Woolridge, Orlando
83Star/NBA-180
84Star/CrtKg-38
84Star/NBA-112
84Star/PolASG-34
84Star/SlamD-10
85Bull/Interlake-2
85Star/Gator-9
85Star/NBA-123
85Star/SlamD-9
85Star/TmSuper-CB2
86F-130
87F-129
89Hoops-279A
89Hoops-279B
90F-96
90F/Up-U27
90Hoops-162
90Hoops/II-411
90NotreDame-27
90SkyBox-142
90SkyBox/II-382
91F-56
91F/Up-283
91Hoops/I-58
91Hoops/II-364
91Hoops/Super-26
91Panini-51
91Piston/Unocal-13
91SkyBox/I-77
91SkyBox/II-628
91UD-352
91UD/Ext-406
92F-71
92Hoops/I-70
92SkyBox/I-75
Woolum, Jerry
89KY/300*-189
Wooten, Ron
90NC/200*-62
90NC/200*-88
Workman, Haywoode
89ProC/CBA-176
91Panini-177
91SkyBox/I-297
91UD-330
91WildCard/Coll-78
Workman, Tom
71T-163
Works, Pierce
91UCLA/144-112
Worley, Joey
89KY/300*-134
Worsley, Larry
89NCSt/Coke-115
89NCSt/Coke-130
Worthen, Sam
82TCMA/CBA-37
Worthington, Charles
89KY/300*-241
Worthy, James
82Lakers/BASF-12
83Lakers/BASF-13
83Star/All-R-10
83Star/NBA-25
84Lakers/BASF-11
84Star/Arena-D8
84Star/Celt-9
84Star/CrtKg-49
84Star/NBA-184
85JMS-23
85Prism-1M
85Star/NBA-33
85Star/TmSuper-LA3
86F-131
86Star/CrtKg-33
87F-130
88F-70
88Fourn/St-10
89F-80
89Hoops-210
89Hoops-219AS
89NC/Coke-114
89NC/Coke-19
89NC/Coke-20
89NC/Coke-21
89NC/Coke-22
89NC/Coke-23
90F-97
90Hoops-163
90Hoops-26AS
90Hoops/CollB-48
90Hoops/Super-50
90NC/200*-104
90NC/200*-152
90NC/200*-5
90NC/200*-78
90Panini-5
90Panini-EAS
90SkyBox-143
91F-104
91F/Up-384TL
91Hoops/I-106
91Hoops/I-272AS
91Hoops/II-474SC
91Hoops/II-515Ar
91Hoops/II-539M
91Hoops/McDon-22
91Hoops/Super-50
91Panini-17
91SkyBox/Blister-5M
91SkyBox/Canada-26
91SkyBox/I-143
91SkyBox/II-471TW
91SkyBox/Proto-143
91UD-146
91UD-49AS
91UD-85TC
91UD/Ext-473AS
91UD/McDon-M9
92F-114
92F/AS-24
92F/TmLeader-13
92Hoops/I-115
92Hoops/I-318AS
92SkyBox/I-121
Wosley, Larry
89NCSt/Coke-57AS
Wright, Bill
90AZ/125*-45AS
Wright, Brad
91UCLA/144-23AS
Wright, Gerry
90ProC/CBA-52
Wright, Harold
91ProC/CBA-129
Wright, Howard
71Col/Mara-11
71Pacer/Mara-9
Wright, Joby
86IN/GreatI-35
Wright, Joey
91Classic-40
91Classic/DPColl*-188
91Crtside-43
91FrRow/100-34
91FrRow/50-34
91FrRow/Premier-58
91StarPic-27
Wright, Larry
77T-112
Wright, Lonnie
71Flor/McDon-9
71T-206
Wright, Orville
48T/Magic*-L9
Wright, Poncho
81Louville/Pol-19
88Louville/194-123
88Louville/194-30
89Louville/300*-261
89Louville/300*-43
Wright, Steve
91ProC/CBA-168
Wright, Tyler
91Classic/DPColl*-10
Wright, Wilbur
48T/Magic*-L9
Wrightson, Bernie
90AZSt/200*-177
Wulk, Ned
90AZSt/200*-128
Wyatt, Horace
82TCMA/CBA-29
90Clemson/200*-76
Wyatt, Jane
48T/Magic*-J41
Wylie, Joe
91Classic-28
91Classic/DPColl*-176
91Crtside-44
91FrRow/100-36
91FrRow/50-36
91FrRow/Premier-56
91StarPic-42
91WildCard/Coll-10
Wynder, A.J.
90ProC/CBA-139
90ProC/CBA-26
91ProC/CBA-39
Yarborough, Bill
90Clemson/200*-168
Yardley, George
57T-2
57Union-31
81TCMA-25
85Star/Schick-25
Yates, George
89KY/300*-88
Yates, Wayne
61Lakers/Bell-10
Yates, Tony
80IL/Arby's-14CO
81IL/Arby's-15CO
Yelverton, Charlie
72T-133
Yeoman, Felix
91George/100-71
Yeomans, Tony
90FLSt/200*-33
Yepremian, Garo
81T/Thirst-29
Yerina, Pat
82Fairf-17
Yessin, Humzey
89KY/300*-66
Yessin, Rudy
89KY/300*-242
Yewcic, Tom
90MISt/200*-48
Yoder, Steve
89WI/Smok-14CO
Yoest, Mike
90ProC/CBA-193
Yokley, John
89NC/Coke-173
Yonakor, Rich
81TCMA/CBA-55
89NC/Coke-155
90NC/200*-146
York, Cliff
89Louville/300*-215
York, Smedes

BUY - SELL - TRADE

ST. LOUIS CARDINALS SPECIALIST

B. A. MURRY CARDS

BASEBALL - BASKETBALL

709 TAYLOR DRIVE
CARBONDALE, IL 62901

(618) 457-8278

SPORTSNET IL-202

FIRST BASE

A Sports Nostalgia Shop
Baseball, Football and Other Sports Cards
Memorabilia and Souvenirs

LBJ 635
Central 75
Skillman
Audelia

11-6 Mon.-Sat.
Closed Sun.

10729 Audelia Rd. #110
Audelia Plaza
Dallas, TX 75238
(214) 341-9919

SPECIALIZING IN BASKETBALL CARDS & MEMORABILIA

BUYING/SELLING QUALITY BASKETBALL FOR THE COLLECTOR & INVESTOR.

STAR KAHNS TOPPS POLICE SETS COLLECTIONS
REGIONAL ISSUES FLEER COLLEGE SETS BOWMAN

CALL (805) 773-2744 FOR FRIENDLY ANSWERS TO ANY QUESTIONS.

Service and Satisfaction is our specialty. All transactions handled professionally and discreetly.

Best time to call is 5-10pm PST

ED TAYLOR'S BASEBALL DREAMS

195 WAVE AVE., PISMO BEACH, CA 93449